INTERNATIONAL LAW IN DOMESTIC COURTS

International Law in Domestic Courts

A Casebook

Edited by
ANDRÉ NOLLKAEMPER
AUGUST REINISCH
with
RALPH JANIK
FLORENTINA SIMLINGER

OXFORD
UNIVERSITY PRESS

OXFORD
UNIVERSITY PRESS

Great Clarendon Street, Oxford, OX2 6DP,
United Kingdom

Oxford University Press is a department of the University of Oxford.
It furthers the University's objective of excellence in research, scholarship,
and education by publishing worldwide. Oxford is a registered trade mark of
Oxford University Press in the UK and in certain other countries

First Edition published in 2018

Published in the United States of America by Oxford University Press
198 Madison Avenue, New York, NY 10016, United States of America

British Library Cataloguing in Publication Data
Data available

Library of Congress Control Number: 2018952553

ISBN 978–0–19–873975–3 (pbk.)
ISBN 978–0–19–873974–6 (hbk.)

Foreword

International Law in Domestic Courts—ILDC, the OUP database that assembles judicial decisions of domestic courts dealing with international law—has become a success story of making international law as applied and understood by non-international courts more accessible to a larger audience. More than ten years ago, when the first ideas were floating around between teams in Amsterdam, Pretoria, Oxford, and Vienna, it seemed an almost insurmountable task to cover the practically infinite varieties how courts in national jurisdictions deal with matters of public international law.

Clearly, domestic court decisions have figured prominently in many national journals, yearbooks, or reviews of international law, mostly in the sections on the judicial practice of the various states.

To make this very important 'material' of international law more accessible and at the same time more easily understood through some 'light' annotation was the major idea that has subsequently led to the creation of the ILDC. Instead of publishing the cases annually in judicial practice collections, the idea was to have an ever-growing electronic database which offers the opportunity to add not only recent but also older cases in order to provide a general overview that may become easily searchable across jurisdictions and timeframes by relying on the technical opportunities of looking for issue areas and by also providing some explanation and guidance to the cases.

Thus, the idea of the specific ILDC template was born, which was so successful that it has been modified in various ways and adopted by other Oxford Reports on International Law (ORIL) modules as well. Each ILDC reported case starts with a brief summary of the facts that led to a judicial decision, which is then paraphrased in a so-called held section. In the analysis, ILDC reporters provide some explanation of the decisions, commenting both on the international law aspects and on the domestic law circumstances that may require explanation in order to understand the way in which the cases are ultimately decided.

After ten yeas we have quite a representative number of cases (some 1,700 reported cases waiting to hit the 2,000 mark soon) that deal with various issues of international law. However, the ILDC, by its very nature, will always remain a 'work in progress'.

It is the aim of this book to demonstrate the diversity and richness of this body of domestic court cases. It thus contains various chapters that address both the traditional concepts such as sources and subjects of international law, but also more cross-cutting themes including economic and social rights, terrorism, or amnesties.

Each chapter provides a brief overview of the main issues encountered by domestic courts in their specific area of law, and then presents the most important cases of these areas by quoting from the judgments directly and referring to the ILDC reports.

In total, this ILDC Casebook aims at illustrating both the richness of the existing jurisprudence of domestic courts on matters of international law and the usefulness of the ILDC database for purposes of researching specific international law issues. With the continued growth of the database containing cases from more than ninety countries, its utility is continually increasing and should provide an indispensable tool for all scholars of international law.

The editors wish to thank the many case reporters and commentators who have made the ILDC what it is today, an impressive collection of domestic court practice, and, in particular, the authors of the present seventeen chapters, who undertook the enormous effort to analyse this growing body of case law.

They especially thank Edda Kristjánsdóttir for her contribution to the early conceptual stage not only of this book, but of the ILDC in general, as well as Maria Gavouneli and the University of Athens Law Faculty for hosting and organizing a COST Action Working Group meeting in Athens and Cedric Ryngaert and the University of Leuven for hosting another Working Group meeting, at which central aspects of the present book were developed and discussed.

ANDRÉ NOLLKAEMPER AND AUGUST REINISCH
(with Ralph Janik and Florentina Simlinger)

Table of Contents

Table of Cases

Where the page reference is in **bold** this indicates that the case is discussed at length

INTERNATIONAL AND REGIONAL

Committee on the Elimination of Discrimination against Women

European Court of Human Rights and European Commission of Human Rights

European Union

Inter-American Commission on Human Rights

Inter-American Court of Human Rights

International Arbitration

International Court of Justice

International Criminal Tribunal for Rwanda

International Criminal Tribual for the Former Yugoslavia

International Labour Organisation Administrative Tribunal

Nuremberg International Military Tribunal

Permanent Court of International Justice

UN Human Rights Committee

UN Special Tribunal for Lebanon

World Trade Organisation

DOMESTIC

Albania

Argentina

Benin

Botswana

Brazil

Bulgaria

Canada

Gambia

Germany

Ghana

Greece

Hong Kong

Hungary

Iceland

India

Ireland

Israel

Italy

Japan

Kenya

Kosovo

Latvia

Luxembourg

Macao

Malawi

Mexico

Netherlands

New Zealand

Nigeria

Norway

Peru

Philippines

Poland

Portugal

Russia

Spain

Sri Lanka

Suriname

Sweden

Switzerland

Taiwan

Tanzania

Turkey

Turkish Republic of Northern Cyprus

Ukraine

United Kingdom

United States

Uruguay

Venezuela

Uruguay

Venezuela

Table of International Legal Instruments

List of Abbreviations

ACHPR	African Charter on Human and Peoples' Rights
ACHR	American Convention on Human Rights
ADB	African Development Bank
AMF	Arab Monetary Fund
ANC	African National Congress
AQO	Al-Qaida and Taliban Order of 2006
ATS	Alien Tort Statute
AU	African Union
AZAPO	Azanian People's Organization
CAA	Civil Aeronautics Administration
CEDAW	Convention on the Elimination of All Forms of Discrimination against Women
CESCR	Committee on Economic, Social and Cultural Rights
CFI	Court of First Instance
CKGR	Central Kalahari Game Reserve
CND	Campaign for Nuclear Disarmament
CPA	Coalition Provisional Authority
CTA	Cities and Towns Act
DARIO	ILC Draft articles on the responsibility of international organizations
DRET	Democratic Republic of East Timor
ECHR	European Convention on Human Rights
ECJ	European Court of Justice
ECtHR	European Court of Human Rights
ESA	European Space Agency
FSIA	Foreign Sovereign Immunities Act
HMT	Her Majesty's Treasury
HQA	Headquarters Agreement
IACHR	Inter-American Court of Human Rights
IAEA	International Atomic Energy Agency
ICCPR	International Covenant on Civil and Political Rights
ICESCR	International Covenant on Economic, Social and Cultural Rights
ICJ	International Court of Justice
ICTR	International Criminal Tribunal for Rwanda
ICTY	International Criminal Tribunal for the former Yugoslavia
IDF	Israeli Defence Force
IHL	international humanitarian law
ILC	International Law Commission
ILO	International Labour Organization
IOIA	US International Organizations Immunities Act
ISAF	International Security Assistance Force
LTTE	Liberation Tigers of Tamil Eelam
MCA	Military Commissions Act
MNF	multinational force
NGOs	non-governmental organizations
NHRIs	national human rights institutions
NIMT	Nuremberg International Military Tribunal
NTC	National Transitional Council of Libya
OEF	Operation Enduring Freedom
PA	Palestinian Authority
PLO	Palestinian Liberation Organization
PNA	Palestinian National Authority
POW	prisoner of war
PRC	People's Republic of China
RAF	Royal Air Force
SCP	Staff Compensation Plan
SDHR	State Division of Human Rights
SIA	State Immunity Act 1982
SIAC	Special Immigration Appeal Commission
TO	Terrorism Order 2006
TRNC	Turkish Republic of Northern Cyprus

UDHR	Universal Declaration of Human Rights
UK	United Kingdom
UN	United Nations
UN Charter	Charter of the United Nations
UNCLOS	United Nations Convention on the Law of the Sea
UNCSI	UN Convention on Jurisdictional Immunities of States and Their Property 2004
UNHCR	United Nations High Commissioner for Refugees
UNMOVIC	United Nations Monitoring, Verification and Inspection Commission
UNPFCYP	United Nations Peacekeeping Force in Cyprus
UNPROFOR	United Nations Protection Force
UNSC	Security Council of the United Nations
UNSCOM	United Nations Special Commission
UNTSO	UN Truce Supervision Organization
US	United States
VCCR	Vienna Convention on Consular Relations 1963
VCDR	Vienna Convention on Diplomatic Relations 1961
VCLT	Vienna Convention on the Law of Treaties 1969
WFP	World Food Programme

List of Contributors

Rosanne van Alebeek is assistant professor of international law at the University of Amsterdam and a research fellow of the Amsterdam Center of International Law. She specializes in immunity law and hierarchy in international law.

J Craig Barker is dean of the School of Law and Social Sciences and professor of international law at London South Bank University. He is a generalist international lawyer specializing in diplomatic law and diplomatic immunity, as well as international criminal law.

Christina Binder is professor of international law and human rights law at the Bundeswehr University Munich. She is a member of the International Law Association Committees on Implementation of the Rights of Indigenous Peoples and on Human Rights in Times of Emergency. Her research focuses on international human rights, investment arbitration, and on the law of treaties.

Catherine Brölmann is an associate professor of international law at the University of Amsterdam and a member of the Advisory Committee for Public International Law of the Netherlands Government. She is co-editor-in-chief of *Oxford International Organizations*.

Aristoteles Constantinides is associate professor of international law and human rights at the University of Cyprus and a member of the International Law Association Committee on Recognition/Non-recognition in International Law.

Jorian Hamster is an associate at DLA Piper, Amsterdam. He was an intern at the ICC International Court of Arbitration and a junior lecturer on international law at the University of Amsterdam.

Thordis Ingadottir is associate professor at Reykjavik University and is the co-director of the Project on International Courts and Tribunals (PICT). Her research focuses on international courts, international criminal law, and international organizations.

Ralph Janik is a lecturer at the Vienna and Webster University. He focuses on international law and international relations.

Machiko Kanetake is assistant professor of public international law at Utrecht University and editorial board member of the *Leiden Journal of International Law*. She specializes in international security law and the analysis on the 'interfaces' between national and international law.

Claudia Martin is professional lecturer in residence and co-director of the Academy on Human Rights and Humanitarian Law at American University Washington College of Law.

Bea Myers is a lecturer in law at the University of Winchester, researching international criminal law, as well as the death penalty.

André Nollkaemper is professor of public international law at the Faculty of Law of the University of Amsterdam. He is an external legal adviser to the minister of foreign affairs of the Netherlands, a member of the Permanent Court of Arbitration, president of the European Society of International Law, and a member of the Royal Netherlands Academy of Arts and Sciences. He is co-editor-in-chief of ILDC.

Gregor Novak is a J.S.D. candidate at Yale Law School, where his research focuses on customary international law. Until 2016, Gregor was an associate legal officer at the International Court of Justice.

Riccardo Pavoni is associate professor of international and european law at the University of Siena. He is associate editor of the *Italian Yearbook of International Law* and specializes in immunities of state officials, international environmental law, and cultural property law.

August Reinisch is professor of international and european law at the University of Vienna. He is a member of the International Law Commission, of the Institut de droit international, and of the Permanent Court of Arbitration, as well as president of the German Society of International Law. He is co-editor-in-chief of ILDC.

Cedric Ryngaert is professor of public international law and chair of public international law at Utrecht University. He is the author of a large number of publications with respect to jurisdiction and immunities, international organizations, non-state actors, and international criminal law.

Christy Shucksmith is an assistant professor at the University of Nottingham and a member of the American Society of International Law. Her research focuses on humanitarian protection and assistance, as well as the International Red Cross and Red Crescent Movement.

Florentina Simlinger is an assistant at the Section for International Law and International Relations at the University of Vienna, where she specializes in international arbitration and climate change law.

Juan Santos Vara is Jean Monnet chair and professor of public international law and european law at the University of Salamanca. He is one of the co-editors of *European Papers: A journal on Law and Integration*. He specializes in jurisdiction, treaty law, migration, and external relations of the EU.

Nigel D White is professor of public international law at the University of Nottingham. He focuses on the law of international organizations, collective security law and counter-terrorism, and international law.

Harmen van der Wilt is professor at the University of Amsterdam and a member of the editorial board of the Netherlands Yearbook of International Law. He specializes in international criminal law, courts, and tribunals.

I

General Aspects

ANDRÉ NOLLKAEMPER

I. Introduction

The domestic court decisions excerpted in this chapter address general aspects pertaining to decisions of domestic courts on matters of international law that are relevant to the subsequent chapters in the book. These general aspects comprise a rather heterogeneous set of issues that are grouped here into three main sections. The subsections further address certain key concepts—or 'keywords'—that will recur throughout the book.

Section II discusses three conditions for domestic judicial application of international law: the question of whether international law is part of the 'law of the land' (or: is part of the applicable law—section II.1); the question of whether private parties can invoke international law ('standing to invoke international law'—section II.2); and the question of whether, in case of a conflicting outcome in a case, international law can be said to prevail over national law (the question of 'supremacy'—section II.3).

Section III addresses the two techniques that domestic courts commonly use to ensure that a particular international right or obligation is performed at the national level, namely the principle of 'direct effect' (section III.1); and the principle of 'consistent interpretation' (section III.2).

Section IV reviews methods by which domestic courts, rather than giving effect to international law, may block its application (or 'avoid' it).

The topics in these sections are 'preliminary' in a procedural sense: they generally need to be addressed before a court can consider the merits of a claim that is based on international law. This is true in particular for the questions of applicability and private rights, but also for avoidance techniques such as non-justiciability. Note that the issues addressed in this chapter are not exhaustive; several other topics, discussed separately in this book, are also preliminary in nature, in particular the questions of jurisdiction[1] and immunities.[2]

II. Conditions for Domestic Judicial Application of International Law

1. International law as applicable law

The ability of national judges to adjudicate on the basis of international law depends in part on the question of whether international law has been made part of the national legal order in the country in question; in other words, whether it constitutes applicable law in the given jurisdiction. Whether or not it does depends on a political decision of the forum state. International law does not determine its own applicability within national law, nor does international law require domestic applicability.

Some countries have made the decision to make international law automatically part of the 'law of the land' in their national legal orders. Examples of such states, to which reference will be made later in this book, are Argentina, Belgium, Brazil, the Dominican Republic, France, and

1 See C Ryngaert, H van der Wilt, and J Santos Vara, 'Jurisdiction' Chapter 3 in this volume.

2 See R Pavoni, R van Alebeek, 'Immunities of States and their Officials' Chapter 4 in this volume.

the Netherlands. If certain conditions (such as whether or not a rule of international law accords individuals private rights) are satisfied, courts in those countries are thereby able to adjudicate claims on the basis of international law, although the outcome of such adjudication will depend on other factors considered below, such as whether or not in case of inconsistency between an international rule and domestic legislation or precedent, international law has been given supremacy over national law.

(a) Direct applicability of international law

An illustration of a case where international law could be applied as part of law of the land can be taken from the Dominican Republic. In the excerpted judgment, the Supreme Court made clear that Article 3 of the constitution made international law part of the national legal order, rendering it binding on the Dominican Republic. The Court rejected the Superior Land Court's interpretation that the treaties in question were 'foreign legislation' (*legislación extranjera*). By holding that the Superior Land Court should have applied the treaties relied upon by the plaintiff, the Supreme Court clarified that treaties adopted by the Dominican Republic form part of 'Dominican law', and that such treaties are thus applicable in the national legal system without it being necessary to enact specific implementing legislation to that effect.

Casación, Sentencia del 18 de junio de 1997, Gallardo Montilla v Gallardo Concepción and ors, Appeal Judgment, BJ 1039.164, ILDC 1490 (DO 1997), 18th June 1997, Dominican Republic; Supreme Court of Justice [SCJ]

The petitioner, Mr Gallardo Montilla, sought to overturn a judgment by the Superior Land Court, which had confirmed a first instance decision apportioning a plot of land part of his father's estate under a domestic statute that took into account the fact that Mr Montilla had been born out of wedlock. On appeal, Mr Montilla argued that the Superior Land Court had failed to take into account international treaty provisions prohibiting discrimination against children born out of wedlock, including Article 17(5) of the American Convention on Human Rights and Article 26 of the International Covenant on Civil and Political Rights. The Dominican Republic was a party to those treaties at the relevant time. According to Article 3 of the Dominican Constitution (1994): '[t]he Dominican Republic recognises and applies General and American International Law norms insofar as its public powers adopt them'.[3]

> Considering, that international treaties, duly approved by Congress, have the authority of an internal law, insofar as they affect the rights or private interests [which form the] object of the agreement; that therefore, tribunals have not only the right, but [...] the duty to interpret the treaties, insofar as the application of one of their clauses could influence the solution of a private interests [-related] controversy; that this interpretation, like those of laws, is submitted to control of the Supreme Court of Justice, as a Court of Cassation;[4] that as a matter of adjudication, it is also incumbent on tribunals to solve, under the control of cassation, whether an international treaty, like the other laws, are compatible with the Constitution or not;
>
> Considering, that despite the petitioner having argued, that the international treaties [he] adduced had the character of internal laws, by [reason of] having been approved by the National Congress [...] [the Superior Land Court] decided, by contrast, that [these treaties were] foreign legal provisions inapplicable to the case at hand; that in so acting, the [...] [Superior Land] Court disavowed the said treaties, instead of [...] having established that those treaties had received the approval of the National Congress, interpreting their clauses in order to determine whether the

3 'La República Dominicana reconoce y aplica las normas del Derecho Internacional general y americano en la medida en que sus poderes públicos las hayan adoptado.'

4 I.e., a court that only examines points of law.

said [clauses] could or could not influence [. . .] the solution of the controversy; that therefore, the judgment [. . .] [of the Superior Land Court] must be quashed, without it being necessary to examine any other ground of appeal.

(b) Applicability through implementing legislation

Constitutions use differing language to indicate that international law is applicable as law of the land of a given country. The variations in language are significant. In each case it will depend on the construction of the domestic constitution, or other relevant rules of national law, to determine whether or not a court should treat a particular international rule as part of the national legal order.

In states where international law has not been made part of national law, courts will be limited in their possibility to give effect to international law. Many ('dualistic') states require incorporation or implementation of international law in the national legal order.[5] As a general proposition, domestic courts cannot apply international law—notably, treaties[6]—until international law is transformed into domestic law (eg, through an act of parliament or congress).

If a 'dualistic state' adopts legislation to transform a particular treaty, the contents of the treaty becomes part of the law of the land, and courts in principle will be able to apply it—but then as domestic, not international law. This is illustrated by the following case from Nigeria. The African Charter on Human and Peoples' Rights had been incorporated in Nigeria's domestic law, and after that it had the status of domestic law. Mandates enacted by the state could set the inclusion aside.

Abacha and ors v Fawehinmi, Appeal to Supreme Court, Case No SC 45/1997, (2000) 6 NWLR 228, (2002) 3 LRC 296, (2001) 1 CHR 95, ILDC 21 (NG 2000), 28th April 2000, Nigeria; Supreme Court

Chief Gani Fawehinmi was arrested on 30 January 1996 by the state security service. He argued that the arrest and continued detention without charge violated his rights under the 1999 Constitution (Nigeria) and the African Charter on Human and Peoples' Rights, as incorporated in Nigerian legislation.

> 14 I have carefully considered all that has been said by learned counsel for the parties on the status of the Charter as an international treaty entered into by our country. I do not consider it necessary to set out *in extenso* in this judgment their submissions. Suffice it to say that an international treaty entered into by the government of Nigeria does not become binding until enacted into law by the National Assembly. See section 12(1) of the 1979 Constitution which provides:
>
> > 12(1) No treaty between the Federation and any other country shall have the force of law except to the extent to which any such treaty has been enacted into law by the National Assembly (AFRC). [. . .]
>
> 17 Where, however, the treaty is enacted into law by the National Assembly, as was the case with the African Charter which is incorporated into our municipal (i.e. domestic) law by the African Charter on Human and Peoples' Rights (Ratification and Enforcement) Act Cap. 10 Laws of the Federation of Nigeria 1990 (hereafter is referred to simply as Cap. 10), it becomes binding and our courts must give effect to it like all other laws falling within the judicial powers of the courts. By Cap. 10 the African Charter is now part of the laws of Nigeria and like all other laws the courts must uphold it. The Charter gives to citizens of member states of the Organisation of

---

5 G Gaja, 'Dualism: A Review' in J Nijman and A Nollkaemper (eds), *New Perspectives on the Divide between National & International* Law (OUP 2007) 52.

6 In some legal systems, the process of incorporation of customary law differs from the process of incorporation of treaties.

> African Unity rights and obligations, which rights and obligations are to be enforced by our courts, if they must have any meaning. It is interesting to note that the rights and obligations contained in the Charter are not new to Nigeria as most of these rights and obligations are already enshrined in our Constitution. See Chapter IV of the 1979 and 1999 Constitutions.
>
> 18 No doubt Cap. 10 is a statute with international flavour. Being so, therefore, I would think that if there is a conflict between it and another statute, its provision will prevail over those of that other statute for the reason that it is presumed that the legislature does not intend to breach an international obligation. To this extent I agree with their Lordships of the Court below that the Charter possesses "a greater vigour and strength" than any other domestic statute. But that is not to say that the Charter is superior to the Constitution as erroneously, with respect, was submitted by Mr. Adegboruwa, learned counsel for the respondent. Nor can its international flavour prevent the National Assembly, or the Federal Military Government removing it from our body of municipal laws by simply repealing Cap. 10. Nor also is the validity of another Statute necessarily affected by the mere fact that it violates the African Charter or any other treaty. For that matter — see: *Chae Chin Ping v. United States* 130 US. 181 where it was held that treaties are of no higher dignity than acts of Congress, and may be modified or repealed by Congress in like manner, and whether such modification or repeal is wise or just is not a judicial question. [. . .]
>
> 26 It is thus enacted that *all* authorities and persons exercising *legislative, executive* or *judicial* powers in Nigeria are enjoined to give full recognition and effect to the African Charter. That is, the plenitude of the Government of Nigeria cannot do anything inconsistent with the Charter. Section 1 was never suspended or repealed by any of the Constitution (Suspension and Modification) Decrees enacted between 1983 and 1999; it remained in force throughout this period. The position then is that the courts' jurisdiction to give "full recognition and effect" to the African Charter remained unimpaired.

Several examples in other chapters illustrate the dualist position. In *Campaign for Nuclear Disarmament v Prime Minister of the United Kingdom*,[7] treaties and Security Council Resolutions were not considered part of British national law and British courts were therefore not allowed to rule on their meaning.[8]

The UK court in *R v Jones and ors*[9] reasoned that it could not decide matters which entail a crime of aggression, as a crime of aggression is not a crime in the domestic law of the country.[10]

In *Re Habré*[11] the Senegalese Court of Cassation said it could not prosecute a foreigner for acts of torture committed abroad when the provisions of the Convention against Torture and other Cruel, Inhuman or Degrading Treatment of Punishment had not been incorporated into Senegalese domestic law.

(c) Limitations of the monist and dualist labels

While domestic provisions that recognize international law as part of national law create a presumption that a court will be able to adjudicate a claim based on international law, their effect

7 *Campaign for Nuclear Disarmament v Prime Minister of the United Kingdom, Secretary of State for Foreign and Commonwealth Affairs and Secretary of State for Defence* [2002] EWHC 2777 (Admin).

8 ibid, para 22; see C Shucksmith and N White, 'Use of Force' Chapter 12 in this volume.

9 *R v Jones and ors*, England and Wales, House of Lords, 29 March 2006, ILDC 380 (UK 2006).

10 ibid, para 31 of the judgment.

11 *Re Habré*, Appeal Decision, Cassation No 14; (2002) AHRLR 183 (SeCC 2001), Court of Cassation, First Chamber ILDC 164 (SN 2001), 20 March 2001.

is not more than that. There may be several reasons why despite such provisions a court will not be able to adjudicate a claim on the merits, including lack of direct effect.[12]

Conversely, in dualist states courts have been known to give legal effect to a treaty even when the treaty has not been transformed into national law, as illustrated by examples from Iceland and Malawi.

In the Icelandic case, the court cited a treaty in determining the legality of restrictions of a fundamental right protected by the Constitution, ie the freedom of employment. The weight given to UNCLOS was noteworthy, as with respect to the relation between municipal law and international law, Iceland adheres to dualism, and UNCLOS had not been incorporated into Icelandic municipal law.

Vatneyri Case, Public Prosecutor v Kristjánsson (Björn) and ors, Appeal Judgment, Case No 12/2000, H (2000) 1534, ILDC 67 (IS 2000), 6th April 2000, Iceland; Supreme Court

The operator and the captain of a vessel had been indicted for a violation of the Fisheries Management Act, no 38/1990 (Iceland) (Fisheries Act), as the latter had gone fishing without any catch entitlements. The operator and the captain who were charged in this case based one of their defences on section 3(1) of the Fisheries Act as granting the Minister of Fisheries unlimited powers to determine, by administrative provisions, how much may be caught in total from the utilized stocks for which limitation of catch was deemed necessary. They maintained that this arrangement did not fulfil the requirements of Article 75(1) of the 1944 Constitution (Iceland) (Constitution), to the effect that freedom of employment can only be limited by statute. According to the provision, any person was free to pursue the occupation of his choice. This freedom may, however, be limited by law, provided this was required by the public good.

> 9 The provision of Article 75, the first paragraph, of the Constitution, concerning freedom of employment, can be traced to Article 51 of the Constitution on the Particular Affairs of Iceland, of 5 January 1874. According to the provision, any person is free to pursue the occupation of his choice. This freedom may however be limited by law, provided this is required by the public good. [. . .]
>
> 11 It can be inferred from the wording of Section 3, the first paragraph, of Act No. 38/1990, that total allowable catch shall be determined with a view to the optimum yield of utilised stocks, by reference to the best information available on their current condition. This understanding is supported by the explanatory notes to the bill enacted as Act No. 38/1990, and also conforms to the objectives set forth in Section 1 of the Act and in Section 1 of Act No. 57/1996 on Practices Concerning Utilised Stocks of Ocean Life. Accordingly, Section 3, the first paragraph, of Act No. 38/1990, entails an adequately circumscribed standard governing how the Minister shall limit the total allowable catch within each fishing year. Act No. 38/1990 furthermore contains certain rules on how the total allowable catch is to be distributed, and this distribution does not come within the purview of the Minister. The view that the provision in question grants the Minister such unlimited power to limit total available catch as to conflict with the requirement of Article 75, the first paragraph, of the Constitution, to the effect that freedom of employment can only be limited by law, can not be sustained.
>
> 12 Protection and efficient utilisation of the fish stocks of the Icelandic fishing grounds is a matter of important and obvious public interest. Under international law, Iceland has undertaken the obligation of ensuring reasonable utilisation of this resource, as required by Articles 61 and 62 of the United Nations Convention on the Law of the Sea, cf. Announcement No. 7/1985 in Division C of the Law Gazette.

---

12 See section III.1 below.

> Measures to prevent overexploitation by means of catch limits form an indispensable part of the protection and reasonable utilisation of fish stocks. For this reason, the public interest demands that the freedom to fish by way of occupation be made subject to limitations. Article 75 of the Constitution does not prevent law from providing for necessary limitations to total allowable catch from the various utilised stocks [...].

The example from Malawi illustrates that while treaty law is not directly applicable in Malawi unless a domesticating statute had been adopted by parliament, the courts could nevertheless have regard to applicable norms of international law, where appropriate, and as was done in this case, as a guide to interpreting the constitution and other laws. Although not incorporated into national law, the court did rely upon international law to determine the legality of national law.

Adoption of Children Act Chapter 26:01, Re, Ciccone, Decision on merits, Adoption Case No 1 of 2009, [2009] MWHC 3, ILDC 1280 (MW 2009), 3rd April 2009, Malawi; High Court

Madonna Louise Ciccone petitioned the High Court of Malawi, Lilongwe District Registry, for an order to adopt the infant Chifundo James. The High Court dismissed her petition on the basis that she was not resident in Malawi at the time she petitioned the court, as required by the Adoption of Children Act ('Act'), Chapter 26:01 of the Laws of Malawi (Malawi). Ms Ciccone claimed that the decision of the High Court failed to give due regard to the principle of the best interests of the child, which was reflected in the Convention on the Rights of the Child and the African Charter on the Rights and Welfare of the Child, instruments to which Malawi was a party.

> 34 [...]. In doing so the courts will try as much as possible to avoid a clash between what our laws say on the subject and what the international agreements or conventions are saying on the subject, but where this is not possible, the provisions of our Constitution and the laws made under it will carry the day. It should not come as a surprise that this is the state of the law in Malawi because, by their nature, international agreements are a product of compromise arising out of hard bargaining by high contracting parties. They involve a lot of give and take. They are also negotiated by the executive branch of the Government and not by parliament. [...] It is also the executive branch of Government that enters into international conventions. If the executive branch of Government wishes any of the international conventions which it has freely acceded to, to have the force of law, then it should bring such convention before parliament which has the Constitutional mandate to make all laws of this land. In this regard, sections 7, 8 and 9 of the Constitution are not only in tandem with what is contained in section 211 of the Constitution, but are also conclusive on the matter. We do not therefore agree with counsel's submission that the intention of section 211(1) is to make any international convention which Malawi signs automatically part of the law of the country.
>
> 35 Coming to the actual provisions of the CRC we note that Article 3 provides that "the best interest of the child" shall be a primary consideration. Article 21 of the CRC charges the parties who recognize adoptions in their system to ensure that the best interest of the child shall be the paramount consideration and that the adoption is authorized by competent authorities in accordance with the applicable law in those countries. The best interest of the child is also emphasized in Article 24 of the African Charter on the Rights and Welfare of the Child 1990. [...]
>
> 39 Article 24(a) and (b) of the African Charter on the Rights and Welfare of the Child 1999 is for all practical purposes similar to Article 21(a) and (b) of the CRC and the observations we have made in regard to Article 21(a) and (b) are applicable to Article 24(a). All these provisions compliment and amplify the Act. And courts may

take judicial notice of them when they are considering an application under the Act. This is not to say, however, that our own Act is not adequate or comprehensive in dealing with adoption issues, far from it. All we are saying here is that when we look at our Constitution and the Act there is no clash or conflict whatsoever between what is provided for in our own laws and what is provided for in the various conventions that have been referred to us. We will therefore use our own Act and Constitution which are sufficient in deciding this Appeal.

2. Private rights of action

A domestic court that in principle has jurisdiction and will be allowed to apply international law, generally will only be able to adjudicate an international claim if it can, in specific cases, be accessed by persons who are entitled to rely on an international obligation as a basis for their claim. This can be referred to as the requirement of standing,[13] although the terminology differs between countries (other terms used to refer to this requirement are cause of action, invocability, private right of action, or direct effect).

This requirement of standing explains why courts in many jurisdictions allow individuals to bring a claim based on the International Covenant on Civil and Political Rights (ICCPR) or the Convention for the Protection of Human Rights and Fundamental Freedoms (ECHR), but not claims based on Article 2(4) of the Charter of the United Nations (UN Charter),[14] or only rarely on rules of international environmental law.[15] Courts generally take the position that these latter provisions protect rights of states only.[16]

In the practice of national courts, we can identify a procedural and a substantive component of the requirement of a private right of action. On the one hand, the requirement of a private right of action can function as a procedural threshold, preceding consideration on the merits of whether a state acted in breach of a particular international obligation. In that respect, the concept is closely related to and may be an element of the admissibility of claims.

On the other hand, deciding the threshold question may require a determination of the existence of a substantive right.[17] Indeed, 'to bar a case on standing grounds is, realistically, to deny a plaintiff a legal right, so that resolving the jurisdictional question [. . .] requires a close look at the merits'.[18] In *Mora v New York*, the US Court of Appeals for the 2nd Circuit held that Article 36 of the Vienna Convention on Consular Relations (VCCR) did not confer an individual right on the plaintiff and that the plaintiff therefore could not rely on Article 36.[19]

---

13 See in the context of US law C M Vázquez, 'Treaty-Based Rights and Remedies of Individuals' (1992) 92 *Columbia Law Review* 1084, 1133.

14 See, eg, the Netherlands, Supreme Court, *Association of Lawyers for Peace v Netherlands*, C02/217HR, LJN: AN8071; ILDC 152 (NL 2004) para 3.4 (discussing Article 2(4) of the Charter of the United Nations (adopted 26 June 1945, entered into force 24 October 1945) 59 Stat 1031; TS 993; 3 Bevans 1153 (UN Charter) and holding that the prohibition of the use of force was intended to protect states and therefore could not be invoked by a citizen in the national court).

15 D Bodansky and J Brunnée, 'The Role of National Courts in the Field of International Environmental Law' (1998) 7 *Review of European Community & International Environmental Law* 11; M Anderson and P Galizzi (eds), *International Environmental Law in National Courts* (British Institute of International and Comparative Law 2002).

16 See generally L Brilmayer, 'International Law in American Courts: A Modest Proposal' (1991) 100 *Yale Law Journal* 2277, 2292.

17 See Vázquez (n 13) 1135, 1141 (noting that, at least in the US, standing is a function of whether an individual has a primary right under a treaty).

18 Brilmayer (n 16) 2304.

19 *Mora v New York* 524 F 3d 183 (2d Cir 2008); ILDC 1100 (US 2008) [7] (discussing Article 36 of the Vienna Convention on Consular Relations (adopted 24 April 1963, entered into force 19 March 1967) 596 UNTS 261 (VCCR) and holding that 'we conclude that Article 36's obligation to inform detained aliens of the prospect of consular notification and access cannot, when violated, be vindicated by a private action for damages filed in our courts').

An illustration of the application of the private right of action test as a preliminary threshold is the following case from the Netherlands. Even though the Netherlands is a monist jurisdiction, where all rules of international law are part of the law of the land, courts can decline to give effect to rules of international law which do not create private rights. However, judicial practice is far from consistent, and one can witness considerable differences between civil and administrative courts—in the latter the requirement of a private right of action appears to be applied less strictly.

Association of Lawyers for Peace (Vereniging van Juristen voor de Vrede) and ors v Netherlands, Judgment on Appeal in Cassation, C02/217HR, LJN: AN8071, NJ 2004/329, ILDC 152 (NL 2004), 6th February 2004, Netherlands; Supreme Court [HR]

In response to the terrorist attacks on 11 September 2001, the United States (US) and the United Kingdom (UK) began military actions against Taliban and Al-Qaida training camps on 7 October 2001 (Operation Enduring Freedom). Two days later, [the Government of] the Netherlands informed the Dutch Parliament that it supported these military actions on the basis of the principle that the US had the right to act in self-defence. The Association of Lawyers for Peace installed proceedings requesting to prohibit the state to cooperate or engage in the threat or actual use of military force by the US or its allies, so as long as the UN Security Council had not ordered such use of force pursuant Article 42 of the UN Charter. They argued, inter alia, that the use of military force against targets in Afghanistan was a violation of binding principles and rules of international law, and thus that Dutch support for this force constituted a violation of Article 90 of the Dutch constitution, which provides that 'the Government shall promote the development of the international legal order'. Furthermore, the applicants argued that the prohibition on the use of force—including Articles 2(4), 42, and 51 of the UN Charter—as well as the Constitutional obligation enshrined in Article 90, were envisaged to protect fundamental interests of individuals.

> 3.4 Article 2(4) of the Charter of the United Nations includes a provision requiring all Members to refrain from the threat or use of force against the territorial integrity or political independence of any State. This prohibition on the use of force is therefore intended to protect States and a citizen cannot invoke this provision, or the closely related provisions in Articles 42 and 51 of the Charter, before his national courts. [. . .]
>
> Nor is this altered by the argument that the prohibition on the use of force, when viewed in connection with the principle of individual responsibility for crimes against peace, is a rule of international law binding on all persons. Although an individual citizen can be held responsible under this principle for acting in contravention of the prohibition on the use of force, this does not in itself mean that an individual citizen can invoke the prohibition.

The significance of private rights of action as a preliminary question can be illustrated by case law on international humanitarian law (IHL). Lacking a private right of action, individuals who are allegedly victims of IHL violations cannot file suit against states for compensation on the basis of IHL conventions, such as the 1907 Hague Convention or the 1949 Geneva Conventions. For instance, US courts have refused to give direct effect to IHL conventions.

Iraq and Afghanistan Detainees Litigation, Re, Mohammed Ali and ors v Colonel Pappas and ors, Trial court order, 479 F.Supp.2d 85 (D.D.C. 2007), ILDC 812 (US 2007), 27th March 2007, United States; District of Columbia; District Court for the District of Columbia [DDC]

In this litigation, nine plaintiffs alleged that they were innocent civilians who had been tortured and abused while detained by the US military at various locations in Iraq and Afghanistan. Each plaintiff ultimately was released from custody without ever being charged with a crime. The plaintiffs advanced six causes of action, amongst which was the Geneva Convention relative to the Protection of Civilian Persons in Time of War.[20] Citing long-standing US court practice and engaging in a textual analysis of the relevant provisions of Geneva Convention IV, the District Court held that the Geneva Convention IV was not self-executing.

> 58 The Court is not convinced that Geneva Convention IV is self-executing and establishes individual rights that may be judicially enforced via private lawsuits in federal courts. "Absent authorizing legislation, an individual has access to courts for enforcement of a treaty's provisions only when the treaty is self-executing, that is, when it expressly or impliedly provides a private right of action." […] None of the provisions of Geneva Convention IV contain any such express or implied language indicating that persons have individual "rights" that may be enforced under the treaty. Instead, the provisions of Geneva Convention IV state general obligations with regard to the treatment of protected persons that are imposed on signatory States.
>
> 59 Second, the Court's position on this issue is bolstered by the language of the treaty itself. Judge Bork's concurrence in *Tel-Oren*, 726 F.2d at 809, explained that "[a] treaty that provides that party states will take measures through their own laws to enforce its proscriptions evidences its intent not to be self-executing." In this case, Article 146 of Geneva Convention IV, which is located in Part IV titled "Execution of the Convention" states:
>
> The High Contracting Parties *undertake to enact any legislation* necessary to provide effective penal sanctions for persons committing, or ordering to be committed, any of the grave breaches of the present Convention defined in the following Article.
>
> Each High Contracting Party shall be under the obligation to search for persons alleged to have committed, or to have ordered to be committed, such grave breaches, and shall bring such persons, regardless of their nationality, before its own courts. It may also, if it prefers, and in accordance with the provisions of its own legislation, hand such persons over for trial to another High Contracting Party concerned, provided such High Contracting Party has made out a *prima facie* case.
>
> In addition, it is the law of this circuit that a treaty is not self-executing when the rights of individuals are intended to be vindicated through diplomatic recourse. *Holmes v. Laird*, 459 F.2d 1211, 1222 (D.C. Cir. 1972). Article 149 provides that any alleged violation of the treaty shall be subject to an "enquiry" at the request of a party to the conflict, which enquiry shall be undertaken according to procedures negotiated by the parties or determined by an agreed-upon umpire. *Id.* at art. 149. If a violation of the treaty is established, "the Parties to the conflict shall put an end to it and shall repress it with the least possible delay." *Id.* When considered as a whole, it is apparent from these provisions — which make clear that enforcement of Geneva Convention IV is to be left to the legislation and laws of the parties or to diplomatic enquiry — that the treaty is not intended to be self-executing, in which case the plaintiffs are not entitled to pursue private lawsuits against the defendants for alleged violations. This result is consonant with the recognized rule that "international agreements, even those directly benefitting private persons, generally do not create private rights or provide for a private cause of action in domestic courts." Restatement (Third) of the Foreign Relations Law of the United States § 907 cmt. a (1987); *Hamdan I*, 415 F.3d at 39.
>
> 60 Third, other courts that have passed on the question of whether provisions of Geneva Convention IV are self-executing also concluded otherwise. *See Huynh Thi Anh v. Levi*, 586 F.2d 625, 629 (6th Cir. 1978) (stating that general language in Geneva Convention IV offered no evidence that the treaty "was intended to be self-executing

20 Geneva Convention relative to the Protection of Civilian Persons in Time of War (signed 12 August 1949, entered into force 21 October 1950) 75 UNTS 287 (Geneva Convention IV).

or to create private rights or action in the domestic courts of the signatory countries, in the absence of further domestic legislative action"); *Iwanowa v. Ford Motor Co.*, 67 F. Supp. 2d 424, 439 n.16 (D.N.J. 1999) ("Had Iwanowa attempted to assert a claim under the Hague or Geneva Conventions, it would have been dismissed for lack of jurisdiction because only self-executing treaties, *i.e.*, those that do not require legislation to make them operative, confer rights enforceable by private parties."); *American Baptist Churches v. Meese*, 712 F. Supp. 756, 770 (N.D. Cal. 1989) (determining that Article I of Geneva Convention IV is not self-executing because it "does not impose any specific obligations on the signatory nations, nor does it provide any intelligible guidelines for judicial enforcement").

61 Fourth, the recently-enacted Military Commissions Act of 2006, 109 P.L. 366, 120 Stat. 2600, confirms the Court's view that Geneva Convention IV is not self-executing. Section 5 of the Act states that "[n]o person may invoke the Geneva Conventions or any protocols thereto in any habeas corpus or other civil action or proceeding to which the United States, or a current or former officer, employee, member of the Armed Forces, or other agent of the United States is a party as a source of rights in any court of the United States or its States or territories." However, given that the other stated grounds support the Court's conclusion that Geneva Convention IV is not self-executing, it is not necessary to address at this time whether the Military Commissions Act of 2006 has retroactive application to the plaintiffs' lawsuit.

62 Because Geneva Convention IV manifests an intent to be enforced through legislation or diplomacy, it is not a self-executing treaty that provides a private right for the plaintiffs to sue the defendants for money damages. The plaintiffs' cause of action for violations of Geneva Convention IV therefore fails to state a claim for relief and will be dismissed.

US courts also have held that conventions outlawing the use of certain weapons do not create private causes of action. *Stutts and ors* is illustrative in this respect.

Stutts and ors v De Dietrich Group and ors, Stutts and ors v Deutsche Bank AG and ors, District court decision, No 03-CV-4058 (EDNY 2006), ILDC 874 (US 2006), 30th June 2006, United States; New York; District Court for the Eastern District of New York [EDNY]

US military servicemen and civilian employees of contractors who were deployed in the Persian Gulf region during the 1991 Gulf War were allegedly exposed to toxic agents contained in chemical weapons developed or otherwise obtained by the Iraqi government and detonated by the United States and its allies during the Gulf War. The plaintiffs brought suit against foreign corporations that had allegedly sold chemical agents and manufacturing equipment to Iraq that were used to develop the chemical weapons, and had acted as correspondent banks. The servicemen and civilian employees sought compensatory and punitive damages against the bank defendants under, amongst other legal instruments, the Geneva Protocol for the Prohibition of the Use in War of Asphyxiating, Poisonous or Other Gases, and of Bacteriological Methods of Warfare.[21] As in *Goldstar*,[22] the question arose whether there was a private right of action for individuals under the Geneva Protocol.

23 As an initial matter, the Court must determine whether the sources of international law cited in the complaint provide private rights of action. In order for an international treaty such as the Geneva Convention of 1925 to provide for a private

21 Geneva Protocol for the Prohibition of the Use in War of Asphyxiating, Poisonous or Other Gases, and of Bacteriological Methods of Warfare (signed 17 June 1925, entered into force 8 February 1928) 26 UST 571; 94 LNTS 65 (Geneva Protocol).

22 *Goldstar (Panama) SA and ors v United States*, Appeal judgment, 967 F 2d 965 (1992), ILDC 1648 (US 1992), 16th June 1992, United States; Court of Appeals (4th Circuit) [4th Cir].

right of action it must be "self-executing," meaning that a private right of action is explicitly provided for in the treaty or the treaty has been implemented by a U.S. federal statute. […]

25 […] courts hold that the Geneva Conventions are not self-executing treaties and routinely reject private claims brought under them. See, e.g., *Argentine Republic v. Amerada Hess Shipping Corp.,* 488 U.S. 428, 442 (1989) (Geneva Convention on the High Seas, 13 U.S.T. 2312, does not create a private right of action, but sets forth substantive rules of conduct and states that compensation shall be paid for certain wrongs); *United States v. Fort,* 921 F. Supp. 523, 526 (N.D. Ill. 1996) ("The courts have consistently held that the Geneva Conventions ... are not self-executing and, thus, provide no basis for the enforcement of private rights in domestic courts."). Accordingly, since the Geneva Convention is not self-executing and Congress has not passed implementing legislation, plaintiffs have no private right of action under the Convention.

Similar cases have arisen in Japan, notably in the 1990s when several compensation claims were brought by private plaintiffs against the Japanese government relating to civilian suffering during the Second World War. Without exception, Japanese courts have held that such plaintiffs do not have the right to claim compensation under IHL, the Hague Convention in particular, for damages suffered during the Second World War. In the case below, the Tokyo District Court inquired whether, objectively speaking, the content of individual rights was sufficiently clearly defined in the Hague Convention, and whether state parties in fact intended to establish individual rights. Applying Articles 31 and 32 the 1969 Vienna Convention on the Law of Treaties in its customary version, it gave a negative answer to both questions.

Maria Ria Henson et al v State of Japan, Japan, Tokyo District Court Judgment, 9 October 1998, 42 Japanese Annual of International Law 170-183 (1999) (not in ILDC)

In this case, Philippine 'comfort women', who were abused by Japanese soldiers during the occupation of the Philippines by the Japanese Army in the Second World War, brought a suit against the Japanese government claiming compensation for the harm suffered. The claim was partly based on (customary) international humanitarian law, Article 3 of the 1907 Hague Convention respecting the Laws and Customs of War on Land in particular. This article provides: 'A belligerent party which violates the provisions of the said Regulations [the Hague Regulations] shall, if the case demands, be liable to pay compensation. It shall be responsible for all acts committed by persons forming part of its forces'. The question arose whether individual plaintiffs, as opposed to states, could derive rights from the article.

In case of a violation of rights and benefits of individuals, the general principle of international law intends to provide remedies for individual victims indirectly through the exercise of diplomatic protection by the national states of the victims. When individual persons seek to remedy the violation of their rights and benefits directly from foreign States, they need a special norm of international law that provides them rights to claim redress.

[…] The plaintiffs assert that Article 3 of the Hague Convention is a codification of a principle of customary international law which recognizes the right of individual persons to claim compensation for damages directly against other States.

[…] In view of the purpose of the clauses of the Hague Convention and Regulations, Article 3 of the Convention should be understood as imposing liability for reparations on a belligerent party as a sanction against the violation of the Hague Regulations committed by its army or persons forming part of its army in order to secure observance of the Convention. It does not provide any right for individuals to demand compensation for damages and injury caused by the violation of the Regulations directly against belligerent State parties.

> The following facts will support the interpretation of the Court. First, the general principle of international law provides that international law is a law governing relations between States. Secondly, Article 3 of the Hague Convention prescribes that the provisions of the Regulations and the Convention "do not apply except between Contracting Powers, and then only if all the belligerents are parties to the Convention". Thirdly, there is no statement in Article 3 of the Convention referring to individuals as the subject to whom wrongdoing States are liable and obliged to pay compensation.
>
> […] the Regulations, as examined above, are nothing more than rules of conduct for the military and its members, and Article 3 of the Convention provides nothing more than State responsibility as a sanction against the State of a wrongdoer. Therefore, it is not possible to recognize that the article provides the right to individuals to claim directly against an occupying State. […] even if the article imposes payment of compensation on the belligerent parties, it does not lead directly to the recognition of the right of individuals to file claims.
>
> To summarize, according to the ordinary meaning to be given to the terms in their context, Article 3 of the Hague Convention cannot be understood as a clause that entitles individual victims to bring a claim for compensation directly against a wrongdoing State. Accordingly, it is impossible to recognize that the article is a codification of a rule of customary international law.

A reasoning similar to that made by US and Japanese courts was made in the following German court case, brought by Serb victims of the NATO military operation in Serbia (1999), notably the bombardment of a bridge, in which Germany had participated. The legal question was again whether the Hague and Geneva Conventions conferred rights on individuals to claim compensation from an allegedly responsible state (Germany in this case) for IHL violations of which those individuals were victims.

Varvarin Bridge Case, 36 citizens of the Former Federal Republic of Yugoslavia v Germany, Appeal judgment, III ZR 190/05, BGHZ 166, 384, JZ 2007, 532, BeckRS 2006, 14043, LSK 2007, 100071, RIW 2007, 137, VersR 2007, 1368, DÖV 2007, 429, ILDC 887 (DE 2006), 2nd November 2006, Germany; Federal Court of Justice [BGH]

> 6 1. a) The traditional concept of international law as law between States does not classify the individual as a subject of international law, but grants only indirect international protection to the individual. With regard to violations of international law based on actions against foreign citizens, the person affected was not entitled to bring a claim, but rather his or her native country was. In the area of diplomatic protection, the State obtained vindication of its own rights through respect for international law vis-à-vis its citizen (senate decision BGHZ (Bundesgerichtshof (Federal High Court) 155, 279, 291). The State acted as an intermediary for the person in question, i.e. all relations under international law were exclusively a matter for States, which in this respect also included the interests of the individuals. Consequently the individuals could not request the establishment of the wrong or the remedy of the wrong (Senate, aaO). […]
>
> 8 b) [Not] every rule originating from treaty-protected human rights also confers actual individual rights. Some conventions merely contain protective duties in the sphere of human rights without granting individual rights at the same time (Hobe/Kimminich, aaO p. 161). In particular, the rule still applies that, irrespective of a primary claim by the affected people for the observance of international law, the country of nationality is still basically only entitled to a secondary claim for compensation for the unlawful acts of a foreign State against its citizens (cf. Article 3 of the Hague Convention

(Haager Landkriegsordnung) BVerfGE (Bundesverfassungsgericht-German Federal Constitutional Court) 112, 1, 32 and following; Federal Constitutional Court NJW (Neue Juristische Wochenschrift) 2004, 3257, 3258; Federal Constitutional Court NJW 2006, 2542, 2543). Thus, it is for every international treaty which confers benefits on individuals to determine through interpretation whether and to what extent it should confer individual rights, i.e. whether it confers an independent right (a subjective right) — including, if applicable, a right to damages — or whether it only confers a general right (Dörr JZ (Juristische Zeitung-Law Journal) 2004, 574, 575; Herdegen aaO §22 note. 5). [. . .]

9 2. According to these principles, the plaintiffs are neither able to bring claims for compensation at the international level on the basis of Article 3 of the Hague Convention respecting the Laws and Customs of War on Land of 18 October 1907 (Hague Convention), or on the basis of Article 91 of the first Additional Protocol of 8 June 1977 to the Geneva Convention relative to the Protection of Civilian Persons in Time of War (AP I) of 12 August 1949 (BGBl. (Bundesgesetzblatt-Federal Law Gazette), 1990 II p. 1551; in the following: AP (Additional Protocol I). Other primary grounds for their claim — under international law — are not evident. [. . .]

10 a) Article 3 of the Hague Convention, which originally, undoubtedly, only had an intergovernmental character due to the earlier legal position of lack of rights and obligations for individuals (cf. Senate BGHZ 155, 279, 291), supports no direct individual claim for compensation for a war crime under international law, taking into account that the view of rights for individuals in the international law changed in the meantime (BVerfGE 112, 1, 32 and following; Federal Constitutional Court NJW 2006, 2542, 2543). While the origin of the provision illustrates that it concerns the protection of individuals and, consequently and indirectly, protects human rights, it does not follow that the regulation can be a basis for a direct claim under international law against a State for damages for the affected individual. According to the jurisprudence of the Federal Constitutional Court, to this day only the State of nationality is liable for secondary claims for compensation based on unlawful acts of a foreign State against its citizens, in spite of the development of the level of protection of human rights which resulted in the recognition that individuals could partly be subjects of international law and to the establishment of individual claim cases based on treaties (Federal Constitutional Court NJW 2004, 3257, 3258; 2006, 2542, 2543). [. . .]

11 b) The legal status of Article 91 of AP I cannot, ultimately, be considered to be different. It could be that the regulations of the law of armed conflict in the Additional Protocols of 1977 for the protection of the civilian population which are considered here — particularly Article 51 of AP I — justify the subjective rights of the affected individuals (civilians) for the purposes of a (primary) claim for observance of the provisions of international humanitarian law (cf. Article 3 Federal Constitutional Court HLKO NJW 2004, 3257, 3258; Dörr JZ 2004, 574, 575; id JZ 2005, 905, 908). An individual (secondary) restitution claim in the case of a violation of these provisions arises from this text, but in no case from practice under the international law, or from its history or the prior interpretation of Article 91 of AP I. [. . .]

12 aa) (1) According to Article 91 of AP I "A Party to the conflict which violates the provisions of the Conventions or of this Protocol shall, if the case demands, be liable to pay compensation. It shall be responsible for all acts committed by persons forming

part of its armed forces." This provision corresponds almost literally to Article 3 of the Hague Convention. It corresponds accordingly to the general view that Article 91 of AP I (merely) confirms pre-existing regulations in accordance with Article 3 of the Hague Convention, and extends them to four (Red Cross) Geneva Conventions and the Additional Protocol. Article 91 of AP I has the same meaning as Article 3 of the Hague Convention (Heintschel v. Heinegg, in: Heintschel v. Heinegg, among others, Entschädigung nach bewaffneten Konflikten (Restitution after armed conflicts) [2001], 1, 38; Wolfrum, in: Fleck, Handbuch des humanitären Völkerrechts in bewaffneten Konflikten (Handbook of Humanitarian Law in Armed Conflicts), additional note 1214). The reports on the conference in which the Additional Protocols were drafted do not support the assumption that the contracting parties sought to add meaning to Article 91 of AP I beyond the meaning of the Article 3 of the Hague Convention (cf. Official Records of the Diplomatic Conference on the Reaffirmation and Development of International Humanitarian Law applicable in Armed Conflicts, Geneva in 1974–1977, Vol. III, p. 347; Vol. IX, p. 355ff., 397; Kalshoven, in: International and Comparative Law Quarterly Vol. 40 [1991], 827, 844ff.). If, at the time, the contracting parties had wanted to provide a basis for individual claims for damages in the area concerned, they could have turned to Article 5(5) of the European Convention for the Protection of Human Rights and Fundamental Freedoms (European Convention on Human Rights (ECHR)) dated 4 November 1950, which was in effect at the time of the negotiations of the Additional Protocols and which explicitly foresees a claim for compensation for the person whose human rights have been violated; nothing suggests that a similar regulation was intended for the responsibility of the State for violations of international humanitarian law in armed conflicts. [. . .]

13 (2) The fact that the Geneva Additional Protocols only supported intergovernmental rather than direct individual restitution claims, according to the principles of State responsibility, is confirmed, *inter alia*, by the fact that the draft Articles of the International Law Commission of the United Nations (ILC) on State responsibility of 2001 (cf. attached to resolution 56/83 of the General Assembly of the United Nations on 12 December 2001; printed in Sartorius II No. 6) only foresee in Article 42 the entitlement of an injured State to invoke the responsibility of another State and no individual claims of injured individuals. That is to say, these Articles constitute binding international law only to the extent that they codify customary international law (Schröder, in: Graf Vitzthum, aaO, paragraph 7, note 7). In any case, they are an indication of the fact that the contrary position has not yet developed. In the future, claims of violations of international law are to be considered as a basis for (substitute) proceedings between States (Heintschel v. Heinegg, aaO p. 25). In particular, also because of the specialist nature of international humanitarian law in relation to general human rights (cf. Heintze HuV-I 2003, 172, 174 and following), an individual right cannot be derived from the interpretation of Article 91 of AP I merely on the basis that in certain cases people whose human rights were violated can be granted the right to file a complaint against the violating State (for examples, see Article 34 of the ECHR) [. . .]

14 bb) Furthermore, the commentary on the Additional Protocols to the Geneva Conventions (de Preux, in: Sandoz/Swinarski/Zimmermann, Commentary on the Additional Protocols [1987] Ln. 3657) arrives at the conclusion that under Article 91 of AP I, with the exception of special cases, foreign nationals who were harmed by unlawful acts of a warring party would have to turn to their own government to take up their complaints on their behalf and present it to the responsible party. As far

as de Preux (aaO) simultaneously points to a "trend" that has been developing since 1945, i.e., to recognition of the exercise of rights by individual people, this trend represents — as with similar interpretations or analysis in international law literature (cf. Kleffner, in: 15 LJIL [2002], 235, 244 and following, 250; Zegveld, in: 85 IRRC [2003], 497, 505 and following; Dörr JZ 2005, 905, 909) — no more than the statement of an ideal in the area of international humanitarian law, to be achieved in the future but not yet incorporated in the practice of international law. In this area the general criminal law principle that the violation of a primary obligation normally leads to a secondary claim for the holder of the injured right (Dörr aaO p. 909), receives only limited actual recognition. [...]

17 3. Regarding the above-mentioned question, denied by the Senate, of whether a directly applicable individual right can be derived from Article 3 of the Hague Convention or from Article 91 of AP I, or from another rule of the international law, no consideration is necessary for the Federal Constitutional Court according to Article 100(2) of the Basic Law. The obligation for consideration applies only when the concerning question is "dubious", i.e. the court finds serious doubts in jurisprudence and the literature (Federal Constitutional Court NJW 2006, 2542, 2544). The above interpretation suggests that, according to the general understanding of international law, the individual concerned claim restitution in cases like this, as desirable as this is for some individual voices in the literature of international law. In particular, there are no (international or national) court orders which unambiguously affirm the right to bring proceedings for damages through such an individual (international law) claim for compensation and which can be used as the basis for a decision. Furthermore, there are no suggestions that such individual claims for compensation would have been recognised against the responsible State under current international law.

3. Supremacy

If a court is permitted to apply international law, it might occur that the rule conflicts with national legislation. The question here is to determine whether international law prevails over national law, or to put differently, whether international law has supremacy above national law.

From the perspective of international law, states cannot plead provisions of their municipal legal systems to evade an obligation laid down by international law. That is, the lawfulness of conduct under municipal law does not excuse a breach of international law by states. If an international obligation is to be honoured, all state organs (eg parliaments, courts, municipalities, etc) must act in conformity with what that obligation requires of the state.

Practice at domestic level is diverse. The following cases illustrate the position that international law is, also in the domestic sphere, supreme over national law. The first two cases are noteworthy, as they rely as support for that position on international rather than on domestic law. Even though many states considered international norms to prevail over national legislation, such hierarchy of norms was usually introduced by means of national constitutional law, rather than by recognizing supremacy of international law as an international obligation.

In the example from Chile, supremacy is given to international law on the basis of international law. The court noted that '[u]sing a domestic norm to justify not applying an international treaty breached Art 27 of the Vienna Convention on the Law of Treaties [...]'.

Peru v Chile, Appeal decision, Rol No 2242-06, ILDC 1443 (CL 2007), 21st September 2007, Chile; Supreme Court

Alberto Fujimori served as President of Peru from 28 July 1990 to 14 November 2000. In November 2000 Fujimori fled to Japan, facing corruption and human rights violation charges in Peru relating to his mandate. On 6 November 2005, Fujimori arrived in Santiago, Chile, apparently intending to return to Peru. During this visit, Fujimori was detained under Interpol's arrest warrant. Peru requested his extradition on thirteen charges, alleging that Fujimori had established criminal groups involving various members of his government with the purpose of carrying out crimes against Fujimori's opponents. The request for extradition was initially considered by a single judge of the Supreme Court of Chile, who ruled against extraditing Fujimori based on insufficient evidence to grant the request. Peru appealed the decision, presenting additional evidence supporting the former president's links to human rights abuses.

> H1 Under the Extradition Treaty (Chile/Peru) (5 November 1932), each party agreed to extradite to the other any person who was wanted in the requesting state for prosecution for an extraditable offence. The Procedural Criminal Code, 1997 (Chile) ('Procedural Code') required that for extradition to be sought a person had to be charged in a criminal proceeding. The extradition of former President Fujimori could not be rejected in application of the Procedural Code because that would have violated the Extradition Treaty. Also, using a domestic norm to justify not applying an international treaty breached Article 27 of the Vienna Convention on the Law of Treaties,[23] which provided that a state could not invoke municipal laws to justify non-compliance with the duties arising out of a treaty.

A similar approach was taken by the Constitutional Court of Latvia. The court applied the principle of supremacy within the domestic legal order and concluded that a national norm conflicting with an international treaty was invalid.

Linija v Latvia, Judgment of the Constitutional Court of the Republic of Latvia on a request for constitutional review, Case No 2004-01-06, Latvian Herald, No 108, 3056, ILDC 189 (LV 2004), 7th July 2004, Latvia; Constitutional Court

The Latvian Parliament adopted the law 'On the International Convention for the Facilitation of International Maritime Traffic' (the Convention) on 11 September 1997, thereby ratifying the said Convention. The Convention provides that 'public authorities shall not impose any penalty upon ship-owners in the event that any control document in possession of a passenger is found by public authorities to be inadequate, or if, for that reason, the passenger is found to be inadmissible to the State'. In 1998, the Parliament amended the Administrative Penalties Code. The amended Article 114 of this Code now imposed a fine on natural and legal persons who transported a person lacking the proper travel documents into Latvia through maritime and airport traffic. In 2003, such a fine was imposed on a shipping company that brought a Swedish national, whose passport was about to expire, to Latvia. The shipping company contested this fine in the district court, arguing that Article 114 of the Administrative Penalties Code constituted a violation of the FIMT Convention. The district court referred the case to the Constitutional Court, asking whether the Code of Administrative Penalties was compatible with Standard 3.15 of the FIMT Convention and whether the respective provision of the Code of Administrative Penalties was valid.

> 6 [. . .] On April 6, 1993 the Supreme Council of the Republic of Latvia with a decision "On accession to Vienna Convention on the Law of Treaties of May 23, 1969" ratified the Vienna Convention on the Law of Treaties, of May 23, 1969 (further—the Vienna Convention). The Vienna Convention foresees that states parties recognize the ever-increasing importance of treaties as a source of international law and as a means of developing peaceful co-operation among nations, whatever their constitutional and social systems. Article 26 of the Vienna Convention provides that "every treaty in force is binding upon the parties to it and must be performed by them

23 (adopted on 22 May 1969, entered into force 27 January 1980) 1155 UNTS 331; 8 ILM 679 (1969); 63 AJIL 875 (1969) (Vienna Convention, VCLT).

> in good faith". Consequently, every state must observe its obligations under international treaties and other sources of international law. Therefore, a State may not conflict national law with international law. State's national law may not contradict international obligations (law).
>
> Article 68 of the Constitution of the Republic of Latvia provides inter alia that all international agreements which settle legislative matters need to be ratified by the Saeima. When the Constitutional Assembly included this norm into the Constitution, it did not envisage it to be possible that Latvia shall not perform its international obligations. The requirement to have the respective international agreements ratified by the Saeima was included into the Constitution with an objective to preclude such international obligations, which regulate legislative matters, without the approval of the Saeima. Thus, it is evident that the Constitutional Assembly has been guided by the presumption that international obligations "settle" issues and that they must be fulfilled.
>
> The Law "The Procedure by which Laws and Other Acts, adopted by the Saeima, the President and the Cabinet of Ministers are Promulgated, Published and are Valid" does not specify what is the position of international agreements in the hierarchy of normative acts. However, this law has been adopted after the adoption of the law "On International Agreements of the Republic of Latvia". Article 13 of the law "On International Agreements of the Republic of Latvia" provides that "if an international agreement approved by the Saeima foresees provisions that conflict with legislative acts of the Republic of Latvia, the rules of the international agreement are to be applied". Also paragraph 6 of Article 16 of the Law on the Constitutional Court provides that the Constitutional Court hears cases on the compatibility of national legislation with international agreements, which are not breaching the Constitution.
>
> Therefore, it is evident from the national legislation as well as from the international obligations of the Republic of Latvia under the Vienna Convention on the Law of Treaties, in particular, the obligation to perform treaties in good faith, that in case of a contradiction between rules of international law, which have been approved by the Parliament, and national legislation, provisions of international law must be applied. Moreover, international obligations, which Latvia has undertaken by international agreements approved by the Saeima are binding also on the Saeima. It may not adopt legislation that contradicts these obligations.
>
> The applier of legal norms, also a court, when faced with a conflict between the international norm and national legislation of Latvia, must apply the international norm.

While international law claims, but cannot ensure, supremacy at the international level, many states have prioritized domestic law over conflicting rules of international law. The impact of domestic supremacy rules on the possibility that domestic courts apply particular rules of international law is evidenced in several chapters in this volume.

The District Court of The Hague addressed the question of whether treaty law prohibited the Netherlands from exercising universal jurisdiction over violations of Common Article 3 of the Geneva Conventions. In its answer, the District Court gave supremacy to Common Article 3 of the Geneva Conventions on the basis of Article 94 of the Dutch Constitution.[24]

In its decision in *WEU v Siedler*,[25] the Belgian Court of Cassation emphasized the primacy of directly applicable provisions of international law over provisions of domestic law.

24 *Public Prosecutor v F, First instance*, Criminal procedure, LJN: BA9575, 09/750001–06, District Court of The Hague, ILDC 797 (NL 2007), 25 June 2007.

25 *Western European Union v Siedler*, Court of Cassation of Belgium (3rd Chamber), 21 December 2009, Cass No S 04 0129 F; ILDC 1625 (BE 2009).

The Greek Supreme Court stated in *Germany v Prefecture of Voiotia*[26] that international custom forms an integral part of national law and prevails over any statutory provisions.[27]

The following cases illustrate the effect of a lack of domestic supremacy. In *Canada v Edelson*[28] the Israeli Supreme Court gave primacy to national law above international customary law on state immunity when qualifying the concerned state behaviour of Canada as sovereign or non-sovereign.

In *Bouzari and ors v Iran*[29] the Canadian Court expressly stated the superiority of its State Immunity Act (SIA) over international law: 'Canada has clearly legislated so as not to create this exception to state immunity whether it has an international law obligation to do so or not'.[30]

In *Fernandez v Fernandez*[31] the US Supreme Court gave primacy to the US constitution over conflicting international law obligations: 'As a general rule, a treaty provision that contravenes "any of the prohibitions or limitations of the Constitution applicable to the exercise of authority by the United States" is null and void. 1 Restatement (Third), the Foreign Relations Law of the United States (1987) § 302 (2) [. . .]The United States Supreme Court has "regularly and uniformly recognized the supremacy of the Constitution over a treaty"'.[32]

The Italian Supreme Court in *Drago v International Plant Genetic Resources Institute (IPGRI)*[33] refrained from invoking international law while applying substantively equivalent principles of domestic law. In this case, the principle of constitutional supremacy was upheld:

> It is necessary to determine whether this measure, which unequivocally recognises the body's immunity from Italian jurisdiction and extends to employment relations with its employees, complies with the constitutional principle of judicial protection, as referred to under Article 24 of the Constitution, which constitutes a cardinal principle of the legal order (see Court of Cassation, All Civil Sections, no 12614, 17 December 1998, and no. 149/1999 cit.). This cardinal principle is overridden by the customary principle par in parem non habet iurisdictionem in relation to states, as the principle reflects the sovereign equality of state organisations that is a rule universally recognised by the international community to which our Constitution conforms (Article 10). But this prevalence is no longer justified when the sacrifice of the "cardinal principle" of the Constitution arises not from the international system but from a commitment freely entered into by our Republic through the ratification of a convention. In this case, the requirement that the commitment undertaken be translated into a ratifying law for it to become binding upon the courts brings to the fore the fundamental principles of the Constitution, with which the undertaking must be compatible for the ratifying law to be valid (see Constitutional Court judgement no 223 of 1996).[34]

In *Horgan v An Taoiseach and ors*[35] the Irish High Court ruled that 'one can only conclude therefore that principles of international law enter domestic law only to the extent that no

26 Greece, Supreme Court (Areios Pagos), *Germany v Prefecture of Voiotia*, No 11/2000, 4 May 2000, ILDC 287 (GR 2000).

27 ibid, para 8.

28 Israel, Supreme Court, *Canada v Edelson*, 3 June 1997, 131 ILR 279, ILDC 577 (IL 1997).

29 Canada, Ontario Court of Appeal, *Bouzari and ors v Iran*, 30 June 2004, ILDC 175 (CA 2004).

30 ibid, para 67.

31 US, Supreme Court of Connecticut, *Fernandez v Fernandez*, 19 July 1988, 545 A2d 1036 (Conn 1988), ILDC 1385 (US 1988).

32 ibid, para 25.

33 *Drago v International Plant Genetic Resources Institute (IPGRI)*, Final appeal judgment, no 3718; ILDC 827 (IT 2007) Italy, Court of Cassation, All Civil Sections, 19 February 2007.

34 ibid, para 6.5.

35 *Edward Horgan v An Taoiseach and ors*, Application for Declaratory Relief, (2003 No 3739P); (2003) 2 IR 468; (2003) IEHC 64.

constitutional, statutory or other judge made law is inconsistent with the principle in question. Where a conflict arises, the rule of international law must in every case yield to domestic law'.[36]

The Dutch Supreme Court judged in *Bouterse*[37] that customary international law could not supersede an Act of Parliament, hereby referring to Article 94 of the Constitution.

In *H v Prosecutor*[38] the Dutch Supreme Court ruled that Article 94 of the Dutch Constitution implicitly precluded courts from testing Acts of Parliament against rules of customary international law (ie unwritten international law).

III. Techniques

This section will discuss two techniques that national courts have resorted to in applying international law: direct effect (section 2.1) and consistent interpretation (section 2.2).

1. Direct effect

Courts can give effect to international obligations in two ways: indirect (that is, through national law), or direct. There is no doubt that indirect effect is the most common way to give effect to international obligations. Courts then secure the performance of an international obligation by applying domestic law that substantively incorporates or encompasses that obligation. This will be the situation when domestic law may pre-exist and substantively overlap with an international obligation. Unless international law provides more protection, the courts can in principle confine themselves to applying national law.

Courts may also give indirect effect to an international obligation by applying a law that has implemented (or: 'transformed') that obligation in national law. Such indirect effect is the normal situation in the many states that require transformation of international obligations into domestic law. But also states where international law in principle is the law of the land resort to such implementing legislation, because they may seek to make such obligations more coherent with national law, because these obligations are incomplete, or because legal certainty is enhanced if they are expressly made subject to legislation.

In contrast, a court gives '*direct* effect' to an obligation if it enforces that obligation as such, not in a domesticated form. The effect is 'direct' in the sense that it does not depend on an intervening legislative step. The defining feature of direct effect—enforcement of an international obligation without being dependent on implementing legislation—is caught by the term 'self-executing'. A treaty provision can execute itself, without requiring additional legislation. That is: without intervening legal step by the state, the international norm becomes operative for individual state organs and indeed for private individuals.[39]

The classic reference for direct effect is the US case *Foster v Nelson*. This case involved a treaty-based land-grant dispute between the United States and Spain. The US district court held that it could not give direct effect to the treaty in question and explained the criterion for self-executing international law. By making a distinction between self-executing and not self-executing treaties, it states that courts are empowered to rely on international law and thereby control executive power, when it is regarded as equivalent to a legislative act and operates as legislation.

36 ibid, para 135.

37 *Bouterse*, Judgment on Appeal, HR 00749/01 CW 2323; ILDC 80 (NL 2001) The Netherlands, Supreme Court, 18 September 2001.

38 *H v Public Prosecutor*, Appeal judgment, LJN: AZ7143; Judgment on merits, Case No 07/10063 (E); LJN BG1476, Court of Appeal and Supreme Court, ILDC 636 (NL 2007) 29 January 2007 and ILDC 1071 (NL 2008) 8 July 2008.

39 T Buergenthal, 'Self-Executing and Non-Self-Executing Treaties in National and International Law' (1992) IV *Recueil des Cours* 303, 317.

Foster and Elam v Neilson, Appellate judgment, 27 US (2 Pet) 253 (1829), ILDC 2021 (US 1829), 7 L Ed 415 (1829), 1st January 1829, United States; Supreme Court [US]

207 A treaty is, in its nature, a contract between two nations, not a legislative act. It does not generally effect, of itself, the object to be accomplished, especially so far as its operation is infra-territorial, but is carried into execution by the sovereign power of the respective parties to the instrument.

208 In the United States, a different principle is established. Our Constitution declares a treaty to be the law of the land. It is consequently to be regarded in courts of justice as equivalent to an act of the Legislature whenever it operates of itself, without the aid of any legislative provision. But when the terms of the stipulation import a contract, when either of the parties engages to perform a particular act, the treaty addresses itself to the political, not the Judicial, Department, and the Legislature must execute the contract before it can become a rule for the Court.

209 The article under consideration does not [...] say that those grants are hereby confirmed. Had such been its language, it would have acted directly on the subject, and would have repealed those acts of Congress which were repugnant to it; but its language is that those grants shall be ratified and confirmed to the persons in possession, &c. By whom shall they be ratified and confirmed? This seems to be the language of contract; and if it is, the ratification and confirmation which are promised must be the act of the Legislature. Until such act shall be passed, the Court is not at liberty to disregard the existing laws on the subject. Congress appears to have understood this article as it is understood by the court. [...]

The important role of direct effect can be seen in those cases where a court declines to give direct effect to an international obligation, as in the Swiss example below. Although the Federal Supreme Court expresses the monist tradition of the Swiss legal system, the Federal Supreme Court's decision that the ICESCR in general does not grant individuals any subjective or legally enforceable rights in effect ensures that in the case at hand the openness to international law did not help the plaintiffs. According to the Federal Supreme Court, the ICESCR Articles 13(2)(b) and (c), in particular, are not specific enough for granting direct effect in their national legal system.

A and B v Government of the Canton of Zurich, Appeal against a Regulation of 15 September 1999 adopted by the Canton of Zurich on the Tuition at Schools of Higher Education, Case No 2P.273/1999, BGE 126 I 242, ILDC 350 (CH 2000), 22nd September 2000, Switzerland; Federal Supreme Court [BGer]

On 15 September 1999 the Government of the Canton of Zurich adopted a new Regulation on Tuition for Students of the Schools of Higher Education (Regulation). Before the Regulation, these schools did not require any registration and tuition fees. A and B challenged this new Regulation before the Federal Supreme Court. They claimed that this new Regulation, by introducing new registration and tuition fees, violated Article 13(2)(b) and Article 13(2)(c) of the International Covenant on Economic, Social and Cultural Rights.[40]

2b Switzerland was a country with a monist tradition: an international treaty ratified by the Federal Council formed part of federal law from the time of its entry into force for Switzerland; it was immediately binding on the authorities without need for it to be incorporated in the internal legal system through the adoption of a special law. However, the provisions of an international treaty could only be invoked by

40 (ICESCR) (signed 16 December 1966, entered into force 3 January 1976, entered into force for Switzerland on 18 September 1992) 993 UNTS 3.

individuals before the national courts if they were self-executing, that is: if they had a sufficiently clear and tangible content to form the basis of a decision. Treaty provisions of a programmatic character could not be considered as self-executing: they did not establish individual rights that could be invoked before national courts, but needed to be elaborated and given appropriate form by the legislator.

2c Subject to certain exceptions, the International Covenant on Economic, Social and Cultural Rights (ICESCR) is not regarded in the jurisprudence of the Federal Court of Justice as directly applicable [...]. The international law obligations assumed by Switzerland under this Covenant are consequently of a programmatic nature; the provisions of the Treaty are directed — contrary to the directly applicable guarantees of the International Covenant of 16 December 1966 on Civil and Political Rights (ICCPR; SR 0.103.2), to which Switzerland also acceded at the same time — are not aimed at the individual but (primarily) at the Parliaments of the Contracting States, which must regard them as a guideline for their activities (according to the Statement from the Federal Council of 30 January 1991 concerning Switzerland's accession to the two international human rights treaties of 1966, BBl 1991 I 1193 and 1202). The Federal Council and Parliament have consequently assumed that the provisions of the ICESCR essentially grant the individual no subjective or legally enforceable rights, apart from a few exceptions, that the citizen could invoke before Swiss administrative and legal authorities (BBl 1991 I 1202; AB 1991 Note 1494, p. 930). [...]

2g [...]. The question at issue is therefore how obligations of treaty law undertaken must be executed and whether and to what extent the provisions of this Covenant can be invoked within a state as "self-executing" by an individual in connection with an individual objection procedure (see Yvo Hangartner, Principles of Swiss National Law, Vol. I: Organisation, Zurich 1980, pp. 42–43; Ulrich Häfelin/Walter Haller, Swiss Federal Law, 4th edition, Zurich, 1998, Note 1038; Jeanine de Vries Reilingh, L'application des Pactes des Nations Unies relatifs aux droits de l'homme de 1966, Dissertation Neuenburg, Basel and Geneva 1998, Notes 104 et seq.; Manfred Nowak, Contents, Significance and implementing mechanisms of the two UN Human Rights Treaties, in: Switzerland and the UN Human Rights Treaties, 2nd edition, Basle 1997, p. 19; Gebert, op. cit., pp. 122–123; Künzli, op. cit., p. 532).

3 Article 13(2)(b) and (c) of the ICESCR do not contain, as will be shown, any enforceable guarantees concerning rights of the individual, that might be invoked in the present case on the basis of Article 84(1)(c) Constitution by Constitutional Objection.

The significance of direct effect is illustrated by several cases in this volume. In relation to international criminal law, the following cases can be noted. In *Public Prosecutor v Arklöf*[41] the Swedish court granted criminal responsibility to Jackie Arklöf for war crimes in the Yugoslavia Wars on the basis of a reference in a domestic penal code to customary international law. Several rules in international humanitarian law were directly applied.

In *Military Prosecutor v Bongi Massaba*[42] the Military Tribunal of Ituri, Democratic Republic of Congo (DRC), applied self-executing norms of international criminal law directly. Blaise Massaba, captain in the Congolese army, was charged with the war crimes of wilful killing and pillaging, as provided for in Article 8(2)(b)(xvi) and 8(2)(a)(i), respectively, of the Rome Statute

41 *Public Prosecutor v Arklöf*, Judgment, Case No B 4084-04 District Court of Stockholm, 18 December 2006, ILDC 633 (SE 2006).

42 *Military Prosecutor v Bongi Massaba*, Criminal trial judgment and accompanying civil action for damages, RP No 018/2006; RMP No 242/PEN/06, 24 March 2006, ILDC 387 (CD 2006).

of the International Criminal Court and the Congolese military penal code. The DRC had ratified the Rome Statute in 2002. The Congolese court applied the Rome Statute in order to fill the gaps in domestic law (also supremacy of international law on the basis of Article 215 the DRC constitution).

In *US v Smith*[43] the US Supreme Court found provisions in international criminal law sufficiently precise to be self-executing.

Conversely, in *Movement Against Racism and for Peoples' Friendship v Aussaresses*[44] the French Court of Cassation ruled that customary international law as such could not palliate the lack of explicit domestic provisions, and could therefore never serve as an adequate basis for prosecution and conviction within the French legal order.

2. Consistent interpretation

Apart from direct application of international legal obligations, international law can also be made effective in the national legal order by ways of consistent interpretation of national law. Domestic courts ensure compliance with international law by interpreting or applying their national laws in conformity with the standards or conditions laid down in international law. This section exemplifies how the concept of consistent interpretation is applied by national judges.

Interpretation No 27, Re, Judicial interpretation, [2002] no 27, ILDC 263 (CN 2002), 27th August 2002, China; Supreme People's Court

On 27 August 2002, at the 1239th Meeting of the Judicial Committee of the Supreme People's Court, the Committee adopted Provisions of the Supreme People's Court on Several Issues Concerning the Hearing of International Trade Administrative Cases. The Provisions were promulgated on the same day as Interpretation No 27 (Supreme People's Court), 2002 (Interpretation 27), and entered into force on 1 October 2002.

The preamble of Interpretation 27 stated the purpose of the Provisions as follows: 'In order to hear international trade administrative cases justly and duly pursuant to law, these Provisions are formulated in accordance with the Administrative Procedure Law of the People's Republic of China ("Administrative Procedure Law")[...], the Legislation Law of the People's Republic of China [...], and other relevant laws'.

The Supreme People's Courts judged upon the question of whether China is required to choose an interpretation consistent with the relevant provisions of international treaty obligations of the People's Republic of China (PRC).

> 13 Article 7 of Interpretation 27: According to Paragraph 1 of Article 52 of the Administrative Procedure Law and Paragraphs 1 and 2 of Article 63 of the Legislation Law, a people's court shall, in the hearing of international trade administrative cases, follow the laws and administrative regulations of the People's Republic of China, as well as the local regulations, which relate to or affect the international trade, enacted by the local legislatures within the statutory legislative authority. [...]
>
> 15 Article 9 of Interpretation 27: If there are two or more reasonable interpretations for a specific clause of the law or administrative regulation applied by a people's court in the hearing of an international trade administrative case, and among which one interpretation is consistent with the relevant provisions of the international treaty that the PRC concluded or entered into, such interpretation shall be chosen, with the exception of the clauses on which the PRC claims reservation.

43 *United States v Smith*, Appeal judgment, 18 US 5 Wheat 153 (1820) US Supreme Court, 2 February 1820, ILDC 1053 (US 1820).

44 *Movement Against Racism and for Peoples' Friendship v Aussaresses*, Appeal judgment, Appeal No 02-80719; Decision No 122 France, Court of Cassation, Criminal Chamber, 17 June 2003, ILDC 775 (FR 2003).

Teoh's case, Minister of State for Immigration and Ethnic Affairs v Teoh, Final appeal judgment, Case No FC 95/013, ILDC 779 (AU 1995), (1995) 183 CLR 273, (1995) 128 ALR 353, (1995) 69 ALJR 423, (1995) EOC 92-696 (extract), [1995] HCA 20, 7th April 1995, Australia; High Court [HCA]

In May 1988, Mr Ah Hin Teoh, a Malaysian citizen, came to Australia. He entered Australia on a temporary visa. He subsequently married Mrs Jean Lim, an Australian citizen, in July 1988. Mr Teoh and his wife had three children together. Prior to the expiry of his temporary visa, Mr Teoh applied for a permanent resident status. Whilst his application was being processed, Mr Teoh was convicted for the importation and possession of heroin. This conviction led to the refusal of Mr Teoh's permanent resident status. Teoh applied for a review of this decision, referring to the rights of his children not to be separated from their parents, but this application was rejected by the Immigration Review Panel in July 1991. The Australian immigration minister accepted the decision of the panel and ordered that Mr Teoh be deported. Teoh brought the case before the Federal Court. The court subsequently dismissed the case. On appeal, the full bench of the Federal Court found that the decisions of the immigration minister had been an improper exercise of power, because the minister had failed to investigate the effects of deportation on Mr Teoh's family. The immigration minister appealed this decision to the High Court of Australia.

> 23 The [United Nations] Convention [on the Rights of Children] was ratified by the Commonwealth Executive on 17 December 1990 and it entered into force for Australia on 16 January 1991. [. . .]
>
> 24 Articles 3 and 9 of the Convention provide as follows: [. . .]
>
> > Article 9
> >
> > "1. States Parties shall ensure that a child shall not be separated from his or her parents against their will, except when competent authorities subject to judicial review determine, in accordance with applicable law and procedures, that such separation is necessary for the best interests of the child. Such determination may be necessary in a particular case such as one involving abuse or neglect of the child by the parents, or one where the parents are living separately and a decision must be made as to the child's place of residence."
>
> 25 It is well established that the provisions of an international treaty to which Australia is a party do not form part of Australian law unless those provisions have been validly incorporated into our municipal law by statute. [. . .] In this case, it is common ground that the provisions of the Convention have not been incorporated in this way. [. . .]
>
> 26 But the fact that the Convention has not been incorporated into Australian law does not mean that its ratification holds no significance for Australian law. [. . .]
>
> 34 [. . .] ratification by Australia of an international convention is not to be dismissed as a merely platitudinous or ineffectual act, particularly when the instrument evidences internationally accepted standards to be applied by courts and administrative authorities in dealing with basic human rights affecting the family and children. Rather, ratification of a convention is a positive statement by the executive government of this country to the world and to the Australian people that the executive government and its agencies will act in accordance with the Convention. That positive statement is an adequate foundation for a legitimate expectation, absent statutory or executive indications to the contrary, that administrative decision-makers will act in conformity with the Convention and treat the best interests of the children as "a primary consideration". It is not necessary that a person seeking to set up such a legitimate expectation should be aware of the Convention or should personally entertain the expectation; it is enough that the expectation is reasonable in the sense that there are adequate materials to support it. [. . .]

> 36 The existence of a legitimate expectation that a decision-maker will act in a particular way does not necessarily compel him or her to act in that way. That is the difference between a legitimate expectation and a binding rule of law. To regard a legitimate expectation as requiring the decision-maker to act in a particular way is tantamount to treating it as a rule of law. It incorporates the provisions of the unincorporated convention into our municipal law by the back door. [. . .]
>
> 37 But, if a decision-maker proposes to make a decision inconsistent with a legitimate expectation, procedural fairness requires that the persons affected should be given notice and an adequate opportunity of presenting a case against the taking of such a course. So, here, if the delegate proposed to give a decision which did not accord with the principle that the best interests of the children were to be a primary consideration, procedural fairness called for the delegate to take the steps just indicated.

A, Amnesty International (intervening) and Commonwealth Lawyers Association (intervening) v Secretary of State for the Home Department, Appeal judgment, [2005] UKHL 71, [2006] 2 AC 221, [2005] 3 WLR 1249, [2006] 1 All ER 575, ILDC 363 (UK 2005), 8th December 2005, United Kingdom; House of Lords [HL]

After the terrorist attacks of 11 September 2001, the United Kingdom adopted the Anti-terrorism, Crime and Security Act ('the 2001 Act'). This 2001 Act allowed for the indefinite detention of persons who were not British citizens but who were suspected of being terrorists and whose presence in the UK the secretary of state for the Home Department reasonably believed to be a risk to the national security.

The secretary of state applied this rule to ten foreign nationals whom he suspected of being terrorists. These persons could leave the country or be detained for an indefinite period without a trial. Eight out of these ten people chose to stay and challenge their detention. Among other things, the detainees claimed that the evidence against them was obtained through torture, inflicted upon them by foreign officials. In 2003, the Special Immigration Appeals Committee (SIAC) held that the fact that some of the evidence might have been obtained through torture did not render it inadmissible. The detainees appealed this decision at the Court of Appeals claiming that the SIAC erred in its application of Article 15 of the Convention against Torture. The Court of Appeals held that it could not apply the Convention against Torture because it had not been incorporated in British law. The detainees subsequently appealed to the House of Lords. Counsel for the detainees argued that English common law prohibited the admission of evidence that was obtained under torture. It was also argued that, even if English law did not require the exclusion of such evidence, the European Convention on Human Rights did require it. Furthermore, the 2001 Act should be construed as intending to comply with the UK's treaty obligations.

> 30 The preamble to the United Nations Charter (1945) recorded the determination of member states to reaffirm their faith in fundamental human rights and the dignity and worth of the human person and to establish conditions under which justice and respect for the obligations arising from treaties and other sources of international law can be maintained. The Charter was succeeded by the Universal Declaration of Human Rights 1948, the European Convention 1950 and the International Covenant on Civil and Political Rights 1966, all of which (in articles 5, 3 and 7 respectively, in very similar language) provided that no one should be subjected to torture or inhuman or degrading treatment. [. . .]
>
> 33 It is common ground in these proceedings that the international prohibition of the use of torture enjoys the enhanced status of a *jus cogens* or peremptory norm of general international law. For purposes of the Vienna Convention, a peremptory norm of general international law is defined in article 53 to mean "a norm accepted

and recognized by the international community of States as a whole as a norm from which no derogation is permitted and which can be modified only by a subsequent norm of general international law having the same character". In *R v Bow Street Metropolitan Stipendiary Magistrate, Ex p Pinochet Ugarte (No 3)* [2000] 1 AC 147, 197–199, the *jus cogens* nature of the international crime of torture, the subject of universal jurisdiction, was recognised. [. . .]

There can be few issues on which international legal opinion is clearer than on the condemnation of torture. Offenders have been recognised as the "common enemies of mankind" [. . .]

34 As appears from the passage just cited, the jus cogens erga omnes nature of the prohibition of torture requires member states to do more than eschew the practice of torture. [. . .] There is reason to regard it as a duty of states, save perhaps in limited and exceptional circumstances, as where immediately necessary to protect a person from unlawful violence or property from destruction, to reject the fruits of torture inflicted in breach of international law. [. . .]

52 I accept the broad thrust of the appellants' argument on the common law. The principles of the common law, standing alone, in my opinion compel the exclusion of third party torture evidence as unreliable, unfair, offensive to ordinary standards of humanity and decency and incompatible with the principles which should animate a tribunal seeking to administer justice. But the principles of the common law do not stand alone. Effect must be given to the European Convention, which itself takes account of the all but universal consensus embodied in the Torture Convention. The answer to the central question posed at the outset of this opinion is to be found not in a governmental policy, which may change, but in law.

Baker v Canada, Canada, Supreme Court, 9 July 1999, 2 SCR 817 (not in ILDC)

The appellant, a woman with Canadian-born dependent children, was ordered to be deported. She then applied for an exemption, based on humanitarian and compassionate considerations under section 114(2) of the Immigration Act, from the requirement that an application for permanent residence be made from outside Canada. A senior immigration officer replied by letter stating that there were insufficient humanitarian and compassionate reasons to warrant processing the application in Canada.

The Federal Court (Trial Division), dismissed an application for judicial review but certified the following question pursuant to section 83(1) of the Act: 'Given that the Immigration Act does not expressly incorporate the language of Canada's international obligations with respect to the International Convention on the Rights of the Child, must federal immigration authorities treat the best interests of the Canadian child as a primary consideration in assessing an applicant under section 114(2) of the Immigration Act?' The Court of Appeal limited its consideration to the question and found that the best interests of the children did not need to be given primacy in assessing such an application. The order that the appellant be removed from Canada, which was made after the immigration officer's decision, was stayed pending the result of this appeal.

1 L'HEUREUX-DUBÉ J. — Regulations made pursuant to s. 114(2) of the Immigration Act, R.S.C., 1985, c. I-2, empower the respondent Minister to facilitate the admission to Canada of a person where the Minister is satisfied, owing to humanitarian and compassionate considerations, that admission should be facilitated or an exemption from the regulations made under the Act should be granted. [. . .].

69 Another indicator of the importance of considering the interests of children when making a compassionate and humanitarian decision is the ratification by Canada of the Convention on the Rights of the Child, and the recognition of the importance of children's rights and the best interests of children in other international instruments

ratified by Canada. International treaties and conventions are not part of Canadian law unless they have been implemented by statute: *Francis v. The Queen*, [1956] S.C.R. 618, at p. 621; *Capital Cities Communications Inc. v. Canadian Radio-Television Commission*, [1978] 2 S.C.R. 141, at pp. 172-73. I agree with the respondent and the Court of Appeal that the Convention has not been implemented by Parliament. Its provisions therefore have no direct application within Canadian law.

70 Nevertheless, the values reflected in international human rights law may help inform the contextual approach to statutory interpretation and judicial review. As stated in R. Sullivan, Driedger on the Construction of Statutes (3rd ed. 1994), at p. 330: [T]he legislature is presumed to respect the values and principles enshrined in international law, both customary and conventional. These constitute a part of the legal context in which legislation is enacted and read. *In so far as possible, therefore, interpretations that reflect these values and principles are preferred.* [Emphasis added.] The important role of international human rights law as an aid in interpreting domestic law has also been emphasized in other common law countries: see, for example, *Tavita v. Minister of Immigration*, [1994] 2 N.Z.L.R. 257 (C.A.), at p. 266; *Vishaka v. Rajasthan*, [1997] 3 L.R.C. 361 (S.C. India), at p. 367. It is also a critical influence on the interpretation of the scope of the rights included in the *Charter: Slaight Communications, supra; R. v. Keegstra*, [1990] 3 S.C.R. 697.

71 The values and principles of the Convention recognize the importance of being attentive to the rights and best interests of children when decisions are made that relate to and affect their future. In addition, the preamble, recalling the Universal Declaration of Human Rights, recognizes that "childhood is entitled to special care and assistance". A similar emphasis on the importance of placing considerable value on the protection of children and their needs and interests is also contained in other international instruments. The United Nations Declaration of the Rights of the Child (1959), in its preamble, states that the child "needs special safeguards and care". The principles of the Convention and other international instruments place special importance on protections for children and childhood, and on particular consideration of their interests, needs, and rights. They help show the values that are central in determining whether this decision was a reasonable exercise of the H & C power. […]

76 Therefore, both because there was a violation of the principles of procedural fairness owing to a reasonable apprehension of bias, and because the exercise of the H & C discretion was unreasonable, I would allow this appeal.

Several other cases in this volume illustrate the technique of consistent interpretation. In the *Jorgic Case*[45] the German Criminal Code, §6 Number 1, is interpreted in light of the Genocide Convention and the Rome Statute. By doing so, the German Federal Constitutional Court has come to the decision that international law does not preclude states from exercising universal jurisdiction.

In *Menchu and ors v Two Guatemalan Government Officials and ors*[46] the Spanish Constitutional Court overturned the restrictive interpretation of the principle of universal jurisdiction as provided for in Article 23.4 of the Organic Law of the Judicial Power (LOPJ), which is consistent with international law. As stated in the judgment: '[…] The concept of universal jurisdiction

45 *Jorgic Case*, Individual constitutional complaint, BVerfG, 2 BvR 1290/99, Federal Constitutional Court, (Second Senate), 4th Chamber, ILDC 132 (DE 2000), 12 December 2000.

46 *Guatemala Genocide Case, Menchú Tumn (Rigoberta) and ors v Two Guatemalan Government Officials and Six members of the Guatemalan Military*, Constitutional Appeal, Case No 237/2005, ILDC 137 (ES 2005), 26 September 2005, Spain; Constitutional Court.

in current international law is not configured around links of connections founded on particular state interests, as shown by article 23.4 LOPJ [. . .]'.[47]

The *Couso* case[48] deals with the exercise of universal jurisdiction by Spanish courts over crimes of war committed during the Iraq war. The Spanish Supreme Court declared that the Fourth Geneva Convention and Article 23.4 of the LOPJ granted universal jurisdiction to Spanish courts, meaning that under the terms of international law the crime is permitted to be prosecuted in Spain on the basis of Article 23.4 of the LOPJ. However, the Spanish Supreme Court denied absolute universal jurisdiction as it defended the need for connection with Spanish interests.

In *Empagran*[49] the US Supreme Court referred to the customary international law principle of non-intervention when applying US antitrust laws to foreign anti-competitive conduct and gave a restrictive interpretation to its Sherman Antitrust Act.

Alcoa[50] introduced the 'effects doctrine' in antitrust matters: 'Pursuant to this doctrine, which is a variation on the objective territoriality principle, States have jurisdiction over anticompetitive conduct that produces adverse effects within their territory.'[51] By reaching this conclusion, the US court interpreted its statutory laws in line with international law.

In *Bouzari and ors v Iran*,[52] the Canadian court referred to consistent interpretation when stating that domestic law should be interpreted, as far as possible, consistently with conventional and customary international law.

IV. Avoidance

Domestic courts have devised a variety of avoidance techniques, which allow them to escape the implications of constitutional requirements to apply international legal provisions. These include the doctrine of non-justiciability (wherein one might include the political question doctrine) and the act-of-state doctrine. Also denials of standing, and the doctrine of non-self-execution of treaties (discussed above) can be seen as belonging to this category. The following case is the most famous act-of-state doctrine case, which provides that '[e]very sovereign state is bound to respect the independence of every other sovereign state, and the courts of one country will not sit in judgment on the acts of the government of another done within its own territory'.[53]

Banco Nacional de Cuba v Sabbatino and Farr, Whitlock & Company, Decision of Supreme Court on the Grant of Certiorari, No 16, 376 US 398 (1964), 11 L.Ed.2d 804 (1964), 84 S.Ct. 923 (1964), ILDC 391 (US 1964), 23rd March 1964, United States; Supreme Court [US]

> 23 The classic American statement of the act of state doctrine, which appears to have taken root in England as early as 1674, Blad v. Bamfield, 3 Swans. 604, 36 Eng. Rep. 992, and began to emerge in the jurisprudence of this country in the late eighteenth and early nineteenth centuries [. . .] is found in Underhill v. Hernandez, 168 U.S. 250, where Chief Justice Fuller said for a unanimous Court (p. 252):
>
> > "Every sovereign State is bound to respect the independence of every other sovereign State, and the courts of one country will not sit in judgment on the acts of

47 ibid, para 9.

48 *Jiménez Sánchez and ors v Gibson and ors*, Appeal judgment, Case No 1240/2006, ILDC 993 (ES 2006), 11 December 2006, Spain; Supreme Court.

49 *F Hoffmann-La Roche Ltd et al v Empagran SA et al*, 124 S Ct 2359 (2004).

50 *United States v Aluminium Corp of America*, 148 F 2d 416 (2d Cir 1945) (Alcoa).

51 See C Ryngaert, H van der Wilt, and J Santos Vara, 'Jurisdiction' Chapter 3 in this volume.

52 Canada, Ontario Court of Appeal, *Bouzari and ors v Iran*, 30 June 2004, ILDC 175 (CA 2004).

53 *Banco Nacional de Cuba v Sabbatino and Farr, Whitlock & Company*, Decision of Supreme Court on the Grant of Certiorari, No 16, 376 US 398 (1964), 11 L Ed 2d 804 (1964), 84 S Ct 923 (1964), ILDC 391 (US 1964), 23 March 1964, United States; Supreme Court [US], para 416.

the government of another done within its own territory. Redress of grievances by reason of such acts must be obtained through the means open to be availed of by sovereign powers as between themselves." [. . .]

29 Preliminarily, we discuss the foundations on which we deem the act of state doctrine to rest, and more particularly the question of whether state or federal law governs its application in a federal diversity case.

30 We do not believe that this doctrine is compelled either by the inherent nature of sovereign authority, as some of the earlier decisions seem to imply, see Underhill, supra; American Banana, supra; Oetjen, supra, at 303, or by some principle of international law. If a transaction takes place in one jurisdiction and the forum is in another, the forum does not by dismissing an action or by applying its own law purport to divest the first jurisdiction of its territorial sovereignty; it merely declines to adjudicate or makes applicable its own law to parties or property before it. The refusal of one country to enforce the penal laws of another (supra, pp. 413–414) is a typical example of an instance when a court will not entertain a cause of action arising in another jurisdiction. While historic notions of sovereign authority do bear upon the wisdom of employing the act of state doctrine, they do not dictate its existence.

31 That international law does not require application of the doctrine is evidenced by the practice of nations. Most of the countries rendering decisions on the subject fail to follow the rule rigidly. No international arbitral or judicial decision discovered suggests that international law prescribes recognition of sovereign acts of foreign governments, see 1 Oppenheim's International Law, 115aa (Lauterpacht, 8th ed. 1955) and apparently no claim has ever been raised before an international tribunal that failure to apply the act of state doctrine constitutes a breach of international obligation. If international law does not prescribe use of the doctrine, neither does it forbid application of the rule even if it is claimed that the act of state in question violated international law. The traditional view of international law is that it establishes substantive principles for determining whether one country has wronged another. Because of its peculiar nation-to-nation character the usual method for an individual to seek relief is to exhaust local remedies and then repair to the executive authorities of his own state to persuade them to champion his claim in diplomacy or before an international tribunal. See United States v. Diekelman, 92 U.S. 520, 524. Although it is, of course, true that United States courts apply international law as a part of our own in appropriate circumstances, Ware v. Hylton, 3 Dall. 199, 281; The Nereide, 9 Cranch 388, 423; The Paquete Habana, 175 U.S. 677, 700, the public law of nations can hardly dictate to a country which is in theory wronged how to treat that wrong within its domestic borders.

32 Despite the broad statement in Oetjen that "The conduct of the foreign relations of our Government is committed by the Constitution to the Executive and Legislative [. . .] Departments," 246 U.S., at 302, it cannot of course be thought that "every case or controversy which touches foreign relations lies beyond judicial cognizance." Baker v. Carr, 369 U.S. 186, 211. The text of the Constitution does not require the act of state doctrine; it does not irrevocably remove from the judiciary the capacity to review the validity of foreign acts of state.

33 The act of state doctrine does, however, have "constitutional" underpinnings. It arises out of the basic relationships between branches of government in a system of separation of powers. It concerns the competency of dissimilar institutions to make and implement particular kinds of decisions in the area of international relations. The doctrine as formulated in past decisions expresses the strong sense of the Judicial

> Branch that its engagement in the task of passing on the validity of foreign acts of state may hinder rather than further this country's pursuit of goals both for itself and for the community of nations as a whole in the international sphere. Many commentators disagree with this view; they have striven by means of distinguishing and limiting past decisions and by advancing various considerations of policy to stimulate a narrowing of the apparent scope of the rule. Whatever considerations are thought to predominate, it is plain that the problems involved are uniquely federal in nature. If federal authority, in this instance this Court, orders the filed of judicial competence in this area for the federal courts, and the state courts are left free to formulate their own rules, the purposes behind the doctrine could be as effectively undermined as if there had been no federal pronouncement on the subject. [...]
>
> 38 If the act of state doctrine is a principle of decision binding on federal and state courts alike but compelled by neither international law nor the Constitution, its continuing vitality depends on its capacity to reflect the proper distribution of functions between the judicial and political branches of the Government on matters bearing upon foreign affairs. It should be apparent that the greater the degree of codification or consensus concerning a particular area of international law, the more appropriate it is for the judiciary to render decisions regarding it, since the courts can then focus on the application of an agreed principle to circumstances of fact rather than on the sensitive task of establishing a principle not inconsistent with the national interest or with international justice. It is also evident that some aspects of international law touch much more sharply on national nerves than do others; the less important the implications of an issue are for our foreign relations, the weaker the justification for exclusivity in the political branches. The balance of relevant considerations may also be shifted if the government which perpetrated the challenged act of state is no longer in existence, as in the Bernstein case, for the political interest of this country may, as a result, be measurably altered. Therefore, rather than laying down or reaffirming an inflexible and all-encompassing rule in this case, we decide only that the Judicial Branch will not examine the validity of a taking of property within its own territory by a foreign sovereign government, extant and recognized by this country at the time of suit, in the absence of a treaty or other unambiguous agreement regarding controlling legal principles, even if the complaint alleges that the taking violates customary international law.

A different type of avoidance strategy is found in the example below from the Netherlands, based on considerations of separation of powers. The Supreme Court found that the claims of the Association of Lawyers for Peace and the other organizations were related to questions concerning the policy of the state in matters of foreign affairs and defence. This policy will strongly depend on political considerations connected to the context of the case. It was not up to the civil courts to weigh these political considerations and to prohibit the state at the request of a citizen from carrying out certain acts in performance of political decisions in matters of foreign affairs or defence or to order a particular conduct in such matters.[54]

Association of Lawyers for Peace (Vereniging van Juristen voor de Vrede) and ors v Netherlands, Judgment on Appeal in Cassation, C02/217HR, LJN: AN8071, NJ 2004/329, ILDC 152 (NL 2004), 6th February 2004, Netherlands; Supreme Court [HR]

The Association of Lawyers for Peace and four other organizations requested the Supreme Court to prohibit the state, by way of injunctive relief, to cooperate or engage in the threat or actual

---

54 J Fleuren, *Association of Lawyers for Peace (Vereniging van Juristen voor de Vrede) and ors v Netherlands*, Judgment on Appeal in Cassation, C02/217HR, LJN: AN8071, NJ 2004/329, ILDC 152 (NL 2004), 6 February 2004, Netherlands; Supreme Court [HR], H3.

use of military force by the US or its allies against persons the US associated with the attacks of 9/11, so long as the UN Security Council had not ordered the use of force.

> 3.4 Article 2(4) of the Charter of the United Nations includes a provision requiring all Members to refrain from the threat or use of force against the territorial integrity or political independence of any State. This prohibition on the use of force is therefore intended to protect States and a citizen cannot invoke this provision, or the closely related provisions in Articles 42 and 51 of the Charter, before his national courts.
>
> Article 90 of the Constitution does not lead to a different opinion. Although this article directs the government to promote the international legal order, neither this article nor any other article determines how this should be done. The Supreme Court observes in this connection that the present claims of the Association and Others relate to questions concerning the policy of the State in matters of foreign affairs and defence, and that such policy depends to a large extent on political considerations in connection with the circumstances of the case. It is not up to the civil courts to make these political decisions, even as regards the prohibition on the use of force, or to prohibit the State at the request of a citizen from carrying out certain acts in performance of political decisions in the field of foreign policy or defence or to order it to follow a particular course of action in this field.

In the Israeli case below, petitioners had requested the Israeli Defence Forces not to replace and bury the bodies of casualties of fighting in the occupied territories. Although only as a final remark, the Israeli High Court noted that '[c]learly this Court will take no position regarding the manner in which combat is being conducted. As long as soldiers' lives are in danger, these decisions will be made by the commanders'.[55]

Barake v Minister of Defence of Israel and ors, Original petition to the high court of justice, HCJ 3114/02, ILDC 369 (IL 2002), 14th April 2002, Israel; Supreme Court; Supreme Court as High Court of Justice

> 12. It is good that the parties to these petitions have reached an understanding. This understanding is desirable. It respects the living and the dead. It avoids rumors. Of course, the law applies always and immediately. Respondents informed us that, in all their activities, the military authorities are advised by the Chief Military Attorney. This is how it should be. Even in a time of combat, the laws of war must be followed. Even in a time of combat, all must be done in order to protect the civilian population. *See* HCJ 2901/02 [1]; HCJ 2936/02 [2]; HCJ 2977/02 [3]; and HCJ 3022/02 [4]. Clearly this Court will take no position regarding the manner in which combat is being conducted. As long as soldiers' lives are in danger, these decisions will be made by the commanders. In the case before us, it was not claimed that the arrangement at which we arrived endangered the lives of soldiers. Nor was it claimed that the temporary order endangered the lives of soldiers. On the contrary; the arrangement at which we arrived is an arrangement in which all are interested.

Presidency of the Council of Ministers v Markovic and ors, Application for preliminary order on jurisdiction, 8157, 85 Rivista di diritto internazionale 799 (2002), ILDC 293 (IT 2002), 8th February 2002, Italy; Supreme Court of Cassation

Relatives of victims of NATO bombardments in Belgrade brought a civil claim before the Tribunal of Rome seeking compensation from the Italian Government. The Court of Cassation found that the choice of methods of warfare was to be regarded as an 'act of government', which

55 *Barake v Minister of Defence of Israel and ors*, Original petition to the High Court of Justice, HCJ 3114/02, ILDC 369 (IL 2002), 14 April 2002, Israel; Supreme Court; Supreme Court as High Court of Justice, para 12.

in turn was the manifestation of a political function. Similar acts were, by their very nature, non-justiciable. With respect to 'acts of government', no judicial review was admissible.

2. — The application holds the Italian State responsible for an event resulting from an act of war, in particular the method of conducting hostilities of aerial combat.

The choice of a means of conducting hostilities is an act of Government.

These are acts that constitute the manifestation of a political function with regard to which the Constitution requires attribution to a constitutional body: an act which by its nature is not such that a situation of protected interests can arise in respect thereof, whereupon the actions in which it is manifested assume or do not assume a particular content — Joined Divisions 12 July 1968 No. 2452; 17 October 1980 No. 5583; 8 January 1993 No. 124.

With regard to actions of this type, no court has the power to sanction the method by which the action has been put into effect.

2

Statehood and Recognition

ARISTOTELES CONSTANTINIDES

I. Introduction

International law lays down the factual criteria for statehood, that is, the conditions that must be fulfilled for an entity to qualify as a state and exist as a person in international law. Once an entity attains statehood, it possesses all the capacities of an international legal person, the entire range of powers and responsibilities on the international plane, including rights and obligations under international law. It is therefore paramount to ascertain when a territorial entity qualifies as a state.

The most common starting point for discussing the criteria for statehood is Article 1 of the 1933 Inter-American (Montevideo) Convention on the Rights and Duties of States which requires: (a) permanent population, (b) defined territory, (c) government, and (d) capacity to enter into relations with other states.[1] The Montevideo formula was 'a child of its time' and did not reflect the self-determination, democracy, and legitimacy concerns that characterized relevant debates later in the twentieth century.[2] Despite its wide acceptance in the practice of states (far beyond its sixteen parties),[3] it has come under scholarly criticism, especially the fourth element ('capacity to enter into relations with other states').[4] Many scholars do not include that condition among the elements of statehood,[5] considering such capacity to be a consequence, not a condition, of statehood,[6] or holding that the essence of that capacity is independence.[7] Indeed, there is no doubt that the entity exercising control over territory and population should be sovereign and enjoy (formal) independence, in the sense that it is not in law dependent on or under the sovereign authority of another state.[8]

The controversies surrounding statehood are exemplified in those contested cases of effective entities that aspire to statehood but whose claim is recognized by none, one, a few or many states and/or international organizations (eg Abkhazia, Kosovo, Palestine, Puntland, Saharan Arab Democratic Republic, Somaliland, South Ossetia, Taiwan, Turkish Republic of Northern Cyprus, etc). The reasons for their non-recognition may vary, but it is widely accepted today—albeit not without controversy—that statehood (and recognition) is denied to effective entities meeting the factual/effectiveness criteria of statehood but having emerged in breach of peremptory norms of international law.[9]

---

1 (1933) 49 Stat 3097, TS 881, 165 LNTS 19, 3 Bevans 145.

2 V Lowe, *International Law* (OUP 2007) 153.

3 See ILA Committee on Recognition/Non-recognition in International Law, 'First Report' in *ILA Report of the Seventy-Fifth Conference held in Sofia* (ILA 2012) 170–71.

4 See, eg, T D Grant, 'Defining Statehood: The Montevideo Convention and its Discontents' (1998) 37 *Columbia Journal of Transnational Law* 403.

5 See, eg, R Jennings and A Watts (eds), *Oppenheim's International Law* Vol I (9th edn, Longman 1992) 120–23.

6 J Crawford, *The Creation of States in International Law* (2nd edn, OUP 2006) 61.

7 M N Shaw, *International Law* (7th edn, CUP 2014) 147.

8 Crawford (n 6) 62ff; Jennings and Watts (n 5) 122.

9 Crawford (n 6) 148; J Dugard, *Recognition and the United Nations* (CUP 1987) 131; E Milano, *Unlawful Territorial Situations in International Law* (Martinus Nijhoff 2006) 64; R Portman, *Legal Personality in International Law* (CUP 2010) 252–53; T Christakis, 'L'obligation de non-reconnaissance des situations créées par le recours illicite à la force ou d'autres actes enfreignant des règles fondamentales' in C Tomuschat and

As to recognition, there are two theories on its relevance for statehood. The constitutive theory holds that recognition is a precondition of statehood; states become international persons through recognition by other states. On the other hand, the declaratory theory maintains that a territorial entity is a state by fulfilling the criteria for statehood regardless of recognition, which is a political act falling within the discretion of states. Neither theory in its strong form satisfactorily explains modern practice,[10] but it is common ground that the declaratory theory enjoys wider support, especially in academic writings.[11] In any case, recognition maintains an important role in providing strong evidence that the statehood criteria have been met and in making the state effective outside its own borders.[12]

In addition to states, recognition has traditionally also been conferred to governments. This practice was in decline in the past decades but has recently resurged, as evidenced during the conflicts in Libya and Syria.

Questions of statehood and recognition are for the most part a matter for diplomatic intercourse. They are also, albeit less frequently, dealt with by international judicial and other bodies. When they arise before domestic courts, they often involve determinations by the Executive. In many states, particularly common law jurisdictions, courts have developed doctrines of judicial deference to the Executive and avoid making their own determinations.

The first section of this chapter deals with cases concerning the contested statehood of various territorial entities. The second section focuses on questions of (non-)recognition of states and governments and the third section surveys cases involving interrelated questions of secession, legitimacy, occupation/annexation, and state continuity.

II. Statehood Criteria

Duchy of Sealand, Re, A German citizen by birth, First instance, Case no 9 K 2565/77, (1978) Deutsches Verwaltungsblatt 510, (1989) 80 ILR 683, ILDC 2119 (DE 1978), 3rd May 1978, Germany; North Rhine-Westphalia; Cologne; Administrative Court [VG]

This case concerned the citizenship of the so-called 'Duchy of Sealand', a self-proclaimed 'state' established in 1967 on an abandoned anti-aircraft platform, which was attached by concrete pillars to the seabed eight nautical miles off the southern coast of England. The 'Duchy' was permanently inhabited by thirty to forty persons and had started to issue passports. The plaintiff sought a declaration that acquisition of the Duchy's citizenship had resulted in loss of his German citizenship. His action was dismissed on the ground that the 'Duchy of Sealand' did not constitute a state and he had therefore not acquired foreign nationality.

> 15 International law lays down three essential attributes for Statehood. The State must have a territory, that territory must be inhabited by a people and that people must be subject to the authority of a Government [. . .].
>
> 16 The 'Duchy of Sealand' fails to satisfy even the first condition as it does not possess a State territory within the meaning of international law.

J M Thouvenin (eds), *The Fundamental Rules of the International Legal Order: Jus Cogens and Obligations Erga Omnes* (Martinus Nijhoff 2005) 127–66. *Contra* J Verhoeven, *La reconnaissance internationale dans la pratique contemporaine: les relations publiques internationales* (Pedone 1975) 607–17; A Tancredi, 'A Normative "Due Process" in the Creation of States through Secession' in M Kohen (ed), *Secession: International Law Perspectives* (CUP 2006) 171, 198.

10 Crawford (n 6) 5; T Grant, *The Recognition of States: Law and Practice in Debate and Evolution* (Praeger 1999) 19.

11 B Roth, *Governmental Illegitimacy in International Law* (OUP 1999) 126; J van der Vyver, 'Statehood in International Law' (1991) 5 *Emory International Law Review* 9, 12.

12 Shaw (n 7) 150; Milano (n 9) 63.

> 17 The former anti-aircraft platform is not situated on any fixed point of the surface of the earth. [...]
>
> 18 [...] [O]nly those parts of the surface of the earth which have come into existence in a natural way can be recognized as constituting State territory. A man-made artificial platform, such as the so-called "Duchy of Sealand", cannot be called either "a part of the earth's surface" or "land territory" because it does not constitute a segment of the earth's sphere. [...]
>
> 24 [...] The formation of land by the erection of dykes or dams and similar structures on the sea-shore or in coastal waters is not comparable to the construction of artificial islands such as 'Sealand'. The positioning of dykes results in the enlargement of existing State territory by the acquisition of a new piece of the surface of the earth directly adjacent to existing State territory, which assumes the same status as that territory. By contrast, the artificial island of 'Sealand' did not involve the creation of any new piece of the earth's surface.
>
> 25 In addition to the lack of State territory, the so-called 'Duchy' also lacks a State people within the meaning of international law. At present the 'Duchy' has 106 'citizens'. [...] [T]he size of a people is irrelevant to the question of whether or not it constitutes a State [...]. Nevertheless, in the case of the 'Duchy of Sealand' it cannot be accepted that there is a 'people' within the meaning of international law since the life of a community is lacking.
>
> 26 The State, as an amalgamation of many individuals, complements the family, which consists of only a few members, and has the duty to promote community life. This duty does not merely consist of the promotion of a loose association aimed at the furtherance of common hobbies and interests. Rather it must be aimed at the maintenance of an essentially permanent form of communal life in the sense of sharing a common destiny [...].
>
> 27 The so-called 'nationals' of the 'Duchy of Sealand' do not satisfy these criteria for community life. Apart from the 30 to 40 persons permanently living on the platform, who are responsible for its defence and the maintenance of its installations, the presence of the other so-called 'nationals' is limited to occasional visits. [...] [A] State community must play a more decisive role in serving the other vital human needs of people from their birth to their death. These needs include education and professional training, assistance in all the eventualities of life and the provision of subsistence allowances where necessary. The so-called 'Duchy of Sealand' fails to satisfy any of these requirements.
>
> 28 Regardless of the material prerequisites which an entity must have in order to constitute a 'people' under international law, the 'nationals' of the 'Duchy' themselves fail to satisfy an essential condition for their classification as a people. These 'nationals' have not acquired their 'nationality' in order to live with one another and handle all aspects of their lives on a collective basis, but on the contrary they continue to pursue their individual interests outside the 'Duchy'. The common purpose of their association is limited to a small part of their lives, namely their commercial and tax affairs. This degree of common interest cannot be regarded as sufficient for the recognition of a 'people' within the meaning of international law.

The decision in this unusual case relied on German publicists for identifying three essential attributes of statehood, thus ignoring the controversial fourth one listed in the Montevideo Convention ('capacity to enter into relations with other states'). As noted by the ILDC reporter, this omission was consistent with German state practice.[13] In any case, this would have played

---

13 P Staubach, Analysis, *Duchy of Sealand, Re, A German citizen by birth*, ILDC 2119 (DE 1978) A1.

no role in deciding the case, since the court's analysis of the criteria of territory and people were sufficient to deny the 'Duchy of Sealand' any claim to statehood.

East Timor and ors v Netherlands, Decision on admissibility, ILDC 2118 (NL 1980), (1992) 87 ILR 73, 21st February 1980, Netherlands; The Hague; District Court

The Democratic Republic of East Timor (DRET) and the Revolutionary Front for an Independent East Timor (Fretilin) brought a claim against the Netherlands concerning the export of two corvettes to Indonesia in August 1975. The claim was brought a few years after Indonesia had invaded and annexed East Timor. The Netherlands challenged the *locus standi* of the plaintiffs, arguing that the DRET did not exist as a state and that the Fretilin Liberation Movement had no legal personality.

> H1 The question as to whether the Democratic Republic of East Timor could be considered an independent state had to be answered on the basis of the law as it stood at the time of the institution of proceedings before the Court, and more specifically on the basis of the factual criteria for statehood prevailing in international law. (paragraph 3)
>
> H2 It was not decisive that the Netherlands, as with almost the entire international community, had not recognized the Democratic Republic of East Timor as a state. However, the lack of recognition of statehood by the majority of the international community did create a presumption that the requirements for statehood had not been fulfilled. (paragraphs 3 and 4)
>
> H3 In order to qualify as a state, a mere proclamation of independence was not sufficient. (paragraph 4)
>
> H4 Both Fretilin and the Netherlands appeared to proceed from the assumption that at the time of the institution of proceedings the territory of East Timor was entirely under the control of the Indonesian government, with the possible exception of certain actions by groups of Fretilin supporters, and that the pretender state (ie the Democratic Republic of East Timor) did not exercise effective and stable authority. (paragraph 6)
>
> H5 In *NV Koninklijke Paketvaartmij v Republic of South Maluku, Judgment on appeal, Amsterdam Court of Appeal, 8 February 1951 ('Republic of South Maluku')* the statehood of the Republic of South Maluku was accepted by the Court, even though it could have been anticipated that the authority of that state would not be maintained in the long run. However, Fretilin could not rely on this ruling because the Republic of South Maluku had fulfilled the requirements of statehood, notably stability and effective control, at the time of the outset of the proceedings. (paragraph 8)
>
> H6 The Democratic Republic of East Timor did not fulfil the requirements for statehood at the time of the summons, nor at the time of this judgment. The claim was therefore inadmissible. (paragraph 7)

Fretilin's claim was apparently premised on the assumption that DRET had achieved statehood upon its declaration of independence on 28 November 1975 and had retained statehood, notwithstanding Indonesia's invasion of the territory on 7 December 1975 and its subsequent occupation and annexation, which was ongoing at the time of the proceedings. Indeed, it is an established rule of international law that belligerent occupation does not affect the continuity of a state.[14] Permanence is also not an indispensable attribute of statehood but may be highly relevant when fulfilment of the statehood criteria is uncertain; states may have brief existence, provided of course that they have an effective independent government.[15] Fretilin's claim to DRET's

14 Crawford (n 6) 688.

15 ibid, 90–91.

ten-day statehood would have been more fully answered if that aspect had also been addressed in view of Portugal's partial (but not yet complete) withdrawal from East Timor earlier in 1975 and the domestic unrest and opposition to Fretilin during its short-lived authority. Against this background, it is doubtful whether the effective authority criterion and/or that of formal/legal independence were met. Indeed, shortly after Indonesia's invasion, both the General Assembly and the Security Council reaffirmed the status of East Timor as a non-self-governing territory and continued to consider Portugal as the administering Power until the late 1990s, when the Indonesian troops withdrew and East Timor came under UN administration before achieving statehood in 2002.

The court summarily dismissed the claim to statehood based solely on Fretilin's declaration of independence and focused its assessment on the situation at the time of the proceedings, when it was obvious that Fretilin was lacking effectiveness due to Indonesia's on-going occupation of East Timor. The decision also followed the declaratory approach and regarded the non-recognition of DRET as indicative and not decisive of its claim to statehood. Interestingly as well, as noted by the ILDC reporters, there was no reference to the Montevideo Convention.[16]

Morgan Guaranty Trust Company of New York and ors v Palau, Appeal judgment, Docket No 89-7096, Case No 1427, ILDC 2011 (US 1991), 924 F 2d 1237 (2d Cir 1991), 4th February 1991, United States; Court of Appeals (2nd Circuit) [2d Cir]

Palau is a Pacific island state that used to be part of the US Trust Territory of the Pacific Islands. Since 1981 Palau has enjoyed substantial self-government and, following a series of inconclusive plebiscites, it ultimately ratified a Compact of Free Association with the US in 1986, marking its *de jure* independence in 1994. When the plaintiff banks claimed US$35 million under a loan agreement concluded with Palau in 1983, Palau pleaded sovereign immunity. In 1986, the District Court for Southern New York (at a moment when, admittedly, Palau's independence appeared imminent) held that Palau had *de facto* sovereignty and was a foreign state within the meaning of the US Foreign Sovereign Immunity Act (FSIA) but was not protected by sovereign immunity in that particular instance. Palau appealed.

> 36 [. . .] Under international law, a state is said to be an entity possessed of a defined territory and a permanent population, controlled by its own government, and engaged in or capable of engaging in relations with other such entities. Restatement (Third) of the Foreign Relations Law of the United States § 201 (1987) ('Restatement 3d') [. . .]
>
> 37 According to international law, a sovereign state has certain well accepted capacities, rights and duties:
>
> (a) sovereignty over its territory and general authority over its nationals;
>
> (b) status as a legal person, with capacity to own, acquire, and transfer property, to make contracts and enter into international agreements, to become a member of international organizations, and to pursue, and be subject to, legal remedies;
>
> (c) capacity to join with other states to make international law, as customary law or by international agreement. [Restatement 3d § 206] [. . .]
>
> 42 Palau simply does not have the attributes of statehood, and cannot be considered a foreign sovereign. [. . .] The Trusteeship Agreement, of course, confers upon the United States 'full power of administration, legislation and jurisdiction over the territory,' as well as the right to apply 'such of the laws of the United States as it may deem appropriate.' A more wide-ranging authority to govern is hard to imagine. The United States exercised that authority at the time of the transactions giving rise to this action, and continues to exercise it. [. . .]

16 C Brölmann and M Ooms, Analysis, *East Timor and ors v Netherlands*, ILDC 2118 (NL 1980) A4.

43 [Palau] is the sole remaining part of the Pacific Trust Territory remaining under the trusteeship. It seems clear that Palau must continue as a trust territory until the United Nations Security Council acts to relieve the United States of its responsibilities under the trust [...]. [...]

46 [...] It seems to us that a political entity whose laws may be suspended by another cannot be said to be possessed of sovereignty of any kind, de facto or de jure. That is the case with respect to the United States and Palau. Moreover, the Palauan courts are not independent of the United States. The Justices of the High Court of Palau are appointed by the Secretary of the Interior, and the court is constrained to apply the law of the United States in effect in the territory, including the executive orders of the Secretary of the Interior. [...] This, too, is inconsistent with the concept of sovereignty. [...] The reality is that the United States has ultimate authority over the governance of Palau, [...] and it therefore cannot be said that Palau is an entity 'under the control of its own government,' Restatement 3d § 201. Neither can it be said to be sovereign over its own territory, with general authority over its nationals in the manner contemplated by *Restatement 3d* § 206(a). [...]

48 [...] Although it is true that Palau has entered into some fisheries and marine resources treaties and has sent representatives to international conferences, it has done so with the approval of the United States, at whose sufferance it conducts foreign relations under the provisions of the Palauan Constitution. Palauan laws and treaties may not be inconsistent with United States treaties or international agreements, and this has been the case during the entire period of trusteeship. [...] Under the present Executive Order, even communications with foreign governments by the Republic of Palau must follow consultation with, and approval by, the Department of State. The power to maintain diplomatic ties with other sovereigns and to make international agreements and treaties, [...] and the capacity to join with other states to make international law, Restatement 3d§ 206(c), are rights of sovereignty not possessed by Palau. [...]

53 Our conclusion in this case well may have been different had the Compact of Free Association been fully approved by the parties to the Compact. Such approval would have marked the entry of Palau into the final stage of its transition to self-government and would have signalled the certain and unavoidable termination of the Trusteeship. [...] Subject to the control of its internal and external affairs by the United States, deficient in all the major attributes of statehood, its Compact of Free Association remaining unapproved after seven plebiscites, the Republic of Palau concedes its lack of sovereignty. We are constrained to agree.

The Court of Appeals relied on the Restatement (Third) of Foreign Relations Law and stressed the numerous factors that pointed to Palau's lack of independence at the material time, when Palau was still a Trust territory. The court made a proper assessment of the statehood criteria and considered that independence was among the essential components of a sovereign state. This was crucial in dismissing Palau's claim to *de facto* sovereignty, which was admittedly short of the FSIA requirement of *de jure* statehood.

The proper meaning of independence in relation to so-called 'micro-states' (or 'mini-states') had been debated for some time before their admission to the UN,[17] since some of them emerged under some form of legal dependence from their former colonial powers.[18] This was

17 Liechtenstein was admitted in 1990, Micronesia and Marshall Islands in 1991, San Marino in 1992, Andorra and Monaco in 1993, Kiribati, Nauru, and Tonga in 1999, and Tuvalu in 2000.

18 T Grant, 'States Newly Admitted to the United Nations: Some Implications' (2000) 39 *Columbia Journal of Transnational Law* 177, 182.

also the case with Palau; its formal independence in 1994 was coupled with a Compact of Free Association with the US, which deprived Palau, as an 'associated state', of the final say in several important issues. That said, it is well accepted that such a state of affairs does not necessarily affect statehood unless foreign control 'overbear[s] the decision-making of the entity concerned on a wide range of matters of high policy and doing so systematically and on a permanent basis'.[19]

Kadić and ors v Karadžić (Radovan), Appeal judgment, Docket No 94-9035, Docket No 94-9069, Case No 1541, Case No 1544, ILDC 814 (US 1995), 70 F 3d 232 (2d Cir 1995), 64 USLW 2231 (1995), (1997) 104 ILR 135, 13th October 1995, United States; Court of Appeals (2nd Circuit) [2d Cir]

This case involved an ATS suit for genocide and other international humanitarian law violations against Radovan Karadžić, the leader of Srpska, the self-proclaimed (and unrecognized) state of the Bosnian Serbs within Bosnia and Herzegovina during the country's civil war. Karadžić was served with process outside the UN headquarters in New York while visiting the US upon UN invitation in early 1993. Some of the issues raised in the case revolved around whether Karadžić had acted as a private individual or a state official. The District Court of Manhattan for the state of New York had found that the alleged violations required state action and that the 'Bosnian-Serb entity' headed by Karadžić did not meet the definition of a state. Upon appeal, appellants contended that Srpska satisfied the definition of a state.

> 36 (a) Definition of a state in international law. The definition of a state is well established in international law: Under international law, a state is an entity that has a defined territory and a permanent population, under the control of its own government, and that engages in, or has the capacity to engage in, formal relations with other such entities. [Restatement (Third) § 201] [. . .]
>
> 38 Although the Restatement's definition of statehood requires the capacity to engage in formal relations with other states, it does not require recognition by other states. [. . .] Recognized states enjoy certain privileges and immunities relevant to judicial proceedings, [. . .] but an unrecognized state is not a juridical nullity. Our courts have regularly given effect to the "state" action of unrecognized states. [. . .]
>
> 39 The customary international law of human rights, such as the proscription of official torture, applies to states without distinction between recognized and unrecognized states. See Restatement (Third) §§ 207, 702. It would be anomalous indeed if non-recognition by the United States, which typically reflects disfavor with a foreign regime—sometimes due to human rights abuses—had the perverse effect of shielding officials of the unrecognized regime from liability for those violations of international law norms that apply only to state actors.
>
> 40 Appellants' allegations entitle them to prove that Karadzic's regime satisfies the criteria for a state, for purposes of those international law violations requiring state action. Srpska is alleged to control defined territory, control populations within its power, and to have entered into agreements with other governments. It has a president, a legislature, and its own currency. These circumstances readily appear to satisfy the criteria for a state in all aspects of international law. Moreover, it is likely that the state action concept, where applicable for some violations like "official" torture, requires merely the semblance of official authority. The inquiry, after all, is whether a person purporting to wield official power has exceeded internationally recognized standards of civilized conduct, not whether statehood in all its formal aspects exists.

19 I Brownlie, *Principles of Public International Law* (7th edn, OUP 2008) 72. See also Crawford (n 6) 492.

The court's conclusion that Srpska satisfied the statehood criteria was hasty and apparently driven by its quest to overcome the state/official action concept and hold Karadžić liable. On the other hand, the court's reliance on the Restatement's declaratory approach to recognition was in line with the prevailing view in international law.

Knox and ors v Palestinian Liberation Organization and ors, Trial judgment, No 03 Civ 4466, ILDC 1984 (US 2004), 306 F Supp 2d 424 (SDNY 2004), 1st March 2004, United States; New York; District Court for the Southern District of New York [SDNY]

The plaintiffs were US victims of a terrorist attack in Israel in 2002. They sued the defendants under the US Anti-Terrorism Act, alleging that the Palestinian Liberation Organization (PLO) and the Palestinian Authority (PA) were implicated in the attacks by instructing or materially supporting the attacker. The PLO and the PA claimed sovereign immunity, arguing that Palestine was a state.

> 27 […] "[A] state is an entity that has [1] a defined territory and a [2] permanent population, [3] under the control of its own government, and that [4] engages in, or has the capacity to engage in, formal relations with other such entities." Restatement (Third) § 201. The PLO and PA do not meet, nor are they part of any entity which meets, these criteria because, first, the PLO and PA do not sufficiently "control" Palestine and, second, they do not have sufficient capacity to engage in foreign relations.
>
> 28 Defendants argue that, at least since the United Nations called for a partition of British-mandated Palestine, Palestine has had a defined territory. While acknowledging that the borders have occasionally changed and that there is some dispute as to their exact contours, Defendants maintain that it is commonly recognized that Palestine today consists of the West Bank, Gaza Strip, and East Jerusalem. Moreover, Defendants remind the Court of what is an indisputable historical fact: that there has been a permanent population in Palestine for over two millennia.
>
> 29 Plaintiffs' briefing purports to challenge these first two requirements, but their arguments in this regard are, in essence, that neither the PLO nor PA has a defined territory *under its control*, nor a permanent population *under its control*. Accordingly, the Court moves directly to the third prong of the Restatement (Third) definition and addresses whether there is a government in Palestine in control of a defined territory and permanent population.
>
> **4. Control Over Territory And Population**
>
> […]
>
> 32 It is well-accepted under international law that, to meet the governmental control requirement, the entity "must be capable of acting independently of foreign governments." […] In other words, the entity must be "independent from direct orders from other State powers." […]
>
> 34 An examination of the [1995 Interim Agreement on the West Bank and the Gaza Strip] confirms that the Oslo Accords have not created a Palestinian state because the Interim Agreement substantially circumscribes the PA's authority in many spheres of governance. […]
>
> 35 In short, the PA's authority is subordinate to Israel's sovereign control, in many fundamental ways that conflict with and negate a claim of the existence of independent statehood for the Palestinian territory over which the PA exercises the limited governmental power specified in the Oslo Accords. […]
>
> 37 Defendants do not dispute any of these limitations on the PA's control, except to point out that they are the result of Israel's illegal and oppressive occupation. It is true that "belligerent occupation does not affect the continuity of the state." […]

However, the predicate for this principle is that a sovereign entity satisfying all of the prerequisites for statehood existed prior to the occupation. In this case, Defendants have not argued that there was an independent state of Palestine immediately before Israel's allegedly illegal occupation. Under international law, a state will *maintain* its statehood during a belligerent occupation, […] but it would be anomalous indeed to hold that a state may achieve sufficient independence and statehood in the first instance while subject to and laboring under the hostile military occupation of a separate sovereign. In light of the preceding discussion, the Court concludes that neither the PLO nor PA possesses sufficient control over the disputed Palestinian territories to satisfy the "control" criterion of statehood.

5. Capacity To Conduct Foreign Relations

38 "An entity is not a state unless it has competence, within its own constitutional system, to conduct international relations with other states, as well as the political, technical, and financial capabilities to do so." Restatement (Third) § 201 cmt. e. The capacity of a state to engage in foreign relations with other sovereigns depends, in part, "on the entity concerned being separate for the purpose of [international] relations so that no other entity both carries out and accepts responsibility for them." […] Under the Interim Agreement, the PA is expressly prohibited from conducting foreign relations:

In accordance with the [1993 Declaration of Principles on Interim Self-Government Arrangements], the [PA] will not have powers and responsibilities in the sphere of foreign relations, which sphere includes the establishment abroad of embassies, consulates or other types of foreign missions and posts or permitting their establishment in the West Bank or the Gaza Strip, the appointment of or admission of diplomatic and consular staff, and the exercise of diplomatic functions. Interim Agreement, art. IX […]. The Interim Agreement permits the PLO to negotiate and enter into international agreements regarding certain economic development plans, as well as certain cultural, scientific and educational agreements, "for the benefit of" the PA. See Interim Agreement, art. IX(b) […]. However, the Interim Agreement explicitly declares that these limited activities "shall not be considered foreign relations." *Id.* More importantly, the Interim Agreement provides no mechanism by which the PLO could actually implement any international commitments in the spheres of power delegated to the PA. […] Furthermore, neither the PLO nor the PA would be able to implement any international commitments in the spheres of authority which, as discussed above, remain with Israel, such as those relating to external threats, border control, and the movement of persons into the Palestinian territories. For this independent reason, Defendants have failed to carry their burden to demonstrate that the PLO or PA, even in combination, have sufficient capacity to conduct international relations to satisfy that criterion of statehood.

The statehood criteria under the Restatement, which was relied upon by the court, are identical to those of the Montevideo Convention. Hence, the court examined separately the third (Palestine's control over territory and population) and the fourth (Palestine's capacity to conduct foreign relations) criteria. It is not common to find judgments discussing the latter element. Admittedly, the limitations of the PA in the sphere of foreign relations under the Oslo Accords were a good opportunity for applying that test. As pointed out in the introductory note of this Chapter, the relevance of the fourth Montevideo element is seriously questioned by scholars as well as in state practice. In any case, as noted by the ILDC reporter, the court's analysis of the statehood criteria as applied to Palestine was *dicta* because the court held that Palestine's non-recognition by the US was conclusive for the immunity question.[20]

20 R Mayor, Analysis, *Knox and ors v Palestinian Liberation Organization and ors*, ILDC 1984 (US 2004) A1. See below for the court's examination of the question of recognition.

Ungar v Palestine Liberation Organization [PLO] and Palestinian Authority, Appeal Judgment, Docket No 04-2079, 402 F.3d 274 (1st Cir. 2005), ILDC 124 (US 2005), 31st March 2005, United States; Court of Appeals (1st Circuit) [1st Cir]

Yaron and Efrat Ungar, a US couple, were killed by members of the Hamas Islamic Resistance Movement during a terrorist attack in Israel in 1996. The administrator of the Ungar's estates and other plaintiffs filed a suit in the US under the Anti-Terrorism Act, alleging that the PLO and the PA had engaged in international terrorism within the meaning of the Act. The district court denied the PLO and PA's motions to dismiss and ordered a default judgment against them. On appeal, the PLO and the PA claimed sovereign immunity, arguing that Palestine was a state.

> 22 […] The district court had access to judicially manageable standards for resolving the issue before it […] and those standards did not require the court to make nonjudicial policy determinations. Both sides agreed that the definition of a "state" under the relevant statutes was informed by an objective test rooted in international law and articulated in the Restatement (Third) of Foreign Relations. Under these circumstances, the determination of whether the defendants have adduced sufficient evidence to satisfy that definition is quintessentially appropriate for a judicial body. […]
>
> 56 International law defines a state as "an entity that has a defined territory and a permanent population, under the control of its own government, and that engages in, or has the capacity to engage in, formal relations with other such entities." Restatement (Third) of Foreign Relations § 201. This definition derives from the Montevideo Convention of 1933. […] In applying this definition, some courts have subdivided the analysis into four parts, asking whether the putative state (i) has a defined territory and (ii) a permanent population, which (iii) is under the control of its own government, and (iv) has the capacity to engage in foreign relations. […]
>
> 57 In practice, the third element is the most salient factor in the statehood calculus. […] The Restatement's explanation of this element is rather sparse; it notes only that "[a] state need not have any particular form of government, but there must be some authority exercising governmental functions and able to represent the entity in international relations." Restatement (Third) of Foreign Relations § 201 cmt. d. To satisfy these requirements, a state's government must, at a bare minimum, be independent and in general control of its territory, maintaining at least a modicum of law and order. […] Its government must speak for the state as a whole; the mere presence of independent tribes or factions within a territory, lacking common institutions, cannot constitute a government in control. […]
>
> 58 The first, second, and fourth elements are dependent on (or, sometimes, subsumed by) the third. As to the first — defined territory — the "only requirement is that the State must consist of a certain coherent territory effectively governed." […] So too the second element, which typically is satisfied by showing a permanent population within the defined territory. […] The relationships of these elements with the all-important third element is readily evident. As one court put it, the question is essentially whether the entity claiming statehood has a "defined territory *under its control*" and a "permanent population *under its control*." *Knox*, 306 F. Supp. 2d at 434 (emphasis in original).
>
> 59 The fourth element — "capacity to engage in foreign relations" — focuses on "competence, within [a state's] own constitutional system, to conduct international relations with other states, as well as the political, technical, and financial capabilities to do so." Restatement (Third) of Foreign Relations § 201 cmt. e. Again, this is a

function of independence and effective government control. [...] In that sense, then, it too is dependent on the third element.

60 We add that the party who alleges sovereign immunity has the burden of proving that status. [...]

61 The defendants argue that the state of Palestine exists; that they constitute core elements of that state; and that, therefore, they are immune from suit under the FSIA (and, thus, under the ATA). This argument has a quicksilver quality: it is hard to pin down exactly when or how the defendants assert that Palestine achieved statehood. At various points in their briefs, they hint at three possibilities: (i) the period from the beginning of the mandate through the 1967 Arab-Israeli war; (ii) the period from the end of that war up until the creation of the Palestinian Authority (1994); and (iii) the period from 1994 forward. In an abundance of caution, we consider whether the defendants have made a prima facie showing of statehood at any such juncture.

62 [...] [T]he focus shifts to the third prong of the test for statehood. At that stage, the question becomes whether the defendants have shown that the identified territory and population are self-governing. In answering this question, we look separately at each period.

63 **1. The Initial Period.** As to the pre-1967 period, the defendants' argument seems to be that the territory that comprised the Palestinian portion of the mandate was a state prior to, during, and after the mandate. Their support for this thesis is very weak; they assert only that throughout this interval there were local governmental institutions in place that catered to the Palestinian populace.

64 This assertion is manifestly insufficient to make the defendants' prima facie case of statehood. The third element of the test requires governmental independence and control of a defined territory. That element plainly was not satisfied while the defined territory was part of the Ottoman Empire; even if the Palestinian people exercised operating control over domestic governmental functions in the region — and the defendants offer nothing to support such a claim — that would not be sufficient to show the existence of an independent political unit that *controlled* the territory.

65 The same is true for the latter portions of the period. During the currency of the mandate, the United Kingdom exercised suzerainty over the administration and laws of the defined territory. [...] Following the United Kingdom's relinquishment of the mandate and the onset of the 1967 Arab-Israeli war, the Israelis occupied much of the land designated for a future Arab state, and the Egyptians and Jordanians seized the rest. The net result is that, at all times, other states had control over the defined territory.

66 The defendants resist the obvious conclusion. In particular, they rely upon United Nations General Assembly Resolution 181(II), noting that it called for an independent Arab state to come into existence no later than October 1, 1948, and that this became a reality in the sense that "Palestinian government institutions continued to function under Egyptian and Jordanian occupation much as they had under the Mandate." [...] These assertions are insufficient to show that a political unit was in control of the defined territory and populace. The mere fact that the United Nations conceived an aspirational plan for Palestinian statehood does not establish the existence of a state. Nor does the fact that the Egyptians and Jordanians occupied and controlled a significant portion of the defined territory immediately following the end of the mandate aid the defendants' cause. To the contrary, the fact is a stark reminder that no state of Palestine could have come into being at that time. [...]

67 **2. The Middle Period.** The interval following the occupation of the West Bank and the Gaza Strip by Israel in 1967 is no more promising. With respect to this time span, the defendants rely heavily on Security Council Resolution 242 and its hortatory call for Israeli withdrawal from "territories occupied in the recent conflict" and for all states to respect and acknowledge "the sovereignty, territorial integrity and political independence of every State in the area." That reliance is mislaid. There is a vast difference between what should be and what is; the fact that some political leaders recognize that particular territory should comprise a state does not make that territory a state under the prevailing principles of international law.

68 What counts is that the defendants have not presented *any* evidence indicating that Palestine actually became a state following Israel's conquest of the lands previously occupied by Jordan and Egypt. The one circumstance to which the defendants advert — that the Israelis did not dismantle the local governmental institutions in the region — is wholly inadequate to show that there was a Palestinian state underlying the Israeli occupation. The territory went directly from Jordanian/Egyptian control to Israeli control, thus undermining the defendants' statehood argument. [...]

69 To be sure, the defendants point proudly to the U.N.'s 1974 recognition of the PLO. We do not minimize the political significance of that event. The fact remains, however, that neither political recognition of the PLO nor United Nations support for self-governance is sufficient to signify that the Restatement's conditions for statehood have been met. [...]

70 **3. The Most Recent Period.** The defendants' argument for current statehood posits that Palestine's changing status over the last decade marked the emergence of the defined territory from Israeli control and the establishment of a Palestinian government in its place. The PLO's 1988 declaration of independence adumbrated the inception of this period. The period itself commenced, however, in 1994, the signal event being the creation of the PA as an entity having some lawful authority in the West Bank and Gaza. The defendants suggest that this development signified the birth of a government sufficiently in control of the defined territory to satisfy the third element of the Restatement test. We reject the suggestion.

71 Undoubtedly, the agreements to which the defendants allude vested some autonomy in the newly created PA. But the authority so transferred was limited and, during and after that transition, Israel explicitly reserved control over all matters not transferred. [...]. Several of these reserved powers are incompatible with the notion that the PA had independent governmental control over the defined territory. To illustrate, the interim agreement expressly denied the PA the right to conduct foreign relations [...]; left Israel with an undiminished ability to defend and control the territorial borders [...]; denied the PA the right to create or maintain either an army or a navy [...]; retained Israeli control over the territorial airspace [...]; and placed severe restrictions on the PA's lawmaking ability (declaring, inter alia, that any laws passed in contravention of the DOP would be void ab initio) [...]. These restrictions remain in effect. It is, therefore, transparently clear that the PA has not yet exercised sufficient governmental control over Palestine to satisfy the third element of the Restatement test. [...]

72 The defendants do not deny that these limitations are incompatible with statehood, but, rather, contend that they were imposed by force and that the Israeli occupation is all that is preventing the full exercise of the prerogatives of statehood. The problem with this contention is that it presupposes that Palestine was a state *before* the Israeli occupation — and the defendants have not shown that it was. [...]

> 73 We recognize that the status of the Palestinian territories is in many ways sui generis. Here, however, the defendants have not carried their burden of showing that Palestine satisfied the requirements for statehood under the applicable principles of international law at any point in time. In view of the unmistakable legislative command that sovereign immunity shall only be accorded to states — a command reflected in both the FSIA and the ATA — the defendants' sovereign immunity defense must fail.

As observed by the ILDC reporter, unlike in *Knox*, the court did not decide the case based on Palestine's non-recognition by the US because the US government had abandoned the 'recognition test' in the case at hand.[21] The court stressed the 'all-importance' of the control over territory and population requirement, which it conflated with independence, and found that the exercise of authority by the Palestinians in all instances fell short of that requirement. Citing this decision as well as *Knox*, Crawford has concluded that an entity claiming statehood but created during a period of foreign military occupation will be presumed not to be independent.[22] A less stringent test has led others to conclude that Palestine was a state.[23] In the meantime, however, significant progress has been made towards Palestinian state-building under the auspices of various international organizations, which has reinforced the argument that the Palestinian Authority seems to meet—at least by a minimum standard—the criterion of government.[24] In a related development, by resolution 67/19 of 29 November 2012, the UN General Assembly accorded Palestine 'non-member observer state' status in the United Nations.

Basha (Association of the Elon Moreh College) v Israel and ors, Administrative Decision, Case No 4049/02, ILDC 453 (IL 2006), 23rd April 2006, Israel; Jerusalem (disputed); District Court

The issue in this case, decided in the aftermath of Israeli disengagement from Gaza, was whether it was possible to sue the authorities of the Palestinian National Authority (PNA) for failure to enforce Israeli judgments in areas under the PNA's control, as was provided in the 1995 interim agreement between Israel and the PNA. This involved a judgment on whether the PNA enjoyed sovereign immunity, hence the inquiry into the status of the PNA.

> **The status of the "Territories"—from territory held by Israel to territory under quasi-sovereignty**
>
> 5. Area A was never part of the territory of the State of Israel. It was part of territories held by the State of Israel. […] Israel had effective control of the territories. This control was attained by military means. As a result, the powers of the government that had applied to these territories prior to their seizure by Israel were suspended, and the commander of the military forces took over the responsibilities of the previous government […].
>
> 6. […] The area held was not itself part of the territory of the State of Israel and the procedures in that area were outside the jurisdiction of Israeli courts […].
>
> 7. This has been the situation since 1967. This does not amount to grant of rights to Israeli governmental authorities to operate in the territories without express instruction under the internal law of the territories, and a corresponding provision in Israeli law.

21 A McDonnell, Analysis, *Ungar v Palestine Liberation Organization [PLO] and Palestinian Authority*, ILDC 124 (US 2005) A1.

22 Crawford (n 6) 148.

23 For a powerful argumentation in favour of Palestine's statehood see J Quigley, *The Statehood of Palestine* (CUP 2010).

24 T Megiddo and Z Nevo, 'Revisiting Lessons on the New Law of Statehood: Palestinian Independence in a Post-Kosovo World' in D French (ed), *Statehood and Self-Determination: Reconciling Tradition and Modernity in International Law* (CUP 2013) 187, 199.

8. […] [T]he Interim Agreement changed the status of the Palestinian National Authority in Israeli law, by virtue of recognition of its jurisdiction over some of the territories. Recognition of this status carries with it considerable legal significance. In fact, the Palestinian National Authority acquired the status of a quasi-sovereign entity, ruling over part of a political nation, de facto. One of the clear indicators of such is the creation of a Palestinian police force (see section 1 of the Schedule to the Legal Assistance Law). Another indicator is a provision that limits Israeli judicial powers, transferring powers of governance over persons who are not Israeli, even if this is not stated explicitly, to the Palestinian legal authorities (section 2(d) of the Schedule to the Legal Assistance Law).

9. The Palestinian National Authority's status crystallized further when Israel exited the Gaza Strip, leaving governing of the area in the hands of the Palestinian National Authority […]. In fact, the Palestinian National Authority meets the requirements that make up a state, being territory, population and government (or sovereign enforcement on population), albeit in a disjointed and unstable manner. Despite this, the Authority is not recognized by most countries of the world as being a country. But the question of recognition is mainly one of declaratory significance. What is more, international law is concerned more with substance than with form. Therefore, the more indicators of sovereignty the Palestinian National Authority might have, including having particular institutions, international status, territory under exclusive control, police forces, independent currency, etc., the more alike it will be to a political entity, and the greater the tendency will be to apply laws relating to a state to the Authority, even in the absence of formal recognition of such.

Par in parem non habet imperium

10. Recognition of the Palestinian National Authority as having the capacity of a sovereign over part of the territories needs to be answered in terms of customary international law as well. The Palestinian National Authority exercises policing and judicial responsibilities in the territories under the control of the Palestinian National Council, pursuant to the Interim Agreement. It exercises these authorities in the Gaza Strip as well. Imposition of this responsibility almost means the affording of powers. It would not be plausible for the Palestinian National Authority to be caught in a grey area in which it was under responsibility, but without the power to exercise authority or the right to claim a sovereign status vis-à-vis any other sovereignty. The claim for such powers stems from the very fact of providing these sovereign indicators. […]

These rules do not apply to the Palestinian National Authority directly, so long as it has not been recognized as a state. However, it is not possible to disregard the aspects of sovereignty that have been granted to the Authority and its territories. Some of these are stated expressly in the Interim Agreement and in the Implementation Law, by virtue of qualification of Israeli legal powers in the territories. Also, even those powers that remain, for instance in criminal law, do not originate from either the military commander or Israeli law, but rather, from the Interim Agreement. The significance of this is that even without recognition of full sovereignty, the Interim Agreement has, with regard to the relationship between Israel and the Palestinian National Authority, in fact adopted the customary international law principle of *par in parem non habet imperium* — one sovereign state does not control nor have jurisdiction over another sovereign entity. Although there is no express adoption of this rule in the Interim Agreement, it is the starting point for requiring Palestinian consent to any act on the part of Israel which might harm sovereignty, including execution or enforcement of criminal judgments.

> 11. [...] We might say that since immunity is a right of a state, the rule applies only to states. However, the status of the Palestinian National Authority, and the fact that it is a quasi-sovereign over the territories or part of them, are what cause the logic of immunity to be applied to it. [...] Accordingly, a political unit within a state has also been recognized as a state for the purpose of acquiring immunity. The functional test gives rise to the result that even where a country does not recognize another entity as a country, it will not be exempt from recognizing such other entity under international law. [...] This examination shows that the Palestinian Authority enjoys immunity. This would have been the case even without the Interim Agreement, and it is certainly the case by virtue of the Agreement. The Agreement itself states that the powers of the State of Israel over the areas in question are, from now on, the results of the arrangement that the parties reached, and that is the legitimate source of Israel's actions in these territories (alongside other rules of international law). This is the necessary conclusion of all of the sovereign indicators in the actions of the Palestinian National Authority, which are expressed in effective control in at least certain parts of the territories (supra, paragraph 9).
>
> 12. In summary of this point: the territories were not under Israeli sovereignty. They were under Israeli military control. The military commander was the sovereign. The Interim Agreement altered the situation of the territories. It transferred part of them into the control of the Palestinian National Authority. This control is accompanied by indicators of sovereignty. The Implementation Law afforded Israeli recognition to this status of the Palestinian National Authority. This recognition does not amount to recognition of the Palestinian National Authority as a state. Such recognition requires a formal act by the government of Israel, which has not been put into effect [...]. However, even without such recognition, the Palestinian National Authority enjoys application of the relevant provisions of customary international law, including immunity. Application of this rule is not connected to answering the question of whether the Palestinian National Authority is a state or not. It is sufficient that it be a sovereign or quasi-sovereign entity, which controls territory that is deemed to be "abroad" as far as Israel is concerned. Application of this rule is the result of a purposive reading of the Interim Agreement, and of the Implementation Law. [...]

The court acknowledged that the PNA met the criteria of statehood but fell short of considering it as a state, partly due to its non-recognition, even though such non-recognition was not taken to be determinative. It rather considered the PNA as a quasi-sovereign entity with numerous sovereignty indicators, which was sufficient to grant it immunity and decided the case accordingly. As pointed out by the ILDC reporter, the court applied a functional test of sovereignty and reached a controversial conclusion, leaving many questions unanswered.[25] However, since this decision was issued by a district court, it was not binding on the Supreme Court or other district courts.

SMZ v Khamis Ali and Others, The Revolutionary Government of Zanzibar v Khamis Ali (Machano), Appeal judgment, [2000] TZCA 1, ILDC 922 (TZ 2000), 21st November 2000, Tanzania

The main issue in this case was whether the crime of treason, which implied the breach of allegiance owed to one's state, could be committed in Tanzania against the Revolutionary Government of Zanzibar, which was—along with Tanganyika—a constituent part of Tanzania. Tanganyika and Zanzibar merged on 26 April 1964 to become the United Republic of Tanzania.

25 T Kritzman, Analysis, *Basha (Association of the Elon Moreh College) v Israel and ors*, ILDC 453 (IL 2006) A4–A5.

The court thus inquired into the status of Zanzibar under Tanzania's Constitution as well as under international law.

> 12 [...] To focus the matter squarely to the matter before us, the questions are: is Zanzibar a state and is the Revolutionary Government of Zanzibar sovereign? [...]
>
> 17 [...] [T]here are four conditions that need to be satisfied for a state to exist. [...]
>
> 18 The first of the four conditions is that there must be a people. This is an aggregate of individuals of both sexes, regardless of race or colour or creed, together as a community. Secondly, there must be a country in which the people have settled down. The size of the country is immaterial. Thirdly, there has to be a Government i.e. a person or persons who are the representatives of the people who rule according to the law of the land. Lastly, the Government has to be sovereign.
>
> 19 What is sovereignty? Oppenheim says at page 113, "Sovereignty is supreme authority, an authority which is independent of any other earthly authority. Sovereignty in the strict and narrowest sense of the term implies, therefore, independence all-round, within and without the borders of the country". [...]
>
> 29 [T]he constitutional set-up of the United Republic is unique. It is a union but with some elements of federalism. [...]
>
> 30 We can in all fairness say that The United Republic of Tanzania closely resembles a real union but for the stipulation that a real union is not itself a state. There is no speck of doubt that the United Republic of Tanzania is a state. The two parts forming the United Republic of Tanzania can neither separately go to war against a foreign power nor can war be made against one of them separately as was amply demonstrated in the war against Idi Amin Dada of Uganda. The whole of Tanzania went to war and each part contributed towards the cost of that war. The United Republic of Tanzania is the treaty-making power. This was illustrated by the abortive attempt of Zanzibar to join the Organization of Islamic Conference.
>
> 31 May be this is the proper juncture to turn to the question [...]: is Zanzibar a sovereign state in international law?
>
> 32 After the above exposition, we have no difficulty at all to answer that question in the negative. The International Persons called Tanganyika and Zanzibar ceased to exist as from 26th April, 1964 because of the Articles of Union. The two states merged to form a new international person called the United Republic of Tanzania.
>
> 33 [...] [B]oth Tanganyika and Zanzibar, and not Zanzibar alone, surrendered their treaty-making powers to the United Republic of Tanzania.
>
> 34 Thus, Zanzibar, just like its sister Tanganyika, is neither a state nor is it sovereign. The state and the sovereign is the United Republic of Tanzania.

After analysing relevant provisions of the Constitution, the court held that treason can only be committed against the sovereign, which was the United Republic of Tanzania and not the Revolutionary Government of Zanzibar, because treason was a breach of security, which was a Union (that is, a federal) matter under Tanzania's Constitution. The court reached the right conclusion on the status of Zanzibar, by emphasizing (formal) independence as the statehood criterion (in the court's words, 'the Government has to be sovereign'), which was missing since Zanzibar was a constituent entity of Tanzania. The court's emphasis on the treaty-making power resting on Tanzania, however, was rather misplaced since many constituent entities of federations do possess such power without any impact on their status or on the federal state's statehood, as the following case also demonstrates. Lastly, there was again no reference to the Montevideo Convention and the court relied largely on publicists. The Court accepted four conditions for statehood, the fourth one being that the Government has to be sovereign.

Italy v D M, Final Appeal on Preliminary Question, Case No 49666, Diritto e giustizia 30 (11/2005), (2006) 2 Riv Dir Int 568, ILDC 74 (IT 2004), 28th December 2004, Italy; Supreme Court of Cassation

This case also related to the legal status of a constituent entity of a federation. The issue was whether Milo Djukanović—at the relevant time the President and then the Prime Minister of Montenegro—was entitled to head of state immunity even though Montenegro was not at that time a sovereign state, but part of the Union of Serbia and Montenegro (Montenegro became an independent state in 2006). The Tribunal of Naples granted him head of state immunity, based on Montenegro's high degree of autonomy within the Union with Serbia as well as on the fact that Montenegro was party in international agreements, some of which had been concluded with Italy. The prosecutor's office appealed.

> 13) [. . .] [T]he Court disagrees with the opinion [. . .] that it is necessary for a State to be recognised as sovereign by Italy and other States before that State can be considered as sovereign for the purposes of the immunity of its top-ranking authorities under our law. In fact, under the general rules of international law [. . .] a government which exercises its power over a territorial community effectively and independently automatically becomes subject to international law. Therefore, a sovereign State exists as an autonomous subject of international law where there are the three elements territory—people—government and the requirements of effectiveness and independence are satisfied. However, recognition of this governmental entity by other States is not necessary. Indeed, the recognition of one State by another has no legal consequences (nor does non-recognition), and belongs in the political sphere, since it demonstrates nothing more than an intention to pursue friendly relations, to exchange diplomatic representatives and to establish cooperation of varying strength through the conclusion of agreements. Recognition therefore does not create legal personality under international law. As international legal doctrine notes, if it were otherwise, once a new government entity with characteristics of effectiveness and independence is created, pre-existing States would be able to operate a sort of power of admission to the international community over it through recognition.
>
> 14) Therefore, in the present case, whether Italy (like other States) has recognised Montenegro as a sovereign State is totally irrelevant for the purposes of granting immunity from criminal jurisdiction to its top-ranking officials. [. . .]
>
> 17) Although they do not create legal personality, significant factors to be considered in resolving this problem are the Constitutions of Montenegro and the Union of Serbia–Montenegro, the behaviour of other States towards Montenegro and vice versa, and in particular its participation in international treaties or conventions or intergovernmental organisations and the opinion of the Italian Ministry of Foreign affairs, which is the authority our law designates for international relationships and the observing and collection of data and relevant matters under international law. [. . .]
>
> 32) It therefore emerges from the Constitution of the Union of Serbia and Montenegro that the Union is the only entity which can possess legal personality under international law and which can be a member of international organisations for which legal personality is a membership requirement. The two member States may maintain international relationships, conclude international agreements, establish representative offices abroad and participate in universal and regional organisations, but only if this does not require or imply legal personality under international law (which is reserved to the Union alone) and in any event does not conflict with the powers of the Union or interests of the other State.

> 33) When compared with these decisive factors, the individual participation of Serbia in the Vienna negotiations on Kosovo and the joint request of the two States to be admitted separately to Interpol [...] are completely irrelevant. In fact, these are marginal and insignificant matters which are certainly insufficient for the acquisition of autonomous international legal personality, and which in any event fall completely within those international relations which are granted to the individual Member State under arts. 14 and 15 of the Constitution of the Union precisely because they do not presuppose international legal personality and do not interfere with the powers of the Union or the interests of the other member States.
>
> 34) Equally irrelevant, for the same reasons, are other agreements [...], such as agreements between Montenegro and Macedonia, between Montenegro and Albania, and between a public security department of the Italian Interior Ministry and a public security department of the Montenegrin Interior Ministry. Indeed, the fact that the Defendant was only able to give these marginal and limited examples of international agreements to which Montenegro is a party is clear confirmation of the lack of sovereignty and autonomous international legal personality of that State.
>
> 35) In conclusion, according to the evidence given in the proceedings it must be held that the State of Montenegro does not currently qualify as a sovereign State within the international community or as an autonomous and independent entity under international law. Therefore the conditions do not exist for applying [head of State immunity] to D.

This was another decision affirming the declaratory theory of recognition. In fact, as observed by the ILDC reporter, the clear statement of the court on this point represented a departure from its previous rulings.[26] It is also noteworthy that, unlike other (mostly common law) courts, Italian courts did not generally seek statements or certificates from the Executive clarifying whether or not a given entity was considered to be a state.[27] The court did so in the case at hand, but clarified at the same time that it did not consider itself bound by the views of the Executive. The court relied on the constitution of the Union of Serbia and Montenegro to rightly downplay any manifestations of independent treaty making and participation in international affairs by Montenegro as indications of independence and statehood.

III. Recognition/Non-recognition

1. Unrecognized states

The legal status of unrecognized states or other (unlawful) territorial entities and their instrumentalities has given rise to rich case law by domestic courts in past decades.[28] One category of cases related to the politically motivated Cold War practice of not granting recognition to entities that obviously fulfilled the criteria of statehood (eg East Germany).[29] Another category related to the non-recognition of racist regimes such as that of Ian Smith in South Rhodesia[30]

26 P Palchetti, Analysis, *Italy v D M*, ILDC 74 (IT 2004) A3.

27 ibid, A4.

28 For case law during the inter-war period see, *inter alia*, N D Houghton, 'The Validity of the Acts of Unrecognized De Facto Governments in the Courts of Non-Recognizing States' (1928–29) 13 *Minnesota Law Review* 216; E Borchard, 'The Unrecognized Government in American Courts' (1932) 26 *American Journal of International Law* 261.

29 See, *inter alia*, *Carl Zeiss Stiftung v Rayner and Keeler Limited* [1967] 1 AC 853, [1966] 2 All ER 536, [1966] 3 WLR 125, [1967] RPC 497, 18 May 1966, Civil Division [EWCA Civ]; *Upright v Mercury Business Machines*, 213 NYS (2d) 417 (1961); 32 ILR 65; *Federal Republic of Germany v Elicofon*, 358 F Supp 747 (EDNY 1970).

30 *Madzimbamuto v Lardner-Burke* [1968] UKPC 18, [1969] AC 645, 23 July 1968.

or the Homelands/Bantustans created by South Africa in furtherance of its apartheid policy.[31] Another issue is what acts may amount to (implied) recognition and which authority may grant it. There are common threads in the relevant jurisprudence of domestic courts but there is also room for variations. The point of departure is that unrecognized states/entities or governments do not have *locus standi* in domestic courts and any (governmental) acts of such entities are in principle denied recognition. However, this is not an absolute conclusion and, depending on the factual and legal context of each case, there can be space for different outcomes. In any case, any certificates by the Executive, especially in common law jurisdictions, are by and large determinative and binding on courts although some domestic courts may have more leeway than others. These issues are discussed in the following cases, with a focus on Taiwan.

Knox and ors v Palestinian Liberation Organization and ors, Trial judgment, No 03 Civ 4466, ILDC 1984 (US 2004), 306 F Supp 2d 424 (SDNY 2004), 1st March 2004, United States; New York; District Court for the Southern District of New York [SDNY]

As noted *supra*, although the court in this case examined and dismissed the statehood claim of the PLO and the PA, it held that even if there existed a sovereign state of Palestine the defendants would still not be entitled to immunity because such a state was not recognized by the United States. In doing so, the court dwelled on recognition and the treatment of unrecognized entities before US courts.

> B. Unrecognized State
>
> 43 [. . .] [B]ecause comity is often a function of recognition, matters concerning who is recognized as the sovereign or government of a particular territory, and whether and to what extent comity is accorded to its acts and officials, are political questions uniquely within the domain and prerogatives of the executive branch. [. . .] *Guaranty Trust,* 58 S.Ct. at 791 ("What government is to be regarded here as representative of a foreign sovereign state is a political rather than a judicial question, and is to be determined by the political department of the government."); *see also Sabbatino,* 376 U.S. at 410, 84 S.Ct. 923 (noting that "[p]olitical recognition is exclusively a function of the Executive" and that the Court "would hardly be competent to undertake assessments of varying degrees of friendliness or its absence") [. . .].
>
> 44 Recognition of a foreign entity of a sovereign state, or of a regime as the government of a state, may be effectuated by express declaration of the executive branch, by bilateral agreement with the foreign state, by the presentation of credentials by the United States to the authorities of the state and by the United States receiving the credentials of the diplomatic representatives of the foreign state. [. . .] Recognition may also be found to be implied, for example, through a vote by the United States to admit a foreign entity to membership in an international body open only to sovereign states. [. . .] While recognition is a matter of which courts may take judicial notice, [. . .] the "possible incongruity of judicial 'recognition' [. . .] would constitute an unwarranted arrogation of power. This constraint on judicial authority is especially compelling because the political discretion to recognize foreign states and governments carries with it "the power to determine the policy which is to govern the question of recognition." [. . .] Hence, "recognition is not always absolute; it is sometimes conditional." [. . .] Accordingly, the manner, means and timing that define the terms of any such conditions of recognition of a purported sovereign or its representatives are matters clearly beyond the realm of judicial competence.

31 *Achievers Investments Incorporated and South Africa (intervening) v Karalekas and McCahill,* Appeal judgment, 675 A2d 946 (DC App 1996), ILDC 943 (US 1996), 29th April 1996, Court of Appeals [DC App]; *Gur Corporation v Trust Bank of Africa* [1987] 1 QB 599; 75 ILR 675.

45 By the same token, the effects of political nonrecognition are whatever the states involved intend the consequences to be. [...] In addressing claims of sovereign or governmental immunity or disputes concerning the legitimacy of the actions of unrecognized foreign states, courts have taken divergent approaches. Some have enunciated as a categorical rule that "[i]n the absence of recognition no comity exists." *Cibrario,* 139 N.E. at 262 (holding that a government not recognized by the United States is not entitled to bring suit in courts in this country); [...].

46 This proposition is grounded on the premise that actual recognition serves as a prerequisite for a United States court to exercise jurisdiction over a claim concerning the existence of a foreign state or the legitimacy of an act of such a state. Thus, following this course, the executive branch's decision to withhold or reject recognition would be dispositive of the judicial proceeding; regardless of the nature of the dispute, the court would not venture beyond the status of the foreign entity as an unrecognized state. [...].

47 More specifically, according to this doctrine, nonrecognition may result in denial of access to courts in this country. [...]

48 Under another approach, other courts have not been beholden solely to the status of nonrecognition and, without relying only on the executive branch's ultimate determination in that regard, have not categorically nullified the official actions or disregarded the sovereignty claims of unrecognized entities. *See Kadic,* 70 F.3d at 244. Rather, in adjudicating these questions they generally have endeavored to draw certain pragmatic distinctions. First, these courts take cognizance of the difference between recognition of the existence of a particular unrecognized foreign state and the scope of any privileges and immunities that may be conferred upon it in a given case, including the treatment accorded to the purported government and representatives of the entity. Hence, while as a factual and juridical matter an unrecognized foreign entity may satisfy the criteria for statehood under the Restatement (Third)'s definition in a specific judicial proceeding, it does not follow that all of the privileges and immunities that ordinarily accompany sovereign status will necessarily be extended to the entity or its designated rulers. [...]

49 Second, the unrecognized foreign state is accorded *de facto* existence with respect to adjudications of strictly commercial transactions, adjustments of private rights, and effectuation of juridical and ministerial acts properly taken by it within the ambit of its territory incidental to sovereign or governmental functions that are deemed judicially cognizable; however, no such presumptive effect is generally given to circumstances involving political questions that fundamentally implicate the status of the foreign entity in its formal relations with the United States and that thus necessarily demand an expression from the executive branch concerning the United States foreign policy consequences of a legal determination regarding the matter at issue. [...]

50 A third approach adopted by the courts in some unrecognized state cases is to defer to an expression of United States foreign policy with regard to the appropriateness of entertaining the assertion of immunity or giving effect to the foreign act in question. *See Sabbatino,* 376 U.S. at 410, 84 S.Ct. 923 (permitting access to United States courts to a foreign entity where the executive had clearly expressed its support for the granting of such privilege) [...].

51 Fourth, in some cases where the executive branch has not interposed any suggestion of foreign policy interest in the prosecution of an action involving an unrecognized state, the courts have exercised jurisdiction to consider the matter if adjudication

of the controversy would not violate domestic public policy or otherwise conflict with the interests of justice. […]

52 Whatever doctrinal differences may distinguish the courts' treatment of rights and duties asserted in claims by or against unrecognized states or governments, a reconciling principle may be discerned threading through the various approaches, either expressed or implied, about which there appears to be no judicial dispute. When the executive branch, either by word or deed, does manifest its political determination that the courts' exercise of jurisdiction over a particular matter involving actions or privileges and immunities of unrecognized states or governments would be inimical to United States foreign policy interests or relations with the unrecognized sovereign, or when the court on its own, from demonstrable matters of public record, may readily ascertain such fundamental conflict with public policy were it to give effect to the invocation of sovereign status of the unrecognized state or government, the courts generally accept as conclusive such declared or ascertained expression of United States international relations policy. […]

54 The courts have also declared, in a doctrine especially germane to the issues at hand, that an unrecognized state cannot assert its sovereign status to immunize its acts or its representatives from exercise of "jurisdiction in [actions] alleging violations of basic human rights or international law." *See Kadic*, 70 F.3d at 245 (holding that customary international law of human rights "applies to states without distinction between recognized and unrecognized states"); *Klinghoffer*, 937 F.2d at 49 (noting that "there is no bar to suit where an unrecognized regime is brought into court as a defendant"); *see also* Shaw, *supra*, at 262 ("[A]n unrecognized state must be deemed subject to the rules of international law. It cannot consider itself free from restraints as to aggressive behaviour. …").

The court made a very wide and useful survey of (non-)recognition in US courts and discerned various approaches to unrecognized entities: denial of access to US courts; limited (*de facto*) juridical personality for non-sovereign matters such as commercial transactions or private rights; deference to the Executive, especially when dealing with immunity; and, absent any direction by the Executive, acceptance of jurisdiction unless it violated public policy or the interests of justice. These approaches are, to a greater or lesser extent, also found in other jurisdictions.

Civil Aeronautics Administration v Singapore Airlines Limited, Appeal Decision, [2004] SGCA 3, [2004] 1 SLR 570, ILDC 86 (SG 2004), 14th January 2004, Singapore; Supreme Court; Court of Appeal

This case was an appeal from *Woo v Singapore Airlines Limited and Civil Aeronautics Administration (joining)*.[32] The plaintiff in that case had sued Singapore Airlines Limited (SAL) for the crash of a Singapore Airlines plane at Taipei's Airport in Taiwan in 2000. SAL joined Civil Aeronautics Administration (CAA) of Taiwan's Ministry of Transport and Communications as a third party. CAA claimed immunity under Singapore's State Immunity Act (SIA). The Singapore's Ministry for Foreign Affairs was 'unable' to issue a certificate confirming that Taiwan was a state for the purposes of the SIA and CAA's application was rejected. On appeal, CAA claimed immunity even if there was no official recognition of Taiwan. It contended that Singapore had recognized Taiwan *de facto, inter alia* by signing a double-taxation treaty with it. CAA also argued that the court could hold its own enquiry as to the question of *de facto* recognition. The High Court held that the certificate was conclusive in stating that Taiwan was not a state, either *de facto* or *de jure*, for the purposes of SIA and dismissed the appeal. Upon further appeal, the ruling was confirmed and the Court of Appeal in the decision at hand took pains in finding that Singapore's dealings with Taiwan did not amount to either *de jure* or *de facto* recognition and reaffirmed that Taiwan did not enjoy immunity.

32 Appeal judgment, [2003] SGHC 190, (2003) 3 SLR 688, ILDC 547 (SG 2003), 28 August 2003, High Court.

11 [...] To our mind, the effect of the negative answer from the Ministry is clear, ie, Taiwan is not a State for the purposes of the Act. If she is, the certificate would have been issued by the Ministry. [...] [T]he two replies by the Ministry to the parties are therefore conclusive on the point in issue, that is, that Taiwan is not a State to which the Act would apply. [...] There is no ambiguity in the answer from the Ministry of Foreign Affairs that the Republic of China is not a state, whether *de facto* or *de jure*, for the purposes of the Act. No reasons were given and none is required under the Act. [...]

Question within the exclusive province of the Executive

15 The above should dispose of this appeal. However, even if one were to take the view that the replies from the Ministry were ambiguous, it is not for the court to embark on an independent examination of the evidence adduced to determine whether Taiwan is a State for the purposes of the Act. The correct approach would be for the court to revert to the Ministry for a more specific answer. On a question such as this, which is a matter wholly within the Executive's domain, it is essential that the Judiciary does not act in a manner inconsistent with the approach of the Executive. [...]

22 A question such as that which arises in the present case, whether an entity is a State so as to enjoy sovereign immunity in Singapore, is eminently a matter within the exclusive province of the Executive to determine, as what are involved in the question are not only matters of fact but also matters of policy. The courts are not in the best position to decide such a question. [...]

25 [...] [T]he question of sovereign immunity is special and should be treated differently from the general question whether a State has come into being. It is incongruous to say that a State is required to accord sovereign immunity to another State when the latter is not recognised by the former. Bearing in mind the pre-eminence given to recognition by virtue of s 18 of the Act, the question of sovereign immunity clearly stands on a different footing from other questions in which the existence of a State comes into issue.

Position under customary international law

29 [...] Assuming the reply of MFA is vague and, contrary to the views we have earlier expressed, the court has the competence to independently determine whether Taiwan is a State, has Singapore, through various transactions with Taiwan, in fact, regarded the latter as a State? In short, is there *de facto* recognition by conduct? [...]

32 The starting point in considering whether Singapore has, in fact, regarded Taiwan as a sovereign State, must be the sort of representation which each country has, by mutual consent, established in the territory of the other. [...]

33 It would be noted that, unlike other sovereign States, Taiwan does not have a diplomatic representation in Singapore. It only has a trade representation here, or as the representation was earlier called, "Trade Mission". It is not an Embassy. As the website indicated, the functions of the Representative Office are only in respect of specific areas of co-operation. There is no exchange of "ambassadors". This use of the institution of trade representation is wholly in line with the practice among States of dealing with a political subdivision of another State. It is significant to note that when Singapore established a mission in Taiwan in 1979, it was a Consulate Office to deal with consular and trade matters.

34 This approach reflects the one-China policy which has been adopted by Singapore even before formal relations were established with mainland China, the People's

> Republic of China ("PRC") in 1990. Singapore has not treated Taiwan in the same manner as other sovereign States. That has been its consistent stand. Thus, in 1989, when President Lee Teng-Hui of Taiwan was in Singapore for a visit, there were no flags, no guard of honour, no ceremonial trappings which would normally come with a visit by a head of State. Of course, he was accorded other courtesies of a guest. Later, in 1990, when Singapore established diplomatic relations with the PRC, the Taiwan mission in Singapore was no longer allowed to use the title "the Republic of China".
>
> 35 Counsel for CAA is quite right to point out that Singapore has, through its departments and agencies, entered into various agreements or memoranda of understanding with similar entities in Taiwan on specific areas, ranging from air services agreements to avoidance of double taxation, the promotion and protection of investment, and tourism. There is no denying that in those areas there is close co-operation between the two territories. But co-operation with an entity in a specific area does not imply recognition as sovereign State. […]
>
> 36 We agree with the submission of SIA's counsel, that what emanates from the dealings between Singapore and Taiwan is that Singapore "has always been careful to maintain the stand of not recognising, whether formally or informally, Taiwan's status in any way that may suggest that it is a State, consistent with its one-China policy". For there to be implied recognition, the acts must leave no doubt as to the intention to grant it. […]
>
> 49 As we see it, there is nothing seriously inconsistent with the stand of not granting recognition to an entity for purposes of state immunity and yet permitting that entity to be sued for its acts. […] [N]on-recognition does not deny the existence of a foreign government: it simply denies its competence to represent the state concerned on the international plane. […]
>
> 50 Reverting to the present case, once it is appreciated that the non-recognition of Taiwan is only in respect of the Act there is no reason why its effect should or need be extended to other respects. That would be completely unwarranted. The existence of Taiwan is a fact and the government of Taiwan exercises control over a specified area. The accident happened at an airport within the control of CAA and, as it does not enjoy immunity under Singapore law, it must answer the allegations made against it of having caused or contributed towards the tragedy.

Apart from being loyal to the 'one voice' doctrine, this decision was also interesting in relation to implied recognition (which, however, it seemed to conflate with *de facto* recognition).[33] In line with established practice, it affirmed that cooperation by means of maintaining a representation office or even concluding agreements in specific areas did not amount to (implied) recognition in the absence of a clear intention to do so. Indeed, it is well accepted that no recognition of statehood is implied by such acts in the absence of unequivocal intention to the contrary.[34]

Parent and ors v Singapore Airlines Ltd and Civil Aeronautics Administration, Decision of Superior Court of Quebec, 2003 IIJ Can 7285 (QC CS), ILDC 181 (CA 2003), 22nd October 2003, Canada; Quebec; Superior Court [QCCS]

This case also arose from the air crash of Singapore Airlines in Taiwan in 2000. The court had to determine whether Taiwan was a state and thus entitled to immunity under Canada's State

33 According to Jennings and Watts (n 5) 155, *de facto* recognition is 'a lesser degree of recognition, taking into account on a provisional basis of present realities' when, in the view of the recognizing state, the new authority, although actually independent and effective, has not acquired sufficient stability, whereas implied recognition 'takes place through acts which, although not referring expressly to recognition, leave no doubt as to the intention to grant it'. See Jennings and Watts (n 5) 169.

34 H Lauterpacht, *Recognition in International Law* (CUP 1947) 406; Jennings and Watts (n 5) 170–71.

Immunity Act. As in the previous case, the Canadian Ministry of Foreign Affairs did not issue a certificate confirming that Taiwan was or not a foreign state for the purposes of the Act.

Findings of fact: CAA and Taiwan

52 By giving the courts the power to determine whether a party to a dispute qualifies as a "foreign state" for the purposes of the Act in the light of the evidence provided (which may or may not include a certificate), the Canadian legislature separates the legal aspect from the political and the diplomatic. [...]

54 [...] [W]hen the situation cannot be officially recognised politically and diplomatically or the minister refrains from issuing a certificate, the task of evaluating the facts, and drawing the necessary legal conclusions then falls to the court dealing with the claim. [...]

58 The existence of a State implies the presence of four elements: "these elements are identified in Article 1 of the Montevideo Convention on the Rights and Duties of States; they are: The presence of a defined territory; The presence of a permanent population; The presence of an effective government; The capacity to enter into relations with other States.

Furthermore, to have the greatest effect in the international community, the existence of a State must be recognised by other States. This recognition is principally, but not exclusively, linked to the presence of constituent elements of the State." [citation omitted]

59 The recognition of a State by the other States does not create the State: the birth and the existence of a State is a question of fact. [...]

60 The evidence in the present file is conclusive as to the four constituent elements of the State: (1) the island of Taiwan constitutes a defined territory; (2) the island of Taiwan is occupied by a permanent population; (3) an effective government exists in Taiwan and (4) the government of Taiwan enters into relations with other states. [...]

63 [...] [I]n conclusion, the Tribunal concurs with the following statement by the author Hugh M. Kindred:

> "In pursuing this course [of independent judicial inquiry], the courts may find themselves granting a degree of respect or even immunity for a foreign regime that superficially may seem wholly out of accord with the government's declarations of diplomatic distance. But the illusion will be in the denials of recognition by the government for diplomacy's sake and no longer in the fictions of the courts." [citation omitted]

As observed by the ILDC reporter, absent a certificate by the Executive, this was the first case in which a Canadian court took an independent course and made its own enquiry into the issue of (Taiwan's) statehood.[35] What is more, the court's conclusion was at variance with Canada's policy of not recognizing Taiwan. This approach was also at variance with that of Singapore's courts (also due to different wording of the respective Immunity Acts) and undermined the 'one voice' doctrine. However, when the Canadian government issues a certificate, it is conclusive proof of its content.[36]

Wang (Chuan Pu Andrew) and ors v Office of the Federal Prosecutor, Final Appeal Judgment, Case No 1A.3/2004, ILDC 90 (CH 2004), 3rd May 2004, Switzerland; Federal Supreme Court [BGer]

This case concerned cooperation by means of mutual legal assistance in criminal matters between Switzerland and Taiwan during criminal proceedings against the appellant suspects in

35 H M Kindred, Analysis, *Parent and ors v Singapore Airlines Ltd and Civil Aeronautics Administration*, ILDC 181 (CA 2003) A2.

36 ibid, A3.

Switzerland. The Taiwanese suspects alleged that Switzerland's non-recognition of Taiwan as a state should block any legal assistance in criminal matters between Switzerland and Taiwan.

> 5.2 Statehood under international law is defined according to three criteria: a territory; a population; and an effective and independent government […]. With regard to the case in question, the Republic of China cannot claim to exercise sovereignty over mainland China, because her Government does not exercise effective authority over the territory and the population that makes up the People's Republic of China […]. With regard to the island of Taiwan on the other hand, the Republic of China presents all the attributes of a State: it has occupied this territory since 1945; it has a significant population (consisting of ethnic Taiwanese, mainland Chinese and their descendants, and an aboriginal minority); and Taiwan is undeniably independent, including with regard to the People's Republic of China […].
>
> 5.3 […] The majority view in international law is that recognition only has a declaratory effect and is not a condition for statehood as such, in the sense that it only confirms that the criteria of existence of a State are met. International recognition, however, is not required to gain the status of a State existing in its own right […].
>
> Up until Taiwan's exclusion from the UN on 25th October 1971, most countries recognised the Republic of China as the sole Chinese State. After 1979, a large number of them, falling in line with the United States, recognised the People's Republic of China and broke off diplomatic relations with the Republic of China. Today only some twenty States maintain diplomatic relations with Taiwan. The status of the Republic of China is therefore ambiguous. She enjoys limited international recognition, but not so limited as to reduce Taiwan to the status of an international pariah State (such as, the Turkish Republic of Northern Cyprus, for example, which is only recognised by Turkey). Taiwan's status is more similar to that of States whose recognition is contested by a section of the international community without this casting doubt over their status as an international legal entity (for example: Israel or the former German Democratic Republic […]).
>
> Since 1950, Switzerland has held the People's Republic of China to be the sole legitimate representative of the Chinese people, and has established diplomatic relations with the People's Republic of China and broken off links with Taiwan […]. […] Only the Swiss Federal Council (*Conseil Fédéral*), which has remained intransigent on this issue since 1950, can modify Switzerland's position […]. It cannot be maintained in this respect that requesting or granting mutual legal assistance in criminal matters to Taiwan equates to recognition, even implicit, of the Republic of China. This proves therefore that the argument whereby carrying out the request could be interpreted as a hostile act towards the People's Republic of China is unfounded.
>
> The absence of recognition and the absence of diplomatic relations does not mean that all relations relating to mutual aid with Taiwan are proscribed. The fact that the Republic of China does not belong to the UN is not crucial here. Just taking this one example, the Federal Republic of Germany was only admitted to the UN in 1973, but this did not prevent Switzerland from concluding several dozen treaties with the Federal Republic of Germany in the meantime (including treaties regarding mutual legal assistance in criminal matters).
>
> 5.4 […] Furthermore the concept of Taiwan as a dissident province of the People's Republic of China poses a delicate problem in terms of international law, because looking beyond this request, it is the government in Taipei (and not in Beijing) which exercises effective authority over the island of Taiwan. The request for mutual legal assistance relates to facts which took place within the compass of power of the Taiwanese authorities. Those charged are Chinese from Taiwan and some of them are being detained

> there. Criminal proceedings have been commenced which might lead to the accused being brought before the legal authorities in Taiwan. The mechanisms of operation of the Taiwanese institutions, especially those of her judicial institutions, are guaranteed on a continuous basis. Even if Switzerland cannot, by definition, conclude treaties with the Republic of China, which it does not recognise as a State, this does not prevent occasional co-operation between authorities, as is the case in the matter at hand. [...]
>
> 5.5 To conclude, the Swiss authorities can request and grant mutual legal assistance in criminal matters to the Taiwanese authorities, without this modifying the position of the People's Republic of China, the sole Chinese State recognised by Switzerland. Because the Republic of China is not recognised, there is no contact with Switzerland on a diplomatic level. Consequently the request was not transmitted through an official representation in Switzerland, but via a cultural and economic delegation, established in the form of an association in accordance with Article 60 ff of the Swiss Civil Code (*Code Civil*). This unusual *modus operandi*, brought about by force of circumstances, does not alter in any way the official nature of the actions of the Taiwanese authorities and does not cast doubt on the validity of the request from this respect. For the rest, contrary to what the appellants say, the requesting State can appoint a representative in Switzerland for procedural needs: this has been the case notably with Pakistan and Ethiopia. The law does not, moreover, prohibit this. The Swiss Federal Office of Justice (*Office fédéral de la justice*) and the Investigating Magistrate cannot therefore be reproached for communicating with the Taiwanese authorities via an informal channel.

Citing several publicists, the Swiss Supreme Court held that Taiwan fulfilled the conditions for statehood, irrespective of its non-recognition by Switzerland and most states, thus following the declaratory theory of recognition. The court identified three criteria for statehood: a territory, a population, and an effective and independent government, in disregard of the Montevideo Convention and its fourth condition. The court also affirmed the established view that (unofficial) cooperation with an unrecognized state in the form of mutual legal assistance in criminal matters did not amount to (implied) recognition.

2. Recognition of governments

Occasions for recognition of governments arise usually in cases of civil war and/or unconstitutional assumption of power and may involve a choice between two (or more) rival authorities. Recognition of governments had been in decline, as prominently evidenced by the UK's decision in 1980 no longer to confer such recognition.[37] In such a case, there will probably be no certificate with controlling effect on the issue and it may fall to the courts to rule which entity should enjoy governmental status and lawfully bind the state in its international relations. This is what happened in the first case discussed in this section. However, the conflicts in Libya and Syria have witnessed several states (including the UK) reverting to their past practice of recognizing governments and issuing relevant certificates, as occurred in the last case of this section.

Sierra Leone Telecommunications Company Limited v Barclays Bank plc, Trial judgment, ILDC 1740 (UK 1998), [1998] All ER (D) 66, 6th February 1998, United Kingdom; England and Wales; High Court [HC]; Queen's Bench Division [QBD]; Commercial Court

The plaintiff company (Sierratel) was a state-owned company of Sierra Leone whose board of directors was appointed by the Government of Sierra Leone. Sierratel had a bank account with the defendant bank in London and had authorized four signatories to sign payment requests on its behalf. In May 1997, there was a military *coup* in Sierra Leone and the democratically

37 51 *BYBIL* (1980) 367.

elected government fled into exile. The new regime dismissed the board of directors of Sierratel, suspended three of the original signatories, and instructed the bank not to honour payment instructions issued by them. The High Commissioner of Sierra Leone in London, who continued to act on behalf of the exiled Government, instructed lawyers to bring an action in the name of Sierratel, seeking a declaration that the bank account remained subject to instructions of the original signatories. Counsel for Sierratel argued that the military regime was not the Government of Sierra Leone and, as a result, the instructions given to the bank by the new regime were ineffective.

> 35 The factors to be taken into account in deciding whether a government exists as the government of a state are set out [in *Republic of Somalia v. Woodhouse Drake & Carey (Suisse) S.A. and Others*] by Hobhouse J as follows: [. . .]
>
> **(a) Whether it is the constitutional government of the state**
>
> 38 On 28 November 1997 the Foreign and Commonwealth Office wrote to Messrs Stephenson Harwood as follows:
>
> "[. . .] The British Government welcomed the election in Sierra Leone of President Ahmad Tejan Kabbah in February 1996. We have consistently condemned the military coup of 25 May 1997 which overthrew the democratically elected government of Sierra Leone. We look forward to the restoration of constitutional order in that country. We continue to deal with the democratically elected government of Sierra Leone under President Kabbah. We have no dealings with the military junta in Freetown." [. . .]
>
> **(b) The degree, nature and stability of administrative control, if any, that it of itself exercises over the territory of the state**
>
> 42 According to the Sierra Leone High Commissioner the military junta presently has no control whatsoever over the country outside of Freetown and there are civil unrest problems in Freetown. There are still defence units loyal to President Kabbah throughout the country. [. . .] The junta has very little real control over the administrative affairs of the country. [. . .]
>
> 43 According to the affidavit of Mr Berewa, Attorney General and Minister of Justice in President Kabbah's government, it is precisely because there is in fact no semblance of order in Freetown that the expatriate community and diplomatic missions, which were evacuated following the coup, still remain out of the country. [. . .] It has been the clear aim of the junta to coerce the civil population to collaborate with them. They have failed in this aim, and to such an extent that there has been a very significant defection by members of the Sierra Leone army and civilian police to the forces of the West African Peace Keeping Force ECOMOG, and the Civil Defence Militia, which is loyal to President Kabbah.
>
> 44 Of the three tiers of superior courts (the High Court, Court of Appeal and Supreme Court), none are sitting or hearing cases. Over 80 per cent of the judges of the superior courts have fled the country since the coup. [. . .]
>
> 46 [. . .] The majority of the citizens of Sierra Leone are waiting for the democratically elected government to be restored. The infrastructure of the country has collapsed. Basic amenities such as water and electricity are virtually non-existent. Owing to the embargo on postal activities by the Universal Postal Union there is no postal communication between Sierra Leone and the outside world. Hospitals function only at the behest of Médecin Sans Frontières or the International Red Cross. The junta itself is not providing medical services. Despite strenuous attempts by the junta to reopen schools, the majority of schools have remained closed since the coup because

parents do not co-operate with the junta and are afraid that their children may be kidnapped, harmed or raped. Petrol is in extremely short supply [. . .]. The junta has no control over more than two-thirds of the country. They do not control the country's only international airport situated at Lungi, near Freetown, nor the main internal airfield at Hastings. Both these airfields are controlled by the forces of ECOMOG. The Port of Freetown at Queen Elizabeth II Quay is also under the control of the ECOMOG Forces. Similarly ECOMOG controls the main routes to and from the capital city, Freetown, and even members of the junta are not allowed to move freely from Freetown to the provinces and back. The civil defence units which remain loyal to President Kabbah and which are fighting for the restoration of democracy are in control of a very significant portion of the territory up-country. [. . .] The most recent reports show that forces loyal to President Kabbah are in control of the most important areas up-country.

(c) Whether Her Majesty's government has any dealings with it and if so what is the nature of those dealings

47 See under (a) above.

(d) In marginal cases, the extent of international recognition that it has as the government of the state

48 The United Nations has imposed sanctions relating to the supply of arms and petroleum products to Sierra Leone: see United Nations Resolution SCR 1132 of 8 October 1997. [. . .] In addition the coup has also been condemned by the Commonwealth, the Organisation of African Unity and the European Community. [. . .] [An] ECOWAS peace plan for Sierra Leone [. . .] provides for the reinstatement of the legitimate government of President Kabbah within a period of six months. The peace plan remains operative and it is fully expected that the legitimate government of President Kabbah will be reinstated in Sierra Leone within the stated timeframe.

49 [. . .] I conclude that the military junta are not "the Government of Sierra Leone". The mandate to Barclays of 31 July 1996 stands. Nothing that the military junta has purported to do since May 1997 affects that mandate. The letters of 22 December 1997 and 31 December 1997 from those associated with the junta to the bank are of no effect. The military junta is not the government of Sierra Leone. The "new directors" were not validly appointed. It follows that Sierratel is entitled to the declaration sought and I order accordingly.

In traditional international law, as famously held in the *Tinoco Arbitration*,[38] governmental status was allocated to the entity enjoying effective control of the territory,[39] with the apparent acquiescence of the population under its control.[40] As observed by the ILDC reporter, the case at hand was not decided on that basis but considered the additional factors required by UK law,[41] as these were set out in *Woodhouse*, a decision of 1992 concerning the legal status of the interim government of Somalia during the country's civil war. By considering legitimacy and international recognition, the decision at hand was in line with a trend to do away with effective control as the sole factor determining governmental status as a matter of international law,[42] even though it

38 [1923] 1 *RIAA* 369.

39 Lauterpacht (n 34) 98.

40 Jennings and Watts (n 5) 151.

41 M Saul, Analysis, *Sierra Leone Telecommunications Company Limited v Barclays Bank plc*, ILDC 1740 (UK 1998) A3.

42 See B Roth, 'Secessions, Coups and the International Rule of Law: Assessing the Decline of the Effective Control Doctrine' (2010) 11 *Melbourne Journal of International Law* 1.

may still be difficult to identify sufficient state practice and *opinio juris* to confirm a development in the law in that direction.[43]

British Arab Commercial Bank plc v National Transitional Council of the State of Libya, ex parte Foreign and Commonwealth Office, Declaratory judgment, [2011] EWHC 2274 (Comm), ILDC 1807 (UK 2011), 26th August 2011, United Kingdom; England and Wales; High Court [HC]; Queen's Bench Division [QBD]

The issue in this case was whether the National Transitional Council of Libya (NTC) or the Qadhafi government was Libya's government during the country's civil war and could thus control the accounts of the Libyan Embassy in the British Arab Commercial Bank in London. Following the UK government announcement on 27 July 2011 that it recognized and would deal with the NTC as the sole governmental authority in Libya, the Bank was receiving conflicting instructions from the two rivalries concerning the operation of the accounts and initiated proceedings against the NTC, asking for urgent declaratory relief.

> 22. I should make one point plain at the outset. The Bank invited me to indicate that the court would be assisted by a certificate from the Foreign & Commonwealth Office. It also submitted however that absent such certificate, the court should nevertheless investigate the factual position for itself. This would have involved consideration of issues such as whether the NTC is the constitutional government of Libya, the degree, nature and stability of administrative control that it of itself exercises over the territory of the state, whether HMG has any dealings with it and, if so, what is the nature of those dealings, and the extent of international recognition that it has as the government of the state. Reliance was placed on the approach taken by Hobhouse J in *Republic of Somalia v Woodhouse & Carey (Suisse) S.A.* [1993] QB 54, and adopted by Cresswell J in *Sierra Leone Telecommunications Co Ltd v Barclays Bank plc* [1998] All ER 821. That might be a difficult exercise given the conditions that appear to prevail in Libya at the time of this judgment (26 August 2011).
>
> 23. However it is clear that the *Somalia* and *Sierra Leone* cases are different, because the issue did not concern the position of a government recognised by Her Majesty's Government as the government of the state in question. In any event, in the present case this submission has been overtaken by events. I indicated that the court would be assisted by a certificate as to the recognition status of the NTC and the Qadhafi regimes, and at the hearing counsel for the FCO produced a certificate dated 24 August 2011 signed by the Foreign Secretary as follows: [. . .]
>
> (1) Her Majesty's Government recognise the National Transitional Council as the Government of Libya.
>
> (2) Her Majesty's Government do not recognise any other Government in Libya. In particular, they no longer recognise the former Qadhafi regime as the Government of any part of Libya. [. . .]
>
> 24. In the present case, there has been no investigation of the factual position in Libya as in the *Somalia* or *Sierra Leone* cases, or indeed any factual investigation other than as set out in this judgment. I should however note that the witness statement of Mr Nacua is to the effect that since the creation of the NTC, a growing number of states have recognised it as the legitimate government of Libya, and this is made out clearly in the evidence. However, for present purposes, the important point is that the government of the United Kingdom recognises it as the legitimate government of Libya. I now come to the questions for decision.

43 M Saul, Analysis, *Sierra Leone Telecommunications Company Limited v Barclays Bank plc*, ILDC 1740 (UK 1998) A5, citing S Talmon, 'Recognition of the Libyan National Transitional Council' (2011) 15(16) *ASIL Insights*.

(1) Is the court satisfied that the NTC is, and the Qadhafi regime is not, the Government of Libya?

25. There can only be an affirmative answer to this question. In so far as it goes, the Foreign Secretary's certificate of 24 August 2011 is conclusive, because in the field of foreign relations, the Crown in its executive and judicial functions speak with one voice [. . .].

(5) Should the hearing be adjourned to enable the Qadhafi regime to be present? [. . .]

32. Further, both parties submit that the matter is academic, since the formerly recognised Libyan Government would have no *locus standi* in the English courts to challenge the NTC's claim as regards the accounts. The Bank points out, I think rightly, that such adverse claim as has been made in relation to these accounts has been made on the basis that the Qadhafi Government remains the lawful government of the state of Libya. Following the Foreign Secretary's certificate, no such proposition can be advanced in the English courts. Thus, it is established that an unrecognised state cannot sue or be sued in an English court [. . .]. As a general matter, an unrecognised government has no *locus standi* in the English courts [. . .]. There would, therefore, be no purpose in adjourning the hearing.

This decision illustrates the conclusive effect of a certificate by the Executive on matters of recognition. Had it not been for such certificate, it would have been extremely difficult for the court to make its own factual investigation into the complex situation then unfolding in Libya. The court also reiterated the settled doctrine that unrecognized or formerly recognized governments have no *locus standi* in the English courts.

IV. Statehood—Secession, Legitimacy, Occupation/Annexation, Continuity

Secession of Quebec, Re, Reference to Supreme Court, [1998] 2 SCR 217, (1998) 161 DLR (4th) 385, (1998), 55 CRR (2d) 1, ILDC 184 (CA 1998), 20th August 1998, Canada; Supreme Court [SCC]

Quebec is the only province of Canada with a predominantly francophone population. In response to the separatism movement in the province, the Government of Quebec held a referendum in 1995 to determine whether the population was in favour of secession from Canada. A narrow majority favoured remaining part of Canada. In the wake of the referendum, the Federal Government sent three questions to the Supreme Court of Canada with a view to clarifying whether Quebec had a unilateral right of secession under Canadian law or international law.

(5) Suggested Principle of Effectivity

106 [. . .] Although under the Constitution there is no right to pursue secession unilaterally, that is secession without principled negotiation, this does not rule out the possibility of an unconstitutional declaration of secession leading to a *de facto* secession. The ultimate success of such a secession would be dependent on effective control of a territory and recognition by the international community. [. . .]

107 In our view, the alleged principle of effectivity has no constitutional or legal status in the sense that it does not provide an *ex ante* explanation or justification for an act. In essence, acceptance of a principle of effectivity would be tantamount to accepting that the National Assembly, legislature or government of Quebec may act without regard to the law, simply because it asserts the power to do so. So viewed, the suggestion is that the National Assembly, legislature or government of Quebec could purport to secede the province unilaterally from Canada in disregard of Canadian and international law. It is further suggested that if the secession bid was successful, a

new legal order would be created in that province, which would then be considered an independent state.

108 Such a proposition is an assertion of fact, not a statement of law. It may or may not be true; in any event it is irrelevant to the questions of law before us. If, on the other hand, it is put forward as an assertion of law, then it simply amounts to the contention that the law may be broken as long as it can be broken successfully. Such a notion is contrary to the rule of law, and must be rejected.

B. Question 2

Does international law give the National Assembly, legislature or government of Quebec the right to effect the secession of Quebec from Canada unilaterally? In this regard, is there a right to self-determination under international law that would give the National Assembly, legislature or government of Quebec the right to effect the secession of Quebec from Canada unilaterally? […]

110 […] While our response to Question 2 will address considerations raised by [the] alternative argument of "effectivity", it should first be noted that the existence of a positive legal entitlement is quite different from a prediction that the law will respond after the fact to a then existing political reality. These two concepts examine different points in time. The questions posed to the Court address legal rights in advance of a unilateral act of purported secession. […]

(1) Secession at International Law

111 It is clear that international law does not specifically grant component parts of sovereign states the legal right to secede unilaterally from their "parent" state. […] Given the lack of specific authorization for unilateral secession, proponents of the existence of such a right at international law are therefore left to attempt to found their argument (i) on the proposition that unilateral secession is not specifically prohibited and that what is not specifically prohibited is inferentially permitted; or (ii) on the implied duty of states to recognize the legitimacy of secession brought about by the exercise of the well-established international law right of "a people" to self-determination. The *amicus curiae* addressed the right of self-determination, but submitted that it was not applicable to the circumstances of Quebec within the Canadian federation, irrespective of the existence or non-existence of a referendum result in favour of secession. We agree on this point with the *amicus curiae*, for reasons that we will briefly develop.

(a) Absence of a Specific Prohibition

112 International law contains neither a right of unilateral secession nor the explicit denial of such a right, although such a denial is, to some extent, implicit in the exceptional circumstances required for secession to be permitted under the right of a people to self-determination, e.g., the right of secession that arises in the exceptional situation of an oppressed or colonial people, discussed below. As will be seen, international law places great importance on the territorial integrity of nation states and, by and large, leaves the creation of a new state to be determined by the domestic law of the existing state of which the seceding entity presently forms a part […]. Where, as here, unilateral secession would be incompatible with the domestic Constitution, international law is likely to accept that conclusion subject to the right of peoples to self-determination, a topic to which we now turn.

(b) The Right of a People to Self-determination

113 While international law generally regulates the conduct of nation states, it does, in some specific circumstances, also recognize the "rights" of entities other than nation states — such as the right of a *people* to self-determination.

114 The existence of the right of a people to self-determination is now so widely recognized in international conventions that the principle has acquired a status beyond "convention" and is considered a general principle of international law. [. . .]

(i) Defining "Peoples"

123 International law grants the right to self-determination to "peoples". Accordingly, access to the right requires the threshold step of characterizing as a people the group seeking self-determination. However, [. . .] the precise meaning of the term "people" remains somewhat uncertain.

124 It is clear that "a people" may include only a portion of the population of an existing state. The right to self-determination has developed largely as a human right, and is generally used in documents that simultaneously contain references to "nation" and "state". The juxtaposition of these terms is indicative that the reference to "people" does not necessarily mean the entirety of a state's population. To restrict the definition of the term to the population of existing states would render the granting of a right to self-determination largely duplicative, given the parallel emphasis within the majority of the source documents on the need to protect the territorial integrity of existing states, and would frustrate its remedial purpose.

125 While much of the Quebec population certainly shares many of the characteristics (such as a common language and culture) that would be considered in determining whether a specific group is a "people", as do other groups within Quebec and/or Canada, it is not necessary to explore this legal characterization to resolve Question 2 appropriately. Similarly, it is not necessary for the Court to determine whether, should a Quebec people exist within the definition of public international law, such a people encompasses the entirety of the provincial population or just a portion thereof. Nor is it necessary to examine the position of the aboriginal population within Quebec. As the following discussion of the scope of the right to self-determination will make clear, whatever be the correct application of the definition of people(s) in this context, their right of self-determination cannot in the present circumstances be said to ground a right to unilateral secession.

(ii) Scope of the Right to Self-determination

126 The recognized sources of international law establish that the right to self-determination of a people is normally fulfilled through *internal* self-determination — a people's pursuit of its political, economic, social and cultural development within the framework of an existing state. A right to *external* self-determination (which in this case potentially takes the form of the assertion of a right to unilateral secession) arises in only the most extreme of cases and, even then, under carefully defined circumstances. *External* self-determination can be defined as in the following statement from the Declaration on Friendly Relations as

> [t]he establishment of a sovereign and independent State, the free association or integration with an independent State or the emergence into any other political status freely determined by a *people* constitute modes of implementing the right of self-determination by *that people.* [Emphasis added.]

127 The international law principle of self-determination has evolved within a framework of respect for the territorial integrity of existing states. The various international documents that support the existence of a people's right to self-determination also contain parallel statements supportive of the conclusion that the exercise of such a right must be sufficiently limited to prevent threats to an existing state's territorial integrity or the stability of relations between sovereign states.

128 The Declaration on Friendly Relations, the Vienna Declaration and the Declaration on the Occasion of the Fiftieth Anniversary of the United Nations are specific. They state, immediately after affirming a people's right to determine political, economic, social and cultural issues, that such rights are *not* to be construed as authorizing or encouraging any action that would dismember or *impair, totally or in part, the territorial integrity or political unity of sovereign and independent States conducting themselves in compliance with the principle of equal rights and self-determination of peoples* and thus possessed of a Government representing the whole people belonging to the territory without distinction. ... [Emphasis added.] [...]

130 [...] There is no necessary incompatibility between the maintenance of the territorial integrity of existing states, including Canada, and the right of a "people" to achieve a full measure of self-determination. A state whose government represents the whole of the people or peoples resident within its territory, on a basis of equality and without discrimination, and respects the principles of self-determination in its own internal arrangements, is entitled to the protection under international law of its territorial integrity.

(iii) Colonial and Oppressed Peoples

[...]

132 The right of colonial peoples to exercise their right to self-determination by breaking away from the "imperial" power is now undisputed, but is irrelevant to this Reference.

133 The other clear case where a right to external self-determination accrues is where a people is subject to alien subjugation, domination or exploitation outside a colonial context. [...]

134 A number of commentators have further asserted that the right to self-determination may ground a right to unilateral secession in a third circumstance. Although this third circumstance has been described in several ways, the underlying proposition is that, when a people is blocked from the meaningful exercise of its right to self-determination internally, it is entitled, as a last resort, to exercise it by secession. The Vienna Declaration requirement that governments represent "the whole people belonging to the territory without distinction of any kind" adds credence to the assertion that such a complete blockage may potentially give rise to a right of secession.

135 Clearly, such a circumstance parallels the other two recognized situations in that the ability of a people to exercise its right to self-determination internally is somehow being totally frustrated. While it remains unclear whether this third proposition actually reflects an established international law standard, it is unnecessary for present purposes to make that determination. Even assuming that the third circumstance is sufficient to create a right to unilateral secession under international law, the current Quebec context cannot be said to approach such a threshold. As stated by the *amicus curiae* [...]:

[TRANSLATION]

15 The Quebec people is not the victim of attacks on its physical existence or integrity, or of a massive violation of its fundamental rights. The Quebec people is manifestly not, in the opinion of the *amicus curiae*, an oppressed people.

16 For close to 40 of the last 50 years, the Prime Minister of Canada has been a Quebecer. During this period, Quebecers have held from time to time all the most important positions in the federal Cabinet. During the 8 years prior to June 1997,

the Prime Minister and the Leader of the Official Opposition in the House of Commons were both Quebecers. At present, the Prime Minister of Canada, the Right Honourable Chief Justice and two other members of the Court, the Chief of Staff of the Canadian Armed Forces and the Canadian ambassador to the United States, not to mention the Deputy Secretary-General of the United Nations, are all Quebecers. The international achievements of Quebecers in most fields of human endeavour are too numerous to list. Since the dynamism of the Quebec people has been directed toward the business sector, it has been clearly successful in Quebec, the rest of Canada and abroad.

136 The population of Quebec cannot plausibly be said to be denied access to government. Quebecers occupy prominent positions within the government of Canada. Residents of the province freely make political choices and pursue economic, social and cultural development within Quebec, across Canada, and throughout the world. The population of Quebec is equitably represented in legislative, executive and judicial institutions. In short, to reflect the phraseology of the international documents that address the right to self-determination of peoples, Canada is a "sovereign and independent state conducting itself in compliance with the principle of equal rights and self-determination of peoples and thus possessed of a government representing the whole people belonging to the territory without distinction".

137 The continuing failure to reach agreement on amendments to the Constitution, while a matter of concern, does not amount to a denial of self-determination. In the absence of amendments to the Canadian Constitution, we must look at the constitutional arrangements presently in effect, and we cannot conclude under current circumstances that those arrangements place Quebecers in a disadvantaged position within the scope of the international law rule.

138 In summary, the international law right to self-determination only generates, at best, a right to external self-determination in situations of former colonies; where a people is oppressed, as for example under foreign military occupation; or where a definable group is denied meaningful access to government to pursue their political, economic, social and cultural development. In all three situations, the people in question are entitled to a right to external self-determination because they have been denied the ability to exert internally their right to self-determination. Such exceptional circumstances are manifestly inapplicable to Quebec under existing conditions. Accordingly, neither the population of the province of Quebec, even if characterized in terms of "people" or "peoples", nor its representative institutions, the National Assembly, the legislature or government of Quebec, possess a right, under international law, to secede unilaterally from Canada.

139 We would not wish to leave this aspect of our answer to Question 2 without acknowledging the importance of the submissions made to us respecting the rights and concerns of aboriginal peoples in the event of a unilateral secession, as well as the appropriate means of defining the boundaries of a seceding Quebec with particular regard to the northern lands occupied largely by aboriginal peoples. However, the concern of aboriginal peoples is precipitated by the asserted right of Quebec to unilateral secession. In light of our finding that there is no such right applicable to the population of Quebec, either under the Constitution of Canada or at international law, but that on the contrary a clear democratic expression of support for secession would lead under the Constitution to negotiations in which aboriginal interests would be taken into account, it becomes unnecessary to explore further the concerns of the aboriginal peoples in this Reference.

(2) Recognition of a Factual/Political Reality: the "Effectivity" Principle

140 As stated, an argument advanced by the *amicus curiae* on this branch of the Reference was that, while international law may not ground a positive right to unilateral secession in the context of Quebec, international law equally does not prohibit secession and, in fact, international recognition would be conferred on such a political reality if it emerged, for example, via effective control of the territory of what is now the province of Quebec.

141 It is true that international law may well, depending on the circumstances, adapt to recognize a political and/or factual reality, regardless of the legality of the steps leading to its creation. However, as mentioned at the outset, effectivity, as such, does not have any real applicability to Question 2, which asks whether a right to unilateral secession exists.

142 No one doubts that legal consequences may flow from political facts, and that "sovereignty is a political fact for which no purely legal authority can be constituted ...", [citation omitted]. Secession of a province from Canada, if successful in the streets, might well lead to the creation of a new state. Although recognition by other states is not, at least as a matter of theory, necessary to achieve statehood, the viability of a would-be state in the international community depends, as a practical matter, upon recognition by other states. That process of recognition is guided by legal norms. However, international recognition is not alone constitutive of statehood and, critically, does not relate back to the date of secession to serve retroactively as a source of a "legal" right to secede in the first place. Recognition occurs only after a territorial unit has been successful, as a political fact, in achieving secession.

143 As indicated in responding to Question 1, one of the legal norms which may be recognized by states in granting or withholding recognition of emergent states is the legitimacy of the process by which the *de facto* secession is, or was, being pursued. The process of recognition, once considered to be an exercise of pure sovereign discretion, has come to be associated with legal norms. See, e.g., European Community Declaration on the Guidelines on the Recognition of New States in Eastern Europe and in the Soviet Union, 31 I.L.M. 1486 (1992), at p. 1487. While national interest and perceived political advantage to the recognizing state obviously play an important role, foreign states may also take into account their view as to the existence of a right to self-determination on the part of the population of the putative state, and a counterpart domestic evaluation, namely, an examination of the legality of the secession according to the law of the state from which the territorial unit purports to have seceded. As we indicated in our answer to Question 1, an emergent state that has disregarded legitimate obligations arising out of its previous situation can potentially expect to be hindered by that disregard in achieving international recognition, at least with respect to the timing of that recognition. On the other hand, compliance by the seceding province with such legitimate obligations would weigh in favour of international recognition. The notion that what is not explicitly prohibited is implicitly permitted has little relevance where (as here) international law refers the legality of secession to the domestic law of the seceding state and the law of that state holds unilateral secession to be unconstitutional.

144 As a court of law, we are ultimately concerned only with legal claims. If the principle of "effectivity" is no more than that "successful revolution begets its own legality" [citation omitted], it necessarily means that legality follows and does not precede the successful revolution. *Ex hypothesi*, the successful revolution took place outside the constitutional framework of the predecessor state, otherwise it would not be characterized as "a revolution". It may be that a unilateral secession by Quebec

> would eventually be accorded legal status by Canada and other states, and thus give rise to legal consequences; but this does not support the more radical contention that subsequent recognition of a state of affairs brought about by a unilateral declaration of independence could be taken to mean that secession was achieved under colour of a legal right. [...]
>
> 146 The principle of effectivity operates very differently. It proclaims that an illegal act may eventually acquire legal status if, as a matter of empirical fact, it is recognized on the international plane. [...] In this way, a change in the factual circumstances may subsequently be reflected in a change in legal status. It is, however, quite another matter to suggest that a subsequent condonation of an initially illegal act retroactively creates a legal right to engage in the act in the first place. The broader contention is not supported by the international principle of effectivity or otherwise and must be rejected.

This is one of the most celebrated decisions issued by a domestic court. It was also influential on other courts.[44] It is widely cited for reaffirming that international law neither allows nor (explicitly) prohibits secession. It was the first to clarify the law of self-determination outside the colonial context and did so on the question of Quebec's secession, which was widely considered as unsupported by law.[45] The court held that external self-determination was a right of colonial peoples and, outside a colonial context, a right of peoples that were subject to alien subjugation, domination, or exploitation. As also noted by the ILDC reporter, the judgment reflected the general preference in international law for the territorial integrity and stability of states.[46] After some hesitation ('it remains unclear whether this third proposition actually reflects an established international law standard'), the court seemed to embrace the so-called 'remedial secession', at least as a last resort in the rarest of circumstances where a definable group is denied internal self-determination, in the sense of 'meaningful access to government to pursue their political, economic, social and cultural development'. This decision is indeed among the authorities cited in support of remedial secession although that theory remains highly controversial and it is still not established that it is accepted by positive law.[47] In any case, it was easy to find that Quebec's situation within Canada by and large failed to reach the very high threshold of such an entitlement, even if applicable.

As to the principle of effectivity in the context of international law, despite expressing some disfavour ('the existence of a positive legal entitlement is quite different from a prediction that the law will respond after the fact to a then-existing political reality'), the court acknowledged the important role it can play if a secession is successful and is recognized by states ('Secession of a province from Canada, if successful in the streets, might well lead to the creation of a new state'). This explains the conclusion that international law does not ultimately prohibit secession,[48] unless of course such secession has resulted from a serious breach of a *jus cogens* norm. Such a breach triggers the obligation of non-recognition,[49] which vitiates and obliterates effectivity since effectivity in this sense requires and depends on recognition ('the viability of a would-be state in the

44 See, eg, *The Province of North Cotabato et al v The Government of the Republic of the Philippines et al*, Supreme Court of the Philippines, 14 October 2008, which followed and reproduced large parts of *Re Secession of Quebec* to decide the case.

45 See, eg, A Cassese, *Self-Determination of Peoples: A Legal Reappraisal* (CUP 1995) 253.

46 G MacNeil, Analysis, *Secession of Quebec, Re*, ILDC 184 (CA 1998) A7.

47 For a convincing rejection of remedial secession in the period following Kosovo's declaration of independence and the ICJ Advisory Opinion on Kosovo see K Del Mar, 'The Myth of Remedial Secession' in French (n 24) 79–108.

48 See P Dumberry, 'Lessons Learned from the *Quebec Secession Reference* Before the Supreme Court of Canada' in Kohen (n 9) 416, 437.

49 ibid, 440 n 131; Crawford (n 6) 158; Christakis (n 9) 142; Milano (n 9) 64.

international community depends, as a practical matter, upon recognition by other states'). This is further illustrated in the following cases discussed in this section.

Another legacy of this landmark judgment was the controversial proposition that the legality of the secession under domestic (constitutional) law would/should be taken into account by states when considering recognition of the seceding entity. This judicious proposition was criticized for being at variance with established law and practice on recognition, still falling within the discretion of states.[50]

Lastly, since it concluded that Quebec was not entitled to unilateral secession, the court left unresolved the question of defining the boundaries of a seceding Quebec with particular regard to the northern lands occupied largely by aboriginal peoples. The contentious issue here was whether Quebec would have been entitled to retain its federal boundaries and thus incorporate the aboriginals, based on controversial application of the *uti possidetis* principle outside its original colonial context, or the affected aboriginal peoples could opt to remain part of Canada.[51] *Uti possidetis* has given rise to thorny issues in the context of non-decolonization territorial disputes.[52] In *One Third of the National Assembly Deputies*, the Constitutional Court of Slovenia accepted the application of *uti possidetis* as a general principle of international law applicable for determination of the borders of the states created upon the dissolution of the former Yugoslavia absent an agreement on border delimitation.[53]

Autocephalous Greek-Orthodox Church of Cyprus and Cyprus v Goldberg and Feldman Fine Arts Incorporated and Goldberg, Appeal judgment, 917 F2d 278 (7th Cir 1990), ILDC 1676 (US 1990), 24th October 1990, United States; Court of Appeals (7th Circuit) [7th Cir]

This case concerned the return of four Byzantine mosaics stolen from the Kanakaria church in Turkish-occupied northern Cyprus in the late 1970s. The defendant, an art dealer from Indiana, purchased them in 1988. The US District Court for the Southern District of Indiana awarded possession of the mosaics to the Church of Cyprus as the rightful owner. Upon appeal, one of the arguments was that the District Court had erred in not giving effect to several confiscatory decrees issued in 1975 by the Turkish Federated State of Cyprus (the forerunner of the TRNC) that had divested the church of title to the mosaics.

> 49 What Goldberg is claiming is that the TFSC's confiscatory decrees, adopted only one year after the Turkish invasion, should be given effect by this court because the TFSC and its successor TRNC should now be viewed as the "*de facto*" government north of the Green Line. This we are unwilling to do. We draw on two lines of precedent as support for our decision. First, we note that, contrary to the New York court's decision in *Salimoff*, 262 N.Y. 220, 186 N.E. 679, several courts of the same era refused to give effect to the nationalization decrees of the as-yet-unrecognized Soviet Republics. These courts relied on a variety of grounds, including especially the fact that the political branches of our government still refused to recognize these entities. [. . .] Similarly, as regards the Turkish administration in northern Cyprus, the United States government (like the rest of the non-Turkish world) has not recognized its legitimacy, nor does our government "recognize that [the Turkish administration]

50 Dumberry (n 48) 438–40.

51 ibid, 443–46. See also S Lalonde, 'Quebec's Boundaries in the Event of Secession' (2003) 3 *Macquarie Law Journal* 129.

52 For recent thorough reviews of the debate see A Peters, 'The Principle of Uti Possidetis Juris: How Relevant Is It for Issues of Secession?' in C Walter, A von Ungern-Sternberg, and K Abushov (eds), *Self-Determination and Secession in International Law* (OUP 2014) 68–94; T Christakis and A Constantinides, 'Territorial Disputes in the Context of Secessionist Conflicts' in M Kohen and M Hebie (eds), *Research Handbook on Territorial Disputes in International Law* (Edward Elgar Publishing 2018) 343–95.

53 *One Third of the National Assembly Deputies*, Constitutional Review, Rm-1/00-29, Official Gazette of Slovenia, No 43/2001, ILDC 402 (SI 2001), 19 April 2001, Constitutional Court, para 24.

has functioned as a de facto or quasi government . . ., ruling within its own borders." *Salimoff*, 186 N.E. at 682 (relying on the fact that the U.S. government had so "recognized" the Soviet government).

50 Second, we are guided in part by the post-Civil War cases in which courts refused to give effect to property-affecting acts of the Confederate state legislatures. In one such case, *Williams v. Bruffy*, 96 U.S. 176, 24 L. Ed. 716 (1878), the Supreme Court drew a helpful distinction between two kinds of "*de facto*" governments. The first kind "is such as exists after it has expelled the regularly constituted authorities from the seats of power and the public offices, and established its own functionaries in their places, so as to represent in fact the sovereignty of the nation." *Id.* at 185. This kind of *de facto* government, the Court explained, "is treated as in most respects possessing rightful authority, . . . [and] its legislation is in general recognized." *Id.* The second kind of *de facto* government "is such as exists where a portion of the inhabitants of a country have separated themselves from the parent State and established an independent government. The validity of its acts, both against the parent State and its citizens or subjects, depends entirely upon its ultimate success. . . . If it succeeds, and becomes recognized, its acts from the commencement of its existence are upheld as those of an independent nation." *Id.* at 186. (The Court held that the Confederacy was a government of the second type that ultimately failed.) Goldberg argues that the TFSC and its successor TRNC have achieved the level of "ultimate success" contemplated by this standard, because they have maintained control of the territory north of the Green Line for over fifteen years. We will not thus equate simple longevity of control with "ultimate success." The Turkish forces, despite their best efforts, did not completely supplant the Republic nor its officers. Instead, the TFSC and the TRNC, neither of which has ever been recognized by the non-Turkish world, only acceded to the control of the northern portion of Cyprus. The Republic of Cyprus remains the only recognized Cypriot government, the sovereign nation for the entire island. Rejecting Goldberg's invitation to delve any further into facts and current events which are not of record in this proceeding, we conclude that the confiscatory decrees proffered by Goldberg do not divest the Church of its claim of title.

The court's conclusion that the Republic of Cyprus remains the sovereign nation for the entire island reaffirmed the established rule that occupation does not affect the continuity of the state and illegal intervention does not extinguish the formal or even the actual independence of the state.[54] That said, the post-Civil War case law that was applied seemed rather odd in terms of (contemporary) international law. Following that case law, the court could seem to have suggested that the Goldberg claim would have been successful if the Turkish forces had occupied the entire island of Cyprus, displaced the legitimate government altogether, and received recognition, in what could perhaps be reminiscent of *debellatio*, which is considered as inconsistent with contemporary international law.[55] Yet, in contemporary international law there is a legal duty to withhold recognition in this kind of unlawful territorial situations resulting from the violation of peremptory rules of international law such as the prohibition of the use of force.[56]

54 Crawford (n 6) 73.

55 E Benvenisti, *The International Law of Occupation* (2nd edn, OUP 2013) 163.

56 See ILC Articles on State Responsibility, Article 41 para 2, Report of the International Law Commission on the Work of its Fifty-Third Session, UN GAOR 56th Sess, Supp No 10 (2001) 43 ('No State shall recognize as lawful a situation created by a serious breach [of an obligation arising under a peremptory norm of general international law], nor render aid or assistance in maintaining that situation'). See also Crawford (n 6) 148; Milano (n 9) 64.

Republic of Cyprus and ors v Dikmen, Appeal judgment, 19 U 4878/10, ILDC 2236 (DE 2013), 18th March 2013, Germany; Bavaria; Munich; Higher Regional Court [OLG]

This case also concerned restitution of cultural objects plundered from churches in northern Cyprus after the 1974 Turkish invasion. The Greek Orthodox, Armenian, and Maronite Churches of Cyprus lodged a complaint seeking restitution of many of the cultural objects found in the collection of the defendant, a Turkish antique dealer residing in Munich. The Republic of Cyprus joined the complaint, seeking restitution of the prehistoric artefacts in the same collection. Restitution was possible under German law if title to the objects was proven. In this regard, one of the issues raised was whether the occupation of northern Cyprus since 1974 and the establishment of the TRNC in 1983 had any impact on the ownership rights of the Churches.

> H4 The artworks could be considered as having come from the location in northern Cyprus as asserted by the churches. The churches could prove the origins of the artworks and so could lawfully invoke their title to the property. Dikmen could neither bring any title to the goods nor prove their acquisition by any legal method. However, this was only valid for the artworks that had been plundered in the churches and monasteries, but not for the excavated prehistoric materials. Even if they had also come from the part that was controlled by the *de facto* authorities of the TRNC, the first instance judgment constituted an incomplete decision and the question of the prehistoric objects had not been decided. The first instance decision had not succeeded in establishing that the objects found in a territory that belonged *de jure* to the Republic of Cyprus, but were *de facto* out of its control, could be considered as the property of the legal government of Cyprus. The TRNC was not considered as a subject of international law. No state except Turkey had recognized the TRNC as a state. (paragraphs 46-48)
>
> H5 The self-proclaimed TRNC declared its independence on 15 November 1983 and was recognized as a state on the same day by the Republic of Turkey. Northern Cyprus still belonged *de jure* to the Republic of Cyprus. The Security Council of the United Nations ('UNSC') had stated in its Resolution 541, UN Doc S/RES/541, 18 November 1983 'that the attempt to create a "Turkish Republic of Northern Cyprus" is invalid', that 'the declaration referred to above is legally invalid and calls for its withdrawal'. Furthermore, it '(c)alls upon all States not to recognize any Cypriot State other than the Republic of Cyprus'. This call was followed by the European Union. (paragraph 49)

The court held that the occupation of northern Cyprus since 1974 and the establishment of the TRNC in 1983 had not resulted in any lawful transfer of property rights and thus the Churches had not been deprived of their rights. As noted by the ILDC reporter, this was in line with the relevant case law of the European Court of Human Rights (ECtHR) on the property rights of displaced Greek Cypriots, which, however, the court did not cite.[57]

The court affirmed that the northern part of Cyprus, which is *de facto* administered by the TRNC, belongs *de jure* to the Republic of Cyprus even though the latter does not exercise *de facto* control over that part since 1974. As commented by the ILDC reporter, the court denied any legal personality under international law to the self-proclaimed TRNC,[58] considering its non-recognition by the international community of states, except for Turkey. This could have alluded to the constitutive approach to recognition but the court also invoked Security Council

57 R Caballero, Analysis, *Republic of Cyprus and ors v Dikmen*, ILDC 2236 (DE 2013) A4–A6.
58 ibid, A1.

Resolution 541, which had declared the proclamation of the TRNC as legally invalid and called upon all states not to recognize it.

A better view on the matter is that the TRNC is denied statehood (and hence recognition) due to its illegal creation, that is, as a result of Turkey's unlawful use of force in 1974 and continued occupation of northern Cyprus since then.[59] Non-recognition of the TRNC is thus a collective duty, a consequence of the breach of an obligation arising under a peremptory norm of general international law (prohibition of the use of force) in the sense of Articles 40 and 41 of the ILC Articles on State Responsibility. As stated by the ILC, 'where a serious breach [...] has resulted in a situation that might otherwise call for recognition, this has nonetheless to be withheld'.[60] This duty originated in the inter-war period as the so-called 'Stimson doctrine' in response to illegal annexation of territories,[61] such as in the case that follows.

Border Treaty, Re, Kariņš and ors v Parliament of Latvia and Cabinet of Ministers of Latvia, Constitutional Review, Case No 2007-10-0102, ILDC 884 (LV 2007), 29th November 2007, Latvia; Constitutional Court

This case was brought by 21 members of the Latvian Parliament, asking the Constitutional Court to declare that the Law authorizing the conclusion of the 2007 Border Treaty between Latvia and Russia was not in conformity with Latvia's Declaration of Independence of 1990, and that the Border Treaty, modifying Latvia's borders, and the Ratification Law were unconstitutional. The Preamble of the Declaration of Independence established the basis of the doctrine of legal continuity of Latvia. Latvia became independent in 1920; it was then occupied and annexed by the Soviets in 1940, before regaining independence in 1990. In examining the application, the Constitutional Court made a very extensive and thorough analysis of the factual and legal background of Latvia's statehood. The focus here is on the illegality and non-recognition of Latvia's annexation and the continuity of the state.

> 29.1. [...] According to the general legal principle *ex iniuria ius non oritur* (unlawful acts do not create rights), annexation carried out as a result of an unlawful use of force could not enjoy international legality. [...]
>
> Initially being developed in the form of the so-called Stimson's doctrine, the principle along with its application was recognized also in other situations. [...]
>
> One can agree with the evaluation given in the doctrine that in the late 30s of the XX century from different international treaties and state practice, an international obligation of non-recognition of acquisition of territory, which is a result of unlawful use of force, had developed. [...]
>
> 32. [...] As the principle of self-determination of people, as well as prohibition of the unlawful use of force or threat thereof developed, additional legal criteria crystallised in international law in accordance with the principle *ex injuria ius non oritur*. The effect of these rules could be different. Sometimes the principle *ex injuria ius non oritur* precluded

59 See, eg, Crawford (n 6) 133, 159–61; A Constantinides, 'The Cyprus Problem in the United Nations Security Council' (2014) 19 *Austrian Review of International and European Law* 29, 51. This was also confirmed by the ICJ in *Accordance with International Law of the Unilateral Declaration of Independence in Respect of Kosovo* (Advisory Opinion) [2010] ICJ Rep 403, where the Court stated (at para 81, with reference to, *inter alia*, northern Cyprus) that 'the illegality attached [by the Security Council] to the declarations of independence thus stemmed [...] from the fact that they were, or would have been, connected with the unlawful use of force or other egregious violations of norms of general international law, in particular those of a peremptory character (*jus cogens*)'.

60 ILC, 'Report of the International Law Commission on the Work of its Fifty-Third Session: Commentary to Article 41 of the Articles on Responsibility of States for Internationally Wrongful Acts' (2001) UN Doc A/56/10, p 115, para 8.

61 D Turns, 'The Stimson Doctrine of Non-Recognition: Its Historical Genesis and Influence on Contemporary International Law' (2003) 2 *Chinese Journal of International Law* 105.

the existence of a State in the cases when although the Montevideo criteria were met other important rules of international law were violated (e.g. in respect to observance of the rights of self-determination, racial discrimination and unlawful use of force) [. . .]. In other cases the principle *ex injuria ius non oritur* meant the existence or continued existence of a State when it did incompletely fulfill the Montevideo criteria (e.g. in respect to exercising the rights of self-determination or unlawful annexation) [. . .].

32.1. [. . .] The principle *ex injuria ius non oritur* imposes obligations on subjects of international law not to recognize unlawful situations, including unlawful annexation of territories to other states if the annexation has taken place in breach of rules of international and domestic law or by force. The abovementioned principle raises the obligation of the international community to at least react to the illegal annexation of a State or its part to the territory of another State and not to recognize such changes as legally complete (the so-called collective non-recognition duty) [. . .] The international community does not recognize illegal annexation of a State or a part thereof to the territory of other state as accomplished. It means that the unlawfully destroyed state *de iure* continues existing and there consequently also exists a legal possibility to restore the respective state *de facto* in accordance with the rules of international law. If such state is *de facto* restored, it does not form a new State but continues its *de facto* interrupted statehood. This is the essence of the doctrine of legal continuity in international law that follows from the use of force or threat of the use of force according.

32.2. [. . .] State continuity describes the continuity or identity of States as legal persons in international law. The basis of State continuity is subject to relevant claims and recognition of those claims determined, in principle, in accordance with the applicable international law rules or procedures when statehood is at issue [. . .].

If a state, independence of which has been illegally terminated, restores its statehood, it can under the doctrine of continuity recognize itself as the same State which had been illegally terminated. In this case it is necessary that the state itself establishes its continuity and acts in accordance with the claims of this doctrine both in international relations and domestic policy, and it is also necessary that such self-assessment of the state is accepted by the international community. [. . .]

International law does not require a restitution of international rights and obligations of the State, but instead to carry out their re-evaluation on the basis of an *a priori* existence, through *ad hoc* agreements on the necessity to terminate, amend them or by concluding their invalidity as a result of the *rebus sic stantibus* doctrine. In other words, changes have to take place within the framework of the doctrine of continuity, rather than outside it.

As a result of such fundamental changes, not only the self-assessment of the State is important, but also the reaction of the international community; the international community is entitled not to recognize the position of the State regarding its continuity. [. . .]

33.1. Latvia has never recognized the conduct of the USSR against Latvia in 1940 as lawful [. . .]

The protests of [the] ambassadors of Latvia expressed the official viewpoint of Latvia, because the government of the Republic of Latvia terminated its work as a result of the aggression and occupation by the USSR. Having regard to these reports, Latvian diplomatic and consular agencies in foreign States continued their activities up to the restoration of independence of the Republic of Latvia without recognizing the annexation of Latvia to the USSR and by representing interests of the Republic of Latvia as organs of the State [. . .]. [. . .]

33.2. The struggle of the citizens of Latvia for the restoration of the statehood of Latvia began soon after the occupation of Latvia. [. . .] This movement involved almost all residents of Latvia and was concluded by the passage of the Declaration on Independence on May 4, 1990 and passage of the Constitutional Law on August 21, 1991. [. . .]

The Declaration on Independence establishes the *de facto* renewal of the Latvian independence of the Republic of Latvia, confirming the doctrine of Latvian State continuity. [. . .]

The restored Republic of Latvia identifies itself with the pre-war Latvia. The constitutional institutions of Latvia justify their position with the fact that after the events of 1940 Latvia as a subject of international law had not lost its status. After restoration of independence, Latvia continues its statehood (*integratio ad integrum*) [. . .].

34. Continuity of Latvia has also been recognized by the international community. Initially this recognition manifested itself as non-recognition of the illegal incorporation of Latvia into the USSR, but after restoration of independence of Latvia it turned into recognition of continuity of the State of Latvia, namely, the international community recognized the State restored on May 4, 1990 to be the same State, independence of which had been unlawfully terminated in 1940.

34.1. [. . .] Unlawful annexation of the Baltic States to the USSR were not recognised, along with the US, by the FRG, France, Italy, Canada, Japan and more than 50 other States of the world [. . .].

Consequently one can justifiably conclude that the international community did not recognize occupation and annexation of Latvia, as well as confirmed the *de facto* restoration of independence of Latvia. This position was expressed in the practice of both States and international organization, in respect to bilateral and multilateral agreements and financial and human rights obligations [. . .].

34.2. After 1990, when the Baltic States regained their independence, most States that had never recognized their incorporation into the USSR, declared the re-establishment of their diplomatic relations. [. . .]

The most important international organizations recognized the continuity of the Baltic States [. . .]. [. . .]

The international society supported the claim of the Baltic States for their State continuity, which followed from the non-recognition of occupation and annexation by these States.

34.3. [. . .] International law does not require all other States to recognize the State continuity. Taking into account the factual context of the unlawful annexation, almost always at least one State will consider the situation to be lawful, and it would be absurd to confer veto rights to this State or to these states of absolute minority. Approval of state continuity claim can be established when assessing reaction of the international society in general. When assessing the practice of the states in 1940 – 1990, it is possible to identify isolated opposite or contradictory opinions of States, however it is necessary to consider these exceptions in their broader legal context. The scope and content of the duty of collective non-recognition of unlawful situations has been controversial also in the later cases when it was assessed in the framework of the UN and in the International Court [. . .]. Regarding Latvia and other Baltic States, the duty of non-recognition of unlawful situations followed largely from the customary international law and it was not concretized in the framework of international organizations, therefore the precise scope, content and way of implementation of this duty

> *de facto* remained in the discretion of the specific states. Taking into account the decentralized model of non-recognition, the practice of the absolute majority of States, international organizations and case law has during 50 years consistently retained the position of non-recognition, in legally essential moments confirming the non-recognition of unlawful annexation and the continuation of the statehood of Latvia, that the European Court of Human Rights also recognised in the form of a judgment.

This was a quite elaborate exposition of the principle *ex iniuria ius non oritur* and the effects of recognition/non-recognition on a state's claim to continuity. As noted by the ILDC reporter, the court's conclusions were generally in line with the prevailing scholarly opinion that due to the Soviet aggression against Latvia, followed by its unlawful occupation and annexation, Latvia's statehood only ceased *de facto* and Latvia continued to exist *de jure*.[62] The obligation of non-recognition was considered as applying back to the Second World War when Latvia and the other Baltic states were annexed to the USSR. The court downplayed the opposite or contradictory views of some states toward the Soviet annexation of the Baltic states by emphasizing the reaction of the international community at large. In view of that diversity, some scholars have been more cautious on whether there was a customary obligation of non-recognition back in 1940.[63]

John Doe v United States, Trial judgment, ILDC 1868 (US 2010), 95 Fed.Cl. 546 (Fed. Cl. 2010), 10th November 2010, United States; Court of Federal Claims [Fed Cl]

The Iraqi plaintiff filed a suit in the US concerning the temporary occupation, due to 'military necessity', of his home in Fallujah, Iraq, by members of the US Marine Corps and Coalition Forces fighting Iraqi insurgents in March 2004. He alleged that the conduct of the Coalition Forces constituted a 'taking of property without either due process or fair compensation', as protected by the Fifth Amendment to the US Constitution, which was guaranteed to inhabitants of territories 'in which the United States exercises sovereign power'. The plaintiff argued that he had standing as a non-US resident because, *inter alia*, the United States was at the time exercising sovereign authority over Iraq through the Coalition Provisional Authority (CPA) following the invasion of Iraq by the US and its allies in 2003. The US denied those claims, arguing that the US had not acquired *de jure* sovereignty over Iraq during the occupation.

> 56 Plaintiff cannot overcome the weight of law against the propositions that the United States was the sovereign in Iraq or that Iraq was an unincorporated territory of the United States at the time of the occupation of his house. First, plaintiff does not rely on any precedent, or even a single case, that establishes that the United States acquires de jure sovereignty over a country because United States military forces temporarily occupy it, even if those forces exercise some form of governmental authority during that time. […] The United States may acquire territory by discovery, by agreement or treaty, and by conquest. […] However, the mere possession of a territory, even by treaty, does not translate automatically into an exercise of sovereign authority. […]
>
> 58 In *Boumediene*, trumpeted by plaintiff, Justice Kennedy distinguished between de jure and de facto sovereignty, explaining that "it is not altogether uncommon for a territory to be under the *de jure* sovereignty of one nation, while under the plenary control, or practical sovereignty, of another." […] Plaintiff seizes on this distinction to argue that the United States exercised de facto sovereignty over Iraq. […]
>
> 59 The Court in *Boumediene* rejected the Government's argument that, "as applied to noncitizens, the Constitution necessarily stops when *de jure* sovereignty ends," […] and concluded that "by virtue of its complete jurisdiction and control," […] over the United

62 E Broks, Analysis, *Border Treaty, Re, Kariņš and ors v Parliament of Latvia and Cabinet of Ministers of Latvia*, ILDC 884 (LV 2007) A6.

63 ibid, A20, with further reference to Jennings and Watts (n 5) 186.

States Naval Station at Guantanamo Bay, Cuba, the United States "maintains *de facto* sovereignty over this territory" while Cuba retains de jure sovereignty […]. Any factual counterpart, however, is absent in the present controversy. […]

60 Unlike the unique "complete jurisdiction and control" exercised by the United States over Guantanamo Bay—which is provided for by treaty—or other United States territories, at no time was Iraq "acquired" by the United States or any of its Coalition partners. […] Nor can plaintiff point to any UN resolution or act of Congress that recognizes the United States or the CPA as the sovereign power in Iraq. See S.C. Res. 1483, at 1 (reaffirming "the sovereignty and territorial integrity of Iraq"). Plaintiff cannot escape the reality that, while the CPA indeed may have exercised governmental and administrative functions, that role does not translate into an exercise of sovereignty because the CPA was a multinational organization. […] As defendant has shown, the documents themselves cited by plaintiff attest to the multinational composition of the CPA. See S.C. Res. 1483, at 2 (recognizing that nations comprising the CPA acted as "occupying powers under unified command," and calling upon "the Authority, ... to promote the welfare of the Iraqi people through the effective administration of the territory" (emphasis added)). Nor did Iraq ever come under the "complete jurisdiction and control" of the United States the way Guantanamo Bay did following the end of the Spanish American War. […]

61 In fact, defendant points to actions taken by the United States that persuasively demonstrate that neither Congress nor the President ever intended the United States to exercise sovereign power in Iraq. […]

As observed by the ILDC reporter, the court's decision relied on domestic law and jurisprudence without any discussion of international law apart from the references to Security Council Resolution 1483.[64] It involved an interesting discussion of sovereignty, a concept with notoriously various meanings.[65] Indeed, the circumstances surrounding the adoption of Resolution 1483 and subsequent ones on Iraq in the aftermath of the country's invasion and occupation by the US and its allies showed that Iraqi sovereignty was central to those debates and was used in different ways by different actors.[66] The court's conclusion that the United States did not exercise sovereignty over Iraq was consistent with international law and with the presumption that occupation was considered as a temporary condition that did not bring about changes in the sovereignty of the occupied state.[67]

V. Conclusion

The survey of these representative cases demonstrates that certificates issued by the Executive on statehood and recognition are by and large conclusive for domestic courts in common law jurisdictions. In other jurisdictions, as well as in exceptional cases when courts in common law jurisdictions must make their own determinations, there is space for conflicting outcomes, as illustrated by the cases concerning Taiwan, where domestic courts reached different conclusions on the statehood of Taiwan, which were even at variance with their government's policy.

64 R Mayor, Analysis, *John Doe v United States*, ILDC 1868 (US 2010) A5–A6.

65 Crawford (n 6) 32.

66 T Grant, 'The Security Council and Iraq: An Incremental Practice' (2003) 97 *American Journal of International Law* 823, 836.

67 R Mayor, Analysis, *John Doe v United States*, ILDC 1868 (US 2010) A7. Cf Crawford (n 6) 689, observing that, absent a competing government-in-exile, an occupation government regulated under Chapter VII of the UN Charter, such as the CPA, 'may possess general status as an entity authorised to act on behalf of the State, even though it is not an indigenous government and has not been elected or otherwise chosen by the people of the State'.

It is also noteworthy that domestic courts in Germany, the Netherlands, Switzerland, and Tanzania did not refer to the Montevideo Convention when making pronouncements on statehood but mostly relied on publicists, whilst the US courts relied on the Restatement, which reproduces the Montevideo formula. Thus, in most non-US cases reviewed in this chapter there is notable absence of the fourth Montevideo element of statehood (capacity to enter into relations with other states), which seems to corroborate the scholarly opinion about its irrelevance for statehood and, in its lieu, the preponderance of (formal) independence as an attribute of statehood.

The case law of domestic courts also confirms the long-established rules on implied recognition. As to recognition of governments, the elaborate criteria set out by lower courts in the United Kingdom in the 1990s were an interesting move towards upsetting the traditional predominance of effective control as the sole factor for recognition. However, the renewed practice of the UK to confer recognition on governments has put on ice that judicial venture.

When it comes to questions of legitimacy, a central theme in many decisions was the interplay between legality and effectiveness in unlawful territorial situations. The outcome is by and large a vindication for the principle of legality, corroborating the prevailing view that statehood in contemporary international law is no longer a monopoly of effectiveness.

From the viewpoint of international law, the quality of domestic decisions on statehood and recognition varies. Many courts have produced lengthy and pertinent judgments of high quality (eg, on Quebec's secession, on Latvia's annexation etc). Other times, when complex questions of international law were decided without much international law analysis or on purely domestic doctrines, the decisions are more relevant in terms of their outcome, as a matter and indication of state practice, rather than for the value of their analysis.

3
Jurisdiction

CEDRIC RYNGAERT, HARMEN VAN DER WILT,
AND JUAN SANTOS VARA

I. Introduction

The law of jurisdiction is concerned with the delimitation of states' powers to adopt and enforce their laws regarding situations beyond, or partly beyond, their own borders.

Domestic courts have played a particularly prominent role in the law of jurisdiction. Frequently, they have been requested to review the reach of domestic laws in light of international law; in so doing, they have contributed to the crystallization of norms of customary international law on jurisdiction. In fact, *international* courts have offered only scant guidance as to the law of jurisdiction: the 1927 Permanent Court of International Justice's *Lotus* judgment still stands as an authoritative decision, despite its obvious flaws.[1] By and large, domestic courts have not followed the liberal *Lotus* rule of jurisdiction, pursuant to which any jurisdictional assertion is presumptively lawful, absent evidence of a prohibitive rule to the contrary. Instead, they have tended to apply the Draft Convention on Jurisdiction designed at Harvard in 1935.[2] This convention rejects the *Lotus* approach and only allows the exercise of jurisdiction if the asserting state grounds its jurisdictional assertion on a *permissive* principle of jurisdiction: territoriality, nationality/personality, security, or universality.

The law of jurisdiction has been developed in particular in criminal law and, to a lesser extent, in economic law (antitrust and competition law in particular). Section II discusses a number of recent criminal cases, with a particular focus on the contentious universality principle (which does not require a nexus with the state exercising jurisdiction)—although it starts with two cases that gave an expansive interpretation to the territoriality and personality principles. Section III discusses the reach of states' economic laws, the enforcement of which is often quasi-criminal and thus considered as subject to public international law rules of jurisdiction developed in the field of criminal law.

II. Criminal Jurisdiction

Traditionally, criminal jurisdiction is strongly wedded to the state's territory, because criminal law is an asset of sovereignty. The exercise of extraterritorial jurisdiction easily generates conflicts

1 PCIJ, *SS Lotus (France v Turkey)* [1927] PCIJ Reports, Series A No 10, p 19: 'It does not [. . .] follow that international law prohibits a State from exercising jurisdiction in its own territory, in respect of any case which relates to acts which have taken place abroad, and in which it cannot rely on some permissive rule of international law. Such a view would only be tenable if international law contained a general prohibition to States to extend the application of their laws and the jurisdiction of their courts to persons, property and acts outside their territory, and if, as an exception to this general prohibition, it allowed States to do so in certain specific cases. But this is certainly not the case under international law as it stands at present. Far from laying down a general prohibition to the effect that States may not extend the application of their laws and the jurisdiction of their courts to persons, property and acts outside their territory, it leaves them in this respect a wide measure of discretion which is only limited in certain cases by prohibitive rules; as regards other cases, every State remains free to adopt the principles which it regards as best and most suitable'. The *Lotus* dictum is undesirable, as it allows for an inflation of possible assertions of concurrent jurisdiction by different States. See C Ryngaert, *Jurisdiction in International Law* (OUP 2008).

2 Harvard Research on International Law, 'Draft Convention on Jurisdiction with Respect to Crime' (1935) 29 AJIL 439, 468.

between states and is therefore suitable for international legal regulation. Universal jurisdiction, which does not require any links between the crime/offender and the forum state, is a particularly sensitive issue. In this survey, case law of the Western European states that have been most active in the realm of universal jurisdiction features prominently.

Al-Shami v Ayalon, Appeal Judgment, No K08/0386 Rechtspraak.nl: BK7374 (translation of BK1478), ILDC 673 (NL 2009), 26 October 2009, Netherlands; The Hague; Court of Appeal

On 16 May 2008, counsel for Al-Shami, a resident of the Occupied Palestinian Territory of Gaza, registered a complaint of torture at the National Public Prosecutor's Office allegedly committed in the period from 31 December 1999 until February 2000 by Ayalon, who at the time was head of Shin Bet, the Israeli Security Agency. Ayalon was present in the Netherlands between 16 and 20 May 2008.

The complaint of 16 May 2008 included evidence of the alleged torture and made reference to state obligations in terms of the Convention Against Torture and Cruel, Inhuman and Degrading Treatment. Al-Shami's counsel requested the public prosecutor to inform her as soon as possible as to whether a criminal investigation against Ayalon would take place, stressing the urgent nature of the complaint.

The public prosecutor decided not to start criminal proceedings, after which Ayalon had left the country, whereupon Al-Shami lodged a complaint with the Court of Appeal in order to challenge the Prosecutor's decision.

The question to be decided was whether the Netherlands had jurisdiction, following Ayalon's departure from the Netherlands, in respect of the offences allegedly committed by him.

> 11. The question to be decided by the Court of Appeal is whether the Netherlands now has jurisdiction — following the complainee's departure from the Netherlands — in respect of the offences allegedly committed by him. To answer this question, it may be relevant in certain circumstances to know whether the Netherlands had jurisdiction at the time of the complainee's stay in the Netherlands. [. . .]
>
> 12.1 The Court of Appeal cannot determine with sufficient certainty from the information and the accompanying explanatory notes whether the complainee was classified as a suspect at the time of his stay in the Netherlands. Indeed, in view of the submissions and the available data, it may even be doubted whether there was the slightest suspicion against the complainee. Nor is this altered by the documents accompanying the information, which quote statements by the complainee to the effect (in essence) that, generally speaking, he approved of the interrogation methods used by his service.
>
> The Court of Appeal considers the classification as a 'verdachte' (suspect) to be of importance since under the Torture Convention (and, by extension, section 2 of the International Crimes Act) there has to be a suspect if jurisdiction is to be established. In the Bouterse judgment the Supreme Court used the term 'vermoedelijke dader', which was evidently based on the English text of the Convention. Articles 5 (2) and 6 (1) of the English text refer to the 'alleged offender' and 'a person alleged to have committed any offence' respectively. The French text of the Convention uses the term 'une personne soupçonnée'.
>
> In the opinion of the Court of Appeal this disparity with the English text is of relatively minor importance since article 6 (1) also provides that the custody and other legal measures 'shall be as provided in the law of that State'. The Court of Appeal assumes that custody and other legal measures are possible in the Netherlands only if there is a person who can be treated as the suspect, certainly in cases not involving extradition. In the opinion of the Court of Appeal the terms 'alleged offender' and 'vermoedelijke dader' can to this extent — and in so far as relevant here — be equated with the term 'verdachte' as used in the Dutch translation of the Torture Convention, which corresponds with the French text.

> Article 6 (1) of the Torture Convention also provides that a State Party should take a suspect into custody or take other legal measures to ensure his presence once it is satisfied, after an examination of information available to it, that the circumstances so warrant. The Court of Appeal considers — to put it mildly — that the possibility cannot by any means be excluded that further investigation was needed if the complainee was to be treated as a suspect, i.e. as someone reasonably suspected of an offence. The Court of Appeal is not aware of any such investigation. The Court of Appeal therefore doubts whether the complainee was already a suspect and could have been interviewed or arrested as such in the Netherlands. [. . .]
>
> 15. In the opinion of the Court of Appeal the Netherlands does not now have jurisdiction over the complainee since the Public Prosecution Service carried out no investigation whatever into the complainee's alleged role or share in the torture of the complainant (and was indeed unable to carry out an investigation given the shortness of the complainee's stay in the Netherlands) and also since the complainee was not arrested at that time and is no longer in the Netherlands. The Court of Appeal also notes here that the wording used in the Convention and the Act is 'is present', not 'was present' or 'has been present'. Nor, by the way, does the Court of Appeal consider it likely that the complainee will return to the Netherlands at some time in the future.
>
> 16. The Court of Appeal refers in this connection to the Explanatory Memorandum to the International Crimes Bill, which also used that wording: 'There are good reasons for limiting universal jurisdiction to suspects present in the territory of the state. First, trial in absentia, without any connection with the case [. . .], is generally seen as inappropriate. And, second, trial in absentia can easily give rise to conflicts of jurisdiction [. . .].' The Court of Appeal therefore notes that it was, above all, the wish to prevent trials in absentia (and such a trial would almost certainly have occurred in the present case if proceedings had been instituted by the Public Prosecution Service) which was decisive in the inclusion of a provision in the Act limiting universal jurisdiction to cases in which the person concerned is present in the Netherlands.
>
> 17. As regards the expediency of prosecuting the complainee in the Netherlands, the Court of Appeal would observe for the record that, quite apart from the lack of jurisdiction, the further investigation that would be necessary in Israel would not seem possible at first sight since it is unlikely that the Israeli authorities would consent to this.
>
> 18. In view of the above, the Court of Appeal considers that it was reasonable for the public prosecutor to decide not to institute criminal proceedings against the complainee after he left the Netherlands.

In this case, the Court of Appeal was confronted with one of the dismal consequences of the familiar construction under international law, requiring the presence of the suspect as a prerequisite for the exercise of universal jurisdiction. The pertinent question was whether jurisdiction would *persist* when the suspect had left the territory of the state. Logic dictates that the court would first inquire whether the Netherlands had ever possessed jurisdiction when the suspect still resided in the Netherlands. However, an affirmative answer was dependent on the question of whether Ayalon could be qualified as a suspect. This line of reasoning—dictated by the UN Convention against Torture itself—inevitably drew the court into a vicious circle. For, in order to exercise jurisdiction, one must have a suspicion. However, to buttress a suspicion, one usually requires criminal jurisdiction, because only in that case can enforcement measures, including the arrest of the suspect, be taken.[3]

3 For further analysis see also J Handmaker, Analysis, *Al Shami v Ayalon*, ILDC 673 (NL 2009).

United States v Ali, Appeal judgment, 718 F3d 929 (DC Cir 2013), No 12-3056, ILDC 2265 (US 2013), 11th June 2013, United States; Court of Appeals (DC Circuit) [DC Cir]

The *CEC Future*, a Danish ship carrying the cargo of a US Corporation, had been captured by Somalian pirates and had been forced to change course and enter Somalia's territorial waters. Ali Mohamed had boarded the ship, had assumed the role of interpreter, and had negotiated with the owners for the release of the ship, its crew, and its cargo. In 2011, US prosecutors had lured Ali into US territory where he was arrested on charges of conspiracy to commit piracy and aiding and abetting piracy and conspiracy to commit hostage taking and aiding and abetting hostage taking. The intriguing question was whether the US courts could exercise (universal) jurisdiction, now that Ali had not performed his criminal activities on the high seas but in Somalia's territorial waters:

> 20. Explicit geographical limits—"on the high seas" and "outside the jurisdiction of any state"—govern piratical acts under article 101(a)(i) and (ii). Such language is absent, however, in article 101(c), strongly suggesting a facilitative act need not occur on the high seas so long as its predicate offense has. *Cf. Dean v. United States*, 556 U.S. 568, 573 (2009) ("[W]here Congress includes particular language in one section of a statute but omits it in another section of the same Act, it is generally presumed that Congress acts intentionally and purposely in the disparate inclusion or exclusion." (internal quotation marks omitted)). So far, so good; *Charming Betsy* poses no problems.
>
> 21. Ali endeavors nonetheless to impute a "high seas" requirement to article 101(c) by pointing to UNCLOS article 86, which states, "The provisions of this Part apply to all parts of the sea that are not included in the exclusive economic zone, in the territorial sea or in the internal waters of a State, or in the archipelagic waters of an archipelagic State." 1833 U.N.T.S. at 432. Though, at first glance, the language at issue appears generally applicable, there are several problems with Ali's theory that article 86 imposes a strict high seas requirement on all provisions in Part VII. For one thing, Ali's reading would result in numerous redundancies throughout UNCLOS where, as in article 101(a)(i), the term "high seas" is already used, and interpretations resulting in textual surplusage are typically disfavored. *Cf. Babbitt v. Sweet Home Chapter of Communities for a Great Or.*, 515 U.S. 687, 698 (1995). Similarly, many of the provisions to which article 86 applies explicitly concern conduct outside the high seas. *See, e.g.*, UNCLOS, art. 92(1), 1833 U.N.T.S. at 433 ("A ship may not change its flag during a voyage or while in a port of call ...."); *id.* art. 100, 1833 U.N.T.S. at 436 ("All States shall cooperate to the fullest possible extent in the repression of piracy on the high seas or in any other place outside the jurisdiction of any State."). Ali's expansive interpretation of article 86 is simply not plausible.
>
> 22. What does article 86 mean, then, if it imposes no high seas requirement on the other articles in Part VII of UNCLOS? After all, "the canon against surplusage merely favors that interpretation which *avoids* surplusage," not the construction substituting one instance of superfluous language for another. *Freeman v. Quicken Loans, Inc.*, 132 S. Ct. 2034, 2043 (2012). We believe it is best understood as definitional, explicating the term "high seas" for that portion of the treaty most directly discussing such issues. Under this interpretation, article 86 mirrors other prefatory provisions in UNCLOS. Part II, for example, concerns "Territorial Sea and Contiguous Zone" and so opens with article 2's explanation of the legal status of a State's territorial sea. 1833 U.N.T.S. at 400. And Part III, covering "Straits Used for International Navigation," begins with article 34's clarification of the legal status of straits used for international navigation. 1833 U.N.T.S. at 410. Drawing guidance from these provisions, article

> 86 makes the most sense as an introduction to Part VII, which is titled "High Seas," and not as a limit on jurisdictional scope. *Cf. FDA v. Brown & Williamson Tobacco Corp.*, 529 U.S. 120, 133 (2000) ("It is a fundamental canon of statutory construction that the words of a statute must be read in their context and with a view to their place in the overall statutory scheme." (internal quotation marks omitted)).

In this case, the US court harbours an expansive interpretation of criminal universal jurisdiction in respect of persons who aid and abet the crime of piracy. As long as the predicate offence is committed on the high seas, jurisdiction extends over acts performed by accessories in the territorial waters of another state. The District Court reaches this conclusion by an *a contrario* interpretation of the relevant provision of the UN Convention on the Law of the Seas which is, though bold, acceptable under the Vienna Convention on the Law of Treaties, as the commentator correctly observes.[4] The decision deviates from previous US case law that required both the predicate and the ancillary offence to have been committed on the high seas.

H v Public Prosecutor, Judgment on Merits, Case No 07/10063 (E), Decision No LJN: BG1476, ILDC 1071 (NL 2008), 8th July 2008, Netherlands; Supreme Court [HR]

The defendant, who in the 1980s was a high-ranking Afghan officer in Kabul, had sought asylum in the Netherlands. His application was rejected on the basis of the exclusion clause in Article 1F of the Convention relating to the Status of Refugees, and the matter came to the attention of the public prosecutor. The defendant was charged with co-perpetration of war crimes and torture and with superior responsibility in respect of war crimes.

The Dutch courts—in three instances—had to answer the question of whether the Netherlands was allowed to exercise universal jurisdiction over war crimes committed in a non-international armed conflict.

> 6.1. The ground of appeal is directed against the rejection of the defence that the Dutch courts have no jurisdiction in respect of the offences in count 3.
>
> 6.2. It should be noted at the outset that since the entry into force of the Convention, acts in breach of article 3 of the Convention have constituted the crime described in section 8 of the Wartime Offences Act and that in such a case [. . .] the Dutch courts are entitled under section 3 (old) of the Wartime Offences Act to exercise what is termed universal jurisdiction.
>
> 6.3. The defence and the ground of appeal are essentially based on the position that the Dutch courts, which do not have primary jurisdiction in respect of the charges in count 3, also do not have secondary jurisdiction based on the principle of universality in this respect. This position is based on the view that since this concerns an offence committed in an armed conflict which, at the time of the acts of which the defendant is accused (1985–1988), was not of an international character (referred to below as an internal armed conflict) and that at that time there was no — written or unwritten — mandate under international law to create universal jurisdiction with regard to such offences, section 3 (old) of the Wartime Offences Act should not be applied in the absence of such a mandate.
>
> 6.4. Article 94 of the Constitution provides that statutory regulations in force within the Kingdom shall not be applicable if such application is in conflict with provisions of treaties that are binding on all persons or of decisions of international organisations. It is implicit in this provision that the courts should determine whether statutory regulations are in compliance with treaties and decisions of international organisations, but may not test them for compliance with unwritten international law [. . .].

4 E Gladman, Analysis, *United States v Ali*, ILDC 2265 (US 2013) A2.

> 6.5. In view of the above finding at 6.4, the Court of Appeal was correct to hold that it was not competent to test the jurisdictional provision of section 3 (old) of the Wartimes Offences Act for compliance with unwritten international law.
>
> 6.6. Contrary to what was submitted at the appeal hearing and in the ground of appeal, article 8 of the Criminal Code provides no basis for not applying the jurisdiction provision of section 3 (old) of the Wartime Offences Act on these international law grounds. Although article 8 of the Criminal Code does indeed provide that the applicability of the Dutch provisions on jurisdiction is limited by the exceptions recognised in international law, this does not amount – partly as a result of the legislative history of this provision […] – to more than a statutory recognition of immunity from jurisdiction derived from international law.

In this case, defence counsel argued that the establishment and exercise of universal jurisdiction in non-international armed conflicts required an explicit mandate under international law. The Supreme Court—in full agreement with the Court of Appeal—interpreted this defence as a claim to a rule of customary international law, prohibiting states to create universal jurisdiction without such a mandate, and they found that Article 94 of the Dutch Constitution implicitly precluded courts from testing Acts of Parliament against rules of customary international law. An appeal to Article 8 of the Dutch Criminal Code which introduces international law as a check on jurisdictional over-expansion by the back door did not help defence counsel either, as the Supreme Court gave a restrictive interpretation of this provision. It only served to remind states of their international obligations to observe immunities.[5]

KS and PC v RT and RD, Appeal Judgment, Case No P.07.0216.F, ILDC 1118 (BE 2008), 30th May 2007, Belgium; Court of Cassation

Criminal proceedings were brought in Belgium against two foreign nationals, RT and RD, on the basis of a civil party petition by two minors of foreign nationality, KS and PC. KS and PC had been the victims of alleged sexual offences committed outside Belgium by RT and RD. Article 10ter, para 2, of the Preliminary Title of the Code of Criminal Procedure allowed for the exercise of extra-territorial, universal jurisdiction over persons who had committed sexual offences against minors. Article 12(1) of the Preliminary Title provided that prosecution of these persons could only take place when the accused were found in Belgium. The legal issue before the court was whether this implied that the accused had to be present in Belgium at the time criminal proceedings were initiated against them.

> 14 Article 10ter, 2 of the preliminary title of the Code of Criminal Procedure allows the prosecution in Belgium of every person who has allegedly committed, outside the territory of the Kingdom, one of the offences which are provided in articles 372–377 and 409 of the Penal Code against a minor. However, such prosecution will only take place, by virtue of Article 12, 1st part, of the preliminary title, if the accused is found in Belgium.
>
> 15 It is not required that, the suspect being on the territory at the beginning of the prosecution, he still resides there at the moment of the judgement. It suffices, but is also mandatory, that after having committed the crime of which he is suspected, the perpetrator has come to Belgium, even if he has left the territory before the first acts of the procedure have started.
>
> 16 This condition, being linked to the admissibility of public action, must be complied with at the moment on which such action is put in motion. Later presence of the suspect on Belgian territory cannot have the effect of making admissible a prosecution that was not allowed at the moment that it started.

---

5 For further analysis see C Ryngaert, Analysis, *KS and PC v RT and RD*, ILDC 1118 (BE 2008).

The interesting aspect of this judgment was that universal jurisdiction in Belgium is apparently not restricted to international crimes *stricto sensu*, but applies to sexual offences against minors as well. The Court of Cassation found that the suspect need not be present on Belgian territory at the time of the judgment (corroborated in *FE alias NY v DS*, ILDC 1117 (BE 2007)). However, the court specified that the presence of the suspect was required at the time of the initiation of criminal proceedings, thus flouting the broader interpretation of the Advocate General Vandermeersch that presence at any moment would suffice.

Niyonteze and Military Prosecutor of the Military Tribunal of First instance 2 v Military Appeals Tribunal 1A, Cassation judgment, ILDC 349 (CH 2001), 27th April 2001, Switzerland; Military Supreme Court

Starting on 3 July 1996, criminal investigations were undertaken in Switzerland against Fulgence Niyonteze, a Rwandan citizen then residing in Geneva as a refugee, for acts allegedly committed in Rwanda during the civil war in 1994.

On 30 April 1999, the Military Tribunal of First Instance found Niyonteze guilty of homicide, instigation of homicide and attempted homicide, as well as of serious violations of international treaty provisions regarding warfare and the protection of persons and goods, and sentenced him to life in prison.

After appellate proceedings, the case reached the Military Supreme Court, where Niyonteze claimed in particular that there was no sufficient link between the acts he was charged with and the conflict in Rwanda and therefore these acts could not be judged as violations of international humanitarian law. For the purpose of the topic under scrutiny, it was relevant that the Military Supreme Court addressed the issue whether Niyonteze could be prosecuted on the charge of serious violations of international humanitarian law allegedly committed in a non-international armed conflict.[6]

> 3.c) [. . .] Nor is there any doubt that a foreign perpetrator of violations of the laws on war, who acted against foreign persons within the context of a non-international conflict in a foreign territory, can be prosecuted under the Swiss jurisdiction under Article 109 CPM, as ordinary Swiss criminal law does not contain comparable legislation. This extension of the territorial application of the criminal law in Switzerland is a consequence of Article 2(9) CPM, which determines that "civilians (to be understood as persons not subject to military service in Switzerland) are subject to the military criminal code if, during an armed conflict, they are found guilty of offences under the law (Articles 108 to 114)"; this standard must be applied in conjunction with Article 9 CPM, which states that the CPM is applicable "to offences committed in Switzerland, and those committed abroad" [. . .]. The Military Tribunals are competent, since Article 218 CPM provides that any person to whom military law is applicable is subject to the military tribunals (paragraph 1), including when the offence was committed abroad (paragraph 2). [. . .]
>
> d) Moreover it was not in dispute in the exchanges between the parties that in Rwanda, during the months of April to July 1994, a non international armed conflict within the meaning of Common Article 3 took place in the territory of that country involving the government army (the Rwandan Armed Forces — FPR). This conflict also falls under the definition of Article 1 of Protocol II. The Court of Appeal arrived at this conclusion by referring to the case law of the International Criminal Tribunal for Rwanda (or the International Criminal Tribunal for the Prosecution of Persons Responsible for

6 For further analysis of the case see M Sassoli, 'Le génocide rwandais, la justice militaire suisse et le droit international' (2002) 12 *Revue Suisse de droit international et européen* 151; L Reydams, 'Niyonteze v Public Prosecutor' (2002) 96 *American Journal of International Law* 231.

> Genocide and Other Serious Violations of International Humanitarian Law Committed in the Territory of Rwanda and Rwandan Citizens responsible for genocide and other such violations committed in the territory of neighbouring States, between 1 January 1994 and 31 December 1994; hereafter ICTR). Indeed in decisions of its trial chambers where the issue had to be resolved, the ICTR has accepted that the events or massacres of the population in Rwanda between April and July 1994 fell within the context of an internal armed conflict covered by Common Article 3 and Protocol II [. . .]

Like their Dutch colleagues in the cases against Afghan asylum-seekers,[7] the Swiss (military) courts took for granted that their domestic law provided for universal jurisdiction in respect of suspects of war crimes committed in a non-international armed conflict. However, unlike the Dutch courts, the Swiss Military Court did not explicitly predicate this jurisdictional authority on Common Article 3 of the Geneva Conventions.

The commentators suggested that customary international law could be invoked as an adequate source for this position: 'Although the concept of grave breaches does not extend to armed conflicts not of an international character and hence does not apply to violations of Common Article 3 of the Geneva Conventions and of Additional Protocol II, one can argue that customary international law requires, or at least allows, states to exercise universal jurisdiction also in regard to serious violations of the law applicable to non-international armed conflicts'.[8]

Jorgic Case, J (a bosnian Serb), Individual Constitutional Complaint, 2 BvR 1290/99, ILDC 132 (DE 2000), 12th December 2000, Germany; Constitutional Court [BVerfG]

In the *Jorgic* case, the complaint, lodged at the Constitutional Court, concerned the conviction by a German court of a Bosnian Serb—Jorgic—for various crimes, including genocide, committed during a Serbian ethnic-cleansing campaign in the newly independent Bosnia and Herzegovina in 1992. Before the Constitutional Court, Jorgic argued that certain constitutional rights under the Basic Law had been violated, which also applied to foreign nationals. Among other things, he claimed that the lower courts had overstepped constitutional boundaries by applying the principle of universality to the allegations against him.

> 37 6. The challenged decisions do not violate the constitution by assuming the applicability of German criminal law pursuant to § 6 Number 1 of the German Criminal Code in conjunction with Article VI of the Genocide Convention, to the charged actions of the complainant. [. . .]
>
> 38 a) Out of respect for the prohibition on interference with state sovereignty that is anchored in customary and treaty law (Article 2, Number 1 of the UN Charter), the Federal Constitutional Court has required some sensible nexus with Germany when subjecting acts to German law that have occurred in a foreign territory and therefore outside the German territory [. . .]. What constitutes a sensible nexus is dependent on the particular nature of the subject of regulation. [. . .]
>
> [. . .] For criminal law, the principle of universal or world jurisdiction constitutes such a sensible nexus, along with the principles of territoriality, protection, active and passive personality, and the principle of the substituting criminal law jurisdiction [. . .]. Universal jurisdiction applies only to specific crimes which are viewed as threats to the legal interests of the international community of states. It is distinguishable from the principle of the substituting criminal law jurisdiction, codified in §7.2 Number 2 of the German Criminal Code, in that it is not dependent on whether the

7 ILDC Nos 636, 797, and 1071.

8 C Bergmann and A Ziegler, Analysis, *Niyonteze and Military Prosecutor of the Military Tribunal of First instance 2 v Military Appeals Tribunal 1A*, ILDC 349 (CH 2001) A4.

act is punishable in the territory where it occurs or whether or not there is a possibility for extradition. [...]

39 b) Whether the Genocide Convention contains such a rule providing for universal jurisdiction must be determined by interpretation of the Convention. Treaties in international law are generally interpreted in accordance with the ordinary meaning of the terms of the treaty, in light of the treaty's object and purpose, and with consideration given to general international law [...]. The courts' interpretation and application regarding the field of application of the German provisions concerning genocide found in § 6 Number 1 of the German Criminal Code in conjunction with Article VI of the Genocide Convention, are, in any event, neither obviously untenable [...] nor arbitrary, in that, pursuant to no conceivable aspect, they can be considered legally justifiable [...].

40 aa) In the course of interpreting the treaty in accordance with the meaning of its terms, courts have concluded, with no reservations concerning possible constitutional law violations, that Article VI of the Genocide Convention in no case contains a ban on the application of the German criminal jurisdiction. The Convention's explicit treatment of the jurisdictional element is, however, not exhaustive because the active or passive personality principle as the basis for criminal jurisdiction is also not identified. [...] Pursuant to its object and purpose, the courts have interpreted Article I of the Genocide Convention such that the Convention strives for effective criminal prosecution of genocide. Therefore, the absence of a rule concerning universal jurisdiction only means that the states that are parties to the Convention are under no obligation to prosecute, although they have the opportunity to pursue criminal prosecutions on this basis. There is no reservation when, in justifiable cases, priority is given to the systematic-teleological interpretation of international treaties over the interpretation of a treaty in accordance with the meaning of its terms [...]. This is especially the case with respect to prosecution of foreign criminal acts on the basis of international treaties, which often do not clearly identify which jurisdictional nexus will be regulated. Genocide is, as the most severe violation of human rights, [...] the classic case for application of universal jurisdiction, the purpose of which is to make possible the most thorough prosecution of crimes perpetrated against the especially important legal interests of the international community of states.

41 bb) Furthermore, on the basis of Article 31.3, Letter b of the Vienna Convention on the Law of Treaties, the Federal Court of Justice relied upon the Rome Statute of the International Criminal Court, which has not yet come into force and has not yet been ratified by Germany. The Rome Statute, however, addresses only the jurisdiction of the International Criminal Court. The national courts only come into consideration in so far as the relationship between the national court with presumptive jurisdiction and the International Criminal Court is at issue. With respect to the jurisdiction of the national courts over genocide, the Rome Statute also raises questions because it requires, for the jurisdiction of the International Criminal Court, the ratification of the Statute by the State where the crime occurs or the State of the perpetrator. This contradicts the idea behind universal jurisdiction, which does not require such a nexus. Germany failed, during the negotiations over the Rome Statute, in its attempt to derive the automatic jurisdiction of the International Criminal Court from the national courts' jurisdiction over the relevant crimes, a competence which has universal jurisdiction as its basis. This proposal was founded on the competence of all states, which can transfer to the international court the authority to prosecute to which they are entitled pursuant to universal jurisdiction. The German proposal was, however, rejected on the basis of the *pacta tertiis* argument (cf. Article 34 of the

> Vienna Convention on the Law of Treaties) and not because the applicability of universal jurisdiction to the crimes identified in Article 6 et seq. of the German Criminal Code should be called into question. [. . .]

The Constitutional Court thoroughly substantiated its opinion that international law in no way precluded Germany's universal jurisdiction over the crime of genocide. It probably could have sufficed by declaring that it adhered to the well-known *Lotus* formula, observing that the jurisdiction clause in the Genocide Convention was not exhaustive and that international law, absent an explicit prohibition, left states a margin of appreciation to establish and exercise extraterritorial jurisdiction. However, the court took pains to elaborate on the wording and history of both the Genocide Convention and the Rome Statute. With respect to the latter, the court suggested that, while universal jurisdiction for the International Criminal Court itself had been unattainable, the Rome Statute did by no means preclude states from exercising universal jurisdiction.[9]

Guatemala Genocide Case, Menchú Tumn (Rigoberta) and ors v Two Guatemalan Government Officials and Six members of the Guatemalan Military, Constitutional Appeal, Case No 237/2005, ILDC 137 (ES 2005), 26th September 2005, Spain; Constitutional Court

On 2 December 1999, Rigoberta Menchú and a group of non-governmental organizations filed a suit before the National Court (*Audiencia Nacional*) against eight senior Guatemalan government officials. The complaint charged the defendants with terrorism, genocide, and systematic torture committed during the Guatemalan civil war, which lasted from 1978 to 1986. The criminal proceedings were based on Article 23(4) of the former Organic Law of the Judicial Power (*Ley Orgánica del Poder Judicial*, OLJP).

The Supreme Court had previously held that a connection with a national interest was necessary to permit the extraterritorial extension of Spanish jurisdiction (ie the nationality of the victims, the presence of the accused in Spanish territory or any other direct connection with national interests). The judgment of the Supreme Court thus allowed investigations for the torture and killing of Spanish citizens in Guatemala but threw out the claims concerning Guatemalan victims.

The claimants filed a constitutional appeal (*recurso de amparo*) against the judgment of the Supreme Court, challenging the restrictive interpretation of the principle of universal jurisdiction as provided for in Article 23(4) of the OLJP.

> 8. Together with the presence on national territory of the assumed perpetrator, the Ruling under appeal introduces two further connecting links: that of the personality of the victim, so that universal competency depends on the Spanish nationality of the victims; and that of the connection of the crimes committed with other relevant Spanish interests, which is nothing more nor less than a generic reformulation of the so-called real principle of protection or defence. These restrictions appear to have been drawn once again from international customary law, referring, without further details,

9 For further analyses, compare J E Wetzel, Analysis, *Jorgic Case, J (a bosnian Serb)*, ILDC 132 (DE 2000); K Ambos, 'Case note to the decision of the Federal Court of Justice' (1999) *Neue Zeitschrift für Strafrecht* 404; M Bungenberg, 'Extraterritoriale Strafrechtsanwendung bei Verbrechen gegen die Menschlichkeit und Völkermord' (2001) *Archiv des Völkerrechts* (AVR) 170; S Kadelbach, 'Case note to the decision of the Federal Constitutional Court' (2001) *Juristenzeitung* (JZ) 981; C Hoss and R A Miller, 'German Federal Constitutional Court and Bosnian War Crimes: Liberalizing Germany's Genocide Jurisprudence' (2001) 44 *German Yearbook of International Law* 576; M Kotzur, 'Weltrecht ohne Weltstaat—die nationale (Verfassungs-) Gerichtsbarkeit als Motor völkerrechtlicher Konstitutionalisierungsprozesse?' (2002) *Die Öffentliche Verwaltung* 195; R Rissing-van Saan, 'The German Federal Supreme Court and the Prosecution of International Crimes Committed in the Former Yugoslavia' (2005) 3 *Journal of International Criminal Law* 354; C Kress, 'Versailles-Nuremberg-The Hague: Germany and International Criminal Law' (2006) 40 *International Lawyer* 15.

to the fact that "a significant part of legal doctrine and some national courts" have tended to recognise the relevance of certain connecting links.

9. In this way the restriction based on the nationality of the victims incorporates an additional requirement not contemplated in the law, which furthermore has no teleological basis and therefore, in particular with regard to genocide, contradicts the nature of the crime itself and the shared aspiration to achieve universal prosecution, something which would effectively be curtailed by such a restriction. As stipulated by art. 607 of the Criminal Code the legal nature of genocide is characterised by the membership of the victim or victims of a national, ethnic, racial or religious group, together with the fact that the acts perpetrated have the specific aim of destroying this group, precisely with regard to their links of belonging. The exegesis employed by the Ruling of the Supreme Court would imply, as a result, that the crime of genocide would only be of relevance to the Spanish Courts when the victim was of Spanish nationality and, furthermore, when the conduct was motivated by the aim of destroying the Spanish national group. The improbability of this possibility should be sufficient to show that this was not the purpose which the Legislator sought with the introduction of universal jurisdiction in art. 23.4 OLJP and that this interpretation cannot be in accordance with the purpose in establishing this institution.

And the same must be concluded with relation to the criterion of national interest. Apart from the fact, noted by the Public Prosecutor in his report, that the reference to the national interest in the Ruling under appeal is nominal, and lacks even the minimum elaboration which would make it possible to specify its content, what is clear is that the inclusion of paragraph 4 of Article 23 OLJP renders it practically bereft of content, by referring back to the rule of jurisdictional competency contained in the preceding paragraph. As has already been stated, the decisive issue is that submitting competency for the adjudication of international crimes such as genocide or terrorism to competition between national interests, in the terms proposed in the Ruling, is not fully reconcilable with the basis of universal jurisdiction. The international and cross-border prosecution which the principle of universal justice seeks to impose is based exclusively on the specific characteristics of the crimes which are subject to it, where the damage (typically in the case of genocide) transcends the specific victims and affects the international community as a whole. Consequently, the prosecution and punishment of these constitute not just a shared commitment but also a shared interest of all the States (as we had occasion to affirm in the Constitutional Court Ruling 87/2000, of 27 March, FJ 4), and the legitimacy of this, as a consequence, does not depend on further particular interests of each of the States. By the same token, the concept of universal jurisdiction in current international law is not configured around links of connection founded on particular state interests, as shown by art. 23.4 OLJP, the aforementioned German Law of 2002 or, to give yet more examples, the Resolution adopted by the Institute of International Law in Krakow on 26 August 2005, in which, after setting out the aforementioned commitment of all States, universal jurisdiction in criminal affairs is defined as "the competence of a State to prosecute alleged offenders and to punish them if convicted, irrespective of the place of commission of the crime and regardless of any link of active or passive nationality, or other grounds of jurisdiction recognized by international law."

In this interesting case, the Spanish Constitutional Court gave a wide understanding of the universal jurisdiction principle. The judgment of the Constitutional Court dismantled the prior doctrine of the Spanish Supreme Court and thereby eliminated the previously existing limitations to the application of the principle of universal jurisdiction. The decision stated that Spanish Courts have jurisdiction over crimes of international significance, regardless of the nationality of the victims and perpetrators. Such crimes include torture, crimes against humanity, and genocide.

The *Guatemala* decision has had important consequences over the last years. As a result of the *Guatemala* decision, the Spanish National Court has initiated investigations regarding international crimes committed in different regions of the world (Tibet, China, Iraq, Gaza, El Salvador, and Rwanda). From a political point of view, the wide understanding of universal jurisdiction has triggered diplomatic conflicts between Spain and the countries concerned. As a result, Spain decided in 2009 to amend Article 23(4) of the LOPJ reducing the scope of universal jurisdiction (Organic Law No 1/2009). Furthermore, Organic Law No 1/2014 introduced a very restrictive approach to the concept of universal jurisdiction.[10]

Jiménez Sánchez and ors v Gibson and ors, Appeal Judgment, Case No 1240/2006, ILDC 993 (ES 2006), 11th December 2006, Spain; Supreme Court

The *Couso* case deals with the exercise of universal jurisdiction by Spanish courts over crimes of war committed during the Iraq war. On 23 April 2003, a US tank fired on the Palestine Hotel in Baghdad from where several international journalists were reporting on the Iraq war. As a result, José Couso, a Spanish cameraman who was filming from the hotel, was severely wounded and died in hospital a few hours later. A Reuters cameraman, Taras Protsyuk, was also killed and others journalists were injured. A few weeks later, José Couso's family and the Free Association of Lawyers and the Association of Television and Video Cameramen brought criminal charges for war crimes and murder against three US officers involved in Couso's death (Sergeant Thomas Gibson, Captain Philip Wolford, and Lieutenant-Colonel Philip de Camp). The US authorities maintained that the attack had been in response to a previous attack originating from the area where the Palestine Hotel was located and denied any fault on the part of US soldiers.

In October 2003, the complaint was accepted by the Central Judge nº 1 of the Spanish National Court (*Audiencia Nacional*), who issued international arrest warrants for the three US officers, requesting their extradition to Spain. However, on 8 October 2006, the Criminal Chamber of the National Court overruled the decision of the Central Judge and stated that the Spanish courts had no jurisdiction to investigate the facts and set aside the international arrest warrants for the US officers. Couso's family and the other claimants appealed against the National Court's ruling before the Supreme Court, claiming that it had infringed the right to effective judicial protection.

> EIGHT. At this point, it is necessary to highlight the serious problems that may arise in the interpretation and application of the law called into question in this appeal (Article 23.4 of the OLJP). To do this, it is necessary to highlight the scope of the terms that define the ambit of Spanish jurisdiction in areas such as terrorism, counterfeiting, drug trafficking and, in particular, reference to any other crime that, under the terms of international treaties and conventions, must be prosecuted in Spain [letter h) of the abovementioned Article in the OLJP]. Without doubt, this was the main reason for the demarcation carried out by this court in the judgments handed down on 25 February and 20 May 2003 (on the so-called Guatemala Case and Peru Case,

10 For further analyses see B Montejo, Analysis, *Guatemala Genocide Case, Menchú Tumn (Rigoberta) and ors v Two Guatemalan Government Officials and Six members of the Guatemalan Military*, ILDC 137 (ES 2005); H Ascensió, 'The Spanish Constitutional Tribunal's Decision in Guatemalan Generals Unconditional Universality is Back' (2006) 4 *Journal of International Criminal Jurisdiction* 586; R Bermejo García and C Ruiz Miguel, 'Jurisprudencia en materia de Derecho internacional público: una Sentencia incongruente, restrictiva e irresponsable (nota a la Sentencia 237/2005 del Tribunal Constitucional)' (2005) 57 *Revista Española de Derecho Internacional* 911; N Roht Arriaza, 'Guatemala Genocide Case' (2006) 100 *American Journal of International Law* 207; J Santos Vara, 'La jurisdicción de los tribunales españoles para enjuiciar los crímenes cometidos en Guatemala' (2006) 11 *Revista Electrónica de Estudios Internacionales* 1; H van der Wilt, 'Universal Jurisdiction under Attack: An Assessment of the African Misgivings of International Criminal Justice, as Administered by Western States' (2011) 5 *Journal of International Criminal Justice* 207.

> respectively) which, in short, merely served to highlight the need for a legitimating point of connection, without which one could with some justification refer to a disproportionate expansion of the national criminal jurisdiction, in particular if one considers that the principle of opportunity is not recognised in our legal system. At the same time, popular action is recognised free of any particular limitation (see Article 125 C.E. and Articles 100, 101 and 270 LCP).
>
> In any event, the intervention of the Spanish courts in respect of acts committed outside Spain can give rise to unquestionable disputes from an international relations perspective for Spain (a competence that belongs to the government) (see Article 97 C.E.), a matter that is thus beyond the judiciary but of which the courts, no doubt, cannot be totally unaware.
>
> [...] In a specific reference to the interpretation of the rule that attributes jurisdiction in Article 23.4 of the OLJP, the Constitutional Court states that "the ultimate foundation of this rule attributing jurisdiction lies in the universalisation of the jurisdiction of states and their bodies for knowledge of certain acts in whose prosecution and ruling all states have an interest ... ". In this regard, it has declared that "in principle, Article 23.4 of the LOPJ grants very broad scope to the principle of universal justice, given that the sole express limitation to the same is the principle of *res judicata.*" The Constitutional Court — the last word on constitutional guarantees (see Article 123 C.E.) — also concludes that "the OLJP establishes a principle of absolute universal jurisdiction" (see STC 237/2005; FJ 3.).
>
> The weight of the conclusion reached above by the Constitutional Court and the irregular legal basis of the resolution which is the object of the appeal on the specific issue of the scope of Spanish jurisdiction in relation to the matter, provide resounding justification for the finding of a breach of the law cited on the grounds specially cited, despite the founded observations made in the first legal grounds of this resolution.

In this case, the Supreme Court accepted the line of argument developed by Couso's family and the other claimants in the sense that the Fourth Geneva Convention and Article 23(4) of the OLJP granted universal jurisdiction to Spain's judges and courts to investigate and judge the facts.

Even though the Supreme Court accepted the possibility for Spain to investigate the facts, it criticized the broad interpretation of the principle of universal jurisdiction made by the Spanish courts. The Supreme Court highlighted the problems that could arise within the sphere of international relations as a result of the involvement of Spanish courts in events occurring beyond Spain's borders. There was no doubt, though, that the basic reason why the Supreme Court had accepted jurisdiction in this case was due to the fact that one of the victims was a Spanish national.[11]

III. Jurisdiction in Economic Matters

Jurisdictional issues do not only arise in criminal matters but also in economic matters, in particular in the law of restrictive business practices—which is termed 'antitrust law' in the United States and 'competition law' in Europe.[12]

---

11 For further analyses see J Santos Vara, M Candela Soriano, Analysis, *Jiménez Sánchez and ors v Gibson and ors*, ILDC 993 (ES 2006); J Santos Vara, 'Crónica sobre la aplicación judicial del Derecho internacional público' (2007) 14 *Revista Electrónica de Estudios Internacionales* 1; H Olásolo Alonso, 'Análisis del caso Couso a la luz del Estatuto de Roma' (2007) 5 *Revista Electrónica del Departamento de Derecho de la Universidad de la Rioja* 1; C Fernández Liesa, 'El asunto Couso en los tribunales nacionales y en las relaciones internacionales' (2011) 63 *Revista Española de Derecho Internacional* 145.

12 G W Haight, 'International Law and Extraterritorial Application of the Antitrust Laws' (1953–54) 63 *Yale Law Journal* 639; R Y Jennings, 'Extraterritorial Jurisdiction in the United States Antitrust Laws' (1957) 33

The United States has been the first state to extend the long arm of its antitrust statutes (*Alcoa*, 1945). The exercise of jurisdiction over foreign conspiracies, and any limitations on such exercises, have been justified on various grounds, such as economic necessity, legislative intent but also international law. The analysis in this section will concentrate on the international law issues raised by a number of leading judgments in the field, of both US and European courts.[13] No relevant non-Western judgments have been identified. This may, at least in part, be attributed to the absence of a strong antitrust competition law framework or its timid enforcement outside the US and Europe.

United States v Aluminium Corp of America, 148 F2d 416 (2d Cir 1945) (Alcoa) (not in ILDC)

In *Alcoa*, foreign aluminium companies had formed a cartel in Switzerland by agreeing to pay royalties to each other if their aluminium production exceeded a certain level. This arrangement could have had an inflationary effect on aluminium prices and caused aluminium import shortages in the United States. The question arose whether the United States could exercise jurisdiction over a wholly foreign conspiracy affecting the American market. The Court answered as follows:

> [I]t is settled law [...] that any state may impose liabilities, even upon persons not within its allegiance, for conduct outside its borders that has consequences within its borders which the state reprehends; and these liabilities other states will ordinarily recognize [...]

Alcoa is the seminal judgment introducing the 'effects doctrine' in antitrust matters. Pursuant to this doctrine, which is a variation on the objective territoriality principle, states have jurisdiction over foreign anti-competitive conduct that produces adverse effects within their territory. As the quotation above makes clear, the *Alcoa* principle is not only the result of statutory construction, guided by the presumption against Congress legislating extraterritorially, but is also determined by international law. Indeed, the court unambiguously cites the 'limitations customarily observed by nations upon the exercise of their powers', which suggests that *international law* regulates states' jurisdictional assertions. It is not fully clear, however, whether the requirement that US antitrust law only extends to agreements that actually produce adverse effects, and not to agreements that only intend to produce such effects, flows from statutory interpretation, international law constraints or a combination of both.

Ölfeldrohre, WuW/E BGH 1276, Bundesgerichtshof (BGH), 12 July 1973 (not in ILDC)

In Europe, the effects doctrine in competition matters came to fruition in Germany. Admittedly, in the early days of competition law, the German Federal Cartel Office, which administers the German Competition Act, was reluctant to assert its jurisdiction over foreign members of international conspiracies. Instead, it only focused on the German members. German law scholars nevertheless argued that international law authorized the exercise of effects-based jurisdiction over foreign-based conspiracies as early as 1965.[14] In the 1973 *Ölfeldrohre* judgment, the German Supreme Court (*Bundesgerichtshof*) eventually held that § 130 (2), then § 98 (2),

---

British Yearbook of International Law 146; C T Oliver, 'Extraterritorial Application of United States Legislation Against Restrictive or Unfair Trade Practice' (1957) 51 *American Journal of International Law* 380; D Rishikesh, 'Extraterritoriality Versus Sovereignty in International Antitrust Regulation' (1991) 14 *World Comp* 33; W D Whitney, 'Sources of Conflict Between International Law and the Antitrust Laws' (1953–54) 63 *Yale Law Journal* 655; J H W Verzijl, 'The Controversy Regarding the So-Called Extraterritorial Effect of the American Antitrust Laws' (1961) 8 *Netherlands International Law Review* 3.

13 The analysis of the majority of cases is, at least in part, drawn from C Ryngaert, *Jurisdiction over Antitrust Violations in International Law* (Intersentia 2008).

14 Eg E Rehbinder, *Extraterritoriale Wirkungen des deutschen Kartellrechts* (Nomos 1965).

GWB authorized effects-based jurisdiction but only if the foreign restrictive practices concerned violated 'the area of protection of the particular substantive rule [at issue]':

> In light of the variety of conceivable effects of foreign restraints on competition on the domestic market, a limitation and concretization of the concept of domestic effects is required in order to prevent the unlimited expansion of the international application of the substantive rules. [...] As § 98 (2) is not a substantive law rule, but rather a conflict of laws principle, [...] clarity concerning [...] which foreign-related effects fall within the [German Competition Act] can only be achieved by construing § 98 (2) in relation to the general protective purpose of the statute as a whole and the protective purpose of the relevant substantive rules. Thus, the consequences of foreign-related restraints on competition can be viewed as "domestic effects" only when they constitute a domestic violation of the area of protection of the particular substantive rule.[15]

Accordingly, the German Supreme Court required there to be a violation of the protective purpose (*Schutzzweck*) of a particular GWB provision before § 98 (2) GWB could apply. If jurisdiction is tied to the protective purpose of a substantive antitrust provision, the jurisdictional threshold for one provision (eg pre-merger notification) could be higher than for another (eg merger prohibition). The *Ölfeldrohre Schutzzweck* doctrine enabled the Federal Cartel Office and the courts to shape the effects principle in particular cases by defining its specific elements in relation to the protective purpose of a specific provision.[16]

Timberlane Lumber Co v Bank of America, 549 F 2d 597 (9th Cir 1976) (not in ILDC)

In *Timberlane*, the plaintiff, the American lumber company Timberlane, sued defendants in Honduras and the Bank of America, alleging that all the defendants had conspired to prevent it from exporting to the United States. The case could have been perfectly dealt with under the *Alcoa* effects doctrine, but the court saw the drawbacks of the doctrine and chose another avenue.

> What we prefer is an evaluation and balancing of the relevant considerations in each case in the words of Kingman Brewster, a "jurisdictional rule of reason." Balancing of the foreign interests involved was the approach taken by the Supreme Court in Continental Ore Co. v. Union Carbide & Carbon Corp., 370 U.S. 690, 82 S.Ct. 1404, 8 L.Ed.2d 777 (1962), where the involvement of the Canadian government in the alleged monopolization was held not to require dismissal. The Court stressed that there was no indication that the Canadian authorities approved or would have approved of the monopolization, meaning that the Canadian interest, if any, was slight and was outweighed by the American interest in condemning the restraint. [FN30] Similarly, in Lauritzen v. Larsen, 345 U.S. 571, 73 S.Ct. 921, 97 L.Ed. 1254 (1953), the Court used a like approach in declining to apply the Jones Act to a Danish seaman, injured in Havana on a Danish ship, although he had signed on to the ship in New York.[17]

Under *Timberlane*, the interest-balancing test is an integral part of the jurisdictional analysis.[18] Interest-balancing does not merely mitigate pre-existing effects-based jurisdiction: it is instead

15 BGH, July 12, 1973, WuW/E BGH 1276, 1278–1279 (Ölfeldrohre), translation available in D J Gerber, 'The Extraterritorial Application of the German Antitrust Laws' (1983) 77 AJIL 756, 765.

16 D J Gerber, 'The Extraterritorial Application of the German Antitrust Laws' (1983) 77 AJIL 756, 781.

17 *Timberlane Lumber Co v Bank of America*, 549 F 2d 613-14 (9th Cir 1976).

18 For an analysis see L Kestenbaum, 'Antitrust's "Extraterritorial" Jurisdiction: a Progress Report on the Balancing of Interests Text' (1982) 18 *Stanford Journal of International Law* 311; S A Kadish, 'Comity and International Application of the Sherman Act: Encouraging the Courts to Enter the Political Arena' (1982) 4 *Northwestern Journal of International Law & Business* 130; E A Rosic Jr, 'The Use of Interest Analysis in the Extraterritorial

constitutive of such jurisdiction. This test was later laid down as a 'rule of reason' in Section 403 of the Restatement (Third) of US Foreign Relations Law, the drafters of which believed that it constituted international law.

Hartford Fire Insurance Co and ors v California and ors, Decision not subject to appeal, 509 US 764 (1993), ILDC 1448 (US 1993), 28th June 1993, United States; Supreme Court [US]

In *Hartford Fire Insurance v California*, a case concerning a London-based reinsurance cartel affecting the US market, the lower court had, along the lines of *Timberlane*, declined to exercise jurisdiction under the principle of international comity. It believed that 'application of [American] antitrust laws to the London reinsurance market would lead to significant conflict with English law and policy' and that '[s]uch a conflict, unless outweighed by other factors, would by itself be reason to decline exercise of jurisdiction'.[19] The US Supreme Court, however, unambiguously rejected the application of *Timberlane* in this case.

> 41. [. . .] international comity would not counsel against exercising jurisdiction in the circumstances alleged here.
>
> 42. The only substantial question in this litigation is whether "there is in fact a true conflict between domestic and foreign law." Société Nationale Industrielle Aérospatiale v. United States Dist. Court for Southern Dist. of Iowa, 482 U.S. 522, 555, 107 S.Ct. 2542, 2562, 96 L.Ed.2d 461 (1987) (BLACKMUN, J., concurring in part and dissenting in part). [. . .] We have no need in this litigation to address other considerations that might inform a decision to refrain from the exercise of jurisdiction on grounds of international comity.

Under the *Hartford Fire* standard, if a foreign country merely allows anti-competitive conduct adversely affecting the US market, the Sherman Act would apply—as there is no 'true conflict'.[20] A true conflict, barring application of the Sherman Act, will only arise if the foreign state requires an activity which the US prohibits or, conversely, when the foreign state prohibits an activity which the US requires. There are few, if any, references to international law in *Hartford Fire*. To be true, there are references to the US Restatement of Foreign Relations, but it is unclear whether the relevant provisions of the Restatement (on sovereign compulsion) also constitute international law. Of note is, in any event, that the Supreme Court in *Hartford Fire* abandoned *Timberlane*'s wide concept of comity, a concept requiring the balancing of various interests, including governmental interests. In practice, almost inevitably, application of the 'true conflict' doctrine as espoused by the Supreme Court risks encroaching to a much greater extent on the interests of other nations, and thus possibly violates the international law principle of non-intervention.

Application of United States Antitrust Law' (1983) 16 *Cornell International Law Journal* 147; P M Roth, 'Reasonable Extraterritoriality: Correcting the 'Balance of Interests' (1992) 41 *International and Comparative Law Quarterly* 245; M Sornarajah, 'The Extraterritorial Enforcement of US Antitrust Laws: Conflict and Compromise' (1982) 31 *International and Comparative Law Quarterly* 127.

19 Restated in *Hartford Fire Insurance Co and ors v California and ors*, Decision not subject to appeal, 509 US 764 (1993), ILDC 1448 (US 1993), 28 June 1993, United States; Supreme Court [US], 40.

20 For an analysis see D Park, Analysis, *Hartford Fire Insurance Co and ors v California and ors*, ILDC 1448 (US 1993); R P Alford, 'The Extraterritorial Application of Antitrust Laws: A Postscript on Hartford Fire Insurance Co. v. California' (1993) 34 *Virginia Journal of International Law* 213; V Gupta, 'After Hartford Fire: Antitrust and Comity' (1996) 84 *Georgetown Law Journal* 2287; A F Lowenfeld, 'Conflict, Balancing of Interests, and the Exercise of Jurisdiction to Prescribe: Reflections on the Insurance Antitrust Case' (1995) 89 *American Journal of International Law* 42; J A Trenor, 'Jurisdiction and the Extraterritorial Application of Antitrust Laws After Hartford Fire' (1995) 62 *University of Chicago Law Review* 1583; R J Weintraub, 'Hartford Fire Insurance Co., Comity and the Extraterritorial Reach of United States Antitrust Laws' (1994) 29 *Texas International Law Journal* 427.

Wood Pulp, Osakeyhtiö and ors v Commission of the European Communities, Final judgment, 89/85, 104/85, 114/85, 116/85, 117/85, 125/85, 126/85, 127/85, 128/85, 129/85, (1988) ECR 5193, ILEC 035 (CJEU 1988), 27th September 1988, Court of Justice of the European Union [CJEU]; European Court of Justice [ECJ]

In the *Wood Pulp* case, the European Commission had imposed fines on 41 foreign suppliers of wood pulp, as well as two of their trade associations, on the ground that they had fixed the price of wood pulp sales to purchasers in the Common Market. The undertakings concerned were not established in the EC, nor was their cartel agreement concluded there. In the Commission's view, the effect of the agreements and practices on prices announced and/or charged to customers and on resale of pulp within the Community was not only substantial but also intended, and was the primary and direct result of the agreements and practices. On the basis of these direct, substantial, and reasonably foreseeable *effects* on sales to customers in the Common Market, the Commission established its jurisdiction over the foreign companies (ie the 'effects doctrine' as set out in the *Alcoa* case discussed above). The wood pulp conspirators thereupon challenged the Commission's exercise of jurisdiction before the European Court of Justice (ECJ) on the grounds that it would violate international law.

> 17 The producers in this case implemented their pricing agreement within the common market. It is immaterial in that respect whether or not they had recourse to subsidiaries, agents, sub-agents, or branches within the Community in order to make their contacts with purchasers within the Community.
>
> 18 Accordingly the Community's jurisdiction to apply its competition rules to such conduct is covered by the territoriality principle as universally recognized in public international law.

In *Wood Pulp*, the court distinguished between the *extraterritorial* formation of the pricing agreement, and the *territorial* implementation thereof.[21] The court did not clarify the term 'implementation', which is not based on previous case law or legal doctrine, but it is clear that it refers to the sales through which the conspirators put their agreement into effect. As, for jurisdictional purposes, it suffices that the undertakings make sales in the Community, '[i]t is immaterial in that respect whether or not they had recourse to subsidiaries, agents, sub-agents, or branches within the Community in order to make their contacts with purchasers within the Community'.[22] Importantly, from the viewpoint of international law, the court held that, since the implementation was territorial, the anti-competitive conduct 'is covered by the territoriality principle as universally recognised in public international law'.[23]

It is conspicuous that, unlike the Commission, the ECJ refused to adopt the *Alcoa* effects doctrine in competition matters, apparently believing that this doctrine was 'extraterritorial' in nature, and thus impermissible under international law. In the court's view, jurisdiction should be based on territorial 'implementation' for there to be legitimate jurisdiction under the territoriality principle, a traditional ground of jurisdiction under public international law. It remains somewhat elusive, however, to what extent the implementation doctrine differs from the effects doctrine in practical terms.

21 For an analysis see J E Ferry, 'Towards Completing the Charm: The Woodpulp Judgment' (1989) 19 *European Intellectual Property Law Review* 21; J J Friedberg, 'The Convergence of Law in an Era of Political Integration: The Wood Pulp Case and the Alcoa Effects Doctrine' (1991) 52 *University of Pittsburgh Law Review* 289; M Friend, 'The Long Arm of Community Law' (1989) 14 *European Law Review* 169; M Jeffrey, 'The Implications of the Woodpulp Case for the European Communities' (1991) 4 *Leiden Journal of International Law* 75; D G F Lange and J B Sandage, 'The Woodpulp Decision and its Implications for the Scope of EC Competition Law' (1989) 26 *Common Market Law Review* 137; F A Mann, 'The Public International Law of Restrictive Practices in the European Court of Justice' (1989) 38 *International and Comparative Law Quarterly* 375.

22 *Wood Pulp*, para 17.

23 ibid, para 18.

Gencor Limited v European Commission, Application for annulment of Commission Decision, Case T-102/96, ECLI:EU:T:1999:65, [1999] ECR II-753, ILEC 077 (GCEU 1999), [1999] All ER (EC) 289, [1999] 4 CMLR 971, 25th March 1999, Court of Justice of the European Union [CJEU]; General Court of the European Union [EGC]; General Court (5th Chamber)

In 1996, the European Commission had determined that a concentration between the South African platinum mining companies Gencor and Lonrho would be incompatible with the Common Market.[24] Although the South African competition authorities did not object to the merger,[25] the Commission found that it would create a position of collective dominance between Gencor and Lonrho, and Anglo American Corporation (another competitor in the platinum market). Thereupon, Gencor brought an action for annulment of the decision, alleging that the Merger Control Regulation only concerned concentrations which take effect within the Common Market and, accordingly, not the concentration at issue, which related to economic activities conducted within South Africa, outside the Common Market.

Assessing the territorial scope of the Merger Control Regulation, the European Court of First Instance (CFI) in *Gencor Ltd v Commission of the European Communities* confirmed that 'Article 1 does not require that, in order for a concentration to be regarded as having a Community dimension, the undertakings in question must be established in the Community or that the production activities covered by the concentration must be carried out within Community territory'.[26] Accordingly, the Regulation could have an extraterritorial scope, and apply to foreign undertakings having sales within the Community, if the proposed merger at least met the substantive turnover criteria of Article 1 (2) of the Regulation (which it did in this case).[27] The question arose whether this would be in accordance with public international law and, in particular, with the ECJ's interpretation of the territoriality principle in the 1988 *Wood Pulp* case.

> 90 Application of the [Merger] Regulation is justified under public international law when it is foreseeable that a proposed concentration will have an immediate and substantial effect in the Community.
>
> 91 In that regard, the concentration would, according to the contested decision, have led to the creation of a dominant duopoly on the part of Amplats and Implats/LPD in the platinum and rhodium markets, as a result of which effective competition would have been significantly impeded in the common market within the meaning of Article 2(3) of the Regulation. […]
>
> 101 It follows that the application of the Regulation to the proposed concentration was consistent with public international law.
>
> 102 It is necessary to examine next whether the Community violated a principle of non-interference or the principle of proportionality in exercising that jurisdiction.
>
> 103 The applicant's argument that, by virtue of a principle of non-interference, the Commission should have refrained from prohibiting the concentration in order to avoid a conflict of jurisdiction with the South African authorities must be rejected, without it being necessary to consider whether such a rule exists in international law.

24 Case IV/M619, decision 97/26/EC of 24 April 1996, [1997] OJ L11/30.

25 The clearance by the South African government was obvious as consumption was predominantly abroad and the South African economy would accordingly have gained more than South African consumers would lose. See E Fox, 'The Merger Regulation and its Territorial Reach: Gencor Ltd v. Commission' (1999) *European Competition Law Review* 334, 335. See also *Gencor* (n 24) para 71, addressing the consideration by the Commission that the concentration could be compared to an export cartel.

26 *Gencor* (n 24) para 79.

27 ibid, para 80.

In *Gencor*, the court found that the defendants sold goods in the Community, and as sales amount to implementation, the Commission would have jurisdiction under the *Wood Pulp* jurisdictional standard, which the ECJ held to be compatible with public international law.[28] It is conspicuous, however, that the CFI, unlike the ECJ in *Wood Pulp*, seemed to embrace the American effects doctrine, pursuant to which jurisdiction obtains as soon as substantial, direct, and reasonably foreseeable effects on domestic commerce could be established.[29] The effects doctrine as espoused by the CFI in *Gencor* may not necessarily have supplanted the implementation doctrine established by the ECJ in *Wood Pulp*, however. International mergers differ from international cartels (*Wood Pulp*); the former almost inevitably have repercussions within the Community as part of the worldwide market in which the merging companies trade.

E*** v Bundeskartellanwalt and Bundeswettbewerbsbehörde, Appeal judgment, 16 Ok 49/05, ILDC 1593 (AT 2006), 27th February 2006, Austria; Supreme Court of Justice [OGH]**

Not only EU competition law but also EU member states' competition laws may apply to cross-border mergers, thereby raising issues of possibly *extraterritorial* merger control. As domestic competition laws, like EU competition law, ordinarily remain silent on their territorial scope, courts have further developed the reach of those laws in light of international law, in particular the 'effects principle'. A fine example is offered by the following Austrian judgment in *Re Erste Bank*, which precluded the application of Austrian merger control law to a proposed merger on the grounds that the requirements of direct and substantial anti-competitive effects were not satisfied:

> H1 The 1988 Cartel Act did not provide a clear rule on its territorial scope of application. However, domestic legislation could be said to have applied a modified version of the 'effects principle'.
>
> H2 The purpose of Austrian merger control legislation was the protection of the domestic market. Assuming overly broad jurisdiction in matters of merger control would be questionable on grounds of international law. Therefore, it was only applicable when the circumstances restricting competition produced their effects within Austrian territory.
>
> H4 The fact that the financial position of a domestic undertaking had improved due to the acquisition of the foreign undertakings did not have an immediate or direct effect on the domestic market. Rather, the acquisitions could only have had a very indirect effect.

F Hoffmann-La Roche Ltd et al v Empagran SA et al, 124 S Ct 2359 (2004) (not in ILDC)

Empagran, a case decided by the US Supreme Court in 2004, concerned the question of whether foreign plaintiffs had standing in US courts for foreign harm caused by a global vitamins producers' cartel that also caused some domestic harm. The question had major international law significance. As the situation had only a tenuous nexus with the United States, exercising jurisdiction could boil down to a regulation of the competitive conditions of other nations. Thus, it could possibly violate the international law principle of non-intervention.

> No one denies that America's antitrust laws, when applied to foreign conduct, can interfere with a foreign nation's ability independently to regulate its own commercial

---

28 For further analyses see M P Broberg, 'The European Commission's Extraterritorial Powers in Merger Control: The Court of First Instance's Judgment in Gencor v. Commission' (2000) 49 *International and Comparative Law Quarterly* 172; G P Elliott, 'The *Gencor* Judgment: Collective Dominance, Remedies and Extraterritoriality under the Merger Regulation' (1999) 24 *European Law Review* 638; A Ezrachi, 'Limitations on the Extraterritorial Reach of the European Merger Regulation' (2001) 22(4) *European Competition Law Review Journal* 137; P J Slot, 'Case T-102/96, Gencor Ltd v. Commission' (2001) 38(6) *Common Market Law Review* 1573; Y van Gerven and L Hoet, '*Gencor*: Some Notes on Transnational Competition Law Issues' (2001) 28(2) *Legal Issues of Economic Integration* 195.

29 *Gencor* (n 24), para 90.

> affairs. But our courts have long held that application of our antitrust laws to foreign anticompetitive conduct is nonetheless reasonable, and hence consistent with principles of prescriptive comity, insofar as they reflect a legislative effort to redress domestic antitrust injury that foreign anticompetitive conduct has caused.
>
> But why is it reasonable to apply those laws to foreign conduct insofar as that conduct causes independent foreign harm and that foreign harm alone gives rise to the plaintiff's claim? Like the former case, application of those laws creates a serious risk of interference with a foreign nation's ability independently to regulate its own commercial affairs. But, unlike the former case, the justification for that interference seems insubstantial.

In *Empagran*, the US Supreme Court prevented US courts from being overwhelmed by antitrust suits filed by foreign-based plaintiffs, and from upsetting foreign governments, by giving a restrictive interpretation to relevant provision of the Sherman Antitrust Act. The court ultimately held that US courts did not have jurisdiction over significant foreign anti-competitive conduct causing adverse domestic effects and independent foreign harm, where the plaintiff's claim rests solely on the independent foreign harm.[30]

The Supreme Court in *Empagran* relied heavily on considerations of reasonableness and international comity, which caution jurisdictional restraint. The court construed the legislative intent underlying the applicable legislation (the Foreign Trade Antitrust Improvements Act) not only in light of its language and history but also in light of international law: referring to the *Charming Betsy* doctrine of consistent interpretation,[31] it pointed out that it should be assumed that 'Congress ordinarily seeks to follow [...] the principles of customary international law'.[32] In particular, it paid close consideration to the customary international law principle of non-intervention in the internal affairs of another state, stating that it is to be assumed that Congress takes 'the legitimate sovereign interests of other nations into account'[33] when assessing the reach of US law and avoids extending this reach when that would create a 'serious risk of interference with a foreign nation's ability independently to regulate its own commercial affairs'.[34] By emphasizing the role of the customary international law principle of non-intervention and the jurisdictional rule of reason, the Supreme Court apparently reversed the very narrow interpretation it had given to the rule of reason in its 1993 *Hartford Fire* judgment (the 'true conflict' doctrine), and it returned to the *Timberlane* approach.

30 For further analysis see S E Burnett, 'US Judicial Imperialism Post "Empagran v. F. Hoffmann-La Roche"?: Conflicts of Jurisdiction and International Comity in Extraterritorial Antitrust' (2004) 18 *Emory International Law Review* 555; H L Buxbaum, 'National Courts, Global Cartels: F. Hoffmann-La Roche Ltd. v. Empagran, S.A.' (2004) 5 *German Law Journal* 1095; L M Donovan, 'Importing Plaintiffs: The Extraterritorial Scope of the Sherman Act after *Empagran*' (2006) 91 *Iowa Law Review* 719; S Fernandes, 'F. Hoffmann-La Roche, Ltd. v. Empagran and the Extraterritorial Limits of United States Antitrust Jurisdiction: where Comity and Deterrence Collide' (2005) 20 *Connecticut Journal of International Law* 267; S F Halabi, 'The Comity of *Empagran*: the Supreme Court Decides that Foreign Competition Regulation Limits American Antitrust Jurisdiction over International Cartels' (2005) 46 *Harvard International Law Journal* 279; C Ryngaert, 'Foreign-to-Foreign Claims: the US Supreme Court's Decision (2004) v. the English High Court's Decision (2003) in the Vitamins Case' (2004) 25 *European Competition Law Review* 611; C Sprigman, 'Fix Prices Globally, Get Sued Locally? US Jurisdiction Over International Cartels' (2005) 72 *University of Chicago Law Review* 265; A Stanger, 'Analyzing U. S. Antitrust Jurisdiction over Foreign Parties After Empagran S. A. v. F. Hoffmann-La Roche, Ltd' (2003) *Brigham Young University Law Review* 1453; W Wurmnest, 'Foreign Private Plaintiffs, Global Conspiracies, and the Extraterritorial Application of US Antitrust Law' (2005) 28 *Hastings International & Competition Law Review* 205.

31 *Murray v The Schooner Charming Betsy*, 6 US 64 (US 1804).

32 *F Hoffmann-La Roche Ltd et al v Empagran SA et al*, 124 S Ct 2359 (2004), 2366.

33 ibid.

34 ibid, 2367.

Morrison and ors v National Australia Bank Limited and ors, Appeal judgment, 130 S Ct 2869, 177 L Ed 2d 535 (US 2010), ILDC 1567 (US 2010), 24th June 2010, United States; Supreme Court [US]

Questions of international jurisdiction do not only arise in antitrust/competition matters but also in securities (financial) law. Traditionally, lower US courts had liberally established US jurisdiction over transnational securities transactions by requiring proof of some effect or conduct in the United States. This liberal approach was repudiated, however, by the 2010 judgment of the US Supreme Court in *Morrison*.

In this case, Australian shareholders sued National Australia Bank (National), an Australian bank whose 'ordinary shares' were not traded on any exchange in the United States. The only link with the US was that National had purchased HomeSide Lending, a Florida-based company, after which National's share prices had fallen. The plaintiffs alleged that HomeSide's officers had manipulated financial models, conduct which violated US securities legislation, and that National and its chief executive officer were aware of this deception, notably §10(b) of the 1934 Securities and Exchange Act. The question arose as to whether US courts had jurisdiction over such a situation which had only tenuous links with the United States.

> 20 [. . .] The results of judicial-speculation-made-law – divining what Congress would have wanted if it had thought of the situation before the court – demonstrate the wisdom of the presumption against extraterritoriality. Rather than guess anew in each case, we apply the presumption in all cases, preserving a stable background against which Congress can legislate with predictable effects. (slip op. p. 12) [. . .]
>
> 29. There is no affirmative indication in the Exchange Act that §10(b) applies extraterritorially, and we therefore conclude that it does not. (slip op. p. 16) [. . .]
>
> 35 [. . .] The probability of incompatibility with the applicable laws of other countries is so obvious that if Congress intended such foreign application "it would have addressed the subject of conflicts with foreign laws and procedures." (slip op. p. 20)

Morrison contains few references to international comity or international law. Instead, the analysis is centered almost entirely on ascertaining the intent of the US Congress. The court presumes that Congress does not legislate extraterritorially, unless a contrary intent appears—ie, the long-standing presumption against extraterritoriality as a canon of statutory construction—but it also notes that this presumption is not 'a limit upon Congress's power to legislate' and that it 'applies regardless of whether there is a risk of conflict between the American statute and a foreign law'.[35] Accordingly, theoretically at least, Congress can go beyond the restraints imposed by international law, at least if there is an explicit statement to this effect ('clear statement rule').[36] Admittedly, towards the end of the opinion, the Supreme Court does refer to the interests of foreign nations (by notably citing a number of their *amicus curiae* briefs which voiced concern over possible conflicts between US and foreign law), without however going as far as invoking the *Charming Betsy* principle of consistent interpretation or raising the specter of US law conflicting with the international law principle of non-intervention.[37]

35 Slip op p 5.

36 ibid, p 20.

37 E Cosenza, 'Paradise Lost: 10 (b) after Morrison v. the Australia Bank' (2011) 11(2) *Chicago Journal of International Law* 343; K M White, 'Is Extraterritorial Jurisdiction Still Alive?: Determining the Scope of U.S. Extraterritorial Jurisdiction in Securities Cases in the Aftermath of Morrison v. National Australia Bank' (2012) 37(4) *North Carolina Journal of International Law and Commercial Regulation* 1187; M Ventoruzzo, 'Like Moths to a Flame? International Securities Litigation after Morrison: correcting the Supreme Court's "Transactional Test"' (2012) 52(2) *Virginia Journal of International Law* 405.

Kiobel v Royal Dutch Petroleum Co., 133 S Ct 1659 (2013) (not in ILDC)

The strict application of the presumption against extraterritoriality in *Morrison* was reaffirmed in *Kiobel*,[38] a seminal case pertaining to the geographic scope of the Alien Tort Statute. The Alien Tort Statute[39] provides that '[t]he district courts shall have original jurisdiction of any civil action by an alien for a tort only, committed in violation of the law of nations or a treaty of the United States'. In *Kiobel*, the question arose whether, under the ATS, US courts had 'extraterritorial' jurisdiction over cases brought against Shell, an Anglo-Dutch corporation present in the United States, by Nigerian victims in respect of harm done in Nigeria. Relying on the presumption against extraterritoriality rather than international law proper, the Supreme Court refused to give a wide extraterritorial reach to the ATS for the following reasons:

> [A]ll the relevant conduct took place outside the United States. And even where the claims touch and concern the territory of the United States, they must do so with sufficient force to displace the presumption against extraterritorial application [...] Corporations are often present in many countries, and it would reach too far to say that mere corporate presence suffices. If Congress were to determine otherwise, a statute more specific than the ATS would be required.[40]

Kiobel seems to sound the death knell for the 'universal civil jurisdiction' which the ATS had come to epitomize, ie, adjudicatory jurisdiction in tort matters absent a territorial or national link to the forum state.[41] The 'touch and concern' standard espoused by the Supreme Court points to a *US national interest* that needs to be vindicated by offering an ATS remedy.[42] While dissenting Justice Breyer considered not providing a safe harbor for an enemy of all mankind to be a distinct American interest,[43] this argument has not had much traction in the lower courts post-*Kiobel*. At most, probably, the ATS could be resorted to with respect to extraterritorial harm caused by US-based corporations, and even that is hardly certain.[44] Post-*Kiobel* ATS decisions are, in any event, decidedly conservative. Application of the requirements that the relevant conduct take place in the US and touch and concern the US has typically resulted in the plaintiffs' claim being barred.[45]

IV. Conclusion

Domestic courts have assumed a rather prominent role in the further development of the international law of jurisdiction. They have at times embraced expansive interpretations of jurisdictional principles that have redefined the field. In particular, as regards antitrust or competition law, high courts in the United States and Europe have introduced the effects and implementation

38 *Kiobel v Royal Dutch Petroleum Co*, 133 S Ct 1659 (2013).

39 28 USC § 1350; ATS.

40 133 S Ct 1669.

41 See C Ryngaert, 'Universal Tort Jurisdiction over Gross Human Rights Violations' (2007) 38 *Netherlands Yearbook of International Law* 3.

42 For an analysis see R Altman, 'Extraterritorial Application of the Alien Tort Statute After Kiobel' (2016) 24 *University of Miami Business Law Review* 111; S H Cleveland, 'After "Kiobel"' (2014) 12(3) *Journal of International Criminal Justice* 551; A Grear and B H Weston, 'The Betrayal of Human Rights and the Urgency of Universal Corporate Accountability: Reflections on a Post-Kiobel Lawscape' (2015) 15(1) *Human Rights Law Review* 21; G L Skinner, 'Beyond Kiobel: providing Access to Judicial Remedies for Violations of International Human Rights Norms by Transnational Business in a New (Post-Kiobel) World' (2014) 46(1) *Columbia Human Rights Law Review* 158.

43 Slip op p 15.

44 See *Mujica v AirScan Inc*, 771 F 3d 580, 594 (9th Cir 2014); *Cardona v Chiquita Brands Int'l Inc*, 760 F 3d 1185, 1189 (11th Cir 2014).

45 See, apart from the aforementioned cases, *Mastafa v Chevron Corp*, 770 F 3d 170, 182 (2d Cir 2014); but see contra *Sexual Minorities Uganda v Lively*, 960 F Supp 2d 304, 312 (D Mass 2013).

doctrines as variations on the territoriality principle, and in so doing redefined transnational competition law (*Alcoa*, US; *Wood pulp*, and *Gencor*, EU).

Domestic courts have also pushed the envelope with respect to universal criminal jurisdiction. The Spanish Constitutional Court, for instance, eliminated all limitations to the application of the universality principle, thereby enabling domestic courts to hear a larger number of international crimes cases (*Menchú Tumn*, Spain). Such bold action has sometimes led to diplomatic conflict and political pushback, to which the legislative rolling back of the universality principle in Spain testifies.

However, domestic courts are not necessarily unaware of the potential for international strife to which their exercise of jurisdiction can give rise. For instance, in an international crimes case, the Spanish Supreme Court highlighted the international problems that could arise in case of Spanish courts' involvement in extraterritorial events (*Jimenez Sanchez*, Spain). Also, some US courts, especially those hearing antitrust cases, have conducted an interest-balancing test, based on international comity or even the principle of non-intervention, to preclude jurisdictional overreach that could upset foreign nations (*Timberlane, Empagran*, US).

Nonetheless, by and large, domestic courts are reluctant to review the reach of domestic law in light of the international law of jurisdiction. Especially in criminal law, domestic courts will not normally review statutory law provisions on jurisdiction in light of customary international law of jurisdiction (*H v Public Prosecutor*, Netherlands; *N v Military Prosecutor*, Switzerland). Still, in case domestic law happens to be in accordance with international law, courts may well embark on justificatory analysis (*Jorgic*, Germany).

In the US, determining the acceptable reach of US law is typically a function of congressional intent rather than of international law. US courts may then review, or rather interpret, statutory law in light of the presumption against extraterritoriality, a US foreign relations-based canon of statutory construction which presumes that Congress only legislates with domestic concerns in mind. On the basis of the presumption, the US Supreme Court has restricted the geographical reach of securities law and the Alien Tort Statute (*Morrison, Kiobel*, US). As it happens, reliance on the presumption may serve the same purpose as reliance on the international law of jurisdiction, namely the prevention of international discord.

4

Immunities of States and their Officials

ROSANNE VAN ALEBEEK AND RICCARDO PAVONI

I. Introduction

International immunity rules have first and foremost developed through domestic jurisprudence. Domestic court decisions are the primary source of state practice to which regard must be had when establishing the scope of a particular immunity rule under customary international law. The law of diplomatic and consular immunity is codified in the 1961 Vienna Convention on Diplomatic Relations (VCDR)[1] and the 1963 Vienna Convention on Consular Relations (VCCR),[2] whereas treaty rules relating to the law of state immunity may be found in the 1972 European Convention on State Immunity[3] and the not-yet-in-force 2004 UN Convention on Jurisdictional Immunities of States and Their Property (UNCSI).[4] Immunity rules are generally considered the example *par excellence* of domestic courts playing a central role in the application and development of international law.[5] In *Jurisdictional Immunities of the State* (*Germany v Italy: Greece intervening*), the International Court of Justice (ICJ) emphasized that a survey of domestic court practice was indispensable for the identification of the scope of the rule of state immunity:

> [s]tate practice of particular significance is to be found in the judgments of national courts faced with the question whether a foreign State is immune, the legislation of those States which have enacted statutes dealing with immunity, the claims to immunity advanced by States before foreign courts and the statements made by States, first in the course of the extensive study of the subject by the International Law Commission and then in the context of the adoption of the UNCSI. *Opinio juris* in this context is reflected in particular in the assertion by States claiming immunity that international law accords them a right to such immunity from the jurisdiction of other States; in the acknowledgment, by States granting immunity, that international law imposes upon them an obligation to do so; and, conversely, in the assertion by States in other cases of a right to exercise jurisdiction over foreign States.[6]

---

1 Vienna Convention on Diplomatic Relations (adopted 18 April 1961, entered into force 24 April 1964) 500 UNTS 95.

2 Vienna Convention on Consular Relations (adopted 24 April 1963, entered into force 19 March 1967) 596 UNTS 261.

3 European Convention on State Immunity (adopted 16 May 1972, entered into force 11 June 1976) 1495 UNTS 182. Only 8 States are parties to this convention.

4 United Nations Convention on Jurisdictional Immunities of States and Their Property (UNCSI) (16 December 2004) UN Doc A/RES/59/38, annex. The Convention will enter into force after 30 ratifications or accessions by states (Article 30). At the time of writing, 22 states have ratified or acceded to the Convention.

5 Eg A Nollkaemper, *National Courts and the International Rule of Law* (OUP 2011) 10.

6 *Jurisdictional Immunities of the State* (*Germany v Italy: Greece intervening*) [2012] ICJ Rep 99 para 55.

While there is by now widespread consensus on the broad contours of the international rules, their interpretation has varied across, and often even within, domestic jurisdictions. One explanation for these conflicting interpretations of the requirements of international law in domestic immunity decisions is the impact of domestic law conceptions on domestic judges. In addition, immunity rules have often been codified in domestic legislation, mostly in common law countries, thereby severing them from the developments in international law. United States (US) case law, making up over half of domestic immunity decisions,[7] deserves special mention in this regard. While the 1976 Foreign Sovereign Immunities Act[8] set out to codify international law,[9] US courts approach immunity as a matter of grace and comity on the part of the US rather than as a matter of right.[10] A more mundane explanation can finally be found in the lack of experience with and knowledge of international law that sometimes characterizes domestic immunity decisions. International law rules are often muddled when applied by domestic judges. It is consequently both difficult and unhelpful to identify 'leading cases' in the field of immunity law, and caution is required to draw inferences from any single case. Every decision must be approached in a critical vein and, as Lady Fox once put it, it is always necessary carefully to 'extract its relevance in establishing the rule in international law'.[11]

This chapter will discuss the principal immunity rules—state immunity (section III); diplomatic immunity and head of state immunity (section IV); functional immunity and consular immunity (section V)—through a selection of domestic immunity decisions. In addition, domestic decisions on two thematic issues will be discussed: immunity as a rule of international or domestic law, and the impact of domestic immunity legislation (section II); and the tension between international immunity rules and the fundamental rights of individuals under domestic constitutional law or international human rights and criminal law (section VI).

While the chapter addresses all different immunity rules applicable to states and their officials, it does not address all issues that arise within the context of the application of these rules. For questions as to the relation between immunity and jurisdiction,[12] the

7 According to H Fox and P Webb, *The Law of State Immunity* (3rd edn, OUP 2013) 98: US federal courts 'until recently, provided over half of all the case-law on State immunity'.

8 US, Foreign Sovereign Immunities Act 1976, Public Law 94-583, 90 Stat 2891, reproduced in (1976) 15 ILM 1388.

9 See, eg, United States, Supreme Court, *Samantar v Yousuf and Ors*, 1 June 2010, ILDC 1505 (US 2010) para 23.

10 See section II.3 below.

11 H Fox, *The Law of State Immunity* (2nd edn, OUP 2008) 23.

12 One question that for example arises is that of the definition of 'jurisdiction' which triggers immunity rules. In *Djibouti v France*, the ICJ ruled that 'the determining factor in assessing whether or not there has been an attack on the immunity of the Head of State lies in the subjection of the latter to a constraining act of authority'; *Certain Questions of Mutual Assistance in Criminal Matters* (*Djibouti v France*) [2008] ICJ Rep 177 para 170. The French Court of Cassation has held that investigation of a crime does not necessarily entail the exercise of jurisdiction, France, Court of Cassation, Criminal Division, *Lydienne X v Prosecutor*, 19 March 2013, ILDC 2035 (FR 2013) para 15. See also Belgium, Brussels Labour Court of Appeals, *BS and KG v AR and AR*, 25 November 2002, ILDC 50 (BE 2002) paras 74 ff.

definition of state,[13] *ex officio* application,[14] and waiver,[15] we direct the reader to the ILDC database.

II. Immunity as a Rule of International or National Law, and the Impact of Domestic Immunity Legislation

In *Jurisdictional Immunities of the State*, the ICJ emphasized that 'whether in claiming immunity for themselves or according it to others, States generally proceed on the basis that there is a right to immunity under international law, together with a corresponding obligation on the part of

13 On the one hand, there are cases in which the question of statehood is central. In this sense domestic courts have *inter alia* assessed whether the Holy See benefited from state immunity (see, eg, United States, Court of Appeals for the Sixth Circuit, *O'Bryan and ors v Holy See (Vatican City State)*, 10 February 2009, ILDC 1234 (US 2009)); whether a Palestinian state existed (United States, Court of Appeals for the First Circuit, *Ungar and ors v Palestine Liberation Organization and Palestinian Authority, Estate of Efrat Ungar and ors v Palestine Liberation Organization and Palestinian Authority*, 31 March 2005, ILDC 124 (US 2005); Israel, District Court of Jerusalem, *Basha, Association of the Elon Moreh College v Israel and ors*, 23 April 2006, ILDC 453 (IL 2006); Israel, Supreme Court, *Palestinian National Authority and ors v Dayan and ors*, 17 July 2007, ILDC 784 (IL 2007)); whether Taiwan was a state (Singapore, High Court, *Woo v Singapore Airlines Limited*, 28 August 2003, ILDC 547 (SG 2003); Singapore, Court of Appeal, *Civil Aeronautics Administration v Singapore Airlines Ltd*, 14 January 2004, ILDC 86 (SG 2004); Canada (Quebec), Superior Court of Quebec, *Parent and ors v Singapore Airlines Ltd and Civil Aeronautics Administration*, 22 October 2003, ILDC 181 (CA 2003)); whether the European Community was a foreign state, a political subdivision of a foreign state, or an agency or instrumentality of a state (United States, District Court for the Eastern District of New York, *European Community and Ors v RJR Nabisco Incorporated and Ors*, 13 May 2011, ILDC 1828 (US 2011)). On the other hand, there are cases in which the link between an entity and a foreign state is central. In this context, domestic courts have *inter alia* assessed whether an airline which was owned for ninety-one per cent by a state was an agent of the state (United States, District Court for the District of Minnesota, *Shirobokova v CSA Czech Airlines, Inc and Delta Airlines*, 24 August 2004, ILDC 717 (US 2004)); whether a state-supported museum was an agency of the state (United States, District Court for the Central District of California, *Cassirer v Spain and Thyssen-Bornemisza Collection Foundation*, 30 August 2006, ILDC 720 (US 2006)); whether a school created and owned by a foreign state enjoyed immunity from jurisdiction (France, Court of Cassation, *X v Saudi School in Paris and Saudi Arabia*, 20 June 2003, ILDC 777 (FR 2003)); whether a rail company, owned by a foreign state, that sold tickets through a third party in the United States enjoyed immunity (United States, Court of Appeals for the 9th Circuit, *Sachs v Republic of Austria and Others*, 6 December 2013, ILDC 2230 (US 2013)); whether—and by the application of which criteria under domestic and international law—state-owned companies retained their separate personality such that their assets could not be equated with those of the state (United Kingdom, Privy Council, *La Générale des Carrières et des Mines v FG Hemisphere Associates LLC*, 17 July 2012, ILDC 2043 (UK 2012)); whether the Vatican Radio was a 'central body of the Catholic Church', so as to be entitled to immunity (Italy, Court of Cassation, *Public Prosecutor of the Rome Tribunal v Tucci and Ors*, 21 May 2003, ILDC 295 (IT 2003) para 25)); whether the Pontificio Collegio Americano del Nord was a 'central body of the Catholic Church', so as to be entitled to immunity (Italy, Court of Cassation, *Cruz v Pontificio Collegio Americano del Nord*, 1 August 2011, ILDC 1783 (IT 2011) paras 8–10)).

14 See, eg, Austria, Supreme Court, *Elisabeth von P v Karl Johannes von S*, 12 June 2007, ILDC 463 (AT 2007) para 1; Finland, District Court of Helsinki, *Carrasco v Venezuela*, 14 November 2000, ILDC 167 (FI 2000); Switzerland, Federal Supreme Court, *X v North Korea and ors*, 3 September 2007, ILDC 1293 (CH 2007); Netherlands, Haarlem District Court, *JSP and ors v Spain*, 19 April 2006, ILDC 545 (NL 2006) para 2.12. See also *Certain Questions of Mutual Assistance in Criminal Matters* (n 12), para 196; see also UNCSI (n 4) Article 6.

15 See, eg, *Elisabeth von P v Karl Johannes von S* (n 14); United States, District Court for the District of Columbia, *John Doe and ors v Israel and ors*, 10 November 2005, ILDC 318 (US 2005); France, Court of Cassation, *Iraqi State v Corporation Dumez GTM (SA)*, ILDC 771 (FR 2006); *Carrasco v Venezuela* (n 14); Germany, Higher Regional Court, *Former consular employee at the Consulate General of Croatia in Stuttgart v Croatia*, 23 October 2014, ILDC 2428 (DE 2014); Belgium, Court of Appeal, *NML Capital Ltd v Argentina*, 21 June 2011, ILDC 1803 (BE 2011); Belgium, Court of Cassation, *Argentina v NML Capital Limited*, 22 November 2012, ILDC 2055 (BE 2012); United States, District Court for the District of Columbia, *Ashraf-Hassan v Embassy of France in the United States*, 17 April 2014, ILDC 2206 (US 2014); South Africa, Constitutional Court, *Zimbabwe v Fick and ors*, 27 June 2013, ILDC 2083 (ZA 2013); Germany, Federal Court of Justice, *Insolvency administrator of W AG v Thailand*, 30 January 2013, ILDC 2177 (DE 2013).

other States to respect and give effect to that immunity'.[16] In general, domestic courts do indeed recognize that the immunity of a foreign state or its officials concerns rights and obligations under international law.[17] The grant of immunity flows from the international law obligation to refrain from exercising jurisdiction, when to do so would be necessary to respect state sovereign equality, dignity, and rights. This does not mean that courts always have regard to international law when deciding immunity questions. Several states have enacted domestic immunity legislation, purportedly codifying the international rules in domestic law, and courts in these states tend to apply the domestic immunity statute rather than engaging in a careful analysis of international law. The US takes the 'nationalization' of the immunity rule even one problematic step further. US immunity (case) law proceeds from the premise that state immunity is a matter of grace and comity rather than a matter of right and obligation, and denies therewith the international law character of the rule altogether (although courts sometimes have regard to international law when deciding cases before them).

This section will first give an example of a domestic court establishing the scope of, and directly applying, the rule of state immunity under customary international law (1). Then an example of the prevalence of domestic immunity law over international law will be given (2). The section concludes with a couple of cases illustrating the unilateralist approach to immunity rules taken by the US (3).

1. State immunity as a rule of international law

Her Majesty the Queen in Right of Canada v Edelson and ors, Final appeal judgment, PLA 7092/94, 51(1) PD 625, ILDC 577 (IL 1997), 3rd June 1997, Israel; Supreme Court

Canada claimed state immunity in a dispute over the rental of premises that were intended to serve as its ambassadorial residence.

> 11. [. . .] Israel, for its part, does not have any specific legislation concerning the immunity of foreign states [. . .] What, then, is the law in this case?
>
> 12. The answer is that the rules of sovereign immunity are part of customary international law. [. . .] This Court has consistently held that Customary international law is part of the Law of the Land, subject to Israeli legislation providing otherwise. [. . .]
>
> 15. [. . .] The immunity of a state from the jurisdiction of the courts of another state is an undisputed principle of customary international law. [. . .]
>
> 16. What is the scope of state immunity? There has been a transition in customary international law in this regard. Originally, state immunity was recognized as applying to all state acts, regardless of their nature. Later, towards the end of the 19th century, a distinction emerged between those states which followed the common law and those which followed the continental approach. While the former continued to recognize comprehensive and "absolute" state immunity, their continental counterparts, on the other hand, recognized only restricted and "relative" state immunity. [. . .]
>
> In the 20th century, this gap began to narrow. Indeed, most states in which absolute immunity had previously been practiced adopted "relative" immunity in one form or another. The theory of restricted immunity is based on the premise that state immunity does not apply when the foreign state acts in a commercial capacity in the

16 *Jurisdictional Immunities of the State* (n 6) para 56.

17 See, eg, Italy, Supreme Court of Cassation, *Académie de France à Rome v Galamini di Recanati*, 17 June 2014, ILDC 2437 (IT 2014) para 4; Germany, Higher Regional Court, *German holder of Greek state bonds v Hellenic Republic*, 4 December 2014, ILDC 2427 (DE 2014); Philippines, Supreme Court, *Arigo v Smith, Arigo and Ors v Swift and Ors*, 16 September 2014, ILDC 2315 (PH 2014) para 22; Poland, Supreme Court, *Natoniewski case, Natoniewski v Germany*, 29 October 2010, ILDC 1996 (PL 2010) para 10.

private law sphere (*jure gestioni*). Immunity will apply only when the state exercises sovereign authority in the public law sphere (*jure imperii*). [...]

22. The assertion that state immunity is restricted under Israeli law requires that we determine this restriction's parameters. This is not a simple undertaking by any means. Indeed, while it is one thing to reject the absolute application of immunity, it is quite another to determine restricted immunity's scope.

23. [...] [I]f the decision respecting the issue of state immunity was subject to my own personal discretion, I would consider the possibility of establishing a rule—subject to very few exceptions, [...]—that the doctrine of state immunity does not apply in Israel, and that the relationship between the foreign state and the Israeli judiciary is identical to that of the State of Israel to its own judiciary. We are, however, not at liberty to rule as such. Rather, in all matters that touch upon customary international law, the courts must rule in accordance with the rules of customary international law, and we cannot invent our own laws. The rule of law means that the judge too is subject to it. We must therefore act in accordance with the rules of customary international law, which recognize the restricted immunity of foreign states with respect to affairs of state. However, from the various possible alternatives offered by customary international law, we may choose the alternative most consistent with the basic principles of international law, on the one hand, and the basic values of Israeli Law on the other. Within this framework, we can choose the option, which most restricts state immunity and consequently broadens the scope of the rule of law.

24. The accepted approach to state immunity in customary international law differentiates between two categories of acts of state. The first deals with the foreign state's acts in its sovereign capacity *acta jure imperii*. This category includes, for example, the confiscation of property for national needs, or the revoking of licenses on grounds of public welfare. [...] The foreign state enjoys immunity with respect to all these acts. The second category includes the foreign state's "private acts." This includes a contractual agreement whereby, for example, a foreign state agrees to sell its shares in a government owned company. Regarding the latter, the foreign state does not enjoy immunity. The difficulty, of course, is in drawing the line between these two categories. The dividing line must be drawn in a way which maintains a proper balance between two sets of opposing interests. The first relates to the individual's civil rights, the principle of equality under the law and to ensuring the rule of law. The other regards the foreign state's interest in fulfilling its political goals without being subject to another state's judicial supervision. [...]

25. The accepted criterion used in customary international law for the purpose of determining State immunity distinguishes between acts of state and private (or commercial) acts. An important question in this context is the following: In determining whether an act is of a sovereign or private nature, do we consider the nature of the act—that is to say, its legal structure—or its purpose? [...]

26. The generally, though not universally, accepted approach of customary international law is that the determinant, though not exclusive, criterion is the legal nature of the state's act rather than its purpose. [...]

29. The distinction between sovereign and private acts is by no means clear-cut. Thus, different states may adopt different guidelines in this context. It seems to me that, pending the development of a standard international practice regarding this issue, it is inevitable that each state will apply its own locally accepted criteria in accordance with its existing national jurisprudence. [...]

> The qualification of state activity as sovereign or non-sovereign must in principle be made by national (municipal) law, since international law, at least usually, contains no criteria for this distinction.
>
> Needless to say, as customary international criteria evolve, we will act accordingly.
>
> 30. [...] It is incumbent upon us to formulate a distinction that accounts for basic values such as individual rights, equality before the law and the rule of law. This having been said, we will allow the foreign state to realize its sovereign objectives, without subjecting them to judicial review in a foreign state's courts.
>
> The balance struck between these conflicting considerations is far from simple and is certainly not immutable. It would seem that, for the time being, it is sufficient to determine that, when in doubt, we must rule in favor of recognizing internal jurisdiction. In any case, the tendency should be towards restricting immunity. This is our practice regarding any domestic matter. [...] This will also be our policy regarding "external" questions. State immunity should only be recognized in clear-cut cases. Such cases are characterized by state immunity being geared towards preventing judicial proceedings in one particular state concerning the acts of another state, the dominant element of which is of [sic] the sovereign nature of the acts in question [...]
>
> 33. Does the dispute in the case at bar fall under the category of state immunity, in its restricted and relative sense? The answer is no. The legal nature of the state's act is that of a rental contract. It is an act, which, according to its nature and character, belongs to the realm of private law. It bears no sovereign aspects, nor is there any exercise of statutory authority. Any private individual could have performed a similar act. On the strength of the facts presented before the magistrate court, there are no special aspects which justify abandoning consideration of the transaction's form, in favor of considering the purposes it was intended to serve. The fact that Canada, rather than a private individual, is a party to the transaction does not affect our understanding of the transaction or its ramifications in any way. The magistrate court's [sic] correctly remarked that the lease for the residence for the ambassador and his family boasts no "sovereign" indication. State immunity simply does not apply.

A couple of observations can be made. In the first place, it is interesting to note that in 2008 Israel adopted domestic immunity legislation, the Foreign States Immunity Law.[18] Israeli courts are therefore no longer to apply customary international law when deciding state immunity claims, but will have to apply the domestic statute instead.[19]

The decision above reflects due respect for international law. The court revealed that it would rather not grant foreign states immunity from its jurisdiction and that it would prefer to treat foreign states on equal footing with the own state. However, with some regret, the court considered that 'we cannot invent our own laws' and that it should 'rule in accordance with the rules of customary international law'. This consideration appears in an interesting light when placed in the discussion on, eg, the development of a possible 'human rights exception' to state immunity, discussed in section VI below.

The Israeli Supreme Court did, however, see room for manoeuvre within the bounds set by international law. With the observation that the distinction between sovereign and non-sovereign acts is not clear-cut and that 'pending the development of a standard international practice regarding this issue, it is inevitable that each state will apply its own locally accepted criteria in accordance with its existing national jurisprudence', the court touched upon a

18 Foreign States Immunity Law 5769-2008.

19 See section II.2 below.

well-known discussion. The reliance on national law standards—the *lex fori*—in the application of the international rule has been a common response to the elusive nature of the restrictive rule of state immunity. In the *Claim against the Empire of Iran* the German *Bundesverfassungsgericht* considered that 'the classification of a State's function (according to the legal nature of the act) as governmental or non-governmental must be determined according to current domestic law, as international law does not, as a rule, include criteria for such a delineation',[20] and many courts have followed its example. Conversely, in a 2014 judgment the Austrian Supreme Court of Justice held that the distinction was to be made by reference to international law, not national law.[21] That latter position is convincing. As Crawford rightly pointed out, the *lex fori* principle can only mean that international law 'does not *require* immunity to be accorded to foreign State defendants [...] in any case'.[22] He argued that: 'as soon as it is conceded that [...] international law does require some immunity, then international law distinguishes to that extent between immune and non-immune transactions, and the question becomes on what basis it is doing so. [...] The initial assumption should be that international law does allow such distinctions to be drawn, that it does not leave them to the uneven discretion of forum States'.[23] The criticism is compelling and it is indeed often pointed out by the supporters of the principle that:

> [n]ational law can only be employed to distinguish between a sovereign and a non-sovereign activity of a foreign State insofar as it cannot exclude from the sovereign sphere, and thus from immunity, such State dealings as belong to the field of State authority in the narrow and proper sense, according to the predominantly-held view of States. In this generally recognizable field of sovereign activity are included transactions relating to foreign affairs, and military authority, the legislature, the exercise of police authority, and the administration of justice.[24]

In other words, domestic courts may only have regard to national law when international law leaves them discretion in the exact application. Once there is consensus on the qualification of certain activity as either sovereign or non-sovereign, qualification under national law is irrelevant. The assertion of the Israeli Supreme Court that international law usually 'contains no criteria' for distinguishing sovereign from non-sovereign activity is arguably too pessimistic: there seems to be little controversy as to the core content of the sovereign activity of a state; it is just the outer limit of the concept that is frayed.

The court indicated that the discretion left by international law to national courts should be used to restrict state immunity as far as possible. It emphasized in this regard 'basic values such as individual rights, equality before the law and the rule of law' and considered that it could 'choose the option, which most restricts state immunity and consequently broadens the scope of the rule of law', and by later stating that 'when in doubt, we must rule in favor of recognizing internal jurisdiction', it indicated that Israeli law imposed an obligation to do so. We will see in sections III and VI below that the tension between the rights of individuals and the rights of states in this field of law has played, and continues to play an important role in the development of international immunity rules.

---

20 Germany, Federal Constitutional Court, *Claim against the Empire of Iran Case*, 30 April 1963, 45 ILR 57, 80. See also Germany, Federal Supreme Court, *Church of Scientology Case*, 26 September 1978, 65 ILR 193, 196–97; Germany; Higher Regional Court, *German holder of Greek state bonds v Hellenic Republic*, 4 December 2014, ILDC 2427 (DE 2014) paras 45–47.

21 Austria, Supreme Court, *RB and TB v Hellenic Republic*, 20 May 2014, ILDC 2214 (AT 2014) para 2.

22 J Crawford, 'International Law and Foreign Sovereigns: Distinguishing Immune Transactions' (1983) 54 *British Yearbook of International Law* 75, 78.

23 ibid; see also C H Schreuer, *State Immunity: Some Recent Developments* (Grotius Publications 1988) 33.

24 *Claim against the Empire of Iran Case* (n 20) 81.

2. Domestic immunity legislation

Several states have codified immunity rules in statute law. The lead was taken by the US in 1976 with the Foreign Sovereign Immunities Act (FSIA).[25] The list of states with domestic immunity legislation includes the United Kingdom (1978); Singapore (1979); Pakistan (1981); South Africa (1981); Canada (1982); Australia (1985); Argentina (1995); Israel (2008); and Japan (2009).[26] Whereas these statutes for the most part purport to codify international law, and domestic courts in these states adopt the principle of interpretation in conformity with international law, in case of a clear contradiction between international law and the domestic statute, the domestic statute is bound to prevail. While this depends on the status of international law in any specific domestic system, the fact is that many of the countries with domestic immunity legislation listed above recognize the superiority of domestic statutes over international law.

Bouzari (Houshang) and ors, Amnesty International (Canadian Section) (intervening) and ors (intervening) v Iran, Appeal decision, 71 OR (3d) 675 (Ont CA), 2004 CanLII 871 (ON CA), (2004) 243 DLR (4th) 406, 2004 CarswellOnt 2681, 122 CRR (2d) 26, (2004) OJ No 2800, ILDC 175 (CA 2004), 30th June 2004, Canada; Ontario; Court of Appeal [ONCA]

Mr Bouzari sued Iran in the Canadian courts on allegations of torture committed in Iran. The Ontario Court of Appeal had to decide the Iranian claim to immunity under the 1982 State Immunity Act (SIA).

> [60] [The public international law] issue takes the appellant beyond the exceptions to state immunity which are expressly enacted in the SIA. He argues that the SIA must be read in conformity with Canada's public international law obligations and that both by treaty and by peremptory norms of customary international law, Canada is bound to permit a civil remedy against a foreign state for torture committed abroad. He says that Canada's obligations under international law require that the SIA be interpreted to provide an exception to state immunity for such a claim.
>
> [61] The motion judge dismissed this argument. She carefully analyzed both Canada's treaty obligations and its obligations under customary public international law and found that neither extends to the obligation contended for by the appellant.
>
> [62] I agree with her analysis and will return to it in more detail. First, however, it is useful to turn to a preliminary point about the interplay between Canada's obligations at public international law and its domestic legislation.
>
> [63] Canada's international law obligations can arise as a matter of conventional international law or customary international law.
>
> [64] Where Canada has undertaken treaty obligations, it is bound by them as a matter of conventional international law. Parliament is then presumed to legislate

25 US, Foreign Sovereign Immunities Act 1976, Public Law 94-583, 90 Stat 2891, reproduced in (1976) 15 ILM 1388.

26 UK, State Immunity Act 1978, reproduced in (1978) 17 ILM 1123; Singapore, State Immunity Act 1979, reproduced in UN Doc ST/LEG/SER.B.20, 28; Pakistan, State Immunity Ordinance 1981, reproduced in UN Doc ST/LEG/SER.B.20, 20; South Africa, Foreign States Immunity Act 1981, reproduced in UN Doc ST/LEG/SER.B/20, 34; Canada, State Immunity Act 1982, reproduced in (1982) 21 ILM 798; Australia, Foreign Sovereign Immunities Act 1985, reproduced in (1986) 25 ILM 715; Argentina, La Ley 24.488, Inmunidad Jurisdiccional de los Estados Extranjeros ante los Tribunales Argentinos (1995), reproduced in A Dickinson, R Lindsay, and J P Loonan (eds), *State Immunity: Selected Materials and Commentary* (OUP 2004); Israel, Foreign States Immunity Law 5769-2008; Japan, Act on Civil Jurisdiction over Foreign States 2009, reproduced in (2010) 53 *Japanese Yearbook of International Law* 830. See also s 86(1) of the Indian Code of Civil Procedure and the interpretation thereof in India, Supreme Court, *Mirza Ali Akbar Kashani v United Arab Republic* (1965) 64 ILR 489.

consistently with those obligations. [...] Thus, so far as possible, courts should interpret domestic legislation consistently with these treaty obligations.

[65] The same is true where Canada's obligations arise as a matter of customary international law. As acknowledged by the Attorney General in this case, customary rules of international law are directly incorporated into Canadian domestic law unless explicitly ousted by contrary legislation. So far as possible, domestic legislation should be interpreted consistently with those obligations. This is even more so where the obligation is a peremptory norm of customary international law, or *jus cogens*. [...]

[66] However, [...] whether Canada's obligations arise pursuant to treaty or to customary international law, it is open to Canada to legislate contrary to them. Such legislation would determine Canada's domestic law although it would put Canada in breach of its international obligations.

[67] This discussion is important in this case because the SIA so clearly provides the code for according state immunity as a matter of Canadian domestic law. Even if Canada's international law obligations required that Canada permit a civil remedy for torture abroad by a foreign state, Canada has legislated in a way that does not do so. Section 3 of the *SIA* accords complete state immunity except as provided by the *SIA*. And, as we have seen, none of the relevant exceptions in the SIA permits a civil claim against a foreign state for torture committed abroad. Canada has clearly legislated so as not to create this exception to state immunity whether it has an international law obligation to do so or not.

[68] However, the more fundamental question is whether Canada has the international law obligation contended for by the appellant. [...]

As the ILDC reporter on this case aptly notes 'the case was a strong reminder that, even in the event of a breach, it was not open to domestic courts to second guess Parliament and provide a remedy which had been clearly excluded. Absent constitutional constraint, Parliament was free at the domestic level to abrogate its international commitments'.[27] While arguably the reasoning of the court only applies to abrogation of pre-existing international obligations, the fact that the case turned on an alleged violation of the 1984 Convention against Torture[28] suggests a more general principle: in case of divergence or clash between the international and the national rule, the courts have to apply the domestic statute.

3. United States: the apparent denial of any international legal obligation

US case law frequently evidences a unilateral approach to immunity questions, based on the assumption that these questions lie within the complete discretion of the state.[29] In view of the fact that until recently half of all domestic immunity decisions stemmed from US courts,[30] it is important to reflect briefly on the relevance of this jurisprudence for the rules under international law.

Austria and Austrian Gallery v Altmann, On Writ of Certiorari, Docket No 03-13, 541 US 677 (2004), 327 F 3d 1246 (2004), 124 S Ct 2240 (2004), 159 L Ed 2d 1 (2004), ILDC 114 (US 2004), 7th June 2004, United States; Supreme Court [US]

The heiress of the owner of six Klimt paintings confiscated by the Nazis or expropriated by the Austrian government after the Second World War filed an action against Austria to recover the

27 G MacNeil, Analysis, *Bouzari and ors v Iran*, ILDC 175 (CA 2004) A3.

28 Convention against Torture and Other Cruel, Inhuman and Degrading Treatment or Punishment (adopted 10 December 1984, entry into force 26 June 1987) 1465 UNTS 85.

29 See J Finke, 'Sovereign Immunity: Rule, Comity, or Something Else?' (2010) 21 *EJIL* 853.

30 See n 7.

paintings. Austria invoked state immunity from US jurisdiction. The case turned on the question of whether the 1976 FSIA could be given retroactive application.

> 19 In accordance with Chief Justice Marshall's observation that foreign sovereign immunity is a matter of grace and comity rather than a constitutional requirement, this Court has "consistently [. . .] deferred to the decisions of the political branches—in particular, those of the Executive Branch—on whether to take jurisdiction" over particular actions against foreign sovereigns and their instrumentalities. *Verlinden B. V. v. Central Bank of Nigeria*, 461 U. S. 480, 486 (1983) (citing *Ex parte Peru*, 318 U. S. 578, 586–590 (1943); *Republic of Mexico v. Hoffman*, 324 U. S. 30, 33–36 (1945)). Until 1952 the Executive Branch followed a policy of requesting immunity in all actions against friendly sovereigns. [. . .]. In that year, however, the State Department concluded that "immunity should no longer be granted in certain types of cases." [. . .]. In a letter to the Attorney General, the Acting Legal Adviser for the Secretary of State, Jack B. Tate, explained that the Department would thereafter apply the "restrictive theory" of sovereign immunity [. . .]
>
> 28 [. . .] Prior to 1976 foreign states had a justifiable expectation that, as a matter of comity, United States courts would grant them immunity for their public acts (provided the State Department did not recommend otherwise), but they had no "right" to such immunity. [. . .]
>
> 30 [. . .] [T]he principal purpose of foreign sovereign immunity has never been to permit foreign states and their instrumentalities to shape their conduct in reliance on the promise of future immunity from suit in United States courts. Rather, such immunity reflects current political realities and relationships, and aims to give foreign states and their instrumentalities some *present* "protection from the inconvenience of suit as a gesture of comity." [. . .] Throughout history, courts have resolved questions of foreign sovereign immunity by deferring to the "decisions of the political branches [. . .] on whether to take jurisdiction." [. . .]

Because before the enactment of the FSIA in 1976 foreign states only had a 'justifiable expectation that, as a matter of comity, United States courts would grant them immunity' but 'no "right" to immunity', the FSIA could be given retroactive effect. Whereas in 1976 the FSIA was meant to 'codify the so-called "restrictive" principle of sovereign immunity as presently recognised in international law',[31] the US judiciary is now of the opinion that '[f]oreign sovereign immunity is, and always has been, "a matter of grace and comity on the part of the United States, and not a restriction imposed by the Constitution"'.[32] The emphasis of the ICJ on the obligatory, international law character of the rule in *Jurisdictional Immunities of the State* seems a silent rebuke of the US position.[33]

Ye and ors v Former President Jiang Zemin and Falun Gong Control Office (also known as Office 6/10), United States Department of State (intervening) and United States Department of Justice (intervening), Appeal Judgment, Docket No 03-3989, 383 F.3d 620 (7th Cir. 2004), ILDC 683 (US 2004), 8th September 2004, United States; Court of Appeals (7th Circuit) [7th Cir]

A group of practitioners of Falun Gong, a spiritual movement of Chinese origin, sued the then President of China, Jiang Zemin, and the Falun Gong Control Office established by him during his presidency, on allegations of torture, genocide, arbitrary arrest, and imprisonment, as well

31 See n 9.

32 United States, Supreme Court, *Argentina v NML Capital, Limited*, 16 June 2014, ILDC 2201 (US 2014) para 12 (referring to *Verlinden BV v Central Bank of Nigeria*, 461 US 480 (1983)).

33 See text with n 16.

as violations of freedom of conscience, movement, and religion. The US government moved to intervene in the proceedings on behalf of Jiang Zemin entering a so-called 'suggestion of immunity'.[34]

> 15 The FSIA does not [...] address the immunity of foreign heads of states. The FSIA refers to foreign states, not their leaders. The FSIA defines a foreign state to include a political subdivision, agency or instrumentality of a foreign state but makes no mention of heads of state. 28 U.S.C. § 1603(a). Because the FSIA does not apply to heads of states, the decision concerning the immunity of foreign heads of states remains vested where it was prior to 1976 — with the Executive Branch. [...]
>
> 19 The appellants' position [...] is that, in at least a particular class of cases (those involving *jus cogens* norms), a court cannot defer to the position of the Executive Branch with respect to immunity for heads of states. The Supreme Court has held, however, that the Executive Branch's suggestion of immunity is conclusive and not subject to judicial inquiry. [...]
>
> 20 The appellants present their argument as one of international law — under customary international law, a state cannot provide immunity to a defendant accused of violating *jus cogens* norms. Our first concern, however, is to ascertain the proper relationship between the Executive and Judicial Branches insofar as the immunity of foreign leaders is concerned. The obligation of the Judicial Branch is clear — a determination by the Executive Branch that a foreign head of state is immune from suit is conclusive and a court must accept such a determination without reference to the underlying claims of a plaintiff. [...]
>
> 21 Our deference to the Executive Branch is motivated by the caution we believe appropriate of the Judicial Branch when the conduct of foreign affairs is involved. [...] The determination to grant (or not grant) immunity can have significant implications for this country's relationship with other nations. A court is ill-prepared to assess these implications and resolve the competing concerns the Executive Branch is faced with in determining whether to immunize a head of state. [...]
>
> 22 Although our decision in *Sampson* [*Sampson v. Federal Republic of Germany*, 250 F.3d 1145, 1149–50 (7th Cir. 2001)] was one of statutory interpretation, we believe it is also instructive here. In *Sampson* we held that the FSIA did not include an implied exception to its general grant of sovereign immunity to foreign states where a foreign state was accused of violating *jus cogens* norms. [...] Because the FSIA contained no such exception, Germany was immune from suit brought by a survivor of Auschwitz in the Northern District of Illinois.
>
> 23 Our interpretation of the FSIA confirmed that Congress could grant immunity to a foreign state for acts that amounted to violations of *jus cogens* norms. Just as the FSIA is the Legislative Branch's determination that a nation should be immune from suit in the courts of this country, the immunity of foreign leaders remains the province of the Executive Branch. The Executive Branch's determination that a foreign leader should be immune from suit even when the leader is accused of acts that violate *jus cogens* norms is established by a suggestion of immunity. We are no more free to ignore the Executive Branch's determination than we are free to ignore a legislative determination concerning a foreign state. [...] Pursuant to their respective authorities, Congress or the Executive Branch can create exceptions to blanket immunity. In such

34 See for the letter of the Legal Advisor of the Department of State (the so-called 'Taft letter'), L S Yelin, 'Head of State Immunity as Sole Executive Lawmaking' (2011) 44 *Vanderbilt Journal of Transnational Law* 911, 997 (Annex B). In addition, the government issued an Amicus brief to the Seventh Circuit Court.

> cases the courts would be obliged to respect such exceptions. In the present case the Executive Branch has recognized the immunity of President Jiang from the appellants' suit. The district court was correct to accept this recognition as conclusive.

US courts consider the executive's directions on head of state immunity questions to be binding.[35] Whether the same is true for executive suggestions in respect of foreign state officials who are not covered by the head of state immunity rule is not yet settled. Whereas some lower courts have regarded the Executive suggestion dispositive also in those cases,[36] the 4th Circuit Court of Appeals held in the 2012 *Samantar* case that: '[u]nlike head-of-state immunity and other status-based immunities, there is no equivalent constitutional basis suggesting that the views of the Executive Branch control questions of foreign official immunity. Such cases do not involve any act of recognition for which the Executive Branch is constitutionally empowered; rather, they simply involve matters about the scope of defendant's official duties'. According to the Circuit Court '[t]hese immunity decisions turn upon principles of customary international law and foreign policy, areas in which the courts respect, but do not automatically follow, the views of the Executive Branch'.[37] Also, in FSIA-controlled cases[38] and in diplomatic immunity cases,[39] statements of the executive may exert considerable, or even decisive influence.

III. State Immunity

As stated in the Introduction, the UNCSI is not yet in force, and therefore issues of state immunity continue to be regulated by uncodified customary international law, with the exception of the few states that have ratified the ECSI (which is only applicable to the relations between the same states) and of those which primarily refer to their domestic legislation and/or to considerations of grace and comity.[40]

There currently exists a virtually universal acceptance[41] of a customary rule which accord states restrictive immunity from the jurisdiction of other states, ie, immunity only shields acts

35 See, eg, also United States, Court of Appeals for the 10th Circuit, *Habyarimana and Ntaryamira v Kagame, President of Rwanda*, 10 October 2012, ILDC 2162 (US 2012) para 5; United States, District Court for the District of Columbia, *Manoharan and ors v Rajapaksa*, 29 February 2012, ILDC 2020 (US 2012) para 8.

36 See United States, District Court for the District of Columbia, *Li and United States (intervening) v Bo*, 1 August 2008, ILDC 1155 (US 2008); United States, Court of Appeals for the 2nd Circuit, *Matar and ors v Dichter*, 16 April 2009, ILDC 1392 (US 2009); United States, District Court for the Eastern District of New York, *Rosenberg and ors v Lashkar-e-Taiba and ors*, 30 September 2013, ILDC 2223 (US 2013). See also United States, Court of Appeals for the 10th Circuit, *Habyarimana and Ntaryamira v Kagame, President of Rwanda*, 10 October 2012, ILDC 2162 (US 2012) para 5, where the principle is stated in broader terms.

37 United States, Court of Appeals for the 4th Circuit, *Yousuf and ors v Samantar*, 2 November 2012, ILDC 1958 (US 2012) paras 24–26. See also United States, District Court for the District of Columbia, *Balcero Giraldo and ors v Drummond Company Incorporated and ors*, 8 September 2011, ILDC 1835 (US 2011), where the Court did consider executive suggestions to be decisive, but since the executive suggestion recognized immunity 'as to information relating to acts taken or obtained in his official capacity as a government official', it left it to itself to apply that standard.

38 See United States, District Court for the District of Columbia, *Agudas Chasidei Chabad of the United States v Russian Federation and ors*, 16 January 2013, ILDC 2004 (US 2013); *Rosenberg and ors v Lashkar-e-Taiba and ors* (n 36).

39 See United States, District Court for the District of Columbia, *Montuya v Chedid and Chedid*, 26 April 2011, ILDC 2195 (US 2011) para 14.

40 See sections II.2 and II.3 above.

41 For residues of absolute immunity, see *Democratic Republic of the Congo and ors v FG Hemisphere Associates LLC*, 8 June 2011, ILDC 1970 (HK 2011); *Skarphéðinsdóttir v Embassy of the United States*, 15 September 1995, ILDC 1021 (IS 1995); *Aerotrade Inc v Bezzi ex p Haiti*, BJ 863 1735, 1 October 1982, ILDC 1204 (DO 1982); *Twictor Investments Ltd v United States*, Civil Suit No 1309/2001, 23 May 2003, ILDC 927 (KE 2003); *(Anonymous) Foreign State v (Anonymous) Russian Construction Company*, Information Letter No 58, s 5, 18 January 2001, ILDC 24 (RU 2001) (however, Russian practice has now shifted to restrictive immunity; see ECtHR, *Oleynikov v Russia*, App No 36703/04 (14 March 2013)).

which are a manifestation of sovereign authority (*acta jure imperii*) as opposed to acts of a private law nature (*acta jure gestionis*).

Given the massive volume of cases involving substantive aspects of the law of state immunity, the following subsections concern a few decisions made in the areas which appear most relevant in practice, while continuing to show divergences of approaches and solutions on the part of domestic courts. These are: (1) commercial activities undertaken by foreign states, especially when such activities are part of complex transactions also denoted by elements of governmental authority (so-called 'mixed state activities'); (2) labour disputes brought by employees of foreign states; (3) non-commercial territorial torts causing personal injury or damage to property which are attributable to foreign states; and (4) immunity from execution, ie, state property immunity from measures of constraint.

1. Commercial activities

This subsection discusses a few domestic court decisions dealing with the so-called 'commercial activity exception' to state immunity. Historically, this exception was the first to emerge as a result of the increasing involvement of states and their agencies in private law transactions (*acta jure gestionis*), with the associated need to ensure fairness and justice to individuals who enter into such transactions.

The exception has thus been the primary driver for the shift from a doctrine of absolute state immunity to a doctrine of relative state immunity, ie, one which can only be successfully claimed for *acta jure imperii* as opposed to *acta jure gestionis*.

While 'some form'[42] of the commercial transaction exception may safely be considered as part of customary international law, doubts remain as to its precise contours. Two problems stand out in this connection: (i) whether the determination that a given state conduct represents a commercial transaction should be made by reference to its *nature* or its *purpose* or both, where the first option is evidently the more favourable to the loss of immunity;[43] and (ii) whether so-called 'mixed activities' of foreign states, ie, composite state conduct denoted both by elements of governmental authority and by private law aspects, should attract immunity.

The three following decisions addressed mixed activities of foreign states. In considering the latter's immunity claims, the courts concerned also made significant findings on the issue whether regard should be had to the nature or purpose of the conduct at stake. The different outcomes evidence persistent uncertainties on these matters.

Such uncertainties are not dispelled by the UNCSI. First, the commercial transaction exception set out in Article 10 UNCSI contains an enigmatic paragraph 3 upholding state immunity when the relevant proceedings concern transactions by state enterprises or entities having an independent legal personality. Secondly, the definition of 'commercial transaction' in Article 2(1)(c) is not precise, as it includes an open-ended clause referring to 'any other contract or transaction of a commercial, industrial, trading or professional nature', the only explicit exclusion being 'a contract of employment of persons'. Thirdly, and most importantly, Article 2(2) reads: 'In determining whether a contract or transaction is a "commercial transaction" [. . .], reference should be made primarily to the nature of the contract or transaction, but its purpose should also be taken into account if the parties to the contract or transaction have so agreed, or if, in the practice of the State of the forum, that purpose is relevant to determining the non-commercial character of the contract or transaction'. This provision, which makes room for the 'purpose test' whenever this is in line with the practice of the forum state, is inconsistent with the practice of a large number of states which are firmly anchored to the 'nature test'. Therefore, the *dictum* by

42 S Wittich, 'Article 10' in R O'Keefe and C J Tams (eds), *The United Nations Convention on Jurisdictional Immunities of States and Their Property: A Commentary* (OUP 2013) 167, 182.

43 See also Israel, Supreme Court, *Canada v Edelson*, section II.1 above.

the European Court of Human Rights (ECtHR) in *Oleynikov*[44] that the UNCSI's provisions on the commercial transaction exception reflect customary law, and are as such binding on states irrespective of their ratification of the UNCSI, is highly questionable and problematic.[45]

New Zealand, Court of Appeal, Controller and Auditor-General v Sir Ronald Davison, 16 February 1996, (1997) 36 ILM 728 (not in ILDC)

The applicant sought judicial review of the power of the defendant to order the production of documents allegedly providing evidence of a scheme of tax fraud and evasion carried out by several New Zealand companies with the complicity of the Cook Islands Government. The issue of sovereign immunity arose because the Cook Islands were considered a fully sovereign and independent state and because the applicant, while a New Zealand official, was also acting as an auditor for the Cook Islands.

In order to decide whether the disclosure of the documents was barred by sovereign immunity, the Court of Appeal enquired into whether the scheme of tax fraud and evasion at stake could be classified as a commercial transaction. This complex scheme was indeed a prototype of composite conduct on the part of the foreign state, encompassing both elements of governmental authority (the operation of the tax system) and commercial aspects, ie sham sales and purchases of financial products aimed at repaying the taxes owed by the companies, while extracting a fee for the tax benefits thus accruing to the same companies. Four judges out of five, albeit with different reasoning, concluded that sovereign immunity was to be ruled out.

> Cooke P:
>
> Seen in isolation, the issuing of a tax credit is an act which could only be performed by a state. At least on the surface, it would by itself attract sovereign immunity. […] Dealing in promissory notes is an activity which any private citizen can perform. As a whole the transactions may be called the sale of tax credits, but, if that description is too loose, it is at least clear that there is apparently strong evidence of ostensibly commercial sale-and-purchase contracts as a key component of the arrangements. […] [T]he Cook Islands Government and its instrumentalities were engaged to a major extent in such mixed-up activities. […] Their commercial aspect is so significant that one can have no doubt that the doctrine of sovereign immunity must be excluded in relation to the whole inquiry. A government which descends to this extent into the market place cannot fairly expect total immunity. (at 730)
>
> Richardson J:
>
> The operation of a tax system is a quintessential example of governmental activity that should ordinarily be immune from intrusive scrutiny by the agencies of another state. […] The exercise of the tax function may constitute an abuse of power but that does not change the character of the power which is exercised. (at 734)
>
> I do not see how the […] transactions, dependent as they were on the exercise of the sovereign taxing power, could be characterised differently. It follows that any demand for documents which are held in New Zealand on behalf of the Cook Islands Government is an intrusion on the public or sovereign activities of the Cook Islands. (at 735)
>
> Thomas J:
>
> I propose to advance an alternative and, I consider, preferable approach. […] Under this approach, no single criteria or test for determining whether the claim of a foreign state for sovereign immunity should be granted would be adopted. Rather, regard

44 *Oleynikov v Russia* (n 41) paras 61, 66, 68.

45 See R van Alebeek, 'Oleynikov Judgment on State Immunity' http://echrblog.blogspot.it/2013/03/oleynikov-judgment-on-state-immunity.html (last accessed 16 October 2017).

> would be had to all relevant factors in the light of any criteria which are applicable in the circumstances. Where the criteria are in conflict, it will be necessary to balance one against the other in reaching a decision as to whether or not sovereign immunity is applicable. (at 740)
>
> [I]t would seemingly subvert the intention of Parliament if the Courts were to grant sovereign immunity to the Cook Islands in the present circumstances. (at 741)
>
> The Cook Islands' interference with New Zealand's sovereign right to tax, provides a sound reason for not granting it sovereign immunity. [...] [T]he enquiry being undertaken is not directed at the Cook Islands Government itself. It is not directly "impleaded" in the process. [...] Nor is the Cook Islands Government exposed to any enforcement procedures in respect of its involvement in the transactions under enquiry. [...] The Auditor-General and the documents in issue are within New Zealand. [...] The physical presence of the property reinforces the state's full and absolute territorial jurisdiction. [...] [T]o insist on the production of the documents in issue [...] should be justified under international law having regard to the fact that the documents are believed to contain evidence of a conspiracy, to which the Cook Islands Government was a party [...]. (at 742)
>
> [T]his is not a case where the dispute would be best dealt with politically or through diplomatic channels. [...] Finally, it is relevant to assess whether sovereign immunity should be granted having regard to the principles underlying the doctrine. [...] [I]t cannot be validly claimed that, once the Cook Islands Government chose to enter into the arrangements in issue with the ramifications which that had for the New Zealand tax regime, it is an affront to the dignity of that nation to have its actions examined in the course of an enquiry in New Zealand. [...] [I]t can hardly be said that New Zealand is seeking to intervene in the internal or external affairs of the Cook Islands [...]. [I]t cannot be properly suggested that refusing to waive its jurisdiction in the present circumstances would demonstrate a lack of comity or goodwill on New Zealand's part. [...] Nor, again, can the maintenance of the international order be used to shelter behind when conduct is undertaken by the foreign state which is itself damaging to that international order. (at 743)

This case is a remarkable example of the difficulties facing domestic courts in the interpretation of the commercial transaction exception to sovereign immunity when mixed or composite conduct by foreign states is at issue. Indeed, there was no unanimity of the court in recognizing that the contested tax-fraud scheme was alien to sovereign immunity, with Richardson J dissenting on this point and Thomas J preferring a different, multi-pronged test for finally adjudicating the immunity claim.

By contrast, all five judges basically agreed with an alternative ground for denying immunity in this case, one which this decision is especially noted for, namely reliance on public policy as a matter of 'fundamental values' or 'fundamental principles of justice' of the forum state (see the judgment by Richardson J, at 736–37). Various commentators have therefore highlighted this decision as an embryonic recognition on the part of a supreme court, as the Court of Appeal is in the New Zealand system, of the priority of human rights over the principle of state immunity.[46]

Airport L, LLC (GmbH) v United States, Final appeal/cassation, 2 Ob 156/03k, ILDC 3 (AT 2003), 28th August 2003, Austria; Supreme Court of Justice [OGH]

The company operating Linz-Hörsching Airport sued the US in order to recover certain landing fees and airport charges allegedly owed in connection with the use of the said airport by US air force flights carried out in the context of the UN-authorized NATO IFOR/SFOR mission in

46 See, eg, M Byers, 'Introductory Note' (1997) 36 ILM 721. See section VI below.

Bosnia Herzegovina. Although the elements of governmental authority involved in the overall conduct by the foreign state were glaringly paramount, the Supreme Court agreed to discuss the applicability of the commercial exception to state immunity, considering that the use of a civilian airport for intermediate landings was an activity that could also be undertaken by private parties. The court upheld the conclusion of the lower courts and accorded state immunity to the US.

> 4) [...] NATO's IFOR and SFOR mission are operations included in the Dayton Peace Treaty and are enshrined under international law by corresponding United Nations Resolutions [...], entrusting NATO with the task of bringing peace to Bosnia Herzegovina and then keeping the peace there [...]. There is therefore no doubt that the deployment of the defendant's troops and aircraft as part of the IFOR or SFOR missions ordered by the UN can only be, by its very nature and also in the light of international law, a sovereign act, implemented by and enshrined in treaties under international law and UN Security Council Resolutions. Actions by a State under the terms of a treaty under international law constitute sovereign acts.
>
> [...] Although the Supreme Court is of the firm view that the operations by the defendant's aircraft over the course of the IFOR/SFOR mission in principle constituted sovereign acts, it must be examined whether intermediate landing at an Austrian civil airport is to be categorised as an act under private law or not, because the operations could, for instance, have merely been escort operations or auxiliary operations assisting performance of the sovereign operations, and, as specified above, the nature of the act itself is used rather than the object or purpose of the act when differentiating between sovereign acts and acts under private law. The question to be asked is whether a subject under private law could also have performed the act in question. [...]
>
> 9) [...] In any case the military operations of a State's air-force are sovereign acts of State [...]. If a State has acted according to the terms of a treaty under international law, then this also constitutes sovereign action [...]. The same must apply for Resolutions of the Security Council of the United Nations having binding legal effect. [...] If the defendant's flights were being used for these sovereign purposes [...], then not only did these "State aircrafts" enjoy full immunity [...], but so too did the foreign State responsible (as the owner and dispatcher) as a subject under international law, irrespective of the cargo these aircraft[s] were carrying (aid for example, as claimed here). This therefore constituted sovereign State action [...]. Not even the plaintiff claims that the landings by US military aircraft at an Austrian civil airport at issue in the proceedings were purely "private" operations and not part of the UN approved mission. [...]

This decision is testimony of persistent uncertainties, even among courts in Europe, over the distinction between acts *jure imperii* and acts *jure gestionis*. This is especially so when, as it frequently happens, mixed activities by foreign states are at stake. In this case, the critical activity, which tilted the balance in favour of upholding sovereign immunity, was identified in the deployment of military flights in the context of a UN-authorized peacekeeping mission. The intermediate landings of the US aircrafts at a civilian airport and the pecuniary obligations thereby allegedly assumed were only prima facie private in nature. These private law activities were, however, ancillary to the predominantly governmental nature of the foreign state's overall conduct and had to be viewed as serving sovereign purposes. However, the Supreme Court's uncertainty in dealing with the situation at stake is *inter alia* evidenced by its reference to the 'purpose test' when seeking to characterize the disputed military flights (paragraph 9). Its findings ultimately bring support to retaining the 'purpose test' as part and parcel of the overall appraisal of complex patterns of conduct by foreign states.[47]

47 See case report by S Wittich (2005) 99 AJIL 248.

Borri v Argentina, Request for a Ruling on Jurisdiction, Case No 11225, (2005) 88 Riv Dir Int 856, ILDC 296 (IT 2005), 27th May 2005, Italy; Supreme Court of Cassation[48]

Mr Borri brought a dispute against the Republic of Argentina in order to obtain the reimbursement of certain 'Argentinean global bonds' that he had purchased on the international stock market. In the context of the 2002 emergency measures addressing its economic breakdown, Argentina had frozen such bonds and rescheduled their repayment. This is a typical example of mixed conduct of foreign states. The Italian Supreme Court unexpectedly granted state immunity.

> 4. [T]he applicant's arguments cannot be accepted […] because, while the issuing and placing in the international market of the securities concerned are undeniably of a private law nature, the subsequent moratorium adopted by the Argentinean government […] [is] not of an analogous character. […]
>
> 4.2 [The Argentinean] laws are clear manifestations of the sovereign power of the State […]. This is both because they are budgetary laws and, above all, because of their purposes […] which are manifestly public and pursued to regulate finances for the protection of the primary needs of the economic survival of the population in the context of a serious national emergency.

Whereas the issuance of bonds and similar financial instruments by foreign states is a historical manifestation of *jure gestionis* conduct, the adoption of legislative measures is a commonly accepted example of *jure imperii* activity. The question is whether a foreign state may displace the *jure gestionis* nature of the former activity, and thus successfully rely on immunity before domestic courts, through the enactment of subsequent laws which repudiate its contractual obligations.

The affirmative answer given by the Italian Supreme Court in the *Borri* decision was unsound, because in this case considerations of fairness and justice to individuals entering into financial transactions with foreign states strongly militated in favour of denying immunity. Unlike the New Zealand and Austrian decisions reviewed in this subsection, it must be underscored that the *original* foreign state's activity at issue in the *Borri* case was of a squarely commercial nature.

The court's decision is also troubling given the opposite solution espoused by various domestic courts in respect of identical or very similar situations.[49] Given the absence of references by the court to foreign jurisprudence or legal materials, this case is thus a telling example of the shortcomings arising from the absence of transnational judicial dialogue on international law issues.[50]

2. Labour disputes

The extent to which labour disputes are covered by state immunity is one of the most controversial questions in this area of the law. The traditional *jure imperii* v *jure gestionis* dichotomy is not readily applicable to contracts of employment with foreign states. For instance, when providing a definition of 'commercial transaction', Article 2(1)(c) UNCSI expressly excludes 'a contract of employment of persons' therefrom. As recalled below, contracts of employment are indeed covered by a specific exception in Article 11 UNCSI. Another element to be taken into account is that, in this area, human rights considerations are more prominent than in others (just think of sex discrimination in employment issues or workers' health and safety cases).

48 Compare with Italy, Court of Cassation, *Italian Ministry of Foreign Affairs v Immobiliare Villa ai Pini s.r.l. and People's Republic of China*, 17 July 2008, ILDC 1371 (IT 2008).

49 See, eg, United States, Supreme Court, *Republic of Argentina v Weltover*, 12 June 1992, 504 US 607, ILDC 1924 (US 1992). See B Bonafé, 'State Immunity and the Protection of Private Investors: The *Argentine Bonds* Case Before Italian Courts' (2006) 16 *Italian Yearbook of International Law* 165.

50 R Pavoni, 'A Decade of Italian Case Law on the Immunity of Foreign States: Lights and Shadows' (2009) 19 *Italian Yearbook of International Law* 73, 78–80.

Practice shows that these circumstances have resulted in the progressive relaxation of the rule of state immunity in employment disputes. However, the precise boundaries of the employment exception remain uncertain. Domestic court practice evidences a variety of positions whereby different subjective and objective criteria are relied upon to decide whether the specific case attracts immunity (eg, employment at embassies *vel non*, rank of the employee, nature of the claim, nationality of the employee). Article 11 UNCSI confirms such uncertainties. It does not provide for a simple rule of non-immunity.[51] Instead, after proclaiming that employer states are not immune in labour disputes relating to work performed in the forum state, Article 11 lists a number of exceptions to the exception, most of which raise difficult interpretative issues. These counter-exceptions basically concern suits relating to: (i) employees involved in the exercise of governmental functions; (ii) persons enjoying diplomatic or consular immunities; (iii) recruitment or reinstatement; (iv) dismissal, provided that the relevant proceedings jeopardize the security interests of the employer state, *as determined by that state*; and (v) nationals of the employer state.

In a line of recent cases,[52] the ECtHR boosted the status of Article 11 UNCSI by considering it as a codification of customary international law, thus binding upon a state irrespective of its ratification of the UNCSI (with the only caveat that the same state had not objected to the adoption of Article 11). In all such cases, the ECtHR concluded that the respondent states had violated Article 6 of the European Convention on Human Rights (ECHR) on the right of access to a court by upholding state immunity contrary to (its interpretation of) Article 11 UNCSI. A plethora of arguments can be advanced against the proposition that Article 11 reflects customary law (such as, elementarily, the substantial inconsistencies in state practice) and against the methodology used by the ECtHR for that finding.[53] At any rate, the impact of the ECtHR's UNCSI jurisprudence on states that are parties to the ECHR is likely to yield uniformity in the decisions of courts across the broad 'ECHR European region'.[54] By contrast, it

51 Compare with ECSI, Article 5.

52 ECtHR, *Cudak v Lithuania*, App No 15869/02 (23 March 2010); ECtHR, *Guadagnino v Italy and France*, App No 2555/03 (18 January 2011); ECtHR, *Sabeh El Leil v France*, App No 34869/05 (29 June 2011); ECtHR, *Wallishauser v Austria*, App No 156/04 (17 July 2012); ECtHR, *Radunović and Others v Montenegro*, App Nos 45197/13, 53000/13, and 73404/13 (25 October 2016); ECtHR, *Naku v Lithuania and Sweden*, App No 26126/07 (8 November 2016). For an earlier decision, (at least) partially overruled by the preceding jurisprudence, where the ECtHR denied instead a violation of Article 6 ECHR allegedly arising from a grant of state immunity in a dispute involving recruitment at a foreign embassy, see ECtHR, *Fogarty v United Kingdom*, App No 37112/97 (21 November 2001). See R Garnett, 'State and Diplomatic Immunity and Employment Rights: European Law to the Rescue?' (2015) 64 *ICLQ* 783.

53 See R Pavoni, 'The Myth of the Customary Nature of the United Nations Convention on State Immunity: Does the End Justify the Means?' in A van Aaken and I Motoc (eds), *The European Convention on Human Rights and General International Law* (OUP 2018) 264.

54 Two prominent examples of recent adherence to the ECtHR *Cudak* jurisprudence come from Italian and United Kingdom courts: for the UK, see Supreme Court, *Benkharbouche v Secretary of State for Foreign and Commonwealth Affairs*, [2017] UKSC 62, 18 October 2017; for the Italian Court of Cassation, see *Embassy of Spain to the Holy See v de la Grana Gonzales*, 18 April 2014, ILDC 2436 (IT 2014); *Académie de France à Rome v Galamini di Recanati*, 18 September 2014, ILDC 2437 (IT 2014); *Lasaracina v Embassy of the United Arab Emirates*, 27 October 2014, ILDC 2438 (IT 2014). For scholarly analyses, see the commentary by P Rossi, (2014) 24 *Italian Yearbook of International Law* 468; P Webb, 'The Immunity of States, Diplomats and International Organizations in Employment Disputes: The New Human Rights Dilemma?' (2016) 27 *EJIL* 745; K S Ziegler, 'Immunity *versus* Human Rights: The Right to a Remedy after *Benkharbouche*' (2017) 17 *Human Rights Law Review* 127. Examples of the divergence of national court practice in Europe, predating the ECtHR jurisprudence in question, include: France, Court of Cassation, *X v Saudi School in Paris and Saudi Arabia* (n 13); Norway, Supreme Court, *A v B*, 3 April 2004, ILDC 23 (NO 2004); Italy, Court of Cassation, *Vespignani v Bianchi*, 22 July 2004, ILDC 556 (IT 2004); Portugal, Supreme Court of Justice, *AA v Austrian Embassy*, 18 February 2006, ILDC 826 (PT 2007); The Netherlands, The Hague Court of Appeal, *X v Morocco*, 27 July 2007, ILDC 548 (NL 2007).

remains extremely interesting to follow developments in non-European jurisdictions, especially those that are withholding their ratification of the UNCSI.

García de Borrisow v Embassy of Lebanon, Decision on Admissibility, Case No 32096, ILDC 1009 (CO 2007), 13th December 2007, Colombia; Supreme Court of Justice [CSJ]

The plaintiff in this case, a former secretary of the Embassy of Lebanon in Colombia, was dismissed from her post when she reached the age of 60. She brought proceedings against the Embassy (as legal representative of the State of Lebanon) to recover certain sums of money to which she was entitled under Colombian labour law by reason of unfair dismissal.

> 10 There is now an urgent need for this chamber to re-examine the issue [of State immunity in labour disputes]; in the last 20 years, numerous arguments have emerged in favour of a re-examination of current considerations concerning immunity from the jurisdiction of states in relation to labour issues, which, due to their importance, cannot be disregarded since they are part of the dialectic process created to give workers' rights a sense of realism and effectiveness in all areas. […]
>
> 26 It is well-known that treaties codify the fundamental principles established by states through international custom, or [through] *ius cogens*, resulting in a situation where despite the fact that said Convention [UNCSI] has not been [ratified by Colombia], it is at present the ideal instrument for advocating that the jurisdictional immunity of states has been reassessed in the praxis of nations […]
>
> 27 This new direction brings with it the need to answer to the citizens of the State, when, as in this case, despite being nationals and having provided services to diplomatic missions of other countries, this court has ruled out the possibility of ascertaining by process whether they have a right to a wage or benefit, based on respect for the inviolable sovereignty of states. In fact, at present there are no constitutional or legal grounds for persisting with this thesis, since in this way the stated benefits and labour laws may not be recognised. This is the case given that, in light of a labour relationship that is in keeping with the employment laws of the receiving state […], [the employment activities at stake are] distinct from the activities of the foreign country within the scope of its sovereign functions, i.e. they are not government activities.

This decision is significant because it demonstrates the determination of a state's highest court to reverse its earlier jurisprudence on state immunity in labour matters in the light of the fundamental right to work (paras 11–15) and the 2004 UNCSI, thereby denying such immunity in the case at hand. What is most important is that, although unratified by Colombia, the court relied on the UNCSI as an instrument reflecting customary law.

However, the precedential value of the decision on this point is dubious, given that the court did not even cite Article 11 UNCSI and did not therefore test its findings against the provisions of this norm. Indeed, its final conclusion at paragraph 27 was simply that contracts of employment were not *jure imperii* activities, thereby implying that they were not covered by the customary rule of restrictive state immunity. As such, that conclusion was wrong, because contracts of employment cannot either be considered as *jure gestionis* activities in the traditional meaning. They are rather a *sui generis* species of state activities. This is plainly demonstrated by Article 11 UNCSI itself, which endorses a much more nuanced and sophisticated solution than what is implied by the Colombian court. In particular, Article 11(2)(d) would apply to the facts of this case, ie, the employer state would lose immunity in relation to the dismissal proceedings at hand, *provided* it had not determined that such proceedings would interfere with its security interests.

Bah v Libyan Embassy, Application to Industrial Court, case no IC 956/2005, ILDC 154 (BW 2005), 28th November 2005, Botswana; Industrial Court

A Guinean national's contract of employment with the Libyan Embassy in Botswana was terminated by the Embassy without notice. The ex-employee sued the Embassy (as representative of the Libyan State) and claimed various sums of money, such as severance pay.

> [25] On the basis of the authorities cited above, I have no hesitation whatsoever in holding that an action and or [sic] legal suit arising out of breach of the employment contract [. . .] involves a private law transaction and is justiciable.
>
> [26] In my considered view there is no reason why the respondent should be immune from a legal suit of this nature. The applicant in this matter is not in anyway challenging a governmental act, but is merely seeking compliance with the [Botswana] Employment Act in so far as he is merely claiming payment of severance pay, notice pay and the payment of wrongfully withheld wages.

This decision shows the increasing universal acceptance of the erosion of the rule of state immunity in relation to employment disputes, including those involving embassy employees (at least junior employees, as this seems to be the post held by the plaintiff within the administrative staff of the Libyan embassy). Although characterizing contracts of employment as 'private law transactions', this decision should be distinguished from the Colombian judgment discussed earlier, as the Botswana court relied upon further criteria for denying immunity, eg the exclusively pecuniary nature of the claims advanced by the plaintiff.[55]

The Botswana court did not mention the UNCSI. Despite the aforementioned ECtHR case law, it must be noted that it is questionable that the UNCSI removes immunity in labour disputes involving the administrative and technical staff of embassies. As the ILDC reporter succinctly and acutely put it: 'Article 11(2)[b](iv) [UNCSI] provided that Article 11(1) did not apply to any person enjoying diplomatic immunity. Under Article 37 of the Vienna Convention [on Diplomatic Relations], administrative and technical staff members of an embassy enjoyed immunity if they were not nationals [of] or permanent residents in the receiving State. That meant that if the UN Convention had been applicable, the embassy would have enjoyed immunity if Mr Bah was not a permanent resident of Botswana'.[56]

Finally, this case is an interesting example of transjudicial dialogue in the area of state immunity. Botswana follows the common law tradition, but the court did not only rely on common law authorities. It especially accorded significant weight to the decisions of the Swiss Federal Tribunal.[57]

Dube and Rabasha v American Embassy/Botusa, First instance judgment, Case No IC 897/2006, ILDC 1347 (BW 2008), 30th October 2008, Botswana; Industrial Court

The plaintiffs brought various pecuniary claims against the United States (via its embassy and one of its agencies in Botswana) on the ground that their employment at the embassy and the agency had been terminated unfairly.

> [16] [. . .] In this particular instance, it is important to examine the impact of the international labour standards not only on the domestic situation, but in their applicability to foreign sovereigns on local or extraterritorial soil. [. . .]

---

55 Botswana, Industrial Court, *Bah v Libyan Embassy, Application to Industrial Court*, 28 November 2005, ILDC 154 (BW 2005), para 26.

56 M Killander, Analysis, *Bah v Libyan Embassy*, ILDC 154 (BW 2005) A4. In addition, VCDR, Article 38(2) provides that also members of the staff of the mission who are nationals of or permanently resident in the receiving State shall enjoy immunities 'to the extent admitted by the receiving State'.

57 See particularly, Swiss Federal Tribunal, *S v India*, 22 May 1984, 82 ILR 14.

> [21] In view of the judicial pronouncements and the international labour standards that this court applies under its equity jurisdiction, it is clear that the doctrine of sovereign immunity applicable in Botswana is that of restrictive immunity as opposed to absolute immunity. In other words, a foreign sovereign enjoys immunity from suit and legal process where […] the basis of the claim is an act 'jure imperii' […]. On the other hand, the sovereign will not enjoy such immunity if […] the basis of the claim is an act 'jure gestionis' […]; particularly where fundamental rights are concerned.
>
> [22] It is also clear that when a State decides to become a Member of the ILO, which the respondent is, it accepts the fundamental principles embodied in the Constitution of the ILO and the Declaration of Philadelphia; and that a State has an obligation to give effect to the fundamental principles of international labour standards in its embassies, consulates and other offices. An employment contract being a matter of private law, the court finds that this matter is justiciable under the restrictive immunity doctrine.

This decision of the Botswana Industrial Court upheld the essential conclusion the same court had reached a few years earlier in the *Bah* case, ie that employment contracts were not caught by the rule of state immunity as they were to be regarded as private law transactions.

However, the court introduced a novel argument for justifying its assertion of jurisdiction over the dispute at hand, namely the fundamental nature of workers' rights. After a very interesting résumé of pertinent ILO practice, the court ruled that foreign states were under an obligation to secure the enjoyment of workers' rights to all persons employed in their diplomatic missions. Although the court did not explain what this ruling exactly had to do with the law of state immunity, the decision was a significant example of the growing impact of human rights considerations on employment disputes involving foreign states, as recalled in the introduction to this subsection.

3. Territorial torts

Article 12 UNCSI reads: 'Unless otherwise agreed between the States concerned, a State cannot invoke immunity from jurisdiction before a court of another State […] in a proceeding which relates to pecuniary compensation for death or injury to the person, or damage to or loss of tangible property, caused by an act or omission which is alleged to be attributable to the State, if the act or omission occurred in whole or in part in the territory of that other State and if the author of the act or omission was present in that territory at the time of the act or omission'.[58]

The purpose of this (rather convoluted) provision is to codify the so-called 'territorial tort exception' to state immunity, which removes immunity in respect of 'personal injury' and 'damage to property' caused by a foreign state in the territory of another state (ie, the forum state). The rationale of this exception is thus the appropriateness of the forum state's assertion of jurisdiction over civil claims arising from torts presenting a close connection to its territory (in accordance with the criterion of *locus commissi delicti*).

A provision similar to Article 12 UNCSI is included in all of the existing domestic immunity statutes, with the exception of the Pakistani legislation.[59] The tort exception was primarily intended to cover claims resulting from road traffic accidents involving vehicles owned by states and comparable 'insurable risks';[60] in other words, it was essentially meant to cover tortious state conduct that could be viewed as included in the notion of *acta jure gestionis* (such as the stipulation of an insurance policy). However, certain ground-breaking national court decisions have

58 cf ECSI, Article 11.

59 See *Jurisdictional Immunities of the State* (n 6) para 70.

60 ibid, para 64.

applied the tort exception to state activities that are properly characterized as *acta jure imperii*, such as abuses by police officers and political assassinations by intelligence officers, namely acts which may also constitute violations of human rights under international law. Historically, this key development has been inaugurated by the jurisprudence of US courts.

The decisions selected below provide a representative sample of outstanding problems in domestic court case law as regards the applicability of the tort exception to *jure imperii* activities, in general, and human rights breaches, in particular. They concern two interconnected, yet distinct, sub-issues: (i) whether the tort exception covers *jure imperii* acts, in the first place; and (ii) whether, at any rate, actions performed by the armed forces of a state, particularly in time of war, fall outwith the scope of the tort exception (in other words, whether military activities constitute an exception to the tort exception).

US, District Court for the District of Columbia, Letelier v Chile, 11 March 1980, 488 F.Supp. 665 (1980) (not in ILDC)

In the US, the territorial tort exception is enshrined in section 1605(a)(5) of the FSIA. This section provides that a foreign state shall not be immune from the jurisdiction of US courts in any case 'in which money damages are sought against a foreign state for personal injury or death, or damage to or loss of property, occurring in the United States and caused by the tortious act or omission of that foreign state or of any official or employee of that foreign state while acting within the scope of his office or employment'. The same provision contemplates exceptions to the tort exception. Most notably, the latter does not apply to 'any claim based upon the exercise or performance or the failure to exercise or perform a discretionary function regardless of whether the discretion be abused'. The case under consideration arose from the assassination of former Chilean ambassador and foreign minister Orlando Letelier and his American assistant Ronnie Moffitt in Washington DC on 21 September 1976 by a car bomb. Relatives of the victims brought an action for damages against Chile and Chilean officials in the US District Court for the District of Columbia. Chile pleaded immunity by arguing that the FSIA's exceptions in no way cover acts of political assassination because of their governmental character. The plaintiffs counterargued that the tort exception did apply on the facts of the case. The court ruled in favour of the plaintiffs and asserted jurisdiction.

> Nowhere is there an indication that the tortious acts to which the Act makes reference are to only be those formerly classified as "private", thereby engrafting onto the statute [...] the requirement that the character of a given tortious act be judicially analyzed to determine whether it was of the type heretofore denoted as *jure gestionis* or should be classified as *jure imperii*. (at 671)
>
> As its language and the legislative history make apparent, the discretionary act exemption [...] corresponds to the discretionary exception found in the Federal Tort Claims Act. [...] [A]n act that is discretionary is one in which "there is room for policy judgment and decision." [...] While it seems apparent that a decision calculated to result in injury or death to a particular individual or individuals, made for whatever reason, would be one most assuredly involving policy judgment and decision and thus exempt as a discretionary act [...], that exception is not applicable to bar this suit. [...] There is no discretion to commit, or to have one's officers or agents commit, an illegal act [...]. Whatever policy options may exist for a foreign country, it has no "discretion" to perpetrate conduct designed to result in the assassination of an individual or individuals, action that is clearly contrary to the precepts of humanity as recognized in both national and international law. (at 673)

Letelier is a pioneering precedent to the extent that it is the first known domestic court decision in any jurisdiction applying the tort exception to a quintessential *jure imperii* act of a foreign state, ie political assassination by state agents. The court mostly relied on a textual reading of the FSIA and emphasized that the relevant provision did not contain any distinction between 'private torts' and 'sovereign torts'. Significantly, the court refused to reintroduce that distinction in the FSIA through the back door of the 'discretionary function' counter-exception,[61] which could be interpreted as a bar to jurisdiction over torts arising from governmental acts. In doing so, it notably referred to the blatant unlawfulness of similar acts of assassination under national and *international* law. This decision has constituted guidance and authority both for the work of such bodies as the International Law Commission and for subsequent jurisprudence in the US[62] and other countries in the area of state immunity.

Ireland, Supreme Court, McElhinney v Williams and Her Majesty's Secretary of State for Northern Ireland, 15 December 1995, 104 ILR 691 (not in ILDC)

Ireland does not have a domestic immunity statute, nor is it a Party to the ECSI or the UNCSI. Accordingly, Irish courts address issues of state immunity on the basis of customary international law, which Ireland accepts as the rule of conduct in its relations with other states by virtue of Article 29, section 3 of its constitution.

In *McElhinney*, the plaintiff brought an action for damages against the UK (via its Secretary of State for Northern Ireland) for assault and personal injuries allegedly committed on Irish territory by a UK soldier in the exercise of official duties. The plaintiff argued that the tort exception applied to this case as a norm of customary international law as evidenced by the immunity statutes and practice of several states (UK, US, Australia, and Canada) and by the ECSI. He submitted that the *jure imperii* character of the contested conduct was irrelevant. The Supreme Court rejected these arguments and upheld the immunity of the UK.

> There can be no doubt but that the first named defendant [the soldier] in carrying out his duties at the said checkpoint was acting within the sphere of governmental or sovereign activity and the acts complained of must be regarded as jure imperii even though alleged to have been committed within this jurisdiction. (at 699-700)
>
> Distinction must be drawn between the provisions of legislation in a number of States and the provisions of public international law and the principles set forth in individual State legislation cannot be regarded as establishing principles of public international law.
>
> The provisions of statutes cannot be used as evidence of what international law is: statutes are evidence of the domestic law in the individual States and not evidence of international law generally. [. . .]
>
> I do not have to decide, in the circumstances of this case, whether the terms of the [ECSI] are part of the domestic law of this State because even if they were, the appellant's claim herein would fail by virtue of the terms of Article 31 of the said Convention, which [. . .] recognize that as a matter of international law immunities and privileges in respect of anything done or omitted to be done by, or in relation to armed forces when on the territory of another Contracting State, exist. (at 701)
>
> Despite the Herculean efforts of the appellant's legal advisers in making available to the Court, copies of all relevant decisions, articles, and draft conventions and the cogent arguments of counsel, I am not satisfied that it is a principle of public international law that the immunity granted to sovereign States should be restricted by making them liable in respect of tortious acts committed on their behalf by their servant or agent causing personal injuries to the person affected by such act or omission when such act or omission is committed jure imperii and I would dismiss the appeal on this point. (at 702–703)

61 Duly noted in *Jurisdictional Immunities of the State* (n 6) para 71.

62 See, most famously, US Court of Appeals for the Ninth Circuit, *Liu v Republic of China*, 29 December 1989, 892 F 2d 1419 (1989).

This decision is remarkable for several reasons. First, it denied that, as a matter of customary international law, the tort exception excluded state immunity in respect of *jure imperii* activities. In doing so, it dismissed the relevance of domestic immunity statutes, the text of which does not contain any saving clause for such activities, on the ground that domestic legislation (and related practice) does not constitute evidence of what international law is. This is obviously wrong, as state legislation is a prime manifestation of the state practice necessary for the emergence of customary international law. An authoritative confirmation thereof comes from the *Jurisdictional Immunities* judgment where the ICJ thoroughly examined immunity statutes with a view to identifying the principles governing the law of state immunity.[63]

Secondly, while militating in favour of the general proposition that customary law does not withhold immunity for *jure imperii* torts, this decision alluded to a narrower counter-exception to the tort exception, ie, one which only shielded torts committed by the armed forces of a foreign state while on the territory of another state. This 'military activities counter-exception', which is provided for in Article 31 of the ECSI but *not* in the UNCSI, was relevant on the facts of the case as the latter involved an assault by gun by a UK soldier on duty. It was in this connection that the ICJ relied on the *McElhinney* decision in *Jurisdictional Immunities*.[64]

Thirdly, this case gave rise to an application against Ireland before the ECtHR which rejected, by a vote of twelve to five, the applicant's allegation that the defendant state had breached Article 6 ECHR on the right of access to justice by upholding the UK's immunity.[65] The ECtHR was quite dubious of the emergence of a customary rule corresponding to the tort exception. It stated that the exception was merely a 'trend in international and comparative law'[66] reflected in a practice which was 'by no means universal'.[67] Most significantly, the ECtHR considered the exception as primarily applicable 'to "insurable" personal injury, that is incidents arising out of ordinary road traffic accidents, rather than matters relating to the *core area of State sovereignty such as the acts of a soldier on foreign territory* which, of their very nature, may involve sensitive issues affecting diplomatic relations between states and national security'.[68]

Schreiber and Amnesty International (intervening) v Attorney-General of Canada and Germany, Appeal from Ontario Court of Appeal, [2002] 3 SCR 269, (2002) 216 DLR (4th) 513, 2002 SCC 62, ILDC 60 (CA 2002), 12th September 2002, Canada; Supreme Court [SCC]

In Canada, the tort exception is contained in section 6 of the SIA, according to which: 'A foreign state is not immune from the jurisdiction of a court in any proceedings that relate to (*a*) any death or personal or bodily injury, or (*b*) any damage to or loss of property that occurs in Canada.' The plaintiff in this case invoked such provision so as to overcome a plea of immunity advanced by Germany in proceedings that he had instituted to recover damages arising from his alleged wrongful arrest and detention carried out by the Canadian authorities upon an arrest warrant issued by that foreign state.

> 30 The intervener, the United States of America, brought up an argument that neither of the respondents raised which would severely restrict the scope of application of the exception. The United States asserts that a distinction must be made between *acta jure imperii* and *acta jure gestionis* in determining whether any of the exceptions to immunity under the *State Immunity Act* are applicable. [. . .]

63 For the statement of principle, see *Jurisdictional Immunities of the State* (n 6) para 55.
64 ibid, paras 68 and 72.
65 ECtHR, *McElhinney v Ireland*, App No 31253/96 (21 November 2001).
66 ibid, para 38.
67 ibid.
68 ibid, emphasis added.

> 32 I accept the appellant's argument on the irrelevance of the *jure imperii/jure gestionis* distinction for a number of reasons. First, the wording of s. 6(*a*) clearly states that this exception applies to all torts committed by a foreign state which cause death or personal injury. [. . .]
>
> 34 Furthermore, most of the international law authorities cited by the parties appear to accept that the personal injury exception does not distinguish between *jure imperii* and *jure gestionis* acts. [. . .]
>
> 37 In addition, the interpretation advanced by the United States would deprive the victims of the worst breaches of basic rights of any possibility of redress in national courts. Given the recent trends in the development of international humanitarian law enlarging this possibility in cases of international crime, as evidenced in the case before the House of Lords, *R. v. Bow Street Metropolitan Stipendiary Magistrate (No. 3)*, [1999] 2 W.L.R. 827 (U.K. H.L.), such a result would jeopardize at least in Canada a potentially important progress in the protection of the rights of the person.

Coming from a supreme court, this is a very authoritative precedent on the irrelevance of the distinction between *jure imperii* acts (such as the one at stake here, ie, an arrest warrant) and *jure gestionis* acts for the purposes of the tort exception.[69] The Canadian Supreme Court reached that conclusion on the basis of a textual reading of the SIA, an overall appraisal of pertinent materials (with the ECSI and the ILC work on state immunity being expressly cited) *and* the need to offer a remedy to victims of human rights violations.

This human rights rationale for the decision (paragraph 37) is, however, unclear. It seems to broadly refer to any human rights violation, wherever committed, even though the court was perfectly aware that the exception at stake only applied to territorial torts. That the court had in mind a broad human rights rationale seems confirmed by its citation of the UK House of Lords *Pinochet No 3* decision,[70] which entailed systematic torture committed in a state other than the forum state (the UK in that case). However, this citation is misleading to the extent that *Pinochet* involved the functional immunity from criminal jurisdiction of an ex-head of state. It is now widely accepted that, in the case of international crimes, a parallelism between the immunity of state officials and the immunity of the state itself is improper.[71] At any rate, Canadian court decisions subsequent to *Schreiber*,[72] including—lately—the *Kazemi* decision of the Supreme Court,[73] have dismissed the existence of a broad human rights exception to state immunity.

It is most interesting that the argument of the inapplicability of the tort exception to *jure imperii* acts was put forward by the US Government as an intervener. In the light of the *Letelier* decision and its aftermath, this makes clear that in the US there exists disagreement over this matter between the judiciary and the executive.[74] This may weaken the precedential value of the US case law considered above.

Summing up, although many manifestations of practice seems to indicate that the tort exception does apply to *jure imperii* activities, states are divided in this respect. This may contribute to understanding why, in *Jurisdictional Immunities of the State*, the ICJ controversially refrained from taking position on this key point.[75]

---

69 See *Jurisdictional Immunities of the State* (n 6) para 64.

70 UK, House of Lords, *R, ex parte Pinochet v Bartle and ors*, section VI.2(b) below.

71 See *Jurisdictional Immunities of the State* (n 6) paras 87 and 91.

72 Such as in the *Bouzari* case (n 27), section II.2 above.

73 Canada, Supreme Court, *Estate of the late Zahra (Ziba) Kazemi and Hashemi, Canadian Lawyers for International Human Rights (intervening) and ors (intervening) v Iran and ors*, 10 October 2014, ILDC 1721 (CA 2014).

74 See, indeed, *Jurisdictional Immunities of the State* (n 6) para 64; cf R Pavoni, 'An American Anomaly? On the ICJ's Selective Reading of United States Practice in *Jurisdictional Immunities of the State*' (2011) 21 *Italian Yearbook of International Law* 143, 153.

75 *Jurisdictional Immunities of the State* (n 6) para 65.

Germany v Prefecture of Voiotia (Representing 118 persons from Distomo village), Petition on cassation against default, no 11/2000, (2000) 49 Nomiko Vima 212, ILDC 287 (GR 2000), 4th May 2000, Greece; Supreme Court

This case, better known as the *Distomo* case,[76] involved an action for compensation for damage brought against Germany by the relatives of victims of a massacre of civilians committed in Greece during the Second World War by occupying Nazi troops. The Hellenic Supreme Court concluded, by an overwhelming majority, that Germany was not entitled to immunity, thereby confirming an award of damage in the amount of roughly €20 million as determined by a lower court. The chief argument of the Supreme Court was the existence of a customary norm removing immunity in respect of territorial torts, regardless of whether such torts originated in *jure imperii* acts, including crimes against humanity perpetrated in times of armed conflict. Greece applies the rules of state immunity as a matter of customary law, which in turn enjoys primacy over any inconsistent domestic legislation (Article 28(1) of the Constitution of Greece).

> 8 […] [A] general practice by the states of the international community that is accepted as law is established, *i.e.* the formation of international custom […], according to which state courts, by way of exception from the principle of immunity, have […] jurisdiction to adjudicate on actions for reparations (including pecuniary damage) caused by tort and committed against persons and their property in the territory of the *forum* by organs of the foreign state that were present in the same territory at the time of commission of the torts, even if these were *acta jure imperii.* […]
>
> 10 […] [T]he [tort] exception from the rule of immunity does not cover claims for reparation of damages resulting from armed conflict, the core of which is usually comprised of a conflict between states, which necessarily strikes non-combatant populations. […] [H]owever, […] the abovementioned exception from immunity is applied […] in relation to claims for damages arising out of offences (usually crimes against humanity) that strike […] persons of a limited circle and specified place that have no relation to the armed conflict and take no part whatsoever, either directly or indirectly […], in warfare operations. […]
>
> 12 […] [C]onsidering that the torts in question (murders that also constitute crimes against humanity) were directed against specific persons limited in number who resided in a specific place, who had nothing to do with the resistance activity resulting in the death of German soldiers taking part in a terror operation against the local population, that the said homicides constituted hideous murders that objectively were not necessary in order to maintain the military occupation of the area or subdue the underground action, carried out in the territory of the *forum* by organs of the German Third Reich in an abuse of sovereign power, the relevant claims for reparation and pecuniary damage fell under the […] jurisdiction of the Court adjudicating on the merits, since they are exempt from the privilege of immunity in accordance with the international customary law that has been developed as illustrated above.

Although generally quoted as the first ever supreme court precedent denying a foreign state immunity for serious human rights and humanitarian law violations, this decision was especially important for the narrower proposition that it existed a customary territorial tort exception applicable to *jure imperii* acts, including unlawful warfare operations by a hostile, occupying army. The Supreme Court cited a wealth of materials confirming the inapplicability of the distinction between *jure imperii* and *jure gestionis* to the tort exception, including the US *Letelier* and *Liu* jurisprudence examined earlier. On the other hand, the Supreme Court held that the crimes at stake were not exempted from the tort exception, even though they were part of military

76 See the case report by M Gavouneli and I Bantekas (2001) 95 AJIL 198.

activities carried out in the course of an armed conflict. The court's reasoning on this point is, however, problematic. It seemed to only rule out certain grave crimes directed against non-combatant civilians and not justified by military necessity from the scope of the military activities/armed conflict counter-exception. In this connection, the dissenting judges, including the Chief Justice, spoke of an artificial distinction and a 'legalist invention'[77] on the part of the majority.

In the face of Germany's refusal to honour the damages award made in this case, the plaintiffs sought execution against certain German property located in Greece. However, the Greek Minister of Justice withheld its authorization to institute the relevant enforcement proceedings, a rather outdated requirement which is still present in the Greek legal system and which was, however, upheld by the Supreme Court in this case (judgments Nos 36/2002 and 37/2002 of 28 June 2002). This situation led to an application before the ECtHR against Germany and Greece complaining of a violation of the right to a court and the right to property. By a majority of its members, the ECtHR rejected the application. It upheld its *Al-Adsani* decision and declared that it was not established 'that there is yet acceptance in international law of the proposition that states are not entitled to immunity in respect of civil claims for damages brought against them in another State for crimes against humanity'.[78] The ECtHR did not accord any relevance to the fact that the crime at stake was perpetrated on Greek soil. It seems that it only intended to reiterate its broad view on the non-existence of a human rights exception to state immunity under customary international law. It is also to be noted that, at that stage, the *Distomo* case involved immunity from execution, not from adjudication, an important aspect which the ECtHR overlooked.

The plaintiffs in the *Distomo* case have also sought recognition and enforcement of the damages award in Germany and Italy. The execution proceedings in Italy are still ongoing,[79] despite the ICJ's condemnation of Italy for having granted *exequatur* to the *Distomo* decision[80] and having allowed measures of constraint against German sovereign property, ie, the registration of a legal charge (*ipoteca giudiziale*) over Villa Vigoni, immovable property owned by Germany and located in northern Italy.[81]

Germany v Margellos and 18 other natural and legal persons (intervening), Petition for Cassation, Case No 6/2002, (2003) 1 AED 11, (2003) 56 RHDI 199, ILDC 87 (GR 2002), 17th September 2002, Greece; Special Supreme Court

Margellos was another case involving compensation claims for WWII atrocities by Nazi troops brought before the Greek courts in the aftermath of the 2000 *Distomo* decision examined earlier. The plaintiffs were victims (or their successors) of crimes committed in 1944 by Nazi occupying forces, when they burned to the ground the village of Lidoriki, in the Prefecture of Fokis.

In light of persistent uncertainties over whether state immunity applied to the legal situation at stake and given the absence of a rule of *stare decisis* in Greece, the Supreme Court referred the *Margellos* case to the Special Supreme Court. A peculiar feature of the Greek legal system is indeed that, under the circumstances prevailing in the *Margellos* case, the courts may refer cases to the Special Supreme Court, which has jurisdiction over 'the settlement of controversies regarding the determination of generally recognized rules of international law' (Article 100 of

77 Greece, Supreme Court, *Germany v Prefecture of Voiotia (Representing 118 persons from Distomo village)*, 4 May 2000, ILDC 287 (GR 2000) para 11.

78 ECtHR, *Kalogeropoulou and Others v Greece and Germany*, App No 59021/00 (12 December 2002).

79 On the other hand, such proceedings were dismissed by the German Federal Court of Justice, *Greek Citizens v Germany* (*Distomo* case), 26 June 2003, ILDC 389 (DE 2003).

80 See especially, Italy, Court of Cassation, *Germany v Autonomous Prefecture of Vojotia*, No 11163/2011, 20 May 2011, ILDC 1815 (IT 2011).

81 See *Jurisdictional Immunities of the State* (n 6) paras 109–33. Note, however, that Villa Vigoni's immunity has recently been upheld by the Italian Court of Cassation, *Sterea Ellada Region v Presidency of the Council of Ministers and Germany*, No 14885/2018, 8 June 2018.

the Constitution of Greece). The ensuing decisions are especially authoritative, since Greek courts must abide by them, unless they take the view that the relevant international law has changed.

The Special Supreme Court held that Germany was entitled to immunity under customary international law, in fact overruling the opposite decision made by the Supreme Court two years earlier in the *Distomo* case.

> 14. [. . .] [T]he Court [. . .] concludes that in the current stage [. . .] of international law, a generally accepted rule of this law has not been formed that would allow, by exception from the principle of immunity, to lawfully prosecute a State before the Court of another State for compensation for all kinds of offenses which took place on the territory of the forum State and in which armed forces of the defendant State were involved in any manner, either in time of war or in time of peace. [. . .] To the contrary, it results from all evidence, without exception, that the foreign State continues to enjoy the immunity when it is prosecuted for acts which took place on the territory of the forum State and in which its armed forces were involved in any manner, without the distinction of whether these acts were in violation of *jus cogens* or whether these armed forces were involved in a conflict with other armed forces. Indeed [. . .] Article 31 of the European Convention [is] formulated exhaustively and [is] not subject to this distinction. This rule is justified by the need to respect the sovereignty of the foreign State, of which the primary manifestation is the action of its armed forces [. . .].

This decision of the Special Supreme Court may be seen as a repudiation of the 2000 *Distomo* decision of the Supreme Court, although, as we know, the same decision was not technically overturned and the judgment holders are still seeking to enforce the related damages award. This repudiation was fatal to Italy's reliance on Greek practice in the *Jurisdictional Immunities* case. According to the ICJ, 'Greek State practice taken as a whole actually contradicts, rather than supports, Italy's argument'.[82] The ICJ's finding was especially based on the *Margellos* decision and the absence of any later deviation from that decision by the Greek courts. What the ICJ did not recall is that the decision in question was the result of a bare majority of six judges versus five dissenting judges.

The key argument of the majority was that the territorial tort exception does not apply to acts committed on the forum state's territory by the armed forces of a foreign state, regardless of whether such acts were carried out in times of peace or war, or whether they constituted war crimes prohibited by *jus cogens*. This endorsement of a sweeping 'armed conflict counter-exception' to the tort exception was essentially upheld by the ICJ.[83] The majority of the Special Supreme Court heavily relied on Article 31 ECSI, evidently considered as a reflection of customary law, given that Greece was not a party thereof. Unlike the UNCSI, a form of the armed forces counter-exception may be found in Article 31 ECSI: 'Nothing in this Convention shall affect any immunities or privileges enjoyed by a Contracting State in respect of anything done or omitted to be done by, or in relation to, its armed forces when on the territory of another Contracting State.' The dissenting judges took a radically different view. According to them, Article 31 only shielded acts by armed forces of a state which were present in the territory of another state upon consent of the latter; in any case, they continued, such acts could not include war crimes which were prohibited by *jus cogens*.

There are sound reasons for believing that, *Jurisdictional Immunities* judgment notwithstanding,[84] the scope and extent of the armed forces counter-exception to the tort exception will be subject to further developments in practice and academic debates.

---

82 ibid, para 76. See also ibid, para 83.

83 ibid, paras 77–79.

84 cf Pavoni (n 74) 152–58.

4. Enforcement immunity

Enforcement immunity (or immunity from execution) shields certain state property located on the territory of the forum state from measures of constraint, such as attachment or seizure, aimed at the satisfaction of judgments rendered against foreign states. The rules governing enforcement immunity are distinct and separate from those concerning jurisdictional immunity from suit *stricto sensu*.[85] This means that, irrespective of the legality of the underlying assertion of jurisdiction over a foreign state, a domestic court must still decide whether enforcement immunity subsists and accordingly assess whether the property targeted by the judgment holder may lawfully be levied upon for the execution of a judicial decision against that state.

More concretely, the separate nature of enforcement immunity is shown by the fact that a waiver by a state of its jurisdictional immunity does not entail a waiver of its immunity from execution, which requires a specific manifestation of consent.[86] Moreover, the rules on enforcement immunity are more protective of states than those relating to immunity from suit, since a denial of the former immunity is deemed a greater interference with sovereign functions. In short, under contemporary international law, a successful and full execution of a judgment against a foreign state remains a rather exceptional occurrence.

There can be no doubt, however, that under customary law immunity from execution has evolved into a restrictive rule. That is, in addition to the uncontested cases of consent to execution and earmarking of property for the satisfaction of specific claims, states do not enjoy enforcement immunity when the property against which execution is sought is used or intended for use for commercial purposes (*jure gestionis* property). This 'purpose test' evidently implies more deference towards state sovereignty as compared to the test of the nature of the activity that normally applies with respect to the commercial exception to immunity from jurisdiction.

Significantly, the UNCSI foresees a commercial property exception only for post-judgment measures of constraint and not for pre-judgment measures, ie, interim measures taken before the judgment on the merits in order to ensure satisfaction of an eventual award of damages.[87] It further requires a connection between the targeted property and the entity against which the claim was lodged.[88] It is uncertain whether these prescriptions reflect customary law, and both the ICJ[89] and the ECtHR[90] have refrained from such an enquiry.

A notable feature of the UNCSI is that it singles out specific categories of state property[91] which by definition, and 'in particular',[92] must be considered as non-commercial property exempt from execution proceedings. These basically are: (i) diplomatic and consular property, including any bank account, 'used or intended for use in the performance of the functions of the

85 As confirmed by the ICJ in *Jurisdictional Immunities of the State* (n 6) paras 113–14.

86 See for instance UNCSI, Article 20. Moreover, according to the UNCSI and unlike immunity from suit, consent by a state to the taking of measures of constraint against its property can only be explicit, cf UNCSI, Articles 18(a) and 19(a). For the sake of precision, the UNCSI also allows measures of constraint against state property which a state has allocated or earmarked for the satisfaction of specific claims (Articles 18(b) and 19(b)). This hypothesis may be regarded as a case of implicit consent.

87 UNCSI, Article 19(c).

88 ibid.

89 *Jurisdictional Immunities of the State* (n 6) para 117. However, the court made clear that the essence of the UNCSI provisions at stake, ie the commercial property exception, is a manifestation of customary law, ibid, para 118; cf C Brown and R O'Keefe, 'Article 19' in R O'Keefe and C J Tams (eds), *The United Nations Convention on Jurisdictional Immunities of States and Their Property: A Commentary* (n 42) 308, 327.

90 ECtHR, *Wallishauser v Austria (No 2)*, App No 14497/06 (20 June 2013) para 72 ('even if it were established that the content of Articles 18 to 21 of the 2004 Convention were applicable as rules of customary international law [. . .]').

91 UNCSI, Article 21(1).

92 ibid.

diplomatic mission of the State or its consular posts [...]';[93] (ii) military property;[94] (iii) central bank property;[95] and (iv) cultural property.[96] The following are examples of national court practice involving some of these items. Many decisions show outstanding uncertainties in the application of the general principle of restrictive execution immunity to actual disputes.

(a) Embassy bank accounts

Germany, Federal Constitutional Court, *Philippine Embassy Bank Account Case*, 13 December 1977, 65 ILR 146 (not in ILDC)

An individual was creditor of a judgment against the Philippines awarding him/her 95,000 Deutsche Marks roughly in respect of arrears of rent and repair expenses relating to a building that he/she had rented to that foreign state. He/she obtained an attachment order from a lower court against the bank account of the Embassy of the Philippines held at the Deutsche Bank in Bonn. The Philippines claimed that the bank account was covered by enforcement immunity since, *inter alia*, it was intended to provide the funds necessary for running its embassy in Germany. The question of the legality of the attachment order under customary international law was submitted to the German Constitutional Court.

> There exists the following general rule of international law: Forced execution of judgment by the State of the forum under a writ of execution against a foreign State which has been issued in respect of non-sovereign acts (*acta iure gestionis*) of that State, on property of that State which is present or situated in the territory of the State of the forum is inadmissible without the consent of the foreign State if, at the time of the initiation of the measure of execution, such property serves sovereign purposes of the foreign State. Claims against a general current bank account of the embassy of a foreign State which exists in the State of the forum and the purpose of which is to cover the embassy's costs and expenses are not subject to forced execution by the State of the forum. (at 164)
>
> Because of the difficulties of delimitation involved in judging whether th[e] ability to function [of a diplomatic mission] is endangered, and because of the potential for abuse, general international law makes the area of protection enjoyed by the foreign State very wide and refers to the typical abstract danger, but not to the specific threat to the ability of the diplomatic mission to function posed by measures on the part of the receiving State. (at 186)
>
> [F]or the executing authorities of the receiving State to require the sending State, without its consent, to provide details concerning the existence or the past, present or future purposes of funds in such an account would constitute interference, contrary to international law, in matters within the exclusive competence of the sending State. On the other hand, general international law does not prohibit asking the sending State to substantiate the fact that a given account is one that is used for the continued performance of the functions of its diplomatic missions. As regards the substance and form of such substantiation, the State of the forum must of course, in accordance with international law, be satisfied with due assurances from a competent authority of the sending State. (at 189)
>
> This Chamber fully appreciates that the immunity accorded to claims arising out of a general current account of the embassy of a foreign State might in some cases be used as a shield for financial transactions through such an account which were not directly related to the functions of a diplomatic mission. Should such a case occur

93 ibid, Article 21(1)(a).
94 ibid, Article 21(1)(b).
95 ibid, Article 21(1)(c).
96 ibid, Article 21(1)(d) and (e).

> [. . .] it would be for the competent authorities of the Federal Republic of Germany to counter a "non-functional" use of the immunity of diplomatic missions by diplomatic and other means admissible under international law. (at 190)

Philippine Embassy Bank Account is no doubt one of the most famous domestic court decisions in the field of state immunity. This is probably due to the rigorous methodology used by the German Constitutional Court for identifying customary law in the area of immunity from execution, with specific reference to the controversial issue of embassy (mixed) bank accounts.[97] The court quoted at length the case law of international courts, domestic courts (both European and non-European), the works of international institutions, international and national legal instruments, and legal writings. In addition, the solid foundations of this decision spurred a line of domestic jurisprudence which, either expressly or implicitly, heavily relied upon it.[98] Accordingly, *Philippine Embassy Bank Account* has been duly identified as a milestone judgment paving the way for transnational judicial dialogue.[99]

At the same time, domestic courts have refined the approach of the German Constitutional Court by clarifying that so-called 'mixed accounts', ie accounts used for both public and commercial purposes, are also covered by immunity, while however speaking of a rebuttable presumption of immunity[100] open to the provision of evidence that the account at hand was in fact *exclusively* employed for *jure gestionis* transactions.

(b) Cultural property

Rubin (Jenny) and ors v Iran and ors, Decision on Post-Judgment Claim to Collect Damages Awarded, 456 F.Supp.2d 228 (D. Mass. 2006), ILDC 892 (US 2006), 30th September 2006, United States; Massachusetts; District Court for the District of Massachusetts [D Mass]

Relying on the terrorism exception to state immunity under the US FSIA,[101] several survivors and relatives of victims of a 1997 suicide bombing in Jerusalem carried out by Hamas with the support of Iran had obtained a judgment against that state and certain officials of that state from the District Court for the District of Columbia awarding them compensatory damages in the amount of US$71.5 million.[102] Amongst other assets, they sought execution of that judgment on various collections of Persian antiquities and cultural heritage property allegedly owned by Iran. In the present case, they requested the attachment of artifacts housed by the Museum of Fine Arts in Boston and several Harvard University's museums. These institutions (so-called 'trustee process defendants') intervened in the proceedings and asserted the immune status of the works of art at stake.

> 8 The property within the possession of the trustee process defendants is thus immune from execution and attachment unless one of the exceptions in §§ 1610

97 It is therefore unsurprising that the ICJ has referred to this decision as an illustration of state practice in the field of enforcement immunity, see *Jurisdictional Immunities of the State* (n 6) para 118.

98 See, eg, UK, House of Lords, *Alcom Ltd v Colombia*, 12 April 1984, 74 ILR 1970; Austria, Supreme Court, *L-W Verwaltungsgesellschaft mbH & Co KG v DVA*, 30 April 1986, 77 ILR 489; Italy, Constitutional Court, *Condor and Filvem v Ministry of Justice*, 15 July 1992, (1994) 33 ILM 596; Botswana, High Court, *Angola v Springbok Investments (Pty) Ltd*, 12 October 2003, ILDC 7 (BW 2003).

99 A Reinisch, 'The International Relations of National Courts: A Discourse on International Law Norms on Jurisdictional and Enforcement Immunity' in A Reinisch and U Kriebaum (eds), *The Law of International Relations: Liber Amicorum Hanspeter Neuhold* (Eleven 2007) 289, 293–97.

100 The burden-of-proof issue is not well settled, however, with some courts showing a more progressive approach towards a shared burden between the foreign state and its creditors: see especially Belgium, Brussels Court of Appeals, *M v Democratic Republic of the Congo and ors*, 26 April 2010, ILDC 1623 (BE 2010) (denying immunity to the technical bank account of the Congolese Embassy in Belgium), and compare with Belgium, Brussels Court of Appeals, *Iraq v Vinci Constructions Grands Projets SA*, 4 October 2002, ILDC 49 (BE 2002).

101 Presently codified at s 1605A of the FSIA.

102 *Campuzano v Islamic Republic of Iran*, 10 September 2003, 281 F Supp 2d 258 (2003).

and 1611 applies […]. Only one of those exceptions — that which is set forth in § 1610(a)(7) — is potentially relevant in this case. Section 1610(a)(7) provides:

> The property in the United States of a foreign state […] *used for a commercial activity* in the United States, shall not be immune from […] execution … if … the judgment relates to a claim for which the foreign state is not immune under [the FSIA terrorism exception], regardless of whether the property is or was involved with the act upon which the claim is based.
>
> 28 U.S.C. § 1610(a)(7) (emphasis added).

9 The parties dispute the scope of this "commercial use" exception. The plaintiffs contend that it encompasses the commercial use of the property by any party, not just the foreign sovereign. In contrast, the trustee process defendants argue that the exception applies only where the foreign sovereign itself has made commercial use of the property within the United States. This is the better view. First and foremost, the plain language of FSIA, read in its entirety, warrants such a conclusion […].

10 […] It is further evident from the legislative history of FSIA that […] well-established principles of international law informed Congress' decisions regarding the proper scope of immunity to be granted to a foreign sovereign's property […].

11 Taken together, the plain language of the statute, its legislative history, and generally accepted principles of international law establish that the "commercial use" exception […] applies only where it is the foreign sovereign who engages in the commercial activity. Here, it is the trustee process defendants, not Iran, who possess and make use (commercially or otherwise, an issue that need not be decided here) of the disputed antiquities. For this reason, §1610(a)(7) is inapplicable, and the property remains immune under FSIA.

12 The property's immunity under FSIA notwithstanding, the plaintiffs may still be able to obtain the antiquities pursuant to […] the Terrorism Risk Insurance Act of 2002 ("TRIA") […]. Section 201 of the TRIA provides:

> […] [I]n every case in which a person has obtained a judgment against a terrorist party on a claim based upon an act of terrorism, or for which a terrorist party is not immune under [the FSIA terrorism exception], the blocked assets of that terrorist party shall be subject to execution or attachment in aid of execution […].

16 […] [T]he trustee process defendants have repeatedly and emphatically argued that none of the antiquities in their possession belong to the Republic of Iran […]. Because ownership of the property is contested, the antiquities […] remain blocked […]. Thus, if the plaintiffs are able to establish that the antiquities are indeed the property of Iran, those assets will be subject to attachment and execution […].

Despite various references to international law, this decision is yet another glaring example of US judicial unilateralism in matters of state immunity. This is unsurprising as the background of the case at hand is the controversial terrorism exception to sovereign immunity included in the US FSIA.[103]

---

103 See also, most recently, the Justice Against Sponsors of Terrorism Act (JASTA), a statute passed by the US Congress on 28 September 2016 despite an earlier veto by President Obama. JASTA, which is codified at s 1605B of the FSIA, removes any legal obstacle to compensation claims against foreign states arising from their complicity in terrorist acts in the US carried out 'on or after September 11, 2001'. It paves the way for litigation against states allegedly involved in the Twin Towers attacks of 11 September 2001 (such as Saudi Arabia).

The District Court dismissed the applicability of the commercial property exception to immunity from execution *only* because it was not the defendant state's commercial activities that were at stake, but those of the museums holding the property and allegedly engaged in the selling of books and academic publications arising from research on the artefacts. However, and most importantly, the court declared that the immune status of the antiquities could be removed under the 2002 Terrorism Risk Insurance Act (TRIA) if, in further proceedings, the plaintiffs were able to prove that such antiquities belonged to Iran.[104]

Absent from the court's analysis is any consideration of the inherently immune status which should attach to cultural objects by reason of the governmental purposes that they, by definition, fulfil. There indeed exists growing evidence of a customary rule exempting cultural heritage property,[105] as well as any property intended for use for cultural and educational purposes,[106] from measures of constraint.[107]

TRIA is a piece of terrorism-related legislation which generally allows the satisfaction of judgments against terrorist states upon the latter's 'blocked assets' (ie, assets blocked by the US administration under a variety of sanctions programs against foreign states). It is part of a series of legislative enactments and judicial decisions[108] which paved the way for execution on Iranian

---

104 Subsequent to this decision, attachment of the antiquities has been avoided following the District Court's determination that they did not belong to Iran, but to the museums, see *Rubin v Iran*, 15 September 2011, 810 F Supp 2d 402 (2011), affirmed on other grounds (the assets at stake were not contested/blocked assets under the TRIA) by the US Court of Appeals for the First Circuit, 27 February 2013, 709 F 3d 49 (2013). Parallel proceedings targeting a number of collections of ancient Persian artifacts in the possession of the University of Chicago and Chicago's Field Museum of Natural History have lately been dismissed by the US Supreme Court, *Rubin v Iran*, 21 February 2018, 138 S Ct 816 (2018) (affirming Court of Appeals for the Seventh Circuit, *Rubin v Iran*, 19 July 2016, 830 F 3d 470 (2016)). The Supreme Court held that a distinct provision of the FSIA—s 1610(g)—which broadly allows satisfaction of judgments under the terrorism exception was not a free-standing exception to execution immunity, as it still required that one the specific exceptions under the FSIA applied.

105 Purportedly codified by UNCSI, Article 21(1)(d) and (e). See also Declaration on Jurisdictional Immunities of State Owned Cultural Property, drafted under the aegis of the Council of Europe Committee of Legal Advisers on Public International Law, available at https://rm.coe.int/declaration-on-immunities-en/168071bb2d (last accessed 16 July 2018). As of 16 July 2018, there are twenty signatories, including the Holy See, to the Declaration. On the other hand, under s 1611 of the US FSIA only the assets of foreign central banks or monetary authorities and property of a military character are singled out as categories of state property exempted from execution (diplomatic and consular property has to be added to the list as a result of the US legislation incorporating the VCDR and VCCR).

106 Such as cultural centres and buildings dedicated to cultural activities: see *Jurisdictional Immunities of the State* (n 6) para 119 (declaring unlawful the registration of a legal charge on Villa Vigoni by Italy, because the Villa is a cultural centre promoting cultural exchanges between Italy and Germany). But see, most recently, the opposite conclusion of Canadian courts in yet another case against Iran arising under Canada's terrorism exception to state immunity, *Tracy v The Iranian Ministry of Information and Security*, 2016 ONSC 3759 (Ontario Superior Court of Justice, 9 June 2016), *affirmed* 2017 ONCA 549 (Court of Appeal for Ontario, 30 June 2017) (allowing execution against Iranian cultural centres located in Canada).

107 This seems especially correct on the facts of the *Rubin* case, where the property at stake had nothing to do with the underlying claim. Less clear-cut are cases concerning property unlawfully confiscated or retained by foreign states. For exhaustive accounts of the practice, especially in the US, involving immunity and cultural property, see N van Woudenberg, *State Immunity and Cultural Objects on Loan* (Martinus Nijhoff 2012); A Gattini, 'The International Customary Law Nature of Immunity from Measures of Constraint for State Cultural Property on Loan' in I Buffard, J Crawford, A Pellet, and S Wittich (eds), *International Law between Universalism and Fragmentation*. Festschrift *in Honour of Gerhard Hafner* (Martinus Nijhoff 2008) 421; C A Caprio, 'Artwork, Cultural Heritage Property, and the Foreign Sovereign Immunities Act' (2006) 13 *International Journal of Cultural Property* 285; R Pavoni, 'Sovereign Immunity and the Enforcement of International Cultural Property Law' in F Francioni and J Gordley (eds), *Enforcing International Cultural Property Law* (OUP 2013) 79, and, most recently, R Pavoni, 'State Immunity and Cultural Heritage' in F Francioni and A F Vrdoljak (eds), *The Oxford Handbook of International Cultural Heritage Law* (OUP forthcoming).

108 See lately, Supreme Court, *Bank Markazi v Peterson*, 20 April 2016, 136 S Ct 1310. For comments, see K Daugirdas and J D Mortenson, 'Contemporary Practice of the United States Relating to International Law' (2016) 110 AJIL 555, 555–62.

property in the US of a multitude of judgments against Iran awarding damages totalling, as of 12 June 2016, over US$56 billion.[109] On 14 July 2016, Iran filed an application against the US with the ICJ, claiming a number of violations of the 1955 Iran–US Treaty of Amity arising from the legislation and judicial practice in question.[110]

(c) Central bank property

AIG Capital Partners Incorporated and CJSC Tema Real Estate Company Limited v Kazakhstan, National Bank of Kazakhstan (intervening) and ors (intervening), Enforcement Decision, [2005] EWHC 2239, [2006] 1 All ER 284, [2006] 1 WLR 1420, [2006] 1 All ER (Comm) 1, [2006] 1 Lloyd's Rep 1, ILDC 94 (UK 2005), 20th October 2005, United Kingdom; England and Wales; High Court [EWHC]; Queen's Bench Division [QBD]; Commercial Court

This case originated from a decision by an arbitral tribunal under the auspices of the International Centre for Settlement of Investment Disputes (ICSID), whereby the claimants were awarded a total of approximately US$10 million as compensation for the repudiation of a contract for the development of a residential housing complex and ensuing expropriatory actions by Kazakhstan. In the face of Kazakhstan's refusal to honour the award, the claimants sought execution against London-based cash and securities managed by the National Bank of Kazakhstan, ie Kazakhstan's central bank.

Kazakhstan invoked the immunity of the funds at hand by relying on section 14(4) of the UK SIA, according to which '[p]roperty of a State's central bank or other monetary authority shall not be regarded […] as in use or intended for use for commercial purposes'. The purpose of this provision is to foreclose the application of the commercial property exception from enforcement immunity to central banks' funds and other property.

> 57. […] [T]he wording of *section 14(4)* is clear and imperative […]. All "*property*" of a State's central bank or other monetary authority is covered […]. It does not matter whether the central bank is a department of the State or a separate entity. In all cases the central bank's property "*shall not be*" regarded as in use or intended for use for commercial purposes. […] [T]hen the property of a State's central bank (or other monetary authority) must enjoy complete immunity from the enforcement process in the UK courts. […]
>
> 79. […] [T]he restriction on the right of a party to enforce a judgment on the property of a central bank or other monetary authority that is imposed by *section 14(4)* is both legitimate and proportionate [and thus compatible with Article 6(1) ECHR] […].
>
> 80. […] I regard the UN Convention on Jurisdictional Immunities of States and their Property […] as a most important guide on the state of international opinion on what is, and what is not, a legitimate restriction on the right of parties to enforce against State property generally. I accept that the Convention does not constitute a *jus cogens* in international law. I recognise that the Convention has not yet been adopted by any States. But its existence and adoption by the UN […] powerfully demonstrates international thinking on the point. It suggests that the grant of immunity to all the property of a State's central bank is, in the eyes of the international community of States, legitimate […].
>
> 81. […] [I]n the existing legislation of States there is no consensus which grants only limited immunity as to enforcement procedures against the property of a State's

109 *Certain Iranian Assets (Iran v United States of America)*, Application of 14 July 2016, Table 2.

110 *Certain Iranian Assets* (n 109).

> central bank. Some States' legislation permits enforcement against a central bank's property if used for commercial purposes; other States' legislation does not.
>
> 82. […] The wording of *section 14(4)* provides a sensible rule which is easy to apply and thereby assists the promotion of comity and good relations between States. […] The overwhelming presumption must be that a central bank's work is for sovereign purposes and that its property is used for sovereign purposes. But if there had to be a more restrictive provision than *section 14(4)* then there could be much scope for litigation. A party could obtain a legitimate judgment against a State. It might wish to enforce it in the UK and that State's central bank may maintain funds in the UK. Those funds would be the obvious target for enforcement. Such an attempt could lead to a dispute over whether the funds are for use or intended for use for commercial purposes, with the need for disclosure, statements and a hearing. That is not conducive to comity and good relations between States. The interpretation of *section 14(4)* I have adopted avoids all that.
>
> 83. […] [T]he fact that the Claimants would not be able to enforce the ICSID award against the London Assets does not mean that the award is ineffective and a nullity. I do not know what other assets might be available for enforcement purposes. But there is no evidence before me to indicate that the Claimants would be left without a remedy worldwide.

This decision is interesting for two reasons. First, the court's conclusion on the absolute nature of immunity from execution for central bank property was found to be supported by the UNCSI, which 'powerfully demonstrate[d] international thinking on the point',[111] despite the fact that at the time the Convention had just been adopted and had not been ratified by any states. UNCSI's sweeping clause[112] completely exempting central bank property from enforcement proceedings was thus used as a tie-breaker in an area where domestic legislation and court practice is diversified and does include examples of denial of immunity to funds of central banks, when they are not held for the bank's own account (but rather in the name of and/or for the account of the state) and especially when they are proven to be used or intended for use for non-governmental activities.[113] It is therefore rather dubious that the UNCSI reflects customary law (also) in this respect.[114]

Secondly, the decision is notable for its treatment of the issue of the compatibility of enforcement immunity of central bank property with ECHR rights, ie the right to a court and the right to property. The English court accepted that these rights were engaged by the granting of absolute immunity to central bank assets. Nevertheless, the UNCSI was again crucial in showing the legitimacy and proportionality of the resulting restriction on these rights. Most interestingly, the court deemed necessary to add that this restriction did not imply that the ICSID award was 'ineffective' and a 'nullity',[115] as the plaintiffs had apparently other assets against which—and venues 'worldwide' where—they could seek execution of the arbitral decision. This implies that, according to some courts, a tension between international immunities

111 United Kingdom, England and Wales, High Court, *AIG Capital Partners Incorporated and CJSC Tema Real Estate Company Limited v Kazakhstan, National Bank of Kazakhstan (intervening) and ors (intervening)*, Enforcement Decision, 20 October 2005, ILDC 94 (UK 2005) para 80.

112 UNCSI, Article 21(1)(c).

113 See, eg, s 1611(b)(1) US FSIA, s 11(4) Canada's SIA, and s 32 Australia's FSIA. For the divergences in court practice, see A Reinisch, 'European Court Practice Concerning State Immunity from Enforcement Measures' (2006) 17 *EJIL* 803, 826–27.

114 See C Brown and R O'Keefe, 'Article 21' in R O'Keefe and C J Tams (eds), *The United Nations Convention on Jurisdictional Immunities of States and Their Property: A Commentary* (n 42) 334, 346–47.

115 *AIG Capital Partners Incorporated and CJSC Tema Real Estate Company Limited v Kazakhstan, National Bank of Kazakhstan (intervening) and ors (intervening)* (n 111) para 83.

and human rights is also present in the field of enforcement immunity and that proportionality of rights' restrictions under the guise of an 'alternative remedy test' is a pertinent consideration in state immunity cases as well.[116] At the same time, it is clear that this court's alternative remedy test is rather illusory, because it implies that enforcement immunity can never be removed insofar as it is possible to identify foreign states' assets located anywhere in the world and potentially available for the satisfaction of judicial debts.

IV. Personal Immunity

A limited number of foreign state officials enjoy almost absolute immunity from foreign jurisdiction during their terms of office. Since the immunity attaches to the status of the office-holder rather than to a particular act, this type of immunity is called personal immunity (or status immunity). Two subtypes must be distinguished: diplomatic immunity, which shields (ad hoc) diplomatic agents from the criminal jurisdiction of the receiving state, as well as from most of its civil jurisdiction (1), and personal immunity of certain high-ranking officials, which applies *erga omnes* and shields these officials from all foreign criminal jurisdiction and grants them extensive immunity from civil jurisdiction (2). Personal immunity ends when the term of office expires. Former officials continue, however, to be protected by functional immunity, as discussed in section V below.[117]

1. Diplomatic immunity

In the *Hostages* case, the ICJ underlined the importance of diplomatic immunity rules: 'there is no more fundamental prerequisite for the conduct of relations between States than inviolability of diplomatic envoys and embassies, so that throughout history nations of all creeds and cultures have observed reciprocal obligations for that purpose; and [...] the obligations thus assumed, notably those for assuring the personal safety of diplomats and their freedom from prosecution, are essential, unqualified, and inherent in their representative character and their diplomatic function'.[118] Diplomatic privileges and immunities, the Court considered, are 'an instrument essential for effective co-operation in the international community, and for enabling States, irrespective of their differing constitutional and social systems, to achieve mutual understanding and to resolve their differences by peaceful means'.[119]

These privileges and immunities are by and large codified in the VCDR.[120] In view of the variety of privileges and immunities under diplomatic law domestic jurisprudence touches upon a broad array of questions. This section singles out a couple of cases concerning the scope of the immunity from jurisdiction of diplomatic agents (a) and the issue of 'ad hoc' diplomatic missions (b).

First, it has to be noted that domestic courts are sometimes confused about the distinction between the rules on diplomatic immunity and those on state immunity. At times embassies or ambassadors are named as parties to a dispute, while in fact the complaint is directed against the foreign state itself. In such cases, the applicable immunity regime is, in principle, state immunity, not diplomatic immunity.[121]

---

116 See section VI.1(b) below.

117 See, eg, VCDR, Articles 39.2: 'When the functions of a person enjoying privileges and immunities have come to an end, such privileges and immunities shall normally cease at the moment when he leaves the country, or on expiry of a reasonable period in which to do so, but shall subsist until that time, even in case of armed conflict. However, with respect to acts performed by such a person in the exercise of his functions as a member of the mission, immunity shall continue to subsist'.

118 *United States Diplomatic and Consular Staff in Tehran* (*United States of America v Iran*) (Provisional Measures) [1979] ICJ Rep 7 para 38.

119 ibid, para 39.

120 ibid, para 41.

121 See *Skarphéðinsdóttir v Embassy of the United States* (n 41); Taiwan, High Court, *Panamanian Embassy in Taipei, Taiwan v Collins Company Limited*, 17 February 2004, ILDC 554 (TW 2004); Latvia, Supreme Court,

Of course, the fact that a dispute in which a foreign state is a party concerns the diplomatic mission or its personnel may be relevant to the application of the state immunity rule. Article 11 of the UNCSI, for example, evidences that the diplomatic status of an employee is a crucial factor in the qualification of a labour dispute as immune or non-immune. Moreover, when courts take the purpose of an act into account for determining whether state immunity must be recognized, acts that may normally qualify as non-governmental may be seen as governmental when they concern a diplomatic mission.[122]

Exceptionally, diplomatic immunity rules may, however, apply in cases in which the state rather than a diplomatic agent is a party.[123] In this respect it is interesting to note that the Understandings annexed to the UNCSI recall in relation to Article 11 the obligation of a receiving state under Article 38.2 VCDR to exercise its jurisdiction over nationals and permanent residents that are not members of the diplomatic staff, 'in such a manner as not to interfere unduly with the performance of the functions of the mission'.[124] In addition, proceedings against a foreign state concerning diplomatic property may in exceptional circumstances violate the inviolability of that property under diplomatic law. Apart from the inviolability of embassy bank accounts as discussed in section III.4(a) above, certain disputes concerning mission premises or residences of diplomatic agents may be incompatible with the inviolability of these properties. While most disputes will be able to proceed normally,[125] a claim to evacuate mission buildings would for example be incompatible with the inviolability of the mission under diplomatic law.[126] It is unsettled whether disputes over the ownership of mission premises must be seen to threaten the mission's inviolability. The German Federal Constitutional Court considered that a dispute over the ownership of mission premises would not interfere with the performance of the diplomatic duties of a foreign state and was hence allowed,[127] but the Swedish Supreme Court has recognized immunity in a comparable ownership dispute.[128]

VČ v Embassy of the Russian Federation to Latvia, 12 December 2007, ILDC 1063 (LV 2007); Botswana, *Bah v Libyan Embassy*, above section III.2; Botswana, Industrial Court, *Dube and Rabasha v American Embassy/Botusa*, above section III.2; Israel, Supreme Court, *Her Majesty the Queen in Right of Canada v Edelson*, above section II.1; United Kingdom, Employment Appeals Tribunal, *Military Affairs Office of the Embassy of Kuwait v Caramba-Coker*, 10 April 2003, ILDC 251 (UK 2003); United States, *Pradhan and Pradhan v Al-Sabah, Ambassador to the Embassy of Kuwait and Hermina, Counsel for the Embassy of Kuwait*, 5 January 2004, ILDC 718 (US 2004); United States, Court of Appeals for the 2nd Circuit, *USAA Casualty Insurance Company (on the application of Adelman) v Permanent Mission of the Republic of Namibia and ors*, 25 May 2012, ILDC 2225 (US 2012). See for a problematic confusion of state and diplomatic immunity, Colombia, Supreme Court of Justice, *García de Borrisow v Embassy of Lebanon*, above section III.2. See for the application of the rule of state immunity in a case against a consular officer, Italy, Court of Cassation, *Vespignani v Bianchi*, 22 July 2004, ILDC 556 (IT 2004). See for a case where the court failed to recognize the applicability of the law of state immunity, Ukraine, *Private Entrepreneur Individual—4 and Private Entrepreneur Individual—5 v Consulate General of Romania in Chernivtsi and Embassy of Romania in Ukraine*, 2 July 2013, ILDC 2279 (UA 2013).

122 Japan, *Interquest Co v Saudi Arabia*, 27 December 2005, ILDC 1020 (JP 2005); see section III.1.

123 Notably, UNCSI, Article 3.1 provides that: 'The present Convention is without prejudice to the privileges and immunities enjoyed by a State under international law in relation to the exercise of the functions of: (*a*) its diplomatic missions, consular posts, special missions, missions to international organizations or delegations to organs of international organizations or to international conferences; and (*b*) persons connected with them'.

124 Understanding with respect to Article 11, Annex to the UNCSI.

125 See Austria, Regional Court for Civil Matters, *E AG v S*, 23 January 2001, ILDC 357 (AT 2001); Latvia, Supreme Court, *VČ v Embassy of the Russian Federation to Latvia*, 12 December 2007, ILDC 1063 (LV 2007); Israel, Supreme Court, *Her Majesty the Queen in Right of Canada v Edelson*, above section II.1.

126 See, eg, United States, Court of Appeals for the 2nd Circuit, *767, Third Avenue Associates and Another v Permanent Mission of the Republic of Zaire to the United Nations*, 988 F 2d 295 (1993).

127 Germany, Federal Constitutional Court, *Jurisdiction over Yugoslav Military Mission (Germany) Case*, 30 October 1962, 38 ILR 162.

128 Sweden, Supreme Court, *Beckman v Chinese People's Republic*, 1 March 1957, 24 ILR 221.

(a) The ratione materiae *scope of diplomatic immunity from jurisdiction*

Article 31.1 VCDR reads: 'A diplomatic agent shall enjoy immunity from the criminal jurisdiction of the receiving State. He shall also enjoy immunity from its civil and administrative jurisdiction, except in the case of: (*a*) A real action relating to private immovable property situated in the territory of the receiving State, unless he holds it on behalf of the sending State for the purposes of the mission; (*b*) An action relating to succession in which the diplomatic agent is involved as executor, administrator, heir or legatee as a private person and not on behalf of the sending State; (*c*) An action relating to any professional or commercial activity exercised by the diplomatic agent in the receiving State outside his official functions'.

The notion of 'civil' jurisdiction is usually interpreted broadly, thus as extending to *inter alia* family law disputes, like divorce,[129] custody,[130] alimony or paternity proceedings.[131] A Dutch court recently ruled that issuing a speeding ticket is an administrative sanction which entails the exercise of jurisdiction and is hence not allowed under diplomatic law.[132]

The exceptions to the rule must be construed narrowly. Domestic courts at times use inventive reasoning to interpret the rule restrictively so as to avert the adverse consequences of the application of the rule on the course of justice. These narrow interpretations of the rule are, however, contentious.

Public Prosecutor v LC, Appeal Judgment, (2002-2003) 8 Rechtskundig Weekblad 301, ILDC 46 (BE 2002), 1st March 2002, Belgium; Brussels; Court of Appeal

The Brussels Court of Appeal was asked to decide whether the Juvenile Court of Brussels had jurisdiction over, and could impose educational measures on, the daughter of the first secretary of the Zambian embassy in Brussels.

> 3. By virtue of Articles 31 and 37 of the Vienna Convention of 18 April 1961 on Diplomatic Relations, [...] both diplomatic officers and their resident family members enjoy immunity from criminal, civil and administrative jurisdiction in the host State. However, these provisions cannot be interpreted as meaning that legal authorities in the host State are unable to apply compulsory supervisory or protective measures in the case of children in a situation of troubled upbringing if such children "enjoy" diplomatic immunity. This interpretation does not conflict with Article 29 of the said Convention, which in combination with Article 37, clearly imposes the obligation on the host State to take all suitable steps to prevent the dignity, freedom or values of resident family members of diplomatic officers from being jeopardised.
>
> 4. If the provisions of the Vienna Convention of 18 April 1961 are to be assumed to be incompatible with the initiation of legal proceedings to protect diplomats' children, then these provisions will be in conflict with the New York Convention of 20 November 1989 on the Rights of the Child. According to Article 19 of this Convention, State parties will take all suitable steps to protect the child against all forms of physical or mental violence, injury or abuse, neglect or neglectful treatment, mishandling or exploitation, including sexual abuse, and these measures must include suitable procedures for tracing, reporting, referring, examining, treating and the

129 United States, Supreme Court of Connecticut, *Fernandez v Fernandez*, 19 July 1998, ILDC 1385 (US 1988) paras 9–11.

130 Belgium, Brussels Court of Appeals, *Mr C v Mrs M*, 28 February 2008, ILDC 1501 (BE 2008).

131 Russia, Supreme Court, *O v L*, 1 February 2005, ILDC 959 (RU 2005).

132 The Netherlands, Court of Appeal, 26 September 2014, ECLI:NL:GHARL:2014:7398. As a consequence of this judgment, the Netherlands is no longer issuing speeding tickets to individuals with diplomatic status. It will shift to a system where diplomats receive a notification and an invitation to pay the fine. See also cases in n 12 on the definition of jurisdiction.

> following up of cases of child abuse and, where applicable, procedures for involving legal authorities.
>
> 5. Article 2 of this Convention emphasises that State parties guarantee the rights described in the Convention for each child under their legal authority without discrimination of any kind whatsoever.
>
> 6. Both Belgium and Zambia are party to the Convention on the Rights of the Child […]
>
> 7. The conflict between the two said Conventions, ascertained on the assumption that the provisions of the Vienna Convention of 18 April 1961 must be taken as incompatible with the initiation of legal proceedings to protect diplomats' children, must be resolved in favour of the Convention on the Rights of the Child. After all, the rule should be applied that provisions of the former Convention only apply insofar as these are compatible with those of the later Convention, notwithstanding the fact that Article 30 of the Vienna Convention on the Law of Treaties of 23 May 1969, and transposed by the Act of 10 June 1992, only applies to treaties concluded by States following the date it came into effect in those States (cf. Article 4 of this Convention). This rule is in fact only a confirmation of the previously established principle of "*lex posterior derogat priori*" […]
>
> 8. Therefore, the Vienna Convention of 18 April 1961 is unable under any circumstance to prevent legal proceedings from being instigated to protect diplomats' children. The lower court therefore also erred in declaring it had no jurisdiction to consider applications from the Public Prosecution Service.

The court held that diplomatic immunity under Article 31 VCDR does not preclude the imposition of judicial child protection measures in regard to children of diplomatic agents since Article 29 in conjunction with Article 37 VCDR obliges the receiving state to protect the person, freedom or dignity of these children. The court further argued that Article 31 was incompatible with the obligation under Article 19 of the UN Convention on the Rights of the Child (CRC). In view of the *lex posterior derogat legi priori* principle, it held that Article 31 could not find application to the facts of this case.

The decision can be criticized from the perspective of diplomatic immunity law as well as from that of treaty law. Foreign diplomats are inviolable (Article 29 VCDR) and immune from the jurisdiction of the receiving state (Article 31 VCDR), and these rules apply to their family members as well (Article 37 VCDR). The inviolability of a diplomatic agent, his family and his private residence does not prevent temporary emergency measures by the receiving state in case a child is in danger, as Denza points out: 'a very limited exception […] may be implied on a basis of self-defence or an overriding duty to protect human life'.[133] The subjection of a diplomat to child care measures imposed by the host state would be a continuous violation of his inviolability and immunity that cannot be qualified as a temporary emergency measure. Admittedly, the obligations of the receiving state under Article 29 to protect individuals with diplomatic status may be at odds with the obligations under that same article to respect the inviolability of another person with diplomatic status, and under Article 31 to respect that person's immunity from jurisdiction. Reliance on the obligations under Article 29 to Article 37 as regards the child, in order to circumscribe the inviolability and immunity of the diplomat in general terms contravenes, however, the essence of diplomatic immunity law. If the sending state refuses to agree to the subjection of its diplomatic agent to the jurisdiction of the receiving state, the removal of the

133 See E Denza, *Diplomatic Law, Commentary on the Vienna Convention on Diplomatic Relations* (4th edn, OUP 2016) 223.

diplomat from one's territory through a *persona non grata* declaration seems more in line with the object and purpose of the VCDR.

Also, the argument based on the CRC is not convincing. The *travaux préparatoires* of the Convention in fact reveal that the scope *ratione personae* of the Convention was changed exactly to ensure the special status of children of diplomats. Originally, states were to ensure the rights under the Convention to each child 'within their territories or subject to their jurisdiction', while Article 2.1 now provides that the rights have to be ensured to each child 'within their jurisdiction'.[134]

Papavassilopoulos v Barone, Appeal judgment, Case no 27044, (2009) Giustizia civile 604, ILDC 1343 (IT 2008), 13th November 2008, Italy; Supreme Court of Cassation

A Greek diplomat accredited to the Greek Embassy in Rome used the services of an Italian lawyer in a dispute concerning compensation for damage resulting from personal activities of the diplomat. The lawyer subsequently brought a claim against the diplomat for the recovery of an unpaid bill. The diplomat invoked diplomatic immunity from the jurisdiction of Italian courts. The lawyer argued that the exception of Article 31(1)(c) applied.

> 22 [...] [W]ith reference to the specific position of the foreign State acting jure privatorum, one may conclude that a more general principle exists in accordance with which not only the State, but also the subject/natural person both actively and passively establishing professional, commercial or working relationships (of a purely private nature) in Italy is required to accept the jurisdiction of the Italian State, both in proceedings and (as in this case) in the context of executive procedures legitimately brought against it.
>
> 23 Therefore, also in this respect, given the groundlessness of the further arguments made by the applicant concerning the interpretation of Art. 31 of the Vienna Convention, the following legal principle is articulated: regarding the jurisdiction of the Italian Courts, Art. 31, paragraph 1, letter c) of the Vienna Convention of April 24, 1963, ratified by Law No. 804 of August 9, 1967, must be interpreted as meaning that immunity from jurisdiction is excluded for diplomats, both in the event that they are the active subject of professional or commercial activity not exercised as part of their official duties (as provided for by the law in question), and in the event that the diplomat is the passive subject of these relationships, if entered into *jure privatorum* in State territory, i.e. entirely outside of their official duties and responsibilities.

The court was mistaken to rely on the restrictive approach to the law of state immunity for the interpretation of the scope of the exception of Article 31(1)(c) VCDR. The two rules are fundamentally distinct, and the rationale behind the exception of Article 31(1)(c) VCDR is in no way related to the rationale behind absence of state immunity for *acta jure gestionis*. Hence, the scope of the article cannot be informed by the scope of the law of state immunity.

The exception of Article 31(1)(c) VCDR has evolved in reaction to 'the problem of the merchant ambassador'[135] and ensures that diplomats and especially family members of diplomats that engage in professional or commercial activity in the receiving state can be held accountable for those activities.[136] The exception only applies to continuous activity, not to single professional

134 United Nations Commission on Human Rights, 'Report of the Working Group on a Draft Convention on the Rights of the Child' (1989) UN Doc E/CN.4/1989/48, paras 160–63; S L Detrick, *A Commentary on the United Nations Convention on the Rights of the Child* (Martinus Nijhoff 1999) 70–71.

135 Denza (n 133) 248.

136 Diplomatic agents are in principle prohibited from practising 'for personal profit any professional or commercial activity' in the receiving State (Article 42 VCDR) and the exception of Article 31(1)(c) would hence only arise in exceptional circumstances in regard to the diplomatic agent himself, see Denza (n 133) 250–51.

or commercial acts, and does hence not allow analogous interpretation with the *acta jure gestionis* exception to state immunity. As Denza explains: '[o]rdinary contracts incidental to life in the receiving State, such as purchase of goods, medical, *legal* or educational services, or agreements to rent accommodation do not constitute "commercial activities"'.[137] Also, contracts with domestic staff are generally considered not to fall under the exception.[138] While a diplomat that contracts a lawyer to give him continuous advice in regards to professional activities carried out in the receiving state would come within the ambit of the exception, the diplomat who consults a lawyer on legal questions that are incidental to his day to day life would not.

The interpretation of this article by the Italian court defies the common understanding on the scope of the exception. The broad interpretation of the exception as excluding immunity for all commercial and professional activity unrelated to official functions contravenes the generally accepted interpretation of the article.

(b) The ratione personae *scope of diplomatic immunity from jurisdiction*

The rule of diplomatic immunity extends to family members of the diplomatic agent.[139] Since it is up to the receiving state to define the notion of 'family member',[140] the scope of application may differ slightly from state to state. Treaties constituting an international organization, as well as headquarters agreements, commonly extend the rules of diplomatic immunity to state representatives to permanent missions to international organizations, as well as to certain staff members of those organizations.[141]

A question that is not completely settled is to what extent foreign officials on ad hoc diplomatic missions—'special missions'—enjoy diplomatic immunity in the receiving state. The 1969 Convention on Special Missions has not received wide support,[142] but it seems generally accepted that diplomatic immunity rules apply to at least some special missions, as recognized by several domestic courts. In the 1984 *Tabatabai* case, the German Federal Supreme Court held that irrespective of the Convention on Special Missions there is 'a customary rule of international law based on State practice and *opinio juris* according to which it [is] possible for an *ad hoc* envoy, who has been charged with a special political mission by the sending State, to be granted immunity for that mission by individual agreement with the receiving State. Envoys engaged on such a mission could thereby be placed on the same footing as the members of the permanent missions of States, who were protected by international treaty law'.[143] Interestingly, in the course of the proceedings before the ICJ in the *Arrest Warrant* case, Belgium emphasised that it recognized the immunity of 'representatives of foreign States who visit Belgium on the basis of an official invitation'.[144] A couple of recent cases may be recalled to confirm this position.

---

137 Denza (n 133) 251 (emphasis added).

138 ibid, 251–52; United States Court of Appeals for the 4th Circuit, *Tabion v Mufti* 73 F 3d 535 (1996); United States, District Court for the District of Columbia, *Sabbithi and ors v Major Al Saleh and ors,* 20 March 2009, ILDC 1652 (US 2009); United States, District Court for the District of Columbia, *Montuya v Chedid and Chedid*, 26 April 2011, ILDC 2195 (US 2011); United Kingdom, High Court of Justice, *Wokuri v Kassam*, 30 January 2012, [2012] EWHC 105; United Kingdom, Court of Appeal, *Reyes v Al-Malki*, 5 February 2015, [2015] EWCA Civ 32.

139 VCDR, Article 37.

140 Denza (n 133) 319 ff.

141 See for an example: United States, District Court for the Southern District of New York, *Devi and Sivam v Silva*, 9 April 2012, ILDC 2781 (US 2012).

142 United Nations Convention on Special Missions, New York, 8 December 1969, 1400 UNTS 231; at the time of writing, 39 states are party to this convention.

143 Germany, Federal Supreme Court, *Tabatabai*, 27 February 1984, 80 ILR 388, 394. See also Austria, Supreme Court, *Syrian National Immunity*, 12 February 1998, 127 ILR 88, 92; United States, *Kilroy v Windsor*, 7 December 1978, 81 ILR 605, 606–07.

144 See Counter Memorial of the Kingdom of Belgium, 28 September 2001, para 1.12, http://www.icj-cij.org/files/case-related/121/8304.pdf (last accessed 8 July 2018).

Li and United States (intervening) v Bo, Motion to Dismiss for Lack of Jurisdiction, 568 F.Supp.2d 35 (D.D.C. 2008), ILDC 1155 (US 2008), 1st August 2008, United States; District of Columbia; District Court for the District of Columbia [DDC]

The Minister of Commerce of the People's Republic of China had travelled to the US to participate in a US–China Joint Commission on Commerce and Trade, at the invitation of the US authorities. When a group of practitioners of the Falun Gong movement sued the Minister for human rights abuses that allegedly occurred while he served as governor of the Liaoning Province, the US Department of State submitted a Suggestion of Immunity and Statement of Interest, asking the court to find the Minister immune from service of process and therefore not subject to the court's jurisdiction.

> 8 The logic that underlies deference to the Executive's assertion regarding a head of state or diplomatic agent is, in this Court's view, equally applicable to a foreign minister who is part of a special diplomatic mission. Indeed, the Executive's authority to assert such immunity derives from customary international law and the President's powers to conduct foreign affairs and receive foreign ministers. Restatement (Third) of Foreign Relations Law § 464, cmt. i. ("High officials of a foreign state and their staffs on an official visit or in transit … enjoy immunities like those of diplomatic agents when the effect of exercising jurisdiction against the individual would be to violate the immunity of the foreign state.") […]

Even though this case turned on the 'suggestion of immunity' issued by the Executive, the court cared to point out that the suggestion was in accordance with customary international law rules on diplomatic immunity, therewith supporting the position that ad hoc diplomats, at least in case of high-level special missions, are covered by these rules.

Khurts Bat and Mongolia (intervening) v Investigating Judge of the German Federal Court and Secretary of State for Foreign and Commonwealth Affairs (intervening), Appeal decision, [2011] EWHC 2029 (Admin), [2012] 3 WLR 180, [2011] All ER (D) 293, [2011] ACD 111, ILDC 1779 (UK 2011), 29th July 2011, United Kingdom; England and Wales; High Court [HC]; Queen's Bench Division [QBD]; Administrative Court

The head of the Mongolian Intelligence Service was arrested by the UK police following an arrest warrant issued by Germany. Bat was accused of abducting a Mongolian national in Germany and transferring him to Mongolia where he was subsequently imprisoned and tortured. Bat argued, *inter alia*, that he enjoyed diplomatic immunity because he visited the UK on official government business. Neither the UK nor Mongolia are parties to the Special Missions Convention.

> 22. […] It was agreed that under rules of customary international law Mr Khurts Bat was entitled to inviolability of the person and immunity from suit if he was travelling on a Special Mission sent by Mongolia to the United Kingdom with the prior consent of the United Kingdom. […]
>
> 26. It is important to appreciate that the status of immunity conferred by a Special Mission is that which is conferred on a permanent Diplomatic Mission. Under customary international law those accredited to a permanent Diplomatic Mission enjoy inviolability of the person and immunity from suit. […] A Special Mission performs temporarily those functions ordinarily taken care of by a permanent mission. The Special Mission represents the sending State in the same way as a permanent Diplomatic Mission represents the State who sends it […].
>
> 27. The essential requirement for recognition of a Special Mission is that the receiving State consents to the mission, as a Special Mission. […]
>
> 29. It is vital to bear in mind that the consent which must be previously obtained is consent to a Special Mission. A State which gives such consent recognises the special

> nature of the mission and the status of inviolability and immunity which participation in that Special Mission confers on the visitors. Not every official visit is a Special Mission. Not everyone representing their State on a visit of mutual interest is entitled to the inviolability and immunity afforded to participants in a Special Mission.

This case equals the immunity of special missions to which a receiving state has consented to that of permanent missions. Since Mr Khurts Bat was not considered to be protected by such immunity, the court turned to the more general question of functional immunity, discussed in section V.1 below.

2. Personal immunity of certain high-ranking state officials

(a) *The* ratione materiae *scope of personal immunity from jurisdiction*

The immunity of heads of state[145] in office[146] from foreign criminal jurisdiction is absolute. When a civil suit is instigated against a foreign head of state it must first be ascertained whether he or she is in fact sued in the capacity as representative of the state—the case is then in fact one against the state and the rule of state immunity applies.[147] Only when the personal responsibility of the head of state under civil law is at stake, the rule of head of state immunity applies. The scope of that rule is, however, uncertain.

The 2001 Resolution on Immunities from Jurisdiction and Execution of Heads of State and of Government in International Law adopted by the *Institut de droit international* provides in Article 3 that '[i]n civil and administrative matters, the Head of State does not enjoy any immunity from jurisdiction before the courts of a foreign State, unless that suit relates to acts performed in the exercise of his or her official functions. [...] Nonetheless, nothing shall be done by way of court proceedings with regard to the Head of State while he or she is in the territory of that State, in the exercise of official functions'.[148] Other interpretations of the rule have, however, been advanced. In the UK, for example, foreign heads of state enjoy the same immunity as ambassadors,[149] and the Austrian Supreme Court has even held head of state immunity from civil jurisdiction to be absolute.[150] Also, the Canadian Supreme Court appeared to proceed from an absolute immunity from civil jurisdiction in its 2014 judgment in the *Kazemi* case.[151] It held: 'Under customary international law, there is a distinction between the blanket immunity *ratione personae* of high-ranking individuals such as the head of state, and the immunity *ratione materiae* for former

145 For US cases in which executive suggestions of immunity controlled the grant of personal immunity, see section II.3 above, under US, Court of Appeals for the Seventh Circuit, *Ye and Others v Zemin and Falun Gong Control Office*, 8 September 2004, ILDC 683 (US 2004).

146 See section IV.2(b) below for other office-holders covered by this rule.

147 See, eg, the commentary to UNCSI, Draft Article 2(1)(b)(iv), ILC, 'Draft Articles on Jurisdictional Immunities of States and their Property, with commentaries' (1991) Yearbook of the International Law Commission, Vol II, Part Two, p 13 ff, UN Doc A/CN.4/L.457, para 17: 'The fifth and last category of beneficiaries of State immunity encompasses all the natural persons who are authorized to represent the State in all its manifestations, as comprehended in the first four categories mentioned in paragraphs 1(*b*)(i) to (iv). Thus, sovereigns and heads of State in their public capacity would be included under this category as well as in the first category, being in the broader sense organs of the Government of the State'. The commentary further explained at para 18: '[a]ctions against such representatives or agents of a foreign Government in respect of their official acts are essentially proceedings against the State they represent'.

148 Institut de Droit International, Resolution on the Immunities from Jurisdiction and Execution of Heads of State and of Government in International Law (2001), (2000–2001) 69 *Annuaire de l'Institut de droit international* 743.

149 Section 20(1) of the 1978 UK State Immunity Act.

150 Austria, Supreme Court, *W v Prince of Liechtenstein and ors*, ILDC 1 (AT 2001) para 11. See, however, section VI.1(b) for discussion of the finding of the Supreme Court that human rights law may under certain circumstances limit the application of this immunity.

151 *Kazemi* (n 73). See also United States, District Court for the Eastern District of New York, *Gomes v ANGOP, Angola Press Agency and ors*, 22 August 2012, ILDC 2224 (US 2012) para 24.

heads of state and lower-ranking officials which applies only in respect of official acts performed for or on behalf of the state. These doctrines recognize the unique role and responsibility of heads of state. Immunity *ratione personae* shields individuals in the state's highest positions of authority and, in so doing, preserves their ability to carry out the governance of the state'.[152]

(b) The ratione personae *scope of personal immunity from jurisdiction*

The personal immunity of incumbent heads of state does not apply to heads of entities that do not qualify as sovereign states,[153] nor does it apply to the heads of constituent units of federal states.[154] The rule may, on the other hand, extend to family members but the extent of that inclusion is not settled.[155] Another contentious issue is what other office-holders are covered by personal immunity. In *Arrest Warrant*, the ICJ ruled that 'certain holders of high-ranking office in a State, such as the Head of State, Head of Government and Minister for Foreign Affairs, enjoy immunities from jurisdiction in other States, both civil and criminal',[156] and therewith extended the personal immunity recognized in respect of heads of state to other high-ranking office-holders. This aspect of the decision has received fierce criticism since all relevant state practice as well as logic militate in favour of a distinct treatment of the head of state from other office-holders.[157] Not surprisingly, however, domestic courts have followed the ICJ on this point.[158] The *Arrest Warrant* judgment triggered the question of whether other office-holders than the ones explicitly mentioned by the ICJ would be covered by the personal immunity rule. In 2008 the ILC Special Rapporteur Kolodkin noted that the ICJ 'clearly confirmed that the category of such officials is not limited to the three mentioned',[159] but in 2013 Special Rapporteur Escobar Hernández held that the applicability of the rule 'to other senior State officials cannot be demonstrated at the present stage in the development of international law'.[160] Nevertheless, some national courts have extended the *ratione personae* scope of the rule. Apart from the application to heads of government,[161] domestic courts have also granted personal immunity to a minister

152 *Kazemi* (n 73) para 186. Notably, in Canada, Superior Court of Québec, *Kazemi (Estate of) and Hashemi v Iran, Ayatollah Ali Khamenei and ors*, 25 January 2011, 2011 QCCS 196, the issue of head of state immunity was completely overlooked.

153 See references given in n 13 for case law concerning the definition of 'state' for immunity purposes.

154 Italy, Court of Cassation, *Italy v D M (Djukanović)*, 28 December 2004, ILDC 74 (IT 2004) para 13; United Kingdom, Administrative Court, *R (on the application of Alamieyeseigha) v Crown Prosecution Service*, 25 November 2005, ILDC 93 (UK 2005).

155 See J Verhoeven (Rapporteur Institut de Droit International), *Les immunités de juridiction et d'exécution du chef d'Etat et de gouvernement en droit international, Rapport provisoire (2000)*, (2000–2001) 69 *Annuaire de l'Institut de droit international* 482, 530. See also Austria, Supreme Court, *Anita W v Johannes Adam II, Prince of Liechtenstein*, ILDC 1 (AT 2001) in which it was held that the immunity only extended to 'closest family members of a Head of State forming part of his/her household', para 11.

156 *Arrest Warrant of 11 April 2000* (*Democratic Republic of the Congo v Belgium*) [2002] ICJ Rep 3, para 51. Notably, the ICJ underlined in *Djibouti v France* (n 12) that the *Procureur de la République* and the Head of National Security did not enjoy personal immunity, para 194. Djibouti had abandoned that argument in the course of the proceedings, changing it for a functional immunity argument instead, see paras 185–87. For the exclusion of the head of the national security from the *ratione personae* scope of the rule, see also United Kingdom, Administrative Court, *Khurts Bat and Mongolia (intervening) v Investigating Judge of the German Federal Court and Secretary of State for Foreign and Commonwealth Affairs (intervening)*, section IV.1(b) above, para 61.

157 See, eg, R Jennings and A Watts (eds), *Oppenheim's International Law* (9th edn, Longman 1992) 1033, para 445; A Watts, 'The Legal Position in International Law of Heads of State, Heads of Government and Foreign Ministers' (1994-III) 247 *Recueil des Cours* 13, 102.

158 See *Italy v D M (Djukanović)* (n 154) para 10.

159 ILC, 'Preliminary report on immunity of State officials from foreign criminal jurisdiction, by Mr. Roman Anatolevich Kolodkin, Special Rapporteur' (2008) UN Doc A/CN.4/601, p 60, para 117.

160 ILC, 'Second report on the immunity of State officials from foreign criminal jurisdiction, by Ms. Concepción Escobar Hernández, Special Rapporteur' (2013) UN Doc A/CN.4/661, p 22, para 66.

161 Belgium, Court of Cassation, *Re Sharon and Yaron, HSA v SA (Ariel Sharon) and YA (Amos Yaron)*, 12 February 2003, ILDC 5 (BE 2003).

for commerce and international trade[162] and to a minister of defence in the case discussed below. In its judgment on preliminary objections in *Immunities and Criminal Proceedings* (*Equatorial Guinea v France*), the ICJ held that it lacked jurisdiction to entertain the claim whether the Second Vice-President of Equatorial Guinea was entitled to personal immunity.[163] Equatorial Guinea had argued that he was, since he represented the country, had the capacity to act on behalf of the state in its relations with other states and international organizations, and had to travel abroad to exercise his functions effectively.[164]

Mofaz, Re, First Instance, ILDC 97 (UK 2004), 12th February 2004

Relatives of victims of military operations conducted by the Israel Defence Forces in the Occupied Palestinian Territories sought the issuance of a warrant by the Bow Street Magistrates' Court for the arrest of General Shaul Mofaz, the Defence Minister of Israel, who was visiting the United Kingdom at the time.

> 11 There appears to be no statutory basis for a claim of immunity in this case. The House of Lords in *Pinochet (No 3)* 2000 1 AC 119 accepted the principle that United Kingdom law would give effect to immunity under customary international law in the absence of a statutory requirement not to do so. State immunity has only to date been recognized to shield the conduct of certain individuals. The International Court of Justice in the *Arrest Warrant* case (*Congo v Belgium*) held that such immunity extended to the serving Head of State, Head of Government and the Foreign Minister. However, what is clear from paragraph 51 of the judgment is that the [C]ourt did not need to consider immunity in relation to any other minister. Paragraph 51 reads:
>
> The [C]ourt would observe at the outset that in international law it is firmly established that, as also diplomatic and consular agents, certain holders of high-ranking office in a State, such as the Head of State, Head of Government and Minister for Foreign Affairs, enjoy immunities from jurisdiction in other States, both civil and criminal. For the purposes of the present case, it is only the immunity from criminal jurisdiction and the inviolability of an incumbent Minister for Foreign Affairs that fall for the Court to consider.
>
> Two points arise from that. The use of the words 'such as' the Head of State, Head of Government and Minister for Foreign Affairs indicate to me that other categories could be included. In other words, those categories are not exclusive. Additionally, the last line made it absolutely clear that it was only the Minister of Foreign Affairs that fell to the Court to consider—no other office holder.
>
> 12 The basis for saying that a Foreign Minister should have [S]tate immunity was to enable him effectively to fulfil his function which would include travel or diplomatic missions on behalf of the State. Would such immunity extend to any other Minister of State, including a Defence Minister?
>
> 13 The function of various Ministers will vary enormously depending upon their sphere of responsibility. I would think it very unlikely that ministerial appointments such as Home Secretary, Employment Minister, Environment Minister, Culture Media and Sports Minister would automatically acquire a label of [S]tate immunity. However, I do believe that the Defence Minister may be a different matter.

162 United Kingdom, Bow Street Magistrates' Court, *Re Bo Xilai*, 8 November 2005, 129 ILR 713, 714.

163 See *Immunities and Criminal Proceedings* (*Equatorial Guinea v France*) (Preliminary Objections), ICJ, 6 June 2018, paras 91–103 http://www.icj-cij.org/files/case-related/163/163-20180606-JUD-01-00-EN.pdf (last accessed 8 July 2018).

164 See *Immunities and Criminal Proceedings* (*Equatorial Guinea v France*) (Application) paras 17–19 http://www.icj-cij.org/docket/files/163/19036.pdf (last accessed 8 July 2018).

> 14 Although travel will not be on the same level as that of a Foreign Minister, it is a fact that many [S]tates maintain troops overseas and there are many United Nations missions to visit in which military issues do play a prominent role between certain States. It strikes me that the roles of defence and foreign policy are very much intertwined, in particular in the Middle East.
>
> 15 I recognize that I am working in somewhat unchartered waters but having given the matter very considerable consideration overnight and today I conclude that a Defence Minister would automatically acquire [S]tate immunity in the same way as that pertaining to a Foreign Minister. Given that finding, I decline to issue the warrant requested.

As mentioned above, the extension of head of state immunity to ministers of foreign affairs in the *Arrest Warrant* case received strong criticism. There are very cogent arguments indeed for the position that, apart from the head of state, foreign office-holders are only protected by absolute immunity on their official travels abroad. The case, and the offspring thereof in domestic jurisprudence, have however created a new reality through the emergence of a general state practice and *opinio juris* in favour of the application of head of state immunity to certain high-level office-holders.

V. Functional Immunity and Consular Immunity

1. Functional immunity

Functional immunity shields all (former) state officials from foreign jurisdiction in respect of 'official acts', or 'acts performed in the exercise of their functions', or, as the ILC puts it 'act[s] performed by a State official in the exercise of State authority'.[165] Domestic courts encounter three principal controversies on the scope of the rule: the definition of 'official act'; the question of whether it applies in the face of criminal jurisdiction; and the question of whether the rule shields officials suspected of international crimes from jurisdiction.

The latter issue will be dealt with in section VI below. The question of the definition of 'official act' has led to diverging domestic court decisions. Many domestic courts approach this rule as an extension of the rule of state immunity to individual state officials. In *Jones v Saudi Arabia* the UK House of Lords recalled that the basic rationale underlying functional immunity is that 'the foreign state is entitled to claim immunity for its servants as it could if sued itself. The foreign state's right to immunity cannot be circumvented by suing its servants or agents'.[166] According to the House of Lords, functional immunity applies whenever an individual is sued in respect of an act that is attributable to the state, and the state itself could invoke state immunity had it been sued instead.[167] The courts of New Zealand,[168] Australia,[169] and Canada[170] have followed the House of Lords on this point, and also the following Swiss case seems to proceed from it.

165 Draft Article 2f, as provisionally adopted, ILC, 'Report on the Work of the of the International Law Commission on the Sixty-Eighth Session' (2016) UN Doc A/71/10, 352.

166 United Kingdom, House of Lords, *Jones, Redress (intervening) and ors (intervening) v Ministry of the Interior of Saudi Arabia and Lieutenant Colonel Abdul Aziz*, 14 June 2006, ILDC 521 (UK 2006) para 10 (see also section VI.2(a)).

167 ibid, eg para 74.

168 New Zealand, High Court, *Fang and ors and Attorney-General (intervening) v Jiang and ors*, 21 December 2006, ILDC 1226 (NZ 2006).

169 Australia, Supreme Court New South Wales, *Cuiying Zhang v Jiang Zemin and ors and Attorney-General of the Commonwealth (intervening)*, 5 October 2010, ILDC 2024 (AU 2010).

170 *Kazemi* (n 73).

Adamov (Evgeny) v Federal Office of Justice, Appeal Judgment, Case No 1A 288/2005, ILDC 339 (CH 2005), 22nd December 2005, Switzerland; Federal Supreme Court [BGer]

Adamov is the former Head of the Russian Institute for Nuclear Research and the former Minister of Atomic Energy of the Russian Federation. When he travelled to Switzerland the United States requested his extradition in relation to criminal proceedings concerning conspiracy to transfer stolen money and securities, conspiracy to defraud the US, money laundering, and tax evasion. The acts related to funds obtained from US sources during his term of office. Subsequently, the Russian Federation requested his extradition in relation to criminal proceedings partly concerning the same facts. In the course of the proceedings, the question of functional immunity arose.

> 3.4.2 [...] Immunity under public international law should notably prevent a state from limiting the sovereignty of another state by extending its jurisdiction to apply to the sovereign acts of the second state and its organs of state [...] One of the main functions of the immunity from criminal and enforcement proceedings granted to (current) members of government is the guarantee of political stability which this provides. This privilege granting immunity from criminal proceedings is supposed to prevent a government's actions from being hindered by politically motivated criminal actions brought against holders of high office. The purpose of immunity from criminal proceedings on the other hand is not to guarantee immunity from criminal prosecution for corruption (or even for private law offences) for former members of government for an unspecified period of time (or for life). Even the "personal" absolute immunity attached to highly ranking institutions of the state essentially evolves after departure from office into purely "functional" immunity for official office-related executive acts [...].

The court limits functional immunity to the 'sovereign acts' of the organs of a state and therewith equates it to the rule of state immunity.[171] While the court implies that corruption does not qualify as an official act for functional immunity purposes,[172] it does not squarely draw that conclusion. Instead, it decides to give priority to the Russian request because the US is only an indirectly affected state while the Russian Federation is the directly affected state. Curiously, the Russian insistence on the functional immunity of its former minister from US jurisdiction in respect of the alleged crimes seems to have influenced the court in its decision.[173]

Other domestic courts have approached the rule of functional immunity differently. In the Philippines the functional immunity of state officials is also cast in terms of the law of state immunity, but domestic courts do not regard all acts that are attributable to the state as official acts. In *Arigo v Smith*,[174] for example, the Philippine Supreme Court held that 'if the judgment against [...] officials will require the state itself to perform an affirmative act to satisfy the same, such as the appropriation of the amount needed to pay the damages awarded against them, the suit must be regarded as against the state itself'[175] but pointed out that 'the doctrine of immunity from suit will not apply and may not be invoked where the public official is being sued in his private and personal capacity as an ordinary citizen'.[176] According to the court: 'a public official may be liable

171 See also Switzerland, Federal Supreme Court, *A v B*, 21 November 2003, ILDC 342 (CH 2003) para 10.

172 See for this position eg United States, Court of Appeals for the 5th Circuit, *Jimenez v Aristeguieta*, 12 December 1962, 311 F 2d 547 (1962); Switzerland, Federal Tribunal, *Marcos and Associates v Chambre d'Accusation*, 1 July 1987, 82 ILR 53.

173 See paras 3.4.3 and 3.4.4.

174 Philippines, Supreme Court, *Arigo v Smith, Arigo and ors v Swift and ors*, 16 September 2014, ILDC 2315 (PH 2014).

175 ibid, para 25.

176 ibid, para 33.

in his personal private capacity for whatever damage he may have caused by his act done with malice and in bad faith, or beyond the scope of his authority or jurisdiction'.[177] However, claims against the commander of a US Navy Ship in respect of the environmental damage caused by the running aground of the ship on the Tubbataha Reefs in the Philippines, was considered to regard the commander in his official capacity as an officer of the US Navy.[178]

When the US Supreme Court ruled in the 2010 *Samantar* case that foreign state officials are not covered by the FSIA but that their immunity claims are to be decided under the common law, it did recognize that 'some actions against an official in his official capacity should be treated as actions against the foreign state itself, as the state is the real party in interest'.[179] Since then lower courts have indeed concluded in several cases that the foreign state officials before it were in fact sued in their official capacities. This has either led to dismissal of the case because the defendants were 'not the real parties in interest',[180] or to treating the case as one instigated against the foreign state, and application of the FSIA.[181]

In sum, whereas some courts regard any claim against a foreign state official in respect of acts attributable to the state as a case against the state, other courts perform a substantive test, determining whether the individual is sued in an official or private capacity. While domestic courts may usually not establish the scope of the authority of a foreign official when he or she has acted within the territory of his own state, the case law relating to acts of foreign officials on the territory of the forum state evidences that the courts regularly establish the personal responsibility of the official for acts that clearly can also be attributed to the state under the law of state responsibility.

This latter approach makes sense, and is also supported by the definition of functional immunity as adopted by the Appeals Chamber of the International Tribunal for the Former Yugoslavia in *Prosecutor v Blaškić*.[182] According to the Appeals Chamber state officials enjoy functional immunity because they 'are mere instruments of a State and their official action can only be attributed to the State. They cannot be the subject of sanctions or penalties for conduct that is not private but undertaken on behalf of a State. In other words, State officials cannot suffer the consequences of wrongful acts *which are not attributable to them personally* but to the State on whose behalf they act: they enjoy so-called "functional immunity"'.[183] Under this definition, functional immunity turns on the question of whether the individual bears individual responsibility for the vexed act and hence indeed on the capacity in which the individual can be sued. Notably, however, the 'attribution' approach of the UK House of Lords in the *Jones* case discussed above, has been sanctioned by the ECtHR in the 2014 decision in *Jones v United Kingdom*.[184]

Finally, it is to be noted that a couple of recent domestic court decisions expressed support for the position that functional immunity does not generally apply outside the civil law context of state immunity. We consider two of such judgments, each with a slightly different take on the issue.

177 ibid.

178 ibid, para 34.

179 *Samantar v Yousuf* (n 9) para 28.

180 See, eg, *Gomes v ANGOP, Angola Press Agency and ors* (n 151).

181 See, eg, United States, District Court for the District of Columbia, *Mohammadi and ors v Khamenei and ors*, 31 May 2013, ILDC 2261 (US 2013).

182 *Prosecutor v Blaškić*, IT-95-14, Judgment on the Request of the Republic of Croatia for Review of the Decision of Trial Chamber II of 18 July 1997.

183 *Prosecutor v Blaškić* IT-95-14, Judgment on the Request of the Republic of Croatia for Review of the Decision of Trial Chamber II of 18 July 1997 (ICTY, Appeals Chamber, 1997) para 38 (emphasis added).

184 ECtHR, *Jones and others v United Kingdom*, App Nos 34356/06 and 40528/06 (14 January 2014), paras 203, 204, 213.

'Abu Omar' case, General Prosecutor at the Court of Appeals of Milan v Adler and ors, Final appeal judgment, No 46340/2012, ILDC 1960 (IT 2012), 29th November 2012, Italy; Supreme Court of Cassation; 5th Criminal Section

The case results from the criminal prosecution of, *inter alia*, twenty-six US agents accused of having actively cooperated in the abduction of an Egyptian cleric who had been granted political asylum by Italy. The cleric was brought to a US airbase in Italy and flown to Germany, and then to Cairo, Egypt, where he was allegedly tortured by Egyptian authorities during his detention. Two were members of the US consular staff in Italy and they presented a request for acquittal on the grounds of, *inter alia*, the functional immunity they enjoyed.

> 23.2. […] the rules of the *Vienna Convention*, given that the treaty was ratified and made executive in Italy by law no. 804/67, are provisions of Italian legislation and as such are interpreted and applied by the Italian judge, and it is not possible to share the view put forward by petitioner De Sousa who, on this point, has also cited authoritative theory and judgments reached by the UN's International Law Commission, that these rules could not be interpreted by the judges because it would rest solely with the originating State to determine whether or not the activities actually engaged in come under the heading of *consular functions*. […]
>
> 23.7. […] [I]nternational law cannot be seen as including a customary principle of [functional immunity]; there is a principle of sovereign states' immunity from civil jurisdiction, and this principle is codified in many treaties, but it is not possible to derive from this immunity an immunity from criminal jurisdiction which, obviously, cannot refer to States, but to individuals … To argue the existence of a customary rule in these circumstances is incorrect because there is no consolidated case law, there are no identifiable, progressive and concurring official statements by States and there is no unequivocal interpretation of legal theory […] It may be concluded therefore that the treatment applied in this area is characterised by such discontinuity that it is not possible to recognise a generally applicable rule; and indeed removal from foreign jurisdiction in the case of deployed State entities is contemplated in specific treaties, while in their absence functional immunity is not normally recognised by national jurisdictional bodies.

According to the court, the rule of functional immunity does not extend to criminal law, except when provided for in a specific treaty like the VCCR, VCDR, or Status of Forces agreements. The court herewith changes its position as set out in the 2008 *Lozano* case.[185] The court also rejected the defendants claim to consular immunity, as discussed in section V.2 below.

In a later case concerning the same facts, the court held that the CIA agents that were posted as US diplomats to Italy at the time of the alleged crimes could not rely on the functional immunity of Article 39(2) VCDR. First, the court again pointed out that the question of whether acts were committed in the exercise of diplomatic functions fell within the exclusive domain of the judiciary, and that the Italian courts should not rely on the opinion of the sending state.[186] It then held that the kidnapping did not qualify as the exercise of diplomatic functions since the kidnapping had been done in the capacity as CIA agents and the entire operation had been planned and implemented through the organizational structure of the CIA.[187]

185 Italy, Court of Cassation, *Lozano (Mario Luiz) v Italy*, 24 July 2008, ILDC 1085 (IT 2008) para 5.

186 Italy, Supreme Court of Cassation, *In the matter of criminal proceedings against Medero and ors, Medero and ors v Nasr (aka Abu Omar) and Ghali*, 25 September 2014, ILDC 2239 (IT 2014) paras 2.1–2.2.

187 ibid, para 2.2.

Khurts Bat and Mongolia (intervening) v Investigating Judge of the German Federal Court and Secretary of State for Foreign and Commonwealth Affairs (intervening), Appeal decision, [2011] EWHC 2029 (Admin), [2012] 3 WLR 180, [2011] All ER (D) 293, [2011] ACD 111, ILDC 1779 (UK 2011), 29th July 2011, United Kingdom; England and Wales; High Court [HC]; Queen's Bench Division [QBD]; Administrative Court

The head of the Mongolian Intelligence Service was arrested by the UK police following an arrest warrant issued by Germany. Bat was accused of abducting a Mongolian national in Germany and transferring him to Mongolia, where he was subsequently imprisoned and tortured. Bat argued, *inter alia*, that he enjoyed functional immunity in relation to the alleged crimes. The court had regard to the position of ILC Special Rapporteur Kolodkin.

> 70. [...] there is a dearth of cases which have decided that an official acting on behalf of a State is entitled to immunity from criminal prosecution in respect of an offence committed in the forum state. [...]
>
> 96. [...] But the question whether immunity *ratione materiae* exists where a crime is perpetrated in the territory of the State which exercises jurisdiction is a separate question. The Special Rapporteur's conclusion in that respect is: "A situation where criminal jurisdiction is exercised by a State in whose territory an alleged crime has taken place, and this State has not given its consent to the performance in its territory of the activity which led to the crime and to the presence in its territory of the foreign official who committed this alleged crime, stands alone in this regard as a special case. It would appear that in such a situation there are sufficient grounds to talk of an absence of immunity." (page 59) (and see paragraph 90)
>
> 97. The Special Rapporteur, Roman Kolodkin, takes the view that consent of the receiving State, not only to the discharge of function, but the presence of the foreign official in its territory, is crucial (see paragraph 82). He draws the distinction between those cases where the receiving State consents in advance to the presence of a foreign official operating in the receiving State's territory and those cases where the State has not given its consent to the presence of a foreign official and his presence is unknown. Where a State has consented to the presence and activity of a foreign official in its territory in advance, it has also consented in advance to the immunity of that person in connection with his official activity. He continues: "If, though, there was no such consent, and the person is not only acting illegally but is present in the State territory illegally, then it is fairly difficult to assert immunity. Examples of this type of situation include espionage, acts of sabotage, kidnapping etc." [...]
>
> 101. For those reasons, I conclude there is no customary international law which affords this appellant immunity *ratione materiae* [...].

The take of the UK court on the limited scope of functional immunity differs from that of the Italian court. It held that functional immunity does not extend to the alleged crimes committed on the territory of the forum state in the course of activity to which that forum state did not consent. In other words, functional immunity in respect of crimes committed outside the forum state or within the forum state in the course of activity to which that state had consented was left untouched. The case thereby supports the position that domestic courts can identify the limits of authority of a foreign official when he or she has acted within the territory of the forum state, as discussed above, although it limits this position explicitly to the criminal law sphere. It is to be noted that the current ILC Rapporteur working on the topic approaches the issue in terms of an exception to functional immunity, akin to the territorial tort exception in the realm of the law of state immunity. The 2016 proposal for Draft Article 7 ('Crimes in respect of which immunity does not apply') reads: '1. Immunity shall not apply in relation to the following crimes: […] (iii) Crimes that cause harm to persons, including death and serious injury, or to property, when such crimes are committed in the territory of the forum State and the State official is present in said territory at the time that such crimes are committed'. In 2017, the Drafting Committee decided, however, to delete territorial crimes from Draft Article 7. The explanation of the chairperson does little to clarify the matter: 'the United Nations Convention on Jurisdictional Immunities does not contain such an exception for crimes, and that in any case the exception could not apply to acts *jure imperii*. Since it would only cover acts not performed in official capacity, some members considered the provision superfluous. Some members expressed the view that this was not an issue covered by 'exceptions' because there would be no immunity at all. Therefore there was no need to create an exception to something that did not exist in the first place. For these reasons, the Drafting Committee did not incorporate the proposed provision in draft article 7. Instead the commentaries will clarify that to the extent that these acts are subjected to the principle of territorial sovereignty, they do not enjoy immunity *ratione materiae*'.[188]

It is clear that international law on this point is in a state of flux.

2. Consular immunity

Article 43 VCCR[189] provides:

> 1. Consular officers and consular employees shall not be amenable to the jurisdiction of the judicial or administrative authorities of the receiving State in respect of acts performed in the exercise of consular functions.
>
> 2. The provisions of paragraph 1 of this article shall not, however, apply in respect of a civil action either: (*a*) arising out of a contract concluded by a consular officer or a consular employee in which he did not contract expressly or impliedly as an agent of the sending State; or (*b*) by a third party for damage arising from an accident in the receiving State caused by a vehicle, vessel or aircraft.

When the functions of a consular officer come to an end, his/her immunity terminates as well. As Article 53.4 VCCR stipulates, however, with respect to acts performed by a consular officer or a consular employee in the exercise of his/her functions, immunity from jurisdiction shall continue to subsist without limitation of time. Since the immunity of the consular officer during his/her term of office is limited to these functional acts anyhow, the difference between the immunity of an incumbent and a former consular officer is minimal.

The most contentious issue in regard to the scope of consular immunity is to what extent the commission of (serious) crimes may qualify as 'acts performed in the exercise of consular functions'. The following two cases serve to illustrate this point.

Commonwealth of Massachusetts v Jerez (Rafael), Appeal decision, 390 Mass 456 (Mass 1983), ILDC 1450 (US 1983), 17th November 1983, United States; Massachusetts

A consular officer, who on his way to a cultural event stopped at his consular offices to collect his national flag and some promotional literature entered a dispute with the building's security guard when leaving his office. When a police officer stepped in, a fight between the police officer and the consular officer followed. The consular officer was arrested for assault and battery on a police officer.

188 A Rajput, 'Immunity of State Officials from Foreign Criminal Jurisdiction', statement, International Law Commission, 69th Session, 20 July 2017, 11 http://legal.un.org/docs/?path=../ilc/documentation/english/statements/2017_dc_chairman_statement_iso.pdf&lang=E (last accessed 8 July 2018).

189 Consular officers may at time be sued as representatives of the state; in that case, the rule of state immunity applies.

> 6 […] The language of art. 5(b) [VCCR] defines "[c]onsular functions" in general terms inviting flexible construction. The clear import of such language as "furthering the development of […] cultural […] relations" is that it not be construed restrictively. "[A] narrow reading of the treaty would be inconsistent with its apparent purpose to eliminate the last vestiges of the notion that a consul was simply a 'commercial representative.'" *Heaney v. Government of Spain*, 445 F.2d 501, 505 (2d Cir. 1971). Applying art. 5(b) in a manner consistent with this clear import is appropriate, since doing so will foster the underlying purposes of the Vienna Convention to promote harmonious international relations.
>
> 7 The judge was warranted in concluding that Jerez was seeking to further cultural relations between the Dominican Republic and the United States, and engaged in his consular capacity, at the time of the alleged assault and battery. […]
>
> 13 To determine whether the intentional tort of an employee occurred within the scope of his employment "[w]hat must be shown is that the employee's assault was in response to the plaintiff's conduct which was presently interfering with the employee's ability to perform his duties successfully." *Miller v. Federated Dep't Stores, Inc.*, supra at 350. While Miller addressed employers' liability for acts by employees, we think that the standard set forth there applies in the context of the present case as well. […] The police officer's actions interfered with Jerez's unimpeded ability to attend the scheduled cultural gathering. Accordingly, Jerez's alleged wrongful conduct occurred in response to conduct which was presently interfering with his ability to exercise his consular functions successfully. Under the agency principle established in *Miller*, therefore, Jerez was acting within the scope of his authority when the altercation occurred […]

The court arguably construed the functional immunity of consular officers too broadly. It is without a doubt accepted that violations of (criminal) law of the receiving state may qualify as official acts for consular immunity purposes. A prominent example is provided by the Italian *Rissmann* case.[190] The case concerned a German Consul that had issued a passport and travel documents for a minor resident in Italy and assisted her to leave Italy in order to join her father, a German national resident in Germany. While the minor was a German national under German law and a German court had entrusted guardianship to her father, under Italian law she was an Italian national and an Italian court had entrusted her to her mother, resident in Genoa. Criminal proceedings were instituted against the Consul. In an official memorandum, the German Embassy in Rome objected that Rissmann had acted in the exercise of his functions and invoked consular immunity on his behalf. In response to the claim of immunity the Italian court first considered the nature of the concept of consular immunity. It held that 'functional immunity … finds its justification in the general principle according to which the consul's acts, even though they may be valid within the legal system of the receiving State and thus produce legal consequences therein, constitute an activity of the sending State and not of the consul personally, since, in the exercise of his office he is accountable to his government. Such an immunity is not, therefore, merely procedural. It is based on a principle of substantive law and continues even after his tour of office has terminated'.[191] With regard to the acts violating Italian criminal law the court considered that 'there can be no doubt that Rissmann, in issuing her with a German passport, was carrying out a true and proper official act as Consul … It should not be forgotten that Consuls, being State agents operating abroad, do not exceed

190 Italy, Tribunal of Genoa, *Re Rissmann*, 6 May 1970, (1971) 54 RDI 702; Court of Cassation, 28 February 1972, (1973) 9 RDIPP 121; see 71 ILR 577 for both judgments.

191 Tribunal of Genoa, 71 ILR 577, 581.

the scope of their functions when they act in accordance with the laws of their country which they must comply with in so far as these laws are to be applied abroad. ... There can be no doubt that the German Federal Republic, in the aforementioned memorandum of its Embassy in Rome had fully assumed responsibility for the Consul's action, as it complied with the provisions of the German legal system to which Rissmann's conduct was required to conform'.[192] The Court of Cassation affirmed the decision underlining that the agent had acted 'within the limits of his functions' carrying out 'acts proper to his office'.[193]

However, the facts of the *Jerez* case are markedly different. The assault of the police officer did as such not qualify as a consular function. Rather, the court held that since the assault was in reaction to conduct impeding the consular officer to perform his functions, it was performed in the exercise of consular functions[194] and hence immune under Article 43 VCCR.

Notably, in 1987 another US court came to a very different conclusion in a case strikingly similar on the facts. *Gerritsen v De La Madrid* concerned a civil suit against several Mexican consular officers on allegations of having unlawfully impeded a protest against the Mexican President near the Consulate in Los Angeles.[195] The allegations included striking with a heavy metal object, threatening with a club and gun, kidnapping and interrogating the protester, and forcibly taking his leaflets and camera. The officers' claim that the alleged acts qualified as official acts for which they enjoyed immunity was rejected. The court considered that the consular functions at issue in the case were explicitly circumscribed by normative limits in Article 5 VCCR. Subsections (a) and (m) of this article provide that consular functions consist of 'protecting in the receiving State the interests of the sending State and its nationals [...], within the limits permitted by international law' and 'performing any other functions entrusted to a consular post by the sending State which are not prohibited by the laws and regulations of the receiving State'. The court concluded that since the suppressing of the freedom of speech on political matters violates international law, and assault with a deadly weapon and kidnapping violate US penal laws, the alleged acts could not have been performed in the exercise of consular functions.[196]

'Abu Omar' case, General Prosecutor at the Court of Appeals of Milan v Adler and ors, Final appeal judgment, No 46340/2012, ILDC 1960 (IT 2012), 29th November 2012, Italy; Supreme Court of Cassation; 5th Criminal Section

For the facts of this case, see section V.1 above. The two members of the US consular staff also based their requests for acquittal on the grounds of the consular immunity they enjoyed. The court set out to interpret the notion of 'consular functions' in Article 43, in accordance with Article 5 VCCR.

> 23.4. [...] [I]n general terms the first paragraph [of article 5] states an obvious fact, i.e. that consular officials must act in the interests of their State of origin and its citizens, in the sense that, being representatives of that State, they cannot and must not take any action that might cause it harm.
>
> This is a general rule, the significance of which is that consular officials must pursue the interests of their State of origin in all the activities demanded of them and that this is stated in the successive paragraphs of art. 5.

192 ibid, 582–83.

193 ibid, 583.

194 VCCR, Article 5.b provides: 'Consular functions consist in furthering the development of commercial, economic, cultural and scientific relations between the sending state and the receiving state and otherwise promoting friendly relations between them in accordance with the provisions of the present Convention'.

195 United States, Court of Appeals for the 9th Circuit, 1987, *Gerritsen v De La Madrid*, 18 June 1987, 101 ILR 478.

196 ibid, 481–82.

> Certainly the provision cannot be interpreted in the sense that its consuls are permitted to carry out any action provided it is in the interests of their State of origin.
>
> Indeed, the following paragraphs of art. 5 state clearly what consular functions are permitted, examples of which range from promoting the development of commercial, economic, cultural and scientific relations between the State of origin and that of residence, to obtaining information on commercial conditions, the issuing of travel documents and passports, providing assistance to the citizens of the State of origin, and performing notary functions,
>
> Two aspects are highlighted: the first is that they involve typically administrative tasks, aimed primarily at promoting the commercial activities of the represented country and at providing assistance to the citizens thereof who are in difficulties in the country of residence; the second aspect worthy of note is that many activities — for example, those referred to in letters f), g), h), i), j), k) and l) of art. 5 — are governed by the specific rule that the various functions must be performed *"with respect to the laws and regulations of the State of residence"*.
>
> Moreover, letter m) of art. 5 of the *Vienna Convention* permits consuls to exercise any other function required of a consular official by the State of origin *"that is not forbidden by the laws and regulations of the State of residence, or which the State of residence does not oppose to* [...]."
>
> This is a so-called final regulation which, very clearly, stipulates that the interests of the Country of origin may be protected by the consul exercising the functions listed in art. 5 of the *Convention* within the limits permitted not only by the laws, but also by the regulations, of the State of residence, unless the latter has also given consent to the performance of illegal actions, or *actions against the law*, on its own territory.
>
> 23.5. From what has been said above it can be seen quite clearly that the detention of a person in order to then take him/her to a place where it is possible to submit him/her to interrogation using brutal methods — torture — does not come under the consular functions and is contrary to Italian law, so Lady and De Sousa cannot be recognised as having any consular immunity.

The Court of Cassation did not follow the highly problematic reasoning of the lower court that had concluded from Articles 41 and 43 VCCR that the Convention did not provide consular immunity for 'grave crimes'.[197] The Court of Cassation correctly pointed out that the 'grave crime' exception of Article 41 only relates to inviolability and does not in any way detract from the immunity provided for in Article 43.[198] Consular officers are amenable to suit for all acts performed outside the exercise of their functions. Article 41 provides that as a rule, they can nevertheless not be arrested and detained during trials in respect of these acts, except in case of a grave crime.

Since there was no immunity under the VCCR, the court turned to the more general question of functional immunity, discussed in section V.1 above.

VI. Tension between Immunity Rules and Fundamental Rights under Domestic Constitutional Law or International Human Rights and Criminal Law

The tension between immunity from jurisdiction and the right of individuals to have their case heard in court is unmistakable. Indeed, 200 years ago, when the US Supreme Court heard the *Schooner Exchange* case, the lawyer of the original owners of the ship exclaimed: 'Your own

197 Italy, Tribunal of Milan, *Public Prosecutor v Adler and Ors* (*'Abu Omar'* case), 1 February 2010, ILDC 1492 (IT 2010).

198 Italy, Supreme Court of Cassation, *'Abu Omar' case, General Prosecutor at the Court of Appeals of Milan v Adler and Ors*, 29 November 2012, ILDC 1960 (IT 2012) paras 23.3–23.4.

citizens plundered. Your national rights violated. Your courts deaf to the complaints of the injured. Your government not redressing their wrongs, but giving a sanction to their spoliators.'[199] The 'access to court' argument against immunity rules is still regularly invoked in judicial proceedings. In recent years, a different type of human rights based argument against immunity rules has been brought before the courts. It has been argued that states that violate *jus cogens* norms, or state officials that commit international crimes, cannot successfully invoke the immunity defense in proceedings before foreign domestic courts.

This section will first discuss domestic court practice concerning the right of access to court (1), both in terms of a right under constitutional law (a) and in terms of a right under international human rights law (b). Subsequently, the case law concerning the question of the applicability of immunity rules in cases concerning alleged *jus cogens* violations or international crimes will be discussed (2), both as regards states (a) and state officials (b).

1. Access to court

(a) Domestic constitutional law

There is considerable tension between immunity rules and fundamental rights of individuals. That tension partly explains the abandonment or rejection of the absolute state immunity rule. Courts around the world agreed that 'it is necessary in the interest of justice to individuals having transactions with states to allow them to bring such transactions before the courts'.[200] The Indian Supreme Court explicitly invoked domestic constitutional norms in order to circumscribe the discretion granted to the government by domestic legislation in deciding state immunity questions. Section 86(1) of the Indian Code of Civil Procedure provides that '[n]o Ruler of a foreign state may be sued in any court otherwise competent to try the suit except without the consent of the Central Government certified in writing by the Secretary of State'—and this provision has been interpreted to apply to proceedings against foreign states as well.[201] In *Harbhajan Singh Dhalla v Union of India*, the Indian Supreme Court held that the exercise of jurisdiction over non-sovereign acts of foreign states 'would be in conformity with the principles of international law as recognised as part of our domestic law and in accordance with our Constitution and human rights, the power given to the central Government must not be exercised arbitrarily or on whimsical grounds but upon proper reasons and grounds'. The court added that such exercise of jurisdiction would moreover 'be in consonance with human rights'.[202]

With the adoption of a restrictive approach to the rule of state immunity the discussion has not come to an end. For one, there are still immunity rules that are almost absolute, like the personal immunity protecting diplomats or heads of state. French courts have recognized in a handful of cases that in exceptional circumstances the application of the law of diplomatic immunity may engage the responsibility of the receiving state towards the individual whose access to court is barred.[203] The responsibility is framed in terms of a breach of the principle of equality of citizens in bearing public burdens in cases where the application of customary international law causes a serious and special harm. In a 2011 judgment, the French Council of State again confirmed the principle and held the French state responsible for the damage to an individual as a result of the application of the rule of immunity from execution.[204] A German court avoided answering the question of whether the forum state could be held responsible by an individual

199 United States, Supreme Court, *Schooner Exchange and Bonaparte (on the application of United States) v McFaddon and Greetham*, 24 February 1812, ILDC 1378 (US 1812), for the quote see 11 US 116 (US 1812) 128.

200 United Kingdom, House of Lords, *I Congreso del Partido* (1983) 1 AC 244, 262.

201 India, Supreme Court, *Mirza Ali Akbar Kashani v United Arab Republic* (1965) 64 ILR 489.

202 India, Supreme Court, *Harbhajan Singh Dalla v Union of India* (1986) 92 ILR 530, 536–37.

203 France, Council of State, *Dame Burgat et autres*, 1976, 104 (1977) JDI 630; *Tizon et Millet*, 1984, 31 (1985) AFDI 928; Administrative Court of Appeals of Paris, 16 July 1992, (1992) RGDIP 238.

204 France, Council of State, *Om Hashem D (Saleh) and Others v France*, 14 October 2011, ILDC 2074 (FR 2011).

whose access to court is blocked by the diplomatic immunity rule. Since the limitation is a territorial and temporal one, not an absolute one, the court ruled, the question of the responsibility of the forum state did not have to be addressed.[205] In the following 1988 case, a US court refused to find a clash between constitutional due process guarantees and diplomatic immunity, but on such limited grounds that it could be seen to in fact support the argument.

Fernandez v Fernandez, Appeal judgment, 545 A.2d. 1036 (Conn 1988), ILDC 1385 (US 1988), 19th July 1988, United States; Connecticut; Supreme Court [Conn]

Mozambique waived the immunity of one of its diplomats so as to allow the US courts to entertain the request of the diplomat's wife to dissolve their marriage. The waiver did not, however, regard monetary claims arising out of the marital dissolution.

> 24 The final question is whether, on remand, the trial court will have authority to award the plaintiff support payments and whatever ancillary monetary relief seems appropriate. In support of jurisdiction over her claims, the plaintiff relies not on a specific treaty provision, as was the case regarding real property, but instead on her alleged due process right of access to a judicial forum for a resolution of all disputes arising out of a marital dissolution. She maintains that the residual immunity conferred upon the defendant in this case must give way to her right of access guaranteed by the fourteenth amendment to the United States constitution. *See Boddie v. Connecticut*, 401 U.S. 371, 377–79, 91 S. Ct. 780, 28 L. Ed. 2d 113 (1971).
>
> 25 This claim raises serious concerns about the interrelationship of two equally valid federal laws: constitutional principles safeguarding individual rights and treaty provisions preserving the inviolability of diplomatic agents. As a general rule, a treaty provision that contravenes "any of the prohibitions or limitations of the Constitution applicable to the exercise of authority by the United States" is null and void. 1 Restatement (Third), The Foreign Relations Law of the United States (1987) § 302(2) […] The United States Supreme Court has "regularly and uniformly recognized the supremacy of the Constitution over a treaty." […] The reason for this rule is that the federal government, as a creature of the constitution, must exercise its authority within the limitations proscribed by its charter. […]
>
> 26 Presumably, the right enunciated in *Boddie*, which springs from the due process clause of the fourteenth amendment, applies against the federal government through the due process clause of the fifth amendment. *Boddie* thus constitutes, in the language of the Restatement, a limitation "applicable to the exercise of authority by the United States." We nevertheless face a troubling uncertainty as to the scope of *Boddie*: Does the right of access to dissolve a marriage include the right of access to obtain proprietary relief incident to divorce? We think not. The focus of the Supreme Court in *Boddie* was squarely on the "fundamental human relationship" of marriage. […] "The denial of access to the judicial forum in *Boddie* touched directly […] on the marital relationship and on the associational interests that surround the establishment and dissolution of that relationship." […] The plaintiff offers no direct authority to the contrary and we have found none. We therefore decline to expand the holding of *Boddie* beyond its factual boundaries of the marital status. Accordingly, no conflict exists between the federal constitution and the Vienna Convention in this case.

The court avoided a clash between the Constitution and the VCDR by a restrictive interpretation of the right of access to court. One cannot but wonder what would have been the outcome had the state *not* waived immunity for the dissolution of the marriage.

205 Germany, Higher Regional Court, *Diplomatic immunity for alleged labour exploitation case, Pfarr (on behalf of National of Indonesia) v Anonymous*, 9 November 2011, ILDC 1903 (DE 2011) para 25 ff.

Individuals do at times argue that also the restrictive state immunity rule infringes their constitutional rights. Courts are, however, generally reluctant to find a clash between the restrictive rule of state immunity and constitutional rights of individuals. A notable exception is the following 2014 judgment of the Italian Constitutional Court.

Simoncioni and ors v Germany and President of the Council of Ministers of the Italian Republic (intervening), Constitutional review, Judgment No 238/2014, ILDC 2237 (IT 2014), 22nd October 2014, Italy; Constitutional Court

Italian nationals sued Germany before the Tribunal of Florence in respect of war crimes committed by Germany in Italy during WWII. After the ICJ Judgment in *Jurisdictional Immunities*,[206] Italian courts, including the Court of Cassation, had felt compelled to grant immunity to Germany in similar cases. The Tribunal of Florence, however, raised a question of constitutionality with the Constitutional Court: is the international law rule affording state immunity for war crimes and crimes against humanity compatible with Articles 2 and 24 of the Italian Constitution?

> 3.2 […] [T]here is no doubt that the fundamental principles of the constitutional order and inalienable human rights constitute a "limit to the introduction […] of generally recognized norms of international law, to which the Italian legal order conforms under Article 10, para. 1 of the Constitution" […] and serve as 'counter-limits' [*controlimiti*] to the entry of European Union law […] as well as limits to the entry of the Law of Execution of the Lateran Pacts and the Concordat […] In other words, they stand for the qualifying fundamental elements of the constitutional order. […]
>
> 3.4 […] Article 10, para. 1 of the Constitution […] requires that this Court ascertain whether the customary international norm of immunity from the jurisdiction of foreign States, as interpreted in the international legal order, can be incorporated into the constitutional order, as it does not conflict with fundamental principles and inviolable rights. [On the contrary], if there were a conflict, "the referral to the international norm [would] not operate" (Judgment No. 311/2009). Accordingly, the incorporation, and thus the application, of the international norm would inevitably be precluded, insofar as it conflicts with inviolable principles and rights. […]
>
> This Court has repeatedly observed that the fundamental principles of the constitutional order include the right to appear and to be defended before a court of law in order to protect one's rights guaranteed by Article 24, i.e. the right to a judge. This is especially true when the right at issue is invoked to protect fundamental human rights. […]
>
> Nonetheless, precisely with regard to cases of immunity from jurisdiction of States envisaged by international law, this Court has recognized that, in cases involving foreign States, the fundamental right to judicial protection can be further limited, beyond the limitations provided by Article 10 of the Constitution. However, this limit has to be justified by reasons of public interest potentially prevailing over the principle of Article 24 Constitution, one of the "supreme principles" of the constitutional order (Judgment No. 18/1982). Moreover, the provision that establishes the limit has to guarantee a rigorous assessment of the [public] interest in light of the concrete case (Judgment No. 329/1992).

206 *Jurisdictional Immunities of the State* (n 6). See R Pavoni, '*Simoncioni v. Germany*: Italian Constitutional Court Decision on Law Implementing Immunity of Foreign States from War Crimes Compensation Claims in Accordance with 2012 ICJ Judgment' (2015) 109 AJIL 400.

In the present case, the customary international norm of immunity of foreign States, defined in its scope by the ICJ, entails the absolute sacrifice of the right to judicial protection, insofar as it denies the jurisdiction of [domestic] courts to adjudicate the action for damages put forward by victims of crimes against humanity and gross violations of fundamental human rights. This has been acknowledged by the ICJ itself, which referred the solution to this issue, on the international plane, to the opening of new negotiations, diplomatic means being considered the only appropriate method (para. 102, Judgment of 3 February 2012).

Moreover, in the constitutional order, a prevailing public interest that may justify the sacrifice of the right to judicial protection of fundamental rights (Articles 2 and 24 Constitution), impaired as they were by serious crimes, cannot be identified.

Immunity from jurisdiction of other States can be considered tenable from a legal standpoint, and even more so from a logical standpoint, and thus can justify on the constitutional plane the sacrifice of the principle of judicial protection of inviolable rights guaranteed by the Constitution, only when it is connected — substantially and not just formally — to the sovereign functions of the foreign State, i.e. with the exercise of its governmental powers.

Respect for fundamental principles and inviolable human rights, identifying elements of the constitutional order, is the limit that indicates (also with a view to achieving the goal of maintaining good international relations, inspired by the principles of peace and justice, for whose realization Italy agrees to limitations of sovereignty by virtue of Article 11 of the Constitution) the receptiveness of the Italian legal order to the international and supranational order (Articles 10 and 11 of the Constitution), as this Court has repeatedly upheld [. . .]. This in itself rules out that acts such as deportation, slave labor, and massacres, recognized to be crimes against humanity, can justify the absolute sacrifice in the domestic legal order of the judicial protection of inviolable rights of the victims of those crimes.

The immunity of the foreign State from the jurisdiction of the Italian judge granted by Articles 2 and 24 Constitution protects the [sovereign] function [of State]. It does not protect behaviors that do not represent the typical exercise of governmental powers, but are explicitly considered and qualified unlawful, since they are in breach of inviolable rights, as was recognized, in the present case, by the ICJ itself, and — before that Court — by the FRG [. . .]. These rights are deprived of an effective remedy, as acknowledged in the ICJ Judgment. The ICJ stated that it was not unaware "that the immunity from jurisdiction of Germany in accordance with international law may preclude judicial redress for the Italian nationals concerned" (para. 104), thus hoping for the re-opening of negotiations.

Therefore, in an institutional context characterized by the centrality of human rights, emphasized by the receptiveness of the constitutional order to external sources (Judgment No. 349/347), the denial of judicial protection of fundamental rights of the victims of the crimes at issue (now dating back in time), determines the completely disproportionate sacrifice of two supreme principles of the Constitution. They are indeed sacrificed in order to pursue the goal of not interfering with the exercise of the governmental powers of the State even when, as in the present case, state actions can be considered war crimes and crimes against humanity, in breach of inviolable human rights, and as such are excluded from the lawful exercise of governmental powers.

3.5 [. . .] [I]nsofar as the law of immunity from jurisdiction of States conflicts with the aforementioned fundamental principles [of the Constitution], it has not entered the Italian legal order and, therefore, does not have any effect therein.

While the Italian Court of Cassation had earlier ruled that there was no choice but to follow the 2012 ICJ judgment in *Germany v Italy*,[207] the Constitutional Court relied on the counter-limits doctrine[208] to protect the Italian domestic legal order from international rules that are incompatible with fundamental constitutional principles. In the subsequent *Flatow* case[209] and *Podrute Massacre case*,[210] the Court of Cassation followed the Constitutional Court, and even broadened the scope of applicability of the counter-limits doctrine in immunity cases by ruling that it applies irrespectively of the question of whether other judicial remedies were available or not.[211]

Denying effect to international law in the domestic legal order on the basis of domestic constitutional law may lead to violation of the international legal rule, and hence to international responsibility. The recourse to counter-limits in domestic law as a shield against international immunity rules follows earlier, unsuccessful attempts to formulate similar limits in terms of the right of access to court under *international* law.

(b) *International human rights law*

The tension between immunity rules and fundamental rights of individuals can also be cast in terms of a conflict of *international* norms, namely immunity rules on the one hand and international human rights obligations on the other. Notably, in 2012 the ICJ held in *Jurisdictional Immunities* that it could 'find no basis in the State practice from which customary international law is derived that international law makes the entitlement of a State to immunity dependent upon the existence of effective alternative means of securing redress. Neither in the national legislation on the subject, nor in the jurisprudence of the national courts which have been faced with objections based on immunity is there any evidence that entitlement to immunity is subjected to such a precondition'.[212] However, the question of whether a customary international law exception to the rule of state immunity has developed through state practice is fundamentally distinct from the question of whether the rule of state immunity *clashes* with the right of access to court.

In 2001 the ECtHR addressed the question of the relation between Article 6 ECHR and state immunity in the cases of *Al-Adsani v United Kingdom, McElhinney v Ireland*, and *Fogarty v United Kingdom*.[213] Applicants in all three cases had argued that the refusal of domestic courts to entertain their claims because of the state immunity rule had violated their right of access to court under Article 6 ECHR. The ECtHR rejected the argument. It held that the Convention could not 'be interpreted in a vacuum' and that it 'should so far as possible be interpreted in harmony with other rules of international law of which it forms part, including those relating

---

207 Italy, Court of Cassation, *Military Prosecutor v Albers and ors and Germany (joining)*, 9 August 2012, ILDC 1921 (IT 2012); Italy, Court of Cassation, *Frascà v Germany and Giachini (guardian of Priebke) and Italy (joining)*, 21 February 2013, ILDC 1998 (IT 2013).

208 See more generally G Martinico, 'National Courts and Judicial Disobedience to the ECHR: A Comparative Overview' in O Mjöll Arnardóttir and A Buyse (eds), *Shifting Centres of Gravity in Human Rights Protection: Rethinking Relations between the ECHR, EU and National Legal Orders* (Routledge 2016) 59–78.

209 Italy, Court of Cassation, *Flatow and ors v Iran and Iranian Ministry of Information and Security and Ministry of Foreign Affairs of Italy (intervening)*, 28 October 2015, ILDC 2459 (IT 2015).

210 Italy, Court of Cassation, *Podrute Massacre case*, 29 October 2015, ILDC 2536 (IT 2015). For an earlier case where the argument at stake was denied in the context of an employment dispute, see Italy, Court of Cassation, *Cargnello v Italy*, 20 June 2005, ILDC 557 (IT 2005).

211 *Podrute Massacre case* (n 210) para 5.2.7. In *Flatow* (n 209), the principle was also stated in such broad terms: 'This judgment [No 238/2014 of the Constitutional Court] barred the entry into our system of the customary rule of state immunity, to the extent that it extends immunity to actions for damages resulting from acts or behaviors recognized as war crimes and crimes against humanity which are detrimental to inviolable rights of the person' (para 4). See R Pavoni, 'How Broad Is the Principle Upheld by the Italian Constitutional Court in Judgment No. 238?' (2016) 14 *Journal of International Criminal Justice* 573.

212 *Jurisdictional Immunities of the State* (n 6) para 101.

213 ECtHR, *Al-Adsani v United Kingdom*, App No 35763/97 (21 November 2001); *McElhinney* (n 65); *Fogarty* (n 52).

to the grant of State immunity'.[214] 'It follows', the court reasoned, 'that measures taken by a High Contracting Party which reflect generally recognised rules of public international law on State immunity cannot in principle be regarded as imposing a disproportionate restriction on the right of access to a court as embodied in Article 6 § 1. Just as the right of access to a court is an inherent part of the fair trial guarantee in that Article, so some restrictions on access must likewise be regarded as inherent, an example being those limitations generally accepted by the community of nations as part of the doctrine of State immunity'.[215] Since the court, with a very narrow majority, concluded that under international law state immunity continues to apply to *jus cogens* violations (see section VI.2 below), the access to court argument also failed. By contrast, the cases of *Cudak v Lithuania*,[216] *Guadagnino v Italy and France*,[217] and *Sabeh El Leil v France*[218] evidence that the court *will* find a violation of Article 6 if a domestic court grants state immunity in excess of the requirements under international law.

In a couple of pre-*Al-Adsani* domestic cases, such as the Austrian case discussed below, relevance *was* given to the question of whether remedies alternative to those of the forum were available to the individual claimants. However, since the *Al-Adsani* judgment, domestic courts tend to follow the ECtHR on this point.[219]

Anita W v Johannes Adam II, Prince of Liechtenstein, Final Appeal/Cassation, 7 Ob 316/00x, ILDC 1 (AT 2001), 14th February 2001, Austria; Supreme Court of Justice [OGH]

The head of state of Liechtenstein, his sister, and his two brothers were sued by an Austrian national claiming to be their child and sister, respectively, and applying for an affiliation order before the Austrian courts.

> 16) [. . .] [A]ny litigation on the said issues, exclusively relating to constitutional and civil rights, should be brought before a domestic court in the home country of the foreign Head of State, i.e. a court in Liechtenstein [. . .] These issues, however, cannot override the issue of (absolute) immunity under international law, which takes precedence here, and so cannot, as a rule, permit litigation abroad [. . .] In the light of the statements by the authors quoted (Martiny and Delbrück/Wolfrum), only if such an (affiliation) suit were barred and the (illegitimate) child was denied this option in the home country of the Head of State, for reasons of legal procedure for example, would the civil rights issues override those of international law and thereby (be able to) possibly override an exemption based on immunity. Only in such a case would the plaintiff in these proceedings be entitled to a judicial ruling on the claim under the terms of obligations under human rights law, to which, under certain circumstances, immunity regulations have to defer (Lüke, loc. cit. 384). However not even the Plaintiff

214 *Al-Adsani* (n 213) para 55.

215 ibid, para 56.

216 *Cudak* (n 52).

217 *Guadagnino* (n 52).

218 *Sabeh El Leil* (n 52).

219 Belgium, Brussels Court of Appeal, *Iraq v Vinci Constructions* (n 100); UK, High Court, Queen's Bench Division, Commercial Court, *AIG Capital Partners Inc and CJSC Tema Real Estate Co Ltd v Kazakhstan and ors*, 21 October 2005, ILDC 94 (UK 2005), see section III.4(c) above; France, Court of Cassation, Civil Division, *Société NML Capital v Argentina*, 28 March 2013, ILDC 2075 (FR 2013); Belgium, Court of First Instance, *V and 39 other plaintiffs v Holy See and ors*, 1 October 2013, ILDC 2739 (BE 2013); Italy, Court of Cassation, *Lasaracina* (n 54); Italy, Court of Cassation, *Embassy of Spain to the Holy See v de la Grana Gonzales* (n 54). For a controversial application of the principle upheld by the ECtHR, see Albania, Supreme Court, *Haxhiaj v Chemonics International Incorporated*, 10 June 2011, ILDC 2507 (AL 2011). UK courts have expressed doubts as to the approach of the ECtHR, by evoking the possibility that 'there is not even a prima facie breach of article 6 if a state fails to make available a jurisdiction which it does not possess': *Jones v Ministry of the Interior of Saudi Arabia* (n 165) para 64, following the reasoning of Lord Millett in United Kingdom, House of Lords, *Holland v Lampen-Wolfe*, 20 July 2000, ILDC 223 (UK 2000).

herself argued that recourse to legal proceedings in Liechtenstein was barred and nor is there any other documentary evidence for this.

According to the court, the right of access to justice may prevail over head of state immunity should the plaintiff be barred from legal proceedings in the head of state's home state. The argument recalls the 'reasonable alternative means' doctrine that the ECtHR introduced in *Waite and Kennedy v Germany* in the context of the immunity of international organizations.[220]

As said, however, the ECtHR has in 2001 clarified that the *Waite and Kennedy* doctrine does not apply to the immunity of states and their officials, and many domestic courts have followed suit. Yet one Belgian court seemed to argue in 2008 that it did consider the availability of reasonable alternative means relevant to assessing the relation between diplomatic immunity and the right of access to court.[221]

2. Immunity for alleged international crimes/*jus cogens* violations

This section includes a selection of cases concerning the existence and/or emergence of 'human rights/international crimes exceptions or derogations' to the immunities enjoyed by states and state officials, which in recent times is no doubt the most debated topic in this area of the law. The two subsections below respectively address (a) state immunity for *jus cogens* violations, and (b) foreign official immunity for international crimes. While the general issue appears the same, ie whether international immunities may be denied by domestic courts when the defendant is accused of egregious breaches of fundamental human rights, it is, however, necessary to distinguish the treatment of foreign official immunity from that of state immunity. This is certainly a consequence of the fact that these two types of immunities are best viewed as autonomous doctrines of international law. Unlike states, it should be recalled that individual state officials: (i) enjoy different types of immunities, according to their status (immunity *ratione materiae* and immunity *ratione personae*); (ii) may be subject to both criminal and civil foreign jurisdiction; and (iii) are accountable before domestic courts under the customary law principle of individual criminal responsibility for international crimes. As shown by the cases discussed below, these distinctive features imply that, unlike state immunity, a single, across-the-board solution is inapplicable in the field of foreign official immunity for international crimes.

(a) State immunity for jus cogens *violations*

The argument that states cannot rely on the rule of state immunity when they stand accused of *jus cogens* violations first surfaced in US courts. While the argument met with some sympathy of the courts, it was invariably dismissed as incompatible with the US FSIA. In *Siderman de Blake v Argentina*, where the defendant state was accused of torture, the Ninth Circuit Court of Appeals held for example that '[a]s a matter of international law, the [. . .] argument carries much force. [. . .] Unfortunately, we do not write on a clean slate. We deal not only with customary international law, but with an affirmative Act of Congress, the FSIA'.[222]

The question of whether indeed under customary international law such a *jus cogens* exception to state immunity exists has been dealt with differently in a number of jurisdictions. The ECtHR concluded in its 2001 judgment in *Al-Adsani* that: '[n]otwithstanding the special character of the prohibition of torture in international law, the Court is unable to discern in the international instruments, judicial authorities or other materials before it any firm basis for concluding that, as a matter of international law, a State no longer enjoys immunity from civil suit in the courts

---

220 ECtHR, *Waite and Kennedy v Germany*, App No 26083/94 (18 February 1999) para 68.

221 Belgium, Brussels Court of Appeals, *Mr C v Mrs M* (n 130) paras 40–41. See also Belgium, Brussels Labour Court of Appeals, *BS and KG v AR and AR* (n 12).

222 United States, Court of Appeals for the 9th Circuit, *Siderman de Blake and ors v Argentina and ors*, 22 May 1992, ILDC 2171 (US 1992) para 49.

of another State where acts of torture are alleged'.[223] Several domestic courts that have dealt with this question have taken the same position.[224] In recent times, only Italian courts forcefully and consistently argued in a different vein. A joined commentary, which takes stock of the 2012 ICJ judgment in *Jurisdictional Immunities*,[225] will follow the extracts of two prominent cases representative of both schools—the Italian *Ferrini* case and the UK *Jones* case.

Ferrini v Germany, Appeal decision, Cass no 5044/04, ILDC 19 (IT 2004), 11th March 2004, Italy; Supreme Court of Cassation[226]

An Italian national claimed compensation from Germany for damages he had suffered as a result of his forced deportation and forced labour during the Second World War. The plaintiff's principal argument was that the rule on state immunity was inapplicable because the crimes imputed to Germany amounted to *jus cogens* violations. After recalling that the norms prohibiting forced labour and forced deportation are indeed non-derogable and that various other consequences—such as universal jurisdiction—are connected to the commission of international crimes, the Italian Supreme Court accepted the plaintiff's argument and concluded that state immunity had to be denied in the case at hand.

> 9.1. The recognition of immunity from jurisdiction for States that are responsible for such offences is in blatant contrast with the normative framework outlined above, since this recognition obstructs rather than protects such values, the protection of which is rather to be considered […] essential for the entire international community […] [T]here can be no doubt that this *antinomy* must be resolved by giving precedence to the higher-ranking norms […] This therefore rules out the possibility that in such hypotheses the State could enjoy immunity from foreign jurisdiction […]
>
> 9.2. […] Respect for inviolable human rights has by now attained the status of a fundamental principle of the international legal system […] And the emergence of this principle cannot but influence the scope of other principles that traditionally inform this legal system, particularly that of the "sovereign equality" of States, which constitutes the rationale for the recognition of State immunity from foreign civil jurisdiction. Indeed, legal rules should not be interpreted in isolation since they complement and integrate each other, and the application of one is dependent on the others […] [These] criteria [also] apply to the interpretation of customary norms, which like the others are part of a system and therefore may only be correctly understood in relation to other norms that form an integral part of the same legal system […].

Jones, Redress (intervening) and ors (intervening) v Ministry of the Interior of Saudi Arabia and Lieutenant Colonel Abdul Aziz, Appeal judgment, [2006] UKHL 26, [2006] 2 WLR 1424, [2007] 1 AC 270, [2007] 1 All ER 113, ILDC 521 (UK 2006), 14th June 2006, United Kingdom; House of Lords [HL]

Mr Jones and other claimants sued Saudi Arabia and certain Saudi officials in the UK courts on allegations of torture committed in that foreign state. They argued that the grant of state immunity (and of foreign official immunity) to Saudi Arabia (and its officials) violated their right

223 *Al-Adsani* (n 213) para 61.

224 See, eg, *Bouzari and ors v Iran* (n 27); Canada, Superior Court of Justice, 28 February 2005, *Arar v Syrian Arab Republic and Jordan (joining)*, ILDC 639 (CA 2005); *Jones v Ministry of the Interior of Saudi Arabia* (n 166); Poland, Supreme Court, *Natoniewski v Germany*, 29 October 2010, ILDC 1996 (PL 2010); *Cuiying Zhang v Jiang Zemin* (n 169).

225 *Jurisdictional Immunities of the State* (n 6).

226 For other Italian cases see, eg, Court of Cassation, *Germany v Mantelli and ors*, 29 May 2008 ILDC 1037 (IT 2008); *Lozano (Mario Luiz) v Italy* (n 184); *Germany v Autonomous Prefecture of Vojotia* (n 80).

of access to court under Article 6(1) ECHR. To demonstrate that the restriction on this right arising from the grant of immunity was illegitimate and/or disproportionate, they submitted that the ban on torture and the associated right to compensation for the victims amounted to international *jus cogens* norms. The House of Lords dismissed these claims and afforded immunity to both Saudi Arabia and its officials.

> 22 […] The *Ferrini* decision cannot in my opinion be treated as an accurate statement of international law as generally understood; and one swallow does not make a rule of international law. The more closely-reasoned decisions in *Bouzari* […] are to the contrary effect. […]
>
> 26 […] [T]he UN Immunity Convention of 2004 provides no exception from immunity where civil claims are made based on acts of torture […] Despite its embryonic status, this Convention is the most authoritative statement available on the current international understanding of the limits of state immunity in civil cases, and the absence of a torture or jus cogens exception is wholly inimical to the claimants' contention […]
>
> 27 […] [T]here is no evidence that states have recognised or given effect to an international law obligation to exercise universal jurisdiction over claims arising from alleged breaches of peremptory norms of international law, nor is there any consensus of judicial and learned opinion that they should. This is significant, since these are sources of international law. But this lack of evidence is not neutral: since the rule on immunity is well-understood and established, and no relevant exception is generally accepted, the rule prevails. […]
>
> 43 […] [T]here is no doubt that the prohibition on torture is a norm [of jus cogens] […] But the question is whether such a norm conflicts with a rule which accords state immunity […]
>
> 44 The jus cogens is the prohibition on torture. But the United Kingdom, in according state immunity to the Kingdom, is not proposing to torture anyone. Nor is the Kingdom, in claiming immunity, justifying the use of torture. It is objecting in limine to the jurisdiction of the English court to decide whether it used torture or not […].
>
> 63 […] [T]he Italian *Ferrini* case […] exhibits the same bare syllogistic reasoning as the judgment of the minority in *Al-Adsani* […] [T]he *Ferrini* case should be seen rather as giving priority to the *values* embodied in the prohibition of torture over the values and policies of the rules of state immunity. I think that this is a fair interpretation of what the court was doing and, if the case had been concerned with domestic law, might have been regarded by some as "activist" but would have been well within the judicial function. […] [T]he ordering of competing principles according to the importance of the values which they embody is a basic technique of adjudication. But the same approach cannot be adopted in international law, which is based upon the common consent of nations. It is not for a national court to "develop" international law by unilaterally adopting a version of that law which, however desirable, forward-looking and reflective of values it may be, is simply not accepted by other states […].

The controversy between the *Jones* and the *Ferrini* courts has been said to pivot on their different conception of the role of domestic courts in the international legal order.[227] Academic

227 A Roberts, 'Comparative International Law? The Role of National Courts in Creating and Enforcing International Law' (2011) 60 *ICLQ* 57.

doctrine is split along the same lines. In *Jurisdictional Immunities*,[228] the ICJ has firmly positioned itself in the *Jones* camp, and it is to be expected that this judgment will guide domestic court practice for the years to come.[229] The judgment has also been followed by the ECtHR in the 2014 case of *Jones v UK*.[230]

In a straightforward reliance on the two-pronged test for customary international law the ICJ first engaged in a detailed examination of state practice and *opinio juris*,[231] concluding that 'under customary international law as it presently stands, a State is not deprived of immunity by reason of the fact that it is accused of serious violations of international human rights law or the international law of armed conflict'.[232] Secondly, the Court addressed the argument that hierarchically higher *jus cogens* norms trump the rule of state immunity. Its rejection of the argument repeats the reasoning well rehearsed in doctrine over the years. The Court noted that the argument 'depends upon the existence of a conflict between a rule, or rules, of *jus cogens*, and the rule of customary law which requires one State to accord immunity to another', while 'no such conflict exists'.[233] According to the Court '[t]he two sets of rules address different matters. The rules of State immunity are procedural in character and are confined to determining whether or not the courts of one State may exercise jurisdiction in respect of another State. They do not bear upon the question whether or not the conduct in respect of which the proceedings are brought was lawful or unlawful'.[234] Finally, the Court rejected the argument that immunity should be denied because the proceedings brought before the Italian courts were the only outstanding remedy available to the victims.[235]

Of the twenty-two states that have until now ratified or acceded to the UNCSI, six have done so with a declaration referring to human rights.[236] In 2006 and 2009 respectively, Norway and Sweden declared that they 'understand [...] that the Convention is without prejudice to any future international development in the protection of human rights'. Switzerland stated in 2010 that the convention is 'without prejudice' to developments in international law in regards to serious human rights violations committed outside the state of the forum. Italy, acceding in 2013, announced that 'the Convention will be interpreted and applied in accordance with the principles of international law and, in particular, with the principles concerning the protection of human rights from serious violations', and Finland, ratifying in 2014, stated 'that the Convention is without prejudice to any future international legal development concerning the protection of human rights', a formulation more or less repeated by Liechtenstein when acceding in 2015.

(b) Foreign official immunity for international crimes

Criminal jurisdiction—personal immunity

In the *Arrest Warrant* case the ICJ held that it cannot be deduced from state practice 'that there exists under customary international law any form of exception to the rule according immunity from criminal jurisdiction and inviolability to incumbent Ministers for Foreign Affairs, where they are suspected of having committed war crimes or crimes against humanity'.[237] This has

228 *Jurisdictional Immunities of the State* (n 6).

229 See indeed Netherlands, Supreme Court, *Stichting Mothers of Srebrenica and Others v Netherlands and United Nations*, 13 April 2012, ILDC 1760 (NL 2012); *Kazemi* (n 73).

230 *Jones* (n 184) para 198.

231 *Jurisdictional Immunities of the State* (n 6) paras 83–90.

232 ibid, para 91.

233 ibid, para 93.

234 ibid.

235 See text with n 212.

236 All the following information is taken from https://treaties.un.org/Pages/ShowMTDSGDetails.aspx?src=UNTSONLINE&tabid=2&mtdsg_no=III-13&chapter=3&lang=en#EndDec (last accessed 8 July 2018).

237 *Arrest Warrant of 11 April 2000* (n 156), para 58.

been confirmed by domestic courts in cases against, for example, the then Libyan head of state Qadhafi;[238] the then Israeli head of government Sharon;[239] and the Sudanese head of state Al-Bashir.[240]

Criminal jurisdiction—functional immunity

The situation is less clear, however, in regards to state officials who are not (or no longer) protected by personal immunity rules. In the *Arrest Warrant* case the ICJ held that these officials can be sued for acts committed 'in a private capacity',[241] without giving guidance as to what acts qualify as such. And also in *Jurisdictional Immunities* the ICJ did not express an opinion on the scope of functional immunity in criminal proceedings. Several commentators have interpreted the *Arrest Warrant* case as an 'implicit rejection'[242] of an international crimes exception to functional immunity, since international crimes are, they argue, commonly committed in an official capacity. Without entering this debate here in any detail, it is good to note that that position follows from a particular conception of the rule of functional immunity. It was explained in section V.1 above that there is extensive state practice supporting the position that, for functional immunity purposes, official acts should be understood as acts for which an individual can only be sued in an official capacity since he or she bears no individual responsibility for their performance.[243] In any case, a number of domestic court decisions *have* recognized limits to functional immunity in respect of international crimes, and that position is now also the basis on which the ILC proceeds in its work on the topic of immunity of state officials from foreign criminal jurisdiction. We discuss below a couple of high profile cases in this area.

In its 1962 judgment in the *Eichmann* case, Israel's Supreme Court held that crimes against humanity 'are completely outside the "sovereign" jurisdiction of the State that ordered or ratified their commission, and therefore those who participated in such acts must personally account for them and cannot shelter behind the official character of their task or mission'. 'International law', the court continued, 'postulates that it is impossible for a State to sanction an act that violates its severe prohibitions, and from this follows the idea which forms the core of the concept of "international crime", that a person who was a party to such a crime must bear individual responsibility for it. If it were otherwise, the penal provisions of international law would be a mockery'.[244] After the *Eichmann* case, the question of functional immunity for international crimes was squarely addressed by English courts in the *Pinochet* case.

R., ex parte Pinochet v Bartle and ors, Appeal, [1999] UKHL 17, [2000] 1 AC 147, [1999] 2 All ER 97, [1999] 2 WLR 827, (1999) 38(3) ILM 581, (2002) 119 ILR 135, ILDC 1736 (UK 1999), 24th March 1999, United Kingdom; House of Lords [HL]

The former head of state of Chile, General Pinochet, was arrested by UK police when he visited the country for medical treatment. The UK acted upon a warrant for his arrest issued by a Spanish magistrate who wished to prosecute Pinochet for human rights abuses committed

238 France, Court of Cassation, *Re Qadhafi*, 13 March 2001, ILDC 774 (FR 2001).

239 *Re Sharon and Yaron* (n 161).

240 South Africa, Supreme Court of Appeal, *Minister of Justice and Constitutional Development and ors v The Southern African Litigation Centre*, 15 March 2016, ILDC 2533 (ZA 2016) para 84. See for other examples: United Kingdom, *Application for a Warrant for the Arrest of Robert Mugabe*, 14 January 2004, ILDC 96 (UK 2004); Sierra Leone, Supreme Court, *Sesay (Issa) and ors v President of the Special Court for Sierra Leone and ors, Original*, 14 October 2005, ILDC 199 (SL 2005); Netherlands, District Court, *The Hague City Party (De Haagse Stadspartij) and ors v Netherlands and ors*, 4 May 2005, ILDC 849 (NL 2005); Benin, *Legal Opinion*, Case No 029-C, 25 July 2003, ILDC 844 (BJ 2003); *Fang and ors v Jiang and ors* (n 168).

241 *Arrest Warrant* (n 156) para 61.

242 R O'Keefe, *International Criminal Law* (OUP 2015) 442–43. See also Fox and Webb (n 7) 558–61.

243 See for a more detailed discussion of this position eg R van Alebeek, 'National Courts, International Crimes and the Functional Immunity of State Officials' (2012) 59 *Netherlands International Law Review* 5.

244 Israel, Supreme Court, *Attorney-General of Israel v Adolf Eichmann*, 36 ILR 277, 309–10.

during his dictatorship. Pinochet challenged the arrest and extradition, arguing that he enjoyed immunity in respect of the alleged crimes.

Lord Hutton:

212 The crucial question for decision is whether, if committed, the acts of torture [. . .] alleged against Senator Pinochet were carried out by him in the performance of his functions as head of state. [. . .]

242 [. . .] [S]ince the end of the second world war there has been a clear recognition by the international community that certain crimes are so grave and so inhuman that they constitute crimes against international law and that the international community is under a duty to bring to justice a person who commits such crimes. Torture has been recognised as such a crime. [. . .]

253 [. . .] I do not consider that Senator Pinochet or Chile can claim that the commission of acts of torture after 29 September 1988 were functions of the head of state. The alleged acts of torture by Senator Pinochet were carried out under colour of his position as head of state, but they cannot be regarded as functions of a head of state under international law when international law expressly prohibits torture as a measure which a state can employ in any circumstances whatsoever and has made it an international crime. [. . .]

262 [. . .] I consider that under international law Chile is responsible for acts of torture carried out by Senator Pinochet, but could claim state immunity if sued for damages for such acts in a court in the United Kingdom. Senator Pinochet could also claim immunity if sued in civil proceedings for damages [. . .]

Lord Saville of Newdigate:

273 [. . .] [U]nless there exists, by agreement or otherwise, any relevant qualification or exception to the general rule of immunity ratione materiae, Senator Pinochet is immune from this extradition process. The only possible relevant qualification or exception in the circumstances of this case relates to torture. I am not persuaded that before the Torture Convention there was any such qualification or exception [. . .] [A]s between the states who are parties to the Convention, there is now an agreement that each state party will establish and have [. . .] jurisdiction over alleged torturers from other state parties [. . .]

278 It is important to bear in mind that the Convention applies (and only applies) to any act of torture "*inflicted by or at the instigation of or with the consent or acquiescence of a public official or other person acting in an official capacity*" [. . .]

279 To my mind it must follow in turn that a head of state, who for state purposes resorts to torture, would be a person acting in an official capacity within the meaning of the Convention [. . .]

280 It does not follow from this that the immunity enjoyed by a serving head of state, which is entirely unrelated to whether or not he was acting in an official capacity, is thereby removed in cases of torture. In my view it is not, since immunity ratione personae attaches to the office and not to any particular conduct of the office holder.

281 On the other hand, the immunity of a former head of state does attach to his conduct whilst in office and is wholly related to what he did in his official capacity.

282 So far as the states that are parties to the convention are concerned, I cannot see how, so far as torture is concerned, this immunity can exist consistently with the terms of that Convention. Each state party has agreed that the other state parties can exercise jurisdiction over alleged official torturers found within their territories . . . and

> thus, to my mind, can hardly simultaneously claim an immunity from extradition or prosecution that is necessarily based on the official nature of the alleged torture.
>
> Lord Millett:
>
> 333 […] In my opinion there was no immunity to be waived. The offence is one which could only be committed in circumstances which would normally give rise to the immunity. The international community had created an offence for which immunity ratione materiae could not possibly be available. International law cannot be supposed to have established a crime having the character of a jus cogens and at the same time to have provided an immunity which is coextensive with the obligation it seeks to impose.

All seven Law Lords issued an individual opinion and, while it is difficult to identify the *ratio decidendi* of the denial of immunity to the former head of state of Chile, most commentators agree that most of the six majority opinions rely in one way or the other on the specific terms of the 1984 Torture Convention.[245] The fact that torture in the sense of the Convention is by definition committed by a state official, and the fact that the Convention obliges states to exercise jurisdiction over suspected torturers also on the basis of the universality principle, were considered incompatible with continued functional immunity from criminal jurisdiction. In other words, the *Pinochet* case does not recognize an exception to functional immunity for all international crimes as a matter of principle.

Nevertheless, hopes were that the judgment would push a movement for a broader exception for international crimes generally. The Resolution on Immunities from Jurisdiction and Execution of Heads of State and of Government in International Law adopted by the *Institut de droit international* in 2001, provides that former heads of state 'may be prosecuted and tried when the acts alleged constitute a crime under international law'.[246] But the promise held by the *Pinochet* case did only slowly materialize in domestic court practice. A handful of courts recognized a limit to functional immunity on the basis of *jus cogens* reasoning,[247] which have scant precedential value in light of the ICJ *Arrest Warrant* judgment. A couple of other courts recognized the broader exception in *obiter dicta*.[248]

In spite of the limited practice and the lack of uniformity in the judicial reasoning in the cases that *are* there, the ILC Rapporteur found that 'the majority trend is to accept the existence of certain limitations and exceptions to such immunity, either in view of the gravity of the crimes, because they violate peremptory norms or undermine values of the international community as a whole, or because the crimes in question cannot be regarded as acts performed in an official capacity since they go beyond or do not correspond to the ordinary functions of the State'.[249] The Rapporteur's proposal to exclude functional immunity for international crimes[250] met with a mixed reception. While there was some support for it,[251] several members pointed out that it did not codify customary international law, but rather was an exercise of progressive development.[252] The disagreement within the Commission was evidenced by the adoption of Draft Article 7 by

245 Convention against Torture and Other Cruel, Inhuman or Degrading Treatment or Punishment (adopted 10 December 1984, in force 26 June 1987) 1465 UNTS 85.

246 Resolution IDI (n 148), Article 13.2.

247 See Italy, Court of Cassation, *Lozano (Mario Luiz)* (n 185); Switzerland, Federal Criminal Court, *A v Swiss Federal Public Prosecutor, B, and C*, 25 July 2012, ILDC 1933 (CH 2012).

248 See Austria, Supreme Court, *W v Prince of Liechtenstein and ors* (n 150) para 13; Netherlands, Court of Appeal, *In re Bouterse*, 20 November 2000, LJN: AA8395.

249 ILC, 'Fifth report on immunity of State officials from foreign criminal jurisdiction, by Concepción Escobar Hernández, Special Rapporteur' (2016) UN Doc A/CN.4/701, para 121.

250 ibid para 95.

251 ILC, 'Report of the International Law Commission on the Work of the Sixty-Eight Session' (2016) UN Doc A/71/10 para 235.

252 ibid, paras 214–16 and 238.

recorded vote. With twenty-one members voting in favour and eight members voting against, the following Draft Article was provisionally adopted.[253]

> Article 7
> Crimes under international law in respect of which immunity ratione materiae shall not apply
> 1. Immunity ratione materiae from the exercise of foreign criminal jurisdiction shall not apply in respect of the following crimes under international law:
>   (a) crime of genocide;
>   (b) crimes against humanity;
>   (c) war crimes;
>   (d) crime of apartheid;
>   (e) torture;
>   (f) enforced disappearance.
> 2. For the purposes of the present draft article, the crimes under international law mentioned above are to be understood according to their definition in the treaties enumerated in the annex to the present draft articles.

Since the majority of the members voting in favour reasoned in terms of progressive development rather than codification,[254] the adoption of Draft Article 7 does not as such support the position that there is no functional immunity for international crimes under international law.

Civil jurisdiction

There is a clear tendency to restrict the influence of international criminal law to immunity from criminal jurisdiction. In its judgment in *Jurisdictional Immunities*, the ICJ implicitly, and possibly inadvertently, provided support for the distinction between criminal and civil jurisdiction by stating that it was 'addressing only the immunity of the State itself from the jurisdiction of the courts of other States; the question of whether, and if so to what extent, immunity might apply in criminal proceedings against an official of the State is not in issue in the present case'.[255] The proclaimed dichotomy seems to leave no room for the separate category of civil proceedings against state officials. This is also the position of the House of Lords advanced in *Jones v Saudi Arabia*.

Jones, Redress (intervening) and ors (intervening) v Ministry of the Interior of Saudi Arabia and Lieutenant Colonel Abdul Aziz, Appeal judgment, [2006] UKHL 26, [2006] 2 WLR 1424, [2007] 1 AC 270, [2007] 1 All ER 113, ILDC 521 (UK 2006), 14th June 2006, United Kingdom; House of Lords [HL]

For the facts of this case, see section VI.2(a) above. The claimants argued that the immunity applicable to the foreign state in civil proceedings should be distinguished from the immunity applicable to the officials of that state in the same proceedings.

> 10 […] There is […] a wealth of authority to show that […] the foreign state is entitled to claim immunity for its servants as it could if sued itself. The foreign state's right to immunity cannot be circumvented by suing its servants or agents. […] In the UN Convention of 2004 […] this matter is expressly addressed in article 2 where "State" is defined in (1)(b)(iv) to mean "representatives of the State acting in that capacity". It is further provided, in article 6(2)(b), that "A proceeding

253 ILC, 'Report of the International Law Commission on the Work of the Sixty-Ninth Session' (2017) UN Doc A/71/11 p 177.

254 See for an overview of the positions of individual ILC members R van Alebeek, 'The "International Crime" Exception in the ILC Draft Articles on the Immunity of State Officials from Foreign Criminal Jurisdiction: Two Steps Back?' (2018) 112 AJIL Unbound 27.

255 *Jurisdictional Immunities of the State* (n 6) para 91.

> before a court of a State shall be considered to have been instituted against another State if that other State [...] (b) is not named as a party to the proceeding but the proceeding in effect seeks to affect the property, rights, interests or activities of that other State". [...]
>
> 11 In some borderline cases there could be doubt whether the conduct of an individual, although a servant or agent of the state, had a sufficient connection with the state to entitle it to claim immunity for his conduct. But these are not borderline cases. Colonel Abdul Aziz is sued as a servant or agent of the Kingdom and there is no suggestion that his conduct complained of was not in discharge or purported discharge of his duties as such. The four defendants in the second action were public officials. The conduct complained of took place in police or prison premises and occurred during a prolonged process of interrogation concerning accusations of terrorism (in two cases) and spying (in the third). There is again no suggestion that the defendants' conduct was not in discharge or purported discharge of their public duties.
>
> 12 International law does not require, as a condition of a state's entitlement to claim immunity for the conduct of its servant or agent, that the latter should have been acting in accordance with his instructions or authority. A state may claim immunity for any act for which it is, in international law, responsible, save where an established exception applies. [...]

If suits in respect of acts that can be attributed to the state automatically trigger the application of the law of state immunity, civil claims against foreign state officials based on international crimes allegations will normally be covered by the rule of state immunity. Hence, under the conception of the rule of functional immunity espoused by the House of Lords in the *Jones* case and later sanctioned by the ECtHR these claims will normally be dismissed on state immunity grounds. However, if one recognizes that functional immunity is directly related to the concept of individual responsibility under international law, a different picture emerges. It is hard to see how the individual responsibility for international crimes could be limited to the criminal realm.[256]

US doctrine is too nuanced and diverse to discuss in detail here, but it is notable that some lower courts have excluded *jus cogens* violations from the rule of functional immunity in civil proceedings,[257] while other courts have disagreed.[258] Moreover, even after *Samantar* the FSIA has occasionally been applied to such a suit, where the court was of the opinion that the officials were sued in their official capacity and that hence the state was the real party in interest.[259]

The picture that emerges in this section is a blurred one: this area of law is clearly in flux. While the support for an international crimes exception to functional immunity from criminal jurisdiction is increasing, the immunity of the state itself in respect of such crimes stands strong, and there is a deep divide in judicial and academic thinking as to the position of state officials in civil proceedings regarding international crimes. The recourse to domestic constitutional law as a barrier against international immunity rules, as most vividly illustrated by the Italian *Simoncioni* case discussed in section VI.1(a), may inspire other domestic courts, thus eventually generating the case law necessary for the identification of change in the scope of customary international

256 Note that also Article 13 of the IDI Resolution (n 148) formulates the exception both in terms of criminal and civil law.

257 *Yousuf and ors v Samantar* (n 37); United States, District Court for the Eastern District of Virginia, *Warfaa v Ali*, 29 July 2014, ILDC 2253 (US 2014).

258 *Balcero Giraldo* (n 37); *Matar* (n 36); *Rosenberg and ors v Lashkar-e-Taiba and ors* (n 36).

259 *Mohammadi and ors v Khamenei and ors* (n 181).

law. Of course, this would imply that such domestic courts rely on international rules, and not (only) on their constitutional norms.

VII. Conclusion

The case law discussed in this chapter elicits three concluding remarks. First, the pivotal role of domestic courts in the development of international immunity rules translates into an interplay of domestic law and international law in domestic immunity decisions, and partly explains the many controversies on the precise parameters of the various rules of this area of the law. While there may be a convergence of practice in respect of some issues, divergence of domestic courts' interpretations of immunity rules is an inherent characteristic of immunity law. Secondly, domestic immunity decisions at times rest on feeble grounds, with judges mixing up different immunity rules, misreading precedents, and displaying a lack of expert knowledge in the field of international law. On the other hand, the judgment of the House of Lords in the *Jones* case illustrates how a single domestic court decision which rests on a dubious interpretation of precedent and principle may gain ground rapidly. A critical approach by other courts is hence warranted at all times. And, thirdly, while there is a clear trend towards restricting immunity so as to impact least the rights and interests of private parties, unabated heed is usually paid to the core rationale for immunity rules: the need to protect the sovereign rights of states and to secure the effective performance of the functions of certain office-holders who conduct interstate relations.

5

International Organizations

AUGUST REINISCH AND GREGOR NOVAK

I. Introduction

International organizations do not regularly appear before domestic courts.[1] Most of their activities take place on the international level and concern their powers, including their treaty-making powers, their relations with members or non-members, or involve questions of international responsibility or liability. All of these issues are intrinsically related to the international legal personality of international organizations.[2] However, in a growing number of situations, international organizations need to act as subjects of domestic law.[3] It is their domestic legal personality which permits them, for example, to enter into procurement contracts, to own movable and immovable property, and to sue before domestic courts. Yet, in most domestic cases involving international organizations, courts do not deal with their legal personality as such but with the legal basis and extent of their immunities from legal process.

International organizations are sued before domestic courts mostly on the basis of alleged violations of private law obligations. Sometimes, claimants also seek to secure their accountability under international law, which may raise issues of international responsibility. This development is partly attributable to the fact that, especially since the second half of the 20th century, the number and scope of activities of international organizations has greatly expanded.[4] This increase has been accompanied by a corresponding risk that their activities may cause harm to others. At the same time, many international organizations have provided for mechanisms giving individuals or companies the opportunity to have their complaints heard. These means include judicial or quasi-judicial bodies or tribunals, eg administrative tribunals for staff members,[5] arbitration for contractors or (non-staff) consultants, or more informal mechanisms, such as 'ombudsperson' procedures for others, eg subcontractors.[6] Where such alternative legal

---

1 For such cases see *Oxford Reports on International Law in Domestic Courts* (headnotes and analysis) http://www.oxfordlawreports.com/ (last accessed 16 October 2017), *International Law Reports*, or *International Legal Materials*.

2 See C F Amerasinghe, *Principles of the Institutional Law of International Organizations* (2nd edn, CUP 2005) 69–77, 315–51; R-J Dupuy (ed), *Manuel sur les organisations internationales/A Handbook on International Organizations* (2nd edn, Martinus Nijhoff 1998); F L Kirgis Jr, *International Organizations in Their Legal Setting* (2nd edn, West 1993); J Klabbers, *An Introduction to International Institutional Law* (3rd edn, CUP 2015) 46–50, 130–51; J Klabbers and Å Wallendahl (eds), *Research Handbook on the Law of International Organizations* (Edward Elgar Publishing 2011) 33–56 (T Gazzini), 132–55 (A Reinisch); P Sands and P Klein, *Bowett's Law of International Institutions* (6th edn, Sweet & Maxwell 2009); H G Schermers and N M Blokker, *International Institutional Law* (5th edn, Martinus Nijhoff 2011) 985–1079.

3 See generally and with further references eg A Reinisch, 'Contracts between International Organizations and Private Law Persons' in R Wolfrum (ed), *The Max Planck Encyclopedia of Public International Law, Vol II* (OUP 2012) 754–57.

4 See, on the number of IOs, eg, Amerasinghe (n 2) at 6; see, on the scope of activities of IOs, eg, J E Alvarez, *International Organizations as Law-Makers* (OUP 2006).

5 See generally C F Amerasinghe, *The Law of the International Civil Service, Two Volumes* (Clarendon Press 1994); see on the case of the United Nations UN Office of Administration of Justice, *Third activity report of the Office of Administration of Justice for the period 1 July to 31 December 2010* (2011).

6 See, eg, the European Space Agency's 'Industrial Ombudsman' procedure in the area of procurement, which was discussed in *SA Energies Nouvelles et Environnement v Agence Spatiale Européenne (European Space Agency)*, First

redress is unavailable or considered inadequate, affected persons have sometimes attempted to bring international organizations before domestic courts. It seems likely that this trend will continue where the possible benefits of litigation outweigh its costs. However, it needs to be kept in mind that the likelihood of success and the costs of litigation against international organizations before domestic courts vary across jurisdictions and depend on the rules applicable with regard to particular international organizations.

Generally, the most important bar to legal action against international organizations is the jurisdictional immunity accorded to them. This immunity is usually granted to international organizations in their constituent treaties, in general multilateral privileges and immunities treaties, or in bilateral headquarters or host agreements. There is an ongoing debate and a diversity of domestic courts' views as to whether and to what extent international organizations enjoy immunity as a matter of customary international law.[7] In addition, national legislation may provide a legal basis for the immunity of international organizations. While most international organizations enjoy some form of immunity, the immunity standards are often substantively different, including most importantly 'absolute' and 'functional' immunity standards. However, courts have usually interpreted even functional immunity as barring legal process in all cases, thus assimilating it to 'absolute' immunity. Nevertheless, the interpretation of seemingly identical immunity standards can diverge across jurisdictions. Moreover, some domestic courts have become increasingly willing to balance jurisdictional immunity with the right to access to justice.

The following cases illustrate the ways in which domestic courts have addressed problems related to the domestic legal personality of international organizations (section II), the sources of immunities of international organizations (section III), the scope of immunities of international organizations (section IV), the tension between immunities and the right of access to justice (section V), as well as the question of attribution of internationally wrongful conduct to and the responsibility of international organizations (section VI).

II. The Domestic Legal Personality of International Organizations

International organizations require domestic legal personality in order to engage in various legal acts necessary for their functioning. They may need to enter into procurement contracts, own movable and immovable property, or sue third parties before domestic courts. Usually, these legal capacities—forming the most important facets of legal personality under domestic law—are expressly stipulated in either the constituent instruments of an international organization,[8]

Instance Decision, 2006 6216 JdT 171, ILDC 1229 (BE 2005), 1 December 2005, Belgium, Brussels, Court of First Instance and in *SA Energies Nouvelles et Environnement v European Space Agency*, Appeal judgment, no 2011/2013, 2006/AR/1480, ILDC 1729 (BE 2011), 23 March 2011, Belgium, Brussels, Court of Appeal.

7 See the overview of the debate in A Reinisch, *International Organizations before National Courts* (CUP 2000) 145 ff; M Wood, 'Do International Organizations Enjoy Immunity Under Customary International Law?' (2014) 10 *International Organizations Law Review* 287.

8 See, eg, Articles of Agreement of the International Monetary Fund (adopted 22 July 1944, entered into force 27 December 1945) 2 UNTS 40, art IX s 2 and Articles of Agreement of the International Bank for Reconstruction and Development (signed 27 December 1945, entered into force 27 December 1945) 2 UNTS 134 (IBRD Articles of Agreement), art VII s 2, which provide: 'The Fund/Bank shall possess full juridical personality and, in particular, the capacity: (i) to contract; (ii) to acquire and dispose of immovable and movable property; and (iii) to institute legal proceedings'. TFEU art 335 (TEC ex art 282), Rome (25 March 1957), as amended, provides: 'In each of the Member States, the Union (Community) shall enjoy the most extensive legal capacity accorded to legal persons under their laws; it may, in particular, acquire or dispose of movable and immovable property and may be a party to legal proceedings'. See also the similar provisions in International Convention relating to Co-operation for the Safety of Air Navigation (adopted 13 December 1960, entered into force 1 March 1963) 523 UNTS 117, art 4.

in general privileges and immunities treaties between states,[9] or in headquarters agreements between an international organization and a state.[10] The extent to which such treaty-based obligations are directly applicable in the domestic legal order of states differs across jurisdictions.[11] In the absence of a relevant treaty-based obligation, member states of an international organization, and especially a host state, are often considered to be under a customary international obligation to recognize its domestic legal personality.[12] A more difficult question arises with respect to the basis for domestic legal personality of an international organization in third states. Such states will generally not be under a customary international obligation to recognize the domestic legal personality of an international organization of which they are not members.[13] However, even absent a customary rule, domestic law, including principles of 'comity', or more generally of private international law (conflict of laws), may be applicable.

Arab Monetary Fund v Hashim (No 3), [1991] 1 All ER 871, 21 February 1991, United Kingdom; House of Lords [HL] 872 (not in ILDC)

Private international law principles were relevant most prominently in the case of *Arab Monetary Fund v Hashim*.[14] In this case the appellant, the Arab Monetary Fund (AMF), which had been created by a 1976 treaty between twenty Arab states and the Palestine Liberation Organization (PLO), attempted to bring an action before English courts against Mr Hashim and others in order to recover assets that had allegedly been misappropriated by Mr Hashim. The respondents argued that the AMF lacked capacity to sue in English courts. Finally, the House of Lords pronounced itself in favour of the AMF's legal personality on the basis of comity. The court held that:

> [a]lthough when sovereign states entered into an agreement by treaty to confer legal personality on an international organisation the treaty did not create a corporate body with capacity to sue and be sued in English courts, the registration of that treaty in one of the sovereign states conferred legal personality on the international organisation and thus created a corporate body which the English courts could and should recognise, since by comity the courts of the United Kingdom recognised corporate bodies created by the law of a foreign state recognised by the Crown. [. . .]

This case illustrates that even if the forum state is neither under a treaty-based nor a customary obligation to accord domestic legal personality to an international organization, its courts may nevertheless recognize such personality based on private international law (conflict of laws) principles, such as the common law principle of comity.

III. The Legal Basis of the Immunities of International Organizations

An initial task faced by domestic courts in cases involving an international organization is to identify the legal basis for its immunity. It remains controversial whether the immunity of international organizations, in contrast to state immunity, is based exclusively on treaty law, as well

9 See, eg, Convention on the Privileges and Immunities of the United Nations (adopted 13 February 1946, entered into force 17 September 1946) 1 UNTS 15, art I s 1.

10 See, eg, Headquarters Agreement between the International Criminal Court and the Host State (done 7 June 2007, entered into force 1 March 2008) ICC-BD/04-01-08, art 3.

11 See Amerasinghe (n 2) 69 ff.

12 T Gazzini, 'Personality of International Organizations' in J Klabbers and Å Wallendahl (eds), *Research Handbook on the Law of International Organizations* (Edward Elgar Publishing 2011) 45.

13 ibid; Amerasinghe (n 2) 76 (holding that the existence of such a general custom 'cannot be assumed').

14 *Arab Monetary Fund v Hashim (No 3)* [1991] 1 All ER 871, 21 February 1991, United Kingdom, House of Lords [HL] 872.

as domestic implementing legislation,[15] or also on customary international law, which may be directly applicable in some domestic legal systems.[16] Usually, domestic courts can decide immunity cases involving international organizations on the basis of applicable treaty law, ie the law applicable by courts in light of the respective provisions of domestic (constitutional) law relating to the domestic validity and direct applicability of treaty law.[17] Additionally, especially in some common law jurisdictions, legislation has been adopted that permits the executive to pass implementing measures according a certain scope of immunities to specific international organizations.[18]

Spaans v Iran-United States Claims Tribunal, Final appeal judgment, Case No 12627, Decision No LJN: AC9158, NJ 1986, 438, (1987) 18 NYIL 357, ILDC 1759 (NL 1985), 20th December 1985, Netherlands; Supreme Court [HR]

A case where a domestic court clearly affirmed the existence of a customary international rule providing for the jurisdictional immunity of international organizations was *Spaans v Iran-United States Claims Tribunal.*[19] In that case, an interpreter at the Iran–US Claims Tribunal tried to sue his employer, the tribunal, which for practical purposes was considered to enjoy the status of an international organization in the Netherlands. However, at the time of the litigation the host state had no obligation, based on a host agreement or another treaty, to accord immunity to the tribunal. After the lower courts expressed diverging views on the matter, the Dutch Supreme Court concluded that:

> H3 [a]ccording to unwritten international law as it stands at present, an international organization is in principle not subject to the jurisdiction of the courts of the host State in respect of all disputes which are immediately connected with the performance of the tasks entrusted to the organization in question.

Similarly, in a 1985 decision by the Italian Court of Cassation, *Christiani v Italian Latin-American Institute*, the court held that an organization with legal personality benefited from immunity for 'all acts and relationships entered into in the exercise of essential functions of the organization'.[20] However, in subsequent cases, such as *Drago v International Plant Genetic Resources Institute (IPGRI)*[21] and *Pistelli v European University Institute*,[22] Italian courts distinguished between the sources of state immunity and international organizations' immunities. Also, other domestic courts have either not accepted a customary international law basis for international organizations' immunities[23] or have decided to avoid addressing this question. *Drago v International Plant Genetic Resources Institute (IPGRI)*[24] was based on an action over an

15 See n 7.

16 See generally I Brownlie, *Principles of Public International Law* (OUP 2008) 47 ff; see also A Nollkaemper, 'General Aspects' Chapter 1 in this volume.

17 See R Pavoni, R van Alebeek, 'Immunities of States and Their Officials' Chapter 4 in this volume.

18 For example, in the UK the International Organisations Act 1968 [UK] 6 and 7 Eliz 2 c 48.

19 *Spaans v Iran-United States Claims Tribunal*, Final appeal judgment, Case No 12627, Decision No LJN: AC 9158, NJ 1986, 438, (1987) 18 NYIL 357, ILDC 1759 (NL 1985), 20 December 1985, Netherlands, Supreme Court [HR].

20 *Christiani v Italian Latin-American Institute*, Corte di Cassazione, 25 November 1985 [1992] 87 ILR 21, 25.

21 *Drago v International Plant Genetic Resources Institute (IPGRI)*, Final appeal judgment, Case No 3718, Giustizia Civile Massimario, 2007, 2, ILDC 827 (IT 2007), 19 February 2007, Italy, Supreme Court of Cassation.

22 *Pistelli v European University Institute*, Appeal judgment, No 20995, Guida al diritto 40 (3/2006), ILDC 297 (IT 2005), 28 October 2005, Italy, Supreme Court of Cassation.

23 See, eg, *Internationale Nederlanden Aviation Lease BV and Others v Aviation Authority and the European Organization for the Safety of Air Navigation (Eurocontrol)* [1997] 1 Lloyd's Rep 80, 11 June 1996, United Kingdom, Queen's Bench Division (Commercial Court); *Irish Aerospace (Belgium) NV v European Organization for the Safety of Air Navigation (Eurocontrol)* [1992] 1 Lloyd's Rep 383, 6 June 1991, United Kingdom, Queen's Bench Division (Commercial Court).

24 *Drago v International Plant Genetic Resources Institute (IPGRI)* (n 21).

employment dispute brought by a former employee of the IPGRI, an international organization based in Italy. After the court of first instance had declined to exercise jurisdiction and that decision had been upheld by the Rome Court of Appeals, the applicant challenged the judgment before the Court of Cassation. That court discussed the distinction between state immunity and the immunities accorded by states to international organizations and rejected the argument that customary rules on state immunity have been extended to international organizations.

Pistelli v European University Institute, Appeal judgment, No 20995, Guida al diritto 40 (3/2006), ILDC 297 (IT 2005), 28th October 2005, Italy; Supreme Court of Cassation

In *Pistelli v European University Institute*,[25] the Italian Court of Cassation also dealt with the question of the sources of the immunities of international organizations, equally distinguishing them from the customary law origin of state immunity.[26] The Court of Cassation did not find it 'clear' that the law of state immunity had been 'extended by customary law to all international organisations with specific legal personality under international law'. It elaborated as follows:

> 4. [b]y virtue of Article 10(1) of the Constitution, the Italian legal order conforms to generally recognised rules of international law and it is on the basis of these rules that case law recognises the immunity of foreign States from Italian jurisdiction, based on a customary international rule on respect for other countries' sovereignty. This immunity concerns legal relations outside the Italian legal order, either when foreign States act as subjects of international law or when they act as sovereign powers in their own legal order, namely as sovereign entities. [. . .]
>
> 6. States are afforded immunity from jurisdiction for acts carried out *iure imperii* in their capacity as sovereign entities, but not those carried out *iure gestionis*. [. . .]
>
> 8. The problems summarised above have become more complex, especially recently, as an increasing number of subjects operating with varying degrees of independence from States have appeared in the sphere of international law. These international organisations were mainly founded by States after the Second World War to satisfy the requirements of the international community that had not previously been addressed, or at least not sufficiently addressed.
>
> The first problem associated with these entities is whether they should be granted legal personality under international law and consequently the ability to establish legal relations with States. In the absence of specifically agreed definitions, their legal personality is often characterised by the immunities and privileges conferred on them. However, the capacity to participate in certain relations and to be subject to international law, on the basis of provisions contained in their constitutive treaties does not always make such organisations of equal status to that of States. It may be that such bodies are not necessarily guaranteed immunity from national jurisdiction (this was the case for the European School in Varese — Ispra, formed by certain E.U. member States [. . .]).
>
> 9. This view is founded on the fact that it is not clear that the principle *par in parem non habet iurisdictionem*, which operates between States and is implicitly referred to in Article 10(1) of the Constitution, has been extended by customary law to all international organisations with specific legal personality under international law.
>
> As it is impossible to place States and international organisations on the same level, the privileges and immunities the latter enjoy can only arise from specific agreements, through Article 11 of the Constitution.

25 *Pistelli v European University Institute* (n 22).

26 On the sources of the law of state immunity see, eg, H Fox and P Webb, *The Law of State Immunity* (3rd edn, OUP 2013) 101 ff.

These sources are not only agreements between States, namely between those who establish the organisation, referred to as Contracting States, but also the so-called "headquarters agreements", drawn up between an organisation without its own territory and the State in which it establishes its principal or secondary headquarters.

Such agreements concern the overall legal status of the organisation and better guarantee its self-regulation, in addition to giving certainty in its relationships with the host State, but they do not necessarily establish immunity, or else limit such immunity with reference to institutional functions or property destined for official use. [. . .]

Mahalwas v United Nations Truce Supervision Organization and Attorney General (intervening), Appeal Decision, PLA 3093/07, ILDC 1070 (IL 2007), 15th August 2007, Israel; Jerusalem (disputed); District Court

The legal basis for the immunities of the United Nations (UN) and its subsidiary bodies was an issue in the Israeli case *Mahalwas v United Nations Truce Supervision Organization*.[27] The claimant had previously obtained a judgment *in absentia* from the Jerusalem Magistrates' Court ordering the UN Truce Supervision Organization[28] (UNTSO) to pay damages for personal injuries he had allegedly suffered while working for UNTSO. The case arose when the claimant attempted to obtain execution of this judgment. After the competent execution office ordered the closure of the execution case owing to the immunity enjoyed by the UNTSO, the claimant appealed to a district court. The court discussed the scope of immunities granted to the UNTSO, elaborated on its specific sources both in international and domestic law, confirmed the execution office's decision, and also stated that the immunities of international organizations did not find a basis in customary international law. The court held as follows:

10. [F]ollowing the [UN] Charter, a Convention on the Privileges and Immunities of the United Nations was adopted by the United Nations in 1946 [. . .]. Israel became a party to this Convention in 1949. [. . .]

This immunity had been anchored in internal legislation even prior to the establishment of the State of Israel, in the Privileges and Immunities of the United Nations Ordinance, 1947 [. . .], which authorizes the Minister of Foreign Affairs to prescribe in an order that the immunities and privileges set out in Part I of the Schedule to the Ordinance be afforded to the United Nations. By virtue of his authority under the Ordinance, the Minister of Foreign Affairs enacted the Immunities and Privileges of the United Nations Order, 1947 [. . .], which provides, inter alia, that the United Nations shall have "immunity against lawsuits and legal actions".

11. According to counsel for the Attorney General, due to the provisions of the Ordinance and the Order, the United Nations is immune against any "legal action", including execution of judgment. The State of Israel is a party to the Convention and is bound to act in accordance with the provisions of it and to respect the status of the United Nations, and therefore, it is not possible to institute execution proceedings against the United Nations in the State of Israel. [. . .]

[T]he reliance placed by counsel for the Applicant on the Canada ruling[[29]] cannot assist him since the issue discussed therein was that of the immunity of the applicant

27 *Mahalwas v United Nations Truce Supervision Organization and Attorney General (intervening)*, Appeal Decision, PLA 3093/07, ILDC 1070 (IL 2007), 15 August 2007, Israel, Jerusalem (disputed), District Court.

28 UNSC Res 73 (11 August 1949) SCOR 4th Year 8.

29 *Her Majesty the Queen in Right of Canada v Edelson and ors*, Final appeal judgment, PLA 7092/94, 51(1) PD 625, ILDC 577 (IL 1997), 3 June 1997, Israel, Supreme Court.

> [. . .] which is in fact the state of Canada [. . .], i.e., the immunity of a foreign nation. What is more, the laws of immunity of foreign states are part of customary international law. However, as we have seen, the question of the immunity of the United Nations is part of treaty-based international law (the Convention), which has been anchored in the internal legislation of the State of Israel (the Ordinance). It should also be noted that the Canada ruling dealt with the question of immunity of a foreign sovereign against lawsuits. [. . .]

IV. The Scope of Immunities of International Organizations

The immunity of an international organization from suit may range from none to absolute. If an international organization voluntarily submits to the jurisdiction of the forum state it may be deemed to have waived its immunity from suit. Questions related to a waiver of immunity will need to be addressed by domestic courts in cases where the existence, the form in which it was given, or the extent of the waiver are in dispute. Moreover, sometimes claimants have attempted to link the question of a waiver with the issue of balancing immunities with access to justice questions, such as in the case *Bisson v United Nations and ors*, discussed below.[30] In such instances, the existence of an implicit waiver is alleged.

The permissibility of a waiver was discussed in *Mahalwas v UNTSO*, whose facts are related above. In that case, an Israeli district court applied Article II section 2 of the UN General Convention, which prohibited a waiver of immunity with respect to 'any measure of execution' against the organization.[31]

Company Baumeister Ing Richard L v O, Final appeal/cassation, 10 Ob 53/04y, ILDC 362 (AT 2004), 14th December 2004, Austria; Supreme Court of Justice [OGH]

An Austrian court dealt with the question of the proper form of a waiver in *Company Baumeister Ing Richard L v O*.[32] In the case, the claimant, a construction company, argued that an international organization, seated in Austria, had implicitly waived its immunity by having raised an objection to a payment order. For, in a 'note verbale' addressed to the Austrian Ministry of Foreign Affairs, the international organization had rejected the claim raised by the company on the merits without having explicitly expressed a waiver. While the Austrian Supreme Court accepted in principle the possibility of an implicit waiver, it did not specify its conditions, as there was no need to do so for the case at hand. The court found:

> 19 [I]mmunity can be waived in accordance with Article IX Paragraph 2 Case 1 of the Introductory Act to the Austrian Jurisdiction Code (Einführungsgesetz zur Jurisdiktionsnorm). "With regard to an international organisation, the body responsible for external representation of the organisation is responsible for submitting the declaration of waiver". The waiver must be declared explicitly and is only binding for the case for which it is issued [. . .]. The acceptance of judicial settlements does not, in its own right, constitute a waiver of immunity [. . .]. The waiver can be declared both before and after the origin of the litigation or during pendency of legal proceedings. A waiver issued for the trial proceedings does not encompass the enforcement proceedings (Matscher [. . .]). It is uncontested that there has been

30 *Bisson v United Nations and ors*, Decision on a Report and Recommendation of a US Magistrate Judge, Case No 06-6352, ILDC 889 (US 2008), 11 February 2008, United States, New York, District Court for the Southern District of New York [SDNY]. See also text at n 64 below.

31 See *Mahalwas v United Nations Truce Supervision Organization and Attorney General (intervening)* (n 27) para 11.

32 *Company Baumeister Ing Richard L v O*, Final appeal/cassation, 10 Ob 53/04y, ILDC 362 (AT 2004), 14 December 2004, Austria, Supreme Court of Justice [OGH].

> no explicit waiver of immunity by the defendant. According to Matscher […], with regard to the principle of good faith, which also applies under international law, immunity can also be waived by implicit behaviour. Purely passive behaviour, however, (such as the receipt of the claim or of a summons, non-appearance at a court hearing) cannot constitute an implicit waiver of immunity. Actions implying a waiver of immunity can be performed by the immune legal entity itself or by one of the latter's authorised representatives. For declarations of waiver issued during pendency of proceedings or for declarations of waiver issued to the court, the regulations regarding mandatory legal counsel also take effect. From this point of view as well, however, the objection against the payment order does not necessitate submission to domestic jurisdiction (Matscher loc. cit., note 165). In the light of these statements there has therefore been no effective waiver by the defendant of its immunity. The defendant also explicitly refused to waive its immunity in its "note verbale" of 31/3/2004.
>
> 20 Because there has therefore been no waiver of immunity by the defendant, the illegal service of process in accordance with Article 7 of the Austrian Act on the Service of Documents under Administrative Procedure (Zustellungsgesetz) has not been remedied. Legally valid service of process has not been effectuated on the international organisation and the process has therefore not yet been legally concluded. Consequently the claim was rightly rejected by the lower instance courts due to lack of jurisdiction in accordance with Article 42 Paragraph 1 of the Austrian Law on Court Jurisdiction (Jurisdiktionsnorm). […]

In the absence of a waiver of immunity, a domestic court will need to interpret any applicable rule in order to determine the precise scope of the respective international organization's immunity. As pointed out above, such rules can be contained in treaties or domestic statutes or, less commonly, arise under customary international law. Often, relevant treaties will provide for absolute[33] or functional immunity: whereas the former implies immunity from every form of legal process, the latter provides for immunity only where this is necessary for the fulfilment of the respective international organizations' functions.[34] However, judicial practice in several jurisdictions shows that the application of 'absolute' or 'functional' immunity usually largely leads to the same scope of immunity, ie absolute or quasi-absolute immunity, because any activity of an international organization, other than one performed ultra vires, can be

33 See, eg, Convention on the Privileges and Immunities of the United Nations (adopted 13 February 1946, entered into force 17 September 1946) 1 UNTS 15, art II s 2. See also A Reinisch, 'Immunity of Property, Funds and Assets (General Convention, art II s 2)' in A Reinisch (ed), *The Conventions on the Privileges and Immunities of the United Nations and its Specialized Agencies: A Commentary* (OUP 2016) 63–98.

34 See, eg, Constitution of the International Labour Organization (Part XIII Treaty of Peace between the Allied and Associated Powers and Germany) (signed 28 June 1919, entered into force 10 January 1920, as amended 20 April 1948) 15 UNTS 40, art 40. Many constituent documents of international organizations follow the 'prototype' of functional privileges and immunities, found in the Charter of the United Nations (adopted 26 June 1945, entered into force 24 October 1945) 1 UNTS XVI, art 105(1); see, eg, Constitution of the World Health Organization (adopted 22 July 1946, entered into force 7 April 1948) 14 UNTS 185, art 67(a); Charter of the Organization of American States (adopted 30 April 1948, entered into force 13 December 1951) 119 UNTS 3, art 133; Statute of the Council of Europe (adopted 5 May 1949, entered into force 3 August 1949) ETS No 1, art 40(a). On the prevailing functionalist rationale for immunities of international organizations see also Kirgis (n 2); Reinisch (n 7) 234; Amerasinghe (n 2) 316; Schermers and Blokker (n 2) 252; M Singer, 'Jurisdictional Immunity of International Organizations: Human Rights and Functional Necessity Concerns' (1995) 36 *Virginia Journal of International Law* 53; C H Brower, 'International Immunities: Some Dissident Views on the Role of Municipal Courts' (2000) 41 *Virginia Journal of International Law* 1; E Gaillard and I Pingel-Lenuzza, 'International Organizations and Immunity from Jurisdiction: To Restrict or to Bypass' (2002) 51 *International & Comparative Law Quarterly* 1.

understood as functionally necessary, given the delegated nature of international organizations' powers.[35]

The distinction between absolute and functional immunity is relevant also in the context of domestic statutes, most notably the US International Organizations Immunities Act (IOIA), which appear to equalize the scope of international organizations' immunity to that of states.[36] Traditionally, state immunity was considered as absolute, following the principle of *par in parem non habet imperium*. However, absolute jurisdictional immunity of states has today given way to the customary distinction between *acta iure imperii* and *acta iure gestionis*, with immunity from suit only accorded with respect to the former. But even where such an express reference to state immunity is not apparent, some domestic courts tend to interpret the scope of immunity enjoyed by international organizations to be 'restrictive', like that of states. In particular, Italian courts have traditionally approximated functional immunity to restrictive immunity.[37] The following case excerpts concern the scope of immunities of international organizations. As indicated above, one important conclusion is that most courts accord a quasi-'absolute' immunity to international organizations, even if specific approaches adopted by courts differ. In this process, however, many domestic courts have struggled with the correct interpretation of the scope of 'functional' immunity. Moreover, for a specific category of international organizations, mostly international financial institutions,[38] a much more limited immunity from legal process is provided for in the relevant legal instruments.[39]

Hunter v United Nations and ors, Judicial Review of Administrative Order, 800 N.Y.S.2d 347 (Sup. Ct. N.Y. County 2004), ILDC 693 (US 2004), 15th November 2004, United States; New York; New York City; 1st District (New York County); Supreme Court [NY Sup]

The scope of the immunities of the UN under US law was discussed, for example, in *Hunter v United Nations and ors*.[40] This case was prompted by a complaint filed by a UNICEF employee following the non-renewal of her fixed-term position before the New York State Division of Human Rights (SDHR), alleging *inter alia* racial discrimination. After the SDHR dismissed the complaint on the basis of lack of jurisdiction, Ms Hunter appealed to the New York State Supreme Court. The court discussed the sources of UN immunities and elaborated as follows:

> 13 Article 105, section 2, of the United Nations Charter states, "Representatives of the Members of the United Nations and officials of the Organization shall similarly enjoy such privileges and immunities as are necessary for the independent exercise of their functions in connection with the Organization" (59 Stat. 1033 [1945]).

---

35 See, eg, also *Trempe v Staff Association of the International Civil Aviation Organization and ors*, Judgment on jurisdiction, 2003 CanLII 44121, ILDC 1748 (CA 2003), 20 November 2003, Canada, Quebec, Superior Court [QCCS].

36 See, eg, US International Organizations Immunities Act [29 December 1945] [1937–1945] 59 Stat 669. See for a leading interpretation of the IOIA *Atkinson v Inter-Am. Dev Bank*, 156 F 3d 1335, 1341 (DC Cir 1998), as amended 28 October 1998, United States, Court of Appeals (noting that '[i]n light of this text and legislative history, we think that despite the lack of a clear instruction as to whether Congress meant to incorporate in the IOIA subsequent changes to the law of immunity of foreign sovereigns, Congress' intent was to adopt that body of law only as it existed in 1945—when immunity of foreign sovereigns was absolute').

37 Also in the field of state immunity, Italian courts, together with Belgian ones, were among the first to develop the concept of restrictive immunity accorded only to *iure imperii* activities, which implied that foreign states may be sued for their *iure gestionis* acts. See, eg, Fox and Webb (n 26) 152 ff.

38 See further A Reinisch and J Wurm, 'International Financial Institutions before National Courts' in D D Bradlow and D B Hunter (eds), *International Financial Institutions and International Law* (Kluwer 2010) 103–35.

39 ibid.

40 *Hunter v United Nations and ors*, Judicial Review of Administrative Order, 800 NYS 2d 347 (Sup Ct NY County 2004), ILDC 693 (US 2004), 15 November 2004, United States, New York, New York City, 1st District (New York County), Supreme Court [NY Sup].

> 14 The Agreement Between the United Nations, June 26, Nov. 21, 1947, 61 Stat. 3416 ("the UN Headquarters Agreement"), Public Law 80–357, Article III, Section 7 (b) states "except as otherwise provided in this agreement or in the General Convention, the federal, state and local law of the United States shall apply within the headquarters district."
>
> 15 The Convention on the Privileges and Immunities of the United Nations ("Convention"), 21 U.S.T. 1418, T.I.A.S. No. 6900, which was adopted by the General Assembly on February 13, 1946 and acceded to by the United States on April 29, 1970, confers on the United Nations a broad immunity from suit. Section 2 of the Convention provides: "The United Nations … shall enjoy immunity from every form of legal process except insofar as in any particular case it has expressly waived its immunity" (21 U.S.T. 1418, 1422).
>
> 16 The General Convention, Article II, Section 3, states, "The premises of the United Nations shall be inviolable. The property and assets of the United Nations, wherever located and by whoever held, shall be immune from search, requisition, confiscation, expropriation and any other form of interference, whether by executive, administrative, judicial or legislative action" (21 U.S.T. 1418).
>
> 17 The General Convention, Article V, Section 18, states, "Officials of the United Nations shall be immune from legal process in respect of words spoken or written and all acts performed by them in their official capacity" (21 U.S.T. 1418).
>
> 18 A similar immunity exists pursuant to the International Organizations Immunities Act ("Act"), 22 U.S.C. §§ 288–228f-2. Section 2(b) of the Act says that "[i]nternational organizations … shall enjoy the same immunity from suit and every form of judicial process as is enjoyed by foreign governments, except to the extent that such organizations may expressly waive their immunity for the purpose of proceedings or by the terms of any contract" (22 U.S.C. § 288a(b)). The United Nations is an "international organization" within the meaning of the Act's definition thereof, 22 U.S.C. § 288, by virtue of Executive Order No. 9698, Feb. 19, 1946, 11 Fed. Reg. 1809.
>
> 19 There seems to be little question that UNICEF, as a United Nations agency, is treated as an international organization under § 288(a) […].

The court then went on to interpret the IOIA in order to determine the scope of immunities accorded to the UN and its agencies, quoting from leading cases dealing with this question, such as *Broadbent v Organization of American States*[41] and *Mendaro v World Bank*:[42]

> 20 It is unclear whether the Act, by granting to international organizations immunity co-extensive with that of foreign governments, confers the absolute immunity foreign governments enjoyed at the time of the Act's passage, or the somewhat restrictive immunity provided for the Foreign Sovereign Immunities Act of 1976, 28 U.S.C. § 1602 et seq., withholding immunity from claims based on among other things, a foreign government's 'commercial activity' (see e.g. *Broadbent v. Organization of American States*, 628 F.2d 27, 30–35 [D.C. Cir. 1980]; *Boimah v. United Nations General Assembly*, 664 F.Supp., at 71). However, this Court need not decide the issue. Under the Convention the United Nations' immunity is absolute, subject only to the organization's express waiver thereof in particular cases. Moreover, even if the Foreign Sovereign Immunities Act applies so as to limit the Act's grant of immunity, an international organization's employment relationship with its internal staff is not

41 *Broadbent et al v Organization of American States et al*, 628 F 2d 27 (DC Cir 1980), 8 January 1980, United States, Court of Appeals, 34–35.

42 *Mendaro v World Bank*, 717 F 2d 610 (DC Cir 1983), 27 September 1983, United States, Court of Appeals.

"commercial activity" (see *Tuck v. Pan American Health Organizations*, 668 F.2d 547, 550 [D.C. Cir. 1981]; *Broadbent v. Organization of American States*, 628 F.2d, at 34–35; *Boimah v. United Nations General Assembly*, 664 F.Supp., at 72).

21 The question under both the Convention and the Act is whether the United Nations has ever "expressly waived" its immunity to employee actions. This Court can find no evidence of an express waiver. The Court is aware of what is known as the Headquarters Agreement of the United Nations, 61 Stat. 756 (1947), reprinted following 22 U.S.C. § 287, section 19 of which reads: "It is agreed that no form of racial or religious discrimination shall be permitted within the headquarters district" (61 Stat. 756, 764 [1947]). But this language hardly constitutes an "express" waiver of immunity from racial, nationality or sex based employment suits (*Boimah v. United Nations General Assembly*, 664 F.Supp., at 72).

22 Moreover, article 105(1) of the Charter reads: "The Organization shall enjoy in the territory of each of its Members such privileges and immunities as are necessary for the fulfillment of its purposes" (59 Stat. 1033, 1053 [1945]). It appears clear from the case law that an international organization's self-regulation of its employment practices is an activity essential to the "fulfillment of its purposes," and thus an area to which immunity must extend (see e.g. *Boimah v. United Nations General Assembly*, 664 F.Supp., at 72).

23 In *Broadbent v. Organization of American States* [. . .] the Court of Appeals for the D.C. Circuit held that the defendant was immune under the Act from a suit brought by its employees alleging breach of their employment contracts. The Court reasoned: The United States has accepted without qualification the principles that international organizations must be free to perform their functions and that no member state may take action to hinder the organization. The unique nature of the international civil service is relevant. . . . An attempt by the courts of one nation to adjudicate the personnel claims of international civil service would entangle those courts in the internal administration of those organizations. Denial of immunity opens the door to divided decisions of the courts of different member states passing judgment on the rules, regulations, and decisions of the international bodies. Undercutting uniformity in the application of staff rules or regulations would undermine the ability of the organization to function effectively. (*Broadbent v. Organization of American States*, 628 F.2d, at 34–35).

24 Similarly, in *Mendaro v. World Bank*, 717 F.2d 610 (D.C. Cir. 1983), the same court held that the defendant was immune under the Act from an employee's Title VII suit alleging sex discrimination: [T]he purpose of immunity from employee actions is rooted in the need to protect international organizations from unilateral control by a member nation over the activities of the international organization within its territory. The sheer difficulty of administering multiple employment practices in each area in which an organization operates suggests that the purposes of an organization could be greatly hampered if it could be subjected to suit by its employees worldwide. (*Mendaro v. World Bank*, 717 F.2d, at 615–616).

25 This policy underlying the immunity of an international organization also suggests that the Court should be slow to find an "express" waiver. As the *Mendaro* court noted, "courts should be reluctant to find that an international organization has inadvertently waived immunity when the organization might be subjected to a class of suits which would interfere with its functions" (*Mendaro v. World Bank*, 717 F.2d, at 617; see also *Boimah v. United Nations General Assembly*, 664 F.Supp., at 72; *Tuck v. Pan American Health Organization*, 666 F.2d 547).

26 Absent an express waiver of immunity the complaint against the United Nations and UNICEF cannot stand. [. . .]

OSS Nokalva Incorporated, 617 F.3d 756 (3d Cir. 2010), ILDC 1580 (US 2010), 16th August 2010, United States; Court of Appeals (3rd Circuit) [3d Cir]

In contrast to *Hunter*, in 2010 the US Court of Appeals for the Third Circuit did address the question of whether the immunities accorded to international organizations under the IOIA were to be interpreted retroactively or dynamically in *OSS Nokalva*.[43] This case concerned a dispute between the European Space Agency (ESA) and one of its contractors. The court examined the question of whether the IOIA was to be interpreted in light of the extent of state immunity at the time of the IOIA's adoption in 1945, or rather in line with subsequent changes in the law of state immunity. The court held:

> 28 [W]e find no compelling reason why a group of states acting through an international organization is entitled to broader immunity than its member states enjoy when acting alone. Indeed, such a policy may create an incentive for foreign governments to evade legal obligations by acting through international organizations [...] For these reasons, we conclude that ESA is not entitled to immunity as it stood for foreign sovereigns in 1945.
>
> 29 [T]he FSIA grants foreign governments immunity from the jurisdiction of United States courts, except when, inter alia, "the action is based upon a commercial activity carried on in the United States" [...] It is undisputed that the Agreements at issue here constituted such "commercial activity" and, because we construe the IOIA to incorporate the exceptions to immunity set forth in the FSIA, we will affirm the District Court's order denying ESA's motion to dismiss.[44]

While the Third Circuit of the US Federal Judiciary thus seems to have opened the door to a reconsideration of the traditional 'absolute' understanding of international organizations' immunities under the IOIA,[45] the absolute understanding of such immunities as reflected in *Atkinson*[46] remains good law in the DC Circuit, as suggested by two recent cases,[47] as well as in the Second Circuit. For example, in *Nyambal v International Monetary Fund*, the DC Circuit affirmed *Atkinson* and rejected the plaintiff's reliance on *OSS Nokalva*—however, that case mainly turned on the court's understanding of the 'dual protections conferred by the [IMF's] Articles of Agreement and the IOIA', immunities which the court held to be 'though unusually expansive [...] [limited] by a showing of express waiver'.[48]

V. The Balancing of Immunities with Access to Justice Concerns

Since the late 1990s some domestic courts have challenged the broad understanding of the immunity of international organizations. This challenge was based on a concern for the implications of immunity for the right of access to justice by affected parties. The underlying argument

43 *OSS Nokalva Incorporated*, 617 F 3d 756 (3d Cir 2010), ILDC 1580 (US 2010), 16 August 2010, United States, Court of Appeals (3rd Circuit) [3d Cir].

44 ibid, 764–65.

45 See the chapter on the relevant case law from the United States by C H Brower, II, in A Reinisch (ed), *The Privileges and Immunities of International Organizations in Domestic Courts* (OUP 2013).

46 See n 36.

47 *Jam v Int'l Fin Corp.*, 172 F Supp 3d 104 (DDC 2016), 24 March 2016, United States, District Court (likewise affirming Atkinson and refusing to adopt the position expressed in *OSS Nokalva*); see also *Jam v Int'l Fin Corp.*, 860 F 3d 703 (DC Cir 2017); see most recently *Jam v Int'l Fin Corp.*, 138 S Ct 2026 (US 2018) (petition for writ of certiorari granted); *Nyambal v International Monetary Fund*, 772 F 3d 277, 281 (DC Cir 2014), 25 November 2014, United States, Court of Appeals (noting that 'Atkinson remains vigorous as Circuit law; international organizations "enjoy the same immunity from suit and every form of judicial process as is enjoyed by foreign governments, except to the extent that such organizations [...] expressly waive their immunity" ').

48 *Nyambal v International Monetary Fund* (n 47) 281.

was that international organizations, when exercising powers affecting individuals or other private parties, should not be considered free from effective mechanisms to ensure their accountability. This argument had already been acknowledged by international courts and tribunals, especially the ICJ in its Advisory Opinion on the *Effect of Awards*[49] and administrative tribunals, eg the ILOAT in *Chadsey v Universal Postal Union.*[50] Domestic courts further reasoned that the immunity accorded to international organizations could only be justified where at least alternative accountability mechanisms were made available to affected persons. The idea that granting immunities was linked to the availability of adequate and effective alternative means of dispute settlement emerged first in the jurisprudence of the German Federal Constitutional Court[51] and was later expressed in the judgment of the European Court of Human Rights (ECtHR) in the *Waite and Kennedy* case in 1999.[52] Subsequently, this reasoning emerged in a number of other domestic court decisions, which can be seen as part of a trend seeking to restrain the immunity of international organizations when it unduly conflicts with the rights of individuals of access to justice.[53] Yet, this reasoning is not limited to the right of access to justice. Thus, the ECtHR dealt with other alleged human rights violations of EU Member States based on EC/EU law and found that Member States remained responsible for European Convention on Human Rights (ECHR) violations if 'equivalent legal protection', eg for the right to property, was not available within the respective international organization mandating certain action.[54] Nonetheless, the ECtHR has recently clarified that it does not follow from its reasoning in *Waite and Kennedy*

49 *Effect of Awards of Compensation Made by the United Nations Administrative Tribunal* [1954] ICJ Rep 47, at 57, stating that it would '[. . .] hardly be consistent with the expressed aim of the Charter to promote freedom and justice for individuals [. . .] that [the United Nations] should afford no judicial or arbitral remedy to its own staff for the settlement of any disputes which may arise between it and them'.

50 See, eg, in *Chadsey v Universal Postal Union*, ILO Administrative Tribunal, 15 October 1968, Judgment No 122, the ILOAT found that especially the 'principle that [. . .] employees were entitled, in the event of a dispute with their employers, to the safeguard of some appeals procedure' was a 'general principles of civil service law'.

51 *Hetzel v EUROCONTROL*, 2 BvR 1058/79, BVerfG 59, 63; NJW (1982), 512, DVBl (1982), 189, DÖV (1982), 10 November 1981, Germany, Federal Constitutional Court, Second Chamber, 404. See also on the background of *Hetzel v EUROCONTROL* and the related case of *Strech v EUROCONTROL*, A Bleckmann, *Internationale Beamtenstreitigkeiten vor nationalen Gerichten* (Duncker & Humblot 1981); I Seidl-Hohenveldern, *Die Immunität internationaler Organisationen in Dienstrechtsstreitfällen* (Duncker & Humblot 1981).

52 ECtHR, *Waite and Kennedy*, App No 26083/94 (18 February 1999) para 53. See also A Reinisch and U Weber, 'In the Shadow of Waite and Kennedy: The Jurisdictional Immunity of International Organizations, the Individual's Right of Access to Courts and Administrative Tribunals as Alternative Means of Dispute Settlement' (2004) 1 *International Organizations Law Review* 59; N Angelet and A Weerts, 'Les immunités des organisations internationales face à l'article 6 de la Convention européenne des droits de l'homme' (2007) 1 *Journal du droit international* 1; A Reinisch, 'The Immunity of International Organizations and the Jurisdiction of their Administrative Tribunals' (2008) 7 *Chinese Journal of International Law* 285.

53 See *Siedler v Western European Union*, Appeal judgment, JT 2004, 617, ILDC 53 (BE 2003), 17 September 2003, Belgium, Brussels, Labour Court of Appeal, 4th Chamber. See also *Manderlier v Organisation des Nations Unies and État Belge (Ministre des Affaires Étrangères)*, Tribunal Civil de Bruxelles, 11 May 1966, *Journal des tribunaux*, 10 December 1966, No 4553, 121; *Pasicrisie Belge* (1966) III, 103, (1966) UNJYB 283, (1972) 45 ILR 446; *Istituto Universitario Europeo v Piette*, Italian Court of Cassation, 18 March 1999, No 149, in RDIPP, 2000, 475–76; *Consortium X v Switzerland*, Final appeal judgment, BGE 130 I 312, ILDC 344 (CH 2004), 2 July 2004, Switzerland, Federal Supreme Court [BGer]; *UNESCO v Boulois*, Tribunal de grande instance de Paris (ord Réf), 20 October 1997, Rev Arb (1997) 575; Cour d'Appel Paris (14ème Ch A), 19 June 1998 (1999) 24 *Yearbook of Commercial Arbitration* 294; *SA Energies Nouvelles et Environnement v Agence Spatiale Européenne*, first instance and Court of Cassation decisions (n 6); *Cultier v Organisation Européenne de Télécommunications par Satellite (Eutelsat)*, 98-44996, 5 June 2001, France, Court of Cassation; *African Development Bank v X*, Appeal judgment, 04-41012, ILDC 778 (FR 2005), 25 January 2005, France, Court of Cassation [Cass]; *B and ors*, Final judgment, 2 BvR 1458/03, BVerfGK 8, 325–31, ILDC 1751 (DE 2006), 3 July 2006, Germany, Constitutional Court [BVerfG]; *Jananyagam v Commonwealth Secretariat*, Appeal judgment, Appeal No UKEAT/0443/06/DM, ILDC 1763 (UK 2007), 12 March 2007, United Kingdom, Employment Appeals Tribunal [EAT].

54 ECtHR, *Bosphorus Hava Yollari Turizm ve Ticaret Anonim Şirketi v Ireland*, App No 45036/98 (30 June 2005); ECtHR, *Denise Matthews v United Kingdom*, App No 24833/94 (18 February 1999).

'that in the absence of an alternative remedy the recognition of immunity is *ipso facto* constitutive of a violation of the right of access to a court'.[55]

Domestic courts have been and to a large extent remain reluctant to question the adequacy of available alternative dispute settlement mechanisms. This reluctance is based on the valid arguments for upholding the immunity of international organizations: that immunity guarantees the independence of international organizations and prevents undue interference in their work. Nevertheless, some courts have started to deprive international organizations of their jurisdictional immunity where no alternative remedy was available or where the alternative redress did not seem to conform to certain minimum standards of independence or fairness.

Drago v International Plant Genetic Resources Institute (IPGRI), Final Appeal Judgment, Case No 3718, Giustizia Civile Massimario, 2007, 2, ILDC 827 (IT 2007), 19th February 2007, Italy; Supreme Court of Cassation

The Italian Supreme Court's decision in *Drago v International Plant Genetic Resources Institute (IPGRI)*[56] is illustrative of a number of domestic court decisions which refrain from expressly invoking an international standard on the access to court, while applying substantively equivalent principles of domestic law. The Italian constitution, like many others, contains a right of access to court.[57] The Italian Supreme Court elaborated as follows:

> 6.4. Through Law no. 67 of 15 January 1994 an agreement was ratified between the Italian Republic and the International Plant Genetic Resources Institute (IPGRI) regarding the headquarters of IPGRI, signed in Rome on 10 October 1991, as well as an exchange of notes between these parties on 8/9 February 1993. Article 5 of the agreement states that "the Institute shall enjoy jurisdictional immunity of all types, with reference to any deed of a public or private nature, except in those specific cases in which it has been specifically waived by the Director General".
>
> 6.5. It is necessary to determine whether this measure, which unequivocally recognises the body's immunity from Italian jurisdiction and extends to employment relations with its employees, complies with the constitutional principle of judicial protection, as referred to under Article 24 of the Constitution, which constitutes a cardinal principle of the legal order (see Court of Cassation, All Civil Sections, no 12614, 17 December 1998, and no 149/1999 cit.). This cardinal principle is overridden by the customary principle *par in parem non habet iurisdictionem* in relation to States, as the principle reflects the sovereign equality of state organisations that is a rule universally recognised by the international community to which our Constitution conforms (Article 10). But this prevalence is no longer justified when the sacrifice of the 'cardinal principle' of the Constitution arises not from the international system but from a commitment freely entered into by our Republic through the ratification of a convention. In this case, the requirement that the commitment undertaken be translated into a ratifying law for it to become binding upon the courts brings to the fore the fundamental principles of the Constitution, with which the undertaking must be compatible for the ratifying law to be valid (see Constitutional Court judgement no 223 of 1996). Consequently, the complete exclusion of the right to jurisdictional protection before an independent organ for legal disputes arising from

55 ECtHR, *Stichting Mothers of Srebrenica and Others against the Netherlands*, App No 65542/12 (11 June 2013) para 164.

56 See n 21.

57 Article 24 of the Italian constitution provides as follows: 'Anyone may bring cases before a court of law in order to protect their rights under civil and administrative law. Defense is an inviolable right at every stage and instance of legal proceedings. The poor are entitled by law to proper means for action or defense in all courts. The law shall define the conditions and forms of reparation in case of judicial errors'.

specific relationships must raise doubts about the constitutional legitimacy of the law ratifying conventions containing such provisions, or, where possible, encourage interpretations of the provisions in line with the Constitution. In accordance with such criteria, in its case law, the Court of Cassation, All Civil Sections, has taken the view that the immunity granted to an international entity does not raise doubts as to constitutional legitimacy when the convention that transfers those situations away from Italian jurisdiction nevertheless ensures jurisdictional protection of the same situations before an impartial, independent judge, albeit chosen according to procedures and criteria other than those in national legislation: see Cassation, All Civil Sections, no 5942, 18 May 1992, and no 1237, 23 January 2004, in relation to the referral to the Administrative Tribunal of the International Labour Organisation (ILO) of proceedings brought by FAO employees against their employer for the protection of their rights; see also Cassation, All Civil Sections, no 20995/2005 cit., in relation to the enactment of the statute of the European University Institute through the provision of an instrument for resolving disputes before an appropriate committee (which does not merely constitute an internal remedy, in part because the competence of such a committee may be substituted by that of the European Court of Justice.)

6.6. In the case at hand, the conditions for such a guarantee do not exist with regard to the employment relationship in question. Indeed, it is self-evident that it was not until January 2001 that the IPGRI joined the ILO and the jurisdiction of the Administrative Labour Tribunal, to which therefore the dispute could not be referred, given that this organisation's rules provide for the inadmissibility of appeals centred on rights whose facts predate membership of the body. The body's internal rules (known as the Personnel Policy Manual) state that disciplinary measures are to be re-examined by a body known as the Appeals Committee, which may also consider appeals of a non-disciplinary nature. This merely constitutes an internal remedy, which does not provide jurisdictional protection in the aforesaid sense. It should nevertheless be noted that this Manual (para 144.02) expressly excludes the possibility of that body examining appeals relating to the expiry of an employee's contract of employment ("action based on expiration of an appointment by its own terms is not disciplinary in character, nor may such action form the basis of grievance").

6.7. The incompatibility of the rules in question with the aforementioned constitutional principle, due to the exclusion of the right of the body's employees to jurisdictional protection before an independent organ, makes it necessary to ascertain whether an adaptive interpretation of this law is possible, according to the prevailing tenet of interpretation that requires courts to choose, among other hypothetically possible solutions, the one that renders the measure compliant with the Constitution (see Constitutional Court judgements 113/2000, 277/2000, 316/2001, 198/2003). This interpretation may be reached, in accordance with the principle of constitutional supremacy, on the basis of the point provided by Article 17 of the agreement ratified with Law no 67/1994, which states the following: "The Institute shall establish suitable procedures for resolving disputes with its employees." The Institute signing the agreement therefore undertakes a specific obligation, in compliance with the fundamental constitutional guarantee, to create instruments for jurisdictional protection before an impartial and independent body. On the basis of the same principle it must be held that compliance with this obligation is a prerequisite for the application of jurisdictional immunity pursuant to Article 5 of the agreement.

6.8. Therefore, it must be held that the failure to fulfil the obligation in question in this period (precluding recourse to any form of jurisdictional protection of subjective situations by the Institute's employees, as noted under 6.6) prevented the application of immunity; and therefore related disputes, including that brought by Drago, must fall within Italian jurisdiction.

7. Italian jurisdiction must therefore be confirmed, while incorporating the other criticisms. The disputed sentence must be quashed and the case remitted to the court of first instance, which should also reach a decision regarding the costs of the whole proceedings.

A notable shift can also be observed from a series of early decisions of French courts in which the immunities of international organizations were regularly upheld on the basis of protecting international organizations' independence[58] to more recent cases in which French courts have found immunities inapplicable in the absence of legal remedies available to international organizations' staff members. Even in cases where an administrative tribunal was available to aggrieved staff members, the French Court of Cassation has begun examining its design and conformity with the right of access to justice and to a fair trial.[59]

African Development Bank v X, Appeal judgment, 04-41012, ILDC 778 (FR 2005), 25th January 2005, France; Court of Cassation [Cass]

In *African Development Bank v X*,[60] the French Court of Cassation, invoking the 'international ordre public',[61] endorsed the jurisdiction of French courts over an international organization which had been granted immunity under a headquarters agreement when the latter had not made appropriate legal remedies for aggrieved staff members available. The claimant in the case was a civil servant employed by the African Development Bank (ADB), an international organization. After having been dismissed, he tried to obtain damages against the ADB before a French court. France was a party to the relevant treaty granting near absolute immunity to the ADB and the treaty had also been implemented domestically. After the claim was deemed admissible by the lower instance courts, the Court of Cassation was called to decide whether immunities granted to the ADB were applicable in a case where the lack of an internal complaints procedure for aggrieved employees meant that the lack of French jurisdiction left the claimant without any access to legal process. The court chose to deny the ADB immunity on the following basis:

1 According to the judgment under appeal (Paris, 7 October 2003), Mr. X, employed in 1992 by the African Development Bank was dismissed by a letter dated 20 November 1995 from the chairman of this international organisation;

2 It is claimed that the judgment wrongly declared admissible the action for payment of compensation and bonuses, brought by a former international employee (Mr X) against his former employer, an international organisation, the African Development Bank, whose headquarters are in the Ivory Coast, whereas the court of appeal held that the claimant was employed by an international organisation conducting its business in Africa, as a result of which, at the time of the events, this did not fall within the jurisdiction of a contracting party to the European Convention on Human Rights. He could therefore not have recourse to the rights and freedoms provided in that Convention. In proceeding, nonetheless, on an alleged infringement of the substance

58 See A Reinisch, 'Privileges and Immunities' in Klabbers and Wallendahl (n 2) 60; see, eg, *Hintermann v Union de l'Europe Occidentale* (1997) Clunet 141, 14 November 1995, France, Court of Cassation.

59 *X v Organisation for Economic Co-operation and Development*, Appeal judgment, No 09-41030, ILDC 1749 (FR 2010), 29 September 2010, France, Court of Cassation [Cass].

60 *African Development Bank v X* (n 53).

61 See on this concept in French case law Y Kerbrat, Analysis, *African Development Bank v X*, ILDC 778 (FR 2005).

of the right of a court to refuse to apply immunity from jurisdiction, the court of appeal had acted *ultra vires* with regard to Article 52 of the Agreement of 4 August 1963 establishing the African Development Bank, together with Article 1 of the European Convention on Human Rights;

3 However, the African Development Bank cannot invoke immunity from jurisdiction in a lawsuit from an employee who it dismissed, as at the time of the events it had not set up within the organisation a court competent to consider disputes of this kind, making it impossible for a party to approach a court eligible to find on his claim and to exercise a right that falls within international public policy, constituting a denial of justice, which establishes jurisdiction for the French courts if a link with France exists;

4 The court of appeal, on the one hand, correctly held that in the absence of any industrial tribunals set up within the African Development Bank, the immunity from jurisdiction established for the benefit of this bank in Article 52 of the Agreement signed in Khartoum on 4 August 1963, published in decree No. 86-1039 of 12 September 1986, makes it impossible for the employee to exercise his right to have a court consider his case. On the other hand, it found that the link with France was the French nationality of the person concerned, thus the court of appeal did not act ultra vires in holding that the French court was competent to consider the dispute;

However, not all domestic courts have denied immunity to international organizations in situations where no alternative remedy was made available to affected individuals.[62]

Bisson v United Nations and ors, Decision on a Report and Recommendation of a US Magistrate Judge, Case No 06-6352, ILDC 889 (US 2008), 11th February 2008, United States; New York; District Court for the Southern District of New York [SDNY]

In *Bisson v United Nations and ors*[63] the claimant had argued that, like the UN, the World Food Programme (WFP) had waived its immunity by failing to provide an appropriate mode of settlement for her dispute. Specifically, she claimed that the organization's Staff Compensation Plan (SCP) provided no mechanism for compensating general damages and, thus, the remedies available under the SCP were inadequate. The first instance judge had noted that the remedies available under the SCP were similar to most state workers' compensation schemes, which also excluded recovery for pain and suffering. Bisson had also claimed that since Section 29(a) of the UN General Convention[64] conferred a mandatory obligation on the UN to provide an appropriate mode of settlement for her dispute, the absence of such a mechanism was to be construed as an explicit waiver of immunity. The judge concluded that Bisson's dissatisfaction with the compensation policy did not make the policy inadequate and did not constitute waiver of immunity, quoting *Mendaro v World Bank*.[65] In her objection to the first instance judge's report and recommendation (R&R), Bisson claimed that the UN's and WFP's failure to provide for appropriate modes of settlement denied her

62 See, eg, *Georges v United Nations*, 834 F 3d 88 (2d Cir 2016), 18 August 2016, United States, Court of Appeals, discussed below.

63 *Bisson v United Nations and ors* (n 30). Bisson had been reimbursed by the WFP's Staff Compensation Plan (SCP) for medical, hospital, and other expenses directly associated with her injuries and had also been offered compensation in the amount of US$104,000 for permanent partial incapacity, which she had incurred in the course of her employment for the World Food Programme (WFP). She claimed general damages stemming from the defendants' gross negligence and intentionally torturous conduct.

64 Art VIII s 29(a) of the UN General Convention provides that '[t]he United Nations shall make provisions for appropriate modes of settlement of: (a) disputes arising out of contracts or other disputes of a private law character to which the United Nations is a party'.

65 '[E]mployee dissatisfaction with the efficacy of the administrative remedy is insufficient to dissolve the immunity of international organizations.' *Mendaro v World Bank* (n 42).

her rights under the International Covenant on Civil and Political Rights (ICCPR).[66] The higher court rejected all arguments and upheld the WFP's immunity, arguing as follows:

A. Objection as to the Employment Dispute

[. . .]

19 Bisson suggests that if the IOIA did in fact incorporate the FSIA commercial activity exception, her claim might have merit. The Court disagrees. As Magistrate Judge Peck noted, the FSIA commercial activity exception is limited to commercial activity in the United States or that causes a direct effect in the United States. (R&R 24 n.18.) Bisson's injury occurred during her WFP employment in Iraq, and, as a resident of Italy, she has not alleged any effect in the United States. Thus, even assuming *arguendo* that the exception were incorporated, it would not apply to Bisson.

20 More importantly, Magistrate Judge Peck's R&R does not rest upon the claim that Bisson's injuries occurred during her WFP employment; it rests upon the UN and WFP's broad immunity under the UN Convention and the organizations' failure to expressly waive that immunity. As Magistrate Judge Peck noted, "What Bisson misunderstands is that her relationship to the defendants is irrelevant. Even if she were not an employee of the WFP or the UN, both organizations would still be immune from suit by her, and § 29(a) still would not constitute an express waiver." (R&R 27 n.22.)

21 Bisson also raises this objection with regard to the WFP, arguing that her claim extends beyond a mere employment dispute with the WFP to a claim of gross negligence and intentionally tortuous conduct. The argument is based on the same misunderstanding. Regardless of the character of the organization's acts and the context in which they occurred, the WFP, as a part of the UN and entitled to the same organizational immunity, remains immune from Bisson's claims.

B. Objection as to the Workers Compensation Analogy

22 [. . .] Magistrate Judge Peck concluded that employee dissatisfaction with administrative remedies is insufficient to dissolve organizational immunity. Bisson conceded in her Objections that she is an employee of the WFP and has failed to point to anything other than personal dissatisfaction with the SCP to support a claim for general damages.

C. Objection as to § 29(a) of the UN Convention

23 [. . .] Magistrate Judge Peck concluded that § 29(a) contains no language effecting an express waiver under any circumstances and that, even assuming *arguendo* that the UN failed to provide an adequate settlement mechanism, such failure did not constitute waiver because express waiver may not be inferred from conduct. (R&R 26.) That conclusion is correct.

D. Objection as the UN and WFP's Treaty Obligations

24 Bisson claims that the UN's and WFP's failure to provide for appropriate modes of settlement denies her rights under the International Covenant on Civil and Political Rights ("ICCPR"). The ICCPR addresses the "right to self-determination," that is, the right to "freely determine [one's] political status and freely pursue [one's] economic, social and cultural development." ICCPR, Art. 1, § 1. According to the treaty,

66 International Covenant on Civil and Political Rights (adopted 19 December 1966, entered into force 23 March 1976) 999 UNTS 171.

> state parties should "ensure that any person whose rights or freedoms as herein recognized are violated shall have an effective remedy." ICCPR, Art 2, § 3(a)
>
> 25 This objection lacks merit for two reasons. First, Bisson's right to "self-determination" is not implicated in this case. She is not seeking redress from political or civil oppression, but rather recovery of damages for allegedly tortuous conduct. Second, assuming *arguendo* that this case does implicate the rights addressed by the treaty, the ICCPR does not create any judicially enforceable individual rights. When the Senate ratified the ICCPR in 1992, it declared that "Articles 1 through 27 of the Covenant are not self-executing." 138 Cong. Rec. S4781-01, S4784 (Apr. 2, 1992). Moreover, "the ICCPR[] came with attached [Reservations, Understandings, and Declarations] declaring that the ICCPR is not self-executing. This declaration means that the provisions of the ICCPR do not create a private right of action or separate form of relief enforceable in United States courts." *Guaylupo-Moya v. Gonzales*, 423 F.3d 121, 137 (2d Cir. 2005); see also *Igartua De La Rosa v. United States*, 32 F.3d 8, 10 n.1 (1st Cir. 1994) (per curiam), *cert. denied*, 514 U.S. 1049 (1995) (noting that the ICCPR does not give rise to "privately enforceable rights under United States law"). Therefore, even if Bisson has rights under the ICCPR that are implicated here, this Court cannot enforce them.

The issue of balancing immunities with access to justice arose again in *Georges v United Nations*, a 2016 case that came before the Second Circuit of the US Federal Judiciary. The claimants' attempt to bring a class action against the UN, among others, for its alleged role in the spread of a cholera epidemic that affected Haiti in 2010[67] failed after the District Court affirmed the UN's immunity from suit.[68] On appeal, the plaintiffs argued that the UN and the UN Stabilization Mission in Haiti should not benefit from immunity on a number of grounds, among others the alleged violation of the UN's obligation to provide for appropriate dispute resolution mechanisms and due to an alleged violation of plaintiffs' constitutional rights of access to the US federal courts. However, on this crucial question, the court found that the UN's 'fulfilment of an obligation under the [Convention on Privileges and Immunities of the United Nations] to make provisions for appropriate modes of settlement of certain disputes [was] not a condition precedent to its immunity' under that convention.[69]

Where claimants have access to an alternative remedy, national courts are less likely to exercise jurisdiction over the respective international organization. In such cases, alternative remedies are sometimes scrutinized, but often in a deferential and abstract way.[70]

Pistelli v European University Institute, Appeal judgment, No 20995, Guida al diritto 40 (3/2006), ILDC 297 (IT 2005), 28th October 2005, Italy; Supreme Court of Cassation

An example of this approach is found in *Pistelli v European University Institute*,[71] where the Italian Court of Cassation found that the immunities granted to the European University Institute, an international organization, were to be upheld since the internal legal remedy available to individual staff members complied with the Italian constitutional standards of access to court and fair trial:

> 14. [T]he complete exclusion of the right to jurisdictional protection before an independent organ for legal disputes arising from specific relationships must raise doubts about

67 See, eg, E Grinberg and R Roth, 'UN apologizes for Haiti cholera spread in plan to eradicate disease' CNN Online (1 December 2016) http://www.cnn.com/2016/12/01/health/haiti-cholera-un-apology/ (last accessed 1 March 2017).

68 *Georges v United Nations*, 84 F Supp 3d 246 (SDNY 2015), 9 January 2015, United States, District Court.

69 *Georges v United Nations* (n 62) at 90.

70 See also eg the recent practice of the German Federal Constitutional Court: *Company P*, Final judgment, 2 BvR 1848/07, [2010] Gewerblicher Rechtsschutz und Urheberrecht 1031-32, ILDC 1750 (DE 2010), 27 April 2010, Germany, Constitutional Court [BVerfG]; *B and ors* (n 54); BVerfG, Entscheidung vom 28.11.2005 – 2 BvR 1751/03, 2 BvR 1751/03, BVerfGK 6, 368, 28 November 2005, Germany, Constitutional Court [BVerfG].

71 *Pistelli v European University Institute* (n 22).

the constitutional legitimacy of the law ratifying conventions containing such provisions, or, where possible, encourage interpretations of the provisions in line with the Constitution.

14.1 However, the situation is different for a convention which only excludes such disputes from Italian courts, while nevertheless ensuring the jurisdictional protection of the same situations before an impartial and independent judge, even if chosen with procedures and criteria other than those in national legislation. In this case there is no violation of the "cardinal principles" of our Constitution and no reason not to apply the convention, in the form of the ratifying law.

From an examination of the constitutive convention of the EUI it appears that there are adequate instruments for jurisdictional protection, alongside the explicit conformation of immunity from Italian jurisdiction with respect employment relations with non-local personnel.

14.2 The provision in the convention (art 6(5)(c)) under which the statute must define the mechanism for the resolution of disputes between the Institute and the beneficiaries of the statute, has been enacted as, once internal claims have been exhausted the interested party can take disputes to a Commission, whose members are chosen by the High Council from a list compiled by an international judicial organ.

The provision of the Convention appears sufficient to draw the conclusion that the instrument for settling disputes was envisaged as excluding national jurisdiction, and not as a mere internal remedy. In any event, definitive confirmation is provided by Annex 2 of the same Convention, where it states that the provisions of Article 6(5)(c) do not prevent the High Council from designating the Court of Justice of the European Communities, after consultation with the President of that Court, as the body appointed to settle disputes between the Institute and its staff.

The possibility of substituting the competence of the Committee with the Court of Justice of the European Communities definitely reveals the intention for the procedure not to be merely an interim remedy, following which is the possibility of access to jurisdictional protection, but rather the exclusive jurisdictional means of settling disputes with staff.

It is possible to contrast the approach in *Pistelli*, based on an abstract interpretation of the relevant provisions, without examining the actual quality of the available remedy,[72] with the approach taken by the Belgian courts in *Siedler v Western European Union*.[73]

Siedler v Western European Union, Appeal Judgment, JT 2004, 617, ILDC 53 (BE 2003), 17th September 2003, Belgium; Brussels; Labour Court of Appeal; 4th Chamber

Siedler v WEU is a prominent case in which a domestic court engaged in a balancing of immunities with access to justice and fair trial concerns by engaging more comprehensively than most other courts with the particular design of the available remedy.[74] It found that the internal procedure for the settlement of employment disputes within the WEU,[75] an international organization headquartered in Belgium, did not offer the guarantees necessary to

72 M Iovane, Analysis, *Pistelli v European University Institute*, ILDC 297 (IT 2005) A3: 'The Court limited itself to quoting a couple of articles where the setting up of this system is envisaged in principle. However, there is no further analysis on the composition of the commission, on its procedural rules, on the substantive norms it applies, or on the possibility of challenging its decisions before an appellate mechanism'.

73 *Siedler v Western European Union* (n 53).

74 Also engaging in this type of balancing is *Illemassene v OECD*, Cour de cassation, Chambre Sociale, No de pourvoi: 09-41030, 30 November 2010.

75 The WEU was 'effectively closed' in 2010. See Western European Union, 'Statement of the Presidency of the Permanent Council of the WEU on behalf of the High Contracting Parties to the Modified Brussels Treaty: Belgium, France, Germany, Greece, Italy, Luxembourg, The Netherlands, Portugal, Spain and the United Kingdom' (31 March 2010).

secure a fair trial and denied immunity to the organization. The appellate court examined the WEU's Appeals Commission as follows:

> 59 The WEU appeals commission was properly vested with a jurisdictional role competent to settle a dispute, to announce the annulment of a challenged decision brought before it should the event arise, and to order the organization to repair the damage caused by a challenged decision and to reimburse the costs (art. 59). The adversarial character of procedure is guaranteed. However, there is no provision as regards the implementation of its decisions.
>
> 60 On the other hand, the public character of the debates is not guaranteed—the hearings of the appeals are secret indeed (art. 57)—nor is the publication of the decisions guaranteed (art. 5). The designation of members is assigned to an intergovernmental Council, which appoints members of the Commission for a period of two years.
>
> 61 The method of designation and the short period of the mandate carry the risk of linking the members of the commission too closely with the organization. Permanence is a necessary precondition of the notion of independence. There is no provision for the eventuality of challenging impartiality.
>
> 62 The recourse provided by the WEU personnel stature does not offer all the guarantees inherent in the notion of due process, with some of the most important conditions being flawed.
>
> 63 It is thus established that the limitation on the access to the normal courts by virtue of the jurisdictional immunity of the WEU is incompatible with art. 6, paragraph 1 of the European Convention on Human Rights (ECHR).

Thus, examining the WEU's Appeals Commission, the Belgian appellate court preliminarily concluded that this internal body was properly vested with a jurisdictional role competent to settle a dispute in an adversarial manner, to announce the annulment of a challenged decision brought before it should the event arise, to order the organization to repair the damage caused by a challenged decision, and to reimburse costs.[76] However, it found fault in the fact that no provisions regarding the implementation of the Appeals Commission's decisions existed. Moreover, the appellate court admonished the Appeals Commission that the public nature of the debates was not guaranteed as the hearings of the latter were secret, the publication of the decisions was not guaranteed, and the appointment of the Commission's members for a period of two years was entrusted to an Inter-governmental Council. In the appellate court's view, the latter was seen to carry the risk of linking the members of the Commission too closely to the organization since it violated permanence as a necessary precondition of the notion of independence. Moreover, no provision existed to permit challenges concerning the impartiality of individual members. As the procedure provided by the WEU personnel statute thus did not offer all the guarantees inherent in the notion of fair trial, 'with some of the most important conditions being flawed', the court finally concluded that the limitation on the access to the normal courts by virtue of the jurisdictional immunity of the WEU was incompatible with Article 6(1) of the ECHR.

On 21 December 2009, the Court of Cassation delivered its decision in *Siedler*,[77] as well as in another case[78] relating to the immunity of an international organization which also arose from

76 *Siedler v Western European Union* (n 53), para 59.

77 *Western European Union v Siedler*, Appeal judgment, Cass No S 04 0129 F, ILDC 1625 (BE 2009), 21 December 2009, Belgium, Court of Cassation.

78 *Secrétariat Général du Groupe des États d'Afrique, des Caraïbes et du Pacifique contre Lutchmaya*, Cour de cassation de Belgique, 21 December 2009, C03/0328F/1. This judgment is related to *Lutchmaya v General Secretariat of the ACP Group*, Appeal decision, *Journal des Tribunaux* 2003, 684, ILDC 1363 (BE 2003), 4 March 2003, Belgium, Brussels, Court of Appeal. In *Lutchmaya v General Secretariat of the ACP Group* a Belgian appellate

a staff dispute. In *WEU v Siedler*, the Court of Cassation approved the legal qualification made by the appellate court, particularly quoting the appellate court's finding that the mode of appointment of the members of the Appeals Commission and the short duration of their mandate entailed the risk that its members would be too closely tied to the organization and emphasizing that the irremovability of the Commission's members was a necessary corollary to the notion of independence.[79] However, the appeal raised by the WEU was granted insofar as it concerned the application of domestic provisions of labour law. The Court of Cassation held that these were not applicable in the concrete case in light of the general principle of law providing for the primacy of directly applicable provisions of international law over provisions of domestic law.[80]

Balancing immunities of international organizations with access to justice concerns was also an issue in *SA Energies Nouvelles et Environnement v Agence Spatiale Européenne*, a case in which the Belgian Court of Cassation confirmed lower instance judgments that had affirmed the immunity of Agence Spatiale Européenne, an international organization, in light of a claim by an unsuccessful subcontractor, SA Energies Nouvelles et Environnement. The lower instance courts had considered a (non-judicial) ombudsman procedure, a judicial remedy of the subcontractor towards the prime contractors as well as arbitration, in combination or by themselves, to have provided one or more reasonable alternative remedies. While this case seems more deferential than *Siedler*, it does not in fact mark a move away by the Belgian Court of Cassation from a focus on the availability of reasonable alternative remedies and fair trial concerns. Rather, the Court of Cassation explained its conclusion by the particular context of the case, which involved a subcontractor who was only indirectly affected by the respective international organization's activities and who did have at least one judicial remedy at its disposal, namely towards the prime contractors.[81]

The Association of Citizens Mothers of Srebrenica et al v The State of the Netherlands and the United Nations, Appeal Court in The Hague, Case-list number 200.022.151/01, 30 March 2010 (not in ILDC)

A comparable reasoning is found in the Dutch case *Mothers of Srebrenica et al v State of the Netherlands and the United Nations.*[82] In this case, the Appeal Court in The Hague upheld the immunity of the UN in a case involving the alleged shared responsibility of a state and an international organization also on the ground that the individuals concerned had at least two other entities to hold accountable. The court found that:

> [i]t cannot be said in this case that the right of access to a court of law of the Association et al. is violated if the UN's invocation of immunity from prosecution is allowed. The

court had decided to deny immunity based on the reasoning that an international organization could only invoke its immunity in domestic proceedings, provided that the plaintiff had access to other reasonable available means to protect his or her rights guaranteed by art 6(1) of the ECHR. In contrast to *Siedler v WEU* (n 53), the lack of any complaints mechanism whatsoever made the court's task easier. Moreover, the court found that the reasoning of the ECtHR in *Waite and Kennedy* was also applicable to the immunity from execution, since execution was seen to form an integral part of a fair trial. An appeal by the ACP Group Secretariat led to a decision of the Court of Cassation handed down on the same date as the *WEU v Siedler* cassation decision. Therein, the Court of Cassation upheld the appellate court's judgment, which had given precedence to art 6(1) of the ECHR over the relevant seat agreement. The court again essentially referred to the jurisprudence of the ECHR and stressed that it was necessary to examine whether the person against whom immunity from execution was invoked had other reasonable means effectively to protect the rights guaranteed to him or her by the Convention. See also on the Belgian jurisprudence C Ryngaert, 'The Immunity of International Organizations Before Domestic Courts: Recent Trends' (2010) 7 *International Organizations Law Review* 121.

79 See *Western European Union v Siedler* (n 77) at 21 and 22.

80 ibid, 23.

81 *SA Energies Nouvelles et Environnement v Agence Spatiale Européenne* (n 6).

82 *The Association of Citizens Mothers of Srebrenica et al v The State of the Netherlands and the United Nations*, Case-list number 200.022.151/01, 30 March 2010, Netherlands, Appeal Court in The Hague, Commerce section.

> Court of Appeal refers to the decision in the case of the European Court of 21 September 1990 *Fayed v. United Kingdom*, no. 17101/90, which shows that the European Court considers even fairly far-reaching restrictions to access to a court of law acceptable. There is no question of such far-reaching restrictions in this case, as the Association et al. can hold two categories of parties liable for the damages incurred by the mothers of Srebrenica, namely the perpetrators of the genocide and the State. Seen in this light the Court of Appeal does not hold decisive, although it regrets, the fact that the UN has not instigated an alternative course of proceedings in conformity with their obligations under article VIII § 29 in the preamble and under (a) of the Convention for claims as this in order to waive the immunity from prosecution. [. . .] The conclusion must be that there is no unacceptable violation of article 6 ECHR or article 14 ICCPR if a Netherlands court of law in this case upholds the immunity from prosecution granted to the UN. [. . .][83]

Stichting Mothers of Srebrenica and ors v Netherlands and United Nations, Final appeal judgment, LJN: BW1999, ILDC 1760 (NL 2012), 13th April 2012, Netherlands; Supreme Court [HR]

On appeal before the Supreme Court, however, the Dutch Supreme Court invoked the ICJ's *Jurisdictional Immunities* case[84] in order to hold that the UN enjoyed immunity from jurisdiction, regardless of the availability of alternative redress and regardless of the seriousness of the alleged wrongdoing:

> H6. In *Jurisdictional Immunities of the State* [. . .] the ICJ held that it could 'find no basis in the State practice from which customary international law is derived that international law makes the entitlement of a State to immunity dependent upon the existence of effective alternative means of securing redress'. The difference between the immunity of states and the immunity of international organizations did not justify a different assessment of the relation between the immunity of the UN and the right of access to court than of the relation between the immunity of the state and that right. The immunity of the UN applied irrespective of the gravity of the allegations.[85]

In other words, even if the claimants had only one party, the UN, to hold accountable, the Supreme Court's reasoning would lead to an absolute understanding of the UN's immunity in this case. This reasoning by the Dutch Supreme Court was later confirmed by the ECtHR in its judgment in the case *Stichting Mothers of Srebrenica and Others against the Netherlands*. Among others, the court there had to 'decide whether the Netherlands violated the applicants' right of "access to a court", as guaranteed by Article 6 of the Convention, by granting the United Nations immunity from domestic jurisdiction'.[86] Given the powerful impact of the ECtHR's judgments regionally, and sometimes beyond, its reasoning on the point is worth citing in full:

> 163. As the applicants rightly pointed out, in *Waite and Kennedy* (cited above, § 68)—as in *Beer and Regan* (cited above, § 58)—the Court considered it a 'material factor', in determining whether granting an international organisation immunity from domestic jurisdiction was permissible under the Convention, whether the applicants had available to them reasonable alternative means to protect effectively their rights under the Convention. In the present case it is beyond doubt that no such alternative means existed either under Netherlands domestic law or under the law of the United Nations.

83 ibid, paras 5.13–5.14.

84 *Jurisdictional Immunities of the State* (*Germany v Italy: Greece intervening*) [2012] ICJ Rep 99.

85 *Stichting Mothers of Srebrenica and ors v Netherlands and United Nations*, Final appeal judgment, LJN: BW1999, ILDC 1760 (NL 2012), 13 April 2012, Supreme Court [HR] H6.

86 *Stichting Mothers of Srebrenica and Others against the Netherlands* (n 55) para 137.

> 164. It does not follow, however, that in the absence of an alternative remedy the recognition of immunity is ipso facto constitutive of a violation of the right of access to a court. In respect of the sovereign immunity of foreign States, the ICJ has explicitly denied the existence of such a rule (*Jurisdictional Immunities of the State (Germany v. Italy: Greece intervening)*, § 101). As regards international organisations, this Court's judgments in *Waite and Kennedy* and *Beer and Regan* cannot be interpreted in such absolute terms either.
>
> 165. There remains the fact that the United Nations has not, until now, made provision for "modes of settlement" appropriate to the dispute here in issue. Regardless of whether Article VIII, section 29 of the Convention on the Privileges and Immunities of the United Nations can be construed so as to require a dispute settlement body to be set up in the present case, this state of affairs is not imputable to the Netherlands. Nor does Article 6 of the Convention require the Netherlands to step in: as pointed out above, the present case is fundamentally different from earlier cases in which the Court has had to consider the immunity from domestic jurisdiction enjoyed by international organisations, and the nature of the applicants' claims did not compel the Netherlands to provide a remedy against the United Nations in its own courts. [. . .]
>
> 169. The above findings lead the Court to find that in the present case the grant of immunity to the United Nations served a legitimate purpose and was not disproportionate.[87]

VI. Responsibility of International Organizations

Both domestic and international cases dealing directly with the responsibility of international organizations remain scarce, as was also acknowledged in the General Commentary of the International Law Commission (ILC) to its Draft Articles on the Responsibility of international organizations.[88] For example, the reports presented by the ILC's Special Rapporteur on the topic identified only a small number of domestic cases, some European Court of Justice (ECJ) cases, and some cases decided by international tribunals, many of them by the ECtHR.[89] One of the domestic cases mentioned by the ILC's Special Rapporteur was *Nissan v Attorney-General*,[90] which concerned the alleged responsibility of the United Kingdom (UK) for damage caused by its troops as part of the United Nations Peacekeeping Force in Cyprus (UNPFCYP). In particular, the opinion expressed in the judgment by Lord Morris of Borth-y-Gest implies *a contrario* that the UN could incur responsibility. Lord Morris found that:

---

87 ibid, paras 163–69.

88 ILC, 'Draft articles on the responsibility of international organizations, with commentaries' (2011) UN Doc A/66/10; see also ILC, 'Titles and texts of the draft articles on the responsibility of international organizations adopted by the Drafting Committee on second reading in 2011' (Statement of the Chairman of the Drafting Committee) (2011) UN Doc A/CN.4/L.778.

89 ILC, 'First report on responsibility of international organizations, by Mr Giorgio Gaja, Special Rapporteur' (2003) UN Doc A/CN. 4/532; ILC, 'Second report on responsibility of international organizations, by Mr Giorgio Gaja, Special Rapporteur' (2004) UN Doc A/CN.4/541; ILC, 'Third report on responsibility of international organizations, by Mr Giorgio Gaja, Special Rapporteur' (2005) UN Doc A/CN.4/553; ILC, 'Fourth report on responsibility of international organizations by Mr Giorgio Gaja, Special Rapporteur' (2006) UN Doc A/CN.4/564; ILC, Fifth report on responsibility of international organizations by Mr Giorgio Gaja, Special Rapporteur' (2007) UN Doc A/CN.3/583; ILC, 'Sixth report on responsibility of international organizations by Mr Giorgio Gaja, Special Rapporteur' (2008) UN Doc A/CN.4/596. See also for an analysis G Hafner, 'Is the Topic of Responsibility of International Organizations Ripe for Codification? Some Critical Remarks' in U Fastenrath and others, *From Bilateralism to Community Interest: Essays in Honour of Bruno Simma* (OUP 2011) 695–717.

90 *Nissan v Attorney-General* [1968] 1 QB 286 (CA), [1969] 1 All ER 629 (HL).

> [t]hough national contingents were under the authority of the United Nations and subject to the instructions of the commander, the troops as members of the force remained in their national service. The British forces continued, therefore, to be soldiers of Her Majesty. Members of the United Nations force were subject to the exclusive jurisdiction of their respective national state in respect of any criminal offences committed by them in Cyprus.

Some domestic courts have addressed the question of whether a certain internationally wrongful act was attributable to an international organization or to a state or states in order to determine whether it had jurisdiction. Thus, in the case *HN v Netherlands (Ministry of Defence and Ministry of Foreign Affairs)*, Dutch courts were asked to examine the responsibility of the Netherlands and the UN for allegedly wrongful conduct committed by 'Dutchbat', a Dutch battalion sent to participate in the United Nations Protection Force (UNPROFOR) in order to protect the Srebrenica safe haven in Bosnia and Herzegovina, where an act of genocide was committed against the Bosnian Muslims in 1995.[91] In the first instance, the district court,[92] relying on the ECtHR's judgment in joined cases *A Behrami and B Behrami v France and Saramati v France, Germany and Norway (Behrami and Saramati)*,[93] concluded that the allegedly wrongful acts were attributable exclusively to the UN. Therefore, the claim by the applicant survivor had to be denied. However, upon appeal, and later before the Supreme Court, this reasoning was not upheld. Rather, the Dutch Supreme Court supported a theory of a 'possibility of dual attribution of given conduct' under certain circumstances. Thus, the Supreme Court held that:

> [i]nternational law, in particular article 7 [of the ILC Draft articles on the responsibility of international organizations (DARIO)] in conjunction with article 48 (1) DARIO, does not exclude the possibility of dual attribution of given conduct. It follows that the Court of Appeal was able to leave open whether the United Nations had effective control over Dutchbat's conduct in the early evening of 13 July 1995. Even if this was the case, it does not necessarily mean that the United Nations had exclusive responsibility.[94]

R (on the application of Al-Jedda) v Secretary of State for Defence, Appeal judgment, (2007) UKHL 58, (2008) 1 AC 332, [2008] 3 All ER 28, [2008] HRLR 13, [2008] UKHRR 244, ILDC 832 (UK 2007), 12th December 2007, United Kingdom; House of Lords [UKHL]

The case of *R (on the application of Al-Jedda) v Secretary of State for Defence*[95] also concerned the question of attribution of allegedly wrongful acts either to a state or to an international

---

91 In 2007, the ICJ ruled that 'the acts of those who committed genocide at Srebrenica cannot be attributed to the Respondent under the rules of international law of State responsibility: thus, the international responsibility of the Respondent is not engaged on this basis'. See *Application of the Convention on the Prevention and Punishment of the Crime of Genocide* (*Bosnia and Herzegovina v Serbia and Montenegro*) [2007] ICJ Rep 43, para 415.

92 *HN v Netherlands* (Ministry of Defence and Ministry of Foreign Affairs), First Instance Judgment, Decision No LJN: BF0181, Case No 265615, ILDC 1092 (NL 2008), 10 September 2008, Netherlands, The Hague, District Court (finding that 'it must be concluded that the reprehended Dutchbat actions must be attributed exclusively to the United Nations, so that the State's primary defence succeeds. This means that the State cannot be held responsible for any breach of contract or wrongful act committed by Dutchbat. As follows from 4.4 of this ruling, neither is the State liable for wrongful action taken by those in charge of the armed forces or members of National Government').

93 ECtHR, *Agim Behrami and Bekir Behrami v France and Ruzhdi Saramati v France*, Germany and Norway (Decision on Admissibility) App Nos 71412/01 and 78166/01 (2 July 2009).

94 *Netherlands v Nuhanović*, 6 September 2013, Supreme Court of the Netherlands, First Chamber, 12/03324, LZ/TT, paras 3.11.2.

95 *R (on the application of Al-Jedda) v Secretary of State for Defence*, Appeal judgment, (2007) UKHL 58, (2008) 1 AC 332, [2008] 3 All ER 28, [2008] HRLR 13, [2008] UKHRR 244, ILDC 832 (UK 2007), 12 December 2007, United Kingdom, House of Lords [UKHL].

organization. The acts had been committed by UK forces in the framework of the multinational task force (MNF), which had been authorized by the UN Security Council through Resolution 1511[96] in order to support the security situation in Iraq following the intervention by the US and its allies. Distinguishing the case at hand from *Behrami and Saramati*, the House of Lords affirmed jurisdiction but found the UK not responsible. The House of Lords described the approach of the ECtHR in *Behrami and Saramati*, summarizing the court's finding and distinguishing the case from the one at hand as follows:

> 21. [T]he [ECtHR, in *Behrami and Saramati*] accordingly concluded (para 151) that, since UNMIK was a subsidiary organ of the UN created under Chapter VII and KFOR was exercising powers lawfully delegated under Chapter VII by the Security Council, their actions were directly attributable to the UN, an organisation of universal jurisdiction fulfilling its imperative collective security objective. The applicants' complaints were accordingly incompatible *ratione personae* with the provisions of the Convention.
>
> 22. Against the factual background described above a number of questions must be asked in the present case. Were UK forces placed at the disposal of the UN? Did the UN exercise effective control over the conduct of UK forces? Is the specific conduct of the UK forces in detaining the appellant to be attributed to the UN rather than the UK? Did the UN have effective command and control over the conduct of UK forces when they detained the appellant? Were the UK forces part of a UN peacekeeping force in Iraq? In my opinion the answer to all these questions is in the negative.
>
> 23. The UN did not dispatch the coalition forces to Iraq. The CPA was established by the coalition states, notably the US, not the UN. When the coalition states became occupying powers in Iraq they had no UN mandate. Thus when the case of Mr Mousa reached the House as one of those considered in *R(Al-Skeini and others) v Secretary of State for Defence) (The Redress Trust intervening)* [2007] UKHL 26, [2007] 3 WLR 33 the Secretary of State accepted that the UK was liable under the European Convention for any ill-treatment Mr Mousa suffered, while unsuccessfully denying liability under the Human Rights Act 1998. It has not, to my knowledge, been suggested that the treatment of detainees at Abu Ghraib was attributable to the UN rather than the US. Following UNSCR 1483 in May 2003 the role of the UN was a limited one focused on humanitarian relief and reconstruction, a role strengthened but not fundamentally altered by UNSCR 1511 in October 2003. By UNSCR 1511, and again by UNSCR 1546 in June 2004, the UN gave the multinational force express authority to take steps to promote security and stability in Iraq, but (adopting the distinction formulated by the European Court in para 43 of its judgment in *Behrami and Saramati*) the Security Council was not delegating its power by empowering the UK to exercise its function but was authorising the UK to carry out functions it could not perform itself. At no time did the US or the UK disclaim responsibility for the conduct of their forces or the UN accept it. It cannot realistically be said that US and UK forces were under the effective command and control of the UN, or that UK forces were under such command and control when they detained the appellant.
>
> 24. The analogy with the situation in Kosovo breaks down, in my opinion, at almost every point. The international security and civil presences in Kosovo were established at the express behest of the UN and operated under its auspices, with UNMIK a subsidiary organ of the UN. The multinational force in Iraq was not established at

96 UNSC Res 1511 (16 October 2003) UN Doc S/RES/1511.

> the behest of the UN, was not mandated to operate under UN auspices and was not a subsidiary organ of the UN. There was no delegation of UN power in Iraq. It is quite true that duties to report were imposed in Iraq as in Kosovo. But the UN's proper concern for the protection of human rights and observance of humanitarian law called for no less, and it is one thing to receive reports, another to exercise effective command and control. It does not seem to me significant that in each case the UN reserved power to revoke its authority, since it could clearly do so whether or not it reserved power to do so.
>
> 25. I would resolve this first issue in favour of the appellant and against the Secretary of State.

While accepting the jurisdictional arguments of the claimant, the House of Lords had decided that, owing to Article 103 of the UN Charter, the relevant UN Security Council resolutions prevailed over the UK's obligations under the ECHR, and therefore found no violation of the right to security and liberty of the person under Article 5(1) of the ECHR. Subsequently, the applicant brought a case before the ECtHR, where the Grand Chamber confirmed the House of Lords' reasoning with respect to jurisdiction, but found a violation of the applicants' rights under the ECHR by the UK and ordered compensation.[97]

VII. Conclusion

Two broad factual developments have strongly motivated affected persons to seek to bring international organizations before domestic courts: on the one hand, the extent of the activities of international organizations that can negatively affect these persons and, on the other, the possible lack of alternative remedies available to such affected persons to secure their interests or rights. Domestic court cases involving international organizations reflect the diversity of the sources of the institutional law of international organizations, various traditions of incorporating international law into the domestic legal order, and the increasing tendency of some courts to adopt a more restrictive reading of international organizations' immunities or to deny them altogether in order to uphold the right of access to justice and to a fair trial of all those affected.

97 ECtHR, *Al-Jedda v UK*, App No 27021/08 (7 July 2011) and ECtHR, *Al-Skeini v UK*, App No 55721/07 (7 July 2011).

6

The Law of Treaties

CHRISTINA BINDER AND CATHERINE BRÖLMANN*

I. Introduction

The current chapter does not aim at repeating the several books and treatises on the law of treaties[1]—that is, the international legal rules governing the conclusion, application, termination, and so forth, of treaties. Rather, it focuses on how the law of treaties is used and applied in domestic courts. This perspective is increasingly relevant as a growing body of substantive international rules and norms is enshrined in treaties (or treaty law), with normative effect in domestic legal orders.

Domestic courts may be faced with the entire range of rules codified in the Vienna Convention on the Law of Treaties (VCLT),[2] the Vienna Convention on Succession of States in respect of Treaties[3] and the Vienna Convention on the Law of Treaties between States and International Organizations or between International Organizations (1986 VCLT).[4] Judging from the case law collected in the ILDC it seems, however, that certain questions are especially urgent: notably those revolving around consent, entry into force, termination, interpretation, and self-executing character of treaties. The sections in this chapter then in a general sense correspond to themes and stages in the 'life of a treaty' that play a role in domestic case law: conclusion and entry into force (II); self-executing character (III); binding force and observance (IV); reservations and declarations (V); interpretation (VI); scope (VII); successive treaties (VIII); amendment and modification (IX); and termination and suspension (X).

This is not the only possible classification. To some extent, the terms are a matter of choice, which, if consistently maintained, does not always correspond to the terms chosen by the various domestic courts. For example, as—in accordance with the regime of the Vienna Conventions—we do not distinguish between bilateral and multilateral treaties, we do not observe a distinction between 'termination' (used mostly in relation to bilateral treaties) and 'withdrawal' (used mostly in relation to multilateral treaties). We use the term 'self-executing' interchangeably with 'directly applicable' or 'directly effective'. On the other hand, for terminological clarity, the following terms are to be distinguished: 'application' of a rule means it is being put to use on a legal case or question; 'implementation' refers to the creation of additional (international and—mostly—national) legal rules to flesh out a given treaty rule. 'Bindingness' of a treaty refers to its legal effect vis-à-vis a particular party, while 'entry into force' signifies the treaty instrument as such takes normative effect.

* Our gratitude is due to Mr Robin Peeters (LLM) as well as to Mrs Isabella Brunner for their valuable research assistance.

1 See, eg, commentaries: Oliver Dörr and Kirsten Schmalenbach (eds), *Vienna Convention on the Law of Treaties: A Commentary* (Springer 2012); Olivier Corten and Pierre Klein (eds), *The Vienna Conventions on the Law of Treaties: A Commentary* (Oxford University Press 2011).

2 Vienna Convention on the Law of Treaties (VCLT) (adopted on 22 May 1969, entered into force 27 January 1980) 1155 UNTS 331.

3 Vienna Convention on Succession of States in respect of Treaties (adopted 23 August 1978, entered into force on 6 November 1996) 1946 UNTS 3.

4 Vienna Convention on the Law of Treaties between States and International Organizations or between International Organizations (adopted 21 March 1986, not yet in force) 25 ILM 543.

A central feature in the treatment of law of treaties questions in domestic case law is the interaction (and occasional confusion) between the domestic and international law levels. This interaction often adds a particular dimension to the legal questions addressed by national courts—such as when the domestic approval and the international expression of consent are combined to appraise the conclusion of a treaty, or when the normative scope of the international rule as such is linked to domestic law rules for incorporation to appraise its applicability in domestic law.

Leaving aside the interplay of international and domestic law, the question as to how a treaty formally takes effect within a domestic order is for the pertinent constitutional system to decide. That topic is treated in Chapter 1 of this volume. In this chapter we will therefore not discuss the incorporation of international law into national systems, nor address their 'monist' and 'dualist' characteristics. We will, on the other hand, look at the possible 'self-executing' character of treaties, as this relates to the normative quality of the international rule as such. More generally, we only marginally address topics of the law of treaties, as, eg, state succession, that are treated in other parts of this book.

The basis for this chapter is constituted by selected case law from domestic courts in different jurisdictions. In the ILDC database, as of January 2017, some 500 cases were identified as containing issues related to the law of treaties.[5] Of those, some forty cases with highly relevant content were used.[6] The remaining cases with law of treaties aspects are not *per se* without relevance. On the contrary, many contain relevant elements or, while placed in one law of treaties category, have significance for at least one other category.[7] This is why footnotes may refer to cases in addition to those mentioned in the main text. Occasionally the chapter includes a reference to decisions of non-national human rights bodies, where this may provide relevant context.

II. Conclusion and Entry into Force

Questions relating to the conclusion and entry into force of a treaty, as with the law of treaties in general, most often arise alongside an issue of substantive law. These questions may refer to rules of domestic law (eg, the requirement of parliamentary approval for the government to bind the state to a treaty), or of international law (eg, the need of 'full powers' for the state representative to perform international legal acts in relation to treaty-making—ultimately the 'expression of consent to be bound' as envisaged in Articles 11 ff of the VCLT). Domestic courts are often

5 In addition to these cases classified in the *law of treaties* section, we have added several cases to the list that had been placed in the *sources, foundations and principles of international law* section but were labelled with a 'law of treaties' keyword.

6 The limited number necessarily implies that cases are referred to by way of example. The following criteria were applied for case selection. The choice of certain cases rather than others was made in first place with respect to their relevance for the topics discussed. However, certain topics came up more frequently than others, with eg the category of interpretation containing approximately thirty cases while the category of *fundamental change of circumstances* has only one. Since it seemed important to include a maximum of categories in the present contribution, this necessarily meant that for the smaller categories such as *fundamental change of circumstances* or *entry into force*, sometimes cases had to be chosen even though their content was not always in every way substantial. For the bigger category of *interpretation*, conversely, this led to deselecting several interesting cases, as to leave space for cases of other categories.

7 For example, cases in the category of *scope* were often relevant for *interpretation* too; those in *binding force and observance* also raised questions of *conclusion and entry into force* or the *self-executing character of treaties*. On the other hand, some ILDC categories did not appear helpful for the systemization of the cases—this was in any way the case with the category of *application*. The categories of *breach* and *effect for third states* comprised one and zero cases respectively. Those three categories were therefore deleted from the final list and the cases placed under categories where they were more suited. Other categories were joined and will be treated in one section because of their intrinsic relatedness, namely 'binding force' and 'observance'; 'termination and suspension' and 'fundamental change'.

faced with questions that touch upon both the domestic and the international law level. Possible confusion is furthered by the terminological ambiguity of words such as 'approval', 'adoption', and 'ratification' which, depending on the commentator and on the constitutional system concerned, may refer to a domestic legal act or to an international legal act. Conclusion and entry into force together give the treaty full legal effect at the international level. How the treaty then takes effect within a particular domestic order is for the pertinent constitutional system to decide.[8]

1. Conclusion

'Conclusion' of a treaty is a much-used but imprecise term, which, depending on the context, may comprise several stages, ranging from negotiation of the text to the treaty taking legal effect by 'entry into force'. In this chapter we take as the prime element of 'conclusion' the act by which a state (or other legal actor) expresses its legal will to be bound by an agreement. Such an 'expression of consent to be bound' (Articles 11 ff of the VCLT) may take different legal shapes and forms, notably that of 'simplified signature' (expressing consent by one single signing action—Article 12 of the VCLT) and 'ratification' (the confirmation of an earlier, non-definitive signature—Article 14 of the VCLT).

In the context of treaty conclusion, domestic courts generally face questions of the validity and the applicability of treaties in the domestic order. This involves, eg, the legal conditions for expression of consent. Some conditions pertain to international and some to domestic law, with an occasional intertanglement in the legal reading of the facts.

Thus, the 'consent' of a competent state organ at the domestic level and the 'consent' of a state at the international level may become linked in an intricate manner. This happened in the case *Harksen v President of South Africa and Others*,[9] where it was claimed that the consent of the president to extradite Mr Harksen to Germany in the absence of an extradition treaty amounted to an international agreement as such, and that in concluding this agreement the president had infringed the South African constitution. The Constitutional Court, however, observed a strict separation between the international and the domestic law levels and reasoned that the president's consent pertained only to the latter:

Harksen v President of South Africa and ors, Appeal to Constitutional Court, Case CCT 41/99, 2000 (2) SA 825 (CC), ILDC 659 (ZA 2000), 30th March 2000, South Africa; Constitutional Court [CC]

> [14] Although presidential consent under section 3(2) [of the Extradition Act 67, 1962], may eventually have international resonance, the Act governs applications for extradition on the domestic plane only. This is true whether there is a treaty or not. Where South Africa is bound by an extradition treaty, its terms will govern the international obligations of this country to the foreign State. Nonetheless, as far as domestic law is concerned the implementation of those international obligations is expressly made subject to the provisions of the Act. Similarly, in a non-treaty extradition, the surrender of the person sought is subject to the requirements of the Act. [. . .]
>
> [21] Although the judicial determination of the existence of an international agreement may require the consideration of a number of complex issues, the decisive factor is said to be whether "the instrument is intended to create international legal rights and obligations between the parties". [. . .] the consent given by the President served merely to bring the appellant within the purview of the Act. It was a domestic act

8 See T Ingadottir, 'Enforcement of Decisions of International Courts at the National Level' Chapter 10 in this volume.

9 *Harksen v President of South Africa and ors*, Appeal to Constitutional Court, Case CCT 41/99; ILDC 659 (ZA 2000) 2000 (2) SA 825 (CC), 30 March 2000.

> never intended to create international legal rights and obligations. It was not an agreement at all: neither an international agreement as maintained by the appellant nor an "informal agreement" as suggested by the High Court.

An interplay of the international and the national law level was at issue also in *Bayan v Romulo, Muna v Romulo and Ople, Petition for certiorari, mandamus, and prohibition.*[10] In this case the Philippine Supreme Court held that an exchange of notes on non-surrender of US nationals to the ICC constituted a valid treaty between the Philippines and the US; such first of all under Philippine law, as the president had validly expressed consent to be bound on behalf of the state without involvement of the Senate since for its subject matter the agreement could lawfully fall in the category of 'executive agreements'; and secondly under international law, which after all recognized both 'exchanges of notes' and the domestic law category of 'executive agreements' as regular treaties. As for substance, and incidentally, bilateral non-surrender treaties were admissible, in accordance with Article 98 of the ICC Statute.

Bayan v Romulo, Muna v Romulo and Ople, Petition for certiorari, mandamus, and prohibition, GR no 159618, ILDC 2059 (PH 2011), 1st February 2011, Philippines; Supreme Court

> 22 [...] An exchange of notes falls "into the category of inter-governmental agreements," which is an internationally accepted form of international agreement. The United Nations Treaty Collections (Treaty Reference Guide) defines the term as follows:
>
> An "exchange of notes" is a record of a routine agreement, that has many similarities with the private law contract. The agreement consists of the exchange of two documents, each of the parties being in the possession of the one signed by the representative of the other. Under the usual procedure, the accepting State repeats the text of the offering State to record its assent. The signatories of the letters may be government Ministers, diplomats or departmental heads. The technique of exchange of notes is frequently resorted to, either because of its speedy procedure, or, sometimes, to avoid the process of legislative approval.
>
> 23 In another perspective, the terms "exchange of notes" and "executive agreements" have been used interchangeably, exchange of notes being considered a form of executive agreement that becomes binding through executive action. On the other hand, executive agreements concluded by the President "sometimes take the form of exchange of notes and at other times that of more formal documents denominated 'agreements' or 'protocols'." As former US High Commissioner to the Philippines Francis B. Sayre observed in his work, The Constitutionality of Trade Agreement Acts:
>
> The point where ordinary correspondence between this and other governments ends and agreements — whether denominated executive agreements or exchange of notes or otherwise — begin, may sometimes be difficult of ready ascertainment. [...]
>
> 24 It is fairly clear from the foregoing disquisition that E/N BFO-028-03 — be it viewed as the Non-Surrender Agreement itself, or as an integral instrument of acceptance thereof or as consent to be bound — is a recognized mode of concluding a legally binding international written contract among nations.
>
> 25 Article 2 of the Vienna Convention on the Law of Treaties defines a treaty as "an international agreement concluded between states in written form and governed by international law, whether embodied in a single instrument or in two or more related instruments and whatever its particular designation." International agreements may be in the form of (1) treaties that require legislative concurrence after executive

10 *Bayan v Romulo, Muna v Romulo and Ople, Petition for certiorari, mandamus, and prohibition*, GR no 159618, ILDC 2059 (PH 2011), 1 February 2011, Philippine Supreme Court.

ratification; or (2) executive agreements that are similar to treaties, except that they do not require legislative concurrence and are usually less formal and deal with a narrower range of subject matters than treaties.

26 Under international law, there is no difference between treaties and executive agreements in terms of their binding effects on the contracting states concerned, as long as the negotiating functionaries have remained within their powers. Neither, on the domestic sphere, can one be held valid if it violates the Constitution. Authorities are, however, agreed that one is distinct from another for accepted reasons apart from the concurrence-requirement aspect. As has been observed by US constitutional scholars, a treaty has greater "dignity" than an executive agreement, because its constitutional efficacy is beyond doubt, a treaty having behind it the authority of the President, the Senate, and the people; a ratified treaty, unlike an executive agreement, takes precedence over any prior statutory enactment.

27 Petitioner parlays the notion that the Agreement is of dubious validity, partaking as it does of the nature of a treaty; hence, it must be duly concurred in by the Senate. Petitioner takes a cue from Commissioner of Customs v. Eastern Sea Trading, in which the Court reproduced the following observations made by US legal scholars: "[I]nternational agreements involving political issues or changes of national policy and those involving international arrangements of a permanent character usually take the form of treaties [while] those embodying adjustments of detail carrying out well established national policies and traditions and those involving arrangements of a more or less temporary nature take the form of executive agreements."

28 Pressing its point, petitioner submits that the subject of the Agreement does not fall under any of the subject-categories that are enumerated in the Eastern Sea Trading case, and that may be covered by an executive agreement, such as commercial/consular relations, most-favored nation rights, patent rights, trademark and copyright protection, postal and navigation arrangements and settlement of claims. [. . .]

30 We are not persuaded.

On the other hand, the Polish Customs Chamber proceeded from a strict separation between legal orders when in *SP SA v Director of the Customs Chamber in Lódz*[11] the question was brought whether a treaty that was being provisionally applied without having been ratified or promulgated could have binding effect in the Polish legal order. The Customs Chamber answered in the negative.

SP SA v Director of the Customs Chamber in Lódz, Complaint procedure, I SA/ Ld 1707/ 2002, ILDC 270 (PL 2003), 26th March 2003, Poland; Supreme Court

12 [. . .] Binding effect of the agreement in international relations is not identical with its binding effect within the domestic legal order of the country which is a party to such agreement. Therefore, the opinion issued in response to the claim that the Agreement, in its wording, constituted a source of law before it was promulgated, cannot be shared. The provisional application of a treaty on a temporary basis before it enters into force, pursuant to Article 25(1) of the Vienna Convention on the Law of Treaties done at Vienna on 23 May 1969 (Journal of Laws, 1990, No 74, item 439),

11 *SP SA v Director of the Customs Chamber in Lódz*, Complaint procedure, I SA/ Ld 1707/2002; ILDC 270 (PL 2003), 26 March 2003. See also *Ushakov v Russian Federation*, Constitutional proceedings, No 8-п, Sobranie zakonodatel'stvo Rossiiskoi Federatsii, 9 April 2012, No 15 item 1810, ILDC 1930 (RU 2012), 27 March 2012, in which the Russian Constitutional Court held that provisionally applied treaties could not be implemented at the national level unless they were officially published, in the same way as treaties that had formally entered into force.

> applies to international law and does not entail any binding provisions of the international agreement within the domestic [legal] order.

In the employment dispute *League of Arab States v TM*,[12] a blend of international and national law arguments was at issue. The Belgian Supreme Court decided that the *League of Arab States* (League), although constituting an international organization, did not enjoy immunity from jurisdiction, *inter alia* on the ground that the federal parliament had failed to approve the Headquarters Agreement (HQA) between Belgium and the League, which provided for such immunity. The League argued that parties had given their consent to be bound to the HQA by way of so-called simplified signature (as envisaged for inter-governmental organizations in Article 12 of the 1986 VCLT)—from which it would follow that under Belgian law parliamentary approval was not required. The Supreme Court framed the question as one of international law and dismissed the possibility of simplified signature on the ground that the 1986 Vienna Convention with its Article 12 was not yet in force. This was a problematic argument as the court did not broach the question of whether customary law of treaties allowed for this form. In fact, as appears from the *travaux préparatoires* of the 1969 Vienna Convention, which contain an identical Article 12, the procedure of simplified signature had existed for a long time.

In many states, judicial practice includes a 'rule of construction' (see below) or 'treaty-conform interpretation', which allows the court to take into account a treaty which has not (yet) taken effect at the domestic law level, because it has not been ratified by the state or 'transformed' into domestic law, as the case may be. In *Englaro, as guardian of Englaro v Office of the Public Prosecutor at the Tribunal of Milan and ors*[13] the Italian Supreme Court held that the 1997 Convention for the Protection of Human Rights and Dignity of the Human Being with regard to the Application of Biology and Medicine,[14] which had not yet been ratified by Italy (although such had been authorized and requested by the Parliament) could be used as an interpretative tool so as to give the domestic rules a meaning most consistent with that treaty.[15] The difference with genuine 'reception' or 'incorporation' of the international treaty norm into the domestic order (see Part I) is of course that in case of a conflict, domestic law would prevail.

Finally, domestic courts may be faced with a question that in essence is preliminary—this is the question as to whether they are dealing with a treaty or a treaty framework at all. This has come up both in international (see ICJ 1994 *Qatar v Bahrain*[16]) and domestic cases. In *Dutch Seamen's Welfare Foundation v Minister of Transport, Public Works, and Water Management*[17] that question hinged on the distinction between a treaty and an institutional act. The Dutch Seamen's Welfare Foundation argued that adoption of the text of ILO Convention No 163 concerning Seafarers' Welfare at Sea and in Port (ILO Treaty) in the ILO Plenary Conference equalled 'signature' on the part of the member states in the sense of Article 14 of the VCLT. It would follow that the Netherlands by terminating a subsidy to the Seamen's Welfare Foundation had breached its legal obligation under Article 18 of the Vienna Convention[18] not to defeat the

12 *League of Arab States v TM*, Appeal judgment, Case No S.99.0103.F; ILDC 42 (BE 2001), 12 March 2001.

13 *Englaro, as guardian of Englaro v Office of the Public Prosecutor at the Tribunal of Milan and ors*, Appeal judgment, No 21748; ILDC 1431 (IT 2007) (2007) Foro italiano I-3025, 16 October 2007.

14 (signed 4 April 1997, entered into force 1 December 1999) ETS No 164.

15 See *Englaro, as guardian of Englaro v Office of the Public Prosecutor at the Tribunal of Milan and ors* (n 13) para 7.2—no English translation available.

16 *Maritime delimitation and territorial questions between Qatar and Bahrain (Qatar v Bahrain)* (Jurisdiction and Admissibility) [1994] ICJ Rep 112, 120 ff.

17 *Dutch Seamen's Welfare Foundation v Minister of Transport, Public Works, and Water Management*, Higher appeal judgment, Case No 200410468/1; ILDC 852 (NL 2005) LJN No AU0095; AB (2006) No 17727, 27 July 2005.

18 VCLT (n 2) Article 18 reads: 'A State is obliged to refrain from acts which would defeat the object and purpose of a treaty when: (a) it has signed the treaty or has exchanged instruments constituting the treaty subject to ratification, acceptance or approval, until it shall have made its intention clear not to become a party to the treaty; [. . .]'.

object and purpose of the ILO Treaty prior to its final consent to be bound. The Dutch council of state dismissed this reasoning and considered adoption of the text rather as a legal act of member states in an institutional framework.

Dutch Seamen's Welfare Foundation v Minister of Transport, Public Works, and Water Management, Higher appeal judgment, Case No 200410468/1, Decision No LJN: AU0095, AB (2006) No 17727, ILDC 852 (NL 2005), 27th July 2005, Netherlands; Council of State [RvS]

> 2.3. The appellant has argued that the Court has failed to appreciate that, since the State signed the ILO Treaty, this fact leads to direct treaty obligations for the State. [. . .].
>
> 2.3.1 However, this argument is rejected. The text of the ILO Treaty was endorsed by the ILO conference on 8 October 1987. The ILO Statute does not provide for separate signature of ILO treaties by member states, rather it provides solely for ratification of a treaty. Therefore the ILO Treaty cannot be said to have been 'signed' by the Netherlands. Article 19(5) e. of the ILO Statute provides that a member state has no additional obligations other than providing periodic reports as indicated, as long as the Statute has not been ratified by the member state. It is a fact that the ILO Treaty has not been ratified by the Netherlands. There are, therefore, no other treaty obligations, other than the obligation to provide reports. Even where actual arrangements correspond to the objectives of the ILO Treaty, these nevertheless do not give rise to any treaty obligations, nor to any legally binding expectations that future arrangements will accord with the ILO Treaty. [. . .]
>
> 2.4 The appellant has also argued in vain that the Court failed to appreciate that article 18 of the Treaty of Vienna had been violated. No situation arises as described in article 18, preamble and in (a) and (b), of the Vienna Convention on the Law of Treaties regarding the ILO Treaty. Contrary to the considerations of the Court, the State is not therefore obliged to refrain from actions which would conflict with the object and purpose of the ILO Treaty. [. . .]

2. Entry into force

The entry into force of a treaty (Article 24 of the VCLT) signifies the treaty instrument taking legal effect at the international level. That moment rarely coincides with the moment of taking effect in the domestic legal order. This discrepancy is a regular cause for questions brought before domestic courts. In the decision in *National Federation of Guardianship Associations v France*[19] the French council of state examined whether the legality of a Ministerial order could be assessed according to the revised European Social Charter, in case the Charter had entered into force in international law before the date of issuance of the Ministerial order, but had taken legal effect within the domestic legal order *after* that date of issuance. The Council held that the date of entry into force mentioned in the Charter solely governed the effects of the treaty at the international level. Its taking effect within the domestic legal order was subject to publication according to Article 55 of the French constitution.[20]

III. Self-executing Character of Treaties

Another fundamental question with which domestic courts are faced on a regular basis is whether a treaty provision is self-executing (also: 'directly applicable' or 'directly effective'). That

19 *National Federation of Guardianship Associations v France*, Decision on annulment for abuse of power, No 213461; ILDC 765 (FR 2000), 7 July 2000.

20 See para 28—no English translation available.

is, whether the treaty can be applied in the domestic legal order without additional regulation of an international or national character. The issue came up, eg, in *Bug river claims, Czesław S v State Treasury and Minister of the State Treasury*, where the Polish Constitutional Court held that the reference to domestic measures in the text of the agreement concerned testified to the fact that they were not self-executing.[21]

This is to be distinguished from the question as to whether a domestic legal system allows for a rule to be invoked directly by an individual, or to be applied without 'transformation' into domestic statute law (see Chapter 1 in this volume). To be sure, self-executingness or direct applicability of a treaty (provision) is all the more relevant in countries with a predominantly 'monist' constitutional system for the reception of international law. For instance, in the United States, in order to allow a *civil* claim for a violation of a treaty provision, a court would have to find that the treaty (provision) was self-executing and conferred individual rights.[22] This is similar in many legal systems of Latin American countries, as well as, eg, in the domestic legal orders of Switzerland and the Netherlands.

In *Commonwealth of Pennsylvania v Judge*[23] the court stressed how direct applicability of the relevant treaty provision was a necessary condition for a treaty provision to be invoked before a domestic court. As the US Supreme Court had declared the ICCPR in its entirety (!) to be non-self-executing,[24] *in casu* the appellant was unsuccessful in his invoking of Article 6 of the ICCPR.

Commonwealth of Pennsylvania v Judge (Roger), Appeal Judgment, 916 A.2d 511 (Pa 2007), 591 Pa 126, ILDC 1218 (US 2007), 21st February 2007, United States; Pennsylvania; Supreme Court [Pa]

> 28 We believe that Appellant, in arguing that this Court must enforce the Committee's determinations, has misapprehended the law of treaties. In asserting that all international agreements ratified by the Senate have binding force upon the courts of this country, Appellant ignores the distinction between self-executing and non-self-executing treaties. Indeed, contrary to Appellant's assertion that ratification of the ICCPR rendered the treaty the supreme law of the land, with binding force on both the state and federal governments, ratification is not by itself sufficient to mandate enforcement of a non-self-executing treaty. See Sanchez-Llamas, __ U.S. at __, 126 S.Ct. at 2680; Sosa, 542 U.S. at 735, 124 S.Ct. at 2767; Auguste v. Ridge, 395 F.3d 123, 133 n.7 (3d Cir. 2005) ("Treaties that are not self-executing do not create judicially enforceable rights unless they are first given effect by implementing legislation").
>
> 29 [...] Further, the United States Supreme Court has stated that the ICCPR is not self-executing and, thus, does not create obligations that are enforceable in domestic courts. [...]

21 *Bug river claims, Czesław S v State Treasury and Minister of the State Treasury*, Cassation judgment, I CK 323/02; ILDC 268 (PL 2003) OSNC 2004/6/103, 21 November 2003, para 27—no English translation available.

22 On such a treaty violation amounting to a deprivation of rights see *Cornejo v County of San Diego and ors*, Appeal judgment, 504 F 3d 853 (9th Cir 2007); ILDC 1080 (US 2007), 24 September 2007. See also the text accompanying n 79 below.

23 *Commonwealth of Pennsylvania v Judge (Roger)*, Appeal judgment, 916 A 2d 511 (Pa 2007); 591 Pa 126; ILDC 1218 (US 2007), 21 February 2007.

24 'Several times [...] the Senate has expressly declined to give the federal courts the task of interpreting and applying international human rights law, as when its ratification of the International Covenant on Civil and Political Rights declared that the substantive provisions of the document were not self-executing. [...] [A]lthough the Covenant does bind the United States as a matter of international law, the United States ratified the Covenant on the express understanding that it was not self-executing and so did not itself create obligations enforceable in the federal courts.' *Sosa v Alvarez-Machain*, 542 US 692 (2004), IV. A and C.

In *A and B v Government of the Canton of Zurich*[25] the question arose as to whether Articles 13(2)(b) and 13(2)(c) of the International Covenant on Economic, Social and Cultural Rights were *to some extent* self-executing. Without using the expression, the court was looking for a possible directly applicable 'minimum core content' (as defined by the ICESCR Committee in 1994 General Comment no 3) of the treaty, but in the case at hand found none.

A and B v Government of the Canton of Zurich, Appeal against a Regulation of 15 September 1999 adopted by the Canton of Zurich on the Tuition at Schools of Higher Education, Case No 2P.273/1999, BGE 126 I 242, ILDC 350 (CH 2000), 22nd September 2000, Switzerland; Federal Supreme Court [BGer]

> 2.— [...] c) Subject to certain exceptions, the International Covenant on Economic, Social and Cultural Rights ICESCR) is not regarded in the jurisprudence of the Federal Court of Justice as directly applicable. [...]
>
> d) As far as the provision of Article 13 (2) c. of the ICESCR now in question is concerned, the Federal Court clearly denied its direct applicability [...] There is no reason for departing from this Statement. It is not as such questioned by the petitioners. The only point can be whether Article 13 (2) c. (or b.) of the Covenant also has enforceable, directly applicable substance insofar as it prevents the national parliament from increasing or reintroducing charges, because this will mean a step back from the recognised constitutional objective (cf. on this Gebert, op. Cit., pp. 457–8; Jörg Künzli/Walter Kälin, The Importance of the UN Covenant on Economic, Social and Cultural rights to Swiss law, in Switzerland and The UN Human Rights Covenants (Die Schweiz und die UNO-Menschenrechtspakte), 2nd edition, Basel 1997, pp. 110 and 147–148). [...]
>
> 3.— Article 13 (2) (b) and (c) of the ICESCR do not contain, as will be shown, any enforceable guarantees concerning rights of the individual, that might be invoked in the present case on the basis of Article 84 (1) c. Constitution by Constitutional Objection.

In *S Y Q C v Government of the City of Buenos Aires*,[26] the Argentinian Supreme National Court more explicitly found that, while there was a wide margin of discretion by the individual state, a reasonableness test was called for in order to identify to what extent the obligation had to be fulfilled. The case dealt with the question of whether the international obligation to provide adequate housing was relative to a state's available resources. In reliance especially on the UN Economic and Social Council's statement to take steps to the maximum of available resources, the court held that every right entailed a core obligation that had to be satisfied by the state.[27] Only then would the international human rights commitments be met by Argentina.

While the self-executing character of a treaty is a condition for application of a treaty or some of its provisions, in the domestic legal order, such application would generally still be dependent on publication.[28] Thus, in *Preventive Review of Unconstitutionality of Statute,*

25 *A and B v Government of the Canton of Zurich*, Appeal judgement, Case No 2P.273/1999; ILDC 350 (CH 2000) partly published as BGE 126 I 242, 22 September 2000.

26 *S Y Q C v Government of the City of Buenos Aires*, Review of facts motion before the Supreme Court, Q 64 XLVI, ILDC 2384 (AR 2012), 24 April 2012, Argentina; Supreme Court.

27 ibid, para 14: 'Where the available resources are demonstrably inadequate, the obligation remains for a State party to ensure the widest possible enjoyment of economic, social and cultural rights under the prevailing circumstances. [E]ven in times of severe resource constraints, State parties must protect the most disadvantaged and marginalized members or groups of society by adopting relatively low-cost targeted programmes'. Quotation taken from UNCESCR: 'An evaluation of the obligation to take steps to the "maximum of available resources" under an optional Protocol to the Covenant' (2007) UN Doc E/C 12/2007/1, para 4.

28 cf *8 December Murders case, Public Prosecutor v Bouterse and Others*, 11 May 2012, ILDC 1892 (SR 2012).

Determination of Unconstitutional Omission to Legislate, Case No 7/2005 (III 31),[29] the Hungarian Constitutional Court concluded *inter alia* that a promulgating act which provided that a self-executing treaty had been applicable from a date before the promulgation of the treaty, violated the prohibition of retroactivity and hence the Hungarian constitution. In its reasoning, the court set out the mechanism for establishing direct applicability in the—dualist—Hungarian system.

Madl, Preventive review of unconstitutionality of statute, Mádl, President of Hungary, Determination of Unconstitutional Omission to Legislate, Case No 7/2005 (III 31), Decision No 41/2005, ILDC 828 (HU 2005), 29th March 2005, Hungary; Constitutional Court

> 3. Pursuant to Article 16 of Act XI of 1987 on Legislation, incorporation and publication of the treaty in domestic law are also required in the case of so-called self-executing treaties. If an international legal obligation becomes part of domestic law after incorporation without a specific statement from participant states or domestic legislators regarding direct applicability of the treaty, the law enforcement body decides in the case at hand whether the particular provision of the international treaty is applicable with regard to the given case. The precondition for applicability is that those subject to the international treaty are precisely defined private legal entities and that the rights and obligations included in the treaty are specific enough so that the treaty is enforceable without any further domestic legislative action.
>
> 4. [...] However, courts are authorised to make a final decision as to whether they classify as self-executing an international treaty or its individual provisions applicable to the given case. Hungarian law enforcement practice considers the Warsaw Convention as directly applicable when deciding legal disputes between private legal entities. {Courts have applied the Warsaw Convention in civil actions in the following cases: Judicial Decisions BH 1977. 436, BH 1982. 482, BH 1982. 531, BH 1983. 246, BH 1996. 332 and BH 1997. 197.) Furthermore, the Montreal Protocol amends several provisions previously classified as self-executing, including for example Articles 18 and 22 of the Warsaw Convention.

Incidentally, the court also determined a particular domestic Law Decree (No 27) to be inconsistent with the provisions of the VCLT; such as, eg, in the arguably confusing use of the term 'ratification' to refer to the domestic law process of Parliamentary approval, rather than to the international legal act of expressing consent.[30]

In *X v University of Lucerne*,[31] the Swiss Federal Supreme Court held that Article IV(1) of the Convention on the Recognition of Qualifications concerning Higher Education in the European Region (Lisbon Treaty) concerning the recognition of qualifications regarding access, mobility, and degrees in higher education, was self-executing and directly applicable also at the lower administrative levels of the Swiss state, following from the fact that *in casu* the Confederation as well as the cantons, and—by delegation—the universities, were competent to make decisions on recognition, in accordance with the Lisbon Treaty.

29 *Preventive Review of Unconstitutionality of Statute, Determination of Unconstitutional Omission to Legislate*, Case No 7/2005 (III 31); [41/2005] Hungarian Official Gazette, 1989–1998; ILDC 828 (HU 2005), 29 March 2005.

30 ibid, para V2.

31 *X v University of Lucerne, Student Administration Office and Department of Education and Culture of the Canton of Lucerne*, Final appeal judgment, 2C_457/2013, BGE 140 II 185 (partly published as), ILDC 2370 (CH 2014), 13 March 2014, Switzerland; Federal Supreme Court [BGer]; Public Law Chamber II.

X v University of Lucerne, Student Administration Office and Department of Education and Culture of the Canton of Lucerne, Final appeal judgment, 2C_457/2013, BGE 140 II 185 (partly published as), ILDC 2370 (CH 2014), 13th March 2014, Switzerland; Federal Supreme Court [BGer]; Second Public Law Division

> 4.2 Rightly, the applicant criticizes the view that the Lisbon Convention was — as is the case with the Council of Europe Convention No 15 — not self-executing for present purposes: According to relevant case law, a treaty norm is directly applicable if its content is sufficiently precise and clear to form the basis of a decision in a particular case. The norm thus has to be justiciable, ie define the rights and obligations of an individual and be directed at the competent authorities. The latter determines whether the norm can be directly applied (BGE 136 I 297 para 8.1; 133 I 286 para 3.2; 124 III 90 para 3a). The Lisbon Convention as a joint treaty within the framework of the Council of Europe and UNESCO is based through its Article IV(1) on the principle of acceptance of qualifications acquired abroad. Since its entry into force, states parties have had the obligation to show that recognition decisions were transparent and fair, justified, non-discriminatory and within the scope of the Convention. Indeed, each state party retains the competence to determine the substantial differences that exist between foreign qualification programmes and its own study system and to require that the applicants undertake additional training where necessary. However, the responsibility to demonstrate that an application does not meet the presumed equivalence respectively the correspondent requirements between the states parties lies with the body undertaking the assessment (Article III(3)). Procedural guarantees safeguard the rights accorded by the Convention (cf Article III(5). It is, therefore, generally assumed that the principle of acceptance respectively of (mutual) recognition — substantial differences in programmes aside — may be directly invoked and that Article IV(1) has self-executing effect within the meaning of the case law. This also applies in cases such as the present where the responsibility to make recognition decisions lies within the competence of the member states, ie the Cantons and their institutions (Article II(1)).

IV. Binding Force and Observance

1. Binding force

An intrinsic characteristic of treaties is their binding force, which has international as well as domestic dimensions. The 'bindingness' at the international plane is linked to the conclusion and entry into force of the treaty. The legal effects in the domestic legal order, on the other hand, depend on a treaty's domestic incorporation and are for the respective constitutional systems to determine.[32]

In this sense, the Russian Constitutional Court held in *Constitutionality of Part 3 of Article 1244 of the Civil Code of the Russian Federation*,[33] concerning the Russian legal system that certain treaties were directly applicable, unless they contained a state's obligation to change its domestic law.[34] The Russian Constitutional Court ultimately found, however, that it had no competence to decide whether the specific international provision had supremacy over national law.

32 In Aust's terms, for example, the international and national laws of treaties thus operate at different planes. See A Aust, *Modern Treaty Law and Practice* (3rd edn, CUP 2013) 159.

33 *On the Constitutionality of Part 3 of Article 1244 of the Civil Code of the Russian Federation*, Constitutional Proceedings, No 2531-O, ILDC 2448 (RU 2014), Russian Constitutional Court, 6 November 2014.

34 ibid, ref 5, p 9.

Especially in case of treaties which are supposed to create immediate effects at the national level, eg human rights treaties, the distinction between both planes is frequently blurred. This was evidenced in *Denton v Director General National Intelligence Agency and ors*,[35] where the High Court of Gambia had to deal with human rights treaties (the African Charter on Human and Peoples' Rights and the ICCPR), which had been ratified by Gambia but not given effect in the domestic legal order. Despite them not having been 'domesticated', the court found that the treaties created legal obligations and applied them to the case.

Denton v Director General National Intelligence Agency and ors, Decision on Application for Declaratory Relief, Civil HC 241/06/MF/087/F1, ILDC 881 (GM 2006), 24th July 2006, Gambia; High Court

> 19 From the onset, I wish to refer to the case of Caso Loyaza Tamago v Peru, 3rd June 1999, Inter American Court Series C Number 53 (1999). In this case, Peru had refused to implement the decision of the Inter American Court, and the Court observed that Article 27 of the Vienna Convention on the Law of Treaties of 1969 prohibits parties from invoking internal law to justify non-compliance with Treaty obligations.
>
> 20 I am bringing this up to address the Respondent's contention that since the Gambia has not domesticated the African Charter [. . .] the Applicant cannot rely on the Charter. It is a fact that once a country signs a treaty, it should, strictly speaking, put into effect measures to domesticate it immediately on ratification. But there is no time limit to this; some countries do it faster than others. [. . .] But the fact that a country has not domesticated an international instrument, but has ratified it only, does not exonerate it from its obligations under that instrument.
>
> 21 This has been demonstrated fully with particular reference to the African Charter on Human and Peoples' Rights, and in particular by the Government of the Gambia, which has rightly subjected itself to the jurisdiction of the African Commission on Human and Peoples' Rights in many instances, where the Commission has ruled, for and against Gambia [. . .] If I am to agree that non domestication of the Treaties by the Gambia exonerates the government from its responsibilities under the Charter and the ICCPR, then I would seek to defeat the whole purpose of ratification and what it means to the Gambian government and her people. [. . .][36]

2. Observance

An implication of the binding force of treaties is their observance and due performance by the parties.[37] This duty is most prominently expressed in the ***pacta sunt servanda*** rule in Article 26 of the VCLT, which, together with the corollary duty in Article 27 of the VCLT (stating that a party may, in principle, not invoke the provisions of its internal law as justification for its failure to perform a treaty), operates as a bridge between the international and the domestic plane. Not surprisingly, domestic courts often refer to these rules when appraising the position

---

35 *Denton v Director General National Intelligence Agency and ors*, a 2006 decision of the High Court of Gambia. Decision on Application for Declaratory Relief, Civil HC 241/06/MF/087/F1; ILDC 881 (GM 2006), 24 July 2006. The case concerned the arrest and detention of a woman who had been held *incommunicado* for three months without any charges being pressed against her.

36 See also para 60: 'Given the above analysis, I find that the arrest and continuous detention of the petitioner, can therefore be termed arbitrary, and be regarded as a violation of her right to freedom of liberty as contained in Article 19(3) of the Gambian Constitution, Article 6 of the African Charter on Human and Peoples' Rights and Article 9 of the International Covenant on Civil and Political Rights'.

37 According to Reuter: 'treaties are made to be performed'. See P Reuter, *Introduction to the Law of Treaties* (2nd edn, Kegan 1995) para 44 or P Reuter, *Introduction to the Law of Treaties* (Routledge 2012) para 44.

of international law in the domestic legal order.[38] While this clearly involves the reception of treaty law in the domestic legal order, some judgments put strong emphasis on the international legal obligations and seemingly make these, rather than the domestic rules on the reception of treaty law, the deciding factor. Some of those judgments are reported here as an illustration of how domestic courts employ the international obligation of treaty performance and observance as the guiding norm.

In *Linija v Latvia*[39] the Latvian Constitutional Court—seized in last instance with fines imposed on shipping companies in contravention of Latvia's international obligations—maintained that in case of any contradiction between international law and domestic legislation, international law prevailed and had to be applied; a national norm conflicting with an international treaty was, according to the court, null and void.[40] To reach its conclusion, the court strongly relied on the necessary performance of treaties in good faith as envisaged in Article 26 of the VCLT.

Linija v Latvia, Judgment of the Constitutional Court of the Republic of Latvia on a request for constitutional review, Case No 2004-01-06, Latvian Herald, No 108, 3056, ILDC 189 (LV 2004), 7th July 2004, Latvia; Constitutional Court

> 6. [...] The Vienna Convention foresees that states parties recognize the ever-increasing importance of treaties as a source of international law and as a means of developing peaceful co-operation among nations, whatever their constitutional and social systems. Article 26 of the Vienna Convention provides that "every treaty in force is binding upon the parties to it and must be performed by them in good faith". Consequently, every state must observe its obligations under international treaties and other sources of international law. Therefore, a State may not conflict national law with international law. State's national law may not contradict international obligations (law). [...]
>
> Therefore, it is evident from the national legislation as well as from the international obligations of the Republic of Latvia under the Vienna Convention on the Law of Treaties, in particular, the obligation to perform treaties in good faith, that in case of a contradiction between rules of international law, which have been approved by the Parliament, and national legislation, provisions of international law must be applied. Moreover, international obligations, which Latvia has undertaken by international agreements approved by the Saeima [Parliament] are binding also on the Saeima. It may not adopt legislation that contradicts these obligations. [...]

Similarly, in *On the Constitutionality of Part 3 of Article 1244 of the Civil Code of the Russian Federation*,[41] the Russian Constitutional Court referred to the *pacta sunt servanda* principle of Article 26 of the VCLT, to answer the question of whether domestic law contradicted an international treaty. It moreover underlined the domestic legal provisions that stipulated the supremacy of international principles and treaties over Russian domestic law, such as Article 15(4) of the Russian Constitution, Article 5 of the Federal Law on international treaties and Article 7 of the Russian Civil Code.[42]

38 In addition to the cases mentioned below see also *Ray Sigorta AS v Nunner Lojistik Ticaret Limited Sti*, Appeal decision, E 2007/2970; K 2008/4599; ILDC 1034 (TR 2008), 7 April 2008, where the court deals with the question of how to observe the *pacta sunt servanda* principle.

39 *Linija v Latvia*, Judgment of the Constitutional Court of the Republic of Latvia on a request for constitutional review, Case No 2004-01-06; ILDC 189 (LV 2004), 7 July 2004.

40 ibid, operative para 1.

41 *On the Constitutionality of Part 3 of Article 1244 of the Civil Code of the Russian Federation* (n 33).

42 At para 3.0, page 8 of the judgment; Unfortunately, the Constitutional Court decided to leave open the question of whether a national law conflicted with international law, stating that such an interpretation was not within its competence.

Whether non-observance of obligations incurred by the Czech Republic in a bilateral extradition treaty was permissible on the ground of an alleged violation of domestic human rights obligations was the question in the constitutionality complaint re: *Recognition of a Sentence Imposed by a Thai Court.*[43] The Czech Constitutional Court referred to the *pacta sunt servanda* rule, recognizing it as a general principle of natural law and detailing the reasons to uphold it.

On the Constitutionality of Part 3 of Article 1244 of the Civil Code of the Russian Federation, Constitutional proceedings, No 2531-O, ILDC 2448 (RU 2014), 6th November 2014, Russian Federation; Constitutional Court

> 34. The Constitutional Court submits that the Czech Republic is bound by international agreements, as follows from Article 1, Paragraph 2 of the Constitution, according to which "The Czech Republic shall observe its obligations under international law." The corollaries of this clause include the general principle of natural law recognised by the international community of *pacta sunt servanda*, i.e. agreements must be kept. [. . .]
>
> The extent to which the state in question respects this principle not only has a role to play in strengthening that state's own legal environment, through fostering citizens' confidence in the law, but also offers a yardstick of the confidence with which the state is viewed in the international community. The extent to which the principle is respected provides a measure for some form of predictable conduct by subjects of international law and permits the mutual bona fide expectation that commitments arising from international agreements will be met, within the norms of international ius cogens. The order arising to some measure from international agreement appears to be the best environment for international cooperation and for the protection of a state's interests — whether cultural, economic, political, or humanitarian — within that environment. A breach of international commitments therefore does not only bring with it international responsibility as specified under international law, but also a loss of confidence amongst the international community and a deterioration in cooperation between states.

On this basis, the court decided in favour of the legal obligation of observance of treaties to the detriment of the individual applicant and denied the constitutionality complaint.[44] Also in its conclusions, the court upheld the principles of *pacta sunt servanda* and good faith as cornerstones of the international law of treaties:

> 58. The Czech authorities cannot therefore rule on objections which are essentially directed against Thai convictions, because the Czech Republic would run foul of the two principles which represent cornerstones of international treaty law and whose importance has been underlined by their incorporation in the Preamble of the UN Charter: the principle of pacta sunt servanda and the principle of good faith. The principle of good faith is a basic rule for interpreting the text of international commitments. Under the terms thereof, such commitments must be interpreted in good faith, taking into account the overall context of the respective treaty and in the light of the aim and purpose for which the treaty was concluded. The aim and purpose of the treaty concluded between the Kingdom of Thailand and the Czech Republic was to transfer the petitioner, at his own request, to his home environment, closer to his family and friends, and to enable him to serve the remainder of his sentence at home, in his native land. In light thereof, the Constitutional Court is unable to agree to the petitioner's request that, due to a procedural defect, which falls well

43 *Recognition of a Sentence Imposed by a Thai Court*, Constitutional Complaint, I ÚS 601/04; ILDC 990 (CZ 2007), 21 February 2007.

44 ibid, para 57.

> short of constitutional level, the Constitutional Court should annul the decisions by the Czech courts of general jurisdiction and release the petitioner. By granting the petitioner's request the Constitutional Court would not only be breaching Article, 1 Paragraphs 1 and 2 of the Constitution of the Czech Republic, but also the credibility which the Czech Republic enjoys in international relations.

The international legal duty to perform treaty obligations was also the principal argument in *President of the Turkish Republic of Northern Cyprus v Assembly of the Turkish Republic of Northern Cyprus*,[45] which was decided at the first and last instance by the Northern Cyprus Supreme Court sitting as the Constitutional Court. In this case, a constitutional review of treaties in the abstract was at stake. When addressing the question of whether provisions of the 2000 Framework Protocol on the Establishment of a Campus in the Turkish Republic of Northern Cyprus (TRNC) could unilaterally be modified, the Northern Cyprus court similarly upheld the supremacy of international law. Overruling an older decision, the court stated that treaty provisions could not be altered through constitutional review.[46] In order to reach that conclusion, it relied on the principles of equality and reciprocity between states:

President of the Turkish Republic of Northern Cyprus v Assembly of the Turkish Republic of Northern Cyprus, First instance, D 4/2005 [9/2005], ILDC 500 (TCc 2005), 25th November 2005, Cyprus

> 48 The most important principles applied in relations between states are the principles of equality and reciprocity. States, like persons or legal entities, expect that all parties to an agreement will follow its terms and conditions. If a party to an agreement reached after substantial negotiations says: "I am going to sign this agreement but if the Constitutional Court annuls any of its articles, it will not be executed in full", this will create multiple problems because such a reservation will lead to another reservation by another party. With great probability, other articles of the agreement will also be annulled by the Constitutional Court of the other country. The resulting document will turn out to be quite a different agreement. [...]

The court also considered it a 'worldwide principle' that treaties were not subject to constitutional review:

> 66 It is a worldwide principle that international agreements are not subject to constitutional review. Saying "I am not reviewing the international agreement as a whole, I am just reading one of its articles along with an article from my Constitution and interpreting it in a different way" is no different from direct and open review of such agreement, because the consequences of both are the same. The agreement shall be rendered ineffective unilaterally, and the other party will not be able to execute the agreement under the principles of equality and reciprocity. No state would then wish to enter into agreements with a state which changes an international agreement through a unilateral decision.[47]

---

45 *President of the Turkish Republic of Northern Cyprus v Assembly of the Turkish Republic of Northern Cyprus*, First and last instance, D 4/2005 (9/2005); ILDC 500 (TCc 2005), 25 November 2005.

46 '[...] We may say that our country is about to face rather complicated legal problems due to this decision [(Decision No 11/93; Docket No 9/94, Constitutional Court)]. The Court held that the mentioned precedent, which had accepted the Constitutional Court's power to declare a statutory provision unconstitutional where that provision originated from a treaty obligation, was dangerous for the foreign relations of TRNC—which were in any case very limited due to the unrecognized status of the entity' (ibid, para 48).

47 See also '[...] A universal principle dictates not to appeal to the Constitutional Court claiming violation of the constitution in international agreements. First, we need to analyse its scope and as to why this principle is adapted. [...]' (ibid, para 47).

In *Legal Opinion on the Compatibility of the Bilateral Agreement Between the Governments of the United States and Benin with Article 98 of the Rome Statute of the International Criminal Court*,[48] the Benin Supreme Court dealt with conflicting *international* obligations. More particularly, it had to decide whether a so-called 'Article 98 Agreement'[49] between Benin and the United States, which would oblige Benin not to surrender US nationals to the International Criminal Court, was compatible with Benin's obligations under the Rome Statute of the International Criminal Court (Rome Statute). To reach its conclusion that Benin was prevented from signing the Bilateral Agreement,[50] the court referred to Benin's obligations arising from Articles 26 and 18 of the VCLT under the general law of treaties as well as to its specific obligations resulting from the Rome Statute (while it did not rely on Article 30 of the VCLT and the conflict clause of Article 98 of the Rome Statute):

Benin, Legal Opinion, Case No 029-C, ILDC 844 (BJ 2003), 25th July 2003, Benin

> With regard to the general principles governing international treaties
>
> 34 It shall be recalled that the pacta sunt servanda rule confirmed in the Vienna Convention of 23 May 1969 to which Benin is also a party states that "[e]very treaty in force is binding upon the parties to it and must be performed by them in good faith" (Article 26).
>
> 35 The corollary of this provision appears in Article 18 of the Vienna Convention, which lays down that "[a] State is obliged to refrain from acts which would defeat the object and purpose of a treaty".
>
> 36 The result is that Benin, which has freely consented to the Rome Statute, places loyalty and trust in the commitment made, especially with regard to its specific obligations under this Treaty.
>
> With regard to the specific obligations resulting from the Rome Statute
>
> 37 Benin has ratified the Rome Statute which imposes obligations on it such as those regarding cooperation with the International Criminal Court; obligations whose scope is limited by the draft agreement put forward for signature.
>
> 38 Benin cannot withdraw from it by recourse to the exemptions under Article 98 of the Rome Statute. As there is no reservation, as article 120 strictly prescribes, any agreement that is made subsequent to the Rome Statute can only be taken as an evasion of the proper execution of its obligations.

As to economic, social, and cultural rights, the question often arises to what extent these rights are binding upon the state parties. In *S Y Q C v Government of the City of Buenos Aires*,[51] the

48 *Legal Opinion on the Compatibility of the Bilateral Agreement Between the Governments of the United States and Benin with Article 98 of the Rome Statute of the International Criminal Court*, Legal opinion, Case number 029-C; ILDC 844 (BJ 2003), 25 July 2003.

49 Article 98 of the Rome Statute: 'Cooperation with respect to waiver of immunity and consent to surrender. 1. The Court may not proceed with a request for surrender or assistance which would require the requested State to act inconsistently with its obligations under international law with respect to the State or diplomatic immunity of a person or property of a third State, unless the Court can first obtain the cooperation of that third State for the waiver of the immunity. 2. The Court may not proceed with a request for surrender which would require the requested State to act inconsistently with its obligations under international agreements pursuant to which the consent of a sending State is required to surrender a person of that State to the Court, unless the Court can first obtain the cooperation of the sending State for the giving of consent for the surrender'.

50 'Having regard to the above comments, the Government of Benin cannot sign the bilateral agreement proposed by the American Government without compromising its obligations under the Rome Statute establishing the International Criminal Court […]' *Legal Opinion on the Compatibility of the Bilateral Agreement Between the Governments of the United States and Benin with Article 98 of the Rome Statute of the International Criminal Court* (n 48) para 45.

51 *S Y Q C v Government of the City of Buenos Aires*, Review of facts motion before the Supreme Court, Q 64 XLVI, ILDC 2384 (AR 2012), 24 April 2012, Argentina; Supreme Court. The case dealt with the question of whether the international obligation to provide adequate housing was relative to a state's available resources.

Argentinian Supreme National Court found that, while there was a wide margin of discretion by the individual state, the obligations had to undergo a reasonableness test to identify to what extent the obligation had to be fulfilled. It moreover held that every right entailed a core obligation that had to be satisfied by the state. It noted: 'Where the available resources are demonstrably inadequate, the obligation remains for a State party to ensure the widest possible enjoyment of economic, social and cultural rights under the prevailing circumstances. [E]ven in times of severe resource constraints, State parties must protect the most disadvantaged and marginalized members or groups of society by adopting relatively low-cost targeted programmes'.[52] Only then would the international human rights commitments be met by Argentina.

V. Reservations and Declarations

Immediately relevant to the binding force and observance of treaties are reservations and interpretative declarations, by which a state may adjust the scope of its treaty obligations at the time of expressing consent to be bound. Frequently, domestic courts are faced with questions of admissibility of reservations. In this context, also the distinction between reservations (which modify the scope of treaty obligations)[53] and interpretative declarations (which specify but cannot alter the extent of treaty obligations) was prominently at issue.

The (non-)admissibility of reservations to bilateral treaties was a primary question in *Kariņš and ors v Parliament of Latvia and Cabinet of Ministers of Latvia*[54] where the Latvian Constitutional Court had to decide, *inter alia*, whether the phrase 'observing the principle of inviolability of frontiers established by the Organization of Security and Cooperation in Europe' in Article 1 of the Law on the Republic of Latvia and the Russian Federation Treaty on the State Border of Latvia and Russia (Latvian Ratification Law) constituted a reservation, and a permissible one, to the Treaty on the State Border of Latvia and Russia. The court held that the reference was an impermissible reservation to a bilateral treaty.[55] To reach its conclusion, the Latvian Constitutional Court started out with a detailed distinction between reservations and interpretative declarations:

Border Treaty, Re, Kariņš and ors v Parliament of Latvia and Cabinet of Ministers of Latvia, Constitutional Review, Case No 2007-10-0102, ILDC 884 (LV 2007), 29th November 2007, Latvia; Constitutional Court

> 77.2. International law does not prohibit States from making reservations when undertaking international obligations by amending specific rules of the treaty, as well as by attaching interpretative declarations or unilateral statements of different nature.
>
> In accordance with Article 2 (d) of the Vienna Convention, "reservation" means a unilateral statement, however phrased or named, made by a State, when signing, ratifying, accepting, approving or acceding to a treaty, whereby it purports to exclude or to modify the legal effect of certain provisions of the treaty in their application to that State. [. . .]
>
> International law permits that States attach interpretative declarations to the treaties. Interpretative declarations, according to the definition provided by the International Law Commission, are a unilateral statement, however phrased or named, made by a State or by an international organization whereby that State or that organization purports to specify or clarify the meaning or scope attributed by the declarant to a treaty or to certain of its provisions. [. . .]

52 ibid, para 14.

53 See VCLT (n 2) Article 2(1)(d).

54 *Kariņš and ors v Parliament of Latvia and Cabinet of Ministers of Latvia, and joined case*, Constitutional review, Case No 2007-10-0102; ILDC 884 (LV 2007), 29 November 2007.

55 See ibid, substantive part, para 4.

> Both reservations and interpretative declarations are the instruments of international law, with which a State can affect the international obligations that it itself undertakes in a favourable manner, provided that the respective amendments or explanations do not come into conflict with the object and purpose of the specific treaty. Similarly, these instruments are to be used not in the way that the State itself wants but by observing the rules of international law of treaties and customary law.

According to generally accepted doctrine, domestic statute law would not *per se* constitute a legal act at the international level and modify treaty relations with a co-contracting party. The Latvian Constitutional Court found, however, that the reference in the Latvian Ratification Law could have the character of a reservation, as it factually narrowed the preamble of the Border Treaty. Proceeding from there, the court held that the reservation was impermissible for a bilateral treaty:

> 77.3. Any unilateral statement whereby a State indicated the manner in which it intended to implement the treaty as a whole should be viewed as a reservation. [...]
>
> The reference to the principle of inviolability of borders made in Article 1 of the Ratification Law narrows the Preamble of the Border Treaty, which refers to the UN and OSCE principles.
>
> In the view of the Constitutional Court, such a reference in Article 1 of the Ratification Law can have the character of a reservation.
>
> 78. Expression of such a separate position that does not coincide with the position of the other State established in the Ratification Act and is not coordinated with the text of the concluded Border Treaty can considerably affect the fulfilment of the obligations undertaken in the particular Treaty and the international law opinion of the other party [...]
>
> 78.2. International law does not permit formulating reservations to all international treaties. The Vienna Convention, as its preparatory materials show, deals with formulating reservations to multilateral international treaties. [...]
>
> It is not possible to formulate reservations that affect the content or application of bilateral international treaties [...] If a State still decides to do it, this means that it does not agree to the concluded treaty and proposes to reopen the negotiations [...]

While the Latvian Constitutional Court examined the substance of the assumed reservation to decide upon its permissibility, in *Public Prosecutor v Belgium and Others*[56] the focus of attention of the Ghent Court of Appeal was on the domestic procedures required under domestic law (*in casu* parliamentary consent and publication) for reservations to be valid in the Belgian domestic legal order.

In *FEMOSPP and the Federal Prosecutor v Echeverría and Others*,[57] the Mexican Supreme Court had to deal with the admissibility of a Mexican 'interpretative declaration' to the 1968 Convention on the Non-Applicability of Statutory Limitations to War Crimes and Crimes against Humanity (Convention on War Crimes), which determined that the non-applicability of statutory limitations would only concern crimes committed after the entry into force of the Convention for Mexico in June 2002.

When examining whether Mexico's 'interpretative declaration' was in fact a reservation, the Mexican Supreme Court started with an analysis of the difference between interpretative declarations and reservations:

56 *Public Prosecutor v Belgium and ors*, Appeal judgment, T Strafr 2001, 267; ILDC 40 (BE 2001), 19 January 2001.

57 *FEMOSPP and the Federal Prosecutor v Echeverría and others*, Appeal decision, Appeal No 1/2004-PS, Appeal No 8/2004-PS ILDC 76 (MX 2005), 15 June 2005.

Federal Prosecutor assigned to the Special Office of the Attorney General for Federal Crimes Committed by Public Servants against Persons Related to Past Social and Political Movements and Federal Prosecutor assigned to the Second District Federal Court for Criminal Proceedings in the Federal District v Echeverria (Luis) and Moya-Palencia (Mario), Appeal Decision, Appeal No 1/2004-PS, Appeal No 8/2004-PS, ILDC 76 (MX 2005), 15th June 2005, Mexico; Supreme Court of Justice of the Nation

> 174 In light of the foregoing, we should determine the legal nature of the "interpretative declaration" issued by the Mexican State when approving the analyzed Convention. The characteristics of these declarations are not defined in written rules of international law, such as the Vienna Convention; rather, in practice the States have understood them as unilateral declarations, made outside a treaty, which perform functions different from the "reservations". In this regard, the interpretative declarations may not in any case "exclude or modify" the legal effects of a treaty for a signatory state. In this sense, the declarations are clarifying or explanatory declarations for the scope of the rules of the treaty for the purposes of domestic law. [. . .]
>
> 176 From the foregoing [reference to Art 2.1.d VCLT] it is clear that there are substantial differences between interpretative declaration and reservation in international legislation, and that the term reservation or declaration does not depend on the designation or pronouncement with which it identifies, but rather on the material characteristics of the unilateral declaration issued by the State, the essence of the distinction being the exclusion or modification of the legal effects of certain provisions of a treaty in the application within the territory of the issuing State. [. . .]

Turning to Mexico's 'interpretative declaration', the court decided that the declaration could be considered a reservation only if it modified the scope of application of the Convention on War Crimes, which it found to be the case.

> 178 In those terms, the interpretative declaration issued by the Mexican State would have to be considered as a reservation if it were to modify in any way the scope of the effect of the analyzed Convention, which in the case in question would be the period of effect. [. . .]
>
> 179 It could be submitted, as the Federal Prosecutor does, that the intention of the Convention is to rule even on acts carried out prior to its effective date within domestic law, which could be inferred from the wording of the Convention itself, which literally provides that:
>
>> "Article I. No statutory limitation shall apply to the following crimes, irrespective of the date of their commission [. . .]".
>
> 180 In this case, the intention of the Convention would be to govern all crimes committed, regardless of their date. Therefore, the interpretative declaration issued by the Mexican State would actually modify the period of effect of the Convention, and would thus have to be qualified as a reservation. This designation, in principle would force the court to evaluate the reservation with regards to the object and purpose of the treaty, pursuant to article 19 c) of the Vienna Convention.

Somewhat surprisingly, however, the Mexican Supreme Court ended with a purely domestic consideration, finding Mexico's 'interpretative declaration' valid for being in line with Mexico's constitutional limitations.[58]

58 ibid, paras 181, 182, and 193; critical also M Cortina-Borja, Analysis, *FEMOSPP and the Federal Prosecutor v Echeverría and Others*, ILDC 76 (MX 2005) A6.

In *GE v Germany*[59] the substantial question was whether the reservation made by Germany to Article 26 of the International Covenant on Civil and Political Rights was applicable to the communication. Letter (c) of Germany's reservation to the Optional Protocol stated that the Committee shall not be competent for communications 'by means of which a violation of article 26 of the [ICCPR] is reprimanded, if and insofar as the reprimanded violation refers to rights other than those guaranteed under the aforementioned Covenant'. In the instant case, the complainant claimed that his right to freely exercise or choose an occupation was violated by Germany. Germany pointed out that work-related rights were not covered in the ICCPR and thus concerned rights 'other than those guaranteed under the aforementioned Covenant', meaning that the Human Rights Committee was not competent owing to Germany's reservation.[60]

GE v Germany, Admissibility, UN Doc CCPR/C/104/D/1789/2008, Communication No 1789/2008, IHRL 3817 (UNHRC 2012), 26th March 2012, United Nations General Assembly [UNGA]; Office of the High Commissioner for Human Rights [OHCHR]; United Nations Human Rights Committee [UNHRC]

> 7.3 The Committee notes the State party's argument contesting the Committee's competence in this case due to paragraph (c) of its reservation to the Optional Protocol [...] The State party, in its submission, construes the claim by the author as basically referring to an alleged violation of his right to choose or exercise an occupation, which is indeed not covered by the Covenant on Civil and Political Rights. The Committee, however, considers the present communication as related to an alleged violation of the autonomous rights to equality and non-discrimination enshrined in article 26 of the Covenant. The Committee is thus not precluded from proceedings to examine whether the admissibility requirements have been met.

The finding of the Committee was criticized by some of its members for not adequately interpreting Germany's reservation. In the individual opinion by Committee member Mr Neuman, joined by members Mr O'Flaherty, Sir Nigel Rodley, and Mr Iwasawa, it says:

> The majority [...] takes the occasion, in paragraph 7.3 of its decision, to address one of the State party's reservations to the Optional Protocol, and gives the reservation an untenable interpretation.
>
> Part (c) of Germany's reservation to the Optional Protocol denies the competence of the Committee with respect to communications "by means of which a violation of article 26 of the [Covenant] is reprimanded, if and insofar as the reprimanded violation refers to rights other than those guaranteed under the aforementioned Covenant." From its language and context, it is clear that this reservation purports to limit the Committee's competence over article 26 claims to situations in which an author alleges discrimination with respect to some other right contained in the Covenant, in a provision other than article 26 itself. Thus, the reservation would reduce the Committee's competence to cases where article 26 serves an "accessory" function, similar to the function of the non-discrimination norm in article 14 of the European Convention for the Protection of Human Rights and Fundamental Freedoms.
>
> I fully agree with the majority's position that the rights to equality and non-discrimination enshrined in article 26 of the Covenant are autonomous, not merely accessory. [...]
>
> The Federal Republic of Germany did not make a reservation to article 26 when it ratified the Covenant, and therefore is substantively bound by the full meaning of

---

59 *GE v Germany*, Admissibility, UN Doc CCPR/C/104/D/1789/2008, Communication No 1789/2008, IHRL 3817 (UNHRC 2012), 26 March 2012, United Nations General Assembly [UNGA]; Office of the High Commissioner for Human Rights [OHCHR]; United Nations Human Rights Committee [UNHRC].

60 ibid, para 4.2.

> article 26. When, however, Germany ratified the Optional Protocol to the Covenant in 1993, it sought to prevent communications based on this autonomous character of Article 26 from being brought before the Committee, by articulating the reservation quoted above.
>
> The Committee maintains in paragraph 7.3 of its decision that the reservation does not apply to the author's claim of age discrimination, because the author's claim asserts a violation of the autonomous rights to equality and non-discrimination enshrined in article 26. This interpretation not only contradicts the clear meaning of the reservation, but appears to deprive the reservation of any content whatsoever. Every claim of discrimination […] can be described as relating to the autonomous right enshrined in article 26.
>
> I do not see how such a nullifying interpretation can be justified. To the contrary, the reservation (if permissible) would exclude the author's claim of discrimination from the Committee's competence precisely because the claim is autonomous and not accessory – that is what the reservation means. Germany's reservation might be impermissible, but the majority does not address that question, construing the reservation instead as inapplicable to the author's claim, on grounds that would render it inapplicable to every claim.

Although Mr Neuman and the other committee members disagreed with the majority's finding and addressed the possibility of the reservation to be impermissible, they nevertheless decided not to go into detail with the question of permissibility:

> I will not explore the permissibility of the reservation here, because I do not see sufficient reason to reach that question, given that the communication is already inadmissible on grounds of lack of exhaustion of domestic remedies. […] Having responded to the majority's interpretation, I would postpone analysis of the more difficult question of the permissibility of the reservation until a communication is presented that genuinely requires it.

Similarly, Mr Salvioli notes in his individual opinion:

> 1 I am not satisfied with the way in which the Committee has handled the E. v. Germany case […]. The Committee has found the complaint inadmissible on the grounds of non-exhaustion of domestic remedies without first having resolved the issue of its competence, which is called into question by the State party on the basis of its reservation to the Optional Protocol. […]
>
> 4 I cannot, however, agree with the line of reasoning that appears at the end of paragraph 7.3 of the decision, in which the Committee concludes that there is no connection between subparagraph (c) of Germany's reservation, formulated when it ratified the Optional Protocol, and the author's complaint, for the reason that the communication refers exclusively to a possible violation of his stand-alone rights to equality and non-discrimination. […]
>
> 6 The right to work and other workplace rights are not covered by the International Covenant on Civil and Political Rights […]; for that reason the argument put forward by Mr. G. E. in the communication under consideration is directly related to the reservation formulated by the State party on ratifying the Optional Protocol. The Committee resolved the matter of its competence using an unconvincing line of argument and avoiding what it should have done, which was to consider the case in the light of whether or not Germany's reservation was valid.
>
> 7 The Committee's first competence with regard to individual communication is its "competence with respect to its competence", whereby an international body is deemed competent to decide whether or not it is competent. In my view, therefore,

> it would not have been right either on the one hand to find that subparagraph (c) of Germany's reservation applies to Mr. G. E.'s case (which is correct though for a different reason from that put forward by the Committee in paragraph 7.3 of its decision) but on the other hand to decide not to examine the validity or otherwise of the reservation simply because the domestic remedies had not been exhausted. The first issue of admissibility to be resolved is that of the Committee's competence, and all the more so when that competence is questioned by the State.
>
> 8 [...] Addressing other matters of admissibility ahead of the competence issue may well offer a less thorny path, but runs counter to the legal logic that should guide an international protection body like the Human Rights Committee.

Unlike Mr Neuman, however, Mr Salvioli expressly addresses the question of the validity of Germany's reservation:

> 10 The subparagraph in question constitutes a reservation that directly affects a provision of the Covenant, namely article 26. However, at the time the State ratified the Covenant, in 1973, it formulated no reservation to the aforementioned article. Under article 19 of the Vienna Convention on the Law of Treaties (1969), a State may, when signing, ratifying, accepting, approving or acceding to a treaty, formulate a reservation.
>
> 11 Only in 1993, when it ratified the Optional Protocol, did Germany formulate the reservation in question [...]
>
> 12 In the instant case, the Committee should have declared itself competent to resolve the matter, but not for the reasons set forth in the last part of paragraph 7.3 of the Views. [...] Firstly, subparagraph (c) of the German reservation has no validity, as it constitutes a reservation to article 26 of the International Covenant on Civil and Political Rights that was made not when it should have been, at the time of ratification, but 20 years subsequently. A careful reading of the reservation leads one to conclude that it refers in fact not only to the competence of the Committee but also to the actual content of article 26, which it aims to circumscribe.
>
> 13 Secondly, the Committee's competence to deal with this case rests on the complementary argument that the reservation in question is also incompatible with the substance of the Protocol, and is thus equally invalid, since it attempts to oblige the Committee to interpret the article, which touches on a fundamental tenet of international human rights law (nothing less than the principles of equal protection of the law and non-discrimination) in a manner that is restrictive and contrary to the Committee's understanding.
>
> 14 Only once the issue of the Committee's competence had been resolved on the grounds of the non-validity of subparagraph (c) of Germany's reservation, should the Committee have proceeded to conclude that the complaint filed by Mr. G. E. was inadmissible because of his failure to exhaust all domestic remedies.

María Cruz Achabal Puertas v Spain[61] dealt with a reservation made by Spain when ratifying the Optional Protocol to the ICCPR excluding the Human Rights Committee's competence with regard to cases that have already been 'examined' under another international investigation or settlement procedure. In the case at hand, the European Court of Human Rights had already dealt with the matter and declared the complaint inadmissible. However, the Human

61 *María Cruz Achabal Puertas v Spain*, Merits, UN Doc CCPR/C/107/D/1945/2010, IHRL 3809 (UNHRC 2013), 27 March 2013, United Nations Human Rights Committee [UNHRC].

Rights Committee practically circumvented this reservation, by acknowledging its existence, but noting that 'in the particular circumstances' the reservation posed 'no obstacle to its examining the present communication'.[62]

This was criticized by committee members Ms Seibert-Fohr, Mr Iwasawa, Ms Motoc, Mr Neuman, Mr Shany, and Mr Vardzelashvili in their dissenting opinion:

María Cruz Achabal Puertas v Spain, Merits, UN Doc CCPR/C/107/D/1945/2010, IHRL 3809 (UNHRC 2013), 27th March 2013, United Nations General Assembly [UNGA]; Office of the High Commissioner for Human Rights [OHCHR]; United Nations Human Rights Committee [UNHRC]

> We are unable to agree with the admissibility decision rendered by the Committee in this case [. . .]. When the Spanish Government acceded to the Optional Protocol to the International Covenant on Civil and Political Rights, it did so "on the understanding that the provisions of article 5, paragraph 2, of that Protocol mean that the Human Rights Committee shall not consider any communication from an individual unless it has ascertained that the same matter has not been or is not being examined under another procedure of international investigation or settlement."
>
> According to the Committee's established jurisprudence [. . .], this condition is not fulfilled if a case has been dismissed only on procedural grounds. [. . .] However, when the European Court of Human Rights has based a declaration of inadmissibility not solely on procedural grounds but also on reasons that include "a certain consideration of the merits of the case", then, according to the Committee's jurisprudence, a matter should be deemed to have been "examined" within the meaning of the reservation to article 5, paragraph 2 (a) of the Optional Protocol. [. . .] The Committee has recognized that "even limited consideration of the merits" of a case constitutes an examination within the meaning of the respective reservation. [. . .]
>
> We see no reason to depart from this long-standing interpretation in the case before us. The European Court based its inadmissibility decision on the argument that it did not find "any appearance of violation of the rights and freedoms guaranteed by the Convention and its Protocols." We fail to see how this could be interpreted other than as an even limited consideration of the merits.
>
> [. . .] It is not for the Human Rights Committee to assess whether the examination of a case has been sufficiently careful under a procedure which enforces a norm affording an equivalent level of protection to that provided by article 7 of the Covenant, and which was invoked unsuccessfully by the author of a communication before the matter was brought to the Committee.[63]

---

62 ibid, para 7.3.

63 Contrary to that statement, committee members Mr Flinterman and Mr Salvioli stated in their opinion: '1 We agree with the Committee's finding that the reservation introduced by Spain on its ratification of the Optional Protocol in the particular circumstances of the case cannot be regarded as an obstacle to the examination of the merits of the communication of the author under article 5, paragraph 2 (a), of the Optional Protocol. It would have been important, however, if the Committee would have highlighted the particular circumstances of the case in more detail. This would have made it clear that the Committee would only deviate from its general respect for reservations [. . .] in exceptional circumstances. [. . .] 4 [. . .] In such cases where the physical integrity, yes indeed the right to life, of the individual complainant has been at stake, it should be clear from the record of the (inadmissibility) decision of the European Court of Human Rights that the Court has sufficiently given attention to the merits of the case in order to constitute an examination for purposes of the preclusionary effect of a reservation, like the Spanish one, to article 5, paragraph 2 (a), of the Optional Protocol. If that is not the case, the Committee may legitimately declare the communication admissible despite the reservation, like it did in the present case'.

In *X and ors*,[64] the French Court of Cassation reaffirmed that it was the judge's duty to interpret any treaty invoked by the parties, including any reservation or declaration related to such a convention. The question of the power to interpret treaties arose because the investigative Chamber in the instant case had relied on material of the indicted persons, which they were not allowed to use owing to reservations made by Luxembourg on the European Convention on Mutual Assistance in Criminal Matters and the Additional Protocol to that Convention.

VI. Interpretation

A central task that comes with the application of treaties, as of domestic statute law, is the interpretation of written provisions. Courts may be asked to interpret treaty rules as such, or domestic rules that are an explicit translation of the treaty, or independent domestic rules against the backdrop of a particular treaty (see above on treaty-conform interpretation). In all cases, courts appear to rely at least to some degree on the *international* canon of rules for treaty interpretation as codified in Articles 31 and 32 of the VCLT. It helps that the VCLT framework for interpretation is famously broad, subsidiary, and not very hierarchically structured.[65] The reasoning of national and international courts often seems to touch upon as many interpretive tools as are applicable, to then use an interpretive tool of their choosing as the decisive factor. Traditionally, treaty interpretation conducted by international courts gives considerable weight to the aspect of consent as a basis of the treaty. Hence, Articles 31 and 32 of the VCLT emphasize a textual approach, whether alone or in concert with a focus on 'intention'; a similar method may be gleaned from the ICJ's practice.[66] Although mentioned in the VCLT, there is generally less concern for 'object and purpose' as a tool to establish the text's meaning.[67] In contrast, the interpretation of treaties by domestic courts appears more often inspired by the principle of effectiveness, or a teleological approach, to the text. As with 'intent' in treaty interpretation by domestic courts, the 'purpose' of the treaty may be found not only in the international context but also in national law or policy considerations. Naturally, in jurisdictions where the rule of precedent is observed, such as the US and, when it applies common law, Canada, judicial

64 *X and ors*, Appeal judgment, no 13-84.778, ILDC 2376 (FR 2014), 15 January 2014, France; Court of Cassation [Cass]; Criminal Division.

65 VCLT (n 2) Article 31 addresses the VCLT's general rules of treaty interpretation: '1. A treaty shall be interpreted in good faith in accordance with the ordinary meaning to be given to the terms of the treaty in their context and in the light of its object and purpose. 2. The context for the purpose of the interpretation of a treaty shall comprise, in addition to the text, including its preamble and annexes: (*a*) any agreement relating to the treaty which was made between all the parties in connection with the conclusion of the treaty; (*b*) any instrument which was made by one or more parties in connection with the conclusion of the treaty and accepted by the other parties as an instrument related to the treaty. 3. There shall be taken into account, together with the context: (*a*) any subsequent agreement between the parties regarding the interpretation of the treaty or the application of its provisions; (*b*) any subsequent practice in the application of the treaty which establishes the agreement of the parties regarding its interpretation; (*c*) any relevant rules of international law applicable in the relations between the parties. 4. A special meaning shall be given to a term if it is established that the parties so intended'. M Herdegen, 'Interpretation in International Law' in R Wolfrum (ed), *Max Planck Encyclopedia of Public International Law* (OUP 2008) http://www.mpepil.com (last accessed 26 January 2018); R Gardiner, *Treaty Interpretation* (OUP, reprint 2010); following the ILC itself, such interpretation is frequently described as 'an art not an exact science'.

66 See, eg, S Torres Bernárdez, 'Interpretation of Treaties by the International Court of Justice Following the Adoption of the 1969 Vienna Convention on the Law of Treaties' in G Hafner and others (eds), *Liber Amicorum Professor Seidl-Hohenveldern* (Martinus Nijhoff 1998) 721–48.

67 cf VCLT 1969 (n 2) Articles 31–33 and the identical language found in 1986 VCLT (n 4) Articles 31–33; cf I Sinclair, *The Vienna Convention on the Law of Treaties* (2nd edn, MUP 1984) 131 ('there is also the risk that the placing of undue emphasis on the "object and purpose" of a treaty will encourage teleological methods of interpretation').

decisions as interpretive instruments have a more central role than envisaged in the Articles 31 and 32 of the VCLT (in which they go unmentioned).

In *Pushpanathan v Canada*[68] the Canadian Supreme Court examined whether trafficking in narcotics was 'contrary to the purposes and principles of the *United Nations*' in the sense of Article 1(F)(c) of the Convention relating to the Status of Refugees (Refugee Convention), which describes a ground for exclusion from the protection of the Convention. The court referred to a 'textual analysis' (para 56) of the Convention, but overall it focused on the purpose of the treaty linked with the intent of the parties. Specifically, the court used the purpose of Article 1(F) of the Refugee Convention (that is, to prevent persons having caused persecution and refuge of others from subsequently enjoying refugee protection) to delimit and meaningfully interpret 'the purposes and principles of the UN Charter'.

The court expressly employed international rules for treaty interpretation, both with regard to 'incorporated' and 'translated' treaty norms.[69]

Pushpanathan and Canadian Council for Refugees (intervening) v Minister of Citizenship and Immigration, Appeal to Supreme Court, [1998] 1 SCR 982, (1998) 160 DLR (4th) 193, (1998) 11 Admin LR (3d) 1, ILDC 182 (CA 1998), 4th June 1998, Canada; Supreme Court [SCC]

> 51 [...] Since the purpose of the Act incorporating Article 1F(c) is to implement the underlying Convention, the Court must adopt an interpretation consistent with Canada's obligations under the Convention. The wording of the Convention and the rules of treaty interpretation will therefore be applied to determine the meaning of Article 1F(c) in domestic law (Ward, supra, at pp. 713–16). [...]
>
> 54 [...] I am bound to approach the application of the exclusion clause, first, by reference to the existing jurisprudence of this Court and, second, by reference to the clear intent of the signatories to the Convention. Where, however, there is an unresolved ambiguity or issue, the construction most agreeable to justice and reason must prevail. [...]
>
> 56 The starting point of the interpretative exercise is, first, to define the purpose of the Convention as a whole, and, second, the purpose and place of Article 1F(c) within that scheme. [...]
>
> 57 [...] This overarching and clear human rights object and purpose is the background against which interpretation of individual provisions must take place. [...]
>
> 63 What is crucial, in my opinion, is the manner in which the logic of the exclusion in Article 1F generally, and Article 1F(c) in particular, is related to the purpose of the Convention as a whole. The rationale is that those who are responsible for the persecution which creates refugees should not enjoy the benefits of a Convention designed to protect those refugees. [...]
>
> 65 Determining the precise content of this phrase ["Contrary to the Purposes and Principles of the United Nations"] is significantly easier having defined a discrete purpose which Article 1F(c) was intended to play within the structure and purposes of the Convention. [...] The guiding principle is that where there is consensus in international law that particular acts constitute sufficiently serious and sustained violations of fundamental human rights as to amount to persecution, or are explicitly

68 *Pushpanathan v Canada* (Minister of Citizenship and Immigration), Appeal to Supreme Court, (1998) 1 SCR 982; ILDC 182 (CA 1998) as amended by (1998) 1 SCR 1222, 4 June 1998.

69 ibid, para 53, G MacNeil, Analysis, *Pushpanathan v Canada*, ILDC 182 (CA 1998) A6.

> recognized as contrary to the purposes and principles of the United Nations, then Article 1F(c) will be applicable. [. . .]

Thus, ultimately the deciding factor was political consensus rather than interpretation of the text in the strict sense:

> 74 There is no rational connection between the objectives of the Convention and the objectives of the limitation on Article 1F(c) as stated by the respondent. Until the international community makes clear its view that drug trafficking, in one form or another, is a serious violation of fundamental human rights amounting to persecution, then there can be no rationale for counting it among the grounds of exclusion. [. . .]

The dissenting opinion held that drug trafficking could, as in this case, fall under that category, based on and depending on the scale and gravity of the acts.

Article 1F of the Refugee Convention was also at issue in *Febles v Canada*,[70] with the specific question as to whether Article 1F(b) was applicable to deny the protection of the Convention to persons who had committed serious non-political crimes outside a country of refuge prior to admission to that country, even if these persons had had served their sentence(s) in full, as in the present case, or only if such persons were fugitives from justice. By systematically applying the instrumentarium of Article 31 of the VCLT, the Supreme Court found nothing in the ordinary meaning, the context, or the object and purpose of the provision indicated that it should be given a narrow interpretation so as to refer only to fugitives. The Supreme Court expressly noted the auxiliary nature of Article 32 of the VCLT and the absence of a need to consult the *travaux préparatoires* for further clarification in the case at hand.

Febles v Canada (Citizenship and Immigration), Febles, Amnesty International (intervening) and ors (intervening) v Minister of Citizenship and Immigration, Appeal decision, 2014 SCC 68, [2014] 3 SCR 431, 376 DLR (4th) 387, Case No 35215, ILDC 2285 (CA 2014), 30th October 2014, Canada; Supreme Court [SCC]

> The ordinary meaning of Article 1F(b)'s terms "has committed a serious . . . crime" refers only to the crime at the time it was committed and not to anything subsequent to the commission of the crime. There is nothing in the text of the provision suggesting that Article 1F(b) only applies to fugitives, or that factors such as current lack of dangerousness or post-crime expiation or rehabilitation are to be considered or balanced against the seriousness of the crime.
>
> The context around Article 1F(b) supports this interpretation. The immediate context of Article 1F(b) is Article 1F as a whole. There is nothing in the wording of Articles 1F(a) and 1F(c) to support the view that the exclusion from refugee protection under Article 1F(b) is confined to fugitives. Nor does Article 33(2) of the Refugee Convention support the view that Article 1F(b) is confined to fugitives. The reason Article 33(2) applies only to particularly serious crimes, and has the additional requirement that "danger to the community" be demonstrated, is because it authorizes removal of a person whose need for protection has been recognized.
>
> Likewise, the object and purposes of the Refugee Convention do not support the contention that Article 1F(b) is confined to fugitives. The Refugee Convention has twin purposes: it aims to strike a balance between helping victims of oppression by allowing them to start new lives in other countries, while also protecting the interests

70 *Febles v Canada (Citizenship and Immigration), Febles, Amnesty International (intervening) and ors (intervening) v Minister of Citizenship and Immigration*, Appeal decision, 2014 SCC 68, [2014] 3 SCR 431, 376 DLR (4th) 387, Case No 35215, ILDC 2285 (CA 2014), 30 October 2014, Canada; Supreme Court [SCC].

of receiving countries, which they did not renounce simply by negotiating specific provisions to aid victims of oppression. The Refugee Convention is not itself an abstract principle, but an agreement among sovereign states in certain specified terms, negotiated by them in consideration of the entirety of their interests. Accordingly, exclusion clauses should not be enlarged in a manner inconsistent with the Refugee Convention's broad humanitarian aims, but neither should overly narrow interpretations be adopted which ignore the contracting states' need to control who enters their territory. Ultimately, the purpose of an exclusion clause is to exclude, and broad purposes do not invite interpretations of exclusion clauses unsupported by the text. Article 1F(b) is not directed solely at fugitives and neither is it directed solely at some subset of serious criminals who are undeserving at the time of the refugee application. Rather, in excluding all claimants who have committed serious non-political crimes, Article 1F(b) expresses the contracting states' agreement that such persons by definition would be undeserving of refugee protection by reason of their serious criminality.

Excluding people who have committed serious crimes may support a number of subsidiary rationales — it may prevent people fleeing from justice; it may prevent dangerous and particularly undeserving people from entering the host country. It may help preserve the integrity and legitimacy and ultimate viability of the refugee protection system. It may deter states from exporting criminals as refugees. It may allow states to reduce danger to their society from serious criminality cases as a class, given the difficult task and potential for error when attempting to determine the ongoing dangerousness of criminals from abroad on whom they may often have limited reliable information. Whatever rationales for Article 1F(b) may or may not exist, its purpose is clear in excluding persons from protection who previously committed serious crimes abroad.

With respect to the Travaux préparatoires, the Vienna Convention conditions for their use in interpretation are not present in this case. The meaning of Article 1F(b) is clear, and admits of no ambiguity, obscurity or absurd or unreasonable result. Therefore, the Travaux préparatoires should not be considered. Further, even if they were considered, the Travaux préparatoires do not support the contention that Article 1F(b) is confined to fugitives.

King v Bristow Helicopters Ltd[71] addressed the question of whether a psychiatric condition constituted 'bodily injury' under Article 17 of the Warsaw Convention on International Carriage by Air (Warsaw Convention), for the purpose of claiming damages.

M, Re, King v Bristow Helicopters Limited, Appeal judgment, [2002] UKHL 7, [2002] 2 AC 628, [2002] WLR 578, [2002] 2 All ER 565, ILDC 242 (UK 2002), 28th February 2002, United Kingdom; House of Lords [HL]

Lord Steyn:

16. [. . .] It is irrelevant what bodily injury means in other contexts in national legal systems. The correct inquiry is to determine the autonomous or independent meaning of "bodily injury" in the Convention: *R v Secretary of State for the Home Department, Ex p Adan* [2001] 2 AC 477. And the premise is that something that does not qualify as a "bodily injury" in the Convention sense does not meet the relevant threshold for recovery under it. [. . .]

71 *M, Re, King v Bristow Helicopters Limited*, Appeal judgment, [2002] UKHL 7, [2002] 2 AC 628, [2002] WLR 578, [2002] 2 All ER 565, ILDC 242 (UK 2002), 28th February 2002, United Kingdom; House of Lords (HL).

> Lord Hope, with Lords Steyn and Mackay:
>
> 82. The meaning that is to be given to the words used in the Convention must be the meaning which was to be attributed to them when the Convention was entered into in 1929. But it must always have been intended that the application of that meaning to the facts would depend on the evidence. The proper approach is to make use of the best current medical and scientific knowledge that is available. […]
>
> Lord Hobhouse:
>
> 141. The word bodily is simpler. It means pertaining to the body. There must be an injury to the body. It is, as it must be, accepted that the brain, the central nervous system and the glands which secrete the hormones which enable the brain and the rest of the central nervous system to operate are all integral parts of the body just as much as are the toes, heart, stomach and liver. They are all susceptible to injury. […] The medical science of diagnosis exists to enable the appropriate inferences to be drawn from the observed evidence. Medicinal treatments (as with drugs) are prescribed on the basis that there is a physical condition which can be reversed or alleviated by physical means. […]
>
> 148. […] Therefore, it is the unadorned language of the article to which attention must be directed. It is again a descent into unprincipled subjectivism to use, as do the Court of Appeal (§§50 and 96) and others have done before them, the absence of travaux préparatoires as a tool of construction. Thus the Court of Appeal say: "We consider that it is highly significant that no mention was made of liability for mental injury [sic] in the course of the negotiations that resulted in the Warsaw Convention." This is reasoning which speculates about the subjective intentions of the delegates and is not directed to the objective autonomous meaning of the words used. […]
>
> 149. Secondly it is also mistaken to interpret a convention such as the Warsaw Convention, or the various amended versions of it, as if they were intended to be historical documents frozen in time. […] The principle is more simple. Words have a meaning which does not change but the application of those words to the decision of any question depends on the facts and circumstances of the case in which that question arises. It is the facts and circumstances of the cases that change, not the meaning of the contractual words. […]

The Lords ran by all the interpretative instruments offered by the international law of treaties. Ultimately, it was found that a psychiatric condition could qualify as a 'bodily injury' for the purposes of Article 17 of the Warsaw Convention in those cases if and when it triggered, or was linked to, some physical condition.[72] The temporal factor in the case was neutralized by the emphasis on the 'ordinary meaning of the terms'; there was no hint to an evolutive interpretation or 'living instrument' doctrine.

The following case, on the other hand, appears as a textbook case of intertemporal law and shows how the date of conclusion of a treaty informed the interpretation of some of its provisions, as the 'critical date' for determining the current legal situation lay in the past. The case of *Sea Hunt Inc and Commonwealth of Virginia v Unidentified Shipwrecked Vessel or Vessels and ors*[73] concerned two Spanish Royal Naval vessels, *La Galga* and *Juno*, which had been lost off the shores of present-day Virginia in 1750 and 1802, respectively. Both Spain and Virginia asserted ownership and salvage rights over the shipwrecks. A central question was whether Spain had—as was required—'expressly

72 ibid; see R O'Keefe, Analysis, *M, Re, King v Bristow Helicopters Limited*, ILDC 242 (UK 2002).

73 *Sea Hunt Incorporated and Commonwealth of Virginia v Unidentified Shipwrecked Vessel or Vessels and ors*, Appeal judgment, 221 F 3d 634 (4th Cir 2000); ILDC 940 (US 2000), 21 July 2000.

abandoned' *La Galga* by the Definitive Treaty of Peace between France, Great Britain, and Spain of 10 February 1763 (the 1763 Treaty). The court held this was not the case.

Sea Hunt Incorporated and Commonwealth of Virginia v Unidentified Shipwrecked Vessel or Vessels and ors, Appeal judgment, 221 F.3d 634 (4th Cir. 2000), ILDC 940 (US 2000), 21st July 2000, United States; Court of Appeals (4th Circuit) [4th Cir]

> 19 Under the terms of the 1902 Treaty, Spanish vessels can likewise be abandoned only by express renunciation. Both Spain and the United States agree that this treaty provision requires that in our territorial waters Spanish ships are to be accorded the same immunity as United States ships. They also agree that such immunity requires application of the express abandonment standard [...] We cannot therefore adopt an implied abandonment standard in the face of treaties and mutual understandings requiring express abandonment. Such a standard would supplant the textual framework of negotiated treaties with an unpredictable judicial exercise in weighing equities. [...]
>
> 25 The plain language of this treaty provision contains no evidence of an express abandonment. First, Article XX does not include any of the common nouns that could refer to LA GALGA. Notably absent are the terms "shipwreck," "vessels," "frigates," or "warships." Other provisions of the treaty mention these terms explicitly. [...]. Without any mention of shipwrecks or any seagoing vessels it is hard to read Article XX as an express abandonment of LA GALGA.
>
> 26 Second, the cession of state property in Article XX is limited to all that Spain possesses "on the continent of North America." The plain meaning of this is that Spain ceded to Great Britain only what was located on land. Spain did not cede possessions in the sea or seabed. [...]
>
> 28 [I]n light of eighteenth century understandings, this "on the continent" language would hardly amount to clear and convincing evidence of an express abandonment of property in coastal waters. In fact, the three-mile coastal belt, well-recognized today, had no clear counterpart in eighteenth century international law. Ownership of the three-mile belt in the eighteenth century was but a "nebulous suggestion." *United States v. California*, 332 U.S. at 32. When "in 1776 the American colonies achieved independence and when in 1783 the Treaty of Paris was concluded, neither the British crown nor the colonies individually had any right of ownership of the seabed of the sea adjacent to the American coast." Report of Special Master Maris, O.T. 1973, No. 35 Orig. at 47, adopted by *United States v. Maine*, 420 U.S. 515 (1975). Sovereign rights to the territorial sea were not established in international law until some time in the nineteenth century. See California, 322 U.S. at 33; accord Maine, 420 U.S. at 524. Nineteenth century and present-day views of territorial cession are hardly dispositive of what mid-eighteenth century treaty signatories intended. See *Shively v. Bowlby*, 152 U.S. 1, 57 (1894); *United States v. Ancgog*, 190 F. Supp. 696, 698 (D. Guam 1961).

In *Anonymous v Public Prosecutor*,[74] the Netherlands Supreme Court decided that Article 105 of the United Nations Convention on the Law of the Sea, in combination with relevant United Nations Security Council resolutions, provided a 'procedure prescribed by law' as required by Article 5 of the European Convention on Human Rights and hence sufficed as a legal basis for detention at sea in the context of a counter-piracy mission. The court interpreted the requirement 'a procedure prescribed by law' from a conceptual angle, and found a legal basis in

74 *Anonymous v Public Prosecutor*, Judgment on merits, Case No 14/01783, ECLI:NL:HR:2015:3640, ILDC 2571 (NL 2015), 22 December 2015, Netherlands; Supreme Court [HR].

international law, tied in with European human rights law. Lawfulness meant that detention had to rest on a legal basis, which must be pre-existing and meet certain requirements of quality. *In casu* the court found that Article 105 UNCLOS sufficed as a legal basis for deprivation of liberty as it satisfied general principles of rule of law, legal certainty (clarity and foreseeability of the law), proportionality, and protection against arbitrariness.

In the case *Register of Wills for Baltimore County v Arrowsmith and ors*[75] two factors additional to the regular catalogue of interpretive tools entered the interpretation process: equity and the division of competences between the federal and the state level within the state. The US Court of Appeals decided that the Convention for the Avoidance of Double Taxation with Respect to Taxes on Estates, Inheritance, and Gifts between Germany and the United States did not render inapplicable the state of Maryland's statute of limitations with respect to filing a claim for refund of inheritance taxes, even if this resulted in an unfair situation of *de facto* double taxation.

Register of Wills for Baltimore County v Arrowsmith and Others, Court of Appeals judgment, 778 A 2d 364 (Md 2001), ILDC 1246 (US 2001), 15th August 2001, United States; Maryland

> 36 We must interpret our State laws and the provisions of the Treaty as a court of law, not as a court of equity. While we recognize the unfortunate result that may befall appellees, we will not subvert the clear intention of those who drafted and ratified this Treaty on behalf of the United States, nor will we dismiss our Legislature's mandate in establishing guidelines for prompt and efficient administration of estates. [...]

The court put considerable emphasis on the *travaux préparatoires* of the Tax Treaty as evidence of the intention of the contracting parties, and the treaty's object and purpose.

> 7 [...] The express purpose of the Treaty was to prevent the double taxation of the estates of citizens or residents of the two countries. [...]
>
> 19 Appellees argue that the scope of the Treaty must necessarily encompass state as well as federal taxes because viewed otherwise, the express purpose of the Treaty — to avoid double taxation — would be defeated. [... but ...] Had the drafters intended the Treaty to "necessarily" apply to state estate and inheritance taxes, there would be no need for a separate provision that unequivocally refers to the credits afforded for state taxation. [...]
>
> 21 [...] With respect to the Treaty under scrutiny today, the Senate Committee on Foreign Relations provided an express declaration of understanding that is supportive of this Court's conclusion. [...] Thus, not only does a textual reading of the Treaty clearly indicate that it exclusively applies to Federal death taxes, but the Senate's express language, e.g. "the proposed treaty does not apply to ... taxes imposed by state or local governments," impedes the ability to put forth any rational challenge to such application. [...]

The court then went on to consider the findings of other US courts on similar tax treaties, which in international law is accepted (eg for the purpose of determining customary international law), as constituting general evidence, even though consisting of several bilateral treaties.

Register of Wills for Baltimore County v Arrowsmith and Others, Court of Appeals judgment, 778 A 2d 364 (Md 2001), ILDC 1246 (US 2001), 15th August 2001, United States; Maryland

> 26 While we are one of a small number of courts to consider the impact of federal estate tax treaties on state probate proceedings, we are not the first. Given that the

75 *Register of Wills for Baltimore County v Arrowsmith and ors*, Court of Appeals judgment, 778 A 2d 364 (Md 2001); ILDC 1246 (US 2001), 15 August 2001.

> substance and purpose of these bilateral agreements are virtually identical, given that other bodies of authority, intimately involved in the making and implementation of these treaties (e.g. the Department of Treasury and the Senate Committee on Foreign Relations) have expressly asserted the inapplicability of the treaty provisions to state probate proceedings, and given the outcome of other similar judicial claims, we find significant support for our holding today that the United States-Germany Estate Tax Treaty does not impose on Maryland any duty or obligation to alter its probate proceedings to accommodate the appellees. [. . .]

Next to interpretation of binding treaty norms, courts may adopt an interpretive discourse and refer to treaties without legal force in the domestic legal order, in order to support and legitimize a particular reading of a domestic legal provision. One example of such 'treaty-conform interpretation' is the *Englaro* case mentioned above.[76] Another is the judgment in *Frudenthal v Israel*,[77] where the Israeli Supreme Court interpreted domestic law—the criminal offence of trafficking in persons in an Israeli Statute—in conformity with international treaties, namely the 2000 Convention against Transnational Organized Crime and the Protocol to Prevent, Suppress and Punish Trafficking in Persons, Especially Women and Children, which supplemented the Convention. It held that, although Israel had not ratified these international instruments, by signing them it had expressed its willingness to take part in an international effort to abolish trafficking and the Israeli Statute was therefore to be interpreted in accordance with the spirit of the convention and the protocol.[78]

Frudenthal (Michael) v Israel, Appeal judgment, CA 11196/02, ILDC 364 (IL 2003), 3rd August 2003, Israel; Supreme Court; Supreme Court as Court of Appeal; Criminal Division

> 5. I will add that the offense involved in trafficking in persons has become a phenomenon of global concern, and many countries have declared war on it. As part of its efforts to join the international struggle against trafficking in persons, Israel signed the United Nations Convention Against Transnational Organized Crime, including the Protocol to Prevent, Suppress, and Punish Trafficking in Persons which supplements the Convention. The Convention and the Protocol, which will enter into force shortly, have yet to be ratified in Israel, but Israel's joining the Convention expresses its aspiration to take an active part in the norms that the family of nations has created around this issue. [. . .]
>
> In amending the Penal Law, Israel's legislature sought to take part in the international struggle against trafficking in persons — at this stage, trafficking for the purpose of prostitution — because the phenomenon has already infiltrated Israel. Consequently, the purposes of the legislation are identical to the purpose of the above-mentioned protocol. We therefore should interpret the provisions of the Israeli statute in accordance with the spirit of the Convention, which seeks to prevent the exploitation of power in the form of transferring people and trafficking in them for the purpose of prostitution or slavery. We should, therefore, interpret the statute according to its purpose, and in a way that will not defeat the goal of the legislation.

Finally, a particular category of interpretive questions is whether a treaty creates individual rights, even if not explicitly addressed to individuals in the way of a human rights treaty. A well-known subject of debate is Article 36 of the Convention on Consular Relations, according to which local authorities must notify all detained foreigners 'without delay' of their right to have

76 *Englaro, as guardian of Englaro v Office of the Public Prosecutor at the Tribunal of Milan and ors*, Appeal judgment, No 21748; ILDC 1431 (IT 2007) (2007) Foro italiano I-3025, 16 October 2007; see para 7.2—no English translation available.

77 *Frudenthal v Israel*, Appeal judgment, CA 11196/02; ILDC 364 (IL 2003), 3 August 2003.

78 ibid, para 5.

their consulate informed of their detention. In *Cornejo v County of San Diego and ors*[79] the court held that this provision entailed no individual right.

Cornejo v County of San Diego and ors, Appeal Judgment, 504 F3d 853 (9th Cir 2007), ILDC 1080 (US 2007), 24th September 2007, United States; Court of Appeals (9th Circuit) [9th Cir]

> 3 We agree with the district court that Article 36 does not create judicially enforceable rights. Article 36 confers legal rights and obligations on States in order to facilitate and promote consular functions. Consular functions include protecting the interests of detained nationals, and for that purpose detainees have the right (if they want) for the consular post to be notified of their situation. In this sense, detained foreign nationals benefit from Article 36's provisions. But the right to protect nationals belongs to States party to the Convention; no private right is unambiguously conferred on individual detainees such that they may pursue it through § 1983. [. . .]

The court placed strong emphasis on intention, taking a national law perspective (referring to the domestic legal act of 'ratification' by parliament) as much as an international perspective (referring to the drafters of the Convention). The seminal pronouncement by an ***international*** court on Article 36 of the Convention on Consular Relations is the International Court of Justice's judgment in the *LaGrand* case in 2001. It is remarkable that in *Cornejo* the US court referred to *LaGrand* only once, in relation to the functionalist rationale of the law on consular relations (para. 19). It did not, however, mention that the ICJ *in casu* had found Article 36(1)(b) to 'create [. . .] individual rights for the detained person'.[80] This was pointed out only in the dissenting opinion.[81]

> 9[2] Therefore, the question here is whether Congress, by ratifying the Convention, intended to create private rights and remedies enforceable in American courts through § 1983 by individual foreign nationals who are arrested or detained in this country. It is an open question for us. [. . .]
>
> 13 [. . .] Cornejo's most compelling argument is that Article 36 textually uses the word "rights" in reference to a detainee's being informed that he can, if he wants, have his consular post advised of his detention and have communications forwarded to it. This use of the word in paragraph 1(b) "arguably confers on an individual the right to consular assistance following arrest." *Breard*, 523 U.S. at 376. However, it says nothing about the nature of "his rights" or how, if at all, they may be invoked. This language, therefore, must be considered in light of what the Convention, and Article 36, are all about. Restatement § 325(1) (noting that treaty terms are to be construed in their context and in the light of the treaty's object and purpose). [. . .]
>
> 24 Given that Article 36 does not unambiguously confer a right in individual detainees to support a cause of action under § 1983, we see no need for resort to the travaux préparatoires. [. . .] To the extent the travaux préparatoires is susceptible to different interpretations, it is too ambiguous under domestic law — which controls the exercise of rights pursuant to paragraph 2 of Article 36 — to create a privately enforceable right not explicitly found in the text.

See also *Doe v Doe*,[82] in which the Israeli Supreme Court based its decision as to whether Article 15 of the Hague Convention on the Civil Aspects of International Child Abduction conferred an

---

79 *Cornejo v County of San Diego and ors* (n 22). (Paragraph numbers have been added to this decision by OUP/ILDC.)

80 *LaGrand Case* (*Germany v US*) [2001] ICJ Rep 466, paras 77 and 89.

81 D W Nelson, Senior Circuit Judge, dissenting, paras 27–52 of the *Cornejo* decision (n 22), reference to *LaGrand* in para 44.

82 *Doe v Doe*, Motion for leave to appeal, ILDC 2319 (IL 2014), 1930/14, 5 June 2014, Israel; Supreme Court.

individual right of legal action, ultimately on the object and purpose of the Convention. The court held that, while Israeli law allowed an individual to file an application under Article 15 to Israeli courts, the application would need to be appropriate in light of such object and purpose of the Hague Convention: that is, it would support the main proceedings through a clarification of Israeli law as required by the foreign court.

VII. Scope

The determination of a treaty's scope is intrinsically linked to treaty interpretation. It has a temporal and a territorial dimension. The temporal scope of application refers to the time-span covered by the operation of a treaty. The territorial scope, on the other hand, concerns the geographic area of treaty application. While this is usually a state's territory,[83] some treaties provide for extraterritorial extension (eg to overseas territories)[84] or apply only to parts of a state's territory as in certain instances of state succession.

In *Hans-Jürgen Hartman M/S Kvitnes GmbH & Co KG v Ministry of Fisheries and Coastal Affairs*[85] the Norwegian Supreme Court had to answer the question of whether a 1996 Protocol ratified by Germany, but not in force at the time of a shipwreck, was applicable to that shipwreck rather than the previously existing 1976 Convention on Limitation of Liability for Maritime Claims. The court found that the 1996 Protocol was binding for Germany only after it entered into force in May 2004, irrespective of the fact that Germany had ratified it already in September 2001.[86]

Reederei Hans-Jürgen Hartman M/S Kvitnes GmbH & Company KG v Ministry of Fisheries and Coastal Affairs, Final Decision on Civil Interlocutory Appeal, Case No HR-2007-00325-A, ILDC 818 (NO 2007), 15th February 2007, Norway; Supreme Court

> (24) When the Rocknes was lost, Germany was a party to the 1976 Convention. The 1996 Protocol entered into force in Germany on the same day as it entered into force internationally — on 13 May 2004. […]
>
> (26) […] The 1996 Protocol was, for Germany's part, binding from the moment it came into force on 13 May 2004. With regard to Section 170 of the Norwegian Maritime Code, Germany cannot be considered to be a party in terms of international law from the date of ratification, namely 3 September 2001. […]
>
> (31) With regard to liable parties from states who are party to the 1976 Convention, the 1996 Protocol can therefore only be invoked for incidents which occurred after the date on which it came into force internationally. […]

83 See VCLT (n 2) Article 29: 'Unless a different intention appears from the treaty or is otherwise established, a treaty is binding upon each party in respect of its entire territory'.

84 For details see Aust (n 32) 178 ff.

85 *Hans-Jürgen Hartman M/S Kvitnes GmbH & Co KG v Ministry of Fisheries and Coastal Affairs*, Final decision on civil interlocutory appeal, Case No HR-2007-00325-A; ILDC 818 (NO 2007), 3 August 2003. See in this context also *National Federation of Guardianship Associations v France*, Decision on annulment for abuse of power, No 213461; ILDC 765 (FR 2000), 7 July 2000
(n 19) and accompanying text.

86 *Hans-Jürgen Hartman M/S Kvitnes GmbH & Co KG v Ministry of Fisheries and Coastal Affairs* (n 85) para 31. The Norwegian Supreme Court's findings—that a treaty applies only after its entry into force for the respective state—is in line with VCLT (n 2) Article 18, which limits a state's obligation prior to a treaty's entry into force to the duty not to defeat the object and purpose of the treaty; see also *Peru—Agricultural Products, Guatemala v Peru*, Panel report, WT/DS457/R, ITL 081 (WTO 2014), 27 November 2014, World Trade Organisation [WTO]—under binding force. See also VCLT (n 2) Article 24.

Another case dealing with the temporal scope of a treaty was *Kell v Canada*.[87] In this case, an indigenous woman named Ms Kell alleged violation of the Convention on the Elimination of All Forms of Discrimination against Women (CEDAW), because she had been denied legal relief after having been arbitrarily evicted from her property by her abusive partner. Canada claimed that the facts relevant to the communication had occurred before the entry into force of the Optional Protocol of the Convention. Thus, the temporal scope had not been met (paras 4.2, 4.3, and 6.1). The Committee nevertheless found that the claim was admissible *ratione temporis* as the discrimination of Ms Kell had continued after the entry into force of the Optional Protocol, thus constituting a pending continuing claim.

Kell v Canada, Merits, UN Doc C/51/D/19/2008, IHRL 1971 (CEDAW 2012), 28th February 2012, Committee on the Elimination of Discrimination against Women [CEDAW]

> 7.5 The Committee found that since the author's claim had not been barred by limitation in any of the proceedings before the domestic courts after ratification of the Protocol, and since the author's claim had already been pending before the courts at the time of ratification and entry into force of the Protocol, her claim constituted a pending claim. The Committee was of the view that the subject matter and discriminatory effect of the alleged violation did not cease to exist, as the claim was a pending continuing claim not barred by limitation. The Committee considered the facts that are the subject of the communication to be of a continuous nature, and found that admissibility ratione temporis is thereby justified, and declared the communication admissible under article 4, paragraph 2(e), of the Optional Protocol.

A special issue concerning the territorial scope of the application of treaties in case of state succession arose in *Ltd Partnership Z v High Court of the Canton of Thurgau*.[88] The question was whether the notification of bankruptcy directly to the domicile of an addressee in Baden was permissible in accordance with the 1825/1826 Agreement between the Swiss Confederation and the crown of the State of Württemberg, which established the national treatment of their citizens in cases of insolvency and provided for the direct sending through postal channels. Since the agreement was restricted to the territory of former Württemberg and had never been extended to Baden as a consequence of the merger of the two territories in 1952, the Swiss Federal Court declined its applicability.[89] The court decided that in case of a unification of two territories a treaty is only applicable to the territory of the original treaty party, without extending to the entire unified territory.[90]

---

87 Merits, UN Doc C/51/D/19/2008, IHRL 1971 (CEDAW 2012), 28 February 2012, Committee on the Elimination of Discrimination against Women [CEDAW].

88 *Ltd Partnership Z v High Court of the Canton of Thurgau*, Appeal judgment; ILDC 341 (CH 2005), 15 June 2005.

89 To reach its conclusion, the court referred to the Ministry of Justice's information as to the territorial scope of application: '[. . .] The Ministry for Justice, Federal and European Affairs for Baden-Württemberg also assumed in the above-mentioned opinion that the treaty remains in force now as before. However, from a territorial viewpoint it considered that it only applied to the territory of the former kingdom of Württemberg (including the former Hohenzollern lands) which had concluded the treaty and that the unification of the Lands of Württemberg-Baden, Württemberg-Hohenzollern and (south)Baden (situated in the S.______) in 1952 did not extend of the scope of its validity [. . .]' (Translation; ibid, para 2.2.2).

90 Compare the rule stipulated in Art 31 of the 1978 Vienna Convention on the succession of States in respect of Treaties: '*Effects of a uniting of States in respect of treaties in force at the date of the succession of States.* 1. When two or more States unite and so form one successor State, [. . .] 2. Any treaty continuing in force in conformity with paragraph 1 shall apply only in respect of the part of the territory of the successor State in respect of which the treaty was in force at the date of the succession of States unless: [. . .] (*c*) in the case of a bilateral treaty, the successor State and the other State party otherwise agree. [. . .]'. Note however that Switzerland is not a party to the Convention, which moreover relates to states and not territories.

A similar question arose in *Azra Basic v United States*.[91] In this case, Azra Basic, subject to charges of war crimes committed against civilians, first filed a motion to dismiss the complaint owing to the fact that the 1901 Treaty between the United States and the Kingdom of Serbia for the Mutual Extradition of Fugitives from Justice (Extradition Treaty) did not apply to Bosnia and Herzegovina.[92] She alleged that Bosnia and Herzegovina had not been under Serbian governance at the time of entry into force of the Extradition Treaty. Moreover, Bosnia and Herzegovina had not directly succeeded to that treaty. Later, Ms Basic recognized the validity of the Extradition Treaty, but challenged its application on the grounds that the crimes she was charged with were not within the scope of the Extradition Treaty. With regard to both arguments, the court held as follows.

Azra Basic v United States, Trial judgment, 2012 WL 3067466 (ED KY), ILDC 1990 (US 2012), 27th July 2012, United States; Kentucky

> 15 […] c) The treaties named in the Complaint are in full force and effect, meaning the extradition mechanics apply. […] The Court found in its prior order on Basic's motion to dismiss that BiH succeeded to Yugoslavia's position as a party to the treaty between the United States and Serbia. […] Further, both the United States and BiH are bound by the CAT. […] BiH succeeded to the CAT and provided a formal instrument of succession to the UN Secretary-General on September 1, 1993 with "effect from 6 March 1992." […] The CAT, by its terms, operates to incorporate torture as an extraditable offense under the Treaty. CAT, Art. 8
>
> […] e) The Complaint charges Basic with a crime or crimes that fall within the scope of the Treaty's extradition ambit. The Complaint […] cites a request to extradite Basic to face a charge of "war crimes against civilians" under Article 142 of the criminal code applicable in the Republika Srpska (a BiH subdivision) and Article 173 of the general criminal code of BiH. Those statutes appear variously in the record. […] The war crimes statutes referenced place under the rubric of "war crimes" various specific acts. These include, as pled, the underlying alleged acts of murder and torture by Azra Basic. […]
>
> 15.1 The Treaty does not list "war crimes" per se, but it does expressly direct extradition for "murder". Treaty, Art. II ("Extradition shall be granted for the following crimes and offences: 1. Murder[.]"). The CAT, which binds both BiH and the United States, inserts "torture" as an extraditable category. Per the CAT, acts of torture (a defined term) must be criminal offenses under the laws of each "State Party." CAT, Art. 4, Sec. 1 (emphasis added). All such offenses further "shall be deemed to be included as extraditable offences in any extradition treaty existing between States Parties." Id. at Art. 8, Sec. 1. The CAT thus requires criminalization of "torture," and requires that torture be extraditable. The BiH statutes tie the torture scope to the international range of illegality. The Treaty and the CAT combine to establish that the war crimes specified in the Complaint – murder and torture in violation of the code sections alleged – are within the extradition scope of the Treaty. The Court must interpret treaty language liberally […]. A treaty that includes "murder" and (via the CAT) "torture" surely, under any reasonable construction, includes as extraditable predicates war crimes premised on the same specific categories of criminal allegations. See also In re Extradition of Handanovic, 829 F. Supp. 2d 979, 989 (D. Or. 2011) ("When

91 *Azra Basic v United States*, Trial judgment, 2012 WL 3067466 (ED KY), ILDC 1990 (US 2012), 27 July 2012, United States; Kentucky.

92 Treaty between the United States of America and the Kingdom of Servia for the Mutual Extradition of Fugitives from Justice (signed 25 October 1901, entered into force 12 May 1902) 32 Stat 1890, 1902 WL 17946. The Extradition Treaty subsequently applied to the successor states of the Kingdom of Serbia, namely the Kingdom of Serbia, Croatia, Slovenia, and subsequently also to Yugoslavia.

determining whether crimes not included in a list treaty by name are nonetheless extraditable, courts have followed the well-established rule that treaties are to be construed liberally to favour the obligation to surrender fugitives.") (citation omitted).

Swiss Compensation Office v M[93] dealt with the question of whether there was a customary international law rule according to which treaties with a predecessor state were automatically in force with the successor state. Specifically, a Social Security Agreement was concluded between Switzerland and the Federal People's Republic of Yugoslavia in 1962. It entered into force in 1964, and continued to be in force with Serbia. When the Republic of Kosovo seceded from Serbia, Switzerland recognized Kosovo as an independent state. The question thus arose whether the bilateral agreement between Serbia and Switzerland would also apply to the newly established Republic of Kosovo. The Swiss Federal Supreme Court stated as follows.

BGer, Urteil vom 19.06.2013 - 9C_662/2012, Swiss Compensation Office v M, Decision of the Swiss Federal Supreme Court, 9C_662/2012, ILDC 2371 (CH 2013), 19th June 2013, Switzerland; Federal Supreme Court [BGer]; Social Chamber II

> 3 It is clear and undisputed that the Agreement of 8 June 1962 between the Swiss Confederation and the Former (Socialist) Federal Republic of Yugoslavia on Social Security ([…] hereinafter: Social Security Agreement […]) continued to be in effect with regard to the Republic of Serbia […]. On 17 February 2008 the Serbian province of Kosovo declared its independence. The Swiss Federal Council recognized Kosovo as an independent state on 27 February 2008. […]. The Federal Supreme Court also referred to Kosovo as a sovereign state […].
>
> 4.1 When the territorial sovereignty over a certain area changes, i.e. when a new state takes the place of another state as a sovereign over certain territory, the question of treaty succession arises. It concerns the question whether and when a newly established state may continue to apply treaties initially concluded with the predecessor state.
>
> 4.2.1 For the present case concerning the secession of Kosovo – the separation and creation of a new state while the old territorially reduced state continues to exist […] – the Social Security Agreement does not contain any rules.
>
> 4.2.2 The Vienna Convention of 23 May 1969 on the Law of Treaties (Vienna Convention, VCLT […]), which entered into force in Switzerland on 6 June 1990, shall not, according to Article 73, prejudge any question that may arise in regard to a treaty from a succession of States.[94]

As regards the question of customary international law and state succession, the Swiss Federal Court stated as follows.

> 4.2.3 The Vienna Convention on Succession of States in Respect of Treaties of 1978 (hereinafter: Vienna Convention), which entered into force in 1996 and regulates what should happen with already existing international treaties in the event of state succession, has not been ratified by the Swiss Confederation […]. In some part, rules were codified which deviate from customary international law […], which might explain the low acceptance and lack of practical relevance […]. In addition, the Swiss Confederation criticized that, according to the Vienna Convention, bilateral treaties automatically continue to apply in the case of dismemberment and secession (Article

93 *Swiss Compensation Office v M*, BGer, Urteil vom 19.06.2013—9C_662/2012, *Swiss Compensation Office v M*, Decision of the Swiss Federal Supreme Court, 9C_662/2012, ILDC 2371 (CH 2013), 19 June 2013, Switzerland; Federal Supreme Court [BGer]; Social Chamber II.

94 Translation by authors since there was no English translation by ILDC.

34 of the Vienna Convention) […]. Such automatism does not find support in customary international law […].

4.2.4 Pursuant to long-standing case-law of the Federal Supreme Court, there is no rule of customary international law according to which treaties concluded with the predecessor state were automatically in force in the relationship with a newly established state and the opposite party of the predecessor state […].

4.4 As long as the concerned states have not agreed upon an explicit provision […], there are essentially three principles for the assessment of the question whether and under which requirements a successor state may continue the treaties of the predecessor state: continuity, continuity ad interim and tabula rasa. […] Depending on the concerned subject matter (cf. for example human rights or border treaties) and the concerned (third) party and its international obligations […] they are applied in different ways […].

5.1 In the Swiss Confederation, regarding the question of (bilateral) treaty succession through a successor state, a certain practice has evolved, which is featured primarily by the discontinuity (no automatic duplication of treaty relations) of treaties.

5.2 In *BGE 105 Ib 286* E. 1c S. 291 […] the Federal Supreme Court held that it cannot be suggested that a rule of customary international law exists according to which treaties concluded with the predecessor state were automatically in force in the relationship with the newly established state and the opposite party of the predecessor state. A bilateral treaty only remains in force, if the newly established state and the opposite party agree to continue the treaty; either through explicit or conclusive action. […]

5.3 [T]he Federal Supreme Court considered in *BGE 132 II 65* E. 3.5.2 S. 73 f. […]: "In a document by the Directorate of Public International Law of the Swiss Federal Department of Foreign Affairs of 30 March 1992 it was inter alia held with regard to Ukraine […] that there are no generally recognized principles in the area of treaty succession; nor do successor states automatically succeed to the rights and obligations of the original state. It must be examined for each treaty, whether the succession of the rights and obligations of the original state through the newly established state meets the needs of both parties to the treaty. This examination often takes a lot of time. In the meantime, the concerned treaties should continue to apply temporarily, not so much for legal reasons, but rather for practical reasons […].

Concerning Kosovo's secession and the question of treaty succession, the Swiss Federal Court held as follows.

6.1 The secession of Kosovo by definition requires that the Republic of Serbia remains a subject of international law […]. The Social Security Agreement therefore continues to be in effect with regard to Serbia […].

6.4 Regarding the question of the continuity of bilateral treaties, it appears from the reproduced facts that Switzerland has, also in relation with Kosovo, chosen a pragmatic approach. It is of crucial importance that, also in this case, there has been no automatic treaty succession. It was decided to continue to apply the bilateral treaties, taking into account the interests of the newly established state as well as Switzerland through negotiations. In the meantime, the treaties in question were applied temporarily, not for legal reasons, but for practical reasons – especially due to reasons of legal certainty to prevent a legal "interruption" in the event of definitive treaty succession. In other words, the bindingness of the treaty ended – in the relationship with the (former Serbian) state territory of the Kosovo – in principle with the establishment

> and recognition of the Republic of Kosovo as a successor state […]; with its declaration of independence, Kosovo has given up its legal identity with Serbia […]. Accordingly, a formal termination of the agreement was not required […]. Neither the current state of international law (the law of treaties) […] nor its practice[…] in the context of successor states – especially in recent times – is opposed to the handling and approach of Switzerland. The fact that Switzerland continued to apply the Social Security Agreement temporarily does not lead to a different result. The Republic of Kosovo was at all times aware that a consensus with Switzerland was needed for a definite treaty succession […]. It was therefore aware that the treaty would continue to apply conditionally. With the final decision of Switzerland not to transfer any agreements between itself and the Republic of Serbia onto the Republic of Kosovo, solely the state of suspension was ended and not the Social Security Agreement itself. […] Apart from that, with the pragmatic continuity of the treaty it becomes apparent that treaties can have not only a prenatal, but also a post-mortem existence. The former is regulated in Article 25 VCLT as a provisional application of a treaty not yet in force […]. By contrast, in this case the application of a treaty not any longer in force is under consideration. […] Under these circumstances, the dogmatics call for an analogous application of Article 25 VCLT, which, in its paragraph 2, stipulates that the state of suspension can be terminated unilaterally through notification – without any negative consequences […].

As regards the non-continuance of the Social Security Agreement, the Swiss Federal Court held as follows.

> 8 As an interim result it should therefore be held that the former Serbian province, and of today the Republic of Kosovo, has, with its secession, brought about – with respect to its territory as well as its treaty obligations – an effective change under international law and that the non-continuance of the Social Security Agreement by Switzerland on the new territorial authority as of 1 April 2010 is lawful.

Concerning the extraterritorial scope of treaties, in *MEN v Denmark*[95] a Burundian asylum-seeker alleged that Denmark had violated her rights under the CEDAW. Denmark had rejected MEN's claim for asylum and had prepared her deportation to Burundi. This, even though she claimed that she would face a real risk of persecution in Burundi, being a member of the opposition party, and 'as a woman, could be subjected to rape or other forms of bodily harm upon her return'.[96] Denmark was of the opinion that the communication should be declared inadmissible *ratione loci* and *ratione materiae*, as the author's claims related to violations that might be possibly committed by Burundi, not by Denmark:

> 4.6 The State party submits that the return of the author to Burundi will not lead to a violation of the provisions of the Convention, as claimed by the author. […] The State party further submits that the alleged violations in the author's complaint relate to Burundi and not to Denmark. The State party argues that the Committee lacks jurisdiction over the relevant violations in respect of Denmark, and therefore, the communication is incompatible with the provisions of the Convention. The author's claims are based not on any treatment that she will suffer at the hands of the State party, but on consequences that she may suffer if she is returned to Burundi. […]
>
> 4.7 The State party submits that the concept of jurisdiction for the purposes of article 2 of the Optional Protocol must be considered within the general meaning of the

95 *MEN v Denmark*, Admissibility, UN Doc CEDAW/C/55/D/35/2011, IHRL 3847 (CEDAW 2013), 26 July 2013, Committee on the Elimination of Discrimination against Women [CEDAW].

96 ibid, para 3.

term in public international law. Thus, the words "under the jurisdiction of a State party" must be understood to mean that a State's jurisdictional competence is primarily territorial and that State jurisdiction is presumed to be exercised throughout its territory. Only in exceptional circumstances can certain acts of a State party produce effects outside its territory, triggering its responsibility ("extraterritorial effect"). The State party submits that no such exceptional circumstances exist in this case.

4.8 The State party further submits that there is no jurisprudence by the Committee that indicates that the provisions of the Convention have extraterritorial effect. […]

4.9 […] The State party argues that it is responsible only for obligations vis-à-vis individuals under its jurisdiction and cannot be held responsible for discrimination in another country. Returning a person who comes to the State party simply to escape from discriminatory treatment in her own country, however objectionable that treatment may be, cannot constitute a violation of the Convention by that State party.

The CEDAW Committee eventually held that the communication was inadmissible under article 4(1) of the Optional Protocol (failure to exhaust local remedies).[97] However, regarding the extraterritorial application of the convention, it noted that if there was a 'real, personal and foreseeable risk' that gender-based violence would occur even in another country and jurisdiction, states had a positive duty to protect women from such a risk:

8.9 As to the State party's argument that nothing in the Committee's jurisprudence indicates that any provisions of the Convention have extraterritorial effect, the Committee recalls that, under article 2(d) of the Convention, States parties undertake to refrain from engaging in any act or practice of discrimination against women and to ensure that public authorities and institutions shall act in conformity with this obligation. This positive duty encompasses the obligation of States parties to protect women from being exposed to a real, personal and foreseeable risk of serious forms of gender-based violence, irrespective of whether such consequences would take place outside the territorial boundaries of the sending State party: if a State party takes a decision relating to a person within its jurisdiction, and the necessary and foreseeable consequence is that that person's rights under the Convention will be violated in another jurisdiction, the State party itself may be in violation of the Convention. For example, a State party would itself be in violation of the Convention if it sent back a person to another State in circumstances in which it was foreseeable that serious gender-based violence would occur. The foreseeability of the consequence would mean that there was a present violation by the State party, even though the consequence would not occur until later […].

The committee thus acknowledged that a state had duties to protect women from harm that occurred outside its territorial boundaries. However, it nevertheless held that the allegations made by the complainant were not sufficiently substantiated.

8.9 What amounts to serious forms of gender-based violence will depend on the circumstances of each case and would need to be determined by the Committee on a case-by-case basis at the merits stage, provided that the author had made a prima face case before the Committee by sufficiently substantiating such allegations. In the present case, the author failed to sufficiently substantiate her allegations for purposes of admissibility and the Committee need not examine them further.[98]

97 ibid, para 8.3.

98 See also *MS (on behalf of MS's husband and their two minor children) v Denmark*, Admissibility, UN Doc CEDAW/C/55/D/40/2012, IHRL 3844 (CEDAW 2013), 22 July 2013, Committee on the Elimination of

VIII. Successive Treaties

Frequently linked to conclusion and entry into force, as well as to termination of treaties, are cases of successive treaties. Here the temporal order of treaties on the same subject matter may determine the applicability of an agreement internationally and domestically. In *Question of law regarding the interpretation of Article 17(2) of Treaty on Extradition between the Republic of Poland and Australia, Re, Reference to Supreme Court on Preliminary Question* [99] the Supreme Court found for applicability of an extradition treaty to proceedings initiated while a previous extradition treaty was still in force. Such on the ground that the previous treaty had been terminated by the conclusion of a new treaty by the same parties, as envisaged in Article 59 of the VCLT:

> 15 [...] The provisions of Article 17(2) of the Treaty of 1998 stipulate that on the date of this Treaty entry into force, the Treaty of 1932 shall cease to be in force. This is the general rule lex posterior derogat priori. Article 17(3) of the 1998 Treaty regulates only a limited scope of intertemporal problems stipulating that extradition requests submitted after the entry into force of this Treaty shall be governed by this Treaty regardless of the date of the commission of the offence for which extradition is requested. This provision also allows for the application of new regulations.
>
> 20 [...] A treaty is thus considered to be no longer in force if there is a treaty concluded later, concerning the same subject matter (Article 59 of the Convention). Unless the treaty stipulates otherwise, its expiration releases the parties of their duties of any further fulfillment of their obligations thereunder (Article 70 of the Convention).

Whether the earlier or the later treaty was applicable to extradition requests submitted before the later treaty entered into force could neither be determined on the basis of the text of the two treaties, nor on the basis of the general law of treaties. The court henceforth resorted to national law and went on to decide that also in these cases the new treaty would apply:

> 21 As far as the domestic legal norms regulating procedural matters are concerned, it is generally accepted that the proceedings are being conducted in accordance with the law in force. In case of doubt, the rule dubio lex nova should be applied.

IX. Amendment and Modification

The process of agreeing on amendments and bringing them into force can be as difficult as negotiating and concluding the original treaty. On the other hand, because of their long life, many multilateral treaties are likely to need amendment. In view of these difficulties, states parties often resort to informal means in lieu of formal amendment procedures—subsequent agreements and practice being one of them. This is reflected in domestic case law.

Discrimination against Women [CEDAW], which also concerned the extraterritorial application of provisions in the CEDAW. However, in that case the Committee decided to leave out the question of admissibility *ratione loci* and *ratione materiae* entirely and only referred to its deliberations on the 'foreseeability principle' in another decision (*MNN v Denmark, Communication No 33/2011*). See also *YC v Denmark*, Admissibility, UN Doc CEDAW/C/59/D/59/2013, IHRL 3848 (CEDAW 2014), 24 October 2014, Committee on the Elimination of Discrimination against Women [CEDAW], where the question of extraterritoriality arose as well, but the Committee decided not to address this specific issue, since the communication was already inadmissible on other grounds.

99 *Question of law regarding the interpretation of Article 17(2) of Treaty on Extradition between the Republic of Poland and Australia, Re, Reference to Supreme Court on Preliminary Question*, I KZP 47/02, ILDC 19 February 2003, 273 (PL 2003).

The judgment of the German Constitutional Court *Parliamentary group of the Party of Democratic Socialism in the German Federal Parliament v Federal Government*[100] concerned the 1999 NATO New Strategic Concept, that is NATO's 'roadmap' for the following decade adopted at the NATO Summit meeting in Lisbon and which extended the organization's scope of (self-defence) operation to territories of non-member states. The court first examined the Concept's legal status and found that it did not amount to a formal amendment to the original NATO Treaty.

New Strategic Concept Case, Parliamentary group of the Party of Democratic Socialism in the German Federal Parliament v Federal Government (represented by the Federal Chancellor), Constitutional dispute between federal organs (Organstreitverfahren), 2 BvE 6/99, ILDC 134 (DE 2001), 22nd November 2001, Germany; Constitutional Court [BVerfG]

> 137 It cannot be concluded, based exclusively on the highly political character of the 1999 Strategic Concept, that the new Strategic Concept demonstrates the consent to amend the existing treaty. The new Strategic Concept of April 23 and 24, 1999, is a consensus paper that describes NATO's new tasks and instruments only in general terms; thus, the new tasks and instruments are characterised by a high degree of flexibility and are open to a wide variety of interpretations. [...]
>
> 138 In particular, the wording of the new 1999 Strategic Concept indicates that it is not a treaty. It is true that in particular, the central passages about the missions that do not fall under Article 5, and about the Security Council's mandate for such missions, contain legal concepts and legal terms. The text, however, mostly consists of descriptions and analyses of the present political situation in the Euro-Atlantic area and of the new threats that result from this situation, and of declarations of intention that are too general to create, from the new Strategic Concept as such, obligations that would arise from a treaty.

The court affirmed that a treaty could also be amended without an explicit manifestation of intent, but with sufficiently clear objective circumstances pointing to the existence of a consenting will to amend the treaty:

> 139 2. The content of the new 1999 Strategic Concept also cannot be regarded as an amendment of the Treaty that can be inferred from acts of the parties. A treaty can be amended without an explicit manifestation of an intent to amend the treaty if objective circumstances that are sufficiently clear point to the existence of a consenting will to amend the treaty (cf. ICJ, Maritime Delimitation and Territorial Questions, loc. cit., [paras. 25 et seq.]). If commitments that are made in the 1999 Strategic Concept are, in an insurmountable and clearly discernible manner, inconsistent with the area of operation that is defined in the Treaty, or if they contain an expansion of the Treaty beyond the scope that has been binding to this point, this indicates the parties' consent to amend the Treaty. If there are no indications of a corresponding subjective consent of the parties to be bound by the document and of a consent to amend the Treaty, the inconsistency with the existing Treaty must, however, be sufficiently clear in the new 1999 Strategic Concept in order to trigger the procedure pursuant to Article 59.2(1) of the Basic Law. This is not the case here. In particular, the issue that is at the centre of the Organstreit [Constitutional Dispute between federal organs] proceedings, i.e., the expansion of the Alliance's security policy approach to crisis response operations, constitutes only a further development of the NATO

100 *Parliamentary group of the Party of Democratic Socialism in the German Federal Parliament v Federal Government*, Constitutional dispute between federal organs (Organstreitverfahren), BverfG, 2 BvE 6/99; ILDC 134 (DE 2001), 22 November 2001.

> Treaty, which cannot be interpreted, at any rate with the degree of certainty required for assuming the existence of a consent to amend the Treaty that can be inferred from acts of the parties, as an inconsistency with, or as an expansion of, the content of the existing Treaty.

In the absence of a formal amendment, the German Constitutional Court referred to other forms of legally relevant acts, especially in the area of treaty interpretation:

> 148 [. . .] If the new 1999 Strategic Concept is interpreted accordingly, such commitments under international law [resulting from the consent to the new 1999 Strategic Concept for the Federal Republic of Germany below the level of the conclusion of the Treaty] can take the shape of: (1) a binding concretisation of the content of the Treaty by the competent NATO organs; or (2) an authentic interpretation of the NATO Treaty by the parties to the Treaty; but also (3) a joint enhancement, outside the Treaty, of a practice under international law (Article 31.3, letters [a] and [b] of the Vienna Convention on the Law of Treaties, cf. ICJ, Case concerning Kasikili/Sedudu Island [Botswana/Namibia], Judgement, paras. 49 et seq.; Heathrow Airport User Charges Arbitration, in: American Journal of International Law 88 [1994], pp. 738 and 742). [. . .]

The German Constitutional Court's decision thus reflected the difficult dividing line(s) between interpretation, informal modification and formal amendment. Altogether, the court chose a traditional approach to treaty amendment and law-making, in line with the VCLT's and the ICJ's position, finding that the NATO New Strategic Concept was to be regarded neither as an international treaty nor as an amendment of the NATO Treaty.[101]

Occasionally the notion of amendment appears to be mixed with that of successive treaties on the same subject matter. This is shown in *Attorney-General v Zaoui and Inspector-General of Intelligence and Security*.[102] In the case at issue, a refugee seeking judicial recourse against expulsion had argued *inter alia* that by virtue of Article 30 of the VCLT relating to the application of successive treaties, Article 33(2) of the 1951 Convention relating to the Status of Refugees (1951 Convention) had been 'amended' by the more absolute prohibitions of refoulement contained in Article 3(1) of the CAT and Articles 6(1) and 7 of the ICCPR. The New Zealand Supreme Court rejected the applicant's position and clarified that Article 30 of the VCLT dealt with successive treaties relating to the same subject matter rather than with treaty amendments.[103]

Attorney-General v Zaoui and Inspector-General of Intelligence and Security and Human Rights Commission (intervening), Appeal to Supreme Court, [2005] NZSC 38, (2006) 1 NZLR 289, (2005) 7 HRNZ 860, ILDC 81 (NZ 2005), 21st June 2005, New Zealand; Supreme Court

> [50] Those provisions [Art 30(3, 4.a) VCLT] are designed for treaties that create bilateral rights and obligations. They do not easily apply to the present situation where the obligations of article 33 are in substance unilateral as well as being owed erga omnes (to all the other parties collectively). More significantly in the present context, the provisions do not, contrary to the submissions, regulate the amendment of treaties. That is a matter dealt with in articles 39–41 which are not applicable in the present case. Rather, as the heading to article 30 shows, its provisions concern the

101 For criticism of this 'anachronistic' point of view see, eg, H Sauer, 'Die NATO und das Verfassungsrecht—neues Konzept, alte Fragen' 62 *Zeitschrift für ausländisches öffentliches Recht und Völkerrecht* (2002) 317, 336; see generally B Schlütter, Analysis, *Parliamentary group of the Party of Democratic Socialism in the German Federal Parliament v Federal Government*, ILDC 134 (DE 2001) A3–A5.

102 *Attorney-General v Zaoui and Inspector-General of Intelligence and Security*, Appeal to Supreme Court, (2005) NZSC 38; ILDC 81 (NZ 2005), 21 June 2005.

103 It may be criticized, however, in that the court did not refer to the principle of maximum protection, which is generally applicable in the case of human rights treaties. See, eg, ICCPR, Article 5.

> application of successive treaties relating to the same subject matter. That is to say, article 33.2 of the 1951 Convention has not itself been amended by the later ICCPR and Torture Convention. Rather, they have to be applied in a successive way. [...]

X. Termination and Suspension of Treaties

Invalidity, termination, and suspension are much discussed in literature,[104] but seem to have less practical relevance. Case law, both international and domestic, is limited. Out of the 110 cases, a mere four dealt with termination and suspension, and none with invalidity.

The British case *R (Kibris Türk Hava Yollari) v Secretary of State for Transport (and the Republic of Cyprus as an interested party)*[105] discussed in much detail the VCLT's termination, withdrawal, and suspension provisions (Articles 57–62 of the VCLT) and their procedural complements laid down in Articles 65–68 of the VCLT. Such in order to decide on the extension of a Turkish Airline's operating permit between the United Kingdom and Northern Cyprus. Since the granting of permits as requested would have constituted a breach of the UK's obligations vis-à-vis the Republic of Cyprus (RoC) under the 1944 Chicago Convention on International Aviation,[106] the British court examined, *inter alia*, whether the Convention had been suspended as between the UK and the RoC with respect to Northern Cyprus because of the RoC's loss of control over Northern Cypriotic territory. The judges analysed especially whether there was a case of supervening impossibility of performance (Article 61 of the VCLT), which in the end they denied.

R (Kibris Türk Hava Yollari and CTA Holidays Limited) v Secretary of State for Transport (and the Republic of Cyprus as an interested party), Court of Appeal (Civil Division) on Appeal from the Queen's Bench Division administrative Court, [2010] EWCA Civ 1093, 12 October 2010 (not in ILDC)

> 37. That provision [Article 61 VCLT] is very narrow in scope, relating to termination or suspension in consequence of the permanent or temporary disappearance or destruction of an object indispensable for its execution. That is not this case. In any event, (a) this is not a case of impossibility of performance of the treaty, and (b) no party has invoked impossibility of performance as a ground for suspending the operation of the treaty.
>
> 38. As to (a), the RoC's rights under the Chicago Convention are capable of being exercised in respect of northern Cyprus even without effective control over the territory itself. The rights may not be fully effective and enforceable, but they can be exercised effectively, as has been done in practice, by withholding permission for, or imposing limitations on, flights over the territory and by the non-designation of airports in the territory. The RoC is entitled to rely on other states to honour their obligations under international law to respect its decisions on such matters; and the effectiveness of the exercise of its rights is evidenced most

104 See, eg, F Capotorti, 'L'extinction et la suspension des traités' (1971-III) 134 *Recueil des Cours* 427; G Haraszti, 'Treaties and the Fundamental Change of Circumstances' (1975-III) 146 *Recueil des Cours* 1; N Kontou, *Termination and Revision of Treaties in the Light of New Customary International Law* (Clarendon Press 1994); C Feist, *Kündigung, Suspendierung und* Rücktritt *von völkerrechtlichen Verträgen* (Duncker & Humblot 2001); M M Gomaa, *Suspension or Termination of Treaties on Grounds of Breach* (Martinus Nijhoff 1996); D W Greig, *Invalidity and the Law of Treaties* (BIICL 2006); C Binder, *Die Grenzen der Vertragstreue im Völkerrecht am Beispiel nachträglicher Umstandsänderung* (Springer 2013).

105 *R (Kibris Türk Hava Yollari and CTA Holidays Limited) v Secretary of State for Transport (and the Republic of Cyprus as an interested party)*, Court of Appeal (Civil Division) on Appeal from the Queen's Bench Division administrative Court, [2010] EWCA Civ 1093, 12 October 2010.

106 ibid, para 45. The RoC had refused to grant permission for scheduled flights operated by the claimant.

> obviously by the fact that all states other than Turkey have in practice respected those decisions.
>
> 39. As to (b), suspension pursuant to Article 61(1) does not occur automatically but has to be invoked. Articles 65-68 lay down formal procedures to be followed and make provision for judicial settlement, arbitration and conciliation. Far from having exercised the right to invoke suspension of the convention, however, the RoC continues to rely on the treaty as having full force and effect; and there is no evidence that any other contracting state has invoked suspension of the treaty in relation to northern Cyprus.

The judges, moreover, found that the VCLT set out an exhaustive list of grounds and consequences regarding suspension, termination, and withdrawal.

> 41. [...] The general principle asserted by the appellants is said to result in the automatic suspension of sovereign rights, including treaty rights, without any invocation of suspension as required under the provisions of the Vienna Convention. [...]
>
> 42 [...] the preamble to the Vienna Convention takes the matter no further forward: the rules of customary international law continue to govern questions not regulated by the Convention, but the circumstances in which treaty rights may lawfully be suspended are regulated by the Convention, as Article 42(2) (quoted above) makes clear. [...]

This considered, the judges felt it necessary to look for answers outside the VCLT's scope as indicated in Article 73 of the VCLT, notably in the areas of state responsibility (especially *force majeure*) and the outbreak of hostilities between the treaty parties.[107] Having found none of them applicable, they also rejected that the 'RoC's entitlement to exercise its rights under the Chicago Convention had been suspended in relation to northern Cyprus even though the rights themselves had not been suspended'.[108]

> 68. [...] The RoC remains the relevant state party to the convention, and the Government of the RoC continues to represent the RoC under the convention and is recognised by the ICAO as the only legitimate government of the state. The authorities of the TRNC have no status under the convention. Indeed, they purport to represent not the RoC but the TRNC, which is not recognised as a state and is on no view a party to the convention. [...] The authorities of the TRNC may purport to exercise, in relation to northern Cyprus, the rights of the RoC under the convention but neither under the convention itself nor by virtue of any principle of customary international law can they be said to have displaced the Government of the RoC as the body entitled to exercise the convention rights of the RoC. [...] the argument as to suspension of entitlement to exercise the convention rights, as distinct from suspension of the convention rights themselves, gets the appellants nowhere.

The judges concluded, accordingly, that 'the grant of the permits sought by the appellants would constitute a breach of the United Kingdom's obligation to respect the rights of the RoC under the Chicago Convention and would in consequence be unlawful as a matter of domestic law'.[109]

In *X and Y v Government and Administrative Tribunal of the Canton of Zurich*[110] the Federal Supreme Court of Switzerland discussed, among others, the legal effects of the termination of the 1872 Treaty on Establishment and Commerce between Russia and Switzerland (1872 Treaty) after the October revolution in 1917 by the then Russian government, which had not

107 ibid, paras 43–67 and 69.

108 ibid, para 68.

109 ibid, para 69.

110 *X and Y v Government and Administrative Tribunal of the Canton of Zurich*, Appeal judgment, Case No ATF 132 II 65; ILDC 340 (CH 2005), 22 November 2005—no English translation available.

been recognized *de jure* but only *de facto* by Switzerland. In the course of its considerations, the Swiss court referred to the division of competences between the government and courts concerning treaty termination. Only political organs would be in the position to terminate international treaties whereas it was for courts to decide upon the legal question of whether a treaty was still in force in a particular case.[111] In order to find that the 1872 Treaty had been—at least—suspended, the court referred to subsequent practice, affirming that despite the normalization of the relationship between Switzerland and the Soviet Union after 1946, the treaty had never been invoked by either state party.[112]

In *RD v Belgium*[113] the Belgian Court of Cassation analysed whether the EU Council Framework Decision of 2002 on the European arrest warrant had terminated the 1962 Treaty on Extradition and Mutual Assistance in Criminal Matters between Belgium, Luxembourg, and the Netherlands (1962 Treaty). The court found that the unanimous approval of the Framework Decision constituted a 'consultation' in the sense of Article 54(b) of the VCLT and thus amounted to treaty termination by consent.

RD v Belgium, Final Appeal/Cassation, Case No P.04.1211.N, JT 2005, 322, ILDC 6 (BE 2004), 24th August 2004, Belgium; Court of Cassation

> 48) Whereas the unanimous approval by the European Union Member States of the Council Framework Decision on 13 June 2002 constitutes a consultation as defined in Article 54 (b) of the Vienna Convention of 23 May 1969; [. . .]
>
> 50) Whereas in implementing the Framework Decision of the Council of 13 June 2002 into their national law, Belgium and Luxembourg, Member States of the European Union, withdrew, in accordance with Article 54 (b) of the Vienna Convention of 23 May 1969, from the Treaty of 27 June 1962 on Extradition and Mutual Assistance in Criminal Matters concluded between them, insofar as this treaty concerns extradition and subject to the provision of Article 10.4 of Luxembourg Law; [. . .]

However, the judgment may be criticized. It seems indeed problematic to imply termination by consent (Article 54(b) of the VCLT) as the Belgian court did. The EU Council Framework Decision and the 1962 Extradition Treaty do not necessarily have the same scope[114] and one may wonder whether it truly was the intention of the parties to remove the Extradition Treaty from the international legal order.[115]

The most-tried ground for unilateral termination and suspension of treaties is the 'fundamental change of circumstances' or so-called *rebus sic stantibus* clause. The Supreme Court of Macao decision *A v B and Others*[116] addressed treaty termination in an alleged case of fundamental change of circumstances. At stake was the applicability of the 1930 Convention

111 ibid: '4.2.3 The question is therefore, whether the termination from the year 1917 has led to the extinction of the Settlement Treaty. While the political authorities are solely competent to terminate a treaty (*BGE 49 I 188* E. 3 S. 194 f.), it is the courts which decide independently on the legal question, whether a treaty is still valid (*BGE 81 II 319* E. 4 S. 330; 78 I 124 E. 3 S. 130). [. . .]'.

112 ibid, para 4.2.5.

113 *RD v Belgium*, Final appeal/Cassation, No P041211N; ILDC 6 (BE 2004); (2005) *Journal des Tribunaux* 322, 24 August 2004.

114 The 1962 Extradition Treaty contained—contrary to the EU Council Framework Decision—also provisions on 'small judicial assistance' between the states parties. What is more, the European arrest warrant only applied to relatively serious crimes, while the Extradition Treaty was also applicable to minor offences. For details see C Ryngaert, Analysis, *RD v Belgium*, ILDC 6 (BE 2004) A5–A7.

115 It might have been more appropriate for the court to refer to Article 30 of the VCLT (n 2) on successive treaties relating to the same subject matter which affirms in paragraph 3 '[w]hen all the parties to the earlier treaty are parties also to the later treaty but the earlier treaty is not terminated or suspended in operation under Article 59 [of the VCLT], the earlier treaty applies only to the extent that its provisions are compatible with those of the latter treaty'. See also C Ryngaert, Analysis, *RD v Belgium*, ILDC 6 (BE 2004) A8.

116 *A v B and ors*, Appeal judgment, Case No TUI-S-2/2004; ILDC 626 (MO 2004), 2 June 2004—no English translation available.

Providing a Uniform Law for Bills of Exchange and Promissory Notes, which established a lower interest rate than Macanese laws.[117] The applicant company, asking for a higher interest rate in accordance with Macanese domestic provisions, argued *inter alia* that the Asian economic crisis constituted a fundamental change of circumstances, which had terminated or suspended the 1930 Convention. Having confirmed the superior hierarchical position of international treaty law over the laws of Macao,[118] the Macanese Supreme Court affirmed the solid normative status of the *rebus sic stantibus* rule,[119] but did not find it to be applicable in the case at hand. The court based this, first of all, on a factual argument, as there was no proof that the required change of circumstances had actually taken place. Most importantly, however, the court stated that it would have been for the treaty parties—Portugal or, after 19 December 1999, the Central People's Republic of China—to invoke changed circumstances. Since neither of the parties had done so, the court found that the Macanese Decree Law regarding commercial interest rates violated the 1930 Convention and was thus inapplicable.[120]

117 As regards the new legal order established through the creation of the Macau Special Administrative Region: International treaties where China was not a party but which had been implemented by Macao, as the 1930 Convention, were permitted to remain applicable in Macao in accordance with Article 138 of the Basic Law which entered into force on 20 December 1999. See A Zimmermann, *Staatennachfolge in internationale Verträge* (Springer 2000) 852. The Central People's Republic of China notified the UN Secretary General in 1999 thus of the 1930 Convention's continued applicability. See *A v B and ors*, ILDC 626 (MO 2004) F3–F4.

118 *A v B and ors* (n 116) para 58.

119 ibid, para 63.

120 ibid, paras 77–78.

7

Customary International Law

JORIAN HAMSTER

I. Introduction

Finding and applying rules of customary international law places the domestic judge in an intriguingly complex position. On the one hand, he is the guardian of the law in the national legal order.[1] On the other hand, he is just as much an agent of the international legal order, entrusted with the task to effectuate rules of international law. Scelle's theory of ***dédoublement fonctionnel*** describes the 'role-splitting' of the domestic judge as agent of both the domestic and international legal order.[2] In this context, the concept of an 'agent' often presupposes a one-way direction: rules of international law exist, and it is up to the agents of the international legal order to make sure they are applied.[3] And more than any other agent of the international legal order operating on the domestic level he is bound by the obligation to state what the law *is*, not what it should be.[4] However, international scholars are gradually paying more attention to a different understanding of the role of domestic courts as agents of international law. Under this perspective, domestic courts are not just agents in the *application* of international law, but also agents in the *development* of international law.[5] Especially in the context of customary international law it is an oversimplification to state that domestic courts just apply international law, as this selection of cases from the ILDC database demonstrates. Domestic courts sometimes find rules of customary nature, and sometimes play a vital role in the emergence of new rules. In order to discern this pattern, it is necessary to abandon a strictly formalistic perspective. Domestic court judgments are indeed just facts for the ICJ, and their role in the sources of international law is limited to being constitutive of state practice (and *opinio juris*).[6] Thus, the development of custom by a single domestic court is impossible. On the other hand, if we go beyond this formalistic, source-based approach, an analysis of national court decisions often demonstrates

---

1 E Benvenisti and G W Downs, 'National Courts, Domestic Democracy and the Evolution of International Law'(2009) 20 *EJIL* 60, 61.

2 G Scelle, 'Règles Générales du Droit de la Paix' (1933) 46 *Recueil des Cours* 327, 356; A Cassese, 'Remarks on Scelle's Theory of 'Role Splitting' (*dédoublement fonctionnel*) in International Law' (1990) 1 *EJIL* 210, 212.

3 In Scelle's own words: '[. . .] *pour assurer l'efficacité* des normes d'un autre ordre juridique privé des organes nécessaires a cette réalisation' (emphasis added). G Scelle, 'Règles Générales du Droit de la Paix' (1933) 46 *Recueil des Cours* 331; A-M Slaughter and W Burke-White, 'The Future of International Law Is Domestic (or, The European Way of Law)' (2006) 47 *Harvard International Law Journal* 327, 350.

4 Which is why the ILA considers statements by the executive and legislative branches of government more relevant state practice: International Law Association (ILA), Committee on Formation of Customary (General) International Law, Statement of Principles Applicable to the Formation of General Customary International Law, Final Report (2000) Principle 9, 18.

5 See generally the issue of the *Leiden Journal of International Law* dedicated to the symposium on domestic courts as agents in the development of international law: (2013) 26(3) *Leiden Journal of International Law* 531; and further A Tzanakopoulos and C J Tams, 'Introduction: Domestic Courts as Agents of Development in International Law' (2013) 26 *Leiden Journal of International Law* 531, 534.

6 ILA, Committee on Formation of Customary (General) International Law, Statement of principles Applicable to the Formation of General Customary International Law, Final Report (2000) Principle 9; *Certain German Interests in Polish Upper Silesia* (*Germany v Poland*) (Merits) PCIJ Rep Series A No 7, 19: 'From the standpoint of International Law and of the Court which is its organ, municipal laws are merely facts which express the will and constitute the activities of States, in the same manner as do legal decisions or administrative measures'.

a different picture. National court decisions pronouncing upon the existence of a customary rule of international law can create what some authors have called *ripple effects*.[7] Some domestic courts are indeed aware of the effect their findings might have for the development of a rule of custom.[8] As Tzanakopoulos and Tams noted: 'first, within the regime of sources of international law, decisions by domestic courts have a very limited formal impact; and, second, this does not preclude them from exercising an important role in practice'.[9] It follows that domestic courts dealing with international legal rules of customary nature do not just have a double role in respect of their function as agent of the international and/or domestic legal order. Also within international law, they function both as agents of the application of law and as agents of the development of law.[10]

A second introductory remark is necessary at this point. It would be a simple task for the international lawyer to criticize every single case involving customary international law.[11] They often display methodological deficits, or contain conclusions that are not shared by the majority of scholars. As will be discussed in section III, such deficits relate to the inherent difficulties of the theory of custom and are not limited to domestic court decisions on custom.[12] Instead, there is a wealth of interesting material in these judgments for the international legal scholar. First, research on customary international law could seriously benefit from analysing how domestic courts find and apply custom, as this would enormously increase the existing 'pool' of cases dealing with the formation and existence of custom. Secondly, it may reveal a lot of about the interplay between the national and international legal order, and the position of courts as actors in the international legal order.[13] Many of the court judgments here discussed cite other court judgments, either as a confirmation of their finding or as evidence of a rule of custom.[14] These 'conversations' between courts, also between national and international courts, reveal a certain awareness by domestic courts about their position as actors in and enforcers of the international legal order.[15]

Another interesting characteristic of the judgments here discussed is their daring and progressive reasoning, especially when compared to international courts' approach to custom.[16] And whereas Stirling-Zanda could still write in 2004 that courts in continental Europe showed caution and restraint with respect to the determination of customary international law, cases from the last decade

7 R van Alebeek, 'Domestic Courts as Agent of Development of International Immunity Rules' (2013) 26 *Leiden Journal of International Law* 559, 577; G M Badr, *State Immunity: An Analytical and Prognostic View* (Martinus Nijhoff Publishers 1984) 135.

8 See, eg, the two cases discussed below: Italy, *Lozano v Italy*, Court of Cassation, 24 July 2008, ILDC 1085 (IT 2008); Italy, *Germany v Mantelli and ors*, Court of Cassation, 29 May 2008, ILDC 1037 (IT 2008).

9 Tzanakopoulos and Tams (n 5).

10 See R van Alebeek, 'Domestic Courts as Agent of Development of International Immunity Rules' (2013) 26 *Leiden Journal of International Law* 559, 574; A Roberts, 'Comparative International Law? The Role of National Courts in Creating and Enforcing International Law' (2011) 60 *International & Comparative Law Quarterly* 57, 68.

11 See for articles with this critical tone: M Mendelson, 'The Effect of Customary International Law on Domestic Law: an Overview' (2004) 4 *Non-State Actors and International Law* 75, 79, 82; J Wouters, 'Customary International Law before Domestic Courts: Some Reflections from a Continental European Perspective' (2004) 4 *Non-State Actors and International Law* 25, 35, 36.

12 See section III below.

13 Roberts (n 10) 58; Y Shany, 'National Courts as International Actors: Jurisdictional Implications' (2009) 15 *Federalismi* 1; A Tzanakopoulos, 'Domestic Courts in International Law: The International Judicial Function of National Courts' (2011) 34 *Loyola of Los Angeles International and Comparative Law Review* 133, 134.

14 For example: Israel, *Public Committee against Torture v Israel*, High Court of Justice, 14 December 2006, ILDC 597 IL (2006); *Canada Ltée (Spraytech, Société d'arrosage) and Services des espaces verts Ltée/Chemlawn v Hudson (Town)*, Judgment of the Supreme Court, (2001) 2 SCR 241; ILDC 185 (CA 2001), 28 June 2001.

15 See on the concept of the transnational judicial dialogue/conversations: A-M Slaughter, 'A Global Community of Courts' (2003) 44 *Harvard International Law Journal* 191; M A Waters, 'Mediating Norms and Identity: The Role of Transnational Judicial Dialogue in Creating and Enforcing International Law' (2005) 93 *Georgetown Law Journal* 487; K G Young, 'The World, through the Judge's Eye' (2009) *Australian Year Book of International Law* 27.

16 See *C and ors v Director of Immigration*, 18 February 2008, ILDC 1119 (HK 2008).

have demonstrated that such a statement cannot be easily upheld nowadays.[17] This development begs questions as to the hierarchy of domestic and international courts: are international courts and tribunals the more dogmatic and conservative ones—as higher courts domestically often are—since they perceive themselves as legitimate guardians of international legal orthodoxy?[18] Moreover, it begs for a reassessment of the perception that the common law—civil law divide can explain for much of the differences in reasoning on customary international law in domestic courts.[19]

This chapter contains a selection of interesting cases from the ILDC database, chosen from jurisdictions all over the world.[20] They are an example of the way domestic courts apply custom and provide an example of the problems domestic courts encounter. The first paragraph focuses on the way courts find and apply custom, and highlights methodological questions. The second paragraph pays attention to the above-mentioned position of domestic courts as developers and even creators of international custom and the progressive reasoning they use. It is important to understand that all these cases at least demonstrate a willingness of domestic courts to engage in difficult questions of international law. Rather than simply criticizing these courts, it is vital to realize the important role that these courts can play in the development of international law.

II. Domestic Courts' Methodology in Determining Customary International Law

An analysis of domestic courts' methodology in determining customary international law reveals many of the conceptual and practical deficits in the theory of international custom. First, it is noteworthy that in these domestic judgments the requirements of *opinio juris* and state practice are paid lip service to at its best—often they are not even mentioned. The ILDC database contains very few examples of a domestic court classifying arguments and evidence of custom as either one of these categories.[21] Another difficulty lies in the *Continental Shelf*-requirement that state practice should be extensive and virtually uniform.[22] There are huge differences in what domestic courts consider sufficient state practice (or *opinio juris*, for that matter) for a norm to exist.[23] As it is evidently a Sisyphean task, for any court, to establish the existence of sufficient state practice by seriously analysing state practice of all states, this requirement is often replaced by an analysis of international legal scholarship on the matter, or a reference to international judgments as evidence of custom,

---

17 S Stirling-Zanda, 'The determination of customary international law in European courts (France, Germany, Italy, The Netherlands, Spain, Switzerland)' (2004) 4 *Non-State Actors and International Law* 3, 7. For an Italian example see *Ferrini v Germany*, Appeal decision, Cass No 5044/04, ILDC 19 (IT 2004), 11 March 2004, Supreme Court of Cassation. Greece provides another example: Greece, Supreme Civil and Criminal Court (Areios Pagos), *Germany v Prefecture of Voiotia*, representing 118 persons from Distomo village, 4 May 2000, ILDC 287 (GR 2000).

18 A von Bogdandy and I Venzke, 'On the Functions of International Courts: An Appraisal in Light of their Burgeoning Public Authority' (2013) 26 *Leiden Journal of International Law* 49, 57, 64; P A Nollkaemper, 'Conversations among Courts: International and Domestic Adjudicators' in C Romano, K Alter, and Y Shany, *The Oxford Handbook of International Adjudication* (OUP 2013) 523, 533.

19 Mendelson (n 11) 75.

20 Also with a view to countering criticism that scholarship on customary international law is often focused too much on Western-European and North-American Jurisdictions, see A T Guzman, 'Saving Customary International Law' (2005–2006) 27 *Michigan Journal of International Law*, 115 150–51; Mendelson (n 11); D P Fidler, 'Challenging the Classical Concept of Custom: Perspectives on the Future of Customary International Law' (1996) 39 *German Yearbook of International Law* 198, 203–04.

21 A notable exception is *State v Petane*, Supreme Court Decision, 1988 3 SA 51 (C); ILDC 1348 (ZA 1987) in which case the South African Supreme Court during the apartheid era used the distinction between *usus* and *opinio juris* to argue that general assembly resolutions and state declarations should only be classified as *opinio juris*, thus rendering several supposedly customary international human rights obligations void of the necessary state practice.

22 *North Sea Continental Shelf (Federal Republic of Germany/Netherlands, proceedings joined with Federal Republic of Germany/Denmark)* [1969] ICJ Rep 3, para 75.

23 As will be discussed in section III of this chapter.

as several cases in this chapter demonstrate.[24] This approach, however understandable, has its obvious weaknesses from an academic point of view.[25] Moreover, the open nature of many norms of customary international law, which are by their very nature less precise than other norms of international law, provide national courts with ample opportunity to arrive at different conclusions than international courts or scholars.

However, it would be all too easy to criticize domestic courts for these deficiencies. As mentioned, these weaknesses are part and parcel to the concept of customary international law. Academic discussions still linger on as to what should be qualified as *opinio juris* or state practice.[26] The International Court of Justice is not a saint in abiding by its own *continental shelf* requirements, and the ethical and moral content of some of these norms seem to play an important role in the ICJ's findings on whether related state practice qualifies as extensive or not.[27] Other international tribunals also demonstrate rather peculiar approaches when applying custom.[28] Although it is obviously true that domestic courts are less experienced in finding custom than international courts, they can hardly be blamed for not being able to analyse all state practice and *opinio juris* as to the existence of a norm of custom. In this light it is understandable that judges tend to conduct their research based on, so to say, 'ready-made' evidence such as academic opinions, international court judgments and conventions. This approach will be discussed further in the analyses to the cases.

1. Constitutive elements of customary international law

Kiobel and ors (on behalf of Kiobel and Tusima) v Royal Dutch Petroleum Co and ors, Appeal judgment, Docket No 06-4800-cv, Docket No 06-4876-cv, 623 F3d 111 (2d Cir. 2010), ILDC 1552 (US 2010), 17th September 2010, United States; Court of Appeals (2nd Circuit) [2d Cir]

Nigerian national Kiobel and others sued Shell under the Alien Tort Statute (ATS), bringing claims against Shell for aiding and abetting crimes against humanity by the Nigerian government. The ATS was at the time considered to give US courts jurisdiction over tort claims brought by foreign nationals for violations of the law of nations, including customary international law, whether they had occurred in the United States or elsewhere.[29] Therefore, the Court of Appeals had to analyse whether tort actions could be brought against corporations under customary international law.

> 9 [. . .] As Judge Friendly carefully explained, customary international law includes only "those standards, rules or customs (a) affecting the relationship between states

24 See *C and ors v Director of Immigration*, 18 February 2008, ILDC 1119 (HK 2008); *Kiobel and ors v Royal Dutch Petroleum and ors*, 17 September 2010, ILDC 1552 (US 2010).

25 Guzman (n 20) 125–27; D P Fidler, 'Challenging the Classical Concept of Custom: Perspectives on the Future of Customary International Law' (1996) 39 *German Yearbook of International Law* 198, 202.

26 See A D'Amato, *The Concept of Custom in International Law* (Cornell University Press 1971) 49; M Akehurst, 'Custom as a Source of International Law' (1975) 47 *British Yearbook of International Law* 1; J P Kelly, 'The Twilight of Customary International Law' (2000) 40 *Virginia Journal of International Law* 449, 450.

27 *Arrest Warrant of 11 April 2000 (Democratic Republic of the Congo v Belgium)* [2002] ICJ Rep 3, Dissenting opinion of Judge ad hoc Van den Wyngaert 170, 55; T Treves, 'Customary International Law' Max Planck Encyclopedia of International Law, para 20; A Roberts, 'Traditional and Modern Approaches to Customary International Law: A Reconciliation' (2001) 95 AJIL 757, 759, 767.

28 See the criticism on the *Taylor* judgment by the Appeal Chamber of the Special Court for Sierra Leone by M Milanović, 'SCSL Appeals Chamber Affirms Charles Taylor's Conviction' 26 September 2013, *EJILTalk!* http://www.ejiltalk.org/scsl-appeals-chamber-affirms-charles-taylors-conviction/ (last accessed 30 October 2017) and especially J Heller, 'The SCSL's Incoherent—and Selective—Analysis of Custom' 27 September 2013 *Opinio Juris* http://opiniojuris.org/2013/09/27/scsls-incoherent-selective-analysis-custom/?utm_source=feedly (last accessed 30 October 2017).

29 In the subsequent Supreme Court proceedings, the Supreme Court found that the ATS does not apply extraterritorially: *US Supreme Court, Kiobel and ors v Royal Dutch Petroleum Co*, 17 April 2013, ILDC 2082 (US 2013).

or between an individual and a foreign state, and (b) used by those states for their common good and/or in dealing *inter se*."

10 Our recognition of a norm of liability as a matter of *domestic law*, therefore, cannot create a norm of customary international law. In other words, the fact that corporations are liable as juridical persons under domestic law does not mean that they are liable under international (and therefore, under the ATS). Moreover, the fact that a legal norm is found in most or even all "civilized nations" does not make that norm a part of customary international law. […]

16 […] Looking to international law, we find a jurisprudence, first set forth in Nuremberg and repeated by every international tribunal of which we are aware, that offenses against the law of nations (*i.e.*, customary international law) for violations of human rights can be charged against States and against individual men and women but not against juridical persons such as corporations. As a result, although international law has sometimes extended the scope of liability for a violation of a given norm to individuals, it has *never* extended the scope of liability to a corporation. […]

44 To attain the status of a rule of customary international law, a norm must be "specific, universal, and obligatory." *Sosa*, 542 U.S. at 732 (quoting with approval the statement of a lower court) (internal quotation marks omitted); *see also Flores*, 414 F.3d at 248 ("[C]ustomary international law is composed only of those rules that States universally abide by, or accede to, out of a sense of legal obligation and mutual concern."); Restatement (Third) § 102(2) ("Customary international law results from a general and consistent practice of states followed by them from a sense of legal obligation."). Defining such norms "is no simple task," as "[c]ustomary international law is discerned from myriad decisions made in numerous and varied international and domestic arenas." *Flores*, 414 F.3d at 247. The sources consulted are therefore of the utmost importance. As the Supreme Court re-emphasized in *Sosa*, we look to "those sources we have long, albeit cautiously, recognized":

> "[W]here there is no treaty, and no controlling executive or legislative act or judicial decision, resort must be had to the *customs and usages of civilized nations*; and, as evidence of these, to the works of jurists and commentators, who by years of labor, research and experience, have made themselves peculiarly well acquainted with the subjects of which they treat. Such works are resorted to by judicial tribunals, not for the speculations of their authors concerning what the law ought to be, but for trustworthy evidence of what the law really is." […]

46 A. International Tribunals

Insofar as international tribunals are established for the specific purpose of imposing liability on those who violate the law of nations, the history and conduct of those tribunals is instructive. We find it particularly significant, therefore, that no international tribunal of which we are aware has *ever* held a corporation liable for a violation of the law of nations. […]

47 […] The London Charter and the trials at Nuremberg that followed are collectively the single most important source of modern customary international law concerning liability for violations of fundamental human rights. […]

B. International Treaties

59 Treaties "are proper evidence of customary international law because, and insofar as, they create *legal obligations* akin to contractual obligations on the States parties to them." *Flores*, 414 F.3d at 256. Although all treaties ratified by more than one State provide *some* evidence of the custom and practice of nations, "a treaty will only constitute *sufficient proof* of a norm of *customary international law* if an overwhelming

majority of States have ratified the treaty, *and* those States uniformly and consistently act in accordance with its principles." *Id.* (second emphasis added). Moreover, as one distinguished scholar of international law has explained:

> "The ordinary treaty by which two or more states enter into engagements with one another for some *special* object can very rarely be used even as evidence to establish the existence of a rule of *general law*; it is more probable that the very reason of the treaty was to create an obligation which would not have existed by the general law, or to exclude an existing rule which would otherwise have applied."

Brierly, *ante*, at 57 (emphases added). That a provision appears in one treaty (or more), therefore, is not proof of a well-established norm of *customary* international law. [...]

61 Even if those specialized treaties had been ratified by an "overwhelming majority" of states, *id.* at 256—as some recent treaties providing for corporate liability have been, *see, e.g.*, Convention Against Transnational Organized Crime, art. 10(1), *adopted* Nov. 15, 2000, S. Treaty Doc. 108-16; Convention on Combating Bribery of Foreign Public Officials in International Business Transactions, art. 2, *done* Dec. 17, 1997, S. Treaty Doc. No. 105-43—the fact that those treaties impose obligations on corporations in the context of the treaties' particular subject matter tells us nothing about whether corporate liability for, say, violations of *human rights*, which are not a subject of those treaties, is universally recognized as a norm of *customary international law*. Significantly, to find that a treaty embodies or creates a rule of customary international law would mean that the rule applies beyond the limited subject matter of the treaty and *to nations that have not ratified it*. *See* 1 *Oppenheim's International Law* § 626, at 1261. To construe those treaties as so-called "law-making" treaties—that is, treaties that codify existing norms of customary international law or crystalize an emerging rule of customary international law—would be wholly inappropriate and without precedent. *See id.* § 583, at 1203–04 (discussing "law-making" treaties).

62 [...] Furthermore, even if, as a general rule, treaties on a specialized subject matter could be viewed as crystalizing a norm of customary international law (which they generally cannot), it would be inappropriate to do so in this case in light of the recent *express rejection* in major multilateral treaties of a norm of corporate liability in the context of human rights violations. *See, e.g.*, Rome Statute, *ante*, art. 25.

63 Finally, the few specialized treaties imposing liability on corporations have not had such influence that a general rule of corporate liability has become a norm of customary international law. The ICJ in 1969 described the process by which that might occur in the well-known *North Sea Continental Shelf Cases*. There, Denmark and the Netherlands had argued that the Federal Republic of Germany was bound by a particular provision of a treaty, which Germany had not ratified, because the rule embodied in the multilateral treaty had become a norm of customary international law. According to the ICJ, accepting that view would require treating [a particular provision of the 1958 Geneva Continental Shelf Convention] as a norm-creating provision which has constituted the foundation of, or has generated a rule which, while only conventional or contractual in its origin, has since passed into the general *corpus* of international law, and is now accepted as such by the *opinio juris*, so as to have become binding even for countries which have never, and do not, become parties to the Convention. There is no doubt that this process is a perfectly possible one and does from time to time occur: it constitutes indeed one of the recognized methods by which new rules of customary international law may be formed. At the same time this result

is not lightly to be regarded as having been attained. *North Sea Continental Shelf Cases*, [1969] 8 I.L.M. 340, 373–74. For a treaty provision to attain the status of a norm of customary international law, the ICJ explained, "[i]t would in the first place be necessary that the provision concerned should, at all events potentially, be of a *fundamentally norm-creating character* such as could be regarded as forming the basis of a general rule of law." *Id.* at 374 (emphasis added). Provisions on corporate liability in a handful of specialized treaties cannot be said to have a "fundamentally norm-creating character." Moreover, as the history of the Rome Statute demonstrates, "still unresolved controversies as to the exact meaning and scope of this notion" of corporate liability "raise further doubts as to the potentially norm-creating character of the rule." *Id.*

Accordingly, provisions imposing corporate liability in some recent specialized treaties have not established corporate liability as a norm of customary international law. […]

C. Works of Publicists

67 Although the works of publicists (*i.e.*, scholars or "jurists") can be a relevant source of customary international law, "[s]uch works are resorted to by judicial tribunals, not for the speculations of their authors concerning what the law ought to be, but for trustworthy evidence of what the law really is." *Sosa*, 542 U.S. at 734 (quoting *The Paquete Habana*, 175 U.S. at 700); *see also* ICJ Statute, *ante*, art. 38(1)(d), 59 Stat. at 1060 (directing the ICJ to apply "judicial decisions and the teachings of the most highly qualified publicists of the various nations, as *subsidiary means for the determination of rules of law*." (emphasis added)); *see* note 47, *post.*

68 In light of the evidence discussed above, it is not surprising that two renowned professors of international law, Professor James Crawford and Professor (now Judge) Christopher Greenwood, forcefully declared in litigation argued before this panel on the same day as this case, that customary international law does not recognize liability for corporations that violate its norms. According to Professor Crawford, "no national court [outside of the United States] and no international judicial tribunal has so far recognized corporate liability, as opposed to individual liability, *in a civil or criminal context* on the basis of a violation of the law of nations or customary international law." *See* Declaration of James Crawford ¶ 10, *Presbyterian Church of Sudan v. Talisman Energy, Inc.*, No. 07-0016 (2d Cir. Jan. 22, 2009) (emphasis added); *see also* Second Declaration of Christopher Greenwood ¶ 13, *Presbyterian Church of Sudan v. Talisman Energy, Inc.*, No. 01 Civ. 9882 (S.D.N.Y. July 10, 2002) ("[T]here is not, and never has been, any assertion of the criminal liability of corporations in international law."); Michael Koebele, *Corporate Responsibility Under the Alien Tort Statue* 196 (2009) ("[D]espite trends to the contrary, the view that international law primarily regulates States and in limited instances such as international criminal law, individuals, but not [transnational corporations], is still the prevailing one among international law scholars."). 47 Even those who favor using the ATS as a means of holding corporations accountable for human rights violations reluctantly acknowledge that "the universe of international criminal law does not reveal any prosecutions of corporations per se." Ratner, note 43, *ante*, at 477.48

69 Together, those authorities demonstrate that imposing liability on corporations for violations of customary international law has not attained a discernible, much less universal, acceptance among nations of the world in their relations *inter se*. Because corporate liability is not recognized as a "specific, universal, and obligatory" norm, *see Sosa*, 542 U.S. at 732 (internal quotation marks omitted), it is not a rule of customary international law that we may apply under the ATS.

Owing to the extraordinary international subject matter jurisdiction over violations of 'the law of nations' the ATS provides for, rediscovered in the notorious *Filartiga* judgment, US courts have had ample opportunities to analyse customary international law.[30] The Court of Appeals for the Second Circuit deciding this case has dealt with seven ATS cases since 2000, which certainly explains to a certain extent the quality of the judgment in the way it deals with customary international law compared to ATS judgments by other US courts and the judgments dealing with customary international law in the ILDC database in general.[31] The court's approach to custom is based upon two requirements: on the one hand, the court repeats neatly the elements of state practice and *opinio juris*. On the other hand, the court's interpretation of custom is transformed through the specific requirement under the ATS, first expressed in the *Sousa* judgment, that the norm relied upon must be specific, universal, and obligatory.[32] This criterion limits the scope of customary rules that can be applied: it is very well possible to find examples of custom that are not specific, and the concept of regional custom contradicts the idea that it should be universal.[33] Even custom without an obligatory character could be envisaged.[34] Thus, custom is analysed through the prism of the specific ATS requirements.

A second remarkable feature of this judgment is found in the sources of evidence discussed by the court. First, it looks at the judgments of international tribunals, arguing that courts are often established for the specific purpose of imposing liability, and that its findings are therefore instructive in relation to this issue, which is, after all, a liability question. The court then considers it relevant that no international tribunal has ever held a corporation liable for a violation of international law. Although this might be true as a matter of fact, its relevance is limited, given that no international court was ever presented with that issue. In the same vein, it seems doubtful whether it can indeed be said that the Nuremberg tribunals are 'the single most important source' of custom regarding liability for human right violations. This approach stands also out because US courts have often dismissed claims under the ATS for the reason that claimants are merely citing international court decisions as evidence of custom whereas this is deemed to be insufficient and even irrelevant.[35] Lastly, the opening statement of the court in paragraph 9, citing Judge Friendly, is an anachronism: One of the essential findings of the Supreme Court in *Sosa* was after all that international custom in relation to human rights does not only contain 'those standards, rules or customs [...] affecting the relationship between states or between an individual and a foreign state' but also standards in respect of the relation between a state and its own nationals.[36]

30 The ILDC database contains over 60 entries of cases brought under the ATS.

31 The important ATS cases of the Second Circuit: *Filartiga*, 630 F 2d 876, ILDC 681 (1980); *Kadić v Karadžić*, 70 F 3d 232 (2d Cir 1995), *Wiwa v Royal Dutch Petroleum Co.*, 226 F 3d 88 (2d Cir 2000); *Bigio v Coca-Cola Co.*, 239 F 3d 440 (2d Cir 2000); *Flores and ors v Southern Peru Copper Corporation*, 414 F 3d 233 (2d Cir 2003), 29 August 2003, ILDC 303 (US 2003); *Khulumani v Barclay Nat'l Bank Ltd.*, 504 F 3d 254 (2d Cir 2007) ILDC 686 (US 2007); *Viet. Assoc. for Victims of Agent Orange v Dow Chem. Co.*, 517 F 3d 104 (2d Cir 2008) ILDC 1040 (US 2008); *Abdullahi v Pfizer, Inc.*, 562 F 3d 163 (2d Cir 2009) ILDC 1232 (US 2009); *Presbyterian Church of Sudan v Talisman Energy, Inc.*, 582 F 3d 244 (2d Cir 2009).

32 *Sosa v Alvarez-Machain*, Decision of Supreme Court, 542 US 692 (2004); ILDC 117 (US 2004), 29 June 2004, para 732.

33 *Right of Passage over Indian Territory* (*Portugal v India*) (Judgment) [1960] ICJ Rep 6, 39; ICJ, *Asylum case* (*Colombia v Peru*) (Judgment) [1950] ICJ Rep 266, 276.

34 Roberts (n 10); D'Amato (n 26) 61-63.

35 See *Flores and ors v Southern Peru Copper Corporation*, Appeal judgment from the Court of Appeals for the Second Circuit; ILDC 303 (US 2003), 29 August 2003 para 84: 'Plaintiffs also rely on judicial decisions of international tribunals in support of their claims. In particular, they rely on decisions of the International Court of Justice, and on the European Court of Human Rights, a regional institution. But neither of these tribunals is empowered to create binding norms of customary international law'.

36 *Sosa v Alvarez-Machain*, Decision of Supreme Court, 542 US 692 (2004); ILDC 117 (US 2004), 29 June 2004, para 60.

C v Director of Immigration, First instance, HCAL 132/2006, [2008] 2 HKC 165, [2008] HKCFI 109, ILDC 1119 (HK 2008), 18th February 2008, Hong Kong; High Court; High Court as Court of First Instance [HKCFI]

The applicants in this case had sought protection as refugees. Their claims were dismissed, but upon the Director of Immigration's decision to repatriate the applicants, they filed a claim arguing that the principle of non-refoulement prohibited their repatriation. As the application of the Refugee Convention, signed by mainland China, was not extended to Hong Kong, Judge Hartmann had to look into the question of whether the principle of non-refoulement was part of customary international law.

> 65. Academic writers are agreed that a rule of customary international law has three fundamental elements. First, the rule should be of a norm-creating character, capable therefore of forming the basis of a general rule of law. Second, there must be a settled and consistent practice by states; not by all states, but by states generally. Third, the practice must be followed because it is accepted as being legally obligatory. […]
>
> 68. Accordingly, a settled and consistent practice among states, if it is to develop into a rule of customary international law, must be accompanied by conduct on the part of states—including those which are specially affected—acknowledging that the practice has acquired the force of law. […]
>
> 70. In its 1950 judgment in the *Asylum Case (Columbia/Peru)* ICJ Reports (1950) 266, at 277, the International Court of Justice recognised that a rule of customary international law, even if proved, would not be binding on a state which had, by evidence of its actions, repudiated it:
>
> > "But even if it could be supposed that such a custom existed between certain Latin-American States only, it could not be invoked against Peru which, far from having by its attitude adhered to it, has, on the contrary, repudiated it by refraining from ratifying the Montevideo Conventions of 1933 and 1939 … "
>
> 71. On behalf of the Director, it is argued that Hong Kong has never recognised any form of legal obligation to adhere to a norm of international custom concerning the refoulment of refugees. In this regard, it is said, Hong Kong is no different from many other—indeed the majority—of jurisdictions in Asia. This persistent non-recognition is evident inter alia from the fact that the Refugee Convention has never been extended to Hong Kong, from other reservations in our laws and from numerous statements made by the Hong Kong Government.
>
> 72. But that being said, the fact that the Refugee Convention has never been extended to Hong Kong, while a relevant factor, is not decisive. I say that because a rule of customary international law maintains its independent existence even though that rule has partially or even exactly been codified in a treaty.
>
> 73. A rule of customary international law may exist before a treaty has been created or may emerge from the terms of a treaty. In *Nicaragua v. United States of America (Case Concerning Military And Paramilitary Activities In And Against Nicaragua)* ICJ Reports (1986) p.14, para.175, the International Court of Justice rejected the argument that it should refrain from applying rules of customary international law because they had been 'subsumed' or 'supervened' by those of international treaty law. It concluded: "… even if a treaty norm and a customary norm relevant to the present dispute were to have exactly the same content, this would not be a reason for the Court to take the view that the operation of the treaty process must necessarily deprive the customary norm of its separate applicability."

74. Of particular relevance to the reservation applied to Hong Kong in respect of the Refugee Convention, the International Court of Justice went on to say: "Nor can [a] multilateral treaty reservation be interpreted as meaning that, once applicable to a given dispute, it would exclude the application of any rule of customary international law the content of which was the same as, or analogous to, that of the treaty-law rule which had caused the reservation to become effective." […]

94. In this regard, it is to be remembered that, while the importance of academic opinions have long been accepted in issues of international law, common law courts have recognised that such opinions alone, while they may point to the true state of the law, cannot make the law. As Cockburn CJ said in *R. v. Keyn* (1876) 2 Ex D 63, 202: " … even if entire unanimity had existed in respect of the important particulars to which I have referred, in place of so much discrepancy of opinion, the question would still remain, how far the law as stated by the publicist had received the assent of the civilized nations of the world. For writers on international law, however valuable their labours may be in elucidating and ascertaining the principles and rules of law, cannot make the law. To be binding, the law must have received the assent of the nations who are to be bound by it. This assent may be express, as by treaty or the acknowledged concurrence of governments, or may be implied from established usage …" […]

98. In short, it may be said that, certainly among academic writers, there has not been—and is not now—a universal consensus on the issue. […]

103. Of particular authority, in my view, is an opinion completed in 2001 by Sir Elihu Lauterpacht QC and Daniel Bethlehem QC (both noted scholars in the field of international law) entitled: The Scope and Content of the Principle of Non-Refoulment. The authors of the opinion conclude that "non-refoulment must be regarded as a principle of customary international law". […]

104. In the same year; that is, in 2001, a 'round table' of some 35 international law experts, meeting at the Lauterpacht Research Centre for International Law at the University of Cambridge, concluded that non-refoulment is a principle of customary international law. […]

106. But, as I have indicated earlier, the prevailing opinion is not universally accepted. There exists a body of academic opinion to the effect that—at this time—there is insufficient evidence to justify the assertion that the duty to avoid refoulment of refugees has evolved beyond the scope of the Refugee Convention. […]

113. I have taken note of the dissenting voices. I have reminded myself of the dangers of legal wishful thinking: considering it right that it should be so and therefore making it so. On balance, however, it seems to me that today it must be recognised that the principle of non-refoulment as it applies to refugees has grown beyond the confines of the Refugee Convention and has matured into a universal norm of customary international law.

114. I recognise that a good many states have not acceded to the Refugee Convention itself and, by their actions, have been unambiguous in their repudiation of the norm as it has evolved in customary international law. But that being said, the International Court of Justice, the primary judicial body of the United Nations, has emphasised that universal adherence is not required for a rule of customary international law to come into being. In *Nicaragua v. United States of America (Case Concerning Military And Paramilitary Activities In And Against Nicaragua)* ICJ Reports (1986) p.14, para.186, the Court put it in the following terms:

"The Court does not consider that, for a rule to be established as customary, the corresponding practice must be in absolutely rigorous conformity with the rule. In order to deduce the existence of customary rules, the Court deems it sufficient that the conduct of States should, in general, be consistent with such rules, and that instances of State conduct inconsistent with a given rule should generally have been treated as breaches of that rule, not as indications of the recognition of a new rule."

115. In my judgment, doing the best I can in an area where there are strongly conflicting opinions, it seems to me, on balance, that today states generally do adhere to the norm and do so out of recognition that it creates an obligation in law. Most states that are specially affected with refugee-related problems recognise the binding effect of the norm.

116. In coming to my finding, I have also taken into account the present recognition by states generally that fundamental humanitarian considerations have themselves evolved into a humanitarian law, that law linking and, to a greater or lesser degree, binding the conduct of states. [. . .]

133. In recognition of its humanitarian ideal, it may be said that the principle of non-refoulment should today be incapable of derogation or repudiation. But that, to my understanding, is not the basis upon which a norm of jus cogens is formed. One must look to the practice of states generally and why it is that they adhere to the practice. [. . .]

135. While, on balance, I am drawn to the conclusion that the rule against refoulment is a rule of customary international law, I think it goes too far to hold—at this time—that the rule has acquired the status of a peremptory norm. Put another way, the ideal does not accord with present reality and, if the ideal is to prevail, it may bring the norm itself into disrepute.

Judge Hartmann's analysis of customary international law is a case in point for the previously mentioned difficulties a domestic court encounters when it has to decide whether a rule exists as customary international law. It is for a domestic judge plainly impossible to review all state practice and *opinio juris* on such a debated matter as the non-refoulement principle, concerning which there is an abundance of worldwide state practice to be analysed. In this respect, it is only logical that Judge Hartmann resorts to academics in order to decide the matter. As the US Supreme Court already stated in 1900 in the *Paquete Habana* case, '[n]ot for the speculations of their authors concerning what the law ought to be, but for trustworthy evidence of what the law really is'.[37]

However, this leads to a series of new questions: what is decisive in finding that scholars agree on the existence of a customary rule? Is agreement amongst the substantial majority of scholars required, or only amongst a minority, if this minority consists of some influential and pre-eminent scholars in the field? Or is the mere fact that serious disagreement exists enough to conclude that a rule has not come into being? The Hong Kong Judge decided eventually that, despite strongly conflicting positions, non-refoulement is a norm of customary character according the prevailing academic opinion, which position he subsequently adopted in his judgment. The ILDC database contains examples where judges, confronted with strongly conflicting academic opinions, decided that this was strong evidence that the academic opinion could not be taken into account. In *Flores*, the US District Court dismissed the evidentiary value of statements by academic experts provided for by the plaintiffs as 'even less probative [than plaintiffs' documentary evidence] of the existence of universal norms, especially considering the vigorous academic debate over the content of international law'.[38] The Court of Appeals dismissed these affidavits even more vehemently, stating that article 38 of the ICJ

37 *The Paquete Habana and The Lola*, Decision of the Supreme Court, 175 US 677; ILDC 392 (US 1900) para 68.
38 *Flores and ors v Southern Peru Copper Corporation* (n 35) para 86.

statute does not recognize 'as a source of customary international law the policy-driven or theoretical work of advocates that comprises a substantial amount of contemporary international law scholarship'.[39] In this light, it is no exaggeration to state that scholarship on the principle of non-refoulement may indeed be policy-driven from time to time-of which Judge Hartmann is, however, mindful when he states that: 'I have reminded myself of the dangers of legal wishful thinking: considering it right that it should be so and therefore making it so.'

Germany v Margellos and 18 other natural and legal persons (intervening), Petition for Cassation, Case No 6/2002, (2003) 1 AED 11, (2003) 56 RHDI 199, ILDC 87 (GR 2002), 17th September 2002, Greece; Special Supreme Court

Mr Margellos and other villagers of Lidoriki, a village destroyed by German forces in the Second World War sued Germany in the aftermath of the famous *Distomo* case (ILDC 287 (GR 2000)), claiming indemnities for the destruction of their property and the physical injuries suffered. The Greek Supreme Court (Areios Pagos), having been petitioned for cassation by Germany after two default judgments against it, decided to refer the case to the Special Supreme Court, which had the power to give an opinion as to whether a rule invoked in litigation indeed qualifies as a generally accepted rule of international law.

> 14. Whereas, regardless of what has been argued in the three judgments presented in the previous judgment, the Court, following the examination of all above evidence, concludes that in the current stage of progression of international law, a generally accepted rule of this law has not been formed that would allow, by exception from the principle of immunity, to lawfully prosecute a State before the Court of another State for compensation for all kinds of offenses which took place on the territory of the *forum* State and in which armed forces of the defendant State were involved in any manner, either in time of war or in time of peace, while this response is not sufficient for dealing with the issues that are presented in the indicting judgment. To the contrary, it results from all evidence, without exception, that the foreign State continues to enjoy the immunity when it is prosecuted for acts which took place on the territory of the *forum* State and in which its armed forces were involved in any manner, without the distinction of whether these acts were in violation of jus cogens or whether these armed forces were involved in a conflict with other armed forces. Indeed the relative provisions of Article 31 of the European Convention are formulated exhaustively and are not subject to this distinction. This rule is justified by the need to respect the sovereignty of the foreign State, of which the primary manifestation is the action of its armed forces, as this respect is the foundation of the equality of States and, hence, of the smooth functioning of international relations at which all principles and rules of international law are aimed.
>
> [. . .] As the rule of non-applicability of immunity in the case of civil liability of States in armed conflicts is not laid down in any text or evidence, the Court is not permitted, despite what was found in the previous judgment, to formulate such a rule or to infer its existence without invoking specific evidence from international practice, or to derive through interpretation on its own the principle of the obligation of States to compensate violations of its law during war on land [. . .]
>
> This case concerns war crimes, which are explicitly prohibited by the Hague Convention and create a direct obligation for compensation to the injured persons by the State responsible for these crimes committed by its organs. In light of these facts, according to the minority opinion, the provisions of Article 11 of the 1972 European

39 ibid, para 90.

> Convention on State Immunity, which provide for the non-applicability of immunity and, in any case, establish the absence of an international obligation on a State to grant sovereign immunity to another State for crimes committed in the territory of the *forum* State by a perpetrator present on its territory (independently of whether sovereign acts of the defendant State are concerned), also reflect general international practice that is accepted as a rule of law, namely a generally accepted rule of customary international law. The aforementioned rule is not vitiated when dealing with acts of armed forces or relevant to the armed forces of a State which constitute war crimes; in no case do these acts fall within the meaning of armed conflict.
>
> 15. Whereas, further to the above, the Supreme Court finds that at the current stage of development of international law a generally accepted rule of this law continues to exist, according to which a State cannot be lawfully prosecuted before the court of another State for compensation for all kinds of offenses committed on the territory of the *forum* State and in which armed forces of the defendant State are involved in any manner, either in time of war or in time of peace.

The Greek Special Supreme Court found itself in a difficult position in this case. On the one hand, the 'normal' supreme court had already ruled in the famous *Distomo* case that Germany could under similar circumstances not rely on immunity.[40] On the other hand, that judgment had been met with criticism by foreign states.[41] The court's approach therefore seems to combine two approaches: on the one hand, it contains an explanation of the *rationale* behind the international rules on state immunity, which perhaps serves an explanatory function towards the Greek public opinion. At the same time, the judgment demonstrates a technical approach to the determination of customary international law, arguing that it is as a matter of law plainly impossible to prove at the current stage of international law the existence of a customary rule excluding the application of the immunity of states for crimes committed on the territory of the forum state.

The majority emphasizes that the existence of a customary international law cannot be inferred, constructed, or derived through interpretation. Although this is a clear criticism of the reasoning in the *Distomo* judgment, the main legal issue that distinguishes both cases is the relevance attached to the European Convention on State Immunity and its number of ratifications. As mentioned before, the determination of custom by domestic courts often boils down to analysing court judgments (see *Kiobel*), academic opinions (see *C v Hong Kong*) or conventions.[42] However, there are some serious problems attached to inferring custom from treaty ratifications. First, the fact that states decide that a treaty is necessary to regulate a certain issue could just as well indicate that 'the very reason of the treaty was to create an obligation which would not have existed by the general law [...] evidence of the fact that it is not yet a norm of customary international law'.[43] The US Court of Appeals in *Kiobel* for that reason stated that the fact that '[a] provision appears in one treaty (or more), therefore, is not proof of a well-established norm of *customary* international law'.[44] Therefore, just as is the case with other evidence of state practice, ratification of a treaty as evidence of state practice has to be extensive, which is eventually what made the special supreme court in this case decide that the European Convention on State Immunity, with its eight ratifications, did not constitute convincing evidence of the existence of a norm of customary international law.

40 As discussed below in Supreme Civil and Criminal Court (Areios Pagos), *Germany v Prefecture of Voiotia, representing 118 persons from Distomo village*, 4 May 2000, ILDC 287 (GR 2000).

41 'Westerwelle empört über Griechische Klage' *Die Welt*, 13 January 2011 http://www.welt.de/politik/ausland/article12140825/Westerwelle-empoert-ueber-griechische-Klage.html (last accessed 30 October 2017).

42 M Mendelson 'The formation of customary international law' in (1998) 272 *Recueil des Cours* 296.

43 J L Brierly, *The Law of Nations* (6th edn, OUP 1963) 57.

44 *Kiobel and ors v Royal Dutch Petroleum and ors*, 17 September 2010, ILDC 1552 (US 2010), para 59.

2. Interpreting broad norms of customary international law

Public Committee against Torture in Israel and Palestinian Society for the Protection of Human Rights and the Environment v Israel and ors, Original Petition to the High Court of Justice, HCJ 769/02, ILDC 597 (IL 2006), 13th December 2006, Israel; Supreme Court; Supreme Court as High Court of Justice

Two human rights organizations challenged the Israeli targeted killings policy of preventive strikes by the Israeli Defence Forces (IDF) in the Occupied Territories aimed at killing individuals involved in terrorist attacks against Israel. Therefore the Israeli High Court of Justice had to analyse the rules of customary international law regarding belligerent occupation and international humanitarian law.

4. [. . .] The prohibition of arbitrary killing which is not necessary for self defense is entrenched in the customary norms of international law. Such a prohibition stems also from the duties of the force controlling occupied territory toward the members of the occupied population, who are protected persons according to IV Geneva Convention Relative to the Protection of Civilian Persons in Time of War 1949 (hereinafter—the *Fourth Geneva Convention*), as well as the two additional protocols to the conventions signed in 1977. All of this law reflects the norms of customary international law, which obligate Israel.

19. Substantial parts of international law dealing with armed conflicts are of customary character. That customary law is part of Israeli law, "by force of the State of Israel's existence as a sovereign and independent state" (*S.Z. Cheshin*, J., CrimApp 174/54 *Shtempfeffer v. The Attorney General*, 10 PD 5, 15; *see also* CrimApp 336/61 *Eichmann v. The Attorney General*, 17 PD 2033; CApp 7092/94 *Her Majesty the Queen in Right of Canada v. Edelson*, 51(1) PD 625, 639 and the caselaw referred to within, and Ruth Lapidoth, *The Status of Public International Law in Israeli Law*, 19 Mishpatim 809 (5750) [*Mikumo shel haMishpat haBeinleumi haPombi beMishpat haYisraeli*]; R. Sable, International Law 29 (2003) [Mishpat Beinleumi]). *Shamgar P.* expressed that well, stating:

> "According to the consistent caselaw of this Court, customary international law is a part of the law of the country, subject to Israeli statute determining a contrary provision" (HCJ 785/87 *Afu v. The Commander of IDF Forces in the West Bank*, 42(2) PD 4, 35). The international law entrenched in international conventions which is not part of customary international law (whether Israel is party to them or not), is not part of the internal law of the State of Israel [. . .] Indeed, the "geometric location" of our issue is in customary international law dealing with armed conflict. It is from that law that additional law which may be relevant will be derived according to our domestic law. International treaty law which has no customary force is not part of our internal law. [. . .]

23. A central consideration affecting the balancing point is the identity of the person harmed, or the objective compromised in armed conflict. That is the central principle of the distinction (*see* Dinstein, at p. 82; Ben-Naftali & Shani, at p. 151). Customary international law regarding armed conflicts distinguishes between combatants and military targets, and non-combatants, in other words, civilians and civilian objectives (see *The Legality of Nuclear Weapons*, at p. 257; *The First Protocol*, art. 48). [. . .]

25. [. . .] The Imprisonment of Unlawful combatants Law, 5762-2002 authorizes the chief of the general staff of the IDF to issue an order for the administrative detention of an "unlawful combatant". That term is defined in the statute as "a person who took part in hostilities against the State of Israel, whether directly or indirectly, or is part of a force which commits hostilities against the state of Israel,

who does not fulfill the conditions granting prisoner of war status in international humanitarian law, as determined in article 4 of III Geneva Convention relative to the Treatment of Prisoners of War, 12 August 1949." Needless to say, unlawful combatants are not beyond the law. They are not "outlaws". God created them as well in his image; their human dignity as well is to be honored; they as well enjoy and are entitled to protection, even if most minimal, by customary international law (Neuman, *Humanitarian Law and Counterterrorist Force*, 14 Eur. J. Int'l L. 283 (2003); Georg Nolte, *Preventative Use of Force and Preventative Killings: Moves into a Different Legal Order*, 5 Theoretical Inquiries In Law 111, 119 (2004), hereinafter "Nolte"). That is certainly the case when they are in detention or brought to justice (*see* §75 of *The First Protocol*, which reflects customary international law, as well as Knut Dormann, *The Legal Situation of 'Unlawful/Unprivileged' Combatants*, 85 IRRC 45, 70 (2003), hereinafter "Dormann"). [. . .]

26. Customary international law regarding armed conflicts protects "civilians" from harm as a result of the hostilities. The International Court of Justice discussed that in *The Legality of Nuclear Weapons*, stating: "states must never make civilians the object of attack" (p. 257). That customary principle is expressed in article 51(2) of *The First Protocol*, according to which: "The civilian population as such, as well as individual civilians, shall not be the object of attack".

From that follows also the duty to do everything possible to minimize collateral damage to the civilian population during the attacks on "combatants" (*see* Eyal Benvenisti, *Human Dignity in Combat: the Duty to Spare Enemy Civilians*, 39 Isr. L. Rev. 81 (2006). Against the background of that protection granted to "civilians", the question what constitutes a "civilian" for the purposes of that law arises. The approach of customary international law is that "civilians" are those who are not "combatants" (*see* §50(1) of *The First Protocol*, and Sable, at p. 432). In the *Blaskic* case, the International Criminal Tribunal for the former Yugoslavia ruled that civilians are—"Persons who are not, or no longer, members of the armed forces" (*Prosecutor v. Blaskic* (2000) Case IT-95-14-T, para 180).

27. In the oral and written arguments before us, the state asked us to recognize a third category of persons, that of unlawful combatants [. . .] 28. The literature on this subject is comprehensive (Richard R. Baxter, *So-Called 'Unprivileged Belligerency': Spies, Guerrillas and Saboteurs*, 28 Bri. Y. B. Int'l L. 323 (1951); Kenneth Watkin, *Warriors without Rights? Combatants, Unprivileged Belligerents, and Struggle over Legitimacy*, 11 Harvard Program on Humanitarian Policy and Conflict Research (2005), hereinafter "Watkin"; Calle, *Unlawful Combatants and the Geneva Conventions*, 44 Va. J. Int'l L. 1025 (2004); Michael H. Hoffman, *Terrorists Are Unlawful Belligerents, Not Unlawful Combatants: a Distinction With Implications for the Future of International Humanitarian Law*, 34 Case W. Res. J. Int'l L. 227 (2002); Shlomy Zachary, *Between the Geneva Conventions: Where Does the Unlawful Combatant Belong*, 38 Isr. L. Rev. 378 (2005); Nolte; Dormann). We shall take no stance regarding the question whether it is desirable to recognize this third category. The question before us is not one of desirable law, rather one of existing law. In our opinion, as far as existing law goes, the data before us are not sufficient to recognize this third category. That is the case according to the current state of international law, both international treaty law and customary international law (*see* Cassese, at pp. 408, 470). It is difficult for us to see how a third category can be recognized in the framework of the Hague and Geneva Conventions. It does not appear to us that we were presented with data sufficient to allow us to say, at the present time, that such a third category has been recognized in customary international law. However, new reality at times requires new

interpretation. Rules developed against the background of a reality which has changed must take on dynamic interpretation which adapts them, in the framework of accepted interpretational rules, to the new reality (*see Jami'at Ascan*, at p. 800; *Ajuri*, at p. 381). In the spirit of such interpretation, we shall now proceed to the customary international law dealing with the status of civilians who constitute unlawful combatants. [. . .]

30. The basic principle is that the civilians taking a direct part in hostilities are not protected from attack upon them at such time as they are doing so. This principle is manifest in §51(3) of *The First Protocol*, which determines: "Civilians shall enjoy the protection afforded by this section, unless and for such time as they take a direct part in hostilities." As is well known, Israel is not party to *The First Protocol*. Thus, it clearly was not enacted in internal Israeli legislation. Does the basic principle express customary international law? The position of The Red Cross is that it is a principle of customary international law (Henckaerts & Doswald–Beck, at p. 20). That position is acceptable to us. It fits the provision Common Article 3 of *The Geneva Conventions*, to which Israel is party and which, according to all, reflects customary international law, pursuant to which protection is granted to persons "[T]aking no active part in the hostilities." The International Criminal Tribunal for the former Yugoslavia determined that article 51 of *The First Protocol* constitutes customary international law (*see* Struger ICTY IT-OT-42-T-22 (2005)). In military manuals of many states, including England, France, Holland, Australia, Italy, Canada, Germany, the United States (Air Force), and New Zealand, the provision has been copied verbatim, or by adopting its essence, according to which civilians are not to be attacked, unless they are taking a (direct) part in the hostilities. The legal literature sees that provision as an expression of customary international law (*see* Dinstein, at p. 11; Kretzmer, at p. 192; Ben–Naftali & Michaeli, at p. 269; Cassese, at p. 416; and Marco Roscini, *Targeting and Contemporary Aerial Bombardment*, 54 Int'l and Comp L. Q. 411, 418 (2005), hereinafter "Roscini"; Vincent-Jöel Proulx, *If the Hat Fits Wear It, if the Turban Fits Run for your Life: Reflection on the Indefinite Detention and Targeted Killings of Suspected Terrorists*, 56 Hastings L.J. 801, 879 (2005); Adrich, *The Laws of War on Land*, 94 Am. J. Int'l L. 42, 53 (2000)).

33. Civilians lose the protection of customary international law dealing with hostilities of international character if they "take . . . part in hostilities." What is the meaning of that provision? The accepted view is that "hostilities" are acts which by nature and objective are intended to cause damage to the army. Thus determines Commentary on the Additional Protocols, published by the Red Cross in 1987:

"Hostile acts should be understood to be acts which by their nature and purpose are intended to cause actual harm to the personnel and equipment of the armed forces" (Y. Sandoz et al. Commentary on the Additional Protocols 618 (1987)).

A similar approach was accepted by the Inter-American Commission on Human Rights, and is positively referred to in Henckaerts & Doswald-Beck (p. 22).

34. Civilians lose the protection against military attack, granted to them by customary international law dealing with international armed conflict (as adopted in *The First Protocol*, §51(3)), if "they take a direct part in hostilities." That provision differentiates between civilians taking a direct part in hostilities (from whom the protection from attack is removed) and civilians taking an indirect part in hostilities (who continue to enjoy protection from attack). What is that differentiation? A similar provision appears in Common Article 3 of *The Geneva Conventions*, which uses the wording "active part in hostilities." The judgment of the International Criminal Tribunal for Rwanda determined that these two terms are of identical content (*see The Prosecutor v. Akayesu*, case no. ICTR-96-4-T (1998)). What is that content? It seems accepted in

the international literature that an agreed upon definition of the term "direct" in the context under discussion does not exist (*see* Direct Participation In Hostilities Under International Humanitarian Law, Report Prepared by the International Committee of the Red Cross (2003); Direct Participation in Hostilities Under International Humanitarian Law (2004)). Henckaerts & Doswald-Beck rightly stated that—"It is fair to conclude ... that a clear and uniform definition of direct participation in hostilities has not been developed in state practice" (p. 23).

In that state of affairs, and without a comprehensive and agreed upon customary standard, there is no escaping going case by case, while narrowing the area of disagreement (compare *Tadic*). [...]

40. [...] On the one hand, a civilian who took a direct part in hostilities once, or sporadically, but detached himself from them (entirely, or for a long period) is not to be harmed. On the other hand, the "revolving door" phenomenon, by which each terrorist has "horns of the alter" (1 Kings 1:50) to grasp or a "city of refuge" (Numbers 35:11) to flee to, to which he turns in order to rest and prepare while they grant him immunity from attack, is to be avoided (*see* Schmitt, at p. 536; Watkin, at p. 12; Kretzmer, at p. 193; Dinstein, at p. 29; and Parks, at p. 118). In the wide area between those two possibilities, one finds the "gray" cases, about which customary international law has not yet crystallized. There is thus no escaping examination of each and every case. [...]

45. [...] As we have seen, this requirement of proportionality is employed in customary international law regarding protection of civilians (*see* Cassese, at p. 418; Kretzmer, at p. 200; Ben-Naftali & Michaeli, at p. 278; see also Gardam; as well as §51(2)(III) of *The First Protocol*, which constitutes customary law). When the damage to innocent civilians is not proportional to the benefit of the attacking army, the attack is disproportionate and forbidden. [...]

53. [...] the types of questions examined by this Court have also been decided by international courts. International law dealing with the army's duties toward civilians during an armed conflict has been discussed, for example, by the international criminal tribunals for the former Yugoslavia and Rwanda (*see* paragraphs 26, 30 & 34 above). These courts have examined the legal aspects of the conduct of armies. Why can't an Israeli court perform that same examination? Why do those questions, which are justiciable in international courts, cease to be justiciable in national tribunals? [...]

60 [...] The examination of the "targeted killing"—and in our terms, the preventative strike causing the deaths of terrorists, and at times also of innocent civilians—has shown that the question of the legality of the preventative strike according to customary international law is complex [...] The result of that examination is not that such strikes are always permissible or that they are always forbidden. The approach of customary international law applying to armed conflicts of an international nature is that civilians are protected from attacks by the army. However, that protection does not exist regarding those civilians "for such time as they take a direct part in hostilities" (§51(3) of *The First Protocol*). Harming such civilians, even if the result is death, is permitted, on the condition that there is no other means which harms them less, and on the condition that innocent civilians nearby are not harmed. Harm to the latter must be proportional. That proportionality is determined according to a values based test, intended to balance between the military advantage and the civilian damage. As we have seen, we cannot determine that a preventative strike is always legal, just as we cannot determine that it is always illegal. All depends upon the question whether the standards of customary international law regarding international armed conflict allow that preventative strike or not.

This case dealt with a highly sensitive issue in Israeli politics, the targeted killings policy. Caught between international disapproval and strong approbation in Israeli politics, President Barak of the Israeli Supreme Court had to navigate through a political minefield to find a solution to a legal question which was firmly entrenched in customary international law, or, in his own words: 'the "geometric location" of our issue is in customary international law dealing with armed conflict'.[45]

The reason for this was that, under Israeli domestic law, international conventions are not part of the internal law of Israel, but rules of customary international law are.[46]

A couple of elements of the court's methodology stand out. First, the judgment does not contain a single mention of the requirements of state practice and *opinio juris*, which is remarkable for a judgment whose reasoning depends entirely on the existence and content of customary international law. Instead, the court consistently follows a different approach: it analyses consecutively all rules pertinent to the solution of the issue, starting with the prohibition on arbitrary killing, moving on to the protection of civilians in armed conflict, finally reaching the rule that civilians taking a direct part in hostilities are not protected by this rule. When discussing a rule, the court first looks at the existence of that rule in a convention. Secondly, it turns to international case law and legal literature, in that order, to analyse whether the rule of the convention is customary. Special importance is attached to the position of the Red Cross in its commentaries to the Geneva Conventions and its volume on customary international humanitarian law.[47] Given the difficulties for domestic courts in analysing state practice and *opinio juris* themselves, the relevance of such volumes, the result of a phenomenal scholarly effort to indeed collect and analyse worldwide state practice, is beyond doubt. Special importance is also attached to the special expert opinion by Antonio Cassese that claimants had submitted, which is cited throughout the judgment, although the court does not follow its final conclusion.

Secondly, the court adopts an interesting, although peculiar approach to the interpretation of broad, undefined customary norms. It states in paragraph 26 that '[...] new reality at times requires new interpretation. Rules developed against the background of a reality which has changed must take on dynamic interpretation which adapts them, in the framework of accepted interpretational rules, to the new reality'.[48] The pivotal issue here was the interpretation of the term 'direct' in the rule that civilians taking a direct part in hostilities are not protected as civilians under the laws of armed conflict. The court reasoned that, as international custom had 'not yet crystallized', what constitutes direct participation should be assessed on a case by case basis. Admittedly, the precise boundaries of what constitutes direct participation and what not are not crystal clear. However, emphasizing the fact that there is a large area of 'grey cases' in combination with the aforementioned dynamic interpretation allowed the court not to discuss the requirement that strikes against civilians can only take place at the moment that civilians indeed directly participate in armed attacks.[49] President Barak could subsequently conclude that the IDF could continue their strikes, while simultaneously maintaining judicial oversight

45 *Public Committee against Torture in Israel and Palestinian Society for the Protection of Human Rights and the Environment v Israel* (n 14) para 19.

46 See *Her Majesty the Queen in Right of Canada v Edelson and ors*, Final appeal judgment, PLA 7092/94, 51(1) PD 625, ILDC 577 (IL 1997), 3 June 1997.

47 J Pictet, *Commentary on the Geneva Conventions of 12 August 1949. Volume I* (ICRC 1952); J M Henckaerts and L Doswald-Beck, *Customary International Humanitarian Law* (CUP 2005).

48 *Public Committee against Torture in Israel and Palestinian Society for the Protection of Human Rights and the Environment v Israel* (n 14) para 26.

49 Which would most probably have meant that the Israeli preventive strikes would have been illegal: See E Peled, Analysis, *Public Committee against Torture in Israel and Palestinian Society for the Protection of Human Rights and the Environment v Israel*, ILDC 597 (IL 2006) A2; Y Sandoz and ors, *Commentary on the Additional Protocols of 8 June 1977 to the Geneva Conventions of 12 August 1949* (Martinus Nijhoff 1987) 618.

over the legality of such attacks. A different decision would most likely have caused public outrage among Israeli policy-makers and the general public.

This case emphasizes that domestic courts remain agents of the national legal order as well. It demonstrates that even within rather sound methodological boundaries, the nature of customary international law allows for a great deal of domestic policy considerations, as will be extensively discussed in the next chapter.

III. Domestic Courts as Agents in the Development of Customary International Law

Customary international law is probably the source of international law most attacked and discussed, criticized and praised, and academics struggle with its circular and contradictory character. [50] As mentioned above, it lacks a convincing theoretical underpinning, is hardly ever properly established, even by the World Court, and is open to constant debate. There is one particular issue which encapsulates and highlights all this criticism: the question of the emergence of new rules of custom.[51] As D'Amato already recognized in 1971: 'The question of how custom comes into being and how it can be changed or modified are wrapped in mystery and illogic'.[52] Or as Gavouneli put it in her ILDC analysis of the *Distomo* case: 'It is often said that the formation of custom requires at least three judgments: the first one is wrong; the second sets a trend; the third confirms the new rule'.[53] For the pivotal, contradictory, or, if one opines less critically, at least paradoxically essence of the formation of new custom is that 'each deviation contains the seeds of a new rule'.[54] As all would agree that international law allows for custom to be altered, this premise necessarily entails that deviations of existing rules are necessary for new custom to emerge. Consequently, one might argue that courts 'engage in a legitimate function when contributing to custom formation through breaches of existing rules'.[55] Some domestic courts indeed refer to the notion of emerging custom and their position in the development of new customary rules.[56] Whereas, as a matter of sound logic, it can indeed be argued that deviations of existing customary international norms in light of the emergence of new norms are not to be considered mistakes by definition, this does not mean that every court judgment referring to this notion is to be endorsed. This will be discussed further in the commentary to some cases that explicitly refer to emerging custom.

Apart from the domestic courts constructing their reasoning around the notion emerging custom, another, more heterogeneous category of cases is discernible in which courts engage in daring and sometimes clearly mistaken findings of custom. First, some courts apply a sound methodology as to the existence of a norm, but take extensive liberties in interpreting this norm, as was the case in the above discussed case of *Public Committee against Torture*.[57] A second pattern does still apply the *continental shelf* criteria, but stretches the requirement of *extensive* and *virtually uniform* state practice to its utter limits. The *Distomo* case, which will be discussed below, is a prime example of this approach. A third approach attaches great importance to very limited but deliberately chosen state practice and *opinio juris* it considers particularly relevant.

---

50 Kelly (n 26) 450; A Roberts, 'Traditional and Modern Approaches to Customary International Law: a Reconciliation' (2001) 95 AJIL 757, 757; Guzman (n 20) 117.

51 Guzman (n 20) 124; R Kolb, 'Selected Problems in the Theory of Customary International Law' (2003) 50 *Netherlands International Law Review* 119, 130–36.

52 D'Amato (n 26) 4.

53 M Gavouneli, Analysis, *Germany v Prefecture of Voiotia*, ILDC 287 (GR 2000) A6.

54 D'Amato (n 26) 98.

55 Roberts (n 10) 70.

56 See *Germany v Mantelli and ors*, Preliminary Order on Jurisdiction, No 14201/2008, 29 May 2008, ILDC 1037 (IT 2008), para 11; *Lozano v Italy* (n 8) para 6.

57 See, eg, *Public Committee against Torture in Israel and Palestinian Society for the Protection of Human Rights and the Environment v Israel* (n 14).

This is mostly the practice and *opinio* of the forum state, as is the case in *Chile v Aranciabel*, discussed later in this paragraph, but other focal points are found too.[58] Lastly, the ILDC database contains examples of 'construing' and 'deducting' custom rather than applying the essentially inductive approach required by the *continental shelf* criteria.[59] A fascinating example is the case of *Italia Nostra v Ministry of Cultural Heritage and Libyan Arab Jamahiriya*, in which case the Italian Council of State found that there was a customary obligation to return works of art taken wrongfully in times of wartime occupation.[60] It based its reasoning on a) the customary obligation on the use of force, b) the existence of restitution as a form of compensation, combined with c) the customary principle of self-determination.[61] It can thus be concluded that domestic courts can be very creative in moulding customary international law in their favour. In this respect it should be kept in mind that the domestic judge always remains an agent of the domestic legal order too. All issues in the following cases were subject to fierce debate in society and politics, and the court judgments performed an important domestic function.[62] At the same time, their burgeoning international relevance should not be underestimated. It seems that the often-used metaphor of the 'double hats' may prove too weak to describe the pharaonic double crown some courts have put on.

1. 'Sufficient' state practice and opinio juris

Germany v Prefecture of Voiotia (Representing 118 persons from Distomo village), Petition on cassation against default, no 11/2000, (2000) 49 Nomiko Vima 212, ILDC 287 (GR 2000), 4th May 2000, Greece; Supreme Court

The Greek village of Distomo was burned to the ground during the Second World War by German forces. After the end of the War, 118 villagers brought suit against Germany, claiming indemnities for destruction of their property and the atrocities committed by the occupation troops. After a default judgment of the court of first instance, Germany waived its right to appeal and brought a petition for cassation. The applicants argued that under customary international law an exception from state immunity existed in case of tortuous liability for grave breaches of international law.

> 7 Whereas, in accordance with article 38 paragraph 1 of the Statute of the International Court [of Justice] at The Hague (1946), international custom, as a source of international law, is a general practice accepted as law. Therefore, in order for international custom to exist, two elements are required: (a) one that is factual and external, i.e. a constant and uniform practice and (b) one that is psychological, i.e. the conviction that the said practice corresponds to a defined legal obligation

58 In *Canada v Edelson*, in which case the Israeli supreme court, called upon to decide on the application of customary immunity law in respect of the Canadian ambassadorial residence attached special importance to Canadian state practice: (n 46) para 19.

59 See, eg, *Ferrini v Germany*, Appeal decision, Cass No 5044/04, ILDC 19 (IT 2004), 11 March 2004, Supreme Court of Cassation; R Kolb, 'Selected Problems in the Theory of Customary International Law' (2003) 50 *Netherlands International Law Review* 119, 126; Roberts (n 10) 758.

60 *Italia Nostra v Ministry of Cultural Heritage and Libyan Arab Jamahiriya*, Appeal judgment, Case No 3154/2008; ILDC 1138 (IT 2008).

61 ibid, para 4.4.

62 'Greece to intervene in reparations trial' *Kathimerini*, 12 January 2011 http://www.ekathimerini.com/4dcgi/_w_articles_wsite1_1_12/01/2011_372930 (last accessed 30 October 2017); 'L'imam rapito a Milano dalla Cia I silenzi e la complicità con Washington' *La* Repubblica, 28 Juni 2005 http://www.repubblica.it/2005/e/sezioni/cronaca/islamici/inchiestazoppa/inchiestazoppa.html (last accessed 30 October 2017); 'Plan Cóndor: Arancibia Clavel, condenado a 12 años de prisión' *La Nacion*, 30 September 2004 http://www.lanacion.com.ar/640898-plan-condor-arancibia-clavel-condenado-a-12-anos-de-prision (last accessed 30 October 2017); 'Lozano non si può processare in Italia' *Corriere della Sera*, 19 Juni 2008 http://www.corriere.it/cronache/08_giugno_19/lozano_cassazione_fd6bae40-3de5-11dd-9c4b-00144f02aabc.shtml (last accessed 30 October 2017).

or right (*opinio juris sive necessitatis*). Therefore, when states follow a certain practice, either positive or negative, in international relations, with the belief that the said practice constitutes a lawful action according to international law, they create custom. From the nature of things, greater importance is attributed to states closely connected with the formation of international custom. In assessing the value of state practice the element of time is also considered, since duration attests to consistency in application and also confirmation of the value of the customary rule, without, however, excluding cases in which long practice is not necessary for the creation of a customary rule. The verification of international custom is of vital importance, since, in accordance with article 28 paragraph 1 of the Constitution, international custom as a generally recognised rule of international law constitutes an integral part of Greek law and prevails over any contrary provision of law. In relation to the methods of verification of custom, the United Nations International Law Commission drew up, in 1951, an indicative list including judgments by international but also national courts, diplomatic correspondence, expert opinions by legal councillors to states, international conventions, national laws as well as the practice of international organisations. The importance of codifying conventions, through which a customary rule already in force is crystallised or subsequently to the conclusion of which such rule is created, as well as [the importance of] judgments of international and also national courts of states contributing to the determination of the existence and contents of international customary law, should be underlined. Finally, the conclusions reached by the doctrine and especially the teachings of distinguished international publicists of various countries (article 38 paragraph 1(d) of the ICJ Statute) constitute auxiliary means to this regard.

8 [. . .] the tendency at the international level to further limit the immunity of foreign states led, within the framework of the Council of Europe, to the conclusion of the European Convention on State Immunity (Basle, 16 May 1972). The said Convention constitutes a codification of the pre-existing customary law in continental Europe and has been ratified by eight member-states to the Council of Europe: the United Kingdom, the Federal Republic of Germany, Austria, Belgium, Cyprus, Luxemburg, the Netherlands and Sweden. Lack of ratification by other European states up to the present time does not express, in itself, disagreement with the general principles thereof, since the European countries in their totality accept and apply by way of custom the system of limited immunity and in particular some of them are pioneers in the application thereof, as is the case (apart from Belgium, which has already ratified the Convention) with Italy, France and Greece. According to article 11 of the above codifying Convention, a contracting state cannot claim immunity from the jurisdiction of a court of another contracting state in relation to its civil liability for the reparation of damages (including pecuniary damage) caused by tort against persons or property (intentional or negligent bodily damage, homicide, damage to alien property, arson, etc), irrespective of whether the tort was committed by the contracting state jure imperii or jure gestionis. The necessary condition for the affirmation of tortuous liability of the foreign state is the existence of a connection with the *forum* state. In particular, it is required: a) that the act or omission was committed in the territory of the *forum* state and b) that the perpetrator was present in the same territory at the time of commission. Furthermore, the said European Convention of 1972 inspired and influenced important foreign states that adopted national laws on foreign state immunity and excluded from immunity, *inter alia*, tortuous liability of foreign states upon the same conditions as above, thus affirming the principle of territoriality (tort committed in the territory of the *forum* by a perpetrator who was present in the same territory at the time of commission). Thus, such exception from immunity is provided by the laws of the United States [of America] (Foreign Sovereign

Immunities Act—FSIA of 1976, article 1605(a)(5)), the United Kingdom (Sovereign Immunity Act—SIA of 1978, article 5), Canada (SIA of 1982, article 6), Australia (FSIA of 1985, article 13), South Africa (FSIA of 1981, article 6) and Singapore (SIA of 1979, article 7). Moreover, the United Nations International Law Commission (ILC), comprised of 34 representatives of member-states to the United Nations, among which the USA, Canada, Brazil, Egypt, the United Kingdom, Germany, France, Italy, Greece, the former Soviet Union, China, India and Japan, submitted to the General Assembly, in 1991, the final draft articles on Jurisdictional Immunities of States and their Property, for which work had begun in 1978. This important document, reflecting the views of the international community on issues of immunity, inspired in addition by the principles of the European Convention on state immunity, provides in broader and thorough wording (article 12) an exception from immunity for the tortuous liability of a foreign state under the exact same conditions, […] Identical to the abovementioned draft of the International Law Commission is the draft by the Institut de droit international of the same year (1991), providing (article 2 paragraph 2 under e) an exception to immunity and an affirmation of the jurisdiction of the *forum* courts in relation to offences involving death or bodily injury of persons or loss or damage of property caused by the activity of a foreign state and the organs thereof in the territory covered by the jurisdiction of the *forum*. At the same time, state courts in the international community, with the courts of the USA being the first among them, issued judgments by which it was found that they had jurisdiction to adjudicate on actions brought by persons against foreign states concerning reparations for tortuous acts committed *jure imperii* in the territory of the *forum* by perpetrators who were present in that territory at the time of commission thereof. Indicative reference is made to *Letelier v. Republic of Chile* (488 F. Supp. 665 (DDC 1980)), where the American courts ruled in favour of their jurisdiction to adjudicate on this case that regarded the assassination of former Chilean ambassador Orlando Letelier in a bombing attack in the USA that was ordered by the then Chilean government and committed by its organs, i.e. an act *jure imperii* committed in violation of human rights within the USA and contrary to the principles of international law. Similarly, the US Court of Appeals of the 9th Circuit ruled in favour of its jurisdiction in *Liu v. Republic of China* (642 F. Supp. 297 (N.D. Cal. 1986)), a case regarding the execution (by gunshot on American soil) of Taiwanese dissident Henry Liu by agents of China, which acted in the exercise of its sovereign power (*jure imperii*). The said exception from immunity is also adopted by a large number of distinguished publicists. In light of the above, a general practice by the states of the international community that is accepted as law is established, i.e. the formation of international custom constituting, in accordance with article 28 paragraph 1 of the Constitution, an integral part of national law prevailing over any contrary statutory provision, according to which state courts, by way of exception from the principle of immunity, have international jurisdiction to adjudicate on actions or reparations (including pecuniary damage) caused by tort and committed against persons and their property in the territory of the *forum* by organs of the foreign state that were present in the same territory at the time of commission of the torts, even if these were *acta jure imperii*. […]

9 A dissenting opinion by five (5) members of the Court, i.e. Areios Pagos President St. Matthias and Justices A. Krommydas, G. Rigos, Th. Bakas and K. Vardavakis accepts the following: "The European Convention on State Immunity of 1972 is not a codification of previously developed customary law in its entirety. The exception from exterritoriality (state immunity) for offences committed in the territory of the *forum* state by a perpetrator who was present in that territory, as sovereign acts (*jure imperii*), neither corresponded then (in 1972) nor corresponds today to a generally acknowledged

(customary) rule of international law. Apart from the mere 8 states that have ratified the said Convention, no other international agreement provides for such exception. The fact that the abovementioned common law states subsequently introduced the exception, by way of a national law restricting the immunity of other states before their own courts, is irrelevant in so far as the formation of customary law is concerned. The above laws are not products of the international legal order but national (internal) law, through which state immunity is regulated solely as a jurisdictional issue between the national courts of the abovementioned common law states and other states exclusively and not reciprocally. It is for this reason that the abovementioned two US court judgments invoked by the majority do not attest to the existence of international custom, since they apply US national law and not an international law rule. Moreover, the draft articles that the United Nations International Law Commission (ILC) began drawing up in 1978 and submitted to the United Nations General Assembly in 1991 (Draft on Jurisdictional Immunities of States and their Property) remain, to this date, a simple draft, just like the respective Draft of the International Law Institute. Their drafting indicates lack of a customary rule exempting from state immunity offences committed in the territory of the *forum* state as *acta jure imperii*. The discord, to which the lack of further development in the abovementioned plans is due, barring them from obtaining binding force, affirms the fact that their provisions, particularly in relation to the exception in question before us, are not a generally acknowledged rule of international law, i.e. international custom. Furthermore, in the draft on state immunity between American States of the Interamerican Juridical Committee of 1983, the exception on offences committed in the territory of the *forum* is limited only to those committed "in the framework of commercial activities" and therefore does not extend to offences *jure imperii* (article 6 under e in conjunction with article 5 paragraph 1). Additionally, the case law of the House of Lords is equally distinctive, as it accepts an objection on the immunity of foreign states with the integral reasoning that it refers to offences committed *jure imperii* (House of Lords: Congresso del Partido, 1983; *Kuwait Airways Corporation v. Iraqi Airways Co*, 1995. Generally: Académie de droit international, *Recueil des Cours*, 1980 II, tome 167, Sir Ian Sinclair, p. 141 et seq.)".

This case—preceding the above-mentioned *Margellos* case—stirred international debate as to the territorial tort exception in customary international immunity law. The Greek claimants decided to have this judgment enforced in Italy, which, together with the previous Italian *Ferrini* case, eventually led Germany to start proceedings against Italy before the ICJ.[63] The case is also interesting from the perspective of customary law. The majority starts by carefully describing the requirements of state practice and *opinio juris* in paragraph 7. However, it stretches its interpretation of both norms to their utter limits; firstly, by stating that 'when states follow a certain practice, either positive or negative, in international relations, with the belief that the said practice constitutes a lawful action according to international law, they create custom'. The latter statement is an ingenious twist: *opinio juris* does not mean that the practice simply has to be considered lawful. For example, the fact that states allow tourists to visit their territory is definitely a lawful action under international law, but that does not make it custom. What matters is whether states consider themselves *obliged* to do so by a norm of international law.[64]

Secondly, the Court's interpretation of state practice is rather creative. While international law indeed attributes more relevance to the practice of states closely connected with the subject matter

63 *Germany v Prefecture of Voiotia*, Corte di Cassazione [Italian Court of Cassation], No 14199/2008, 29 May 2008, reported in (2009) 92 *Rivista di diritto internazionale* 594.

64 *North Sea Continental Shelf* (*Federal Republic of Germany/Netherlands, proceedings joined with Federal Republic of Germany/Denmark*) (Judgment) [1969] ICJ Rep 3, para 77.

of the norm, but that does not mean that a selection can be made of states that adhere to the newly formed rule, as if they were more closely connected to it. The same goes for the court's statement that the European Convention on State Immunity influenced 'important' foreign states, without explaining why these states are more important than others. Moreover, the court constantly frames the European Convention on State Immunity of 1972 as a 'codifying' convention without demonstrating that the drafters of the convention indeed were under the impression they were merely codifying customary law in respect of the territorial tort exception. The hazards of taking conventions as evidence of custom have been discussed elsewhere in this chapter.[65] The same goes for the *Areios Pagos*' approach to national court judgments. It merely cites two US cases, a state of which it had already been demonstrated that its legislation allowed for the territorial tort exception. Although there might definitely be an argument in favour of the territorial tort exception, the Supreme Court's decision is not to be applauded for its pseudo-inductive approach in determining custom.

'Abu Omar' case, General Prosecutor at the Court of Appeals of Milan v Adler and ors, Final appeal judgment, No 46340/2012, ILDC 1960 (IT 2012), 29th November 2012, Italy; Supreme Court of Cassation; 5th Criminal Section

This case followed in the aftermath of the infamous kidnapping by the CIA in Milan of Abu Omar, an Egyptian cleric who had been granted asylum in Italy. After the kidnapping, the CIA put him on a plane and transferred him to Egypt, where he was reportedly tortured. The tribunal of Milan convicted 22 CIA agents for participation in this operation—part of the US 'extraordinary renditions' programme—two of which were employed at the US Consulate in Milan. These two agents claimed in cassation that they enjoyed functional immunity under customary international law as the acts were committed in the performance of their official duty.

> 23.7 The so-called *functional immunity*
>
> But the applicants and especially Sabrina De Sousa have asserted that one must recognise that the regulations on Consular immunity are nothing more than the implementation of general customary law regulation, by which *par in parem non habet jurisdictionem*, such that the individual-body of a sovereign State could not be subject to the jurisdiction of another State for the actions carried out *iure imperii*; therefore the *CIA* agents that had allegedly in theory, participated in the kidnapping of Abu Omar, would be subjects on a *special mission* and their conduct, based on the above stated principles, would be immune from the jurisdiction of the *host* country; therefore involving functional immunity.
>
> The theory cannot be accepted, because as also found by authoritative case law, a customary law principle of this kind is not recognised in international law; there exists a principle of immunity from the civil jurisdiction of sovereign States, with this principle codified in numerous treaties. But immunity from criminal jurisdiction cannot derive from this immunity, which obviously does not refer to countries, but to single individuals.
>
> And in actual fact, never before quite a recent judgment handed down by the Supreme Court (Section 1, 19 June-24July 2008, Lozano, No. 31171), as it was authoritatively found, had Italian jurisprudence had any doubts regarding the country's freedom to exercise criminal jurisdiction in respect of foreign State entities, in the absence of specific regulations provided to protect them such as those referring to the immunity of Diplomatic and Consular officials (which according to international customary law are the equivalent to the highest offices of countries—heads of state, head of the government and Minister of Foreign Affairs; see International Court of Justice, 14 February 2002, Democratic Republic of the Congo c. Belgium), or to the

65 See text to n 42.

> divisions of jurisdiction between the sending and resident country for the military stationed in foreign countries.
>
> The problem therefore consists of checking whether there effectively exists a customary law regulation under international law that also guarantees criminal immunity to the individual-entity of a sovereign State, even when it does not involve Diplomatic and/or Consular officials and high appointments of State.
>
> On this point, jurisprudence is divided, because alongside those authorities that recognise the existence of a customary law regulation of this kind, there are others that recognise this only in respect of the activities authorised by the foreign country where these take place, while there are still others that maintain that the benefit of immunity is recognised according to specific regulations only to certain categories of entities in exercising the functions that are typical of their office.
>
> This Court believes that this last interpretation is the more correct one, because it takes into account the developments in international relations, which as already stated, the *Nato Convention and Vienna Convention on Consular immunity* are valid examples.
>
> Already the disparity shown above in jurisprudence makes one understand that it is very difficult to speak of a customary law regulation that can only be guessed at when a standard and extended practice can be discerned over time, which in the case in point, is not totally undisputed.
>
> Even a review of jurisprudence practices supports the conclusion that has been reached, because from a careful examination of the jurisprudence conducted by the *Lozano* judgment, only two previous precedents in fact emerge on criminal matters: the very distant McLeod case of 1847, regarding the destruction of the steamship *Caroline* that had been providing aid to Canadian rebels, and the more recent *Djibouti vs France* case, in which however the International Court of Justice in The Hague did not accept Djibouti's requests.
>
> In Italy, the criminal immunity of a foreign entity has been recognised only in cases governed by specific agreements of a constitutional nature, such as the Lateran Agreements; this is understood to relate to the well-known Marcinkus case (Section V, 17 July 1987, Marcinkus, CED no. 180349).
>
> So then in holding that a customary law regulation exists in this situation does not appear correct, because there is no consolidated jurisprudence, there is no recognition of continual and consistent official statements by countries, and there is no unequivocal interpretation of the jurisprudence.
>
> On the other hand, due to the uncertainty that characterises this sensitive aspect of international relations—and more so to make an example—countries normally govern their jurisdiction over military officials based on the *SOFA Status of Forces Agreement.*
>
> We can conclude then that the treatment applied on this issue presents such disparities that it does permit us to recognise a regulation with a standard extent; and in fact, the removal of foreign jurisdiction in respect of sending State entities is provided for in specific treaties, while where this is lacking, functional immunity is generally not accorded by the national jurisdictional bodies.

This is the first of three Italian judgments discussed in this chapter, which all have in common that they demonstrate a very progressive approach to customary international law.[66] The court's

66 Italian courts generally demonstrate an eagerness to engage in international legal issues, as can be seen from the large number of Italian cases discussed in this volume. See R van Alebeek, R Pavoni, 'Immunities of States and Their Officials' Chapter 4; A Reinisch, G Novak, 'International Organizations' Chapter 5; C Binder, C Brölmann, 'Law of the Treaties' Chapter 6; A Constantinides, '*Jus cogens*' Chapter 8 in this volume.

decision that the CIA agent could be prosecuted essentially hinges upon a rather astute distinction it created between immunity from civil law suits and immunity from penal prosecution. It states that whereas there is clear custom upholding the former immunity, this has to be independently analysed for the latter. In this analysis, the court is rather flexible in its treatment of custom. Instead of stating that such functional immunity had existed and seeking to prove that new custom had emerged, it started from scratch. It commenced with the premise that the existence of the criminal immunity rule had to be proven, thereby departing from previous case law such as the *Lozano* case, in which the Supreme Court, though ruling in favour of the 'emerging rule', found that there had existed such an immunity rule.[67]

Thus, in analysing whether a rule of criminal immunity existed, the court found that doctrine was divided on the issue—although it merely cited Italian doctrine—as a result of which the existence of the rule could *not* be presumed. This demonstrates once again the difficulties domestic courts encounter in respect of the level of evidence required for finding in respect of (varying) doctrinal opinions. The court's reasoning on relevant case law is rather flawed: whereas it argued that the fact that it could only find two cases that dealt with criminal immunities for state officials, this might very well be because it never came to a case or judgment as a result of the existence of criminal immunity for state officials. And whereas the court states that it there is no official state practice on the matter, the reality is that an abundance of such state practice exists.[68] The last paragraph is also a case in point for the above-mentioned problem of treaty and custom. Whereas many court judgments in this chapter rely—sometimes mistakenly—on the notion of treaties as codification of custom, the Italian Court of Cassation considers the conclusion of specific Status Of Forces Agreements (SOFAs) as evidence that no custom on criminal immunity existed yet. Although, as discussed above, this is a theoretically sound approach, the fact that SOFAs deal with a variety of issues, combined with the fact that international doctrine and international case law in fact do recognize this immunity, renders it rather doubtful in this context. However, the CIA abductions had been subject to fierce criticism in politics and society, and whereas the court of first instance, the appeal court, and the court of cassation all applied different argumentations to come to their judgments, their findings were still the same: the CIA behaviour was unacceptable and could therefore not go unpunished.[69]

Chile v Arancibia Clavel (Enrique Lautaro), Appeal Judgment, Case No 259, A 533 XXXVIII, ILDC 1082 (AR 2004), 24th August 2004, Argentina; Supreme Court [CSJ]

Mr Arancibia Clavel was convicted by the Argentinian court of first instance for being a member of the Direction of National Intelligence of Chile, in which function he participated in the persecution, torture and murder of opponents to the Pinochet regime residing in Chile. In cassation, the Supreme Court of Justice had to consider whether statutory limitations applied to war crimes and crimes against humanity. According to the Convention on the Non-Applicability of Statutory Limitations to War Crimes and Crimes against Humanity, signed and ratified by Argentina, this was not the case. However, this Convention had only become effective in the domestic legal order of Argentina after the period in which Mr Arancibia Clavel committed his crime. In light of the principle of non-retroactivity, the court therefore had to analyse whether there existed in 1974–1978 a principle of non-applicability of statutory limitations to war crimes in customary international law.

67 See below discussion of *Lozano v Italy* (n 8).

68 A Caligiuri, Analysis, *'Abu Omar' case, General Prosecutor at the Court of Appeals of Milan v Adler and ors*, ILDC 1960 (IT 2012) A7; ILC, 'Immunity of State officials from foreign criminal jurisdiction' (2008) UN Doc A/CN.4/596, para 154.

69 First instance judgment: *General Prosecutor at the Court of Appeals of Milan v Adler and ors*, Tribunal of Milan, Fourth Criminal Section, No 12428/09; ILDC 1492 (IT 2010), 4 November 2009; Appeal judgment; *General Prosecutor at the Court of Appeals of Milan v Adler and ors*, Court of Appeals of Milan, No 3688, (2011) 21 *Italian Yearbook of International Law* 351, 15 December 2010.

26) That the preamble of the Convention on the Imprescriptibility of War Crimes and Crimes Against Humanity states that one of the reasons for the establishment of the rule of imprescriptibility was the "serious concern among the global public" regarding the application to war crimes and crimes against humanity of the rules of national law concerning the prescription of ordinary crimes, "as it impedes the prosecution and punishment of the people responsible for these crimes". In addition, the text of article IV, according to which the State Parties "in compliance with their own respective constitutional procedures, undertake to adopt any legislative measures, or measures of another kind, necessary for the prescription of the criminal proceedings or of the punishment, established in law or by another means, not to apply to the crimes mentioned in articles I and II of this Convention and, in the event that it exists, for it to be abolished". These statements, although they are not categorical in terms of the retroactivity of the convention, indicate the need for an examination of the issue of differentiated prescription, depending on whether or not it is a crime against humanity.

27) That the aforementioned convention constitutes the culmination of a long process that began in the early 60s, when prescription threatened to become a source of impunity for the crimes carried out during the second world war, as it was close to being twenty years since those crimes were committed.

28) This Convention [The Convention on the Prevention and Punishment of the Crime of Genocide] only confirms imprescriptibility which involves the recognition of a rule that is already in existence (ius cogens) as part of customary international law. In this way, the prohibition on the retroactive application of criminal law is not violated, but rather a principle of customary international law is reaffirmed as being already in existence at the time of the commission of the acts.

29) That indeed, it is not actually a matter of the retroactive validity of the international conventional regulations, as long as, prior to the ratification of the 1968 convention, its status as a customary regulation of international law was ius cogens, whose key function "is to protect States from agreements concluded against some of the general values and interests of the international community of States as a whole, in order to ensure that those general rules of law whose inobservance may affect the very essence of the legal system are respected" (Judgements: 318:2148, vote of judges Nazareno and Moliné O'Connor). From this perspective, as well as being possible to state that international custom already considered crimes against humanity to be imprescriptible prior to the convention, this custom was also common material in international law prior to the incorporation of the convention into national law.

30) That the clauses of the modern treaties benefit from the assumption of their operability, "as they are, in the main, clear and complete for their direct application by the State parties and individuals without any need for direct implementation", and also, "the means of express acceptation through conventional adhesion or ratification is not exclusive for the purposes of determining the existence of the ius cogens. In the majority of cases, it is configured from the tacit acceptation of a specific practice" (Judgements: 318:2148, vote of Judge Bossert).

31) At the time of the acts, the Argentine State had already contributed to the formation of international custom in favour of the imprescriptibility of crimes against humanity (see. Decisions: 318:2148, opinion of Judge Bossert, recital 88 et seq.).

32) In accordance with the above, and as part of this evolution of international human rights law, it could be said that the Convention on the Non-Applicability of Statutory Limitations to War Crimes and Crimes Against Humanity merely represented the codification of principles already in force in our State as part of the international community.

> 33) As a result, the acts for which Arancibia Clavel was sentenced were already prohibited under international law at the time they were committed. Consequently, the Convention cannot be applied retroactively; rather, this was already the rule as a consequence of international custom in force since the 1960s, by which Argentina was bound.

This decision meant an important breakthrough for the possibility to prosecute crimes committed during the Pinochet and Videla regimes.[70] In its analysis of the customary nature of the imprescriptibility of crimes against humanity, the problem of 'entangled treaty and custom' again plays a role, and again, just as in *Distomo*, a convention with a fairly limited number of ratifications (only nine) is considered evidence of codification of pre-existing customary norms, partly on the ground that its preamble 'affirmed' the principle of imprescriptibility.[71]

This judgment's most remarkable feature in its analysis of customary international law is the importance it attaches to the fact that Argentina contributed to the development of this norm of customary international law. Strictly speaking, this should not be of any relevance from an international law perspective, apart from the limited notion of *persistent objector* in respect of which the national position does play a role.[72] However, for the Argentinian Supreme Court, this is a separate argument in order to come to its finding that a rule of customary international law existed. Apart from the fact that this is from an international law perspective incorrect reasoning, it begs the more fundamental question of whether these judgments with an overtly domestic content should be considered international law proper. Roberts has stated in this respect that we could and maybe should speak of 'hybrid international/national norms', and Tzanakopoulas and Tams refer to it as 'domesticated international law'.[73] It might be relevant from a domestic perspective whether Argentina had contributed to the emergence of a rule, from the perspective of international law it is not. Such decisions might be a point in case for those authors arguing that the relevance of 'domesticated international law' is necessarily limited.[74] On the other hand, such clear positions on the existence of a, from a human rights perspective, important customary international rule might very well influence the further development of such a rule.[75] It seems that at the current stage of research on this topic, both positions are defendable, as has been noted: 'it is a matter of perspective and assumption, not one of "right or wrong"'.[76]

2. The notion of 'emerging custom'

Lozano (Mario Luiz) v Italy, Appeal Judgment, Case No 31171/2008, ILDC 1085 (IT 2008), 24th July 2008, Italy; Supreme Court of Cassation; 1st Criminal Section

The US soldier Mr Lozano had opened fire at a car approaching a checkpoint in Iraq where Lozano was stationed on duty. He killed an Italian national and injured two others, leading the Italian public prosecution to initiate criminal proceedings against him. Mr Lozano's defence was based on the argument that the US as sending state had exclusive jurisdiction and, subsidiarily, that he enjoyed immunity as the incident occurred during the exercise of *acta jure imperii*, acting

70 F Raimondo, Analysis, *Chile v Arancibia Clavel*, ILDC 1082 (AR 2004) A8.

71 ibid para A3.

72 J I Charney, 'The Persistent Objector Rule and the Development of Customary International Law' (1985) 56 *British Yearbook of International Law* 1, 16.

73 Roberts (n 10) 60; Tzanakopoulos and Tams (n 5).

74 R O' Keefe, 'Domestic Courts as Agents of Development of the International Law of Jurisdiction' (2013) 26 *Leiden Journal of International Law* 541, 549.

75 Or lead to fragmentation: see A Kunzelmann, 'An Australian International Law: The Impact of Australian Courts on the Fragmentation of International law' (2008) 27 *Australian Yearbook of International Law* 225; J d'Aspremont, 'The Systemic Integration of International Law by Domestic Courts: Domestic Judges as Architects of the Consistency of the International Legal Order' in O Fauchald and A Nollkaemper (eds), *The Practice of International and National Courts and the (De-)fragmentation of International Law* (Hart Publishing 2012) 141.

76 Tzanakopoulos and Tams (n 5).

as organ of the United States. In cassation, the Italian Court of Cassation had to analyse whether a rule of customary international law existed assigning exclusive jurisdiction to a sending state, and whether a rule existed providing for immunity against charges of homicide in customary international law.

> 3. […] Thus, faced with the multinational, multifunctional organisational features of the peace mission authorised by the United Nations in Iraq described above, which are difficult to relate to the classic schemes of wartime occupation drawn up in the past, it seems totally inappropriate, in order to paralyse the applicability of a criterion of jurisdiction, such as the passive personality principle, which links the jurisdiction of the Italian State to the nationality of the victims of the criminal deed Articles 8 and 10 Criminal Code; Law Decree n. 3 of 19 January 2005, Article 13, converted into Law n. 37 of 18 March 2005), to refer, as the Court of Assisi [sic! The Corte d'Assise] in Rome did, to an alleged customary international principle (the so-called "law of the flag"), which is universally recognised and directly applicable by virtue of Article 10(1) of the Constitution, under which the State sending the military contingent abroad, in the event of wartime or other occupation, the transit and stationing of foreign troops within the territory of a State, is exclusively subjected to the civil and criminal jurisdiction for offences committed by its personnel within that territory.
>
> Even aside from the doubts expressed by the Permanent Court of International Justice in its classic decision of 1 September 1927 in the *S.S. Lotus* case, concerning actual evidence of the existence of "a rule of customary international law which established the exclusive jurisdiction of the State whose flag was flown on board a merchant ship on the high seas", since "the principle is not universally accepted", the All Criminal Sections of this Court had already observed, in the judgment dated 28 November 1959, in *Meitner* (in Giustizia penale, 1960, III, 481; to which can be added Cassation Section II, 30/1/1959, Public Prosecutor in Parker proceedings, ibid, 1959, III, 424 and Section II, 15/4/1959, *Knopich*, ibid, 1960, III, 22), that the development of international relations after the Second World War, with permanent bases consequently being created within the territory of other States, " … brought about a progressive restriction of the principle of the so-called jurisdiction of the flag ("ubi signa et jurisdictio", "la loi suit le drapeau"), under which the right to exercise jurisdiction over a State's own troops located on foreign territory and thus exempt from the jurisdiction of the occupied or host State was recognised to be that of the State of origin, or of the flag, "ne impediatur officium", in order to ensure that it had competence over its own units".
>
> 4 […] Yet, despite the jurisdictional trend in favour of the sending State revealed by international practice, we cannot yet find in existence a recognised customary international principle or ad hoc agreements or SOFAs which dictate special, explicit rules on the "horizontal" partition of jurisdiction between States which are party to the Coalition or the Multinational Force operating within the territory of another State. […]
>
> 5 […] Instead, this court believes that the basis for the exclusive pre-eminence of the "active" jurisdiction of the USA is to be found in the customary principle of international law which provides for "functional immunity" (*ratione materiae*), from the domestic jurisdiction of the foreign State, in the case in point from the jurisdiction of the Italian State, of the individual who, like the accused Lozano, a soldier in the United States military contingent which is part of the Multinational Force, operating in Iraq under the aegis of the United Nations Security Council but under the "effective control" of the command structure of the sending State (see, in this regard, European Court of Human Rights, 31 May 2007, in the cases of *Behrami and Saramati v. France*), acted iure imperii in exercising the functions of guard and control at a road block.

The principle whereby facts and acts carried out *iure imperii* by individuals acting as organs of another State in exercising duties and public functions attributed to them are removed from the civil or criminal jurisdiction of a foreign State constitutes a principle from a customary international source, which is universally accepted by prevalent doctrine and by both national and international case law, incorporated into the Italian legal order as a pre-existing general rule of international law (Constitutional Court, n. 48 of 1979), by virtue of the automatic incorporation procedure set down in Article 10(1) of the Constitution, and, as such, taking priority over the criteria for jurisdiction laid down under domestic rules also of a criminal character.

The existence of such a customary rule of international law and its effectiveness in our legal order cannot be called into question, since the principle of functional immunity, even in the "restricted" or "relative" notion, in other words restricted to purely those activities which, as opposed to "*iure gestionis*" activities, are the direct and immediate expression of the sovereign function of States, under which activities carried out in the course of military operations ontologically fall, has found broad and undisputed recognition, from as far back as the ancient, famous *McLeod* case of 29 December 1837, in both doctrine and jurisprudence, domestic and international.

In support of the theory of the persistent validity of the principle of immunity from civil jurisdiction for acts of this type it is not only the constant national jurisprudence on legitimacy that can be called upon, but also (Cassation Civil Section One, nos. 14199 and 14201 of 2008, n. 11255 of 2005, n. 5044 of 2004, n. 8157 of 2002 and n. 530 of 2000), judgments by other European Supreme Courts (17 July 2002 by the Greek Supreme Court, 26 June 2003 by the German Federal Court of Cassation, 16 December 2003 by the French Court of Cassation, 14 June 2006 by the English House of Lords, in the Jones case), the judgments by the European Court of Human Rights (21 November 2001, *Al Adsani v. United Kingdom*, 12 December 2002, *Kalogeropoulou v. Greece and Germany*, 14 December 2006, *Markovic v. Italy*), the decision of 29 October 1997 by the International Criminal Tribunal for the former Yugoslavia in *Blaškić* (subpoena) and, finally, the more recent judgment by the International Court of Justice of 4 June 2008 in *Djibouti v. France*, §§ 185, 194–196 (to which can be added, by the same Court, the judgment of 14 February 2002 in *Democratic Republic of Congo v. Belgium*, and the *Arrest Warrant* case of 11 April 2000 against the former Foreign Minister Yerodia, § 58).

6 [. . .] However, a more recent trend can be discerned, both in international law doctrine and in still a minority part of domestic jurisprudence, which is intended to dispute the wider application of the customary rule on the immunity of the foreign State, which relates to civil liability resulting from the unlawful activity carried out iure imperii by one of its organs, as well as to the immunity from criminal jurisdiction of the individual author, acting as organ of the State, of the same unlawful act, positing the existence of an exception to immunity where the acts have been carried out in violation of peremptory rules of international law, as in the field of the protection of fundamental human rights, if the individual is guilty of "international crimes", as a guarantee of the values underlying the international community as a whole.

Moreover, although having to note the prevalence of the opposing thesis, which, "as the current rule of public international law" (House of Lords, 14 June 2006, in the *Jones* case, and 24 March 1999, in the *Pinochet III* case; Irish Supreme Court, 15 December 1995, in the McElhinney case; Supreme Court of Ontario, 1 May 2002, in the *Bouzari* case; European Court of Human Rights, 21 November 2001, *Al*

> *Adsani v. United Kingdom*, 21 November 2001, *McElhinney v. Ireland*, 12 December 2002, *Kalogeropoulou v. Greece and Germany*, 14 December 2006, *Markovic v. Italy*; ICJ, 14 February 2002, *Arrest Warrant* case, § 58; International Criminal Tribunal for the former Yugoslavia, 10 December 1998, the *Furundzija* case), at most only allows derogations from the doctrine of State immunity when this is provided for by a treaty, such as for genocide or torture, it is worth stressing that in the more careful decisions of the European Court of Human Rights (21 November 2001, *Al Adsani* and 12 December 2002, *Kalogeropoulou*, citt.) it is, however, advised that this "does not preclude a development in customary international law in the future".
>
> It can, therefore, be held (agreeing, on this point, with the lucid arguments of the more recent judgments of the Court of Cassation, All Civil Sections: n. 5044 del 2004 and nos. 14199 and 14201 of 2008, citt.) that an international custom is "in the process of being formed" which, in consideration of the cogent, imperative nature of the norms of humanitarian international law ("peremptory norms of general international law", in the wording of Article 53 of the Vienna Convention on the Law of Treaties of 23 May 1969), which impose respect for fundamental human rights, and in consideration of the actual harmfulness of "universal values which transcend the interests of the individual State communities", is intended to limit the immunity from civil liability of a foreign State, whose organ, while exercising an iure imperii activity, such as in situations of war, has, however, made itself the author of acts of such severity so as to "undermine the very foundations of co-existence between peoples" (Constitutional Court of Hungary, n. 53 of 1993), which can therefore constitute "international crimes".

This decision is squarely rooted at the centre of the debate on emerging custom. As discussed in the introduction to this paragraph, the paradoxical, contradictory nature of the emergence of new custom becomes even more problematic when it has to be addressed by domestic courts, as it touches upon the question what their role is. On the one hand, one might argue that they are, or, from a normative perspective, should be mere enforcers of international law. On the other hand, they could be seen as agents in the developments of international law, which entitles them to perform a legitimate function in the development of international custom. Italian courts have, over the last decades, continuously positioned themselves as legitimate agents in the development of international custom.[77]

It is important to note that the Italian Court of Cassation is not ignorant as to international law, and it has a long history of applying it.[78] In this case, it cited twenty-one international documents, five European Court of Human Rights (ECtHR) decisions, three International Court of Justice (ICJ) decisions, one International Criminal Tribunal for Rwanda (ICTR) decision and eleven cases from foreign jurisdictions, while it heard expert evidence from three international legal experts during the course of the proceedings. The quintessential difference with the cases discussed under paragraph 2.A. is its use of the concept of emerging custom. Contrary to the same court's reasoning in *Adler*, it did not engage in astute reasoning to circumvent certain difficulties in proving custom, nor did it—as the Greek courts in *Distomo*—claim to have proven the clear existence of a well-established rule of custom by stretching the requirements of custom to its outer limits. The court accepts and even discusses the existence of an abundance of case law from the ICJ, the ECtHR, and national courts pointing at an opposite conclusion than the one it finally reached. By using the concept of emerging custom, it

---

77 See *Ferrini v Germany*, Appeal decision, Cass No 5044/04, ILDC 19 (IT 2004); *General Prosecutor at the Court of Appeals of Milan v Adler and ors*, Final appeal judgment, No 46340/2012, ILDC 1960 (IT 2012); *Italia Nostra v Ministry of Cultural Heritage and Libyan Arab Jamahiriya*, Appeal judgment, Case No 3154/2008; ILDC 1138 (IT 2008); *Germany v Mantelli and ors*, LDC 1037 (IT 2008); *De Guglielmi v Germany*, First Instance Judgment, 46 Rivista di diritto internazionale private e processuale 1006 (2010); ILDC 1784 (IT 2010).

78 Stirling-Zanda (n 17) 12–14.

condones the existence of evidence pointing at contrary conclusions, and allows for a less strict burden of proof in the establishment of this emerging custom. From a theoretical perspective, this evidently makes more sense than bluntly arguing that there is extensive state practice when there clearly is not.

Germany v Mantelli and ors, Preliminary Order on Jurisdiction, Case No 14201/2008, (2008) Riv Dir Int 896, ILDC 1037 (IT 2008), 29th May 2008, Italy; Supreme Court of Cassation

During the Second World War, hundreds of thousands of Italians were deported to Germany and forced to work for German enterprises. In 2004, Mantelli and 13 other Italian victims of the deportation and their descendants instituted civil proceedings for pecuniary compensation at the Tribunal of Turin against Germany and Daimler-Chrysler.

> 10 Having noted also that, in today's appeal, in further support of the theory of the permanent validity of the principle of immunity from the civil jurisdiction of the foreign state for "*iure imperii*" acts:
>
> — recent judgments by other Supreme European Courts are recalled. Such as, in particular, the decisions of 17 September 2002 by the Greek Supreme Court, 26 June 2003 by the German Federal Court of Cassation, 16 December 2003 by the French Court of Cassation and 14 June 2006 by the House of Lords (in the case of *Jones v. Ministry of Interior Al-Mamlaka Al-Arabiya AS Saudiya and others*);
>
> — a 2002 judgment by the Superior Court of Justice for Ontario is also reported (in the *Houshang Bouzari* case);
>
> — also recalled are judgments of the ECtHR (21 November 2001 *Al-Adsani v. the Government of the United Kingdom, Great Britain and Northern Ireland*; 12 December 2002 *Kalogeropoulou v. Greece and Germany*; 14 December 2006 *Markovic v. Italy*);
>
> — it is also made clear that the decisions by the United States courts cited in judgment n. 5044/04 exclusively concern, in so far as they are based on an express normative provision (1996 amendment to the Foreign Sovereign Immunities Act of 1976), those states which "sponsor" terrorism, whilst in numerous other United States decisions the traditional principle of immunity has been reaffirmed.
>
> 11 Considering, however, that, firstly, the provisions contained in the treaties of 1947 and 1961 recalled earlier are of no use in excluding the jurisdiction of the Italian judge, given that: as worded, they refer to substantive law relationships and not to jurisdiction (it being up to any judge in charge to decide on the merits concerning the demands subject of the waiver and, in the first place, concerning the date at which the right was acquired); if it were thought otherwise, it could not explain the commitment undertaken by the Republic of Italy to "hold the Federal Republic of Germany indemnified against any and all potential actions or other legal claims", nor the fact that the same F.R.G. had set up, with the participation of those German companies which had used the labour of the deportees, a Foundation ("Remembrance, Responsibility and the Future") to also ensure an indemnity for the victims;
>
> — that neither can the lack of jurisdiction of this Court be said to be implicated by the principles of international law concerning the immunity of States from civil jurisdiction;
>
> — that, from this point of view, the decisions of national and European Supreme Courts invoked by the petitioner demonstrate only that these Plenary Sessions, in judgment n. 5044 of 2004, had declared themselves already "aware" of: the

fact, that is, that, *at present,* no *certain and explicit* international custom exists whereby the principle of the immunity of the foreign State from civil jurisdiction for acts carried out *iure imperii* [. . .] can be held to be derogated in view of acts of such severity as to constitute "crimes against humanity";

— that, moreover, the above decisions [. . .] can definitely not even be deemed expressive of a custom *in the opposite direction;*

— that indeed—as, inter alia, emerges from the minority opinion attached to the ECtHR judgment of 21 November 2001, in the case of Al-Adsani v. United Kingdom [. . .] and from a significant *obiter* in the subsequent judgment, by the European Court, of 12 December 2002, in the case of Kalogeropoulou and others v. Greece and Germany—a principle restricting immunity of a State which has become the author of crimes against humanity can be presumed to be *"in the process of formation"*;

— that, in fact, the customary principle of immunity from the civil jurisdiction of a foreign State [. . .] therefore *co-exists,* in the international legal order, with the other parallel principle, of equal general scope, whereby *international crimes "threaten all of humanity and undermine the very bases for co-existence between peoples"* (thus, literally, for example, the Constitutional Court of Hungary 1993 n. 53; and, similarly, *inter alia*, the International Criminal Tribunal for the former Yugoslavia, 10 December 1998 and 14 January 2000; ECtHR 21 November 2001, A. V. United Kingdom). As such—that is as a crime against humanity—being in particular, again at international community level, considered *"the deportation and subjection of the deportees to forced labour"* [as can be seen unequivocally, *inter alia*, from the United Nations Charter signed in London on 8 August 1945, at Article 6 b); from Resolution 95 of 11 December 1946 by the UN's General Assembly, from the Principles of International Law adopted in June 1950 by the UN Commission, sub. VI, from Security Council Resolutions n. 827/93 and n. 955/94, which adopted, respectively, the Statute of the International Criminal Tribunal for the former Yugoslavia (Articles 2 and 5) and the Statute of the International Criminal Tribunal for Rwanda (Article 3); and, finally, from the Statute establishing the International Criminal Court, which was signed in Rome on 17 July 1998 by as much as 139 States (120 of them ratifying) and which came into force on 1 July 2002 (Articles 7–8)];

— that the undeniable conflict between the principles—which are both automatically incorporated into our legal order due to the (production) norm at Article 10 of the Constitution—at the time these are, as in the case in point, simultaneously and antagonistically applicable, cannot be resolved otherwise—that this Plenary Session remain persuaded—*on the systematic level,* giving priority to higher-ranking norms (according to the criterion already posited by the minority judges in the above-cited ECHR 21 November 2001);

— that, in fact, as already emphasised in this Court's judgment n. 5044 of 2004, respect for the inviolable rights of the person has acquired, also in the international legal order, the nature of a fundamental principle . . .

— that, in now confirming the conclusions already reached in the above precedent, this Court is *aware* of thus contributing to the *emergence* of a conformative rule of the immunity of the foreign State, which is, however, considered to already *be inherent in* the international legal system.

— that, moreover, as also stressed by the international legal doctrine most relevant to the matter at hand, it would be "incongruous" to say the least for civil jurisdiction to be asserted in respect of a foreign State in the case of violations of contractual obligations ascribable to it, and by contrast to be excluded in the case of much more serious violations, such as those which constitute *crimes* even *against humanity*, which also mark the *breaking point* of the tolerable exercise of sovereignty;

— that all of this confirms that the Federal Republic of Germany does not have the right to be recognised, in this dispute, as immune from the civil jurisdiction of the Italian Judge—which is therefore to be declared—also by virtue of the fact that the unlawful conduct partly occurred in Italy;

— that all questions relating to the existence of the right invoked in this case and to the admissibility of the present application remain naturally unprejudiced (Article 386 Code of Civil Procedure);

FOR THESE REASONS

12 The Court, in its Plenary Session, having joined the appeals, declares that the Italian Judge has jurisdiction in respect of the claim for compensation submitted against the F.R.G. and a lack of such jurisdiction in respect of the parallel demand for indemnity against the Daimlerchrysler company. Expenses offset.

In the (in)famous *Ferrini* case, the Italian Court of Cassation had held that Germany could in certain cases not be said to enjoy immunity for atrocities committed during the second world war. Although *Ferrini* was decided in 2004 and had been met with a lot of criticism, the Italian court in this case from 2008 confirmed the main finding, having omitted some of the more controversial parts of the *Ferrini* reasoning.[79] Two issues related to custom deserve to be discussed here. First, the court of cassation, just as it did previously in *Adler* and *Lozano* discussed national case law from other jurisdictions. Above it was mentioned that the phenomenon by which domestic courts refer to each other in deciding international law issues might highlight an interesting transnational judicial dialogue between domestic courts as agents of the international order. It could also lead to a strengthening of the importance and effects of domestic courts pronouncing upon international law. However, this does not mean that they should always be applauded.

IV. Conclusion

Van Alebeek remarks that many domestic courts in the context of immunity law 'limit the discussion of foreign precedent to a handful of examples at most, and transnational judicial dialogue on immunity questions generally does not serve the purpose of discovering the rule, but that of corroborating the preferred outcome with foreign precedent'.[80] The relevance of referring to other domestic court judgments in the manner described by Van Alebeek is not just a matter of concern for academics. Lord Bingham of the House of Lords dismissed invocation of the *Ferrini* case in the case of *Jones v Saudi Arabia* with the catchy phrase: 'one swallow does not make a rule of international law'.[81] However, the difference between *Jones* and *Kiobel* on the one hand and *Ferrini* and *Mantelli* on the other are more fundamental than this little taunt by the House of Lords reveals. It relates to the very essence of the domestic court's position in the international legal order. In *Mantelli*, the Italian court stated that it was 'aware of the fact that it thus contributed to the emergence of a confirmative rule of foreign state immunity'. The

79 A Chechi and R Pavoni, Analysis, *Germany v Mantelli and ors*, ILDC 1037 (IT 2008) A4.

80 R van Alebeek, 'Domestic Courts as Agent of Development of International Immunity Rules' (2013) 26 *Leiden Journal of International Law* 559, 563–44.

81 *Jones v Saudi Arabia* [2006] UKHL 26, Opinion by Lord Bingham of Cornhill, para 22.

Supreme Court claims its, in its own opinion, legitimate role of an agent in the development of international custom, as it considers it necessary that these rules are developed.[82]

At the other end of the spectrum, we find Lord Hoffmann's unequivocal condemnation of such a stance: '[i]t is not for a national court to 'develop' international law by unilaterally adopting a version of that law which, however desirable, forward-looking and reflective of values it may be, is simply not accepted by other states'.[83] It is this transnational judicial conversation which demonstrates aptly that, despite their limited role in the theory of the source of international law, the legitimate position of domestic courts in the development of international custom remains more than academic theorization, but subject to debate among the very courts which, either as international law enforcers or international law creators, are no longer to be ignored in the study of international law.[84] As one of the judgments discussed in this chapter rhetorically wonders: 'Why do those questions, which are justiciable in international courts, cease to be justiciable in national tribunals?'[85] It seems, in a twist to Lauterpacht's vision of the future of international law, that domestic courts will prove capable of indeed becoming the guardians of *customary* international law.[86]

82 Similar statements on the necessity to arrive at the 'better' position can be found in, for example, *Office of the Prosecutor v Priebke*, P/457/XXXI, ILDC 1599 (AR 1995), stating that it acted in the interest of the global community; *Polyukhovich v Commonwealth (War Crimes Act Case)* [1991] HCA 32, (1991) 172 CLR 501, para 66; Lord Sankey, *In re Piracy Jure Gentium* [1934] AC 586, 588–89.

83 *Jones v Saudi Arabia* [2006] UKHL 26, Opinion by Lord Hoffmann, para 63.

84 Tzanakopoulos and Tams (n 5) 535.

85 *Public Committee against Torture v Israel* (n 14) para 45.

86 H Lauterpacht, 'Decisions of Municipal Courts as a Source of International Law' (1929) 10 *British Yearbook of International Law* 65, 93.

8

Jus Cogens

ARISTOTELES CONSTANTINIDES

I. Introductory Note

Jus cogens runs counter to state voluntarism and the consensual character of international law and has always been controversial.[1] The concept has come under attack on various institutional, structural, pragmatic, and political grounds.[2] The definition of a peremptory norm of general international law (*jus cogens*) in Article 53 of the Vienna Convention on the Law of Treaties (VCLT) as 'a norm accepted and recognized by the international community of States as a whole as a norm from which no derogation is permitted and which can be modified only by a subsequent norm of general international law having the same character' has added to the controversy by exposing the difficulties in identifying the substance of the concept and a procedure for its determination. Indeed, the full content of *jus cogens* was left by the International Law Commission (ILC) 'to be worked out in State practice and in the jurisprudence of *international* tribunals'.[3] Article 66 of the VCLT provided for judicial determination of disputes concerning *jus cogens* by the International Court of Justice (ICJ) or arbitration. The ICJ, however, avoided any explicit reference to *jus cogens* until 2006.[4]

Other international courts and tribunals were more willing to endorse the concept and elaborate on its content, scope, and effects.[5] They played a crucial role in detaching *jus cogens* from the law of treaties, following a path first taken by domestic courts. Meanwhile, scholarly interest has been unremitting and shows an overwhelming support for the concept.

The lively academic debate reveals various approaches on the place and role of *jus cogens* in the international legal order. Apart from the avowed positivists still denying the concept and its role in international law, scholars range from those viewing *jus cogens* as centred on the effect of non-derogability,[6] most of them linking it with public policy,[7] to those who consider *jus*

1 It has been observed that '*jus cogens* was perhaps the most strenuously debated item at the Vienna Conference'. See R Jennings, 'Treaties' in M Bedjaoui (ed), *International Law: Achievements and Prospects* (UNESCO/Martinus Nijhoff 1991) 135, 154.

2 See, *inter alia*, P Weil, 'Towards Relative Normativity in International Law?' (1983) 77 *American Journal of International Law* 413; S Sur, 'La créativité du droit international' (2012) 363 *Recueil des Cours de l'Academie de Droit International* 197 ff; M Glennon, 'De l'absurdité du droit impératif (*jus cogens*)' (2006) 110 *Revue Générale de Droit International Public* 529.

3 ILC, 'Yearbook of the International Law Commission' (1966) Vol II, UN Doc A/CN.4/SER.A/1966/Add 1, 248 (emphasis added).

4 *Armed Activities on the Territory of the Congo (New Application: 2002)* (*Democratic Republic of the Congo v Rwanda*) (Jurisdiction and Admissibility, Judgment) [2006] ICJ Rep 31, para 64. It did, however, allude to the concept in the *Nicaragua* case (referring to the prohibition of the use of force as being 'not only a principle of customary international law but also a fundamental or cardinal principle of such law'), *Military and Paramilitary Activities in and against Nicaragua* (*Nicaragua v United States of America*) (Merits, Judgment) [1986] ICJ Rep 100, para 190 and in the *Nuclear Weapons* Advisory Opinion (referring to 'intransgressible principles of humanitarian law'), *Legality of the Threat or Use of Nuclear Weapons* (Advisory Opinion) [1996] ICJ Rep 266, para 79.

5 See especially the ICTY decision in *Prosecutor v Furundžija* (Judgment) [1999] 38 *International Legal Materials* 317. See also the numerous references to *jus cogens* by the Inter-American Court of Human Rights as summarized in G Neuman, 'Import, Export, and Regional Consent in the Inter-American Court of Human Rights' (2008) 19 *European Journal of International Law* 101, 117–18.

6 R Kolb, *Peremptory International Law—Jus Cogens: A General Inventory* (Bloomsbury 2015) 40.

7 See, *inter alia*, L Hannikainen, *Peremptory Norms (Jus Cogens) in International Law: Historical Development, Criteria, Present Status* (Finnish Lawyers' Pub Co 1988) 1–4.

cogens as substantive rules of higher hierarchical status and as constitutional norms protecting the fundamental values of the international community.[8] An important consequence of the latter constitutionalist approach is the perception of *jus cogens* as the ultimate limit to any state and international legislative, executive, or judicial acts, well beyond its non-derogability effect.[9] Under this approach, any legislative, executive, or judicial act contrary to *jus cogens* should be without legal effect as a logical consequence and by proper operation of *jus cogens* and its inherent qualities. The opposite approach stresses the need to establish that the content, scope, and effects of a *jus cogens* rule have acquired customary status through state practice and *opinio juris*.

These two approaches pervade most of the relevant international and domestic case law on *jus cogens*. A leading example of the controversy in international case law is the European Court of Human Rights (ECtHR) judgment in *Al-Adsani*, where a majority of nine judges denied 'that there is yet acceptance in international law of the proposition that States are not entitled to immunity in respect of civil claims for damages for alleged torture committed outside the forum State',[10] whereas a strong dissenting opinion argued that '[d]ue to the interplay of the *jus cogens* rule on prohibition of torture and the rules on State immunity, the procedural bar of State immunity is *automatically* lifted', and that the distinction made between civil and criminal proceedings was not consonant 'with the *very essence of the operation* of the *jus cogens* rules'.[11]

The possible effects of the *jus cogens* character of the prohibition against torture were spelled out by the International Criminal Tribunal for the former Yugoslavia (ICTY) in *Furundžija* as including setting aside amnesty laws; civil suits for damages in foreign courts;[12] the exercise of universal jurisdiction;[13] and excluding torture from a statute of limitations.[14] *Al-Adsani* and *Furundžija* feature heavily in many domestic decisions discussed in this chapter.

In *Jurisdictional Immunities of the State*, the ICJ stressed that it must 'inquire whether customary international law has developed to the point where a State is not entitled to immunity in the case of serious violations of human rights law or the law of armed conflict'[15] and engaged in detailed examination of state practice and *opinio juris*, including numerous decisions of domestic courts (many of which are discussed in the present chapter and in the chapter on immunities).[16] It concluded that 'under customary international law as it presently stands, a State is not deprived of immunity by reason of the fact that it is accused of serious violations of international human rights law or the international law of armed conflict'.[17] Significantly, the ICJ also stated that there is nothing inherent in the concept of *jus cogens* that would require the modification or would displace the application of the customary rules on jurisdictional immunities.

Against this background, this chapter presents some of the most representative cases in which domestic courts have made pronouncements on the concept of *jus cogens* (section II); referred,

8 See, *inter alia*, A Cançado Trindade, 'International Law for Humankind: Towards a New *Jus Gentium*' (2005) 316 *Recueil des Cours de l'Academie de Droit International* 336 ff; E de Wet, 'The International Constitutional Order' (2006) 55 *International and Comparative Law Quarterly* 51; A Orakhelashvili, *Peremptory Norms in International Law* (OUP 2008) 7 ff.

9 In the words of the ICTY in *Furundžija*: '[*jus cogens*] serves to internationally de-legitimise any legislative, administrative or judicial act authorising torture' (para 155).

10 *Al-Adsani v United Kingdom* [2001] ECHR 752, para 61.

11 ECtHR, *Al-Adsani v United Kingdom*, App No 35763/97 (21 November 2001), Joint Dissenting Opinion of Judges Rozakis and Caflisch joined by Judges Wildhaber, Costa, Cabral Barreto, and Vajic, para 3 (emphasis added). Judge Loucaides and Judge Ferrari-Bravo issued separate dissenting opinions.

12 *Prosecutor v Furundžija* (n 5) para 155.

13 ibid, para 156.

14 ibid, para 157.

15 *Jurisdictional Immunities of the State (Germany v Italy: Greece intervening)* (Merits, Judgment) [2012] ICJ Rep 41, para 83.

16 See R van Albeek and R Pavoni, 'Immunities' Chapter 4 in this volume.

17 *Jurisdictional Immunities of the State* (n 15) 44, para 91.

often in *obiter dictum*, to specific rules as (not) being of *jus cogens* nature and, less frequently, to the process of identifying them (section III); and passed judgment on the effects of *jus cogens* (section IV).

II. Concept

Siderman de Blake and ors v Argentina and ors, Appeal judgment, Case No 85-5773, 965 F2d 699 (9th Cir 1992), ILDC 2171 (US 1992), 60 USLW 2771 (1992), (1992) 103 ILR 454, 22nd May 1992, United States; Court of Appeals (9th Circuit) [9th Cir]

The plaintiffs brought a suit in the United States (US) against the government of Argentina and various Argentinian military officials, alleging, *inter alia*, acts of torture and argued that Argentina was not covered by the Foreign Sovereign Immunities Act (FSIA) with respect to violations of *jus cogens* rules, such as the prohibition of torture.

> 40 *Jus cogens* is related to customary international law […]. Courts seeking to determine whether a norm of customary international law has attained the status of *jus cogens* look to the same sources, but must also determine whether the international community recognizes the norm as one "from which no derogation is permitted." *Committee of U.S. Citizens Living in Nicaragua v. Reagan*, 859 F.2d 929, 940 (D.C.Cir. 1988) [hereinafter "CUSCLIN"] (quoting Vienna Convention, art. 53). In CUSCLIN, the only reported federal decision to give extended treatment to *jus cogens*, the court described *jus cogens* as an elite subset of the norms recognized as customary international law. *Id.*
>
> 41 While *jus cogens* and customary international law are related, they differ in one important respect. Customary international law, like international law defined by treaties and other international agreements, rests on the consent of states. […] International agreements and customary international law create norms known as *jus dispositivum*, the category of international law that "consists of norms derived from the consent of states" and that is founded "on the self-interest of the participating states." Klein, *A Theory for the Application of the Customary International Law of Human Rights by Domestic Courts*, 13 Yale J. Int'l L. 332, 351 (1988) [hereinafter "*Human Rights in Domestic Courts*"]. *Jus dispositivum* binds only "those states consenting to be governed by it." *Id.*
>
> 42 In contrast, *jus cogens* "embraces customary laws considered binding on all nations," *id.* at 350-51, and "is derived from values taken to be fundamental by the international community, rather than from the fortuitous or self-interested choices of nations," *id.* at 351. Whereas customary international law derives solely from the consent of states, the fundamental and universal norms constituting *jus cogens* transcend such consent, as exemplified by the theories underlying the judgments of the Nuremberg tribunals following World War II. [citation omitted] The legitimacy of the Nuremberg prosecutions rested not on the consent of the Axis Powers and individual defendants, but on the nature of the acts they committed: acts that the laws of all civilized nations define as criminal. […] The universal and fundamental rights of human beings identified by Nuremberg – rights against genocide, enslavement, and other inhumane acts […] – are the direct ancestors of the universal and fundamental norms recognized as *jus cogens*. In the words of the International Court of Justice, these norms, which include "principles and rules concerning the basic rights of the human person," are the concern of all states; "they are obligations *erga omnes*." *The Barcelona Traction, Light & Power Co. (Belgium v. Spain)*, 1970 I.C.J. 3, 32.
>
> 43 Because *jus cogens* norms do not depend solely on the consent of states for their binding force, they "enjoy the highest status within international law." CUSCLIN,

859 F.2d at 940. For example, a treaty that contravenes *jus cogens* is considered under international law to be void *ab initio*. See Vienna Convention, art. 53; Restatement 102 Comment k. Indeed, the supremacy of *jus cogens* extends over all rules of international law; norms that have attained the status of *jus cogens* "prevail over and invalidate international agreements and other rules of international law in conflict with them." Restatement 102 Comment k. A *jus cogens* norm is subject to modification or derogation only by a subsequent *jus cogens* norm. *Id.*

This was the first decision by a US Court of Appeals to elaborate on the concept of *jus cogens* (there have been earlier decisions by District Courts, most notably the *Committee of US Citizens Living in Nicaragua v Reagan*, cited therein). It referred extensively to the third Restatement of the Foreign Relations Law of the United States and scholarly writings and has been relied upon in most US cases that followed.[18] Relying on scholars, the court's discussion of *jus cogens* reflected the influence of natural law thinking, referring to the 'nature of the acts' and to universal norms of a highest status transcending state consent.

Bouzari (Houshang) and ors, Amnesty International (Canadian Section) (intervening) and ors (intervening) v Iran, Appeal decision, 71 OR (3d) 675 (Ont CA), 2004 CanLII 871 (ON CA), (2004) 243 DLR (4th) 406, 2004 Carswell Ont 2681, 122 CRR (2d) 26, (2004) OJ No 2800, ILDC 175 (CA 2004), 30th June 2004, Canada; Ontario; Court of Appeal [ONCA][19]

[86] A peremptory norm of customary international law or rule of *jus cogens* is a higher form of customary law. It is one accepted and recognized by the international community of states as a norm from which no derogation is permitted. Not only does the rule of *jus cogens* override other rules of customary international law in conflict with it, but, by the *Vienna Convention on the Law of Treaties*, a treaty obligation which conflicts with a rule of *jus cogens* is of no force or effect in international law.

In this decision, the court accepted that the overriding effect of *jus cogens* extended beyond the Vienna Convention to cover also rules of customary law (in the instant case, state immunity). There is overwhelming support for this proposition.[20] The reference to 'higher' form of customary law is more controversial but accords with the prevalent scholarly approach.

Riveros v Office of the Public Prosecutor, Recourse of cassation and unconstitutionality, M 2333 XLII, ILDC 1084 (AR 2007), 13th July 2007, Argentina; Supreme Court [CSJN]

This case concerned the pardon granted in 1989 to Argentinian military officials for crimes committed during Argentina's 'dirty war'.

15) There is a system of rights protection which is mandatory regardless of the express consent of the nations, which is now known in this evolutionary process as *jus cogens*. It is the highest source of international law, which is imposed on states and which prohibits the commission of crimes against humanity, including in times of war. It may not be derogated by contrary treaties and must be applied by domestic courts of states irrespective of its eventual express acceptance.

18 See, eg, *Kane v Winn*, District Court judgment, 319 F Supp 2d 162 (D Mass 2004), ILDC 694 (US 2004), 27 May 2004, District Court for the District of Massachusetts [D Mass]; *Khouzam v Hogan and ors*, Habeas Corpus Petition, 529 F Supp 2d 543 (MD Pa 2008), ILDC 933 (US 2008), 10 January 2008, District Court for the Middle District of Pennsylvania [MD Pa]; *Estate of Anastacio Hernandez-Rojas and ors v United States and 50 US government officials*, Decision on motion to dismiss, 2013 WL 5353822 (SD Cal 2013), ILDC 2149 (US 2013), 24 September 2013, United States; California; District Court for the Southern District of California [SD Cal].

19 For the facts of this case see section IV.2(a) below.

20 See, eg, Orakhelashvili (n 8) 340; K Zemanek, 'The Metamorphosis of Jus Cogens: From an Institution of Treaty Law to the Bedrock of the International Legal Order?' in E Cannizaro (ed), *The Law of Treaties Beyond the Vienna Convention* (OUP 2011) 381, 394. *Contra* Kolb (n 6) 64–72.

One of the controversies surrounding *jus cogens* is whether, strictly speaking, it is a source of international law, as it is considered to be according to the constitutionalist approach.[21] In the same vein, the court's reference to the 'highest source' hints to a hierarchy in international law with *jus cogens* at the top. Doing away with express acceptance of states goes to the same direction. This line of argument was crucial for the court's ruling in the case at hand that the presidential pardons for crimes committed during Argentina's dictatorship were invalid as contrary to *jus cogens*.

In his dissenting opinion in that case, Judge Fayt rightly emphasized that 'not every customary norm of general international law has the peremptory character which is by definition required for a *jus cogens* norm'. There is the so-called 'double consent' requirement, ie, acceptance of the rule not only as customary but also as peremptory; a rule of *jus cogens* is first and foremost a rule of customary law, but not every rule of customary law is a rule of *jus cogens*. In *Stutts and ors v De Dietrich Group and ors*, the court got it right:

This Court has ruled that plaintiffs fail to establish that prohibition on the development, manufacture, and stockpiling of chemical weapons is a rule of customary international law. *A fortiori*, plaintiffs are unable to establish that the prohibition they advance rises to the level of a *jus cogens* norm of international law.[22]

Re Víctor Raúl Pinto, Re, Pinto (Víctor Raúl) v Relatives of Tomás Rojas, Decision on Annulment, Case No 3125-04, ILDC 1093 (CL 2007), 13th March 2007, Chile; Supreme Court

The pertinent issue in this case was whether Chile's 1978 Amnesty Law for crimes committed during Pinochet's dictatorship was in conformity with international law.

> THIRTY-THREE: [A]t the time of the commission of the criminal acts under review, there was a compulsory system in place for the protection of rights in Chile, irrespective of the express consent of the other nations concerned, which system is known as a set of peremptory rules of international law, or *ius cogens*. Such standards are imposed on States and prohibit crimes against humanity, including those committed in the course of international and non-international conflicts. This peremptory international law implies the rejection *in limine* by civilized nations of injustices that offend human conscience and which constitute crimes against humanity.

This statement is interesting in that it implicitly held that the concept of *jus cogens* existed in international (customary) law and was applicable in 1973 (which was the time of the commission of the crimes), that is, before the entry into force of the VCLT in 1980 and before Chile became a party (Chile signed the Convention in 1969 and ratified it in 1981).

Association France-Palestine Solidarité (AFPS) and Palestine Liberation Organization (PLO) v Société Alstom transport SA and ors, Appeal judgment, No 11/05331, ILDC 2036 (FR 2013), 22nd March 2013, France; Île-de-France; Versailles; Administrative Court of Appeal

This French judgment stands out for casting doubt to the notion of *jus cogens* and denying it any recognition in the domestic law of France. The applicant organizations sued the respondent French companies for having set up a company with Israeli corporations to construct and operate a transport service in Jerusalem, arguing that the concession contract was null and void because its 'cause' breached several provisions of international humanitarian law.[23]

21 See, eg, *Al-Adsani* (n 11), Joint Dissenting Opinion of Judges Rozakis and Caflisch joined by Judges Wildhaber, Costa, Cabral Barreto, and Vajić, para 1 ('the basic characteristic of a *jus cogens* rule is that, *as a source of law* in the now vertical international legal system, it overrides any other rule which does not have the same status') (emphasis added).

22 District court decision, No 03-CV-4058 (EDNY 2006), ILDC 874 (US 2006), 30 June 2006, United States; New York; District Court for the Eastern District of New York [EDNY] para 35, fn 18.

23 A Glazewski, Facts, *Association France-Palestine Solidarité (AFPS) and Palestine Liberation Organization (PLO) v Société Alstom transport SA and ors*, ILDC 2036 (FR 2013) F3.

The claims were rejected both at first instance and on appeal for lack of direct effect of the international humanitarian law provisions at stake, which could not therefore be invoked against the respondent companies; such lack of direct effect could not be overcome by either customary law, *jus cogens*, or the international public order. The Court of Appeal held that *jus cogens* was not recognized by domestic law, even in the limited sense of the VCLT; France has not signed the Convention, considering that the vagueness of *jus cogens*, its content and formation has not diminished since 1969, whereas its abusive invocation can risk disregarding the *pacta sunt servanda* norm.[24] The court also held that the applicants did not demonstrate the existence of a superior international public order qualified as *jus cogens*, which could be imposed on non-state actors such as the French companies in the domestic legal order of France.[25] This decision reflects the strong French scepticism against *jus cogens*, which is widely shared among some of the country's eminent scholars.[26]

III. Content and Identification

This section presents an illustration of decisions in which domestic courts held that certain rules of international law were (not) of a *jus cogens* nature. Most of the decisions recognizing a rule as *jus cogens* have done so in *dicta* without much analysis and explanation, and involve rules that are widely considered as *jus cogens* (III.1). On the other hand, most of the decisions denying a rule the status of *jus cogens* are more elaborate on the process of identifying *jus cogens* and are therefore quoted at some length (III.2).

1. Rules identified as *jus cogens*

(a) International crimes

Although the origins of *jus cogens* are rather unclear,[27] it is widely considered that the norms and crimes identified at Nuremberg are the direct ancestors of the fundamental norms recognized as *jus cogens*.[28] Thus, the rules prohibiting genocide, crimes against humanity, and war crimes are generally accepted as *jus cogens*. Domestic courts have taken this for granted in relevant cases without any further explanation or analysis, as the following illustrative excerpts show.[29]

Germany v Margellos and 18 other natural and legal persons (intervening), Petition for Cassation, Case No 6/2002, (2003) 1 AED 11, (2003) 56 RHDI 199, ILDC 87 (GR 2002), 17th September 2002, Greece; Special Supreme Court

> 14. […] War crimes […] are explicitly prohibited by rules of international law of *jus cogens* character, which hierarchically are above any other rule of international law. As is generally acknowledged, the provisions contained in the above-cited Hague Regulations attached to the Hague Convention IV of 1907 have become customary rules of international law of *jus cogens* character, which are generally accepted. (para. 14, dissenting opinion) […]

24 *Association France-Palestine Solidarité (AFPS) and Palestine Liberation Organization (PLO) v Société Alstom transport SA and ors*, Appeal judgment, No 11/05331, ILDC 2036 (FR 2013), 22 March 2013, France; Île-de-France; Versailles; Administrative Court of Appeal, para 125.

25 ibid, paras 131, 132.

26 See Weil (n 2); Sur (n 2).

27 L Henkin, 'International Law: Politics, Values and Functions' (1989) 216 *Recueil des Cours de l'Academie de Droit International* 9, 60.

28 See, eg, E de Wet, 'The Prohibition of Torture as an International Norm of *Jus Cogens* and Its Implications for National and Customary Law' (2006) 15 *European Journal of International Law* 97, 111.

29 The facts of these cases are stated in section IV.2(a) below.

Federal Prosecutor assigned to the Special Office of the Attorney General for Federal Crimes Committed by Public Servants against Persons Related to Past Social and Political Movements and Federal Prosecutor assigned to the Second District Federal Court for Criminal Proceedings in the Federal District v Echeverria (Luis) and Moya-Palencia (Mario), Appeal Decision, Appeal No 1/2004-PS, Appeal No 8/2004-PS, ILDC 76 (MX 2005), 15th June 2005, Mexico; Supreme Court of Justice of the Nation

> 555. The prohibition of genocide forms part of the general principles of International Law, as a norm of *jus cogens*, and, therefore, exists as binding Law since before the facts of the case.

Riveros v Office of the Public Prosecutor, Recourse of cassation and unconstitutionality, M 2333 XLII, ILDC 1084 (AR 2007), 13th July 2007, Argentina; Supreme Court [CSJN]

> 15) *Jus cogens* prohibits the commission of crimes against humanity, including in times of war.

(b) Prohibition of torture

Most domestic courts have concluded that the prohibition of torture is a rule of *jus cogens* without much analysis, based on the overwhelming consensus in the international community and among scholars.[30] The following decisions are a little more elaborate.

Siderman de Blake and ors v Argentina and ors, Appeal judgment, Case No 85-5773, 965 F2d 699 (9th Cir 1992), ILDC 2171 (US 1992), 60 USLW 2771 (1992), (1992) 103 ILR 454, 22nd May 1992, United States; Court of Appeals (9th Circuit) [9th Cir]

> 46 [W]hile not all customary international law carries with it the force of a *jus cogens* norm, the prohibition against official torture has attained that status. In [*Committee of U.S. Citizens Living in Nicaragua v. Reagan*], the D.C. Circuit announced that torture is one of a handful of acts that constitute violations of *jus cogens*. In *Filartiga*, though the court was not explicitly considering *jus cogens*, Judge Kaufman's survey of the universal condemnation of torture provides much support for the view that torture violates *jus cogens*. In Judge Kaufman's words, "[a]mong the rights universally proclaimed by all nations, as we have noted, is the right to be free of physical torture." 630 F.2d at 890. Supporting this case law is the Restatement, which recognizes the prohibition against official torture as one of only a few *jus cogens* norms. Restatement 702 Comment n (also identifying *jus cogens* norms prohibiting genocide, slavery, murder or causing disappearance of individuals, prolonged arbitrary detention, and systematic racial discrimination). Finally, there is widespread agreement among scholars that the prohibition against official torture has achieved the status of a *jus cogens* norm. [...]
>
> 47 Given this extraordinary consensus, we conclude that the right to be free from official torture is fundamental and universal, a right deserving of the highest status under international law, a norm of *jus cogens*. The crack of the whip, the clamp of the thumb screw, the crush of the iron maiden, and, in these more efficient modern times, the shock of the electric cattle prod are forms of torture that the international order will not tolerate. To subject a person to such horrors is to commit one of the most egregious violations of the personal security and dignity of a human being. That states engage in

---

30 Eg, *A (FC) and ors (FC) v Secretary of State for the Home Department, A and ors (FC) v Secretary of State for the Home Department (joined appeals)*, Appeal judgment, [2005] UKHL 71, ILDC 363 (UK 2005), [2006] 2 AC 221, [2005] 3 WLR 1249; [2006] 1 All ER 575, 8 December 2005 (para 33, Lord Bingham), referring to *R, ex parte Pinochet v Bartle and ors*, Appeal, [1999] UKHL 17, [2000] 1 AC 147, [1999] 2 All ER 97, [1999] 2 WLR 827, (1999) 38(3) ILM 581, (2002) 119 ILR 135, ILDC 1736 (UK 1999), 24 March 1999, House of Lords (HL).

official torture cannot be doubted, but all states believe it is wrong, all that engage in torture deny it, and no state claims a sovereign right to torture its own citizens. [...] Under international law, any state that engages in official torture violates *jus cogens*.

Suresh, United Nations High Commissioner for Refugees (intervening) and ors (intervening) v Canada (Minister of Citizenship and Immigration) and Attorney-General of Canada, Decision, Docket No 27790, 2002 SCC 1, [2002] 1 SCR 3, (2002) 37 Admin LR (3d) 159, (2002) 90 CRR (2d) 1, (2002) SCJ No 3, 281 NR 1, (2002) 208 DLR (4th) 1, (2002) 18 Imm LR (3d) 1, 2002 Carswell Nat 8, 2002 Carswell Nat 7 (SCC), ILDC 186 (CA 2002), 11th January 2002, Canada; Supreme Court [SCC]

Suresh, a Sri Lankan of Tamil descent, applied for judicial review of the decision ordering his deportation to Sri Lanka on the ground that he was a danger to the security of Canada. Suresh argued that he would face a serious risk of torture if deported to Sri Lanka.

62 In the case at bar, there are three compelling indicia that the prohibition of torture is a peremptory norm. First, there is the great number of multilateral instruments that explicitly prohibit torture [...].

63 Second, Amnesty International submitted that no state has ever legalized torture or admitted to its deliberate practice and that governments accused of practising torture regularly deny their involvement, placing responsibility on individual state agents or groups outside the government's control. Therefore, it argues that the weight of these domestic practices is further evidence of a universal acceptance of the prohibition on torture. Counsel for the respondents, while not conceding this point, did not refer this Court to any evidence of state practice to contradict this submission. However, it is noted in most academic writings that most, if not all states have officially prohibited the use of torture as part of their administrative practices [...].

64 Last, a number of international authorities state that the prohibition on torture is an established peremptory norm: [...] Others do not explicitly set it out as a peremptory norm; however, they do generally accept that the protection of human rights or humanitarian rights is a peremptory norm [...].

65 [...] [T]he fact that such a principle is included in numerous multilateral instruments, that it does not form part of any known domestic administrative practice, and that it is considered by many academics to be an emerging, if not established peremptory norm, suggests that it cannot be easily derogated from.

(c) Other (non-derogable) human rights

Apart from the prohibition of torture, other human rights are also widely considered as *jus cogens*. A strong indication for such status is their non-derogability, that is, their non-suspension in times of emergency. However, there are non-derogable rights (eg, the right to life) that are not absolute and can be subject to limitations.[31] Thus, non-derogable rights should not be automatically identified with *jus cogens*. Again, most decisions of domestic courts do not elaborate on their conclusions.

Sarei and ors v Rio Tinto PLC and Rio Tinto Limited, Judgment on Motion to Dismiss, ILDC 604 (US 2002), 221 F.Supp.2d 1116 (C.D. Cal. 2002), 9th July 2002, United States; California; District Court for the Central District of California [CD Cal]

This was a class action filed in the US by inhabitants of Papua New Guinea's island of Bougainville, under the US Alien Tort Statute (ATS). The plaintiffs asserted that Rio Tinto's

31 On limitations and derogations in international human rights law see, eg, F Mégret, 'Nature of Obligations' in D Moeckli, S Shah, and S Sivakumaran (eds), *International Human Rights Law* (2nd edn, OUP 2014) 110–14.

mining operation in Bougainville had destroyed the island's environment, harmed the health of its people and that these and other harmful and illegal acts were, at least in part, motivated by racial discrimination. The court held that racial discrimination could form the basis of a claim under the ATS but eventually dismissed all claims on grounds of the act of state and political question doctrines.

> 77 [...] [I]t is well-settled that racial discrimination is a violation of the law of nations. Many courts, indeed, have held that practicing racial discrimination violates a *jus cogens* norm. [...] See [...] *Siderman de Blake, supra*, 965 F.2d at 717 [...]; [...] *Hirsh v. State of Israel*, 962 F.Supp. 377 (S.D.N.Y. 1997) at 381 ("A foreign state violates *jus cogens* when it participates in such blatant violations of fundamental human rights as 'genocide, slavery, murder, torture, prolonged arbitrary detention, and racial discrimination,'" quoting *Committee of U.S. Citizens in Nicaragua v. Reagan*, 859 F.2d 929, 941 (D.C. Cir. 1988)); *Denegri v. Republic of Chile*, Civ. A. No. 86-3085, 1992 WL 91914, *4 (D.D.C. Apr. 6, 1992) ("*jus cogens* comprises the fundamental human rights law that prohibits genocide, slavery, murder, torture, prolonged arbitrary detention, and racial discrimination"); [...] Clearly, a claim under the ATS may be based on the violation of a *jus cogens* norm such as racial discrimination. [...]

RM v Attorney General, JK (on the application of RM) v Attorney General, Application brought by way of original summons to high court, Civil Case 1351, ILDC 699 (KE 2006), 1st December 2006, Kenya; Nairobi; High Court

> 43 A consistent pattern of gross violations of internationally recognized human rights if practiced encouraged or conducted by the government of a state as official policy—constitutes a violation in the category of *jus cogens*.

This *dictum* was stated by the court when discussing (and rightly dismissing) the main argument in that case, which was that the Kenyan Children Act discriminating against children born out of wedlock by not placing any parental responsibility for them on the child's father was a violation of *jus cogens*. The latter argument also shows how the concept of *jus cogens* can be subject to abuse in an effort by litigants to make a strong(er) case.

Germany v Mantelli and ors, Preliminary Order on Jurisdiction, Case No 14201/2008, (2008) Riv Dir Int 896, ILDC 1037 (IT 2008), 29th May 2008, Italy; Supreme Court of Cassation

> H4 [...] Deportation and forced labour were included among the serious violations of fundamental rights and of *ius cogens* [...]

Adhikari and ors v Daoud & Partners and ors, Decision on motion to dismiss, ILDC 1562 (US 2009), 697 F.Supp. 2d 674 (S.D. Tex. 2009), 3rd November 2009, United States; Texas; District Court for the Southern District of Texas [SD Tex]

> 29 [...] It is apparent from the findings of both judicial and academic authorities [...] that human trafficking and forced labor, whether committed by states or private individuals, have been recognized as violations of jus cogens norms, and therefore fall within the jurisdictional grant of the ATS.

(d) Other norms

On the constitutionality of provisions of Russian domestic law establishing the obligation to implement judgments of the European Court of Human Rights, Group of Deputies of the State Duma of the Russian Federation, Constitutional proceedings, Judgment No 21-P, ILDC 2455 (RU 2015), 14th July 2015, Russian Federation; Constitutional Court

A main issue in this case was whether implementation of ECtHR judgments was mandatory in the Russian legal order if such implementation conflicted with the constitution. The court's judgment included a *dictum* that the principle of equality, respect of rights, and state sovereignty, as well as non-interference with the domestic affairs of a state was a *jus cogens* norm.[32] This was apparently stated to corroborate the court's main conclusion that Russia had the right to reject implementation of a judgment by the ECtHR that goes beyond the ordinary meaning of the European Convention on Human Rights (ECHR) and could lead to violation of its object and purpose, such judgment being outside the obligations undertaken upon ratification.[33] This outlier ruling is interesting, as it is reminiscent (or a resurgence) of the Soviet conception of *jus cogens* as a shield against coercive outside interference in the domestic affairs of states that would oblige them to undertake inconvenient international legal obligations.[34]

2. Rules denied the status of *jus cogens*

(a) Derogable human rights (right to property, right to fair trial, right to remedy)

Nada (Youssef) v State Secretariat for Economic Affairs and Federal Department of Economic Affairs, Administrative appeal judgment, Case No 1A 45/2007, BGE 133 II 450, ILDC 461 (CH 2007), 14th November 2007, Switzerland; Federal Supreme Court [BGer]

The applicant's assets in Switzerland were frozen in implementation of UN Security Council sanctions against a list of individuals associated with Al-Qaida and Osama bin Laden. He complained that the refusal of the Swiss authorities to remove his name from the list infringed his rights to property, fair trial, and effective remedy. The court held that the obligation to apply Security Council resolutions was only limited by *jus cogens* and thus examined whether the rights invoked fell under *jus cogens*.

> 7.3 […] In general, *jus cogens* includes elementary human rights such as the right to life, the protection from torture and humiliating treatment, the freedom from slavery and human trafficking, the prohibition on collective punishment, the principle of personal responsibility in criminal prosecution, and the principle of non-refoulement […]. Going one step further, it is sometimes argued that protection from arbitrary imprisonment and certain related procedural guarantees also belong to *jus cogens* […].
>
> By contrast, other fundamental rights, even if they are of great importance for Switzerland, do not necessarily belong to peremptory international law […]. This holds true in particular for the fundamental rights of right to property and to commercial freedom of action invoked by the petitioner […]. But even the procedural guarantees asserted by the petitioner (right a to legal hearing and a fair trial pursuant to Article 6(1) of the ECHR and Article 14(1) of the International Covenant on Economic, Social, and Cultural Rights; right to an effective appeal pursuant to Article 13 of the ECHR and Article 2(3) of the International Covenant on Civil and Political Rights) do not belong to the inalienable core of the international conventions on human rights (see Article 15(2) of the ECHR and Article 4(2) of the International Covenant on Civil and Political Rights) and thus do not belong categorically to jus cogens […].

The court's ruling on which human rights are (not) considered as *jus cogens* largely relied on the writings of scholars. The main reason for denying the status of *jus cogens* to the right to fair trial

32 *On the constitutionality of provisions of Russian domestic law establishing the obligation to implement judgments of the European Court of Human Rights, Group of Deputies of the State Duma of the Russian Federation*, Constitutional proceedings, Judgment No 21-P, ILDC 2455 (RU 2015), 14 July 2015, Russian Federation; Constitutional Court, H9.

33 ibid.

34 See P Stephan, 'The Political Economy of *Jus Cogens*' (2011) 44 *Vanderbilt Journal of Transnational Law* 1073, 1085–86.

and the right to effective remedy was that they were not among the non-derogable rights in both the ECHR and the International Covenant on Civil and Political Rights (ICCPR). This position is, however, not uncontroversial. The Human Rights Committee has opined that 'the category of peremptory norms extends beyond the list of non-derogable provisions as given in article 4, paragraph 2' [of the ICCPR] and includes the 'fundamental principles of fair trial, including the presumption of innocence'.[35]

Nada was followed by *A v Federal Department of Economic Affairs*,[36] with similar factual and legal background, involving the confiscation of the applicant company's assets in Switzerland, in implementation of UN Security Council sanctions against a list of individuals and entities associated with the former Iraqi government of Saddam Hussein. The company's request to the UN Security Council's Sanctions Committee to have its name removed from the UN list was unsuccessful. The company appealed against the confiscation decision, arguing that the listing procedure under Security Council Resolution 1483 was in breach of fundamental guarantees of procedure and the right to a remedy, which are recognized in international law. Following *Nada*, the court held that the obligation to apply Security Council resolutions was only limited by *jus cogens* and found that neither the fundamental guarantees of procedure nor the right to remedy belonged to *jus cogens*. As in *Nada*, the court's conclusion was largely based on the fact that the human rights in question were not among the non-derogable rights in the ECHR and the ICCPR.[37]

East German Expropriation Case, Mr von der M, Joint constitutional complaint, 2 BvR 955/00, BVerfGE 112, 1, NVwZ 2005, 560, ILDC 66 (DE 2004), 26th October 2004, Germany; Constitutional Court [BVerfG][38]

> 116 At the date that was decisive for creating standards, the date of the expropriations [1945-1949], there was no general legal conviction that the protection of property of the state's own citizens was part of universally applicable public international law in the sense of ius cogens.
>
> 117 Nor can it be established that at a later date a rule of peremptory public international law arose that excludes ex nunc the possibility of treating the existing situation as lawful (ius cogens superveniens). [. . .]
>
> 118 [. . .] Universal public international law has not contained and does not contain a guarantee of the property of a state's own citizens as a protective standard for human rights. It is true that in the year 1948, in Article 17.2 of the Universal Declaration of Human Rights, the General Assembly of the United Nations [. . .] laid down that "(n)o-one" may be "arbitrarily deprived of his or her property", but the Universal Declaration is not binding public international law. By reason of differences of opinion between West and East, property was also not mentioned in the International Covenant on Civil and Political Rights of 19 December 1966 [. . .]. In view of this hesitation on the part of the international community to enter into a binding agreement, there can be no question of a customary norm of the legal protection of property as a human right applying worldwide, that is, in favour not only of the citizens of foreign states, but also of a state's own citizens. The significance of property for the dignity and the freedom of humanity—as part of the minimum protection of human rights—was recognised only later; the process of discussion on the level of public international law has not been completed even today [. . .].

35 UNCHR, 'General Comment No. 29: Article 4 (Derogations during a State of Emergency)' (2001) UN Doc CCPR/C/21/Rev.1/Add 11, para 11.

36 Administrative first instance judgment, No 2A 783/2006; ILDC 1200 (CH 2008) 23 January 2008, Federal Supreme Court.

37 ibid, paras 8.3–8.4.

38 For the facts of the case see section IV.1 below.

This decision seemed to conflate the identification of a universally binding customary rule and a *jus cogens* rule. Be that as it may, it was rightly held that the right to property was not *jus cogens* because it was not a customary rule in the first place (at least not in the past decades, on which the court focused its analysis).

(b) Death penalty

Buell (Robert A.) v Mitchell (Betty), Appellate Decision, App No 99-4271, 274 F 3d 337 (6th Cir 2001), ILDC 300 (US 2001), 30th January 2001, United States; Court of Appeals (6th Circuit) [6th Cir]

The applicant was sentenced to death and argued on appeal that the Ohio death penalty violated, *inter alia*, the customary and *jus cogens* norm of international law proscribing capital punishment.

> 118. There is no indication that the countries that have abolished the death penalty have done so out of a sense of legal obligation, rather than for moral, political, or other reasons. Moreover, since the abolition of the death penalty is not a customary norm of international law, it cannot have risen to the level that the international community as a whole recognizes it as *jus cogens*, or a norm from which no derogation is permitted. Therefore, we cannot conclude that the abolition of the death penalty is a customary norm of international law or that it has risen to the higher status of *jus cogens*.

Although the large majority of states worldwide have either officially abolished the death penalty or refrain from implementing it—partly as a result of a powerful campaign by the human rights movement—there are still a few dozens of 'retentionist' states which are unwilling to follow this trend. It is thus questionable whether a customary rule has developed to the effect of an unconditional abolition of death penalty. By holding that the abolition of the death penalty was not a customary norm of international law, the court properly gave effect to the 'double consent' requirement and rightly found that, *a fortiori*, it could not be a rule of *jus cogens*.

(c) Non-refoulement

C v Director of Immigration, First instance, HCAL 132/2006, [2008] 2 HKC 165, [2008] HKCFI 109, ILDC 1119 (HK 2008), 18th February 2008, Hong Kong; High Court; High Court as Court of First Instance [HKCFI]

This case concerned the removal of six refugee claimants from Hong Kong. The applicants argued, *inter alia*, that non-refoulement had become a rule of *jus cogens*.

> 117. On behalf of the applicants, considerable reliance is placed on a pronouncement of the UNHCR Executive Committee made in 1996 that the "principle of *non-refoulment* is not subject to derogation": that it has therefore acquired the status of a norm of *jus cogens*. [. . .]
>
> 118. I note, however, that the conclusion was made by the Executive Committee (consisting then of only 51 members) against the backdrop of "widespread violations of the principle of *non-refoulement*".
>
> 119. In an article published in 2001 [. . .], Jean Allain writes that the rule against refoulment has acquired the status of a peremptory norm. [. . .]
>
> 121. In approaching the question, the author speaks of the need to consider the current practice of states but, on my reading, his underlying rationale appears to be why it is so important that the principle of *non-refoulment* should have its enhanced status; the desired end result therefore colouring present reality. [. . .]
>
> 123. What is telling, in my view, is that the opinion—*The Scope and Content of the Principle of Non-Refoulment*—completed in 2001 by Sir Elihu Lauterpacht and

> Daniel Bethlehem makes no assertion that the rule against *refoulment* has attained the status of a peremptory norm. Nor, to my understanding, did the subsequent 'round table' meeting of some 35 international law experts. […]
>
> 125. If the doctrinal origins of *jus cogens* are uncertain it appears to me that its substantive content is equally open to debate. […]
>
> 130. [T]he 'Cartagena Declaration on Refugees' adopted in 1984 by the Colloquium on the International Protection of Refugees in Central America, Mexico and Panama declared that the principle of *non-refoulment* was a rule of *jus cogens*. […]
>
> 131. However, as Goodwin-Gill and McAdam, the authors of *The Refugee In International Law*, Oxford University Press, 3rd Ed., page 38, say of this declaration:
>
> > "[…][The Cartagena Declaration] emerged not from within a regional organization, but out of an *ad hoc* group of experts and representatives from governments in Central America […]." […]
>
> 133. In recognition of its humanitarian ideal, it may be said that the principle of *non-refoulment* should today be incapable of derogation or repudiation. But that, to my understanding, is not the basis upon which a norm of *jus cogens* is formed. One must look to the practice of states generally and why it is that they adhere to the practice.
>
> 134. Torture has been recognised as being so abhorrent that *refoulment* is not subject to exception. Even a person who was a principal torturer himself, while he may be brought to justice by other means, may not be *refouled* if it places him at risk of the very torture he once practised. Refugee law, however, is subject to exceptions. Issues, for example, going to the mass influx of refugees pose profound problems.
>
> 135. While, on balance, I am drawn to the conclusion that the rule against *refoulment* is a rule of customary international law, I think it goes too far to hold—at this time—that the rule has acquired the status of a peremptory norm. Put another way, the ideal does not accord with present reality and, if the ideal is to prevail, it may bring the norm itself into disrepute.

This is one of the few decisions elaborating at length on whether a customary rule amounted to *jus cogens*. The court was eager to identify the practice of states to that effect and was unwilling to rely on the views expressed by scholars. From a positivist viewpoint, such a scrutiny is to be welcomed if *jus cogens* were not to degenerate to arbitrary statements leading to contradictory judgments and undesirable fragmentation. In a similar vein, a few years earlier the Supreme Court of New Zealand held that '[w]hile there is overwhelming support for the proposition that the prohibition on torture itself is *ius cogens*, there is no support in the state practice, judicial decisions or commentaries to which we were referred for the proposition that the prohibition on refoulement to torture has that status'.[39]

IV. Effects

1. Invalidity of treaties

Claims of invalidity of treaties due to conflict with *jus cogens* are scarce in state practice.[40] The following two cases are examples of such claims put forward in domestic judicial proceedings,

39 *Attorney-General v Zaoui and Inspector-General of Intelligence and Security and Human Rights Commission (intervening)*, Appeal to Supreme Court, [2005] NZSC 38, (2006) 1 NZLR 289, (2005) 7 HRNZ 860, ILDC 81 (NZ 2005), 21 June 2005, New Zealand, para 51 (concerning the deportation of an Algerian recognized refugee from New Zealand on national security grounds).

40 For an overview see Orakhelashvili (n 8) 153–64.

although only the first one involves an inter-state dispute. Interestingly, they both involve claims of conflict with peremptory norms that have emerged after the conclusion of the treaties concerned (*jus cogens superveniens*).

Goran U, Foreign judgment execution procedure, No 1768/1998, Aranzadi RJ (Referencia de Jurisprudencia) 2001/3968, ILDC 130 (ES 2001), 20th February 2001, Spain; Supreme Court

This case concerned Mr Goran U's request before the Supreme Court of Spain for execution of a judgment issued by the Supreme Court of Gibraltar. According to the Spanish court, foreign judgments could only be recognized if issued by the courts of a state with sovereignty and jurisdiction over the territory. Sovereignty over Gibraltar is disputed between the United Kingdom (UK) and Spain. Spain asserts that the 1713 Treaty of Utrecht by which Gibraltar was ceded to the UK did not transfer title over the entire territory. The argument was also put forward that the 1713 Treaty might conflict with *jus cogens superveniens*.

> 5. [...] Principles particular to intertemporal law in the area of international law, and in particular in the area of the law of treaties, obscure the validity of British rights derived from the Treaty of Utrecht, inasmuch as they allow their laws to be interpreted in light of current events; even the provisions of the Vienna Convention of 1969 obscure this validity. Although Article 64 of the Convention provides for the termination of opposing treaties in existence with a new imperative norm of international law, and Article 71(2) dispenses with compliance with the Treaty and maintains rights, obligations and legal situations to the extent that their continued presence is not in itself opposed to a new imperative norm of international law, the granting of sovereignty as a result of a use of force now lacks legitimacy and would only be respected where there is no violation of the principle of territorial integrity that constitutes the aim of the process and the right to decolonisation.
>
> 6. [...] [I]f the granting of territory in 1713 [...] included this transfer of territorial sovereignty, its current legitimacy is in question according to the law of treaties, current decolonisation law and, finally, the fact that the current statute of Gibraltar is derived from the use of force and that the effects and consequences of this statute contradict the principles of the territorial integrity and self-determination that constitute the aim of the decolonisation process.

This was the fourth argument put forward by the court to deny the request for execution of the Gibraltar judgment. The court questioned the continued validity of the 1713 Treaty under the *jus cogens* provisions of the VCLT, but did so in such a laconic way that evoked more questions than it tried to answer. This interesting argument required much more elaboration to make it tenable in light of the principles of intertemporal law, which were only mentioned *en passant*.

East German Expropriation Case, Mr von der M, Joint constitutional complaint, 2 BvR 955/00, BVerfGE 112, 1, NVwZ 2005, 560, ILDC 66 (DE 2004), 26th October 2004, Germany; Constitutional Court [BVerfG]

The complainants were heirs of former landowners whose property had been expropriated by the Soviets during the Land Reform in post-War East Germany. They argued, *inter alia*, that the exclusion of the restitution of expropriated land under the 1990 Germany Unification Treaty was contrary to peremptory norms of public international law.

> 98 The concept of peremptory rules of public international law has recently been confirmed and further developed in the articles of the International Law Commission (ILC) on the law of state responsibility [...]. This field of law is a central area of general international law that governs the (secondary) legal consequences of a state's violation of its (primary) obligations under international law. Article 40.2 of the ILC Articles on the responsibility of states contains the definition of a serious violation of ius cogens and obliges the community of states to

cooperate in order to terminate the violation by use of the means of public international law. In addition, a duty is imposed on the states not to recognise a situation created in violation of ius cogens.

99 In the cases to be decided, there is no violation of this duty of respect by German state bodies. The expropriations were the responsibility of the Soviet occupying power (a). On German unification, the Federal Republic of Germany attained the sovereign competence to decide on the reversal of the measures on the basis of sovereign acts by occupying powers. Public international law does not require the Federal Republic of Germany to make restitution. Nor did it have a duty to attach the legal consequence of voidness to the expropriations. The Federal Republic of Germany had merely a duty of cooperation with regard to the consequences (b). It fulfilled this duty by bringing about German unification peacefully by way of negotiations. Only by doing this did it achieve the de facto possibility to correct the situation, which was determined by history. The Federal Republic of Germany was allowed to come to the conclusion that dealing cooperatively with German unification would be incompatible with treating the expropriations as void (c). [. . .]

110 The Federal Republic of Germany is subject to no duty derived from public international law to make restitution to the persons affected by the expropriations. In connection with the Two-Plus-Four Talks, it impliedly and admissibly waived the right to any claims it had to damages under public international law (1). There are no rules of mandatory public international law preventing this (2). [. . .]

115 (2) In the case of a violation of peremptory norms of public international law by the Soviet occupying power, the Federal Republic of Germany was not obliged even under general public international law to attach the legal consequence of voidness to the expropriations.

116. At the date that was decisive for creating standards, the date of the expropriations, there was no general legal conviction that the protection of property of the state's own citizens was part of universally applicable public international law in the sense of ius cogens.

117 Nor can it be established that at a later date a rule of peremptory public international law arose that excludes ex nunc the possibility of treating the existing situation as lawful (ius cogens superveniens). The institution of newly developed peremptory international law overtaking older law has been laid down in positive contract law. Under Article 53 of the Vienna Convention on the Law of Treaties, treaties that conflict with a peremptory norm of general international law are void. Under Article 64 of the Convention, a treaty entered into earlier that to date has been unobjectionable becomes void if it is in conflict with a peremptory norm of general international law that comes into existence later.

118 Accordingly, what is important is not so much the obligations to which the occupying power was subject in the period from 1945 to 1949 as the obligations to which the Federal Republic of Germany was subject when it entered into the Unification Treaty. [. . .]

119 Modern public international law is characterised by a continuous increase in the severity of the legal consequences which it attaches to the violation of particular central norms; the states are increasingly subjected to a duty to terminate and remove grave violations of peremptory international law. [. . .]

121 The ILC Articles contain a Chapter III, dealing separately with a duty to act on the part of third-party states (Articles 40 et seq.), but this treats only serious violations of peremptory international law. A breach is serious if it is gross or systematic in

> nature (Article 40.2). The states must cooperate in order to bring an end to any such breach (Article 41.1). In addition, no state may recognise as lawful a situation created by such a breach or render aid or assistance in maintaining it (Article 41.2).
>
> 122 However, these provisions do not give rise to the legal consequence that the expropriations on the basis of sovereign acts by occupying powers—assuming they violated mandatory international law—are to be treated as void. Instead, the legal consequence of voidness is laid down only to the extent that duties under treaties are directed precisely to performance that is prohibited by a peremptory norm. Apart from this, however, and all the more so if a factually established situation and differing political interests are involved, the states have merely a duty to cooperate with regard to the consequences. Behind this duty of cooperation is the consideration that it is urgently necessary to create a situation that, while safeguarding the interests on both sides, does actually mitigate the breach of peremptory law as far as possible.

The crucial pronouncement in this decision for present purposes was that there was no violation of *jus cogens* either when the expropriations were carried out by the Soviets in 1945–1949 or when they were not reversed under the 1990 Germany Reunification Treaty. This would suffice to dispense with the argument of the claimants. Nonetheless, the court went further and held that, even if the expropriations had violated peremptory rules of international law, the 1990 Treaty provision not reversing them would still not be void. The reasons given were rather obscure and seemed to conflate the effect of invalidity of a treaty due to a conflict with *jus cogens* under Articles 53 and 64 of the VCLT with the consequences of a serious breach of a *jus cogens* norm under the ILC Articles on State Responsibility. Under the latter, there is both a duty of states to cooperate with a view to terminating the consequences of such breach, which the court held that Germany had satisfied, and a duty not to recognize a situation resulting from a *jus cogens* violation, which the court did not adequately address.

2. Immunities

This section should be read in conjunction with the chapter on immunities in this volume.[41]

(a) Immunities of states

Germany v Prefecture of Voiotia (Representing 118 persons from Distomo village), Petition on cassation against default, no 11/2000, (2000) 49 Nomiko Vima 212, ILDC 287 (GR 2000), 4th May 2000, Greece; Supreme Court

The case involved a compensation claim against Germany brought by 118 claimants, represented by the Prefecture of Voiotia in Greece, for indemnity for atrocities committed by the German occupation forces in the village of Distomo in June 1944. The court of first instance had held that a state could not invoke immunity when the act attributed to it was in breach of *jus cogens*. It also held that a state committing such a breach has indirectly waived immunity. The Supreme Civil and Criminal Court (*Areios Pagos*) followed a different reasoning (the so-called tort exception[42]) but in effect upheld the essence of the decision of the court of first instance by ruling that:

> [the Court of First Instance's] different reasoning, *i.e.* that the plaintiff could not invoke its right of immunity as it had resigned therefrom indirectly, since the acts for which the defendants complain in their original action were committed by its organs in breach of rules of peremptory international law (article 46 of the Regulations

41 R van Alebeek, R Pavoni, 'Immunities of States and their Officials' Chapter 4 in this volume.

42 ibid, where this case is also discussed.

annexed to the 1907 Hague IV Convention) and they were not acts *iure imperii*, ruled in effect correctly in relation to the issue of its international jurisdiction. (para. 12)

In a joint dissenting opinion, five judges disagreed:

[A]n exception to the immunity of the German State may not be founded on the violation of international *jus cogens* rules, since there is no customary rule according to which such a breach would engender a tacit waiver of sovereign immunity. (para. 13)

The relevance of this decision on the effect of *jus cogens* is rather limited, since the court did not dwell on the issue at any length but in effect upheld (in fact, it did not overrule) the decision of the court of first instance, which had articulated the *jus cogens* exception argument. The dissenting opinion was also laconic in rejecting that argument. In any case, this decision was among the first by a highest court to deal with the broader issue of the exceptions from state immunity and it has been quoted in numerous other decisions.

Germany v Margellos and 18 other natural and legal persons (intervening), Petition for Cassation, Case No 6/2002, (2003) 1 AED 11, (2003) 56 RHDI 199, ILDC 87 (GR 2002), 17th September 2002, Greece; Special Supreme Court

The facts of this case were similar to those of the previous case, concerning compensation claims against Germany for atrocities committed in 1944.

14. […] [I]t results from all evidence, without exception, that the foreign State continues to enjoy the immunity when it is prosecuted for acts which took place on the territory of the forum State and in which its armed forces were involved in any manner, without the distinction of whether these acts were in violation of *jus cogens* or whether these armed forces were involved in a conflict with other armed forces. Indeed the relative provisions of Article 31 of the European Convention [on State Immunity] are formulated exhaustively and are not subject to this distinction. […]

As the rule of non-applicability of immunity in the case of civil liability of States in armed conflicts is not laid down in any text or evidence, the Court is not permitted […] to formulate such a rule or to infer its existence without invoking specific evidence from international practice, or to derive through interpretation on its own the principle of the obligation of States to compensate violations of its law during war on land.

As in the previous case, the court did not discuss the *jus cogens* exception to state immunity at any length; in effect, it refused to infer the existence of such an exception 'without invoking specific evidence from international practice' or to derive such exception through its own interpretation.

Ferrini v Germany, Appeal decision, Cass no 5044/04, ILDC 19 (IT 2004), 11th March 2004, Italy; Supreme Court of Cassation

Mr Ferrini brought a civil claim against Germany for compensation for the material and moral injuries he had suffered during his capture, deportation, and forced labour by German armed forces in 1944–1945. Germany argued that his suit was precluded by state immunity.

9. It is commonly stated that international crimes "threaten humanity as a whole and undermine the very foundations of international coexistence". […] Indeed, these are crimes that consist of the particularly intense or systematic violation of basic human rights, […] which are protected by non-derogable norms that stand at the apex of the international legal system, taking precedence over all other norms, whether of conventional or customary nature […] and therefore also over those norms governing immunity.

9.1. The recognition of immunity from jurisdiction for States that are responsible for such offences is in blatant contrast with the normative framework outlined above,

> since this recognition obstructs rather than protects such values, the protection of which is rather to be considered, in accordance with such norms and principles, essential for the entire international community, so that in the most serious cases it should justify mandatory forms of response. Moreover, there can be no doubt that this antinomy must be resolved by giving precedence to the higher-ranking norms, as pointed out in the dissenting opinions expressed by the minority judges (eight against nine) appended to the *Al-Adsani* decision. This therefore rules out the possibility that in such hypotheses the State could enjoy immunity from foreign jurisdiction. This would appear to be borne out by the *Furundzija* decision, which lists the possibility of victims "bringing civil suits for compensation before the Courts of a foreign state" among the effects of the violation of norms of this type at "an inter-State level".

This was the most influential decision of a domestic court accepting that the operation of *jus cogens* as higher-ranking norms should take precedence over any customary rules, such as state immunity, which were in 'blatant contrast' with this normative framework. *Ferrini* was confirmed in numerous decisions of Italian courts involving Second World War claims against Germany[43] and gave rise to the *Jurisdictional Immunities of the State* case (*Germany v Italy, Greece intervening*) before the ICJ, which was, however, decided with an overwhelming majority in favour of Germany.

Bouzari (Houshang) and ors, Amnesty International (Canadian Section) (intervening) and ors (intervening) v Iran, Appeal decision, 71 OR (3d) 675 (Ont CA), 2004 CanLII 871 (ON CA), (2004) 243 DLR (4th) 406, 2004 Carswell Ont 2681, 122 CRR (2d) 26, (2004) OJ No 2800, ILDC 175 (CA 2004), 30th June 2004, Canada; Ontario; Court of Appeal [ONCA]

Mr Bouzari sued Iran in the Canadian courts on allegations of torture committed in Iran. One of his arguments against Iran's claim to immunity was that Canada was bound by peremptory norms of customary international law to permit a civil claim against a foreign state for torture committed abroad.

> 88. The motion judge conducted a careful review of the decisions of domestic and international tribunals and state immunity legislation and concluded that the peremptory norm prohibiting torture does not carry with it such an obligation [to provide the right to a civil remedy for torture committed abroad by a foreign state]. She put her conclusion succinctly at para. 63 of her reasons:
>
> An examination of the decisions of national courts and international tribunals, as well as state legislation with respect to sovereign immunity, indicates that there is no principle of customary international law which provides an exception from state immunity where an act of torture has been committed outside the forum, even for acts contrary to *jus cogens*. Indeed, the evidence of state practice, as reflected in these and other sources, leads to the conclusion that there is an ongoing rule of customary international law providing state immunity for acts of torture committed outside the forum state.

43 See, eg, *Germany v Mantelli and ors*, Preliminary order on jurisdiction, No 14201/2008; ILDC 1037 (IT 2008) 29 May 2008; *Criminal proceedings against Milde*, Appeal judgment, Case No 1072/2009; ILDC 1224 (IT 2009), Italy, Court of Cassation, First Criminal Section, 13 January 2009. Interestingly, however, in *United States v Tissino and ors*, Preliminary order on jurisdiction, Case No 4461/2009; ILDC 1262 (IT 2009) Italy, Court of Cassation, All Civil Sections, 25 February 2009 (involving US immunity from civil jurisdiction for damages incurred as a result of deployment of nuclear weapons at a military base on Italian territory), the court referred to the ICJ decisions on the *Arrest Warrant* and *the Armed Activities* cases and refused to exercise jurisdiction by stating, *inter alia*, that a *jus cogens* violation could not provide by itself a basis for exercising jurisdiction in respect of a foreign state. In effect—and in contrast to previous Italian case law—this was a denial of the *effet utile* of *jus cogens*.

[. . .]

90. [. . .] The extent of the prohibition against torture as a rule of *jus cogens* is determined not by any particular view of what is required if it is to be meaningful, but rather by the widespread and consistent practice of states. As the motion judge found, that practice reflects the customary international law principle that state immunity is provided for acts of torture committed outside the forum state, not the obligation contended for by the appellant.

[. . .]

94. The second answer is that as a matter of practice, states do not accord a civil remedy for torture committed abroad by foreign states. The peremptory norm of prohibition against torture does not encompass the civil remedy contended for by the appellant.

This decision clearly rejected any inherent qualities of a bold version of *jus cogens* not supported by widespread and consistent state practice. Such practice was carefully examined by the lower court and was not reproduced in the decision.

Jones, Redress (intervening) and ors (intervening) v Ministry of the Interior of Saudi Arabia and Lieutenant Colonel Abdul Aziz, Appeal judgment, [2006] UKHL 26, [2006] 2 WLR 1424, [2007] 1 AC 270, [2007] 1 All ER 113, ILDC 521 (UK 2006), 14th June 2006, United Kingdom; House of Lords [HL]

In two separate actions, Mr Jones and other petitioners claimed damages in the UK against the Ministry of Interior of Saudi Arabia and senior Saudi officers for, *inter alia*, torture committed in Saudi Arabia. The claims involved consideration of immunity both of Saudi Arabia and the individual defendants. The Court of Appeal held that Saudi Arabia was entitled to state immunity under the UK State Immunity Act but there was no blanket immunity for the Saudi officials for acts of systematic torture. The House of Lords reversed the Court of Appeal's decision, holding that state immunity applied also to the individual officials. Lord Bingham and Lord Hoffmann delivered the leading speeches, in which they made extensive references to relevant international and domestic case law.

Lord Bingham

22. The *Ferrini v Federal Republic of Germany* decision cannot in my opinion be treated as an accurate statement of international law as generally understood; and one swallow does not make a rule of international law. The more closely-reasoned decisions in *Bouzari v Islamic Republic of Iran* [. . .] are to the contrary effect.

[. . .]

24. [. . .] [I]n the light of the decision of the International Court of Justice in *Democratic Republic of the Congo v Belgium* (*Case concerning Arrest Warrant of 11 April 2000*) [. . .] state immunity *ratione personae* can be claimed for a serving foreign minister accused of crimes against humanity. Thus, even in such a context, the international law prohibition of such crimes, having the same standing as the prohibition of torture, does not prevail. It follows that such a prohibition does not automatically override all other rules of international law. The International Court of Justice has made plain that breach of a *jus cogens* norm of international law does not suffice to confer jurisdiction (*Democratic Republic of the Congo v Rwanda* (3 February 2006), [. . .] para 64). [. . .] Where state immunity is applicable, the national court has no jurisdiction to exercise.

[. . .]

26. Thirdly, the UN Convention provides no exception from immunity where civil claims are made based on acts of torture. The Working Group in its 1999 Report makes plain that such an exception was considered, but no such exception was agreed.

Despite its embryonic status, this Convention is the most authoritative statement available on the current international understanding of the limits of state immunity in civil cases, and the absence of a torture or *jus cogens* exception is wholly inimical to the claimants' contention. [...] It may very well be that the claimants' contention will come to represent the law of nations, but it cannot be said to do so now.

Lord Hoffmann

45. To produce a conflict with state immunity, it is therefore necessary to show that the prohibition on torture has generated an ancillary procedural rule which, by way of exception to state immunity, entitles or perhaps requires states to assume civil jurisdiction over other states in cases in which torture is alleged. Such a rule may be desirable and, since international law changes, may have developed. But, contrary to the assertion of the minority in *Al-Adsani v UK*, it is not *entailed* by the prohibition of torture. [...]

48. In *Democratic Republic of the Congo v Belgium* (*Case concerning Arrest Warrant of 11 April 2000*) [...] [t]he International Court of Justice accepted that the law prohibiting the commission of such crimes was *jus cogens* but held that this did not entail an exception to the rule of state immunity for a head of state and certain other high state officials including a foreign minister. [...]

49. What this case shows is that the *jus cogens* nature of the rule alleged to have been infringed by the state or one of its officials does not provide an automatic answer to the question of whether another state has jurisdiction. [...]

59. I turn next to the decisions of national courts. In *Siderman de Blake v Republic of Argentina* (1992) 965 F 2d 699 the United States Court of Appeals [...] left open the possibility that there might be such an exception in customary international law, derived from the *jus cogens* nature of the prohibition on torture ('the ... argument carries much force') but held that the court was bound by the unequivocal terms of the Foreign Sovereign Immunities Act 1976 ('the FSIA'). While *Siderman de Blake v Republic of Argentina* turned upon the terms of national legislation, the legislation itself is evidence against a state practice of having an exception to state immunity in torture cases.

60. In *Bouzari v Islamic Republic of Iran* (2002) 124 ILR 427 [...] the Superior Court [...] concluded [...] that

> 'the decisions of state courts, international tribunals and state legislation do not support the conclusion that there is a general state practice which provides an exception from state immunity for acts of torture committed outside the forum state.'

61. This conclusion was upheld by the Ontario Court of Appeal (see (2004) 71 OR (3d) 675 at 694-696).

62. The decision of the Greek Court of Cassation in *Prefecture of Voiotia v Federal Republic of Germany* Case No 11/2000 [...] went upon a theory of implied waiver which has received no support in other decisions. It was undermined by the court's own refusal to order enforcement of the judgment and held to be wrong by a judgment of a special Supreme Court (the Anotato Eidiko Dikasterio) convened to decide cases involving the interpretation of international law: *Margellos v Germany* [...]. The original judgment was coldly received by the German Supreme Court when the claimants attempted to enforce it directly in Germany: *Greek Citizens v Federal Republic of Germany* (*The Distomo Massacre Case*) (2003) 42 ILM 1030. The court said (at 1033):

> 'There have recently been tendencies towards a more limited principle of state immunity, which should not apply in case of a peremptory norm of international law (*ius cogens*) has been violated ... According to the prevailing view, this is not international law currently in force.'

> 63. That leaves the Italian *Ferrini* case, *Ferrini v Federal Republic of Germany*, which exhibits the same bare syllogistic reasoning as the judgment of the minority in *Al-Adsani v UK* (2001) 12 BHRC 88. […] It is not for a national court to 'develop' international law by unilaterally adopting a version of that law which, however desirable, forward-looking and reflective of values it may be, is simply not accepted by other states. […]
>
> 84. The notion that acts contrary to *jus cogens* cannot be official acts has not been well received by eminent writers on international law. […]
>
> 85. In principle, therefore, I would reject the argument that torture or some other contravention of a *jus cogens* cannot attract immunity *ratione materiae* because it cannot be an official act.

From a positivist viewpoint, this decision made the most extensive and elaborate analysis of available legal sources to deny any operation of *jus cogens* not supported by state practice. Its ruling was followed by other courts. For instance, in *Fang and ors and Attorney-General (intervening) v Jiang and ors*, the New Zealand High Court held that: '[t]he House of Lords has comprehensively and persuasively rejected the proposition that the practice of torture may be an exception to the principle of state immunity for the purposes of the potential civil liability of individual officials or servants of the state'.[44] In a similar vein, relying on *Jones*, the parties in *Habib v Australia*[45] agreed that Habib would be unable to sue any foreign states or their agents, as sovereign immunity would act as a procedural bar on the claim.

Military Prosecutor v Albers and ors and Germany (joining), Final appeal judgment, No 32139/2012, ILDC 1921 (IT 2012), 9th August 2012, Italy; Supreme Court of Cassation; 1st Criminal Section

This Italian case also concerned Germany's immunity for crimes committed during the Second World War. It was the first judgment issued by the Supreme Court of Cassation in the aftermath of the ICJ's pronouncement that Italy was in breach of Germany's immunity.[46] As noted by the ILDC reporter, the court did abandon its previous case law but this was not an unconditional surrender since the dismissal of the *Ferrini* approach was qualified by various considerations.[47]

> 5. Now, it is immediately obvious, and with particular clarity that, in the context of the International Court's thorough analysis of *jus cogens*, it is acknowledged that there is no conflict between the binding provisions of international law and the customary law that grants the State immunity, since these operate at *two different levels*, the first, of a substantive nature, serving to attribute a value to the State's actions and the second defined by its procedural nature, such that they do not interfere with one another (with the logical consequence that it is not possible to deduce from the inadmissibility of the claim the lawfulness of the conduct of the State in violation of human rights). This assertion raises certain doubts in the mind of the Court with regard to its compatibility

44 Ex parte application for leave to serve statement of claim and notice of proceeding outside New Zealand, Case No CIV 2004-404-5843, [2007] NZAR 420, ILDC 1226 (NZ 2006), 21 December 2006, New Zealand; High Court [HC], para 62.

45 Decision on justiciability, (2010) FCAFC 12, [2010] 183 FCR 62, (2010) 265 ALR 50, (2010) 113 ALD 469, ILDC 1518 (AU 2010), 25 February 2010, Australia; Federal Court [FCA]; Full Court [FCAFC].

46 Subsequent relevant cases include *Frascà v Germany and Giachini (guardian of Priebke) and Italy (joining)*, Preliminary order on jurisdiction, No 4284/2013, ILDC 1998 (IT 2013), 21 February 2013, Italy; *Alessi and ors v Germany and Presidency of the Council of Ministers of the Italian Republic (intervening)*, Referral to the Constitutional Court, Order No 85/2014, ILDC 2725 (IT 2014), 21 January 2014, Italy; Tuscany, Florence; Court of First Instance; *Simoncioni and ors v Germany and President of the Council of Ministers of the Italian Republic (intervening)*, Constitutional review, No 238, Decision No 238/2014, ILDC 2237 (IT 2014), 22 October 2014, Italy; Constitutional Court.

47 D Amoroso, Analysis, *Military Prosecutor v Albers and ors and Germany (joining)*, ILDC 1921 (IT 2012) A1.

with the general principles applying to the interpretation of the rules, in that it seems unduly limiting to confine the category of *jus cogens* to its substantive scope alone, overlooking the fact that its actual *effectiveness* is measured precisely on the basis of the legal consequences derived from violation of the binding rules. Furthermore, it would not seem a consideration of minor importance that the stated distinction between the "substantive" and "procedural" rules results in nothing other than the impunity of the subjects and ends by reaffirming the unconvincing inclusion, under the scope of jurisdictional exemption, typical of acts performed *jure imperii*, of acts such as crimes against humanity which some endeavour to include under that heading.

Nevertheless, account must be taken of the decision of 3 February 2012, both because of its undisputable authoritative nature and because of the factors that indicate its persuasive nature [. . .].

6. The Court takes the view that it must assess the effect that the said pronouncement has had on the status of the "living principles" governing jurisdiction, and thus examining it as a *dictum* of the international Court rather than as a highly plausible source of a judicial solution: we refer in particular to the assertion that, as international law currently stands, it is necessary to rule out the possibility that violations of *jus cogens* should have an effect on the law on immunity enjoyed by States and one must, instead, assert that these are relevant solely for the preservation of sovereignty, in which context no conduct—however detestable—can achieve the status of a "*breaking point for an acceptable exercise of national sovereignty*". Alongside this *dictum* one must also juxtapose the fact that, as shown by the decision of 3 February 2012, no Supreme Court has made pronouncements inspired by the same principles as those assumed by the Combined Sections of this Court as a basis for the decisions of 2004 and 2008.

Accordingly, if it is true that one cannot deduce from the position adopted by the International Court arguments that could repudiate the persuasiveness and judicial soundness of the principles that have always been affirmed by this Court, that position, in the context of the essential isolation of the position adopted by the Italian Court, certainly makes it advisable to assess the 2004 and 2008 judgments—expressly seen as sources of a contribution "*to the emergence of a rule in conformity with the immunity of the foreign State*"—as an attempt, dictated by the need to affirm principles of judicial civilisation which, in the absence of its "ratification" by the International Community, of which the Hague Court is the highest jurisdictional representation, has not or has not yet received the necessary agreement and which, for this inescapable reason, cannot be extended to further applications. The expressions of full agreement with the Italian Court's positions on the part of an authoritative section of legal theory and the symptomatic emergence of differing opinions in the International Court's pronouncements do not rule out the possibility that, in the future, the principle of the necessary withdrawal of the immunity of States acting *jure imperii*, when such acts are contrary to basic human rights for citizens, may be wholly or partially adopted by the international Community. But this situation has not yet become a reality.

(b) Immunities of state officials

R., ex parte Pinochet v Bartle and ors, Appeal, [1999] UKHL 17, [2000] 1 AC 147, [1999] 2 All ER 97, [1999] 2 WLR 827, (1999) 38(3) ILM 581, (2002) 119 ILR 135, ILDC 1736 (UK 1999), 24th March 1999, United Kingdom; House of Lords [HL]

This was one of the most famous cases on head of state immunity. It concerned a request by the Spanish authorities to the UK to extradite Augusto Pinochet, a life-long senator in Chile and Chile's former head of state, to be tried in Spain for torture and other crimes committed against Spanish nationals during his dictatorship. The pertinent issue for present purposes was whether Senator Pinochet—as a former head of state—was entitled to immunity *ratione materiae* for torture and other serious violations of international law of a *jus cogens* character. The *jus cogens* argument was discussed by three of the Lords that issued the majority (6:1) decision, which held that Senator Pinochet had lost his immunity owing to (and since) the entry into force of the Convention against Torture, which was considered as an implied waiver of immunity by the states parties.

Lord Browne-Wilkinson

51 Can it be said that the commission of a crime which is an international crime against humanity and jus cogens is an act done in an official capacity on behalf of the state? I believe there to be strong ground for saying that the implementation of torture as defined by the Torture Convention cannot be a state function.

[...]

54 I have doubts whether, before the coming into force of the Torture Convention, the existence of the international crime of torture as jus cogens was enough to justify the conclusion that the organisation of state torture could not rank for immunity purposes as performance of an official function. At that stage there was no international tribunal to punish torture and no general jurisdiction to permit or require its punishment in domestic courts. Not until there was some form of universal jurisdiction for the punishment of the crime of torture could it really be talked about as a fully constituted international crime. But in my judgment the Torture Convention did provide what was missing: a worldwide universal jurisdiction. Further, it required all member states to ban and outlaw torture: Article 2. How can it be for international law purposes an official function to do something which international law itself prohibits and criminalises? [...]

Lord Hope of Craighead

184 [...] The principle of immunity ratione materiae protects all acts which the head of state has performed in the exercise of the functions of government. The purpose for which they were performed protects these acts from any further analysis. There are only two exceptions to this approach which customary international law has recognised. [...] The second relates to acts the prohibition of which has acquired the status under international law of jus cogens. This compels all states to refrain from such conduct under any circumstances and imposes an obligation erga omnes to punish such conduct. As Sir Arthur Watts Q.C. said in his Hague Lectures [...], in respect of conduct constituting an international crime, such as war crimes, special considerations apply.

185 But even in the field of such high crimes as have achieved the status of jus cogens under customary international law there is as yet no general agreement that they are outside the immunity to which former heads of state are entitled from the jurisdiction of foreign national courts. [...]. As [Lord Slynn of Hadley] said [...], except in regard to crimes in particular situations where international tribunals have been set up to deal with them and it is part of the arrangement that heads of state should not have any immunity, there is no general recognition that there has been a loss of immunity from the jurisdiction of foreign national courts.

Lord Millett

333 My Lords, the Republic of Chile was a party to the Torture Convention, and must be taken to have assented to the imposition of an obligation on foreign national courts to take and exercise criminal jurisdiction in respect of the official

> use of torture. I do not regard it as having thereby waived its immunity. In my opinion there was no immunity to be waived. The offence is one which could only be committed in circumstances which would normally give rise to the immunity. The international community had created an offence for which immunity ratione materiae could not possibly be available. International law cannot be supposed to have established a crime having the character of a jus cogens and at the same time to have provided an immunity which is co-extensive with the obligation it seeks to impose.

This decision was issued in 1999, at a time when important developments on jurisdictional immunities and related issues were unfolding and there were high expectations about the possibility and promise of a bold version of *jus cogens*. Yet, both Lord Browne-Wilkinson and Lord Hope stopped short of holding that the *jus cogens* character of the prohibition of torture was in itself sufficient to deprive a head of state of immunity *ratione materiae* before foreign national courts. Lord Hope stressed that such loss of immunity only applied where international tribunals were in place to try heads of state and Lord Browne-Wilkinson held that loss of head of state immunity required some form of universal jurisdiction for the crime of torture, which he did not find to exist before the adoption of the Convention against Torture. This reasoning has been criticized as 'inherently flawed' from the point of view of a bold version of *jus cogens*; under such a reading of the concept, the 'inevitable conclusion' should have been that the customary rule of head of state immunity could not derogate from the *jus cogens* nature of the prohibition of torture.[48] Lord Millett was more in line with consequential *jus cogens* by denying head of state immunity in view of the *jus cogens* prohibition of torture, irrespective of the Convention against Torture.

Ye and ors v Former President Jiang Zemin and Falun Gong Control Office (also known as Office 6/10), United States Department of State (intervening) and United States Department of Justice (intervening), Appeal Judgment, Docket No 03-3989, 383 F.3d 620 (7th Cir. 2004), ILDC 683 (US 2004), 8th September 2004, United States; Court of Appeals (7th Circuit) [7th Cir]

The plaintiffs sued the former President of China, Jiang Zemin, under the Alien Tort Statute for, *inter alia*, acts of torture, genocide, and arbitrary arrest. The US intervened asserting head of state immunity.

> 19. The appellants' position, therefore, is that, in at least a particular class of cases (those involving *jus cogens* norms), a court cannot defer to the position of the Executive Branch with respect to immunity for heads of states. The Supreme Court has held, however, that the Executive Branch's suggestion of immunity is conclusive and not subject to judicial inquiry.
>
> [...]
>
> 23. Our interpretation of the FSIA confirmed that Congress could grant immunity to a foreign state for acts that amounted to violations of *jus cogens* norms. Just as the FSIA is the Legislative Branch's determination that a nation should be immune from suit in the courts of this country, the immunity of foreign leaders remains the province of the Executive Branch. The Executive Branch's determination that a foreign leader should be immune from suit even when the leader is accused of acts that violate *jus cogens* norms is established by a suggestion of immunity. We are no more free to ignore the Executive Branch's determination than we are free to ignore a legislative determination concerning a foreign state.

48 See A Bianchi, 'Immunity versus Human Rights: The Pinochet Case' (1999) 10 *European Journal of International Law* 237, 245, fn 32.

As noted by the ILDC reporter, this decision was in line with other decisions by US courts on this issue, as well as with the ICJ decision in *Arrest Warrant*.[49] The court did not say that heads of state could escape liability for *jus cogens* violations; rather, it deferred to the executive to make what in effect was the dispositive determination about that claim.

John Doe and ors v Israel and ors, Motion disposition, 400 F Supp 2d 86, 95-96 (DDC 2005), ILDC 318 (US 2005), 10th November 2005, United States; District of Columbia; District Court for the District of Columbia [D.D.C.]

This was a civil suit filed by Palestinians living in the West Bank or in the US (most of whom were US citizens or permanently resident aliens) under the Alien Tort Statute alleging various personal and financial injuries caused by the actions of Israel and various Israeli government officials in their official and personal capacities, regarding settlement activities in the West Bank, including injuries sustained in the US, some of which were allegedly in violation of *jus cogens* rules. The Israeli defendants invoked various defences, including immunity under the FSIA and head of state immunity.

> 31. But even assuming that the Israeli defendants have engaged in *jus cogens* violations, plaintiffs still cannot state a claim under § 1605(a)(1) [of the FSIA] because their argument is foreclosed by controlling precedent. *Jus cogens* violations, without more, do not constitute an implied waiver of FSIA immunity. *Princz v. Fed. Republic of Germany*, 26 F.3d 1166, 1173–75 (D.C. Cir. 1994); *accord Smith v. Socialist People's Libyan Arab Jamahiriya*, 101 F.3d 239, 242–45 (2d Cir. 1997). Section 1605(a)(1) is construed narrowly; the judiciary is not to re-draft the FSIA so as to force an exception that Congress did not craft. *See Princz*, 26 F.3d at 1173; *Smith*, 101 F.3d at 242–45.

The court dismissed the claim that *jus cogens* violations could implicitly waive FSIA immunity on the ground that such violations were not among the exceptions enumerated in the FSIA. The court refused to construe the FSIA in a way that would denote any specific implications of the *jus cogens* character of the violations out of respect for the legislative authority of the Congress.

Iraq and Afghanistan Detainees Litigation, Re, Mohammed Ali and ors v Colonel Pappas and ors, Trial court order, 479 F.Supp.2d 85 (D.D.C. 2007), ILDC 812 (US 2007), 27th March 2007, United States; District of Columbia; District Court for the District of Columbia [DDC]

The plaintiffs brought claims against the former US Secretary of Defence Donald Rumsfeld and other US officials for alleged torture during their detention in Iraq and Afghanistan. The defendants argued, *inter alia*, that they were absolutely immune from liability pursuant to the Federal Employees Liability Reform and Tort Compensation Act of 1988 (Westfall Act). The plaintiffs relied on the *jus cogens* character of the alleged violations to argue that the Westfall Act did not cover the torts allegedly committed by the defendants and that the defendants had acted outside their scope of employment since *jus cogens* violations could never fall within the scope of employment.

> 45 [. . .] [T]he plaintiffs' argument that the statute does not cover intentional torts is contrary to the plain meaning of the statute ["negligent or wrongful act or omission"] as well as precedent concluding otherwise. This Court therefore finds that the Westfall Act applies to the intentional torts alleged by the plaintiffs in their Amended Complaint.
>
> [. . .]

49 J Heyman-Kantor, Analysis, *Ye and ors v Former President Jiang Zemin and Falun Gong Control Office (also known as Office 6/10), United States Department of State (intervening) and United States Department of Justice (intervening)*, ILDC 683 (US 2004) A1.

> 52 […] [T]he parties [dispute] whether violations of *jus cogens* international law ever can be deemed to be within the scope of employment. […]
>
> 54 […] [T]he proper inquiry for this Court's purpose is whether detaining and interrogating enemy aliens were the kinds of conduct the defendants were employed to perform or were incidental to the conduct the defendants were employed to perform. The Court finds that they were. As military officials commanding Armed Forces serving our country during a war, there can be no credible dispute that detaining and interrogating enemy aliens would be incidental to their overall military obligations. […]
>
> 55 […] [T]he defendants are entitled to absolute immunity pursuant to the Westfall Act for the alleged international law violations.

This was another decision in which the court interpreted applicable domestic law and followed previous case law in a way that denied any consequential effects to *jus cogens*.

Lozano (Mario Luiz) v Italy, Appeal Judgment, Case No 31171/2008, ILDC 1085 (IT 2008), 24th July 2008, Italy; Supreme Court of Cassation; 1st Criminal Section

Mr Lozano, while on duty as a US soldier in Iraq, killed an Italian national and injured two others. He pleaded immunity from the criminal jurisdiction of the Italian courts.

> 6. [A] more recent trend can be discerned, both in international law doctrine and in still a minority part of domestic jurisprudence, which is intended to dispute the wider application of the customary rule on the immunity of the foreign State, which relates to civil liability resulting from the unlawful activity carried out *iure imperii* by one of its organs, as well as to the immunity from criminal jurisdiction of the individual author, acting as organ of the State, of the same unlawful act, positing the existence of an exception to immunity where the acts have been carried out in violation of peremptory rules of international law, as in the field of the protection of fundamental human rights, if the individual is guilty of "international crimes", as a guarantee of the values underlying the international community as a whole.
>
> Moreover, although having to note the prevalence of the opposing thesis, […] it is worth stressing that […] this "does not preclude a development in customary international law in the future".
>
> It can, therefore, be held […] that an international custom is "in the process of being formed" which, in consideration of the cogent, imperative nature of the norms of humanitarian international law ("peremptory norms of general international law", in the wording of Article 53 of the Vienna Convention on the Law of Treaties of 23 May 1969), which impose respect for fundamental human rights, and in consideration of the actual harmfulness of "universal values which transcend the interests of the individual State communities", is intended to limit the immunity from civil liability of a foreign State, whose organ, while exercising an *iure imperii* activity, such as in situations of war, has, however, made itself the author of acts of such severity so as to "undermine the very foundations of co-existence between peoples" (Constitutional Court of Hungary, n. 53 of 1993), which can therefore constitute "international crimes".
>
> From the parallel and contradictory co-existence of the two principles in the international legal order, both of which are general in scope, it follows, as a logical corollary, that, where both principles are simultaneously applicable, the eventual conflict must be resolved on the systematic level of co-ordination and on the basis of the criterion of balancing interests, priority being given to the principle of higher rank and of *jus cogens* character, and therefore to the guarantee that the most serious crimes which violate the inviolable rights of the freedom and dignity of the human being,

> "due to its assiological meta-value content" within the international community, in respect of the interests of States in sovereign equality and non-interference, the violation of those fundamental rights representing "the breaking point of the tolerable exercise of sovereignty", in other words the "abuse of sovereignty" of the State, shall not go unpunished.

The court acknowledged that the prevailing view in international and domestic jurisprudence would grant immunity even in case of *jus cogens* violations. However, in line with Italian jurisprudence, it sided with the minority view seeking change in customary law by emphasizing the 'logical corollary' of the higher rank of *jus cogens*, which should be given priority in case of conflict with the rules on immunity (including, in the case at hand, immunity of state officials).

3. Diplomatic protection

Diplomatic protection was traditionally regarded as an exclusive right of states, in the sense that a state exercised diplomatic protection in its own right because an injury to a state's national was considered to be an injury to the state itself.[50] This approach was reaffirmed by the ICJ in *Barcelona Traction*.[51] It reflects the inter-state character of international law, which was absolutely the case when diplomatic protection was taking shape in the early times of international law. Even though this fiction is nowadays rather anachronistic, not much has changed in the law and jurisprudence on diplomatic protection to reflect the contemporary enhanced position of individuals in international law. The discretion of states to exercise diplomatic protection is not even bypassed in cases involving alleged violations of *jus cogens*; the ILC did not ultimately go further than recommending that states 'should give due consideration to the possibility of exercising diplomatic protection, especially when a significant injury has occurred'.[52]

The following three domestic cases were decided along these lines and did not recognize any automatic right of diplomatic protection in cases of *jus cogens* violations; they held that such a development should be supported by state practice (which was found to be lacking) and develop into customary law. In *Kaunda*, however, the Court found such a right in South Africa's Constitution.

R (on the application of Abbasi (Feroz Ali) and Abbasi) v Secretary of State for Foreign and Commonwealth Affairs and Secretary of State for the Home Department, Original application for judicial review, [2002] EWCA Civ 1598, ILDC 246 (UK 2002), 6th November 2002, United Kingdom; England and Wales; Court of Appeal [CA]

Mrs Abbasi brought proceedings on behalf of her son, a UK national, who was held at Guantánamo Bay without charge and without access to a court. The claimants sought an order to require the UK government to make representations to the US government or to take other appropriate action on Abbasi's behalf to redress the situation.

> 41. […] [T]he *First Report on Diplomatic Protection* by Professor Dugard […] proposed that a State should have legal duty (under general international law) "to exercise diplomatic protection on behalf of the injured [national] upon request, if the injury results from a grave breach of a jus cogens norm attributable to another State" (draft Article 4(1)). It suggested that such a duty (and the corresponding right of the national) should exist where the national was unable to bring a claim before a competent international court or tribunal. Mr Blake recognised that this proposal

50 ILC, 'Report of the International Law Commission on the Work of its Fifty-Eighth Session: Commentary to Article 1 of the Draft articles on Diplomatic Protection' (2006) UN Doc A/61/10, p 25, para 3.

51 [1970] ICJ Rep 44, paras 78–79.

52 ILC, 'Report of the International Law Commission on the Work of its Fifty-Eighth Session: Article 19(a) of the Draft articles on Diplomatic Protection' (2006) UN Doc A/61/10, p 94.

had not yet been accepted by all states parties (including the US and the UK). Indeed Professor Dugard himself had accepted that his proposal would not in fact go forward. He later said:

> "The Special Rapporteur recognised that he had introduced Article 4 *de lege ferenda*. [...] It was thus an exercise in the progressive development of international law. But the general view was that the issue was not yet ripe for the attention of the Commission and that there was a need for more state practice and, particularly, more *opinio juris* before it could be considered." (ILC Report, 2000, para. 456).

[...]

69. It is clear that international law has not yet recognised that a State is under a duty to intervene by diplomatic or other means to protect a citizen who is suffering or threatened with injury in a foreign State.

Kaunda v President of South Africa and ors, Appeal to Constitutional Court, Case No CCT23/04, 2005 (4) SA 235 (CC), 2004 (10) BCLR 1009 (CC), ILDC 89 (ZA 2004), 4th August 2004, South Africa; Constitutional Court [CC]

The applicants were arrested in Zimbabwe and feared that they would be extradited to Equatorial Guinea to face charges in connection with an alleged coup attempt. They sought orders to require the South African government to make representations on their behalf to both Zimbabwe and Equatorial Guinea to ensure that their fundamental rights would be respected.

28. It had been suggested that the traditional approach to diplomatic protection, such as that set out in the *Barcelona Traction* case, should be developed to recognise that in certain circumstances where injury is the result of a grave breach of a *jus cogens* norm, the state whose national has been injured, should have a legal duty to exercise diplomatic protection on behalf of the injured person. As a corollary to that, states would be obliged to make provision in their municipal law for the enforcement of this right before a competent court or other independent national authority.

29. It appears from the ILC report [on diplomatic protection] that although there was some support for this development, and some recent national constitutions made provision for such an obligation, presently this is not the general practice of states. Currently the prevailing view is that diplomatic protection is not recognised by international law as a human right and cannot be enforced as such. To do so may give rise to more problems than it would solve. Diplomatic protection remains the prerogative of the state to be exercised at its discretion. It must be accepted, therefore, that the applicants cannot base their claims on customary international law. No contention to the contrary was addressed to us in argument.

[...]

69. There may [...] be a duty on government, consistent with its obligations under international law, to take action to protect one of its citizens against a gross abuse of international human rights norms. A request to the government for assistance in such circumstances where the evidence is clear would be difficult, and in extreme cases possibly impossible, to refuse. It is unlikely that such a request would ever be refused by government, but if it were, the decision would be justiciable, and a court could order the government to take appropriate action.

70. There may even be a duty on government in extreme cases to provide assistance to its nationals against egregious breaches of international human rights which come to its knowledge. The victims of such breaches may not be in a position to ask for

assistance, and in such circumstances, on becoming aware of the breaches, the government may well be obliged to take an initiative itself.

Judge Ngcobo, concurring: It is not unreasonable [...] to require a State to react by way of diplomatic protection to measures taken by a State against its nationals which constitute the grave breach of a norm of *jus cogens*. (para. 169)

R and Office of the United Nations High Commissioner for Refugees (intervening) (on the application of Al-Rawi and ors) v Secretary of State for Foreign and Commonwealth Affairs and Secretary of State for Home Affairs, Appeal decision, [2006] EWCA Civ 1279, [2008] QB 289, [2007] 2 WLR 1219, (2007) 2 LRC 499, [2006] All ER (D) 138 (Oct), [2006] HRLR 42, [2007] UKHRR 58, (2006) 103(41) LSG 33, ILDC 729 (UK 2006), 12th October 2006, United Kingdom; England and Wales; High Court [HC]

The claimants appealed to the UK government to request their immediate release from Guantánamo Bay, where they were allegedly being tortured. They argued, *inter alia*, that the *jus cogens* status of the prohibition of torture ought to take priority over other concerns.

102. [The *Furundzija* decision] shows that, as a matter of international law, (1) the status of *ius cogens erga omnes* empowers but does not oblige a state to intervene with another sovereign to insist on respect for the prohibition of torture [...].

103. But none of this imposes a duty on states, sounding in international law, of the kind for which the appellants must here contend. [...]

107 The *Kaunda* case is plainly, with great respect, a powerful and important authority. But it cannot in our judgment be treated as an engine to drive a significant change in the law of human rights or in any general principle of international law. In essence it was a domestic constitutional case. It does not push out the edges of *jus cogens erga omnes*. [...]

4. International crimes

Office of the Prosecutor v Priebke (Erich), Ordinary appeal judgment, request of extradition, P/457/XXXI, ILDC 1599 (AR 1995), 2nd November 1995, Argentina; Supreme Court [CSJ]

Italy requested Priebke's extradition from Argentina to stand trial in Italy for the execution of 335 people in Rome in March 1944. The Federal Court of Appeals denied the extradition, holding that Priebke's acts constituted the crime of homicide and were subject to Argentina's statute of limitations and could not be characterized as war crimes *ex post facto*. Upon appeal, the prosecutor argued that Priebke's acts amounted to crimes against humanity, which were not subject to the statute of limitations.

4. The characterization of a crime as a crime against humanity does not depend on the willingness of either the requesting or the requested states during the procedure of extradition, but on the international law principles of ius cogens.

5. In such circumstances, crimes against humanity are not subject to the application of statutory limitations and the requested extradition has to be granted.

This was one of the first domestic decisions to rule on the effects of *jus cogens* and bypass domestic legislation that would have resulted in the non-extradition and thus non-trial of Priebke for international crimes. The lack of analysis in the reasoning of the majority was partially compensated by the elaborate opinions of the concurring Judges Nazareno, and Moliné O'Connor[53] and Bossert.[54] However, as noted by the ILDC reporter, none succeeded in proving the existence

53 Paras 66–71, 76–77.

54 Paras 88–91.

of a customary rule precluding the application of statutory limitations to international crimes.[55] Thus, in effect, the ruling and the outcome were based on the consequential effects of *jus cogens*. This decision was particularly influential on subsequent Argentinian cases.[56]

In the landmark case *Simón (Julio Héctor) v Office of the Public Prosecutor*,[57] concerning Argentina's Amnesty Laws of 1986 and 1987, which precluded the prosecution of the crimes committed during Argentina's dictatorship, one of the main arguments of the accused was that his prosecution violated the principle of legality and constituted an *ex post facto* application of the law. The Supreme Court held that Argentina had an obligation under international human rights law to prosecute the perpetrators of crimes against humanity and paved the way to justice for the victims of crimes committed during Argentina's 1976–83 military dictatorship. *Jus cogens* arguments were absent in the majority decision but were prominent in the concurring opinions of some judges, in an apparent effort to buttress the outcome against objections related to the principle of legality. For example, in his concurring opinion, Judge Boggiano held that it was inherent in *jus cogens* norms that in case of a conflict between the principle of non-retroactivity, which would favour the perpetrator of international crimes, and the principle of retroactivity, which was found in conventions on non-application of statutory limitations, the latter ought to prevail.[58]

Similarly, in *Riveros v Office of the Public Prosecutor*, a case concerning the pardon granted in 1989 to Argentinian military officials for crimes committed during Argentina's 'dirty war', the Supreme Court held that the peremptory international system ('un sistema internacional imperativo') and the international human rights system rejected any idea of impunity and entailed that the decision to close the criminal proceedings undermined the international obligations relating to investigation of crimes, identification of their perpetrators, accomplices, and accessories, and imposition of corresponding sanctions, as well as the right of victims to an effective remedy.[59]

Public Prosecutor's Office, de Lois (Graciela) (intervening) and ors (intervening) v Manzorro (Adolfo), Final Appeal Judgment, Case No 16/2005, Aranzadi JUR 2005/132318, ILDC 136 (ES 2005), 19th April 2005, Spain; National Court; Criminal Chamber

This case concerned criminal proceedings against Adolfo Scilingo, an Argentine officer, for crimes against humanity committed by the military regime in Argentina since 1976, and the jurisdiction of Spanish courts over those crimes. One of the main issues was whether subjecting Scilingo to the Spanish criminal provisions penalizing crimes against humanity, which were in force since 2004, was in breach of the principle of legality.

> B.1. […] [T]he conduct prosecuted is also subject to international criminal law, specifically constituting a crime against humanity […].
>
> [I]n a way these laws [prohibiting crimes against humanity] are not autonomous (or not totally autonomous at any rate), inasmuch as to a large extent they represent the incorporation of pre-existing international criminal law in domestic law, which, due to its characteristics and objectives […] is part of international *ius cogens* and, therefore, has binding effect *erga omnes*, both in terms of criminal conduct and the application of consequences. […]
>
> We believe that the *ius cogens* status of the international law incorporated in or represented by domestic law, the compulsory nature of which it recognised therein,

55 R Mattassini de Hill, Analysis, *Office of the Prosecutor v Priebke (Erich)*, ILDC 1599 (AR 1995) A7–A9.

56 ibid, A1.

57 Appeal judgment, S 1767 XXXVIII; ILDC 579 (AR 2005), 14 June 2005, Argentina; Supreme Court (CSJ).

58 ibid, para 43.

59 Recourse of cassation and unconstitutionality, M 2333 XLII, ILDC 1084 (AR 2007), 13 July 2007, Supreme Court [CSJ], para 32.

> prevents it from going against its essential content or limiting its intended temporal, subjective or territorial scope of application. With pre-existing international law having been incorporated into domestic law in order to facilitate the application of the former, it is not logical for domestic law to overlook the fact that international law was already compulsory *per se* or that, due to its characteristics and universal nature, this law is organised, not in one specific State, but in all of humanity and all States in order to protect higher values of humanity, which have an equal interest in the prosecution and punishment of the abovementioned crimes.

The judgment was the first ever conviction in Spain for crimes against humanity.[60] The court resorted to the *jus cogens* character of the prohibition of crimes against humanity to overcome limitations of (domestic) criminal law relating to the principle of criminal legality referring to the characterization, precise nature, accessibility, predictability, and certainty of the criminal law, and ultimately established that the Spanish courts could exercise universal jurisdiction by holding that the criminalization of a conduct in international customary law was sufficient to satisfy the principle of legality. This construction was not without controversy and was criticized on the ground that international law lacked sufficient precision to satisfy the principle of legality.[61]

Gypsy International Recognition and Compensation Action v International Business Machines Corp, Final appeal judgment, 4c.113/2006, BGE 132 III 661, ILDC 352 (CH 2006), 14th August 2006, Switzerland; Federal Supreme Court [BGer]

GIRCA claimed that actions by IBM in Geneva between 1935 and 1945 constituted complicity in crimes against humanity committed by the Nazis. The pertinent issue was whether statutory limitation prevented the enforcement of the claims.

> 4.4.2 GIRCA loses sight of the object of the litigation when it bases its claim on *opinio juris* and submits that the non-applicability of the statute of limitations to crimes against humanity falls under *ius cogens*, and should, as customary international law, prevail over positive law. In fact, governing Swiss law recognises that the nature of such crimes is not subject to time limitations in Article 75*bis* CP, which the decision being appealed from does not call into question. The sole issue is the question of any retroactive effect of this provision to a crime which was already time-barred when such provision entered into force, and which Swiss law expressly precludes. It does not appear that such bar would be contrary to the *opinio juris*, or prohibited by *ius cogens*. Further, international law similarly guarantees the principle of prohibiting the retroactive effect of laws, subject to the application of the more favourable law [. . .]. Applying Article 75*bis* CP retroactively in this case would mean precisely to disregard the principle of *lex mitior*. Under these circumstances, the appeal must be dismissed.

As noted by the ILDC reporter, the outcome of this judgment, albeit without adequate analysis, was tenable from the perspective of international criminal law since it was doubtful whether, before 1983, when the provision of the Swiss Penal Code excluding the statutory limitation of crimes against humanity entered into force, customary international law or *jus cogens* required that crimes against humanity were not subject to statutory limitation.[62]

Overall, these cases show that there is considerable controversy surrounding statutory limitations of international crimes and the relevant impact of *jus cogens*. Domestic courts have come to

60 L Paradell and B Montejo, Analysis, *Public Prosecutor's Office, de Lois (Graciela) (intervening) and ors (intervening) v Manzorro (Adolfo)*, ILDC 136 (ES 2005) A2.

61 ibid, A4.

62 T Burri, Analysis, *Gypsy International Recognition and Compensation Action v International Business Machines Corp*, ILDC 352 (CH 2006) A1.

different conclusions, some being more prone than others to recognize the consequential effect of *jus cogens* in that regard.

5. Inadmissibility of evidence obtained through torture

The prohibition of invoking any statement procured by torture as evidence in judicial proceedings is well established in international law (eg, in Article 15 of the Convention against Torture) and is a corollary to the absolute prohibition of torture.[63] There is, however, some controversy with regard to the (in)admissibility of foreign torture evidence, which came to the fore in the post-9/11 fight against terrorism. Litigants in some cases have linked the admissibility of torture evidence to the *jus cogens* prohibition of torture.

A, Amnesty International (intervening) and Commonwealth Lawyers Association (intervening) v Secretary of State for the Home Department, Appeal judgment, [2005] UKHL 71, [2006] 2 AC 221, [2005] 3 WLR 1249, [2006] 1 All ER 575, ILDC 363 (UK 2005), 8th December 2005, United Kingdom; House of Lords [HL]

The issue in this case was whether UK courts may receive evidence which had, or may have been, procured by torture inflicted by officials of a foreign state without the complicity of the British authorities. The Special Immigration Appeal Commission (SIAC) and the Court of Appeal by a 2:1 majority had held that the alleged use of torture under such circumstances was relevant to the weight of the evidence but did not render it legally inadmissible. Upon appeal to the House of Lords, one of the arguments of the applicants was that foreign torture evidence was precluded by the *jus cogens* character of the prohibition of torture.

> Lord Bingham
>
> 34. As appears from [*Furundzija*, paras 147-157], the *jus cogens erga omnes* nature of the prohibition of torture requires member states to do more than eschew the practice of torture. In *Kuwait Airways Corporation v Iraqi Airways Co (Nos 4 and 5)* [2002] UKHL 19, [2002] 2 AC 883, paras 29, 117, the House refused recognition to conduct which represented a serious breach of international law. This was, as I respectfully think, a proper response to the requirements of international law. In General Comment 20 (1992) on article 7 of the ICCPR, the UN Human Rights Committee said, in para 8:
>
> > "The Committee notes that it is not sufficient for the implementation of article 7 to prohibit such treatment or punishment or to make it a crime. States parties should inform the Committee of the legislative, administrative, judicial and other measures they take to prevent and punish acts of torture and cruel, inhuman and degrading treatment in any territory under their jurisdiction."
>
> Article 41 of the International Law Commission's draft articles on Responsibility of States for internationally wrongful acts (November 2001) requires states to cooperate to bring to an end through lawful means any serious breach of an obligation under a peremptory norm of general international law. [. . .]
>
> There is reason to regard it as a duty of states, save perhaps in limited and exceptional circumstances, as where immediately necessary to protect a person from unlawful violence or property from destruction, to reject the fruits of torture inflicted in breach of international law. As McNally JA put it in *S v Nkomo* 1989 (3) ZLR 117, 131:

63 See, eg, *Mthembu (Bongani) v State*, Appeal judgment, Case No 379/07, (2008) ZASCA 51, ILDC 958 (ZA 2008), 10 April 2008, Supreme Court of Appeal [SCA], para 32 ('The absolute prohibition on the use of torture in both our law and in international law therefore demands that "any evidence" which is obtained as a result of torture must be excluded "in any proceedings" ').

> "It does not seem to me that one can condemn torture while making use of the mute confession resulting from torture, because the effect is to encourage torture."

Lord Bingham was the only Lord to refer to the *jus cogens* nature of the prohibition against torture to reach his conclusion on the inadmissibility of foreign torture evidence, which was, however, short of unambiguous ('save perhaps in limited and exceptional circumstances'). He relied rather on the common law and constitutional principles to 'give a very clear negative answer' to the admissibility of foreign torture evidence.[64] He could not, however, convince the majority, which ruled that the SIAC could admit such evidence if it concluded that there was no more than a possibility that the information was obtained by torture.[65]

V. Conclusion

This survey of cases on *jus cogens* from more than a dozen states shows that—with the apparent exception of French courts—domestic courts have generally endorsed the concept. In most cases, they have, however, treated the relevant issues briefly. Nonetheless, as instances of state practice, they can provide some evidence on various features of the concept. Significantly, some decisions stem from courts of states that are not party to the Vienna Convention on the Law of Treaties, such as the US and Kenya. If anything, a blunt and wholesale denial of *jus cogens* as useless and not recognized in the (judicial) practice of states can be laid to rest.

With few exceptions, domestic jurisprudence has not elucidated the definitional issues and has largely reproduced the views of scholars as to which norms fall within this category. The role of domestic courts was more influential in spelling out the effects of the concept. The overwhelming majority of cases were brought by individuals or groups alleging violations of human rights and/or international humanitarian law and the commission of international crimes. They invoked the *jus cogens* nature of the violations (sometimes by stretching their case too far) either as their main claim or to reinforce their main claim and vindicate their rights by setting aside legal rules that had a constraining effect on those rights: immunities, amnesties, statutes of limitations, and other effects that could conceivably derive as logical and automatic consequences from *jus cogens*. Most domestic courts rejected those arguments and only a minority upheld them, most notably courts in Italy and Argentina. The latter, however, especially the *Ferrini* jurisprudence, were influential in stimulating a heated debate on the possibilities and promise of *jus cogens* and its impact on the very nature of the international legal order. In *Jurisdictional Immunities of States*, the ICJ referred to several of the domestic court judgments discussed in this chapter and adopted a narrow approach, by requiring the effects of any *jus cogens* rule to be supported by state practice, thus putting the relevant debate on ice.

64 Paras 51, 52, where he also stated that 'the principles of the common law do not stand alone. Effect must be given to the European Convention, which itself takes account of the all but universal consensus embodied in the Torture Convention'.

65 This case is further discussed in A Constantinides, 'Terrorism' Chapter 14, section III.2(a) in this volume.

9
Soft Law

MACHIKO KANETAKE

I. Introduction

Article 38(1) of the Statute of the International Court of Justice (ICJ) provides us with a handy catalogue of the recognized sources of international law, namely, conventions, custom, and the general principles of law.[1] Despite the general reliance on the catalogue, questions persist as to whether and to what extent these three sources of international law exhaust the international standards which states consider that they ought to follow.[2] The 'soft' law concept is part of the broad movement since the 1970s—of which this chapter is part—in international legal scholarship to give recognition to international normative standards which do not fall under the recognized sources of international law.[3]

By compiling a selected number of domestic court decisions primarily from the Oxford Reports on International Law in Domestic Courts (ILDC), this chapter aims to provide a glimpse of how domestic courts give recognition, through their judicial reasoning, to soft law.[4] Within the context of the ILDC reports, soft law is understood broadly to embrace a range of standards which states consider that they ought to abide by and which may not yet fall under the three sources of international law. This chapter does not cover a domestic court's reference to foreign law and judgments.

Soft law is typically expressed and developed by way of international instruments adopted by treaty-monitoring bodies and international organizations. Whether or not a normative prescription contained in, for instance, a UN General Assembly resolution, reflects, in substance, the accepted interpretation of treaties or established customary international law is by no means straightforward, owing to the flexibility of treaty interpretation and uncertainties in identifying state practice and *opinio juris* to constitute customary international law. Added also are the absence of centralized authorities to define the existence and scope of international legal rules, as well as the uneasy status of treaty-monitoring bodies and international organizations in the development of supposedly state-centric international law. In this sense, the manner in which domestic judges engage with soft-law instruments would be one indicator to measure the normativity of such international instruments.

This chapter categorizes the selected ILDC case reports primarily according to the *kind of instruments* invoked by domestic courts. As shown by section II of this chapter, the opinions of

1 Statute of the International Court of Justice (signed 26 June 1945, entered into force on 24 October 1945) 39 AJIL Supp 215 (1945), Articles 38(1)(a)-(c).

2 For an overview, see, eg, J Pauwelyn, 'Is It International Law or Not, and Does It Even Matter?' in J Pauwelyn, R Wessel and J Wouters (eds), *Informal International Lawmaking* (Oxford University Press 2012) 125.

3 The term 'soft' law can be used in different ways. In this chapter, the dichotomy of 'soft' and 'hard' law is based on whether a standard qualifies as one of the three sources of international law. However, 'soft' law can also be used to denote treaty provisions which are merely hortatory and not imperative. See R Ida, 'Formation des normes internationales dans un monde en mutation: Critique de la notion de soft law' in *Le droit international au service de la paix, de la justice et du développement: Mélanges Michel Virally* (Pedone 1990) 333.

4 For other cases not covered in this chapter see M Kanetake and A Nollkaemper, 'The Application of Informal International Instruments Before Domestic Courts' (2014) 46 *The George Washington International Law Review* 765. This chapter is in part based on this article.

treaty-monitoring bodies, including those for human rights treaties, have informed judges to construe pertinent treaty provisions. One of the visible examples is judicial reference to General Comments issued by the Human Rights Committee and the Committee on Economic, Social and Cultural Rights for the interpretation of the International Covenant on Civil and Political Rights (ICCPR) and the International Covenant on Economic, Social and Cultural Rights (ICESCR), respectively (as illustrated by *RM and Cradle*). Interestingly, General Comments may instruct domestic courts even if their states are not a party to relevant human rights treaties (*Jaftha v Schoeman*). Recourse is also made to documents prepared by the Office of the United Nations High Commissioner for Refugees (UNHCR) (*Adan*). While the UNHCR is not formally a treaty body for the Refugee Convention, it regularly undertakes refugee status determination according to the Refugee Convention and contributes to the development of its interpretation.

The documents adopted by treaty-monitoring bodies by no means exhaust judicial engagement with soft-law instruments. As illustrated in section III, judges consult documents prepared by a 'conference of parties' (*ADS*). Section IV demonstrates that national courts also refer to the instruments of international organizations, including the UN General Assembly's resolutions (*People's Union for Civil Liberties*). One of the frequently cited resolutions is the Universal Declaration of Human Rights, although its provisions have arguably gained the status of customary international law. As section V suggests, major declarations adopted by intergovernmental forums have also been present in the judicial reasoning, such as the 1990 Bergen Ministerial Declaration on Sustainable Development in order to give meaning to the precautionary principle (*Spraytech*) and the 1972 Stockholm Declaration to interpret the concept of sustainable development (*Fuel Retailers Association*).

Needless to say, these international instruments serve a variety of *purposes* in the reasoning of domestic courts. In the first place, some instruments are invoked for an *evidentiary* purpose. General Assembly resolutions have been invoked as evidence to prove the existence of customary international law (*Filartiga*). Secondly, a more common usage is the *interpretive guide* for customary international law (*Spraytech*), or more frequently, for international treaties, which, especially in the countries with dualist traditions, would be ultimately used to construe domestic law (*RM and Cradle; Adan; ADS*). Finally, soft-law instruments have even been used as *general guidance* that shapes the direction of judicial interpretation. For instance, they have been invoked in order to stress the importance of access to water (*Matsipane Mosetlhanyane*) or to identify an evolving concept of international law and highlight the role of courts in environmental protection (*Fuel Retailers*).

The overview of the selected ILDC cases leads us to the question of *justification*, namely, on what basis domestic courts invoke soft-law instruments in their judicial reasoning. Domestic courts' reference to the instrument can be justified on the basis of formal binding force if declarations or recommendations have been incorporated into domestic law (eg, *Nabori* in section V) or have already been established as customary international law (eg, *Filartiga* in section IV). In such cases, domestic courts find little difficulty in justifying why they can invite UN General Assembly resolutions or other instruments to judicial reasoning. If international instruments are not formally binding, domestic courts' discretionary reference to them may be justified on the basis that the instruments are *persuasive*, or so-called 'persuasive authority' (*Adan*, per Lord Steyn, in Section II). Persuasive authority is contrasted with 'binding authority'. The latter has independent binding force and its authoritativeness stems from its pedigree, as opposed to its merit or substance.[5]

The arena of persuasive authority may appear to be an unregulated sphere, leaving judges wide discretion to pick and choose instruments which support conclusions they have reached

5 See C Flanders, 'Toward a Theory of Persuasive Authority' (2009) 62 *Oklahoma Law Review* 55, 62.

elsewhere. The uncertainty of variables that determine the persuasiveness of an instrument indeed paves the way for domestic courts' purposeful interpretation that support judges' preferred conclusions. Nevertheless, the space of soft-law instruments is not totally without order. From the Oxford Reports on the ILDC cases, it is possible to identify some of the major indicators sustaining the persuasiveness of soft-law instruments.

First, the *systematic association with formal instruments* is one of the factors that determine the persuasiveness of non-treaty instruments. For the purpose of interpreting a particular treaty, the instruments of treaty monitoring bodies and a conference of parties (ie, Sections II-III) are generally more persuasive than those of other bodies (ie, Sections IV-V) owing to the former's institutional linkage to the treaty in question. Secondly, the *nature of the body* and the *procedure according to which instruments are adopted* may also accord persuasiveness on non-treaty instruments. The judicial nature of a body (or of the procedure according to which a particular instrument is adopted) confers persuasiveness on international instruments (as illustrated by *Mansouri-Rad* in section II). Finally, the wider public acceptance, or at least acceptance within the relevant interpretive communities, would render an instrument persuasive before domestic courts (eg, *KwaZulu-Natal v P* in section IV). These indicators by no means exhaust often context-dependent considerations that determine the level of domestic courts' interactions with soft-law instruments. After all, the use of soft-law instruments depends on the discretion of domestic judges, whose level of engagement both augments and diminishes the normativity of international instruments at the international level.

II. Instruments of Treaty-Monitoring Bodies

RM v Attorney General, JK (on the application of RM) v Attorney General, Application brought by way of original summons to high court, Civil Case 1351, ILDC 699 (KE 2006), 1st December 2006, Kenya; Nairobi; High Court

The question the Kenyan High Court encountered in *RM and Cradle* was the compatibility of the Kenyan domestic law, which bestowed parental responsibility for children born out of wedlock only on the mother, with the Kenyan constitution and international covenants. RM, the applicant, was born out of wedlock to a mother and father who were cohabiting before the child's birth, on 16 September 2000, until 3 January 2001. The father disappeared or avoided the mother completely in April 2001, not providing any parental responsibility including support for the child's upkeep. It was argued on behalf of RM that the relevant law, section 24(3) of the Children Act No 8 of 2001 (Kenya), did not place any parental responsibility on a father who was, as in this case, not married to the child's mother.

RM argued that this differentiation, by placing RM and similarly situating children at a disadvantage compared to children born within wedlock, amounted to discrimination contrary to the constitution and international treaties, including the Convention on the Rights of the Child (1989), the African Charter on the Rights and Welfare of the Child (1999), and the Convention on the Elimination of Discrimination Against Women (1979). In upholding the compatibility of the domestic law with the Constitution and the international covenants, the Kenyan High Court invoked a UN General Assembly resolution and the General Comments of the Human Rights Committee.

The following are the excerpts of the relevant parts of the decision. Paragraph numbers have been added to this decision by OUP for the purpose of the ILDC report.

> **Position as Per International Instruments—States Permitted to take into Account Special Circumstances**
>
> [. . .]
>
> 75 It is strikingly clear that Article 2 of the Universal Declaration prohibits distinction of any kind. The obvious interpretation is that no differences at all can be legally

accepted. However the situation on the ground does not support such a restrictive interpretation of the Declaration in that the monitoring bodies have not supported any such interpretation and in some of the constitutions of the member states including that of Kenya do not support the position as stated in Article 2. The Member States have claimed and have been allowed "*a margin of appreciation*" because differences in real life are inevitable and they are not necessarily negative. Indeed, international jurisprudence and supporting case law demonstrates that not all distinctions between persons and groups of persons can be regarded as discrimination in the strict sense or true sense of the term. Thus General Comment No. 18 in the United Nations Compilation of General Comments, p 134 para 1 lays what appears to be a peremptory international norm (jus cogens) in these words:

> "non-discrimination, together with equality before the law and equal protection of the law without any discrimination constitute a basic and general principle relating to the protection of human rights."

76 The second principle which is now generally accepted and which does not support a restrictive interpretation is that *distinctions made between people are justified provided that they are, in general terms reasonable and imposed for an objective and legitimate purpose.*

77 To amplify on this we wish to borrow again from the Human Rights Committee General Comments (supra) at page 135 para 7 in its definition of "discrimination."

> "that the term discrimination as used in the Covenant (International Covenant on Civil and Political Rights) should be understood to imply any distinction, exclusion, restriction or preference which is based on any ground such as race, colour, sex, language, religion, political or other opinion, national or social origin, property, birth or other status, and which has the purpose or effect of nullifying or impairing the recognition, enjoyment or exercise by all persons, on an equal footing of all rights and freedoms"

78 The Human Rights Committee has commented that the enjoyment of rights and freedoms on an equal footing does not mean identical treatment in every instance. Taking the ICCPR as an example Article 6(5) prohibits the death sentence from being imposed on persons below 18 years of age and from being carried out on pregnant women. The other obvious example is affirmative action which is aimed at diminishing or eliminating conditions likely to perpetuate inequality or discrimination in fact. Such a corrective action constitutes or is termed legitimate differentiation under the ICCPR.

79 It is therefore an accepted international principle of law that differentiation based on *reasonable* and *objective criteria* does not amount to prohibited discrimination. A state which complies with this criteria would not be faulted in practice or in its formulation of a supporting law provided this criteria is adhered to. To explain the position further the universality of the 1948 Declaration of Human Rights is based on a common heritage of humankind which is the oneness of the human family and the essential dignity of the individual. It is from these two universally shared traits from which the notion of equality finds its stem or base.

[. . .]

85 Thus we find that since the aim of the section is to provide for parental responsibility locating it initially in the mother and providing for a shared responsibility taking into account all possible relationships that spring from the birth the section has handled the situation with a reasonable proportionality between the difference of the one set of children (generally born within and those born out of wedlock since

> the aim is to provide for parental responsibility in both situations as far as it is practically possible in the later situation. We find that the balance struck by the challenged section cannot be said to be unreasonable or unjust. The difference between the two sets of situations cannot in our view be said not to have an objective *and reasonable justification*.

The General Comments and Recommendations are part of the instruments adopted by human rights treaty-monitoring bodies whose interpretation may guide domestic courts' decisions. Among the monitoring bodies, the Human Rights Committee's General Comments are the most visible ones in the jurisprudence of domestic courts. In this case, the Kenyan High Court consulted the Human Rights Committee's General Comment No 18 (1989)[6] on non-discrimination as interpretive guide as part of international human rights instruments.[7] The Kenyan High Court observed that such restrictive understanding that no distinctions are acceptable is neither supported by member states' practice, nor by the 'monitoring bodies'.[8]

General Comments and Recommendations are formally non-binding instruments adopted by the Human Rights Committee and other monitoring bodies established for UN human rights treaties.[9] General Comments are issued with a view to assisting states parties in preparing their reports, as well as their treaty implementation in general.[10] General Comments are issued as part of the monitoring task to consider and evaluate reports submitted by states parties, and have been regarded 'authoritative' or 'persuasive' by some national courts. For instance, the South African High Court in the *Residents of Bon Vista Mansions v Southern Metropolitan Local* case (2002)[11] referred to General Comment No 12 on the ICESCR for the construction of the international and constitutional right to access to water, and observed that 'General Comments have authoritative status under international law'.[12]

The amenability to General Comments differs, however, according to states or even within one state. For instance, the Tokyo District Court in Japan, in its 15 March 2001 Judgment, regarded the General Comments of the Human Rights Committee as neither authoritative nor legally binding.[13] The differences in terms of the judicial amenability to the documents of monitoring bodies can be ascribed to a number of variables, including: the degree of judges' discretion, the awareness of parties to international human rights documents, and the presence of human rights non-government organizations (NGOs) who are capable of making use of international human rights instruments in their *amici curiae* submissions.

Jaftha and van Rooyen v Schoeman and ors, Appeal decision, CCT74/03, [2004] ZACC 25, ILDC 1846 (ZA 2004), 2005 (2) SA 140 (CC), 2005 (1) BCLR 78 (CC), 8th October 2004, South Africa; Constitutional Court [CC]

Jaftha and Van Rooyen were both unemployed and had few assets. Having been unable to pay their outstanding debt, their homes were sold in a sale of execution. In *Jaftha and van Rooyen v*

6 Human Rights Committee, 'CCPR General Comment No 18: Non-Discrimination' (1989) UN Doc HRI/GEN/1/Rev.1.

7 *RM v Attorney General, JK (on the application of RM) v Attorney General*, Application brought by way of original summons to high court, Civil Case 1351, ILDC 699 (KE 2006) (Kenya, Nairobi, High Court, 1 December 2006), paras 75–78.

8 ibid, para 75.

9 The general comments and recommendations of all human rights treaty bodies are compiled periodically: see, eg, Human Rights Instruments, Volume I, Compilation of General Comments and General Recommendations Adopted by Human Rights Treaty Bodies (2008), UN Doc HRI/GEN/1/Rev.9 (Vol I).

10 For the Human Rights Committee see, eg, UN Doc HRI/GEN/1/Rev.9 (Vol I) (2008) at 172–73.

11 *Residents of Bon Vista Mansions v Southern Metropolitan Local Council* 2002 (6) BCLR 625 (W) (South Africa, High Court Witwatersrand). Cited in: ILA, Committee on International Human Rights Law and Practice, 'Final Report on the Impact of Findings of the United Nations Human Rights Treaty Bodies' (2004) paras 11, 99.

12 *Residents of Bon Vista Mansions v Southern Metropolitan Local Council*, ibid, 629, para 17.

13 Judgment of 15 March 2001, Tokyo District Court, 1784 *Hanrei Jiho* 67.

Schoeman and ors in South Africa, they launched proceedings and sought to set aside the sales in execution. Jaftha and Van Rooyen challenged the constitutional validity of sections 66(1)(a) and 67 of the Magistrates' Courts Act 32 of 1944, which permit the sale in execution of peoples' homes on the basis that they have not paid their debts, and thereby enable the removal of their security of tenure. Jaftha and Van Rooyen argued that these sections of the 1944 Act violate the right to have access to adequate housing, protected in section 26 of the South African constitution. They claimed that both the state and private parties have a duty not to interfere unjustifiably with any person's existing access to adequate housing.

The Cape High Court did not uphold the argument of unconstitutionality.[14] Regarding the content of the right to adequate housing, the High Court was of the view that the right of access to housing does not encompass an entitlement to the ownership of housing. While the High Court acknowledged that the execution process brings the ownership to an end, it held that this does not violate section 26 of the South African constitution because that section does not contain a right to ownership.

The decision of the High Court was appealed in the South African Constitutional Court. The Constitutional Court found the incompatibility of the domestic legislation with the constitutional protection of access to adequate housing. In so holding, the South African Constitutional Court invoked the General Comments of the Committee on Economic, Social and Cultural Rights.

The following are the excerpts of the relevant parts of the decision. Footnotes listed at the end of the extracts are provided in the original document. The texts in square brackets are added by the present author.

> *The right to adequate housing in international law*
>
> 23 Although the concept of adequate housing was briefly discussed in *Government of the Republic of South Africa and Others v Grootboom and Others*[28] this Court has yet to consider it in any detail. This subject has however been dealt with by the United Nations Committee on Economic, Social and Cultural Rights (the Committee) in the context of the International Covenant on Economic, Social and Cultural Rights, 1966 (the Covenant).[29] In terms of section 39(1)(b) of the Constitution, this Court must consider international law when interpreting the Bill of Rights.[30] Therefore, guidance may be sought from international instruments that have considered the meaning of adequate housing.
>
> 24 Article 11(1) of the Covenant reads as follows:
>
> "The States Parties to the present Covenant recognize the right of everyone to an adequate standard of living for himself and his family, including *adequate food, clothing and housing*, and to the continuous improvement of living conditions. The States Parties will take appropriate steps to ensure the realization of this right, recognizing to this effect the essential importance of international co-operation based on free consent." (Emphasis added.)
>
> In its General Comment 4, the Committee, giving content to article 11(1) of the Covenant, emphasised the need not to give the right to housing a restrictive interpretation and to see it as "the right to live somewhere in security, peace and dignity".[31] The position of the Committee reflects the view adopted by this Court in *Grootboom*, that the right to dignity is inherently linked with socio-economic rights.[32] It is important, for the purposes of this case, to point to the Committee's recognition that "the concept of adequacy is particularly significant in relation to the right to housing".[33] While acknowledging that adequacy "is determined in part by social, economic, cultural, climatic, ecological and other factors", it has identified

14 *Jaftha v Schoeman and ors; Van Rooyen v Stoltz and ors* (10) BCLR 1149 (C) (2003).

"certain aspects of the right that must be taken into account for this purpose in any particular context."[34] Of relevance is the focus on security of tenure. The Committee points out that security of tenure takes many forms, not just ownership, but that "all persons should possess a degree of security of tenure which guarantees legal protection against forced eviction, harassment and other threats."[35]

Security of tenure in our historical context

25 The international law concept of adequate housing and its central theme of security of tenure reinforce the notion of adequate housing in section 26 as understood in the light of our particular history of forced removals and racist evictions in South Africa.

[. . .]

52 I have held that section 66(1)(a) of [the Magistrates' Courts Act 32 of 1944] is overbroad and constitutes a violation of section 26(1) of the Constitution to the extent that it allows execution against the homes of indigent debtors, where they lose their security of tenure. I have held further that section 66(1)(a) is not justifiable and cannot be saved to the extent that it allows for such executions where no countervailing considerations in favour of the creditor justify the sales in execution [. . .].

---

28 Id [*Government of the Republic of South Africa and Others v Grootboom and Others* 2001 (1) SA 46 (CC); 2000 (11) BCLR 1169 (CC)] at paras 35-7.

29 South Africa signed the Covenant on 3 October 1994. It has yet to ratify the Covenant.

30 Section 39(1) of the Constitution reads as follows:
"When interpreting the Bill of Rights, a court, tribunal or forum—
(a) must promote the values that underlie an open and democratic society based on human dignity, equality and freedom;
(b) must consider international law; and
(c) may consider foreign law."

31 *The Right to Adequate Housing (Art.11(1)) UNCESCR General Comment 4* (1991) 13 December 1991 E/1992/23 at para 7.

32 See above n 27 [*Government of the Republic of South Africa and Others v Grootboom and Others* 2001 (1) SA 46 (CC); 2000 (11) BCLR 1169 (CC) at para 83].

33 Above n 31 at para 8.

34 Id.

35 Id.

In this case, the South African Constitutional Court sought guidance, not only from Article 11(1) of the ICESCR itself, but also from General Comment No 4 in interpreting the constitutional protection.[15] In South Africa, it is constitutionally required for the court to consider international law when interpreting the Bill of Rights. Noteworthy, however, in this case is that the Constitutional Court consulted the treaty which South Africa had signed but had yet to ratify (fn 29) and the above-mentioned General Comment No 4 adopted by the Committee on Economic, Social and Cultural Rights.

This case is illustrative of the difficulty of identifying the precise 'weight' that courts may give to a soft-law instrument in their judicial reasoning. The extent to which soft-law instruments guide the reasoning of domestic courts varies depending on cases. Some international

---

15 *Jafiha and van Rooyen v Schoeman and ors*, Appeal decision, CCT74/03, [2004] ZACC 25, ILDC 1846 (ZA 2004), 2005 (2) SA 140 (CC), 2005 (1) BCLR 78 (CC) (South Africa, Constitutional Court [CC], 8 October 2004), para 24.

instruments may substantively change the meaning of specific rules or the overall direction of judgment, while others may be treated as confirmatory.

In this case, the South African Constitutional Court situated the concept of adequate housing under international law as something to 'reinforce' the domestic counterpart[16] and made no further reference to international law in the following paragraphs. It is therefore questionable whether the ICESCR and associated General Comment No 4 have substantively guided the interpretation of constitutional provisions by the South African Court. At least within the court's formal narrative, the General Comments had a confirmatory value.

Matsipane Mosetlhanyane and Gakenyatsiwe Matsipane v The Attorney General (Court of Appeal Civil Appeal No CACLB-074-10; High Court Civil Case No MAHLB-000393-09) (Botswana, Court of Appeal, 27 January 2011) (not in ILDC)

The applicants, Matsipane Mosetlhanyane and Gakenyatsiwe Matsipane, were residents of the Central Kalahari Game Reserve (CKGR) in Botswana. They belonged to the 'Basarwa' communities, which used to live on a nomadic basis but over the years formed permanent settlements inside the CKGR whilst continuing with their traditional way of life as hunter-gatherers.

In 2002, the government decided to 'relocate' the Basarwa communities to settlements outside the CKGR. In order to induce the relocation, a pump engine and water tank, which had been installed for the purpose of using a borehole, were dismantled and removed. As a result of this measure, the Basarwa communities encountered a shortage of water. The government also refused to issue special game licences.

Some residents of the Basarwa communities, including Matsipane Mosetlhanyane, instituted proceedings in 2002 against the government.[17] In 2006, the High Court in *Sesana* rendered a decision against the government, holding that the residents were forcibly or wrongful deprived of the lawful possession of the land without their consent, and that the government's refusal to issue special game licences was unlawful and unconstitutional.

What the High Court in *Sesana* did not uphold, however, was the government's obligation to restore the provision of basic and essential services to the Basarwa communities. The government thus continued to refuse to the provision of essential services and did not grant the permission for the abstraction of water. Matsipane Mosetlhanyane and Gakenyatsiwe Matsipane then instituted a new proceeding against the government, claiming their right to abstract and use water. In 2010, the High Court of Botswana held against these two applicants; while it accepted their right to abstract water under section 6 of the Water Act, it held that the abstraction of water may not be done without a permission accordance with section 9 of the Act. The applicants then appealed to the Court of Appeal which decided, in January 2011, in their favour. In reaching the conclusion, the court referred to formally non-binding human rights instruments.

> 8 Quite significantly, the first appellant's account of the human suffering at Mothomelo [in the CKGR] due to lack of water is uncontested. Very often the appellants and other members of the various communities in the reserve do not have enough water to meet their needs. They depend on melons which are either scarce or sometimes non-existent. As a result, life becomes "extremely difficult." They spend a great deal of their time in the bush "looking for any root or other edible matter from which we can extract even a few drops of water." The absence of water frequently makes them "weak and vulnerable to sickness." Some of them suffer from "constipation, headaches or bouts of dizziness." Often they do not sleep well. Young children "cry a great deal." Often they do not have water to cook or

16 ibid, para 25.

17 *Sesana and Others v Attorney-General* [2006] (2) BLR 633 (HC).

to clean themselves. An official report describes them as "very dirty, due to lack of adequate water for drinking and other domestic use." In these circumstances the appellants are "anxious to have use of the borehole, which has now been lying idle for several years." They point to the fact that the borehole is of no use to anyone else but that it is vital to their well-being.

[. . .]

19 It remains then to deal briefly with the appellants' point relating to s 7 (1) of the Constitution . . . Section 7 (1) reads as follows:-

> "7. (1) *No person shall be subjected to torture or to inhuman or degrading punishment or other treatment.*"

[. . .] in my view, the right is absolute and unqualified. Unlike the other rights contained in s3 of the Constitution it is not subject to any limitations "designed to ensure that the enjoyment of the said rights and freedoms of others does not prejudice the rights and freedoms of others or the public interest." I should add that I approach the matter on the basis of the fundamental principle that whether a person has been subjected to inhuman or degrading treatment involves a value judgment. It is appropriate to stress that in the exercise of a value judgment, the Court is entitled to have regard to international consensus on the importance of access to water. Reference to two important documents will suffice:-

(1) On 20 January 2003, the United Nations Committee on Economic, Social and Cultural Rights submitted a report on what it termed Substantive Issues Arising In The Implementation Of The International Covenant On Economic, Social and Cultural Rights. In its introduction it stated the following:-

> "*1. Water is a limited natural resource and a public good fundamental for life and health. The human right to water is indispensable for leading a life in human dignity. It is a prerequisite for the realisation of other human rights...*"

In paragraph 16 (d) of its report the Committee said the following:-

> "*16. Whereas the right to water applies to everyone, States parties should give special attention to those individuals and groups who have traditionally faced difficulties in exercising this right, including women, children, minority groups indigenous peoples, refugees, asylum seekers, internally displaced persons, migrant workers, prisoners and detainees. In particular, States parties should take steps to ensure that:*
>
> *(d) Indigenous people's access to water resources on their ancestral lands is protected from encroachment and unlawful pollution. States should provide resources for indigenous peoples to design, deliver and control their access to water*".

(2) On July 2010, the United Nations General Assembly recognised the right to safe and clean drinking water as a fundamental human right that is essential for the full enjoyment of life and all human rights. Accordingly, the UN General Assembly called upon States:-

> "*(b) To ensure full transparency of the planning and implementation process in the provision of safe drinking water and sanitation and the active, free and meaningful participation of the concerned local communities and relevant stakeholders.*"

20 It was submitted on the appellants' behalf that the Government's refusal to allow them permission to use, at their own expense, the Mothomelo borehole, or any other borehole in the CKGR for that matter, for domestic purposes amounts to degrading treatment contrary to s 7 of the Constitution [. . .]

[. . .]

> 22 [...] As was crisply pointed out to respondent's counsel during argument, the Government seems to be saying to the appellants:- "you can live in your settlement in the CKGR as long as you don't abstract water other than from plants." Surely that cannot be right. Doing the best I can in the exercise of a value judgment in these circumstances I am driven to conclude, therefore, that the factors set out in paragraph [8] above amount to degrading treatment of the appellants. Indeed, I accept that there is a constitutional requirement based on international consensus [...] for Government to refrain from inflicting degrading treatment.

In this case, the Court of Appeal of the Republic of Botswana supported the claims of the applicants primarily based upon the construction of sections 6 and 9 of the Water Act. According to the Court of Appeal, section 6 of the Act does not provide for a right to water as such, but provides a lawful owner or occupier of any land with a right to sink a borehole on such land for domestic purposes without a water right (paras 13–18, not part of the excerpts above).

At the same time, the Court of Appeal touched on the claim submitted by the residents concerning the violation of the right not to be subjected to torture or to inhuman or degrading treatment (as provided in section 7(1) of the Botswana Constitution). In interpreting the constitutional right, the Court of Appeal has drawn on the two documents which are not formally biding in themselves:[18] General Comment No 15 (2002) adopted by the Committee on Economic and Social and Cultural Rights[19] and the resolution of the Human Rights Council.[20]

This case is illustrative of a variety of purposes for which domestic courts may utilize soft-law instruments. In this case, while the above-mentioned General Comment and the resolution were employed in the context of interpreting the constitutional right, the court employed them not necessarily as specific interpretive guides to the constitutional right, but rather to determine the overall normative direction of the judicial reasoning. Having noted that the determination of inhumane or degrading treatment should involve a value judgment, the Court of Appeal observed that '*in the exercise of a value judgment*, the Court is entitled to have regard to *international consensus on the importance of access to water*'.[21] It was for the purpose of highlighting the importance of access to water that the court referred to the General Comment and the Resolution of the Human Rights Council.

Mansouri-Rad v Department of Labour, Appeal decision, Refugee Appeal No 74665/03, [2005] NZAR 60, ILDC 217 (NZ 2004), 7th July 2004, New Zealand

The appellant in *Mansouri-Rad v Department of Labour* was a 25-year-old citizen of Iran. He arrived in New Zealand on 15 March 2003 and sought refugee status. His application was declined by the Refugee Status Branch of the New Zealand Immigration Service. Mansouri-Rad then appealed to the Refugee Status Appeals Authority.

---

18 *Matsipane Mosetlhanyane and Gakenyatsiwe Matsipane v Attorney General* (Court of Appeal Civil Appeal No CACLB-074-10; High Court Civil Case No MAHLB-000393-09) (Botswana, Court of Appeal, 27 January 2011) para 19.

19 Committee on Economic, Social and Cultural Rights, 'General Comment No. 15: The Right to Water (Articles 11 and 12 of the International Covenant on Economic, Social and Cultural Rights)' (2003) UN Doc E/C. 12/2002/11. From the General Comment, the court quoted not only the phrase which stated that the human right to water is indispensable (para 1), but also the special protection for indigenous peoples (para 16(d)).

20 UN Human Rights Council, 'Human Rights and Access to Safe Drinking Water and Sanitation' (2010) UN Doc A/HRC/RES/15/9. The Court of Appeal is referring to the document adopted by the 'UN General Assembly' in 'July 2010' (para 19). Yet it cites the phrase from the Resolution of the Human Rights Council adopted in September 2010. The Human Rights Council's Resolution called upon states '[t]o ensure [...] the active, free and meaningful participation of the concerned local communities and relevant stakeholders therein' (para 8(b)).

21 *Matsipane Mosetlhanyane and Gakenyatsiwe Matsipane v Attorney General* (n 18) para 19 (emphasis added).

The refugee status was to be determined in accordance with Article 1A of the Convention relating to the Status of Refugees (1954).[22] The principal basis for Mansouri-Rad's claim was that he was a homosexual. He argued that in Iran his relationships were conducted furtively and he was always in fear of being reported and arrested. He had attempted suicide on past occasions because of his deep unhappiness at being unable to live a normal life. He said that if he returned to Iran he could not continue to hide his sexual orientation because, for him, homosexuality was not a matter only of sex but of having loving relationships of the kind enjoyed by men and women.

Having considered the meaning of 'being persecuted' under Article 1A of the Refugee Convention, the New Zealand Refugee Status Appeals Authority upheld the refugee status of Mansouri-Rad in its decision of 7 July 2004. In the course of its reasoning, the Appeals Authority referred to the role of a human rights treaty-monitoring bodies and the UN-based human rights body.

The texts in square brackets found in the following excerpts are original.

> **Identifying core human rights**
>
> 62 Recognising that "being persecuted" may be defined as the sustained or systemic violation of basic human rights demonstrative of a failure of state protection, the question which arises is how one identifies "basic human rights".
>
> [...]
>
> 73 The Authority's decisions have ... recognised that in addition to employing the international human rights instruments referred to, it is only appropriate that regard be had to the interpretation of those instruments by the "treaty bodies" set up under the instruments, particularly the Human Rights Committee, the Committee on Economic, Social and Cultural Rights, the Committee on the Elimination of all Forms of Discrimination Against Women, the Committee on the Elimination of Racial Discrimination and of the Committee on the Rights of the Child. The Authority recognises that the binding effect and jurisprudential quality of the decisions of these bodies may be a matter of controversy (see *Refugee Appeal No. 72558/01* (19 November 2002)). Contrast the views expressed by Elizabeth Evatt, a member of the Human Rights Committee, in "The Impact of International Human Rights on Domestic Law" in Huscroft & Rishworth, *Litigating Rights: Perspectives from Domestic and International Law* (Hart Publishing, 2002) at 281, 295, 302 with the views expressed in two other papers published in the same text, namely Paul Rishworth, "The Rule of International Law?" *op cit* 267, 274-279 and Scott Davidson, "Intention and Effect: The Legal Status of the Final Views of the Human Rights Committee" *op cit* 305-321. This is not a controversy we need enter here. The decisions of the Human Rights Committee can be at least of persuasive authority: *R v Goodwin (No. 2)* [1993] 2 NZLR 390, 393 (CA) and *Minister for Immigration and Multicultural and Indigenous Affairs v B* (2004) 206 ALR 130 (HCA) at [148] (Kirby J). See further *Wellington District Legal Services Committee v Tangiora* [1998] 1 NZLR 129, 134-136, 144 (CA) and *Tangiora v Wellington District Legal Services Committee* [2000] 1 NZLR 17, 20-22; [2000] 1 WLR 240, 244-246 (PC). Contrast *Briggs v Baptiste* [2000] 2 AC 40, 53 (PC) where, in the context of the Inter-American system the point made was that while it is to be expected that national courts will give great weight to the jurisprudence of the Inter-American Court, "they would be abdicating their duty if they were to adopt an interpretation of the [American] Convention [on Human

22 Convention relating to the Status of Refugees (adopted 28 July1951, entered into force 22 April 1954) 189 UNTS 137.

Rights, 1969] which they considered to be untenable". For observations as to the binding effect of decisions of the Committee against Torture, see *Ahani v Canada (Attorney General)* (2002) 208 DLR (4th) 66 at paras 34-40 (Ont. CA).

74 On occasion it might also be appropriate to draw on the jurisprudence of the European Court of Human Rights as well as the Inter-American Commission on Human Rights and the Inter-American Court of Human Rights under the American Declaration of the Rights and Duties of Man, 1948 and the American Convention on Human Rights 1969. However, as the European and inter-American systems differ in many ways from each other and from that provided for in the international human rights instruments referred to, caution must be exercised in applying the jurisprudence of these regional organisations outside their proper context. See for example David Harris, "Regional Protection of Human Rights: The Inter-American Achievement" in Harris & Livingstone, "The Inter-American System of Human Rights (Clarendon Press, Oxford, 1998) 1-29 and *Refugee Appeal No. 72558/01* (19 November 2002) at [115]-[119].

75 There are three further cautions. First, in the context of Article 1A(2) of the Refugee Convention, the identification of basic human rights is directed to a single, limited end, namely the illumination of the meaning of the phrase "being persecuted". There is no other purpose. The function of refugee law is palliative. It does not hold states responsible for human rights abuses. The refugee decision-maker does not usurp the jurisdiction of the Human Rights Committee under Article 40 of the International Covenant on Civil and Political Rights (the reporting process) or under Article 41 (the interstate complaints procedure). Nor is it the role of the refugee decision-maker to express "views" as if refugee adjudication were an individual complaint under the First Optional Protocol. The determination of refugee status is no more than an assessment whether, in the event of the refugee claimant returning to the country of origin, there is a real chance of that person "being persecuted" for a Convention reason.

76 Second, it is important to remember why only a highly select group of human rights treaties are to be the point of reference. Not only is there a danger of over-inclusion, new "rights" can be claimed with little thought, debate or agreement: Philip Alston, "Conjuring up new human rights: A proposal for quality control" (1984) Am. J. Int'l L 613. Not everything that may serve to improve the well-being of individuals can or should be accepted as a human right.

77 Third, the intention of the drafters was not to protect persons against any and all forms of even serious harm, but was rather to restrict refugee recognition to situations in which there was a risk of a type of injury that would be inconsistent with the basic duty of protection owed by a state to its own population. As Professor Hathaway explains at op cit 103-104:

> As a holistic reading of the refugee definition demonstrates, the drafters were not concerned to respond to certain forms of harm *per se*, but were rather motivated to intervene only where the maltreatment anticipated was demonstrative of a breakdown of national protection. The existence of past or anticipated suffering alone, therefore, does not make one a refugee, unless the state has failed in relation to some duty to defend its citizenry against the particular form of harm anticipated.

78 It is almost unnecessary to add that we do not see the UN Human Rights Commission as an appropriate point of reference, lying as it does outside the treaty framework earlier described. In addition, the 52-state Commission is highly politicised, as witness the circumstances in which Cuba and China were successful in having the United States lose its seat in 2001. One commentator referred to the observable spectacle of countries

accused of violating human rights being among the most ardent seekers of seats on the Commission in order to be better placed to defend themselves from criticism for violating human rights (see Colum Lynch, "United States loses seat on UN rights body", *Guardian Weekly*, May 10, 2001 p 32) while another commentator concluded that foxes were guarding the chicken coop ("Chickens and foxes", *Economist*, April 21, 2001 p 42). Among the Commission's new members in 2001 were Algeria, Congo, Kenya, Libya, Saudi Arabia, Syria and Vietnam. They were later joined by Pakistan, Sudan and Togo ("Shameful all round", *Economist*, May 12, 2001 p 14). On 23 April 2004 the Commission failed to condemn the crimes against humanity, war crimes and other violations of international humanitarian law committed by the Sudanese government in the western province of Darfur: Human Rights Watch, *Darfur Destroyed: Ethnic Cleansing by Government and Militia Forces in Western Sudan* (May 2004). There is nothing in the assessment of the Human Rights Commission by Tomuschat in *Human Rights: Between Idealism and Realism* (Oxford, 2003) at 115-127 which persuades us that the work of the Commission is relevant to refugee determination.

79 Human rights law is by no means a flawless system. It has many gaps and limitations. But as pointed out by Professor Hillary Charlesworth in "The Challenges of Human Rights Law for Religious Traditions", Janis & Evans (eds), *Religion and International Law* (Martinus Nijhoff, 1999) at 401, 410-411, for all these constraints, it does offer a vocabulary and structure in which claims by marginalised groups can be formulated. It allows dialogue on difficult issues of human existence. Human rights law allows continually changing, negotiated understandings of that which it is most essential to protect in order to defend and to enhance our common humanity. The standards are not perfect: they are simply the best that have been identified and agreed upon thus far.

The New Zealand Refugee Status Appeals Authority recognized the applicant's refugee status on the basis that he had a well-founded fear of being persecuted for reason of his homosexuality. The Appeals Authority defined the notion of 'being persecuted' under the Refugee Convention as the sustained or systemic violations of basic human rights demonstrative of a failure of state protection. In interpreting the terms 'being persecuted' in such a manner, the Appeals Authority not only invoked major human rights treaties but also found it appropriate to consider the interpretation of these treaties by their 'treaty bodies', such as that of the Human Rights Committee.[23]

This case is noteworthy, not because of the Appeals Authority's amenability to the monitoring bodies' instruments, but because of a few remarks the authority made as to *why* it could consult such instruments. The Appeals Authority, while recognizing the controversy over the binding effect of the decisions of human rights treaty monitoring bodies, went on to observe that '[t]he decisions of the Human Rights Committee can be at least of *persuasive authority*'.[24] The Appeals Authority then contrasted the decisions of the human rights treaty monitoring bodies with those of the UN Human Rights Commission (now the UN Human Rights Council) established by the General Assembly. The non-judicial nature of the UN Human Rights Commission, which operates outside the framework of the human rights treaties, seemed to negate the persuasiveness of its decisions before domestic court proceedings. According to the Appeals Authority, 'the 52-state Commission is *highly politicised*, as witness the circumstances in which Cuba and China were successful in having the United States lose its seat in 2001'.[25]

23 *Mansouri-Rad v Department of Labour*, Appeal decision, Refugee Appeal No 74665/03, [2005] NZAR 60, ILDC 217 (NZ 2004) (New Zealand, 7 July 2004), para 73.

24 ibid, emphasis added.

25 ibid, para 78 (emphasis added).

These observations suggest that the persuasiveness of formally non-binding instruments before domestic courts should vary according in part to the existence of systematic association with a specific treaty framework and to the non-political nature of the bodies which adopt international instruments.

R, ex parte Adan v Secretary of State for the Home Department, Appeal decision, [2000] UKHL 67, [2001] 2 AC 477, [2001] 2 WLR 143, [2001] 1 All ER 593, [2001] Imm AR 253, [2000] All ER (D) 2357, ILDC 229 (UK 2000), 19th December 2000, United Kingdom

In *R v Secretary of State for the Home Department, ex parte Adan; R v Secretary of State for the Home Department, ex parte Aitseguer*, Adan, a Somali citizen, and Aitseguer, an Algerian citizen, were asylum-seekers. They both feared persecution by non-state agents. Adan arrived in the United Kingdom (UK) via Germany. She claimed asylum on the basis of the fear of persecution owing to her membership of a minority clan which had been persecuted by the majority clan. Aitseguer arrived in the UK via France. He claimed to be at risk of persecution from a political faction in Algeria and maintained that the Algerian authorities were unable to protect him.

German and French authorities had interpreted Article 1A(2) of the Refugee Convention as applicable only to events of persecution by the state. This interpretation is contrasted with the position of the UK, which includes persecution by non-state actors. Despite these interpretative differences, the secretary of state issued certificates under Article 2(2)(c) of the Asylum Act allowing the return of the asylum-seekers to Germany and France, respectively. Adan and Aitseguer challenged those certificates. The Court of Appeal held that the secretary of state had to be satisfied that the practice in the third country complied with the one true and international meaning of the Refugee Convention, ie that Article 1A(2) applied to situations where persecution was committed by non-state actors.

The secretary of state appealed to the House of Lords, claiming that interpretation of Article 2(2)(c) of the Asylum Act should refer to the Refugee Convention 'as legitimately interpreted by the country concerned'. The decision of the Court of Appeal that Article 1A(2) of the Refugee Convention had only one true and international meaning was also challenged.

The following are the excerpts of the relevant parts of the decision. Paragraph numbers have been added to this decision by OUP for the purpose of the ILDC report.

> **LORD SLYNN OF HADLEY.**
>
> [. . .]
>
> 17 That persecution may be by bodies other than the state, for the purposes of the Geneva Convention, was accepted in *Adan*'s case. Nothing has been said in the present case which suggests that that might be wrong and in my view it was plainly correct. If art 33 of the Geneva Convention had intended his obligation to be limited to cases where a state carried out or tolerated the persecution, art 33 would have said so. The Secretary of State must apply that interpretation to the application of s 2(2)(c) of the Act as he must to his own obligation under art 33 of the Geneva Convention.
>
> [. . .]
>
> **LORD STEYN.**
>
> [. . .]
>
> 54 [. . .] First, it is accepted that the United Kingdom view is shared by the majority of states. It also appears to be gaining ground. Secondly, the *UN Handbook on Procedures and Criteria for Determining Refugee Status* (1979) published by the United Nations High Commission for Refugees (UNHCR), states in para 65:
>
> > 'Persecution is normally related to action by the authorities of a country. It may also emanate from sections of the population that do not respect the standards

established by the laws of the country concerned. A case in point may be religious intolerance, amounting to persecution, in a country otherwise secular, but where sizeable fractions of the population do not respect the religious beliefs of their neighbours. Where serious discriminatory or other offensive acts are committed by the local populace, they can be considered as persecution if they are knowingly tolerated by the authorities, *or if the authorities refuse, or prove unable, to offer effective protection.*' (My emphasis.)

55 Under arts 35 and 36 of the Geneva Convention, and under art II of the protocol, the UNHCR plays a critical role in the application of the Geneva Convention: compare the Statute of the Office of the United Nations High Commissioner for Refugees (UN GA Resolution 428(V) (1950), Doc A/1775) (para 8). Contracting states are obliged to co-operate with the UNHCR. It is not surprising therefore that the *UNHCR Handbook*, although not binding on states, has high persuasive authority, and is much relied on by domestic courts and tribunals (see Aust, *Modern Treaty Law and Practice* (2000) p 191).

56 The relevant autonomous meaning of art 1A(2) of the Geneva Convention is therefore as explained in *Adan*'s case. Like the Court of Appeal I would hold that there is no material distinction between a country where there is no government (like Somalia) and a country when the government is unable to afford the necessary protection to citizens (such as Algeria). Both are covered by art 1A(2).

[. . .]

LORD HUTTON.

[. . .]

72 The essence of the reasoning of the Court of Appeal ([1999] 4 All ER 774 at 794-795, [1999] 3 WLR 1274 at 1295-1296), is:

' . . . the issue we must decide is whether or not, as a matter of law, the scope of art 1A(2) extends to persons who fear persecution by non-state agents in circumstances where the state is not complicit in the persecution, whether because it is unwilling or unable (including instances where no effective state authority exists) to afford protection. We entertain no doubt but that such persons, whose case is established on the facts, are entitled to the convention's protection. This seems to us to follow naturally from the words of art 1A(2): "... is unable or, owing to such fear, is unwilling to avail himself of the protection of that country"; and this involves no technical or over-legalistic reading of the provision. This interpretation is supported by the approach taken in para 65 of the UNHCR Handbook. We have described the Handbook's genesis, to which we attach some importance. While the Handbook is not by any means itself a source of law, many signatory states have accepted the guidance which on their behalf the UNHCR was asked to provide, and in those circumstances it constitutes, in our judgment, good evidence of what has come to be international practice within art 31(3)(b) of the Vienna Convention.'

[. . .]

74–75 Mr Pannick QC, on behalf of the Secretary of State . . . placed reliance on para 5.2 of the joint position of 4 March 1996 (OJ 1996 L63 p 2) of the member states on the harmonised application of the definition of the term 'refugee' in art 1 of the Geneva Convention:

'Persecution by third parties

Persecution by third parties will be considered to fall within the scope of the Geneva Convention where it is based on one of the grounds in Article 1A of that Convention, is individual in nature and is encouraged or permitted by the authorities. Where the official authorities fail to act, such persecution should give rise to individual examination of each application for refugee status, in accordance with national judicial practice, in the light in particular of whether or not the failure to act was deliberate. The person concerned may be eligible in any event for appropriate forms of protection under national law.'

76 He submitted that the wording of the statement shows that it was accepted that the Geneva Convention did not give protection to asylum seekers unless there was complicity by the state in the persecution which they feared.

77 My Lords, I consider that Mr Pannick's second submission relating to comity is of limited weight as the purpose of an English court in determining applications such as the present ones is not to pass judgment on the validity of a decision of a French or German court but to decide if the English Secretary of State has acted lawfully in deciding to remove a claimant for asylum from England.

78 The preamble to the joint position states: 'Having established that the Handbook of the United Nations High Commissioner for Refugees (UNHCR) is a valuable aid to Member States in determining refugee status'; and I think that the weight of Mr Pannick's fourth submission is reduced by the observations in the *UNHCR Handbook*. Paragraph 65 states:

'Persecution is normally related to action by the authorities of a country. It may also emanate from sections of the population that do not respect the standards established by the laws of the country concerned. A case in point may be religious intolerance, amounting to persecution, in a country otherwise secular, but where sizeable fractions of the population do not respect the religious beliefs of their neighbours. Where serious discriminatory or other offensive acts are committed by the local populace, they can be considered as persecution if they are knowingly tolerated by the authorities, or if the authorities refuse, or prove unable, to offer effective protection.'

79 And para 98 states:

'Being *unable* to avail himself of such protection implies circumstances that are beyond the will of the person concerned. There may, for example, be a state of war, civil war or other grave disturbance, which prevents the country of nationality from extending protection or makes such protection ineffective. Protection by the country of nationality may also have been denied to the applicant. Such denial of protection may confirm or strengthen the applicant's fear of persecution, and may indeed be an element of persecution.' (My emphasis.)

In the absence of international adjudicative bodies which systematically interpret treaties, the primary interpretation by each member state can effectively be a definite one and the interpretive differences between states remain unresolved. This holds true in many international treaties, including the Refugee Convention. In this case, while Germany and France restricted 'persecution' to that by a state, the House of Lords confirmed that the UK interpreted persecution broadly to encompass cases in which a person is persecuted from non-state actors and in which a state does not exist or is unable to afford the necessary protection to its citizens. In interpreting the Refugee Convention, Lord Steyn and Lord Hutton referred to the UNHCR Handbook,[26] which does not seem to restrict persecution to that by a state.

26 UNHCR, 'Handbook on Procedures and Criteria for Determining Refugee Status under the 1951 Convention and the 1967 Protocol relating to the Status of Refugees' (1979, and edited in January 1992) UN Doc HCR/1P/4/Eng/Rev.2.

Lord Steyn referred to the nature of the UNHCR Handbook as a 'high persuasive authority'.[27] The body's systematic association with formal international law in terms of law-application seems to be one of the variables that determine persuasiveness. The UNHCR is systematically associated with the Refugee Convention, which acknowledges its critical role, and under which member states are obligated to cooperate with the body.

The UNHCR's Handbook, together with the UNHCR's revised Guidelines on Applicable Criteria and Standards Relating to the Detention of Asylum Seekers (1999),[28] has been referred to by domestic courts to interpret the Refugee Convention and its implementing legislation. The extensive reliance on the UNHCR's Handbook and the Guidelines can be seen, for instance, in the case of *Sarmadi* before the Cyprus Supreme Court in order to interpret the Refugee Convention implemented by national legislation.[29] The Israeli Supreme Court in *Anonymous (Ivory Coast) v Minister of Interior and Head of Administration of Border Crossings, Population and Immigration* also relied on the UNHCR Handbook in interpreting the requirement of persecution under the Refugee Convention, and thereby held that the persecution could arise from the events that occur after an asylum-seeker left the country of origin.[30]

While judges engaged with UNHCR documents, they sometimes made sure to note that the courts are not strictly bound by the positions of the Handbook and Guidelines. For instance, in *Novikov and Chabanyuk v Cyprus*,[31] the Cyprus Supreme Court noted that the UNHCR Handbook containing the best practices is 'soft law' that urges voluntary compliance and is not enforceable law. At the same time, the Cyprus court still regarded the UNHCR Handbook as an international instrument that the competent organs should take into account when examining asylum requests.

III. Instruments of a Conference of Parties

ADS (bvba) and ors v Belgium, Constitutional appeals judgment regarding annulment of the Act of 22 December 2009 concerning a general regulation of smoke-free closed spaces accessible to the public, Case no 37/2011, ILDC 1726 (BE 2011), 15th March 2011, Belgium; Constitutional Court

A Belgian Act of 22 December 2009 on the regulation of smoke-free closed spaces accessible to the public and the protection of employees against tobacco smoke, published in *Moniteur belge* 29 December 2009 (Belgium), prohibited smoking in public places, but made an exception for closed pubs that did not form part of a sports facility (Article 4 of the 2009 Act).

The complainants in *ADS ao, Flemish League Against Cancer and Leo Leys v the Government* argued that the exception contained in the Act was not relevant or proportionate in light of the

27 *R, ex parte Adan v Secretary of State for the Home Department*, Appeal decision, [2000] UKHL 67, [2001] 2 AC 477, [2001] 2 WLR 143, [2001] 1 All ER 593, [2001] Imm AR 253, [2000] All ER (D) 2357, ILDC 229 (UK 2000) (United Kingdom, House of Lords, 19 December 2000) para 55.

28 UNHCR, 'UNHCR's Revised Guidelines on Applicable Criteria and Standards relating to the Detention of Asylum-Seekers' (1999) http://www.unhcr.org/refworld/docid/3c2b3f844.html (last accessed 1 April 2017).

29 *Article 146 of the Constitution, Re, Sarmadi v Cyprus, ex parte Refugee Review Authority, Decision on Judicial Review*, Case No 61/2006, ILDC 835 (CY 2007) (Cyprus, Supreme Court, 3 April 2007) H1–5; A Constantinides, Analysis, *Article 146 of the Constitution, Re, Sarmadi v Cyprus, ex parte Refugee Review Authority*, ILDC 835 (CY 2007) A2.

30 *Anonymous (Ivory Coast) v Minister of Interior and Head of Administration of Border Crossings, Population and Immigration*, Administrative appeal to the Supreme Court, Admin A 4922/12, ILDC 2182 (IL 2013) (Israel, Supreme Court as Court of Appeal, 16 January 2013), H2; A Carmeli, Analysis, *Anonymous (Ivory Coast) v Minister of Interior and Head of Administration of Border Crossings, Population and Immigration*, ILDC 2182 (IL 2013) A1.

31 *Novikov and Chabanyuk v Cyprus*, Case No 681/2008 (Supreme Court of Cyprus, 23 October 2009).

aim pursued, discriminated between comparable situations, and violated the right to health, as laid down in Article 23 of the Belgian Constitution and in the Framework Convention on Tobacco Control (2003),[32] which was ratified by Belgium on 1 November 2005, as well as the right to privacy, as laid down in Article 8 of the European Convention on Human Rights.

In its judgment of 15 March 2011, the Belgian Constitutional Court annulled the provisions of the Belgian Act of 22 December 2009, which provided for the exceptions to a smoking ban in public places.

> [B.6.1.] Regarding exposure to tobacco smoke, as argued by the claimants in case number 4859, it is necessary that the right to health protection referred to in article 23, paragraph 3, section 2, of the Constitution be read in conjunction with the "Framework Convention on Tobacco Control" adopted by the World Health Organisation in Geneva on 21 May 2003, which came into effect on 27 February 2005 and was ratified by the Kingdom of Belgium on 1 November 2005.
>
> Article 8 of the convention states:
>
> "1. The Parties recognise that scientific evidence has shown that exposure to tobacco smoke leads to death, disease and incapacity for work.
>
> 2. Under existing national legal powers, as determined by national legislation, each party adopts appropriate statutory, executive, administrative and/or other measures, implements those measures and promotes them in other areas of its legal powers. These targeted measures must provide for protection against exposure to tobacco smoke in working areas within buildings, in public transport, in public buildings and, as appropriate, in other public places".
>
> Article 18 of the convention states:
>
> "The Parties agree to fulfil their obligations under this Convention in the area of tobacco cultivation and processing in their respective jurisdictions, taking into account protection of the environment and of public health with reference to the environment".
>
> [B.6.2.] In accordance with the Guidelines for Implementation of the Convention, article 8 specified the following obligations:
>
> "Article 8 requires the approval of targeted measures for protecting the population against exposure to tobacco smoke 1) in work places within buildings, 2) in public buildings, 3) in public transport and 4) 'as appropriate' in 'other public places'.
>
> That article prescribes the obligation of providing complete protection by ensuring that each covered public space, each covered work area, all public transport systems and possibly other (uncovered or partially covered) public spaces are free from exposure to secondary tobacco smoke. Exemption on the basis of health and legal arguments are not justified. If exemptions must be considered on the basis of other arguments, then these must be minimal. Moreover, if a Party cannot achieve immediate universal cover, article 8 contains an obligation to remove any exemption as quickly as possible and to make protection complete. Each Party must endeavour to achieve complete protection within five years as from the date on which the Party brings the WHO Framework Convention into effect.
>
> There is no safe level of exposure to secondary smoke and, as recognised by the Conference of Parties in decision FCTC/COP1(15), technical solutions, such as

32 WHO Framework Convention on Tobacco Control (adopted 21 May 2003, entered into force 27 February 2005) 2302 UNTS 166, World Health Assembly Resolution 56.1.

ventilation, air-conditioning and the use of smoking area, do not provide protection against tobacco smoke.

Protection applies to all covered or enclosed work areas, which includes motor vehicles used as work places (e.g. taxis, ambulances and supply vehicles).

The Convention contains protective measures not only for indoor public spaces, but also, where necessary, in other (i.e. uncovered or partially covered) public spaces. In identifying these uncovered and partially covered public spaces for which legislation is required, the Parties must take into account the available data on possible health risks in different situations, and must provide for maximum targeted protection against exposure to tobacco smoke when the factual data show that there is a risk".

[. . .]

[B.6.3.] The provisions must also be read in conjunction with the Recommendations of the European Union Council dated 30 November 2009 regarding smokefree spaces, in which the Council recommends that Member States:

"1. Ensure effective protection against exposure to tobacco smoke in enclosed work places, enclosed public spaces, public transport systems and, where applicable, also in other public spaces where applicable, as determined in article 8 of the WHO Framework Convention on Tobacco Control and on the basis of the other related guidelines for protection against exposure to tobacco smoke that were approved by the second Conference of the Parties to the framework convention, within five years of the convention coming into effect for the Member State in question, or within a maximum of three years following approval of this recommendation;

2. Develop and/or upgrade strategies and measures for preventing the exposure of children and young people to secondary tobacco smoke;

3. To support a 'smokefree' policy with supplementary measures [. . .]".

[B.7.] Consequently hotel and restaurant customers and employees must in the same way be protected against the harmful effects of passive smoking, even if exposure to carcinogenic substances is only minimal. The distinction made in article 2, point 9, and in article 4 § 1, of the contested Act is not at variance with that obligation, since the distinction in question has the consequence that certain hotel and restaurant customers and employees are still exposed to the health risks associated with the use of tobacco products.

[. . .]

[B.9.] The argument in case no. 4859 and arguments one to four in case number 4905 are valid. Article 2, point 9, and article 4, § 1, of the contested law must therefore be declared null and void.

In this case, the Belgian Constitutional Court, in annulling the domestic law which allowed smoking in certain public places, interpreted the constitutional right to health in the light of not only Articles 8 and 18 of the Framework Convention on Tobacco Control but also the following guidelines and instruments: the Guidelines for Implementation of the Framework Convention on Tobacco Control (adopted by the Conference of the Parties of the Tobacco Agreement in 2007),[33] the decision FCTC/COP1(15) of the Conference of the Parties[34] (para B.6.2), and the

33 Guidelines for Implementation of the Framework Convention on Tobacco Control, adopted by the Conference of the Parties of the Tobacco Agreement in 2007, Article 8.

34 Elaboration of Guidelines for Implementation of the Convention (Decision FCTC/COP1(15)) (2007), Article 8: Protection from Exposure to Tobacco Smoke.

Recommendation of the Council of the European Union of 30 November 2009 on smoke-free environments (para B.6.3).[35]

This case is noteworthy precisely because the Guidelines informed the Belgian court's constitutional interpretation to uphold a total ban on smoking in public places, despite the fact that the Convention itself does not categorically mandate universal protection.[36] When domestic courts employ international instruments, they can often be used merely to confirm the meaning of domestic law provisions developed already within the national legal practices. Nevertheless, the Belgian Constitutional Court attached more than a confirmatory value to the Guidelines and the conference of the parties' decision. In this case, the formally non-binding international instruments appear to have given substantive meaning to the content of the constitutional right.

This case illustrates the impact of soft-law instruments, not on the interpretation of relevant treaty provisions, but on the development of constitutional provisions and possibly other domestic law. In other words, the interpretation of domestic law consistent with international law, known as the principle of consistent interpretation, serves not only to find the international affirmation of a particular reading of domestic law, but also to inject new meanings into domestic law.

IV. Instruments of International Organizations

Filártiga and Filártiga and United States (intervening) v Peña-Irala, Appeal Judgment, Docket No 79-6090, Case No 191, 630 F 2d 876 (2d Cir 1980), ILDC 681 (US 1980), 30th June 1980, United States; Court of Appeals (2nd Circuit) [2d Cir]

In *Filartiga v Pena-Irala*, two Paraguayan nationals, Dolly and Joel Filartiga, filed suit in the Eastern District of New York against another Paraguayan national, Americo Norberto Pena-Irala, for the wrongful death by torture of Joelito Filartiga, their brother and son, respectively. The events surrounding the death all took place in Paraguay. The Filartigas alleged that, on 29 March 1976, Pena (the Inspector General of Police in Asuncion at the time) had kidnapped, tortured, and killed Joelito in response to Joel Filartiga's political activities in opposing the government of President Alfredo Stroessner.

The Filartigas first asserted customary international law violations as federal questions, citing the Charter of the United Nations,[37] the Universal Declaration of Human Rights,[38] the Declaration on the Protection of All Persons from Being Subjected to Torture,[39] the American Declaration of the Rights and Duties of Man,[40] and other international instruments evincing a customary norm prohibiting torture. Second, they based their claims on the Alien Tort Statute, 28 USC 1350 (United States) which provided federal district courts with original jurisdiction of any civil action brought by aliens for a tort committed in violation of the law of nations or a treaty of the US.

---

35 Recommendations of the Council of the European Union, Council Recommendation of 30 November 2009 on smoke-free environments, OJ C296/4 (2009).

36 See C Ryngaert, Analysis, *ADS ao, Flemish League Against Cancer and Leo Leys v the Government*, ILDC 1726 (BE 2011) A2-5.

37 Charter of the United Nations (signed 26 June 1945, entered into force 24 October 1945) 1 UNTS XVI.

38 Universal Declaration of Human Rights (adopted 10 December 1948) UNGA Res 217A (III), UN Doc A/810 at 71 (1948).

39 Declaration on the Protection of All Persons from Being Subjected to Torture, UNGA Res 3452(XXX) (9 December 1975) UN Doc A/1034.

40 American Declaration of the Rights and Duties of Man, OAS Resolution, AG/RES 1591 (XXVIII-O/98), Ninth International Conference of American States, (1992) Basic Documents Pertaining to Human Rights in the Inter-American System, OEA/Ser.L.V/II.82 doc.6 rev.1 at 17; (1949) 43 AJIL Supp 133, 1948.

Paragraph numbers in the following excerpts have been added to this decision by OUP for the purpose of the ILDC report.

> 12 Appellants rest their principal argument in support of federal jurisdiction upon the Alien Tort Statute, 28 U.S.C. § 1350, which provides: "The district courts shall have original jurisdiction of any civil action by an alien for a tort only, committed in violation of the law of nations or a treaty of the United States." Since appellants do not contend that their action arises directly under a treaty of the United States, a threshold question on the jurisdictional issue is whether the conduct alleged violates the law of nations. In light of the universal condemnation of torture in numerous international agreements, and the renunciation of torture as an instrument of official policy by virtually all of the nations of the world (in principle if not in practice), we find that an act of torture committed by a state official against one held in detention violates established norms of the international law of human rights, and hence the law of nations.
>
> [. . .]
>
> 14 *The Paquete Habana*, 175 U.S. 677, 20 S. Ct. 290, 44 L. Ed. 320 (1900), reaffirmed that where there is no treaty, and no controlling executive or legislative act or judicial decision, resort must be had to the customs and usages of civilized nations; [. . .].
>
> 15 Habana is particularly instructive for present purposes, for it held that the traditional prohibition against seizure of an enemy's coastal fishing vessels during wartime, a standard that began as one of comity only, had ripened over the preceding century into "a settled rule of international law" by "the general assent of civilized nations." Id. at 694, 20 S. Ct. at 297; accord, id. at 686, 20 S. Ct. at 297. Thus it is clear that courts must interpret international law not as it was in 1789, but as it has evolved and exists among the nations of the world today. See *Ware v. Hylton*, 3 U.S. (3 Dall.) 199, 1 L. Ed. 568 (1796) (distinguishing between "ancient" and "modern" law of nations).
>
> 16 The requirement that a rule command the "general assent of civilized nations" to become binding upon them all is a stringent one. Were this not so, the courts of one nation might feel free to impose idiosyncratic legal rules upon others, in the name of applying international law [. . .]
>
> 17 [. . .] there are few, if any, issues in international law today on which opinion seems to be so united as the limitations on a state's power to torture persons held in its custody.
>
> 18 The United Nations Charter (a treaty of the United States, see 59 Stat. 1033 (1945)) makes it clear that in this modern age a state's treatment of its own citizens is a matter of international concern. It provides:
>
> > With a view to the creation of conditions of stability and well-being which are necessary for peaceful and friendly relations among nations . . . the United Nations shall promote . . . universal respect for, and observance of, human rights and fundamental freedoms for all without distinctions as to race, sex, language or religion. Id. Art. 55. And further:
> >
> > All members pledge themselves to take joint and separate action in cooperation with the Organization for the achievement of the purposes set forth in Article 55. Id. Art. 56.
>
> 19 While this broad mandate has been held not to be wholly self-executing, *Hitai v. Immigration and Naturalization Service*, 343 F.2d 466, 468 (2d Cir. 1965), this observation alone does not end our inquiry. For although there is no universal agreement

as to the precise extent of the "human rights and fundamental freedoms" guaranteed to all by the Charter, there is at present no dissent from the view that the guaranties include, at a bare minimum, the right to be free from torture. This prohibition has become part of customary international law, as evidenced and defined by the Universal Declaration of Human Rights, General Assembly Resolution 217 (III)(A) (Dec. 10, 1948) which states, in the plainest of terms, "no one shall be subjected to torture." The General Assembly has declared that the Charter precepts embodied in this Universal Declaration "constitute basic principles of international law." G.A.Res. 2625 (XXV) (Oct. 24, 1970).

20 Particularly relevant is the Declaration on the Protection of All Persons from Being Subjected to Torture, General Assembly Resolution 3452, 30 U.N. GAOR Supp. (No. 34) 91, U.N.Doc. A/1034 (1975), which is set out in full in the margin. The Declaration expressly prohibits any state from permitting the dastardly and totally inhuman act of torture. Torture, in turn, is defined as "any act by which severe pain and suffering, whether physical or mental, is intentionally inflicted by or at the instigation of a public official on a person for such purposes as … intimidating him or other persons." The Declaration goes on to provide that "(w)here it is proved that an act of torture or other cruel, inhuman or degrading treatment or punishment has been committed by or at the instigation of a public official, the victim shall be afforded redress and compensation, in accordance with national law." This Declaration, like the Declaration of Human Rights before it, was adopted without dissent by the General Assembly. Nayar, "Human Rights: The United Nations and United States Foreign Policy," 19 Harv.Int'l L.J. 813, 816 n.18 (1978).

21 These U.N. declarations are significant because they specify with great precision the obligations of member nations under the Charter. Since their adoption, "(m)embers can no longer contend that they do not know what human rights they promised in the Charter to promote." Sohn, "A Short History of United Nations Documents on Human Rights," in The United Nations and Human Rights, 18th Report of the Commission (Commission to Study the Organization of Peace ed. 1968). Moreover, a U.N. Declaration is, according to one authoritative definition, "a formal and solemn instrument, suitable for rare occasions when principles of great and lasting importance are being enunciated." 34 U.N. ESCOR, Supp. (No. 8) 15, U.N. Doc. E/cn.4/1/610 (1962) (memorandum of Office of Legal Affairs, U.N. Secretariat). Accordingly, it has been observed that the Universal Declaration of Human Rights "no longer fits into the dichotomy of "binding treaty' against "non-binding pronouncement,' but is rather an authoritative statement of the international community." E. Schwelb, Human Rights and the International Community 70 (1964). Thus, a Declaration creates an expectation of adherence, and "insofar as the expectation is gradually justified by State practice, a declaration may by custom become recognized as laying down rules binding upon the States." 34 U.N. ESCOR, supra. Indeed, several commentators have concluded that the Universal Declaration has become, in toto, a part of binding, customary international law. Nayar, supra, at 816–17; Waldlock, "Human Rights in Contemporary International Law and the Significance of the European Convention," Int'l & Comp. L.Q., Supp. Publ. No. 11 at 15 (1965).

In this case, the US Court of Appeals provided civil remedies under the Alien Tort Statute to the victims of torture committed in Paraguay. In this case, the US Court of Appeal employed General Assembly resolutions, namely, the Universal Declaration of Human Rights (1948) and the Declaration on the Protection of All Persons from Being Subjected to Torture (1975), in order to prove customary international law on the prohibition of torture, as well as to interpret the content of the prohibition.

As illustrated by this case, General Assembly resolutions may be invoked by domestic courts to prove the existence of customary international law. In an earlier case of *Eichmann* in 1962, for instance, the Israel Supreme Court invoked General Assembly Resolution 95 (I),[41] which affirmed the Charter of the Nuremberg Tribunal, as evidence that the Nuremberg principles have formed part of the customary law of nations.[42] Also, the First Instance of Brussels in *Re Pinochet*[43] in 1998 referred to General Assembly Resolution 3074 (1973) regarding the detention, arrest, extradition and punishment of individuals guilty of war crimes and crimes against humanity[44] in order to prove the existence of a rule of customary international law that recognized permissive universal jurisdiction over crimes against humanity and authorized national authorities to pursue and prosecute persons suspected of such crimes in all circumstances.[45]

In order for General Assembly resolutions to provide evidence for the existence of customary law, their provisions must be grounded on state practice and *opinio juris*. This is also acknowledged in this case before the US Court of Appeals. While the court observed that 'a [UN] Declaration creates an expectation of adherence',[46] it seems that the court did not regard such expectation as sufficient to validate the invocation of the General Assembly resolution; the US Court of Appeals made sure to observe that '*insofar as the expectation is gradually justified by State practice*, a declaration may by custom become recognized as laying down rules binding upon the States'.[47]

In the light of these requirements, a large part of General Assembly resolutions would not likely be recognized as the articulation of existing customary law. For instance, the evidential value of particular General Assembly resolutions was rejected by the US Court of Appeals in *Flores and ors v Southern Peru Copper Corporation*[48] in 2003, on the ground that the UN General Assembly resolutions invoked by the plaintiffs were not proper sources of customary law but were 'merely aspirational and were never intended to be binding on member States of the United Nations'.[49] While this case was not to leave out the evidentiary value of General Assembly resolutions in general,[50] it suggested that the resolutions in question had not attained the status of customary international law.

Director of Public Prosecutions KwaZulu-Natal v P, Appeal to Supreme Court of Appeal, Case No 363/2005, [2005] ZASCA 127, ILDC 492 (ZA 2005), 1st December 2005, South Africa; Supreme Court of Appeal [SCA]

In *Director of the Public Prosecutions KwaZulu-Natal v P*, the South African Supreme Court of Appeal decided on the question of whether the imprisonment of a child was permissible under the South African Constitution and pertinent international law. In September 2002, P, then

41 Affirmation of the Principles of International Law recognized by the Charter of the Nurnberg Tribunal (11 December 1946) UN Doc A/RES/95(I).

42 *Attorney-General (Israel) v Adolf Eichmann* (1962) 36 ILR 277 (Supreme Court of Israel, Judgment of 29 May 1962).

43 *Re Pinochet* (1998) 119 ILR 345 (Belgium, Court of First Instance of Brussels, Judgment of 6 November 1998).

44 Principles of International Cooperation in the Detention, Arrest, Extradition and Punishment of Persons Guilty of War Crimes and Crimes against Humanity, UNGA Res 3074 (XXVIII) (3 December 1973) UN Doc A/RES/3074. para 1 of the resolution proclaims that war crimes and crimes against humanity shall be subject to investigation 'wherever they are committed'.

45 *Re Pinochet* (n 43) 357; cf *Pinochet* (1999) 119 ILR 360 (Luxembourg, Court of Appeal (Chambre du Conseil), 11 February 1999).

46 *Filártiga and Filártiga and United States (intervening) v Peña-Irala*, Appeal judgment, Docket No 79-6090, Case No 191, 630 F 2d 876 (2d Cir 1980), ILDC 681 (US 1980) (United States, Court of Appeals (2nd Circuit) [2d Cir], 30 June 1980), para 21.

47 ibid, emphasis added.

48 *Flores and ors v Southern Peru Copper Corporation*, Appeal judgment, 414 F 3d 233 (2d Cir 2003) (2003) ILDC 303 (US 2003) (United States, United States Court of Appeals for the Second Circuit, 29 August 2003).

49 ibid, para 71.

50 ibid, para 76 (noting that the court's position is not inconsistent with *Filartiga*).

12 years old, approached two men, and asked them to assist her in killing her grandmother. The two men agreed and entered the house together with P where her grandmother was asleep under the influence of sleeping pills that P had earlier placed in her tea. One of the men strangled P's grandmother to death. P gave the men some household goods and jewellery.

The High Court found P guilty of murder but, considering her age, postponed the passing of sentence for thirty-six months on condition that she would comply with the conditions of a thirty-six-month correctional supervision in accordance with section 276(1)(h) of the Criminal Procedure Act 51, 1977. The conditions included provisions such as house arrest, schooling, therapy, supervised probation (at least four visits by a parole officer per week), and community service.

The state appealed against the High Court decision, claiming that the correctional service provision was too lenient, considering the seriousness of the offence. The Court of Appeal then considered the appropriateness of the sentence, including the imprisonment of the juvenile offender.

In the following excerpts the texts in square brackets are added by the present author.

> **The Issue on Appeal**
>
> 11 In my view the issue on appeal can therefore be narrowed down to whether the sentence imposed by the trial court was appropriate, given that court's duty to have regard to the seriousness of the offence and the interests of society as well as the true character of the accused. This issue must of course now be considered [. . .] with due regard to the sentencing regime foreshadowed in s 28 (1) (g) of the Constitution and international developments as reflected in, for instance, instruments issued under the aegis of the United Nations.
>
> [. . .]
>
> **The Constitution and the International Instruments**
>
> 14 With the advent of the Constitution the principles of sentencing [. . .] must, where a child offender is concerned, be adapted and applied to fit in with the sentencing regime enshrined in the Constitution, and in keeping with the international instruments which lay 'emphasis on *reintegration* of the child into society'. The general principle governing the sentencing of juvenile offenders is set out in s 28 (1) (g) of the Constitution. The section reads:
>
> 'Every child has the right —
>
> (g) not to be detained except as a measure of last resort, in which case, in addition to the rights a child enjoys under sections 12 and 35, the child may be detained only for the shortest appropriate period of time, and has the right to be
>
> —
>
> (i) kept separately from detained persons over the age of 18 years; and
> (ii) treated in a manner, and kept in conditions, that take account of the child's age; . . .'
>
> 15 Section 28 has its origins in the international instruments of the United Nations. Of relevance to this case is the United Nations Convention on the Rights of the Child (1989) which South Africa ratified on 16 June 1995 and thereby assumed an obligation under International Law to incorporate it into its domestic law. Various articles under the convention provide that juvenile offenders under the age of 18 years 'should as far as possible be dealt with by the criminal justice system in a manner that takes into account their age and special needs.' Also of relevance is article 40 (1) of the Convention which recognizes the right of the child offender 'to be treated in a manner consistent with the promotion of a child's sense of dignity and worth, which reinforces the child's respect for human rights and fundamental

freedom of others and which takes into account the child's age and the desirability of promoting the child's reintegration and the child's assuming a constructive role in society.' Section 28 (1) (g) of our Constitution appears to be a replica of s 37(b) of the Convention which provides that children in conflict with the law must be arrested, detained or imprisoned 'only as a matter of last resort and for the shortest appropriate period of time.'

16 The Convention has to be considered in conjunction with other international instruments. Most of these instruments are referred to extensively in *Brandt* [*Brandt v S* [2005] 2 All SA 1 (SCA)]. Of particular relevance in this case, however, is the United Nations *Standard Minimum Rules for the Administration of Juvenile Justice* (1985) ('Beijing Rules'), in particular rule 5 (1). The rule recommends that a criminal justice system should 'ensure that any reaction to juvenile offenders shall always be in proportion to the circumstances of both the offender and the offence'. The rule should, however, not be read in isolation because rule 17 (1) (a) provides that:

> 'The reaction taken shall always be in proportion not only to the circumstances and the gravity of the offence but also to the circumstances and the needs of the juvenile as well as the needs of society'

The commentary notes that it is difficult to formulate guidelines because of the unresolved conflicts of a philosophical nature including rehabilitation versus just deserts, assistance versus repression and punishment, merits of the case versus protection of society in general and general deterrence versus individual incapacitation.

The South African Law Commission

17 In July 2000 the South African Law Commission Project Committee on Juvenile Justice (Project 106) released a Discussion Paper embodying a draft Child Justice Bill. On the sentencing of child offenders there is unqualified support for the principle that 'detention should be a matter of last resort.' It also recommended that 'the sentence of imprisonment for children below a certain age (14) years be excluded.' Following the Beijing Rules, in particular rule 17 (1) (c) thereof the committee recommended that imprisonment should only be imposed upon children who have been convicted of serious and violent offences. These recommendations have not as yet been adopted by Parliament and can have but peripheral value at this stage.

18 Having regard to s 28 (1) (g) of the Constitution and the relevant international instruments, as already indicated, it is clear that in every case involving a juvenile offender, the ambit and scope of sentencing will have to be widened in order to give effect to the principle that a child offender is 'not to be detained except, as a measure of last resort' and if detention of a child is unavoidable, this should be 'only for the shortest appropriate period of time'. This of course applies to a juvenile offender who is under the age of 18 years as provided for in s 28 (1) (g) of the Constitution. Furthermore if the juvenile concerned is a child as described, he or she should be kept separately from persons over the age of 18 years and the sentencing court will have to give directions to this effect, if it considers that the case before it warrants detention. This follows from s 28 (2) of the Constitution which provides that a child's best interests are of paramount importance in every matter concerning the child.

19 It must be remembered that the Constitution and the international instruments do not forbid incarceration of children in certain circumstances. All that it requires is that the 'child be detained only for the shortest period of time' and that the child be 'kept separately from detained persons over the age of 18 years.'

In allowing the imprisonment of child offenders with some conditions, the South African Supreme Court of Appeal drew on the Convention on the Rights of the Child which constituted the basis of section 28 of the constitution.[51] It then moved on to observe that 'the Convention has to be considered in conjunction with other international instruments', including the United Nations Standard Minimum Rules for the Administration of Juvenile Justice (1985) (Beijing Rules) adopted by the General Assembly Resolution.[52]

If an international instrument is *not* systematically linked to a particular treaty, there is greater uncertainty as to why domestic courts can rely on particular instruments as interpretive guide for international or domestic law. The judges' explanation appears necessary in order to justify judicial engagement with soft-law instruments. Yet domestic courts do not often provide an explanation as to why a particular non-treaty instrument would be of relevance to the judges' reasoning. In this case, the Convention on the Rights of the Child was invoked, presumably because the constitutional provision was based on the convention.[53] However, the court did not take steps to explain why the Beijing Rules were of particular relevance in constructing the convention and the constitutional provision on the rights of the child in this case.

This case also suggests that the domestic courts may also refer to the domestic acceptance of non-treaty instruments when the courts employ such instruments as interpretive guide. In this case, the South African Supreme Court, in taking into account the provisions of the Beijing Rules, also referred to the limited domestic relevance of those provisions. While the court observed that the South African Law Commission's recommendations followed the Beijing Rules, it noted that the value of the recommendations is peripheral, as they have not been adopted by the parliament.[54]

People's Union for Civil Liberties v India, Writ petition (civil), AIR 2005 SC 2419, ILDC 458 (IN 2005), 29th April 2005, India; Supreme Court

In *People's Union for Civil Liberties v India*, an Indian human rights organization filed a writ petition under Article 32 of the Indian Constitution in order to challenge the appointment of an individual who used to be the Director of the Central Bureau of Investigation and the Vice President (Asia) of Interpol to the National Human Rights Commission (NHRC). In arguing that such appointment would jeopardize the status of the Commission to strengthen the protection of human rights, the People's Union for Civil Liberties invoked not only the provisions of the Protection of Human Rights Act 1993 and the Constitutional provisions, but also a General Assembly resolution.

In the following excerpts, paragraph numbers have been added to this decision by OUP. The texts in square brackets are added by the present author.

> N. Santosh Hegde, J.
>
> 1 In this writ petition filed under Article 32 of the Constitution, the petitioner is challenging a decision of the first respondent Union of India appointing Respondent 2 as a member of the National Human Rights Commission (the Commission). […] The petitioner urges that such appointment would undermine the status and international recognition of the Commission as an institution for protection of human rights. […] It is submitted that it is also violative of international covenants. For this purpose the petitioner has heavily relied on the

51 *Director of Public Prosecutions KwaZulu-Natal v P*, Appeal to Supreme Court of Appeal, Case No 363/2005, [2005] ZASCA 127, ILDC 492 (ZA 2005) (South Africa, Supreme Court of Appeal [SCA], 1 December 2005), para 15.

52 ibid, para 16; UNGA 'United Nations Standard Minimum Rules for the Administration of Juvenile Justice ("The Beijing Rules")' UNGA Res 40/33 (29 November 1985) UN Doc A/RES/40/33.

53 ibid, para 15.

54 ibid, para 17.

principles laid down in the meeting of representatives of the national institutions in Paris wherein certain principles were evolved in regard to protection of human rights which principles came to be known as "Paris Principles". According to the petitioner, these principles were subsequently endorsed by the UN Commission of Human Rights and the UN General Assembly. The petitioner further contends that the UN Resolution dated 19-12-1993 concerning national institutions for protection of human rights, the compliance with the Paris Principles has become mandatory and since the Paris Principles prohibited the appointment of a civil servant like a police officer to such a Commission, such appointment of the second respondent would send wrong signals to the international community as well as to the United Nations. [. . .]

6 Having heard learned counsel for the parties and on the basis of their pleadings and arguments recorded hereinabove, at the outset we must notice that neither the Paris Principles nor the UN Resolution [. . .] expressly or impliedly exclude the inclusion of a police officer in the Commission. [. . .] Section 3(2)(d) [of the Protection of Human Rights Act, 1993] which refers to two members to be appointed to the Commission reads thus: "3.(2)(d) two members to be appointed from amongst persons having knowledge of, or practical experience in, matters relating to human rights."

7 A plain reading of this section does not give any room for interpretation because the language is quite clear. [. . .]

8 If we apply the said principle of law to the facts of the case, there being no exclusion in Section 3(2)(d) of the Act and the language being clear, we cannot by looking back into the Paris Principles or the UN Resolution interpret an exclusionary clause to keep police officers from being members of the Commission in spite of the Act not providing for the same. [. . .]

16 In the ordinary course the above analysis itself would have been sufficient to dispose of this petition. However, since this matter has been referred to this Bench due to the divergence of views between Hon'ble Sabharwal and Dharmadhikari, JJ. it is in the fitness of things that we note their judgments also and particularly the judgment of Hon'ble Sabharwal, J. as our conclusions are different from his conclusions.

17 In arriving at his decision Hon'ble Sabharwal, J. has treated the Paris Principles and the UN General Assembly Resolution as covenants. Thereafter, he has applied the law applicable to international covenants and imported the obligations under the Paris Principles and the UN General Assembly Resolution as if they are binding as legal obligations on India even in the municipal context. While doing so he has relied upon the judgments of this Hon'ble Court in *Mackinnon Mackenzie & Co. Ltd.* v. *Audrey D'Costa; Sheela Barse* v. *Secy., Children's Aid Society; People's Union for Civil Liberties* v. *Union of India*; and *Vishaka* v. *State of Rajasthan.*

18 Having noted the above we would with respect like to point out that neither the Paris Principles nor the subsequent UN General Assembly Resolution can be exalted to the status of a covenant in international law. Therefore merely because India is a party to these documents does not cast any binding legal obligation on it. Further, all the above cases which Hon'ble Sabharwal, J. has relied upon deal with the obligations of the Indian State pursuant to its being a party to a covenant/treaty or a convention and not merely a declaration in the international fora or a UN General Assembly Resolution.

19 Apart from the above, the fact that the field in relation to the constitution of NHRC is covered by an Act of the Indian Parliament, it follows that neither the Paris

> Principles nor the UN General Assembly Resolution can override the express provisions of the Act. Therefore, we are not in agreement with the decision of Hon'ble Sabharwal, J. After considering the views expressed by Hon'ble Dharmadhikari, J. on this aspect of the case, we are in agreement with the same.
>
> 20 For the reasons stated above this petition fails and is dismissed.

The Paris Principles invoked by the petitioner in this case were adopted in 1991 by the first International Workshop on National Institutions for the Promotion of Protection of Human Rights in Paris and subsequently endorsed by the UN General Assembly in 1993.[55] The Paris Principles have been seen as the 'template' to guide and assess the work of national human rights institutions (NHRIs).[56] In light of the recognition given by the Paris Principles, it is not surprising that the petition in this case relied upon them to augment their opposition to the appointment of a former police officer as a member of the National Human Rights Commission.

In this case, the Indian Supreme Court did not necessarily dismiss the relevance of the UN-backed Paris Principles. The court engaged with the content of the Paris Principles which do not deny the inclusion of a police officer in the commission.[57] At the same time, against the clear language of domestic law, the Supreme Court did not see any interpretive space to accommodate the Paris Principles and the relevant UN resolution.[58] In particular, these international instruments cannot be invoked against the express provisions of the Act of the Indian Parliament.[59] For the court, the fact that the earlier decision treated the Paris Principles and the UN resolution as legally binding overstepped the boundary.[60]

V. Instruments Adopted by Inter-governmental Forums

Nabori and ors v Attorney General and ors, High Court decision, Petition no 466 of 2006, ILDC 1337 (KE 2007), 11th December 2007, Kenya; Nairobi; High Court

In *Nabori and ors v Attorney General and ors*, the Kenyan High Court encountered the question whether Kenya's lack of action against the continued destruction of the ecosystem caused by the introduction of a weed constituted a contravention of internationally acknowledged principles on protection and conservation of the environment.

In 1983–1984, Kenya, following a recommendation of the UN Food and Agricultural Organization, introduced the plant (Prosopis Juliflora) in the Ngambo Location of Marigat Division, Baringo District, Kenya. This was a semi-arid area and prone to desertification. The plant spread very quickly over vast areas of land and, owing to its particular biological characteristics, it displaced both humans and livestock and caused great damage to the lake basin ecosystem.

In 2005, Charles Lekuyen Nabori and others, through the Community Museums of Kenya, filed a complaint with the Public Complaints Commission that was provided for by the Environmental Management and Coordination Act, No 8 of 1999 (Kenya) seeking, *inter alia*, a declaration that the continued decimation of natural biodiversity in the affected area was contrary to Kenya's

55 UNGA, 'Principles Relating to the Status of National Institutions' UNGA Res 48/134 (20 December 1993) UN Doc A/RES/48/134, Annex.

56 G de Beco and R Murray, *A Commentary on the Paris Principles on National Human Rights Institutions* (Cambridge University Press 2014) 3.

57 *People's Union for Civil Liberties v India*, Writ petition (civil), AIR 2005 SC 2419, ILDC 458 (IN 2005) (India, Supreme Court, 29 April 2005), para 6.

58 ibid, para 8.

59 ibid, para 19.

60 ibid, paras 17–18.

obligations as a party to international conventions, in particular the Convention on Biological Diversity (1992).[61]

As part of their claims, they sought awards based on the Stockholm Declaration on the Human Environment 1973[62] and the Rio Declaration on Environment and Development 1992,[63] requesting the issuance of an environmental restoration order against the Attorney General and the other respondents to eradicate the weed and to plant indigenous and environmentally friendly trees and grasses in the affected areas.

In the excerpts, paragraph numbers have been added to this decision by OUP. The text in square brackets has been added by the present author.

> Judgment No. of Ang'awa J
>
> [. . .]
>
> 36 The arguments put forth by the petitioners is that Proposis Juliflora is in effect a noxious weed. It was introduced into the petitioners area of Marigat Division, Baringo District in 1982. The said plant takes 15 years to mature. The 15 – 20 years have come and the plant has wreaked havoc for the people who are basically pastolist, some fisher men and very few do substance farming. The plant has caused flooding and over growing of free areas.
>
> 37 This plant was introduced by the 1st and 2nd respondent [who are the Attorney-General of the Republic of Kenya and the Minister for Environment and Natural Resources of the Republic of Kenya] as a project which in effect is not denied. Realizing the effect of the said plant weed which has had a very negative to the environment and residence as a whole.
>
> [. . .]
>
> 40 The Government of Kenya has failed in its duty by failing to pay attention to the international instruments that Kenya ratified, being The Convention of Biological Diversity 116/92 [. . .].
>
> [. . .]
>
> 42 The petitioners further emphasizes that there are principles that leads the Government of Kenya to apply. The first is:-
>
> i) Public participation and development plans [. . .]
> v) The principles of sustained development and or inter generational and inter generational equity. This means that the present generation should ensure that in excising right to beneficial rise of the environment it be so done for future generations.
> vi) The polluter pay principle should apply. The Government should be held accountable and made to pay for this wrong.
>
> 43 Indeed the three principle were elaborated in the case law of *Waweru v Republic* (2006) I KLR (E & L) 677 (Nyamu, Mohamed Emukulle JJ).
>
> 44 The applicable international instruments relied on case:-
>
> i) Stockholm declaration of Human Environmental 1972.
> ii) The Rio Declaration on Environment and Development 1992.

61 Convention on Biological Diversity (adopted 5 June 1992, entered into force 29 December 1993) 1760 UNTS 79; 31 ILM 818.

62 Stockholm Declaration on the Human Environment (adopted 15 December 1972) UN Doc A/Conf.48/14/Rev.1; 11 ILM 1416 (1972).

63 Rio Declaration on Environment and Development (adopted 14 June 1992) UN Doc A/CONF.151/26 (vol I); 31 ILM 874, 1992.

> Kenya has since enacted the National Environmental Management Co-ordination Act that has domesticated the International Instrument to our National law.
>
> [. . .]
>
> VI: *Finding of the court on the Interpretation of the Constitution of Kenya*
>
> 100 [. . .] ii) *Polluter must pay.*
>
> The principle of polluter must pay is upheld whereby the government of Kenya is held accountable of its actions made twenty years earlier or more knowingly or not. There is a duty of care and accountability by the Government of Kenya to be taken. The government made a mistake in introducing a noxious plant. Though their intentions may have been good the results which has been negative must be remedied by the government of Kenya. [. . .]

In this case, the Kenyan High Court referred to the Stockholm Declaration on the Human Environment 1973[64] and the Rio Declaration on Environment and Development 1992[65] simply on the ground that Kenya has enacted the National Environmental Management Co-ordination Act 1999, that has domesticated these international instruments into the national law. This domestic adoption allowed the domestic court to hold the government's decision-making accountable according *inter alia* to the polluter pays principle with regard to the introduction of the plant, which damaged the regional environment.

As illustrated by this case, insofar as non-treaty instruments are formally or effectively incorporated into domestic legislation, national courts have no difficulties in invoking those instruments as they apply pertinent domestic law, as opposed to the non-treaty instruments themselves. The High Court disregarded the Attorney General and the other respondents' arguments against the application of provisions contained in the Stockholm and Rio declarations by finding that they were now part of domestic law.

In addition, the Kenyan High Court referred to the earlier case of *Waweru v Kenya*. In the *Waweru* case, the High Court of Kenya at Nairobi stated that the principles contained in the National Environmental Management Co-ordination Act (section 3) did constitute part of customary international law and that the courts ought to take cognizance of them in all the relevant situations.[66] Therefore, both domestic law and customary international law may serve as the justification for the reference to the Stockholm and Rio declarations by the Kenyan courts.

114957 Canada Ltée (Spraytech, Société d'arrosage) and Services des espaces verts Ltée/ Chemlawn v Town of Hudson, Federation of Canadian Municipalities (intervening) and ors (intervening), Judgment of the Supreme Court, Docket No 26937, 2001 SCC 40, [2001] 2 SCR 241, ILDC 185 (CA 2001), 28th June 2001, Canada; Supreme Court [SCC]

In *Canada Ltée (Spraytech, Société d'arrosage) and Services des espaces verts Ltée/Chemlawn v Hudson*, the Canadian Supreme Court was seised by the question of whether a by-law regulating the use of pesticides was validly enacted under the relevant statute. The Town of Hudson, Quebec, enacted By-law 270 (1991) to regulate the use of pesticides within the town. Landscaping and lawn-care companies (Spraytech and Chemlawn) operating within the town were served with summons by the town in November of 1992 to respond to charges of having used pesticides in violation of the by-law.

The companies pleaded not guilty and argued that By-law 270 was *ultra vires* in the town's power because it was a complete ban and was discriminatory. They further argued that it was

64 Stockholm Declaration on the Human Environment (adopted 15 December 1972) UN Doc A/Conf.48/14/Rev.1; 11 ILM 1416 (1972).

65 Rio Declaration on Environment and Development (adopted 14 June 1992) UN Doc A/CONF.151/26 (vol I); 31 ILM 874, 1992.

66 (2006) 1 KLR (E & L) 677; C Munyua, Analysis, *Nabori and ors v Attorney General and ors*, ILDC 1337 (KE 2007) A1.

inoperative because it was inconsistent with both federal and provincial legislation which regulated pesticides. The Town of Hudson responded that By-law 270 was validly enacted pursuant to its general power to make by-laws for the health and general welfare of its residents, pursuant to section 410(1) of the Cities and Towns Act (CTA). In its decision of 28 June 2001, the Canadian Supreme Court upheld the validity of the by-law enacted by the Town of Hudson.

Judge L'Heureux-Dubé –

[...]

A. Did the Town Have the Statutory Authority to Enact By-law 270?

[...]

30 To conclude this section on statutory authority, I note that reading s. 410(1) to permit the Town to regulate pesticide use is consistent with principles of international law and policy. My reasons for the Court in *Baker v. Canada (Minister of Citizenship and Immigration)*, 1999 CanLII 699 (S.C.C.), [1999] 2 S.C.R. 817, at para. 70, observed that "the values reflected in international human rights law may help inform the contextual approach to statutory interpretation and judicial review". As stated in *Driedger on the Construction of Statutes, supra*, at p. 330:

> [T]he legislature is presumed to respect the values and principles enshrined in international law, both customary and conventional. These constitute a part of the legal context in which legislation is enacted and read. *In so far as possible, therefore, interpretations that reflect these values and principles are preferred.* [Emphasis added.]

31 The interpretation of By-law 270 contained in these reasons respects international law's "precautionary principle", which is defined as follows at para. 7 of the *Bergen Ministerial Declaration on Sustainable Development* (1990):

> In order to achieve sustainable development, policies must be based on the precautionary principle. Environmental measures must anticipate, prevent and attack the causes of environmental degradation. Where there are threats of serious or irreversible damage, lack of full scientific certainty should not be used as a reason for postponing measures to prevent environmental degradation.

Canada "advocated inclusion of the precautionary principle" during the Bergen Conference negotiations (D. VanderZwaag, CEPA Issue Elaboration Paper No. 18, *CEPA and the Precautionary Principle/Approach* (1995), at p. 8). The principle is codified in several items of domestic legislation: see for example the *Oceans Act*, S.C. 1996, c. 31, Preamble (para. 6); *Canadian Environmental Protection Act, 1999*, S.C. 1999, c. 33, s. 2(1)(*a*); *Endangered Species Act*, S.N.S. 1998, c. 11, ss. 2(1)(*h*) and 11(1).

32 Scholars have documented the precautionary principle's inclusion "in virtually every recently adopted treaty and policy document related to the protection and preservation of the environment" (D. Freestone and E. Hey, "Origins and Development of the Precautionary Principle", in D. Freestone and E. Hey, eds., *The Precautionary Principle and International Law* (1996), at p. 41. As a result, there may be "currently sufficient state practice to allow a good argument that the precautionary principle is a principle of customary international law" (J. Cameron and J. Abouchar, "The Status of the Precautionary Principle in International Law", in *ibid.*, at p. 52). See also O. McIntyre and T. Mosedale, "The Precautionary Principle as a Norm of Customary International Law" (1997), 9 *J. Env. L.* 221, at p. 241 ("the precautionary principle has indeed crystallised into a norm of customary international law"). The Supreme Court of India considers the precautionary principle to be "part of the Customary International Law" (*A.P. Pollution Control Board v. Nayudu*, 1999 S.O.L. Case No. 53, at para. 27). See also *Vellore Citizens Welfare Forum v. Union of India*, [1996]

> Supp. 5 S.C.R. 241. In the context of the precautionary principle's tenets, the Town's concerns about pesticides fit well under their rubric of preventive action.
>
> [. . .]
>
> 43 I have found that By-law 270 was validly enacted under s. 410(1) *C.T.A.* Moreover, the by-law does not render dual compliance with its dictates and either federal or provincial legislation impossible. For these reasons, I would dismiss the appeal with costs.
>
> [. . .]
>
> LeBel J.
>
> [. . .]
>
> 48 [. . .] Interesting as they may be, references to international sources have little relevance. They confirm the general importance placed in modern society and shared by most citizens of this country on the environment and the need to protect it. Nevertheless, no matter how laudable the purpose of the by-law may be, and although it may express the will of the members of the community to protect their local environment, the means to do it must be found somewhere in the law. The issues in this case remain strictly, first, whether the *C.T.A.* authorizes municipalities to regulate the use of pesticides within their territorial limits and, second, whether the particular regulation conforms with the general principles applicable to delegated legislation.

In this case before the Canadian Supreme Court, Judge L'Heureux-Dubé, for the majority, employed paragraph 7 of the Bergen Ministerial Declaration on Sustainable Development (1990)[67] to give meaning to the precautionary principle.[68] While Judge L'Heureux-Dubé did not make an unequivocal statement about the customary law status of the precautionary principle, she noted that a good argument can be made that the precautionary principle is a principle of customary international law.[69] The majority referred to international law on the basis that the legislation is presumed to respect the values and principles enshrined in international law[70] while Judge LeBel, for the minority, tried to confine the judicial reasoning to the construction of domestic law without reference to international sources.[71]

As noted previously (eg, *Jaftha* 2004 and *ADS* 2011), the actual weight that international instruments have in the reasoning of national courts varies according to cases. In this case, even if the consistent interpretation justifies the reference to international law, the precautionary principle, and the Bergen Ministerial Declaration to give meaning to it, appear to have had a confirmatory value, rather than substantively guiding the interpretation of the statute by the court.

Fuel Retailers Association of Southern Africa v Director-General Environmental Management, Department of Agriculture, Conservation and Environment, Mpumalanga Province and ors, Appeal, Case No CCT 67/06, [2007] ZACC 13, 2007 (10) BCLR 1059, ILDC 783 (ZA 2007), 7th June 2007, South Africa; Constitutional Court [CC]

In *Fuel Retailers Association of Southern Africa v Director-General Environmental Management, Department of Agriculture, Conservation and Environment, Mpumalanga Province, and ors*, the South African Constitutional Court decided the questions whether, under domestic law, there

67 Bergen Ministerial Declaration on Sustainable Development in the ECE Region (adopted 16 May 1990) UN Doc A/CONF.151/PC/10, Annex.

68 *114957 Canada Ltée (Spraytech, Société d'arrosage) and Services des espaces verts Ltée/Chemlawn v Town of Hudson, Federation of Canadian Municipalities (intervening) and ors (intervening)*, Judgment of the Supreme Court, Docket No 26937, 2001 SCC 40, [2001] 2 SCR 241, ILDC 185 (CA 2001) (Canada, Supreme Court [SCC], 28 June 2001), para 31.

69 ibid, para 32.

70 ibid, para 30.

71 ibid, para 48.

was an obligation on environmental authorities when making decisions about the construction of a filling to consider its social, economic, and environmental impact, and whether they had complied with the obligation.

Section 22(1) of the Environmental Conservation Act 73, 1989 (ECA) requires that approval be obtained from a competent authority before any activity identified as having the potential to have a substantial detrimental impact on the environment can be undertaken. The ECA empowers the Minister of Environmental Affairs and Tourism to determine activities which, in his or her opinion, could have such effects.

In 2000, a trust applied to the environmental authorities to construct a filling station on its property in accordance with the cited environmental provisions. The environmental authorities approved the application. The Fuel Retailers Association, however, objected to the planned construction and appealed against the decision of the environmental authorities. The Fuel Retailers Association argued that the environmental authorities failed to consider the socio-economic impacts of the proposed petrol station. In its decision of 7 June 2007, the South African Constitutional Court had decided in favour of the Fuel Retailers Association.

> 45 The Constitution recognises the interrelationship between the environment and development; indeed it recognises the need for the protection of the environment while at the same time it recognises the need for social and economic development. It contemplates the integration of environmental protection and socio-economic development. It envisages that environmental considerations will be balanced with socio-economic considerations through the ideal of sustainable development. […] Sustainable development and sustainable use and exploitation of natural resources are at the core of the protection of the environment.
>
> **The concept of sustainable development in international law**
>
> 46 Sustainable development is an evolving concept of international law. Broadly speaking its evolution can be traced to the 1972 Stockholm Conference. That Conference stressed the relationship between development and the protection of the environment, in particular, the need "to ensure that development is compatible with the need to protect and improve [the] environment for the benefit of their population". The principles which were proclaimed at this conference provide a setting for the development of the concept of sustainable development. Since then the concept of sustainable development has received considerable endorsement by the international community. Indeed in 2002 people from over 180 countries gathered in our country for the Johannesburg World Summit on Sustainable Development (WSSD) to reaffirm that sustainable development is a world priority.
>
> 47 But it was the report of the World Commission on Environment and Development (the Brundtland Report) which "coined" the term "sustainable development". The Brundtland Report defined sustainable development as "development that meets the needs of the present without compromising the ability of future generations to meet their own needs". It described sustainable development as—
>
> > "[i]n essence … a process of change in which the exploitation of resources, the direction of investments, the orientation of technological development; and institutional change are all in harmony and enhance both current and future potential to meet human needs and aspirations".
>
> 48 This report argued for a merger of environmental and economic considerations in decision-making and urged the proposition that "the goals of economic and social development must be defined in terms of sustainability". It called for a new approach to development—"a type of development that integrates production with resource conservation and enhancement, and that links both to the provision for all of an

adequate livelihood base and equitable access to resources." The concept of sustainable development, according to the report, "provides a framework for the integration of environment[al] policies and development strategies".

49 The 1992 Rio Conference made the concept of sustainable development a central feature of its Declaration. The Rio Declaration is especially important because it reflects a real consensus in the international community on some core principles of environmental protection and sustainable development. It developed general principles on sustainable development and provided a framework for the development of the law of sustainable development.

50 At the heart of the Rio Declaration are Principles 3 and 4. Principle 3 provides that "[t]he right to development must be fulfilled so as to equitably meet developmental and environmental needs of present and future generations." Principle 4 provides that "[i]n order to achieve sustainable development, environmental protection shall constitute an integral part of the development process and cannot be considered in isolation from it." The idea that development and environmental protection must be reconciled is central to the concept of sustainable development. At the core of this Principle is the principle of integration of environmental protection and socio-economic development.

51 Commentators on international law have understandably refrained from attempting to define the concept of sustainable development. Instead they have identified the evolving elements of the concept of sustainable development. These include the integration of environmental protection and economic development (the principle of integration); sustainable utilisation of natural resources (the principle of sustainable use and exploitation of natural resources); the right to development; the pursuit of equity in the use and allocation of natural resources (the principle of intra-generational equity); the need to preserve natural resources for the benefit of present and future generations (the principle of inter-generational and intra-generational equity); and the need to interpret and apply rules of international law in an integrated systematic manner.

52 The principle of integration of environmental protection and development reflects a—

> "... commitment to integrate environmental considerations into economic and other development, and to take into account the needs of economic and other social development in crafting, applying and interpreting environmental obligations."

This is an important aspect of sustainable development because "its formal application requires the collection and dissemination of environmental information, and the conduct of environmental impact assessments." (Footnote omitted.) The practical significance of the integration of the environmental and developmental considerations is that environmental considerations will now increasingly be a feature of economic and development policy.

53 The principle of integration of environmental protection and socio-economic development is therefore fundamental to the concept of sustainable development. Indeed economic development, social development and the protection of the environment are now considered pillars of sustainable development. As recognised in the WSSD, States have assumed—

> " ... a collective responsibility to advance and strengthen the interdependent and mutually reinforcing pillars of sustainable development—economic development, social development and environmental protection—at the local, national, regional and global levels."

54 The concept of sustainable development has received approval in a judgment of the International Court of Justice. This much appears from the judgment of the International Court of Justice in Gabčíkovo-Nagymaros Project (Hungary/Slovakia) where the Court held—

> "Throughout the ages, mankind has, for economic and other reasons, constantly interfered with nature. In the past, this was often done without consideration of the effects upon the environment. Owing to new scientific insights and to a growing awareness of the risks for mankind—for present and future generations—of pursuit of such interventions at an unconsidered and unabated pace, new norms and standards have been developed, set forth in a great number of instruments during the last two decades. Such new norms have to be taken into consideration, and such new standards given proper weight, not only when States contemplate new activities but also when continuing with activities begun in the past. This need to reconcile economic development with protection of the environment is aptly expressed in the concept of sustainable development."

55 The integration of economic development, social development and environmental protection implies the need to reconcile and accommodate these three pillars of sustainable development. Sustainable development provides a framework for reconciling socio-economic development and environmental protection. This role of the concept of sustainable development as a mediating principle in reconciling environmental and developmental considerations was recognised by Vice-President Weeramantry in a separate opinion in Gabčíkovo-Nagymaros, when he said—

> "The Court must hold the balance even between the environmental considerations and the development considerations raised by the respective Parties. The principle that enables the Court to do so is the principle of sustainable development."

56 It is in the light of these developments in the international law of environment and sustainable development that the concept of sustainable development must be construed and understood in our law.

[. . .]

102 The role of the courts is especially important in the context of the protection of the environment and giving effect to the principle of sustainable development. The importance of the protection of the environment cannot be gainsaid. Its protection is vital to the enjoyment of the other rights contained in the Bill of Rights; indeed, it is vital to life itself. It must therefore be protected for the benefit of the present and future generations. The present generation holds the earth in trust for the next generation. This trusteeship position carries with it the responsibility to look after the environment. It is the duty of the court to ensure that this responsibility is carried out. Indeed, the Johannesburg Principles adopted at the Global Judges Symposium underscore the role of the judiciary in the protection of the environment.

103 On that occasion members of the judiciary across the globe made the following statement—

> "We affirm our commitment to the pledge made by world leaders in the Millennium Declaration adopted by the United Nations General Assembly in September 2000 'to spare no effort to free all of humanity, and above all our children and grandchildren, from the threat of living on a planet irredeemably spoilt by human activities, and whose resources would no longer be sufficient for their needs' "

In addition, they affirmed—

"... that an independent Judiciary and judicial process is vital for the same implementation, development and enforcement of environmental law, and that members of the Judiciary, as well as those contributing to the judicial process at the national, regional and global levels, are crucial partners for promoting compliance with, and the implementation and the enforcement of, international and national environmental law".

104 One of these principles expresses—

"A full commitment to contributing towards the realization of the goals of sustainable development through the judicial mandate to implement, develop and enforce the law, and to uphold the Rule of Law and the democratic process ... "

Courts therefore have a crucial role to play in the protection of the environment. When the need arises to intervene in order to protect the environment, they should not hesitate to do so.

Conclusion

105 The considerations set out above make it clear that the decision of the environmental authorities is flawed [...]. In all the circumstances, the decision by the environmental authorities to grant authorisation for the construction of the filling station under section 22(1) of ECA cannot stand and falls to be reviewed and set aside. [...].

In this case, the South African Constitutional Court invoked non-treaty documents in the following two contexts. First, the court invoked the declarations and report in order to identify an 'evolving concept' of international law.[72] The Constitutional Court's assessment started with the constitutional provision, which recognized the interrelationship between the protection of the environment and the need for social and economic development. According to the court, sustainable development and sustainable use and exploitation of natural resources were at the core of the protection of the environment.[73] The South African Constitutional Court then interpreted the concept of sustainable development in domestic law in the light of international law. Having noted that sustainable development was an 'evolving concept of international law', the court traced the evolution by making reference to several informal international instruments such as the 1972 Stockholm Declaration,[74] the report of the 1987 World Commission on Environment and Development (the Brundtland Report),[75] and the 1992 Rio Declaration.[76]

Secondly, the South African Constitutional Court also referred to the Johannesburg Principles (2002) adopted at the Global Judges Symposium[77] in order to highlight the importance of the

72 *Fuel Retailers Association of Southern Africa v Director-General Environmental Management, Department of Agriculture, Conservation and Environment, Mpumalanga Province and ors*, Appeal, Case No CCT 67/06, [2007] ZACC 13, 2007 (10) BCLR 1059, ILDC 783 (ZA 2007) (South Africa, Constitutional Court [CC], 7 June 2007), para 46.

73 ibid, para 45; D Tladi, Analysis, *Fuel Retailers Association of Southern Africa v Director-General Environmental Management, Department of Agriculture, Conservation and Environment, Mpumalanga Province, and ors*, ILDC 783 (ZA 2007) A1–2.

74 Stockholm Declaration on the Human Environment (adopted 15 December 1972) UN Doc A/Conf.48/14/Rev.1; 11 ILM 1416 (1972).

75 Report of the World Commission on Environment and Development: Our Common Future (1987) UN Doc A/42/427, Annex.

76 *Fuel Retailers Association of Southern Africa v Director-General Environmental Management, Department of Agriculture, Conservation and Environment, Mpumalanga Province, and ors* (n 72) paras 46–50; Rio Declaration on Environment and Development (adopted 14 June 1992) UN Doc A/CONF.151/26 (vol I); 31 ILM 874, 1992.

77 United Nations Environment Programme, 'The Johannesburg Principles on the Role of Law and Sustainable Development adopted at the Global Judges Symposium held in Johannesburg, South Africa on 18–20 August 2002'.

role of courts in the protection of environment.[78] The court observed that if the need arose to intervene in order to protect the environment, the courts should not hesitate to do so.[79]

This case is illustrative of the variance among domestic court decisions with respect to the purposes for which they invoke international law and (formally) non-binding international instruments. In this case, the reference to international instruments (through which the court identified the evolving concept and emphasized the role of courts) may seem to serve the overall 'direction' of the reasoning rather than a concrete interpretive guide to domestic law. In this respect, the purposes for which instruments are employed are akin to those of the above-mentioned *Mosetlhanyane* case (2011), in which the Court of Appeal of the Republic of Botswana made recourse to international instruments in order to stress the importance of access to water.

VI. Conclusion

Domestic courts have the role of sustaining the effectiveness and development of international law, as the subject-matters of international law overlap with those of domestic law. Both international and national law prescribe standards concerning, for instance, human rights, crimes, trade, investment, public health, and environmental conservation. The subject-matter overlaps generate space for national courts to apply, not only domestic legislation which implements international law, but also international treaties and customary international law as a freestanding basis of judicial decisions or as an instrument to supplement the construction of domestic law. Such opportunities for interactions have spread into formally non-binding international instruments. As demonstrated by several cases compiled in this chapter, domestic courts employ a wide range of soft-law instruments despite the lack of formal binding force, presumably due to their persuasiveness. Judges use the documents adopted, for instance, by UN human rights treaty-monitoring bodies, the UNHCR, conference of parties, and the UN General Assembly.

This chapter and the Oxford ILDC reports focus on the cases in which domestic courts proactively employed soft-law instruments. It is reasonable to assume, however, the other side of the interface between national and international law. Domestic courts may also avoid the explicit reference to various soft-law instruments, even if the parties to a dispute have relied on them. Methodologically, it is difficult to trace whether judges have purposely avoided the reference to, for instance, the General Comments or UN General Assembly resolutions. Yet one has to bear in mind that domestic courts, from time to time, deliberately avoid, discount, and explicitly contest soft-law instruments.[80] The cases compiled in this chapter thus present one of multiple interfaces between the domestic and international legal orders.

Whether or not domestic courts' engagement, or lack thereof, with soft-law instruments is desirable depends on normative yardsticks with which to assess judicial engagement. One of the normative questions pertains to the separation of powers between the judiciary and the political branches of the government. The more faithful the judicial organs are to the separation of powers and to the legislative authority of political branches, the less amenable the courts are to soft-law instruments. By applying formally non-binding international instruments without being intermediated by political bodies, domestic courts may interfere with the authority of a legislative body endowed with democratic legitimacy. The extent to which judicial engagement disturbs the separation of powers varies depending on the weight that the instruments carry in judicial reasoning. The authority of political organs may be encroached if domestic

78 *Fuel Retailers Association of Southern Africa v Director-General Environmental Management, Department of Agriculture, Conservation and Environment, Mpumalanga Province, and ors* (n 72) paras 102–04.

79 ibid, para 104.

80 I have separately analysed domestic courts' resistance with regard to UN human rights treaties: see M Kanetake, 'UN Human Rights Treaty Monitoring Bodies Before Domestic Courts' (2018) 67 *International and Comparative Law Quarterly* 201.

courts invoke soft-law instruments, not merely in a confirmatory sense, but also as substantive guide for the interpretation of relevant treaties or domestic law where the standards put forward in soft-law instruments do not fully reflect the established treaty interpretation or customary international law. The methodological challenge lies in the fact that it is often hard to distinguish, from explicit judicial reasoning, to what extent soft-law instruments actually influence the mind-set of judges.

The judicial engagement with soft-law instruments remains a largely unregulated undertaking. The extent to which the instruments permeate domestic courts is often left to litigants' willingness to invoke the instruments, the quality of litigants' arguments, and the awareness and willingness of judges to engage with instruments, despite the lack of formal bindingness. The crux, however, is that the influence of domestic courts' recourse to soft-law instruments is not limited to the outcome of specific court decisions. Judicial reference to soft-law instruments also helps, albeit remotely, to convert those instruments into part of formal international law. Domestic court decisions are after all part of state practices. Domestic judges thus necessarily play a critical dual role in determining the domestic *and* international relevance of soft-law instruments whose effectiveness ultimately relies on acceptance at the national legal order.

10

Enforcement of Decisions of International Courts at the National Level

THORDIS INGADOTTIR

I. Introduction

The international obligation to comply with judgments of international courts is rarely questioned and the compliance record with decisions of those tribunals is relatively good. In the instances of non-compliance, the matter can be brought to an enforcement mechanism at the international level, most often a political process, controlled by states parties to the treaty of the relevant tribunal. In all, the matter is being settled or enforced at the international level. With the development of international courts, the content and remedies of international judgments has changed.[1] Increasingly, decisions of international courts require implementation at the national level, and address not only interests of states but also of individuals. Indeed, today most decisions of international courts come from human rights tribunals, followed by decisions of international criminal tribunals. To some extent, traditional state-to-state courts are following a similar path. For instance, in recent years the International Court of Justice (ICJ) has issued a number of judgments requiring implementation at the national level, and some of them concerned major interests of individuals—even life or death.

This development has put pressure on compliance with decisions of international courts. As a response efforts have been made to strengthen the enforcement mechanism at the international level.[2] Furthermore, as illustrated by the ILDC reports, it can be ascertained that decisions of international courts are increasingly being enforced before domestic courts at the national level.[3] The enforcement has raised various issues, both regarding national and international law. For the purpose of this chapter, national courts have addressed key international law issues, such as the international obligation to comply with decisions of international courts, the possibility of direct effect of decisions of international courts at the national level, the scope of remedies international courts can provide, competing international obligations, and standing. This chapter will present and analyse some of this national jurisprudence. The chosen ILDC cases are enforcement of decisions of the ICJ, international human rights courts, and international criminal tribunals, presented in that order.

1 On the large and growing array of international courts see C P Romano, K J Alter, and Y Shany, 'Mapping International Adjudicative Bodies' in C P Romano, K J Alter, and Y Shany (eds), *The Oxford Handbook of International Adjudication* (OUP 2014).

2 See Protocol No 14 to the Convention for the Protection of Human Rights and Fundamental Freedoms, amending the control system of the Convention (adopted 13 May 2004, entered into force 1 June 2010) *CETS* No 194.

3 For the purposes of this chapter, enforcement of decisions of international courts at the national level refers to proceedings that are commenced before a domestic court in order to have an international judgment complied with.

II. International Court of Justice

Enforcement of decisions of the ICJ before national courts is rare.[4] Various reasons explain this. First of all, decisions of the ICJ are binding on states parties, cf Article 94(1) of the Charter of the United Nations (UN Charter), and the compliance record with decisions of the ICJ is good.[5] Secondly, in the occurrence of non-compliance the UN Charter sets up an enforcement mechanism at the international level via the Security Council, cf Article 94(2) of the UN Charter. Thirdly, parties to cases before the ICJ can only be states, cf Article 34(1) of the Statute of the ICJ, and due to sovereignty and political reality, states are not eager to commence a proceeding before a national court of another state. Finally, in light of carefully framed submissions, many decisions of the ICJ are purely declaratory, being only a milestone in ongoing negotiations between the parties to settle a dispute.

The three ILDC cases discussed below are examples of enforcement of decisions of the ICJ before domestic courts. One of the cases stems from the so-called consular relations cases before the ICJ,[6] which led to several decisions taken by national courts in the United States (US).[7] The consular relations cases before the ICJ all involved the breach of the US to fulfil her obligation under Article 36(1)(b) of the Vienna Convention on Consular Relations by not informing, without delay, foreign nationals of their rights to consular assistance in accordance with the convention, and depriving the relevant foreign state of the right to render diplomatic protection provided for in the convention.[8] In the case discussed, *Medellín v Texas*, the US Supreme Court analyses thoroughly the international obligations to comply with decisions of the ICJ, as well as self-executing character of ICJ decisions in US courts.[9] The analysis is valuable, as at this point in time the binding nature of ICJ orders indicating provisional measures had been confirmed by the ICJ, and final judgment in the case had been delivered.[10] The case also illustrates well the nature of some

---

4 The chapter is limited to cases of enforcement of decisions of the ICJ and does not include cases where national courts are interpreting decisions of the ICJ. For such an effect see discussion in S Ordonez and D Reilly, 'Effect of the Jurisprudence of the International Court of Justice on National Courts' in T M Franck and G H Fox (eds), *International Law Decisions in National Courts* (Brill 1996) 335, 359. Furthermore, the chapter does not include cases regarding Advisory Opinions of the ICJ; see, eg, *Mara'abe and ors v Prime Minister of Israel*, Original Petition, HCJ 7957/04: ILDC 157 (IL 2005); and *Marchiori v Environment Agency and ors*, Appeal judgment, (2002) EWCA Civ 03: ILDC 241 (UK 2002).

5 See C Schulte, *Compliance with Decisions of the International Court of Justice* (OUP 2004); B A Ajibola, 'Compliance with Judgments of the International Court of Justice' in M K Bulterman and M Kuijer (eds), *Compliance with Judgments of International Courts* (Martinus Nijhoff Publishers 1996).

6 *Vienna Convention on Consular Relations* (*Paraguay v United States of America*) (Provisional Measures, Order of 9 April 1998) [1998] ICJ Rep 248, *LaGrand* (*Germany v United States of America*) (Judgment) [2001] ICJ Rep 466, and *Avena and Other Mexican Nationals* (*Mexico v United States of America*) (Judgment) [2004] ICJ Rep 12.

7 Extensive commentaries have been made on these cases, eg, B Simma and C Hoppe, 'From LaGrand and Avena to Medellín: A Rocky Road Towards Implementation' (2005) 14 *Tulane Journal of International and Comparative Law* 7. Other national courts have also interpreted ICJ decisions in the consular relation cases; see, eg, Court of Appeal of Singapore (*Van v Public Prosecutor*, Appeal, (2004) SGCA 47: ILDC 88 (SG 2004)), and Federal Constitutional Court of Germany (*German Consular Notification Case*, Joint constitutional complaint, BVerfG, 2 BvR 2115/01: ILDC 668 (DE 2006)).

8 Vienna Convention on Consular Relations (adopted 24 April 1963, entered into force 18 March 1967) 596 UNTS 261. The jurisdiction of the ICJ in the consular relation cases was based on the Optional Protocol to the Vienna Convention on Consular Relations Concerning the Compulsory Settlement of Disputes (signed 24 April 1963, entered into force 19 March 1967) 596 UNTS 487, Article 1.

9 *Medellín v Texas*, Appeal judgment, Docket No 06-984, ILDC 947 (US 2008), 552 US 491 (2008), 128 S Ct 1346 (2008), 170 L Ed 2d 190 (2008), 76 USLW 4143 (2008), 21 Fla L Weekly Fed S 126 (2008), 2008-1 US Tax Cas (CCH) P50, 242, 25 March 2008, United States; Supreme Court [US]. On self-execution treaties in the US see T Buergenthal, *Self-Executing and non-self-executing treaties in national and international law* (Collected Courses of the Hague Academy of International Law, 1992, IV, 1993) 382.

10 For ILDC commentaries on the earlier cases see: *Breard v Greene*, Application for stay of execution and on writ of certiorari, 523 US 371, 118 S Ct 1352 (1998): ILDC 684 (US 1998), and *Germany and LaGrand v United States and Governor of Arizona*, Application for temporary restraining order or preliminary injunction and on motion for leave to file a bill of complaint, 526 US 111 (1999): ILDC 689 (US 1999).

of the cases before the ICJ, having individuals as major subjects of the decisions of the court. In the second case presented, *Re Member of Parliament*, a member of the Hungarian Parliament tried to enforce a decision of the ICJ before the Hungarian Constitutional Court.[11] Finally, in the last case, *Frascá v Germany*, the Court of Cassation dealt with the question of whether Italian courts could apply an earlier precedent in light of a judgment of the ICJ.[12] With respect to these cases, the discussion in this chapter will be limited to four aspects of enforcement of ICJ decisions: (1) the binding nature of Article 94 of the UN Charter; (2) enforceability of ICJ decisions before domestic courts; (3) remedies; and (4) standing.[13]

1. ILDC cases

Medellín v Texas, Appeal Judgment, Docket No 06-984, ILDC 947 (US 2008), 552 US 491 (2008), 128 S.Ct. 1346 (2008), 170 L.Ed 2d 190 (2008), 76 USLW 4143 (2008), 21 Fla. L. Weekly Fed S 126 (2008), 2008-1 US Tax Cas (CCH) P50, 242, 25th March 2008, United States; Supreme Court [US]

In *Avena and Other Mexican Nationals* the ICJ determined that the US was among others obligated to provide, by means of its own choosing, review and reconsideration of the convictions and sentences of named individuals who had not been informed of their right of consular relations.[14] One of the Mexican individuals referred to in the judgment brought proceedings before US courts arguing that the ICJ decision was binding on US federal and state courts. The ICJ later dealt with the obligation in its decision in *Request for Interpretation of the Judgment of 31 March 2004 in the Case Concerning Avena and Other Mexican Nationals* (*Mexico v United States of America*).[15]

> 19 No one disputes that the Avena decision—a decision that flows from the treaties through which the United States submitted to ICJ jurisdiction with respect to Vienna Convention disputes—constitutes an international law obligation on the part of the United States. But not all international law obligations automatically constitute binding federal law enforceable in United States courts. The question we confront here is whether the Avena judgment has automatic domestic legal effect such that the judgment of its own force applies in state and federal courts.
>
> 20 This Court has long recognized the distinction between treaties that automatically have effect as domestic law, and those that—while they constitute international law commitments—do not by themselves function as binding federal law. … In sum, while treaties "may comprise international commitments … they are not domestic law unless Congress has either enacted implementing statutes or the treaty itself conveys an intention that it be 'self-executing' and is ratified on these terms."
>
> 22 Medellin and his amici nonetheless contend that the Optional Protocol, United Nations Charter, and ICJ Statute supply the "relevant obligation" to give the Avena judgment binding effect in the domestic courts of the United States. Reply Brief for Petitioner 5–6. Because none of these treaty sources creates binding federal law in

11 *Re Member of Parliament, Individual constitutional complaint petition*, Decisions of the Constitutional Court Vol XII No 10 (31 October 2003) pp 1281–91; ILDC 601 (HU 2003).

12 *Frascà v Germany and Giachini (guardian of Priebke) and Italy (joining)*, Preliminary order on jurisdiction, No 4284/2013, ILDC 1998 (IT 2013), 21 February 2013, Italy [i].

13 The term 'direct enforceability' is used by the ICJ in its decision in *Request for Interpretation of the Judgment of 31 March 2004 in the Case Concerning Avena and Other Mexican Nationals* (*Mexico v United States of America*) (Judgment) [2009] ICJ Rep 3, para 44. The ICJ also uses the term 'direct effect'.

14 *Avena and Other Mexican Nationals* (n 6) para 153(9) and (11).

15 *Request for Interpretation of the Judgment of 31 March 2004 in the Case Concerning Avena and Other Mexican Nationals* (n 13).

the absence of implementing legislation, and because it is uncontested that no such legislation exists, we conclude that the Avena judgment is not automatically binding domestic law.

26 The obligation on the part of signatory nations to comply with ICJ judgments derives not from the Optional Protocol, but rather from Article 94 of the United Nations Charter—the provision that specifically addresses the effect of ICJ decisions. … The Executive Branch contends that the phrase "undertakes to comply" is not "an acknowledgement that an ICJ decision will have immediate legal effect in the courts of U. N. members," but rather "a commitment on the part of U. N. Members to take future action through their political branches to comply with an ICJ decision."

27 We agree with this construction of Article 94. The Article is not a directive to domestic courts. It does not provide that the United States "shall" or "must" comply with an ICJ decision, nor indicate that the Senate that ratified the U. N. Charter intended to vest ICJ decisions with immediate legal effect in domestic courts. Instead, "[t]he words of Article 94 … call upon governments to take certain action." … In other words, the U. N. Charter reads like "a compact between independent nations" that "depends for the enforcement of its provisions on the interest and the honor of the governments which are parties to it."

28 The remainder of Article 94 confirms that the U. N. Charter does not contemplate the automatic enforceability of ICJ decisions in domestic courts. Article 94(2)—the enforcement provision—provides the sole remedy for noncompliance: referral to the United Nations Security Council by an aggrieved state.

29 The U. N. Charter's provision of an express diplomatic—that is, nonjudicial—remedy is itself evidence that ICJ judgments were not meant to be enforceable in domestic courts. … And even this "quintessentially international remed[y]," id., at 355, is not absolute. First, the Security Council must "dee[m] necessary" the issuance of a recommendation or measure to effectuate the judgment. Art. 94(2), 59 Stat. 1051. Second, as the President and Senate were undoubtedly aware in subscribing to the U. N. Charter and Optional Protocol, the United States retained the unqualified right to exercise its veto of any Security Council resolution.

31 If ICJ judgments were instead regarded as automatically enforceable domestic law, they would be immediately and directly binding on state and federal courts pursuant to the Supremacy Clause. Mexico or the ICJ would have no need to proceed to the Security Council to enforce the judgment in this case. Noncompliance with an ICJ judgment through exercise of the Security Council veto—always regarded as an option by the Executive and ratifying Senate during and after consideration of the U. N. Charter, Optional Protocol, and ICJ Statute—would no longer be a viable alternative. There would be nothing to veto. In light of the U. N. Charter's remedial scheme, there is no reason to believe that the President and Senate signed up for such a result.

32 In sum, Medellín's view that ICJ decisions are automatically enforceable as domestic law is fatally undermined by the enforcement structure established by Article 94. His construction would eliminate the option of noncompliance contemplated by Article 94(2), undermining the ability of the political branches to determine whether and how to comply with an ICJ judgment.

33 The ICJ Statute, incorporated into the U. N. Charter, provides further evidence that the ICJ's judgment in Avena does not automatically constitute federal law judicially enforceable in United States courts. Art. 59, 59 Stat. 1062. To begin with, the ICJ's "principal purpose" is said to be to "arbitrate particular disputes between national

governments." Sanchez-Llamas, supra, at 355 (citing 59 Stat. 1055). Accordingly, the ICJ can hear disputes only between nations, not individuals. Art. 34(1), 59 Stat. 1059 ("Only states [i.e., countries] may be parties in cases before the [ICJ]"). More important, Article 59 of the statute provides that "[t]he decision of the [ICJ] has no binding force except between the parties and in respect of that particular case." Id., at 1062 (emphasis added). The dissent does not explain how Medellin, an individual, can be a party to the ICJ proceeding.

34 Medellin argues that because the Avena case involves him, it is clear that he—and the 50 other Mexican nationals named in the Avena decision—should be regarded as parties to the Avena judgment. Brief for Petitioner 21–22. But cases before the ICJ are often precipitated by disputes involving particular persons or entities, disputes that a nation elects to take up as its own. ... That has never been understood to alter the express and established rules that only nation-states may be parties before the ICJ, Art. 34, 59 Stat. 1059, and—contrary to the position of the dissent, post, at 23—that ICJ judgments are binding only between those parties, Art. 59, id., at 1062.

43 Our conclusion that Avena does not by itself constitute binding federal law is confirmed by the "postratification understanding" of signatory nations. See Zicherman, 516 U. S., at 226. There are currently 47 nations that are parties to the Optional Protocol and 171 nations that are parties to the Vienna Convention. Yet neither Medellin nor his amici have identified a single nation that treats ICJ judgments as binding in domestic courts.

45 Moreover, the consequences of Medellin's argument give pause. An ICJ judgment, the argument goes, is not only binding domestic law but is also unassailable. As a result, neither Texas nor this Court may look behind a judgment and quarrel with its reasoning or result. (We already know, from Sanchez-Llamas, that this Court disagrees with both the reasoning and result in Avena.) Medellin's interpretation would allow ICJ judgments to override otherwise binding state law; there is nothing in his logic that would exempt contrary federal law from the same fate. See, e.g., Cook v. United States, 288 U. S. 102, 119 (1933) (later-in-time self-executing treaty supersedes a federal statue if there is a conflict). And there is nothing to prevent the ICJ from ordering state courts to annul criminal convictions and sentences, for any reason deemed sufficient by the ICJ. Indeed, that is precisely the relief Mexico requested. Avena, 2004 I. C. J., at 58–59.

51 The dissent worries that our decision casts doubt on some 70-odd treaties under which the United States has agreed to submit disputes to the ICJ according to "roughly similar" provisions. See post, at 4, 16–17. Again, under our established precedent, some treaties are self-executing and some are not, depending on the treaty. That the judgment of an international tribunal might not automatically become domestic law hardly means the underlying treaty is "useless." See post, at 17; cf. post, at 11 (describing the British system in which treaties "virtually always requir[e] parliamentary legislation"). Such judgments would still constitute international obligations, the proper subject of political and diplomatic negotiations. See Head Money Cases, 112 U. S., at 598. And Congress could elect to give them wholesale effect (rather than the judgment-by-judgment approach hypothesized by the dissent, post, at 24) through implementing legislation, as it regularly has.

53 In addition, Congress is up to the task of implementing non-self-executing treaties, even those involving complex commercial disputes. Cf. post, at 24 (Breyer, J., dissenting). The judgments of a number of international tribunals enjoy a different status because of implementing legislation enacted by Congress. ... Such language demonstrates that

Congress knows how to accord domestic effect to international obligations when it desires such a result.

54 Further, Medellin frames his argument as though giving the Avena judgment binding effect in domestic courts simply conforms to the proposition that domestic courts generally give effect to foreign judgments. But Medellin does not ask us to enforce a foreign-court judgment settling a typical commercial or property dispute. ... Rather, Medellin argues that the Avena judgment has the effect of enjoining the operation of state law. What is more, on Medellin's view, the judgment would force the State to take action to "review and reconside[r]" his case. The general rule, however, is that judgments of foreign courts awarding injunctive relief, even as to private parties, let alone sovereign States, "are not generally entitled to enforcement." See 2 Restatement §481, Comment b, at 595.

Member of Parliament, Re, Individual constitutional complaint petition, Decisions of the Constitutional Court Vol XII No 10 [31 October 2003] pp 1281-1291, ILDC 601 (HU 2003), 7th October 2003, Hungary; Constitutional Court

A member of the Hungarian parliament asked the Constitutional Court to declare that the Parliament and the Government had failed to fulfil their legislative tasks arising from the *Gabčíkovo-Nagymaros Project* judgment of the ICJ.[16] In the judgment, the ICJ found that Hungary was not entitled to suspend a treaty and abandon works on the Nagymaros and Gabčíkovo projects, and found among others that Hungary and Slovakia must negotiate in good faith, and must take all necessary measures to ensure the achievement of the objectives of the treaty. Negotiations failed and the case went back to the ICJ.[17] A member of the Hungarian parliament asked the Constitutional Court of Hungary to declare that the Gabcíkovo-Nagymaros problem should have been solved by the legislative organs and the government as required by the ICJ's judgment.

3.3. According to the opinion of the Constitutional Court the judgement of the International Court of Justice in the Hague—when exercising the rules of jurisdiction set forth in the Act on the Constitutional Court (Abtv.)—is not considered a generally recognized principle of international law, neither such an obligation of international law as the obligations contained in international treaties that have become national law. Even though the proceedings of the International Court are based on the consent of the countries involved acknowledging the jurisdiction, as contained in an international treaty, the judgement is not a norm, not a contract, but the resolution of a specific dispute, even if some of its statements gain theoretical content or the value of a precedent.

The International Court has no jurisdiction to annul an internal legal norm, to oblige the participating states to create law. The International Court cannot oblige the state to create law even if the state can only fulfil the obligation contained in the judgement by creating law.

Considering the above the Constitutional Court rejected the petition in this respect due to lack of jurisdiction.

Frascà v Germany and Giachini (guardian of Priebke) and Italy (joining), Preliminary order on jurisdiction, No 4284/2013, ILDC 1998 (IT 2013), 21st February 2013, Italy

The issue in this case was whether Italian courts could apply an earlier precedent on the existence of an exception to state immunity in light of the judgment of the ICJ in *Jurisdictional Immunities*

16 *Gabčíkovo-Nagymaros Project* (*Hungary/Slovakia*) (Judgment) [1997] ICJ Rep 7.

17 *Gabčíkovo-Nagymaros Project* (*Hungary/Slovakia*) Slovakia requests an additional Judgment, Communiqué No 98/28, 3 September 1998.

of the State, Germany v Italy.[18] In its judgment, the ICJ considered that such an exception did not exist in international law and declared that Italy must, by enacting appropriate legislation, or by resorting to other methods of its choosing, ensure that decisions of its courts infringing the immunity which Germany enjoyed under international law ceased to have effect.

H1 Germany was entitled to immunity from jurisdiction for acta iure imperii, regardless of the heinous character of the acts complained of by the plaintiff. As the First Criminal Section of the Court of Cassation had already pointed out in Criminal Proceedings against Albers and ors, Final appeal judgment, No 32139/2012; ILDC 1921 (IT 2012); 9 August 2012 ('Albers'), the Ferrini precedent could not be further applied, since it remained isolated in the international landscape and had been expressly disavowed by the ICJ in Jurisdictional Immunities of the State. (paragraph 4)

H2 This approach had been affirmed by the Italian Parliament with the enactment of Law No 5/2013, 14 January 2013 (Italy) ('Law No 5/2013'). Article 3(1) of Law No 5/2013 compelled Italian courts to declare a lack of jurisdiction whenever 'the International Court of Justice, in a judgment settling a dispute in which Italy is a party, excluded the possibility of subjecting a specific conduct of another State to civil jurisdiction'. (paragraph 5)

2. Commentary

(a) The obligation to comply with ICJ decisions—Article 94 of the Charter of the United Nations

According to Article 94 of the UN Charter, each member of the United Nations undertakes to comply with the decisions of the ICJ in any case to which it is a party. The obligation is a fundamental principle of the law governing litigation before the court. Furthermore, Article 59 of the statute of the court stipulates that the decision of the court has no binding force except between the parties and in respect of that particular case. In *Medellín v Texas* the US Supreme Court firmly stipulated the state's international obligation to comply with decisions of the ICJ. Very different from the US Supreme Court, the Court of Cassation in Italy chose to remain silent on the binding nature of decisions of the ICJ. In its reference to the Italian legislation, excluding Italian courts' jurisdiction based on the decision of the ICJ in *Jurisdictional Immunities of the State*, the Court of Cassation analyses the legislation more as a response to development of customary law, or lack thereof, rather than a response to Italy's international obligation to comply with the decision of the ICJ.

While the US Supreme Court addressed extensively in its decision the international obligation of the US to comply with decisions of the ICJ, it did not seek to interpret domestic law in conformity with that international obligation, nor did it mention the legal consequences of its decision to breach the international obligation.[19] No comments are made on the fundamental principle of international law that a state cannot invoke a provision of its internal law as justification for its failure to perform a treaty, and that conduct of national courts is attributable to a state and can therefore entail the international responsibility of the relevant state.[20]

18 *Jurisdictional Immunities of the State* (*Germany v Italy: Greece intervening*) (Judgment) [2012] ICJ Rep 99.

19 On such interpretation in the US see Third Restatement of the Law of the Foreign Relations Law of the US (1990), 62–69; M N Shaw, *International Law* (6th edn, CUP 2008) 164–65.

20 Vienna Convention on the Law of Treaties (adopted 23 May 1969, entered into force 27 January 1980) 1155 UNTS 331, Article 27; ILC, 'Draft Articles on Responsibility of States for Internationally Wrongful Acts, with commentaries' UN Doc A/56/10, Article 4. Mr Medellín was executed without being afforded the review and reconsideration provided for by paras 138 to 141 of the judgment in *Avena and Other Mexican Nationals*, contrary to what was directed by ICJ in its Order indicating provisional measures of 16 July 2008. The ICJ found that the US did not discharge its obligation under the Court's Order, *Request for Interpretation of the*

Article 94(2) of the UN Charter stipulates the competence and action of the Security Council in the case of non-compliance with judgments of the ICJ. If any party to a case fails to perform the obligations incumbent upon it under a judgment rendered by the court, the aggrieved state may have recourse to the Security Council, 'which may, if it deems necessary, make recommendations or decide upon measures to be taken to give effect to the judgment'. The US Supreme Court views unhesitatingly that the US has the right to use its veto right regarding such enforcement by the Security Council and even considers that this right was a fundamental factor for the state's acceptance of the system, and therefore a condition for US ratification of the UN Charter itself. The US Supreme Court presumption is interesting as the application of veto by a complying state has been questioned in the past, and little practice exists on the matter.[21] The answer to the question depends on the interpretation of Article 27 of the UN Charter, ie whether the matter is a procedural or substantive one. The little practice that exists endorses that the matter is a substantive one and therefor a veto is applicable.[22] That has also been the prevailing view among scholars, and now the US Supreme Court has joined that school of thought.[23]

The US Supreme Court considers international judgments, such as those of the ICJ, being 'the proper subject of political and diplomatic negotiations'.[24] Correctly, in the majority of cases compliance is worked out via diplomatic channels. However, when it fails, attempts have been made to enforce compliance before domestic courts, such as happened in the *Gabčíkovo-Nagymaros Project*. But even when diplomatic negotiations succeed constitutional competences can prevent compliance. Following the judgment of the ICJ in *Avena and Other Mexican Nationals* the US president took measures and called for compliance with the judgment. Those measures did not have any impact on the US Supreme Court's interpretation of the enforceability of the ICJ decisions at the national level—as it construed the president's memorandum not as binding law.[25] The US Supreme Court's view is in line with the understanding that internal 'organs are not directly obliged by virtue of the judgment unless a direct obligation is provided for in the constitutional law of the state concerned'.[26] The ICJ has partly subscribed to this reasoning, as it stated in the *LaGrand* case that the 'order did not require the United States to exercise powers it did not have', and in its analysis of compliance with the order it considered more what the state could have done more, rather than stipulating an obligation of result.[27]

Judgment of 31 March 2004 in the Case Concerning Avena and Other Mexican Nationals (n 13) paras 53 and 61. At the same time, the Court found that Article 60 of the Statute of the Court did not allow it to consider possible violations of the judgment, which it was called upon to interpret: ibid para 56.

21 K Oellers-Frahm, 'Article 94' in B Simma, D E Khan, G Nolte, and A Paulus (eds), *The Charter of the United Nations, A Commentary* (3rd edn, OUP 2012) 1957, 1970.

22 In 1986, when the Security Council voted on a draft resolution calling for full and immediate compliance with the judgment of the ICJ in the case concerning *Military and Paramilitary Activities in and against Nicaragua*, a negative vote of the United States prevented a resolution from being taken, UNSC Draft Res (31 July 1986) UN Doc S/18250.

23 On 28 March 2014, Mexico sent a letter to the Security Council bringing to the attention of the Council the fact that the US had not complied with a judgment of the Court in the *Avena* Case between the two countries. The Council did not consider the letter or take any action; Security Council Report, 'The Rule of Law: Can the Security Council Make Better Use of the International Court of Justice?' *Security Council Report*, 20 December 2016, 6 http://www.securitycouncilreport.org/research-reports/ (last accessed 31 January 2018).

24 *Medellín v Texas* (n 9) para 51 see also *Breard v Greene* (n 10) para 11.

25 On particular weight given to views of executive branch in the US see Restatement of the Law Third the foreign relations law of the United States (1990) 59.

26 H Mosler, 'Article 94' in B Simma (ed), *The Charter of the United Nations, A Commentary* (2nd edn, OUP 2002) 1005, and Oellers-Frahm (n 21) 1962.

27 *LaGrand* (n 6) paras 110–15.

(b) Enforceability of ICJ Decisions before domestic courts—direct effect

In *Medellín v Texas* the US Supreme Court analyses thoroughly the self-executing character of ICJ decisions. The Constitutional Court of Hungary approaches the issue of direct enforceability in a very different manner in *Re Member of Parliament*. The former considers that international judgments can have direct enforceability at the domestic level, given that they were meant to be self-executing or have been made enforceable with implementing legislation. The Constitutional Court of Hungary simply excludes the possibility of decisions of the ICJ to become part of domestic law at all. According to the Constitutional Court of Hungary, decisions of the ICJ can never be customary law or a treaty which has been given the status of national law by an act of parliament. Differently, in *Medellín v Texas* it was uncontested that there had not been implemented a national legislation giving ICJ decisions the status of national law, but the possibility of such a legislation in the future was not excluded by the US Supreme Court, which cited a number of US domestic legislation giving decisions of international courts such a status.[28]

In *Medellín v Texas* the US Supreme Court built its decision on the US distinction between self-executing and non-self-executing treaties, the former being able to operate automatically at the domestic level as opposed to the latter. For this purpose it *inter alia* analysed the wording and purpose of Article 94, the relevance of the enforcement mechanism set up via the Security Council, the intent of the drafters of the UN Charter, and then the intent of the US at the time of ratification, concluding that the Article was not meant to be self-executing. While the analysis is based on principles of US domestic law, its methodology and conclusion may be of relevance for other monist states that have to make this distinction when called upon to apply international agreements (whether they use the term self-executing treaty or not),[29] and for dualist states that need to consider implementing legislation. And from the viewpoint of international law, international courts need at times to consider whether treaties were meant to be directly enforceable or not.[30] In *Jurisdiction of the Court of Danzig*, the Permanent Court of Justice (PCIJ) concluded that '[i]t cannot be disputed that the very object of an international agreement, according to the intention of the contracting Parties, may be the adoption by the Parties of some definite rules creating individual rights and obligations and enforceable by the national courts'.[31] Similarly, in articulating its doctrine of direct effect, the European Court of Justice in *Van Gend en Loos* noted that 'to ascertain whether the provisions of an international treaty extend so far in their effects it is necessary to consider the spirit, the general scheme, and the wording of those provisions', concluding that the Treaty on establishing the EEC created rights having direct effect and creating individual rights which national courts must protect.[32] The ICJ had the opportunity to address the issue of direct effect in its decision in *Request for Interpretation of the Judgment of 31 March 2004 in the Case Concerning Avena and Other Mexican Nationals*. The Court referred to an obligation of result rather than an obligation on the US to give direct enforceability to its decision. The Court also refers to the possibility of domestic law to give its decisions such an effect:

> The *Avena* Judgment nowhere lays down or implies that the courts in the United States are required to give direct effect to paragraph 153(9). The obligation laid down

28 *Medellín v Texas* (n 9) para 51.

29 See discussion by Buergenthal on that the US distinction between self-executing and non-self-executing treaties is not unique to the US, and that the courts of most monist states also apply this distinction; Buergenthal (n 9) 382.

30 In his thorough analysis of self-executing and non-self-executing treaties in national law and international law, Buergenthal concludes that international courts are in general much more reluctant to conclude that a treaty provision is directly applicable than are domestic courts in holding it to be self-executing; Buergenthal (n 9) 340.

31 PCIJ, Ser B, No 15, at 17–18.

32 Case 26/62 *Van Gend en Loos v Nederlandse Administratie der Belastingen* [1963] ECR 1, 12. On this landmark decision see J Weiler, 'The Community System: the Dual Character of Supranationalism' (1981) I *Yearbook of European Law* 267, 274.

> in that paragraph is indeed an obligation of result which clearly must be performed unconditionally; non-performance of it constitutes internationally wrongful conduct. However, the Judgment leaves it to the United States to choose the means of implementation [. . .] Nor moreover does the *Avena* Judgment prevent direct enforceability of the obligation in question, if such an effect is permitted by domestic law.[33]

This arm's length approach and an argued lack of requirement on states by international law to allow their courts to apply international law directly have been commented on as 'perhaps the single greatest limitation of the role of national courts as a systemic force in the protection of the international rule of law'.[34]

(c) Remedies

Both the US Supreme Court and the Constitutional Court of Hungary considered that they have large discretion on how to implement remedial awards by the ICJ. The former court in *Medellín v Texas* notes that it is recognized in international law that implementation of ICJ judgments is left to states.[35] The Constitutional Court of Hungary goes further: 'The International Court of Justice has no jurisdiction to annul an internal legal norm, to oblige the participating states to create law. The International Court cannot oblige the state to create law even if the state can only fulfill the obligation contained in the judgement by creating law'.[36] These views are in line with the position that state sovereignty precludes any specific directions given by international courts on how a state party should implement a decision against it at the national level.[37] This is to some extent in line with practice at the ICJ. As discussed earlier, in its decision in *Request for Interpretation of the Judgment of 31 March 2004 in the Case Concerning Avena and Other Mexican Nationals* the ICJ gave the US flexibility on how to implement its judgment at the national level. State practice has largely followed this school of thinking, and hesitance by litigants to demand specific measures can be ascertained in some cases.[38] However, the ICJ made clear in *Avena and Other Mexican Nationals* that depending on the subject-matter of a dispute, it could make remedies of this kind, citing the example in a cancellation of arrest warrant in *Arrest Warrant of 11 April 2000*.[39] And there are several recent ICJ decisions which are quite specific on performance, despite having to be carried out by 'means of own choosing'. There is *de facto* not much room for any discretion in ICJ orders of stay of execution in *LaGrand* and *Avena and Other Mexican Nationals*,[40] transfer of individuals to International Criminal Tribunal for the former Yugoslavia (ICTY), and cooperation with that tribunal in *Application of the Convention on the Prevention and Punishment of the Crime of Genocide*,[41] prosecution of a named individual in *Questions relating to the Obligation to Prosecute or Extradite*,[42] and ceasing of effect of decisions of Italian courts which infringe the immunity of the Federal Republic of Germany in

33 *Request for Interpretation of the Judgment of 31 March 2004 in the Case Concerning Avena and Other Mexican Nationals* (n 13) 44.

34 A Nollkaemper, *National Courts and the International Rule of Law* (OUP 2011) 126.

35 *Medellín v Texas* (n 9) paras 45, 51; *Breard v Greene* (n 10) para 6.

36 *Re Member of Parliament* (n 11) para 3.3.

37 See C Brown, *A Common Law of International Adjudication* (OUP 2007) 209–16; C Gray, *Judicial Remedies in International Law* (OUP 1987) 98; M N Shaw, 'A Practical Look at the International Court of Justice' in M D Evans (ed), *Remedies in International Law: The Institutional Dilemma* (Hart Publishing 1998') 3–16.

38 T Ingadottir, 'The Role of the International Court of Justice in the Enforcement of the Obligation of States to Investigate and Prosecute Serious Crimes at the National Level' (2014) 47(2) *Israel Law Review* 285, 291–93.

39 *Avena and Other Mexican Nationals* (n 6) para 124.

40 *LaGrand* (n 6) para 59.

41 *Application of the Convention on the Prevention and Punishment of the Crime of Genocide* (*Bosnia and Herzegovina v Serbia and Montenegro*) (Merits) [2007] ICJ Rep 43, para 471.

42 *Questions Relating to the Obligation to Prosecute or Extradite* (*Belgium v Senegal*) (Judgment) [2012] ICJ Rep 442, para 122.

Jurisdictional Immunities of the State.[43] And states have complied with the above remedies, such as the US with respect to *LaGrand* and *Avena and Other Mexican Nationals*,[44] Belgium with respect to *Arrest Warrant of 11 April 2000*,[45] and Italy with respect to *Jurisdictional Immunities of the State*.[46] Certainly, the ICJ is becoming bolder in awarding remedies, while it can be argued that it has still not made full use of them as set out in Draft Articles on State Responsibility.[47]

(d) Standing

The *Medellín v Texas* case illustrates well the changing nature of some of the cases before the ICJ, having individuals as major subjects of its decisions, and how that affects enforcement at the national level. Medellín argued that because the *Avena and Other Mexican Nationals* judgment involved him, he should be regarded as a party to the ICJ judgment, capable of enforcing it before the US courts. The US Supreme Court rejected this argument by referring to Article 59 of the Statute of the ICJ, stipulating that the court's decisions are only binding on the parties to the case. Furthermore, the Supreme Court noted that '[t]he dissent does not explain how Medellín, an individual, can be a party to the ICJ proceedings'.[48] Citing cases before the ICJ regarding diplomatic protection, the Supreme Court continued that '[t]hat has never been understood to alter the express and established rules that only nation-states may be parties before the ICJ'.[49] Similar reasoning was held by the US Court of Appeals for the District of Columbia Circuit in *The Committee of United States Citizens Living in Nicaragua et al, v Reagan et al*.[50] According to the Appellate Court in that case '[n]either individuals nor organizations have a cause of action in an American Court to enforce I.C.J. judgments'.[51]

Indisputably, individuals and legal entities are not parties to a case before the ICJ, cf Article 34(1) of the Statute of the ICJ. Also, in the instances where the enforcement mechanism of Article 94 has been used it has been states that have commenced that process before the Security Council, not individuals or legal entities. And as the US Supreme Court stated, a number of ICJ decisions stem from diplomatic protection, and that does not change who are parties to the case before the ICJ. However, while parties to the cases before the ICJ are states, the cases before

43 *Jurisdictional Immunities of the State* (n 18) para 139(4).

44 *LaGrand* (n 6) para 29; *Avena and Other Mexican Nationals* (n 6) para 59.

45 *Arrest Warrant of 11 April 2000* (*Congo v Belgium*) (Judgment) [2002] ICJ Rep 3. On 15 February 2002, the day after the ICJ delivered its findings in the case, the international arrest warrant for the former Congolese Democratic Republic of Congo foreign minister was withdrawn after consultations between the examining magistrate and Brussels crown prosecutor see discussion in Schulte (n 5) 270.

46 See Law No 5/2013, 14 January 2013, compelling Italian courts to declare a lack of jurisdiction whenever the International Court of Justice, in a judgment settling a dispute in which Italy is a party, excluded the possibility of subjecting a specific conduct of another state to civil jurisdiction.

47 On the remedies of the International Court of Justice see R Higgins, 'Remedies and the International Court of Justice: An Introduction' in M Evans (ed), *Remedies in International Law: The Institutional Dilemma* (Hart Publishing 1998); C Gray, 'Remedies' in C Romano, K J Alter, and Y Shany (eds), *The Oxford Handbook of International Adjudication* (OUP 2014) 875–83. For a criticism that ICJ is not making full use of ILC's Draft Articles on State Responsibility see S Villalpando, 'Editorial: On the International Court of Justice and the Determination of the Rules of Law' (2013) 26 *Leiden Journal of International Law* 243, 250.

48 *Medellín v Texas* (n 9) para 33.

49 ibid, para 34.

50 859 F 2d 929 (DC Cir 1988). The case was an attempt to enforce the ICJ's decision in *Military and Paramilitary Activities in and against Nicaragua* before the US domestic court, in which the US was to stop activities found unlawful in the ICJ decision, including funding for the Contras, and to negotiate a payment of damages to Nicaragua; see *Military and Paramilitary Activities in and against Nicaragua* (*Nicaragua v United States of America*) (Merits) [1986] ICJ Rep 14, paras 292 (12) and 292 (13). Since the ICJ decision and prior to the judgment of the appellate court the US Congress had approved continued funding for the Contras, and in addition, the US had used its veto to block consideration of a resolution of the Security Council concerning enforcement of the ICJ decision, cf Article 94(2).

51 859 F 2d 929 (DC Cir 1988) 934.

the court increasingly deal with individual's rights and obligations under international law. In *LaGrand* and *Avena and Other Mexican Nationals* the ICJ concluded that Article 36(1) of the Vienna Convention created not only a state´s right but also an individual right, rights which the US had violated.[52] Furthermore, this 'interdependence of the rights of the State and of individual rights' led the ICJ to conclude that the duty to exhaust local remedies, which applies to cases of diplomatic protection, did not apply.[53] Furthermore, in *Avena and Other Mexican Nationals*, the ICJ considers remedies both with regard to address the injury done to Mexico and as well its nationals.[54] Thus, the cases became more than one of these 'traditional' diplomatic protection cases listed by the US Supreme Court. Similarly, in its advisory judgment from 2012, the ICJ gives great weight to rights of individuals, having an effect on its consideration of the court´s discretion to decide whether it should give an opinion and on the manner of later proceedings before the court.[55]

While individuals do not have standing before the ICJ, the above cases illustrate how the fast evolving position of the individual in international law is having an impact on the jurisdiction of the court, admissibility of cases before it, its findings and remedial awards. 'While the Court is not in a position to reform this system', in some cases, the Court is attempting to ensure the protection of rights of individuals and mitigate their lack of standing before the Court.[56] In doing so, the court has made attempt to keep pace with established rights of individuals in international law, as well as to contribute to development of the law.[57] Inevitably, this development at the Court and its findings of violations of rights of individuals has had an impact on enforcement before domestic courts, although so far without much success.

III. International Criminal Tribunals

Four of the six cases discussed in this chapter relate to enforcement of arrest warrants and requests for a transfer from two ad hoc criminal tribunals of the United Nations (UN)—the ICTY and the International Criminal Tribunal for Rwanda (ICTR). In these cases, the decision on transfer by a national judicial authority is challenged and appealed by the defendant. In the fifth case the failure of the government of South Africa to arrest the president of Sudan, in accordance with an arrest warrant issued by the International Criminal Court (ICC), gave rise to the litigation. In the last case, the constitutional validity of a degree on cooperation with the ICTY, issued by the executive branch, is reviewed by the Serbian Supreme Court.

The legal framework of the duty of states to enforce decisions of the ICTY and ICTR is strong, both from the international and the domestic point of view. Both tribunals were established by the Security Council of the UN, cf Article 41 of the UN Charter.[58] Statutes of both tribunals, which were annexed to relevant decisions of the Security Council, contain explicit provisions of the duty of states to cooperate with the tribunals (Articles 7 and 29 of the Statute of the ICTY and Articles 8 and 28 of the Statute of the ICTR), and the Security Council has also

52 *LaGrand* (n 6) para 77; *Avena and Other Mexican Nationals* (n 6) para 40. This reading by the Court of Article 36 of the Vienna Convention on Consular Relations has not been followed by courts in the US; see Simma and Hoppe (n 7) 29–30.

53 *Avena and Other Mexican Nationals* (n 6) para 40.

54 ibid, paras 129 and 140.

55 *Judgment No 2867 of the Administrative Tribunal of the International Labour Organization upon a complaint filed against the International Fund for Agricultural Development* (Advisory Opinion) [2012] ICJ Rep 10, para 44.

56 ibid.

57 See, eg, Draft Articles on Diplomatic Protection leave open the question of whether the state exercising diplomatic protection does so in its own right or that of its national, and the draft articles also recommend that the state should give due consideration to the possibility of exercising diplomatic protection and should also transfers to the injured person any compensation obtained; ILC, 'Draft Articles on Diplomatic Protection, with commentaries' (2006) UN Doc A/61/10, Article 1(5) and Article 19.

58 UNSC Res 827 (25 May 1993) UN Doc S/RES/827; UNSC Res 955 (8 November 1994) UN Doc S/RES/955.

called on states to cooperate with the tribunals in accordance with the statutes.[59] Furthermore, citing these provisions, the tribunals' rules of procedure and evidence expressly stipulate that the obligations of the state will prevail over any legal impediment to the surrender or transfer of the accused to the tribunal which may exist under the national law or extradition treaties of the state concerned.[60]

As to the ICC, according to Part 9 of the Rome Statute of the International Criminal Court, states parties shall cooperate fully with the court in its investigation and prosecution of crimes within the jurisdiction of the court. According to Article 98, the court may not proceed with a request for surrender or assistance which would require the requested state to act inconsistently with its obligations under international law with respect to the state or diplomatic immunity of a person of a third state, unless the court can first obtain the cooperation of that third state for a waiver of immunity.

1. ILDC cases

Croatia v N-T, Appeal Judgment, Case No IKž 690/1999-4, ILDC 384 (HR 1999), 13th October 1999, Croatia; Supreme Court

N-T was detained and prosecuted before the county court in Zagreb. The ICTY requested that Croatia would surrender N-T to face charges brought against him there. The county court's decision on the surrender of N-T to the ICTY was appealed to the Supreme Court of Croatia. Among N-T's arguments was that, owing to his nationality, he would not face a fair proceeding before the tribunal. The Constitutional Act on the Cooperation of Croatia with the International Criminal Tribunal was adopted by the Croatian Parliament in 1996 as a legal means for regulating and enabling cooperation with the ICTY. The Act had supremacy over ordinary parliamentary legislation.

> 9. … According to this provision, the chamber of the County Court issued a decision complying with the request for transfer as it established the identity of the person whose transfer was requested (which is not disputable) and that the crimes in question were those over which the International Criminal Tribunal had jurisdiction. The crimes of which M.N. was accused are expressly specified in the provisions of the Statute (Articles 2, 3 and 5). Consequently, the jurisdiction of the International Criminal Tribunal for these crimes is indisputable.
>
> 11. The provisions of the Statute of the International Criminal Tribunal (Articles 7, 29) and the Rules of Procedure and Evidence (Articles 8–13, 58) refer to the primacy of the jurisdiction of the International Criminal Tribunal over national jurisdiction. Rule 58 of the Rules of Procedure and Evidence expressly states that the obligations of the State concerned pursuant to Article 29 of the Statute will prevail over any legal impediment to the transfer of the accused to the Tribunal which may exist under the national law of the State concerned.
>
> 18. The Constitutional Law has been part of the internal legal order of the Republic of Croatia since its adoption (Article 134 of the Constitution of the Republic of Croatia) and, consequently, so have the Statute and Rules of Procedure and Evidence of the International Criminal Tribunal. The provisions of Article 29 of the Statute of the International Criminal Tribunal clearly lay down the obligation of the Republic of Croatia to co-operate with the International Criminal Tribunal and specify that the

59 See, eg, UNSC Res 827 (25 May 1993) UN Doc S/RES/827, para 4.

60 Rule 58 of the ICTY Rules of Procedure and Evidence (adopted 11 February 1994, as amended 10 July 2015) UN Doc IT/32/Rev.50; rule 58 of the ICTR Rules of Procedure and Evidence (adopted 29 June 1995, as amended 13 May 2015).

Tribunal's request for legal assistance must be complied with without delay, which also definitely means the transfer of the accused to the Tribunal. The transfer of the accused to the International Criminal Tribunal upon the execution of its warrant should also be regarded as the implementation of the coercive measures referred to in Article 91 (Chapter VII) of the Charter of the United Nations.

19. The fact that the Republic of Croatia is fulfilling its obligations towards the International Criminal Tribunal—even though the indictment brought by the International Criminal Tribunal mentions the Croatian Army and even the Government of the Republic of Croatia in an extremely negative context arbitrarily and without any arguments—clearly shows that Croatia observes and dutifully carries out its obligations towards the international community assumed under the Constitutional Law on Co-operation with the International Criminal Tribunal.

International Arrest Warrant ('Lukic'), Re, International Criminal Tribunal for the Former Yugoslavia v Lukic (Milan), Decision on arrest, surrender, and extradition, Case No 11807/05, ILDC 1083 (AR 2006), 10th January 2006, Argentina

ML was detained in Argentina pursuant to a warrant of arrest and surrender issued by the ICTY. The following day, Argentina received a request for extradition of ML from Serbia and Montenegro. Argentina had not enacted any law implementing the ICTY statute or ICTY rules into the domestic legal order. Domestic Law No 24767 regulates mutual assistance in criminal matters between Argentina and requesting states in the absence of an applicable treaty. The case was before the National Court on Federal Criminal and Correctional Matters No 8.

51. In that sense it must be stated that in accordance with what was decided in the context of the issue of lack of jurisdiction as formulated in the pleadings, the rules applicable to the surrender application shall be those of international law, including Resolution no. 827 of the Security Council of the United Nations and the Rules on Procedure and Evidence of the ICTY. In addition, the International Cooperation in Criminal Matters Act 24,767 may be applied at a supplementary level to areas that are not covered by the above provisions.

52. Thus, national legislation serves as a support mechanism for checking the requirements an application must contain, as in this case, and also the rights of the defendant and the powers of this court to establish certain relief measures, without losing sight of the guiding principle that favours the overriding interest of the international community which our country is subject to by virtue of the fact that it is part of that community.

53. Following the proposed analysis, and as regards the offences for which the ICTY is bringing charges against Milan Lukic, it should be stated that there is no doubt that he must face punishment, as our country, as a member of the International Community, through its signing of various treaties and conventions, expressly incorporated into its legislation the Geneva Conventions and their respective Additional Protocols, the Rome Statute and the Convention on the Prevention and Punishment of the Crime of Genocide, *inter alia*, which condemn such atrocities.

58. From the foregoing, it is clear that all the requirements needed to grant the application submitted by the International Criminal Tribunal for the former Yugoslavia have been met.

68. It follows from this that the Argentine State, as a founder member of the United Nations, is obliged to enforce applications from the ICTY and to ensure that they

prevail over any other obligation, because failure to do so would involve the Republic's responsibility under international law.

69. Thus, the Statute of the ICTY provides in Articles 9 and 29 that States shall co-operate with the Court in the investigation and prosecution of persons who come within its jurisdiction; that they shall, without delay, process and comply with any application and/or decision made by a Court of First Instance relating to, *inter alia*, the surrender of defendants so as to put them at the disposal of the International Tribunal.

70. Meanwhile, Article 58 of the Rules on Procedure and Evidence of the ICTY provides that the obligations under Article 29 of the Statute shall override all legal obstacles or extradition treaties which the State in question is a party to, or which could obstruct the surrender of a defendant to the Court.

71. In this way, it is clear that by reason of these legal provisions, without prejudice to the provisions of the s. 16 of Act 24,767, there is no doubt that the application submitted by the ICTY overrides the one submitted by the Belgrade Court of First Instance.

75. In that sense, s. 18 of Act 24,767 provides that a person extradited from this country may not be re-extradited to another State without Argentina's prior authorization, save where the extradited person freely and expressly waives that right before an Argentine diplomatic or consular authority, after having had the benefit of legal advice.

Rukundo (Emmanuel) v Federal Office of Justice, Appeal Judgment, Case No 1A.129/2001, Case no 1A.130/2001, ILDC 348 (CH 2001), 3rd September 2001, Switzerland; Federal Supreme Court [BGer]; First Public Law Division

R was arrested in Geneva, following a request for arrest and transfer from the ICTR. R argued before the Federal Supreme Court that he could not be transferred as the ICTR did not guarantee the right to fair trial as contained in European Convention for the Protection of Human Rights and Fundamental Freedoms (ECHR) and the International Covenant on Civil and Political Rights (ICCPR).

H1 Switzerland did not extradite or transfer persons to states or institutions that failed to guarantee the respect of minimal procedural rights, as recognized in democratic states and defined, in particular, by the Convention or the ICCPR; or that violated certain rules accepted as being part of the international *ordre public*. (paragraph 3a).

H2 With regard to the transfer of a person to an international criminal tribunal like the ICTR, however, Switzerland applied a presumption that the above guarantees were fulfilled. The problems existing at the time with regard to the management and the functioning of the ICTR did not reverse this presumption. In view of the various steps taken to improve the functioning of the Tribunal, there was no evidence that the ICTR was not able to execute its tasks in conformity with the guarantees of due process contained in the ICCPR. (paragraph 3b).

Ntawukuriryayo (Dominique), Appeal judgment, Appeal No 08-81262, ILDC 879 (FR 2008), 7th May 2008, France; Court of Cassation [Cass]; Criminal Division

Dominique Ntawukuriryayo appealed an order of transfer to the ICTR before the Court of Cassation in France. He contented, *inter alia*, that his transfer from France was illegal because the completion strategy of the ICTR showed that he would not be tried by the ICTR, but would be transferred to Rwanda to face trial in Rwandan courts, in accordance with rule 11*bis* of the Rules of the Procedure and Evidence.

24 First, the Court is not at present in possession in this particular case of evidence or other elements from which it is able to deduce that the International Criminal Tribunal for Rwanda will be substantively unable to try the person whose extradition is requested, as the Tribunal's completion strategy report to the UN Security Council simply recounts the work of that jurisdiction and defines provisional timetables, from which no legal consequences can be drawn, especially not that Dominique X. is certain to be extradited to Rwanda.

25 Second, be that as it may, the International Criminal Tribunal for Rwanda alone has powers to refer the indictment to another court pursuant to Rule 11bis of its Rules of Procedure and Evidence and determines whether or not to do so in light, in particular, of its conviction 'that the accused will receive a fair trial in the courts of the State concerned and that the death penalty will not be imposed or carried out'; that conviction unequivocally reflects the legitimate concern expressed by counsel for Dominique X. that his trial should be guaranteed by the fundamental principles governing rules of procedure and the rights of the parties.

32 The Court is not in a position to review of the regularity of the evidence adduced by the International Criminal Tribunal for Rwanda.

Minister of Justice and Constitutional Development and ors v The Southern African Litigation Centre, Appeal judgment, 867/15, [2016] ZASCA 17, 2016 (4) BCLR 487 (SCA), [2016] 2 All SA 365 (SCA), 2016 (3) SA 317 (SCA), ILDC 2533 (ZA 2016), 15th March 2016, South Africa; Supreme Court of Appeal [SCA]

South Africa ratified the Rome Statute of the International Criminal Court on 27 November 2000. On 31 March 2005, the Security Council of the UN referred the situation in Darfur, Sudan to the ICC. The ICC issued two warrants of arrest of the Sudanese president Al-Bashir. The 25th Assembly of the African Union (AU) took place in Johannesburg, South Africa, from 7 to 15 June 2015. South Africa was required to enter into a hosting agreement with the Commission of the AU. Sudanese president Al-Bashir was among the guests. On 13 June 2015, the day of Al-Bashir's arrival in South Africa, the ICC's Pre-Trial Chamber II issued an order for the immediate arrest and surrender of Al-Bashir. South Africa argued that the 'special arrangements' made with the AU for hosting the Assembly sought to grant Al-Bashir immunity from arrest and surrender to the ICC for the Assembly's duration and two days thereafter.

56 ... The Security Council referred the situation in Darfur to the Prosecutor in terms of this provision. While there is debate among commentators as to the full effect of such a referral, it is accepted by all that it confers jurisdiction upon the ICC in respect of the actions of a non-party state and its citizens. UN member states are obliged to accept the authority of the decision by the Security Council to refer the situation in Darfur to the Prosecutor. (paragraph 56)

59 Article 27 of the Rome Statute deals with the possibility that the crime being prosecuted is likely in many instances to have been perpetrated by a state actor, ranging from a head of state to a humble official or soldier, and therefore the possibility would exist of the accused person raising a claim to immunity in accordance with long-established principles of customary international law, to be considered later in this judgment. ... The undisputed effect of this provision is that it is not open to a person being prosecuted before the ICC to claim immunity from prosecution or advance a defence of superior orders. It is agreed by all commentators that, because Party States have bound themselves to the Statute including this provision, all Party States have waived any immunity that their nationals would otherwise have enjoyed under customary international law.

62 The Constitution makes international customary law part of the law of South Africa, but it may be amended by legislation. It provides a specific mechanism whereby obligations assumed under international agreements become a part of the law of South Africa. And it decrees that, when interpreting any legislation, the Courts must prefer a reasonable interpretation that is consistent with international law over any alternative interpretation that is inconsistent with international law. …

69 … The argument proceeded, as does this judgment, on the basis that once a head of state has been brought before the ICC no plea of head of state immunity can be invoked. But, as a number of commentators have pointed out, that does not necessarily mean that a state is entitled to ignore head of state immunity when requested to cooperate with the ICC to bring such a person before it. It is in this context that the question of an international crimes exception to head of state immunity arises.

82 … Its current position appears to accept that President Al Bashir would enjoy head of state immunity, were it not, so it believes, for the fact that it has been waived by the Security Council.

90 Some of these features warrant stressing in the light of the fact that there is no dispute that President Al Bashir is subject to the jurisdiction of the ICC and can be prosecuted by it for his alleged crimes. He has been stripped of any immunity when before the ICC. It is therefore important that the purpose of the Implementation Act is to provide a framework to ensure the effective implementation of the Rome Statute. It is to ensure that South Africa conforms to its obligations under the Rome Statute. In that regard there is no doubting its obligation to endeavour to bring President Al Bashir before the ICC for trial. The head of state immunity claimed for him is only a procedural bar to the enforcement of that obligation in this country. It is not an immunity that confers impunity for any wrongdoing on his part.

93 … The section is in a part of the Implementation Act conferring jurisdiction on South African Courts to try international crimes in certain circumstances. It would have been absurd and non-compliant with its international obligations for South Africa in such a case to permit the accused to raise immunity either ratione personae or ratione materiae, or obedience to orders, to avoid conviction or reduce any sentence. In the circumstances the section paraphrased the provisions of Article 27(1) of the Rome Statute and made them applicable in trials for international crimes in South Africa or, as Professor du Plessis expressed matters, it 'trumps' the immunities that would otherwise attach to individuals. The difficulty lies in taking it further to create in South Africa an international crimes exception to head of state immunity. Nevertheless, that does not mean that it is irrelevant to the interpretational exercise. It is a clear indication that South Africa does not support immunities when people are charged with international crimes.

102 DIPA is a general statute dealing with the subject of immunities and privileges enjoyed by various people, including heads of state. The Implementation Act is a specific Act dealing with South Africa's implementation of the Rome Statute. In that special area the Implementation Act must enjoy priority.

103 I conclude therefore that when South Africa decided to implement its obligations under the Rome Statute by passing the Implementation Act it did so on the basis that all forms of immunity, including head of state immunity, would not constitute a bar to the prosecution of international crimes in this country or to South Africa cooperating with the ICC by way of the arrest and surrender of persons charged with such crimes before the ICC, where an arrest warrant had been issued and a request for cooperation made. I accept, in the light of the earlier discussion of head of state

immunity, that in doing so South Africa was taking a step that many other nations have not yet taken. If that puts this country in the vanguard of attempts to prevent international crimes and, when they occur, cause the perpetrators to be prosecuted, that seems to me a matter for national pride rather than concern. It is wholly consistent with our commitment to human rights both at a national and an international level. And it does not undermine customary international law, which as a country we are entitled to depart from by statute as stated in s 232 of the Constitution. What is commendable is that it is a departure in a progressive direction.

Constitutionality and legality of the decree on process of cooperation with the International Criminal Tribunal, Socialist Party of Serbia and ors v Federal Republic of Yugoslavia, Original petition for constitutional review, ILDC 29 (CSXX 2001), 6th November 2001, Serbia and Montenegro (historical); Federal Constitutional Court (historical)

The case before the Federal Constitutional Court of Serbia and Montenegro dealt with the constitutionality and legality of a 2001 degree, issued by the federal government of the Federal Republic of Yugoslavia. The main issues before the court concerned the question of whether the cooperation with the ICTY could be regulated by degree, and whether the Constitution permitted the transfer to the ICTY of FRY nationals.

15. In particular, the challenged Decree is not in accordance with the Constitution of the FRY since under the Decree a body without appropriate authority has regulated the procedure (method) for exercising certain freedoms and rights of man and citizen laid down by the Constitution of the FRY. Namely, pursuant to the provision of Article 67, para 2 of the Constitution of the FRY, the method (procedure) for exercising certain freedoms and rights of man and citizen may only be laid down by law and only if this is envisaged by the Constitution of the FRY or if it is necessary for the exercise of such freedoms and rights. Furthermore, pursuant to the provision of Article 26, para 1 of the Constitution of the FRY, everyone is entitled to equal protection of his or her rights in a procedure prescribed by law. Under the challenged Decree, the Federal Government, as a body with executive power—prescribing the possibility of a procedure for transferring criminal proceedings conducted by a domestic court to the International Criminal Tribunal at the Tribunal's request, prescribing the appropriate application of the provisions of Chapter XXXI of the Criminal Procedure Act, including the arrest of a person whose extradition to the International Criminal Tribunal has been requested, and prescribing the authority of the International Criminal Tribunal to take investigative measures against persons in the territory of the FRY—set down, by means of a sub-law, the method (procedure) for exercising, restricting and safeguarding certain freedoms of man and citizen. As already stated, such a procedure may only be set down by law by a body with legislative power, which, with regard to criminal-law protection, has been done through the Criminal Procedure Act.

25. The Federal Constitutional Court is of the opinion that UN Security Council Resolution 827 concerning the founding of the International Criminal Tribunal cannot be subsumed under the international law that constitutes an integral part of the national legal system referred to in Article 16 of the Constitution of the FRY. The reason for this is that the *ad hoc* measure adopted by the UN Security Council under this Resolution—the setting up of the International Tribunal for the Prosecution of Persons Responsible for Serious Violations of International Humanitarian Law—does not contain international legal norms that produce "validity" or have "binding force". Without those properties, this Resolution is only a political document producing political obligations and acquiring legal validity

only after being given legal force by a legitimate and legal body in the individual legal system of each particular State.

26 Namely, UN Member States, by adopting the Charter of the United Nations, adopted the legal validity of all of its norms, including the legal documents enacted by UN bodies, in accordance with and in the manner specified by the Charter. However, UN Member States did not transfer the judicial powers to UN bodies except, of course, for those powers expressly specified by the Statute of the International Court of Justice, as set down in Chapter XIV of the Charter. The matter under discussion is not such a case. For that reason, Item 4 of UNSC Resolution 827 specifies the political obligation of all States to "cooperate fully with the International Tribunal" and "take any measures necessary under their domestic law to implement the provisions" of the Resolution. In other words, only after investing the obligations from the aforementioned UNSC Resolution with legal norms in accordance with national laws, do the Statute and Rules of Procedure of the International Criminal Tribunal acquire a normative nature which produces legal validity. Without that, they are special political obligations, whose non-fulfilment, of course, may have very serious consequences for individual States.

30. By contrast, as has already been shown, this Court is of the opinion that it does not follow from the substance of the Charter of the United Nations that the Security Council has the express power to create and set up judicial bodies, as a measure to protect peace, for holding accountable citizens of countries that have violated peace and security in the world. It follows from the substance of the quoted provisions of the Charter that such a measure may be considered an international fait accompli binding on any UN Member State. This gives rise to the obligation of legally regulating issues that concern the constitutionally guaranteed freedoms and rights of citizens, the status of state bodies in providing such protection and the activities of national bodies in the provision of legal assistance for the purpose of protecting international peace. One of the rights of a Member State in this case is to make a reasoned appeal to UN bodies to check the regularity of proceedings.

2. Commentary

(a) Article 25 and 41 of the UN Charter, direct effect

The Supreme Court of Croatia and the National Court on Federal Criminal and Correction Matters of Argentina refer to the obligation of the state to cooperate with the ad hoc tribunals, undertaken in Chapter VII of the UN Charter, cf Article 25. The latter court underlines also that failure to cooperate would mean responsibility under international law for the state. Both courts consider this obligation having direct effect in domestic law. In Argentina there was no national implementing legislation, while the Supreme Court of Croatia refers to this obligation in addition to the duty already incorporated in domestic law. In contrast, the Federal Constitutional Court of Serbia and Montenegro considered that the state could not comply with a decision of the UN Security Council unless it had been incorporated into national law, as decisions of the Security Council were not legal norms but rather political decisions. According to the Federal Constitutional Court such implementation would have to take place via the legislator, not the executive branch. Furthermore, the Federal Constitutional Court considered the state not obligated under international law to cooperate with the ICTY as the Security Council had acted *ultra vires* in establishing the tribunal. As the commentator of the case notes, in its deliberation on this point, the Constitutional Court ignores the acceptance of other states of this action of the UN Security Council. The Security Council's authority under Article 41 to order measures regarding prosecutions and judicial cooperation has also been reaffirmed in later practice, eg, the Security Council resolution on the establishment of the ICTR,[61] its resolution on the trial of Charles Taylor in the Netherlands,[62] and its resolutions of a referral of situations to the ICC.[63]

Similarly, in its analysis, the Supreme Court of Appeal of South Africa considers it vital that the jurisdiction of the ICC in the case at hand is based on referral by the Security Council. Citing Article 25 of the UN Charter, it considers member states of the UN, also non-members of the ICC, obliged by the authority of the Security Council's decision. As a result of the referral of the Security Council, Article 27 of the Rome Statute was made applicable to non-state parties and they were therefore unable to rely on Article 98 of the Rome Statute.[64] South Africa, as a member of the UN and of the ICC, was to cooperate fully with the ICC and enforce the arrest warrant issues by the court.

Both the Supreme Court of Croatia and the National Court on Federal Criminal and Correction Matters of Argentina treat the Rules of Procedure and Evidence of the ICTY in the same way as the Statute of the ICTY, and having direct effect in domestic law. This is noteworthy as the Rules of Procedure and Evidence are issued by the judges of the tribunal and not the Security Council.

(b) Competing international obligations

The issues of competing obligations under international law and the supremacy of UN Charter obligations over other international obligations, set out in Article 103 of the UN Charter, are indirectly referred to by the National Court on Federal Criminal and Correction Matters of Argentina. Facing two competing requests of transfer and extradition, the court determines that the state has to ensure the enforcement of application from the ICTY: 'that they prevail over any other obligation, because failure to do so would involve the Republic's responsibility under international law'.[65]

Competing international obligations are also an issue in some of the other cases. This relates to the relations between obligations under Chapter VII of the UN Charter and obligations under human rights treaties, such as the ECHR and the ICCPR. The national courts deliberate whether they can review the procedure at the ad hoc tribunals when deciding on a transfer, and interestingly, reach a different conclusion. In the cases where the transferee raised that he would not receive a fair trial before the ad hoc tribunal in accordance with international human rights treaties, neither the Supreme Court of Croatia nor the Court of Cassation in France considered they could review the proceedings at the relevant tribunal. All they could do was to verify the identity of the relevant person and whether the alleged crimes were within the statute of the ad hoc tribunals. Similarly, the Court of Cassation in France considered that it was not able to review whether the ICTR would re-extradite the relevant person to national proceedings. On the contrary, the National Court on Federal Criminal and Correction Matters of Argentina

61 UNSC Res 955 (8 November 1994) UN Doc S/RES/955.

62 UNSC Res 1688 (16 June 2006) UN Doc S/RES/1688.

63 Regarding the situation in Darfur, UNSC Res 1593 (31 March 2005) UN Doc S/RES/1593; regarding the situation in the Libyan Arab Jamahiriya, UNSC Res 1970 (26 February 2011) UN Doc S/RES/1970.

64 For an opposing view see D Tladi, 'The Duty on South Africa to Arrest and Surrender President Al-Bashir under South African and International Law' (2015) 13(5) *International Criminal Justice* 1027. See also other writings on the case, eg, E De Wet, 'The implications of President Al-Bashir's visit to South Africa for international and domestic law' (2015) 13(5) *Journal of International Criminal Justice* 1049; D Akande, 'The Legal Nature of Security Council Referrals to the ICC and its Impact on Al Bashir's Immunities' (2009) 7(2) *Journal of International Criminal Justice* 342; P Gaeta, 'Does President Al Bashir Enjoy Immunity from Arrest?' (2009) 7(2) *Journal of International Criminal Justice* 328.

65 *International Arrest Warrant ('Lukic'), Re, International Criminal Tribunal for the Former Yugoslavia v Lukic (Milan)*, Decision on arrest, surrender, and extradition, Case No 11807/05, ILDC 1083 (AR 2006), 10 January 2006, Argentina, para 68.

did consider that it was able to do so and when transferring to the ICTY it set the condition that there would not be a re-extradition. Nevertheless, the ICTY extradited the individual to a national court. The Federal Supreme Court in Switzerland stressed that it would not transfer individuals to states or institutions that failed to guarantee the respect of minimal procedural rights. At the same time it made the assumption that as the ICTR was an international tribunal it would fulfil such requirement. The commentator on the Swiss case notes:

> The Federal Supreme Court incidentally reviewed the legality of a Security Council resolution when scrutinizing measures that implemented the resolution. In doing so, it reviewed the actions of the Security Council against the obligations resulting from human rights instruments, such as the Convention or the ICCPR. Thereby, the Court 'affirmed—at least in principle—the normative superiority of both human rights instruments vis-à-vis binding Security Council resolutions'.[66]

The issue of competing obligations between UN Security Council Resolutions and human rights instruments has gained wide attention since the *Kadi* decision of the European Court of Justice.[67] However, the arguments made that a transfer of an individual may give rise to an issue under the human right conventions, due to lack of fair proceedings, and hence engage the responsibility of that state under the conventions, may be hard to sell. Certainly, the jurisprudence of the European Court of Human Rights (ECtHR) in cases regarding deportation and extradition does not support such a claim. It is established in the court's case-law that an issue might exceptionally be raised under Article 6 by an expulsion or extradition decision in circumstances where the fugitive had suffered or risked suffering a flagrant denial of justice in the requesting country.[68] However, that test is very high. As stated by the court in the case of *Othman (Abu Qatada) v United Kingdom*:

> 260. It is noteworthy that, in the twenty-two years since the *Soering* judgment, the Court has never found that an expulsion would be in violation of Article 6. This fact, when taken with the examples given in the preceding paragraph, serves to underline the Court's view that 'flagrant denial of justice' is a stringent test of unfairness. A flagrant denial of justice goes beyond mere irregularities or lack of safeguards in the trial procedures such as might result in a breach of Article 6 if occurring within the Contracting State itself. What is required is a breach of the principles of fair trial guaranteed by Article 6 which is so fundamental as to amount to a nullification, or destruction of the very essence, of the right guaranteed by that Article.[69]

The issue of competing international obligations was also a key element in the debate whether South Africa was obligated to comply with an order of the ICC on arrest of Al-Bashir. The Supreme Court of Appeal considered that the resolution of the Security Council had waived

---

66 A R Ziegler, Analysis, *Rukundo (Emmanuel) v Federal Office of Justice*, ILDC 348 (CH 2001) A2.

67 Joined Cases C-402/05 P & C-415/05 P, *Kadi & Al Barakaat v Council of the European Union and EC Commission* [2008] 3 CMLR 41. For a commentary see, eg, P De Sena and M C Vitucci, 'The European Courts and the Security Council: Between Dédoublement Fonctionnel and Balancing of Values' (2009) 20(1) *EJIL* 193; and M Scheinin, 'Is the ECJ Ruling in Kadi Incompatible with International Law?' (2009) 29(1) *Yearbook of European Law* 637.

68 That principle was first set out in ECtHR, *Soering v UK*, App No 14038/88 (7 July 1989) para 113, and has been subsequently confirmed by the Court in a number of cases (see, *inter alia*, ECtHR, *Mamatkulov and Askarov v Turkey*, App No 46827/99 and 46951/99 (4 February 2005) paras 90–91; ECtHR, *Al-Saadoon and Mufdhi v UK*, App No 61498/08 (2 March 2010) para 149).

69 ECtHR, *Othman (Abu Qatada) v UK*, App No 8139/09 (12 January 2012). See also the judgment of the ECtHR regarding extradition from Sweden to national courts in Rwanda, in which extradition was not considered violation of Article 3 or Article 6 of the ECHR, *Ahorugeze v Sweden*, App No 37075/09 (27 October 2011).

the immunity of Al-Bashir and that therefore it was not faced with any competing international obligations.

IV. Human Rights Courts

The ECtHR and the Inter-American Court of Human Rights (IACHR)[70] have jurisdiction to award reparations to complainants, cf Article 41 of the ECHR,[71] and Article 63 of the American Convention on Human Rights (ACHR).[72] Both human rights instruments have provisions on the binding force of judgments of the respective human rights courts, cf Article 46 of the ECHR and Article 68 of the ACHR.

The ECtHR has reiterated that the general logic of Article 41 on just satisfaction is directly derived from the principles of public international law relating to state responsibility, and that it has to be construed in that context.[73] Furthermore, the ECtHR interprets the provision in accordance with principles of international law on reparations.[74] According to Article 46(1) of the ECHR, member states are obliged to abide by the final judgment of the ECtHR in any case to which they are parties. The ECtHR frequently describes the obligation to comply with its judgments as following:

> It follows, inter alia, that a judgment in which the Court finds a violation of the Convention or its Protocols imposes on the respondent State a legal obligation not just to pay those concerned the sums awarded by way of just satisfaction, but also to choose, subject to supervision by the Committee of Ministers, the general and/or, if appropriate, individual measures to be adopted in its domestic legal order to put an end to the violation found by the Court and make all feasible reparation for its consequences in such a way as to restore as far as possible the situation existing before the breach.[75]

According to Article 68(1) of the American Convention 'State Parties to the Convention undertake to comply with the Court's decisions in any case to which they are parties'. Furthermore, that part of a judgment that stipulates compensatory damages may be executed in the country concerned in accordance with domestic procedure governing the execution of judgments against the state, cf Article 68(2). According to Article 63(1) of the ACHR, if the IACHR finds that there has been a violation, the court shall rule that the injured party be ensured the enjoyment of his right or freedom that was violated. It shall also rule, if appropriate, that the consequences of the measure or situation that constituted the breach of such right or freedom be remedied and

70 National cases regarding enforcement of decisions of human rights bodies, such as of the Human Rights Committee, are not included in the chapter. Different from the IACHR and ECtHR, which decisions are binding under international law, these bodies can only issue views. For discussion on these cases see commentaries in *Hauchemaille v France*, Judicial review, No 238849; ILDC 767 (FR 2001), 11 October 2001; *Commonwealth of Pennsylvania v Judge*, Appeal judgment, 916 A 2d 511 (Pa 2007); 591 Pa 126; ILDC 1218 (US 2007); *Singarasa v Attorney General*, Application for judicial review, SC Spl (LA) No 182/99; ILDC 518 (LK 2006); *Dar v Norwegian Immigration Appeals Board*, Appeal decision, Case No HR-2008-681-A; ILDC 1326 (NO 2008).

71 European Convention for the Protection of Human Rights and Fundamental Freedoms (adopted 4 November 1950, entry into force 3 September 1953) 87 UNTS 103.

72 American Convention on Human Rights (adopted 22 November 1969, entry into force 18 July 1978) 1144 UNTS 123.

73 ECtHR, *Cyprus v Turkey* (just satisfaction) App No 25781/94 (12 May 2014) para 40.

74 ibid, para 41.

75 ECtHR, *Cocchiarella v Italy*, App No 64886/01 (29 March 2006) para 125; ECtHR, *Maestri v Italy*, App No 39748/98 (17 February 2004) para 47; ECtHR, *Menteş and ors v Turkey*, App No 23186/94 (24 July 1998) para 24; ECtHR, *Scozzari and Giunta v Italy*, App No 39221/98 and 41963/98 (13 July 2000) para 249; ECtHR, *Ilaşcu and ors v Moldova and Russia*, App No 48787/99 (8 July 2004) para 487; ECtHR, *Cyprus v Turkey* (just satisfaction), App No 25781/94 (12 May 2014) para 27.

that fair compensation be paid to the injured party.[76] As repeatedly stated by the IACHR, 'to this end, states must ensure the domestic implementation of the provisions of the Court's decision'.[77]

Both human rights regimes have set up an enforcement mechanism with respect to states' compliance with decisions of the courts. With respect to the ECtHR, its the Committee of Ministers of the Council of Europe, which supervises the execution of judgments, cf Article 46(2) of the ECHR.[78] As for decisions of the IACHR, it is the court itself that monitors compliance with its judgments, cf Article 69 of the court's Rules of Procedure.[79]

The ECHR and ACHR enjoy strong standing in national law, in particular the ECHR, which has been incorporated into the law of all its contracting members.[80] However, while the conventions have in many instances been given status of domestic law (or even superior to domestic law), and are directly applicable at the national level, there seems to be a varied practice with respect to the national effect of judgments of the human rights courts.[81] The cases below illustrate how differently domestic courts treat the issue. Furthermore, while decisions of international human rights bodies cannot quash national legislation or annul a decision taken by national authorities, inevitably, a full remedy may require such measures.[82]

1. ILDC cases

Al-Nashif v National Police Directorate at the Ministry of the Interior, Judicial Review, Administrative Case No 11004/2002, Decision No 4332, ILDC 608 (BG 2003), 8th May 2003, Bulgaria; Supreme Administrative Court

Al-Nashif maintained that the rulings at the national level should be revoked pursuant to Article 231(1)(h) of the Civil Procedure Code of Bulgaria, which stated that the interested party might request the revocation of a final decision where a judgment of the ECtHR alleged a violation of the ECHR. In its judgment in *Al-Nashif v Bulgaria* the ECtHR had found a violation of Articles 8 and 13 of the ECHR.[83]

According to Article 13 ECHR, everyone whose rights and freedoms as set forth in this Convention are violated shall have an effective remedy before a national authority, notwithstanding that the violation has been committed by persons acting in an official capacity.

> [ref 9] The person shall have the opportunity to contest the executive claim that this is a matter of national security. Naturally, the judgment of the executive body regarding what poses a threat to national security is of substantial significance; however, the independent body shall be able to respond in cases where the reference to national security has no reasonable grounding in the facts, or exposes an illicit or contrary to

---

76 The language adopted in Article 63(1) is considered broader than Article 41 of the ECHR see Gray (n 47) 894.

77 cf IACHR, *Case of Baena Ricardo et al Competence*, Series C No 104 (28 November 2003) para 60; *Case of the Dismissed Congressional Workers (Aguado Alfaro et al) v Peru* (Order, Monitoring compliance with judgment) (24 November 2010) third considering para, and *Case of Vargas Areco v Paraguay* (Order, Monitoring compliance with judgment) (24 November 2010) third considering para.

78 The recent Protocol 14 to the ECHR strengtens the enforcement mechanism by giving an enforcement role also to the ECtHR. See new Articles 46(3) and 46(4), which empower the Committee of Ministers to seek a further judgment from the court in relation to enforcement.

79 In 2003, the IACHR asserted its competence to monitor the execution of its judgments, *Baena Ricardo and Others v Panama* (Judgment on Jurisdiction) (28 November 2003). In 2011, the IACHR issued 32 orders on monitoring compliance with judgment. On the mechanism see IACHR Annual Report 2011, 13–30.

80 D J Harris, M O'Boyle, E P Bates, and C M Buckley, *Harris, O'Boyle & Warbrick Law of the European Convention on Human Rights* (2nd edn, OUP 2009) 23.

81 Nollkaemper (n 34) 75–76.

82 This is the general view with respect, to the jurisdiction of the ECtHR; *Papamichalopoulos and Others v Greece* (just satisfaction), App No 14556/89 (31 October 1995) para 34; *Le Compte, Van Leuven and De Meyere v Belgium*, Apps No 6878/75 and 7238/75 (18 October 1982) para 13.

83 ECtHR, *Al-Nashif v Bulgaria* (Final Judgment), App No 50963/99 (20 June 2002).

the general meaning of and an arbitrary interpretation of the concept of "national security". Where such guarantees are absent, the police or other state bodies will be able to arbitrarily abuse the rights that the Convention guarantees" (§ 124).

[ref 10] In § 132 of the Decision, the Court reminds that "it has had multiple occasions to state that Article 13 of the Convention guarantees the existence, on the national level, of a remedy that shall enjoin observance of the substance of the rights and freedoms under the Convention, in whatever form they may be guaranteed by the national legislative order... By enabling a direct expression of the obligation of countries to protect human rights first and foremost within the framework of their own legal systems, Article 13 establishes an additional guarantee for the individual in order to guarantee that he or she shall effectively exercise his or her rights.

[ref 11] According to the European Court of Human Rights, "even where it is claimed that a threat to national security exists, the guarantee for an effective remedy requires, at a minimum, that a competent appellate body be informed of the reasons upon which the deportation decision is grounded, even where said reasons are not accessible to the public. The body should be competent to reject the claim of the executive authority that a threat to national security is present, should it find this claim to be arbitrary and groundless. Some form of competitive proceedings should exist if it is necessary for this to be done via a special representative holding a permit to obtain secret information. It is also necessary to examine the question of whether the contested measure would affect the person's right to family life, and if yes, whether the just balance between the public interest affected and the rights of the individual is respected" (§ 137).

[ref 12] In its decision of 20 June 2002, the European Court of Human Rights finds that there has been a violation of Article 8 of the Convention as "Al-Nashif's deportation was ordered pursuant to a legal regime that does not provide necessary safeguards against arbitrariness" (§ 128 and item 3 of the operative part) and there has been a violation of Article 13 of the Convention "as no remedy affording such guarantees of effectiveness was available to the applicants (§ 138 and item 4 of the operative part).

Červeňáková (Margita) and ors v Regional Court in Ústí nad Labem and District Court in Ústí nad Labem and Municipality of Ústí nad Labem (intervening), Decision on Constitutional Complaint, II ÚS 604/02, Sb n u ÚS 7/2004, ILDC 877 (CZ 2004), 26th February 2004, Czech Republic; Constitutional Court

The ECtHR had approved a friendly settlement between the plaintiffs and the Czech Republic and consequently struck out the application from the court's list. However, the plaintiffs partly continued their constitutional complaints.

23 The Constitutional Court therefore began by answering the question of whether the final decision given in this matter by the international court represents an obstacle of res judicata for the Constitutional Court. Article 10 of the Constitution of the Czech Republic incorporates into Czech law a large group of international treaties by which the courts are bound (the principle of monism). However, no provision of Constitutional law incorporates into Czech law a decision given by the international court on the basis of an international treaty which, according to Article 10 of the Constitution, is [already] component to the law. Therefore, within the Czech Republic, this decision does not have effect equal to a decision of Czech courts (the principle of dualism). Hence, neither on the basis of the Constitution nor on the basis of any other component to constitutional order can it be concluded that an obstacle

of res judicata exists for the Constitutional Court due to the fact that the international court has issued a final decision on the case.

[...] 26 The Constitutional Court is in no doubt that the content of the binding judgment of the European Court in the case against the Czech Republic represents an obligation for the Czech Republic arising from international law. The Czech Republic is obliged to observe such obligations, not only under international law, but also with reference to the provision of Article 1 (2) of the Constitution. The Constitutional Court is a constitutional authority of the Czech Republic, and is therefore itself subject to the provision of Article 1 (2) of the Constitution. Consequently, it is the duty of the Constitutional Court, within the scope of its competence, to observe the Czech Republic's obligations arising from the content of a judgment of the European Court. Furthermore, the same conclusion follows from the provision of Article 87 (1) (i) of the Constitution, according to which the Constitutional Court has the jurisdiction to decide on the measures necessary to implement a decision of an international court which is binding on the Czech Republic, should it prove impossible to implement such measures otherwise.

27 In the case in question, the Constitutional Court is not required to 'implement' the judgment, because the government of the Czech Republic has implemented its content within the scope of its competence. However, the above-mentioned provision of the Constitution can only be meaningfully interpreted against the background of the Constitutional Court's general obligation to 'observe' the decisions of international courts, with the understanding that over and above this general obligation, it is actually obligated to 'implement' the content of some of these judgments. A special obligation to 'implement' binding decisions of an international court, without a simultaneous general obligation to 'observe' them as international obligations of the Czech Republic, is conceptually unthinkable.

35 Under the circumstances, the Constitutional Court considers it neither useful nor necessary to dispute or, conversely, to confirm any of the above-mentioned different interpretations by the parties to the settlement. The 'international obligation' that the Constitutional Court is obliged to observe is the binding judgment of the European Court which took into account the settlement reached, accepting it in terms of its compliance with the Convention and the Protocols. Thus the settlement acquired a new legal quality which is distinct from the legal quality of the actual contractual settlement reached between the complainants and the government of the Czech Republic. Hence, the Constitutional Court considers itself competent to interpret the amicable settlement solely in the context of the binding judgment of the European Court dated 29.7.2003, of which such amicable settlement forms a part.

42 The Constitutional Court therefore had to state its opinion on the relevance of the will of the complainants which was expressed at a later date (on 11.6.2003). In a situation where neither the Convention nor the Constitutional Court Act resolves the question, the Constitutional Court was obliged to make appropriate use of Act no. 99/1963, Code of Civil Procedure, as amended (hereinafter the 'CCP'), as provided for in Section 63 of the Constitutional Court Act. Section 99 of the CCP ['Court Settlement'], in paragraph 3, recognises that a settlement approved by the court has the 'effects of a final judgment'. This means that the contents of the Settlement are binding on the parties and on all authorities (Section 159a (4) of the CCP). A settlement constitutes an obstacle of res judicata (Section 159a (5) of the CCP). It is therefore clear that it is legally impossible for a unilateral expression of will by one of the parties to alter the contents of the court settlement.

The complainants' expression of will submitted on 11.6.2003 is therefore irrelevant for the Constitutional Court. The same conclusion must be drawn with reference to Article 1 (2) of the Constitution. The judgment of the European Court dated 29.7.2003, containing an amicable settlement, represents an 'international obligation' for the Constitutional Court. The contents of this 'international obligation' cannot be conceptually changed by a unilateral expression of will submitted under national rather than international law, by a party subject to the jurisdiction of the Czech Republic (by a submission in the course of proceedings relating to a constitutional complaint).

Solicitor General of the Republic v Venezuela, Final Award on Jurisdiction of the Constitutional Chamber, File No 08-1572, No 1939, ILDC 1279 (VE 2008), 18th December 2008, Venezuela; Supreme Tribunal of Justice [TSJ]

In its decision on 5 August 2008, the IACHR found Venezuela in violation of the ACHR and ordered payment of monetary compensation costs and the state to reinstate three judges in their former or similar judicial positions or pay them US$100,000. The IACHR also ordered Venezuela to pass a Code of Judicial Ethics. The Venezuelan Solicitor General requested the Supreme Court of Justice to determine whether Venezuela had to enforce the IACHR's judgment.

35 It must first be noted that the American Convention on Human Rights is a multilateral treaty that has constitutional hierarchy and prevails in the domestic system only "insofar as they contain provisions concerning the enjoyment and exercise [of such rights] that are more favorable" than those established by the Constitution, in compliance with the provisions of Article 23 of our fundamental text.

36 Said Article 23 of the Constitution, reads:

"Article 23.

The treaties, pacts and conventions relating to human rights which have been executed and ratified by Venezuela have a constitutional rank, and prevail over internal legislation, insofar as they contain provisions concerning the enjoyment and exercise of such rights that are more favorable than those established by this Constitution and the laws of the Republic, and shall be immediately and directly applied by the courts and other organs of Government".

44 Now, notice is taken of the failure of the Inter-American Court of Human Rights, in that this body demands that the Venezuelan State indemnify the former judges of the First Court of Administrative Disputes Ana María Ruggeri Cova, Perkins Rocha Contreras and Juan Carlos Apitz, whom it classes as "victims" for having allegedly had their personal rights violated; however in the alleged finding by said Court of the violation of the rights or freedoms protected by the Convention, it laid down compulsory rules on the government and administration of the Legal Power that are the exclusive and excluding competence of the Supreme Court of Justice and established guidelines for the Legislative Power, on matters of legal careers and the liability of judges, violating the sovereignty of the Venezuelan State in the organization of its public powers and the selection of its functionaries, which is inadmissible.

46 Consequently, apart from any antimony there may be between the rules protecting personal rights and those relating to the common good, it is clear that, in failing to merely order an indemnity for the alleged violation of rights, the Inter-American Court of Human Rights used the award analyzed to unacceptably intervene in the government and legal administration that pertains exclusively to the Supreme Court of Justice, in compliance with the Constitution of 1999.

48 On the other hand, the Constitutional Chamber of the Supreme Court of Justice, in its decision No. 1942/2003 specified as follows with regard to Article 23 of the Constitution: "In the opinion of the Chamber, two key elements are clear from Article 23: 1) This concerns human rights that apply to natural persons; 2) It refers to rules that establish rights, not to awards or rulings of institutions, resolutions of organizations, etc., prescribed in the Treaties, but rather only to rules that create human rights. (. . .)

The Chamber repeats that it is the prevailing of the rules forming the Treaties, Pacts and Conventions (synonymous terms) in relation to human rights, but not of the reports or opinions of international organizations, which seek to interpret the scope of the rules of the international instruments, as Article 23 of the Constitution is clear: the constitutional hierarchy of the Treaties, Pacts and Conventions refers to their provisions, which, in being integrated into the current Constitution, means that the only party able to interpret them with respect to Venezuelan Law is the Constitutional Judge, in compliance with Article 335 of the current Constitution, in particular, the recognized interpreter under the 1999 Constitution, and the Constitutional Chamber, and thus is declared (...)

Thus it is the Constitutional Chamber that determines which rules on human rights of these treaties, pacts and conventions shall prevail in the domestic system; in the same way as which human rights not considered in said international instruments shall be valid in Venezuela.

This competence of the Constitutional Chamber for such matters, which stems from the Fundamental Charter, cannot be reduced by additional rules contained in Treaties or any other international texts on Human Rights that may have been signed by the country, which enable the States party to the Treaty to consult international organizations about the interpretation of the rights referred to in the Convention or Pact, as established in Article 64 of the Law Approving the American Convention on Human Rights, the Pact of San José, given that, were this possible, it would be a form of constitutional amendment on the matter, without all the relevant proceedings having been followed, reducing the competence of the Constitutional Chamber and transferring it to these multinationals or transnationals (internationals), who would make them binding interpretations. (. . .)

The decisions of these organizations will be fulfilled in the country, in compliance with that established by the Constitution and the laws, as long as they are not in conflict with the provisions of Article 7 of the current Constitution, which reads: "The Constitution is the supreme law and foundation of the legal order. All persons and organs exercising Public Authority are subject to this Constitution" and as long as they comply with the organic competences recorded in the Conventions and Treaties. Because of this, despite the respect of the Legal Power for the awards or rulings of these organizations, they cannot violate the Constitution of the Bolivarian Republic of Venezuela, just as they cannot infringe the legislation of Treaties and Conventions, which govern these areas or other decisions.

If an international organization, legally recognized by the Republic, should protect anyone, violating the human rights of groups or persons within the country, said decision must be rejected even if issued by international organizations that protect human rights. . . (. . .)

The Chamber considers that there is no legal body above the Supreme Court of Justice and for the purpose of Article 7 of the Constitution, unless the Constitution or law should thus rule, and even in this latter case, any decision in conflict with the rules of the Venezuelan Constitution shall not be applied in the country, and thus declared. (. . .)

Articles 73 and 153 of the Constitution consider the possibility of Venezuelan areas of jurisdiction being transferred to supranational bodies, which are acknowledged as potentially able to compromise national sovereignty.

However, the same Constitution highlights the areas in which this may take place, which are – for example – Latin America and Caribbean integration (Article 153 eiusdem). Different areas to that of Human Rights per se, and where the judgments issued are of immediate application in the territory of the member countries, as specified by Article 91 of the Law Approving the Statute of the Court of Justice of the Andean Community.

The Chamber understands that outside these specific areas, national sovereignty cannot in any case be removed by virtue of Article 1 of the Constitution, which establishes that independence, liberty, sovereignty, immunity, territorial integrity and national self-determination are unrenounceable rights of the Nation. Said constitutional rights are unrenounceable, cannot be relaxed, except where the Fundamental Charter so rules, together with the mechanisms that make it possible, as contemplated by Articles 73 and 336.5 of the Constitution, for example.

The consequence of the foregoing is that, in principle, the enforcement of the awards of Supranational Courts cannot undermine the sovereignty of the country, or the fundamental rights of the Republic" (underlined by this award).

51 In addition to the foregoing, the judgment questioned seeks to disregard the firm nature of the administrative and legal decisions that have acquired the status of res judicata, in ordering the reinstatement of the dismissed judges. In this sense, it must be pointed out that former judge Ana María Ruggeri Cova did not appeal for the reconsideration or any legal review against the deed of dismissal (a fact acknowledged in paragraph 183 of the sentence of the Inter-American Court of Human Rights and at point 10 of chapter X of this same award). On the other hand, the deed of dismissal issued against former judges Perkins Rocha Contreras and Juan Carlos Apitz is final by decision No. 634 of May 21, 2008, issued by the Political Administrative Chamber of the Supreme Court of Justice, whereby it was declared that the administrative dispute of nullity had been abandoned, brought against said deed, as the writ of summons was not collected, published and delivered to the third parties concerned within the terms established in Article 21 of the Organic Law of the Supreme Court of Justice, a situation moreover omitted from the award of the Inter-American Court of Human Rights. Hence, in the opinion of this Constitutional Chamber, it is not possible to disregard the matter of res judicata which involves the deeds of dismissal of the former judges of the First Court of Administrative Dispute, when the administrative or legal resources envisaged by the internal legal system were not urged or were dismissed by definitive ruling by the Highest Court of the Republic, as this would be in conflict with one of the essential values of the Venezuelan Justice System, as is legal safety.

52 It is not a matter of interpreting the content and scope of the judgment of the Inter-American Court of Human Rights, nor of disregarding the treaty validly signed by the Republic, which supports it, or of avoiding the undertaking to enforce decisions in accordance with the provisions of Article 68 of the American Convention on Human Rights, but rather of applying a minimum standard of adjustment of the award to the internal constitutional system, which has occurred in other cases, as when the unenforceability was declared of the award issued by the Inter-American Court of Human Rights on May 30, 1999, in the case: Castillo Petruzzi et al., by the Plenary Chamber of Peru's Supreme Court of Military Justice, for considering, amongst other aspects, that the judicial power "is autonomous and in the exercise

of its functions, its members do not depend on any administrative authority, which shows a blatant disregard for Peruvian legislation on the matter"; that "they seek to disregard Peru's Political Constitution and to subject it to the American Convention on Human Rights in the interpretation that the judges of said Court may make, ad-libitum, in this judgment"; that the award in question, issued by the Special Military Supreme Court, acquired the status of res judicata "and it could not, therefore, be subject to a new ruling as this would constitute an infraction of a constitutional principle"; that "in the hypothetical case that the judgment issued by the American Court should be enforced in accordance with the terms and conditions it contains, there would be a legal impossibility to fulfill it under the demands made by said supranational jurisdiction", as "it would first require the Constitution to be amended" and "the acceptance and enforcement of the sentence of the Court in this matter would seriously endanger the internal security of the Republic".

54 By virtue of the foregoing considerations, this Constitutional Chamber declares the award of the Inter-American Court of Human Rights dated August 5, 2008 unenforceable, resulting in an order for the reinstatement to office of the former magistrates of the First Court of Administrative Disputes, Ana María Ruggeri Cova, Perkins Rocha Contreras and Juan Carlos Apitz B.; based on Articles 7, 23, 25, 138 and 156.32 of Chapter III of Title V of the Constitution of the Republic and case law partially transcribed of the Constitutional and Administrative Policy Chambers. Thus ruled.

56 In the same way, based on the same principle and in compliance with the provisions of Article 78 of the American Convention on Human Rights, the National Executive is asked to denounce this Convention, in view of the clear usurpation of powers committed by the Inter-American Court of Human Rights with the award concerned by this decision; and the fact that this implementation lies institutionally and in terms of competence with the mentioned Treaty. Thus ruled.

58 In light of what has been explained, this Supreme Court of Justice, in its Constitutional Chamber, administering justice in the name of the Republic, by the authority of the law, hereby declares:

1) that the award of the Inter-American Court of Human Rights dated August 5, 2008, whereby the reinstatement to office was ordered of the former magistrates of the First Court of Administrative Dispute, Ana María Ruggeri Cova, Perkins Rocha Contreras and Juan Carlos Apitz B. were ordered, is UNENFORCEABLE, and the Bolivian Republic of Venezuela is ordered to pay the amounts of money and make the publications referred to in the judge disciplinary system.

2) On the basis of the principle of cooperation between authorities (Article 136 of the Constitution of the Bolivarian Republic of Venezuela), and in accordance with the provisions of Article 78 of the American Convention on Human Rights, the National Executive is asked to report this Treaty or Convention in view of the evident usurpation of powers committed by the Inter-American Court of Human Rights, with the award concerned by this resolution.

Dorigo (Paolo), Appeal judgment, No 2800/2007, (2007) Rivista di diritto internazionale 601, ILDC 1096 (IT 2007), 25th January 2007, Italy; Supreme Court of Cassation; 1st Criminal Section

The core issues in the case were whether the judgments of the ECtHR had binding force and enjoyed direct effect within the Italian legal system, and whether final judgments of the ECtHR trumped domestic criminal *res judicata*.

H2 According to Article 670 of the Code of Criminal Procedure, the enforcing judge had to declare unenforceable any final domestic criminal conviction in relation to which the ECtHR had established, first, that the conviction had been pronounced in violation of Article 6 of the ECHR, and, second, that the convicted person had the right to a new trial. This was so even though the legislator had failed to introduce a specific remedy allowing the reopening of the proceedings. (paragraph 8)

H4 The binding force of the judgments of the ECtHR in proceedings to which Italy had been a party could also be inferred from two sources, namely the ratification of Protocol No 14 to the Convention for the Protection of Human Rights and Fundamental Freedoms, amending the control system of the Convention (13 May 2004), and the adoption of Law No 12, 9 January 2006. Protocol No 14 reinforced the obligation deriving from Article 46 of the ECHR, while Law No 12 established that the Prime Minister should promote all government measures which appeared necessary to guarantee the enforcement of the judgments of the ECtHR. (paragraph 5)

H5 Judgments of the ECtHR produced direct effect in the domestic legal order, in the sense that they created rights and obligations, not only for states, but also for individuals. Indeed, when such judgments established a violation of the ECHR's rights, individuals might rely upon a right to reparation, either of a pecuniary nature or as restitution in integrum, which the courts were obligated to enforce. (paragraph 5)

Dorigo and President of the Council of Ministers (intervening), Constitutional review, No 113/ 2011, (2011) 94 RDI 960, ILDC 1732 (IT 2011), 7th April 2011, Italy; Constitutional Court

This case arises from the same events as the case above. The issues before the Constitutional Court were whether the ECHR had constitutional rank within the Italian legal order and whether a decision of the ECtHR against Italy required the reopening of concluded criminal proceedings.

4 .— Art. 46 of the ECHR—cited by the judge in these proceedings as the "interposed law" – imposes an obligation on contracting States, in paragraph 1, "to comply with the final judgments of the Court [European Court of Human Rights] in connection with disputes to which they are parties"; adding, in paragraph 2, that "the Court's final judgment is sent to the Committee of Ministers who oversee its execution".

This is a provision of particular importance in the European system for the protection of fundamental rights, vested in the Court of Strasbourg: indeed, it is clear that the scope of the Contracting States' primary obligation arising out of the ECHR – recognition that each person has the rights and freedoms guaranteed by the Convention (art. 1) – depends, to a large extent, on the specific "nature" of the individual offences identified.

In this regard it must be noted that, subsequent to the ruling for referral to the Constitutional Court, art. 46 of the ECHR has been amended by the implementation (on 1 June 2010) of Protocol no. 14 to the Convention (ratified and made enforceable in Italy by law no. 280 of 15 December 2005). However, this amendment does not cancel the requirements underlying the question of constitutionality, but rather strengthens them. Indeed, by adding a further three paragraphs it is envisaged that the Committee of Ministers may ask the Court of Strasbourg to make an interpretative decision when there are any doubts concerning the content of a previously adopted final judgment, with the effect of preventing its execution (paragraph 3 of art. 46); and, above all, that it may ask the Court to issue a further pronouncement to ascertain a contracting Party's violation of the obligation to comply with its judgments (paragraphs 4 and 5). A specific violation procedure is therefore introduced for the purpose of providing a more incisive means of putting pressure on the defendant State.

With regard to the content of the obligation, art. 46 is to be read systematically in conjunction with art. 41 of the ECHR, according to which, "if the Court declares that there has been a violation of the Convention and its Protocols, and if the other contracting Party's national law only partially permits removing the consequences of the violation, where appropriate the Court will grant the injured party fair redress".

In this regard the most recent consolidated case law of the Court of Strasbourg has affirmed that, "when the Court finds there has been a violation, the defendant State has a legal obligation, not only to pay the interested parties the sums that they are awarded as fair redress, but also to adopt the necessary general measures and/or, if applicable, individual measures" (among many others, Grand Chamber, judgment of 17 September 2009, Scoppola v. Italy, point 147; Grand Chamber, judgment of 1 March 2006, Sejdovi v. Italy, point 119; Grand Chamber, judgment of 8 April 2004, Assanidzé v. Georgia, point 198). The reason for this, in light of art. 41 of the ECHR, is that the sums awarded as fair redress are aimed only at "granting compensation for the damages suffered by the interested parties insofar as these constitute a consequence of the violation that cannot in any case be cancelled" (judgment of 13 July 2000, Scozzari and Giunta v. Italy, point 250).

In contrast, the purpose of the individual measures that the defendant State is required to implement is that defined by the European Court as restitutio in integrum in favour of the interested party. In other words these measures must place "the claimant, where possible, in a situation equivalent to that in which he would have found himself had there not been a violation [. . .] of the Convention" (among many others, Grand Chamber, judgment of 17 September 2009, Scoppola v. Italy, point 151; judgment of 10 November 2004, Sejdovic v. Italy, point 55; judgment of 18 May 2004, Somogyi v. Italy, point 86). With this in mind the defendant State is also called upon to remove the impediments that, at the national legislation level, prevent achievement of the objective: "by ratifying the Convention"; in fact, "the contracting States undertake to ensure that their national law is compatible with the latter" and thus also, "in their own national provisions of law to remove any obstacle to a suitable re-establishment of the claimant's situation" (Grand Chamber, judgment of 17 September 2009, Scoppola v. Italy, point 152; Grand Chamber, judgment of 8 April 2004, Assanidzé v. Georgia, point 198).

With regard in particular to offences associated with the conducting of proceedings, and with criminal proceedings in particular, the Court of Strasbourg, taking the cited premises as its starting point, identified in the re-opening of proceedings the most suitable mechanism for restitutio in integrum, i.e. in cases of an established violation of the guarantees laid down in art. 6 of the Convention. In accordance with the information already provided by the Committee of Ministers, and in Recommendation R (2000)2 of 19 January 2000 in particular, in which the contracting Parties were specifically invited "to examine the respective national legal provisions in order to ensure the existence of adequate scope for the re-examination of a case, including the re-opening of proceedings, when the Court has found a violation of the Convention".

The Strasbourg judges have affirmed, in particular – in what has now become consistent case law – that when a private entity has been found guilty at the end of proceedings characterised by the non-observance of art. 6 of the Convention, the most appropriate means of remedying the identified violation is, as a general rule, "new proceedings or the re-opening of proceedings, at the request of the interested party", in compliance with all the conditions for a fair trial (among many others, the judgment of 11 December 2007, Cat Berro v. Italy, point 46; judgment of 8 February 2007, Kollcaku v. Italy, point 81; judgment of 21 December 2006, Zunic v. Italy, point 74; Grand Chamber, judgment of 12 May 2006, Öcalan v. Turkey, point 210). It is, however, necessary to recognise that the defendant State has a discretionary right to choose the method of fulfilling its obligation, under the scrutiny of the Committee of Ministers and within the limits of the compatibility of pleadings contained in the Court judgment (among many, Grand Chamber, judgment of 17 September 2009, Scoppola v. Italy, point 152; Grand Chamber, judgment of 1 March 2006, Sejdovic v. Italy, points 119 and 127; Grand Chamber, judgment of 12 May 2005, Öcalan v. Turkey, point 210).

[...]

6. —[ref 5] On the other hand the absence of an appropriate remedy for this purpose under Italian law has been censured by the bodies of the European Council, including and most importantly in relation to the case concerning the defendant in the proceedings in question.

In this regard it should be noted first of all – as a correction to what has been stated in the ruling for referral [to the Constitutional Court] – that the European Court of Human Rights has not actually pronounced on the said case. The ruling that the referring judge identifies as the "judgment of 9 September 1998" of the Court of Strasbourg is in fact a report of that same date by the European Commission of Human Rights (a body dissolved by Protocol no. 11): this report was accepted by the Committee of Ministers in its decision of 15 April 1999 (Internal Resolution DH(99)258). Pursuant to art. 32 of the ECHR, in the text that preceded implementation of Protocol no. 11 (which occurred on 1 November 1998, but with application of the previous rules to cases that were pending at that date, under the transitional provision of art. 5), the Committee of Ministers was in fact competent to take decisions on cases submitted to them for examination after the drawing up of a report by the European Commission, which was not followed by deferment of the dispute to the Court of Strasbourg within three months.

The circumstances now presented do not, however, affect the relevance of the question, since under the original art. 32, paragraph 4, of the ECHR, the Committee of Ministers' decisions were binding on contracting States in the same way as the final judgments of the European Court of Human Rights: which means that – retroactively – there is full equivalence of the one type to the other for the purposes under consideration.

With precisely this in mind, both the Committee of Ministers (interim Resolutions ResDH(2000)30 of 19 February 2002, ResDH(2004)13 of 10 February 2004 and ResDH(2005)85 of 12 October 2005), and the Parliamentary Assembly of the Council of Europe (see, among others, Resolution no. 1516(2006) of 2 October 2006) were increasingly critical of Italy's failure to fulfil its obligation to remove the consequences of the violation ascertained in the case in question: default in the specific form of the absence, under national law, of a mechanism appropriate for allowing the re-opening of proceedings declared to be "unfair".

The request to introduce such a mechanism "as quickly as possible" was also sent to the Italian authorities once again, by the Committee of Ministers, on the occasion of the decision to close the monitoring procedure relating to that case: a decision adopted following the said pronouncement of the Court of Cassation which had declared as unenforceable the judgment pronounced against the defendant, ordering its release (Final resolution CM/ResDH(2007)83 of 19 February 2007).

[...]

8. —A different conclusion must be reached regarding the question of constitutional legitimacy now under examination which firstly invests art. 630 of the Code of Criminal Procedure in its entirety, and secondly is proposed with reference to the different and more appropriate parameter specified in art. 117, paragraph one, of

the Constitution, assuming art. 46 (in correlation with art. 6) of the ECHR to be the "interposed law.

As of judgments nos. 348 and 349 of 2007 this Court's case law has consistently adopted the position that the ECHR rules – in the sense ascribed to them by the European Court of Human Rights, specifically instituted for their interpretation and application (art. 32, paragraph 1, of the Convention) – constitute, as "interposed laws", the constitutional parameter referred to in art. 117, paragraph one, of the Constitution, in the part that requires that the national legislation comply with the requirements deriving from the "international obligations" (judgment no. 1 of 2011; judgments nos. 196, 187 and 138 of 2010; judgments nos. 317 and 311 of 2009, and no. 39 of 2008; on the enduring validity of that reconstruction even after the Lisbon Treaty of 13 December 2007 came into effect, judgment no. 80 of 2011). From which perspective, if any difference is found to exist between a national law and the provisions of the ECHR, the ordinary judge must first of all ascertain whether an interpretation of the former in a sense that accords with the Convention is practicable, making use of every hermeneutical instrument at his disposal; and, if this produces a negative result – it not being possible to remedy this by simply not applying the differing national law – he must declare the incompatibility found, proposing a question of constitutional legitimacy with reference to the parameter in question. In its turn the Constitutional Court, which is invested with powers of scrutiny, although it cannot censure the European Court's interpretation of the ECHR, has a legitimate right to ascertain whether the provision of the Convention – which nevertheless occupies a level below that of the Constitution – is in fact in conflict with other provisions of the Constitution: in which case it will be necessary to exclude the suitability of the provision of the Convention for integrating the parameter in question.

In the present case it has already been pointed out (point 4 of the legal Considerations, above) that, in what has now become consistent case law, the Court of Strasbourg takes the view that the obligation to comply with its final judgments, which art. 46, paragraph one, of the ECHR imposes on contracting Parties, also involves the requirement that contracting States permit the re-opening of proceedings, at the request of the interested party, whenever this appears necessary for the purpose of restitutio in integrum in favour of the said party, in cases of violation of the guarantees recognised by the Convention, particularly with regard to fair trials.

This interpretation cannot be seen as conflicting with the forms of protection offered by the Constitution. In particular – albeit in light of the doubtful relevance of the degree of certainty and suitability of the res judicata – it is not possible to regard as contrary to the Constitution the envisaged absence of the corresponding precluding effects in the context of particularly important commitments – such as those determined by the Court of Strasbourg, with regard to the judicial matter in its entirety – in terms of the guarantees relating to fundamental rights of the person: guarantees that, with particular reference to the provisions of art. 6 of the Convention, are amply reflected in the applicable text of art. 111 of the Constitution.

Moreover, the judge has, with good reason, identified the basis for the requested additional intervention in art. 630 of the Code of Criminal Procedure: indeed, in that a review, as an extraordinary means of challenging a decision in general terms, involves the re-opening of proceedings, which requires revisiting the procedural activities of an investigative nature, extended to the gathering of evidence, such a review constitutes the mechanism, among those currently existing in the criminal procedure system, that presents characteristics most in accord with that whose introduction appears necessary for ensuring that the national rules are in accordance with the parameter in question.

Furthermore, contrary to what the Attorney General maintains, acceptance of the matter in dispute cannot be precluded by the fact that – as has been pointed out (point 5 of the legal Considerations, above) – the possible re-opening of proceedings associated with the obligation under the ECHR is found to differ from the other cases of revision currently contemplated in the challenged rules, either because it is contrary to the reasoning adopted in those cases in terms of the nature of the link between "procedural truth" and "historic truth", arising out of factors "outside" the scope of the proceedings already conducted; or because that possibility is at variance with the rigid alternative, contemplated under the existing rules regarding the outcome of the revision judgment, between acquittal and confirmation of the previous judgment.

Faced with a constitutional 'wound' that cannot be resolved by means of interpretation – especially where fundamental rights are involved – the Court is nevertheless required to provide a remedy: and it must do so independent of the fact that the wound is dependent on what the rule provides or, conversely, on what the rule (or, to be more accurate, the rule of most relevance for the matter under discussion) fails to provide. Nor is it possible, in light of this Court's clear findings (judgment no. 59 of 1958), to regard as precluded from a declaration of the constitutional illegitimacy of laws the real or apparent absence of rules that may be derived therefrom, with respect to given relations. Indeed it will, on the one hand, be the responsibility of the ordinary judges to draw from the decision the necessary corollaries in terms of its application, making use of the hermeneutic instruments at their disposal; while, on the other hand, it will be the responsibility of the legislator to make provision, in the most needed and appropriate manner, for aspects that appear to require appropriate regulation.

In the present case, art. 630 of the Code of Criminal Procedure must be declared constitutionally illegitimate precisely because (and in the part where) it fails to contemplate a "different" case for revision, apart from those currently regulated, aimed specifically at permitting (for proceedings resolved by one of the pronouncements referred to in art. 629 of the Code of Criminal Procedure) the re-opening of proceedings – for the purpose, in the latter case, and as a general functional principle, for the re-opening of activities already conducted and, if necessary, for the re-opening of activities necessary for a judgment – when such re-opening is found necessary, in accordance with art. 46, paragraph 1, of the ECHR, in order that it be in conformity with a final judgment of the European Court of Human Rights (which, for the reasons already given, is equated with the decision adopted by the Committee of Ministers under the aforesaid text of art. 32 of the ECHR).

The need for a re-opening will be assessed – in addition to taking account of the objective nature of the violation established (it is thus quite clear that a re-opening will not be triggered by failure to observe the principle of the reasonable duration of the proceedings, contemplated in art. 6, paragraph 1, of the ECHR, since the resumption of procedural activities would determine the details of the offence) – taking account, of course, of the provisions contained in the judgment the execution of which is being considered, and in the "interpretative" judgment required of the Court of Strasbourg by the Committee of Ministers, in accordance with art. 46, paragraph 3, of the ECHR.

Furthermore, it is understood that, when the eventuality being considered occurs, the judge must examine the compatibility of the individual provisions relating to the revision proceedings. It is necessary, in fact, to regard as inapplicable any provisions that appear irreconcilable from the logical/legal perspective, in light of the objective pursued (to place the interested party in the situation in which he would have found himself had the acknowledged violation not occurred, and not to remedy a defective assessment of the facts by the judge, resulting from factors outside the matter being judged), and above all – as already pointed out – those that reflect the traditional intended use of revision proceedings solely for the acquittal of the defendant. Therefore, by way of example, the condition of admissibility, based on the absolute prognosis referred to in art. 631 of the Code of Criminal Procedure, will not apply. Equally inapplicable – in the appropriate cases – will be the provisions of paragraphs 2 and 3 of art. 637 of the Code of Criminal Procedure (according to which, respectively, admission of the request necessarily involves the acquittal of the defendant, and the judge cannot pronounce this exclusively on the basis of a different assessment of evidence admitted in the previous proceedings).

Furthermore, it is necessary to take into account that the possibility of the revision contemplated here necessarily involves a departure – imposed by the need for fulfilling international obligations – from the recognised principle whereby procedural defects remain covered by the matter on which judgment is passed. In this context the revision judge will also assess how the causes of the unfairness of the proceedings, as determined by the European Court, must be defined as defects in the procedural process with reference to national law, adopting all the appropriate measures to eliminate them when pronouncing a new judgment.

2. Commentary

(a) The obligation to comply with decisions of international human rights courts

The constitutional courts in Europe in the above cases firmly underscore the international obligation of their states to comply with decisions of the ECtHR, cf Article 46 of the ECHR. Based on this international obligation, the Bulgarian Constitutional Court concluded that its domestic courts had to apply the ECHR directly as it was interpreted in the ECtHR's judgment in the case, although it would contradict national law. The Constitutional Court of the Czech Republic stated that it was obliged to observe within its competences obligations arising from the content of a binding judgment of the ECtHR. It equated friendly settlement at the ECtHR to such a judgment and therefore ceased national proceedings by the applicants. The Italian courts also gave Protocol 14 considerable weight, considering it strengthened the obligation of states to comply with decisions of the court. The importance that the Court of Cassation gave to the Italian ratification of the protocol is noteworthy as the protocol had not taken effect at the time of decision.

Another interesting conclusion by the Constitutional Court in Italy regards the nature of the decisions of the Committee of Ministers of the Council of Europe. In accordance with the rules of the ECHR at the time, prior to the entry into force of Protocol 11, the Committee of Ministers of the Council of Europe had adopted a report finding a violation of Italy of the convention, through a legally binding decision. The Commission played a different role the entry into force of Protocol 11 to the ECHR. Although former Article 32(4) of the ECHR established the obligation of states to comply with the decisions of the Committee of Ministers, this did not automatically mean that those decisions were to be equated with judicial decisions, such as the judgments of the ECtHR.

(b) Enforceability of ECtHR and IACHR decisions in national courts—direct effect

While the human rights treaties have been given direct effect in national law, there seems to be a varied practice with respect to direct effect of judgments of the relevant human rights courts. In the case of *Dorigo Paolo* the Court of Cassation of Italy concluded that judgments of the ECtHR produced direct effect in the domestic legal order, in the sense that they created rights and obligations, not only for states, but also for individuals. The Bulgarian Constitutional Court noted that while the Bulgarian constitution gave constitutional status to the ECHR it did not afford constitutional status to the decisions of the competent bodies of international organizations, or international jurisdictions and quasi-jurisdictions concerning the implementation of human rights treaties. Similarly, as stated by the Constitutional Court of the Czech Republic, 'none of the provisions of the Constitution incorporated decisions of international courts based on an international treaty which was part of the Czech legal order'. Similarly to the courts in Bulgaria and the Czech Republic, the Supreme Tribunal of Justice in Venezuela distinguished between a direct effect of a treaty and international judgments issued by monitoring bodies supervising that treaty. The court refused to give the same status to international judgments or reports issued by the monitoring bodies supervising human rights treaties as the human rights provisions in those treaties have.

Italy fits into the group of a majority of states described by the Council of Europe as giving direct effect to judgments of the ECtHR.[84] The Czech Republic and Bulgaria do not make it to that category. However, the findings of their constitutional courts, based on the international obligation of their state to comply with the decision of the ECtHR, gave the decisions the same impact as having direct effect.

(c) Remedies

Just as in the case of the ICJ, human rights courts are increasingly leaving less choice to states with respect to remedies. The IACHR has been progressive in this respect, illustrated by its case with respect to Venezuela. In response to that judgment of the IACHR, the Venezuelan court considered it in contradiction with the constitution, to violate the national sovereignty of the country, and to affect the fundamental rights of the state. It even went on, stating that: 'the executive branch should have denounced the ACHR given the IACHR's apparent usurpation of powers when issuing that judgment'. In the last years, the ECtHR has to some extent followed the path of the IACHR as it has become more direct with respect to what means states have to use in their domestic legal order to discharge their obligation to comply with a decision of the court, stating that: '[i]n certain cases, the nature of the violation found may be such as to leave no real choice as to the measures required to remedy it and the Court may decide to indicate a specific measure'.[85] With the same argument, the ECtHR has decided on specific measures, such as a return of a land,[86] a release from custody as soon as possible,[87] that a state must replace detention on remand with other reasonable and less stringent measure of restraint,[88] and to restore title to a flat and to reverse an order for conviction.[89]

The reopening of domestic proceedings has become of fundamental importance for the execution of the ECtHR's judgments. Indeed, in some cases, this is the only form of *restitutio in integrum* possible, ie the only effective means of redressing the violation of the convention. In response to execution problems, caused in certain cases by the lack of appropriate national legislation on the re-opening of proceedings, the Committee of Ministers adopted a recommendation to member states on the re-examination or reopening of certain cases at the domestic level following judgments of the ECtHR, inviting them to ensure that there existed at national level adequate possibilities for achieving, as far as possible, *restitutio in integrum*, including the

84 Council of Europe, Practical impact of the Council of Europe monitoring mechanisms in improving respect for human rights and the rule of law in member states, H/Inf (2010) 7.

85 ECtHR, *Öcalan v Turkey*, App No 46221/9 (12 May 2005) paras 194–95.

86 ECtHR, *Papamichalopoulos and Others v Greece* (just satisfaction), App No 14556/89 (31 October1995) para 38.

87 ECtHR, *Assanidzé v Georgia*, App No 71503/01 (8 April 2004) para 203; *Ilaşcu v Moldova and Russia* (n 75); ECtHR, *Fatullayev v Azerbajdzhan*, App No 40984/07 (22 April 2010) paras 176–77.

88 ECtHR, *Aleksanyan v Russia*, App No 46468/06 (22 December 2008) para 240.

89 ECtHR, *Stolyarova v Russia*, App No 15711/13 (29 January 2015) para 75.

reopening of proceedings.[90] Building on the practice of the committee, the court itself is more and more deciding on such measures.[91]

In *Dorigo Paolo*, the Constitutional Court stated in clear terms that in cases involving violations of Article 6 of the ECHR, the state had an obligation, pursuant to Article 46, to reopen criminal proceedings, as a form of *restitutio in integrum*, in accordance with what was affirmed by the Court of Cassation in its decisions in *Somogyi* and *Dorigo*. A national legislation on re-opening cases is put to a test in *Al-Nashif v Bulgaria*, where the core issues were whether a judgment of the ECtHR against Bulgaria had binding effect in the Bulgarian legal order, and whether a judgment of the ECtHR had primacy over final judgments or rulings rendered by a Bulgarian court and required revocation of the court's final judgments or rulings. Some states have provision in the constitution on implementation of decisions of international courts in general. For instance, in the Czech Republic, according to Article 87(1)(i) of the Constitution the Constitutional Court should decide about implementation of decisions of an international court that are binding on the Czech Republic and which could not be implemented in a different way.

V. Conclusions

The ILDC reports demonstrate that judgments of international courts are being enforced before domestic courts. With respect to judgments of the international criminal tribunals, the ICTY, ICTR, and ICC, and of the international human rights courts, the ECtHR and IACHR, such enforcement has often been successful. The possibility for individuals to enforce decisions of the ICJ before domestic courts has been rejected in the cases covered.

Domestic courts acknowledge the obligation of their relevant states to comply with decisions of international courts. At times, that obligation overrides domestic legal hurdles for enforcement. The cases relating to enforcement of judgment of the international human rights tribunals reflect this. The power of the Security Council and the international obligation by member states of the UN, undertaken in the UN Charter, to comply with its decisions also carried great weight with respect to enforcement of decisions of international criminal courts at the national level; and again, at times prevailed over legal impediments at the national level. The obligation of UN member states, undertaken in the same treaty, to comply with decisions of the ICJ has not has been given the same weight by domestic courts.

Whether decisions of international courts have direct effect in national law is addressed directly by some domestic courts. In many cases, domestic courts consider that international decisions can have such a direct effect. Some domestic courts consider it necessary that the national law explicitly allows such a direct effect, while others *de facto* give decisions of international courts such a direct effect, in order for the state to comply with its international obligations and binding force of international decisions.

Remedies provided by international courts today call for various forms of implementation at the national level, many directed at individuals and other non-state actors. That development has inevitably put the spotlight on compliance of states with decisions of international courts. On the whole, states are complying with international judgments requiring specific remedies at

90 Recommendation No R (2000) 2 of the Committee of Ministers to member States on the re-examination or reopening of certain cases at the domestic level following judgments of the European Court of Human Rights; Explanatory Memorandum on the Recommendation No R (2000) 2 of the Committee of Ministers on the re-examination or reopening of certain cases at domestic level following judgments of the ECtHR.

91 ECtHR, *Gençel v Turkey*, App No 53431/99 (23 October 2003) para 27; ECtHR, *Somogyi v Italy*, App No 67972/01 (18 May 2004) para 86; ECtHR, *Stoichkov v Bulgaria*, App No 9808/02 (24 March 2005) para 81; ECtHR, *Lungoci v Rumania*, App No 62710/00 (26 January 2006); ECtHR, *Claes and Others v Belgium*, Apps No 46825/99, 47132/99, 47502/99, 49010/99, 49104/99, 49195/99, and 49716/99 (2 June 2005); and ECtHR, *Salduz v Turkey*, App No 36391/02 (27 November 2008) para 72.

the national level, and by doing so acknowledging this enhanced power of international courts. At the same time, the practice illustrates how enforcement of international rights and obligations of the individual is dependent on both the international and the national regimes. The practice of who can enforce these remedies before domestic courts is still not settled. With international courts becoming confident in awarding remedies, reparations reflecting international law on state responsibility, and the high interest at stakes for various actors, it can only be expected that enforcement of international decisions before domestic courts will increase. That practice will continue to test compliance of states with decisions of international courts, the enforcement mechanism at the international level, and the relationship between international and domestic law.

II

International Responsibility

RALPH JANIK

I. Introduction

Domestic courts play a twofold (and obviously significant) role in the field of international responsibility. On the one hand, as organs of a state, they may themselves commit or condone an international wrong.[1] This may, for example, happen if the domestic legal framework basically ties their hands and requires them to apply domestic legislation inconsistent with international law—eg if they do not enjoy a sufficient level of judicial discretion to interpret domestic legislation in a manner that conforms to international law, owing to a lack of expertise, judicial independence, or even awareness of international law.

After all, as the House of Lords—the then-highest court in the United Kingdom (UK) (ie until the establishment of the Supreme Court in 2009)—held in *A, Amnesty International (intervening) and Commonwealth Lawyers Association (intervening) v Secretary of State for the Home Department* that the mere 'failure to pass the required implementing legislation has only a potential effect: the wrongful fact occurs only when administrative or judicial measures are taken which, being contrary to international rules due to the lack of implementing legislation, generate State responsibility'. [2] The same holds true for the actual application of pre-existing or newly passed domestic legislation violating international law: As the House of Lords further emphasized—in general terms—'the maintenance or passage of national legislation inconsistent with international rules generates State responsibility and consequently gives rise to a corresponding claim for cessation and reparation (lato sensu) only when such legislation is concretely applied'.[3]

On the other hand, domestic courts can do their utmost to halt or prevent internationally wrongful acts of their states by using harmonization or avoidance techniques.[4] International law can and even *should* accordingly rank among the major factors when applying domestic legislation.[5] Domestic courts have thus at times expressly justified their reasoning and interpretation of international law to prevent their state from committing an international wrong.[6] In particular, judgments by higher-ranking, constitutional, or supreme courts are of utter importance in this regard. As the German Constitutional Court held in the *Yemeni citizens extradition case*,

> [it] is the primary purpose of the verification proceedings to prevent and remedy, whenever possible, violations of international law that are due to the erroneous

1 See C Greenwood, 'State Responsibility for the Decisions of National Courts' in M Fitzmaurice and D Sarooshi (eds), *Issues of State Responsibility before International Judicial Institutions* (Hart Publishing 2004) 55.

2 *A, Amnesty International (intervening) and Commonwealth Lawyers Association (intervening) v Secretary of State for the Home Department*, Appeal judgment, [2005] UKHL 71, [2006] 2 AC 221, [2005] 3 WLR 1249, [2006] 1 All ER 575, ILDC 363 (UK 2005), 8 December 2005, House of Lords [HL], paras 149 and 150.

3 ibid.

4 See D Sloss and M Van Alstine, 'International Law in Domestic Courts' in W Sandholtz and C A Whytock (eds), *Research Handbook on the Politics of International Law* (Edward Elgar Publishing 2017) 79.

5 cf A Nollkaemper, *National Courts and the International Rule of Law* (OUP 2011).

6 A Nollkaemper, 'Grounds for the Application of International Rules of Interpretation in National Courts' in H P Aust and G Nolte (eds), *The Interpretation of International Law by Domestic Courts: Uniformity, Diversity, Convergence* (OUP 2016) 34, 40.

application or to the disregard of rules of international law by German courts, and which can create a responsibility under international law on the part of Germany.[7]

Case law on responsibility covers a wide array of issues, spanning from the scope of responsibility and attribution to the question of aid and assistance, shared responsibility, or state succession. The main cases in this regard will be briefly discussed and quoted in this chapter.

II. State Responsibility and Domestic Law

The hierarchy between international and domestic law has not always been as clear as today. Classical treatises on sovereignty such as those by G W F Hegel famously viewed international law merely as 'external state law' which was only binding, if at all, in a moral but not in a legal sense due to the anarchic nature of the international (inter-state) system.[8] Nowadays states may obviously not rely on their sovereignty or domestic legal order as a justification for violations of international law.[9] Nevertheless, the political atmosphere in a given country may sometimes create pressure on courts to 'preserve the sovereignty of the state'. Constitutions may also create the impression or proceed from the assumption that they rank above international legal obligations. It is sometimes also necessary to rule on or emphasize the role of international law within the domestic legal order.

Constitutionality of the Agreement Establishing an Association between Slovenia and the European Communities, Constitutional Review, Official Gazette RS No 40/97, ILDC 532 (SI 1997), 5th June 1997, Constitutional Court

This was the case in *Constitutionality of the Agreement Establishing an Association between Slovenia and the European Communities*, where the Constitutional Court of Slovenia had to deal with the question of whether the (then-) EC association agreement was in conformity with Slovenia's constitution and whether ratification by the government was allowed even though it required an amendment of the constitution. The court took the opportunity to describe the legal and political character of the Slovenian judicial system and the supremacy of international obligations over constitutional provisions.

> 37. According to article 1 of the Constitution, Slovenia is a democratic republic and a state governed by the rule of law (article 2 of the Constitution). Slovenia enacted its Constitution on the basis of the Basic Constitutional Charter on the Independence and Sovereignty of the Republic of Slovenia and the fact that we Slovenians created our own national identity and attained our nationhood based on the protection of human rights and freedoms, on the fundamental and permanent right of the Slovenian people to self-determination and as a result of our historical and centuries-long struggle for the liberation of our people (Preamble to the Constitution). On this basis and on such grounds it is admissible for the Constitution to be amended in accordance with the procedure specifically set down in Part IX of the Constitution. The procedure for amending the Constitution is on the one hand especially demanding legal procedure and, on the other hand, a procedure subject to the need for legitimacy. And

7 Germany, *Yemeni citizens extradition case*, Anonymous, Individual constitutional complaint, 2 BvR 1506/03, BVerfGE 109, 13, NJW 2004, 141, ILDC 10 (DE 2003), 5th November 2003, Constitutional Court [BVerfG]. The case will be discussed in section IV below.

8 G W F Hegel, *Elements of the Philosophy of Right* (CUP 2003) 368. Seemingly unaware (or in ignorance thereof) of Hegel's far-reaching conceptualization of sovereignty, however, the translators simply translated Hegel's German notion of international law as 'external state law' as 'international law'.

9 See Vienna Convention on the Law of Treaties (VCLT) (adopted on 22 May 1969, entered into force 27 January 1980) 1155 UNTS 331, Article 27 or ILC, Articles on Responsibility of States for Internationally Wrongful Acts ('Articles on State Responsibility') (2001) UN Doc A/56/10, Article 32.

the latter is provided by democratic and public execution of it, which should not be encumbered by any threat that the constitutioner might commit a violation of international law if the procedure were not brought to a successful completion by the same. Precisely for this reason, the constitutioner also instituted the institute of prior review of constitutionality of an international agreement, before the latter has been ratified. If competent authorities who, in accordance with the provision of paragraph 2 of article 160 of the Constitution, may file a motion for the evaluation of conformity of an international agreement in the process of being adopted, with the Constitution, fail to do so, and if the National Assembly—in spite of any such instances of disagreement with the Constitution as may exist—approves the ratification of such agreement, the responsibility with regard to the violation under international law rests with the National Assembly. However, if competent authorities ask for prior evaluation of constitutionality of the international agreement, then, the responsibility for the above mentioned conformity with [. . .] the foundations of the Constitutions rests with the Constitutional Court. This is why the finding of the latter, that individual provisions of the international agreement are in disagreement with the Constitution, can only have the concurrent effect of prohibition of ratification of such provisions of the agreement (if with respect to these reservation [sic!] cannot be applied).

38. Paragraph 2 of article 160 of the Constitution places the public interest, for the State not to commit itself under international law to fulfil obligations which are not in conformity with its Constitution, at the level of a constitutional value. The respect for such public interest, which can also be described as international reputation or credibility of the State (who complies with the principle of pacta sunt servanda and fulfils, in good faith, the obligations undertaken by international agreements) cannot be, as is claimed by the petitioner, exclusively an object of political responsibility of the holders of power with regard to the electorate, for the respect for it should also be deemed to be a question of conformity with the Constitution. The principle of execution in good faith of an international agreement also applies to Europe Association Agreements and requires that provisions of the international agreement be implemented regardless of any obstacles presented by rules of domestic law. In this respect, a contracting party cannot invoke the constitutional provisions of substantive law. The contracting party must assert the right to extensions of time and exclusion from national treatment during the negotiations, but not later than by the time of exchanging the instruments of ratification of the agreement, in the form of reservations, in our case through actual formulation of articles of the basic text, or via Annexes to the basic text or to Protocols, whose content will have the effect of reservation in the sense of the MDKPP. If Slovenia wanted to obtain from the other contracting party additional concessions, which exceed those arrived at during the negotiations prior to the signing of the agreement, it should express these in the form of additional reservations. A reservation, according to international law, is "a unilateral statement drawn up or pronounced at any time, which a State gives when signing, ratifying, adopting or approving an agreement, or acceding to it, and by which it desires to exclude or modify the legal effect of individual contractual provisions when these apply to it" (clause 1.d of article 2 of the MDKPP). However, in such a case the question would arise of legal possibility of a reservation under article 19 of the said Convention, and the key question of a probability that such reservation would be accepted by the other contracting party in accordance with article 20 of the MDKPP. Thus, if subsequent to the signing of the ESP and the approving of the same on the basis of enacting a law on ratification, Slovenia made any further reservation or reservations which would not be accepted by the other contracting party, this could, at most, start a new round of negotiations.

III. Attribution

At times, domestic judges (in particular those at lower levels of the judiciary) show a rather modest level of knowledge in matters of international law in general and state responsibility in particular. If the nature of proceedings and arguably misinformed legal arguments are surprisingly accepted, higher courts need to outline and describe generally-accepted and basically clear rules of international responsibility.

Compagnie Noga D'Importation et D'Exportation SA v Russian Federation, Appeal judgment, 361 F.3d 676 (2d Cir. 2004), ILDC 840 (US 2004), 16th March 2004, United States [US]

In the US case *Compagnie Noga D'Importation et D'Exportation SA v Russian Federation* the Russian Federation argued that the petitioner should have sought the enforcement of an arbitration award against the Russian government instead of the Russian state (since the latter had neither signed the arbitration agreement nor taken part in the proceedings). Since the first instance court did not reject this somewhat crude line of argumentation, the Second Circuit had to clarify the legal personality of states and their different branches or organs, as well as general aspects of attribution.

> 38 The distinction made by the District Court between the acts of a sovereign and the acts of one of its governmental organs also finds no basis in international law. An axiomatic principle of international law is that "[t]he conduct of any State organ shall be considered an act of that State under international law, whether the organ exercises legislative, executive, judicial or any other functions, whatever position it holds in the organization of the State, and whatever its character as an organ of the central government or of a territorial unit of the State." Draft Articles on Responsibilities of States for Internationally Wrongful Acts ("Draft Articles"), art. 4(1) […]. As the commentary to this provision of the Draft Articles explains, "[t]he replies by Governments to the Preparatory Committee for the 1930 Conference for the Codification of International Law were unanimously of the view that the actions or omissions of organs of the State must be attributed to it." Id. art. 4(1) cmt. 4 (footnote omitted), reprinted in ILC Report at 85. "The Third Committee of the Conference adopted unanimously on first reading an article 1, which provided that international responsibility shall be incurred by a State as a consequence of any failure on the part of its organs to carry out the international obligations of the State." Id. (internal quotation marks omitted).
>
> 39 The maxim that the acts of an organ of a sovereign's government are attributable to the sovereign have also been regularly applied in international courts and arbitrations. See Lamm & Aqua, supra, at 730–34. For example, in Texaco Overseas Petroleum Co. v. Government of the Libyan Arab Republic, 53 I.L.R. 393 (1975), the arbitrator rejected the Libyan Government's objections to the tribunal's jurisdiction to arbitrate claims arising out of Libya's nationalization of its oil industry. One of those objections was that the contracts in question had been entered into by the Libyan Minister of Petroleum and thus Libya, "a sovereign State, was not a party to these contracts." Id. at 415. Citing to the 1970 draft of the (as yet unfinished) Draft Articles, the arbitrator overruled this objection, concluding that "it [was] incontestable and uncontested that, if the 'Ministry of Petroleum' or any other qualified organ of the Libyan Government … ha[d] entered into Deeds of Concession, such organ acted as the organ duly qualified and authorized to do so by the Libyan Government." Id. at 416. Thus, it was "the Libyan Arab Republic … and that State alone—which ha[d] become bound by the acts performed by its own organs." Id
>
> 40 In sum, we hold that regardless of whether principles of Russian law, federal common law, or international law are applied, the Russian Federation and the

Government are not separate "parties" for the purposes of confirming and enforcing an arbitral award under the Convention. Accordingly, the judgment of the District Court denying Noga's motion to confirm is vacated.

Iraq and Citizens of the Republic of Iraq v ABB AG and 84 corporations and subsidiaries, Decision on motion to dismiss, ILDC 2163 (US 2013), 920 F Supp 2d 517 (SDNY 2013), 6th February 2013, United States; New York; District Court for the Southern District of New York [SDNY]

Another US case on attribution dealt with the sanctions regime imposed on Iraq after its 1990 attack on Kuwait. As it became increasingly apparent that the sanctions had a tremendous negative impact on the civilian population without weakening the regime of Saddam Hussein (on the contrary, it provided an ideal scapegoat for Hussein's own failures and arguably even increased domestic support),[10] the Security Council designed the so-called 'Oil for Food' programme to alleviate the harm. Owing to Saddam Hussein's efforts to exploit the programme, 'management defects', a lack of adequate supervision and corruption within the UN, it ultimately turned out to be one of the UN's biggest scandals.[11] In the end, a great many foreign companies and Saddam Hussein himself had been able to benefit from the programme.

In 2008, and thus numerous years after the US invasion in Iraq and the establishment of a new—democratic—constitution (in 2005), Iraq filed a complaint in the Southern District of New York against some eighty-five corporations comprising over nine claims, including fraud, corruption, unjust enrichment, breach of contract, or civil conspiracy. Since Hussein's regime lacked legitimacy and since its members had acted for their own personal interest, its actions could not be qualified as governmental, the corporations bore complete liability.

The District Court issued numerous findings on attribution and the nature of governmental actions in the sense of Article 4 of the International Law Commission (ILC) Articles on State Responsibility. For one, it declared that the qualification as exercises of sovereign authority did not hinge on the personal motives of the concerned authorities (although this could be a factor) but rather the nature of the act itself. Furthermore, the lack of legitimacy did not prevent attribution of conduct—what counted was effective control over the state and the government regardless of whether it was coerced by force or not. The nature of a regime did not prevent the responsibility of the state for wrongful conduct.

B. Governmental conduct is conduct taken under color of authority.

74 The U.S. Court of Appeals for the Second Circuit has held that a "governmental [**51] act" is an act "physically taken by persons capable of exercising the sovereign authority of the foreign nation," as long as the persons "purported to act in their official capacity." *Banco de Espana v. Fed. Reserve Bank of N.Y.*, 114 F.2d 438, 444 (2d Cir. 1940). That understanding comports with the International Law Commission's Articles on Responsibility of States for Internationally Wrongful Acts. Those Articles state that when "a person acts in an apparently official capacity, or under colour of authority, the actions in question will be attributable to the State." Articles on Responsibility, art. 4 cmt. 13. Similarly, the Restatement (Third) of Foreign Relations Law of the United States has identified several indicia of attribution: In determining whether an act was within the authority of an official or an official body, or was done under color of such authority ... , one must consider all of the circumstances, including whether the affected parties reasonably considered [*538] the action to be

10 cf P Bennis, S Zunes, and M Honey, 'The Failure of U.S. Policy Toward Iraq and Proposed Alternatives' (2001) 8/3 *Middle East Policy* 101.

11 cf Independent Inquiry Committee into the United Nationals Oil-For-Food Programme, 'Report on Programme Manipulation' https://www.files.ethz.ch/isn/13894/ManipulationReport.pdf (last accessed 3 March 2018).

official, whether the action was for public purpose or for private gain, and whether the persons acting wore official uniforms or used official equipment. Restatement (Third) of Foreign Relations Law § 207 cmt. d [**52] (1987).

75 In the context of an ambassador whose actions injured his or her government, the Second Circuit has concluded that an ambassador binds his or her government when he or she possesses the actual or apparent authority to do so. *First Fid. Bank, N.A. v. Gov't of Antigua & Barbuda-Permanent Mission*, 877 F.2d 189, 192–94 (2d Cir. 1989) (distinguishing the Restatement (Third) of U.S. Foreign Relations Law). In the context of FSIA, however, courts have interpreted that rule to permit apparent authority to bind a sovereign engaged in private conduct but to demand actual authority to bind a sovereign engaged in public conduct. *See Themis Capital*, 2012 U.S. Dist. LEXIS 104453, 2012 WL 3114732, at *13 (reviewing authorities).

76 Neither the *First Fidelity* rule nor its permutations ought to obtain here. Unlike the Hussein Regime, the ambassador in *First Fidelity* was but one person in a larger government. By contrast, there is no entity to answer for Iraq but its government, which necessarily has certain inherent authority to conduct Iraq's affairs. *Cf. First Fid. Bank*, 877 F.2d at 198 (discussing ambassador's inherent agency power in dissent). If a government is alleged to act pursuant to its official duties or for an official [**53] purpose, those acts should be attributed to the sovereign. […]

77 Accordingly, the Court decides that the Hussein Regime's conduct was "governmental" if it was undertaken in the purported or apparent execution of official duties. […]

D. The nature of the Hussein Regime's conduct does not absolve Iraq of responsibility for that conduct.

82 Iraq contends that it does not bear responsibility for the conduct of the Hussein Regime because the Hussein Regime did not act in a way that benefitted the Iraqi people. Rather than ask whether the conduct of the Hussein Regime was governmental, Iraq would have the court ask "Was [Hussein] acting for or against the interests of the Iraqi nation?" (Hr'g Tr. at 22.) Iraq offers three permutations of this argument: (1) Hussein's conduct was private, self-serving conduct and thus not governmental conduct that can be attributed to Iraq; (2) the Hussein Regime was not the legitimate government of Iraq and therefore its actions cannot be imputed to Iraq; and (3) the Hussein Regime committed unlawful conduct that, because [**57] it is unlawful, cannot be attributed to Iraq. The Court rejects each of these arguments because none demonstrates that the alleged conduct of the Hussein Regime is non-governmental. 1. The Complaint does not allege that the Hussein Regime committed acts of personal misconduct as distinct from governmental misconduct.

83 Iraq urges the Court to accept that the Hussein Regime's Programme misdeeds were "personal acts" taken "against the [*540] public interest" and thus, in its view, not attributable to Iraq. Iraq rests its theory on five cases that comment on the private nature of a former governmental leader's corrupt conduct. Those cases analyze whether certain misconduct was "private" or "public" within the rubric of the act of state doctrine or the Foreign Sovereign Immunities Act, 28 U.S.C. § 1602, *et seq.* […]

85 In any event, none of the authorities plaintiff proffers suggest that the alleged misconduct here amounts to private action. In *The Republic of the Philippines v. Marcos*, the Ninth Circuit, sitting en banc, reasoned that the former leader of the government of the Philippines had been accused of committing private misconduct because the complaint stated that he used "his position [**59] of power and authority to convert … to his use and that of his friends, family, and associates, money, funds, and

property belonging to the Philippines and its people." 862 F.2d 1355, 1359 (9th Cir. 1988) (quoting complaint). Similarly, in *Jimenez v. Aristeguieta*, a sovereign accused its former leader of embezzlement and fraud for his private financial benefit. 311 F.2d 547, 557–58 (5th Cir. 1962). And so, too, in *Republic of Haiti v. Duvalier*, where Haiti sought to recover public funds deposited by its former dictator into a personal account. 211 A.D.2d 379, 380–81, 626 N.Y.S.2d 472 (1st Dep't 1995). By contrast, Iraq has not alleged that Hussein funneled money into personal bank accounts in foreign countries, as the Philippines did of the Marcoses, Venezuela did of Jimenez, or Haiti did of Duvalier. Rather, Iraq has alleged that the Hussein Regime directed the kickbacks and bribes into government accounts.

86 The personal bank account fact pattern merely points to the bigger difference: the misconduct in *Marcos, Jimenez,* and *Duvalier* was undertaken by each ruler and his close associates or family; the scheme alleged by Iraq was directed by the entire Hussein *Regime*. Iraq's argument founders on this [**60] fact because it defies reason to label conduct allegedly undertaken by the whole of the public apparatus as "private."

87 Iraq's other authorities have little relevance. In *The Republic of the Philippines v. Westinghouse Electric Corp.*, the court considered a foreign state's suit against a third party for bribing the state's former government. 774 F. Supp. 1438 (D.N.J. 1991). While similar in posture to this action, *Westinghouse* considered whether the Philippines had stated a claim pursuant to Philippine law. *Id.* at 1464. Iraq [*541] has not similarly suggested that it may recover here for defendants' violations of Iraqi law. Last, in *United States v. Noriega*, the defendant failed to persuade the court that the cocaine he trafficked into the United States for his "personal financial enrichment" came within the act of state doctrine. 746 F. Supp. 1506, 1522 (S.D. Fla. 1990), *aff'd*, 117 F.3d 1206 (11th Cir. 1997). Unlike the indictment in the Noriega case, the Complaint here does allege that the Hussein Regime pursued wrongful conduct "in furtherance of [] state policy or to serve some overriding national interest." *Compare id. with* Compl. ¶¶ 2, 7. 2. The legitimacy of the Hussein Regime does not [**61] determine Iraq's responsibility for the Regime's conduct.

88 The legitimacy or illegitimacy of the Hussein Regime's rule does not affect whether the Regime's acts may be attributed to the Republic of Iraq. Indeed, *HN21* Courts have attributed conduct of allegedly unlawful regimes to the states they purported to represent. *E.g., The Sapphire*, 78 U.S. (11 Wall) 164, 167, 20 L. Ed. 127 (1870) (Napoleonic France); Guar. Trust Co. v. United States, 304 U.S. 126, 137, 58 S. Ct. 785, 82 L. Ed. 1224 (1938) (Provisional Government of Russia). And attribution operates independently of diplomatic recognition. "[A] state is responsible for the conduct of its effective government, whether or not that government was recognized by other states." Restatement (Third) of Foreign Relations Law of the United States § 207 cmt. b. What matters is control.

89 Here, Iraq has alleged that the Hussein Regime was "in *de facto* control of the nation" and that control can hardly be disputed. (*See* Compl. ¶ 220 (emphasis original).) This control had legal significance. The parties do not dispute that the Hussein Regime could create rights and obligations within the Programme that reach the Republic of Iraq today. For example, the UN Security Council decided that, "in connection [**62] with the dissolution of the Coalition Provisional Authority, the Interim Government of Iraq and its successors shall assume the rights, responsibilities and obligations relating to the Oil-for-Food-Programme that were transferred to the Authority . . . ." (UN SCOR Res. 1546 (June 8, 2004), Ex. 10 to Bishop Decl.) The Republic of Iraq has entered into a treaty with the

United States of America to settle "certain claims of United States nationals arising from actions of the former Iraqi regime." Claims Settlement Agreement Between the Government of the United States and the Government of the Republic of Iraq (September 2, 2010). The Republic of Iraq has invoked sovereign immunity in response to suits concerning certain Hussein Regime conduct related to the Programme corruption. *E.g., Terenkian v. Republic of Iraq*, 694 F.3d 1122, 1139 (9th Cir. 2012) (sovereign immunity from breach of contract claims concerning contracts canceled due to plaintiff's refusal to pay a bribe); *see also Republic of Iraq v. Beaty*, 556 U.S. 848, 865–66, 129 S. Ct. 2183, 173 L. Ed. 2d 1193 (2009) (invoking sovereign immunity for abuse and mistreatment of American nationals during or after the 1991 Gulf War). And the Republic of Iraq now, by this [**63] action, seeks to recover for harms stemming from oil sales and goods purchases made by the Hussein Regime. 3. The legality of the Hussein Regime's acts does not determine Iraq's responsibility for the Regime's conduct.

90 Iraq next distinguishes the Programme corruption from other Regime acts on the grounds that the challenged conduct was unlawful or against UN regulation. For example, Iraq attempts to exclude from [*542] the definition of "official governmental purposes" any activity or purpose that violated the MOU. (*See* Compl. § 1200.) But "[t]o show that conduct is attributable to the State says nothing, as such, about the legality or otherwise of that conduct. . . ." Articles on Responsibility of States for Internationally Wrongful Acts, art. II cmt. 4.

91 Indeed, if states only bore responsibility for lawful acts they would, perversely, bear no responsibility for unlawful acts. The law is otherwise. A state cannot ordinarily escape liability "for acts of officials and official bodies, national or local, even if the acts were not authorized by or known to the responsible national authorities," or acts "expressly forbidden by law, decree, or instruction." Restatement (Third) of Foreign Relations Law of the United States § 207 cmt. d [**64] (1987). Nor can a state avoid responsibility for acts that violate its own laws. *Banco de Espana v. Fed. Reserve Bank of New York*, 114 F.2d 438, 444 (2d Cir. 1940) ("It should make no difference whether the foreign act is, under local law, partially or wholly, technically or fundamentally, illegal."); *see also Westfield v. Fed. Republic of Germany*, 633 F.3d 409, 418 (6th Cir. 2011) (seizure of property by Nazi regime "governmental" within the meaning of FSIA even though the seizures were voided by subsequent government). Moreover, if courts had to examine whether a government's act was lawful in order to decide whether it was attributable to the state, they would often run afoul of the act of state doctrine; the "lawfulness" of a foreign government's internal acts "is precisely what the act of state doctrine bars United States courts from determining." *Konowaloff*, 702 F.3d at 147; *see also Banco Nacional de Cuba v. Sabbatino*, 376 U.S. 398, 431, 84 S. Ct. 923, 11 L. Ed. 2d 804 (1964) ("[T]he act of state doctrine is applicable even if international law has been violated.").

92 Iraq elsewhere has acknowledged and settled claims against United States nationals for wrongful conduct during the Hussein Regime. *See* U.S.-Iraq [**65] Claims Settlement Agreement; Hr'g Tr. 20 ("We as a nation, the Republic of Iraq, as a nation, have been held responsible for the wrongs of Saddam Hussein just like principals are every day."). Thus, as the Republic of Iraq has itself recognized, it may not avoid responsibility for the Hussein Regime's acts on the basis of their illegality.

93 One final note: To say that Iraq may not avoid responsibility in this action for the Hussein Regime's unlawful conduct is not to deny that the Regime's conduct was unlawful. Unlike Judge Debevoise in *Republic of the Philippines v. Westinghouse Electric*

Corp., 774 F. Supp. 1438, 1452 (D.N.J. 1991), cited by Iraq, the Court does not consider that question, or need to. Nor does holding Iraq responsible for the Hussein Regime's acts imply that Saddam Hussein was the law. It simply accepts what the Complaint alleges—that the Hussein Regime acted as the Iraqi government.

94 The Court concludes that the Programme-related misdeeds of the Hussein Regime alleged in the Complaint may be attributed to the Republic of Iraq. The Complaint alleges that the misconduct occurred pursuant to official policy and in apparent pursuit of political goals. The ethicality, [**66] illegitimacy, or illegality of the acts does not immunize the Republic of Iraq from responsibility. Instead, the Republic of Iraq bears responsibility for the Hussein Regime's conduct alleged here because that conduct was governmental.

IV. Aid and Assistance

Attorney of the Federal Armed Forces v Anonymous (a Major of the Armed Forces), Final appeal, BVerwG 2 WD 12.04, ILDC 483 (DE 2005), 21st June 2005, Federal Administrative Court [BVerwG]

The 2003 invasion in Iraq also triggered a number of significant domestic cases outside of the US. In *Attorney of the Federal Armed Forces v Anonymous (a Major of the Armed Forces)*, Mr Pfaff, a major of the German armed forces, refused to carry out orders because it was not guaranteed that his work on an IT project would not support the unlawful participation of Germany in the illegal aggression against Iraq—namely overflight rights granted to UK and US forces and associated tasks, along with monitoring Turkish airspace.

The court not only stressed the illegality of the war itself but also the '[s]erious legal concerns [...] about the permissibility in international law of these acts of assistance, which in this matter caused the soldier to refuse executing both orders given to him, as he otherwise feared an involvement in the war'.[12] As was noted by the ILDC commentator, the court, while succinctly identifying the relevant substantial legal obligations, nevertheless 'refrained from clarifying the difficult relationships'[13] between the notion of an act of aggression, aid, and assistance, and the law of neutrality. Owing to the presence of the 'required seriousness, depth and inalienability of the soldier's decision of conscience',[14] which was not only based on legal, but also on ethical grounds (the court having also found that he was 'guided by his recognisably strong Christian character'),[15] he was ultimately acquitted.

4.1.4.1.2 The observations of the *Senat* establish as a fact that the federal government of the Federal Republic of Germany made and fulfilled promises in connection with this war, which began on 20 March 2003, to provide the USA and the UK with "overflight rights" for the airspace over German sovereign territory, to enable the use of their "installations" in Germany and to ensure the "protection of these installations" to an extent more closely specified; in addition it agreed in connection with the Iraq war to the further deployment of German soldiers in AWACS aircrafts "to monitor Turkish airspace." The "written statement" which the witness in his then capacity as senior legal advisor of S. had received at his request from the competent office of the

12 *Attorney of the Federal Armed Forces v Anonymous (a Major of the Armed Forces)*, Final appeal, BVerwG 2 WD 12.04, ILDC 483 (DE 2005), 21st June 2005, Federal Administrative Court [BVerwG], para 4.1.4.1.2.

13 H P Aust, Analysis, *Attorney of the Federal Armed Forces v Anonymous (a Major of the Armed Forces)*, ILDC 483 (DE 2005) A3.

14 *Attorney of the Federal Armed Forces v Anonymous (a Major of the Armed Forces)* (n 12) para 4.1.4.2.2.

15 ibid, para 4.1.4.2.1.

Federal Ministry of Defence in the context of his official duties and which he submitted to the *Senat* in the appeal hearing expressly adhered to this fact. The *Senat* has no cause to question the accuracy of the facts represented in this statement, especially as neither the *Bundeswehrdisziplinaranwalt* (federal military prosecutor) nor the soldier raised objections against them in the appeal hearing. Serious legal concerns exist about the permissibility in international law of these acts of assistance, which in this matter caused the soldier to refuse executing both orders given to him, as he otherwise feared an involvement in the war. Therefore, a violation in international law of the prohibition on the use of force cannot be denied *ipso jure* because the government of the Federal Republic of Germany had repeatedly publicly stated (cf. among others statement by Chancellor Schröder on 19 March 2003, 15. legislative period, 34 session, *Verh. des Deutschen Bundestages*, vol. 216 p. 2727 C) "that German soldiers will not participate in fighting." Support to military action contrary to international law can result not only from military participation in fighting, but also in other ways. An offence in international law can be committed by an act or, where a duty to act exists in international law, by omission. (See among others von Münch, *Das völkerrechtliche Delikt*, 1963, p. 134 with further notes). Aiding or assisting in a wrongful act in international law is itself a wrongful act in international law (in particular in the Iraq war cf. in this regard among others Puttler, *HuV-I* 16 (2003), 7 et seq; Bothe, *AVR* 2003, 255 [266] with further notes). Grounds and criteria for answering the question of when the provision of assistance by a nonparticipating party in favour of a belligerent state is contrary to international law arise for the area of support to a military attack contrary to international law by a third state, among others from the "definition of aggression" adopted by the General Assembly of the United Nations on 14 December 1974 without a formal vote by way of general consensus as part of Resolution 3314 (XXIX) (reprinted among others in the collection *"Wehrrecht"* <Beck-Verlag, last revised 1 November 2004> under paragraph 15), from the work of the "International Law Commission" (ILC) of the United Nations and from the law of neutrality in international law. The latter is based on international customary law and Hague Convention V (Hague V) respecting the Rights and Duties of Neutral Powers and Persons in Case of War on Land of 18 October 1907 (RGBl. 1910 p. 151), in force in Germany since 25 October 1910 (cf. Federal Ministry of Justice <eds.>, *Fundstellennachweis B*, last revised: 31 December 2004, p. 238). Art. 3(f) of the aforesaid "definition of aggression" states that an "act of aggression" within the meaning of Art. 39 UN Charter is considered among others as the following: "The action of a State in allowing its territory, which it has placed at the disposal of another State, to be used by that other State for perpetrating an act of aggression against a third State." Even if it is still doubtful today whether the detrimental acts listed in Art. 3 represent not only an "act of aggression" within the meaning of Art. 39 UN Charter, but also a case of "armed attack" within the meaning of Art. 51 UN Charter, an important conviction present in the community of states emerges in any case in Art. 3: if the organs of a territorial state tolerate the execution of acts of aggression by a "foreign state," or omit to prevent military acts of aggression from being carried out from this territory, then the acts of aggression in the case of Art. 3 (f) of the "definition of aggression" are also to be attributed to the territorial state (cf. in this regard among others Kersting, *NZWehrr* 1981, 130 [139]). It certainly must not be overlooked that the General Assembly of the United Nations and the states of all the major legal systems represented therein did not at that time claim with this Resolution adopted in consensus "to lay down [international law] in writing in binding form." The "definition of aggression" however represents at least a not inconsiderable element of the universal consensus of international law, and thereby of the process of formation of law (cf. see

Bruha, *Die Definition der Aggression*, 1980, p. 274 et seq, Fischer in Knut Ipsen <ed.> *Völkerrecht*, op. cit., § 59 margin note 10). In this context, of further significance is also Art. 16 of the Draft Articles on the International Responsibility of States of 26 July 2001 (reproduced in Tomuschat <ed.>, *Völkerrecht*, 2001, p. 97 et seq.), produced by the ILC, which was entrusted by the General Assembly of the United Nations with the task of a corresponding codification (cf. see among others von Münch, op. cit., p. 52 et seq.; Knut Ipsen in: ibid. <ed.>, *Völkerrecht*, op. cit., § 39 margin note 1 et seq.>). This clarification reproduces the relevant basic conception that is present in the various systems of international law and reads as follows: "A State which aids or assists another State in the commission of an internationally wrongful act by the latter is internationally responsible for doing so if: (a) that State does so with knowledge of the circumstances of the internationally wrongful act; and (b) the act would be internationally wrongful if committed by that State." Significant for the determination of the limits in international law regarding provisions of support which a state that is not directly participating in a military conflict renders to a party to the conflict, is moreover and above all Hague V, the provisions of which are also included in the *Zentrale Dienstvorschrift* (central service provisions) (*ZDv*) 15/2 of August 1992 approved by the Federal Ministry of Defence. According to general international law, a state is principally free to decide whether it will participate in a military conflict, although it may only do so on the side of the victim of an armed attack, not on that of the aggressor (cf. no. 1104 *ZDv* 15/2; Bothe in Fleck <ed.>, *Handbuch des humanitären Völkerrechts in bewaffneten Konflikten*, 1994, p. 389). A state that is not participating in an armed conflict between other states has the status of a "neutral state" (cf. no. 1101 *ZDv* 15/2; Bothe, ibidem, s. 386 with further notes). With the exception of the rules already applicable during peacetime in the case of a legally justified "permanent neutrality" (eg, Switzerland and Austria), the duty of neutrality within the meaning of Hague V of a state that is not participating in an armed conflict between other states ("neutral state") begins with the outbreak of the armed conflict (cf. no. 1106 *ZDv* 15/2). The consequences of the neutral status are mutual rights and duties between the neutral state on the one side and the parties to the conflict on the other. According to Art. 1 V. HA the territory of a "neutral" state, thus not participating in the armed conflict, is "inviolable"; any act of war on the same is forbidden (cf. see also no. 1108 *ZDv* 15/2), in particular "leading troops or munitions or supply columns through the territory of a neutral power" (Art. 2 Hague V). A "neutral state," which, with respect to the war against Iraq waged since 20 March 2003 solely by the USA and its allies, also includes the Federal Republic of Germany, must not "support any of the parties to the conflict" on its territory (cf. Nr. 1110 *ZDv* 15/2), in particular it must "not tolerate any of the acts described in articles 2 to 4" (Art. 5 Hague V). This applies both to the carrying of troops, munitions or supply columns (Art. 5(1) in conjunction with Art. 2 Hague V; no. 1115 *ZDv* 15/2: troop or supply transports may not "take place" on neutral state territory; Heintschel von Heinegg in Horst Fischer/Ulrike Froissart/Wolff Heintschel von Heinegg/Christian Raap <eds.>, *Krisensicherung und Humanitärer Schutz—Crisis Management and Humanitarian Protection, Festschrift für Dieter Fleck*, 2004, p. 221 [226]) and for the installation or use of "radiotelegraphy <*"radiotélégraphique"*> stations or any other system that is intended to facilitate communication with the warring land or sea forces" (Art. 5(1) in conjunction with Art. 3(a) and (b) Hague V). The parties to the conflict are further "forbidden to penetrate into neutral airspace with military aircraft, rockets or other flying objects" (no. 1150 *ZDv* 15/2 with reference to Art. 40 the Hague Rules of Air Warfare of 19 February 1923 (*HLKR*—part 14 of *ZDv* 15/3); Bothe, *AVR* 2003, 255 [267]). In relation to a party to the conflict which acts contrary to the prohibitions of

Art. 1 to 4 Hague V, and consequently within the meaning of the Hague V and uses the territory of a neutral state as a base for military operations in the widest sense, the "neutral state" is bound to take positive action and intervene to end the breach of neutrality (cf. see among others no. 1109 *ZDv* 15/2 with reference to Art. 5 Hague V and Art. 2, 9 and 24 Hague XIII; Bothe, ibidem; Heintschel von Heinegg in *Festschrift für Dieter Fleck*, op. cit., p. 224). The "neutral state" is bound under international law "to reject any breach of its neutrality, where necessary by force", although this obligation is limited by the prohibition of the use of force in international law. Armed forces of a party to the conflict situated on the territory of the "neutral state" are to be prevented from participating in action; troops of parties to the conflict "trespassing" on the neutral state territory, thus entering the neutral state territory after the beginning of the armed conflict, are "to be interred" (Art. 11(1) Hague V; no. 1117 clause 1 *ZDv* 15/2; Bothe, ibidem; Heintschel von Heinegg, ibidem, p. 225). Only officers giving their word of honour not to leave the neutral territory without permission may be released (Art. 11(3) Hague V; Heintschel von Heinegg, ibidem, p. 225). The duty to internment arises from the object and purpose of the law of neutrality, since support for fighting from neutral territory and thereby an escalation of the armed conflict by including the neutral state can only be prevented in this way (cf. Heintschel von Heinegg, ibidem, p. 225).

...

4.1.4.1.4 Opinion in international law on military acts of assistance

As emerges from the foregoing explanations (4.1.4.1.1 to 4.1.4.1.3), serious concerns in international law exist about several acts of assistance of the Federal Republic of Germany in favour of the USA and the UK in connection with the war against Iraq begun on 20 March 2003, listed in the "written statement" of the Federal Ministry of Defence and noted by the *Senat* in the appeal hearing. This applies in any case to the granting of overflight rights for military aircraft of the USA and the UK, flying over federal territory on the way to or returning from the war zone in the Gulf region in the framework of the Iraq war. This also applies to the permission for the sending of troops and the transport of weapons and military supplies to the war zone from German territory and for all undertakings which could lead to German state territory serving as starting point or "hub" for military operations directed against Iraq. For, the objective object and purpose of these measures was to facilitate or even promote the military action of the USA and the UK. Because of these objectives grave concerns in international law exist about the conduct of the federal government in this respect, as regards the prohibition on the use of force in international law and the said provisions of Hague V (cf. Bothe, *AVR* 2003, 255 [268]). It is not unequivocal whether these serious concerns in international law also apply to the participation of soldiers of the *Bundeswehr* in deployments of AWACS flights over Turkey and their use for guarding barracks and military and civilian installations of the US armed forces in Germany. For the AWACS flights the answer to the question depends conclusively on whether the data obtained on these deployments was significant for military action in Iraq and whether the USA and UK armed forces had *de facto* access to it. The compatibility with international law of the protection and guarding by the *Bundeswehr* of installations of the US armed forces located in Germany was dependent on whether corresponding tasks of US units moved to the war zone were performed as a deputy, so to say, such as to enable or facilitate moving appropriate troops to the war zone. If this were the case, serious concerns in international law would exist due to this breach of the prohibition laid down in Art. 5(1) in conjunction with Art. 2 Hague V "not to support any of the parties to the conflict" (cf. no. 1110 clause 1 *ZDv* 15/2).

4.1.4.1.5 Possible connection between the IT project SASPF and military support to the USA and its allies

In the context of the war waged against Iraq by the USA and its allies that met serious concerns in international law, and the German military acts of assistance, the soldier found himself—understandably—confronted with the question of whether he himself personally contributed for his part at least indirectly to a facilitation or even promotion of the waging of the war through his continued cooperation on the IT project SASPF in S., which was concretely required from him. In the present context no subsequent examination and decision is hereby required by the investigating *Senat* on the question of whether the soldier would have promoted this or other acts of assistance of the Federal Republic of Germany for the USA and its allies with actual causal effect or at least provided a relevant contribution in this regard by further cooperation—refused by him from 7 April 2003—on the IT project SASPF during the (still ongoing) Iraq war directly or indirectly. The *Truppendienstgericht* (Federal Military Court) denied such a possibility in the judgment under appeal without further justification ("obvious for anyone"). Thus, he had at that time in any case an understandable cause to fear that his work could have promoted or assisted the war. The soldier's superior (at the time), the witness M., in both the trial before the *Truppendienstgericht* and in the appeal hearing before the *Senat*, confirmed that the soldier's submission that he had enquired about the substance of his fears with regards to a possible connection between the IT project SASPF and the German military acts of assistance to the Iraq war. To this particularly pressing question of the soldier the witness M. stated in his capacity as leader of the IT project SASPF in S. that he could not exclude that possibility. In the appeal hearing the witness M. elaborated in this regard by way of explanation that the IT project SASPF among others was supposed to optimise "processes" within the *Bundeswehr* as a whole, above all in the area of logistics. It was not about the use of certain software, but about the optimising of processes. If the envisaged software product SAP proved unsuitable in this regard he believed that an alternative product could be used without great expense. He maintained that since he did not know at the time of the conversations in question with the soldier in the spring of 2003 how long the Iraq war that began on 20 March 2003 would last—and still does not know, he could not honestly exclude that the IT project SASPF would prove relevant for the war in individual areas before its planned final introduction. The *Senat* has no cause to question the substantive accuracy of this evidence or the personal credibility of the witness M. It does not appear that the witness—particularly as leader of the competent IT department in S.—lacked the necessary expert knowledge and professional insight in this regard. The evidence of the witness was understandable and conclusive in and of itself. Despite repeated questioning he adhered in substance to his professional appraisal. Neither concrete indications of contradictions or inconsistencies nor references to the influence of irrelevant considerations were recognised. This is demonstrated above all by the fact that the parties to the proceedings did not raise any substantive concerns against the relevant evidence of the witness, which he had already given in the trial before the *Truppendienstgericht* on 9 February 2004. Indeed the official information obtained by the *Senat* from the Federal Ministry of Defence in September 2004 expressed that the IT project SASPF was still in the testing phase in the spring of 2003; a support of militarily and politically allied states related to SASPF would not (yet) have been possible at that time. The IT project SASPF was designed to support deployments of the *Bundeswehr* armed forces within their "expanded spectrum of tasks", thus beyond the area of defence of the Federal Republic of Germany or (in an alliance case) a NATO ally, and also to make information available to command in this regard from the areas of logistics, personnel, accountancy etc. "online" and "everywhere". It states that this was meant to give the *Bundeswehr* armed forces the capacity of "network operational management" and "interoperability with the armed forces of other nations", because interoperability is the key to joint deployments with complementary division of tasks (burden sharing). As the length of the war was not foreseeable to the soldier—as it wasn't to the competent leader of the IT department in S., the witness M.—at the beginning of the Iraq war in March 2003, it was understandable in this concrete case when the soldier in view of the potential uses of the IT project SASPF that he had become aware of, drew the grave conclusion that under these circumstances he had to reckon with becoming involved himself in the facilitation, ie. the promotion of the Iraq war, by executing the orders given to him on 7 April 2003 and continuing his activities at his post in S. The soldier did not have to expect such a situation either on his joining the *Bundeswehr* nor on his appointment as a professional soldier for which he had applied. Indeed he must have been aware, in particular as a professional soldier, that as a soldier of the *Bundeswehr* he is bound to "loyal service" (s. 7 *Soldatengesetz* (SG) (Act concerning the legal position of soldiers)). This duty requires from the soldier according to the established case law of the *Senat* that he contributes both in and outside of service to the maintenance of the fitness of purpose of the *Bundeswehr* as a military unit and to refrain from anything that could weaken it in its sphere of duties stipulated by the constitution and these acts concretising the same (cf. among others ruling of 28 January 2004—*BVerwG* 2 WD 13.03—<*BVerwGE* 120, 106 [107] = Buchholz 236.1 § 10 SG no. 53 = *NZWehrr* 2004, 169 = *ZBR* 2005, 256>). He had also consciously decided during his career as a soldier to remain a soldier, and in particular not to apply to be recognised as a conscientious objector or to leave the *Bundeswehr* at his own request. The soldier could and should have assumed notwithstanding that in the context of his service he would only be given military orders in compliance with the limits in the *Soldatengesetz* and the German Basic Law and that in a democratic state of law he would only have to execute such orders of his superiors. However, he did not have to anticipate that the government of the Federal Republic of Germany, which is bound to justice and the law (Art. 20(3) Basic Law) and thereby also international law, would decide upon and provide military acts of assistance to the USA and its allies in connection with a war about which serious concerns exist in international law, and that in the specific context of the Iraq war the possibility would arise that he could become involved in such supporting actions with his concrete service activities.

Yemeni citizens extradition case, Anonymous, Individual constitutional complaint, 2 BvR 1506/03, BVerfGE 109, 13, NJW 2004, 141, ILDC 10 (DE 2003), 5th November 2003, Constitutional Court [BVerfG]

Another case dealing with the question of aid and assistance concerned the US extradition request for a suspected terrorist who claimed to be a consultant (at the level of a state secretary) of the Yemeni minister for religious foundations and Imam at the Al-Ihsan mosque in Sanaa (Yemen). The key issue concerned the circumstances of his journey to Germany as he had been prompted to leave Yemen with his secretary after a Yemeni citizen working undercover for the US investigation and prosecution authorities promised to connect him with someone who was ready to donate a large sum of money (whether this money was to be spent to finance terrorist activities or for peaceful purposes remained unclear).

On 10 January 2003, the two Yemenis were detained in Frankfurt pursuant to an arrest warrant issued by the US Federal Court for the Eastern District of New York. The US prosecution authorities accused the claimant of having recruited new members as well as having provided money, weapons and communication equipment to terrorist organizations, in particular Al-Qaeda and Hamas, from October 1997 onwards.

The US embassy delivered an extradition request to the German government on 24 January 2003. The Yemeni embassy claimed that the claimant had been abducted in violation of the prohibition to extradite its own nationals included in Yemen's constitution. It also called on the German government to transfer the claimant back to Yemen. The claimant also stated that he had been abducted and furthermore argued that the facts presented in the extradition request were inadmissible and the request thus had to be declared invalid. He also argued that the interrogation techniques applied by the US authorities when dealing with individuals violated the prohibition of torture in Article 3 of the European Convention on Human Rights (ECHR) and Article 1 of the UN Convention against Torture. The Higher Regional Court of Frankfurt ruled that these concerns were not valid since the US had given assurances to subject the claimant to regular proceedings in front of its domestic courts, where the minimum human rights guarantees were—in contrast to Guantanamo or the Parwan Detention Facility next to the Bagram airfield in Afghanistan—in general upheld.

In contrast to other extradition-related cases (see section VII below), the Constitutional Court refrained from examining the question of extradition to countries where the affected individuals faced a real risk of torture. It rather focused on the legality of luring suspected terrorist outside of their country. If such acts constituted a violation of international law, extradition to the responsible country would by itself constitute a wrongful act by Germany in the sense of Article 16 of the ILC Articles on State Responsibility. The court nevertheless reasoned that the claimant had voluntarily decided to leave Yemen and to travel to Germany since he 'was not subjected to direct force aimed at bending his will, and he was also not threatened with the use of force, and the trickery did not facilitate a subsequent forceful abduction'.[16] In general, 'the circumstances that preceded the arrest' were not regarded 'as an obstacle precluding criminal prosecution in the state of the forum' by state courts.

> 47 Tortious action on the part of the United States would establish their responsibility under international law *vis-à-vis* Yemen. In such a case, there would be the risk that by extraditing the complainant, Germany would support a United States' action that is possibly contrary to international law, which would make Germany itself responsible under international law *vis-à-vis* Yemen. That such state responsibility can, under specific preconditions, be established by the support of third parties' action that is contrary to international law is shown by Article 16 of the International Law Commission's Draft Convention on State Responsibility, which codifies customary international law in this field (on this, cf. Crawford, The International Law Commission's Articles on State Responsibility, 2002, Article 16, pp. 148 *et seq.*).
>
> [...]
>
> 53 b) The examination of state practice shows that the general rule of international law that is alleged by the complainant does not exist. The courts' case-law regarding the question whether the fact that a prosecuted person has been lured out of his or her state of origin becomes an obstacle precluding extradition in the requested state of residence, is heterogeneous. The majority of decisions even does not regard the circumstances that preceded the arrest as an obstacle precluding criminal prosecution in the state of the forum.

16 *Yemeni citizens extradition case*, Anonymous, Individual constitutional complaint, 2 BvR 1506/03, BVerfGE 109, 13, NJW 2004, 141, ILDC 10 (DE 2003), 5th November 2003, Constitutional Court [BVerfG], para 55.

V. Responsibility of States and of International Organizations

The colossal failures of the UN peacekeeping operations and the international community as a whole during the genocides in Rwanda 1994 and Srebrenica 1995 were subject to a large number of decisions on the allocation of responsibility between the UN and the troop-contributing states. In addition, courts also had to rule on eg the EU mission in Somalia (Atalanta) or the overlapping NATO operations in Afghanistan.

Mukeshimana-Ngulinzira and ors v Belgium and ors, First instance judgment, RG No 04/ 4807/A, 07/15547/A, ILDC 1604 (BE 2010), 8th December 2010, Court of First Instance

Mukeshimana-Ngulinzira and ors v Belgium and ors concerned the regrettable role played by Belgium before the April 1994 massacre at the Ecole Technique Officielle in Kigali, where some 2,000 Tutsi (and a number of moderate Hutu) had sought refuge. After the departure of the Belgian troops under Lieutenant Luc Lemaire, followed by the remaining French soldiers, Hutu government troops threw grenades and shot into the crowd, while the Interahamwe (the group known as the driving force behind the genocide) started executions with machetes and bayonets.[17] Eight of the few survivors and relatives of the victims sued Belgium and the military commanders in charge during the evacuation of the troops and foreign nationals.

The court determined that, although the Belgian troops were part of a UN peacekeeping operation, they were still controlled and commanded by the Belgian government which had also given the evacuation order on 11 April 1994.[18] Given that the UN did thus not exercise effective control over the conduct of the Belgian troops, the court seemingly found it unnecessary to apply the rules on the responsibility of international organizations as it focused exclusively on state responsibility instead.[19] While the time limit for such claims had run out, the court left open the possibility of a temporal extension.

> With regards to the fact that the Belgian courts would not have jurisdiction:
>
> 25. For the BELGIAN STATE, the Belgian courts would not have jurisdiction to rule on its responsibility in so far as recognising this would necessarily imply that the court is ruling on the responsibility of the United Nations and other member States of the United Nations.
>
> The argument put forward by the claimants would in fact necessarily assume that the international Community and the United Nations themselves had an obligation to act, an obligation they failed to meet. Therefore, the Court of First Instance has no jurisdiction over the UN and its member States other than Belgium due to their jurisdictional immunity. Therefore, in these circumstances, it would not be possible to rule on Belgian's joint responsibility as claimed.
>
> 26. The court does not share this opinion.
>
> In fact, the argument put forward by the claimant parties is precisely that control of the troops stationed at ETO was withdrawn from the UNAMIR and placed under the sole responsibility of the BELGIAN STATE which alone committed the failures for which it is being criticised, leading to a responsibility which is its own.
>
> This contestation is to be rendered void when the objection to admissibility is scrutinised, asserting the argument of instruction or substantive examination, but as they appear, the claims do not move towards questioning the responsibility of the UN or other member States. We are not working in the conditions of jurisprudence given

17 'When the massacres started, UN troops saved white people' *The Guardian* (19 December 1999) https://www.theguardian.com/world/1999/dec/19/theobserver3 (last accessed 3 March 2018).

18 cf Linda Melvern, 'A People Betrayed: The Role of the West in Rwanda's Genocide' http://www.nytimes.com/books/first/m/melvern-betrayed.html (last accessed 6 March 2018).

19 See C Ryngaert, Analysis, *Mukeshimana-Ngulinzira and ors v Belgium and ors*, ILDC 1604 (BE 2010) A2.

by the BELGIAN STATE where it was criticised for having agreed within NATO to a military operation in Kosovo, decided by NATO, and for having provided it with operational support.

As is made clear by the claimants, "the deeds held against the Belgian State do not originate from its acting in the capacity of a State participating in the UNAMIR". [...]

Knowledge of the identity of the responsible person:

28. Ms. UWIMALI denies that at the outset, she considered the UNAMIR to be responsible (without being able to take action against it due to the immunity of the United Nations).

The responsibility of the BELGIAN STATE (the only party against which she is taking action) would only have become known to her after the facts.

The publication of the report from the Parliamentary Inquiry Commission only allowed her "to sense" a possible responsibility.

It was reading the book by General Dallaire, which came out in December 2003, and even the witness statements produced during the criminal trial of Major Ntuyahaga, in spring of 2007, that showed her that the disputed evacuation order in fact came from Belgium – the peacekeepers having passed under the control of the Belgian army and the evacuation order complying with a decision taken by the Belgian government.

Therefore, the identity of the BELGIAN STATE as the party responsible for her loss only became known to her at the earliest in 2003 and the instruction included in Article 2262 of the Civil Code could only happen at the earliest in 2008, in other words, after she had instigated the action.

29. The question of knowing who, out of the UN and the BELGIAN STATE, bears responsibility for the departure of the Belgian peacekeepers, is, according to the latter, unrelated to Article 2262bis of the Civil Code. It is one of the matters of the proceedings for which the claimants were subject to a time restriction.

30. The Court considers that effectively, following the argument of Ms. UWIMALI would ultimately result, in the case of contestation, in the identity of the responsible party only being known by the judgment ruling on this contestation, and therefore, the instruction, in the majority of cases, would never be able to take place.

At the very least, and disregarding any legal security, the victim could, herself, quite freely locate the moment when a person becomes the appointed responsible party where she is concerned.

It can be assumed in this case that determining the State or Supra-State responsibilities has required putting events into perspective, even if this was done, well before the dates provided by Ms. UWIMALI, during the parliamentary works during the 1997-1998 session, even if these "do not formally establish the responsibility of the BELGIAN STATE".

It should be considered that, as supported by the BELGIAN STATE, the identity of the person whom Ms. UWIMALI wishes to hold responsible was known to her, more than five years before the instigation of her action, independently of the controversies that are still present today, with regard to the respective roles of the BELGIAN STATE or the UNAMIR.

HN [Hasan Nuhanovic] v Netherlands (Ministry of Defence and Ministry of Foreign Affairs), First Instance Judgment, Decision No LJN: BF0181, Case No 265615, ILDC 1092 (NL 2008), 10th September 2008, District Court

Another particularly important (and saddening) case dealing with the interplay between the responsibility of states and international organizations is that of Hasan Nuhanović, a Bosnian

Muslim who worked as an interpreter for the UN and the Dutch troop contingent Dutchbat responsible for the protection of Srebrenica, which had been declared a 'safe area' by the UN Security Council on 16 April 1993 after an eleven-month long siege.[20] Within five days after the beginning of a major offensive against the town on 6 July 1995, Bosnian-Serb forces had essentially overrun the Bosnian army and Dutchbat and taken control of a majority of the enclave causing a flood of approximately 28,000 (Muslim) civilians towards Dutchbat's compound in Potočari. Only a small number (some 3,000 to 4,000), including the parents and the brother of Hasan Nuhanović were admitted inside the UN compound. When the Bosnian-Serb forces started with the mass deportations of the civilians to Bosnian-Muslim controlled territory on 12 July, however, only his father, by virtue of his membership in the committee of refugees representing the Muslim population in negotiations with Ratko Mladić, was allowed to remain. He nevertheless decided to leave with his wife and son.

During this process, the Bosnian Serbs separated the men of military age (sometimes even older and younger) and thus most likely also Hasan Nuhanović's brother and father, from the rest and took them to a building called the 'White House', where summary executions were perpetrated. His mother was also never heard of again. Hasan Nuhanović subsequently tried to claim compensation for the loss of his family, *inter alia* by arguing that the Netherlands was responsible for the wrongful actions of Dutchbat, ie, first and foremost, the failure to put their names on the list of local personnel, sending them away, and abstaining from taking action when his brother and father were separated from his mother.

The District Court in The Hague rejected his claims by holding that the acts by Dutchbat could *only* be attributed to the UN and that the Netherlands could thus not be held responsible for Dutchbat's wrongful acts. Attribution in this sense was thus mutually exclusive—wrongful conduct could only be attributed to the UN *or* to the state placing its troops at the UN's disposal, not to both simultaneously. In addition, the court rejected the claim that the Dutch government had 'cut across the UN command structure'[21] since there was 'no evidence whatsoever that the State gave any instructions as to the manner of evacuation':[22]

> 4.8 If a public body of state A or (another) person or entity with public status (according to the law of state A) is made available to state B in order to implement aspects of the authoritative power of state B, then the actions of that body, person or entity are considered as actions of state B. This rule, considered international common law, is part of the articles accepted by the International Law Commission (ILC) under the auspices of the United Nations concerning the liability of states. According to this rule the attribution should concern acting with the consent, on the authority and 'under direction and control' of the other state and for its purposes. This rule of attribution also applies to the armed forces deployed by a state in order to assist another state, provided that they are placed under the 'command and control' of that other state. In accordance with the existing international practice and the 'draft articles' of the ILC concerning the liability of international organizations, the court applies this rule by means of analogy to the attribution of the actions of armed forces made available by states to the United Nations. (18) The court therefore considers incorrect [N.]'s assertion that the making available of Dutchbat to the United Nations can have no legal consequences under international law for the citizens of Bosnia-Herzegovina.

20 UNSC Res 819 (16 April 1993) UN Doc S/RES/819. See also BBC, 'UN makes Srebrenica "safe haven"' (16 April 1993) http://news.bbc.co.uk/onthisday/hi/dates/stories/april/16/newsid_4253000/4253441.stm (last accessed 6 March 2018).

21 *HN [Hasan Nuhanović] v Netherlands (Ministry of Defence and Ministry of Foreign Affairs)*, First Instance Judgment, Decision No LJN: BF0181, Case No 265615, ILDC 1092 (NL 2008), 10 September 2008, District Court, para 4.14.1.

22 ibid, para 4.14.5.

4.9 In view of the exclusive responsibility of the UN Security Council for maintaining international peace and security, participation in a UN peacekeeping operation on the basis of chapter VII of the Charter implies that the 'operational command and control' over the troops made available is transferred to the UN. This transfer does not include, or at least not necessarily, the personnel matters of the troops and the material logistics of the deployed detachment, nor the decision about whether or not to retreat ('full command', in the Netherlands the supreme command with which the government is invested constitutionally). If transfer is subject to further restrictions then express reservations must be made. [N.] has not submitted anything in this respect. On the other hand, he does invoke the 'Standing Operating Procedures' applying to UNPROFOR and the specific instruction given by Gobillard [substitute-commander of UNPROFOR's headquarters] on July 11, 1995, which could only have pertained to Dutchbat if this battalion ranked within the UN command structure. His challenge, that the Netherlands did not transfer 'operational command and control' in the context of the UN mission in Bosnia-Herzegovina, will therefore not be addressed.

4.10 [M.] and [I. N.] were not employed by Dutchbat. The reproach that Dutchbat offered inadequate protection to them has no bearing on personnel matters reserved to the Netherlands or on the power reserved to the Netherlands to decide whether to withdraw Dutchbat from the authority of the United Nations, for Moreover, the Netherlands' ultimate right to withdraw Dutchbat from Bosnia-Herzegovina should be distinguished from the right at issue here to decide about the evacuation of UNPROFOR units from Srebrenica, which was up to the United Nations. All this means that the acts or omissions Dutchbat is reproached for should be assessed as actions of a contingent of troops made available to the United Nations for the benefit of the UNPROFOR mission.

4.11 To the conclusion that the reprehended acts of Dutchbat should be assessed as those of an UNPROFOR contingent the court attaches the conclusion, with reference to the legal framework for assessment given under 4.6 and 4.8, that these acts and omissions should be attributed strictly, as a matter of principle, to the United Nations. [N.] argued that this principle in their case does not prejudice attribution to the State. The court will address the possible exceptions put forward by them under 4.12, 4.13 and 4.14.

4.12.1 The claimants' assertion, phrased as a general rule, that in the event of violations of standards committed in the execution of powers of control and command transferred to the United Nations, it should still be tested whether the State fulfilled its obligations under the ECHR, the ICCPR, the Genocide Convention and conventions pertaining to international humanitarian law to which the Netherlands is a party, does not hold. When in the execution of powers that are no longer the State's standards are violated then the point of departure must be that those violations cannot be attributed to the State. The same is true when fundamental standards are involved. The question whether obligations from the aforesaid conventions should prevail over the obligations that the State is subject to pursuant to the UN Charter, including the obligation of article 25 concerning the acceptance and implementation of binding decisions by the Security Council is not an issue here, for the making available of troops to the United Nations for a particular mission, as is the case here, is a nonobligatory act. The problem of possibly conflicting contractual obligations ensuing from conventions is therefore not under discussion. The ECtHR jurisprudence relating to this on the question whether an international organization to which sovereignty has been transferred offers equal protection of human rights as the ECHR (19) is irrelevant.

4.12.2 Without detracting from the considerations under 4.12.1 the court will address [N.]'s position under the ECHR, for this convention has a special position amongst the international conventions that the Netherlands is a party to, amongst other things because of the application of the right of complaint of individuals. [N.] argues that Dutchbat's actions should be tested against the ECHR. On the basis of the same jurisprudence of the ECtHR the parties have arrived at opposite conclusions.

4.12.3 First and foremost it must be said that the United Nations are not a contracting party to the ECHR. If the State's primary defence succeeds therefore the ECHR is not applicable. This opinion is supported by rulings of the ECtHR of May 31, 2007 in the cases of A. Behrami and B. Behrami vs. France and Saramati vs. France, Germany and Norway (20), in which actions by citizens of Kosovo were not allowed because the conduct of foreign troops present there was attributable to the United Nations (inadmissibility 'ratione personae'). Without attribution to a signatory of a treaty, of course no violation of an obligation under a treaty could be established. The complaints by A. Behrami, B. Behrami and Saramati did not stand up due to article 34 of the ECHR, in which the right of complaint of individuals is linked to claimed violations by signatory states. In deciding the 'Behrami' and 'Saramati' cases the ECtHR did not address the question whether the citizens of Kosovo, a territory of which the international-law status has been controversial since the falling apart of the former Yugoslavia, were subject to the jurisdiction of the contracting parties to the ECHR. The ECtHR did establish, however, that the international community (in this case NATO and the United Nations) had not only assumed military tasks in Kosovo, but also legislative, executive and judiciary (government) tasks. This was not so in the UNPROFOR mission. The events regarded as violations of the ECHR by [N.] occurred in the sovereign state of Bosnia-Herzegovina. Neither the United Nations nor the State had 'effective overall control' over part of that state's territory. Dutchbat was in Bosnia-Herzegovina with the agreement of the lawful government of that country. The comparison implied by [N.] to the presence of Turkey in northern Cyprus and that of Russia in Transdniestria (Dniester Moldavian Republic) does not hold. Although the compound enjoyed diplomatic protection by the United Nations, the area was not an extraterritorial pocket. The applicability of the ECHR in the case of [N.]'s next of kin who were killed fails already, in the court's opinion, on the ground of article 1 ECHR, in which the scope of the convention is limited to those who come under the jurisdiction of a high contracting party. The term jurisdiction in this article should, according to an ECtHR ruling of December 19, 2001 in the case of Bankovic et al. v. Belgium and sixteen other high contracting parties (21), be interpreted as an essentially territorial concept. In this ruling complaints by citizens of the Federal Republic of Yugoslavia (Serbia and Montenegro) on airborne attacks in their country were disallowed because they were carried out outside the territory of those contracting parties (inadmissibility 'ratione loci'). Later, the ECtHR adopted the same approach in the case of Issa et al. v. Turkey (22). In this case the ECtHR ruled that for the finding that the violations of the convention in the north of Iraq (that were the subject of the complaint) came under the jurisdiction of Turkey it was insufficient that large-scale Turkish military operations took place in the area at the time.

4.13 With his factual assertions [N.] wants to demonstrate that the members of Dutchbat have seriously defaulted and that there was insufficient supervision within Dutchbat on compliance with fundamental standards. On those grounds, according to [N.], the State remains liable. Contrary to [N.]'s suggestion, however, the rule of attribution explained in 4.8 is not set aside. The consequence of attribution to the

United Nations is that even gross negligence or serious failure of supervision on the part of the forces made available to the UN must in principle be attributed exclusively to this organization. In the context of making available troops by member states the United Nations may, however, agree that in the event of gross negligence the state deploying the troops is liable toward the United Nations. (23) The term gross negligence may by extension also include violations of human rights or international humanitarian law. It is also conceivable that on the UN's proposal a stipulation is agreed in which the state deploying the troops assumes thirdparty liability in the event of such violations. No submissions were made on possible exceptions to this rule of exclusive attribution, however, so that the court assumes none occurred. Attribution of acts and omissions by Dutchbat to the United Nations therefore excludes attribution of the same conduct to the State.

4.14.1 The court will now address the question whether the State cut across the United Nations command structure. If Dutchbat was instructed by the Dutch authorities to ignore UN orders or to go against them, and Dutchbat behaved in accordance with this instruction from the Netherlands, this constitutes a violation of the factual basis on which the attribution to the UN rests. This then creates scope for attribution to the State. The same is true if Dutchbat to a greater or lesser extent backed out of the structure of UN command, with the agreement of those in charge in the Netherlands, and considered or shown themselves as exclusively under the command of the competent authorities of the Netherlands for that part. If, however, Dutchbat received parallel instructions from both the Dutch and UN authorities, there are insufficient grounds to deviate from the usual rule of attribution.

4.14.2 In the final report of the Parliamentary Committee of Inquiry on Srebrenica three different moments are mentioned when the Dutch Government, represented by Voorhoeve [the Minister of Defence], affected the commanding of Dutchbat. (24) Two of them relate to the preambles to the fall of Srebrenica. The third moment was discussed above under 4.4.

4.14.3 [N.] based his claim of the State's cutting across the UN command structure mainly on Nicolai's [a Dutch Brigadier General serving as chief of staff of UNPROFOR's headquarters ('HQ') in Sarajevo] double role. In this context he argues as follows. Because in these knife-edge days in July 1995 the United Nations did not function (properly) anymore, the State took over again. Dutch policy and UN policy became separate matters. At the time Nicolai also received instructions from the Netherlands, which he carried out. Karremans [the commander of Dutchbat] had omitted to inform Nicolai about the number of men in the compound. On the basis of this deficient information Nicolai gave orders to co-operate with the Bosnian Serbs on the deportation of the Muslim refugees. No permission was given for this by a higher-ranking UN commander; understandably so, because within the UN organization the evacuation of refugees is a matter for the 'United Nations High Commissioner for Refugees' (UNHCR). In his first meeting with Mladic on July 11, 1995 Karremans said he spoke on behalf of Nicolai and the Dutch authorities. The next morning Karremans on behalf of the Dutch Ministry of Defence offered Mladic assistance by his troops in the evacuation, which can be construed, still according to [N.], as facilitating deportation.

4.14.4 The State argued with regard to this that Nicolai's duty as a liaison officer just entailed passing information on to the Dutch Government. It occurs more often that the UN in peacekeeping operations places militaries of the same nationality as the executive detachments in the command structure in order to leave intact lines of communication as much as possible. Dutchbat's departure from Srebrenica balances between the powers transferred to the UN and those retained by the State, for the State remained responsible for logistic matters in connection with the mission. The assertion that the United Nations were not involved in the evacuation of the refugees is wholly incorrect, according to the State.

4.14.5 There are insufficient grounds for the point of view that Dutchbat by assisting in the evacuation of the citizens of Srebrenica obeyed an order given by the State which should be considered as an infringement of the UN command structure, for even if Nicolai ordered the evacuation of the civilians this does not mean that he did so strictly or for the most part on the authority of the Netherlands. What Nicolai stated as a witness to this court, i.e. that Voorhoeve on July 11, 1995 in a telephone conversation "agreed" that the citizens of Srebrenica who had fled would be evacuated, rather indicates that the UN structure of command was respected. At most, parallel instructions were issued. This does not detract from the fact that, according to the same statement given by Nicolai, Voorhoeve, contrary to UN policies, thus provided political cover for assisting ethnic cleansing, for Nicolai also stated that the basic decision to evacuate came from Sarajevo, so from Gobillard. Nicolai made the same statement to the Parliamentary Committee of Inquiry on Srebrenica. (25) Moreover, Voorhoeve's approval put forward by Nicolai strictly referred to the basic resolution to evacuate, and not to the conditions under which this should take place. Karremans was aware of this approval, considering what he said to Mladic. There is no evidence whatsoever that the State gave any instructions as to the manner of evacuation. On the contrary, Nicolai stated during his provisional examination as a witness that as soon as it became clear the Serbs intended to take charge of the evacuation of the refugees themselves—and the evacuation was not going to be organized and implemented by the United Nations as was assumed originally—"The Hague" worried about the men's fate and was on the phone to say that care should be taken to see to it that the men were under no circumstances treated as a separate group (cf also 4.4 of this ruling). On the basis of all this the court establishes that there can be no matter of any actions taken in contravention of UN policies initiated or approved by the State. In view of the criteria formulated in 4.14.1 for the assessment of the asserted cutting across the UN structure of command, the court concludes that during the evacuation of the Muslim population the factual basis for attribution of Dutchbat actions to the United Nations was fully in place.

4.14.6 It should be recognized that the circumstances in the compound, due to lack of food and medical facilities and with high temperatures were desperate at the time. Nevertheless, the court considers, needless to say, that there are good arguments in support of the claim that the passive attitude of Dutchbat toward the separate deportation on July 12 and 13, 1995 of the able-bodied men by the Bosnian Serbs was not in keeping with the specific instruction to protect civilians and refugees in the altered circumstances to the utmost, an instruction Karremans received from Gobillard—so from the UN structure of command—on July 11, 1995. This is of no avail to [N.], however, because the acts and omissions of Dutchbat during the evacuation should be considered as those of the United Nations. 4.15 From the considerations presented in 4.6 through 4.14 it must be concluded that the reprehended Dutchbat actions must be attributed exclusively to the United Nations, so that the State's primary defence succeeds. This means that the State cannot be held responsible for any breach of contract or wrongful act committed by Dutchbat. As follows from 4.4 of this ruling, neither is the State liable for wrongful action taken by those in charge of the armed forces or members of National Government. This means that [N.]'s claim must be denied.

Nuhanović v Netherlands, Appeal judgment, LJN:BR5388, ILDC 1742 (NL 2011), 5th July 2011, Court of Appeal

The Court of Appeal rejected the District Court's 'command and control' test by applying the effective control standard enshrined in Article 6 of the ILC Articles on the Responsibility of International Organizations. It also emphasized that this control could be exercised by the UN *and* the Netherlands at the same time—as was the case during the relevant period—and the actions of Dutchbat could thus be attributed to both; in this regard, the court described at length the numerous specific orders given by the Netherlands' government in connection with the evacuation and the preceding preparations. It furthermore held that forcing the men to leave, even despite the well-known risks, constituted a breach of the right to life and the prohibition of torture.

> 5.8 In ground 9, Nuhanovic argues that in relation to the criterion for the attribution of the conduct of Dutchbat to the UN or the State, the question should be who had 'effective control' and not, as assumed by the District Court, who exercised 'command and control'. This ground for appeal is correct. In international law literature, as also in the work of the ILC, the generally accepted opinion is that if a State places troops at the disposal of the UN for the execution of a peacekeeping mission, the question as to whom a specific conduct of such troops should be attributed, depends on the question which of both parties has 'effective control' over the relevant conduct. Cf. M. Hirsch, The Responsibility of International Organizations Towards Third Parties: Some Basic Principles (1995) p. 64; F. Messineo, NILR 2009 p. 41–42; A. Sari, Human Rights Law Review 2008 p. 164; T. Dannenbaum, Harvard International Law Journal 2010 p. 140–141. This opinion has also found expression in the draft articles on the Responsibility of international organizations of the ILC, of which Article 6 reads as follows: "The conduct of an organ of a State or an organ or agent of an international organization that is placed at the disposal of another international organization shall be considered under international law an act of the latter organization if the organization exercises effective control over that conduct." Although strictly speaking this provision only mentions 'effective control' in relation to attribution to the 'hiring' international organization, it is assumed that the same criterion applies to the question whether the conduct of troops should be attributed to the State who places these troops at the disposal of that other international organization.
>
> 5.9 The question whether the State had 'effective control' over the conduct of Dutchbat which Nuhanovic considers to be the basis for his claim, must be answered in view of the circumstances of the case. This does not only imply that significance should be given to the question whether that conduct constituted the execution of a specific instruction, issued by the UN or the State, but also to the question whether, if there was no such specific instruction, the UN or the State had the power to prevent the conduct concerned. Moreover, the Court adopts as a starting point that the possibility that more than one party has 'effective control' is generally accepted, which means that it cannot be ruled out that the application of this criterion results in the possibility of attribution to more than one party. For this reason the Court will only examine if the State exercised 'effective control' over the alleged conduct and will not answer the question whether the UN also had 'effective control'.
>
> 5.10 When applying the 'effective control' criterion it is important to establish that it is not disputed that the state that provides the troops keeps control over the personnel matters of the assigned soldiers, who are and will remain employed by the state, as well as the power to take disciplinary action and start criminal proceedings against

these soldiers. It is not disputed either that the state that provides the troops at all times preserves the power to withdraw the troops and to discontinue their participation in the mission.

5.11 Furthermore, the Court attaches importance to the fact that the context in which the alleged conduct of Dutchbat took place differs in a significant degree from the situation in which troops placed under the command of the UN normally operate, as was the issue at stake in the cases Behrami v. France, no. 71412/01 and Saramati v. France, Germany and Norway, no. 78166/01 of the ECtHR (LJN: BB 7360 and BB 3180). After 11 July 1995, the mission to protect Srebrenica had failed. Srebrenica had fallen that day and it was out of the question that Dutchbat, or UNPROFOR in any other composition, would continue or resume the mission. There is no evidence that Resolution 1004 (1995) (see the above under 2.25) resulted in any order to Dutchbat to take up their positions in and around Srebrenica again, nor did the Bosnian Serb Army comply with the Resolution's call to withdraw their troops from Srebrenica. On the contrary, in the evening of 11 July 1995, in joint consultation with Dutch Defence Chief of Staff Van den Breemen, Deputy Commander Van Baal and General Janvier it was decided that there was no sense in using any further violence; see Parliamentary Inquiry Committee Srebrenica, examinations p. 736 (letter from Van den Breemen). The only option was to evacuate Dutchbat and the refugees, and to proceed in such a way that the refugees would not remain unprotected. As Van Baal put it (record of preliminary examination p. 3): "Rather leave all at once, not Dutchbat first, possibly one after the other but under the supervision of Dutchbat." and before the Parliamentary Inquiry Committee (examinations p. 344): "Based on this, a few agreements were made by mutual consultation with General Janvier. Dutchbat was going to evacuate with the battalion. The evacuation of 27.000 people was a major operation." Van den Breemen wrote to the Parliamentary Inquiry Committee (examinations p. 736): "So a cease-fire is needed. Dutchbat stays; humanitarian aid; preparations for evacuation. All this had the purport, given the humanitarian situation and the threat from the Serbs, who were capable of doing anything at any moment, that eventually the refugees as well as Dutchbat had to be evacuated."

5.12 The Court can only conclude that the decision for the evacuation of Dutchbat and the refugees resulting from the consultations between Janvier, Van den Breemen and Van Baal was actually taken by mutual agreement between Janvier on behalf of the UN on the one hand and by Van den Breemen and Van Baal on behalf of the Dutch Government on the other. In the opinion of the Court it is not plausible that two of the highest ranking Dutch military officers had only travelled to Zagreb to be informed about what General Janvier, after being told about their wishes, would decide regarding the evacuation. The Court interprets the background of the consultations of that evening in such a manner that, considering the concerns that existed in The Hague for the safety of both Dutchbat and the refugees, in practice they could only take a decision on the evacuation that not only The Hague but also (the Force Commander of) the UN would approve of. The fact that Gobillard and Nicolai also took the decision to evacuate does not detract from the above conclusion, because what has been decided at the highest level must be decisive. Apparently both the UN and the Dutch Government considered this decision to be of such importance that they left it up to the Force Commander Janvier and two of the highest Dutch military officers. The Dutch Government participated in that decision-making at the highest level. For that matter, as appears from the statement of Nicolai during the preliminary witness examination, the decision taken in Sarajevo only regarded the evacuation of the refugees, not the evacuation of Dutchbat.

5.13 During the preliminary witness examination (court record p. 2), General Nicolai stated the following about the order of 13 July 1995 attached to the court record of his witness examination, which in paragraph 8 refers to Nicolai as "authorized negotiator on behalf of NL Government and UNPROFOR": "It was a turning point; Dutchbat's mission had ended and we were going to focus on getting the battalion back to the Netherlands. In itself this is also a national affair, but apart from that there were additional UN interests and that is why I also acted as the authorized representative for UNPROFOR. In that sense, I kind of had a double role. In this case things went a little further. Normally I did not receive any orders from the Netherlands, but only from the UN. At this moment the Netherlands also participated in the decision-making. I faxed this order to the Infantry Staff and also to DCBC (Crisis Control Centre at the Ministry of Defence) on the 13th in the course of the day, asking whether the Dutch Government could live with this. (…) At that moment, the evacuation of the Bosnian population had already been concluded." Nicolai stated furthermore (court record p. 6): "The Hague phoned me, because The Hague was concerned about the fate of the men and that is why we had to make sure in any case that they would not be treated as an individual group. I told them that we had another priority regarding the order in which the evacuation would have to take place, and that we had not actually taken that into account, but that I would pass it on to Karremans. Subsequently, Karremans said that in fact it was not a relevant problem because there were hardly any men. In my opinion it would [the Court reads: be] completely different if the UN would have been in charge of the transport and not the Serbs. This does not matter, because when the Dutch Government says something like that, as a military officer you just carry it out. By the end of the morning of the 12th it became clear to me that the Serbs would be in charge of the transport."

5.14 Former Minister of Defence Voorhoeve stated as a witness (court record p. 6): "My telephone call with Karremans on 12 July took place around eight o'clock in the morning. Based on the conversations held before that time, I told Karremans to save as much as possible."

5.15 In connection with page 206 of exhibit 4, attached to the court record of the preliminary witness examination (Court: the examination conducted by the Parliamentary Inquiry Committee) the following question was put to Voorhoeve about the subject of the "Double role of Mr. Nicolai, representative of the UN and the Netherlands" (court record of preliminary witness examination p. 8): "You said that the UN command structure did not function. What is the relationship between the double role of Nicolai and the non functioning of the UN command structure?" Voorhoeve answered: "There was no direct relationship. My observation that the command structure did not function was based on a long period, a whole year, of noticing that certain parts of the command structure in particular did not function. Pointing at the highest national military officer is common use, also in peacekeeping operations that are proceeding well. I don't know whether I expressed my concerns about the Muslim men to Colonel Brantz on the 11th. I remember that the conversation was about the refugees, the population of Srebrenica." The aforesaid exhibit 4 (the examination of Voorhoeve by the Parliamentary Inquiry Committee, p. 207), includes the following: "Mr. Rehwinkel: How could Mr. Nicolai in the fax with the guidelines refer to himself as the authorized negotiator for the Netherlands? How was it possible that in the letter to Mladic they spoke of 'a message from the authorities of the Netherlands'? Mr. Voorhoeve: Because Mr. Nicolai was given a double role as a result of the circumstances. He was the highest in rank of all military officers in the UNPROFOR organization who were located close to the problem. The situation in

Srebrenica fell under UNPROFOR Sarajevo. It was logical that the Dutch concerns about the situation were communicated to Mr. Nicolai."

5.16 From what has been established in the above under 2.30 and 2.31 appears furthermore that Karremans received instructions about the evacuation that were jointly issued by Nicolai in his capacity of 'authorized negotiator of the NL Government and UNPROFOR', so also on behalf of the Dutch Government. Karremans also interpreted it in this way, given his fax to Mladic in which he wrote: "(...) I did receive a message from the authorities of the Netherlands thru HQ UNPROFOR in SARAJEVO concerning the evacuation of Dutchbat. I have been ordered (...)". (section underlined by the Court)

5.17 Based on the above, the Court concludes the following. On 11 July 1995, the UN and the Dutch Government took the decision to evacuate Dutchbat together with the refugees. This implied that Dutchbat, after the evacuation had been concluded, would be withdrawn to the Netherlands in the near future. As of 11 July 1995, a transition period started in which matters in Potocari were being completed. An important part of the completion was the aid to and the evacuation of the refugees. Although, as stated by Van Baal during his preliminary witness examination (court record p. 2), at that moment Dutchbat was not being withdrawn from UNPF yet, there could not be any doubt about the fact that this would certainly take place after the evacuation. Nowhere is it suggested in the documents that Dutchbat would have any role to fulfil within UNPF after the evacuation. The distinction made by the District Court between the right invested in the Netherlands to withdraw Dutchbat from Bosnia and Herzegovina and the right of the UN to decide about the evacuation of the UNPROFOR units from Srebrenica is formally correct, but does not do enough justice to the fact that the one formed an integral part of the other.

5.18 An important part of Dutchbat's remaining task after 11 July 1995 consisted of the aid to and the evacuation of the refugees. During this transition period, besides the UN, the Dutch Government in The Hague had control over Dutchbat as well, because this concerned the preparations for a total withdrawal of Dutchbat from Bosnia and Herzegovina. In this respect Nicolai fulfilled a double role because he acted on behalf of the UN and also on behalf of the Dutch Government. The fact that The Netherlands had control over Dutchbat was not only theoretical, this control was also exercised in practice: the Government in The Hague, represented by two of its highest military officers, Van den Breemen and Van Baal, together with Janvier took the decision for the evacuation of Dutchbat and of the refugees, Minister Voorhoeve gave the instruction that Dutchbat was not allowed to cooperate in a separate treatment of the men, and he told Karremans that he had to save as much as possible. Through the intermediary of Nicolai in his double role, the Dutch Government also gave orders to Karremans regarding the evacuation (see 5.16 above). According to the judgment of the Court, in all these cases it was a matter of orders being given and not just transmitting the wishes or expressing the concerns, which Nicolai understood very well ("if the Dutch Government says something like that, as a military officer you just carry it out"). Nicolai sent the order by fax on 13 July 1995 to the Crisis Control Centre at the Ministry of Defence (DCBC) [Defensie Crisisbeheersingscentrum] in The Hague to find out whether the Dutch Government could live with this (see 5.13 above). Karremans also held the view that he was now (jointly) under command of the Dutch Government and acted accordingly (see 5.16 above). In the opinion of the Court it is beyond doubt that the Dutch Government was closely involved in the evacuation and the preparations thereof, and that it would have had the power to prevent the alleged conduct if it had been aware of this conduct at the time. The facts do not leave room for any other conclusion than that, in case the Dutch Government would have given the instruction to Dutchbat not to allow Nuhanovic (as well as his father Ibro Nuhanovic) to leave the compound or to take him along respectively, such an instruction would have been executed. Moreover, in this respect it is important that, as will appear below, the alleged conduct was contrary to the instruction given by General Gobillard to protect the refugees as much as possible, and that the State held it in its power to take disciplinary actions against that conduct.

5.19 The allegations brought against the conduct of Dutchbat by Nuhanovic are directly related to the Dutch Government's decisions and instructions. The allegation that Dutchbat refused to include Nuhanovic on the list of local staff is directly related to the manner in which the evacuation of the refugees was to be carried out, i.e. with respect to the question who would be taken along. This appears, for example, from the fact that Karremans contacted Van Baal because he wanted to take Mandžic along (statement Karremans during the preliminary witness examination, court record of examination, p. 9). The allegation that Dutchbat sent Muhamed Nuhanovic away, and in doing so, Ibro Nuhanovic as well, is related to the way in which the evacuation of the refugees was carried out. The allegation that Dutchbat failed to interfere when Muhamed Nuhanovic and Ibro Nuhanovic were separated from their mother/wife is related to how the instruction given by Minister Voorhoeve to prevent a separate treatment of the men, was carried out. The latter also applies to the allegation that Dutchbat did not report immediately about the separation of the men and women and the other human rights violations that were observed.

5.20 The Court concludes therefore that the State possessed 'effective control' over the alleged conduct of Dutchbat that is the subject of Nuhanovic's claim and that this conduct can be attributed to the State. In so far, grounds 3–9 and 11–13 have been put forward successfully.

Netherlands (Ministry of Defence and Ministry of Foreign Affairs) v Nuhanović, Final appeal judgment, ECLI/NL/HR/2013/BZ9225, ILDC 2061 (NL 2013), 12/03324, 6th September 2013, Supreme Court [HR]

As a consequence of this ruling, the government of the Netherlands rejected both the attribution and the wrongfulness of its acts, arguing that Dutchbat should always have been attributed exclusively to the UN and that the Netherlands had, in any case, not exercised effective control. The Supreme Court then rejected the attribution of Dutchbat under Article 6 of the Articles on the Responsibility of International Organization and applied Article 7 instead. In so doing, it also upheld the possibility of dual attribution and confirmed the Netherlands' effective control over Dutchbat's actions during the transitional period.

Can Dutchbat's conduct be attributed to the State?

3.6.2 The Court of Appeal has rejected Nuhanović's submission that this attribution should take place in accordance with the rules not of international law but of national Bosnian law. It has held in this connection that the question is not whether Dutchbat military personnel acted wrongfully towards Nuhanović but whether the conduct of troops placed at the disposal of the United Nations, whether or not pursuant to an agreement concluded between the State and the United Nations, should be attributed to the State, the United Nations or possibly to both. The question of whether such an agreement has been concluded and, if so, what it involves and what consequences it has, for example in relation to the issue of which party is liable under civil law for Dutchbat's conduct, should be judged according to international law (finding of law 5.3 interim judgment). These rulings have not been disputed in the cassation proceedings. This means that when the State's grounds for challenging the ruling that Dutchbat's disputed conduct must be attributed to the State are assessed it must be assumed that the question of attribution should be answered solely in accordance with the rules of international law.

3.7 In establishing the rules developed in unwritten international law for deciding on what conditions conduct can be attributed to a State or to an international organization, the Supreme Court will refer to two sets of rules drawn up by the International Law Commission (ILC) of the United Nations, namely the Draft Articles on Responsibility of States for Internationally Wrongful Acts of 2001 (below: DARS) and the Draft Articles on the Responsibility of International Organizations of 2011 (below: DARIO).

3.8.1 What is of importance in the first place in determining whether Dutchbat's disputed conduct can be attributed to the State is the provisions of DARS, Part One 'The internationally wrongful act of a State', Chapter II 'Attribution of conduct to a State', of which articles 4 and 8, in so far as relevant here, read as follows: […]

3.8.2 It follows from articles 4 and 8 DARS that Dutchbat's conduct can be attributed to the State if Dutchbat should be considered as an organ of the State (art. 4 (1) DARS) or if Dutchbat in fact acted on the instructions or under the direction or control of the State (art. 8 DARS).

3.9.1 In the proceedings before the Court of Appeal the debate between the parties focused on the question of whether the circumstance that Dutchbat had been placed at the disposal of the United Nations by the State meant that Dutchbat's conduct could be attributed not to the State pursuant to article 4 (1) or article 8 DARS but only to the United Nations. The provisions of the DARIO are of relevance in connection with the latter point.

3.9.2 Articles 6 and 7 DARIO, which are contained in Part Two 'The internationally wrongful act of an international organization', Chapter II 'Attribution of conduct to an international organization', read as follows: […] Article 48 DARIO, which is contained in Part Four 'The implementation of the international responsibility of an international organization', Chapter I 'Invocation of the responsibility of an international organization', reads, in so far as relevant here, as follows:[…]

3.9.3 The commentary on article 7 DARIO (at 1) explains how this provision relates to article 6 DARIO as follows: […]

3.9.4 The Commentary on Part Two, Chapter II DARIO (at 4) notes that articles 6–9 DARIO do not necessarily mean that conduct must be exclusively attributed to an international organization—thereby resulting in exclusive responsibility of the international organization—but instead leave open the possibility of conduct being attributed to an international organization and a State, which would then result in dual attribution to the international organization and the State concerned: 'Although it may not frequently occur in practice, dual or even multiple attribution of conduct cannot be excluded. Thus, attribution of a certain conduct to an international organization does not imply that the same conduct cannot be attributed to a State; nor does attribution of conduct to a State rule out attribution of the same conduct to an international organization. One could also envisage conduct being simultaneously attributed to two or more international organizations, for instance when they establish a joint organ and act through that organ.' Article 48 (1) DARIO therefore expressly leaves open the possibility of more than one State or organization being held responsible for the consequences of an internationally wrongful act.

3.9.5 Finally, the Commentary notes as follows in respect of article 7 DARIO (at 4): 'The criterion for attribution of conduct either to the contributing State or organization or to the receiving organization is based according to article 7 on the factual control that is exercised over the specific conduct taken by the organ or agent placed at the receiving organization's disposal. As was noted in the comment by one State, account needs to be taken of the "full factual circumstances and particular context".'

3.10.1 Part 1 of the cassation appeal submits that in findings of law 5.7 and 5.8 of the interim judgment the Court of Appeal has failed to recognise that a UN troop contingent that has been established in accordance with Chapter VII of the UN Charter and has been placed under the command and control of the United Nations—in this case UNPROFOR, of which Dutchbat formed part—is an organ of the United Nations. This means that attribution of the conduct of such a troop contingent should be made by reference to article 6 DARIO and not by reference to article 7 DARIO. According to this part of the appeal, application of article 6 DARIO means that Dutchbat's conduct should, in principle, always be attributed to the United Nations.

3.10.2 It is apparent from the Commentary on article 7 DARIO (see above at 3.9.3) that this attribution rule applies, inter alia, to the situation in which a State places troops at the disposal of the United Nations in the context of a UN peace mission, and command and control is transferred to the United Nations, but the disciplinary powers and criminal jurisdiction (the 'organic command') remain vested in the seconding State. It is implicit in the findings of the Court of Appeal that this situation occurs in the present case. After all, in finding of law 5.10 of the interim judgment the Court of Appeal has held—and this has not been disputed in the cassation appeal—that it is not at issue that the Netherlands, as the troop-contributing State, retained control over the personnel affairs of the military personnel concerned, who had remained in the service of the Netherlands, and retained the power to punish these military personnel under disciplinary and criminal law. The submission in part 1 of the cassation appeal that the Court of Appeal has failed to apply the attribution rule of article 6 DARIO and has instead wrongly applied the attribution rule of article 7 DARIO therefore fails.

3.11.1 Part 2 of the cassation appeal consists of a series of submissions directed against findings of law 5.8–5.20 of the interim judgment, in which the Court of Appeal has defined the criterion of effective control in applying the attribution rule of article 7 DARIO to the present case.

3.11.2 In so far as these grounds of appeal are based on the submission that international law excludes the possibility that conduct can be attributed both to an international organization and to a State and that the Court of Appeal therefore wrongly proceeded on the assumption that there was a possibility that both the United Nations and the State had effective control over Dutchbat's disputed conduct, they are based on an incorrect interpretation of the law. As held above at 3.9.4, international law, in particular article 7 DARIO in conjunction with article 48 (1) DARIO, does not exclude the possibility of dual attribution of given conduct. It follows that the Court of Appeal was able to leave open whether the United Nations had effective control over Dutchbat's conduct in the early evening of 13 July 1995. Even if this was the case, it does not necessarily mean that the United Nations had exclusive responsibility.

3.11.3 In so far as it is submitted in these grounds of the cassation appeal that the Court of Appeal has applied an incorrect criterion in assessing whether the State had effective control over Dutchbat at the moment of the disputed conduct, they too are based on an incorrect interpretation of the law. For the purpose of deciding whether the State had effective control it is not necessary for the State to have countermanded the command structure of the United Nations by giving instructions to Dutchbat or to have exercised operational command independently. It is apparent from the

Commentary on article 7 DARIO as referred to above at 3.9.5 that the attribution of conduct to the seconding State or the international organization is based on the factual control over the specific conduct, in which all factual circumstances and the special context of the case must be taken into account. In the disputed findings of law the Court of Appeal has examined, in the light of all circumstances and the special context of the case, whether the State had factual control over Dutchbat's disputed conduct. The Court of Appeal has not therefore interpreted or applied the law incorrectly.

3.12.1 Part 3 of the cassation appeal consists of a series of submissions directed against findings of law 5.8–5.20 of the interim judgment that the State had effective control over Dutchbat's disputed conduct.

3.12.2 This finding of the Court of Appeal is based on, among other things, the following facts and circumstances: [. . .]

3.12.3 The Court of Appeal's ruling that the State had effective control over the conduct of which Dutchbat and hence the State as well are accused by Nuhanović does not reveal an incorrect interpretation or application of the law on the concept of effective control. Moreover, the reasons given for this ruling are couched in perfectly clear terms given the findings on which it has been based by the Court of Appeal, as indicated above at 3.12.2. Although the mission had in fact failed and Dutchbat could therefore no longer exert any influence outside the compound, this does not detract from the fact that the State had effective control over Dutchbat's conduct in the compound. The grounds of appeal of part 3 therefore fail for this reason.

3.13 The above findings lead to the conclusion that parts 2 and 3 of the cassation appeal oppose in vain the Court of Appeal's ruling that the State had effective control over the conduct of which Dutchbat—and hence the State as well—is accused by Nuhanović. Given this position, the Court of Appeal was able to find on the basis of the attribution rule of article 7 DARIO, which is applicable to this case, partly in view of what is provided in the attribution rule of article 8 DARS—that Dutchbat's disputed conduct can be attributed to the State.

3.14 Nor can the other grounds of appeal of parts 2 and 3 result in cassation. Pursuant to section 81, subsection 1, of the Judiciary (Organization) Act no further reasons need be given for this, since these grounds of appeal do not warrant the answering of questions of law in the interests of the uniform application of the law or the development of the law.

Mothers of Srebrenica v State of the Netherlands, Court of Appeal of The Hague, 27 June 2017 (not in ILDC)

The closely related case of *Stichting Mothers of Srebrenica and ors v Netherlands and United Nations*[23] is arguably the most well-known and decisive domestic decision on the attribution of responsibility of international organizations and their members. Mothers of Srebrenica, a lobbying group of some 6,000 survivors and relatives of the victims sued both the UN and the Netherlands over their failure to protect the civilians inside the safe area.

In contrast to the case of Hasan Nuhanović, *Stichting Mothers of Srebrenica and ors v Netherlands and United Nations* does not deal with the particular actions of Dutchbat in connection with the relatives of specific persons enjoying a special status but its general behaviour during and after the fall of Srebrenica.

23 *Stichting Mothers of Srebrenica and ors v Netherlands and United Nations*, Final appeal judgment, LJN: BW1999, ILDC 1760 (NL 2012), 13 April 2012, Netherlands; Supreme Court [HR].

The Dutch Supreme Court upheld the absolute immunity of the UN (which refused to take part in the proceedings) even if that amounted to a violation of the right to a fair trial and essentially left the claimants without access to any court.[24] At the same time, however, the possibility of dual attribution as mentioned in the appeal and final judgments in *Nuhanović* left the door open for at least partial responsibility of the Netherlands.[25]

The proceedings subsequently continued against the Netherlands only and, on 27 June 2017, after yet another detailed assessment of the events and communications that had taken place, the Appeals Court of the Hague did indeed allocate a share of the responsibility to the Netherlands since it had also taken part in the decision to evacuate the refugees from and around the UN compound in Potočari.[26] The court first held that Dutchbat was exclusively attributable to the UN (which had, as it normally does during peacekeeping operations, exercised overall control) and there was thus no liability of the Netherlands until the fall of Srebrenica. In line with *Nuhanović* and again applying a restrictive interpretation of Article 8 of the ILC Articles on the Responsibility of International Organizations, however, the Court of Appeals held that the Dutch state's active involvement during the subsequent *transitional period* rendered it responsible for two acts:

First, Dutchbat's efforts to restore calm and avoid chaos among the refugees by forming groups and making them pass through a human corridor towards the buses of the Bosnian Serbs facilitated the separation of the Muslim men. While the court refrained from granting compensation on this ground, it declared that the Netherlands had committed a wrongful act (satisfaction).

Secondly, as Dutchbat knew about the risk of torture, inhumane, or degrading treatment, and even executions, it should have given the men who had already been on their compound the opportunity to stay; even though there was high probability that they would nevertheless have been killed due to a deprivation of water or food or a forced removal by the Bosnian Serbs, there was still a chance to survive, estimated to be at 30 per cent. The Court of Appeals thus held that the Netherlands was 'partially liable' for the losses suffered by the relatives of 350 Muslim men killed during and after the Bosnian Serb forces' deportation of the Muslim population of Srebrenica.

> 11.1 Objection 3 of the C.S. Foundation [the umbrella term for the applicants] focuses on the Court's ruling that the fact the UN has immunity is not relevant for the manner of attribution (Considerations 4.3 and 4.35). In this regard, the C.S. Foundation argues that the ECHR did not declare the C.S. Foundation's complaint concerning the infringement of article 6 ECHR by the UN immunity (the complaint cited above under 4.3) unfounded, but inadmissible, and that it is incorrect to rule that this immunity has no consequences for assessing the State's attributability. According to the C.S. Foundation since it had been ruled that the right to access to the Court had not been affected given the (partial) reasoning that unlike the UN, the State is unable to invoke immunity, the broadest possible attribution to the State must occur. The State contested the objection. The Court's consideration is as follows.
>
> 11.2 For the question of whether and to what extent conduct occurred under the UN flag (and for which the UN, based on the Treaty, is exempt from prosecution with regard to the United Nation's privileges and immunities (Trb. 1948, no. I 224)) should be attributed to the State, the rules of written and unwritten law (international or

24 This case is discussed in detail in A Reinisch, G Novak, 'International Organizations' Chapter 5 in this volume.

25 See R van Alebeek, Analysis, *Stichting Mothers of Srebrenica and ors v Netherlands and United Nations*, ILDC 1760 (NL 2012) A7.

26 See 'The Netherlands partially liable for losses of Mothers of Srebrenica' *De Rechtspraak* (27 June 2017) https://www.rechtspraak.nl/Organisatie-en-contact/Organisatie/Gerechtshoven/Gerechtshof-Den-Haag/Nieuws/Paginas/The-Netherlands-partially-liable-for-losses-of-Mothers-of-Srebrenica.aspx# (last accessed 6 March 2018). For a succinct analysis of this case see C Ryngaert, 'Peacekeepers Facilitating Human Rights Violations: The Liability of the Dutch State in the *Mothers of Srebrenica* Cases' (2017) 64 *Netherlands Law Review* 453.

otherwise), including in particular those set out in the Draft Articles on Responsibility or International Organisations (hereinafter: DARIO) and the Draft Articles on Responsibilities of States for Internationally Wrongful Acts (hereinafter: DARS) by the International Law Organisation. The fact that rules of international law could result in the victims being unable to invoke certain conduct and war crimes committed by the Bosnian Serbs against the UN (due to immunity) and subsequently also against UN member states (due to non-attributability), cannot be attributed to the State and does not mean that more must be attributed to the State than that for which it is responsible according to the applicable rules. The objection is therefore unfounded.

Attribution to the State, effective control (instruction(s))

12.1 Not in dispute is that the conduct of Dutchbat toward the State can be attributed if the State exercised effective control over that conduct. For this purpose, it depends on the State's factual control concerning the specific conduct in question (or neglecting that conduct), with the factual circumstances and the particular context of the case having to be taken into consideration. The Court rightly – and this is also undisputed – considered that the mere fact that Dutch servicemen had been appointed to the UN chain of command, that Dutch UNPROFOR officers in certain cases had direct contact with Dutchbat, and that communication occurred between Dutch UNPROFOR officers and the Dutch government and/or the DCBC, does not entail that the State exercised effective control (court considerations 4.44 – 4.55).

Since the command and control over Dutchbat had been transferred to the UN, in principle the UN exercised effective control over Dutchbat. Whether the exceptional situation – that the State also exercised effective control over aspects of Dutchbat's conduct – arose in one or more specific cases is something the C.S. Foundation must sufficiently substantiate and must prove in the event of a dispute.

12.2 Objection 4 of the C.S. Foundation focuses on the courts conclusions that the State did not provide Dutchbat instructions prior to 9 July 1995, and that those instructions were limited to the blocking positions (court considerations 4.62 – 4.65). According to the C.S. Foundation, the Court failed to understand that the instructions related to giving priority to Dutchbat's own safety in its actions as a whole, and concerned: surrendering observation posts without resistance, surrendering blocking positions, surrendering and ceding weapons and equipment, refusing to return weapons seized to the population, refusing to give the population the necessary medical aid and using resources available for this purpose, and not protecting the population – all contrary to the UN's orders. According to the C.S. Foundation, Dutchbat was already subordinating the UN orders to the safety of the Dutchbat themselves from 8 July 1995. The C.S. Foundation furthermore refers to the statements made by Voorhoeve on 10 July 1995 concerning 'avoiding victims', 'giving the utmost priority to the safety of Dutch servicemen' and 'wanting to see men and women return home unscathed' (for this purpose, see 2.36). The C.S. Foundation argue that these statements reveal a pattern and were not limited to an instruction from the State concerning blocking positions.

12.3 The State contested the objection, and furthermore in particular also disputed that the State exercised effective control by means of an instruction to Dutchbat to avoid unnecessary victims, as considered by the court.

The Court of Justice considers the following in this regard.

12.4 Along with the State and unlike the C.S. Foundation and the Court, the Court of Justice believes it cannot be established that Voorhoeve's statements on or around 10 July 1995 from The Hague concerning 'avoiding victims', 'giving the utmost priority to the safety of Dutch servicemen' and 'wanting to see men and women return home unscathed' can be deemed exercising effective control over specific conduct. This is because the documents offer no point of departure for establishing that factual control was exercised through these statements concerning specific actions of Dutchbat (certain war operations or other specific actions). These statements are general statements that were not focused on specific operational (or other) actions, such as whether or not to abandon certain observation posts or blocking positions at any moment, whether or not to surrender and cede weapons and equipment at specific times or providing medical care, and suchlike. The C.S. Foundation also acknowledges this general nature, stating that the State's instructions were all-encompassing, and that Dutchbat's actions reveal that Voorhoeve's instruction was not restricted to blocking positions, but rather related to every aspect of Dutchbat's actions (statement of grounds of appeal no. 52 and 54). Irrespective of such statements, Dutchbat's factual actions at the site were determined by specific assignments given by the commanders from the UN chain of command, and not by statements by the State. Nothing indicates that the State gave certain orders (specific or otherwise) or instructed them to be given, in the sense that priority had to be given to Dutchbat's safety above any other consideration.

It is furthermore established that before Voorhoeve made the aforementioned statements, a general assignment was explicitly issued on 29 May 1995 from a higher level within the UN chain of command (namely by Lieutenant General Smith) to subordinate the implementation of the mandate to the safety of UN personnel (see 2.27). This was an operational decision by the UN.

The fact that in its statements, the State endorsed the priority on safety since it wished to see the Dutchbat return home unscathed does not therefore mean that the State itself had factual control over the specific operational decisions.

12.5 Unlike the court (Consideration 4.66), the Court of Justice deems that the statements of Voorhoeve, Van den Breemen and Franken referred to by the Court do not support the conclusion that the State received control over operational affairs by means of an instruction, or otherwise exercised effective control. These statements only entail (in brief): the expression of the hope for measures by the commanders (Voorhoeve for the Parliamentary survey commission (hereinafter: PE hearing), p.625), following a meeting with the minister, communicating to the UN that there must be no unnecessary victims (Van den Breemen, PE hearing p.735) and that there should be no Dutch fatalities or wounded (Franken, PE hearing p.67; Hilderink, PE hearing p.212 and 216). This may refer to the communication of a vision and (urgent) wishes, but does not refer to instructions or (other) actual control concerning specific conduct. This does not change if those statements are considered in conjunction with those of Hilderink (cited by the C.S. Foundation in the statement of grounds of appeal under 75 and 76), entailing that the priority was always: the safety of their own troops and the best possible implementation of the mandate within this. Those general statements do not reveal the State's effective control.

12.6 The statements from The Hague should also not be viewed separately from the context within which the command and control over Dutchbat was not only formally transferred to the UN (and thus not assigned to the State but exclusively reserved for the UN), but within which this transfer was also very well implemented in practice with the factual actions and decisions, both in The Hague and at the UN and Dutchbat in Bosnia Herzegovina (still also around 10 July 1995).

[. . .]

12.7 It has been established that the UN provided Dutchbat with specific instructions (including concerning the adoption of blocking positions). There is no evidence of specific instructions from the State to Dutchbat, or of any factual control by the State over the UN instructions, nor of the UN instructions occurring in response to what the State said or did. The fact that certain conduct by Dutchbat followed Voorhoeve's statements chronologically does not mean that actions were prompted (or was partially prompted) by Voorhoeve's statements.

12.8 The intensification of the contact and the clarification of wishes does not mean that the State exercises any control in the sense of effective control over specific actions. Informal consultation is not sufficient for this. There is even less of the control referred to on the grounds that persons were active within the UN chain of command (the C.S. Foundation cite Brantz and Nicolai in particular) who (also) served as the contact persons or even as advocates of the Netherlands. After all, that does not mean the State was to be a part of the UN chain of command or exercise influence over it as the State in such a way that the specific instructions from the UN chain of command (such as an instruction to abandon a blocking position) were in fact given by the State or partly by the State.

12.9 Contrary to the arguments by the C.S. Foundation, the discussions in 'the Tower' concerning the deployment of anti-tank weapons by the blocking positions do not entail any effective control, since the C.S. Foundation has failed to demonstrate sufficiently that instructions from the State were given or could have been given to Dutchbat in response to these discussions. The fact that the DCBC had meetings to arrive at an opinion on situations and to formulate directives and priorities for Dutchbat's actions does not mean that the State exercised or was able to exercise factual control over specific operational actions or omissions by Dutchbat, even if the results of the DCBC consultation were clearly communicated to people within the UN chain of command as the Dutch opinion (such as the NIOD reported on p. 2289).

[...]

12.12 The above demonstrates that no effective control on the part of the State can be derived from statements that victims must be avoided and that their own safety takes priority. This means that the C.S. Foundation's objection – directed against the Court and entailing, in brief, that the Court provided too limited an explanation of the State's instructions (or those it gave) – is unfounded. In view of the above, the question of whether statements as mentioned above were made earlier than 9 July 1995 is not a question for the Court of Justice, since answering this question can in no respect result in a claim being made against the State. The Court of Justice also rejects the C.S. Foundation's assertion that the Court underestimated the importance of giving instructions concerning the blocking positions since, as stated, it cannot be established that instructions were given concerning the blocking positions, from which an effective control by the State can be derived.

[...]

14. The C.S. Foundation furthermore argues that attributing Dutchbat's actions to the State can also occur under certain circumstances if it involves what is known as an "ultra vires act". In the C.S. Foundation's objection, it argues that Dutchbat acted contrary to instruction 9b of the Post Airstrike Guidance (see 2.27), and thus ultra vires, by abandoning the observation posts without a struggle. The C.S. Foundation argues that the Court provided an incorrect interpretation of the Post Airstrike Guidance of 29 May 1995, that the Court made an incorrect estimate of the danger Dutchbat encountered at the observation posts, that the Court unjustly failed to distinguish between the times these posts were abandoned and incorrectly

established factual circumstances, and that the Court failed to consider significant circumstances indicating Dutchbat's collaboration with the Bosnian Serbs. The State has contested this.

15.1 In order to assess the question of whether a case of an ultra vires act that can be attributed to the State existed, the court of justice considers the following.

15.2 In this case, it is not under discussion that a national contingent (such as Dutchbat) made available to the UN for UNPROFOR must be defined as an 'organ' of the UN. Article 7 DARIO stipulates:

> "The conduct of an organ of a State (...) that is placed at the disposal of another international organization shall be considered under international law an act of the latter organization if the organization exercises effective control over that conduct."

Article 8 DARIO stipulates:

> "The conduct of an organ or agent of an international organization shall be considered an act of that organization under international law if the organ or agent acts in an official capacity and within the overall functions of that organization, <u>even if the conduct exceeds the authority of that organ or agent or contravenes instructions.</u>" (underlining by Court of Justice)

This reveals that Dutchbat's actions must be deemed actions of the UN, if occurring 'in an official capacity and within the overall functions' of the UN, even if the actions contradicted instructions.

15.3 It can only be concluded that the actions cannot be attributed to the UN based on article 8 DARIO if the troops acted outside the official capacity' or 'overall functions' of the UN organisation (according to art. 8 DARIO) – thus in the case of Dutchbat: outside the capacity and task of peacekeeper assigned to it by the UN. However, that does not mean any deviation from an order of the UN (or deviation from an interpretation of an order) should be attributed to a member state of the UN as an ultra vires act alongside or instead of the UN itself. Nor can such an intention be derived from the explanation provided by the ILO in article 7 DARIO (referred to by the court in its consideration 4.58). Control by the State of mechanisms such as selection, training and preparation of troops and control by the State of personal matters and retrospective disciplinary procedures, to which the court refers, are not of such a nature that operational decisions arising from them which deviate from the (higher) UN order can be attributed to the State. In terms of operational decisions the State had in principle no further (control) authority following the transfer of command and control.

16.1 In the Court of Justice's opinion, in relation to the operational hostilities, it was not the case that Dutchbat acted outside the 'official capacity' or 'the overall functions' of the UN organisation. The estimation of the situation on site was the UN's concern. Making specific decisions concerning abandoning, reinforcing or recapturing observation posts, concerning the moment at which and the manner in which no resistance (further or otherwise) was offered at the observation posts, concerning whether or not to occupy, move or remove observation posts at any moment, concerning actions involving their own weapons and those seized, concerning requests for aerial support and concerning the deployment of medical resources by servicemen on site, corresponded to the authorities and tasks of the UN peacekeeper and concerned acts in an official capacity and within the overall functions of Dutchbat.

16.2 If the specific operational decisions contradicted the Post Airstrike Guidance of 29 May 1995 or other UN orders (higher or otherwise) – parties are disputing this –, the actions resulting from this cannot therefore be attributed to the State. In relation to the Post Airstrike Guidance, the court of justice furthermore considers the following (in 17.1 – 17.4).

[. . .]

23.1 It is furthermore disputed who (the State or the UN) took the initiative on 11 July 1995 to evacuate the refugees from the mini safe area and to what extent the State exercised control over Dutchbat within this scope. The C.S. Foundation argues that the State initiated the evacuation, in contradiction to Gobillard's order (for this point, refer to 2.45). [. . .]

23.8 Based on this and on other matters, the Court of Justice concludes that the decision to evacuate Dutchbat and the refugees came about by mutual consultation between Janvier on behalf of the UN on the one hand and Van den Bremmen and Van Baal on behalf of the State on the other. Insofar as the C.S. Foundation argues with objection 7 that following the fall of the safe area, the State assumed control from the UN and initiated the evacuation of the refugees contrary to the UN order, the objection fails.

24.1 In the newly arisen situation in which Srebrenica had fallen and the UN mission actually failed at that moment, the State decided in conjunction with the UN to evacuate the population from the mini safe area. The Dutch government participated in this decision-making at the highest level.

24.2 A transition period took effect as a result of this decision, in which the affairs in Potočari were settled and Dutchbat concentrated on its humanitarian task and the preparation for the evacuation of Dutchbat and the refugees from the mini safe area. The State had effective control to this extent. Factual control of the State over other specific actions has not been established. Objection 7 of the C.S. Foundation is unfounded. This also means that the Court of Justice will assume the time established by the Court at which the transition period took effect on 11 July 1995, namely around 23:00. The Court of Justice also agrees with the Court's opinion as follows, that with the decision taken together with the UN to withdraw Dutchbat no earlier than simultaneously with or following the evacuation of the refugees, the State linked the implementation of the authority to withdraw with providing humanitarian aid and the evacuation (or its preparation) of the refugees in the mini safe area in the transaction period (court considerations 4.80–4.85).

24.3 For the sake of clarity, the court of justice notes that the State's control does not in principle exceed the evacuation of the population and the withdrawal of Dutchbat. Whether or not it was feasible and desirable to drive away the Bosnian Serbs by entering into combat in the presence of thousands of refugees involves military estimates and decisions that must also have been made within the UN chain of command, possibly in collaboration with NATO. [. . .]

25. Based on the above, the Court of Justice (as well as the court, consideration 4.87) is of the opinion that in the transition period, the State had effective control over the provision of humanitarian aid and the evacuation (or its preparation) of the refugees in the mini safe area, without it being possible to attribute Dutchbat's actions in this regard to the State, and that the effective control did not concern the flow of refugees commencing prior to the transition period, relocating from the city of Srebrenica to the mini safe area, nor the refugees or Dutchbat's actions outside the mini safe area.

In contrast to the Court, based on the considerations above, the Court of Justice does not therefore attribute the actions contrary to a UN order (such as Gobilliard's order) to the State as an ultra vires act. There is no basis for attributing to the State

> the actions prior to the decision to evacuate on 1 July 1995 and outside the mini safe area.
>
> [...]
>
> 32.1 In consideration of the above, the Court of Justice has determined that Dutchbat's operational (military) operations were conducted without the State's factual control over the specific actions and within 'the official capacity' and 'within the overall functions' of these UN troops. This conduct on the part of Dutchbat cannot therefore be attributed to the State, not even as an ultra vires act, meaning that all objections focused against it due to similar conduct attributable to the State are unfounded.
>
> 32.2 On 11 July 1994 at 11 pm, the State decided together with the UN to allow Dutchbat to provide the humanitarian assistance and evacuation (or its preparation) of the refugees in the mini safe area. The transition period begins at the point, in which the State did indeed have effective control over Dutchbat's conduct relating to humanitarian aid and the evacuation of refugees in the mini safe area.

Arrest of Somali Pirate Suspects Case, Anonymous v Federal Government, Appeal judgment, 4 A 2948/11, (2015) Deutsches Verwaltungsblatt 375, ILDC 2391 (DE 2014), 18th September 2014, Germany; North Rhine-Westphalia; Higher Administrative Court [OVG]

One final case on the allocation of responsibility between international organizations and their member states concerns the European Union Naval Force ATALANTA (EU NAVFOR), established in December 2008 to counter the increased acts of piracy at the Horn of Africa stemming from Somalia. It was tasked with the protection of vessels of the World Food Programme (WFP), the African Union Mission in Somalia (AMISOM), and other vulnerable shipping, deterring and disrupting piracy and armed robbery at sea, monitoring fishing activities off the coast of Somalia, and supporting other EU missions and international organizations working to strengthen maritime security and capacity in the region.[27] Under international law, the operation was based on, among others, Security Council Resolution 1846 (2008) and numerous subsequent resolutions. Its current mandate has been extended until December 2020.

The German Bundestag gave its consent for the participation of the Navy on 19 December 2008; German forces may act against logistical facilities of the pirates at the beach up to a sea depth of 2,000 meters without putting boots on the ground.[28]

On 3 March 2009, nine allegedly Somali pirates were arrested and detained on a German vessel part of the ATALANTA operation. They were subsequently, on the basis of an agreement between the EU and Kenya, handed over to the Kenyan authorities. One of them (X) then instituted proceedings against Germany arguing that his arrest and subsequent detention, as well as the transfer to Kenya and the way he was treated by the Kenyan authorities (owing to the prison conditions) had been unlawful and violated the prohibition of ill-treatment and the right to a fair trial. The German government argued that the actions of the German navy had to be attributed to the EU and that it had trusted the assurances by Kenya to respect human rights law.

The court held that the transfer had to be attributed to Germany and not to the EU (which lacked international legal personality in such matters). Even under the assumption of significant EU involvement in the transfer, Germany would in any case still be co-responsible since neither

27 See 'Mission' European Union Naval Force, 2018 http://eunavfor.eu/mission/ (last accessed 6 March 2018).

28 See Deutscher Bundestag, 'Fortsetzung der Beteiligung bewaffneter deutscher Streitkräfte an der durch die Europäische Union geführten EU NAVFOR Somalia Operation Atalanta zur Bekämpfung der Piraterie vor der Küste Somalias' http://dip21.bundestag.de/dip21/btd/18/116/1811621.pdf (last accessed 6 March 2018).

the EU nor the UN had exercised effective control in the sense of Article 7 of the ILC Articles on the Responsibility of International Organizations.

112 1.3.2 Even assuming that the EU was materially involved in the surrender of the applicant to Kenya, the fact remains that, as an acting Member State, the Federal Republic of Germany was (jointly) responsible for that enforcement, as it always is during the enforcement of Community/Union law.

113 It is possible in principle under general international law within the framework of international organizations to replace the link to German law by a link to the law of the international organization, thereby transferring sole responsibility to the international organization. The legality of action within the framework of the international organization cannot then be reviewed by national courts based on conferral on national bodies.

[...]

117 However, graduated – not alternative – responsibility therefore exists here. There appears to be no reason why this should be any different in the sphere of the CFSP, if sovereign rights were indeed transferred to and administered by the European Union. On the contrary, Union law is transposed by the Member States to an even greater extent than traditional Community law. This is illustrated within the framework of Article 14 TEU, which applies here and which underpinned the Joint Action of 10 November 2008 (2008/851/CFSP), by the fact that it is binding on but not in the Member States. In light of that, there is, however, no reason to give a different answer to the question of responsibility within the framework of the CFSP than under other Union law. On the contrary, it should be assumed, by analogy with that understanding, that national courts have the jurisdiction to provide legal protection against national acts of enforcement. That analogy applies mutatis mutandis to the applicable law. Enforcement is pursued in accordance with the rules of national law, unless that is prevented by an applicable Union law that takes precedence.

119 The above applies a fortiori as – unlike under Community law – no form of legal protection would otherwise be/have been available. According to Article 5 TEU, read in combination with Article 46 TEU (Amsterdam versions), measures under the CFSP were not subject to review by the CJEU. However, according to the case-law of the German Federal Constitutional Court, transfer of sovereign rights ex ante is only permissible and valid domestically if comparable precautions exist to safeguard the law.

[...]

121 These (potential) infringements can be avoided here, however, (only) by a construction in the sense of shared responsibility. In light of Articles 3 and 6 ECHR and Articles 1, 19(4) and 22 of the Basic Law, that construction should be compelling in all cases in which – as here – the question of infringement of fundamental freedoms arises directly.

[...]

122 1.4 That notwithstanding, a construction based on international law, such as that made by the Administrative Court, leads to the same result.

[...]

125 1.4.2 Even disregarding that and assuming that it is possible in principle that the Federal Republic of Germany bears no responsibility due to its integration in

an EU command structure, the prerequisites under international law that must be fulfilled in order for the international organization involved (in this instance the EU and/or the UN) to bear (sole) responsibility have not been fulfilled. According to Article 7 of the International Law Commission (ILC) "Draft articles on the Responsibility of International Organizations", an international organization is (only) responsible for illegal conduct by an organ of State placed at its disposal if it exercised effective control over that conduct. This already established principle of customary international law was 127 the basis, albeit in modified form ("Ultimate Authority and Control/UAAC"), of the judgment of the ECtHR cited by the defendants. The ECtHR, taking a more global viewpoint, draws attention to the overall responsibility for an operation, finding that it does not appear (any longer) to come down to individual action.

[. . .]

129 Which opinion should be endorsed can be left to one side here, as the question of the defendants' responsibility under international law remains in both cases.

[. . .]

131 1.4.2.1 Based on the precedent established in Behrami, the surrender of the applicant to Kenya cannot be ascribed to the UN. Insofar as the ECtHR relevantly considered that UAAC in the case of the NATO intervention in Kosovo rested with the United Nations Security Council and hence the question of the responsibility of the acting States under the European Convention on Human Rights did not arise, the possibility of transfer in this case is undermined by the fact that the relevant UN Security Council resolutions were intended merely to empower the Member States to also fight piracy in the territorial waters of and on mainland Somalia. As the Administrative Court has already rightly held, the measures on the high seas at issue here are, however, already covered by the Convention on the Law of the Sea. There was no need for authorization by the Security Council pursuant to Chapter 7 of the UN Charter.

[. . .]

133 Furthermore, it has neither been argued and there is nothing to suggest that a chain of command ending at the UN Security Council comparable to the intervention in Kosovo existed in respect of the measures to combat piracy, let alone an organizational structure that would have enabled the UN to play a relevant operational role. The mere fact, as argued by the defendant, that there may have been a duty to report to the Security Council does not by any means substantiate influence over specific operational interventions; at best, it allows ex post monitoring.

[. . .]

134 Even disregarding that, there can be no question, based on the precedent established in Behrami, of severing the link between the acting contracting States and the ECHR given that, as stated previously, they played a relevant and independently responsible role within the operation; in fact, the defendant's own sovereign measures had a decisive influence on it.

[. . .]

136 1.4.2.2 The precedent established in Behrami prevents responsibility from being attributed to the EU from the outset. The ECtHR reasoned its judgment primarily on the monopoly of force of the UN and its prominent role in safeguarding world peace. The EU does not have a comparable role.

VI. Domestic Courts and the State of Necessity: The Argentina Debt Crisis

Argentine Necessity Case, K and ors v Argentina (represented by President Néstor Kirchner), Decision of the Federal Constitutional Court, Order of the Second Senate, 2 BvM 1-5/03, 1, 2/06, vol 118, 124, 60 Neue Juristische Wochenschrift (2007), 2610, 138 ILR 1 (2010), ILDC 952 (DE 2007), 8th May 2007, Constitutional Court [BVerfG]

The 1990s Argentine debt crisis[29] and Argentina's ensuing decision to unilaterally impose a so-called haircut on state bonds, and the discontinuation of payments, *inter alia* raised the question of whether states could rely on necessity in the sense of Article 25 of the Articles on State Responsibility vis-à-vis private parties. In a widely discussed landmark judgment, the Federal Constitutional Court of Germany denied this possibility by distinguishing between inter-state necessity and the state of necessity between states and private actors and holding that the latter constituted an overextension not reflected in customary international law.

C.

30 A general rule of international law which entitles a state to temporarily refuse to meet private law payment claims due towards private individuals by invoking state necessity declared because of inability to pay cannot be currently ascertained. [. . .]

34 2. Invocation of state necessity is recognised in customary international law in those legal relationships which are exclusively subject to international law; by contrast, there is no evidence for a state practice based on the necessary legal conviction (*opinio juris sive necessitatis*) to extend the legal justification for the invocation of state necessity to relationships under private law involving private creditors.

35 a) The principle that conduct which does not comply with the respective legal order can be justified under certain circumstances is inherent in both the national legal orders and in international law. In very general terms, national legal orders see both criminal-law and civil-law necessity as a justification for conduct otherwise regarded as wrongful, even though the concrete manifestation of the preconditions for assuming the justification may differ. Von Liszt stated in his international-law manual already in 1898 that the terms "necessary defence" and "necessity", as recognised in criminal and private law, can also preclude the wrongfulness of the violation committed in the arena of international law (von Liszt, *Das Völkerrecht*, 1898, pp. 128–129).

36 b) In connection with the recognition and impact of state necessity under international law and as evidence of its applicability under customary law, reference is made first and foremost to the work on state responsibility and its reception in the judicature of international courts and tribunals done by the United Nations International Law Commission (ILC). After several years of debates and several drafts, the International Law Commission submitted to the United Nations General Assembly in 2001 a draft convention on the topic of Responsibility of States for Internationally Wrongful Acts, the so-called Articles on State Responsibility (Annex to the Resolution of the United Nations General Assembly A/RES/56/83; hereinafter: ILC Articles on State Responsibility).

37 The ILC Articles on State Responsibility are largely concerned with questions of accountability for and consequences of state violations of obligations under international law. This codification draft also covers state necessity under international

29 For an overview of the crisis and its preceding events and decisions see, eg, V A Beker, 'Argentina's Debt Crisis' in B Moro and V A Beker (eds), *Modern International Crises. Argentina, United States and Europe* (Springer 2016) 31.

law (Article 25) as a justification. The draft has not yet led to the conclusion of an international agreement. The document was accepted by the United Nations General Assembly on 12 December 2001. This, however, leads neither *eo ipso* to customary-law application, nor to legally binding application for another reason, but may serve as an indication of a legal conviction as is necessary to form customary law. Ultimately, it is now generally recognised in legal literature and in the view of international courts and tribunals that Article 25 of the ILC Articles on State Responsibility constitutes applicable customary international law. The commentaries of the International Law Commission during the codification process document for this provision the declared objective of identifying and reflecting in the codification the content and scope of the application of the concept under customary law by an evaluation of state practice and of the rulings of international courts, as well as an evaluation of the writings of recognised international-law researchers (International Law Commission, State Responsibility, Yearbook of the International Law Commission 1980, Vol. II, et al. marginal nos. 55 and 78).

[. . .]

45 According to the language of the text, necessity is a justification in a relationship to which international law applies pursuant to Article 25 of the ILC Articles on State Responsibility. If the preconditions apply, necessity only precludes the wrongfulness of an act not in conformity with an international obligation.

[. . .]

49 3. The relevant case-law of international and national courts together with the views expressed in scholarly literature on international law do not permit the positive ascertainment of a general rule of international law, according to which, over and above the area of application of Article 25 of the ILC Articles on State Responsibility, restricted as it is to international-law relations, a state would also be entitled to temporarily refuse to meet payment claims due in private-law relationships towards private creditors after declaring state necessity because of inability to pay. There is no uniform state practice recognising such a justification by force of international law. In the context of proceedings on the constitutionality of a statute, the Federal Constitutional Court is not entitled to expand an existing general rule of international law in terms of its elements.

[. . .]

62 b) An inspection of national case-law on the question of state necessity also fails for lack of agreement to suggest that the recognition of state necessity impacting on private-law relationships is established in customary law. The relevant rulings either only comment on the actual existence of a state of necessity, but not to its legal impact, or they shift the problem to the level of immunity and resulting obstacles to execution. The expert report of Prof. Dr. August Reinisch therefore finds, after evaluating the practice of national courts, that no authoritative conclusions can be drawn from this to justify state inability to pay by pleading state necessity (marginal no. 126).

63 c) In view of the fundamental existence of necessity as a justification in international legal relations, scholarly literature takes the view, in agreement with international and national case-law, that necessity is recognised by customary law (see Baars/Böckel, loc. cit., p. 459 with further references). The relevant literature also distinguishes, however, between recognition in relations between states on the one hand and recognition as a legal justification in relations with private individuals on the other. The views expressed in scholarly literature on the transferability of international-law necessity to relations under private law differ significantly from

one another (see on this Baars/Böckel, loc. cit., pp. 461 et seq. with further references). Scholarly articles indicate that it is desirable in terms of legal policy to recognise state necessity as a plea towards private individuals (see Dolzer, *Staatliche Zahlungsunfähigkeit: Zum Begriff und zu den Rechtsfolgen im Völkerrecht*, in: Jekewitz (ed.), *Des Menschen Recht zwischen Freiheit und Verantwortung:Festschrift für Karl Josef Partsch zum 75. Geburtstag* (1989), p. 550), but the lack of state practice prevents one from reaching the conclusion that customary law is already in force (see Hahn, *Das Völkerrecht der Auslandsschuldenregelungen, Kreditwesen* (1989), p. 314 (318)). The transferability of a legal obligation resulting from a general principle of showing consideration is also discussed in legal literature, but it too is rejected for lack of supporting documentation from state practice (see Ohler, loc. cit., pp. 594–595).

64 Insofar as the scholarly literature indicates that there are, allegedly, domestic legal principles which are common to all legal systems and which thus demand recognition under international law, this can be maintained as to the fundamental principle of compensation between debtors and creditors. This approach is not, however, helpful for a ruling on the submitted question. Were there a general legal principle according to which a debtor state could use the objection of state bankruptcy towards private creditors, state bankruptcy would have to be identifiable in examples from state practice; one would hence have to be able to recognise at least a certain congruency in the various legal systems vis-à-vis the recognition of this principle. This is, however, not the case, as the evaluation of state practice undertaken to verify customary law has revealed. A general legal principle cannot be verified absent a corresponding embodiment in actual legal practice. One may not derive solely from a principle of compensation which is also inherent to the German law of obligations and to the safeguarding of the conflicting interests under procedural law an international rule determining that a state creditor should be placed in a different position than a private individual, and hence could invoke state necessity.

65 4. The question as to recognition, under customary law, particularly of economic or financial state necessity, and as to its preconditions concerning the degree of peril of vital state interests, can remain unresolved here. Because, in any event, an economically or financially defined state of necessity can also not be pled by a state vis-à-vis private individuals so long as there is no rule under international customary law which recognises the transferability of the defence of necessity from relationships under international law to relationships under private law.

Argentine Necessity Case, K and ors v Argentina (represented by President Néstor Kirchner), Decision of the Federal Constitutional Court, Order of the Second Senate, 2 BvM 1-5/03, 1, 2/06, vol 118, 124, 60 Neue Juristische Wochenschrift (2007), 2610, 138 ILR 1 (2010), ILDC 952 (DE 2007), 8th May 2007, Constitutional Court [BVerfG], Dissenting opinion of Judge Lübbe-Wolff on the Order of the Second Senate of 8 May 2007—2 BvM 1-5/03, 1, 2/06

This decision has led to a wave of criticism, not only by various commentators including ILDC reporter Christian Tams[30] but also one of the German judges. In a remarkable and praiseworthy example of horizontal judicial dialogue,[31] Lübbe-Wolff outlined related domestic cases to demonstrate that it was 'wrong to presume that the case-law of national courts also points against the

30 See J A Kämmerer, 'Argentine Debt Crisis' *Max Planck Encyclopedia of Public International Law* (2014) para 18.

31 See, eg, A-M Slaughter, 'A Typology of Transjudicial Communication' (1994) 29 *University of Richmond Law Review* 99, 103 ff; see also A Reinisch (ed), *The Privileges and Immunities of International Organizations in Domestic Courts* (OUP 2013) or A Tzanakopoulos, 'Judicial Dialogue as a Means of Interpretation' in Helmut Philipp Aust and Georg Nolte (eds), *The Interpretation of International Law by Domestic Courts. Uniformity, Diversity, Convergence* (OUP 2016) 72.

existence of a general rule of international law according to which a state can also assert the plea of state necessity before national courts'.[32]

93 The *Corte Suprema di Cassazione* in Italy ruled in April 2005 that the legal acts with which Argentina had declared state necessity and ordered cessation of debt service were expressions of sovereign state power, and ruled that the absolute precedence of the interests of the stateorganised community, which was to be protected by these legal acts, ruled out their evaluation as any possible violation of rights according to the regime of private law applicable to commercial activities; rather, the immunity of the state for *acta iure imperii* was said to apply here (*Corte Suprema di Cassazione, Ordinanza* of 27 May 2005, R.G.N. 6532/04, www). With this ruling of the supreme organ of ordinary Italian jurisdiction, the obligation flowing from international law in the case of state necessity to respect, also in the context of private-law disputes, the precedence of the right of the state in question to avert this necessity is not negated, but, on the contrary, is actually recognised. That the court recognises this at the stage of the immunity question changes nothing in this respect.

94 As to the case-law in the United States of America, which is regarded by some authors as constituting proof of a lack of general recognition of the plea of necessity in private-law relations (see Baars/Böckel, loc. cit., p. 461; Ohler, loc. cit., p. 594 et seq.; see also the expert report of Prof. Dr. August Reinisch on which the Senate's ruling is based, marginal nos. 117 et seq., 125–126), it is in fact true that dispositive importance is not attached to a declared state of necessity *per se*. The opportunity to suspend the proceedings for a limited period of time is, however, used to avert endangering the debt restructuring process of foreign states which are experiencing payment crises (see United States Court of Appeals for the Second Circuit in the cases of *Pravin Banker Associates, Ltd., v. Banco Popular del Peru and the Republic of Peru*, of 25 March 1997, no. 96-713, with reference to the fact that a long-observed practice of recognition of foreign insolvency proceedings by the federal courts was followed therewith, and *EM Ltd. et al. v. Republic of Argentina*, of 13 May 2005, no. 05-1525-cv, with reference to the vital significance of the debt restructuring process for the economic health of a nation). Over and above this, foreign states in general enjoy far-reaching protection against execution measures in the USA. Even if there has been a comprehensive waiver of immunity, the Foreign Sovereign Immunities Act only permits access to assets situated in the U.S.A. which are used for commercial purposes (28 U.S.C. § 1610 (a) (1); concerning this and concerning the interpretation of this provision using its purpose of avoiding a disturbance of public activity of foreign states, see the ruling of the United States Court of Appeals for the Fifth Circuit in the case of *Af-Cap Inc. vs. The Republic of Congo*, of 17 September 2004, no. 03-50506). The funds of foreign central banks are separately protected (28 U.S.C. § 1611 (b) (1)). Accordingly, the United States Court of Appeals for the Second Circuit recently declared impermissible the seizure of monies of the Argentinean Central Bank in accounts held at the Federal Reserve Bank of New York which were wanted by the Argentinean government for payments to the International Monetary Fund, although Argentina had waived its immunity towards the creditors in question to the greatest degree possible under national law: The Foreign Sovereign Immunities Act was said to provide immunity for the funds of foreign central banks against execution and seizure; even if, in the case at hand, these were not funds of the Central Bank, but of the Republic of Argentina, seizure would only have been possible if the funds in question had been used for a commercial purpose, which was said not to be the

32 See the dissenting opinion of Judge Lübbe-Wolff, para 92.

case (see United States Court of Appeals for the Second Circuit, *EM Ltd. v. Republic of Argentina* and *NML Capital Ltd. v. Republic of Argentina*, of 5 January 2007, nos. 06-0403-cv, 06-0405-cv, 06-0406-cv). Thus, protection against enforcement from the more general point of view of immunity according to US law goes beyond the standard of what is required under international law, which is relevant to German law in this respect (see BVerfGE 46, 342 (388–389); 64, 1 (40); Order of the Second Senate of the Federal Constitutional Court of 6 December 2006—2 BvM 9/03 —, *Deutsches Verwaltungsblatt* 2007, pp. 242 et seq.); it aims not to impair the performance of sovereign tasks of a foreign state even if, in the context of commercial activities, the latter had divested itself of its immunity under international law.

96 The ruling of the Senate, by contrast, means that the plea of state necessity under international law, since it is not to be applicable in private-law disputes before national courts, can play a role neither in judgment nor in enforcement proceedings. Accordingly, private creditors—including those who knowingly purchased government bonds with unfavourable risk assessments and correspondingly favourable interest prospects as a speculative investment (in demonstration of this see Frankfurt am Main Higher Regional Court, *Zeitschrift für Versicherungsrecht—VersR* 2005, pp. 797–798; Koblenz Higher Regional Court, *NJW-Rechtsprechungs-Report—NJW-RR* 2004, pp. 1689–1690; Münster Regional Court, *Zeitschrift für Bank—und Kapitalmarktrecht—BKR* 2003, pp. 762 et seq. and pp. 764 et seq.)—can from now on, even in the face of catastrophic domestic breakdowns in the debtor state, not only have their demands recognised in Germany, but can also enforce those demands by way of execution against assets of the debtor state which are intended for sovereign purposes if the corresponding waiver of immunity is present in the loan terms. The US legal situation is much closer to international law.

One additional noteworthy judgment on the Argentine debt crisis issued after that of the Federal Constitutional Court stems from the earlier stages of *NML Capital, Ltd v Republic of Argentina*. Here, the Second Circuit dismissed Argentina's argument that an injunction to pay NML could eventually lead to a state of bankruptcy and thus ultimately deprive NML of all of its claims by declaring itself 'unwilling to permit Argentina's threats to punish third parties to dictate the availability or terms of relief'. Those who had bought Argentine bonds at a later stage, ie when the Argentine debt crisis and the risks associated therewith emerged, had to be paid in full just like the original bondholders.[33]

VII. State Responsibility and Extradition

Settled case law of the European Court of Human Rights (ECtHR) obliges states to refrain from extradition if the concerned individual faces a 'serious risk' of ill-treatment in the sense of Article 3 of the ECHR in the target country.[34] The court also explicitly stated that 'the activities of the individual in question, however undesirable or dangerous, cannot be a material consideration'

33 W M C Weidemaier and A Gelpern, 'Injunctions in Sovereign Debt Litigation' (2014) 31 *Yale Journal on Regulation* 189, 197; see also C G Paulus, 'Debts' *Max Planck Encyclopedia of Public International Law* (2014) para 15.

34 ECtHR, *Soering v United Kingdom*, App No 14038/88 (7 July 1989). The rationale established in the *Soering* case also applies to applications for asylum; see, eg, ECtHR, *Cruz Varas and Others v Sweden*, App No 15576/89 (20 March 1991). In *X against Austria and Yugoslavia*, a case dating back to the 1964, the European Commission of Human Rights held that: '[…] although extradition and the right of asylum are not, as such, among the matters governed by the Convention […] the Contracting States have nevertheless accepted to restrict the free exercise of their powers under general international law, including the power to control the entry and exit of aliens, to the extent and within the limits of the obligations which they have assumed under the Convention'; ECtHR, App No 2143/64 (30 June 1964) 7 *Yearbook of the European Convention on Human Rights* (1964) 314, 328.

and that there was no 'room for balancing the risk of ill-treatment against the reasons for expulsion in determining whether a State's responsibility under Article 3 [. . .] is engaged'.[35] Article 3 as understood and applied by the ECtHR thus sets a higher standard than the principle of non-refoulement enshrined in the 1951 Refugee Convention. After all, Article 33(2) of the latter states that it does not apply to 'a refugee whom there are reasonable grounds for regarding as a danger to the security of the country in which he is, or who, having been convicted by a final judgment of a particularly serious crime, constitutes a danger to the community of that country'.[36]

Domestic courts in states parties to the ECHR have generally accepted the ECtHR's jurisprudence. Extradition cases before the ECtHR nevertheless must not necessarily deal with the level of protection afforded by Article 3 of the ECHR and the impossibility to weigh this obligation against national security interests but also the question of whether the conditions in the target country as such amount to a 'serious' risk of torture, inhumane, or degrading treatment or punishment for virtually everyone or at least do so for the concerned individual (eg because of his or her (past) political affiliation, religious beliefs, or other specific reasons).

Case law also highlights another interesting legal scenario, that of extradition between ECHR countries, namely to Turkey.

The first of two important cases in this regard concerns Metin Kaplan,[37] an Islamic fundamentalist and self-declared 'caliph of Cologne'.[38] He had first travelled to Germany with a tourist visa in 1982 and was asked to leave the country three months after its expiry (whether he had ever left Germany remains unclear). Kaplan then re-entered Germany with another tourist visa in 1986 and requested asylum in 1988. Germany granted asylum in 1992 over fear of criminal prosecution since he was the head of a fundamentalist movement and had to fear criminal prosecution. In July 1996, he called for the murder of his political opponent Ibrahim Sofu, who had also declared himself as a caliph. After Sofu was shot about a year later, Kaplan received a sentence of four years for public incitement to commit crimes in December 2000.

In the following two years, his organization (the 'Caliphate state') was banned, his recognition as a refugee was revoked, and he was due to be expelled to Turkey, which had already requested his extradition in 1999 over accusations that he was working on replacing the democratic order in Turkey in favour of an Islamic theocracy based exclusively on the Quran, having formed a terrorist organization and having planned and directed terror attacks in Turkey. He challenged this decision by claiming that his fair trial rights would be violated in Turkey and that he would furthermore face a risk of being tortured. The Higher Administrative Court in Münster nevertheless found that there was a significantly reduced danger of ill-treatment because the Turkish ministry of foreign affairs had given assurances that he would be transferred directly to the competent court without stopping at any police station; it also held that there was no further evidence that the Turkish authorities would commit any serious human rights violations. Kaplan then appealed to the Federal Administrative Court, which held that he could not rely on the risk of violations of the prohibition of torture and other forms of ill-treatment, the right to fair trial, and the freedom of religion by arguing that he could not rely on the ECHR because he would also be protected within Turkey. The standards of protection in extradition cases between member states to the ECHR was different than in connection with extraditions to non-ECHR members. If violations of his rights under the ECHR should indeed occur, he could

35 ECtHR, *Chahal v United Kingdom*, App No 22414/93 (15 November 1996) para 81.

36 Convention Relating to the Status of Refugees (Refugee Convention) (adopted 28 July 1951, entered into force 22 April 1954) 189 UNTS 137.

37 *Kaplan v Federal State North-Rhine Westphalia*, Appeal judgment, BVerwG 1 C 14/04, ILDC 482 (DE 2004), 7th December 2004, Germany; Federal Administrative Court [BVerwG].

38 See 'Profile: The Caliph of Cologne' *BBC* (27 May 2004) http://news.bbc.co.uk/1/hi/world/europe/1705886.stm (last accessed 6 March 2018).

ultimately issue an individual complaint to the ECtHR, whose interim measures are generally implemented by Turkey. Kaplan thus had to address potential violations within Turkey and there was no particularly high risk of grave and irreparable ill-treatment against which legal protection in Turkey would be too late.

The Dutch Supreme Court came to a somewhat different conclusion regarding extraditions to Turkey in its 2006 judgment in *Minister of Justice v N Kesbir*.[39] Nuriye Kesbir was a former member of the Kurdistan Workers' Party (commonly known as PKK) who was wanted in Turkey owing to her involvement in the organization of attacks on the Turkish military in the Turkish-Kurdish conflict during the 1990s. After the Dutch Supreme Court deemed her extradition lawful at first, Human Rights Watch wrote an open letter to then-Dutch Minister of Justice Piet Hein Donner, arguing that 'any assurances given by the Turkish authorities that Ms Kesbir would not be tortured or ill-treated, and that she would have a fair trial upon return, would not be reliable, particularly in light of Turkey's failure to adequately monitor those responsible for complying with legal safeguards against torture and the authorities' past record in cases where such guarantees have been at issue'.[40] Donner nevertheless continued with the extradition procedure and, after receiving such assurances, approved the extradition on 7 September 2004. After Nuriye Kesbir challenged this decision (Dutch law allowed for such challenges in extradition matters if there is a threat of human rights violations) the district court and subsequently the Court of Appeals both halted the extradition because there still existed a real risk of ill-treatment and, as the latter held, the Turkish assurances were insufficient and too general. Also addressing the inter-relationship between two different obligations (under the ECHR and the extradition request), the Dutch Supreme Court, while referring to the ECtHR's settled jurisprudence on Article 3 of the ECHR, shared the Court of Appeal's assessment. Since Turkey had only given a general guarantee that it would follow its obligations under international treaties, this does not come as a surprise. In a notable difference to the *Kaplan* case, the Supreme Court also broadened its own case law by not only applying the precedence of individual rights in cases of the death penalty and also by applying increased standards between member states to the ECHR.[41]

As is well known, the ECtHR's standard in extradition cases stems from the obligation to refrain from extraditing individuals to countries where they could face the death penalty. In general international law, the situation was somewhat less clear.[42] According to a 2015 report by the Secretary-General, all states that have abolished the death penalty are 'denying extradition to States where the death penalty might be imposed unless assurances were given that the individual concerned could not be sentenced to death or, if sentenced to death, the penalty would not be carried out', while none of these states has extradited individuals absent such assurances.[43]

One example is the Supreme Court of Canada, which, while leaving open the door for possible exceptions, also adopted a similar rationale in *US v Burns* from 2001, when holding that 'in the absence of exceptional circumstances, which we refrain from trying to anticipate, assurances in death penalty cases are always constitutionally required'.[44]

39 *Minister of Justice v N Kesbir*, Extradition Proceedings, Judgment on Appeal in Cassation, Case No C05/120HR, ILDC 851 (NL 2006), 15th September 2006, Supreme Court [HR].

40 'Case of Nuriye Kesbir – Letter to Dutch Ministry of Justice' Human Rights Watch, 23 May 2004 https://www.hrw.org/news/2004/05/23/case-nuriye-kesbir (last accessed 6 March 2018).

41 cf G J Pulles, Analysis, *Minister of Justice v N Kesbir* (n 39) A5.

42 cf V P Nanda, 'Bases for Refusing International Extradition Requests: Capital Punishment and Torture' (1999) 23/5 *Fordham International Law Journal* 1369.

43 *Capital punishment and implementation of the safeguards guaranteeing protection of the rights of those facing the death penalty*, report by the Secretary General, UN Doc E/2015/49, para 57. See also B Malkani, 'The Obligation to Refrain from Assisting the Use of the Death Penalty' (2013) 62(3) *International & Comparative Law Quarterly* 523.

44 Supreme Court of Canada, *US v Burns* [2001] 1 SCR 283, para 65.

Tsebe and Society for the Abolition of the Death Penalty in South Africa and Society for the Abolition of the Death Penalty in South Africa (intervening) v The Minister of Home Affairs and ors, Judgment, 27682/10, ILDC 1782 (ZA 2011), 22nd September 2011, South Africa; Gauteng; Johannesburg; South Gauteng High Court [GPJ-HC]

Another and more recent example is the case of *Tsebe and Society for the Abolition of the Death Penalty in South Africa and Society for the Abolition of the Death Penalty in South Africa (intervening) v The Minister of Home Affairs and ors*. Mr Tsebe had fled to South Africa immediately after an arrest warrant as he was accused of having murdered his wife in Botswana. The South African Minister of Justice refused to extradite him because he could face the death penalty in Botswana (South Africa had abolished the death penalty immediately after the end of the Apartheid regime). The two countries subsequently agreed that Mr Tsebe would be prosecuted in South Africa; however, since South Africa's legal framework did not address jurisdiction for such cases, he was released and was due to be deported to Botswana as an illegal immigrant (until his deportation, he was held in a detention facility for such purposes). His deportation to Botswana was nevertheless halted, raising the question of whether South Africa was permitted to deport him to a country where he could face the death penalty. The South Gauteng High Court stated that state responsibility and the low human rights standards in Botswana concerning the death penalty and the right to life by itself were sufficient to deny extradition to Botswana. It nevertheless went on to elaborate on the domestic legal framework to conclude that an extradition of Mr Tsebe would violate the constitution of South Africa (Article 233) and those international law obligations in conformity with it.

> [67] We would opine that extradition of the applicants to Botswana would be impermissible purely based upon its aforesaid track history in regard to the manner in which it has proven itself to be a flouter of human rights as far as the implementation of the death penalty is concerned. This past conduct by Botswana makes it a pariah state not synchronized with the majority of African countries that have either abandoned or are refusing to implement the death penalty. In our view justice and fairness demands that Botswana should not be the preferred choice to obtain extradition orders from the Republic in circumstances where its past conduct of secretive hangings has led to shock and outrage. In addition, a requested state incurs responsibility if it has reasonable grounds to foresee that violation of human rights will occur in the requesting state and, nonetheless extradites the criminal fugitives. On this basis alone it would be permissible to grant the applications and dismiss the counter applications. However, in view of the importance of the issues at stake it is necessary to canvass them in the light of the domestic constitutional law for human rights and all other relevant statutory law, both national and international. [...]
>
> [119] It is trite that the right to life has limitations in both domestic and international law. Furthermore, it is trite that the death penalty is not outlawed by international law and stands as a limitation to the right to life in certain countries, including Botswana. However, these limitations do not find application in this matter.
>
> [120] The reason for this is that the right to life is being examined through the prism of the South African Constitution in light of the death penalty and the limitation that such penalty imposes on the right. Because the death penalty is absolutely outlawed in South Africa by the Makwanyane decision, any limitations in international law to the right to life are immediately in conflict with our Constitution when applied to this matter, as these limitations can only find application insofar as they form part of the rationale behind the death penalty. As explained in light of Makwanyane, this is a rational that finds no place in South Africa's constitutional democracy.

[121] Therefore, any international law principles that may seek to justify the imposition of the death penalty by Botswana are not binding on this court and any attempt to satisfy them would be unconstitutional. Section 233 of the Constitution does not allow for international law to be applied if it is contrary to the Constitution. However, international law that is in accordance with the Constitution is binding on the Republic.

[122] Bearing this in mind, we refer back to the general international law principles that enunciate the right to life (see paragraphs [114] to [117] above). These parts of international law, insofar as they do not allow for a limitation of life under the death penalty, are binding on the Republic. Therefore, South Africa is bound by its Constitution as well as the international law that conforms with its Constitution, to protect the right to life and should refuse extradition in circumstances such as those faced by this court.

[123] Given that an extradition is performed in terms of domestic law, which is the law of South Africa, and given that the Constitution affirms that it is the supreme law of South Africa, the extraditions of Mr Tsebe and Mr Phale had to conform fully with the Constitution, and thus be accompanied with an assurance from Botswana, despite any international obligations to the contrary.

[124] Therefore, there can be no international law obligations on South Africa to extradite anyone to their possible deaths at the hand of the executive of another state as it would be contrary to our Constitution and invalid. Quite to the contrary, South Africa is bound to honour international obligations that would prevent the extraditions in questions.

VIII. State Responsibility and State Succession

In general, it is commonly assumed that new states enter into life with a clean slate when it comes to liability for acts of their predecessors.[45] Upon closer inspection, however, it is difficult to discern any clear-cut rules of customary international law. Examples range from the Yugoslav wars or the end of the Soviet Union to the peaceful dissolution of Czechoslovakia and the incorporation of the German Democratic Republic into the Federal Republic of Germany. Since actual state practice on this issue is thus scarce and inconclusive, as it was often ultimately dominated by political considerations and horse-trading instead of well-established rules, 'casuistry and ad hocery are unavoidable'.[46] Nevertheless, in contrast to the above-mentioned general finding, it does seem clear that '[t]he wronged state's entitlement to reparation cannot, as a general matter, be wiped out simply because the responsible state has underwent territorial transformations'.[47]

In addition to negotiations on state succession treaties, archives, property, or debts, domestic courts have occasionally also had to deal with issues of state succession to international responsibility.

Yemen v Compagnie d'Enterprises CFE SA, Appeal judgment, No 10717, ILDC 630 (CY 2002), 28th June 2002, Supreme Court [Sup Ct]

In a somewhat atypical case, the Supreme Court of Cyprus had to deal with the doctrine of acquired rights and the 1990 merger of North and South Yemen in *Yemen v Compagnie*

45 See, eg, M N Shaw, *International Law* (6th edn, CUP 2014) 729; J Crawford, *Brownlie's Principles of Public International Law* (8th edn, OUP 2012) 442.

46 M Milanović, 'The Tricky Question of State Succession to International Responsibility' *EJIL:Talk!* (16 February 2009) https://www.ejiltalk.org/the-tricky-question-of-state-succession-to-international-responsibility/ (last accessed 6 March 2018).

47 ibid.

d'Enterprises CFE SA.[48] It concerned a Belgian industrial group (abbreviating and referring to itself as CFE)[49] and a contract to construe and maintain a harbour in South Yemen. In December 1992, CFE filed a request to settle a dispute by arbitration—to be established in Nicosia—with the International Chamber of Commerce. The arbitrator *inter alia* had to decide whether Yemen, as a newly established state, had succeeded into the contract and its provisions relating to the settlement of disputes. Yemen argued that it could not be a party to the arbitration proceedings since it had come into being as an entirely new state and thus free of any preceding (contractual) rights and obligations and that the initial arbitration request addressed South Yemen. In this regard. one needs to bear in mind that South Yemen had indeed ceased to exist after its merger with the north.[50]

As the arbitrator did not accept this argument and after Yemen lost the case, Yemen tried to have the courts of Cyprus annul the award by relying on the same line of arguments as it had during the arbitration proceedings. The Supreme Court qualified the agreement to settle disputes via arbitration as an acquired right and held that such a right did not become extinct owing to state succession.

Relying on a 1968 textbook on international law edited by Max Sørensen,[51] it furthermore held that newly established states benefiting from acts done within the territory of the predecessor—as was the case in this instance—could also be held responsible.

The case stands out in at least two ways. First, the court dealt with the issue at hand under the rubric of state responsibility instead of mere state succession. The proceedings did not concern wrongful acts occurring between states or reparation for such wrongs but the continuation of a contract between a state and a private party as well as, relatedly, standing before a private arbitral tribunal.

Secondly, the court applied the traditional doctrine of acquired rights according to which acquired (private party) rights have to be acknowledged and respected by the successor state. Nevertheless, as the Institut de Droit International stated in Article 25 of its guidelines relating to the succession of property and debts, it does not necessarily have to uphold and guarantee such rights in full but rather 'in so far as is possible'—ie within the limits set by the applicable legal framework (in particular that of the respective investment law regime).[52]

Thirdly, it extensively quoted a rather old textbook instead of more recent works. After all and as stated above, the most pertinent cases on the law of state succession stem from the 1990s, and while the question of state responsibility to state succession is somewhat underexposed, the court should perhaps rather have relied on Patrick Dumberry's treatise on this subject where he explored the principle of unjust enrichment and stated that: 'where the predecessor State *ceases* to exist as a result of the events affecting its territorial integrity (such as cases of dissolution, incorporation and unification of States), what matters is that an internationally wrongful act does not remain unpunished as a result of the disappearance of its perpetrator. We have already concluded that in cases of incorporation and unification of States, the successor State should always take over the obligations arising from the commission of internationally wrongful acts'.[53]

> 14. Below we quote an excerpt from the book of Max Sørensen, "Manual of Public International Law", page 292 and 294, to which the court of first instance referred, which stresses the prevailing view that if the new state benefited from the works of the previous state then it must be responsible for them.

---

48 In fact, the name of the company is Compagnie d'Entreprises CFE, and not as spelled in the ILDC. See http://en.cfe.be/about-cfe/historique.aspx (last accessed 29 July 2018).

49 See the company's description of its history http://en.cfe.be/about-cfe/historique.aspx (last accessed 6 March 2018).

50 cf J Crawford, *The Creation of States in International Law* (2nd edn, OUP 2006) 705.

51 M Sørensen (ed), *A Manual of Public International Law* (MacMillan 1968).

52 Institut de Droit International, 'State Succession in Matters of Property and Debts', Session of Vancouver 2001 http://www.idi-iil.org/app/uploads/2017/06/2001_van_01_en.pdf (last accessed 6 March 2018).

53 P Dumberry, *State Succession to International Responsibility* (Martinus Nijhoff 2007) 278.

"These continue until altered by the new sovereign. They are binding on the new sovereign however, if at the time of the change-over they are vested or acquired. Thus a title to property or a claim to liquidated damages will pass. Damages are liquidated when the issue out of which they arose has been adjudicated and the amount fixed by a competent tribunal.

Some writers consider that any such payments made by the new state in respect of the public debt of its predecessor, are ex gratia; others claim such payments to be due by the operation of the rule *res transit cum suo onere* which is held to apply even if no benefit to the territory exists at all. The better view is that he who takes the benefit must take the burden. So where an identifiable region has benefited by public expenditure to an ascertainable extent, then whoever takes over that part of the territory takes over part of the public debt which corresponds to the benefit. The corollary to this is that no debt is assumed if no benefit attaches, even if the territory is expressly charged with the debt." Therefore, the reason for appeal concerning the claim that the decision of the court of first instance was mistaken in the judgment that the arbitrator examined the issue of state succession at length, is renounced. And so is the allegation that the Court applied the principles regarding the state succession issue in error.

S v Austria, Decision on final appeal, 1Ob149/02x, ILDC 1618 (AT 2002), 30th September 2002, Supreme Court of Justice [OGH]

The Austrian Supreme Court of Justice was also confronted with state succession and the (possible) extinction of a state in *S v Austria*. The case concerned an Austrian citizen (Mr S) who was sentenced to twenty-five years' imprisonment because of espionage by the Soviet occupants in Austria (from 1945 to 1955 Austria had been occupied and split into occupation zones among the Soviet Union, France, the UK, and the United States). He claimed compensation for the inhumane conditions of his 962-day imprisonment in the Soviet occupation zone and later a special prison in the Soviet Union, as well as the confiscation of his property.

Austria argued that there was no legal basis for these claims. After all, upon the end of the occupation it had renounced to act on its own behalf or that of its nationals for any acts that had occurred during this period in Article 24 of the State Treaty for the Re-Establishment of an Independent and Democratic Austria (signed by Austria and the occupying powers) from 1995.[54]

Austria then argued that this had left open the possibility to seek compensation from the Russian Federation, which had enshrined such a right in its 1991 Act on the rehabilitation of victims of political repression. Nevertheless, the deadline set therein had already passed.

The Austrian Supreme Court of Justice held that, since Austria failed to prove that its citizens were not excluded from claiming compensation under the 1991 act owing to the renunciation from 1955, it was presumed that Mr S could not have successfully addressed the Russian Federation.

In this connection, the Austrian Supreme Court of Justice also examined the legal nature of the end of the Soviet Union in light of state responsibility. In general, there are three approaches to this question. It can be interpreted as a series of separations from Russia (which would thus be legally identical with the Soviet Union), a dissolution, or, alternatively, the Russian Federation can be characterized as the 'continuator state' of the Soviet Union, while not being the same

54 State Treaty for the re-establishment of an independent and democratic Austria (signed 15 May 1955, entered into force 27 September 1955) 217 UNTS 223. Article 24 reads as follows:

> 1. Austria waives all claims of any description against the Allied and Associated Powers on behalf of the Austrian Government or Austrian nationals arising directly out of the war in Europe after 1st September, 1939, or out of actions taken because of the existence of a state of war in Europe after that date whether or not such Allied or Associated Power was at war with Germany at the time. This renunciation of claims includes the following: [. . .] (b) Claims arising from the presence, operations or actions of armed forces or authorities of Allied or Associated Powers in Austrian territory.

legal subject in the sense of international law (the latter option seems to have been met with the widest level of support).[55]

The Austrian Supreme Court of Justice held that there was no succession to state responsibility and that the extinction of a state also led to an extinction of its responsibility for its unlawful acts. While the lower court had characterized the end of the Soviet Union as a *dismembratio*, the Austrian Supreme Court of Justice emphasized that the international community—including Austria—had accepted the Russian Federation's declaration to continue the legal personality of the Soviet Union. It nevertheless stated that it was unnecessary to answer the question of whether the Russian Federation was a case of state succession or 'state continuation' because Mr S argued only that he could not seek redress against the Russian Federation because of Austria's renunciation of this right in 1955.

Since the Republic of Austria accepted that the Russian Federation continues the legal personality of the Soviet Union, it accepted the Russian Federation as signatory power of the State Treaty from Vienna. Therefore the waiver agreed upon in Article 24 [State Treaty] nowadays also applies to claims the applicant would have had absent this waiver.[56]

IX. Conclusion

The ILC's work on international responsibility has been met with a wide level of acceptance. Domestic courts routinely cite, discuss, and rely on the Articles on State Responsibility and the Articles on the Responsibility of International Organizations, as well as the respective commentaries. Only in a limited number of cases have they refrained from mentioning these documents, usually to the surprise of the ILDC commentators.[57]

In particular, higher courts do not shy away from lengthy discussions on state practice in general and domestic case law in particular, or the decisions of international courts and organizations or legal scholarship on issues relating to state responsibility. As the various cases on the Srebrenica genocide have shown, such judgments can ultimately also bind their own governments against their express will and line of argumentation.

Louis Henkin's famous finding (shared by many other venerable scholars before and after him) that states do generally not violate international law thus certainly holds true for the rules of state responsibility. Case law also shows that domestic courts are generally keen on respecting international law and doing their utmost to prevent wrongful conduct by their states. Fundamental insights such as the priority of international law over domestic law or the basic rules of attribution are established beyond doubt. States have also accepted that their responsibility could be triggered by extraditing or deporting individuals to countries where they could be subjected to torture, inhumane, or degrading treatment or the death penalty.

The Argentine debt crisis has shown how domestic courts are often not only confronted with similar questions but potentially even the same events. Ideally speaking, they would follow a coherent and uniform approach under such circumstances. The ILDC database can have an additional positive impact in this regard. After all, the law of state responsibility is one of those areas of international law that greatly benefit from additional judicial dialogue at all levels, be it between domestic courts or between domestic and international courts.

55 A Nußberger, 'Russia' *Max Planck Encyclopedia of Public International Law* (October 2009) paras 92-108.

56 *S v Austria*, Decision on final appeal, 1Ob149/02x, ILDC 1618 (AT 2002), 30th September 2002, Supreme Court of Justice [OGH], para 2.1 (author's translation).

57 Examples include H P Aust, Analysis, *Tornado case*, ILDC 819 (DE 2007) A2, or *Mukeshimana-Ngulinzira and ors v Belgium and ors* (n 19).

12

Use of Force

CHRISTY SHUCKSMITH AND NIGEL D WHITE

The selection below is largely confined to domestic cases arising out of recent conflicts (Iraq, Afghanistan, and Kosovo). Cases involving older uses of force have been excluded as they are generally poorly reasoned and do not reflect the heightened debate that recent, often controversial, uses of force have created. The selection is confined to cases that discuss the legality or otherwise of the use of force by states—the *jus ad bellum*—including military actions undertaken in self-defence, or under UN Security Council authority, as well as more contested claims (such as targeted killings). Many domestic cases where conflicts are in issue do not raise *jus ad bellum* matters but concern mistreatment of prisoners, violations of human rights, or international humanitarian law. They have been excluded as they will be dealt with elsewhere in this volume.[1]

The cases are divided into those that amount to a direct challenge to the legality of the use of force by the government of the state, where the court is directly faced with the difficult choice as to whether to get involved in such issues of high politics or whether to decline to exercise review on the basis of the executive, prerogative or non-justiciable nature of the powers being exercised by the government. Very rarely do such cases succeed, the courts being very reluctant to step into areas of foreign policy when potential constitutional crises at the time of decisions to go to war could be very dangerous and have destabilizing effects. The second set of domestic cases concern indirect challenge or review, where the legality of the war or use of force comes up as a defence or excuse for behaviour, or to support a claim of human rights abuse. It might be expected that such cases have a better chance of success since the government is not directly in the dock, but the evidence for this is scant.

I. Direct Legal Challenges

In *The Campaign for Nuclear Disarmament v The Prime Minister of the United Kingdom, The Secretary of State for Foreign and Commonwealth Affairs and The Secretary of State for Defence*,[2] the Campaign for Nuclear Disarmament (CND) sought an advisory declaration as to the true meaning of Security Council Resolution 1441 and, more particularly, as to whether it authorized states to take military action in the event of non-compliance by Iraq with its terms. Security Council Resolution 1441, on the situation between Iraq and Kuwait, was adopted following Iraq's failure to provide full disclosure of its weapons and its obstruction of weapons inspectors from the United Nations Special Commission (UNSCOM) and the International Atomic Energy Agency (IAEA). Security Council Resolution 1441 of November 2002 provided Iraq a final opportunity to comply with its disarmament obligations, and was adopted during the build-up to the invasion of Iraq in March 2003 by the United States (US) and the United Kingdom (UK).

---

1 See C Ryngaert, 'International Humanitarian Law' Chapter 13 in this volume.

2 *The Campaign for Nuclear Disarmament v The Prime Minister of the United Kingdom, The Secretary of State for Foreign and Commonwealth Affairs and The Secretary of State for Defence* [2002] EWHC 2777 (Admin), England and Wales High Court of Justice Queen's Bench Division (Divisional Court) UK, 17 December 2002, ILDC 662 (UK 2002) (*CND*).

Campaign for Nuclear Disarmament v Prime Minister of the United Kingdom and ors, Advisory declaration, Case No CO/5429/2002, (2002) EWHC 2777 (Admin), ILDC 662 (UK 2002), 17th December 2002, United Kingdom; England and Wales; High Court [EWHC]; Divisional Court

Lord Justice Simon Brown:

10 CND point out that an earlier draft of the resolution had provided not merely that non compliance with its terms should constitute a further material breach of Iraq's obligations but also "that such breach authorises Member States to use all necessary means to restore international peace and security in the area". The phrase "all necessary means" is widely recognised to encompass the use of force and indeed this form of words is to be found in Resolution 678 of 29 November 1990 by which Member States were authorised to act following Iraq's invasion of Kuwait. The omission of that clause from Resolution 1441 as adopted is, suggest CND, striking and significant. That consideration, they submit, coupled with ambassadorial statements exemplified by that made by the UK ambassador and, most importantly of all, the express text of the resolution by which any breaches must be reported back to the Council for it to deal with as it may then think appropriate, makes good their contention that breach of the resolution would not of itself authorise the taking of military action. Their case on the true construction of the resolution, they submit, is not merely arguable but strong. They further submit that it raises a sharp-edged question of law involving no considerations of policy, no disputed areas of fact, no consideration of the developing international situation. It is thus an issue upon which the court can and should decide. Such, in a nutshell, is the applicant's contention.

11 The defendants assert to the contrary that there are compelling reasons for the court not to embark upon such an exercise, prominent amongst them considerations of the national interest. It is in this connection that there is before the court a statement dated 5 December 2002 made by Mr Ricketts, Director General for Political Affairs at the Foreign and Commonwealth Office, who draws upon 28 years' experience closely involved in the United Kingdom's conduct of its international relations and diplomatic negotiations with foreign States. I must set out the bulk of this statement in full:

> 3. The claimants have asked that the Government explain its understanding of the legal position with regard to the interpretation of Security Council Resolution 1441 (2002). In the judgment of the Secretary of State and the Foreign & Commonwealth Office, and in my own opinion, however, it would be prejudicial to the national interest and to the conduct of the Government's foreign policy if the Government were to be constrained to make a definitive statement of its legal position under international law in relation to issues concerning the international relations of the United Kingdom. The short point is that it is an unavoidable feature of the conduct of international relations that issues of law, politics and diplomacy are usually closely bound up together. The assertion of arguments of international law by one state is in practice regarded by other states as a political act, and they react accordingly. The UK's international alliances could be damaged by the incautious assertion of arguments under international law which affect the position of those other states.

22 No longer are there any forbidden areas of executive action into which the courts simply cannot look; there are only aspects of decision making which the court must necessarily accept lie properly and solely with the executive, for example questions of policy and the substantive merits of factual decisions in sensitive fields like those of national security, defence and foreign relations. These are fields in which "the court is

> unequipped to judge such merits or demerits" and where in any event respect is properly due to the democratically elected government which is answerable politically for its actions. This case, however, runs the applicants' argument, raises no such considerations. There are no issues which CND seek to have decided here which touch on policy or the merits of any decision. Rather they seek a ruling on a pure point of law in the field of customary international law which is part of English common law. The courts should not refuse this invitation. They cannot justifiably accord to the executive the exclusive right to determine this question; on the contrary, it is a question altogether more appropriate for decision by the court in the exercise of its conventional supervisory jurisdiction: to ensure that those exercising public power have not erred in law in the classic sense of misunderstanding their legal powers.
>
> Skilfully and resourcefully though this argument was advanced it is clearly not without its difficulties. The first is its invocation of the principle that the common law encompasses also customary international law. Correct although this undoubtedly is, I have difficulty in understanding how it avails the applicants here. To engage in war without lawful justification is certainly contrary to the law of nations. The issue which the applicants seek to have determined here, however, is whether in the circumstances postulated war *would* be unlawful and that, of course, involves the interpretation of Resolution 1441 itself, a specific international treaty which clearly is ***not*** part of our domestic law. Ordinarily speaking, English courts will not rule upon the true meaning and effect of international instruments which apply only at the level of international law – see, most recently, *R -v- Lyons* [2002] 3 WLR 1562.
>
> 37 There is no distinction between the position of the United Kingdom and that of all other States to whom Resolution 1441 applies. Why should the English courts presume to give an authoritative ruling on its meaning? Plainly such a ruling would not bind other States. How could our assumption of jurisdiction here be regarded around the world as anything other than an exorbitant arrogation of adjudicative power?
>
> 38 The general rule is that, in the interests of comity, domestic courts do not rule on questions of international law which affect foreign sovereign states.
>
> 43 By constitutional convention the government will always comply with decisions of the court. Whatever the court were to declare the instrument to mean, the government could not ignore that ruling or assert some different meaning in its dealings with other States. And, indeed, the objections go further still. Were the court even to embark upon a hearing of the substantive issue the government would be placed in an impossible position. In practice it would be forced to adopt and argue its position before the court, the very thing that Mr Ricketts indicates would damage the conduct of our international relations. The objection, in short, is not merely to the court ever granting an advisory declaration, but in addition to the court even embarking on the argument.

Shucksmith's Commentary[3] on this case showed that CND brought a direct challenge in the UK as regards potential uses of force against Iraq in 2002. It wanted the Divisional Court to decide whether Security Council Resolution 1441, unanimously adopted on the 8 November 2002, authorized states to take military action in the event of non-compliance with its terms. It sought a declaratory ruling that a potential decision to go to war by the British government would be unlawful without a second Security Council Resolution.[4] Resolution 1441 provided Iraq 'a

3 See C Shucksmith, Analysis, *The Campaign for Nuclear Disarmament v The Prime Minister of the United Kingdom, The Secretary of State for Foreign and Commonwealth Affairs and The Secretary of State for Defence*, ILDC 662 (UK 2002).

4 *CND* (n 2) para 2.

final opportunity to comply with its disarmament obligations' and recalled that the Council had 'repeatedly warned Iraq that it [would] face serious consequences as a result of its continued violations of its obligations'.[5] CND, having heard conflicting statements from the UK Foreign Secretary in the weeks surrounding the adoption of Resolution 1441, stated that there was 'great public interest in ensuring that the government is adequately informed [and not misdirected] on this key question of law'.[6]

The case was brought at a crucial time in 2002, as the situation was still developing and there was no clear indication of British foreign policy that the court could consider. It was brought 'against the backdrop of the UK's military build-up along Iraq's southern border in late 2002'.[7] CND insisted that its claim was a pure question of law as the courts should 'ensure that those exercising public power have not erred in law in the classic sense of misunderstanding their legal powers'. Nevertheless, the court remained unwilling to rule on whether a decision to go to war, if taken, would require a second Security Council resolution.[8]

In this case, the defendant government claimed that British national interests, international relations and its foreign policy could all be detrimentally affected should it outline its legal position as regards use of force against Iraq.[9] First of all, it could have detrimentally affected negotiation of a second resolution. Furthermore, should a second resolution have allowed the use of force against Iraq, the enemy in the ensuing armed conflict would have already known the British legal 'bottom line' and possibly use that information to its advantage. The court agreed with these submissions and would not allow the case to proceed beyond preliminary issues. It stated that there was no sound basis for believing that the government had been wrongly advised as to the true position in international law.[10]

In addition to a consideration of British policy and governmental decisions to go to war, CND argued that prohibition of use of force by one state against another was customary law and is therefore part of UK law. Any use of force not in self-defence, it argued, requires UN Security Council authorization which was not provided by Resolution 1441, and therefore, an advisory declaration to prevent breach of custom 'fell within the court's common law supervisory jurisdiction'.[11]

The court recognized the inherent interface between international law and domestic courts and would have been willing to consider customary international law as it was encompassed in British common law.[12] However, specific treaties, including Security Council resolutions, are not considered part of domestic law and therefore British courts will not rule on their true meaning.[13] The court stated that 'there was no point of reference in domestic law to which the international law issue could be said to have gone; there was nothing susceptible to challenge in the way of the determination of rights, interests or duties under domestic law to draw the court into the field of international law'.[14] The court stated that there was no distinction between the position of the United Kingdom and that of all other states to whom Resolution 1441 applied.[15] The general rule was that, in the interests of comity, domestics courts do not rule on questions of international law which affect foreign sovereign states.[16]

---

5 UNSC Res 1441 (8 November 2002) UN Doc S/RES/1441, paras 2 and 13.
6 *CND* (n 2) para 5.
7 R O'Keefe, 'The Doctrine of Incorporation Revisited' (2009) 79(1) *British Yearbook of International Law* 7, 69.
8 *CND* (n 2) para 22.
9 ibid, para 11(3).
10 ibid, para 47 (iii).
11 O'Keefe (n 7) paras 69–70.
12 *CND* (n 2) para 17.
13 ibid, para 47(i).
14 ibid, para 36.
15 ibid, para 37.
16 ibid, para 38.

From 1958 to 20 September 2001, US military aircraft had the right, under Irish domestic law, of over-flight, landing, and refuelling on condition that the aircraft did not carry arms, explosives, ammunition, or engage in intelligence-gathering. The applicant in *Edward Horgan v Ireland and ors*[17] argued that the decision of the Irish government to allow US military aircraft to over-fly, land and refuel in the period January 2003 to March 2003 in the build up to the invasion of Iraq by the US and UK breached Ireland's obligations as a neutral state by permitting the movement of troops and/or convoys of munitions over its territory. In the statement of claim of 24 March 2003, it was argued that it was against Ireland's neutrality to allow over-flight and transit through Ireland of troops/convoys of either munitions or war supplies. It was argued that to do so equated to participation by Ireland in the war and was in breach of its constitution.

Horgan v Ireland and ors, Application for declaratory relief., 2003 No 3739P, [2003] IEHC 64, (2003) 2 IR 468, ILDC 486 (IE 2003), 28th April 2003, Ireland; High Court

> 32 In the aftermath of September 11th 2001, the Government made clear on the 21st September, 2001 that it would facilitate over flight, landing and refuelling of aircraft engaged "in pursuit of Resolution 1368". Resolution 1368 of the Security Council classified the terrorist attacks of 11th September 2001 as a threat to international peace and security. The resolution called on all States to work together urgently to bring to justice the perpetrators, organisers and sponsors of the attacks and called on the international community to redouble efforts to prevent and suppress terrorist acts.
>
> 33 A memo dated 16th September 2002 from the Political Division of the Department of Foreign Affairs states:—
>
> > "In making this offer of over flight and landing facilities, Ireland is not participating in a war, nor does it mean we have joined a military alliance. Rather, it is simply fulfilling its international legal obligations, acting in accordance with Irish Law, to assist a concerted international response to deal with the threat to international peace and security."
>
> 108 The final portion of para. 11 of the Statement of Claim asserts:—
>
> > "The said military attacks have not been authorised by the Security Council of the United Nations pursuant to Article 42 of its Charter. The attack by the said forces of the United States and of the United Kingdom upon the State of Iraq is contrary to the principles of international law and to the Charter of the United Nations and is unlawful."
>
> 109 Notwithstanding the inclusion of such a claim, the plaintiff has not, in the course of the hearing before this court, invited the court to adjudicate or rule specifically on this issue, asserting that the plaintiff need not do so at this juncture at least. The plaintiff reserved his position to argue the matter further, if necessary.
>
> 110 However, as the issue has been raised before the court and then left to one side, and while the court will not adjudicate upon the issue, it is useful in the context of the remaining issues to be determined to consider a recent, and one might add topical, decision of a Divisional Court in England in *CND v. Prime Minister of the United Kingdom* (judgment delivered on the 17th December 2002).[18] In those proceedings, the plaintiffs sought an advisory declaration as to the true meaning of U.N. Security

17 *Edward Horgan v Ireland and ors*, Application for declaratory relief, (2003 No 3739P); (2003) 2 IR 468; (2003) IEHC 64, Ireland, High Court, 28 April 2003, ILDC 486 (IE 2003) (*Horgan*).

18 *Campaign for Nuclear Disarmament v Prime Minister of the United Kingdom and ors*, Advisory declaration, Case No CO/5429/2002, (2002) EWHC 2777 (Admin), ILDC 662 (UK 2002), 17 December 2002, United Kingdom; England and Wales; High Court [EWHC]; Divisional Court.

> Council Resolution 1441 and more particularly as to whether it authorised States to take military action in the event of non compliance by Iraq with its terms.
>
> 115 The defendants contend, I believe correctly, that this case may be relied upon by the court as emphasising the strictly circumspect role which the courts adopt when called upon to exercise jurisdiction in relation to the Executive's conduct of international relations generally.
>
> 116 Thus, while the legality of the war in Iraq may well be, in the words of a recent article about these proceedings in an Irish national newspaper "the elephant in the room that is impossible to ignore", this case has proceeded in a manner where both sides have given that "elephant" a wide berth, a course which permits, indeed compels, this court to do likewise.
>
> 120 Despite the great historic value attached by Ireland to the concept of neutrality, that status is nowhere reflected in Bunreacht na hEireann, or elsewhere in any domestic legislation. It is effectively a matter of government policy only, albeit a policy to which, traditionally at least, considerable importance was attached.
>
> 121 Ireland is thus in a different position than certain other States, who have incorporated a permanent status of neutrality in their domestic laws.
>
> 122 Without exhaustively requoting from the charters, conventions and writings relied upon by the plaintiff in this case, I am satisfied that there does still exist in international law a legal concept of neutrality whereunder co-relative rights and duties arise for both belligerents and neutrals alike in times of war in circumstances where the use of force is not 'UN led'.
>
> 125 The court is prepared to hold therefore that there is an identifiable rule of customary law in relation to the status of neutrality where under a neutral state may not permit the movement of large numbers of troops or munitions of one belligerent State through its territory en route to a theatre of war with another.
>
> 135 One can only conclude therefore that principles of international law enter domestic law only to the extent that no constitutional, statutory or other judge made law is inconsistent with the principle in question. Where a conflict arises, the rule of international law must in every case yield to domestic law.
>
> 159 I have concluded therefore on this aspect of the case, that international law is only admissible in domestic law to the extent already indicated where in certain limited situations it may be availed of to determine private law claims, absent some contrary or conflicting provision of either the Constitution, statute law or common law. It may also avail other States in their dealings with this State on the international plane. It cannot however impose binding public law obligations on the Executive towards its own citizens under Article 29 for all the reasons stated.
>
> 172 Nonetheless, this court does accept, for all the reasons stated, that some quite egregious disregard of constitutional duties and obligations must take place before it could intervene under Article 28 of the Constitution. This court is not all persuaded that any untoward conduct has occurred such as would even warrant examining further the particular decision and resolution, yet alone making a determination as to their correctness or otherwise.

The challenge failed and it seems that the court was reluctant to hold that customary international law was automatically binding on Ireland, in particular if the constitution held an alternative route. It was also reluctant to judicially review a decision made by elected representatives to allow the use of the airport. The case shows inherent tensions between international law and domestic law. The claim centred on actions amounting to a breach of Ireland's duty as a neutral state and whether those actions actually amounted to participation in the war in Iraq.

It was claimed that under Article 29(3) of the Irish Constitution there was a breach of neutrality, customary international law and general principles of international law. The court would not consider the legality of the war in Iraq.[19] The court felt it was not an appropriate forum for supervising the government's foreign policy. 'It was not for the court to supplant its decision for that of elected representatives'.[20]

In *AWACS/Turkey Case, Parliamentary Group of the Liberal Democratic Party in the German Federal Parliament v The Federal Government*, Turkey requested that NATO member states protect its territory and airspace following a threat by Iraq to attack all US allies in the region in 2003. Approximately one-third of the personnel deployed on the surveillance operations were German. The claim was that the German Federal government failed to obtain a vote in the Bundestag (parliament) before deployment of German military personnel. This was a successful challenge that preparations for war in Iraq required the consent of parliament.

AWACS/Turkey Case, Parliamentary Group of the Liberal Party in the German Federal Parliament v Federal Government, Final judgment, 2 BvE 1/03, DVBl 2008, 770, EuGRZ, 2008, 312, NJW, 2008, 2018, ILDC 956 (DE 2008), 7th May 2008, Germany; Constitutional Court [BVerfG]

> 57 1. a) The Basic Law has entrusted decisions concerning war and peace to the German Bundestag as the representative body of the people. This is expressly laid down with regard to the determination of a state of defence and of tension (Art. 115a (1), Art. 80a (1) GG) and applies, furthermore, generally to the use of the armed forces, even in systems of mutual collective security in the sense of Art. 24 (2) GG. The Federal Constitutional Court has derived a general principle from the general context of the constitutional defense provisions of the Basic Law against the background of the German constitutional tradition since 1918, according to which any use of armed forces essentially requires the prior constitutive consent of the German Bundestag (BVerfGE 90, 286 <381 et seq.>). The provisions of the Basic Law applicable to the armed forces are so drafted as not to entrust the Federal Army as a potential factor of power to the executive authority alone, but to integrate it as a "parliamentary army" into the democratic constitutional arrangement of a state governed by the rule of law (cf. BVerfGE 90, 286 <381–2.>). […]
>
> 68 c) The requirement of parliamentary approval for the deployment of the armed forces (*wehrverfassungsrechtliche Parlamentsvorbehalt*) also and especially grants the Bundestag rights within the framework of this constellation of alliance policy. Not least because of the constitutional scope of the integration authorisation under Article 24 (2) GG, the requirment of parliamentary approval acquires a considerable weight. Since foreign engagements for the Bundeswehr can be based on this provision within the framework and under the rules of the system of mutual collective security, such deployments are constitutionally permissible without prejudice to the material obligations to peace-keeping contained in Art. 24 (2) and Art. 26 (1) 1. GG (cf. BVerfGE 104, 151 <212–3>; 118, 244 <261–2>) in various situations and beyond the limits largely assumed in the constitutional scholarship before 1994 (cf. Bähr, Verfassungsmäßigkeit des Einsatzes der Bundeswehr im Rahmen der Vereinten Nationen, 1994, pp. 175 et seq.; März, Bundeswehr in Somalia, 1993, pp. 13 et seq.).

19 *Horgan* (n 17) para 125.
20 ibid, H2.

69 German cooperation in the strategic overall alignment and decision-taking on concrete engagement of the alliance is very largely in the hands of the Federal Government; it essentially does not conflict with the constitutional allocation of powers that provide special leeway in the area of the government's authority in foreign matters, not least because this complies with the principle of organisationally permitted allocation of functions (cf. BVerfGE 68, 1 <87>; 104, 151 <207>). However the government's freedom to shape alliance policy does not include a decision as to who must decide within the state whether soldiers of the Bundeswehr may participate in a specific engagement decided within the alliance. On account of the political dynamics of an alliance system it is all the more important that the enhanced responsibility for the engagement of armed forces should lie in the hands of the body representing the people.

70 As the Court has already stressed, the Parliament's constitutional reservation on defence forms a substantial corrective as to the limits of parliamentary assumption of responsibility in the area of foreign security policy (cf. BVerfGE 104, 151 <208>; cf. also Röben, op. cit., p. 594). The extensive leeway for the executive power to shape matters in the foreign area ends with the application of military force. With regard to the engagement of armed forces, the German Bundestag not only plays the role of a scrutinising and only indirectly driving and controlling body, but it is required to take basic, constitutional decisions and has responsibility for the armed foreign deployment of the Bundeswehr. The Bundeswehr is accordingly a "parliamentary army", irrespective of the command structure (cf. Article 65a, Article 115b GG), which places operational guidance of the military back in the hands of the executive power. The German Bundestag can preserve its material influence over the use of armed forces only if it possesses effective co-determination rights over the use of such forces before a military enterprise is commenced which then becomes largely a question of military expediency.

This case is controversial as the decision concerned deploying forces to Turkey was part of a wider campaign against Iraq. The German government decided to send troops to Turkey to protect the latter's territory as part of its obligation as a NATO member. This case shows a struggle by the court to balance the requirement of parliamentary consent to military missions and the enhanced role of the executive in the application of its treaty commitments.[21] The German Federal government argued that since the operation was about protecting Turkish territory it was not a decision to go to war and, therefore, not the concern of parliament.

This case also questioned whether 'Operation Display Deterrence' conformed to the spirit and purpose of Article 4 of the NATO Treaty, which states that 'the Parties will consult together whenever, in the opinion of any of them, the territorial integrity, political independence or security of any of the Parties is threatened'. However, it is arguable that the deployment of NATO troops to Turkey, where the US was also building up coalition forces as well as using Turkish airspace to launch attacks against Iraq, could lead to use of force against Turkey by Iraq, perhaps in self-defence:[22] 'As a UN Security Council authorization clears almost all concerns on the lawfulness of the use of the armed forces, at least in terms of the jus ad bellum, deployments

21 *AWACS/Turkey Case, Parliamentary Group of the Liberal Party in the German Federal Parliament v Federal Government*, Final judgment, 2 BvE 1/03, DVBl 2008, 770, EuGRZ, 2008, 312, NJW, 2008, 2018, ILDC 956 (DE 2008), 7 May 2008, Germany; Constitutional Court [BVerfG], paras 68–70.

22 H P Aust, Analysis, *AWACS/Turkey Case, Parliamentary Group of the Liberal Party in the German Federal Parliament v Federal Government*, ILDC 956 (DE 2008) A4.

without such authorization should, in comparison, meet higher standards of parliamentary scrutiny'.[23]

The success of this case in contrast to others is that the focus was on the constitutional dimension under German domestic law, rather than the legality of the use of force under international law. Nevertheless, in the *CND* and *Horgan* cases reviewed above the courts were visibly reluctant to question governmental decisions to go to war, whether under domestic or international law, whereas in this case the court declared that parliament should have been involved in decision-making. According to this view, it is not just the prerogative of the government to make decisions regarding the use of force.

The case of *Association of Lawyers for Peace and ors v Netherlands*[24] dealt with the legal basis for the UK and the US military actions against the Taliban and Al-Qaeda training camps in Afghanistan which started on 7 October 2001. The Netherlands stated that it supported these military actions on the basis of the US/UK right to individual and collective self-defence following the terror attacks of 9/11. The Association of Lawyers for Peace and four other organizations requested the president to prevent any action so long as the UN Security Council had not ordered the use of force. The court was asked whether the UN Charter could be invoked before Dutch courts in the context of the war in Afghanistan.

Association of Lawyers for Peace (Vereniging van Juristen voor de Vrede) and ors v Netherlands, Judgment on Appeal in Cassation, C02/217HR, LJN: AN8071, NJ 2004/329, ILDC 152 (NL 2004), 6th February 2004, Netherlands; Supreme Court [HR]

> 3.4 Article 2(4) of the Charter of the United Nations includes a provision requiring all Members to refrain from the threat or use of force against the territorial integrity or political independence of any State. This prohibition on the use of force is therefore intended to protect States and a citizen cannot invoke this provision, or the closely related provisions in Articles 42 and 51 of the Charter, before his national courts. Article 90 of the Constitution does not lead to a different opinion. Although this article directs the government to promote the international legal order, neither this article nor any other article determines how this should be done.
>
> The Supreme Court observes in this connection that the present claims of the Association and Others relate to questions concerning the policy of the State in matters of foreign affairs and defence, and that such policy depends to a large extent on political considerations in connection with the circumstances of the case. It is not up to the civil courts to make these political decisions, even as regards the prohibition on the use of force, or to prohibit the State at the request of a citizen from carrying out certain acts in performance of political decisions in the field of foreign policy or defence or to order it to follow a particular course of action in this field. Nor is this altered by the argument that the prohibition on the use of force, when viewed in connection with the principle of individual responsibility for crimes against peace, is a rule of international law binding on all persons.
>
> Although an individual citizen can be held responsible under this principle for acting in contravention of the prohibition on the use of force, this does not in itself mean that an individual citizen can invoke the prohibition on the use of force in proceedings brought against the State on the basis of this principle.

---

23 H P Aust and M Vashakmadze, 'Parliamentary Consent to the Use of German Armed Forces Abroad: The 2008 Decision of the Federal Constitutional Court in the AWACS/Turkey Case' (2008) 9 *German Law Journal* 2223.

24 *Association of Lawyers for Peace (Vereniging van Juristen voor de Vrede) and ors v Netherlands*, Judgment on Appeal in Cassation, C02/217HR, LJN: AN8071, NJ 2004/329, ILDC 152 (NL 2004), 6 February 2004, Netherlands; Supreme Court [HR].

What also fails is the submission of the Association and Others that the prohibition on the use of force and Article 90 of the Constitution serves to protect fundamental rights such as the right to a peaceful international order, the right to life and the right to undisturbed enjoyment of personal possessions and that it therefore follows that the civil courts must examine the submissions of the Association and Others to the effect that the State is not observing the obligations resulting from Article 90 of the Constitution and that, as a result, the interests of the Association and Others are being unlawfully prejudiced. This argument fails if for no other reason than what has been held above and also because it fails to recognise that the Association and Others did not base their claims before the court hearing the facts on an infringement of these fundamental rights and that the question whether such an infringement occurred also requires an examination of a factual nature for which there is no place in cassation proceedings.

All arguments in the various parts of ground of appeal II fail in view of what has been held above.

The court stated that the claims of the association and organizations related to questions concerning state policy in matters of foreign affairs and defence, and that such policy depends to a large extent on political considerations in connection with the circumstances of the case. The court held that a citizen cannot invoke Articles 2(4), 42, and 51 of the UN Charter before a national court as the Charter was addressed to states only and may only be invoked by states.[25]

In the *Tornado Case*,[26] it was claimed that by German armed forces taking part in the International Security Assistance Force (ISAF) in Afghanistan since the removal of the Taliban regime in 2001, the German government was in violation of the rule that NATO's activities be geographically limited to the Euro-Atlantic region.

Tornado Case, Parliamentary Group of the PDS/Die Linke in the German Federal Parliament v Federal Government, Dispute between Supreme Federal Bodies (Organstreitverfahren), 2 BvE 2/07, EuGRZ 2007, 331, NVwZ 2007, 1039, NZWehrr 2007, 203, ILDC 819 (DE 2007), 3rd July 2007, Germany; Constitutional Court [BVerfG]

40 b) Under Article 24.2 of the Basic Law in conjunction with Article 59.2 sentence 1 of the Basic Law, the participation of Germany in a system of mutual collective security requires the consent of the legislature. This constitutional requirement of the specific enactment of a statute confers on the *Bundestag* as the legislative body a right of joint decision in the area of foreign affairs and in this respect it creates a right of the *Bundestag* in the meaning of § 64.1 of the Federal Constitutional Court Act (see BVerfGE 90, 286 (351); 104, 151 (194); see also BVerfGE 68, 1 (84–85)).

41 aa) The right of legislation under Article 59.2 sentence 1 of the Basic Law protects the competence of the *Bundestag* to decide jointly on the rights and duties of the Federal Republic of Germany created by international treaties, to the extent that the political relations of the Federal Government or matters of federal legislation are affected. The provision guarantees the legislative function of the legislative bodies in the area of foreign power; their consent in the form of the statute that ratifies a treaty under international law guarantees the domestic application of such treaties and covers the international action of the government within the framework of the treaty (see BVerfGE 58, 1 (37); 90, 286 (357); 104, 151 (194)).

---

25 J Fleuren, Analysis, *Association of Lawyers for Peace and ors v Netherlands*, ILDC 152 (NL 2004) A4.

26 *Tornado Case, Parliamentary Group of the PDS/Die Linke in the German Federal Parliament v Federal Government*, Dispute between Supreme Federal Bodies (Organstreitverfahren), 2 BvE 2/07, EuGRZ 2007, 331, NVwZ 2007, 1039, NZWehrr 2007, 203, ILDC 819 (DE 2007), 3 July 2007, Germany; Constitutional Court [BVerfG] (*Tornado*).

42 The consent of the German *Bundestag* to a treaty is not exhausted in a single act of cooperation when the treaty is entered into; on the contrary, it means the long–term assumption of responsibility for the political programme laid down in the treaty and in the Consent Act. The Consent Act is the foundation not only for the validity and application of the treaty in domestic law, but also for the legally relevant actions of the Federal Government under international law in connection with and on the basis of the treaty (see Wolfrum, *Kontrolle der auswärtigen Gewalt*, in: *Veröffentlichungen der Vereinigung der Deutschen Staatsrechtslehrer—VVDStRL* 56 (1997), p. 38 (54–55); Ress, *Verfassungsrechtliche Auswirkungen der Fortentwicklung völkerrechtlicher Verträge*, in: *Festschrift für Zeidler*, vol. 2, 1987, p. 1775 (1779–1780)). This applies in particular if the treaty is directed either towards integration or towards participation in a system of mutual collective security, as provided by Article 24.1 and 24.2 of the Basic Law in general and Article 23.1 of the Basic Law for the particularly integrated area of the European Union (see BVerfGE 104, 151 (195)).

43 In this connection, political actions on the basis of the treaty and its concretisation, that is the detailing and development in specific terms of the programme laid down in it, is the task of the Federal Government. In the area of foreign policy, the Basic Law has left the Government a broad latitude to carry out its tasks on its own responsibility. Both the role of parliament as the legislative body and also that of the judiciary are restricted in this area, in order that Germany's capacity to act in foreign and security policy is not restricted in a manner that would amount to a functionally inappropriate separation of powers (see BVerfGE 68, 1 (87–88); 104, 151 (207)). The consent of parliament to a treaty therefore at the same time empowers the government to further develop this treaty in the forms of international law, and the Consent Act contains the order for domestic application of the international–law resolutions passed on the basis of the treaty (see BVerfGE 104, 151 (209)).

59 3. The ISAF mission in Afghanistan cannot be seen as such a separation of NATO from its regional connections. For this mission is clearly directed not only to the security of Afghanistan but also and particularly to the security of the Euro–Atlantic area, from future as well as present attacks.

74 The violation of international law by individual NATO military operations, as asserted by the applicant, in particular the violation of the prohibition of the use of military force, may be an indicator that NATO is structurally departing from its constitutionally mandatory orientation towards the maintenance of peace. However, in this connection it must be taken into account that even violations of international law of this nature do not automatically in themselves constitute an infringement of Article 24.2 of the Basic Law that are capable of being challenged in *Organstreit* proceedings. For in the constellation of *Organstreit* proceedings an infringement of the requirement to maintain peace is only significant as the constitutional limit of the integration programme of a system of mutual collective security. The exceeding of this integration programme may be reviewed by the Constitutional Court in *Organstreit* proceedings only because it removes the treaty basis of the alliance from the responsibility of the German *Bundestag* and in doing so infringes the German *Bundestag*'s right under Article 59.2 sentence 1 of the Basic Law in conjunction with Article 24.2 of the Basic Law. Consequently, this supervision does not open the way for a general review as to whether NATO military operations are in conformity with international law. For the *Organstreit* proceedings are not a general review of lawfulness, but consider solely whether NATO's actions, in particular individual operations, show evidence that the alliance is departing from its founding treaty by giving up its orientation towards the

maintenance of peace. It is therefore only to clarify this question that Article 24.2 of the Basic Law enables supervision by the standards of international law, and only as indications of such a change of NATO's structure are such violations of international law constitutionally relevant in *Organstreit* proceedings.

88 But the fact that the operations are largely separate in law and in fact, as set out above, is an obstacle even to this encroachment. In addition, not only the ISAF mission itself, but also the cooperation with the Operation Enduring Freedom has its basis in resolutions of the Security Council under Chapter VII of the Charter of the United Nations; this conformity with the efforts of the United Nations directed to securing peace—independently of a clarification of the question as to whether the Operation Enduring Freedom taking place in Afghanistan at present is in accordance with international law—does not support a departure of NATO from its objective of maintaining peace.

In his commentary on this case,[27] Helmut Aust states that it was claimed that the Federal government contributed to an amendment of the North Atlantic Treaty by informal means, which were outside the statutory framework and infringed Article 59.2 of the Basic Law. The claim concerned whether NATO, in leading ISAF, first in Kabul then over the whole of Afghanistan, had violated the terms of the NATO treaty of 1949. The applicants argued that the 'development' of the NATO treaty by the Federal government following a single act of parliamentary consent given in 1949 was unlawful as true consent would include a 'long-term assumption of responsibility for the political program' by parliament.[28] The applicants contended that the NATO treaty was changed by the German government (and other NATO members) without parliamentary approval and by measures taken under the name of NATO that were in fact unlawful.[29] The German government had failed to involve the Bundestag in a formal legislative process.

In part, the concern of the applicants was that the region ISAF was working on in a mission to help secure Afghanistan was also home to Operation Enduring Freedom (OEF) under which the US was waging a war against terrorism in Afghanistan.[30] The court stated that from the point of view of constitutional law the only question is whether NATO-led ISAF (which had been authorized by Security Council resolutions)[31] was violating international law in Afghanistan through its cooperation with OEF, and whether it manifested a departure from the peace-maintaining objective of the alliance.[32] The court held the two operations—ISAF and OEF—were legally separate.[33]

The court would not discuss whether the 9/11 terrorist attack could be attributed to the Afghan Taliban regime under international law. It failed to decide whether OEF was entitled to continue to operate on basis of self-defence. It also did not rule on the role of the OEF under Security Council Resolutions 1368 and 1373.[34] Nor could it consider whether NATO member states, in particular the US, had breached international law in Afghanistan.

The court stated that it would not rule on these matters because armed actions in Afghanistan were a security issue and, as a failing or failed state, Afghanistan was a dangerous safe haven for

27 H P Aust, Analysis, *Tornado Case, Parliamentary Group of the PDS/Die Linke in the German Federal Parliament v Federal Government*, ILDC 819 (DE 2007) A4.

28 *Tornado* (n 26) para 42.

29 ibid, paras 13(a) and 14.

30 ibid, paras 50–54.

31 UNSC Res 1386 (20 December 2001) UN Doc S/RES/1386 (2001); UNSC Res 1510 (13 October 2003) UN Doc S/RES/1510.

32 *Tornado* (n 26) para 77.

33 ibid, paras 77–79.

34 ibid, para 66(c).

internationally operating terrorist groups.[35] The court appeared more concerned about not restricting actions that maintain the security of Germany rather than ruling on domestic or international legal matters.

The case raised, but did not resolve, wider concerns within the international community that states might be forced into action by virtue of their membership of NATO or the UN, which the state itself had not consented to, or rather the executive may have agreed to but parliament not. While, in the other case from Germany discussed above,[36] the court was prepared to declare that parliamentary approval was required for troop deployments—a clear constitutional requirement in Germany—in this case the more profound issue of interpreting and applying the rights and duties of Germany under the NATO treaty to issues of peace and security was considered not to be reviewable by the German court. The differences in the two cases may also be explained by the presence of a clear international legal basis for the deployment of ISAF in the form of authorizing Security Council resolutions, which were absent in the case of the war in Iraq in 2003.

In the *Kosovo Mission Case*,[37] it was argued that the continuing deployment of German troops to the NATO force (KFOR) in Kosovo was unconstitutional after the declaration of independence of Kosovo on 17 February 2008, owing to the alleged invalidity of Security Council Resolution 1244 of 1999 that had originally mandated the force. It was contended that such factual and legal changes necessitated the further agreement of the German parliament. The arguments presented thus required the Constitutional Court to address the legality of Resolution 1244.

Kosovo Mission Case, Parliamentary Group of the Left Party v Federal Government, Final judgment, 2 BvE 4/08, (2010) Neue Zeitschrift für Verwaltungsrecht-Rechtsprechungsreport 41, (2009) 35 Europäische Grundrechte-Zeitschrift 649, ILDC 1399 (DE 2009), 13th October 2009, Germany; Constitutional Court [BVerfG]

> H6 Resolution 1244 was a necessary condition for the *Bundestag's* decision. It was not evident that the Resolution had become invalid: it was still in force. It had not been revoked by the Security Council, nor had it been superseded by a new Resolution. The Resolution did not provide for a sunset clause or a time limit to the mandate, and the lack of consensus in the Security Council on the Comprehensive Proposal for the Kosovo Status Settlement, UN Doc S/2007/168/Add.1, 26 March 2007 ('Ahtisaari Plan') meant that the Resolution was—at least formally—still in force. (paragraph 26) The claims regarding the substantive validity of the Resolution under international law were not appropriate for decision by the Constitutional Court in '*Organstreit*' proceedings. (paragraph 27)

The court found that Resolution 1244 was still formally valid and therefore dismissed that aspect of the argument. In determining that the factual changes had not reached the threshold necessary to seek further parliamentary approval for continued troop deployed, the Constitutional Court might have been influenced by the 'fact that the International Court of Justice ("ICJ") was already considering a request by the General Assembly for an advisory opinion as to whether Kosovo's declaration of independence violated international law. The International Court of Justice (ICJ) subsequently held that there was no conflict between Kosovo's declaration of independence and Resolution 1244'.[38]

35 ibid, para 67.

36 *AWACS/Turkey Case, Parliamentary Group of the Liberal Party in the German Federal Parliament v Federal Government*, ILDC 956 (DE 2008).

37 *Kosovo Mission Case, Parliamentary Group of the Left Party v Federal Government*, Final judgment, 2 BvE 4/08, (2010) Neue Zeitschrift für Verwaltungsrecht-Rechtsprechungsreport 41, (2009) 35 Europäische Grundrechte-Zeitschrift 649, ILDC 1399 (DE 2009), 13 October 2009, Germany; Constitutional Court [BVerfG].

38 C A Djeffal, Analysis, *Kosovo Mission Case, Parliamentary Group of the Left Party v Federal Government*, ILDC 1399 (DE 2009) A7. See *Accordance with International Law of the Unilateral Declaration of Independence in Respect of Kosovo* (Advisory Opinion) [2010] ICJ Rep 403.

In a country where constitutional restraints and judicial review generally go further into issues of foreign policy than in many others,[39] the German courts are still hesitant when faced with directly questioning the legality of decisions to deploy troops to conflict or post-conflict zones, especially when those operations are multi-national in nature.

II. Indirect Legal Challenges

In *R (Gentle) v Prime Minister*,[40] the mother of a soldier killed in Iraq claimed a right to have an independent inquiry into the wider circumstances surrounding the death of Fusilier Gordon Gentle and his comrades on 24 June 2004, as part of the UK government's obligation to uphold the right to life under Article 2 of the European Convention on Human Rights (ECHR) incorporated into English law by the Human Rights Act 1998.

R (on the application of Gentle and another) v Prime Minister and Others, Appeal judgment, [2008] UKHL 20, [2008] 1 AC 1356, [2008] UKHRR 822, [2008] 3 All ER 1, [2008] 2 WLR 879, [2008] HRLR 27, ILDC 734 (UK 2008), 9th April 2008, United Kingdom; House of Lords [HL]

> Lord Bingham:
> It may be significant that article 2 has never been held to apply to the process of deciding on the lawfulness of a resort to arms, despite the number of occasions on which member states have made that decision over the past half century and despite the fact that such a decision almost inevitably exposes military personnel to the risk of fatalities. There are, I think, three main reasons for this:
>
> (1) The lawfulness of military action has no immediate bearing on the risk of fatalities. Indeed, a flagrantly unlawful surprise attack such, for instance, as that which the Japanese made on the US fleet at Pearl Harbour, is likely to minimise the risk to the aggressor. In this case, as Mr Sumption QC for the respondents pointed out, Fusilier Gentle died after Security Council Resolution 1546 had legitimated British military action in Iraq, so that such action was not by then unlawful even if it had earlier been so.
>
> (2) The draftsmen of the European Convention cannot, in my opinion, have envisaged that it could provide a suitable framework or machinery for resolving questions about the resort to war. They will have been vividly aware of the United Nations Charter, adopted not many years earlier, and will have recognised it as the instrument, operating as between states, which provided the relevant code and means of enforcement in that regard, as compared with an instrument devoted to the protection of individual human rights. It must (further) have been obvious that an enquiry such as the appellants claim would be drawn into consideration of issues which judicial tribunals have traditionally been very reluctant to entertain because they recognise their limitations as suitable bodies to resolve them. This is not to say that if the appellants have a legal right the courts cannot decide it. The respondents accept that if the appellants have a legal right it is justiciable in the courts, and they do not seek to demarcate areas into which the courts may not intrude. They do, however, say, in my view rightly, that in deciding whether a right

39 See G Nolte, 'Germany: Ensuring Political Legitimacy for the Use of Military Forces by Requiring Constitutional Accountability' in C Ku and H Jacobson (eds), *Democratic Accountability and the Use of Force in International Law* (CUP 2002) 231.

40 *R (on the application of Gentle and another) v Prime Minister and Others*, Appeal judgment [2008] UKHL 20, [2008] 1 AC 1356, [2008] UKHRR 822, [2008] 3 All ER 1, [2008] 2 WLR 879, [2008] HRLR 27, ILDC 734 (UK 2008), 9 April 2008, United Kingdom; House of Lords [HL].

exists it is relevant to consider what exercise of the right would entail. Thus the restraint traditionally shown by the courts in ruling on what has been called high policy – peace and war, the making of treaties, the conduct of foreign relations – does tend to militate against the existence of the right .... This consideration is fortified by the reflection that war is very often made by several states acting as allies: but a litigant would be required to exhaust his domestic remedies before national courts in which judgments would be made about the conduct of states not before the court, and even if the matter were to reach the European Court of Human Rights there could be no review of the conduct of non-member states who might nonetheless be covered by any decision.

[...]

Baroness Hale:

47. [...] the Attorney General's written advice of 7 March 2003 was very far from clear and unambiguous. The case for military action rested solely on United Nations authorisation. This in turn depended upon whether non-compliance with UN Security Council Resolution 1441 revived the authorisation "to use all necessary means" given by resolution 678 in 1990. The revival question was controversial enough. But more controversial still was whether revival depended upon a UN Security Council decision that resolution 1441 had not been complied with, or whether it would be sufficient if there were "strong factual grounds" to conclude that Iraq was in breach. The Attorney General judged that a court might well conclude that a further resolution was required, but "equally the counter view can be reasonably maintained". The "safest legal course" would be a further resolution, establishing that the Council had concluded that Iraq had failed to comply with resolution 1441, even if it did not authorise the use of force in so many words. On 17 March 2003, however, having obtained the Prime Minister's unequivocal view that Iraq had committed further material breaches, the Attorney General advised Parliament of his concluded view that "the authority to use force under resolution 678 has revived and so continues to this day". The order to begin the invasion was given the following day.

53. Not surprisingly, the mothers of these young men wanted to know how and why their sons had died. The circumstances surrounding their deaths must have raised many questions in their minds. The Army inquiries took time and they did not feel that they had been kept fully informed. They felt, with some justification, that even in a situation of armed conflict these particular deaths might have been avoided. But on top of those inquiries they wanted to know why their sons had been sent to Iraq at all. What they really want is an inquiry into whether or not the conflict in which their sons died was lawful. The original claim form sought "a declaration that as article 2 ECHR has been violated an independent inquiry must be held and that its remit is to examine all the circumstances of these deaths including whether the decision to use force against Iraq was lawful". If the use of force was lawful, it would be of some comfort to know that their sons had died in a just cause. If it was not, there might at least be some public acknowledgement and attribution of responsibility and lessons learned for the future. If my child had died in this way, that is exactly what I would want. I would want to feel that she had died fighting for a just cause, that she had not been sent to fight a battle which should never have been fought at all, and that if she had then some-one might be called to account.

54. However, the only way to compel such an inquiry is through article 2 of the European Convention on Human Rights. This requires, not only that the state itself shall not take life, and should have a system of laws in place to protect the right to life,

but also "that the authorities [should], do all that can reasonably be expected of them to avoid a real and immediate risk to life of which they have or ought to have knowledge": *Osman v United Kingdom* (1998) 29 EHRR 24, para 116. The duty to respect and protect life can only be made effective by implying an ancillary duty to hold an independent inquiry into deaths where this duty may have been broken: *McCann v United Kingdom* (1995) 21 EHRR 97. There is no point in banning the secret police from killing people in their custody if no-one will ever find out when they do. But there can be no duty to hold an inquiry unless what has happened is at least arguably a breach of the substantive duty to respect and protect life.

55. For the reasons explained earlier, I wish that we could spell out of article 2 a duty in a state not to send its soldiers to fight in an unlawful war. States should protect their soldiers from the consequences of having in practice to obey orders whether or not they are lawful. It might be possible to discover such a duty in the words from *Osman* quoted in the previous paragraph. Sending troops into battle involves a real and immediate risk to their lives, let alone to the lives of others. While it cannot reasonably be expected that states will decline to commit their troops to a lawful war, because states must be allowed to defend themselves and to assist in international efforts to restore peace and stability, it might reasonably be expected that they would decline to commit their troops to an unlawful war. If the European Court of Human Rights in Strasbourg wishes to take article 2 so far, I would be surprised but not at all unhappy.

56. But I do not think that we can go so far. It goes way beyond what member states might have thought that they were committing themselves to in 1950. Although the Convention is a living instrument, not to be interpreted only according to its original intention, we must tread very carefully before implying obligations which are not already there [. . .]. [. . .]

57. I cannot reasonably foresee that Strasbourg would construct out of article 2 a duty not to send soldiers to fight in an unlawful war. The lawfulness of war is an issue between states, not between individuals or between individuals and the state. As already seen, the Statute of the International Criminal Court has not yet changed that. Furthermore, the lawfulness of a war has no direct link with the risk to the soldiers' lives. Soldiers are just as likely to die in a just cause as in an unjust one. Fusilier Gentle died shortly after United Nations Security Council Resolution 1546 of 8 June 2004, which on any view legitimated the multi-national force's attempts to restore security and stability in Iraq: see *R (Al-Jedda) v Secretary of State for Defence* [2007] UKHL 58; [2008] 2 WLR 31. A totally unjustified surprise attack may be much less risky than a properly declared war. It would not meet the real concerns in this case to decide that Trooper Clarke's death required an article 2 inquiry while Fusilier Gentle's did not.

58. A further reason not to spell such a duty out of article 2 is that it would require both the domestic courts of this country, and the European Court of Human Rights in Strasbourg, to rule upon the legality of the use of force against Iraq in international law. This is beyond our competence. The state that goes to war cannot and should not be the judge of whether or not the war was lawful in international law. That question can only be authoritatively decided, not by us or by Strasbourg, but by the international institutions which police the international treaties governing the law of war. But if there were such a right, the domestic courts would have to do their best to decide if it had been broken, because the Human Rights Act 1998 requires us to decide whether or not a public authority has acted compatibly with the Convention rights.

The UK House of Lords (now the Supreme Court) has been reluctant to review decisions of high policy, especially those involving decisions to go to war, whether these arise from direct challenge to the legality of the decision (as in the *CND* case above), or where the challenge indirectly points to a review of the legality of the decision to go to war as in this case, which involved a challenge on the basis of a violation of the right to life of a British soldier killed in the Iraq War.[41]

Despite their ultimate refusal to consider the legality of the war by implying into Article 2 of the ECHR a duty not to send soldiers to fight in unlawful wars, the opinion of Baroness Hale questions the quality and soundness of the legal advice given by the attorney general to the prime minister just before the invasion of Iraq in March 2003, labelling the 'revival' argument' (namely the revival of the authorization to use force given by the Security Council in Resolution 678 of 1990) as 'controversial', and questioning the changes made to the Attorney General's advice so as to remove any doubts he had about such an argument.[42] Nevertheless, Baroness Hale stops short of calling into question the legal basis of the war, and, with Lord Bingham, takes the opportunity to make it clear that whatever the legal basis of the initial invasion, by the time that Fusilier Gentle was killed there was a clear legal basis for the UK presence in southern Iraq, in the form of Security Council Resolution 1546 of 2004.

Although the court did take the opportunity to make clear that the operation was lawful, at least at the time Fusilier Gentle died, the tenor of the judgment is that decisions concerning war and peace are to be dealt with at the international level, although the emphasis placed on the role therein of international courts and other institutions[43] is unconvincing, given Britain's possession of the veto on the UN Security Council and the restricted competence of the ICJ.

In *R v Jones and ors*,[44] anti-(Iraq) war activists broke into a Royal Air Force (RAF) base and committed criminal damage, claiming in their defence that they were justified in that their actions were aimed at trying to prevent a greater crime being committed—the crime of aggression.

R. v Jones (Margaret) and ors, Appeal Judgment, [2006] UKHL 16, [2007] 1 AC 136, [2007] 2 WLR 772, [2006] 2 All ER 741, [2006] 2 Cr App R 9, (2002) 2 CAR 128, ILDC 380 (UK 2006), 29th March 2006, United Kingdom; House of Lords [HL]

> Lord Bingham:
>
> 29. [...] what has become an important democratic principle in this country: that it is for those representing the people of the country in Parliament, not the executive and not the judges, to decide what conduct should be treated as lying so far outside the bounds of what is acceptable in our society as to attract criminal penalties. One would need very compelling reasons for departing from that principle.
>
> 30. [...] A charge of aggression, if laid against an individual in a domestic court, would involve determination of his responsibility as a leader but would presuppose commission of the crime by his own state or a foreign state. Thus resolution of the charge would (unless the issue had been decided by the Security Council or some other third party) call for a decision on the culpability in going to war either of Her Majesty's Government or a foreign government, or perhaps both if the states had gone to war as allies. But there are well-established rules that the courts will be very

41 See further *Smith and Others (FC) v The Ministry of Defence* [2013] UKSC 41. The UK Supreme Court's finding that the UK had jurisdiction for ECHR purposes over soldiers operating in combat situations outside their bases in *Smith v MOD* in 2013 was a major step from the *R (Smith) v Oxfordshire Deputy Coroner* [2010] UKSC 29 in which the UK Supreme Court restricted the application of ECHR to soldiers within their bases. See also the case of Baha Mousa, who died while in a British detention facility in Iraq — *R (Al-Skeini) v Secretary of State for Defence* [2007] UKHL 26 before the UK House of Lords and *Al-Skeini v UK* (2011) 53 EHRR 589 before the European Court of Human Rights.

42 *R (on the application of Gentle and another) v Prime Minister and Others*, Appeal judgment (n 40) para 47.

43 ibid, para 58.

44 *R. v Jones (Margaret) and ors*, Appeal judgment, [2006] UKHL 16, [2007] 1 AC 136, [2007] 2 WLR 772, [2006] 2 All ER 741, [2006] 2 Cr App R 9, (2002) 2 CAR 128, ILDC 380 (UK 2006), 29 March 2006, United Kingdom; House of Lords [HL].

slow to review the exercise of prerogative powers in relation to the conduct of foreign affairs and the deployment of the armed services, and very slow to adjudicate upon rights arising out of transactions entered into between sovereign states on the plane of international law.

31. [. . .] The potential and readily foreseeable problems which might arise if it were permissible to impede military preparations or action by the existing government in this country on the ground of their unlawfulness would not end there. For a person so acting could, at least arguably, on facts more significant than those relied on here, be said to "be adherent to the King's enemies in his realm, giving to them aid and comfort in the realm, or elsewhere" within the meaning of the Treason Act 1351, or to commit the common law offence of sedition by exciting disaffection against the government or the constitution. It has never been a defence to such a charge that the Crown or the government had committed itself to an unjust or unlawful cause. It would be strange if the same conduct could be both a crime and a defence. [. . .]

I am of the clear opinion that the crime of aggression is not a crime in the domestic law of England and Wales within the meaning of section 3.

The reluctance of the UK courts to review the exercise of prerogative powers is very evident here,[45] influencing its decision that the crime of aggression was a crime under international law and not domestic law, in the face of ancient and more recent judicial statements that customary international law was part of UK law.[46] The contention is that parliament is to decide what should be criminal under domestic law, and although the International Criminal Court Act has incorporated war crimes and crimes against humanity into domestic law, the failure to define aggression in the Rome Statute of the ICC meant that it was not part of English law. With the recent definition of aggression by the state parties to the Rome Statute,[47] raising the prospect of its potential incorporation into English law, such a judgment may prove more difficult in the future. If the crime of aggression did become part of UK domestic criminal law then the courts will find it very difficult to hide behind prerogative powers, since the essence of the crime is about the very nature and legality of decisions to go to war.

In *Attorney of the Federal Armed Forces v Anonymous (A Major of the Armed Forces)*, the defendant (an officer in the German armed forces) had been convicted of disobeying orders by refusing to work on operations that he considered might help the prosecution of the invasion of Iraq in March 2003. The defendant claimed that his actions were justified because he held the view that the war against Iraq was illegal under international law—a system of norms he viewed as an ethical minimum, which he argued should be protected by his constitutional right to freedom of conscience. The court felt it necessary to review the legality of the war against Iraq in order to assess the seriousness of the soldier's decision, ultimately upholding his appeal against conviction.

Attorney of the Federal Armed Forces v Anonymous (a Major of the Armed Forces), Final appeal, BVerwG 2 WD 12.04, ILDC 483 (DE 2005), 21st June 2005, Germany; Federal Administrative Court [BVerwG]

4.1.4.1.1 At that time grave legal concerns already existed about the offensive military action initiated by the governments of the USA and the UK on 20 March

45 A Bohm, Analysis, *R. v Jones (Margaret) and ors*, ILDC 380 (UK 2006), A1; N D White, *Democracy Goes to War: British Military Deployments under International Law* (OUP 2009) 22–25, 383–87; See C Villarino Villa, 'The Crime of Aggression before the House of Lords: Chronicle of a Death Foretold' (2006) 4 *Journal of International Criminal Justice* 866.

46 *R v Keyn* (1876) 2 Ex D 63; *R v Bow Street Magistrates, ex parte Pinochet (No 1)* [2001] 1 AC 61 at 91 (Lord Lloyd). See discussion of these cases in *R. v Jones (Margaret) and ors* (n 44) para 23.

47 Review Conference Kampala, Res RC/Res.6, 11 June 1010.

2003 regarding the prohibition of the use of force in the UN Charter and other international law.

In principle "any" threat and use of military force against another state is contrary to international law according to Art. 2(4) of the UN Charter. This strict prohibition of the use of force is in accordance with the established case law of the International Court of Justice (cf. among others *"Military and Paramilitary Activities in and against Nicaragua"* ICJ Reports 1996, pp. 14, 97 et seq., item 183 et seq.) and is at the same time part of international customary law and is counted as *"ius cogens"* (cf. see among others Heintschel von Heinegg in Knut Ipsen <Ed.>, *Völkerrecht*, op. cit., § 15 margin note 53 et seq. [59]; Kadelbach, *Zwingendes Völkerrecht*, 1992, p. 228 et seq with further notes). It is directly binding on all states, regardless of whether they are members of the United Nations or not. The prohibition of the use of force consequently belongs according to s. 25 of the German Basic Law on the "general rules of international law", which according to this constitutional rule are a "part of Federal Law", "take precedence over" interstatal laws and "produce direct rights and duties for the inhabitants of the territory of the Federation."

Under the UN Charter, military force may—exceptionally—be used against the will of the state affected thereby, but only when this is allowed by a legally recognised justification in the individual case.

The UN Charter only provides two such legally recognised justifications. Firstly the UN Security Council can decide on the use of military measures after formally determining an "act of aggression," a "breach of the peace" or at least a "threat to international peace and security" in accordance with Art. 39 of the UN Charter and either carry these out under its own responsibility (Art. 42, 43 UN Charter) or authorise other states (Art. 48 UN Charter) or a "regional system" (Art. 53 UN Charter) to do the same. Furthermore, the use of military force is only allowed if a state alone or in co-operation with its allies is entitled to the right to self-defence in accordance with Art. 51 of the UN Charter.

A state which—for any reason—disregards the prohibition on the use of force in international law and the UN Charter and resorts to military force without such a legally recognised justification, acts contrary to international law. It commits an act of military aggression.

1. a) Contrary to their legal opinion(s) expressed to the UN Security Council in formal diplomatic notes at the beginning of the fighting, the governments of the USA and the UK could not invoke any Resolution(s) of the UN Security Council authorising them in accordance with Art. 39 and 42 of the UN Charter to go to war against Iraq. According to these notes on 21st March 2003 (UN Doc.S/2003/351) the government of the USA relied exclusively and the government of the UK (UN Doc.S/2003/350) referred decisively on Resolutions 678 (1990) and 687 (1991) which had been passed by the UN Security Council after the military occupation of Kuwait by the Iraqi armed forces in 1990 (cf. Bothe, *Archiv des Völkerrechts* <*AVR*> 2003, 255 [259 et seq]). In the Spring of 2003 these did not however represent any effective basis for authorisation for military action against Iraq according to international law.

UN Resolution 678 of 29 November 1990, with which the UN Security Council had authorised Kuwait's allies at that time to employ "all required means" (including military) to liberate Kuwait from the then invading Iraqi troops, could no longer serve as a basis of authorisation for the military action of the USA and its allies against Iraq in the Spring of 2003—thus more than a decade later (cf. see among others Bothe, *AVR*

2003, 255 [263 et seq] with further notes). The objective of this authorisation from 1990, namely to drive the Iraqi aggressors out of Kuwait, had already been achieved in 1990/91. It had thus become obsolete and consequently stopped being a basis for an authorisation of the deployment of military force in 2003. In addition, neither the USA nor its allies had been authorised in 1990/91 to overthrow and disarm the regime of Saddam Hussein in Iraq by military means and bring about a change of political system, which were however the declared (or in any case subsequently conceded) objectives of the war which had begun in the spring of 2003.

Resolution 687 (1991) of 3 April 1991 on the conclusion of an armistice with Iraq, additionally invoked by the governments of the USA and the UK in their notes sent to the UN Security Council at the beginning of their military action against Iraq (UN Doc.S/2003/351 and UN Doc.S/2003/350), was also out of the question as a basis for authorisation of the war in the spring of 2003. The detailed Resolution contained at that time numerous conditions for a formal cease-fire between Iraq and Kuwait and the UN Member States cooperating with Kuwait. Firstly, the text referred to the Resolutions passed earlier by the UN Security Council and established that Kuwait had regained its sovereignty, independence and territorial integrity and that its government had returned. On the other hand Iraq was threatened with "serious consequences" in case of further deployment of gas or bacteriological weapons. Part C of the Resolution recorded Iraq's obligations in relation to its stocks of munitions, subsystems and components and all research, development, support and production facilities. In paragraph 32 of the Resolution the UN Security Council required "Iraq to inform the Security Council that it will not commit or support any acts of international terrorism or allow any organisation directed towards commission of such acts to operate within its territory and to condemn unequivocally and renounce all acts, methods and practices of terrorism." In paragraph 33 of the Resolution the UN Security Council at that time declared "that, upon official notification by Iraq to the Secretary-General and to the Security Council of its acceptance of the provisions above, a formal cease-fire is effective between Iraq and Kuwait and the Member States cooperating with Kuwait in accordance with resolution 678 (1990)." In keeping with this the UN Security Council determined in its further Resolution 707 (1991) passed on 15 August 1991, that considering Iraq's resulting written agreement to fully implement Resolution 687 (1991), the preconditions for a cease-fire stated in paragraph 33 of the said Resolution had been fulfilled. Although the UN Security Council in Resolution 707 (1991) established numerous breaches by Iraq against Resolution 687 (1991), it refrained from lifting the cease-fire. Nor was there any lifting of this legally effected cease-fire at a later time. The claim of some states to be able despite this to decide independently on a termination of this cease-fire consequently conflicted with this. It further conflicted with the declaration by the UN Security Council in Resolution 687 (1991) to decide on further steps in the UN Security Council itself.

The UN Resolutions cited did not represent a legally recognised justification for the initiation of military action—despite the cease-fire legally effected in 1991 — against Iraq by the USA and its allies on 20 March 2003 without prior authorisation by the UN Security Council (in the event likewise among others *Ausarbeitung für die Wissenschaftlichen Dienste des Deutschen Bundestages* of 2 January 2003, in Ambos/Arnold <eds.>, op. cit., p. 224 [227 et seq.]; Bothe, *AVR* 2003, 255 [263 et seq.]).

This also applies for the Resolutions passed by the UN Security Council in the period following the end in 1991 of Iraq's war against Kuwait: 688 (1991) of 5 April 1991, 707 (1991) of 15 August 1991, 715 (1991) of 11 October 1991, 986 (1995) of 14 April 1995 and 1284 (1999) of 17 December 1999. Insofar as the UN Security Council passed these Resolutions on the appointment and sending of a UN inspection team (UNSCOM and since 1999 UNMOVIC) to detect and destroy nuclear, biological and chemical weapons systems possibly present in Iraq, they in particular did not empower the use of military force against Iraq. Neither did they provide that cooperation with the UN inspection team would be enforced by military means nor for the overthrowing of Saddam Hussein's regime by war. This arises directly from the wording of the said Resolutions and requires no further explanation.

All the further Resolutions passed by the UN Security Council on the Iraq conflict in the following period equally contained no authorisation for belligerent action by the government of the USA and its allies against Iraq (also *Ausarbeitung für die Wissenschaftlichen Dienste des Deutschen Bundestages* of 2 January 2003, op. cit. [p. 228 et seq.]; Bothe, *AVR* 2003, 255 [264 et seq.]; Murswiek, *NJW* 2003, 1014 [1015 et seq.]; Bruha in Lutz/Gießmann <eds.>, *Die Stärke des Rechts gegen das Recht des Stärkeren*, 2003, p. 289 et seq. and on the website of the *Deutsche Gesellschaft für die Vereinten Nationen e. V.*, http://www.dgvn.de/publikationen). This applies in particular for Resolution 1441 (2002) which was passed unanimously by the UN Security Council on 8 November 2002 after weeks of negotiations (original text in English at: http://www.un.org./doc; German translation at: VN 2002, 232 et seq). This established a relatively precise regime in terms of content and timing for the demands made on the Iraqi government and the principles for the work of the UNMOVIC inspection team and the International Atomic Energy Authority (IAEA), which was supposed to start activities in Iraq no later than 45 days after the passing of the UN Resolution, thus no later than 23 December 2002, and to conclude the same with a report to the UN Security Council a further 60 days later, thus no later than 21 February 2003. In the case of the Iraqi offices not cooperating fully with the inspection teams on the implementation of the Resolution or impeding them in any way, the head of UNMOVIC, Hans Blix, and the Director General of the IAEA, Mohamed El-Baradei, were directed to report this immediately to the UN Security Council so that the latter could discuss the resulting situation in order to ensure "international peace and security." It remained open what decisions the UN Security Council would pass in such a situation. In paragraph 13 of this Resolution the UN Security Council nevertheless recalled that it had repeatedly warned Iraq in the past and threatened that Iraq should expect "serious consequences as a result of its continued violations of its obligations." It did not specify what these "serious consequences" would consist of. However, after weeks of deliberations the UN Security Council expressed unequivocally in this Resolution 1441 (2002) in paragraph 14 that it would continue to deal with the matter (even after it was passed) itself. It thereby made it clear that it was not prepared to relinquish the matter, but—as provided in the UN Charter—would decide itself (also) in the future what consequences should result from misconduct by Iraq in connection with the implementation of the relevant UN Resolution(s). Consequently, with this Resolution 1441 (2002) and in particular with the wording chosen in paragraph 13 ("serious consequences") it ultimately issued a "mere" unspecified warning, while however consciously refraining from approving or otherwise legitimising the use of force sought by the governments of the USA and the UK. According to the UN Charter measures of military force against Iraq would only have been allowed if the UN Security Council had positively approved the use of force according to the text of the Resolution—within the limits drawn by the UN Charter. Such a "silence" and vagueness about the type of "serious consequences" that the Security Council had used as a threat did not suffice as a basis for authorisation. For in principle "any" threat and use of military force against another state is contrary to international law according to Art. 2 (4) UN Charter, as long as the UN Security Council in accordance with the UN Charter has not decided the contrary as regards the use (and the threat) of force, or in the exceptional case of the right to self-defence in accordance with Art. 51 UN Charter. This cannot be countered by saying that the representatives of the USA and the UK would not have voted in the UN Security Council for the finally passed version of Resolution 1441 (2002) if they had not seen enough opportunities for interpretation in the compromises in wording therein to make their assessment of an authorisation for war against Iraq at least tenable. What state agents "thought" on deliberations and decision-making in the UN Security Council is however not conclusive for determining what the UN Security Council adopted in such a Resolution. It matters rather what made its way into the text of the Resolution passed. If that is missing, the appropriate decision-making process is lacking. Mental reservations of state agents or their superiors are thus not relevant in international law. As evidenced by the text of Resolution 1441 (2002), the UN Security Council did particularly not decide an exception to the fundamental prohibition on the use of force. There is nowhere any talk of authorisation or empowerment of any government or state for the use of force in accordance with chapter VII of the UN Charter. The term "authorisation" does not even appear in the text of the Resolution in this context. The attempt to achieve an authorisation for the use of military means after all through a further Resolution immediately before the start of the war by the governments of the USA, the UK and the Kingdom of Spain did not obtain the majority in the UN Security Council. The relevant draft Resolution was withdrawn to avoid a defeat in voting.

2. b) Neither could the USA and its allies invoke Art. 51 UN Charter for the military action against in Iraq that began in the spring of 2003.

According to its wording Art. 51 UN Charter merely grants the "inherent right" to individual or collective self-defence "if an armed attack occurs" (the English version in this respect shows no deviation from the equally conclusive four other treaty languages according to Art. 111 UN Charter), until the UN Security Council has taken the appropriate measures to guarantee world peace and international security. Even if a number of questions exist as to the scope and limits of this right to self-defence, it applies in any case only "if an armed attack occurs." The use of armed force must have taken place or be taking place by the aggressor, before defensive military strikes are allowed.

Currently, there is admittedly insufficient clarity on when an "armed attack" begins to exist within the meaning of Art. 51 UN Charter (see the references on views in domestic and foreign specialist literature at Nolte in Ambos/Arnold <eds.>, op. cit., p. 303 [306 et seq.]; Bothe in: Graf Vitzthum <ed.>, *Völkerrecht*, 2nd edition 2001, 8. section, margin note 9; Breitwieser, *NZWehrr* 2005, 45 [56 et seq.]).

The governments of some states have repeatedly also claimed a so-called right to "preventive self-defence," invoking Art. 51 UN Charter or international customary law. Here the argument was put forward that due to the state of development and the destructive power of modern weapons as well as the short warning times it would not be appropriate to expect that states must first "wait for" their threatened destruction by the opponent's first deployment of weapons, before they themselves could become militarily active. This has however remained disputed (see on the one hand Randelzhofer in Simma <ed.>, *Charter der Vereinten Nationen*, 1st edition. 1991, Art. 51 margin note 9 to 14 and 34; idem. in Simma <ed.>, *The Charter of the United Nations*, 2nd edition 2002, Art. 51 margin note 39 with further notes; Horst Fischer in Knut Ipsen, *Völkerrecht*, op. cit., § 59 margin note 30, and on the other hand the documentation among others at Murswiek, op. cit., [1016, footnote 12] and Nolte, op. cit. [p. 307]). Despite this some governments

> have admittedly continued in the ensuing period to claim such a right for themselves and others. However, there has been no relevant general acceptance of this in customary law. Such military deployments have until today regularly met with opposition (see the references at Bothe in Graf Vitzthum <ed.>, op. cit., footnote 22; *Ausarbeitung für die Wissenschaftlichen Dienste des Deutschen Bundestages* of 2nd January 2003, op. cit. [p. 227 et seq]).
>
> Even those who advocate a broader interpretation of Art. 51 UN Charter hold the use of military force according to the so-called Webster formula of 24 April 1841 (going back to the then US Foreign Secretary Daniel Webster) at best permissible in an emergency (see the references at Nolte, op. cit. [p. 307]), which is "instant, overwhelming, leaving no choice of means and no moment for deliberation", cf. State Secretary Webster, quoted after Horst Fischer in Knut Ipsen, *Völkerrecht*, op. cit., § 53 margin note 30). The formation of a consistent practice of states in international law and a common legal opinion ("*opinio iuris*") on the existence of a "preventive right of self-defence" going beyond this, and thereby part of customary international law, cannot be established. Even according to the allegations of the governments of the USA and the UK there was no such emergency ("instant, overwhelming, leaving no choice of means and no moment for deliberation") in the spring of 2003. Their diplomatic notes to the UN Security Council of 21 March 2003 already addressed above, do not substantially claim the contrary. The claim originally publicly asserted of a threat by Iraq's weapons of mass destruction as justification for the deployment of military force remained in the realm of political declarations, and was in particular not part of the legal justification to the UN Security Council. In addition it was moderated or even taken back by influential members of the US government (see among others Tomuschat, *Friedenswarte* 78 <2003>, 141 [149], referring to an interview with the deputy US Defence Secretary Paul Wolfowitz in the periodical "Vanity Fair" of 9 May 2003, among others, published by the US Ministry of Defence; Wolfowitz declared that the government's official justification of the war was intended for the public and was developed to overcome "bureaucratic" resistance in the administration and because "it was the one issue that everyone could agree with"; it was more important that a success in the Iraq war would probably make the presence of US troops in the neighbouring Kingdom of Saudi Arabia superfluous [http://www.defenselink.mil/transcripts/2003/tr20030509-depsecdef0223.html]). The decision-makers in the US government—as is also shown by the content of their diplomatic note to the UN Security Council of 21 March 2003—obviously thought that Iraq was not a suitable case for justifying invocation of the right to self-defence according to Art. 51 UN Charter (thus correctly among others Bothe, *AVR* 2003, 253 [261 et seq]; cf. further among others Horst Fischer, *HuV-I* 16 <2003>, 4 et seq., 6; Tomuschat, op. cit. [144 et seq.]; Kurth, *ZRP* 2003, 195 et seq., respectively with further notes).
>
> Accordingly, the Secretary-General of the United Nations, Kofi Annan, also called the military invasion of Iraq, which was carried out in the spring of 2003 by the USA and its allies, an "illegal act" (cf. among others dpa (German Press Agency) report of 16 September 2004).

The court was willing to determine that the war on Iraq was illegal under international law in order to assess the validity of a defence to disobeying orders.[48] This decision should be contrasted not only with the UK decision in *R v Jones*, but also with the parallel UK case when Flight Lieutenant Malcolm Kendall-Smith argued that he could not be obliged to be sent to Iraq to fight what he saw as an illegal war. At his court martial for refusing to obey orders, the Judge

48 *Attorney of the Federal Armed Forces v Anonymous (a Major of the Armed Forces)*, ILDC 483 (DE 2005) H2–H5.

Advocate convicted him, ruling that the order was not unlawful since it was given after UN Resolutions had authorized the presence of a multi-national force in post-invasion Iraq; but the judge also ruled that it was no defence that the defendant believed the order to be unlawful.[49]

The willingness of the German court to accept arguments about the illegality of uses of force in a case, where it is essentially used as a defence, can be contrasted with the courts' hesitation when faced with direct challenge to the legality of decisions to use force. In the other country where the use of forces has been litigated—the UK—the courts in contrast show an unwillingness to discuss the legality of such issues in either type of case.

III. Conclusion

This chapter has shown that the legality of the use of force by the government of the state has been challenged through direct and indirect cases brought before domestic courts. In direct legal challenges, the key concern for the court is whether it is willing and able to reach decisions on the legality of the use of force given its highly-politicized nature. The cases considered in this chapter highlight the overall reluctance of courts to get involved in such matters. In *Edward Horgan v An Taoiseach and ors*, for example, the court felt it was not an appropriate forum for supervising the government's foreign policy: 'It was not for the court to supplant its decision for that of elected representatives'.[50] The Parliamentary Group of the Liberal Democratic Party in the *German Federal Parliament v The Federal Government* case focused on the constitutional dimension under German domestic law, rather than the legality of the use of force under international law and the court declared that parliament should have been involved in decision-making. The chapter considered a number of German Constitutional Court cases and highlighted the nuances in decisions by the court on whether, and to what extent, it was prepared to review decisions to use force.

Indirect challenges concern instances when use of force is defensive or to support a claim of human rights abuse. Even these latter cases are seldom decided by domestic courts. In *R (Gentle) v Prime Minister*, for example, the tenor of the judgment is that decisions concerning war and peace are to be dealt with at the international level. The analysis of the limited case law in this area reveals that domestic courts have made no significant contributions to the application of international law to decisions by states to threaten or use force. The approach seems to be that such fundamental rules of international law concerning the most rudimentary forms of behaviour by states are best left to traditional forms of dispute resolution on the inter-state plane (the ICJ and the UN Security Council), and not within national legal orders.

49 Unreported case summarized in *R (Gentle) v The Prime Minister* [2006] UKHL 20 para 50 (Baroness Hale).
50 *Horgan* (n 17) H2.

13
International Humanitarian Law

CEDRIC RYNGAERT

I. Introduction

Domestic courts typically deal with questions of international humanitarian law (1) when located in a state which is involved in armed conflict or occupation (eg, Israel, but also states deploying troops in out-of-area operations such as the United States (US)), or in which armed conflict has recently taken place (eg, the newly independent republics of the former Yugoslavia); or (2) when located in a third ('bystander') state that is/was not involved in the armed conflict in question but that allows the exercise of universal jurisdiction over war crimes (eg, the Netherlands).

As far as court decisions in (post-)conflict states are concerned, the quantity and quality of such decisions depend heavily on the existence of a functioning and independent judiciary. In many (post-)conflict states, this is not a given. It is no surprise then that the sheer majority of cases (recently made available) come from one jurisdiction: Israel, a state which, while engaged in an armed conflict with the Palestinian side, nonetheless functions very much as a normal rule of law-based state. It boasts independent courts that are willing to censure the state and the military for transgressions of international humanitarian law.

That being said, there are a substantial number of cases available from other jurisdictions, and not only from Western states involved in out-of-area military operations (eg, the US, United Kingdom (UK)).

The individual criminal responsibility of alleged perpetrators of international humanitarian law violations, and the exercise of universal jurisdiction over such perpetrators, are not covered in this chapter, but in the chapters on international criminal law and jurisdiction respectively.

II. The Self-executing Character of International Humanitarian Law Treaties in Domestic Courts

One of the major obstacles to international humanitarian law litigation in domestic courts is the possible lack of a private right of action under international humanitarian law treaties considered as not self-executing. Lacking a private right of action, individuals who are allegedly victims of international humanitarian law violations cannot file suit against states for compensation on the basis of international humanitarian law conventions, such as the 1907 Hague Conventions and the 1949 Geneva Conventions. Notably, US and Japanese courts have refused to give direct effect to international humanitarian law conventions. Some of the leading cases are discussed in this section. In Israel, by contrast, it is accepted that individual plaintiffs can directly rely on applicable international humanitarian law to contest decisions taken by the Israeli Defense Forces and the government. Combined with the ongoing occupation of the Palestine Territories by Israel, there is unsurprisingly a wealth of Israeli case law available, a sizable portion of which is discussed later in this contribution.

United States, Linder et al v Calero Portocarrero et al, Judgment of 17 September 1990, 747 F.Supp. 1452 (S.D. Florida 1990) (not in ILDC)

The case of *Linder et al v Calero Portocarrero et al* concerns a US national (Benjamin Linder) who moved to Nicaragua to aid the Sandinista government. In 1987 he was tortured and killed by a patrol of the Nicaraguan democratic forces, who belonged to the so-called 'contras' who were supported by the US. The plaintiffs thereupon brought suit against three contra organizations and four individuals in a US court. Count IV of the plaintiffs' amended complaint presented a claim for damages resulting from the defendants' alleged violation of common Article 3 of the First Geneva Convention, the Second Geneva Convention and the protocols thereto:

> A treaty will only provide a basis for the enforcement of *private rights* in domestic courts if it is self-executing—that is, if it prescribes rules by which private rights may be determined [...] Whether an international agreement is self-executing is a matter of interpretation to be determined by the courts. [...] "In determining whether a treaty is self-executing courts look to the intent of the signatory parties as manifested by the instrument, and, if the instrument is uncertain, recourse must be had to the circumstances surrounding its execution." [...] Courts which have considered the issue have almost uniformly determined that the Geneva Conventions are not self-executing. [...] The Geneva Conventions expressly call for implementing legislation, and therefore the First and Second Geneva Conventions are not self-executing [...]. While Plaintiffs cite commentary to the Conventions as evidence that the creation of private rights was intended, they cite no language to this effect within the agreement itself. Furthermore, the Plaintiffs fail to cite us to any case law which has held the Geneva Conventions to be self-executing. We can see no reason to find contrary to unanimous precedent on this issue. *(747 F.Supp. 1463)*

Iraq and Afghanistan Detainees Litigation, Re, Mohammed Ali and ors v Colonel Pappas and ors, Trial court order, 479 F.Supp.2d 85 (D.D.C. 2007), ILDC 812 (US 2007), 27th March 2007, United States; District of Columbia; District Court for the District of Columbia [DDC]

That the Geneva Conventions were not self-executing, and thus provided no private cause of action, was reaffirmed by the District Court of Columbia in the 2007 *Iraq and Afghanistan Detainees Litigation*. In this litigation, nine plaintiffs alleged that they were innocent civilians who had been tortured and abused while detained by the US military at various locations in Iraq and Afghanistan. Each plaintiff ultimately was released from custody without ever being charged with a crime. The plaintiffs advanced six causes of action, which included breach of the Geneva Convention relative to the Protection of Civilian Persons in Time of War (Geneva Convention IV).[1] Citing long-standing US court practice and engaging in a textual analysis of the relevant provisions of Geneva Convention IV, the District Court held, not surprisingly, that it was not self-executing.

> 58 The Court is not convinced that Geneva Convention IV is self-executing and establishes individual rights that may be judicially enforced via private lawsuits in federal courts. "Absent authorizing legislation, an individual has access to courts for enforcement of a treaty's provisions only when the treaty is self-executing, that is, when it expressly or impliedly provides a private right of action." [...] None of the provisions of Geneva Convention IV contain any such express or implied language indicating that persons have individual "rights" that may be enforced under the treaty. Instead, the provisions of Geneva Convention IV state general obligations with regard to the treatment of protected persons that are imposed on signatory States.

The idea that the Geneva Conventions are not self-executing was in fact already enunciated in *Johnson v Eisentrager* (1950), in which the US Supreme Court held in a footnote, in respect of a challenge by twenty-one German nationals to their 1945 convictions for war crimes by a

1 Geneva Convention relative to the Protection of Civilian Persons in Time of War (Geneva Convention IV) (signed 12 August 1949, entered into force 21 October 1950) 75 UNTS 287.

military tribunal convened in Nanking, China and to their subsequent imprisonment in occupied Germany:

> 'We are not holding that these prisoners have no right which the military authorities are bound to respect. The United States, by the Geneva Convention of July 27, 1929, 47 Stat. 2021, concluded with forty-six other countries, including the German Reich, an agreement upon the treatment to be accorded captives. These prisoners claim to be and are entitled to its protection. It is, however, the obvious scheme of the Agreement that responsibility for observance and enforcement of these rights is upon political and military authorities. Rights of alien enemies are vindicated under it only through protests and intervention of protecting powers as the rights of our citizens against foreign governments are vindicated only by Presidential intervention'.[2]

Not only may US courts refuse to give direct effect to international humanitarian law treaties regulating the conduct of hostilities or protecting combatants and civilians, they have also held that conventions outlawing the use of certain weapons do not create private causes of action. *Stutts and ors* is illustrative in this respect.

Stutts and ors v De Dietrich Group and ors, Stutts and ors v Deutsche Bank AG and ors, District court decision, No 03-CV-4058 (EDNY 2006), ILDC 874 (US 2006), 30th June 2006, United States; New York; District Court for the Eastern District of New York [EDNY]

US military servicemen and civilian employees of contractors who were deployed in the Persian Gulf region during the 1991 Gulf War were allegedly exposed to toxic agents contained in chemical weapons developed or otherwise obtained by the Iraqi government and detonated by the United States and its allies during the Gulf War. The plaintiffs brought suit against foreign corporations that had allegedly sold chemical agents and manufacturing equipment to Iraq, that were used to develop the chemical weapons, and businesses that had issued letters of credit which has been relied upon for the sale of said goods. The servicemen and civilian employees sought compensatory and punitive damages against the bank defendants under, amongst other legal instruments, the Geneva Protocol for the Prohibition of the Use in War of Asphyxiating, Poisonous or Other Gases, and of Bacteriological Methods of Warfare (Geneva Protocol).[3] As in *Linder*, discussed above, the question arose whether there was a private right of action for individuals under the Geneva Gas Protocol.

> 25 ... courts hold that the Geneva Conventions are not self-executing treaties and routinely reject private claims brought under them. See, e.g., Argentine Republic v. Amerada Hess Shipping Corp., 488 U.S. 428, 442 (1989) (Geneva Convention on the High Seas, 13 U.S.T. 2312, does not create a private right of action, but sets forth substantive rules of conduct and states that compensation shall be paid for certain wrongs); United States v. Fort, 921 F. Supp. 523, 526 (N.D. Ill. 1996) ("The courts have consistently held that the Geneva Conventions ... are not self-executing and, thus, provide no basis for the enforcement of private rights in domestic courts."). Accordingly, since the Geneva Convention is not self-executing and Congress has not passed implementing legislation, plaintiffs have no private right of action under the Convention.

Similar cases have arisen in Japan, notably in the 1990s when a barrage of compensation claims was brought by private plaintiffs against the Japanese government relating to civilian suffering during the Second World War. Without exception, Japanese courts have held that such plaintiffs

2 *Johnson v Eisentrager* 339 US 763 (1950), 789, fn 14.

3 Geneva Protocol for the Prohibition of the Use in War of Asphyxiating, Poisonous or Other Gases, and of Bacteriological Methods of Warfare (Geneva Gas Protocol) (signed 17 June 1925, entered into force 8 February 1928) 26 UST 571, 94 LNTS 65.

do not have the right to claim compensation under international humanitarian law, and the Hague Convention in particular, for damages suffered during the Second World War.

Japan, X et al v the State, Tokyo District Court, Judgment, 27 July 1995; H.T. 894 (197) (1995), 39 Japanese Annual of International Law 265-66 (1996) (not in ILDC)

The Japanese case of *X et al* concerned Korean nationals whose brothers and fathers were allegedly arrested, transported, and murdered by the Japanese military police on accusation of espionage right after the end of the Second World War in a Japanese-occupied territory which is now part of Russia. They filed a claim against the state of Japan for compensatory damages, the publication of an apology and the restoration of their honour. The claims are partly based on international law. See also the similar cases discussed below.

> [Article 3 of the Hague Convention] expressly lays down the responsibility of the belligerents to pay damages. This being so, the purpose of this provision can only be interpreted as to define the state's responsibility and cannot be interpreted to obligate the state to pay damages to each individual of the belligerent state.
>
> [...] Regarding the existence of international customary law as alleged by the plaintiffs, neither the general practice nor the conviction (*opinio juris*) that the state has a duty to pay damages to each individual when that state infringes its obligations under international human rights law or international humanitarian law can be said to exist.

Japan, X et al v the State, Tokyo District Court, Judgment, 30 November 1998; H.T. (991) 262 (1999), 42 Japanese Annual of International Law 143-150 (1999) (not in ILDC)

X et al v the State concerned Dutch nationals who were interned in Japanese detention camps during the Japanese occupation of South East Asia in World War II, and who were allegedly subjected to forced labour, cruel treatment or sex slavery, filed a claim against the Japanese state for compensatory damages. The claim was based on Article 3 of the Hague Convention and on customary international law.

> Article 3 of the Hague Convention only stipulates international responsibility of a State for its violations of the Regulations annexed thereto toward the injured State. It must be stated that in the courts of Japan, individuals who suffered damages by those acts of armed forces members in violation of international humanitarian law cannot claim for compensation against the State to which the offenders belonged. True, according to the evidence, today it is to be admitted that views exist which recognize the possibility of individual claims. Those are all personal views, however, and cannot be upheld by the present Court.
>
> ... since Article 3 of the Hague Convention cannot be a ground to support the claim, it is clear that a rule of international law of the same content, even if it existed, cannot serve as the basis for the claim. Moreover, even if the allegation by the plaintiffs pointed to the existence of international customary law recognizing direct individual claims for compensation against the offending State irrespective of Article 3 of the Hague Convention, there exist no such rules of international customary law to date.

The Tokyo District Court approached the question of whether private plaintiffs could derive individual rights to file suit against a state from Article 3 of the Hague Convention from the angle of the doctrine of direct effect of treaties coupled with an application of various methods of treaty interpretation. The court inquired whether, objectively speaking, the content of individual rights was sufficiently clearly defined in the Hague Convention, and whether state parties in fact intended to establish individual rights. Applying Articles 31 and 32 of the 1969 Vienna Convention on the Law of Treaties as customary law, it gave a negative answer to both questions. Historically, indeed, the treaties were only concerned with inter-state relations and did not confer rights on individuals. Only through the (discretionary) state-to-state mechanism of diplomatic protection could individuals have justice.

Varvarin Bridge Case, 36 citizens of Yugoslavia v Germany, Constitutional complaint, 2 BvR 2660/06, 2 BvR 487/07, ILDC 2238 (DE 2013), EuGRZ 2013, 563, DÖV 2013, 946, 13th August 2013, Germany; Constitutional Court [BVerfG]

A reasoning similar to the one made by US and Japanese courts was made in the *Varvarin Bridge* case,[4] brought by Serb victims of the NATO military operation in Serbia (1999), notably the bombardment of a bridge, in which Germany participated. The legal question was again whether the Hague and Geneva Conventions conferred rights on individuals to claim compensation from an allegedly responsible state (Germany in this case) for international humanitarian law violations of which those individuals were victims. The Constitutional Court answered in the negative.

> H2 There was no rule of customary international law, as applicable in German courts pursuant Article 25 of the Basic Law, according to which victims of armed conflict had an individual right to compensation for violations of international humanitarian law against the alleged wrongdoing state.
>
> H3 Neither Article 3 of the 1907 Hague Regulations nor Article 91 of Additional Protocol I could serve as a legal basis for individual claims. Firstly, these rules were not self-executing … Secondly, neither Article could be understood as providing a right to compensation to individual victims of armed conflict.… Claims for international wrongful acts still had to be taken up by the national state.

Association France-Palestine Solidarité (AFPS) and Palestine Liberation Organization (PLO) v Société Alstom transport SA and ors, Appeal judgment, No 11/05331, ILDC 2036 (FR 2013), 22nd March 2013, France; Île-de-France; Versailles; Administrative Court of Appeal

A French appeals decision demonstrates that, apart from individuals, also *non-governmental organizations* may not be entitled to invoke international humanitarian law conventions in domestic courts, let alone against *corporations*. Unlike states, the latter have no (or at least very limited) international legal personality. In the case, two French corporations had participated in a company which had signed a concession contract with Israel to construct a tramway. The tramway's trajectory included paths over the occupied territories, purportedly in violation of international humanitarian law.

> H2 The international legal norms invoked by the [French-Palestine Solidarity Association] and the PLO did not include the right of individuals or non-state organizations to invoke them before the court. (paragraph 91)
>
> H3 Veolia and Alstom had neither signed these conventions nor were recipients of the obligations contained therein. Therefore they could not be considered as subjects of international law. Since they were deprived of international personality, it was not possible to apply these conventions against them. (paragraph 109)

Japan, Ryuichi Shimoda et al v the State, District Court of Tokyo, 7 December 1963, 8 Japanese Annual of International Law 212 (1964). 32 ILR 626, 640-642 (not in ILDC)

If one does not accept that individuals enjoy private rights of action under the international humanitarian law conventions in the first place, the question of whether states are entitled to waive their rights to bring claims against other states on behalf of the former's aggrieved nationals on the basis of peace treaties becomes moot. A waiver does not violate the rights of individuals, as

4 For a discussion see K F Gärditz, 'Bridge of Varvarin' (2014) 108 *American Journal of International Law* 86; S Mehring, 'The Judgment of the German Bundesverfassungsgericht concerning Reparations for the Victims of the Varvarin Bombing' (2015) 15(1) *International Criminal Law Review* 201.

the state waives *its own* rights, not the rights of individuals. This is borne out by the District Court of Tokyo's decision in *Shimoda*,[5] in which victims of the atomic bombing of Hiroshima and Nagasaki by the US sought to engage the Japanese state's responsibility on the ground that it had waived claims of Japanese nationals against the Allied Powers.

> Article 19(a) of the Treaty of Peace with Japan, which was signed at San Francisco on September 8, 1951, and came into force on April 28, 1952, provides:
>
> > 'Japan waives all claims of Japan and its nationals against the Allied Powers and their nationals arising out of the war or out of actions taken because of the existence of a state of war, and waives all claims arising from the presence, operations or actions of forces or authorities of any of the Allied Powers in Japanese territory prior to the coming into force of the present Treaty.'
>
> [...] it must be pointed out that a State has the power to waive the claims of its nationals under municipal law. A State has, as a function of its sovereignty, the power to create, modify and extinguish rights and duties of its nationals in accordance with the due process of its municipal law; it is therefore possible in theory for a State to undertake, as against another State, to waive the rights of its nationals which have such character in relation to the State, setting aside the question of the propriety of such an undertaking.
>
> [...] Such being the case, the plaintiffs had no rights to lose, and therefore there is no reason for regarding the defendant State as legally responsible to the plaintiffs for an unlawful act.

All foregoing judgments, which did not accept the argument that international humanitarian law conventions provided a private cause of action, are based on a conservative reading of the convention. Israeli case law, however, shows that some domestic courts may be willing to allow private plaintiffs to directly invoke provisions of international humanitarian law treaties. Moreover, the international community has recently pushed for more rights for victims of gross violations of human rights and international humanitarian law. In particular, the Basic Principles and Guidelines on the Right to a Remedy and Reparation for Victims of Gross Violations of International Human Rights Law and Serious Violations of International Humanitarian Law, adopted and proclaimed by the General Assembly in 2005 (the German Constitutional Court refers to an earlier version of this document in the judgment cited above), provides that '[a] victim of a gross violation of international human rights law or of a serious violation of international humanitarian law shall have equal access to an effective judicial remedy as provided for under international law'.[6] The preamble to this document refers to Article 3 of the Hague Convention. While this may not render that provision directly applicable in the domestic legal order, a tendency is clearly discernible to the effect of granting victims of international humanitarian law violations standing in courts and other grievance mechanisms to obtain reparation. This could be done through a domestic statute that confers private rights of action on individuals in respect of violations of international humanitarian law (eg, *habeas corpus* petitions in case of detention),[7] or that refers back to international humanitarian law or international human

5 Japan, *Ryuichi Shimoda et al v the State*, District Court of Tokyo, 7 December 1963, 8 *Japanese Annual of International Law* 212 (1964) 32 ILR 626, 640–42. See also R A Falk, 'The Shimoda Case: a Legal Appraisal of the Atomic Attacks upon Hiroshima and Nagasaki' (1965) 59 *American Journal of International Law* 759; H Fujita, 'Reconsidération de l'affaire Shimoda: analyse juridique du bombardement atomique de Hiroshima et Nagasaki' (1980) 19 *Revue de droit pénal militaire et de droit de la guerre* 49.

6 UNGA, 'Basic Principles and Guidelines on the Right to a Remedy and Reparation for Victims of Gross Violations of International Human Rights Law and Serious Violations of International Humanitarian Law' UNGA Res 60/147 (16 December 2005) UN Doc A/RES/60/147, para 12.

7 See the discussion on the cases dealing with detention below.

rights law. Examples of statutes creating causes of action in respect of international humanitarian law are the US Alien Tort Statute[8] and the US Uniform Code of Military Justice (UCMJ).[9] In *Salim Ahmed Hamdan v Donald H Rumsfeld, Secretary of Defense*, the US Supreme Court held in respect of the UCMJ, Article 21 of which provides that '[t]he provisions of this code conferring jurisdiction upon courts-martial shall not be construed as depriving military commissions, provost courts, or other military tribunals of concurrent jurisdiction in respect of offenders or offenses that by statute or *by the law of war* may be tried by such military commissions, provost courts, or other military tribunals'[10] (emphasis added):

> For, regardless of the nature of the rights conferred on Hamdan, cf. *United States* v. *Rauscher,* 119 U. S. 407 (1886), they are, as the Government does not dispute, part of the law of war. See *Hamdi,* 542 U. S., at 520.521 (plurality opinion). And compliance with the law of war is the condition upon which the authority set forth in Article 21 is granted (slip op. pp. 64-65)

In view of the *renvoi* of a *domestic statute* to the law of war, the court held that the *Eisentrager* footnote, quoted above, was not controlling, thereby overruling the Court of Appeals. Thus, on the basis of the UCMJ, the Geneva Conventions, being part of 'the law of war', *could* create enforceable rights for individuals such as Hamdan, an Al-Qaeda member arrested by US forces in Afghanistan, in the US legal order. Such *renvoi* could, however, easily be withdrawn by the US Congress, as indeed happened when Congress adopted the Military Commissions Act 2006, 120 Stat 2600, section 948b(g) of which provides that '[n]o alien unlawful enemy combatant subject to trial by military commission under this chapter may invoke the Geneva Conventions as a source of rights'.

III. Qualification of Conflict

By its very nature, international humanitarian law only applies in times of armed conflict. The exact qualification of a conflict is therefore crucial, also in light of the fact that different international humanitarian law rules apply to international and non-international conflicts. A number of domestic courts have been asked to qualify certain conflicts for the purpose of applying international humanitarian law—the law of international or non-international armed conflict as the case may be. Two cases, one from the Russian Federation (facing a conflict in Chechnya) and one from the US (fighting a global war on terror against Al-Qaeda), are discussed in this section.

In this judgment,[11] the Russian Constitutional Court tested the constitutionality of a number of Presidential Decrees relating to the conflict in Chechnya in light of the Constitution, including its Article 15, paragraph 4 of which provides that both general and conventional international law shall be part of the Russian legal system. On the basis of this Article, the court reviewed the Decrees in light of Additional Protocol II to the Geneva Conventions.[12]

8 28 US § 1350 ('The district courts shall have original jurisdiction of any civil action by an alien for a tort only, committed in violation of the law of nations or a treaty of the United States').

9 64 Stat 115.

10 548 US 557 (2006).

11 For a longer discussion see P Gaeta, 'The Armed Conflict in Chechnya before the Russian Constitutional Court' (1996) 7 *European Journal of International Law* 563; T G Morshchakova, 'The Chechen War Case and Other Recent Jurisprudence of the Russian Constitutional Court' (1998) 42 *Saint Louis University Law Journal* 743; W E Pomeranz, 'Judicial Review and the Russian Constitutional Court: the Chechen Case' (1997) 23 *Review of Central and East European Law* 9.

12 Protocol Additional to the Geneva Conventions of 12 August 1949, and relating to the Protection of Victims of Non-International Armed Conflicts (Additional Protocol II) (adopted 8 June 1977, entered into force 7 December 1978) 1125 UNTS 609.

Russian Federation, Constitutional Court of the Russian Federation, 31 July 1995, Sobranie zakonodatelstva Rossiyskoy Federatsii, 1995, No. 33, Art. 3424. An unofficial English translation of this judgment has been published by the European Commission for Democracy through Law of the Council of Europe, CDL-INF (96) 1 (see also ICRC website, not in ILDC)

> 5. … The Supreme Soviet of the USSR having ratified Protocol Additional to Geneva Conventions of 12 August 1949 relating to the protection of victims of non-international armed conflicts (Protocol II), have charged the Counsel of Ministers of the USSR to prepare and to submit to the Supreme Soviet of the USSR proposals on appropriate modifications of national law. However the said commission has not been executed. Nevertheless the provisions of the Protocol relative to human treatment of all persons who are not taking part or who are no longer taking part in the hostilities, of wounded and sick, to protection of civilian population, works and installations containing dangerous forces, protection of cultural objects and places of worship shall be applicable by both parties to the armed conflict.
>
> At the same time an unduly national implementation of these provisions was one of the reasons of the failure to respect the rules of the said Additional Protocol which stipulate that the use of force shall be commensurable with the aims and all efforts shall be taken to avoid injuring the interests of civilians and their property.
>
> 6. The Federal Counsel of the Russian Federation shall regularize the legislation on the use of the armed forces of the Russian Federation, as well as the regulation of other matters which can arise in extraordinary situations or during conflicts, including those resulting from the Protocol Additional to Geneva Conventions of 12 August 1949 relating to the protection of the victims of non-international armed conflicts (Protocol II).

Paola Gaeta has observed in respect of this judgment of the Russian Constitutional Court that 'this could well be the first time a national court has been called upon to scrutinize compliance by a state's armed forces with international rules concerning the protection of civilians and the conduct of hostilities during an armed conflict'.[13] Unfortunately, the court did not further justify why precisely Additional Protocol II would be applicable to the conflict in Chechnya. Before applying the rules of Additional Protocol II, the court should have *qualified* the conflict as a non-international armed conflict. It could have held that the conflict rose to the level of an armed conflict of a certain duration and intensity which pitted rebel fighters against government troops, ie, a non-international armed conflict to which Additional Protocol II applies. It could also have held that Chechnyan rebels fought a war of national liberation, to which, pursuant to Article 1(4) of Additional Protocol I,[14] the rules of *international* armed conflicts apply. However, the decision is extremely relevant, not only for the clarification of the law of non-international armed conflict but also in terms of the effect of international law in the Russian legal order.[15]

Hamdan v Rumsfeld and ors, Appeal judgment, 548 US 557, 126 S Ct 2749, 165 L Ed 2d 723 (2006), ILDC 745 (US 2006), 29th June 2006, United States; Supreme Court [US]

In 2001, Salim Ahmed Hamdan, an Al-Qaeda operative, was captured during hostilities between the United States and the Taliban and turned over to the US military. He was

13 Gaeta (n 11) 564.

14 Protocol Additional to the Geneva Conventions of 12 August 1949, and relating to the Protection of Victims of International Armed Conflicts (Additional Protocol I) (adopted 8 June 1977, entered into force 7 December 1978) 1125 UNTS 3.

15 ibid, 574 (concluding that '[t]his decision […] clearly demonstrates that the Russian Constitutional Court has become an important institution promoting compliance with international law in the Russian legal system').

held in custody at the infamous US prison in Guantanamo Bay, Cuba. In 2003, the US President deemed him eligible for trial by military commission for then-unspecified crimes. Before the US Supreme Court the case question arose as to whether Common Article 3 of the Geneva Conventions, which set out some minimal procedural guarantees, applied to the case of Hamdan. The US government and the Court of Appeals believed not, but the Supreme Court thought otherwise:

> The Court of Appeals thought, and the Government asserts, that Common Article 3 does not apply to Hamdan because the conflict with al Qaeda, being… international in scope… does not qualify as a… conflict not of an international character…415 F. 3d, at 41. That reasoning is erroneous. The term 'conflict not of an international character' is used here in contradistinction to a conflict between nations. So much is demonstrated by the 'fundamental logic [of] the Convention's provisions on its application'. *Id.*, at 44 (Williams, J., concurring). Common Article 2 provides that 'the present Convention shall apply to all cases of declared war or of any other armed conflict which may arise between two or more of the High Contracting Parties'. 6 U. S. T., at 3318 (Art. 2, ¶1). High Contracting Parties (signatories) also must abide by all terms of the Conventions vis-à-vis one another even if one party to the conflict is a nonsignatory Power, and must so abide vis-à-vis the nonsignatory if 'the latter accepts and applies. those terms.' *Ibid.* (Art. 2, ¶3). Common Article 3, by contrast, affords some minimal protection, falling short of full protection under the Conventions, to individuals associated with neither a signatory nor even a nonsignatory Power, who are involved in a conflict in the territory of a signatory. The latter kind of conflict is distinguishable from the conflict described in Common Article 2 chiefly because it does not involve a clash between nations (whether signatories or not). In context, then, the phrase 'not of an international character' bears its literal meaning… Commentary on the Additional Protocols to the Geneva Conventions of 12 August 1949, p. 1351 (1987) ('[A] noninternational armed conflict is distinct from an international armed conflict because of the legal status of the entities opposing each other'). (slip op. pp. 67-68)

By characterising the armed conflict between the US and Al-Qaeda as a conflict governed by Common Article 3 of the Geneva Conventions, the US Supreme Court pointed out that US government action in the war on terror was subject to international legal constraints. The Supreme Court read Common Article 3 expansively, and arguably correctly, by holding that the provision applies to *all* armed conflicts, including conflicts pitting a state (the US) against a non-state actor (Al-Qaeda) outside the former's territory. As a result of the applicability of Common Article 3, the Supreme Court could subsequently review the US military commission set up to try Hamdan in light of international humanitarian law (see below 'detention').

IV. Protected Persons

International humanitarian law is a body of law that has as one of its primary aims the protection of persons who do not take part in hostilities, in particular the sick, wounded and shipwrecked, prisoners of war and other detained persons and civilians. With respect to international armed conflicts, Article 4 of the Geneva Convention IV provides that '[p]ersons protected by the Convention are those who, at a given moment and in any manner whatsoever, find themselves, in case of a conflict or occupation, in the hands of a Party to the conflict or Occupying Power of which they are not nationals'.[16]

16 Geneva Convention IV (n 1); a Dutch court held, somewhat enigmatically, that a person was not a protected person 'only if he has actually been incorporated into the opposing party' (ILDC 1071 (NL 2008) para 9.2).

Pursuant to this provision, as traditionally understood, *only* persons who are *not* nationals of a party to a conflict or an occupying power are protected by the Geneva Conventions. The cases discussed in this section concern (1) the question of whether this classic understanding should be maintained, given the changed reality of armed conflicts, and (2) the extent to which protected persons could avail themselves of legal protection of international humanitarian law in case of abuse of protected status or in case considerations of military necessity militate against a broad construction of protection.

Nango and 31 others v Israel and ors, Original Petition to the High Court of Justice, Case No HCJ 7918/05, 59(2) PD 856, ILDC 156 (IL 2005), 22nd August 2005, Israel; Supreme Court; Supreme Court as High Court of Justice

Nango and ors v Israel and ors deals with the 'Disengagement Plan' adopted on 6 June 2004, according to which Israel was to withdraw from the Gaza Strip. The plan included the eviction of all Israelis from the Gaza Strip and from four settlements in the West Bank. Jewish settlers from Gaza claimed that they constituted 'protected persons' under Article 4 of the Geneva Convention IV and, accordingly, that Israel could not permanently evict them from their homes.

> [...] by virtue thereof should be dismissed (858 F-G) 3. [...] the petitioners, who are Israeli citizens living in the evicted areas, do not fall under the definition of the term "protected persons" under the 1949 Geneva Convention for the Protection of Civilians in Times of War, and under the principles of the laws of occupation.

Applying Article 4 of the Geneva Convention IV, the Israeli court refused to consider Jewish settlers in Gaza as protected persons, since they were nationals of Israel (Israel being the Occupying Power of the Palestinian Territories). This traditional nationality requirement has however been relaxed by the ICTY Appeals Chamber in the *Tadic* decision 1999, when the ICTY put forward the criterion of ethnic allegiance to determine the status of the protected person under Article 4 of the Geneva Convention IV.[17] The concept of allegiance espoused by the ICTY in *Tadic* has been cited approvingly in various domestic cases that relate to the ethnic conflict in the former Yugoslavia. Below, the German *Sokolovic* case and the Kosovar *Kolasinac* case are discussed in this respect.

Kosovo, Andjelko Kolasinac case, Case No. AP-KZ 230/2003, Supreme Court of Kosovo, Decision of 9 January 2004 overturning the verdict of 31 January 2003 by the District Court of Prizren, P. No. 226/2001, and remanding the case for retrial, partly reprinted in *Yearbook of International Humanitarian Law* 569 (2004) (not in ILDC)

An allegiance requirement may more accurately capture the reality of ethnic conflict in the former Yugoslavia, where a party to an 'internationalised' armed conflict may well target persons who are formally their own nationals but who, for ethnic reasons, pay allegiance to an adverse party. In *Kolasinac*, a case before the Kosovo Supreme Court, the question arose whether the requirement of allegiance of protected persons also applied to the conflict in Kosovo.

> [...] save Common Article 3 the Fourth Geneva Convention does not cover explicitly the category of protected persons afforded protection in the case before the trial court, i.e. Kosovo Albanians who were Yugoslav nationals and resided on the territory

17 ICTY Appeals Chamber, *Prosecutor v Dusko Tadic* (Judgment) IT-94-1-A (15 July 1999), para 166 ('While previously wars were primarily between well-established States, in modern inter-ethnic armed conflicts such as that in the former Yugoslavia, new States are often created during the conflict and ethnicity rather than nationality may become the grounds for allegiance. Or, put another way, ethnicity may become determinative of national allegiance. Under these conditions, the requirement of nationality is even less adequate to define protected persons. In such conflicts, not only the text and the drafting history of the Convention but also, and more importantly, the Convention's object and purpose suggest that allegiance to a Party to the conflict and, correspondingly, control by this Party over persons in a given territory, may be regarded as the crucial test').

> controlled by Yugoslav government. [. . .] the District Court appears to derive from [the ICTY's] statement that injured parties in their relation with FRY Government had protected status from Geneva Convention IV and both Additional Protocols, despite having been nationals of FRY. The Supreme Court finds that in the light of evidence adduced in the main trial such conclusion was neither factually supported nor sufficiently legally explained. (p. 25)
>
> In the instant case, the Supreme Court finds that the trial court was not right to take the above-quoted ICTY's statement out of its context and use it as basis to automatically import the whole of Geneva Convention's protection of non-combatants to the facts of this case. (p. 25)
>
> [. . .] Rather, the court would need to establish whether between the victims and the party who had control over that group the allegiance based on nationality did not effectively exist, and that, instead, there was an effective allegiance to an adverse party to the international conflict, ethnicity being a possible decisive for the issue of allegiance. Alternatively, it might be considered whether a lack of an effective bond with the party of whom the victims were formally nationals could result in such a situation that the victims who found themselves in the midst of an international conflict were *in substance* treated as stateless persons and therefore, for the purpose of protected status, should be regarded as such. (p. 26)

It is noted that the court did *not* give short shrift to the allegiance concept as set forth by the ICTY regarding the conflict in Bosnia Herzegovina, and thus it is not on a collision course with the ICTY. It only cautioned that the facts of the conflict in Kosovo should be carefully scrutinized: was there really no allegiance whatsoever of the Kosovo Albanian population to the Yugoslav government? In the cases regarding Kosovo, the ICTY did not answer this question, as it qualified the conflict between the KLA and Yugoslav army as a non-international armed conflict.[18] The concept of allegiance in respect of protected persons indeed has its particular relevance only in *international(-ized)* armed conflict to which the Geneva Conventions are applicable in their entirety (and not only Common Article 3).

Physicians for Human Rights v Israeli Defence Force Commander in the West Bank, Original Petition to the High Court of Justice, HCJ 2936/02, ILDC 354 (IL 2002), 8th April 2002, Israel; Supreme Court; Supreme Court as High Court of Justice

Domestic courts, Israeli courts in particular, have tackled many complicated questions as to whether, in specific cases, the military had taken sufficient protective measures with respect to protected persons and (civilian) objects.

A first thorny issue is how the military should react to military personnel and armed groups—who may be protected by the Geneva Conventions—abusing their position. In cases involving shootings by Israeli Defence Forces (IDF) at Red Cross and Red Crescent medical teams working out of ambulances and in hospitals, Israeli courts, while urging caution, have not declared such attacks illegal under international humanitarian law, nor have they affirmed an absolute obligation under international humanitarian law to evacuate the wounded.[19]

18 ICTY Trial Chamber II, *Prosecutor v Limaj, Bala and Musliu* (Judgment) IT-03-66-T (30 November 2005); ICTY Trial Chamber II, *Prosecutor v Djordjevic* (Judgment) IT-05-87/1-T (17 February 2011); ICTY Trial Chamber, *Prosecutor v Milutinovic* (Judgment) IT-05-87-T (26 February 2009).

19 See D Barak-Erez, 'The International Law of Human Rights and Constitutional Law: A Case Study of an Expanding Dialogue' (2004) 2 *International Journal of Constitutional Law* 611, 619; O Ben-Naftali and K R Michaeli, 'Justice-Ability: A Critique of the Alleged Non-Justiciability of Israel's Policy of Targeted Killings' (2003) 1(2) *Journal of International Criminal Justice* 368, 378; O Ben-Naftali and K R Michaeli, 'We Must Not Make a Scarecrow of the Law: A Legal Analysis of the Israeli Policy of Targeted Killings' (2003) 36 *Cornell International Law Journal* 233, 235; L Bilsky, 'Suicidal Terror, Radical Evil, and the Distortion of Politics and Law' (2004) 5(1) *Theoretical Inquiries in Law* 131, 146, 150; G Nolte, 'Preventive Use of Force and Preventive Killings: Moves into a Different Legal Order' (2004) 5(1) *Theoretical Inquiries in Law* 111.

In *Physicians for Human Rights v The Commander of the Israeli Defence Forces in the West Bank*, petitions of an aid organization challenged the legality under international humanitarian law of a number of specific events during a 2002 operation in the Palestinian Territories, namely shootings by IDF at Red Cross and Red Crescent medical teams working out of ambulances and in hospitals, prevention of the evacuation of the wounded and sick to hospitals to receive medical care, and prevention of the evacuation and burial of bodies. The court held as follows:

> 3 Though we are unable to express a position regarding the specific events mentioned in the petition, which are, on the face of things, severe, we see fit to emphasize that our combat forces are required to abide by the rules of humanitarian law regarding the care of the wounded, the ill, and bodies of the deceased. The fact that medical personnel have abused their position in hospitals and in ambulances has made it necessary for the IDF to act in order to prevent such activities but does not, in and of itself, justify sweeping breaches of humanitarian rules. Indeed, this is also the position of the State. This stance is required, not only under the rules of international law on which the petitioners have based their arguments here, but also in light of the values of the State of Israel as a Jewish and democratic state.
>
> 4 The IDF shall once again instruct the combat forces, down to the level of the lone soldier in the field, of this commitment by our forces based on law and morality—and, according to the State, even on utilitarian considerations—through concrete instructions which will prevent, to the extent possible, and even in severe situations, incidents which are inconsistent with the rules of humanitarian law.

Physicians for Human Rights v Israeli Defence Force Commander in the West Bank, Original petition to the High Court of Justice, HCJ 2117/02, ILDC 366 (IL 2002), 28th April 2002, Israel; Supreme Court; Supreme Court as High Court of Justice

This case concerned similar operations where IDF soldiers had fired on ambulances of the Red Crescent and had wounded medical teams travelling in them. As in *HCJ 2936/02*, the High Court reminded the military of its obligation under international humanitarian law to protect medical units and personnel against attacks, while leaving open the option of attack in case of abuse by the enemy.

> 6 [...] the "Medical Service" has the right to full protection only when it is *exclusively* engaged in the search, collection, transport and treatment of the wounded or sick. Note the provisions of Articles 24 of the First Geneva Convention as well as the provisions of article 26, which expands this protection to include the Red Cross and similar voluntary aid societies.

This last decision demonstrates the pragmatic streak of Israeli courts: while IDF Forces should uphold international humanitarian law rules in respect of the treatment of the sick and wounded, and medical personnel, one cannot tolerate that terrorists take advantage of those rules to abuse medical facilities to perpetrate attacks. After all, international humanitarian law is all about striking a precarious balance between military necessity and protection of persons not taking active part in hostilities, a balance which is unhinged when fighters camouflage as medical teams.

Public Committee against Torture in Israel and Palestinian Society for the Protection of Human Rights and the Environment v Israel and ors, Original Petition to the High Court of Justice, HCJ 769/02, ILDC 597 (IL 2006), 13th December 2006, Israel; Supreme Court; Supreme Court as High Court of Justice

As the previously discussed 'medical' cases show, it is sometimes difficult to strike a balance between the imperatives of protecting medical facilities and preventing abuse of such protection. It is equally difficult to give a clear-cut answer to the question of whether the policy of 'targeted killings' employed by states (notably Israel) against members of terrorist organizations is necessarily illegal under international humanitarian law, as this requires striking a difficult balance between the fight against terrorism and the protection of civilians.

In 2006, an Israeli court rendered a nuanced decision in a case brought by two human rights organizations, which challenged the policy of preventive strikes employed by Israel in the Gaza Strip and the West Bank, by which it aimed to kill members of terrorist organizations involved in the planning, launching, or execution of terrorist attacks against Israeli civilians and soldiers. The Israeli court notably clarified the concept of 'direct participation in hostilities'.[20]

> 39. As regarding the scope of the wording "takes a direct part" in hostilities, so too regarding the scope of the wording "and for such time" there is no consensus in the international literature. Indeed, both these concepts are close to each other. However, they are not identical. With no consensus regarding the interpretation of the wording "for such time", there is no choice but to proceed from case to case. Again, it is helpful to examine the extreme cases. On the one hand, a civilian taking a direct part in hostilities one single time, or sporadically, who later detaches himself from that activity, is a civilian who, starting from the time he detached himself from that activity, is entitled to protection from attack. He is not to be attacked for the hostilities which he committed in the past. On the other hand, a civilian who has joined a terrorist organization which has become his "home", and in the framework of his role in that organization he commits a chain of hostilities, with short periods of rest between them, loses his immunity from attack "for such time" as he is committing the chain of acts. Indeed, regarding such a civilian, the rest between hostilities is nothing other than preparation for the next hostility ...
>
> 40. These examples point out the dilemma which the "for such time" requirement presents before us. On the one hand, a civilian who took a direct part in hostilities once, or sporadically, but detached himself from them (entirely, or for a long period) is not to be harmed. On the other hand, the "revolving door" phenomenon, by which each terrorist has "horns of the alter" (1 Kings 1:50) to grasp or a "city of refuge" (Numbers 35:11) to flee to, to which he turns in order to rest and prepare while they grant him immunity from attack, is to be avoided... In the wide area between those two possibilities, one finds the "gray" cases, about which customary international law has not yet crystallized. There is thus no escaping examination of each and every case. In that context, the following four things should be said: first, well based information is needed before categorizing a civilian as falling into one of the discussed categories. Innocent civilians are not to be harmed (*see* Cassese, at p. 421). Information which has been most thoroughly verified is needed regarding the identity and activity of the civilian who is allegedly taking part in the hostilities [...]

Under international humanitarian law, civilians cannot be attacked 'unless and for such time as they take a direct part in hostilities'.[21] The concept of 'direct participation in hostilities' has been

---

20 See, on this case, O Ben-Naftali and K R Michaeli, 'Public Committee Against Torture in Israel v. Government of Israel: Case No HCJ 769/02: Supreme Court of Israel, Sitting as the High Court of Israel, December 13, 2006' (2007) 101 *American Journal of International Law* 459; Ben-Naftali and Michaeli, 'Justice-Ability (n 19) 368; M Lesh, 'The Public Committee Against Torture in Israel v the Government of Israel: the Israeli High Court of Justice Targeted Killing Decision' (2007) 8 *Melbourne Journal of International Law* 373; N Melzer, 'Targeted Killing or Less Harmful Means? Israel's High Court Judgment on Targeted Killing and the Restrictive Function of Military Necessity' (2008) 9 *Yearbook of International Humanitarian Law* 87; H Moodrick-Even Khen, 'Can We Now Tell what "Direct Participation in Hostilities" Is?: HCJ 769/02 the Public Committee against Torture in Israel v. the Government of Israel' (2007) 40 *Israel Law Review* 213; J A Rubel, 'A Missed Opportunity: the Ramifications of the Committee Against Torture's Failure to Adequately Address Israel's Ill-Treatment of Palestinian Detainees' (2006) 20 *Emory International Law Review* 699.

21 Additional Protocol I (n 14) Article 51(3).

further clarified by the ICRC,[22] but both this judgment and the ICRC document do not come up with bright-line rules as regards who is a civilian directly participating in hostilities and thus a legitimate military target. In the final analysis, this determination is to be made on a case-by-case basis. That being said, the Israeli High Court is to be credited with at least advancing a number of criteria that should guide the determination, in particular with respect to the 'for such time' requirement of Article 51(3) of Additional Protocol I.[23] Application of these criteria may offer the Israeli army, and any army for that matter, some leeway to target and kill terrorists who are *planning* terrorist attacks, even though they might not actually be executing them. Such terrorists cannot pass through a 'revolving door' after they have perpetrated an attack and claim that they are no longer directly participating in hostilities. When precisely (alleged) terrorists lose their immunity from targeting is left open by the court.

al–Basyuni Ahmad and ors v Prime Minister and Minister of Defence, Original Petition, Case No HCJ 9132/07, ILDC 883 (IL 2008), 30th January 2008, Israel; Supreme Court; Supreme Court as High Court of Justice

Domestic courts may censure the government and military commanders for having taken actions detrimental to the interests of protected persons. In that sense, the government and the commanders incur negative obligations. At the same time, domestic courts may sometimes also compel commanders to take affirmative protective steps, eg providing humanitarian assistance to civilians and preparing for casualties. In that sense, the state and commanders may incur *positive* obligations under international humanitarian law when conducting military operations or occupying an area. A belligerent's positive obligations vis-à-vis the civilian population are not unlimited, however. This is shown by an Israeli court judgment regarding the legality under international humanitarian law of Israel's decision to restrict the supply of fuel and electricity to the Gaza Strip. At the time, Gaza was no longer effectively controlled by Israel, and Israel feared that fuel and electricity could be used by terrorists targeting Israel. Petitioners claimed that limiting the supply of fuel and electricity would cause certain, severe, and irreversible harm to essential humanitarian systems in the Gaza Strip: to the hospitals, to the water and sewage systems, and to the entire civilian population.

> 22. [W]e reiterate that the Gaza Strip is controlled by a murderous terrorist organization, which acts tirelessly to strike at the State of Israel and its inhabitants, violating every possible rule of international law in its violent acts, which are directed indiscriminately toward civilians—men, women and children. However, as mentioned above, the State of Israel is committed to acting against the terrorist organizations within the framework of the law and in accordance with the provisions of international law, and to refrain from intentional harm to the civilian population in the Gaza Strip. In light of the entirety of information presented before us regarding provision of electricity to the Gaza Strip, we are of the opinion that the amount of industrial diesel that the State announced it will supply, as well as the electricity supplied regularly via power lines originating in Israel, fulfill the basic humanitarian needs of the Gaza Strip at the present time.

This decision again captures well the conflict between the interests of protected persons—in this case the supply of diesel and electricity from Israel to the civilian population in Gaza—and the security needs of the state, which may fear that such a supply is not only used to

22 N Melzer, *Interpretive Guidance on the Notion of Direct Participation in Hostilities under International Humanitarian Law* (ICRC 2009).

23 *Public Committee against Torture in Israel and Palestinian Society for the Protection of Human Rights and the Environment v Israel and ors*, Original Petition to the High Court of Justice, HCJ 769/02, ILDC 597 (IL 2006), 13 December 2006, Israel; Supreme Court; Supreme Court as High Court of Justice, para 40.

fulfil the basic humanitarian needs of the civilian population but is diverted by terrorists. Conspicuous is the almost emotional outburst of the court where it says that Israel is 'a democratic state fighting for its life in the framework of the means that the law puts at its disposal' while 'terrorist organizations [...] rise up against it'.[24] It is hardly surprising then that the court refuses to second-guess decisions of the government—it cites that it only reviews their 'legality'—and that it eventually sides with the government without ascertaining whether the fuel supply is actually abused by terrorists.[25]

V. Detention

In times of armed conflict and occupation, parties to the conflict or occupying powers regularly detain individuals who are seen as posing a security risk. In particular, Israeli and US courts have reviewed the legality of such detentions, which are often of an administrative nature, in light of international humanitarian law. In the course of this review, in some cases questions as to the status of captured fighters have also been raised. Are these fighters, notably irregular fighters involved in 'terrorist activities' entitled to prisoners of war (POW) status pursuant to Article 4A of the Geneva Convention Relative to the Treatment of Prisoners of War (Geneva Convention III),[26] or can they be characterized as 'unlawful/enemy' combatants who do not fall within the ambit of international humanitarian law?

Israeli courts have heard many detention cases in relation to the Israeli-Palestinian conflict. Without exception, they have accepted the authority of the Military Commander to detain any person in occupied territory posing a security risk. However, relying on the Geneva Conventions, they have emphasized the importance of judicial review of executive detention decisions.

Marab and ors v Israeli Defence Force Commander in the West Bank and Judea and Samaria Brigade Headquarters, Final Decision, HCJ 3239/02, ILDC 15 (IL 2003), 5th February 2003, Israel; Supreme Court; Supreme Court as High Court of Justice

The *Marab* case concerned orders of the IDF Commander in the West Bank to allow mass administrative detention of wanted persons for investigative reasons. According to these orders, amongst other things, a detainee could be held in detention for eighteen days without an opportunity to be heard by a judge. In a long but well-reasoned decision that balanced security concerns and individual rights, the High Court ruled that the orders violated international law standards on detention:

---

24 *al-Basyuni Ahmad and ors v Prime Minister and Minister of Defence*, Original Petition, Case No HCJ 9132/07, ILDC 883 (IL 2008), 30 January 2008, Israel; Supreme Court; Supreme Court as High Court of Justice, para 21.

25 ibid, para 20.

26 Geneva Convention Relative to the Treatment of Prisoners of War (Geneva Convention III) (signed 12 August 1949, entered into force 21 October 1950) 75 UNTS 135, Article 4A reads as follows: 'Prisoners of war, in the sense of the present Convention, are persons belonging to one of the following categories, who have fallen into the power of the enemy:

1. Members of the armed forces of a Party to the conflict as well as members of militias or volunteer corps forming part of such armed forces.
2. Members of other militias and members of other volunteer corps, including those of organized resistance movements, belonging to a Party to the conflict and operating in or outside their own territory, even if this territory is occupied, provided that such militias or volunteer corps, including such organized resistance movements, fulfil the following conditions:
   (a) That of being commanded by a person responsible for his subordinates;
   (b) That of having a fixed distinctive sign recognizable at a distance;
   (c) That of carrying arms openly;
   (d) That of conducting their operations in accordance with the laws and customs of war.

21. [on the approach of international law concerning occupation in times of war] On the one hand, the liberty of each resident of occupied territory is, of course, recognized. On the other hand, international law also recognizes the duty and power of the occupying state, acting through the military commander, to preserve public peace and safety; *see* Article 43 of the Annex to the Hague Convention Regulations Respecting The Laws and Customs of War on Land-1907 [hereinafter Hague Regulations]. In this framework, the military commander has the authority to promulgate security legislation intended to allow the occupying state to fulfill its function of preserving the peace, protecting the security of the occupying state, and the security of its soldiers. *See* Article 64 of the Geneva Convention Relative to the Protection of Civilian Persons in Time of War-1949 [hereinafter the Fourth Geneva Convention]. Consequently, the military commander has the authority to detain any person suspect of committing criminal offences, and any person he considers harmful to the security of the area ...

34. [...] we are of the opinion that detention periods of 18 days, under Order 1500, and 12 days, under Orders 1505, 1512 and 1518, exceed appropriate limits. This detention period was intended to allow for initial investigation. However, that is not its proper function. According to the normative framework, soon after the authorized officer carries out the initial detention, the case should be transferred to the track of judicial intervention. The case should not wait for the completion of the initial or other investigation before it is brought before a judge. The need to complete the initial investigation will be presented before the judge himself, and he will decide whether there exists reasonable suspicion of the detainee's involvement to justify the continuation of his detention. Thus, Order 1500, as well as Orders 1505, 1512, and 1518, unlawfully infringes upon the judge's authority, thus infringing upon the detainee's liberty, which the international and Israeli legal frameworks are intended to protect.

In the *Marab* case, the High Court gave concrete application to Articles 43 and 78 of the Geneva Convention IV. These provisions refer to judicial review of administrative detention decisions but do not specify set detention periods or occasions for judicial intervention with regard to detention. Decisions on such detention periods or occasions are indeed best left to the states and their commanders implementing the conventions, who may be confronted with specific security concerns which the drafters of the Geneva Conventions could impossibly have anticipated. It then falls to those states' domestic courts to review the pertinent decisions and to set workable standards as to the length of detention without judicial review. Of note is that the High Court in *Marab* not only relied on international humanitarian law but also on international human rights and Israeli law standards when determining that a period of eighteen days without judicial review violated the law.

A detention issue that in the context of the 'war on terror' has led to heated legal debate was how to categorize, under international humanitarian law, members of organizations proclaimed as 'terrorist', such as Al-Qaeda or Hezbollah, who did not satisfy the requirements of Article 4A of the Geneva Convention III for POW status, the so-called 'unlawful or enemy combatants'. In recent times, mainly Israeli and US courts have tackled this issue, although in the past courts in Singapore, Malaysia, and Nigeria had already given thought to the issue.

Israel v Srur (Muhammad) and ors, Decision on Jurisdiction, Case No 548/06, Case No 549/06, Case No 550/06, ILDC 845 (IL 2007), 4th December 2007, Israel; North District; Nazareth; District Court

The Israeli case of *Srur* concerned the detention of several Hezbollah combatants, captured during the 2006 armed conflict between Israel and Hezbollah (who operated from Lebanon).

When indicted before an Israeli court for murder and attempted murder of IDF soldiers, and engagement in terror, the combatants claimed POW status under Geneva Convention III.

> 8 [. . .] Hezbollah members are not to be deemed to be prisoners of war if only by reason of the fact that the organization operates in violation of the laws of war . . . even though the Hezbollah organization has taken part in various Lebanese governing entities, it still continues to exist as an independent framework and has followed a completely independent policy of its own, as a terrorist organization, without informing even Lebanese governmental concerns of its intentions or its acts.
>
> 10 [. . .] we must perforce understand that the Hezbollah organization does not form part of the armed forces of Lebanon, and that it is not connected with the Government of Lebanon, is not under that body's discipline, either as to receiving executive orders or as to obeying existing orders, either by way of economic ties or supply line ties, whether of combat equipment or other munitions. In fact, Hezbollah constitutes nothing more than an independent military organization, getting orders from its apparatuses, or from entities outside Lebanon (the Government of Teheran).
>
> 12 [. . .] as stated, in view of the evidence now placed before us, we are persuaded that the Defendants ought not to be viewed as prisoners of war even in terms of the provision of Article 4 A (1) of the Convention.

In the *Srur* case, the criminal court engaged in quite a detailed analysis of whether Lebanese Hezbollah fighters fell within the POW definition of Article 4A of the Geneva Convention III, in particular whether they qualified as members of armed forces, militias, and volunteer corps. The case is rather closely argued from a legal point of view. It is notable, however, that at several junctures the court refers to the Iranian overlords of Hezbollah. This statement is probably well received in certain political quarters, but, if it is true that the organization receives orders from Tehran, this raises the question of whether Hezbollah could not qualify as an 'Iranian' militia or volunteer corps. The court believed it did not, as it was not 'united by the central regime'.[27]

The events of 9/11 and the ensuing reaction have also led to significant US jurisprudence on detention. In 2002, US President Bush instituted military commissions to try detainees, including irregular Al-Qaeda fighters captured in the 'war on terror'. Such commissions could possibly characterize irregular Al-Qaeda fighters captured in Afghanistan as unlawful combatants. Subsequently, a criminal court could bring them to justice for their unlawful participation in hostilities against the United States.

Hamdan v Rumsfeld and ors, Appeal judgment, 548 US 557, 126 S Ct 2749, 165 L Ed 2d 723 (2006), ILDC 745 (US 2006), 29th June 2006, United States; Supreme Court [US]

The creation of the special military commissions, and the limited due process guarantees which they offered, sparked a number of legal challenges, most of them based on constitutional grounds. In one of those cases, however, *Hamdan v Rumsfeld*, decided by the US Supreme Court, international humanitarian law played a more prominent role. Having determined that Common Article 3 of the Geneva Conventions was applicable to the armed conflict between the US and Al-Qaeda in Afghanistan, the Supreme Court ascertained whether the mode of establishment of military commissions and their guarantees comported with the Geneva Conventions:

27 *Israel v Srur (Muhammad) and ors*, Decision on Jurisdiction, Case No 548/06, Case No 549/06, Case No 550/06, ILDC 845 (IL 2007), 4 December 2007, Israel; North District; Nazareth; District Court, para 9.

> Common Article 3 [of the Geneva Conventions]... is applicable here and ... requires that Hamdan be tried by a 'regularly constituted court affording all the judicial guarantees which are recognized as indispensable by civilized peoples'. 6 U. S. T., at 3320 (Art. 3, ¶1(d)).
>
> [...] the procedures adopted to try Hamdan deviate from those governing courts-martial in ways not justified by any 'evident practical need', *post*, at 11, and for that reason, at least, fail to afford the requisite guarantees. See *post*, at 8, 11.17. We add only that ... various provisions of Commission Order No. 1 dispense with the principles, articulated in Article 75 and indisputably part of the customary international law, that an accused must, absent disruptive conduct or consent, be present for his trial and must be privy to the evidence against him. See §§6(B)(3), (D). That the Government has a compelling interest in denying Hamdan access to certain sensitive information is not doubted. Cf. *post*, at 47.48 (THOMAS, J., dissenting). But, at least absent express statutory provision to the contrary, information used to convict a person of a crime must be disclosed to him. (slip op. 69-72)

Of note is that the US Supreme Court considered Article 75 of Additional Protocol I to be customary international law (the US not being a party to Additional Protocol I), in keeping with the ICRC's study on customary international law, and to be applicable in *any* armed conflict, not only international armed conflicts. In spite of the court's rather detailed examination of applicable international humanitarian law in *Hamdan*, it is observed, however, that a far larger part of the court's opinion is devoted to an analysis of the compatibility of the establishment and functioning of military commissions with US (constitutional) law.

Following the Supreme Court's ruling, US Congress responded by passing legislation, the Military Commissions Act (MCA).[28] This act did not particularly strengthen the protections offered to detainees: it subjected all alien unlawful enemy combatants to trial by military commission,[29] it deprived federal courts of their jurisdiction to hear *habeas corpus* and other petitions filed by alien enemy combatants,[30] and it excluded the application of a number of due process guarantees under the Uniform Code of Military Justice.[31]

Congress decided for itself in Section 948b(f) that 'a military commission established under this chapter is a regularly constituted court, affording all the necessary "judicial guarantees which are recognized as indispensable by civilized peoples" for purposes of common Article 3 of the Geneva Conventions', a determination which is unlikely to be contested by the courts on the basis of international law, since Section 948b(g) provides that the Geneva Conventions do not establish a source of rights: '[n]o alien unlawful enemy combatant subject to trial by military commission under this chapter may invoke the Geneva Conventions as a source of rights'. Inevitably, however, the MCA raised new legal issues, mostly on constitutional law grounds, including in the further proceedings against Hamdan.

In case of doubt about the exact legal status of a combatant (and accordingly his POW status), in accordance with Article 5 of the Geneva Convention III, such persons 'shall enjoy the protection of the present Convention until such time as their status has been determined by a competent tribunal'. Could military commissions qualify as status determination tribunals pursuant to Article 5 of the Geneva Convention III? Before a military commission established under the MCA, Hamdan claimed entitlement to POW status under Article 4A of the

28 Pub L No 109-399, 120 Stat 2600 (2006) (United States).

29 10 USC s 948b(c).

30 cf, however, *Boumediene and ors v Bush and ors*, Decision, 553 US 723 (2008); ILDC 1039 (US 2008), discussed below.

31 10 USC s 948b(d).

Geneva Convention III, and made a motion for a status determination under Article 5 of the Geneva Convention III.

> 16 The Commission notes the terms of MCA §948b(g), which provide "No alien unlawful enemy combatant subject to trial by military commission under this chapter may invoke the Geneva Conventions as a source of rights." Because the accused has not yet been determined to be an alien unlawful enemy combatant by any tribunal, this section does not apply to defeat his right to rely on the Geneva Conventions for the purposes of determining his status.

In this case, the US military commission hearing the case against *Hamdan* and exercising its *Kompetenz-Kompetenz* characterized itself as a competent status determination tribunal in the sense of Article 5 of the Geneva Convention III, although it is strictly speaking not a tribunal. Much ink has been spilled over the legality and appropriateness of status determination and punishment proceedings before military commissions.[32] Such commissions are however a step forward vis-à-vis the previous Combatant Status Review Tribunals, which failed to conduct a proper Article 5 determination. This decision does obviously not rule out that Al-Qaeda fighters can be qualified as unlawful/enemy combatants and, on that basis, be tried for their unlawful participation in hostilities. A military commission later determined that Hamdan was indeed an 'enemy combatant'.[33] He was convicted in 2008.[34]

In a somewhat related case, *Boumediene and ors v Bush and ors*,[35] the US Supreme Court entertained the question of whether aliens detained as enemy combatants at Guantanamo Bay had the constitutional privilege of habeas corpus to challenge the legality of their detention. A Combatant Status Review Tribunal had determined that each of the aliens in the present suit was an enemy combatant, and, as noted above, the Military Commission Act excluded *habeas corpus* jurisdiction of any court, justice or judge over the Guantanamo detainees. Relying entirely on US constitutional law, and not on international law, the Supreme Court, having granted *certiorari* in light of a circuit split over *habeas corpus* protection, held that the constitutional guarantees of *habeas corpus* extended to the detainees at Guantanamo (as the US maintained *de facto* sovereignty over Cuba) and that the Military Commission Act was an unconstitutional suspension of the writ of *habeas corpus*.

South Africa, S v Petane, Cape Provincial Division, 3 November 1987, 1988 (3) South African Law Reports 51 (not in ILDC)

One final case to be mentioned in this connection is that of *S v Petane*, where a member of the military wing of the African National Congress (ANC) was indicted for terrorism and attempted

32 A C Arend, 'Who's Afraid of the Geneva Conventions? Treaty Interpretation in the Wake of Hamdan v. Rumsfeld' (2007) 22 *American University International Law Review* 709; G P Fletcher, '"Hamdan" Confronts the Military Commissions Act of 2006' (2007) 45 *Columbia Journal of Transnational Law* 427; S Ghoshray, 'Hamdan's Illumination of Article III Jurisprudence in the Wake of the War on Terror' (2007) 53 *Wayne Law Review* 991; G J A Knoops, 'Of the Law of International Criminal Tribunals Within Terrorism and "Unlawful" Combatancy Trials After Hamdan v. Rumsfeld' (2007) 30 *Fordham International Law Journal* 599; F Ní Aoláin, '"Hamdan" and Common Article 3: Did the Supreme Court Get It Right?' (2007) 91 *Minnesota Law Review* 1523; E Shamir-Borer, 'Revisiting Hamdan v. Rumsfeld's Analysis of the Laws of Armed Conflict' (2007) 21 *Emory International Law Review* 601; S Solomon and D Kaye, 'The International Law of Hamdan v Rumsfeld' (2007) 8 *Yearbook of International Humanitarian Law* 149; M Sonn, 'Hamdan v. Rumsfeld: a Bad Decision with the Best Intentions: Why the Court Was Wrong in Interpreting the Geneva Conventions and What Should Be Done' (2007) 19 *Pace International Law Review* 143.

33 *United States v Hamdan* (Salim Ahmed), Ruling on defence motion for Article 5 status determination, ILDC 747 (US 2007), 17 December 2007, United States.

34 For a discussion of the entire proceedings see J C Dehn, 'The *Hamdan* Case and the Application of a Municipal Offence: The Common Law Origins of "Murder in Violation of the Law of War"' (2009) 7 *Journal of International Criminal Justice* 63.

35 *Boumediene and ors v Bush and ors* (n 30).

murder in connection with an attempt to place a bomb in a South African shopping centre. The international law question in this case was whether the accused was entitled to POW status on the basis of Article 1(4) of Additional Protocol I, which extends the legal protection that the Geneva Conventions give in international armed conflicts to (non-international) 'armed conflicts in which peoples are fighting against colonial domination and alien occupation and against racist regimes in the exercise of their right of self-determination'. As South Africa was not a party to Additional Protocol I, the question arose whether its Article 1(4) was binding on South Africa as customary international law.

> On what I have heard in argument I disagree with his assessment that there is growing support for the view that the Protocols reflect a new rule of customary international law. No writer has been cited who supports this proposition. Here and there someone says that it may one day come about. I am not sure that the provisions relating to the field of application of Protocol I are capable of ever becoming a rule of customary international law, but I need not decide that point today. For the reasons which I have given I have concluded that the provisions of Protocol I have not been accepted in customary international law. They accordingly form no part of South African law.

Since this decision, Additional Protocol I has become more widely ratified. That being said, for Article 1(4) to attain customary international law status, it would appear that those states that are 'specially affected' by the rule should recognize it.[36] As the South African court aptly notes, very few countries face a situation of peoples 'fighting against colonial domination and alien occupation and against racist regimes in the exercise of their right of self-determination'. Of those countries that could potentially qualify, few have ratified Additional Protocol I (neither Israel nor Morocco have, but Russia has). The decision also illustrates that domestic courts may be willing to ascertain state practice and *opinio juris* with a view to identifying a rule of customary international law, but that they tend to err on the side of caution.

VI. Occupation

The law of (belligerent) occupation forms part and parcel of international humanitarian law and is governed by the Geneva Convention IV 1949, the Hague Regulations 1907,[37] and applicable customary international law. Domestic courts typically pronounce themselves on questions of occupation law during or in the immediate aftermath of armed conflict and occupation.

As Israel is one of the few (well-functioning) states that occupy another territory—the Occupied Palestinian Territories—most recent decisions on occupation law have been rendered by Israeli courts.[38] The decisions are often well reasoned and rely heavily on international law.

---

36 See *North Sea Continental Shelf Cases* (*Federal Republic of Germany v Denmark; Federal Republic of Germany v Netherlands*) [1969] ICJ Rep 4, 42.

37 Annex to Convention (IV) respecting the Laws and Customs of War on Land: Regulations concerning the Laws and Customs of War on Land (Hague Regulations) (signed 18 October 1907, entered into force 26 January 1910) 36 UST 2277.

38 'Israeli Cases: Beit Sourik Village Council vs. the Government of Israel, Commander of the IDF Forces in the West Bank, 30 June 2004' (2007) 13 *Palestine Yearbook of International Law* 401; 'HCJ 2056/04 Beit Sourik Village Council v. the Government of Israel' (2005) 38(1–2) *Israel Law Review* 83; E Holmila, 'Another Brick in the Wall?: the Decision of the Israeli Supreme Court in the Case of Beit Sourik Village Council v. the Government of Israel and Commander of the IDF Forces in the West Bank (HCJ 2056/04, 30 June 2004)' (2005) 74 *Nordic Journal of International Law* 103; J Litwack, 'A Disproportionate Ruling for All the Right Reasons: Beit Sourik Village Council v. the Government of Israel' (2006) 31 *Brooklyn Journal of International Law* 857; M Pertile, 'Beit Sourik Village Council v. the Government of Israel: a Matter of Principle (and Neglected Rules)' (2005) 65 *Zeitschrift für ausländisches öffentliches Recht und Völkerrecht* 677.

In most cases, they attempt to strike a balance between the government's security needs and the needs of the local population. In striking this balance, it is conspicuous that Israeli courts are not subservient to the government: while they do not second-guess military decisions by the military commander in the occupied territory, they do not shy away from reviewing the government's application of the principle of proportionality—ie, the means to find the balance between security needs and the needs of the local population, and from occasionally finding against the government.

Beit Sourik Village Council v Israel and Israeli Defence Force Commander in the West Bank, Final Decision, HCJ 2056/04, ILDC 16 (IL 2004), 30th June 2004, Israel; Supreme Court; Supreme Court as High Court of Justice

The 2004 *Beit Sourik* decision provides a fine example of the balancing exercise carried out by Israeli courts. The legal question in this case was whether the erection of a separation or security fence between Israel and the Occupied Palestinian Territories, and the fence's route, met the requirements of the law of belligerent occupation. For the purpose of erecting a so-called 'security fence' on West Bank territory, the Israeli Defence Force (IDF) Commander of the West Bank issued eight orders allowing the IDF to seize lands, some of which were privately owned. The fence was erected to prevent the infiltration of terrorists from the West Bank into Israel. Beit Sourik Village Council, representing thousands of village inhabitants, petitioned the High Court of Justice, arguing that the fence, if built along the planned route, would have an excessive impact on many of the basic rights of the Beit Sourik villagers, including under international humanitarian law. As in many international humanitarian law cases heard by Israeli courts, the *Beit Sourik* court was called on to weigh Israel's legitimate security interests and the rights of individuals adversely affected by the construction of the security fence in occupied territory.

> 85. The task of the military commander is not easy. He must delicately balance between security needs and the needs of the local inhabitants. We were impressed by the sincere desire of the military commander to find this balance, and his willingness to change the original plan in order to reach a more proportionate solution. We found no stubbornness on his part. Despite all this, we are of the opinion that the balance determined by the military commander is not proportionate. There is no escaping, therefore, a renewed examination of the route of the fence, according to the standards of proportionality that we have set out.

The *Beit Sourik* case stands out for its clear enunciation of the principle of proportionality as the operating principle of weighing the competing legitimate demands of security and individual rights in times of armed conflict. The principle was recognized as a principle of general international law, international humanitarian law, and Israeli administrative law.

Under international humanitarian law, military commanders in occupied territories do have the authority to seize private lands under Articles 23 and 52 of the Hague Regulations and Article 53 of the Geneva Convention IV, eg, so as to build a security fence, as long as this seizure could be justified by military/security purposes. At the same time international humanitarian law also obliges military commanders to refrain from injuring the local population[39]—thereby emphasizing the local population's rights. The principle of proportionality enables the commanders, as supervised by courts, including domestic courts, to weigh these competing international humanitarian law norms. It is remarkable in this case that, after a lengthy analysis the court, while showing understanding for the military commander's difficult task of weighing the various interests involved, ruled that the balance achieved was not proportionate, and that the commander gave undue priority to the state's security needs. Ultimately, *Beit Sourik* shows how

39 Geneva Convention IV (n 1) Article 27; Hague Regulations (n 37) Articles 43 and 46.

the principle of proportionality, as a principle of law, serves as the tool for domestic courts to review executive military decisions.

Ajuri and ors v Israeli Defence Force Commander in West Bank and ors, Original Petition to the High Court of Justice, Case No HCJ 7015/02, 56(6) PD 352, [2002] Isr L Rep 1, (2003) 97 AJIL 173, ILDC 14 (IL 2002), 3rd September 2002, Israel; Supreme Court; Supreme Court as High Court of Justice

The principle of proportionality has also determined the outcome of other occupation cases pertaining to the collision between security imperatives and individual rights. This outcome has not always been wholly favourable to the Israeli government, as is also exemplified by the *Ajuri* case, another case underlining the independence of Israeli courts vis-à-vis the political branches.

Ajuri[40] revolved around the issuance of orders of residence assignment by the Israeli Defence Force Commander in the West Bank regarding three residents of the West Bank, who were family members of 'suicide bombers'. The orders, which required them to move for two years from the West Bank to Gaza, were issued pursuant to Article 78 of the Geneva Convention IV. The first legal question that arose was whether the assignment of residence from the West Bank to Gaza was not a prohibited deportation, whereas the second was whether the assignment was reasonable in light of the danger represented by the residents.

> 29. The discretion of the military commander to order assigned residence is broad. But it is not absolute discretion. The military commander must exercise his discretion within the framework of the conditions that we have established in this judgment and as prescribed in art. 78 of the Fourth Geneva Convention and the Amending Order. The military commander may not, for example, order assigned residence for an innocent person who is not involved in any activity that harms the security of the State and who does not present any danger, even if the military commander is of the opinion that this is essential for decisive reasons of security. He also may not do so for a person involved in activity that harms the security of the State, if that person no longer presents any danger that assigned residence is designed to prevent. Indeed, the military commander who wishes to make use of the provisions of art. 78 of the Fourth Geneva Convention must act within the framework of the parameters set out in that article. These parameters create a 'zone' of situations—a kind of 'zone of reasonableness'—within which the military commander may act. He may not deviate from them.

Eventually, the court approved the orders with respect to the first two residents, but set aside the orders with respect to the third resident, who was not sufficiently dangerous for purposes of application of Article 78 of the Geneva Convention IV. Conspicuously, in setting aside those orders, the court did not rely on the principle of proportionality as such but on the related requirement of 'reasonableness'. Proportionality could however possibly be seen as making reasonableness operational. After all, the court specifically inquired whether the persons against whom an assignment order was issued posed a real danger to the security of the Israeli state, and thus whether the measure restricting individual rights was proportionate to the security aim pursued. Of note is that the court considered lack of discretion and reasonableness to form an integral part of Article 78 of the Geneva Convention IV, ie, the provision that allows military commanders to issue orders for assigned residence.

40 D Barak-Erez, 'Assigned Residence in Israel's administered Territories: the Judicial Review of Security Measures: Review of H. C. 7015/02, Ajuri v. IDF Commander in the West Bank, 3 September, 2002' (2004) 33 *Israel Yearbook on Human Rights* 303; D Vagts, 'Ajuri v. IDF Commander in West Bank. Case No HCJ 7015/02. (2002) Isr L Rep 1. Supreme Court of Israel, September 3, 2002' (2003) 97 AJIL 173.

Bethlehem Municipality v Ministry of Defence of Israel and Israeli Defence Force Commander in the Judea and Samaria Area, Petition to the High Court of Justice, HCJ 1890/03, PD 59(4) 736, ILDC 368 (IL 2005), 3rd February 2005, Israel; Supreme Court; Supreme Court as High Court of Justice

Another fine example of an—again Israeli—domestic court limiting a military commander's discretion on the basis of a reasonableness/proportionality review of his decisions is offered by the following occupation case regarding the conformity with the law of belligerent occupation of the sequestration of land in the West Bank for paving a secure route to a Jewish holy site close to Bethlehem.[41]

> 21. The Jewish worshippers have the basic right to freedom of worship at Rachel's Tomb, and respondent is responsible for securing the realization of this right, while protecting the security and lives of the worshippers. In examining the means for realization of this purpose, respondent must take into consideration the basic rights of petitioners, including property rights and freedom of movement, and balance properly between them. In this case, the solution adopted by respondent, after he reexamined his original plans and followed the instructions of the caselaw of this Court, indeed ensures the realization of the worshippers' freedom of worship without causing a substantial impingement upon petitioners' freedom of movement and property rights. We therefore have not found that the arrangement made at the end of the proceedings is characterized by unreasonableness which would justify our intervention.

The court also affirmed the commander's authority to take restrictive measures under international humanitarian law, in this case the sequestration of land, but subsequently conducted a reasonableness and proportionality review. In this case, the court used 'reasonableness' and 'proportionality' in the same sentence, without exactly distinguishing between the two.[42] An interesting aspect of the case is that the proportionality-informed balancing exercise pitted two human rights regimes against each other: the right to freedom of worship (freedom of religion) of Jewish worshippers—for whose benefit the sequestration measures were taken—and the freedom of movement and the right to property of the (Palestinian) residents whose position was adversely affected by the measures. Issue may of course be taken with the outcome of the proportionality test, which was clearly favourable to the military commander and indirectly to Jewish worshippers.

National Unity Party v TRNC Assembly of the Republic, First and last instance, D 3/2006, ILDC 499 (TCc 2006), 21st June 2006, Cyprus; Turkish Republic of Northern Cyprus (disputed); Supreme Court; Constitutional Court

While most relevant decisions on occupation are rendered by Israel courts, a limited number of other relevant domestic court cases on occupation are available. Some cases have been decided by Turkish Cypriot courts, which have recognized that Turkey acts as an occupying power in northern Cyprus and have applied the law of occupation to that territory. In one notable decision, a Turkish Cypriot court decided the following with respect to the appropriation of private immovable property by the Turkish Cypriot community after Turkey's 1974 military intervention in Cyprus:

> H1 In international law, immovable private properties in a territory under military control cannot be appropriated by the invading belligerent. However, temporary use of

41 A M Gross, 'Human Proportions: Are Human Rights the Emperor's New Clothes of the International Law of Occupation?' (2007) 18 *EJIL* 35.

42 *Bethlehem Municipality v Ministry of Defence of Israel and Israeli Defence Force Commander in the Judea and Samaria Area*, Petition to the High Court of Justice, HCJ 1890/03, PD 59(4) 736, ILDC 368 (IL 2005), 3 February 2005, Israel; Supreme Court; Supreme Court as High Court of Justice, para 8.

> private lands and buildings was permitted for the purposes required by the necessities of war. If it was necessary, private buildings could be converted into public buildings (such as hospitals) or fortifications. (paragraph 30) In such circumstances, applicable principles of international law did not allow the occupant to change the legal tie between absentees (displaced persons) and their properties (as can be seen from citations in this judgment from Oppenheim, Benvenisti, and the Hague Convention (IV) Respecting the Laws and Customs of War on Land and its annex: Regulations Concerning the Laws and Customs of War on Land (18 October 1907) 36 Stat 2277; 1 Bevans 631; 205 Consol TS 2773; Martens Nouveau Recueil (3d) 461, entered into force 26 January 1910 ('Hague Regulations'). Such persons must still be regarded as the legal owners of the land. (paragraph 32).

This case shows that also Turkish Cypriot courts are not subservient to the government. They are willing to recognize that the Turkish overlords of Turkish Cyprus act as occupying powers, and accordingly to apply the international law of occupation to northern Cyprus. In this case, international humanitarian law and legal literature were amply cited (and arguably correctly applied) to support the rule that immovable private property in occupied territories could not be appropriated, although it could be temporarily used.

VII. Weapons

Portions of international humanitarian law address the lawfulness of the use of certain weapons by belligerents. Some domestic courts have reviewed such use by their own government. A US and a Dutch court decision pertaining to the use of herbicides and chemical weapons respectively are discussed below.

Vietnam Association For Victims Of Agent Orange and ors v Dow Chemical Company and ors, Appeal judgment, 517 F 3d 104 (2d Cir 2008), ILDC 1040 (US 2008), 22nd February 2008, United States; Court of Appeals (2nd Circuit) [2d Cir]

In the United States, private plaintiffs brought a case under the Alien Tort Statute in relation to the US military's use of the defoliant herbicide Agent Orange during the Vietnam War, a herbicide which allegedly caused harm to human health and the environment in Vietnam.[43] The tort case was not brought against the US government but against the defendants who manufactured and supplied the herbicides to the US government. The question arose as to whether the use of Agent Orange constituted a violation of customary international law actionable under the Alien Tort Statute.

> 32 The sources of international law relied on by Plaintiffs do not support a universally-accepted norm prohibiting the wartime use of Agent Orange that is defined with the degree of specificity required by [the U.S. Supreme Court's decision in *Sosa*]. Although the herbicide campaign may have been controversial, the record before us supports the conclusion that Agent Orange was used as a defoliant and not as a poison designed for or targeting human populations. Inasmuch as Agent Orange was intended for defoliation and for destruction of crops only, its use did not violate the international norms relied upon here, since those norms would not necessarily prohibit the deployment of materials that are only secondarily, and not intentionally, harmful to humans. In this respect, it is significant that Plaintiffs nowhere allege that the government intended to harm human beings through its use of Agent Orange.

43 For a discussion of the case see A E A Zierler, 'The Vietnamese Plaintiffs: Searching for a Remedy After Agent Orange' (2007) 21 *Temple International and Comparative Law Journal* 447; M G Palmer, 'Compensation for Vietnam's Agent Orange Victims' (2004) 8 *International Journal of Human Rights* 1.

> 39 Plaintiffs' claims that the use of Agent Orange violated the norm of proportionality and caused unnecessary suffering rely upon international agreements requiring intentionality that Plaintiffs cannot establish. Article 23(e) prohibits the use of "arms, projectiles, or material calculated to cause unnecessary suffering." Article 6 of the Nuremberg Charter proscribes "wanton destruction of cities, towns or villages, or devastation not justified by military necessity." [...] The main problem with the principle of proportionality is not whether or not it exists but what it means and how it is to be applied. It is relatively simple to state that there must be an acceptable relation between the legitimate destructive effect and undesirable collateral effects [...]. It is much easier to formulate the principle of proportionality in general terms than it is to apply it to a particular set of circumstances because the comparison is often between unlike quantities and values.
>
> 40 Plaintiffs have, at best, alleged a customary international norm proscribing the purposeful use of poison as a weapon against human beings that is inapplicable in this case.

The US court's decision in the *Agent Orange Litigation* is interesting in two respects. For one thing, it gives short shrift to (domestic) courts conducting a proportionality-informed review of military decisions. For another, it ruled that only the purposeful use of poison as a weapon against human beings is unlawful under international humanitarian law.

As far as proportionality is concerned, the court held that the principle is too vague and indefinite to satisfy the requirements laid down by the US Supreme Court in the *Sosa* case for a claim under the US Alien Tort Statute (ATS) to be actionable. These requirements do not follow from international law but from statutory interpretation of the ATS. The ATS provides in 28 US § 1350 that '[t]he district courts shall have original jurisdiction of any civil action by an alien for a tort only, committed in violation of the law of nations or a treaty of the United States', but the US Supreme Court later required in *Sosa* that the international norm of which violation was claimed be sufficiently clear and unambiguous and defined with sufficient specificity to render it obligatory and universal.[44] In *Agent Orange*, the court ruled that the international humanitarian law principle of proportionality, which by its very nature is not a bright-line rule but instead requires balancing various interests, does not qualify as such a norm. Compare however the string of Israeli court decisions conducting a proportionality review of decisions of IDF military commanders and of the Israeli government, discussed above.

As far as the second point of interest is concerned, the court required that plaintiffs establish that the US government *intended* to harm human beings through their use of Agent Orange. According to the court, the use of poison that had only secondary harmful effects on human beings—such as the use of the *defoliant* Agent Orange in Vietnam—was not prohibited. As the plaintiffs could not establish the government's intention to harm humans, no international humanitarian law norms were violated. The (older) international humanitarian law treaty norms which prohibit the use of poison, if interpreted restrictively, may indeed only have contemplated outlawing poisonous weapons which *primarily* target humans. However, one may wonder whether a later customary international law norm has not developed to the effect of also outlawing such weapons that, while having another primary purpose, nevertheless cause secondary harm to humans, the civilian population in particular. While the court seemed to entertain this possibility, it swiftly held that any such norm would not be specific enough to be

44 *Sosa v Alvarez Machain*, 542 US 692 (2004). See also *In re Estate of Marcos Human Rights Litigation*, 25 F 3d 1467, 1475 (CA9 1994) ('Actionable violations of international law must be of a norm that is specific, universal, and obligatory').

actionable under the ATS. This may exemplify the reluctance of domestic courts to rely on customary norms that have no foothold in treaty law. That said, a customary norm which prohibits the use of poisonous weapons in all circumstances, even if not directly targeting humans, may be in the process of emerging, or has perhaps already emerged although not in a sufficiently unambiguous form to be actionable under the ATS.

Van Anraat Case, Public Prosecutor and Fifteen anonymous victims v Van Anraat, Case No 2200050906-2, Decision No LJN: BA4676, ILDC 753 (NL 2007), 9th May 2007, Netherlands; The Hague; Court of Appeal

A last case of interest, as far as the legality of using certain weapons in armed conflict is concerned, is the Dutch *van Anraat* case. The court addressed the legality of the use of chemical weapons by the Iraqi regime against the Kurds in northern Iraq between 1984 and 1988 and in the war with Iran, and considered such use to be a clear violation of the 1925 Geneva Gas Protocol.[45] The case was a criminal case brought against the Dutch businessman, van Anraat, who had supplied the chemicals to the Iraqi regime, which according to the prosecutor amounted to complicity in a violation of the laws of war.

> 16 [. . .] As results from the case file (in the period referred to in the charges), the Iraqi regime carried out multiple attacks with (among others) mustard gas during the war with Iran on places in that country, as well as on the border region between Iraq and Iran, where Kurdish population groups lived that were suspected of collaboration with the Iranian enemy. Those attacks caused the death of at least thousands of civilians (that did not participate in the conflict) and caused permanent and severe health problems to very many persons. It is beyond doubt that the regime in Baghdad by doing so committed extensive and extremely gross violations of the international humanitarian law by using a weapon that was already prohibited by the Geneva (Gas) Protocol of 17 June 1925.
>
> The defendant has made an essential contribution to these violations—at a time that many, if not all other suppliers 'pulled out' with regard to the increasing international pressure—by supplying many times in the course of several years (among other matters) very large quantities of a precursor for mustard gas; in doing so the defendant made significant profits. Those supplies enabled the Iraqi regime to (almost) continue their deadly (air) attacks in full force during a number of years. Apparently the defendant did not give his deliberate support to the afore mentioned gross violations out of sympathy for the targets of the regime, but—as it should be assumed—the defendant acted exclusively in pursuit of large gains and fully neglected the consequences of his actions. Even today the defendant does not show any sense of guilt or any compassion for the numerous victims of the mustard gas attacks.

The *van Anraat* case has mainly (international) criminal law relevance,[46] but the criminal court could only rule on van Anraat's complicity in a violation of the laws and customs of war (ie, international humanitarian law) if such a violation were proven. The court did not have to spend much thought on the question of whether the use of mustard gas by Saddam Hussein against the Kurds was prohibited under international law. It was after all the main aim of the 1925 Geneva Gas Protocol to outlaw the use of mustard gas, a weapon that had caused so many casualties during WWI.

45 Geneva Gas Protocol (n 3).

46 See also C Barker, B Myers, and H van der Wilt, 'International Criminal Law' Chapter 15 in this volume.

VIII. Conclusion

The *corpus* of domestic court decisions relevant to international humanitarian law is sizable but not huge. Only a limited number of states have been involved in armed conflict, whereas war crimes trials conducted by third states under the universality principle are few and far between. Importantly, some domestic courts consider international humanitarian law conventions as not self-executing and thus as not conferring a private right of action on individuals and NGOs seeking to challenge governmental action. In spite of these limitations, domestic courts—although to a lesser extent and arguably with lesser authority than international criminal tribunals—have further developed some aspects of international humanitarian law, or at least have clarified the scope of international humanitarian law provisions that lack specificity (eg, regarding administrative detention periods and occasions for judicial review). When so doing, most of the time courts apply international humanitarian law treaty law; they are wary of finding governmental action to be in violation of customary international law.

A large number of pertinent decisions on international humanitarian law stem from Israeli courts. Israeli courts have rendered leading decisions on the notion of participation in hostilities, on security detention, and occupation law. They have demonstrated remarkable independence from the executive branch as they have proved willing to ascertain the reasonableness of military decision-making, notably whether a proper (proportionate) balance has been struck between the government's security imperatives and the needs of the protected persons, in particular civilians. Israeli case law shows that in situations of armed conflict, judges are willing to subject governmental action to international legal constraints.[47] In all states, however, courts remain understandably reluctant to second-guess military decisions when reviewing decisions taken in 'the heat of the battle'.

47 It is of note, however, that in other states, eg the US, judicial review of procedural aspects of governmental conduct in armed conflict could be based on constitutional law rather than international law.

14
Terrorism

ARISTOTELES CONSTANTINIDES

I. Introduction

Terrorism constitutes one of the most serious contemporary threats to international peace and security, human rights, democracy, and the rule of law. The international community stands unanimous in its 'strong and unequivocal condemnation of terrorism in all its forms and manifestations, committed by whomever, wherever and for whatever purposes'.[1] Even though there is an ongoing scholarly debate about whether existing rules of international law (with moderate adjustments) are adequate to respond to terrorism, or whether contemporary terrorism and counter-terrorism responses have led to a new 'international law of terrorism',[2] there is no denial that international law plays a key role in the global fight against terrorism. Yet, the relevant international legal framework has been full of controversies ever since the first international legal instrument to deal with terrorism was adopted by the League of Nations.[3]

The main controversy relates to the very notion of terrorism owing to the notorious inability of the international community to reach a universally accepted generic definition of the term.[4] During the period of decolonization, this was most tellingly verbalized in the famous adage 'one man's freedom fighter is another man's terrorist'. In 2000, the Ad Hoc Committee of the UN General Assembly, which had been tasked to elaborate a comprehensive legal framework of conventions dealing with international terrorism, began working on a draft comprehensive convention but its work was stalled in 2013 following persistent disagreements on the scope of the convention. Since then, a Working Group has been established to overcome the deadlock and finalize the process by addressing the following outstanding thorny issues: a) whether the armed activities of national liberation movements, especially in situations of foreign occupation, should be governed (exclusively) by international humanitarian law and presumably considered as lawful or classify as terrorist and fall within the scope of the convention, and b) whether unlawful activities of state military forces could be considered as terrorist and thus fall within the scope of the convention or should be governed by other rules of international law, most notably international human rights or humanitarian law. The draft convention does not require a political, religious or ideological motivation on the part of terrorists and is limited to physical violence against human beings; hence, violence

1 See UNGA, 'The United Nations Global Counter-Terrorism Strategy Review' UNGA Res 70/291 (19 July 2016) UN Doc A/RES/70/291, para 1. See also the similar wording in the landmark 'Declaration on Measures to Eliminate International Terrorism' UNGA Res 49/60 (9 December 1994) UN Doc A/RES/49/60, para 1.

2 For an excellent overview of the debate see B Saul, *Terrorism* (Hart Publishing 2012) lxvii–lxxxvii. For the traditional view see especially R Higgins, 'The General International Law of Terrorism' in R Higgins and M Flory (eds), *Terrorism and International Law* (Routledge 1997) 13. For a proposition that recent events have triggered a 'Grotian Moment', a fundamental paradigm shift in international law, see M Scharf 'How the War Against ISIS Changed International Law' (2016) 48 *Case Western Reserve Journal of International Law* 1.

3 The 1937 League of Nations Convention for the Prevention and Punishment of Terrorism was subject to various criticisms and did not receive the required number of ratifications to enter into force.

4 See generally B Saul, *Defining Terrorism in International Law* (OUP 2006).

against objects and property is not sufficient. Both these elements are at variance with definitions adopted in other contexts.[5] In the meantime, under the presidency of Antonio Cassese, the Appeals Chamber of the UN Special Tribunal for Lebanon held in 2011 that 'a customary rule of international law regarding the international crime of terrorism, at least *in time of peace*' has emerged.[6] That decision came under attack by scholars who insist that there is no such customary rule.[7]

The absence of a generally accepted comprehensive and precise definition of the crime of terrorism in international law and the resulting infinite variety of definitions in domestic laws could bear on the effective use of extradition and other means of transnational anti-terrorism cooperation and may also give rise to human rights abuses.[8] States have long misused the term to delegitimize political, ethnic, religious, indigenous and other groups they dislike, with the attendant risk that the international community may appear as condoning repressive action against them in the name of counter-terrorism.[9] The first section of this chapter presents several decisions by domestic courts that deal with definitional issues and reflect the uncertainties surrounding the definition and scope of terrorism.

To sidestep the definition conundrum, the international community has long adopted a reactive and so-called 'sectoral' approach, based on transnational cooperation by means of treaties addressing the most common criminal methods used by terrorists such as hijacking of aircraft, hostage taking, bombings, terrorism financing etc. More than a dozen such treaties have been adopted since the 1960s, which largely follow a common pattern, that is, requiring states parties to criminalize in their domestic law the specific (terrorist) acts defined in the treaties; ensure either extradition or prosecution (*aut dedere aut judicare*) with regard to those offences; and engage in mutual cooperation of varying degrees.[10] Parallel developments have taken place in regional organizations.[11]

The political organs of the UN have dealt with terrorism since the early 1970s.[12] The General Assembly has adopted dozens of resolutions condemning terrorism. The shocking attacks of 11 September 2001 and, more recently, the wave of terrorist attacks by ISIS in various parts of the world have further strengthened the determination of the international community to combat terrorism. The Security Council has assumed a leading role with the adoption of legally binding resolutions under Chapter VII of the UN Charter, which have imposed a series of far-reaching obligations on all states including, *inter alia*, to cooperate in various ways, criminalize terrorist acts and implement targeted or 'smart' sanctions against a consolidated list of individuals and

5 See C Walter, 'Terrorism' in R Wolfrum (ed), *Max Planck Encyclopedia of Public International Law* (OUP 2011) para 9.

6 *Interlocutory Decision on the Applicable Law: Terrorism, Conspiracy, Homicide, Perpetration, Cumulative Charging*, Case No STL-11-01/I, 16 February 2011, para 85 (emphasis in the original). The tribunal identified the following three elements of the crime: '(i) the perpetration of a criminal act (such as murder, kidnapping, hostage-taking, arson, and so on), or threatening such an act; (ii) the intent to spread fear among the population (which would generally entail the creation of public danger) or directly or indirectly coerce a national or international authority to take some action, or to refrain from taking it; (iii) when the act involves a transnational element'.

7 See, eg, K Ambos, 'Judicial Creativity at the Special Tribunal for Lebanon: Is There a Crime of Terrorism in International Law?' (2011) 24 *Leiden Journal of International Law* 655; B Saul, 'Legislating for a Radical Hague: The UN Special Tribunal for Lebanon Invents an International Crime of Transnational Terrorism' (2011) 24 *Leiden Journal of International Law* 677.

8 See UNCHR 'Report of the Special Rapporteur on the promotion and protection of human rights and fundamental freedoms while countering terrorism' (2005) UN Doc E/CN.4/2006/98, paras 26, 50.

9 ibid, paras 27, 56.

10 See UN, *International Instruments Related to the Prevention and Suppression of International Terrorism* (United Nations 2008).

11 ibid. See also G Nesi (ed), *International Cooperation in Counter-terrorism: The United Nations and Regional Organizations in the Fight Against Terrorism* (Ashgate 2006).

12 See generally B van Ginkel, *The Practice of the United Nations in Combating Terrorism from 1946 to 2008: Questions of Legality and Legitimacy* (Intersentia 2010).

organizations suspected of terrorism. Such sanctions include the freezing of assets and travel bans of the designated individuals and entities. At the same time, however, these resolutions also stress the need to combat terrorism in accordance with international law, including applicable international human rights, refugee, and humanitarian law,[13] which attests to the various challenges counter-terrorism poses to human rights and the (international) rule of law.[14]

Indeed, the UN sanctions regime was initially unconcerned with the legal protection of the designated individuals and entities, some of which were included in the consolidated list for long, based on apparently weak evidence falling short of due process standards.[15] The listing and delisting regime was gradually improved with the introduction of an Ombudsperson for individual delisting complaints.[16] The harsh impact of the sanctions on the rights and freedoms of designated individuals and entities gave rise to several cases before domestic as well as supranational courts. Some of the most prominent domestic cases are presented in the first part of the second section of this chapter. As discussed below, domestic decisions were largely influenced by the two different approaches adopted by the Court of First Instance of the EU (now the General Court of the EU) and the European Court of Justice (now the Court of Justice of the EU) in the famous *Kadi* case.[17]

The remaining of the chapter presents a dozen cases that exemplify the difficult balance between the need to combat terrorism effectively and the need to uphold (international) human rights standards while doing so. They show how domestic courts in various parts of the world have responded to the attempts by the legislature and the executive to circumvent human rights during the 'war on terror'. The focus is on cases involving the prohibition of torture and non-refoulement as well as the rights to liberty and fair trial, which are endangered by harsh interrogation techniques, admissibility of foreign torture evidence, removals to the risk of torture, prolonged/arbitrary detention, control orders and other measures. Several of these decisions, especially by domestic courts in Europe, also illustrate the interplay between the case law of domestic courts and that of supranational courts or treaty bodies dealing with the same issues.

The main criterion for the selection of cases in this chapter is their discussion and analysis of international norms on terrorism and/or human rights including, in some cases, domestic law implementing international obligations. Thus, it does not include judgments by domestic courts decided purely under domestic law despite their significance from a rule of law perspective.[18]

13 See, eg, UNSC Res 1822 (2008) UN Doc S/RES/1822, preambular para 3.

14 See generally H Duffy, *The 'War on Terror' and the Framework of International Law* (2nd edn, CUP 2015); L Doswald-Beck, *Human Rights in Times of Conflict and Terrorism* (OUP 2011); M Scheinin (ed), *Terrorism and Human Rights* (Edward Elgar Publishing 2013).

15 See especially B Fassbender, 'Targeted Sanctions and Due Process' (2006) 3 *International Organizations Law Review* 437.

16 See P Eden, 'United Nations Targeted Sanctions, Human Rights and the Office of the Ombudsperson' in M Happold and P Eden (eds), *Economic Sanctions and International Law* (Hart Publishing 2016) 135–70.

17 *Yusuf and Al-Barakaat International Foundation v Council of the European Union and Commission of the European Communities and United Kingdom (intervening)*, Judgment, Case T-306/01, [2005] ECR II-3533, 21 September 2005, Court of Justice of the European Union [CJEU]; General Court of the European Union [EGC]; General Court (2nd Chamber); *Kadi v Council of the European Union and Commission of the European Communities*, Judgment, action for annulment, appeal, Case C-402/05 P, Case C-415/05 P, ECLI:EU:C:2008:461, [2008] ECR I-6351, [2009] AC 1225, [2008] 3 CMLR 41, 3 September 2008, Court of Justice of the European Union [CJEU]; European Court of Justice [ECJ]; European Court of Justice (Grand Chamber).

18 See, eg, *Suleiman (on behalf of Suleiman) v Commissioner of Police and ors*, Decision on application for habeas corpus, Misc App 441 of 2010, ILDC 2112 (KE 2010), [2010] eKLR, 30 September 2010, Kenya; Nairobi; High Court, a case of an extraordinary rendition of a Kenyan to Uganda, where the Court relied solely on constitutional law and held (para 9): 'Whether one is a terror suspect or an ordinary suspect, he is not exempted from the ordinary protection of the law. Whatever the security considerations that the Police had in this case, the recognition and preservation of the liberties of this subject was the only way to reinforce this country's commitment to the rule of law and human rights. Police must have the capacity to battle terrorism and enforce human rights at the same time as the two are not, and should not, be incompatible.'

This is particularly so with respect to the US Guantanamo cases in the aftermath of 9/11, which either concerned issues of jurisdiction/sovereignty and/or international humanitarian law or were largely decided under domestic (constitutional) law and doctrine such as the powers of the US President and Congress during armed conflict, with only indirect relevance to international norms on terrorism and/or human rights. In a long *bras de fer* with the executive and the Congress, the US Supreme Court made incremental rule of law gains in *Hamdi v Rumsfeld*,[19] *Rasul v Bush*,[20] and *Hamdan v Rumsfeld*,[21] before ultimately ruling in *Boumediene v Bush* in 2008 that the constitutional guarantees of *habeas corpus* extended to the Guantanamo detainees.[22] Guantanamo litigations continued in lower courts, including on the question of where to resettle the detainees upon release.[23] Similarly, domestic cases arising in the context of counter-terrorism but dealing with the impact of terrorism on other norms of international law, most notably international humanitarian law (including the question of targeted or extra-judicial killings of 'unlawful combatants', which also raises human rights issues) and the use of force, including the controversial question of self-defense against terrorists, are discussed elsewhere in this volume.

II. Terrorism in International Law: Definitional Issues

1. Definition

Suresh, United Nations High Commissioner for Refugees (intervening) and ors (intervening) v Canada (Minister of Citizenship and Immigration) and Attorney-General of Canada, Decision, Docket No 27790, 2002 SCC 1, [2002] 1 SCR 3, (2002) 37 Admin LR (3d) 159, (2002) 90 CRR (2d) 1, (2002) SCJ No 3, 281 NR 1, (2002) 208 DLR (4th) 1, (2002) 18 Imm LR (3d) 1, 2002 CarswellNat 8, 2002 CarswellNat 7 (SCC), ILDC 186 (CA 2002), 11th January 2002, Canada; Supreme Court [SCC]

Mr Suresh, a Sri Lankan of Tamil origin, was recognized by Canada as 'Convention Refugee' in 1990 but a few years later he was subjected to deportation proceedings to Sri Lanka for being a danger to the security of Canada owing to his membership of the Liberation Tigers of Tamil Eelam (LTTE), an organization that, according to the Canadian Security Intelligence Service, was engaged in terrorist activity in Sri Lanka. He argued that he would face torture if deported to Sri Lanka, in breach of Section 7 of the Canadian Charter of Rights and Freedoms. He also argued that the terms 'danger to the security of Canada' and 'terrorism' were unconstitutionally vague.

19 *Hamdi v Rumsfeld*, 542 US 507 (2004) (holding that US citizens have a constitutional right to challenge their detention as enemy combatants before a neutral decision-maker).

20 *Rasul v Bush*, Decision, Docket No 03-334, 542 US 466 (2004), 124 S Ct 2686 (2004), 159 L Ed 2d 548 (2004), 72 USLW 4596 (2004), ILDC 115 (US 2004), 28 June 2004, United States; Supreme Court [US] (holding that US District Courts have habeas corpus jurisdiction to review the legality of detention of the Guantanamo detainees on statutory basis; no discussion of constitutional right of habeas corpus or of relevant international law norms).

21 *Hamdan v Rumsfeld and ors*, Appeal judgment, 548 US 557, 126 S Ct 2749, 165 L Ed 2d 723 (2006), ILDC 745 (US 2006), 29 June 2006, United States; Supreme Court [US] (majority decision holding, *inter alia*, that the military commissions established under the Military Commissions Act of 2006 were subject to judicial review and were unlawful, with extensive discussion of international humanitarian law under domestic law and the Geneva Conventions).

22 *Boumediene v Bush (President of the United States)*, Decision, Docket No 06-1195, 553 US 723 (2008), 128 S Ct 2229 (2008), ILDC 1039 (US 2008), 12 June 2008, United States; Supreme Court [US] (majority decision holding that the US exercised *de facto* sovereignty over Guantanamo, hence the constitutional guarantee of habeas corpus reached those detained there).

23 See, eg, *Kiyemba and ors v Obama and ors*, Appeal judgment, 55 F 3d 1022 (DC Cir 2009), ILDC 1582 (US 2009), 18 February 2009, United States (no discussion of international human rights law).

(b) Are the Terms "Danger to the Security of Canada" and "Terrorism" Unconstitutionally Vague?

(i) "Danger to the Security of Canada"

[. . .]

87 [. . .] International conventions must be interpreted in the light of current conditions. It may once have made sense to suggest that terrorism in one country did not necessarily implicate other countries. But after the year 2001, that approach is no longer valid.

88 First, the global transport and money networks that feed terrorism abroad have the potential to touch all countries, including Canada, and to thus implicate them in the terrorist activity. Second, terrorism itself is a worldwide phenomenon. The terrorist cause may focus on a distant locale, but the violent acts that support it may be close at hand. Third, preventive or precautionary state action may be justified; not only an immediate threat but also possible future risks must be considered. Fourth, Canada's national security may be promoted by reciprocal cooperation between Canada and other states in combating international terrorism. These considerations lead us to conclude that to insist on direct proof of a specific threat to Canada as the test for "danger to the security of Canada" is to set the bar too high. There must be a real and serious possibility of adverse effect to Canada. But the threat need not be direct; rather it may be grounded in distant events that indirectly have a real possibility of harming Canadian security.

90 [. . .] [A] person constitutes a "danger to the security of Canada" if he or she poses a serious threat to the security of Canada, whether direct or indirect, and bearing in mind the fact that the security of one country is often dependent on the security of other nations. The threat must be "serious", in the sense that it must be grounded on objectively reasonable suspicion based on evidence and in the sense that the threatened harm must be substantial rather than negligible.

91 This definition of "danger to the security of Canada" does not mean that Canada is unable to deport those who pose a risk to individual Canadians, but not the country. A different provision, the "danger to the public" provision, allows the government to deport those who pose no danger to the security of the country per se—those who pose a danger to Canadians, as opposed to a danger to Canada—provided they have committed a serious crime. Moreover, if a refugee is wanted for crimes in a country that will not torture him or her on return, the government may be free to extradite him or her to face those charges, whether or not he or she has committed crimes in Canada.

[. . .]

(ii) "Terrorism";

93 The term "terrorism" is found in s. 19 of the *Immigration Act*, dealing with denial of refugee status upon arrival in Canada. [. . .] We do not in these reasons seek to define terrorism exhaustively—a notoriously difficult endeavour—but content ourselves with finding that the term provides a sufficient basis for adjudication and hence is not unconstitutionally vague. We share the view of Robertson J.A. that the term is not inherently ambiguous "even if the full meaning . . . must be determined on an incremental basis" [. . .].

94 One searches in vain for an authoritative definition of "terrorism". The Immigration Act does not define the term. Further, there is no single definition that is accepted internationally. The absence of an authoritative definition means that, at least at the margins, "the term is open to politicized manipulation, conjecture, and polemical interpretation" [. . .].

95 Even amongst those who agree on the definition of the term, there is considerable disagreement as to whom the term should be attached [...]. Perhaps the most striking example of the politicized nature of the term is that Nelson Mandela's African National Congress was, during the apartheid era, routinely labelled a terrorist organization, not only by the South African government but by much of the international community.

96 We are not persuaded, however, that the term "terrorism" is so unsettled that it cannot set the proper boundaries of legal adjudication. The recently negotiated International Convention for the Suppression of the Financing of Terrorism, GA Res. 54/109, December 9, 1999, approaches the definitional problem in two ways. First, it employs a functional definition in Article 2(1)(a), defining "terrorism" as "[a]n act which constitutes an offence within the scope of and as defined in one of the treaties listed in the annex". The annex lists nine treaties that are commonly viewed as relating to terrorist acts [...]. Second, the Convention supplements this offence-based list with a stipulative definition of terrorism. Article 2(1)(b) defines "terrorism" as:

Any [...] act intended to cause death or serious bodily injury to a civilian, or to any other person not taking an active part in the hostilities in a situation of armed conflict, when the purpose of such act, by its nature or context, is to intimidate a population, or to compel a government or an international organization to do or to abstain from doing any act.

97 [...] It is true that the functional approach has received strong support from international law scholars and state representatives – support that is evidenced by the numerous international legal instruments that eschew stipulative definitions in favour of prohibitions on specific acts of violence. While we are not unaware of the danger that the term "terrorism" may be manipulated, we are not persuaded that it is necessary or advisable to altogether eschew a stipulative definition of the term in favour of a list that may change over time and that may in the end necessitate distinguishing some (proscribed) acts from other (non-proscribed) acts by reliance on a term like "terrorism". [...]

98 In our view, it may safely be concluded, following the International Convention for the Suppression of the Financing of Terrorism, that "terrorism" in s. 19 of the Act includes any "act intended to cause death or serious bodily injury to a civilian, or to any other person not taking an active part in the hostilities in a situation of armed conflict, when the purpose of such act, by its nature or context, is to intimidate a population, or to compel a government or an international organization to do or to abstain from doing any act". This definition catches the essence of what the world understands by "terrorism". Particular cases on the fringes of terrorist activity will inevitably provoke disagreement. Parliament is not prevented from adopting more detailed or different definitions of terrorism. The issue here is whether the term as used in the Immigration Act is sufficiently certain to be workable, fair and constitutional. We believe that it is.

The court concluded that the terms 'danger to the security of Canada' and 'terrorism' were not unconstitutionally vague. Applying these terms to the facts of the case, they would permit the deportation of Suresh. The court saw no need to exhaustively define terrorism and relied on the definition of the 1999 International Convention for the Suppression of the Financing of Terrorism for the essence of what is meant by terrorism, which was found to provide a sufficiently well understood basis for adjudication.

Such a rather flexible approach to the definition of terrorism is not only found in cases dealing with immigration proceedings; courts have also taken similar position in criminal and human rights cases. For instance, in *Silva and more than five thousand citizens v Congress of Peru*, the

Constitutional Court of Peru held that a certain margin of imprecision in the definition of terrorism was compatible with the principle of legality, provided that the citizens perceived the content of the prohibition, and could differentiate between what was prohibited and what was permitted.[24] This approach is also consistent with the case law of the European Court of Human Rights (ECtHR), which has held that under (the non-derogable) Article 7 of the European Convention on Human Rights (ECHR), which enshrines the principle of legality, an offence is clearly defined in the law 'where the individual can know from the wording of the relevant provision and, if need be, with the assistance of the courts' interpretation of it, what acts and omissions will make him criminally liable'.[25] That said, there is widespread concern that vague, overbroad, or imprecise definitions of terrorism can be—and often are—overly abusive.[26] The following is a case in point.

Singh and ors v Bihar, Appeal decision, [2004] INSC 225, ILDC 2109 (IN 2004), 2nd April 2004, India; Supreme Court

The appellants in this case were involved in fighting with the police during a raid in the house where they were planning allegedly unlawful activities and where the police seized arms, ammunition, documents, files, letters regarding banned organizations, rifles, cartridges, and carbine. They challenged their conviction for, *inter alia*, offences punishable under India's 1987 Terrorist and Disruptive Activities (Prevention) Act (TADA), arguing that their acts did not fall within its scope. The Supreme Court of India was thus faced with the definition of terrorism.

> 15 […] As noted at the outset, it is not possible to precisely define "terrorism". Finding a definition of "terrorism" has haunted countries for decades. A first attempt to arrive at an internationally acceptable definition was made under the League of Nations, but the one which the convention drafted in 1937 never came into existence. The UN member States still have no agreed-upon definition apparently on account of what at times reveal to be state sponsored terrorism, both at national and international levels. Terminology consensus would, however, be necessary for a single comprehensive convention on terrorism, which some countries favour in place of the present 12 piecemeal conventions and protocols. The lack of agreement on a definition of terrorism has been a major obstacle to meaningful international countermeasures. Cynics have often commended at national and international levels that one State's "terrorist" is another State's "freedom fighter" and that too with the blessings of those in power. […] If terrorism is defined strictly in terms of attacks on non-military targets, a number of attacks on military installations and soldiers' residences could not be included in the statistics. In order to cut through the Gordian definitional knot, terrorism expert A. Schmid suggested in 1992 in a report for the then UN Crime Branch that it might be a good idea to take the existing consensus on what constitutes a "war crime" as a point of departure. If the core of war crimes—deliberate attacks on civilians, hostage-taking and the killing of prisoners—is extended to peacetime, we could simply define acts of terrorism veritably as "peacetime equivalents of war crimes".

24 *Silva and more than five thousand citizens v Congress of Peru*, Original petition, Exp No 010-2002-AI/TC, ILDC 323 (PE 2003), 3 January 2003, Constitutional Court, paras 47 and 77. See also in the same vein *Shining Path Case, Peru v Reinoso (Manuel) and ors*, First instance criminal decision, No 560-03, ILDC 670 (PE 2006), 13 October 2006, National Criminal Court, paras 451–55, with further reference to the case law of the Inter-American Court of Human Rights.

25 Eg, ECtHR, *Cantoni v France*, App No 17862/91 (15 November 1996) para 29. See also A Salinas de Frias, *Counter-Terrorism and Human Rights in the Case Law of the European Court of Human Rights* (Council of Europe Publishing 2012) 117.

26 See, eg, UNCHR, 'Additional progress report prepared by Ms. Kalliopi K. Koufa, Special Rapporteur on terrorism and human rights' (2003) UN Doc E/CN.4/Sub.2/2003/WP.1, para 66.

League of Nations Convention (1937)

16 "All criminal acts directed against a State along with intended or calculated to create a state of terror in the minds of particular persons or a group of persons or the general public."

(GA Res. 51/210—Measures to eliminate international terrorism)

"1. Strongly condemns all acts, methods and practices of terrorism as criminal and unjustifiable, wherever and by whomsoever committed;

2. Reiterates that criminal acts intended or calculated to provoke a state of terror in the general public, a group of persons or particular persons for political purposes are in any circumstances unjustifiable, whatever the considerations of a political, philosophical, ideological, racial, ethnic, religious or other nature that may be invoked to justify them."

[. . .]

22 Terrorism is one of the manifestations of increased lawlessness and cult of violence. Violence and crime constitute a threat to an established order and are a revolt against a civilised and orderly society. "Terrorism" though has not been separately defined under TADA there is sufficient indication in Section 3 itself to identify what it is by an all inclusive and comprehensive phraseology adopted in engrafting the said provision, which serves the double purpose as a definition and punishing provision nor is it possible to give a precise definition of "terrorism" or lay down what constitutes "terrorism". It may be possible to describe it as use of violence when its most important result is not merely the physical and mental damage of the victim but the prolonged psychological effect it produces or has the potential of producing on the society as a whole. There may be death, injury, or destruction of property or even deprivation of individual liberty in the process but the extent and reach of the intended terrorist activity travels beyond the effect of an ordinary crime capable of being punished under the ordinary penal law of the land and its main objective is to overawe the Government or disturb the harmony of the society or "terrorise" people and the society and not only those directly assaulted, with a view to disturb the even tempo, peace and tranquility of the society and create a sense of fear and insecurity.

23 In the aforesaid background, the inevitable conclusion is that the appeals are sans merit and deserve dismissal, which we direct.

The court identified as the key element of terrorism (under the TADA) that the effect and reach of the intended criminal/terrorist activity far exceeded the damage to the immediate victims. As noted by the ILDC reporter, the various international definitions of terrorism reviewed by the court and its reference to the universal difficulty in defining terrorism bolstered its conclusion to uphold TADA's overbroad reach, for which however the Act had been criticized and ultimately lapsed.[27]

Almog and ors v Arab Bank, Public Limited Company, Trial court decision on motions, 471 F.Supp.2d 257 (E.D.N.Y. 2007), ILDC 801 (US 2007), 29th January 2007, United States; New York; District Court for the Eastern District of New York [EDNY]

The plaintiffs were US and foreign nationals, victims or surviving family members of victims of terrorist attacks in Israel. They brought a case against the Arab Bank, claiming that the Bank

27 S Farooq, Analysis, *Singh and ors v Bihar*, ILDC 2109 (IN 2004) A5–A9. Under the TADA definition, any injury, destruction of property, or disruption of essential services could be prosecuted under its much harsher punishment scheme.

knowingly provided banking services to various organizations sponsoring those attacks. The foreign nationals based jurisdiction on the ATS, alleging that the Arab Bank had violated international law by financing suicide bombings and other murderous attacks. Under the ATS's jurisdictional grant, as set out in *Sosa*, federal courts could only recognize private claims for violations of international law if the norm of international law was specific, well-defined and accepted among nations.

> 74 The next issue to be addressed is whether the international norm is of mutual, and not merely several, concern. Suicide bombings and other murderous attacks to intimidate or coerce a civilian population are indisputably of mutual concern. [...] The Bombing Convention states that the occurrence of terrorist attacks by means of explosives or other lethal devices is a matter of grave concern to the international community as a whole. [...] The Financing Convention states that "the financing of terrorism is a matter of grave concern to the international community as a whole." [...]. In addition, Congress has found that "international terrorism affects the interstate and foreign commerce of the United States by harming international trade and market stability, and limiting international travel by United States citizens as well as foreign visitors to the United States." [...]. Indeed, the scope of the nationalities represented by plaintiffs in this very case illustrates one type of impact on the international community that arises when innocent civilians are targeted to be attacked.
>
> 75 In sum, in light of the universal condemnation of organized and systematic suicide bombings and other murderous acts intended to intimidate or coerce a civilian population, this court finds that such conduct violates an established norm of international law. The court further finds that the conduct alleged by plaintiffs is sufficiently specific and well-defined to be recognized as a claim under the ATS. This becomes evident when the conduct alleged here and condemned by the law of nations is viewed in contrast to the conduct alleged in cases where it was found not to be sufficiently specific or well-defined. [...] Here, in contrast, the conduct alleged falls precisely within the norm evidenced by the sources discussed. As already explained, plaintiffs' allegations essentially track the conduct specifically condemned in the Financing and Bombing Conventions, as well as in the ATA sections which implement those Conventions. Thus, the norm is of sufficiently definite content and acceptance among nations of the world as the historical paradigms familiar when § 1350 was enacted.

The District Court in this case found that the prohibition of terrorism financing was a sufficiently well-defined rule of customary international law to allow an ATS claim, largely based on the universal condemnation of suicide bombings and of terrorism financing, as reflected in the two respective conventions of 1997 and 1999. As shown in the following case, this ruling on terrorism financing did not seem to affect the established case law of US courts that terrorism as such was not a well-defined violation of international law for ATS purposes.[28]

As to the issue of complicity liability for terrorism financing, the ILDC reporter remarked that in *Presbyterian Church of Sudan v Talisman Energy Inc*,[29] the Second Circuit had found that there was no international consensus for applying liability for actions undertaken with

28 See, eg, *Tel-Oren v Libyan Arab Jamahiriya and ors*, Appeal judgment, Per Curiam, Docket No 81-1870, Docket No 81-1871, 726 F 2d 774 (DC Cir 1984), 233 US AppDC 384 (1984), ILDC 875 (US 1984), 3 February 1984, United States; Court of Appeals (DC Circuit) [DC Cir]: 'While this nation unequivocally condemns all terrorist attacks, that sentiment is not universal. Indeed, the nations of the world are so divisively split on the legitimacy of such aggression as to make it impossible to pinpoint an area of harmony or consensus" (Judge Edwards, para. 64); "Given such disharmony, I cannot conclude that the law of nations [...] outlaws politically motivated terrorism, no matter how repugnant it might be to our own legal system' (ibid, para 67).

29 582 F 3d 244, 259 (2d Cir), 2 October 2009.

knowledge but without the purpose of aiding and abetting. This would have entailed that the plaintiffs in the case at hand would have to show that the Arab Bank had acted with the purpose of aiding and abetting terrorist organizations to carry out bombings.[30] In contrast, in *Cabello and Cabello-Barrueto v Fernandez-Larios*,[31] the Eleventh Circuit found that the *mens rea* for aiding and abetting in international law was knowledge.[32]

Chiquita Brands International Incorporated and ors v Valencia and ors, Decision on motion to dismiss, Case No 08-01916-MD-MARRA, ILDC 1873 (US 2011), 792 F Supp 2d 1301 (SD Fla 2011), 3rd June 2011, United States; Florida; District Court for the Southern District of Florida [SD Fla]

This case concerned ATS claims against the US multinational corporation Chiquita Brands International Inc for terrorism, torture and other crimes in connection with Chiquita's alleged support of the *Autodefensas Unidas de Columbia* (AUC), the paramilitary units combatting the guerrilla forces in Colombia's civil war, which the US government had classified as a foreign terrorist organization in 1991. The claimants were Colombian family members of victims who had been killed or tortured by the AUC during the late 1990s through 2005. Chiquita moved to dismiss the claims falling within the realm of terrorism or material support of terrorism, arguing that they were not actionable ATS claims.

> 49 [...] the Court rejects Plaintiffs' argument that international-law sources establish a modern, well-defined, universally accepted norm against terrorism. Plaintiffs cite dozens of international treaties, United Nations resolutions and declarations, and regional conventions for this point. [...] Plaintiffs' argument seems to culminate with the International Convention for the Suppression of the Financing of Terrorism, U.N. Doc. A/54/109 (Dec. 9, 1999) ("Financing Convention"), which Plaintiffs contend codified an existing international norm against terrorism created by decades of treaties and conventions. [...]
>
> 50 The Court finds that the Financing Convention neither codifies nor creates an international-law norm against terrorism or financing terrorism. First, the Financing Convention does not establish a *universally accepted* rule of customary international law. An international treaty "will only constitute *sufficient proof* of a norm of customary international law if an *overwhelming majority* of States have ratified the treaty." *Flores*, 414 F.3d at 256 (second emphasis added). [...] In April 2002, when the Financing Convention came into force, only 26 of the 192 nations of the world, or roughly 14%, had ratified it. In February 2004, when Chiquita's alleged payments to the AUC terminated, 111 States, or roughly 58% of the nations of the world, had ratified the Financing Convention. These figures do not constitute the "overwhelming majority" necessary to establish a widely accepted norm of international law prohibiting financial support for terrorism at the time of Chiquita's purported wrongful acts.
>
> 51 Second, the norms in the Financing Convention are not *well-established*. Rather, the signatories to the Financing Convention dispute many of the rules therein, as illustrated by the many declarations and reservations, i.e., non-consents and varying interpretations, appended to the convention. For instance, Egypt declared that it "does not consider acts of national resistance *in all its forms*, including armed resistance against foreign occupation and aggression with a view to liberation and

30 G Crespo, Analysis, *Almog and ors v Arab Bank*, ILDC 801 (US 2007) A3.

31 Appeal judgment, Docket No 99-00528 CV-JAL, Case No 04-10030, 402 F 3d 1148 (11th Cir 2005), ILDC 314 (US 2005), 14 March 2005, United States; Court of Appeals (11th Circuit) [11th Cir].

32 G Crespo, Analysis, *Almog and ors v Arab Bank*, ILDC 801 (US 2007) A3.

self-determination, as terrorist acts." Egypt's declaration prompted an objection by the Czech Republic, which declared that it "considers the declaration to be incompatible with the object and purpose of the Convention." Moreover, a substantial number of states declared that they are not bound to entire subject areas of the Convention. […] Such disagreements, non-consents, and divergent interpretations of the Finance Convention demonstrate that the prohibitions of the convention are disputed and not well-established.

52 Plaintiffs' briefing also provides several footnotes that string cite dozens of other international treaties, United Nations resolutions and declarations, and regional conventions that Plaintiffs contend prohibit specific acts of terrorism. […] The Court further notes that many of these sources address the subject of terrorism, if at all, only at a high level of abstraction and do not provide any definition of terrorism. Thus, like the Financing Convention, these additional sources also fail to provide a well-defined, universally accepted norm of international law against terrorism or material support thereof.

53 Plaintiffs next argue that "nearly every state has incorporated the international prohibition against terrorism in its domestic laws." […] Under *Sosa*, however, a norm of international law sufficient to create a claim under the ATS must be drawn from international, not domestic, laws […] Reliance on domestic laws, even those of the United States, cannot support recognition of an international norm under the ATS. […]

54 Finally, Plaintiffs urge this Court to follow the district court's decision in *Almog v. Arab Bank, PLC*, 471 F. Supp. 2d 257 (E.D.N.Y. 2007), which Plaintiffs contend supports their claim that terrorism is actionable under the ATS. […]

55 To the extent that *Almog* can be read as holding that terrorism, or material support thereof, constitutes a violation of the law of nations, the Court respectfully disagrees with that conclusion for the reasons discussed above. In recognizing an international norm against suicide bombing and other attacks on civilians, the *Almog* court relied largely on the Financing Convention and the International Convention for the Suppression of Terrorist Bombings. […] As discussed above, this Court finds that the Financing Convention fails to establish a universally recognized, well-settled norm of customary international law. Moreover, and as noted above, the Bombing Convention addresses terrorism at a highly abstract level and does not provide any definition of the subject. The Court thus disagrees with *Almog*'s conclusion that these conventions support an international norm, under *Sosa*'s stringent requirements, prohibiting terrorism.

56 *Almog* is also distinguishable in that the court there did not recognize an ATS claim for terrorism in general, as Plaintiffs here urge upon this Court. Rather, *Almog* rested its holding on the specific allegations before it, which the court described as suicide bombings and assassinations of civilians. […] Indeed, the court explained that its holding was limited to the specific factual allegations before it, and not based upon a cause of action for "terrorism" generally. […]

57 For the foregoing reasons, the Court concludes that Plaintiffs' terrorism-based claims are not actionable under the ATS. Like *Tel-Oren, Saperstein*, and *Barboza*, and mindful of *Sosa*'s mandate that courts exercise great caution in recognizing new ATS claims, this Court finds that a claim for terrorism in general, or material support thereof, is not based on a sufficiently accepted, established, or defined norm of customary international law to constitute a violation of the law of nations. Accordingly, the Court lacks subject-matter jurisdiction under the ATS over Plaintiffs' terrorism-based claims and those claims are dismissed.

This decision was an elaborate reaffirmation of established US jurisprudence that terrorism-based claims were not actionable under the ATS and has added to the view that there is no international crime of terrorism in customary law.[33]

Hamdan v United States, Appeal judgment, ILDC 2022 (US 2012), 696 F 3d 1238 (DC Cir 2012), 16th October 2012, United States; Court of Appeals (DC Circuit) [DC Cir]

The Yemeni defendant was a member of Al-Qaeda and bin Laden's personal driver and bodyguard. Since November 2001, he was detained in Guantanamo as an enemy combatant and was convicted before a military commission for providing material support for terrorism, in violation of the Military Commissions Act of 2006 (MCA). The Act gave the military commission jurisdiction for violations of the 'law of war' and listed 'material support for terrorism' as a war crime under international law. Hamdan was convicted and served 66 months in prison, following which he was transferred to Yemen and released. He successfully appealed his conviction, arguing that the MCA could not be retroactively applied to his conduct between 1996 and 2001, and that providing 'material support for terrorism' was not a war crime under international law.

> 57 We turn, then, to the question whether material support for terrorism is an international-law war crime.
>
> 58 It is true that international law establishes at least some forms of terrorism, including the intentional targeting of civilian populations, as war crimes. See, e.g., Rome Statute of the International Criminal Court art. 8(2)(b), July 17, 1998, 2187 U.N.T.S. 90; Geneva Convention Relative to the Protection of Civilian Persons in Time of War (Geneva IV), art. 33, Aug. 12, 1949, 6 U.S.T. 3516, 75 U.N.T.S. 287 […].
>
> 59 But the issue here is whether material support for terrorism is an international-law war crime. The answer is no. International law leaves it to individual nations to proscribe material support for terrorism under their domestic laws if they so choose. There is no international-law proscription of material support for terrorism.
>
> 60 To begin with, there are no relevant international treaties that make material support for terrorism a recognized international-law war crime. Neither the Hague Convention nor the Geneva Conventions—the sources that are "the major treaties on the law of war"—acknowledge material support for terrorism as a war crime. […]
>
> 61 Nor does customary international law otherwise make material support for terrorism a war crime. […]
>
> 62 […] Material support for terrorism was not a recognized violation of the international law of war as of 2001 (or even today, for that matter). As we have noted, the Geneva Conventions and the Hague Convention do not prohibit material support for terrorism. The 1998 Rome Statute of the International Criminal Court, which catalogues an extensive list of international war crimes, makes no mention of material support for terrorism. […] Nor does the Statute of the International Tribunal for the Former Yugoslavia, the Statute of the International Tribunal for Rwanda, or the Statute of the Special Court for Sierra Leone. […] Nor have any international tribunals exercising common-law-type power determined that material support for terrorism is an international-law war crime.
>
> 63 Commentators on international law have similarly explained that material support for terrorism is not an international-law war crime. […] Nor is the offense of material support for terrorism listed in the JAG handbook on the law of war. […]

33 For a forceful argumentation in the same vein see B Saul, *Terrorism* (Hart Publishing 2012) xx–xxiii.

64 In short, neither the major conventions on the law of war nor prominent modern international tribunals nor leading international-law experts have identified material support for terrorism as a war crime. Perhaps most telling, before this case, no person has ever been tried by an international-law war crimes tribunal for material support for terrorism.

65 Not surprisingly, therefore, even the U.S. Government concedes in this case that material support for terrorism is not a recognized international-law war crime. No treaty that the Government has cited or that we are aware of identifies material support for terrorism as a war crime. And the Government further admits: The "offense of providing material support to terrorism, like spying and aiding the enemy, has not attained international recognition at this time as a violation of customary international law." [...]

66 To be sure, there is a strong argument that aiding and abetting a recognized international-law war crime such as terrorism is itself an international-law war crime. And there are other similar war crimes. But Hamdan was not charged with aiding and abetting terrorism or some other similar war crime. He was charged with material support for terrorism. And as the Government acknowledges, aiding and abetting terrorism prohibits different conduct, imposes different mens rea requirements, and entails different causation standards than material support for terrorism. If the Government wanted to charge Hamdan with aiding and abetting terrorism or some other war crime that was sufficiently rooted in the international law of war (and thus covered by 10 U.S.C. § 821) at the time of Hamdan's conduct, it should have done so.

67 The Government latches on to a few isolated precedents from the Civil War era to prop up its assertion that material support for terrorism was a pre-existing war crime as of 2001 for purposes of 10 U.S.C. § 821. There are several independent reasons that those cases fail to support the Government's argument. First, the Civil War cases did not involve any charges of material support for terrorism. Instead, several cases involve guerrillas who were punished for taking up "arms" as "insurgents"—that is, for direct attacks rather than material support. [...] Others were convicted of "joining, aiding and assisting a band of robbers and bandits"—in other words, what we would likely call aiding and abetting, not material support. [...] Second, those Civil War commissions were in part military tribunals governing certain territory—which are a separate form of military commission subject to a separate branch of law, and not the kind of law-of-war military commission at issue here. As others have suggested, their precedential value is therefore limited. [...] Third, and perhaps most to the point, those cases do not establish that material support for terrorism was a war crime recognized under international law as of 1996 to 2001 when Hamdan committed his conduct, which is the relevant inquiry under 10 U.S.C. § 821. The Government contends that those Civil War precedents illuminate what it calls the "U.S. common law of war"—not the international law of war. But the statutory constraint here imposed by 10 U.S.C. § 821 is the international law of war. [...] To be sure, U.S. precedents may inform the content of international law. But those Civil War precedents fail to establish material support for terrorism as a war crime under the international law of war as of 1996 to 2001. And even the Government admits that material support for terrorism was not an international-law war crime as of 1996 to 2001.

68 In short, material support for terrorism was not an international-law war crime under 10 U.S.C. § 821 at the time Hamdan engaged in the relevant conduct.

69 Because we read the Military Commissions Act not to sanction retroactive punishment for new crimes, and because material support for terrorism was not a pre-existing war crime under 10 U.S.C. § 821, Hamdan's conviction for material support for terrorism cannot stand. We reverse the decision of the Court of Military Commission Review and direct that Hamdan's conviction for material support for terrorism be vacated.

This case illustrates one of the major deficiencies of MCA's application: the retroactive prosecution of crimes (particularly the overbroad 'material support for terrorism')[34] that were not prohibited as war crimes triable by military commission under US law at the time the conduct occurred. This was a clear breach of the fundamental principle of legality recognized in international human rights law. The court's decision was in accordance with international law and remedied the violation in that case.

2. The armed conflict exception to terrorism

The controversies surrounding the proper scope of the armed conflict exception to terrorism persist in international law and are echoed in several domestic decisions. Decisions by domestic courts applying domestic legislation present various approaches; some have applied relevant international rules incorporated directly or indirectly in domestic law, while others have ignored them. The following cases illustrate those variations.

Khan v Eric H Holder Jr, Attorney General, Appeal judgment, 584 F 3d 773 (9th Cir 2009), ILDC 1470 (US 2009), 9th September 2009, United States; Court of Appeals (9th Circuit) [9th Cir]

The appellant's application for asylum and withholding of removal under the US Immigration and Nationality Act (INA) was rejected because he was considered as having engaged in terrorist activity owing to his affiliation with the Jammu Kashir Liberation Front (JKLF). He claimed that he was affiliated only with the non-violent political wing of the JKLF, and denied any knowledge of the military wing's activities. He argued that the INA's definition of 'terrorist activity' incorporated international law and thus excluded legitimate armed resistance against military targets from that definition. The Court of Appeals rejected his reading of the statute.

> 4 [. . .] **i . JKLF's Status as a "Terrorist Organization"**
>
> [. . .] Under Khan's proposed definition, actions that are illegal under the laws of the regime in power in the alien's country of origin are "unlawful" within the meaning of § 1108(a)(3)(B)(iii) only if these actions violate the international law of armed conflict. We hold that this is not a permissible reading of the statute.
>
> [. . .]
>
> 6 Khan argues that the BIA's reading of the statute is so broad that it includes within the definition of "terrorist activity" many actions that we generally do not consider to be terrorist in nature. For example, Khan argues that under the BIA's reading, it would include armed resistance by Jews against the government of Nazi Germany. This may be true, but the text does not make an exception for actions that are lawful under international law. An action would be lawful within the meaning of § 1182(a)(3)(B)(iii) if the law of the country in question incorporates international law such that the conduct in question is no longer "unlawful" under the country's domestic law, but Khan has made no argument that that is the case here.
>
> We note that the statute includes a discretionary waiver of the terrorism bar for relief from removal that can be exercised by the Secretary of State or the Secretary of Homeland Security. [. . .]
>
> This waiver weakens Khan's argument that the BIA's reading of the statutory language is overly broad, because the broad statutory definition is combined with a discretionary waiver by executive branch officials. These officials are in a position to

34 See G Fletcher, 'On the Crimes Subject to Prosecution in Military Commissions' (2007) 5 *Journal of International Criminal Justice* 39, 45, considering the offence of material support for terrorism as 'the most aggressive prosecution imaginable' under the MCA.

judge the characteristics of particular groups engaging in armed resistance in their home countries, as well as the implications for our foreign relations in determining whether the actions of these groups are terrorist activities.

[. . .]

c. Summary

12 Given both the text of the statute and Khan's failure to point to any binding international law which would alter our understanding of that text, we hold that the definition of "terrorist activity" under the INA does not provide an exception for armed resistance against military targets that is permitted under the international law of armed conflict. Our reading of the statute accords with the interpretation of both the BIA and the Third Circuit, which have both considered similar questions. In *In re S-K-*, 23 I & N Dec. 936 (BIA 2006), the petitioner had been a member of the Chin National Front ("CNF"), which was involved in armed struggle against the Burmese government and undisputedly had committed violent acts that were unlawful within Burma. *Id.* at 937–38. The petitioner argued, as Khan does here, that the definition of unlawful action as applied to certain regimes and in certain conflicts should not be based solely on the domestic laws of the country where the acts were committed, but should account for whether the regime is in fact "legitimate" under international law or norms. *Id.* at 938. The BIA rejected this argument, holding that the language in the statute was clear:

[. . .] In fact, having reviewed the statutory sections, we find that Congress intentionally drafted the terrorist bars to relief very broadly, to include even those people described as "freedom fighters," and it did not intend to give us discretion to create exceptions for members of organizations to which our Government might be sympathetic. Rather, Congress attempted to balance the harsh provisions set forth in the Act with a waiver, but it only granted the power to make exemptions to the Attorney General and the Secretaries of State and Homeland Security, who have not delegated such power to the Immigration Judges or the Board of Immigration Appeals. . . . [T]here is no exception in the Act to the bar to relief in cases involving the use of justifiable force to repel attacks by forces of an illegitimate regime.

[. . .]

13 Under our reading of the statute, the IJ's holding that the JKLF meets the definition of a "terrorist organization" is supported by substantial evidence. There is documentary evidence in the record, at least some of which is corroborated by Khan's testimony, that members of the JKLF killed politicians, kidnapped the daughter of the Indian Home Minister, and attacked Indian Army convoys. Each of these activities constitutes "terrorist activity" under § 1182(a)(3)(B)(iii). Therefore, substantial evidence supports the IJ's finding that the JKLF, during Khan's affiliation with the organization, constituted a "terrorist organization" under the statute.

As observed by the ILDC reporter, the court ignored international law entirely in interpreting 'terrorist activity', deferring to congress's broad definition and the executive's discretionary waiver, in a way that would not exclude 'bizarre outcomes' such as considering the armed resistance by the Jews against the Nazis as terrorist activities, as also noted by the concurring Judge.[35]

35 C Jill Parmley, Analysis, *Khan v Eric H Holder Jr, Attorney General*, ILDC 1470 (US 2009) A1–A3. In his concurring opinion, Judge Nelson also noted (para 6): 'such anomalous results are not merely hypothetical: the United States military, whose invasions of Afghanistan and Iraq were indisputably "unlawful" under the domestic laws of those countries, would qualify as a Tier III terrorist organization. Accordingly, any individual or

Such unreasonable interpretations could be avoided by allowing an exception in accordance with the customary laws of war.[36] The ILDC reporter further remarked that the court's approach was at variance with the growing terrorism jurisprudence of US courts, which consider the Geneva Conventions when determining the US international legal obligations relating to its policies on holding suspected terrorists.[37]

Her Majesty the Queen (Canada), Attorney General of Ontario (intervening) and ors (intervening) v Khawaja, Final appeal, [2012] 3 SCR 555, 2012 SCC 69, ILDC 2117 (CA 2012), 14th December 2012, Canada; Supreme Court [SCC]

The appellant was convicted of five offences under Canada's Criminal Code, as amended by the 2001 Anti-Terrorism Act (ATA). ATA's definition of 'terrorist activity' excluded acts or omissions committed during an armed conflict, done in conformity with international law. In his appeal to the Supreme Court of Canada, he argued that his involvement in any activities resulting in charges against him fell within the armed conflict exception. His activities in question included extensive communication with and providing money and material support to Omar Khyam, the leader of a terrorist cell who was convicted in the UK of conspiring to bomb targets in the UK and elsewhere. The cell was qualified as a terrorist group for facilitating terrorist activity by supporting the insurgency against the coalition forces in Afghanistan.

> **2. Does the Armed Conflict Exception Apply?**
>
> [. . .]
>
> 100 The critical question in this case is whether the conduct of the appellant, as found by the trial judge, falls within the scope of the armed conflict exception. Like the courts below, I conclude that it did not. The purpose of the armed conflict exception is to exempt conduct taken during an armed conflict in accordance with applicable international law. There is no evidential foundation for the application of this exception in the present case: the conduct cannot be said to have been taken solely in support of an armed conflict, nor was it in accordance with applicable international law.
>
> 101 First, the trial judge expressly found that the appellant knew that the Khyam group's terrorist activities extended beyond the armed conflict in Afghanistan, and supported these terrorist objectives (paras. 130–31). Thus, the appellant's actions were not "directed solely at supporting the insurgency in Afghanistan" (C.A., at para. 168). Even if the appellant's efforts with respect to Afghanistan could be considered part of an armed conflict governed by international law, the verdicts would stand.
>
> 102 Second, the evidence is overwhelmingly contrary to the proposition that the appellant's acts were part of an armed conflict governed by international law. There is no air of reality to the suggestion that the appellant believed that the Khyam group intended to act in compliance with international law, or that he cared if it did. The evidence showed only that "the appellant was a fervent purveyor of hatred, anti-Semitism, religious bigotry and adulation for mass atrocities, who was making detonators, and providing other support, for 'amazing bros ... who felt the same way' " (R.F., at para. 39). The violent jihadist ideology espoused by the appellant in his numerous communications is fundamentally incompatible with international law. The Geneva Conventions prohibit acts aimed at spreading terror amongst civilian populations, which are considered war

group who assisted the U.S. military in those efforts would be ineligible for asylum or withholding of removal. [. . .] This could discourage sympathetic groups from lending support to the U.S. military, knowing it would preclude them from seeking refuge in the U.S. in the future'.

36 C Jill Parmley, Analysis, *Khan v Eric H Holder Jr, Attorney General*, ILDC 1470 (US 2009) A4.

37 ibid, A2.

> crimes. The appellant, by contrast, did what he did in support of a group whose credo was to take arms against whoever supports non-Islamic regimes and that recognized that suicide attacks on civilians may sometimes be justified by the ends of jihad.
>
> 103 This was the evidence before the trial judge. Uncontradicted, it established beyond a reasonable doubt that the appellant's conduct did not fall within the armed conflict exception to the definition of terrorist activity.

As noted by the ILDC reporter, although the decision at hand focused on domestic anti-terror legislation, that legislation had been influenced by international and comparative law.[38] By holding that the armed conflict exception did not apply, the court implicitly recognized that international humanitarian law prohibited acts directed at spreading terror among the civilian population.[39]

Italy v Noureddine Drissi and ors, Decision on preliminary question, No 28491/04 RG NR, N 5774/04 RG GIP, ILDC 20 (IT 2005), 24th January 2005, Italy; Lombardy; Milan; Court of First Instance

This case related to the investigations into the activities of a radical Islamic group operating in Italy with connections to various other countries. Several members of the group were remanded in custody for the crime of association with the aim of committing international terrorism in Italy and abroad under Article 270*bis* of the Italian Criminal Code. They were charged, *inter alia*, with taking part in the recruitment and dispatching to Iraq and other war zones of volunteers to be trained as fighters, mainly within the framework of the Islamic organization Ansar-al-Islam. Because of inadmissible evidence gathered abroad, the judge at that stage of the proceedings had to decide whether there was still justification for maintaining the remand order in respect of the charge of association with the aim of committing international terrorism. She relied on the distinction between terrorism and legitimate guerrilla warfare and decided that there was no such justification.

> 32 The notion of terrorism, as is well known, differs from that of subversion and, similarly, it is not defined in the law. A definition must therefore be derived from the interpretation of international conventions on the subject and, above all, through considering the "rationale" and the genesis of the criminal norm at stake.
>
> 33 The wording of the United Nations Global Convention on Terrorism, drafted in 1999, is emblematic with respect to the first point. Art. 18/2 provides an exemption from the sanctions which it provides, stating that they do not apply to armed forces or armed groups or movements other than armed forces of a State as long as they abide by international humanitarian law.
>
> 34 It may be deduced from this legal instrument, and particularly from the exemption mentioned, that violent activities or guerrilla actions that take place in the context of an armed conflict cannot be prosecuted at the international level, even though carried out by armed forces other than those of the State, unless they violate international humanitarian law—in which case the exemption does not apply.
>
> 35 It can be inferred from this latter limitation that terrorist activities relevant and thus prosecutable under international law are those directed at spreading indiscriminate terror among the civilian population in the name of an ideological and/or religious belief, and which therefore constitute crimes against humanity.

38 G MacNeil, Analysis, *Her Majesty the Queen (Canada), Attorney General of Ontario (intervening) and ors (intervening) v Khawaja*, ILDC 2117 (CA 2012) A1.

39 ibid, A8.

> 39 Having said that, it should be noted that in point of fact it has not been proved on the evidence that the two "cells" in question had objectives beyond the guerrilla activity described above, although they were operating in contexts well-disposed towards terrorism.
>
> 40 In this regard, common membership of a subversive organisation, such as that called "Ansar Al Islam"—moreover bombed and destroyed in the course of this conflict—cannot be said to be a sufficient basis for criminal liability. The composition of such organisation is anything but homogenous and indeed is rather complex and diverse.
>
> 51 Nor does there appear to be criminal links between these groups and those with the same ideological background responsible for attacks of a clearly terrorist nature. In this regard it is not possible to rely on the analogy of "potential operational planning of the movement of men and resources", even less on the asserted "circularity of relationships" between persons moving in the same subversive environment, and therefore on the fact that they knew or met each other.
>
> 52 The fact that the accused were not of Iraqi nationality and therefore could not legitimately fight in a war against the American "enemy" has no effect on the considerations set out above.
>
> 53 In fact, it is evident that the exemption provided under the cited Convention relates to belligerent forces forming part of opposite factions in a war, regardless of the nationality of the individual combatants provided that they fall within a single strategic-ideological background.

The distinction emphasized in this decision between terrorism and legitimate guerrilla warfare was both hailed and criticized. As observed by the ILDC reporter, the decision was controversial; an appeal was immediately lodged, which led to a new remand order a few days later, and Article 270*bis* of the Italian Criminal Code was revised to broaden its scope.[40] The decision was criticized for its reliance on and for its interpretation of—the disputed—Article 18(2) of the Draft UN Comprehensive Convention on International Terrorism.[41] Relying on that provision, the decision accepted that attacks by armed groups or movements directed against military personnel in a situation of foreign military occupation or during an armed conflict were lawful as long as they complied with international humanitarian law. The controversies surrounding the proper scope of the armed conflict exception to terrorism persist to date and have led to an ongoing deadlock in the negotiations of the draft convention. The debate was meant to continue in Italian courts, as shown in the following decision on the same case.

Italy v Abdelaziz and ors, Final Appeal Judgment, No 1072, (2007) 17 Guida al Diritto 90, ILDC 559 (IT 2007), 17th January 2007, Italy; Supreme Court of Cassation; 1st Criminal Section

Upon appeal from the previous decision of the Court of First Instance, the Milan Court of Appeal of Assizes confirmed the acquittal of the accused and upheld the distinction between terrorism and guerrilla warfare in international law.[42] As summarized by the ILDC reporter, the court also held that, while in times of peace even indirect damage to the civilian population was sufficient to qualify an action as a terrorist act, during armed conflict only violent actions directed exclusively against the civilian population could be so labelled.[43] That point was further

40 S Stirling-Zanda, Analysis, *Italy v Noureddine Drissi and ors*, ILDC 20 (IT 2005) A3.

41 ibid, A1, A3–A4.

42 *Italy v Abdelaziz (Bouyahia Maher Ben) and ors*, Appeal against Assizes Decision, Foro Italiano II-343 (2006), 28 November 2005, Italy; Lombardy; Milan; Court of Appeal.

43 M Iovane, Facts, *Italy v Abdelaziz and ors*, ILDC 559 (IT 2007) F8.

appealed to the Supreme Court of Cassation by the Milan Public Prosecutor. In his view, the distinguishing element of international terrorism would lie in the ultimate purpose pursued by means of terrorist acts, and not in the exclusively military or civilian character of the victims.[44]

> 2.1. [...] [I]t must be stressed that from the start, the search for a general definition hinged above all on two international sources namely, firstly, the New York Convention of 1999, passed by the General Assembly of the United Nations to inhibit the funding of terrorism, and, secondly, by the Framework Decision 2002/475/GAI of the European Union. In the absence of global agreement concerning terrorism, consensus on which has been obstructed for decades by disagreement between the Member States of the UN on the question of terrorism committed in the course of wars of liberation and armed struggle to establish self-determination of people, it should be noted that the wording of the Convention of 1999, implemented by the Act of 27 January 2003, No. 7, has sufficiently wide scope to be regarded as a general definition applicable both in peacetime and in wartime and including any kind of behaviour directed against civilian life or security or, in case of war, against "any other person not taking an active part in hostilities in a situation of armed conflict" in order to spread terror amongst the population or to force a state or an international organisation to undertake or refrain from action. In addition to being characterised by such objective and subjective elements and by the identity of the victims (civilians or persons not involved in military operations), it is generally held that in order to be regarded as terrorism, acts must at the psychological level meet further requirements as to political, religious or ideological motivation in accordance with generally accepted international standards as set out in various resolutions of the UN General Assembly and Security Council, and in the Convention of 1997 against terrorist acts committed with the use of explosives. The definition of acts of terrorism under Art. 1 of the European Union's Framework Decision is for its part based on a list of specific crimes considered such under national law, which can cause serious damage to a country or an international organisation and which are committed to seriously intimidate the population or force the public authorities or an international organisation to undertake or abstain from undertaking certain action, or to seriously destabilise or destroy fundamental, economic or social structures of a country or of an international organisation. The defining formula set out in the Framework Decision of 2002 is different from that under the UN Convention of 1999, from which it adopts only the general thrust in respect of the following two aspects. On the one hand, the area of application of crimes of terrorism is more limited, relating only to acts committed in peacetime, as is made clear by introductory "consideration" number 11, which excludes from its scope "activities of the armed forces in times of armed conflict", in accordance with the definitions given to these terms in international humanitarian law: to such a degree that the definition under consideration excludes acts committed in wartime, which are governed by international humanitarian law and, in first instance, by the Geneva Conventions and related Additional Protocols. On the other hand, the Framework Decision has extended the concept of acts of terrorism by providing that these can also be characterised by destructive aims, namely the object of "seriously destabilising or destroying the fundamental, constitutional, economic or social political structures of a country or of an international organisation", absent from the wording of the 1999 Convention. Both definitions therefore include the typical characteristic of acts of terrorism described by the most authoritative commentators as "depersonalisation of

44 ibid, F10.

the victim", meaning the general anonymous nature of persons affected by violent action, the true purpose of which is to spread fear indiscriminately amongst the general public and to force a government or international organisation to take or abstain from pursuing specific action. Finally, the reference to situations of armed conflict—present in the Convention of 1999 and, absent from the Framework Decision—shows the two-sided nature of the provisions on acts of terrorism and the need to differentiate it from the legal provisions concerning the identity of the persons actually concerned and the victims, insofar as the rules of international humanitarian law or ordinary law apply depending on whether the acts are committed by persons who may be regarded as "combatants" and are aimed at civilians or against persons not actively engaged in hostilities. It follows from this that, reframing these subjective requirements, acts of terrorism must fall within the category of war crimes or crimes against humanity.

2.2. In accordance with the obligation to amend domestic rules so as to enable them to conform to the Community's legal provisions, Art. 15 (1) of the Legislative Decree of 27 July 2005, No. 144, adopted by the Act of 31 July 2005, No. 155, upholds the concept contained in the Framework Decision and defines "acts with terrorist aims" as those "which, by their nature or context" may cause serious damage to a country or to an international organisation and which are committed with the purpose of intimidating the population or forcing the public authorities or an international organisation to take or refrain from taking specific action or destabilising or destroying the fundamental, constitutional, economic or social political structures of a country or of an international organisation, and other conduct defined as terrorism or committed with terrorist aims under conventions or other provisions of international law binding upon Italy". The explicit reference to international sources means that adopting the provisions of Art. 270 (e) of the Code of Procedure equals an open definition intended to be extended or restricted as a result not only of the international conventions already ratified but also of future conventions that may be adopted. In this way, provision is made by law for a mechanism that should automatically ensure harmonisation of the laws of the States of the international community in order to ensure that instruments are available for joint action in combating transnational terrorist crime. It must be inferred from the above consideration that the definition under Art. 270 (e) of the Code of Procedure must be read together with that of the Convention of 1999, implemented by Act No. 7 of 2003, and that, by analogy, the elements constituting terrorist acts, referred to in national provisions in the wake of the European Union's Framework Decision, must be incorporated by reference also to the provisions of the said Convention. From this, the conclusion must be drawn that inclusion in the domestic law means that terrorist aims can be thus defined if acts are committed in the context of armed conflict—described as such in international law even in the case of internal civil war—and are committed not only against civilians but also against persons not actively engaged in hostilities, consequently excluding only acts aimed at combatants, which remain subject to the rules of international humanitarian law.

4.1. The submissions by the Attorney General, in which he complained, in accordance with Art. 606 (1) b. of the Code of Criminal Procedure, of the misapplication of criminal law whereby the District Court held that "only acts directed exclusively against the civilian population" are terrorism, consequently indicating that in a situation of armed conflict, so-called Kamikaze suicide actions, when committed against military objectives, cannot be regarded as terrorism, even if causing serious damage and spreading fear amongst the civil population. A statement of this kind cannot be accepted and must be further specified and explained. Above all, the statement is clearly at odds with the explicit provision of the 1999 Convention, even though repeatedly referred to in the impugned judgment, that describes terrorism as "any act aimed at causing death or serious personal injury to a civilian or any other person not actively engaged in hostilities in a situation of armed conflict". Consequently, attacks directed against military personnel engaged in tasks unconnected with hostilities and not in any way attributable thereto, such as, for example, the providing of humanitarian aid, must therefore be included in this class. However, this view cannot be entirely accepted even from this further aspect, since situations may well arise in an atmosphere of armed conflict (between States or in civil war) where acts of violence are directed both against military persons and against the civil population, at a time when—due to the nature of such acts, the means employed and the specific conditions on which they are pursued—they will undoubtedly produce serious injury not only to military persons but also to civilians. It must therefore be said that the wording and the "reasoning" of the international rules, which are aimed at defining the objectives of terrorism in an armed conflict, provide unambiguous interpretative arguments for saying that an act against a military objective must also be regarded as terrorism if the particular circumstances show beyond any doubt that serious harm to the life and physical well-being of the civilian population are inevitable, creating fear and panic amongst the local people. A simple example is an attack using explosives against a military vehicle in a crowded market. In a situation of this kind, an interpretative approach that regards the joint presence of military and civilian victims as an element that is sufficient in itself to deny the terrorist nature of the act undoubtedly lacks consistency and rationality, as it is clear that the certainty (and not simply the possibility or probability) of serious harm inflicted on civilians shows unequivocally that the committing of an intentional and specific act was prompted by a desire to cause the harm and to achieve the particular results that constitute terrorist aims. The relevance of the obvious discrepancy on this point, between the letter of the law and the wrong interpretation of the Court concerned in its the judgment must be reexamined when a reconstruction of the facts is undertaken following a reassessment of the elements of proof.

6.4. The reasoning behind the Court's decisions in this question is wrong, due to an error of law in having found that establishing objectives of international terrorism of the accused persons would decisively depend on the committing of a criminal action against the civil population. In this respect, it has already been made clear that an act against a military objective constitutes terrorism if the particulars and the specific circumstances of the event show that serious harm to life and the physical integrity of civilians are certain and unavoidable, spreading fear and panic amongst the population (see 4.1). It follows from this that an investigation into the objectives of international terrorism could not end with the confirmation of the military nature of the objective of the violence committed, but should have been extended to verifying the underlying causes at the same time, of the harm to civilians and the serious damage to life and physical integrity occurring in situations where this is shown to be the certain and inevitable result of the conduct concerned, through the means employed and the specific circumstances.

7. In conclusion, in light of all the above considerations, the impugned judgment must be set aside and the case referred to another section of the Assize Court of Appeal of Milan which, in a new judgment, must reassess the probatory background and, applying the principles of law mentioned above, will decide whether the three accused should be held responsible for the offence of association as provided by Art. 270(a) of the Criminal Code by way of participation or external complicity.

As noted by the ILDC reporter, the court did not explicitly state that a definition of terrorism existed under customary law but relied on the 1999 Convention for a 'general definition' of terrorism applicable both in times of peace and during armed conflict.[45] In doing so, it did not specifically address the problem of the international character of a terrorist act, but implicitly assumed that an act of international terrorism must show some kind of transnational connections.[46] The approach of the Italian (legislation and) courts to incorporate international law in the domestic definition of terrorism was in sharp contrast to the US approach, as illustrated above in *Khan v Eric H Holder Jr, Attorney General.* As to freedom fighters, the court's position was that their attacks against military targets may amount to terrorist acts when, depending on the circumstances, spreading panic among the public was part of the overall strategy and the harm to civilians was inevitable, such as the bombing of a military vehicle in a crowded market. This ruling was confirmed some years later in the following case.

General Prosecutor of the Court of Appeals of Naples and Prosecutor of the Tribunal of Naples v Legori and ors, Final appeal judgment, No 2843, ILDC 2392 (IT 2014), 21st January 2014, Italy

This case concerned three Sri Lankan nationals accused under Article 270*bis* of the Italian Criminal Code ('associations with the aim of terrorism, including international terrorism') of having associated to provide financial support to the 'Tamil Tigers', an ethnic Tamil organization fighting for independence from Sri Lanka. The first instance Judge pronounced a judgment of non-suit because they were qualified as combatants of a national liberation movement, and therefore their acts were not subject to domestic criminal law, but could at most fall within the domain of international humanitarian law. The Public Prosecutor lodged an appeal with the Court of Cassation citing the ruling of the 2007 judgment in the previous case that terrorism included acts committed during a non-international armed conflict if such acts were directed not only against military targets, but also against civilians or combatants not actively engaged in hostilities.

> H1 The Judge's decision of non-suit was upheld, but its legal basis had to be modified, in part. (paragraph 2)
>
> H2 Article 270bis of the Italian Criminal Code was to be read together with Article 270sexies of the Italian Criminal Code, which implemented into the Italian legal system the European Council Framework Decision on Combating Terrorism, No 2002/475/JHA, entered into force 13 June 2002 ('Framework Decision'). Article 270sexies of the Italian Criminal Code not only provided a definition of terrorism applicable in times of peace, but also contained an opening clause, according to which terrorist acts were those set out in 'conventions and other norms of international law binding on Italy'. (paragraph 2.a)
>
> H3 As stated in the 2007 Judgment, a general definition of terrorism applicable both in times of peace and during armed conflict was to be found in the International Convention for the Suppression of the Financing of Terrorism (9 December 1999) [. . .] ('New York Convention'). This general definition included all acts intended to cause death or bodily injury to civilians, or to any other person, even combatants, not taking an active part in hostilities in a situation of armed conflict. The purpose of the acts must have been to intimidate a population, or to compel a government or an international organization to do or to abstain from doing a certain act. Furthermore, in application of a customary international norm accepted in various United Nations

45 M Iovane, Analysis, *Italy v Abdelaziz and ors*, ILDC 559 (IT 2007) A2.

46 ibid.

resolutions, the acts must have been driven by a political, religious, or ideological motive. (paragraph 2.a)

H4 The interpretation given to Article 21 of the New York Convention by the Judge had to be rejected. Article 21 of the New York Convention provided that nothing in the convention 'shall affect other rights, obligations and responsibilities of States and individuals under international law', in particular international humanitarian law. The Judge had derived from this provision a saving clause, according to which the New York Convention might not apply when a terrorist act was performed during a non-international armed conflict by a national liberation movement. According to the Judge, a terrorist act performed during armed conflict that was gravely in breach of international humanitarian law should be punished as a war crime or a crime against humanity by international courts. (paragraph 2.b)

H5 To the contrary, Article 21 of the New York Convention did not require the non-application of the domestic norm on terrorism whenever the particular act, committed during armed conflict, also fell within the domain of international humanitarian law. The purpose of Article 21 of the New York Convention was to prevent inconsistencies between domestic legislation implementing the New York Convention, on the one hand, and general international law, on the other. In the present case, however, there was no risk of inconsistency, since the Judge's decision had not even indicated the extent to which Legori and ors could have acted consistently with international humanitarian law, and thus could have been shielded from criminal prosecution. Furthermore, this interpretation of Article 21 of the New York Convention found an underpinning in Article 33 of the Geneva Convention Relative to the Protection of Civilian Persons in Time of War (12 August 1949) [...] and Article 4(2) of the Protocol Additional to the Geneva Conventions of 12 August 1949 and Relating to the Protection of Victims of Non-International Armed Conflicts (8 June 1977) [...]. These provisions expressly envisaged, and proscribed, the commission of acts of terrorism in times of war by combatants against persons who were in the power of the adverse party. (paragraph 2.c)

H6 The *ratio decidendi* of the 2007 Judgment therefore had to be upheld. Accordingly, only acts committed during an armed conflict, including by members of non-state organizations, and directed exclusively against combatants, would be excluded from the notion of terrorism. In contrast, the domestic norm on terrorism applied to terrorist acts directed against civilians or against persons not actively participating in hostilities, regardless of the perpetrator's status, provided that the terrorist acts were driven by a political, religious, or ideological motive, and pursued the goal of intimidating a population, or of compelling a government or an international organization to do or to abstain from doing a certain act. (paragraph 2.c)

H7 Nevertheless, the Judge had correctly qualified the crime of 'associations with the aim of terrorism, including international terrorism' pursuant to Article 270bis of the Italian Criminal Code as a *dolus specialis* crime. For this crime to be constituted, the agent had to have shared the goal of the terrorist organization to spread terror among the population, or to compel a state or an international organization to do or to abstain from doing a certain act. The agent's will to support a particular activity of the terrorist organization was not to be regarded as sufficient. In the present case, it had not been established that Legori and ors possessed the *dolus specialis* required. (paragraph 3.d)

The court reaffirmed its reliance on the 1999 Convention for a 'general definition' of terrorism applicable both in times of peace and during armed conflict. Interestingly, it also held that customary law (as 'accepted in various United Nation resolutions') required that terrorist acts be driven by political, religious, or ideological motive. Yet, as recalled by the ILDC reporter, it remains doubtful whether the international community has reached any consensus on a general definition of terrorism.[47]

R v Gul, Appeal judgment, UKSC 64, [2013] 3 WLR 1207, [2014] 1 All ER 463, [2014] 1 Cr App R 14, ILDC 2106 (UK 2013), 23rd October 2013, United Kingdom; Supreme Court [SC]

Gul was condemned for disseminating terrorist publications, which included videos on websites showing attacks by members of Al-Qaeda, the Taliban, and other armed groups in Afghanistan, Iraq, and Chechnya, the use of explosives in Iraq against Coalition forces etc. He appealed arguing that the definition of 'terrorism' in the UK Terrorism Act of 2000 did not cover attacks by non-state armed groups against state armed forces in the context of a non-international armed conflict. His appeal was rejected. He appealed to the Supreme Court arguing that the attacks on Coalition forces in Afghanistan and Iraq, and on military targets in Chechnya, shown on the videos, did not amount to terrorism under international law, even if they did so under the 2000 Act.

The appellant's argument based on international law

Introductory

[. . .]

43. The appellant has two arguments in this connection. The first is that some provisions of the 2000 and 2006 Acts were enacted to give effect to the UK's international obligations arising under treaties concerned with the suppression of terrorism, and that "terrorism" should accordingly be given a meaning in those statutes which accords with the international law norm, and at any rate with the definition in the relevant international document to which effect is intended to be given. The second argument is that, as the 2000 and 2006 Acts criminalise certain "terrorist" actions committed outside the UK, the meaning of "terrorism" in those statutes should not be wider than what is accepted as an international norm.

No international consensus as to terrorism

44. These two arguments each face more than one insuperable obstacle. The common obstacle they both face is that there is no accepted norm in international law as to what constitutes terrorism. [. . .]

45. The appellant seeks to meet this point through the contention that, whereas there is no international agreement as to the meaning of terrorism, there is a general understanding that it does not extend to the acts of insurgents or "freedom fighters" in non-international armed conflicts. The short answer to this point is that, while there is significant support for such an idea, any such support falls far short of amounting to a general understanding which could be properly invoked as an aid to statutory interpretation. [. . .]

46. The United Nations has attempted to identify a comprehensive definition of terrorism, but has so far failed. Indeed, it appears that one of the difficulties has been achieving agreement as to the very point at issue in this appeal. In 2007, the *ad hoc* committee established by General Assembly resolution 51/210 of 17 December 1996

47 S Porro, Analysis, *General Prosecutor of the Court of Appeals of Naples and Prosecutor of the Tribunal of Naples v Legori and ors*, ILDC 2392 (IT 2014) A3. See also *Chiquita Brands International Incorporated and ors v Valencia and ors*, Decision on motion to dismiss, Case No 08-01916-MD-MARRA, ILDC 1873 (US 2011), 792 F Supp 2d 1301 (SD Fla 2011), 3 June 2011, United States; Florida; District Court for the Southern District of Florida [SD Fla], which also rejected the view espoused by the Italian courts.

suggested that it be agreed that "the activities of armed forces during an armed conflict, as those terms are understood under international humanitarian law, which are governed by that law, are not governed by this Convention". However no consensus has been achieved, because various states' delegations were concerned about "(a) the right of peoples to self-determination under international law; (b) the activities of armed forces in armed conflict; and (c) the activities of military forces of a State in peacetime, also taking into account related concerns about State terrorism"—to quote from the committee's 2011 report. In early 2012, the General Assembly established a working group to "finalise" the drafting of a comprehensive international convention on terrorism, but, by the end of that year, the chair of the group reported that there were still disagreements, including as to the precise distinction between terrorism and "legitimate struggle of peoples fighting in the exercise of their right to self-determination".

47. It is true that there are UN Conventions and Council of Europe Conventions concerned with counter-terrorism, which define terrorism as excluding "activities of armed forces during an armed conflict", but there is room for argument as to their precise effect, and, more importantly, it is quite impossible to suggest that there is a plain or consistent approach in UN Conventions on this issue.

48. Thus, the Crown asserts that the UN has adopted fourteen counter-terrorism treaties to date, and of these fourteen treaties (i) seven state that "the activities of armed forces during an armed conflict, as those terms are understood under international humanitarian law, which are governed by that law are not governed by this Convention", (ii) of the seven which have no such statement, six provide that the treaty "does not exclude any criminal jurisdiction exercised in accordance with national law", and (iii) of the seven which include such a statement, at least five contain a provision substantially to the like effect. The appellant contends that the absence of an armed conflict exclusion from a treaty does not mean that that treaty applies in relation to an action at a time of armed conflict. However, it is not normally appropriate to imply a term into an international treaty, and, in any event, the absence of any such express exclusion is scarcely consistent with the contention that there is an internationally accepted norm such as the appellant suggests.

49. Further, as this court pointed out in *Al-Sirri*, para 68, "an attack on [the International Security Assistance Force in Afghanistan] is in principle capable of being an act contrary to the purposes and principles of the United Nations", and such an attack therefore can constitute "terrorism"—see para 3 of the same judgment. Consistently with this, there have been UN resolutions referring to the activities of Al-Qaida and the Taliban as "terrorism", notwithstanding allegations that their actions involved insurgents attacking forces of states and IGOs in non-international armed conflict (eg UN Security Council resolutions 2041, 2069 and 2082 of 2012, and Council Decision 2011/486/CFSP of 1 August 2011).

50. In addition, in international humanitarian law, it appears that insurgents in non-international armed conflicts do not enjoy combatant immunity. […]

51. As for domestic legislation across the world, the Crown states in its argument, without challenge, that of a survey of 42 states it has identified with legislation which defines terrorism, (i) 28 do not exclude armed attacks, (ii) four explicitly include armed attacks, and (iii) seven explicitly exclude armed attacks (which includes the United States, although its position might be said to be ambivalent, as some of the relevant legislation is widely drawn without the exclusion). It is true that none of these legislative provisions explicitly refer to armed attacks during a time of armed conflict, but we would refer back to the point made at the end of para 48 above.

Other problems faced by the appellant's case

52. It appears clear that sections 62–64 of the 2000 Act give effect to the UK's obligations under the International Convention for the Suppression of Terrorist Bombings 1997 and the International Convention for the Suppression of the Financing of Terrorism 1999. It is also fair to say that these two Conventions, particularly the latter, appear to have been drafted so as to exclude insurgent attacks on military forces in non-international armed conflicts from their respective ambits. However, the notion that the meaning of "terrorism" in section 1 of the 2000 Act should be read down, because some of the activities which were rendered offences by that Act were criminalised as a result of the UK's obligations under the two Conventions, runs into two difficulties.

53. First, there is no rule that the UK government cannot go further than is required by an international treaty when it comes to legislating—the exercise is often known as "gold-plating". It is not as if there is anything in either the 1997 or the 1999 Convention which excludes a signatory state going further than the requirements of the Convention, or anything in the 2000 Act which suggests that Parliament intended to go no further. [. . .]

54. Secondly, quite apart from this, if the wide definition of "terrorism" in section 1 of the 2000 Act has to be read down for the purposes of sections 62–64, there is no reason to read it down when it comes to any other provision of the Act—or of the 2006 Act. In *Al-Sirri*, para 36, this court appears to have approved, indeed to have relied on, the proposition that, if application of the wide definition of "terrorism" in section 1 of the 2000 Act led to another provision of the Act conflicting with the UK's obligations under the Geneva Convention, then the definition should be read down when applied to the provision in question, and not generally throughout the Act. To conclude otherwise would be a classic case of letting the tail wag the dog.

55. The 2006 Act takes the appellant's argument no further. It is true that some of its provisions give effect to the UK's obligations under the Council of Europe Convention on the Prevention of Terrorism 2005 and the International Convention for the Suppression of Acts of Nuclear Terrorism 2005. However, section 2 of the 2006 Act was not enacted to give effect to any international Convention, and, even if it had been and had gone further than the Convention concerned required, there is no reason why Parliament should not have gold-plated the legislation, as already explained.

56. The appellant's reliance on the fact that there are provisions of the 2000 and 2006 Acts which criminalise various activities as terrorist offences even if committed abroad, runs into similar problems. Even if it were the case that, because of the need to take into account the UK's international law obligations, the wide definition of terrorism had to be read down when it comes to construing those provisions, that would be of no assistance to a defendant such as the appellant, who is a UK citizen being prosecuted for offences allegedly committed in this country. There is no reason to read down the wide definition of terrorism in a case such as this. The present case does not involve a defendant who has committed acts, which are said to be offences, abroad: the activities said to be offences were committed in the UK—and by a UK citizen.

57. That renders it unnecessary for us to consider whether, as there is no internationally agreed definition of "terrorism", the Court of Appeal was right to decide that there is no reason why Parliament cannot criminalise acts of "terrorism", as defined in section 1 of the 2000 Act, committed outside the UK. [. . .]

58. The appellant contends that the mere fact that certain actions can be characterised as terrorism without offending international law does not mean that those actions can be criminalised by one state if they are carried out in another state. The appellant cites, for example, Brownlie's *Principles of Public International Law* (8th ed 2012), p. 458, which says "if a state wishes to project its prescriptive jurisdiction extraterritorially, it must find a recognised basis in international law for doing so". That raises a point of some importance and some difficulty, and it might be said to represent a shift in focus in international law. Given that we do not have to decide the issue, we should not do so in this appeal: it should await another case.

Conclusion

59. We would accordingly answer the certified question "yes", and consequently we would dismiss this appeal.

60. Before ending this judgment, we would make two further points of a general nature about the 2000 and 2006 Acts.

61. First, we revert to the concern about the width of the definition of "terrorism", as discussed in paras 28–29 and 33–37 above. In his first report, Mr Anderson QC made the point that "the current law allows members of any nationalist or separatist group to be turned into terrorists by virtue of their participation in a lawful armed conflict, however great the provocation and however odious the regime which they have attacked". He went on to say that "other definitions of terrorism choose to exclude activities sanctioned by international law from the reach of terrorist activity", citing the Canadian and South African Criminal Codes as examples. In his second report, Mr Anderson mentioned the "potential application of the Terrorism Acts even to UK forces engaged in conflicts overseas", and referred to the fact that a recent Australian report "recommend[ed] that Australian law be changed so as to provide that the relevant parts of the Criminal Code, as in Canada, do not apply to acts committed by parties regulated by the law of armed conflict."

62. While acknowledging that the issue is ultimately one for Parliament, we should record our view that the concerns and suggestions about the width of the statutory definition of terrorism which Mr Anderson has identified in his two reports merit serious consideration. Any legislative narrowing of the definition of "terrorism", with its concomitant reduction in the need for the exercise of discretion under section 117 of the 2000 Act, is to be welcomed, provided that it is consistent with the public protection to which the legislation is directed.

This decision made an elaborate analysis of the armed conflict exception in international law and its (in)applicability in UK law and in the case at hand. The ILDC reporter took issue with the Supreme Court's inclusion of acts taking place in the context of a non-international armed conflict in the definition of terrorism, citing authorities suggesting that attacks by non-state armed groups against military targets, as opposed to non-combatants (as these terms are defined in international humanitarian law), in non-international armed conflicts do not constitute terrorist acts.[48] It is also noteworthy that, despite upholding the appellant's conviction, the Supreme Court raised concerns on its own motion about the width of the statutory definition of terrorism in UK law, which admittedly however was for the UK Parliament to consider.

48 M Risvas, Analysis, *R v Gul*, ILDC 2106 (UK 2013) A3 (citing the authoritative Commentary by the ICRC to Article 51(2) of Additional Protocol I to the 1949 Geneva Conventions and the ICTY judgment in *Prosecutor v Galić*).

III. Terrorism and Human Rights

1. Security Council anti-terrorism measures and human rights

One of the main issues arising in cases dealing with the impact of Security Council anti-terrorism measures on human rights is whether the (domestic) courts may review them. There is abundant literature and several judicial decisions on the topic.[49] As mentioned in the introduction of this chapter, two main trends emerged in domestic case law, which can be discerned by the approach of the EU courts in the famous *Kadi* case.[50] The CFI (now the GCEU) had initially held that it was not entitled to exercise judicial review of Security Council resolutions unless they violated rules of *jus cogens*, which it considered as the only legal limit to its broad powers. A first wave of domestic decisions followed this path. That ruling was overturned by the Grand Chamber of the ECJ (now the CJEU), which adopted a dualist logic that emphasized the autonomy of the Community legal order, and held that the CJEU, being the judicial body of that legal order, should function within the latter's framework and should therefore review the internal lawfulness of the Community acts giving effect to Security Council resolutions in the light of the Community's constitutional principles, which included fundamental rights. The CJEC found that the contested acts were in breach of fundamental rights and were to be annulled. This decision became influential in the cases that followed.

Italy v Abdelaziz and ors, Final Appeal Judgment, No 1072, (2007) 17 Guida al Diritto 90, ILDC 559 (IT 2007), 17th January 2007, Italy; Supreme Court of Cassation; 1st Criminal Section[51]

> 5.1. [. . .] The Attorney General in his submission argued that the Court concerned failed to take account of the fact the Ansar Al Islam organisation appears on the list of terrorist organisations drawn up under Resolution 1267/99 of the UN Security Council, so that the aims pursued by this group, with which the accused persons had repeated contact, cannot be overlooked. The complaint does not hold water; the argument that inclusion in the lists drawn up by international organisations should in itself be sufficient to demonstrate the terrorist nature of an organisation cannot be upheld, as such a description of the said organisations cannot be binding on the findings made by the judge at his free discretion within proceedings. The lists of "terrorist suspects" or of "prohibited persons" were introduced following a resolution by the UN in 1999, quoted by the Attorney General in Milan, to sanction the Taliban government in Afghanistan for its support for Islamic terrorism, by imposing an embargo and freezing financial resources. The European Union quickly followed this procedure by issuing further regulations, binding on all Member States, which sanctioned the obligation to freeze assets destined for private persons or legal entities included in the list of "prohibited persons", the composition of which was updated by the Commission according to the Resolutions passed by the UN Security Council. In Italy, the task of providing the European Union with information or drawing up lists of a legal nature issued in the course of the preliminary investigations was entrusted to the Financial Security Committee set up by the Ministry of Economic Affairs. On this

49 See, among others, A Reinisch, 'Should Judges Second-Guess the UN Security Council?' (2009) 6 *International Organizations Law Review* 257; A Tzanakopoulos, 'Domestic Court Reactions to UN Security Council Sanctions' in A Reinisch (ed), *Challenging Acts of International Organizations before National Courts* (OUP 2010) 54.

50 See, among others, T Tridimas and J A Gutierrez-Fons, 'EU Law, International Law, and Economic Sanctions against Terrorism: The Judiciary in Distress?' (2008–2009) 32 *Fordham International Law Journal* 660; J Kokott and C Sobotta, 'The Kadi Case: Constitutional Core Values and International Law: Finding the Balance' (2012) 23 *European Journal of International Law* 1015.

51 For the facts of the case see text accompanying n 42 above.

> understanding, it must be stressed that, according to the almost unanimous views of the commentators, inclusion of a group in these lists has purely administrative value and while the imposition of the sanctions is lawful, the effects thereof cannot extend to becoming evidence. The commentators have lucidly stated that to do otherwise would "introduce an item of legal proof into the system, transforming Art. 270 a of the Criminal Code into an absolute criminal measure" and the view has been adopted in the precedents of this Court which, in denying the value as proof of appearance on lists of "prohibited persons", itself referred to the inadmissibility of creating a kind of legal proof that would result in a clear breach of the principles of legality and separation of powers (Cass., Section 1, 15 June 2006, No. 30824, Tartag). Concluding, it must be said that the placing of an organisation on the said lists represents an element of value only as an investigatory starting point and that proof of terrorist aims must necessarily be adduced according to the rules of evidence and probatory assessment laid down in procedural law.

By ruling that the inclusion of an organization in the Security Council consolidating list was not conclusive evidence of its terrorist nature and could not override the principle of free assessment of evidence by an independent judge, the court left the door open for (indirect) judicial review of the relevant Security Council acts. When the Council demands the freezing of assets of specific listed persons, as it did in Resolution 1267, leaving states no margin of appreciation as to the means of implementation, state conduct is strictly conditioned by the Council's binding decision.[52] Thus, reassessing such (domestic) listing under the rules of evidence and evidentiary assessment of domestic procedural law necessarily entails the review of the relevant Security Council act imposing it.

Nada (Youssef) v State Secretariat for Economic Affairs and Federal Department of Economic Affairs, Administrative appeal judgment, Case No 1A 45/2007, BGE 133 II 450, ILDC 461 (CH 2007), 14th November 2007, Switzerland; Federal Supreme Court [BGer]

The Italian and Egyptian applicant was living in a small Italian enclave in Switzerland. His assets in Switzerland were frozen in 2001 under a Swiss Ordinance implementing UN Security Council sanctions against a list of individuals suspected of being associated with Al-Qaida and the Taliban. He was also banned from entry into or transit through Switzerland and as a result he could not leave his town. The UN list was maintained by the Security Council sanctions committee, a political body reaching decisions by consensus of its 15 members, which was tasked with monitoring compliance with the sanctions. De-listing was at the committee's discretion and at the time individuals did not have the right to be heard since the committee did not act as a judicial body. He complained that the refusal of the Swiss authorities to remove him from the Swiss list infringed his rights to liberty, private life, property, fair trial and effective remedy. He also complained that he could not remove his name from the Ordinance even after the accusations against him were found to be unsubstantiated. The Swiss authorities argued that to strike a name from the Swiss list one had to be delisted by the sanctions committee.

> 2.2. [...] As a result of the appearance of the petitioner and his organizations in Appendix 2 of the Taliban Ordinance all his money and financial resources in Switzerland have been seized [...]. Because of this, as well as because of the prohibition of transfers to him or his organizations [...], the employment of the petitioner and his organizations in Switzerland have become impossible. The Taliban Ordinance thus intervenes directly in the non-monetary rights of the petitioner and in his employment. [...] These [measures] have already been in effect for more than five years

52 A Tzanakopoulos, *Disobeying the Security Council: Countermeasures Against Wrongful Sanctions* (OUP 2011) 39.

and no end is in sight. In these circumstances, the Swiss Federal Council correctly affirmed the general applicability of Article 6(1) of the ECHR […].

5. Pursuant to Article 25 of the Charter of the United Nations of 26 June 1945 (UN Charter; SR 0.120) the Member States are obligated to accept and implement the Resolutions of the Security Council consistent with the UN Charter. Hence, the Resolutions of the Security Council (insofar as they are not issued in the form of non-binding recommendations) are also binding on the Member States. […]

5.1 The obligations of the Member States in accordance with the UN Charter do not only take precedence over the domestic laws of the Member States but also over obligations arising from other international agreements. […]

5.3 Even the Security Council is bound by the UN Charter and must act in compliance with its principles and objectives (Article 24(2) of the UN Charter), which includes respect of human rights and fundamental freedoms (Article 1(3) of the UN Charter). This does not mean, however, that a Member State is generally authorized to release itself from an obligation on the ground that a (formally lawful) Resolution of the Security Council is not materially consistent with the UN Charter […].

7. Yet jus cogens, the peremptory rights binding on all subjects of international law, marks the limit of the obligation to apply Resolutions of the Security Council. For this reason, it must be determined whether, as the petitioner asserts, the Resolutions of the Security Council containing the sanctions violate jus cogens.

7.3. We endorse this view.

In general, jus cogens includes elementary human rights such as the right to life, the protection from torture and humiliating treatment, the freedom from slavery and human trafficking, the prohibition on collective punishment, the principle of personal responsibility in criminal prosecution, and the principle of non-refoulement […]

By contrast, other fundamental rights, even if they are of great importance for Switzerland, do not necessarily belong to peremptory international law […] This holds true in particular for the fundamental rights of the right to property and to commercial freedom of action invoked by the petitioner […]. But even the procedural guarantees asserted by the petitioner (right to a legal hearing and a fair trial pursuant to Article 6(1) of the ECHR and Article 14(1) of the International Covenant on Civil and Political Rights; right to an effective appeal pursuant to Article 13 of the ECHR and Article 2(3) of the International Covenant on Civil and Political Rights) do not belong to the inalienable core of the international conventions on human rights (see Article 15(2) of the ECHR and Article 4(2) of the International Covenant on Civil and Political Rights) and thus do not belong categorically to jus cogens […].

7.4. Notably, in the area of sanctions enacted by the Security Council pursuant to Chapter VII of the UN Charter no state consensus is evident that would recognize internationally binding guarantees for proceedings for the protection of the individual.

These sanctions contain drastic economic restrictions for those affected, but the means to maintain a livelihood are free from the restriction (see Resolution 1452 (2002), paragraph 1a), which is why neither danger to life or health nor inhumane or humiliating treatment exists here. The travel ban restricts the freedom of movement of those affected, but generally does not represent a deprivation of freedom. Those affected can move freely in their country of residence (but see E. 10.2 below for more on the particular situation of the petitioner). Furthermore, travel to the country of citizenship is expressly permitted (see Resolution 1734 (2006) paragraph 1b).

> Traditionally, sanctions are enacted by the Security Council without individuals having the chance to speak out on them beforehand or afterward or to lodge appeals to international or national instances. The introduction of the de-listing procedure and the improvements enacted in 2006 (the ability of the individual to appeal to the Sanction Committee directly, specification of the criteria for listing and de-listing, introduction of requirements for listing recommendations, and the obligation of Member States to notify those affected) already represent significant progress compared to the previous situation. Even if this system still shows major shortcomings in terms of fundamental rights (see the Report of the High Commissioner of Human Rights on the protection of human rights and fundamental freedoms while countering terrorism (9 March 2007, A/HRC/4/88) RN 25 ff.; and the Report of the UN Special Rapporteur on the promotion and protection of human rights and fundamental freedoms while countering terrorism (16 August 2006, A/61/267) RN 30 ff.), it does not violate jus cogens.
>
> 8.3. From the above, it is clear that Switzerland is forbidden from independently removing the petitioner's name from Appendix 2 of the Taliban Ordinance. It must be admitted to the petitioner that in this situation there exists no effective possibility of appeal. The Federal Supreme Court can review whether and to what extent Switzerland is bound by the Resolutions of the Security Council, but it is not authorized to remove the sanctions against the petitioner on the basis of violations of his fundamental rights.
>
> Only the Sanction Committee is authorized to remove names from the sanction list. Despite the previously mentioned improvements, the delisting procedures meet neither the requirements of legal protection contained in Article 29(a) BV, Article 6(1) of the ECHR and Article 14(1) of the International Covenant on Civil and Political Rights, nor the requirements of an effective appeal in accordance with Article 13 of the ECHR and Article 2(3) of the International Covenant on Civil and Political Rights [. . .].
>
> This situation can only be alleviated by introducing an effective control mechanism at the UN level. The objective is being actively pursued by the Swiss Federal Council and the Swiss UN permanent representative [. . .].

This was one of the first decisions by a domestic highest court dealing with the legality of Security Council sanctions in a comprehensive way. It held that the obligation to implement binding Security Council resolutions was only limited by *jus cogens*, which comprised some core human rights, but not including those invoked by Nada. Even though the delisting procedure was amended and considerably improved in 2006, it still fell short of international human rights standards but the court ruled that it was not in the position to remedy this situation; this task fell on the UN.

As observed by the ILDC reporter, those findings of the court were largely inspired by the judgment of the GCEU in *Kadi*, which had been issued a year earlier.[53] Swiss courts issued a few other decisions in line with *Nada*.[54] In *A v State Secretariat for Economic Affairs and Federal Department of Economic Affairs*, the court held that Switzerland did not enjoy any margin of appreciation in implementing its obligations under binding Security Council resolutions, which would allow it to strike a name from the Swiss list.[55] It also went a step further in urging the

53 M Lanter, Analysis, *Nada (Youssef) v State Secretariat for Economic Affairs and Federal Department of Economic Affairs*, ILDC 461 (CH 2007) A2.

54 See especially *A v Federal Department of Economic Affairs*, Administrative first instance judgment, No 2A 783/2006, ILDC 1200 (CH 2008), 23 January 2008, Switzerland; Federal Supreme Court [BGer].

55 Administrative first instance judgment, No 1A48/2007, ILDC 1201 (CH 2008), 22 April 2008, 1st Public Law Chamber, H9.

Swiss authorities to support the applicant's delisting request and consider granting him a waiver in respect of restrictions on his freedom of movement, since he was living in a small Italian enclave within Switzerland and such restrictions had harsh consequences on him.[56] The applicant's name was eventually removed from the UN list in September 2009.

The case was brought to Strasbourg. In *Nada v Switzerland*, the Grand Chamber of the ECtHR found that the interference with the applicant's right to private and family life was disproportionate and in breach of Article 8 ECHR because Switzerland had failed to take adequate measures within the constraints of the sanctions regime to adapt that regime to the applicant's harsh individual situation.[57] The court also found a violation of Article 13 ECHR taken in conjunction with Article 8 because the applicant did not have any effective means of obtaining the removal of his name and therefore no remedy in respect of the violations. The ECtHR here followed the CJEU's ruling in *Kadi* that UN law did not preclude judicial review of the Swiss Ordinance implementing UN sanctions.[58] As to Article 5 (right to liberty and security), the court found no violation, ruling, like the Swiss Federal Court, that the prohibition to enter and transit through Switzerland did not amount to deprivation of Nada's liberty.[59] The ECtHR judgment also referred to the two following cases.

Abdelrazik v Minister of Foreign Affairs and Attorney General of Canada, First instance judgment, 2009 FC 580, ILDC 1332 (CA 2009), 4th June 2009, Canada

Mr Abdelrazik, a Sudanese who obtained Canadian citizenship in 1995, was included in the Security Council '1267 Committee' list as an associate of Al-Qaida and was subject to a travel ban in accordance with Security Council Resolution 1822. This occurred in 2006 while he was in Sudan and his Canadian passport had expired, but the Canadian authorities had been obstructing his return to Canada already before his listing. He argued that the Canadian government's actions thwarting his return to Canada were in violation of his right to enter or return to Canada under the Canadian Charter of Rights and Freedoms. The defendants argued that he was prevented from entering Canada because of the Security Council measures and that any actions facilitating his travel back to Canada would breach Canada's international obligations.

> 4 There is a tension between the obligations of Canada as a member of the UN to implement and observe its resolutions, especially those that are designed to ensure security from international terrorism and the requirement that in so doing Canada conform to the rights and freedoms it guarantees to its citizens.
>
> [. . .]
>
> 49 [. . .] Mr. Abdelrazik was listed by the 1267 Committee as being associated with Al-Qaida. Section 2 of Resolution 1822 defines "associated with" as including, but not being restricted to the following:
>
> a. participating in the financing, planning, facilitating, preparing, or perpetrating of acts or activities by, in conjunction with, under the name of, on behalf of, or in support of;
> b. supplying, selling or transferring arms and related materiel to;
> c. recruiting for; or
> d. otherwise supporting acts or activities of;
>
> Al-Qaida, Usama bin Laden or the Taliban, or any cell, affiliate, splinter group or derivative thereof.

56 ibid, H9.2, H10.2.
57 ECtHR, *Nada v Switzerland*, App No 10593/08 (12 September 2012) paras 195–98.
58 ibid, paras 212–13.
59 ibid, para 233.

50 A Study commissioned by the United Nations Office of Legal Affairs, summarizes the lack of legal procedures available to persons listed by the 1267 Committee.

Targeted individuals and entities are not informed prior to their being listed, and accordingly do not have an opportunity to prevent their inclusion in a list by demonstrating that such an inclusion is unjustified under the terms of the respective Security Council resolution(s). There exist different de-listing procedures under the various sanctions regimes, but in no case are individuals or entities allowed directly to petition the respective Security Council committee for de-listing. Individuals or entities are not granted a hearing by the Council or a committee. […] Whether the respective committee, or the Security Council itself, grants a de-listing request is entirely within the committee's or the Council's discretion; no legal rules exist that would oblige the committee or the Council to grant a request if specific conditions are met.

At the same time, no effective opportunity is provided for a listed individual or entity to challenge a listing before a national court or tribunal, as UN Member States are obliged, in accordance with Article 103 of the UN Charter, to comply with resolutions made by the Security Council under Chapter VII of the UN Charter. […]

It has been argued by leading scholars of international law that the present situation amounts to a "denial of legal remedies" for the individuals and entities concerned, and is untenable under principles of international human rights law: "Everyone must be free to show that he or she has been justifiably placed under suspicion and that therefore [for instance] the freezing of his or her assets has no valid foundation."

[footnotes and citations omitted]

51 I add my name to those who view the 1267 Committee regime as a denial of basic legal remedies and as untenable under the principles of international human rights. There is nothing in the listing or de-listing procedure that recognizes the principles of natural justice or that provides for basic procedural fairness. […] [T]he 1267 Committee listing and de-listing processes do not even include a limited right to a hearing. It can hardly be said that the 1267 Committee process meets the requirement of independence and impartiality when, as appears may be the case involving Mr. Abdelrazik, the nation requesting the listing is one of the members of the body that decides whether to list or, equally as important, to de-list a person. The accuser is also the judge.

52 The 1267 Committee process has been amended since its inception to include a requirement that a narrative summary of the reasons for listing be included on the web site of the Consolidated Listing. Notwithstanding that Resolution 1822 provides that such information is also to be provided for those, such as Mr. Abdelrazik, who were previously listed, there is not yet any such narrative provided as regards the rationale for the listing of Mr. Abdelrazik.

53 Originally de-listing requests could only be made by the individual's home State. Again, there has been an amendment to allow a listed individual to make an application personally to the 1267 Committee or to do so through his home State. The *Guidelines of the Committee for the Conduct of Its Work* provide that a petitioner seeking de-listing "should provide justification for the de-listing request by describing the basis for this request, including by explaining why he/she *no longer meets* the criteria described in paragraph 2 of resolution 1617 (2005)..." (emphasis added). Those criteria are the four criteria set out above in paragraph 49. For a person such as Mr. Abdelrazik who asserts that he never met the criteria and was wrongly listed in the first instance, it is difficult to see how he can provide the requested justification, particularly when he has no information as to the basis for the initial listing. Section 7(g)(iii) of the Guidelines further provide that if the request for de-listing is a repeat

> request and if it does not contain any information additional to that provided in the first request, it is to be returned to the petitioner without consideration. It is difficult to see what information any petitioner could provide to prove a negative, i.e. to prove that he or she is not associated with Al-Qaida. One cannot prove that fairies and goblins do not exist any more than Mr. Abdelrazik or any other person can prove that they are not an Al-Qaida associate. It is a fundamental principle of Canadian and international justice that the accused does not have the burden of proving his innocence, the accuser has the burden of proving guilt. In light of these shortcomings, it is disingenuous of the respondents to submit, as they did, that if he is wrongly listed the remedy is for Mr. Abdelrazik to apply to the 1267 Committee for de-listing and not to engage this Court. The 1267 Committee regime is, as I observed at the hearing, a situation for a listed person not unlike that of Josef K. in Kafka's The Trial, who awakens one morning and, for reasons never revealed to him or the reader, is arrested and prosecuted for an unspecified crime.
>
> 54 The UN Security Council itself has recognized the extreme difficulty persons listed have to obtain de-listing. In the Security Council Report *Update Report, April 21, 2008, No. 4* respecting the 1267 Committee it is stated:
>
> It is far easier for a nation to place an individual or entity on the list than to take them off. For example, the US last year wanted to remove Abdul Hakim Monib, a former Taliban minister who switched sides and until recently served as the governor of Afghanistan's Uruzgan province, working with US and NATO troops. But Russia blocked it. In other cases, the US has prevented removal of names and entities it has submitted for *suspected* involvement with Al-Qaida. (emphasis added)
>
> I pause to comment that it is frightening to learn that a citizen of this or any other country might find himself on the 1267 Committee list, based only on suspicion.
>
> 129 [. . .] I find that properly interpreted the UN travel ban presents no impediment to Mr. Abdelrazik returning home to Canada. This interpretation is consistent with the objective of the travel ban as stated by the 1267 Committee in its document *Travel Ban: Explanation of Terms*. There they state that the objective of the travel ban is to "limit the mobility of listed individuals". It is to be noted that the travel ban does not restrict mobility within a country. Its concern is to prevent these individuals from traveling from country to country raising funds and arms and spreading terrorism. Mr. Abdelrazik will have no more mobility, in that sense of the word, if he is in Canada than in Sudan.
>
> 153 I find that the applicant's Charter right as a citizen of Canada to enter Canada has been breached by the respondents in failing to issue him an emergency passport. In my view, it is not necessary to decide whether that breach was done in bad faith; a breach, whether made in bad faith or good faith remains a breach and absent justification under section 1 of the Charter, the aggrieved party is entitled to a remedy. [. . .]
>
> 160 Accordingly, at a minimum, the respondents are to be ordered to provide Mr. Abdelrazik with an emergency passport that will permit him to travel to and enter Canada. [. . .]

This was one of the domestic court decisions that dealt with the effects of sanctions on individuals not by deferring to the (primacy of) Security Council resolutions but by challenging the domestic acts implementing them and by 'interpreting away' Canada's obligations under Resolution 1822 so as to circumvent the travel ban and ensure respect for the constitutional right of Mr Abdelrazik to enter or return to Canada.[60] This approach was in sharp contrast to

60 See Tzanakopoulos (n 52) 135.

that of the Swiss Federal Supreme Court in *Nada* and more in line with that of the CJEU in *Kadi*, which was however not mentioned in the instant decision; the court made no reference to any international or domestic decision in that regard. As noted by the ILDC reporter, although the court's interpretation of the Council's relevant resolutions might be persuasive, it could leave Canada in breach of its international obligations.[61] Abdelrazik returned to Canada on 27 June 2009 as per the court's order.[62]

Ahmed and ors v Her Majesty's Treasury, Appeal decision, [2010] UKSC 2, [2010] 2 AC 534, [2010] 2 WLR 378, [2010] UKHRR 204, [2010] 4 All ER 745, [2010] Lloyd's Rep FC 217, ILDC 1534 (UK 2010), 27th January 2010, United Kingdom; Supreme Court [UKSC]

This case concerned the UK's implementation of Security Council sanctions freezing the assets of the appellants under the Terrorism Order of 2006 (TO) and the Al-Qaida and Taliban Order of 2006 (AQO) enacted under the 1946 United Nations Act. A, K, and M were designated by Her Majesty's Treasury (HMT) owing to reasonable suspicion that they were, or may be facilitating acts of terrorism; G was designated due to his placement in the SC sanctions committee's list at the UK's request; and Hay was designated by HMT because he was in the SC sanctions committee's list, but not at the UK's request. All initiated proceedings to set aside the directions against them. In all cases, the TO and AQO were found to be *ultra vires* the UN Act but remedies varied (in the case of A, K, M, and G, the court quashed the TO and AQO but stayed the orders, whereas in Hay's case the court declined to make a quashing order). HMT appealed. Before the Supreme Court, A, K, and M argued that the TO was *ultra vires* because designated persons could not challenge their designation; G argued that the AQO was *ultra vires* and violated the rights to access to court, private life, and property protected under Articles 6 and 8 of the ECHR and Article 1 of the First Additional Protocol to the ECHR; and Hay argued that the AQO *was ultra vires* because it violated his right of access to a court for an effective remedy.

> Lord Hope, with whom Lord Walker and Lady Hale agree
>
> 38. The effect of the regimes that the TO and the AQO impose is that every transaction, however small, which involves the making of any payments or the passing of funds or economic resources whatever directly or indirectly for the benefit of a designated person is criminalised. This affects all aspects of his life, including his ability to move around at will by any means of private or public transport. To enable payments to be made for basic living expenses a system of licensing has been created. It is regulated by the Treasury, whose interpretation of the sanctions regime and of the system of licensing and the conditions that it gives rise to is extremely rigorous. […] But, taken overall, the regime that is imposed under it remains to a high degree restrictive and, so far as the designated person himself is concerned, just as paralysing.
>
> 56. The TO […] provides in para (2)(a) that the Treasury may give a direction if they have reasonable grounds for suspecting that the person is or may be a person who commits, attempts to commit, participates in or facilitates the commission of acts of terrorism.
>
> 57. The question is whether, by introducing the words "have reasonable grounds for suspecting that the person is or may be", the Treasury exceeded their powers […].
>
> 58. SCR 1373(2001) is not phrased in terms of reasonable suspicion. It refers instead to persons "who commit, or attempt to commit, terrorist acts". The preamble refers

61 L Clarke, Analysis, *Abdelrazik v Minister of Foreign Affairs and Attorney General of Canada*, ILDC 1332 (CA 2009) A6, citing A Tzanakopoulos, 'United Nations Sanctions in Domestic Courts: From Interpretation to Defiance in *Abdelrazik v Canada*' (2010) 8 *Journal of International Criminal Justice* 255.

62 ibid, A7.

to "acts of terrorism". The standard of proof is not addressed. The question how persons falling within the ambit of the decision are to be identified is left to the member states. Transposition of the direction into domestic law under section 1 of the 1946 Act raises questions of judgment as to what is "necessary" on the one hand and what is "expedient" on the other. It was not necessary to introduce the reasonable suspicion test in order to reproduce what the SCR requires. It may well have been expedient to do so, to ease the process of identifying those who should be restricted in their access to funds or economic resources. But widening the scope of the Order in this way was not just a drafting exercise. It was bound to have a very real impact on the people that were exposed to the restrictions as a result of it. The facts of these cases show how devastating their imposition can be on the restricted persons and their families. This raises fundamental questions, such as the standard of proof that should be required, whether the directions should be capable of being challenged by an effective form of judicial review and whether they should last indefinitely or be time limited. The validity of the introduction of the reasonable grounds test must be assessed in the light of the entire system that the TO provides for. Is it acceptable that the exercise of judgment in matters of this kind should be left exclusively, without any form of Parliamentary scrutiny, to the executive?

[…]

61. I would hold that, by introducing the reasonable suspicion test as a means of giving effect to SCR 1373(2001), the Treasury exceeded their powers under section 1(1) of the 1946 Act. This is a clear example of an attempt to adversely affect the basic rights of the citizen without the clear authority of Parliament […]. […] In my opinion the TO is ultra vires section 1(1) of the 1946 Act and, subject to what I say about the date when these orders should take effect, it together with the directions that have been made under it in the cases of A, K, M and G must be quashed.

64. Unlike the TO, the AQO does not rely for its application, at least in the first instance, on a reasonable grounds to suspect test. To this extent it does […] faithfully implement the relevant SCRs. […] Both G and HAY are designated persons because their names are on the list maintained by the 1267 Committee. As they have not been subjected to freezing orders on the basis of a reasonable suspicion, the grounds on which I would hold that the TO was ultra vires do not apply to their designation under the AQO.

65. The question which is common to both G and HAY is whether the AQO is ultra vires section 1 of the 1946 Act because there is no effective judicial remedy against a listing by the 1267 Committee. But I must deal first with Mr Singh's argument that the AQO is unlawful under section 6(1) of the Human Rights Act 1998 […].

66. Mr Singh […] submits that G's rights under article 8 and article 1 of Protocol 1 are obviously interfered with, and that his rights under article 6 are interfered with too as his designation under the AQO interfered with his civil rights but did not give him a meaningful right of access to a court which was capable of granting him an effective remedy. He frankly acknowledged that the decision of the House of Lords in *R (Al-Jedda) v Secretary of State for Defence* [2008] AC 332 was against him on this branch of his argument. But he invited this court to reconsider that decision, especially in the light of the decision of the European Court of Justice in *Kadi v Council of the European Union* (Joined Cases C–402/05P and C-415/05P) [2009] AC 1225.

68. In its judgment the ECJ […] said that the Community was based on the rule of law, inasmuch as neither its member states nor its institutions could avoid review

of conformity of their acts with the EC treaty, that an international agreement could not affect the autonomy of the Community legal system and that according to settled case law fundamental rights formed an integral part of the general principles of law whose observance the Court ensured. In para 285 it said:

> "It follows from all those considerations that the obligations imposed by an international agreement cannot have the effect of prejudicing the constitutional principles of the EC Treaty, which include the principle that all Community acts must respect fundamental rights, that respect constituting a condition of their lawfulness which it is for the Court to review in the framework of the complete system of legal remedies established by the Treaty."

The court went on to say that it did not follow from the principles governing the international legal order under the United Nations that any judicial review of the internal lawfulness of the contested regulation in the light of fundamental freedoms was excluded by virtue of the fact that that measure is intended to give effect to a resolution of the Security Council adopted under Chapter VII of the Charter of the United Nations: para 287. The existence within the United Nations of the re-examination procedure could not give rise to generalised immunity from jurisdiction within the internal legal order of the Community, and the Community judicature must ensure the full review of all Community acts including measures designed to give effect to resolutions adopted by the Security Council under Chapter VII: paras 299 and 326. [. . .]

69. The ECJ is not alone in regarding the way the decisions under the listing system administered by the 1267 Committee are dealt with as incompatible with the fundamental right that there should be an opportunity for a review by an independent tribunal of their lawfulness. In *Abdelrazik v The Minister of Foreign Affairs* [2009] FC 580 Zinn J sitting in the Federal Court of Canada [. . .] found that Mr Abdelrazik's right under the Canadian Charter of Rights and Freedoms to enter Canada, his country of citizenship, which had been denied to him because he was listed and facilitating his return by purchasing an airline ticket on his behalf was precluded by the ban on transferring assets to a listed entity, had been breached.

[. . .]

71. Caution must however be exercised in drawing any firm conclusions from these cases. The decisions of the courts in Canada and the United States were not made under reference to an international human rights instrument such as the European Convention. [. . .] The ECJ was not faced in *Kadi v Council of the European Union* with the problem that article 103 of the UN Charter gives rise to in member states in international law, as the institutions of the European Community are not party to the UN Charter. We must take our guidance from *R (Al-Jedda) v Secretary of State for Defence* [2008] AC 332. In that case the House was unanimous in holding that the obligation under article 25 of the Charter was, by virtue of article 103, to prevail over any other international agreement, including the Convention. [. . .]

72. Lord Bingham gave this explanation for the conclusion that the House had reached in *Al-Jedda's* case:

> "35. Emphasis has often been laid on the special character of the European Convention as a human rights instrument. But the reference in article 103 to 'any other international agreement' leaves no room for any excepted category, and such appears to be the consensus of learned opinion. The decisions of the International Court of Justice (*Questions of Interpretation and Application of the 1971 Montreal Convention Arising from the Aerial Incident at Lockerbie (Libyan Arab Jamahiriya v*

United Kingdom) [1992] ICJ Rep 3, para 39; and *Application of the Convention on the Prevention and Punishment of the Crime of Genocide* [1992] IJC Rep 325, 439–440, paras 99–100 per Judge ad hoc Lauterpacht) give no warrant for drawing any distinction save where an obligation is jus cogens […].

36. I do not think that the European court, if the appellant's article 5(1) claim were before it as an application, would ignore the significance of article 103 of the Charter in international law. …"

In para 39, acknowledging that there was clash between a power or duty to detain exercisable on the express authority of the Security Council and a fundamental human right which the United Kingdom had undertaken to secure to those within its jurisdiction, he said that there was only one way that they could be reconciled. This was by ruling that the United Kingdom might exercise the power of detention authorised by the Security Council but must ensure that the detainee's rights under article 5 were not infringed to any greater extent than was inherent in such detention.

[…]

74. I do not think that it is open to this court to predict how the reasoning of the House of Lords in *Al-Jedda* would be viewed in Strasbourg. For the time being we must proceed on the basis that article 103 leaves no room for any exception, and that the Convention rights fall into the category of obligations under an international agreement over which obligations under the Charter must prevail. The fact that the rights that G seeks to invoke in this case are now part of domestic law does not affect that conclusion. […]

75. But this leaves open for consideration how the position may be regarded under domestic law. Mr Singh submitted that the obligation under article 25 of the Charter to give effect to the SCRs directing the measures to be taken against Usama bin Laden, Al-Qaida and the Taliban had to respect the basic premises of our own legal order. Two fundamental rights were in issue in G's case, and as they were to be found in domestic law his right to invoke them was not affected by article 103 of the UN Charter. One was the right to peaceful enjoyment of his property, which could only be interfered with by clear legislative words […]. The other was his right of unimpeded access to a court […]. As it was put by Viscount Simonds in *Pyx Granite Co Ltd v Ministry of Housing and Local Government* [1960] AC 260, 286, the subject's right of access to Her Majesty's courts for the determination of his rights is not to be excluded except by clear words. As Mr Singh pointed out, both of these rights are embraced by the principle of legality, which lies at the heart of the relationship between Parliament and the citizen. Fundamental rights may not be overridden by general words. This can only be done by express language or by necessary implication. So it was not open to the Treasury to use its powers under the general wording of section 1(1) of the 1946 Act to subject individuals to a regime which had these effects.

76. I would accept Mr Singh's proposition that, as fundamental rights may not be overridden by general words, section 1 of the 1946 Act does not give authority for overriding the fundamental rights of the individual. It does not do so either expressly or by necessary implication. The question is whether the effect of G's designation under the AQO has that effect. To some extent this must be a question of degree. Some interference with the right to peaceful enjoyment of one's property may have been foreseen by the framers of section 1, as it authorises the making of provision for the apprehension, trial and punishment of persons offending against the Order. To that extent coercive steps to enable the measures to be applied effectively can be regarded as within its scope. But there must come a point when the intrusion upon the right to enjoyment of one's property is so great, so overwhelming and so timeless

that the absence of any effective means of challenging it means that this can only be brought about under the express authority of Parliament. Has that point been reached in the case of those who are designated persons under the AQO?

77. The opportunity to seek judicial review under Part 6 of the 2008 Act is not available in the case of persons such as G who are subject to the AQO only because they have been listed by the 1267 Committee. No direction under article 4(1) of the AQO was made in his case. Even if such a direction had been made he would still be a designated person to whom the AQO applied as he has been designated by the Committee [. . .]. In the Court of Appeal Sir Anthony Clarke MR summarised the position in which G found himself in this way [2009] 3 WLR 25, para 108:

> "It is common ground that G is subject to the AQO only because he has been listed by the UN Sanctions Committee ("the committee"). He has never had any contact with the committee, has no idea who precisely made the decision or upon what evidence it was based, although he does now know that it was the UK Government which requested that he be listed. It presumably had some evidential basis for its request. Indeed, it was presumably on the same basis as that relied upon by HMT in making a direction for his designation under the TO and was thus said to be so sensitive that G could not be given details. As to the committee, Mr Singh stresses that there is no information in the public domain that throws any light on who its members are, what degree of independence they enjoy, what evidential test they apply and what, if any, safeguards are in place to protect the rights of the individuals affected."

78. Some further details can be obtained from the *Guidelines of the Security Council Committee established pursuant to Resolution 1267(1999) Concerning Al-Qaida and the Taliban and Associated Individuals and Entities* of 9 December 2008. They state that the committee is comprised of all the members of the Security Council from time to time, that decisions of the committee are taken by consensus of its members and that a criminal charge or conviction is not necessary for a person's inclusion in the consolidated list that the committee maintains, as the sanctions are intended to be preventative in nature. It would appear that listing may be made on the basis of a reasonable suspicion only. It is also clear that, as the committee works by consensus, the effect of the guidelines is that the United Kingdom is not able unilaterally to procure listing, but it is not able unilaterally to procure de-listing either under the "Focal Point" procedure established under SCR 1730(2006). Although the Security Council has implemented a number of procedural reforms in recent years and has sought improvement in the quality of information provided to the 1267 Committee for the making of listing decisions, the Treasury accepted [. . .] that there is scope to further improve the transparency of decisions made by the 1267 Committee and the effectiveness of the de-listing process. On 17 December 2009 the Security Council adopted SCR 1904(2009) which provides in paras 20 and 21 that, when considering de-listing requests, the Committee shall be assisted by an Ombudsperson appointed by the Secretary-General, being an eminent individual of integrity, impartiality and experience, and that the Office of the Ombudsman is to deal with requests for de-listing from individuals and entities in accordance with procedures outlined in an annex to the resolution. While these improvements are to be welcomed, the fact remains that there was not when the designations were made, and still is not, any effective judicial remedy.

81. I would hold that G is entitled to succeed on the point that the regime to which he has been subjected has deprived him of access to an effective remedy. [. . .] What he needs if he is to be afforded an effective remedy is a means of subjecting that listing to judicial review. This is something that, under the system that the 1267 Committee

currently operates, is denied to him. I would hold that article 3(1)(b) of the AQO, which has this effect, is ultra vires section 1 of the 1946 Act. [. . .].

82. I would treat HAY's case in the same way. He too is a designated person by reason of the fact that his name is on the 1267 Committee's list. As has already been observed, the United Kingdom is now seeking that his name should be removed from it. By letter dated 1 October 2009 the Treasury's Sanctions Team informed his solicitors that the de-listing request was submitted on 26 June 2009 but that at the committee's first consideration of it a number of States were not in a position to accede to the request. Further efforts to obtain de-listing are continuing, but this has still not been achieved. So he remains subject to the AQO. In this situation he too is being denied an effective remedy.

83. I would allow the appeals by A, K, M and G. I would declare that the TO is ultra vires and I would quash that Order. I would allow G's appeal as regards the AQO to the extent of declaring that article 3(1)(b) of that Order is ultra vires. [. . .]

84. I would however suspend the operation of the orders that I would make as regards the AQO for a period of one month from the date of the judgment to give the Treasury time to consider what steps, if any, they should now take. [. . .] It is perhaps arguable that suspension of the order relating to the AQO is not needed in HAY's case in view of the steps that are currently being taken for him to be de-listed by the 1267 Committee. But so long as he remains on the list the United Kingdom is bound by article 25 of the Charter to treat him as a designated person and must take steps to subject him to a freezing order in this country. So I think that suspension of the order is needed in his case to enable the Treasury, if so minded, to take the steps to give effect to this obligation pending the proceedings for HAY's de-listing.

The outcome of this case was consciously based on UK domestic law. The court reviewed the domestic measures (the TO and the AQO) implementing the Security Council resolutions under the UN Act of 1947 and found them *ultra vires* the Act because the Act's general wording could not override the applicants' fundamental rights; parliament could do so only by express language or by necessary implication. The court accepted the applicants' strategy to rely on the protection of their human rights under domestic law and not under the ECHR in an obvious attempt to avoid application of Article 103 of the UN Charter, which would have overridden the ECHR as per the unanimous ruling of the House of Lords in *Al-Jedda* a couple of years earlier. In doing so, as commented by the ILDC reporter, the court followed a similar approach to that of the CJEU in *Kadi*, which it cited at some length, by disengaging the UK obligations under the UN Charter and relevant Security Council resolutions from the national implementing measures.[63] Moreover, to preclude any breach of the UK's obligations under the UN Charter, the UK Supreme Court, also like the CJEU in Kadi, suspended the quashing order to give time for enactment of implementing measures compliant with domestic law,[64] which the UK parliament eventually did.

63 K Senior, Analysis, *Ahmed and ors v Her Majesty's Treasury*, ILDC 1534 (UK 2010) A4. See also A Tzanakopoulos, 'Collective Security and Human Rights' in E de Wet and J Vidmar (eds), *Hierarchy in International Law: The Place of Human Rights* (OUP 2012) 42, 59–60.

64 In *Her Majesty's Treasury (Respondent) v Mohammed Jabar Ahmed and Others (FC) (Appellants) Her Majesty's Treasury (Respondent) v Mohammed al-Ghabra (FC) (Appellant) R (on the application of Hani El-Sayed Sabaei Youssef) (Respondent) v Her Majesty's Treasury (Appellant) (No 2), HM Treasury v Ahmed and ors*, Final judgment, [2010] UKSC 5, [2010] 2 AC 534, [2010] WLR 378, [2010] 4 All ER 829, ILDC 1533 (UK 2010), 4 February 2010, Supreme Court, the UK Supreme Court refused to suspend the operation of any part of the court's order any further, as requested by HMT. Lord Hope dissented, arguing that the UK's national interest in resisting threats to the country's security, as well as respect for international obligations, required the Court to do so.

Lord Hope indicated that the ECtHR might come to a different conclusion on the effect of Article 103 in the joint hearing of *Al-Skeini and Al-Jedda v UK* but proceeded, 'for the time being', on the basis that Article 103 left no room for any exception and would thus have prevailed over the ECHR rights. Indeed, the ECtHR took a different approach, that of conforming or harmonious interpretation,[65] and established an interpretative presumption that the Security Council did not intend to impose any obligations on states in breach of fundamental human rights.[66] Applying the ECtHR reasoning in *Al-Jedda* in the case at hand, it would follow that, Article 103 being unavailing, domestic and EU measures implementing Security Council resolutions could be challenged for breaching the ECHR.[67]

Sassi (Nizar) and ors, Cassation Appeal, Pourvoi No 03-84652, Bulletin Criminel 2005 No 1, ILDC 776 (FR 2005), 4th January 2005, France; Court of Cassation [Cass]

This case concerned the applicability of international human rights and humanitarian law in the case of two French nationals detained in Guantanamo Bay without charges and without access to a court or a lawyer from January 2002 until their release and transfer to France in July 2004. In fall 2002, criminal proceedings were initiated in France for their arrest and detention. The examining magistrate refused to investigate, arguing that US agents enjoyed immunity before foreign courts. On appeal, the pre-trial chamber of the Court of Appeal of Lyon confirmed the dismissal of the case, adding that the US operations had to be evaluated in the context of Security Council Resolutions 1368 and 1373 and Article 51 of the UN Charter and that the arrest and detention of the two men were not arbitrary owing to the primacy of those resolutions over French law. The two men appealed to the Criminal Chamber of the Court of Cassation, arguing that even if the right to self-defense and the Security Council resolutions could justify the US intervention in Afghanistan, they could not deprive those captured of the status of prisoners of war under the Third Geneva Convention or of the protection under the ICCPR.

> 11 Whereas […] the examining court when a complaint is referred to it by a plaintiff, must normally investigate regardless of the requisitions of the public prosecutor;
>
> This obligation only ceases […] if, due to reasons affecting the criminal proceedings themselves, the facts cannot legally lead to prosecution or if, on the assumption that the facts are demonstrated, they cannot be given any criminal definition;
>
> 12 Whereas, from the contested judgment and the evidence presented in the proceedings, it appears that Nizar X … and Mourad Z … , French nationals who were detained at Guantánamo Bay, […] report, on the one hand, that they were illegally arrested on account of the armed operations carried out in Afghanistan in response to the attacks carried out on 11 September 2001, and on the other hand, that they were kept in arbitrary detention;
>
> 13 Whereas, to uphold the ruling of the examining judge refusing to investigate these facts, the contested judgment, after having stated the context in which the arrest of the plaintiffs occurred, states that the United States' armed intervention "is connected" on the one hand, to Resolutions 1368 and 1373, adopted unanimously by the United Nations

65 See L Boisson de Chazournes, *Interactions between Regional and Universal Organizations: A Legal Perspective* (Brill Nijhoff 2017) 294–95.

66 ECtHR, *Al-Jedda v United Kingdom*, App No 27021/08 (7 July 2011) para 102: 'Against this background, the Court considers that, in interpreting its resolutions, there must be a presumption that the Security Council does not intend to impose any obligation on Member States to breach fundamental principles of human rights. In the event of any ambiguity in the terms of a Security Council Resolution, the Court must therefore choose the interpretation which is most in harmony with the requirements of the Convention and which avoids any conflict of obligations. In the light of the United Nations' important role in promoting and encouraging respect for human rights, it is to be expected that clear and explicit language would be used were the Security Council to intend States to take particular measures which would conflict with their obligations under international human rights law'.

67 K Senior, Analysis, *Ahmed and ors v Her Majesty's Treasury*, ILDC 1534 (UK 2010) A8. See also M Milanović, 'Al-Skeini and Al-Jedda in Strasbourg' (2012) 23 *European Journal of International Law* 137.

Security Council on 12 and 28 September 2001 and on the other hand, to Article 51 of the United Nations Charter. The judges accept that no international agreement grants competence to the French courts to take cognisance of the situation the plaintiffs are complaining about which is the result of a response to terrorist acts, under the auspices of the United Nations, and may not thus be governed by French law alone. The breaches reported furthermore are not stated in any international covenant or agreement or by French law. They add that it is not for the French courts to recognise the "military order" signed by the President of the United States of America on 12 November 2001;

14 But whereas, by deciding thus, by a single abstract examination of the complaint, without seeking to ascertain, through prior investigation, whether the arrest and conditions of detention of the plaintiffs, that they should have analysed, particularly with regard to the Third Geneva Convention of 12 August 1949 and the International Covenant on Civil and Political Rights of 19 December 1966, were not covered in the provisions of Article 224-1 of the Criminal Code and, as such, due to the French nationality of plaintiffs, did not fall within the competence of the French laws and courts, in application of Articles 113-7 of the Criminal Code and 689 of the Criminal Procedure Code, the examining chamber did not justify its decision;

15 Which resulted in the appeal;

16 On these grounds, the Court

17 QUASHES and REPEALS, all the provisions of the abovementioned ruling of the examining chamber of the Lyon Court of Appeal, of 20 May 2003, so that it is to be tried again, in accordance with the law.

The French court in this case rejected the argument that foreign state actions giving effect to Security Council resolutions in the context of the fight against terrorism was a valid reason for removing the procedural obligation of investigation, which was held to be a right of the detainees under the ICCPR and the Third Geneva Convention.[68] Any ruling to the contrary would have created an immunity of jurisdiction for such acts. However, as rightly observed by the ILDC reporters, the Security Council resolutions had not prejudged the legality of any specific acts performed during such operations under international human rights law and international humanitarian law.[69] Even though it was issued some years earlier, the reasoning and outcome of this decision was in line with the ECtHR approach in *Al-Jedda*, referred to in the previous case, and the Strasbourg court's interpretative presumption that the Security Council did not intend to impose any obligation on member states to breach fundamental principles of human rights. Based on that presumption, Mr Al-Jedda's preventive security detention by the UK forces in Iraq, acting upon a broad Security Council authorization in Resolution 1546, was found to be in breach of Article 5 of the ECHR (admittedly, of course, Al-Jedda is distinguishable from the instant case, where the two men were not detained by the French authorities).

2. Domestic anti-terrorism measures and human rights

(a) Prohibition of torture

Public Committee Against Torture in Israel v Israel and General Security Service, Petition to the High Court of Justice, Case No HCJ 5100/94, ILDC 2115 (IL 1999), 53(4) PD 817, (1999) Is LR 567, 6th September 1999, Israel; Supreme Court

The petitioners challenged the legality of certain investigation methods used by the General Security Service (GSS), the main body responsible for fighting terrorism in Israel. These methods

68 Y Kerbrat and Q Lienard, Analysis, *Sassi (Nizar) and ors*, ILDC 776 (FR 2005) A1.
69 ibid, A2.

included, *inter alia*, the practice of 'shaking', sleep deprivation, excessive tight handcuffs and other kinds of physical pressure, if such pressure was considered as immediately necessary to save human life. These methods, according to the petitioners, constituted 'torture' and were in violation of international law. The state did not deny using such methods but argued that they did not violate international law since they did not cause pain and suffering and offered justifications for their use.

> 23. [...] First, a reasonable investigation is necessarily one free of torture, free of cruel, inhuman treatment, and free of any degrading conduct whatsoever. There is a prohibition on the use of "brutal or inhuman means" in the course of an investigation. [...] This conclusion is in accord with international treaties, to which Israel is a signatory, which prohibit the use of torture, "cruel, inhuman treatment" and "degrading treatment." [...] These prohibitions are "absolute." There are no exceptions to them and there is no room for balancing.
>
> Second, a reasonable investigation is likely to cause discomfort. It may result in insufficient sleep. The conditions under which it is conducted risk being unpleasant. Of course, it is possible to conduct an effective investigation without resorting to violence. Within the confines of the law, it is permitted to resort to various sophisticated techniques. [...] In the end result, the legality of an investigation is deduced from the propriety of its purpose and from its methods. [...]
>
> *From the General to the Particular*
>
> 24. [...] Clearly, shaking is a prohibited investigation method. It harms the suspect's body. It violates his dignity. It is a violent method which can not form part of a legal investigation. It surpasses that which is necessary. [...]
>
> 25. [...] [C]ompelling the suspect to crouch on the tips of his toes for periods of five minutes [...] is a prohibited investigation method. It does not serve any purpose inherent to an investigation. It is degrading and infringes an individual's human dignity.
>
> 26. [...] [W]e accept that the suspect's cuffing, for the purpose of preserving the investigators' safety, is included in the general power to investigate. [...] The cuffing associated with the "Shabach" position, however, is unlike routine cuffing. The suspect is cuffed with his hands tied behind his back. One hand is placed inside the gap between the chair's seat and back support, while the other is tied behind him, against the chair's back support. This is a distorted and unnatural position. The investigators' safety does not require it. Similarly, there is no justification for handcuffing the suspect's hands with especially small handcuffs, if this is in fact the practice. The use of these methods is prohibited. [...].
>
> 27. The same applies to seating the suspect in question in the "Shabach" position. We accept that seating a man is inherent to the investigation. This is not the case, however, when the chair upon which he is seated is a very low one, tilted forward facing the ground, and when he is seated in this position for long hours. This sort of seating is not authorized by the general power to interrogate. [...] All these methods [...] infringe the suspect's dignity, his bodily integrity and his basic rights in an excessive manner. They are not to be deemed as included within the general power to conduct interrogations.
>
> 28. [...] [T]he suspect's head covering—which covers his entire head, rather than eyes alone—for a prolonged period of time, with no essential link to the goal of preventing contact between the suspects under investigation, is not part of a fair interrogation. It harms the suspect and his dignity. It degrades him. It causes him to lose his sense of time and place. It suffocates him. All these things are not included in the general authority to investigate. [...] The covering of the head in the circumstances

described, as distinguished from the covering of the eyes, is outside the scope of authority and is prohibited.

29. […] Being exposed to very loud music for a long period of time causes the suspect suffering. Furthermore, the entire time, the suspect is tied in an uncomfortable position with his head covered. This is prohibited. It does not fall within the scope of the authority to conduct a fair and effective interrogation. […]

30. […] A similar—though not identical—combination of interrogation methods were discussed in the case of *Ireland v. United Kingdom* […]. The Court held that these methods did not constitute "torture." However, since they subjected the suspect to "inhuman and degrading" treatment, they were nonetheless prohibited.

31. […] If the suspect is intentionally deprived of sleep for a prolonged period of time, for the purpose of tiring him out or "breaking" him, it is not part of the scope of a fair and reasonable investigation. Such means harm the rights and dignity of the suspect in a manner beyond what is necessary.

Physical Means and the "Necessity" Defense

33. […] The state maintains that an act committed under conditions of "necessity" does not constitute a crime. Instead, the state sees such acts as worth committing in order to prevent serious harm to human life or limb. These are actions that society has an interest in encouraging, which should be seen as proper under the circumstances. In this, society is choosing the lesser evil. Not only is it legitimately permitted to engage in fighting terrorism, it is our moral duty to employ the means necessary for this purpose. […]

In the course of their argument, the state presented the "ticking bomb" argument. A given suspect is arrested by the GSS. He holds information regarding the location of a bomb that was set and will imminently explode. There is no way to diffuse the bomb without this information. If the information is obtained, the bomb may be neutralized. If the bomb is not neutralized, scores will be killed and injured. Is a GSS investigator authorized to employ physical means in order to obtain this information? The state answers in the affirmative. The use of physical means should not constitute a criminal offence, and their use should be sanctioned, according to the state, by the "necessity" defense.

34. We are prepared to assume, although this matter is open to debate, that the "necessity defense" is available to all, including an investigator, during an interrogation, acting in the capacity of the state. […] Likewise, we are prepared to accept—although this matter is equally contentious—that the "necessity defense" can arise in instances of "ticking bombs," and that the phrase "immediate need" in the statute refers to the imminent nature of the act rather than that of the danger. Hence, the imminence criteria is satisfied even if the bomb is set to explode in a few days, or even in a few weeks, provided the danger is certain to materialize and there is no alternative means of preventing it. […] A long list of arguments, from the fields of ethics and political science, may be raised in support of and against the use of the "necessity defense." […]

35. […] This, however, is not the issue before this Court. […] The question before us is whether it is possible, ex ante, to establish permanent directives setting out the physical interrogation means that may be used under conditions of "necessity." […]

36. In the Court's opinion, the authority to establish directives respecting the use of physical means during the course of a GSS interrogation cannot be implied from the "necessity defense." […]

The "necessity defense" has the effect of allowing one who acts under the circumstances of "necessity" to escape criminal liability. The "necessity defense" does not possess any additional normative value. It can not authorize the use of physical means to allow investigators to execute their duties in circumstances of necessity. The very fact that a particular act does not constitute a criminal act—due to the "necessity defense"—does not in itself authorize the act and the concomitant infringement of human rights. The rule of law, both as a formal and as a substantive principle, requires that an infringement of human rights be prescribed by statute. The lifting of criminal responsibility does not imply authorization to infringe a human right. [...]

37. [...] Granting GSS investigators the authority to apply physical force during the interrogation of suspects suspected of involvement in hostile terrorist activities, thereby harming the suspect's dignity and liberty, raises basic questions of law and society, of ethics and policy, and of the rule of law and security. These questions and the corresponding answers must be determined by the legislative branch. This is required by the principle of the separation of powers and the rule of law, under our understanding of democracy. [...]

38. We conclude, therefore, that, according to the existing state of the law, neither the government nor the heads of the security services have the authority to establish directives regarding the use of physical means during the interrogation of suspects suspected of hostile terrorist activities, beyond the general rules which can be inferred from the very concept of an interrogation itself. Similarly, the individual GSS investigator—like any police officer—does not possess the authority to employ physical means that infringe a suspect's liberty during the interrogation, unless these means are inherent to the very essence of an interrogation and are both fair and reasonable.

An investigator who employs these methods exceeds his authority. His responsibility shall be fixed according to law. His potential criminal liability shall be examined in the context of the "necessity defense." Provided the conditions of the defense are met by the circumstances of the case, the investigator may find refuge under its wings. Just as the existence of the "necessity defense" does not bestow authority, the lack of authority does not negate the applicability of the necessity defense or of other defenses from criminal liability. The Attorney-General can establish guidelines regarding circumstances in which investigators shall not stand trial, if they claim to have acted from "necessity." A statutory provision is necessary to authorize the use of physical means during the course of an interrogation, beyond what is permitted by the ordinary "law of investigation," and in order to provide the individual GSS investigator with the authority to employ these methods. The "necessity defense" cannot serve as a basis for such authority.

A Final Word

39. [...] A democracy must sometimes fight with one hand tied behind its back. Even so, a democracy has the upper hand. The rule of law and the liberty of an individual constitute important components in its understanding of security. At the end of the day, they strengthen its spirit and this strength allows it to overcome its difficulties. [...]

40. [...] We are aware of the harsh reality of terrorism in which we are, at times, immersed. The possibility that this decision will hamper the ability to properly deal with terrorists and terrorism disturbs us. We are, however, judges. We must decide according to the law. [...]

> The GSS does not have the authority to "shake" a man, hold him in the "Shabach" position (which includes the combination of various methods, as mentioned in paragraph 30), force him into a "frog crouch" position and deprive him of sleep in a manner other than that which is inherently required by the interrogation. Likewise, we declare that the "necessity defense," found in the Penal Law, cannot serve as a basis of authority for interrogation practices, or for directives to GSS investigators, allowing them to employ interrogation practices of this kind. Our decision does not negate the possibility that the "necessity defense" will be available to GSS investigators—either in the choice made by the Attorney-General in deciding whether to prosecute, or according to the discretion of the court if criminal charges are brought.

As noted by the ILDC reporter, Israel was a party to the Convention Against Torture since 1991 but there was no domestic law that prohibited the use of torture, using this term, in Israel.[70] The Supreme Court of Israel in this unanimous decision fell short of ruling that the use of interrogation methods involving the use of 'moderate physical pressure' constituted torture in violation of the Convention, but ruled that such methods were illegal under Israeli law, as they infringed on the individual's constitutional right to dignity. That part of the judgment was welcomed by the Committee Against Torture,[71] which however also expressed the following concerns: a) the ruling did not contain a definite prohibition of torture; b) it did not outlaw incidental sleep deprivation but only intentional deprivation—yet, in practice, in cases of prolonged interrogation it is impossible to distinguish between the two conditions; c) it did not reject the availability of the 'defense of necessity' in extreme circumstances (eg, 'ticking bomb' scenario) as defense from criminal liability,[72] although the Convention contains an absolute prohibition on any use of torture or other cruel, inhuman, or degrading treatment and the prohibition of torture is considered a rule of *jus cogens*.[73] Scholars have voiced similar criticisms.[74]

A, Amnesty International (intervening) and Commonwealth Lawyers Association (intervening) v Secretary of State for the Home Department, Appeal judgment, [2005] UKHL 71, [2006] 2 AC 221, [2005] 3 WLR 1249, [2006] 1 All ER 575, ILDC 363 (UK 2005), 8th December 2005, United Kingdom; House of Lords [HL]

This case concerned the admissibility of so-called foreign torture evidence, that is, evidence that was or might have been procured by torture inflicted abroad by foreign officials without the complicity of the British authorities. The case was brought by a group of foreign detainees who were designated as terrorist suspects under the 2001 Anti-Terrorism Act. The Special Immigration Appeal Commission (SIAC) held that the alleged use of torture under such circumstances was relevant to the weight of the evidence but did not render it legally inadmissible, provided that the British government had neither procured the torture nor connived at it. The Court of Appeal by a 2:1 majority upheld that decision. The detainees appealed to the House of Lords, relying on English common law, the ECHR and international law, while the secretary of state insisted that the admission of such evidence was not precluded by law.

---

70 R Hostovsky, Analysis, *Public Committee Against Torture in Israel v Israel and General Security Service*, ILDC 2115 (IL 1999) A1.

71 UNGA, 'Report of the Committee against Torture' (2002) UN Doc A/57/44, para 50.

72 ibid, para 52.

73 See A Constantinides, '*Jus Cogens*' Chapter 8 in this volume.

74 R Hostovsky, Analysis, *Public Committee Against Torture in Israel v Israel and General Security Service*, ILDC 2115 (IL 1999) A3; A Laursen, 'Israel's Supreme Court and International Human Rights Law: The Judgement on "Moderate Physical Pressure"' (2000) 69 *Nordic Journal of International Law* 413; Y Ginbar, *Why Not Torture Terrorists? Moral, Practical, and Legal Aspects of the 'Ticking Bomb' Justification for Torture* (OUP 2008) 200 (referring to the judgment as 'the only model of court-sanctioned interrogational torture in force anywhere in the world at this time').

Lord Bingham

Public International Law

[. . .]

(3) The duty of states in relation to torture.

34. As appears from the passage [in *Prosecutor v Furundzija* [1998] ICTY 3, 10 December 1998, paras. 147-157], the *jus cogens erga omnes* nature of the prohibition of torture requires member states to do more than eschew the practice of torture. [. . .]

Article 41 of the International Law Commission's draft articles on Responsibility of States for internationally wrongful acts (November 2001) requires states to cooperate to bring to an end through lawful means any serious breach of an obligation under a peremptory norm of general international law. An advisory opinion of the International Court of Justice on the Legal Consequences of the Construction of a Wall in the Occupied Palestinian Territory (9 July 2004, General List No 131), para 159 explained the consequences of the breach found in that case. [. . .]

There is reason to regard it as a duty of states, save perhaps in limited and exceptional circumstances, as where immediately necessary to protect a person from unlawful violence or property from destruction, to reject the fruits of torture inflicted in breach of international law. As McNally JA put it in *S v Nkomo* 1989 (3) ZLR 117, 131:

> "It does not seem to me that one can condemn torture while making use of the mute confession resulting from torture, because the effect is to encourage torture."

(4) Article 15 of the Torture Convention.

35. [. . .]

Article 15 of the Torture Convention repeats the substance of this provision, subject to a qualification:

> "Each State Party shall ensure that any statement which is established to have been made as a result of torture shall not be invoked as evidence in any proceedings, except against a person accused of torture as evidence that the statement was made."

The additional qualification makes plain the blanket nature of this exclusionary rule. It cannot possibly be read, as counsel for the Secretary of State submits, as intended to apply only in criminal proceedings. Nor can it be understood to differentiate between confessions and accusatory statements, or to apply only where the state in whose jurisdiction the proceedings are held has inflicted or been complicit in the torture. [. . .]

(5) State practice.

37. [. . .] In France, [. . .] extradition to Spain was refused where allegations that a witness statement had been procured by torture in Spain was judged not to have been adequately answered (*Le Ministère Public v Irastorza Dorronsoro*, Cour d'Appel de Pau, No 238/2003, 16 May 2003). In the Netherlands, it was held by the Supreme Court to follow from article 3 of the European Convention and article 7 of the ICCPR that if witness statements had been obtained by torture they could not be used as evidence: *Pereira*, 1 October 1996, nr 103.094, para 6.2. [. . .]

38. In the United States, [. . .] it had been said to be "unthinkable that a statement obtained by torture or by other conduct belonging only in a police state should be

admitted at the government's behest in order to bolster its case": *LaFrance v Bohlinger* 499 F 2d 29 (1974), para 6.

(6) The rationale of the exclusionary rule.

39. […] It seems indeed very likely that the unreliability of a statement or confession procured by torture and a desire to discourage torture by devaluing its product are two strong reasons why the rule was adopted. But it also seems likely that the article reflects the wider principle expressed in article 69(7) of the Rome Statute of the International Criminal Court, which has its counterpart in the Rules of Procedure and Evidence of the International Criminal Tribunals for the Former Yugoslavia and Rwanda:

> "Evidence obtained by means of a violation of this Statute or internationally recognized human rights shall not be admissible if:
> (a) the violation casts substantial doubt on the reliability of the evidence; or
> (b) the admission of the evidence would be antithetical to and would seriously damage the integrity of the proceedings." […]

(7) The impact of terrorism.

40. The European Court has emphasised that article 3 of the European Convention is an absolute prohibition, not derogable in any circumstances. […]

41. It is true, as the Secretary of State submits, that States Members of the United Nations and the Council of Europe have been strongly urged since 11 September 2001 to cooperate and share information in order to counter the cruel and destructive evil of terrorism. But these calls have been coupled with reminders that human rights, and international and humanitarian law, must not be infringed or compromised. […]

42. […] Security Council resolution 1373 of 28 September 2001 called for cooperation and exchange of information to prevent terrorist acts, but also reaffirmed resolution 1269 of 19 October 1999 which called for observance of the principles of the UN Charter and the norms of international law, including international humanitarian law. By Security Council resolution 1566 of 8 October 2004 states were reminded

> "that they must ensure that any measures taken to combat terrorism comply with all their obligations under international law, and should adopt such measures in accordance with international law, and in particular international human rights, refugee and humanitarian law."

Again, other similar examples could be given. The General Assembly has repeatedly made the same point […]. The Secretary General of the UN echoed the same theme in statements of 4 October 2002, 6 March 2003 and 10 March 2005.

43. […] In its Conclusions and Recommendations on the United Kingdom dated 10 December 2004 (CAT/C/CR/33/3), having received the United Kingdom's fourth periodic report, the Committee [against Torture] welcomed the Secretary of State's indication that he did not intend to rely upon or present evidence where there is a knowledge or belief that torture has taken place but recommended that this be appropriately reflected in formal fashion, such as legislative incorporation or undertaking to Parliament, and that means be provided whereby an individual could challenge the legality of any evidence plausibly suspected of having been obtained by torture in any proceeding.

44. This recommendation followed the judgment of the Court of Appeal in these appeals. Concern at the effect of that judgment was also expressed by the International Commission of Jurists […] and by the Council of Europe Commissioner for Human Rights, Mr Gil-Robles […]. […]

45. The House has not been referred to any decision, resolution, agreement or advisory opinion suggesting that a confession or statement obtained by torture is admissible in legal proceedings if the torture was inflicted without the participation of the state in whose jurisdiction the proceedings are held, or that such evidence is admissible in proceedings related to terrorism.

The Secretary of State's Case

51. [. . .] [T]he English common law has regarded torture and its fruits with abhorrence for over 500 years, and that abhorrence is now shared by over 140 countries which have acceded to the Torture Convention. I am startled, even a little dismayed, at the suggestion (and the acceptance by the Court of Appeal majority) that this deeply-rooted tradition and an international obligation solemnly and explicitly undertaken can be overridden by a statute and a procedural rule which make no mention of torture at all. [. . .] It trivialises the issue before the House to treat it as an argument about the law of evidence. The issue is one of constitutional principle, whether evidence obtained by torturing another human being may lawfully be admitted against a party to proceedings in a British court, irrespective of where, or by whom, or on whose authority the torture was inflicted. To that question I would give a very clear negative answer.

52. I accept the broad thrust of the appellants' argument on the common law. The principles of the common law, standing alone, in my opinion compel the exclusion of third party torture evidence as unreliable, unfair, offensive to ordinary standards of humanity and decency and incompatible with the principles which should animate a tribunal seeking to administer justice. But the principles of the common law do not stand alone. Effect must be given to the European Convention, which itself takes account of the all but universal consensus embodied in the Torture Convention. The answer to the central question posed at the outset of this opinion is to be found not in a governmental policy, which may change, but in law.

Inhuman or degrading treatment

53. The appellants broaden their argument to contend that all the principles on which they rely apply to inhuman and degrading treatment, if inflicted by an official with the requisite intention and effect, as to torture within the Torture Convention definition. It is, of course, true that article 3 of the European Convention (and the comparable articles of other human rights instruments) lump torture and inhuman or degrading treatment together, drawing no distinction between them. The European Court did, however, draw a distinction between them in *Ireland v United Kingdom* (1978) 2 EHRR 25, holding that the conduct complained of was inhuman or degrading but fell short of torture, and article 16 of the Torture Convention draws this distinction very expressly [. . .]

Ill-treatment falling short of torture may invite exclusion of evidence as adversely affecting the fairness of a proceeding under section 78 of the 1984 Act, where that section applies. But I do not think the authorities on the Torture Convention justify the assimilation of these two kinds of abusive conduct. Special rules have always been thought to apply to torture, and for the present at least must continue to do so. It would, on the other hand, be wrong to regard as immutable the standard of what amounts to torture. This is a point made by the European Court in *Selmouni v France* (1999) 29 EHRR 403, paras 99–101 [. . .]

It may well be that the conduct complained of in *Ireland v United Kingdom*, or some of the Category II or III techniques detailed in a J2 memorandum dated 11 October 2002 addressed to the Commander, Joint Task Force 170 at Guantanamo

Bay, Cuba, (see The Torture Papers: The Road to Abu Ghraib, ed K Greenberg and J Dratel, (2005), pp 227–228), would now be held to fall within the definition in article 1 of the Torture Convention.

The burden of proof

59. My noble and learned friend Lord Hope proposes […] a test which, in the real world, can never be satisfied. The foreign torturer does not boast of his trade. The security services, as the Secretary of State has made clear, do not wish to imperil their relations with regimes where torture is practised. The special advocates have no means or resources to investigate. The detainee is in the dark. It is inconsistent with the most rudimentary notions of fairness to blindfold a man and then impose a standard which only the sighted could hope to meet. The result will be that, despite the universal abhorrence expressed for torture and its fruits, evidence procured by torture will be laid before SIAC because its source will not have been "established".

62. I regret that the House should lend its authority to a test which will undermine the practical efficacy of the Torture Convention and deny detainees the standard of fairness to which they are entitled under article 5(4) or 6(1) of the European Convention. […]

Lord Hope

121. […] [T]he exclusionary rule extends to any statement that "is established" to have been made under torture. The rule does not require it to be shown that the statement was not made under torture. It does not say that the statement must be excluded if there is a suspicion of torture and the suspicion has not been rebutted. Nor does it say that it must be excluded if there is a real risk that it was obtained by torture. […] The rule that article 15 lays down looks at what has happened in the past. It applies to a statement that is established to have been made under torture. In my opinion the test that it lays down is the test that should be applied by SIAC. It too must direct its inquiry to what has happened in the past. Is it established, by means of such diligent inquiries into the sources that it is practicable to carry out and on a balance of probabilities, that the information relied on by the Secretary of State was obtained under torture? If that is the position, article 15 requires that the information must be left out of account in the overall assessment of the question whether there were no reasonable grounds for a belief or suspicion of the kind referred to in section 21(1) (a) or (b) of the Anti-terrorism, Crime and Security Act 2001. The same rule must be followed in any other judicial process where information of this kind would otherwise be admissible.

126. […] The exclusionary rule that article 15 of the Torture Convention lays down extends to statements obtained by the use of torture, not to those obtained by the use of cruel, inhuman or degrading treatment or punishment. That is made clear by article 16.1 of the Convention. The borderline between torture and treatment or punishment of that character is not capable of precise definition. […] Views as to where the line is to be drawn may differ sharply from state to state. This can be seen from the list of practices authorised for use in Guantanamo Bay by the US authorities, some of which would shock the conscience if they were ever to be authorised for use in our own country. SIAC must exercise its own judgment in addressing this issue, which is ultimately one of fact. It should not be deterred from treating conduct as torture by the fact that other states do not attach the same label to it. The standard that it should apply is that which we would wish to apply in our own time to our own citizens.

Lord Rodger

138. The courts' deep-seated objection is to torture and to statements obtained by torture. The rejection of such statements is an exception to the general rule that relevant evidence is admissible even if it has been obtained unlawfully. On the other hand, the public interest does not favour SIAC rejecting statements that have not in fact been obtained by torture. More particularly, the public interest does not favour rejecting statements merely because there is a suspicion or risk that they may have been obtained in that way. Reports from various international bodies may well furnish grounds for suspicion that a country has been in the habit of using torture. That cannot be enough. To trigger the exclusion, it must be shown that the statement in question has been obtained by torture.

145. When everything possible has been done, it may turn out that the matter is left in doubt and that, using their expertise, SIAC cannot be satisfied on the balance of probabilities that the statement in question has been obtained by torture. If so, in my view, SIAC can look at the statement but should bear its doubtful origins in mind when evaluating it. My noble and learned friend, Lord Bingham of Cornhill, proposes, however, that the statement should be excluded whenever SIAC is unable to conclude that there is not a real risk that the evidence has been obtained by torture. It respectfully appears to me that this would be to replace the true rule, that statements obtained by torture must be excluded, with a significantly different rule, that statements must be excluded unless there is not a real risk that they have been obtained by torture. In effect, the true rule would be inverted. There is no warrant for Lord Bingham's preferred rule in the common law, in article 15 of the Convention against Torture or elsewhere in international law. [. . .]

The Lords were unanimous in condemning the use of foreign torture evidence but were divided on the standard of proof. Their opinions were largely based on the common law. As in other cases, Lord Bingham's opinion had the strongest internationalist focus, with extensive references to international and comparative sources, a rather normal feature of the post-Human Rights Act jurisprudence in the UK.[75] The majority held that the SIAC should reject the evidence if it found, following diligent investigation and on a balance of probabilities, that it was obtained by torture. If, however, it concluded that there was no more than a possibility that the information was obtained by torture, it should admit it. Lord Bingham opined that the SIAC should reject the evidence if it concluded that there was a real risk that it was obtained by torture, and criticized the test espoused by the majority as impossible to meet and as undermining the effectiveness of the prohibition against torture. Thus, following this decision, which was described as a 'muted' or 'qualified victory' for the rule of law,[76] foreign torture evidence could still be admissible in UK courts. This was confirmed in subsequent cases, most recently in *Youssef v Secretary of State for Foreign and Commonwealth Affairs*, where the UK Supreme Court unanimously held that there was no duty on the UK to inquire into the possible reliance on torture evidence by other states based on mere suspicion of illegality.[77]

The admissibility of evidence potentially obtained through torture (or ill-treatment) of third persons in another country was at issue in two cases before the ECtHR: *Othman v UK*,[78] an

75 D McGoldrick, 'Terrorism and Human Rights Paradigms: The United Kingdom after 11 September 2001' in A Bianchi and A Keller (eds), *Counterterrorism: Democracy's Challenge* (Hart Publishing 2008) 111, 132.

76 S Shah, 'The UK's Anti-Terror Legislation and the House of Lords: The Battle Continues' (2006) 6 *Human Rights Law Review* 416; N Grief, 'The Exclusion of Foreign Torture Evidence: A Qualified Victory for the Rule of Law' (2006) 2 *European Human Rights Law Review* 201.

77 [2016] UKSC 3, 27 January 2016, para 29.

78 ECtHR, *Othman (Abu Qatada) v United Kingdom*, App No 8139/09 (17 January 2012).

expulsion case, and *El Haski v Belgium*, a case on admissibility of foreign torture evidence at a criminal trial (in which, interestingly, the UK government intervened in support of Belgium, inviting the court to confirm that the alleged torture had to be established 'beyond reasonable doubt', citing, *inter alia*, the judgment of the House of Lords in the instant case).[79] In both cases, the Strasbourg court adopted the 'real risk' standard suggested by Lord Bingham and found that there was a violation of Article 6 of the ECHR. In the words of the ECtHR in *El Haski*, 'it is appropriate to follow the approach set out in the *Othman* judgment'; 'where the judicial system of the third State in question does not offer meaningful guarantees of an independent, impartial and serious examination of allegations of torture or inhuman and degrading treatment, it will be necessary and sufficient for the complainant, if the exclusionary rule is to be invoked on the basis of Article 6 § 1 of the Convention, to show that there is a "real risk" that the impugned statement was thus obtained. It would be unfair to impose any higher burden of proof on him'.[80] This approach was also favoured in the following case involving extradition of a Canadian citizen to France.

France v Diab, France, *ex parte* Attorney General of Canada v Diab and Canadian Civil Liberties Association (intervening), Appeal judgment, 2014 ONCA 374, ILDC 2318 (CA 2014), 15th May 2014, Canada; Ontario; Court of Appeal [ONCA]

> 234 [. . .] [I]t is beyond debate that torture-derived evidence may not be used in legal proceedings and cannot be relied upon by a state seeking extradition or being asked to extradite. Article 15 of the *Convention Against Torture*—to which both Canada and France are signatories—makes this clear. [. . .] Section 269.1(4) of the *Criminal Code*, R.S.C. 1985, c. C.46, incorporates this prohibition into Canadian domestic law. To similar effect is s. 83(1.1) of the *Immigration and Refugee Protection Act*, which excludes from evidence in deportation proceedings any information that is believed on "reasonable grounds" to have been obtained as a result of the use of torture.
>
> 235 This exclusion of torture-derived evidence flows from society's abhorrence of torture generally. [. . .] As Lord Hoffman expressed it in *A & Others*, at paras. 82 and 83:
>
>> The use of torture is dishonourable. It corrupts and degrades the state which uses it and the legal system which accepts it. . . . [Its rejection] by the common law has a special iconic importance as the touchstone of a humane and civilised legal system.
>
> 236 The use of torture-derived evidence is also dishonourable. Civilized society rejects both the use of torture itself and the use of torture-derived evidence. In *Othman*, at para. 267, the ECHR concluded that "the admission of torture evidence is manifestly contrary ... to the most basic international standards of a fair trial" and that it would be "a flagrant denial of justice if such evidence were admitted in a criminal trial". At para. 264, the ECHR was forceful in explaining why torture-derived evidence was incompatible with justice: "The trial process is a cornerstone of the rule of law. Torture evidence damages irreparably that process; it substitutes force for the rule of law. . . . Torture evidence is excluded to protect the integrity of the trial process and, ultimately, the rule of law itself."
>
> 237 Canada shares these values. Torture and torture-derived evidence undermine the basic right to a fair trial and their use therefore violates the principles of fundamental justice. This underlying concern for human rights must be accounted for in

79 ECtHR, *El-Haski v Belgium*, App No 649/08 (25 September 2012) para 74.
80 ibid, para 88.

the surrender process because the life, liberty and security interests protected under s. 7 of the *Charter* have to do not only with the act of extraditing but also with the potential consequences of that act [...]. As a result, Canada must neither tolerate resort to torture or the use of torture-derived evidence domestically, nor participate in any action that would clearly permit that to occur in a foreign state.

238 Accordingly, just as the Minister should generally decline to deport refugees where, on the evidence, there is a "substantial risk" they will be tortured if that happens (see *Suresh*, at para. 77) so, too, in our view, should the Minister generally decline to order surrender where there is a substantial risk that torture-derived evidence will be used against the person facing prosecution in the requesting state.

(iv) **"Real risk"**

245 A "real risk", its twin sibling, a "substantial risk", and its cousin "reasonable grounds" or "reasonable basis for belief", all lie in a similar range of the standard of proof spectrum—significantly more onerous than a "plausible connection" but less so than a "balance of probabilities". We see no need to make fine distinctions among them for these purposes. The choice to be made at this stage of the analysis is between "real risk" and "balance of probabilities". Support may be found for both in domestic and international jurisprudence. None of the jurisprudence deals specifically with the requirements relating to the exercise of the Minister's discretion to order or refuse to order surrender under the Act, however.

246 At the end of the day, we adopt "real risk", as opposed to the somewhat higher standard of "balance of probabilities", for this part of the surrender analysis. In our view, the "real risk" threshold is more consistent with the prevailing opinion in the authorities and more appropriately balances the competing tensions between Canada's international comity and extradition obligations, on the one hand, and its constitutional mandate to protect against *Charter* violations, on the other hand.

247 With the exception of the majority in *A & Others* and some other decisions in the United Kingdom, European courts have generally accepted the application of the "real risk" threshold as the ultimate test—recognizing that it involves a lower threshold than "more likely than not"—in cases involving the use of torture-derived evidence and similar problems relating to proceedings tainted by torture. Indeed, in *Othman*, the ECHR rejected the majority view in *A & Others* that a "balance of probabilities" was the ultimate test. It concluded that Mr. Othman's deportation to Jordan would violate his right to a fair trial in Jordan because there was a "real risk" of the admission of evidence obtained through torture of others. The ECHR is responsible for interpreting the *European Convention on Human Rights* for all its signatories, which include the United Kingdom and France.

248 *Othman* is consistent with earlier decisions of the ECHR applying the real risk test: see, for example, *Soering v. The United Kingdom*, Application No. 14038/88 (7 July 1989), at para. 91 (Eur. Ct. H.R.); and *Saadi v. Italy* [GC], Application No. 37201/06 (28 February 2008), at para. 140 (Eur. Ct. H.R.). It is also consistent with the approach taken by international expert bodies in the context of *non-refoulement* to torture or other ill treatment as well as to the risk of the use of torture-derived evidence: United Nations Human Rights Committee, *General Comment No. 31: Nature of the General Legal Obligation Imposed on States Parties to the Covenant*, 80th Sess., U.N. Doc. CCPR/C/21/Rev.1/Add. 13, (2004), at para. 2; and United Nations Committee Against Torture, *Summary Record of the First Part (Public) of the 424th Meeting*, 24th Sess., U.N. Doc. CAT/C/SR.424, (2001), at para. 17.

249 In two reports to the United Nations, in 2006 and 2011, the incumbent UN Rapporteur on torture expressed the view that, once the plausible connection threshold is met, the decision-maker must determine whether there is a "real risk" that the impugned evidence has been obtained by torture: Manfred Nowak, *Report of the Special Rapporteur on Torture and Other Cruel, Inhuman or Degrading Treatment or Punishment*, U.N. Doc. A/61/259, (2006); and Juan E. Méndez, *Report of the Special Rapporteur on Torture and Other Cruel, Inhuman or Degrading Treatment or Punishment*, Human Rights Council, 16th Sess., U.N. Doc. A/HRC/16/52, (2011), at para. 53.

The Court of Appeal of Ontario referred to numerous international sources with a view to justifying its preference for the 'real risk' standard over the 'balance of probabilities' one, which had been espoused by the majority in the House of Lords decision in the previous case. On a factual level, as noted by the ILDC reporter, the court was satisfied that there was no such risk in the case at hand, the extradition request coming from France, a state party to all pertinent human rights treaties, which prohibited the use of torture evidence and had also given (reliable) assurances precluding the use of such evidence.[81]

(b) *Non-refoulement*

Mohamed and Dalvie v President of South Africa, Decision in response to urgent application for leave to appeal, CCT 17/01, [2001] ZACC 18, 2001 (3) SA 893 (CC), 2001 (7) BCLR 685 (CC), ILDC 284 (ZA 2001), 28th May 2001, South Africa; Constitutional Court [CC]

The Tanzanian first applicant was handed over by the South African immigration authorities into US custody for removal to the US, in execution of an arrest warrant to stand trial on various capital charges relating to the 1998 bombing of the US embassy in Tanzania. The High Court had denied him an order declaring that his arrest, detention, interrogation, and handing over to the US was unlawful and unconstitutional, and that the South African authorities had breached his constitutional rights by handing him over to the US custody without obtaining assurances that the death penalty would not be imposed or carried out in the event of conviction. He lodged an urgent application for leave to appeal directly to the Constitutional Court.

Deportation or extradition and the death penalty

43 [...] The procedure followed in removing Mohamed to the United States of America was unlawful whether it is characterised as a deportation or an extradition. Moreover, an obligation on the South African government to secure an assurance that the death penalty will not be imposed on a person whom it causes to be removed from South Africa to another country cannot depend on whether the removal is by extradition or deportation. That obligation depends on the facts of the particular case and the provisions of the Constitution, not on the provisions of the empowering legislation or extradition treaty under which the "deportation" or "extradition" is carried out.

44 [...] Having been identified by the FBI as a suspect for whom an international arrest warrant had been issued in connection with the bombing of the United States embassy in Tanzania, he was apprehended by the South African immigration authorities in a joint operation undertaken in cooperation with the FBI. Within two days of his arrest and contrary to the provisions of the Act he was handed over to the FBI by the South African authorities for the purpose of being taken to the United States to be put on trial there for the bombing of the embassy. On his arrival in the United States he was immediately charged with various offences relating to that bombing and was informed by the court that the death sentence could be imposed on him if

81 G MacNeil, Analysis, *France v Diab, France, ex parte Attorney General of Canada v Diab and Canadian Civil Liberties Association (intervening)*, ILDC 2318 (CA 2014) A7.

he were convicted. That this was likely to happen must have been apparent to the South African authorities as well as to the FBI when the arrangements were made for Mohamed to be removed from South Africa to the United States.

45 Another suspect, Mr Mahmoud Mahmud Salim, alleged to be a party to the conspiracy to bomb the embassies, was extradited from Germany to the United States. Germany has abolished capital punishment and is also party to the European Convention on Human Rights. The German government sought and secured an assurance from the United States government as a condition of the extradition that if he is convicted, Salim will not be sentenced to death. This is consistent with the practice followed by countries that have abolished the death penalty.

49 [. . .] In handing Mohamed over to the United States without securing an assurance that he would not be sentenced to death, the immigration authorities failed to give any value to Mohamed's right to life, his right to have his human dignity respected and protected and his right not to be subjected to cruel, inhuman or degrading punishment.

54 If the South African authorities had sought an assurance from the United States against the death sentence being imposed on Mohamed before handing him over to the FBI, there is no reason to believe that such an assurance would not have been given. [. . .] The fact that Mohamed is now facing the possibility of a death sentence is the direct result of the failure by the South African authorities to secure such an undertaking. The causal connection is clear between the handing over of Mohamed to the FBI for removal to the United States for trial without securing an assurance against the imposition of the death sentence and the threat of such a sentence now being imposed on Mohamed.

55 It is not only sections 10 and 11 of the Constitution that are implicated in the present case. According to section 12 (1)(d) and (e) of our Constitution, everyone has the right to freedom and security of the person, which includes the right not to be tortured in any way and not to be treated or punished in a cruel, inhuman or degrading way. [. . .] South African law considers a sentence of death to be cruel, inhuman and degrading punishment.

59 These cases *Soering v United Kingdom, Hilal v United Kingdom, Chahal v United Kingdom* are consistent with the weight that our Constitution gives to the spirit, purport and objects of the Bill of Rights and the positive obligation that it imposes on the state to "protect, promote and fulfil the rights in the Bill of Rights". For the South African government to cooperate with a foreign government to secure the removal of a fugitive from South Africa to a country of which the fugitive is not a national and with which he has no connection other than that he is to be put on trial for his life there, is contrary to the underlying values of our Constitution. It is inconsistent with the government's obligation to protect the right to life of everyone in South Africa, and it ignores the commitment implicit in the Constitution that South Africa will not be party to the imposition of cruel, inhuman or degrading punishment.

60 The fact that the government claims to have deported and not to have extradited Mohamed is of no relevance. European courts draw no distinction between deportation and extradition in the application of Article 3 of the European Convention on Human Rights. Nor does the Convention Against Torture and Other Cruel, Inhuman or Degrading Treatment or Punishment of which South Africa is a [party] [. . .]. Article 3(1) of this Convention [. . .] makes no distinction between expulsion, return or extradition of a person to another state to face an unacceptable form of punishment. All are prohibited, and the right of a state to deport an illegal alien is subject to that prohibition. That is the standard that our Constitution demands from our government in circumstances such as those that existed in the present case.

> 61 The removal of Mohamed to the United States could not have been effected without the cooperation of the South African immigration authorities. They cooperated well knowing that he would be put on trial in the United States to face capital charges. That he should be arrested and put on trial was clearly a significant and possibly the predominant motive that determined the course that was followed. [...] They must also have known that there was a real risk that he would be convicted, and that unless an assurance to the contrary were obtained, he would be sentenced to death. In doing so they infringed Mohamed's rights under the Constitution and acted contrary to their obligations to uphold and promote the rights entrenched in the Bill of Rights.

This decision was a powerful pronouncement that an abolitionist state such as South Africa was prohibited from removing (by extradition, deportation or related transfers) an individual facing imposition of the death penalty to a retentionist state such as the US, without seeking and obtaining sufficient assurances that the death penalty would not be imposed or, if imposed, would not be carried out. This was done at a time (2001) when this rule was not well established in international law. As rightly pointed out by the ILDC reporter, it was only in 2003 that the Human Rights Committee affirmed this rule in *Judge v Canada*, in a major departure from its earlier jurisprudence in *Kindler v Canada*.[82] The South African Court applied constitutional law but also cited some ECtHR judgments on the matter, which however had prohibited transfers to torture and not to death penalty.

Indeed, the ECtHR was long hesitant to hold that imposition of the death penalty amounted to a violation of the right to life. It was only in 2010, in *Al-Sadoon and Mufdhi v The United Kingdom*, that the Strasbourg court explicitly said so.[83] In *Soering*, the court had famously held that the applicant's exposure to the death row phenomenon, and not to capital punishment per se, would violate Article 3 (prohibition of torture) of the ECHR.[84] The Constitutional Court of South Africa based the prohibition of removal to the death penalty on the government's (positive) obligation to protect the right to life of everyone in South Africa, and on 'the commitment implicit in the Constitution that South Africa will not be party to the imposition of cruel, inhuman or degrading punishment'. Indeed, the various references in the decision to the role played by the South African authorities in knowingly bringing the applicant to US custody and exposing him to the risk of death penalty were pertinent in terms of shared responsibility, by exposing how extradition and similar transfers may serve as aid or assistance by sending states in the commission of internationally wrongful acts by the receiving states.[85]

Suresh, United Nations High Commissioner for Refugees (intervening) and ors (intervening) v Canada (Minister of Citizenship and Immigration) and Attorney-General of Canada, Decision, Docket No 27790, 2002 SCC 1, [2002] 1 SCR 3, (2002) 37 Admin LR (3d) 159, (2002) 90 CRR (2d) 1, (2002) SCJ No 3, 281 NR 1, (2002) 208 DLR (4th) 1, (2002) 18 Imm LR (3d) 1, 2002 CarswellNat 8, 2002 CarswellNat 7 (SCC), ILDC 186 (CA 2002), 11th January 2002, Canada; Supreme Court [SCC][86]

> **2 Are the Conditions for Deportation in the Immigration Act Constitutional?**
>
> **(a) Does the Act Permit Deportation to Torture Contrary to the Charter?**
>
> [...]
>
> 44 Section 7 of the Charter guarantees "[e]veryone ... the right to life, liberty and security of the person and the right not to be deprived thereof except in accordance

82 A Ferreira-Snyman, Analysis, *Mohamed and Dalvie v President of South Africa*, ILDC 284 (ZA 2001) A2.

83 ECtHR, *Al-Saadoon and Mufdhi v United Kingdom*, App No 61498/08 (2 March 2010) para 123.

84 ECtHR, *Soering v United Kingdom*, App No 14038/88 (7 July 1989) para 111.

85 See A Constantinides, 'Extradition' in A Nollkaemper and I Plakokefalos (eds), *The Practice of Shared Responsibility* (CUP 2017) 128, 145.

86 For the facts of the case see above Section II.1.

with the principles of fundamental justice". It is conceded that "everyone" includes refugees and that deportation to torture may deprive a refugee of liberty, security and perhaps life. The only question is whether this deprivation is in accordance with the principles of fundamental justice. If it is not, s. 7 is violated and, barring justification of the violation under s. 1 of the Charter, deportation to torture is unconstitutional.

46 The inquiry into the principles of fundamental justice is informed not only by Canadian experience and jurisprudence, but also by international law, including *jus cogens*. [. . .]

47 Determining whether deportation to torture violates the principles of fundamental justice requires us to balance Canada's interest in combatting terrorism and the Convention refugee's interest in not being deported to torture. Canada has a legitimate and compelling interest in combatting terrorism. But it is also committed to fundamental justice. The notion of proportionality is fundamental to our constitutional system. Thus we must ask whether the government's proposed response is reasonable in relation to the threat. [. . .].

48 With these thoughts in mind, we turn to the question of whether the government may, consistent with the principles of fundamental justice, expel a suspected terrorist to face torture elsewhere: first from the Canadian perspective; then from the perspective of the international norms that inform s. 7.

[. . .]

(ii) The International Perspective

59 We have examined the argument that from the perspective of Canadian law to deport a Convention refugee to torture violates the principles of fundamental justice. However, that does not end the inquiry. The provisions of the Immigration Act dealing with deportation must be considered in their international context [. . .]. Similarly, the principles of fundamental justice expressed in s. 7 of the Charter and the limits on rights that may be justified under s. 1 of the Charter cannot be considered in isolation from the international norms which they reflect. [. . .]

61 It has been submitted by the intervener, Amnesty International, that the absolute prohibition on torture is a peremptory norm of customary international law, or *jus cogens*. [. . .]

65 Although this Court is not being asked to pronounce on the status of the prohibition on torture in international law, the fact that such a principle is included in numerous multilateral instruments, that it does not form part of any known domestic administrative practice, and that it is considered by many academics to be an emerging, if not established peremptory norm, suggests that it cannot be easily derogated from. With this in mind, we now turn to the interpretation of the conflicting instruments at issue in this case.

66 Deportation to torture is prohibited by both the ICCPR, which Canada ratified in 1976, and the CAT, which Canada ratified in 1987. [. . .]

67 [. . .] The clear import of the ICCPR, read together with the General Comment 20, is to foreclose a state from expelling a person to face torture elsewhere.

68 The CAT takes the same stand. [. . .] The CAT's import is clear: a state is not to expel a person to face torture, which includes both the physical and mental infliction of pain and suffering, elsewhere.

70 Article 33 of the Refugee Convention appears on its face to stand in opposition to the categorical rejection of deportation to torture in the CAT. Robertson J.A., faced with this apparent contradiction, attempted to read the two conventions in a way

that minimized the contradiction, holding that the anti-deportation provisions of the CAT were not binding, but derogable.

71 We are not convinced that the contradiction can be resolved in this way. It is not apparent to us that the clear prohibitions on torture in the CAT were intended to be derogable. First, the absence of an express prohibition against derogation in Article 3 of the CAT together with the "without prejudice" language of Article 16 do not seem to permit derogation. Nor does it follow from the assertion in Article 2(2) of CAT that "[n]o exceptional circumstances ... may be invoked as a justification of torture", that the absence of such a clause in the Article 3 refoulement provision permits acts leading to torture in exceptional circumstances. [...]

72 In our view, the prohibition in the ICCPR and the CAT on returning a refugee to face a risk of torture reflects the prevailing international norm. Article 33 of the Refugee Convention protects, in a limited way, refugees from threats to life and freedom from all sources. By contrast, the CAT protects everyone, without derogation, from state-sponsored torture. Moreover, the Refugee Convention itself expresses a "profound concern for refugees" and its principal purpose is to "assure refugees the widest possible exercise of ... fundamental rights and freedoms" (Preamble). This negates the suggestion that the provisions of the Refugee Convention should be used to deny rights that other legal instruments make universally available to everyone.

73 Recognition of the dominant status of the CAT in international law is consistent with the position taken by the UN Committee against Torture, which has applied Article 3(1) even to individuals who have terrorist associations. [...] More particularly, the Committee against Torture has advised that Canada should "[c]omply fully with article 3(1) ... whether or not the individual is a serious criminal or security risk" [...].

74 Finally, we note that the Supreme Court of Israel sitting as the High Court of Justice and the House of Lords have rejected torture as a legitimate tool to use in combatting terrorism and protecting national security [...].

75 We conclude that the better view is that international law rejects deportation to torture, even where national security interests are at stake. This is the norm which best informs the content of the principles of fundamental justice under s. 7 of the Charter.

(iii) Application to Section 53(1)(b) of the Immigration Act

76 The Canadian rejection of torture is reflected in the international conventions to which Canada is a party. The Canadian and international perspectives in turn inform our constitutional norms. The rejection of state action leading to torture generally, and deportation to torture specifically, is virtually categoric. Indeed, both domestic and international jurisprudence suggest that torture is so abhorrent that it will almost always be disproportionate to interests on the other side of the balance, even security interests. This suggests that, barring extraordinary circumstances, deportation to torture will generally violate the principles of fundamental justice protected by s. 7 of the Charter. [...]

77 [...] In Canada, the balance struck by the Minister must conform to the principles of fundamental justice under s. 7 of the Charter. It follows that insofar as the Immigration Act leaves open the possibility of deportation to torture, the Minister should generally decline to deport refugees where on the evidence there is a substantial risk of torture.

78 We do not exclude the possibility that in exceptional circumstances, deportation to face torture might be justified, either as a consequence of the balancing process

mandated by s. 7 of the Charter or under s. 1. (A violation of s. 7 will be saved by s. 1 "only in cases arising out of exceptional conditions, such as natural disasters, the outbreak of war, epidemics and the like" [...]) Insofar as Canada is unable to deport a person where there are substantial grounds to believe he or she would be tortured on return, this is not because Article 3 of the CAT directly constrains the actions of the Canadian government, but because the fundamental justice balance under s. 7 of the Charter generally precludes deportation to torture when applied on a case-by-case basis. We may predict that it will rarely be struck in favour of expulsion where there is a serious risk of torture. However, as the matter is one of balance, precise prediction is elusive. The ambit of an exceptional discretion to deport to torture, if any, must await future cases.

79 In these circumstances, s. 53(1)(b) does not violate s. 7 of the Charter. [...]

3 Are the Procedures for Deportation Set Out in the Immigration Act Constitutionally Valid?

[...]

122 We find that a person facing deportation to torture under s. 53(1)(b) must be informed of the case to be met. Subject to privilege or similar valid reasons for reduced disclosure, such as safeguarding confidential public security documents, this means that the material on which the Minister is basing her decision must be provided to the individual [...]. Furthermore, fundamental justice requires that an opportunity be provided to respond to the case presented to the Minister. While the Minister accepted written submissions from the appellant in this case, in the absence of access to the material she was receiving from her staff and on which she based much of her decision, Suresh and his counsel had no knowledge of which factors they specifically needed to address, nor any chance to correct any factual inaccuracies or mischaracterizations. Fundamental justice requires that written submissions be accepted from the subject of the order after the subject has been provided with an opportunity to examine the material being used against him or her. The Minister must then consider these submissions along with the submissions made by the Minister's staff.

123 Not only must the refugee be informed of the case to be met, the refugee must also be given an opportunity to challenge the information of the Minister where issues as to its validity arise. Thus the refugee should be permitted to present evidence pursuant to s. 19 of the Act showing that his or her continued presence in Canada will not be detrimental to Canada, notwithstanding evidence of association with a terrorist organization. The same applies to the risk of torture on return. Where the Minister is relying on written assurances from a foreign government that a person would not be tortured, the refugee must be given an opportunity to present evidence and make submissions as to the value of such assurances.

124 It may be useful to comment further on assurances. A distinction may be drawn between assurances given by a state that it will not apply the death penalty (through a legal process) and assurances by a state that it will not resort to torture (an illegal process). We would signal the difficulty in relying too heavily on assurances by a state that it will refrain from torture in the future when it has engaged in illegal torture or allowed others to do so on its territory in the past. This difficulty becomes acute in cases where torture is inflicted not only with the collusion but through the impotence of the state in controlling the behaviour of its officials. Hence the need to distinguish between assurances regarding the death penalty and assurances regarding torture. The former are easier to monitor and generally more reliable than the latter.

> 125 In evaluating assurances by a foreign government, the Minister may also wish to take into account the human rights record of the government giving the assurances, the government's record in complying with its assurances, and the capacity of the government to fulfill the assurances, particularly where there is doubt about the government's ability to control its security forces. In addition, it must be remembered that before becoming a Convention refugee, the individual involved must establish a well-founded fear of persecution (although not necessarily torture) if deported.

This was one of the first decisions by a highest court to discuss the relationship between security/terrorism and human rights after the attacks of 9/11, at a time when the shock was still quite severe. The outcome for the rule of law was rather mixed. On the one hand, the court reaffirmed that international law informed the constitutional principle of fundamental justice in Canada and upheld the (virtually categorical) 'rejection of state action leading to torture generally, and deportation to torture specifically'. On the other hand, the court adopted a deferential balancing approach and introduced the infamous exceptional circumstances exception, which did not unequivocally reject deportation to torture and thus undermined the absolute prohibition against torture, at least as a matter of Canadian law (even though the exception has not been used in practice).[87] Unsurprisingly, this ruling led to widespread criticism from UN treaty bodies and other international organs. For instance, the Committee Against Torture expressed its concern at the failure of the Supreme Court of Canada, in *Suresh*, 'to recognise at the level of domestic law the absolute nature of the protection of article 3 of the Convention, which is not subject to any exception whatsoever'.[88]

Lower courts in Canada have followed *Suresh*, as they are duty bound, and reiterated that deportation to torture remained a possibility. For instance, in *Almrei v Minister of Citizenship & Immigration and Solicitor General*, the Federal Court of Appeal acknowledged that the Supreme Court 'did not close the door on a possible deportation to torture' and that 'deportation to torture might be saved by the balancing process mandated under section 7 or might be possible under section 1'.[89]

Attorney-General v Zaoui and Inspector-General of Intelligence and Security and Human Rights Commission (intervening), Appeal to Supreme Court, [2005] NZSC 38, (2006) 1 NZLR 289, (2005) 7 HRNZ 860, ILDC 81 (NZ 2005), 21st June 2005, New Zealand; Supreme Court

The main international law issue before the Supreme Court of New Zealand in this case was whether Article 33(2) of the Refugee Convention called for a proportionality approach requiring an assessment of the possible consequences of deportation for the refugee and a balancing of those consequences against the extent of the danger to New Zealand's security. The applicant argued that Article 33(2) of the Refugee Convention had been amended by Article 3(1) of the Convention Against Torture and Articles 6(1) and 7 of the ICCPR, which contained an absolute prohibition on refoulement. He also argued that the absolute prohibition of refoulement to torture had the status of *jus cogens*, with the consequence that Article 33(2) was void to the extent that it allowed so.

> **1 The meaning of article 33.2; "proportionality" or weighing and balancing**
>
> [...]
>
> **The plain meaning and the purpose**
>
> 25 Article 33, in its plain terms, first places an obligation on the States parties not to expel a refugee whose life or freedom might be threatened in certain circumstances

87 K Roach, *The 9/11 Effect: Comparative Counter-Terrorism* (CUP 2011) 403.

88 UNCHR, 'Report of the Committee against Torture' (2005) UN Doc A/60/44, para 57. See also UNCHR, 'Concluding Observations of the Human Rights Committee on Canada' (2006) UN Doc CCPR/C/CAN/CO/5, para 15.

89 Appeal judgment, 2005 FCA 54, (2005) 3 FC 142, ILDC 638 (CA 2005), 8 February 2005, Federal Court of Appeal [FCA], para 126.

but, second, notwithstanding that prohibition, empowers them to expel a refugee for certain reasons including the endangering of national security. The two considerations are stated distinctly in each paragraph. According to their ordinary meaning, the two provisions operate in sequence. They are not related in any proportionate or balancing way. The second, if satisfied in its own terms, defeats the prohibition in the first. That is so although […] the second operates and must be interpreted in the context of the serious consequences of return to persecution contemplated in the first.

26 The dual purpose of the article is plain enough. The prohibition on exit in para (1) of article 33 mirrors the entry definition in article 1A set out in para [28] but, as with article 1 and its exceptions, the prohibition on exit is not absolute. […]

27 That distinct sequential reading, based as it is on the ordinary meaning of the terms of the two paragraphs of article 33 and their purpose, is supported by a consideration of what the proportionality or sliding scale proposition would require. The decision-maker would have to measure against one another two matters which are very difficult to relate: the level of threat to the life or liberty of an individual, on the one side, and, on the other, the level of reasonably perceived danger to the security of the State. While the law may sometimes appear to require such weighing, such an interpretation is to be avoided unless it is plainly called for.

The context

28 The sequential reading is also supported by the interpretation given to related provisions of the Convention, part of the context in which article 33 is to be read. Article 1A contains the basic definition of a refugee […]. And, as with that provision relating to exit, the entry obligation is subject to limits: under article 1F(b), the Convention does not protect persons with respect to whom there are serious reasons for considering that, among other things, they have committed serious non-political crimes outside their country of refuge before their admission as refugees.

29 In the case of entry, as with expulsion, the argument has been made that the gravity of the crime is to be weighed against the gravity of the possible persecution. That very argument was rejected […]. Article 1F was held to be clear and unambiguous […]

The meaning of article 33.2

42 We accordingly conclude that the judgment or assessment to be made under article 33.2 is to be made in its own terms, by reference to danger to the security, in this case, of New Zealand, and without any balancing or weighing or proportional reference to the matter dealt with in article 33.1, the threat, were Mr Zaoui to be expelled or returned, to his life or freedom on the proscribed grounds or the more specific rights protected by the New Zealand Bill of Rights Act 1990 read with the International Covenant on Civil and Political Rights and the Convention against Torture and other Cruel, Inhuman or Degrading Treatment or Punishment. Paragraph (2) of article 33 of the Refugee Convention states a single standard.

44 One significant feature of para (2) is the contrast between "danger to the security of New Zealand" in its first limb and "danger to the community" in its second, with the second not having a security emphasis but requiring conviction of "a particularly serious crime". Also suggesting a high standard is the consequence of removal to the dangers contemplated by para (1) of article 33. Against those considerations is the wording and drafting history of the provision and its very subject matter which together indicate that the executive has a broad power of appreciation of the relevant facts and considerations.

45 [...] [T]o come within article 33.2, the person in question must be thought on reasonable grounds to pose a serious threat to the security of New Zealand; the threat must be based on objectively reasonable grounds and the threatened harm must be substantial.

Has article 33.2 been amended?

47 So far we have been considering the interpretation of article 33.2 in its own terms. A further argument is that the provision has been amended for those states, including New Zealand, which are also parties to the Convention against Torture. [...] The argument is that the limits on non-refoulement in para (2) of article 33 are overridden in the case where torture is threatened.

48 Much the same argument is made in respect of threats of arbitrary death, as well as of torture, by reference to articles 6(1) and 7 of the ICCPR [...] While those provisions do not expressly deal with state action such as expulsion or deportation which is likely to lead to death or torture in another country, they, like their counterparts in the European Convention on Human Rights, have been applied to such actions by the Human Rights Committee and the European Court of Human Rights.

50 [The provisions of article 30(3) and (4) (a) of the Vienna Convention on the Law of Treaties] are designed for treaties that create bilateral rights and obligations. They do not easily apply to the present situation where the obligations of article 33 are in substance unilateral as well as being owed erga omnes (to all the other parties collectively). More significantly in the present context, the provisions do not, contrary to the submissions, regulate the amendment of treaties. That is a matter dealt with in articles 39–41 which are not applicable in the present case. Rather, as the heading to article 30 shows, its provisions concern the application of successive treaties relating to the same subject matter. That is to say, article 33.2 of the 1951 Convention has not itself been amended by the later ICCPR and Torture Convention. Rather, they have to be applied in a successive way. [...]

Or voided in part by a peremptory norm?

51 A final argument goes a step beyond the amendment contention. It is that the prohibition on refoulement to torture has the status of a peremptory norm or ius cogens with the consequence that article 33.2 would now be void to the extent that it allows for that: see article 64 of the Vienna Convention [...] While there is overwhelming support for the proposition that the prohibition on torture itself is ius cogens, there is no support in the state practice, judicial decisions or commentaries to which we were referred for the proposition that the prohibition on refoulement to torture has that status. [...] So far as state practice and the commentators are concerned the position appears clearly in the legislation mentioned earlier and the papers prepared for, and the statements emerging from, the 2001 UNHCR consultation. They set out the absolute propositions about torture and arbitrary death distinctly from the requirements of article 33: the obligations are successive, not merged.

Conclusion

52 We accordingly conclude that those applying article 33.2 under Part 4A of the Immigration Act are to apply it in its own terms. In particular, to come within article 33.2, the person in question must be thought on reasonable grounds to pose a serious threat to the security of New Zealand; the threat must be based on objectively reasonable grounds and the threatened harm must be substantial.

[...]

3 The protection of the right not to be returned to the risk of torture or the arbitrary taking of life

76 [. . .] [T]he Crown accepts in particular that it is obliged to act in conformity with New Zealand's obligations under articles 6(1) and 7 of the ICCPR and article 3 of the Convention against Torture. [. . .]

77 The question which remains to be considered is the way in which under New Zealand law those obligations may be met, including the question of who is to meet them, given that it is not the Inspector-General.

79 Those provisions do not expressly apply to actions taken outside New Zealand by other governments in breach of the rights stated in the Bill of Rights. That is also the case with articles 6(1) and 7 of the ICCPR. But those and comparable provisions have long been understood as applying to actions of a state party—here New Zealand—if that state proposes to take action, say by way of deportation or extradition, where substantial grounds have been shown for believing that the person as a consequence faces a real risk of being subjected to torture or the arbitrary taking of life. The focus is not on the responsibility of the state to which the person may be sent. Rather, it is on the obligation of the state considering whether to remove the person to respect the substantive rights in issue.

90 [. . .] [T]he right not to be arbitrarily deprived of life and not to be subjected to torture [. . .] are to be interpreted [. . .] so as to be in accordance with international law, both customary and treaty based. [. . .] As already recalled, the relevant provisions of the Covenant have been interpreted to apply to the situation where the state party in question takes action by way of removal of a person to another country if that action means that that person faces a real risk of torture or arbitrary deprivation of life. That removal situation is of course expressly covered in the case of torture by article 3 of the Convention against Torture.

91 [. . .] The power conferred by s 72 is to be interpreted and exercised consistently with the provisions of ss 8 and 9 of the Bill of Rights and with the closely related international obligations in the Covenant and the Convention against Torture. Because the power can be so interpreted and applied, those provisions, as a matter of law, prevent removal if their terms are satisfied even if the threat to national security is made out in terms of s 72 and article 33.2.

93 It is accordingly our view that the Minister, in deciding whether to certify under s 72 of the Immigration Act 1987 that the continued presence of a person constitutes a threat to national security, and members of the Executive Council, in deciding whether to advise the Governor-General to order deportation under s 72, are not to so decide or advise if they are satisfied that there are substantial grounds for believing that, as a result of the deportation, the person would be in danger of being arbitrarily deprived of life or of being subjected to torture or to cruel, inhuman or degrading treatment or punishment.

The court in this case was faced with a normative conflict between the right of a state to deport foreigners who represented a security threat under Article 33 para 2 of the Refugee Convention (and the corresponding domestic legislation of New Zealand) and the obligation of non-refoulement under Article 33 para 1 of the Convention as well as under the CAT and the ICCPR. The Supreme Court clearly disfavoured the proportionality or sliding scale approach espoused by the Court of Appeal, which would require the weighing and measurement by the decision-maker of the human rights/non-refoulement obligations against the level of danger to state security. The court relied on the sequential reading of the two paragraphs and made clear that the provision of Article 33 para 2, which allowed the deportation of an individual presenting a security threat, defeated the prohibition of the preceding provision of Article 33 para 1, thereby resolving the conflict, if any, in Article 33 of the Refugee Convention. However, when it comes to the right to deport an individual under Article 33 para 2 and the non-refoulement obligations under the CAT and the ICCPR, the court was equally categorical in holding that the non-refoulement obligations were absolute and prevailed over the right to deport under Article 33 para 2. This approach contrasted with that of the Supreme Court of Canada in *Suresh*, which had not foreclosed deportation to torture in exceptional circumstances if the threat to the security of Canada required so. As observed by the ILDC reporter, the approach of the Supreme Court of New Zealand, in reliance in part on the common law presumption that statutes should, so far as their text permitted, be interpreted in conformity with international law, entailed that the statutory discretion of the executive had to be exercised in a manner that was consistent with New Zealand's obligations under the CAT and the ICCPR, requiring the executive to conduct a sufficiently wide-ranging inquiry into Mr Zaoui's circumstances to ensure that New Zealand met its international obligations.[90]

RB (Algeria) (FC) and anor v Secretary of State for the Home Department, OO (Jordan) v Secretary of State for the Home Department, RB and U v Secretary of State for the Home Department, Appeal judgment, (2009) UKHL 10, ILDC 1250 (UK 2009), 18th February 2009, United Kingdom; House of Lords [HL]

This case concerned deportation proceedings against a Jordanian (Othman) and two Algerian nationals (RB and U) on the ground of being a danger to the UK's national security. Each contended that deportation would expose them to a real risk of torture or inhuman treatment in breach of their rights under Article 3 ECHR. Othman further contended that, if deported, he would also face a real risk of a flagrant breach of his right to liberty under Article 5 ECHR and his right to a fair trial under Article 6 ECHR. The secretary of state for the Home Department admitted that there was sufficient evidence of the use of torture in both Algeria and Jordan and therefore Her Majesty's Government requested and was given specific assurances that the deportees would be lawfully treated. Each had appealed unsuccessfully to the SIAC and the Court of Appeal. Othman's appeal to the Court of Appeal was allowed on the single ground that his deportation would breach his right to a fair trial under Article 6 ECHR.

Lord Phillips

Reliance on assurances

[...]

114. I do not consider that these decisions [*Chahal v. UK, Mamatkulov v. Turkey, Shamayev v. Georgia and Russia, Saadi v. Italy, Ismoilov and others v. Russia* and *Ryabikin v. Russia* of the ECtHR, and the decision of the UN CAT in *Hanan Attia v. Sweden*] establish a principle that assurances must eliminate all risk of inhuman treatment before they can be relied upon. It is obvious that if a State seeks to rely on assurances that are given by a country with a record for disregarding fundamental human rights it will need to show that there is good reason to treat the assurances as providing a reliable guarantee that the deportee will not be subjected to such treatment. If, however, after consideration of all the relevant circumstances of which assurances form part, there are no substantial grounds for believing that a deportee will be at real risk of inhuman treatment, there will be no basis for holding that deportation will violate article 3.

115. That said, there is an abundance of material that supports the proposition that assurances should be treated with scepticism if they are given by a country where inhuman treatment by State agents is endemic. This comes close to the 'Catch 22'

90 C Geiringer, Analysis, *Attorney-General v Zaoui and Inspector-General of Intelligence and Security and Human Rights Commission (intervening)*, ILDC 81 (NZ 2005) A5.

proposition that if you need to ask for assurances you cannot rely on them. If a State is unwilling or unable to comply with the obligations of international law in relation to the avoidance and prevention of inhuman treatment, how can it be trusted to be willing or able to give effect to an undertaking that an individual deportee will not be subject to such treatment?

117. [...] The only ground upon which [the SIAC's] conclusions [in relation to assurances] can be attacked on an appeal restricted to questions of law is irrationality.

Was SIAC's decision in relation to RB and U irrational?

[...]

123. I have described earlier in this opinion the consideration given by SIAC to the reliance that could be placed on the Algerian assurances. This had particular regard to the general conditions in Algeria at the time that the assurances were given, the attitude of the Algerian authorities to the observance of human rights, the degree of control exercised by the Algerian authorities over the DRS, the internal security service, and the manner in which the performance of the assurances could be verified. SIAC paid careful regard to all relevant matters and applied to them the proper test of whether they amounted to substantial grounds for believing that RB and U would be at real risk of inhuman treatment if returned to Algeria.

124. SIAC gave consideration to the reasons why Algeria was not prepared to agree to monitoring and concluded that this was not indicative of bad faith and that there were alternative ways of ascertaining whether there was compliance with the assurances. These conclusions were not irrational. The contention that the assurances did not, on their true construction, protect against inhuman treatment was not well founded.

125. For these reasons the irrationality challenge to SIAC's conclusions does not succeed. I would reject the appeals brought by RB and U.

Was SIAC's decision in relation to Mr Othman's article 3 challenge irrational?

126. The attack made by counsel for Mr Othman on SIAC's conclusions in relation to article 3 was essentially founded on the weight that SIAC had given to the assurances in the MOU. Just as in the case of Algeria, these assurances were agreed in principle at the highest level in discussions between the Prime Minister and the King of Jordan and between the Foreign Secretary and the Jordanian Foreign Minister. SIAC considered in depth the way that Mr Othman was likely to be treated before his trial, during the trial process and after it. The conclusion reached was that there were not substantial grounds for believing that there was a real risk that Mr Othman would be subjected to inhuman treatment. The MOU was not critical to this conclusion. SIAC commented that the political realities in Jordan and the bilateral diplomatic relationship mattered more than the terminology of the assurances. The former matters, and the fact that Mr Othman would have a high public profile, were the most significant factors in SIAC's assessment of article 3 risk. Study of SIAC's lengthy and detailed reasoning discloses no irrationality.

The additional issues raised in the Othman appeal.

[...]

Risk of violation of article 5

130. In resisting deportation on the ground that his article 5 right will be threatened in Jordan Mr Othman [...] submitted that the risk of being detained without charge for 50 days constituted a real risk of a flagrant violation of article 5.

132. [...] 50 days detention would not constitute a "flagrant breach" of article 5 within the meaning of that phrase as used in foreign Convention rights cases. In that context a "flagrant breach" is a breach whose consequences are so severe that they override the right of a state to expel an alien from its territory. [...] The risk of detention for 50 days falls far short of satisfying the "flagrant breach" test. [...].

"Flagrant breach of article 6"

133. [...] As there is no reported foreign case where article 6 has successfully been invoked, there is a lack of authoritative guidance as to what will amount to a "flagrant breach" of that article.

136. [...] In the first place it is not easy to postulate what amounts to "a complete denial or nullification of the right to a fair trial". [...] What is required is that the deficiency or deficiencies in the trial process should be such as fundamentally to destroy the fairness of the prospective trial.

137. In the second place, the fact that the deportee may find himself subject in the receiving country to a legal process that is blatantly unfair cannot, of itself, justify placing an embargo on his deportation. The focus must be not simply on the unfairness of the trial process but on its potential consequences. An unfair trial is likely to lead to the violation of substantive human rights and the extent of that prospective violation must plainly be an important factor in deciding whether deportation is precluded.

138. [...] If an alien is to avoid deportation because he faces unfair legal process in the receiving state he must show that there are substantial grounds for believing that there is a real risk not merely that he will suffer a flagrant breach of his article 6 rights, but that the consequence will be a serious violation of a substantive right or rights. Quite how serious that violation must be has yet to be made clear by the Strasbourg jurisprudence. Plainly a sentence of death will be sufficient but the ECtHR has expressed doubts as to whether the risk of violation of article 5 can suffice to prevent the expulsion of an alien. [...]

139. In *Mamatkulov* the Grand Chamber was prepared to contemplate, and the minority to find, a violation of article 6 in circumstances where the extradition of the applicants had resulted in lengthy prison sentences. A different approach will, however, be appropriate in an extradition case. There it is the prospective trial that is relied on to justify the deportation. If there is a real risk that the trial will be flagrantly unfair, that is likely to be enough of itself to prevent extradition regardless of the likely consequences of the unfair trial.

141. In summary, the Strasbourg jurisprudence, tentative though it is, has led me to these conclusions. Before the deportation of an alien will be capable of violating article 6 there must be substantial grounds for believing that there is a real risk (i) that there will be a fundamental breach of the principles of a fair trial guaranteed by article 6 and (ii) that this failure will lead to a miscarriage of justice that itself constitutes a flagrant violation of the victim's fundamental rights. I turn to consider, having regard to this test, whether SIAC erred in law in concluding that Article 6 posed no bar to Mr Othman's deportation.

142. The potential consequences to Mr Othman of conviction of the offences for which he will be tried have already been established by the trials that took place in his absence: life imprisonment in the first instance and fifteen years imprisonment in the other. These consequences are, I believe, sufficiently severe to satisfy the second limb of the test. The vital issue that SIAC had to address was whether there were substantial

grounds for believing that Mr Othman faced a real risk of a fundamental breach of the principles of a fair trial as recognised by the Strasbourg court.

[. . .]

The composition of the court

144. As to the composition of the court, the SSCt, it would consist of three judges, of whom the presiding judge and at least one other would be senior military officers, serving in the army as lawyers. The third judge would probably be a civilian. The state prosecutors would also be military officers, part of the same military hierarchy. In Jordan, as in other countries, the prosecutors are considered to be part of the judiciary. The judges would have no security of tenure and would be subject to being replaced by executive decision. They would be subject to the influence of the executive. While not independent there was no reason to suspect them of partiality. Convictions were not a foregone conclusion before the SSCt. There had in the past been a number of acquittals and successful appeals to the Court of Cassation. That was a civil court with jurisdiction to review the decisions of the SSCt on both law and fact.

145. Such a court would not have satisfied the article 6 requirement of an "independent and impartial tribunal". [. . .]

146. While in a domestic case the composition of the SSCt would violate article 6, it does not follow that this would, of itself, constitute a flagrant breach of article 6 sufficient to prevent deportation in a foreign case. The Court of Appeal [. . .] concluded that it would not. I have reached the same conclusion and would endorse the reasoning on this point of the Court of Appeal.

The admission of evidence that may have been obtained by torture

[. . .]

The conclusions of the Court of Appeal

152. SIAC concluded that the shortcomings that I have summarised, when viewed in the context of the trial process as a whole, did not amount to a "total denial of the right to a fair trial". The Court of Appeal held that, in so concluding, SIAC erred in law. The reasoning of the Court of Appeal appears from the following key passages in the judgment of Buxton LJ:

" [. . .] 48. The use of evidence obtained by torture is prohibited in Convention law not just because that will make the trial unfair, but also and more particularly because of the connexion of the issue with article 3, a fundamental, unconditional and non-derogable prohibition that stands at the centre of the Convention protections. [. . .]

49. SIAC was wrong not to recognise this crucial difference between breaches of article 6 based on this ground and breaches of article 6 based simply on defects in the trial process or in the composition of the court. [. . .] That caused it not to recognise the high degree of assurance that is required in relation to proceedings in a foreign state before a person may lawfully be deported to face a trial that may involve evidence obtained by torture."

Conclusions

153. No criticism can be made of Buxton LJ's statement of the fundamental prohibition of the admission of evidence obtained by torture and the reasons for this. I do not accept, however, the conclusion that he has derived from this, namely that it required a high degree of assurance that evidence obtained by torture would not be

used in the proceedings in Jordan before it would be lawful to deport Mr Othman to face those proceedings. As Buxton LJ observed, the prohibition on receiving evidence obtained by torture is not primarily because such evidence is unreliable or because the reception of the evidence will make the trial unfair. Rather it is because "the state must stand firm against the conduct that has produced the evidence". That principle applies to the state in which an attempt is made to adduce such evidence. It does not require this state, the United Kingdom, to retain in this country to the detriment of national security a terrorist suspect unless it has a high degree of assurance that evidence obtained by torture will not be adduced against him in Jordan. What is relevant in this appeal is the degree of risk that Mr Othman will suffer a flagrant denial of justice if he is deported to Jordan. […]

154. The issue before SIAC was whether there were reasonable grounds for believing that if Mr Othman were deported to Jordan the criminal trial that he would there face would have defects of such significance as fundamentally to destroy the fairness of his trial or, as SIAC put it, to amount to a total denial of the right to a fair trial. SIAC concluded that the deficiencies that SIAC had identified did not meet that exacting test. I do not find that in reaching this conclusion SIAC erred in law.

Lord Hoffmann

Article 3: the risk of torture or inhuman or degrading treatment.

187. […] The question of whether assurances obviate the risk is a question of fact, to be decided in the light of all the evidence.

[…]

192. The arrangements with Algeria were negotiated at the highest level and it was plain to the Algerian authorities that what the United Kingdom required was an assurance which would enable it to comply with its obligations under article 3. On the other hand, the assurances had to be expressed in language which would respect the dignity of a sovereign state. […] The main reason why SIAC thought that this assurance would satisfy article 3 was that it was not in the national interest of the Algerians to fail to comply. In those circumstances, the precise language of the assurance was less important than the effect which both sides knew it was intended to have. So far from being irrational, that seems to me an entirely reasonable conclusion which SIAC was entitled to draw from the basic facts it had found to exist about the situation in Algeria.

193. As to external monitoring, a good deal has been written about its importance in enabling a court or other authority to be satisfied that the receiving state is complying with assurances about safety on return. There is no doubt that in the absence of some provision for external monitoring, such assurances may be no more than empty words […]. But there is no rule of law that external monitoring is required. It all depends upon the facts of the particular case and in my opinion SIAC was quite right to say […] that although fulfilment of the assurances must be capable of being verified, external monitoring is only one possible form of verification. In this particular case the Algerian government regarded external monitoring as inconsistent with its sovereign dignity but SIAC considered that there were other ways in which non-compliance was likely to become known and, given the political incentives, these were sufficiently likely to ensure compliance. This was a carefully balanced finding which I think was open to SIAC on the evidence.

194. For these reasons I would dismiss the appeals of RB and U.

Article 6 and Abu Qatada

[. . .]

197. [. . .] Member States are not in a position to regulate the conduct of trials in the foreign countries from which aliens come and to which they may have to be deported. Accordingly, a deporting state will be in breach of article 6 only if there is a real risk that the alien will suffer a "flagrant denial of justice" in the receiving state. [. . .]

201. [. . .] There is in my opinion no authority for a rule that, in the context of the application of article 6 to a foreign trial, the risk of the use of evidence obtained by torture necessarily amounts to a flagrant denial of justice.

203. In addition to the question of using evidence obtained by torture, Abu Qatada also submitted that his trial would be a flagrant denial of justice because it would take place before a military court, which was not for the purposes of article 6 an independent tribunal. SIAC found that although the judges were part of a military hierarchy and the court would therefore not have complied with article 6 in its application to a Member State, they would in fact act judicially and the trial would therefore not be a flagrant denial of justice. The Court of Appeal agreed and on this point I have nothing to add to the reasoning of SIAC and the Court of Appeal.

Lord Hope of Craighead

[. . .]

The article 3 assurances

237. [. . .] The fact that it was thought necessary to obtain the assurances is itself a demonstration that, without them, there was a real risk that treatment contrary to article 3 would be resorted to. There was no question of obtaining a general undertaking that the states concerned would abandon such practices. What was sought were assurances specific to each individual. The context in which they were given was one in which it must be assumed that practices that are objectionable because they are in breach of norms that are agreed internationally are still commonplace. Can it ever be said that, in such circumstances, assurances that particular individuals will not be subjected to them may be accepted as reliable? Is it realistic to expect that the risk of their being subjected to it can be met by monitoring? What sanctions, if any, can be imposed in the event of it being discovered that the assurances have been breached?

238. In *Sing v Canada (Minister of Citizenship and Immigration)* 2007 FC 361, para 136, de Montigny J in the Federal Court of Canada cited with approval a passage from the report of the Special Rapporteur to the United Nations of 1 September 2004, UN Document A/59/324 which states:

> "in circumstances where there is a consistent pattern of gross, flagrant or mass violations of human rights, or of systematic practice of torture, the principle of non-refoulement must be strictly observed and diplomatic assurances should not be resorted to."

It was suggested that this passage showed that assurances were objectionable in principle. But its very language shows, as de Montigny J accepted, that the issue will always be one of fact. As counsel for RB and U accepted, the consistent approach of the Strasbourg court has been to examine any assurances offered in the particular circumstances of the cases before it and to consider whether, in those circumstances, the assurances are sufficient to counter the risk of treatment contrary to article 3.

241. [. . .] The terms in which the assurances were given, the opportunities for monitoring and the extent to which the risks would be reduced all required careful

evaluation. But these were matters for SIAC to resolve, as it did, on a careful consideration of all the evidence.

242. [...] In this field there can be no absolute guarantees that assurances, even at the highest level, will be adhered to. But the Strasbourg jurisprudence does not require them to achieve that standard. The words "substantial" and "real risk" show that the court's approach is essentially a practical one that strikes a balance between the interests of the community and the protection of the individual. [...]

Abu Qatada: article 6

[...]

249. [...] It is plain that in several material respects the circumstances in which the retrial will take place will give rise to the risk of unfairness. [...] But here again, as in the case of the assurances, there is no absolute rule. The question whether or not there will be a flagrant breach must be evaluated. SIAC noted [...] that the retrial will take place within a legally constructed framework and that there was sound evidence that the military court, which is not a mere tool of the executive, appraises the evidence and tests it against the law. I do not think that, looking at the matter overall, SIAC can be faulted on the ground that it failed to subject the issues to anxious scrutiny or that its decision that there would not be a complete denial of a fair trial was one which it was not entitled to reach on the evidence.

Lord Brown

(iii) Article 6 in a foreign case

258. In many parts of the world judicial procedures are markedly different (and to our way of thinking much inferior) to those required by article 6 of the Convention and under other similar constitutional guarantees of due process. No one suggests, however, that people coming from such places are immune from expulsion lest they become subject on return to what we would regard as a defective legal process. True it is that ever since *Soering v UK* (1989) 11 EHRR 439, Strasbourg has contemplated that "an issue might exceptionally be raised under article 6 by an extradition decision in circumstances where the fugitive has suffered or risks suffering a flagrant denial of a fair trial in the requesting country". Not once, however, in the subsequent twenty years has an expulsion or extradition order in fact been held to violate article 6—not even in the somewhat shocking circumstances which arose in *Mamatkulov and Askarov v Turkey* (2005) 41 EHRR 494 where the dissenting minority noted as features of the applicants' terrorist trial in Uzbekhistan that "the applicants were denied the right to be represented by counsel of their own choice, defending counsel being appointed by the public prosecutor; the applicants were held incommunicado until the commencement of their trial in June 1999 [some three months after Turkey had extradited them in the face of a rule 39 order prohibiting such action]; the trial was closed to the general public, to all family members of the applicants and to attorneys hired on behalf of the defence; and the self-incriminating statements used to convict the applicants included those signed during the pre-trial police investigation, while the applicants were in custody and without access to their own lawyers". This, moreover, against the background of an Amnesty International briefing document affording "credible grounds for believing that self-incriminating evidence extracted by torture was routinely used to secure guilty verdicts".

260. [...] Mr Othman is being expelled as an undesirable alien rather than extradited to stand trial and, if returned, tried and convicted, he will plainly suffer ample deprivation of liberty to warrant consideration of his case under article 6 before he comes to be expelled.

> All that said, I find SIAC's judgment on this issue perfectly clear, measured and sensible and the Court of Appeal's criticisms of it misplaced. [. . .] One day, no doubt, a case will come before the courts where, however compelling the security interests of the state which proposes to expel an alien, those interests will fall to be sacrificed to the alien's article 6 right not to be returned to face a flagrantly unjust trial. If, however, as the majority of the Grand Chamber held in *Mamatkulov*, extradition was not unlawful even in the circumstances arising there, in my judgment expulsion most certainly is not unlawful here. [. . .]

This was one of the most elaborate among the dozens of domestic court judgments on diplomatic assurances. Diplomatic assurances have been widely resorted to in the aftermath of 9/11 to circumvent the absolute prohibition of refoulement.[91] The decision at hand was the first issued by the UK highest court, which held that diplomatic assurances gave rise to issues of fact and hence the only legal ground to challenge SIAC's factual conclusions upon appeal was irrationality, which the SIAC's lengthy and detailed reasoning did not disclose. The House of Lords endorsed SIAC's case law that diplomatic assurances could mitigate and reduce the risk of torture to a level at which return would no longer breach the UK's obligations. In their discussion of diplomatic assurances, the Lords made extensive reference to Strasbourg's case law and rightly found that the ECtHR did not support the proposition that assurances were objectionable in principle; indeed, their rejection in the landmark *Chahal* judgment and in a dozen other cases but their acceptance in *Mamatkulov* (heavily relied upon by the Lords in the present case) and a few others showed that assurances may not always be effective but that the legitimacy of their acceptance depended on the facts of each case.

Othman brought his case to the ECtHR, which found, for the first time, a violation of Article 6 in a foreign case because of the real risk of the admission of evidence obtained by torture at his retrial in Jordan.[92] In the same case, the Strasbourg court also formulated a 'checklist' for assessing the quality, credibility, and sufficiency of assurances in their practical application in each case,[93] thus streamlining its approach on diplomatic assurances.

This rather sophisticated judicial approach of courts in Europe is in sharp contrast to that of their US counterparts, as illustrated in the following two cases.

Mohammed (on the application of Munaf) v Geren, Secretary of the Army and ors, Judgment, 128 S.Ct. 2207 (2008), ILDC 1156 (US 2008), 12th June 2008, United States; Supreme Court [US]

The petitioners, a US-Jordanian dual citizen and a US-Iraqi dual citizen, were detained by US military forces operating as part of the UN-mandated Multi-National Force in Iraq for suspected provision of aid to Al-Qaeda and for orchestrating the kidnapping of foreign journalists respectively. They petitioned the US District Court for the District of Columbia to prevent their transfer to Iraqi custody for criminal proceedings, arguing that they had constitutional

91 See extensively A Constantinides, 'Transjudicial Dialogue and Consistency in Human Rights Jurisprudence: A Case Study on Diplomatic Assurances against Torture' in O K Fauchald and A Nollkaemper (eds), *Unity or Fragmentation of International Law: The Role of International and National Tribunals* (Hart Publishing 2012) 267–94; M Giuffré, 'Deportation with Assurances and Human Rights: The Case of Persons Suspected or Convicted of Serious Crimes' (2017) 15 *Journal of International Criminal Justice* 75.

92 *Othman (Abu Qatada) v United Kingdom* (n 78) para 285.

93 ibid, para 189; see also ECtHR, *Labsi v Slovakia* (Judgment), App No 33809/08 (15 May 2012) para 120. The court considered, *inter alia*, the following factors: whether the assurances are specific or general and vague; who has given them and whether that person can bind the receiving state; whether they have been given by a contracting state; the length and strength of bilateral relations between the sending and receiving states, including the receiving state's record in abiding by similar assurances; whether compliance with the assurances can be objectively verified through diplomatic or other monitoring mechanisms; and whether there is an effective system of protection against torture in the receiving state, including whether the state is willing to cooperate with international monitoring mechanisms and non-governmental organizations etc.

due process rights not to be transferred. One of the arguments was that they faced a serious risk of torture. The Court of Appeals affirmed the district court's temporary injunction preventing Omar's transfer as well as the dismissal of Munaf's petition for lack of jurisdiction. The Supreme Court granted *certiorari* and consolidated the two cases.

> 55 Petitioners contend that [...] their transfer to Iraqi custody is likely to result in torture. [...] Such allegations are of course a matter of serious concern, but in the present context that concern is to be addressed by the political branches, not the judiciary. [...]
>
> 57 [...] This recognition that it is the political branches that bear responsibility for creating exceptions to the general rule is nothing new; as Chief Justice Marshall explained in the *Schooner Exchange*, "exemptions from territorial jurisdiction ... must be derived from the consent of the sovereign of the territory" and are "rather questions of policy than of law, that they are for diplomatic, rather than legal discussion." [...]
>
> 58 The Executive Branch may, of course, decline to surrender a detainee for many reasons, including humanitarian ones. Petitioners here allege only the possibility of mistreatment in a prison facility; this is not a more extreme case in which the Executive has determined that a detainee is likely to be tortured but decides to transfer him anyway. Indeed, the Solicitor General states that it is the policy of the United States *not* to transfer an individual in circumstances where torture is likely to result. [...] In these cases the United States explains that, although it remains concerned about torture among some sectors of the Iraqi Government, the State Department has determined that the Justice Ministry—the department that would have authority over Munaf and Omar—as well as its prison and detention facilities have '"generally met internationally accepted standards for basic prisoner needs."' [...] The Solicitor General explains that such determinations are based on "the Executive's assessment of the foreign country's legal system and ... the Executive['s] ... ability to obtain foreign assurances it considers reliable." [...]
>
> 59 The Judiciary is not suited to second-guess such determinations—determinations that would require federal courts to pass judgment on foreign justice systems and undermine the Government's ability to speak with one voice in this area. [...] In contrast, the political branches are well situated to consider sensitive foreign policy issues, such as whether there is a serious prospect of torture at the hands of an ally, and what to do about it if there is. [...]
>
> 60 Petitioners briefly argue that their claims of potential torture may not be readily dismissed on the basis of these principles because the FARR Act prohibits transfer when torture may result. [...] Neither petitioner asserted a FARR Act claim in his petition for habeas, and the Act was not raised in any of the certiorari filings before this Court. [...] Under such circumstances we will not consider the question.
>
> [...]
>
> 64 Munaf and Omar are alleged to have committed hostile and warlike acts within the sovereign territory of Iraq during ongoing hostilities there. Pending their criminal prosecution for those offenses, Munaf and Omar are being held in Iraq by American forces operating pursuant to a U.N. Mandate and at the request of the Iraqi Government. Petitioners concede that Iraq has a sovereign right to prosecute them for alleged violations of its law. Yet they went to federal court seeking an order that would allow them to defeat precisely that sovereign authority. Habeas corpus does not require the United States to shelter such fugitives from the criminal justice system of the sovereign with authority to prosecute them.

Omar and ors v McHugh and ors, Appeal judgment, No 09-5410, ILDC 1773 (US 2011), 646 F.3d 13 (D.C. Cir. 2011), 21st June 2011, United States; Court of Appeals (DC Circuit) [DC Cir]

Omar, one of the petitioners in the previous case, claimed that he had a right to judicial review of the conditions in Iraq before his transfer to Iraqi custody under the Foreign Affairs Reform and Restructuring Act (FARRA) of 1998, which implemented Article 3 of the Convention against Torture, as supplemented by the REAL ID Act of 2005. He also argued that congress could not give immigration transferees a habeas corpus right to judicial review of conditions in the receiving country without extending such right to extradition and military transferees.

> 14 By its terms, the FARR Act provides a right to judicial review of conditions in the receiving country only in the immigration context, for aliens seeking review of a final order of removal. The FARR Act does not give extradition or military transferees—the other two categories in which transfer issues typically arise—a right to judicial review of conditions in the receiving country. Omar is a military transferee, not an alien seeking review of a final order of removal under the immigration laws. Therefore, the FARR Act does not afford him any right to judicial review of conditions in the receiving country. [. . .]
>
> 16 Even if the FARR Act had extended a judicial review right to extradition or military transferees such as Omar, a subsequent statute—the REAL ID Act of 2005—made clear that those kinds of transferees have no such right. The REAL ID Act states that only immigration transferees have a right to judicial review of conditions in the receiving country, during a court's review of a final order of removal. [. . .]
>
> 18 According to Omar, the Constitution's guarantees of habeas corpus and due process grant him a right to judicial review of conditions in Iraq before he is transferred. We disagree with Omar's constitutional argument.
>
> 19 The Supreme Court ruled in Munaf—litigation in which Omar himself was a party—that the Constitution does not grant extradition or military transferees such as Omar a habeas corpus or due process right to judicial review of conditions in the receiving country before they are transferred. [. . .] In so ruling, the Court recognized that there are three principal settings in which the issue arises: (i) extradition, (ii) transfer of military detainees, and (iii) removal of immigration detainees.
>
> 20 Those facing extradition traditionally have not been able to maintain habeas claims to block transfer based on conditions in the receiving country. Rather, applying what has been known as the rule of non-inquiry, courts historically have refused to inquire into conditions an extradited individual might face in the receiving country. In Munaf, the Supreme Court reaffirmed this precise point, stating "we have recognized that it is for the political branches, not the Judiciary, to assess practices in foreign countries." [. . .]
>
> 21 Similarly, military transferees traditionally have not been able to raise habeas claims to prevent transfer based on conditions in the receiving country. Since the Founding, the United States has routinely transferred wartime detainees at the end of hostilities or as part of an exchange, without judicial review of conditions the transferees would face in the other nation. In Boumediene v. Bush, the Supreme Court explained that negotiated exchange of prisoners was "a wartime practice well known to the Framers," and "[j]udicial intervention might have complicated" those negotiations. [. . .]
>
> 22 Therefore, Omar is in a class of would-be transferees who historically have not been able to bring habeas claims to obtain judicial review of conditions in the receiving country before being transferred. Omar is a military detainee captured during war and now facing transfer to the custody of another nation. In addition, because

Omar is facing transfer to the custody of another sovereign that has convicted him of a crime, his situation is analogous to that of an extradition transferee—a point Omar himself acknowledges. [. . .] But neither military detainees nor those facing extradition historically have possessed a right to judicial review of conditions in the receiving country before they were transferred.

26 In short, the inquiry that Omar asks this Court to undertake in this habeas case—reviewing the conditions Omar might face in Iraqi custody—is the precise inquiry that the Supreme Court in Munaf already rejected. As a lower court, even apart from possible res judicata problems with Omar's habeas corpus submission, we have no authority to toss Munaf aside in this manner. [. . .]

27 The Supreme Court has established that there is no freestanding constitutional right for extradition or military transferees to obtain judicial review of conditions in the receiving country before being transferred. And this Court has established that there is no statutory right for extradition or military transferees to obtain such review. No doubt recognizing those obstacles to his submission, Omar strings together a series of quasi-constitutional arguments: He suggests that the Constitution's habeas corpus guarantee somehow combines with the FARR Act to give him a right to judicial review of conditions in the receiving country, even though neither the Constitution nor the FARR Act by itself does so. We disagree with those arguments; indeed, we have some trouble understanding them.

28 First, Omar at times appears to suggest that Congress cannot give immigration transferees a right to judicial review of conditions in the receiving country unless Congress also extends the right to extradition and military transferees. Whatever the merits of that all-or-nothing position as a policy matter, it strikes us as frivolous as a constitutional matter. We see no constitutional reason Congress cannot incrementally or selectively create new rights for transferees beyond the rights guaranteed by the Constitution, at least so long as no suspect classification is employed and the scheme has a rational basis that satisfies equal protection principles.

29 Second, Omar seems to say that the FARR Act violates the Constitution by declaring a statutory "policy" against transfer to torture for all transferees but then affording only immigration transferees the right to judicial review of conditions in the receiving country. We again fail to see how that poses a serious constitutional issue. As a practical and a legal matter, that scenario is no different from Congress creating a right only for immigration transferees to obtain judicial review of conditions in the receiving country. To reiterate, Congress need not proceed in an all or-nothing manner when expanding judicial review for transferees.

31 [. . .] Omar suggests that Congress cannot express a policy for the Executive Branch to follow without also creating a right to judicial enforcement of that policy. No case has ever said that. Under Omar's approach, Congress may not express a general policy regarding transfers and make that policy judicially enforceable only for immigration transferees. Yet Congress could constitutionally achieve the same result simply by declaring that the transfer policy itself applies only to immigration transferees. The Constitution does not turn on such arcane and empty semantics. [. . .]

32 Third, Omar advances a kind of one-way ratchet theory. He suggests that Congress, through the REAL ID Act, could not take away any statutory right it created in the FARR Act of 1998. As an initial matter, as we explained in our statutory analysis above, the REAL ID Act merely confirmed what the FARR Act said—that only immigration transferees may obtain judicial review of conditions in the receiving

> country. But even if the REAL ID Act took away a statutory right that the FARR Act had previously granted, that scenario poses no constitutional problem. Congress does not amend the Constitution, or alter the scope of the constitutional writ of habeas corpus, whenever it amends a statutory right that might be available in a habeas case. Congress thus remains generally free to undo a statute that applies in habeas cases, just as it can undo other statutory rights that it has created. [. . .]
>
> 35 In sum, Congress has no constitutional obligation to grant extradition and military transferees such as Omar a right to judicial review of conditions in the receiving country. The fact that Congress, in the FARR Act, created such a right for immigration transferees does not raise a constitutional problem simply because Congress did not also extend the right to extradition and military transferees. [. . .]
>
> 36 In Munaf, the Supreme Court held that habeas corpus and due process do not give a transferee such as Omar a right to judicial review of conditions in the receiving country. Congress is free to establish additional statutory protections with respect to transfers, whether to correspond U.S. laws to evolving international law norms or for other policy reasons. Indeed, Congress has done so in the immigration context by allowing aliens in removal proceedings to obtain judicial review of conditions in the receiving country before being transferred. But Congress has not created such a right for extradition or military transferees such as Omar. Congress is not constitutionally barred from proceeding in that incremental manner when affording new statutory rights to transferees.

As observed by the ILDC reporter, these decisions affirmed the jurisdictional limitation imposed by Congress on US courts to only review claims under the Torture Convention, as implemented by the FARR Act, in immigration cases but not in cases involving extradition and military transfers, including terrorist suspects challenging their transfer to another country.[94] They also showed that, unlike courts in Europe, US courts adhere to the 'rule of non-inquiry' and do not second-guess the relevant executive's determinations and thus do not inquire into the (prospective) treatment of transferees in another state under the Convention standards without jurisdictional grant by Congress.[95] In *Munaf*, the Supreme Court stated that these were 'sensitive foreign policy issues', which fell on the political branches to assess. Consequently, US compliance with the Torture Convention in non-immigration cases was left solely to the executive, without any meaningful prospect of judicial review. As rightly noted by the ILDC reporter, this excluded the judiciary from the state's 'competent authorities', which are responsible to determine conditions in the receiving country before transferring individuals under Article 3 of the Convention.[96]

(c) Liberty, fair trial, and other human rights

Silva and More than five thousand citizens v Congress of Peru, Original petition, Exp No 010-2002-AI/TC, ILDC 323 (PE 2003), 3rd January 2003, Peru; Constitutional Court

This case involved a 'mass constitutional claim' challenging *in abstracto* the constitutionality of several anti-terrorism Decree Laws issued by the 'Government of Emergency and National Reconstruction', which had taken power in Peru following the 1992 auto-coup. The petitioners challenged the Decree Laws against various human rights protected under the Constitution of Peru as well as treaties ratified by Peru, most notably the Inter-American Convention of Human Rights.

94 H Zarkar, Analysis, *Omar and ors v McHugh and ors*, ILDC 1773 (US 2011) A1.

95 ibid, A2–A3.

96 ibid, A5.

IX. Advocating terrorism and the freedoms of information, expression, opinion and dissemination of ideas

86. The fact that, in abstract terms, the legislator has provided that advocating terrorism is a criminal offense is not, *per se*, unconstitutional, provided that other constitutional rights such as the free development of the personality of students, as well as goods and values protected under the constitution such as the preservation of the constitutional democratic order, without which the exercise of the remaining constitutional rights would not be possible, are pursued, guaranteed and protected. [. . .]

87. However, and as it has been previously held by this Constitutional Court, following the Inter-American Court of Human Rights, the freedoms of information and expression are circumstantial to the constitutional-democratic regime, as they contribute to the formation of free public opinion. Consequently the State, while guaranteeing them, is entitled to repress such behavior that, in its exercise seeks the destruction of the democratic system itself, which is the natural environment where freedom and the exercise of all the fundamental rights of human beings are possible.

Nevertheless, even in these cases criminal repression of these manifestations or expressions must be carried out with scrupulous respect for the limits to which the state *ius puniendi* is subject, such that its intimidating effects do not end up unreasonably denying or hindering the exercise of these preferred freedoms.

88. In this regard, the Constitutional Court considers that section 7 of Executive Order no. 25475 and, by extension, section 1 of Executive Order no. 25880, are unconstitutional insofar as they define the crime of advocating terrorism, in its generic and aggravated forms. Indeed, the said offense definitions do not specifically describe the object of the advocacy, nor what should be understood by advocacy. This constitutes on one hand, a breach of the principle of criminal legality, and simultaneously, a violation of freedom of information and expression, as considered collectively they allow a disproportionate and unreasonable limitation of the said freedoms.

The Constitutional Court is not unaware that the intention behind offense definitions of this nature has occasionally been to silence the expression of minority groups or of groups opposed to the regime in office at the time. The Constitutional Court therefore considers that, in defending these freedoms, the judges of the Judiciary must be especially sensitive in their protection, and thus, shall apply these offense definitions in accordance with article 20 of the International Covenant on Civil and Political Rights and article 13.5 of the American Convention on Human Rights, that is, in the sense that what is prohibited is advocacy that constitutes an incitation to violence or to any other illegal action.

X. The right to due process

§10.2. The right to a judge of competent jurisdiction

a) Trial of civilians by military courts

98. [. . .] [T]he Inter-American Court of Human Rights has, through repeated opinions, indicated that military courts may not be competent to try civilians, because doing so prejudices the right to a judge of competent jurisdiction recognized by article 8, number 1, of the American Convention on Human Rights. [. . .]

99. In the 18 August 2000 judgment, the Court maintained that: "(. . .) the impartiality of the judge is affected by the fact that the Armed Forces have the double function of fighting insurgent groups militarily and of judging and imposing punishments

on said groups" (Cantoral Benavides case. Para 114). According to the Court, where the Armed Forces are in charge of fighting individuals who are subsequently accused of committing the crimes of high treason or terrorism, they may not be competent at the same time to charge and try them, as the former is a "natural" power of the military institution, while the latter is not.

106. In this regard, the Constitutional Court deems that the provisions of the Code of Military Justice which may be included by the law for the purposes of use in the charging of civilians accused of committing the crimes of terrorism and high treason, may *under no circumstance be understood as referring to the "body,"* but rather only to procedural rules to be used by ordinary justice, and provided that said rules, in turn, are consistent with the minimum guarantees of due process provided by the Constitution.

107. In addition, the Constitutional Court considers that the latter possibility should not be understood as a general rule, but rather always as a hypothesis of exceptional nature [. . .]. The terms in which this Constitutional Court has interpreted this constitutional provision have been for the sole purpose of finding it a hermeneutic sense that is not incompatible with the American Convention on Human Rights challenged by the Court, while the legislator adapts article 173 of the Constitution to the aforementioned Convention.

§10.3. The right to a defense

[. . .]

128. For a limitation of a right not to be incompatible with the constitutional rights which it restricts, it should respect its essential content. In this regard, the Constitutional Court does not consider that the limitation on the exercise of the right to the free choice of a defense counsel affects its essence, that is, the possibility for the accused in investigative proceedings or in legal proceedings to have the ability to choose, and thus, not to have an attorney imposed on him. If the challenged provision limits the choice options (the defense counsel of one may not be chosen by another), this, in principle and in general terms, does not generate a lack of defense, as the said choice may be made among other attorneys.

129. This has been the view of the Inter-American Court of Human Rights, when it ruled, in relation to the challenged provision, that "The provision denying the possibility of one single defense counsel assisting more than one defendant limits alternatives with regards to the choice of defense counsel, but does not mean, per se, a breach of article 8.2.d. of the Convention" (Castillo Petruzzi case, para 147).

130. [. . .] [I]n its actual application, especially in a territorial environment where there is no possibility of choice between various legal professionals, due to their absence, the said application—if not the provision—may indeed prejudice the right in question.

§10.4. The presumption of innocence

[. . .]

b) The arrest warrant and the presumption of innocence

140. [. . .] A literal reading of the said provision would appear to imply the obligation of the criminal judge, when ordering the opening of the investigation, to automatically issue an arrest warrant against those charged with the crime of terrorism, without taking into consideration the legal bases provided in article 135 of the Code of Criminal Procedure. [. . .]

141. If that were the meaning of paragraph a of article 13 of Executive Order no. 25475, that is, that remand in custody ordered by the court is to be legitimized based only on the reproachable nature and socially negative consequences of the offense of terrorism, it would contravene the principle of presumption of innocence [. . .].

Remand in custody, which constitutes a restriction of individual freedom despite the fact that during the proceedings it is presumed that the accused is innocent, may only be ordered if, in a specific case, it is deemed indispensable; which consequently assumes that the mandatory nature of such an order may not be established by law. This latter criteria is directly derived from the provisions of article 9.3 of the International Covenant on Civil and Political Rights, according to which "It shall not be the general rule that persons awaiting trial shall be detained in custody," because, as the Inter-American Court of Human Rights has affirmed "This would be tantamount to anticipating a sentence, which is at odds with universally recognized general principles of law."

§10.6. The right to proceedings with a reasonable duration: Art. 1 of Executive Order no. 25708

[. . .]

167. The Constitutional Court considers that proceedings conceived with an extremely summary or rushed duration, with an objective other than that of settling the case in fair terms, or offering a formal ritual for the substantiation of "any criminal charge," infringes the right to proceedings "with due guarantees and within a reasonable time." [. . .] The said scope of the law is further derived directly from article 25(1) of the American Convention on Human Rights, pursuant to which "Everyone has the right to simple and prompt recourse, or any other effective recourse, to a competent court or tribunal for protection against acts that violate his fundamental rights recognized by the constitution or laws of the state concerned or by this Convention (. . .)".

168. In the "Report on Terrorism and Human Rights," of October 22, 2002, the Inter-American Commission stated that "The essential components of the right to due process and to a fair trial also include the right to a hearing within a reasonable time. Although the concept of reasonable time is not easy to define, certain prior requirements have been articulated, in this and in other human rights systems, which are considered necessary in order to duly enforce this right. [. . .]

XIV. The right to nationality

214. The international instruments signed by Peru also declare the right to a nationality. Thus, article XIX of the American Declaration of the Rights and Duties of Man mentions that: "Every person has the right to the nationality to which he is entitled by law." The Universal Declaration of Human Rights, in article 15, states: "Everybody has the right to a nationality. Nobody shall be arbitrarily deprived of his nationality or of the right to change his nationality." In turn, the American Convention on Human Rights refers to this issue in (3), article 20: "No one shall be arbitrarily deprived of his nationality."

216. In our country, the loss of nationality occurs with respect to citizens who are Peruvian by birth and to naturalized foreigners. Article 7 of Executive Order no. 25475 seems to have created a new type of punishment, increasing the list of punishments designed in the Penal Code. Thus, articles 30 and 31 list the cases of punishment. Loss of nationality as a punishment is not provided for by the said articles.

In conclusion, the punishment of loss of nationality violates the provisions of the Political Constitution and international treaties, and it must be declared unconstitutional.

XV. The right to personal integrity

223. [. . .] [T]he Constitutional Court considers that submitting a convict to a punishment that involves absolute isolation during a period of one year constitutes an unreasonable and disproportionate measure, constituting cruel and inhuman treatment. The same occurs with the requirement of maintaining the inmate in one-person cells during his entire period of confinement in a penitentiary. Hence, the aforementioned provisions, to the extent to which they set out the said measures, violate article 2, paragraph 1 of the Constitution and article 5, paragraphs 1, 2 and 6, of the American Convention on Human Rights, as they affect the right to personal freedom.

The court analysed the various human rights at issue in this case under both international law and constitutional law, making extensive reference to the case law of the Inter-American Court of Human Rights. As pointed out by the ILDC reporter, this decision was very important for Peru because it contributed towards the restructuring of democracy in the country by declaring unconstitutional the anti-terrorist legislation enacted during the period of armed violence in the 1980s and 1990s.[97] The decision led to new anti-terrorist legislation as well as retrials of those convicted under the unconstitutional legislation.[98] The court made a refined and welcome analysis of the crime of apology of terrorism in line with international and Inter-American human rights standards and found that the impugned legislation constituted a disproportionate and unreasonable breach of human rights.[99] The decision is also commendable for broadening the temporal scope of the right to a hearing within a reasonable time as aspect of the right to fair trial, which commonly addresses the excessive length of proceedings, to also include trials of unduly brief duration for severe crimes.[100] Another interesting finding of the court, albeit without much analysis, was that loss of nationality as a punishment was unconstitutional and in breach of applicable human rights treaties, hence implying that deprivation of nationality in that context was arbitrary.

Charkaoui v Canada (Citizenship and Immigration), Charkaoui and ors, Attorney General of Ontario (intervening) and ors (intervening) v Minister of Citizenship and Immigration and ors, Appeal judgment, (2007) 1 SCR 350, 2007 SCC 9 (CanLII), 276 DLR (4th) 594, 44 CR (6th) 1, 152 CRR (2d) 17, 54 Admin LR (4th) 1, ILDC 640 (CA 2007), 23rd February 2007, Canada

The appellants were arrested and detained under the 2001 Immigration and Refugee Protection Act (IRPA), which allowed the removal of permanent residents or foreign nationals on various grounds of national security, including involvement in terrorist activities. The period of detention could be, and frequently was, several years. They challenged the Act's detention scheme and review process under Sections 7 (right to life, liberty and security of the person), 9 (protection against arbitrary detention), 10(c) (prompt review of detention), 12 (protection against cruel and unusual treatment), and 15 (equality) of the Canadian Charter of Rights and Freedoms and presented a habeas corpus argument about a 120-day delay for judicial review of continuing detention. The relief sought was to have the relevant IRPA provisions struck out.

97 E Salmón Gárate, Analysis, *Silva and More than five thousand citizens v Congress of Peru*, ILDC 323 (PE 2003) A2.

98 ibid.

99 ibid, A7.

100 ibid, A5.

1 One of the most fundamental responsibilities of a government is to ensure the security of its citizens. This may require it to act on information that it cannot disclose and to detain people who threaten national security. Yet in a constitutional democracy, governments must act accountably and in conformity with the Constitution and the rights and liberties it guarantees. These two propositions describe a tension that lies at the heart of modern democratic governance. It is a tension that must be resolved in a way that respects the imperatives both of security and of accountable constitutional governance.

[. . .]

27 The procedures required to conform to the principles of fundamental justice must reflect the exigencies of the security context. Yet they cannot be permitted to erode the essence of s. 7. The principles of fundamental justice cannot be reduced to the point where they cease to provide the protection of due process that lies at the heart of s. 7 of the Charter. The protection may not be as complete as in a case where national security constraints do not operate. But to satisfy s. 7, meaningful and substantial protection there must be.

3. Relevant Principles of Fundamental Justice

28 The overarching principle of fundamental justice that applies here is this: before the state can detain people for significant periods of time, it must accord them a fair judicial process [. . .]. [. . .]

29 This basic principle has a number of facets. It comprises the right to a hearing. It requires that the hearing be before an independent and impartial magistrate. It demands a decision by the magistrate on the facts and the law. And it entails the right to know the case put against one, and the right to answer that case. Precisely how these requirements are met will vary with the context. But for s. 7 to be satisfied, each of them must be met in substance.

[. . .]

5. Is the Decision Based on the Facts and the Law?

49 The IRPA process at issue seeks to meet this requirement by placing material before the judge for evaluation. [. . .] The normal standards used to ensure the reliability of evidence in court do not apply [. . .]. The named person may be shown little or none of the material relied on by the ministers and the judge, and may thus not be in a position to know or challenge the case against him or her. It follows that the judge's decision, while based on the evidence before him or her, may not be based on all of the evidence available.

51 [. . .] The result is that, at the end of the day, one cannot be sure that the judge has been exposed to the whole factual picture.

52 Similar concerns arise with respect to the requirement that the decision be based on the law. [. . .] The named person is, to be sure, permitted to make legal representations. But without disclosure and full participation throughout the process, he or she may not be in a position to put forward a full legal argument.

[. . .]

6. Is the "Case to Meet" Principle Satisfied?

57 The right to know the case to be met is not absolute. [. . .]

61 In the context of national security, non-disclosure, which may be extensive, coupled with the grave intrusions on liberty imposed on a detainee, makes it difficult, if not impossible, to find substitute procedures that will satisfy s. 7. Fundamental

justice requires substantial compliance with the venerated principle that a person whose liberty is in jeopardy must be given an opportunity to know the case to meet, and an opportunity to meet the case. Yet the imperative of the protection of society may preclude this. Information may be obtained from other countries or from informers on condition that it not be disclosed. Or it may simply be so critical that it cannot be disclosed without risking public security. This is a reality of our modern world. If s. 7 is to be satisfied, either the person must be given the necessary information, or a substantial substitute for that information must be found. Neither is the case here.

63 [. . .] Despite the judge's best efforts to question the government's witnesses and scrutinize the documentary evidence, he or she is placed in the situation of asking questions and ultimately deciding the issues on the basis of incomplete and potentially unreliable information.

64 [. . .] The judge is therefore not in a position to compensate for the lack of informed scrutiny, challenge and counter-evidence that a person familiar with the case could bring. Such scrutiny is the whole point of the principle that a person whose liberty is in jeopardy must know the case to meet. Here that principle has not merely been limited; it has been effectively gutted. How can one meet a case one does not know?

7. Conclusion on Section 7

65 In the IRPA, an attempt has been made to meet the requirements of fundamental justice essentially through one mechanism—the designated judge charged with reviewing the certificate of inadmissibility and the detention. To Parliament's credit, a sincere attempt has been made to give the designated judge the powers necessary to discharge the role in an independent manner, based on the facts and the law. Yet, the secrecy required by the scheme denies the named person the opportunity to know the case put against him or her, and hence to challenge the government's case. This, in turn, undermines the judge's ability to come to a decision based on all the relevant facts and law. Despite the best efforts of judges of the Federal Court to breathe judicial life into the IRPA procedure, it fails to assure the fair hearing that s. 7 of the Charter requires before the state deprives a person of life, liberty or security of the person. I therefore conclude that the IRPA's procedure for determining whether a certificate is reasonable does not conform to the principles of fundamental justice as embodied in s. 7 of the Charter. The same conclusion necessarily applies to the detention review procedures under ss. 83 and 84 of the IRPA.

8. Is the Limit Justified Under Section 1 of the Charter?

66 The Charter does not guarantee rights absolutely. The state is permitted to limit rights—including the s. 7 guarantee of life, liberty and security—if it can establish that the limits are demonstrably justifiable in a free and democratic society. This said, violations of s. 7 are not easily saved by s. 1. [. . .]

The rights protected by s. 7—life, liberty, and security of the person—are basic to our conception of a free and democratic society, and hence are not easily overridden by competing social interests. It follows that violations of the principles of fundamental justice, specifically the right to a fair hearing, are difficult to justify under s. 1[. . .]. [. . .]

68 The protection of Canada's national security and related intelligence sources undoubtedly constitutes a pressing and substantial objective. [. . .] Canada is a net importer of security information. This information is essential to the security and defence of Canada, and disclosure would adversely affect its flow and quality [. . .].

This leaves the question whether the means Parliament has chosen, i.e. a certificate procedure leading to detention and deportation of non-citizens on the ground that they pose a threat to Canada's security, minimally impairs the rights of non-citizens.

69 The realities that confront modern governments faced with the challenge of terrorism are stark. In the interest of security, it may be necessary to detain persons deemed to pose a threat. At the same time, security concerns may preclude disclosure of the evidence on which the detention is based. But these tensions are not new. [...] Nor are these tensions unique to Canada: in the specific context of anti-terrorism legislation, the United Kingdom uses special counsel to provide a measure of protection to the detained person's interests, while preserving the confidentiality of information that must be kept secret. These alternatives suggest that the IRPA regime, which places on the judge the entire burden of protecting the person's interest, does not minimally impair the rights of non-citizens, and hence cannot be saved under s. 1 of the Charter.

[...]

87 I conclude that the IRPA's procedures for determining whether a certificate is reasonable and for detention review cannot be justified as minimal impairments of the individual's right to a judicial determination on the facts and the law and right to know and meet the case. Mechanisms developed in Canada and abroad illustrate that the government can do more to protect the individual while keeping critical information confidential than it has done in the IRPA. Precisely what more should be done is a matter for Parliament to decide. But it is clear that more must be done to meet the requirements of a free and democratic society.

[...]

1. Time Constraints on Review for Foreign Nationals: Breach of Section 9 or Section 10(c)?

91 The lack of review for foreign nationals until 120 days after the reasonableness of the certificate has been judicially determined violates the guarantee against arbitrary detention in s. 9 of the Charter, a guarantee which encompasses the right to prompt review of detention [...]. [...]

93 It is clear that there may be a need for some flexibility regarding the period for which a suspected terrorist may be detained. Confronted with a terrorist threat, state officials may need to act immediately, in the absence of a fully documented case. It may take some time to verify and document the threat. [...] However, this cannot justify the complete denial of a timely detention review. [...]

2. Do Extended Periods of Detention Under the Scheme Violate Section 7 or the Section 12 Guarantee Against Cruel and Unusual Treatment?

96 [...] Detention itself is never pleasant, but it is only cruel and unusual in the legal sense if it violates accepted norms of treatment. Denying the means required by the principles of fundamental justice to challenge a detention may render the detention arbitrarily indefinite and support the argument that it is cruel or unusual. [...].

105 It is thus clear that while the IRPA in principle imposes detention only pending deportation, it may in fact permit lengthy and indeterminate detention or lengthy periods subject to onerous release conditions. The next question is whether this violates s. 7 or s. 12 based on the applicable legal principles.

[...]

110 I conclude that extended periods of detention under the certificate provisions of the IRPA do not violate ss. 7 and 12 of the Charter if accompanied by a process that

provides regular opportunities for review of detention, taking into account all relevant factors, including the following:

(a) Reasons for Detention

111 [...] Detention pursuant to a certificate is justified on the basis of a continuing threat to national security or to the safety of any person. [...] The more serious the threat, the greater will be the justification for detention.

(b) Length of Detention

112 The length of the detention to date is an important factor, both from the perspective of the individual and from the perspective of national security. The longer the period, the less likely that an individual will remain a threat to security [...].

113 A longer period of detention would also signify that the government would have had more time to gather evidence establishing the nature of the threat posed by the detained person. While the government's evidentiary onus may not be heavy at the initial detention review [...], it must be heavier when the government has had more time to investigate and document the threat.

(c) Reasons for the Delay in Deportation

114 When reviewing detentions pending deportation, judges have assessed whether the delays have been caused by the detainees or the government [...]. [...] [A]n unexplained delay or lack of diligence should count against the offending party.

(d) Anticipated Future Length of Detention

115 If there will be a lengthy detention before deportation or if the future detention time cannot be ascertained, this is a factor that weighs in favour of release.

(e) Availability of Alternatives to Detention

116 Stringent release conditions [...] seriously limit individual liberty. However, they are less severe than incarceration. Alternatives to lengthy detention pursuant to a certificate, such as stringent release conditions, must not be a disproportionate response to the nature of the threat.

[...]

123 In summary, the IRPA, interpreted in conformity with the Charter, permits robust ongoing judicial review of the continued need for and justice of the detainee's detention pending deportation. [...] Thus, the IRPA procedure itself is not unconstitutional on this ground. However, this does not preclude the possibility of a judge concluding at a certain point that a particular detention constitutes cruel and unusual treatment or is inconsistent with the principles of fundamental justice, and therefore infringes the Charter in a manner that is remediable under s. 24(1) of the Charter.

124 These conclusions are consistent with English and American authority. Canada, it goes without saying, is not alone in facing the problem of detention in the immigration context in situations where deportation is difficult or impossible. Courts in the United Kingdom and the United States have suggested that detention in this context can be used only during the period where it is reasonably necessary for deportation purposes [...].

IV. Conclusion

138 The scheme set up under Division 9 of Part 1 of the IRPA suffers from two defects that are inconsistent with the Charter.

139 The first is that s. 78(g) allows for the use of evidence that is never disclosed to the named person without providing adequate measures to compensate for this

> non-disclosure and the constitutional problems it causes. It is clear from approaches adopted in other democracies, and in Canada itself in other security situations, that solutions can be devised that protect confidential security information and at the same time are less intrusive on the person's rights. It follows that the IRPA's procedure for the judicial confirmation of certificates and review of detention violates s. 7 of the Charter and has not been shown to be justified under s. 1 of the Charter. I would declare the procedure to be inconsistent with the Charter, and hence of no force or effect.
>
> [. . .]
>
> 140 However, in order to give Parliament time to amend the law, I would suspend this declaration for one year from the date of this judgment. [. . .]
>
> 141 The second defect is found in s. 84(2) of the IRPA, which denies a prompt hearing to foreign nationals by imposing a 120-day embargo, after confirmation of the certificate, on applications for release. [. . .]

This decision was hailed as a victory for the rule of law, for reconciling the state's security claims with the claims to fairness and liberty of individuals suspected of terrorism.[101] It was also hailed as an example of inter-judicial dialogue in the sphere of monitoring counter-terrorism measures.[102] The Supreme Court of Canada presented the British system of security-cleared special advocates as one of the models to be considered by the Canadian Parliament and the latter followed suit by introducing such a special advocates scheme, albeit lacking in robustness.[103] Indeed, that new scheme was also found to be problematic by the Committee against Torture, which recommended that Canada 'reconsider its policy of using administrative detention and immigration legislation to detain and remove non-citizens on the ground of national security', and that terrorism suspects be detained in the framework of criminal procedure and in accordance with the relevant international law safeguards.[104]

Secretary of State for the Home Department v MB, Appeal judgment, [2007] UKHL 46, [2008] 1 AC 440, [2007] 3 WLR 681, ILDC 825 (UK 2007), 31st October 2007, United Kingdom; House of Lords [HL]

This was a joint appeal of two similar cases of non-derogating control orders made against two terrorist suspects, MB and AF, under the 2005 Prevention of Terrorism Act. Under the terms of the orders, the freedom of movement of the suspects was severely restricted and they were, *inter alia*, obliged to live at a specific address (AF was required to remain at his flat for 14 hours each day) with further significant restrictions, to preclude their possible involvement in terrorism-related activities. Both control orders were largely based on secret evidence. The main issues before the House of Lords were whether a) the control orders constituted a criminal charge for the purposes of Article 6 ECHR; b) the withholding of closed material was consistent with the right to fair trial under Article 6 ECHR; and c) the restrictions amounted to a deprivation of liberty within the meaning of Article 5(1) ECHR.

> *Lord Bingham*
>
> 24. I would on balance accept the Secretary of State's submission that non-derogating control order proceedings do not involve the determination of a criminal charge.

---

101 K Roach, 'Section 7 of the *Charter* and National Security: Rights Protection and Proportionality versus Deference and Status' (2012) 42(3) *Ottawa Law Review* 337, 360.

102 E Benvenisti and G Downs, 'National Courts, Domestic Democracy, and the Evolution of International Law' (2009) 20(1) *European Journal of International Law* 59, 67.

103 K Roach, '*Charkaoui* and Bill C-3: Some Implications for Anti-Terrorism Policy and Dialogue between Courts and Legislatures' (2008) 42 *The Supreme Court Law Review: Osgoode's Annual Constitutional Cases Conference* 281, 284.

104 UNGA, 'Report of the Committee against Torture' (2012) UN Doc A/67/44, 118.

Parliament has gone to some lengths to avoid a procedure which crosses the criminal boundary: there is no assertion of criminal conduct, only a foundation of suspicion; no identification of any specific criminal offence is provided for; the order made is preventative in purpose, not punitive or retributive; and the obligations imposed must be no more restrictive than are judged necessary to achieve the preventative object of the order. I would reject AF's contrary submission. [...] But I would accept the substance of AF's alternative submission: in any case in which a person is at risk of an order containing obligations of the stringency found in this case or the cases of *JJ and others* and *E*, the application of the civil limb of article 6(1) does in my opinion entitle such person to such measure of procedural protection as is commensurate with the gravity of the potential consequences. This [...] seems to me to reflect the spirit of the Convention.

32. As the Secretary of State correctly submits, the Strasbourg court has repeatedly stated that the constituent rights embodied in article 6(1) are not in themselves absolute. [...] The court has not been insensitive to the special problems posed to national security by terrorism [...]. It has [...] eschewed the formulation of hard-edged and inflexible statements of principle from which no departure could be sanctioned whatever the background or the circumstances, and has recognised the need for a fair balance between the general interest of the community and the rights of the individual. But even in cases where article 6(1) has not been in issue, the court has required that the subject of a potentially adverse decision enjoy a substantial measure or degree of procedural justice [...].

35. [...] In any ordinary case, a client instructs his advocate what his defence is to the charges made against him, briefs the advocate on the weaknesses and vulnerability of the adverse witnesses, and indicates what evidence is available by way of rebuttal. This is a process which it may be impossible to adopt if the controlled person does not know the allegations made against him and cannot therefore give meaningful instructions, and the special advocate, once he knows what the allegations are, cannot tell the controlled person or seek instructions without permission, which in practice (as I understand) is not given. "Grave disadvantage" is not, I think, an exaggerated description of the controlled person's position where such circumstances obtain.

41. The Council of Europe Commissioner for Human Rights [...] and the Joint Committee on Human Rights [...] had difficulty in accepting that a hearing could be fair if an adverse decision could be based on material that the controlled person has no effective opportunity to challenge or rebut. This is not a case [...] in which the order can be justified on the strength of the open material alone. Nor is it a case in which the thrust of the case against the controlled person has been effectively conveyed to him by way of summary, redacted documents or anonymised statements. It is a case in which, on the judge's assessment which the Court of Appeal did not displace, MB was confronted by a bare, unsubstantiated assertion which he could do no more than deny. I have difficulty in accepting that MB has enjoyed a substantial measure of procedural justice, or that the very essence of the right to a fair hearing has not been impaired.

Lord Hoffman

54. [...] [T]he Strasbourg court has recognised that the right to be informed of the case against one, though important, may have to be qualified in the interests of others and the public interest. The weight to be given to these competing interests will depend upon the facts of the case, but there can in time of peace be no public interest which is more weighty than protecting the state against terrorism and, on the other hand,

the Convention rights of the individual which may be affected by the orders are all themselves qualified by the requirements of national security. There is no Strasbourg or domestic authority which has gone to the lengths of saying that the Secretary of State cannot make a non-derogating control order (or anything of the same kind) without disclosing material which a judge considers it would be contrary to the public interest to disclose. I do not think that we should put the Secretary of State in such an impossible position and I therefore agree with the Court of Appeal that in principle the special advocate procedure provides sufficient safeguards to satisfy article 6.

Baroness Hale of Richmond

65. […] We are all agreed that these are not criminal proceedings for the purpose of article 6; in ordinary civil proceedings it is appropriate to give weight to the interests of each side; nevertheless, the state is seeking to restrict the ordinary freedom of action which everyone ought to enjoy, in some cases seriously. It seems probable that Strasbourg would apply very similar principles to those applicable in criminal proceedings, but would be more inclined to hold that the measures taken by the judicial authorities had been sufficient to protect the interests of the controlled person. It would all depend upon the nature of the case; what steps had been taken to explain the detail of the allegations to the controlled person so that he could anticipate what the material in support might be; what steps had been taken to summarise the closed material in support without revealing names, dates or places; the nature and content of the material withheld; how effectively the special advocate had been able to challenge it on behalf of the controlled person; and what difference its disclosure might have made. All of these factors would be relevant to whether the controlled person had been "given a meaningful opportunity to contest the factual basis" for the order: see *Hamdi v Rumsfeld* 542 US 507 (2004), 509, col 2, O'Connor J.

66. I do not think that we can be confident that Strasbourg would hold that every control order hearing in which the special advocate procedure had been used, as contemplated by the 2005 Act and Part 76 of the Civil Procedure Rules, would be sufficient to comply with article 6. However, with strenuous efforts from all, difficult and time consuming though it will be, it should usually be possible to accord the controlled person "a substantial measure of procedural justice". Everyone involved will have to do their best to ensure that the "principles of judicial inquiry" are complied with to the fullest extent possible. […]

70. […] If, despite all the efforts of the judge and the special advocates to ensure that there is a fair hearing, the judge determines that the hearing cannot be fair unless more material is disclosed, the convention rights require that he be in a position to quash the order. On the face of it, therefore, section 3(13) of the Act may on occasions produce a result which is incompatible with the convention rights. However, this will not be so in every case. Indeed, my view is that the procedures can be made to work fairly and compatibly in many cases. […]

Lord Brown

89. AF's control order subjected him to a fourteen hour curfew. […] I do not regard that as involving a sufficient degree of physical confinement to constitute a deprivation of liberty as opposed to a restriction of AF's freedom of movement. Plainly it is a very severe restriction on that freedom and by virtue of that restriction together with the various additional restrictions inherent in the other conditions and circumstances of AF's order it interferes too with a number of AF's Convention rights (most notably perhaps those under articles 8, 9 and 10). But these are all qualified rights (as too would be AF's right to freedom of movement had the UK in fact conferred it upon

him by ratifying Protocol 4) and it is noteworthy that neither AF nor, indeed, any of the other appellants before your Lordships have sought to challenge the justification for these various restrictions nor their proportionality. I accordingly agree with all your Lordships that the Secretary of State's appeal should succeed on this aspect of AF's case.

90. […] I agree further that the special advocate procedure, highly likely though it is that it will in fact safeguard the suspect against significant injustice, cannot invariably be guaranteed to do so. There may perhaps be cases, wholly exceptional though they are likely to be, where, despite the best efforts of all concerned by way of redaction, anonymisation, and gisting, it will simply be impossible to indicate sufficient of the Secretary of State's case to enable the suspect to advance any effective challenge to it. […] In short, the suspect in such a case would not have been accorded even "a substantial measure of procedural justice" (*Chahal v United Kingdom* (1996) 23 EHRR 413 at para 131) notwithstanding the use of the special advocate procedure; "the very essence of [his] right [to a fair hearing] [will have been] impaired" (*Tinnelly & Sons Ltd and McElduff and others v United Kingdom* (1998) 27 EHRR 249, para 72).

91. I cannot accept that a suspect's entitlement to an essentially fair hearing is merely a qualified right capable of being outweighed by the public interest in protecting the state against terrorism (vital though, of course, I recognise that public interest to be). On the contrary, it seems to me not merely an absolute right but one of altogether too great importance to be sacrificed on the altar of terrorism control. By the same token that evidence derived from the use of torture must always be rejected so as to safeguard the integrity of the judicial process and avoid bringing British justice into disrepute […], so too in my judgment must closed material be rejected if reliance on it would necessarily result in a fundamentally unfair hearing.

Control orders against terrorist suspects, including UK nationals, were enacted in the UK in 2005 as a key anti-terrorism measure when prosecution or deportation appeared not to be available options. They superseded the indefinite detentions without trial of foreign nationals suspected of terrorism, which were introduced in the aftermath of 9/11 in derogation from the right to liberty under Article 5 ECHR. That derogation was found by the House of Lords to be incompatible with the ECHR in the famous *Belmarsh Detainees* case.[105] The control orders scheme was substantially a 'pre-emptive' system operating alongside the criminal justice approach.[106] In effect, the orders amounted to a form of severe punishment (more severe than most criminal penalties), yet imposed without conviction. This entailed that the normal criminal standard of proof (that is, beyond reasonable doubt) was bypassed and reliance was heavily placed on secret evidence, commonly from intelligence sources, while the only remnant of due process—itself dubious—was the special advocates scheme.[107] Despite purporting to be compliant with Article 5 (hence control orders were labelled as *non-derogating*), the scheme was criticized for diluting the rights to liberty and fair trial, and amounting to covert or unacknowledged derogations from Articles 5 and 6 of the ECHR.[108]

Two other judgments on control orders were delivered on the same day: *Secretary of State for the Home Department v JJ*, which concerned an eighteen-hour curfew and other severe

105 *A v Secretary of State for the Home Department*, [2004] UKHL 56, [2005] 2 AC 68.

106 L Zedner, 'Preventive Justice or Pre-punishment? The Case of Control Orders' (2007) 60 *Current Legal Problems* 174.

107 H Fenwick and G Phillipson, 'Covert Derogations and Judicial Deference: Redefining Liberty and Due Process Rights in Counterterrorism Law and Beyond' (2011) 56(4) *McGill Law Journal* 863, 878.

108 ibid, 869, 878.

restrictions,[109] and *Secretary of State for the Home Department v E*,[110] concerning less onerous restrictions, including a twelve-hour curfew. They were followed by *Secretary of State for the Home Department v AF (No 3)*,[111] which revisited the present decision with respect to AF owing to divergent opinions by lower courts, and *Secretary of State for the Home Department v AP*,[112] which was decided by the UK Supreme Court and concerned a 16-hour home confinement and other restrictions.

Turning to the first substantive issue, as observed by the ILDC reporter, the implication of the conclusion that control orders were 'on balance' considered to be preventative measures not involving the determination of a criminal charge, but did engage Article 6 ECHR under its civil head, was that the presumption of innocence under Article 6(2) ECHR did not apply.[113] This conclusion seemed to accord with the case law of the ECtHR but that case law was rather dated and underdeveloped.[114]

Secondly, the key due process issue under Article 6 ECHR was the heavy reliance on secret evidence and the special advocates scheme, the principal deficiency being that the advocates could not take any instructions from the suspects after they have seen the closed material and thus they could not challenge the material based on such instructions.[115] The majority of the Lords in the decision at hand stopped short of considering such scheme as incompatible with Article 6, by holding, somewhat inconclusively, that procedural fairness was fact-specific and could still be achieved in most (but not all) cases even without a minimum disclosure of evidence.[116] This issue was resolved in *A v UK* (the Strasbourg sequel of *Belmarsh Detainees*), where a unanimous Grand Chamber of the ECtHR ruled that a minimum disclosure of the case to the suspect was required and held that due process was not satisfied when 'the open material consisted purely of general assertions and [the] decision […] was based solely or to a decisive degree on closed material';[117] the special advocates could not perform their important function in any useful way 'unless the detainee was provided with sufficient information about the allegations against him to enable him to give effective instructions to the special advocate'.[118] This ruling was unanimously accepted by a nine-judge panel of the House of Lords (albeit reluctantly by some Lords) in *AF (No 3)*.

Lastly, on the impact of control orders on the right to liberty, the House of Lords in the instant case found unanimously that the 14-hour curfew did not amount to a breach of Article 5 ECHR. Indeed, the combined effect of the House of Lords and the UK Supreme Court relevant case law was that control orders imposing daily curfews of 16 hours or less and other restrictions would 'on balance' be compatible with Article 5 ECHR, provided that the overall impact of such restrictions did not have a particularly severe effect on the affected individuals amounting to extreme social isolation.[119] These findings were criticized as incompatible with the ECHR, for focusing too strongly on the idea of physical restraint analogous to an arrest and on specific

109 [2007] UKHL 45, [2008] 1 AC 385.
110 [2007] UKHL 47, [2008] 1 AC 499.
111 [2009] UKHL 28, [2010] 2 AC 269.
112 [2010] UKSC 24, [2010] 3 WLR 51.
113 M Ramsden, Analysis, *Secretary of State for the Home Department v MB*, ILDC 825 (UK 2007) A1.
114 E Bates, 'Anti-Terrorism Control Orders: Liberty and Security Still in the Balance' (2009) 29(1) *Legal Studies* 99, 111.
115 Fenwick and Phillipson (n 107) 892, 897.
116 ibid, 900; Bates (n 114) 113. Lord Bingham was the only one prepared to declare the scheme incompatible with Article 6 ECHR, whereas Lord Hoffmann's dissent fully accepted the position of the government.
117 ECtHR, *A v UK*, App No 3455/05 (19 February 2009) para 220. That judgment found violations of the ECHR in relation to the detention powers under the 2001 anti-terrorism Act, but was of direct relevance to control orders as well.
118 ibid.
119 Fenwick and Phillipson (n 107) 882; Bates (n 114) 105.

periods of house restrictions, and thus disregarding the more holistic notion of degrees of restriction and their overall impact on normal life, as emphasized by the ECtHR in various cases.[120]

Partly because of this domestic and Strasbourg jurisprudence, control orders were superseded in 2012 by the Terrorism Prevention and Investigation Measures (TPIMs), which made improvements to the former scheme and were hailed as a positive development for addressing Strasbourg standards,[121] even though TPIMs remained outside of the criminal justice system. Yet, the enactment of the Counter-Terrorism and Security Act in 2015, which reintroduced some of the repressive measures of the former scheme, has demonstrated that despite judicial efforts since 9/11 the 'pre-emptive' system based on executive measures of dubious compatibility with the ECHR standards continues unabated alongside the various criminal justice responses to terrorism.[122]

IV. Conclusion

This survey of domestic decisions on terrorism focused on the controversial question of the definition and scope of terrorism in international law and the impact of counter-terrorism on human rights. Admittedly, the sample is relatively small compared to the anti-terrorism litigation across the globe and comes mostly from countries with strong independent judiciary. A more complete account of how domestic courts respond to terrorism in other contexts could paint a different picture. Thus, some caution is required before drawing any firm conclusions. What is more, this chapter should be read in conjunction with the terrorism cases in the chapter on international humanitarian law, as well as that on the use of force.

The case law on definitional issues has reaffirmed the divergent approaches on the definition and scope of terrorism and reflects the inability of the international community to reach consensus on a generally accepted precise definition of terrorism. Some courts have relied on the definition of the 1999 International Convention for the Suppression of the Financing of Terrorism for the core elements of terrorism but others have questioned its pertinence. Some courts have also ruled that a certain degree of imprecision in the definition of terrorism is compatible with the principle of legality. Overall, such variety reinforces the need for the speedy adoption of a generally accepted definition of terrorism to help improve counterterrorism cooperation and diminish instances of misusing the term and its adverse consequences on human rights.

When it comes to the impact of terrorism on human rights, there is more clarity, which has been fostered by the case law of supranational courts that have helped refine and clarify the proper scope of human rights and their limitations in the fight against terrorism. This is most notably the case with the impact of Security Council anti-terrorism measures on human rights and the decisive influence of the CJEU as well as the ECtHR. After some ambivalence, it is now established that domestic courts can review domestic implementing legislation under human rights norms. The ECtHR and UN treaty bodies have also cemented the absolute character of the prohibition of torture, which has helped many domestic courts resist efforts to undermine it. This is also the case with non-refoulement although the widespread practice of diplomatic assurances, despite efforts in Europe to streamline it, allows leeway to the executive to make determinations that may put in risk the human rights of affected individuals. This is particularly the case when there is no credible international or domestic monitoring.

The decisions on the impact of terrorism on human rights are illustrative of the role of (domestic) courts and (international) human rights law in highly politicized contexts involving

120 Fenwick and Phillipson (n 107) 885.

121 H Fenwick, 'Designing ETPIMs around ECHR Review or Normalisation of 'Preventive' Non-Trial-Based Executive Measures?' (2013) 76 *Modern Law Review* 876, 907.

122 See also C R G Murray, 'Nudging or Fudging? The UK Courts' Counterterrorism Jurisprudence since 9/11' (2016) 21 *Journal of Conflict and Security Law* 91, 113.

security issues. They exhibit both the emancipatory potential of international human rights law as an effective tool for judicial check on executive action but also the legitimating effect that the law and the judiciary can have in clothing counterterrorism with legal authority through various means such as (excessive) judicial deference to the executive or executive-friendly reading of relevant norms. In this vein, it is noteworthy that, despite the gains from a rule of law perspective, international human rights law has been largely absent from the US decisions concerning the Guantanamo detainees.

As in other fields of international law, the value of the decisions on terrorism (and human rights) for the relevant international norms is rather uneven, some courts having made much more elaborate and sophisticated use and analysis of international (human rights) law than others.

15

Substantive International Criminal Law

HARMEN VAN DER WILT, J CRAIG BARKER, AND BEA MYERS

I. Introduction

This chapter is concerned with the application of international criminal law in domestic courts. The first section concerns the direct application of international criminal law provisions. Whereas national jurisdictions (and human rights provisions in international treaties) require criminal prosecutions and trials to be sustained by explicit standards, the question arises whether international conventional provisions or standards of customary international law can serve that purpose. Closely related to this issue is the question whether the prohibition of the retroactive application of (criminal) law can be mitigated by relying on international sources. This section explores national case law addressing hierarchical relations between the national and international legal order, in connection with the *nullum crimen sine lege* principle.

The second section of the chapter will focus on the application and interpretation of substantive international criminal law in domestic courts. Particular focus will be given to the core crimes of genocide,[1] crimes against humanity,[2] and war crimes,[3] as defined in the Statute of the International Criminal Court. Article 17 of the Rome Statute of the International Criminal Court deals with the issue of complementarity, according to which a case is inadmissible if it 'is being [or has been] investigated or prosecuted by a State which has jurisdiction over it, unless the State is unwilling or unable genuinely to carry out the investigation or prosecution'.[4] The implication of the decision to adopt the principle of complementarity in the Rome Statute is that it is expected that the majority of prosecutions of international criminal law will take place in domestic courts. Nevertheless, although the ICC Statute entered into force with the creation of the ICC in July 2002, the number of domestic prosecutions has not been substantial. Many prosecutions in domestic courts have failed through lack of jurisdiction,[5] and others as a result of other processes such as amnesties and immunities.[6] Furthermore, the prosecution of war crimes within a domestic context are most often undertaken by courts-martial or their equivalent, which are not part of the ILDC process and so do not feature within this chapter. On the other hand, consideration of issues of substantive international criminal law arises not only in criminal proceedings, but can also arise within the domestic context in cases relating, for example, to immigration and deportation. Accordingly, this chapter provides an early analysis of what may become, in the future, a particularly important area of the application of international law in domestic courts.

1 Rome Statute of the International Criminal Court (adopted 17 July 1998, entered into force 1 July 2002) 2187 UNTS 3, Article 6.

2 ibid, Article 7.

3 ibid, Article 8.

4 ibid, Article 17(1)(a).

5 See C Ryngaert, H van der Wilt, and J Santos Vara, 'Jurisdiction' Chapter 3 in this volume.

6 See C Martin, 'Amnesty Laws in Latin-America and the Principles of Accountability developed by the Inter-American Human Rights System' Chapter 16 and R Pavoni, R van Alebeek, 'Immunities of States and their Officials' Chapter 4 in this volume.

II. Direct Application of International Law and the *Nullum Crimen* Principle

Hamdan v United States, Appeal judgment, ILDC 2022 (US 2012), 696 F 3d 1238 (DC Cir 2012), 16th October 2012, United States; Court of Appeals (DC Circuit) [DC Cir]

Hamdan was a member of Al-Qaeda and served as personal driver and bodyguard of Osama bin Laden. After the terrorist attacks on the Twin Towers in September 2001, he was captured in Afghanistan in November 2001 and transferred to the United States. Hamdan was charged and convicted by a military commission for having provided 'material support for terrorism' which was qualified as a war crime under the Military Commission Act of 2006. He was detained at Guantanamo Bay as an 'unlawful enemy combatant'.

Hamdan appealed the verdict. As the Court of Appeals concluded that the Military Commission Act had no retroactive effect and the incriminating acts took place between 1996 and 2001, the court had to ascertain whether 'material support for terrorism' constituted a war crime under international law. Only in this way could the conviction be upheld. The Court of Appeals found that it did not.

> **57** We turn, then, to the question whether material support for terrorism is an international-law war crime.
>
> **58** It is true that international law establishes at least some forms of terrorism, including the intentional targeting of civilian populations, as war crimes. See, e.g., Rome Statute of the International Criminal Court art. 8(2)(b), July 17, 1998, 2187 U.N.T.S. 90; Geneva Convention Relative to the Protection of Civilian Persons in Time of War (Geneva IV), art. 33, Aug. 12, 1949, 6 U.S.T. 3516, 75 U.N.T.S. 287; COMMISSION OF RESPONSIBILITIES, CONFERENCE OF PARIS 1919, VIOLATION OF THE LAWS AND CUSTOMS OF WAR 17 (Clarendon Press 1919) (the Allied Nations condemned Germany for "the execution of a system of terrorism" after World War I).
>
> **59** But the issue here is whether material support for terrorism is an international-law war crime. The answer is no. International law leaves it to individual nations to proscribe material support for terrorism under their domestic laws if they so choose. There is no international-law proscription of material support for terrorism.
>
> **60** To begin with, there are no relevant international treaties that make material support for terrorism a recognized international-law war crime. Neither the Hague Convention nor the Geneva Conventions—the sources that are "the major treaties on the law of war"—acknowledge material support for terrorism as a war crime. See Hamdan, 548 U.S. at 604, 126 S.Ct. 2749 (plurality); Geneva Convention Relative to the Protection of Civilian Persons in Time of War (Geneva IV), Aug. 12, 1949, 6 U.S.T. 3516, 75 U.N.T.S. 287; Hague Convention (IV) Respecting the Laws and Customs of War on Land and Its Annex, Oct. 18, 1907, 36 Stat. 2277.
>
> **61** Nor does customary international law otherwise make material support for terrorism a war crime. Customary international law is a kind of common law; it is the body of international legal principles said to reflect the consistent and settled practice of nations. See RESTATEMENT (THIRD) OF FOREIGN RELATIONS LAW OF THE UNITED STATES § 102(2) (1987) ("Customary international law results from a general and consistent practice of states followed by them from a sense of legal obligation"). It is often difficult to determine what constitutes customary international law, who defines customary international law, and how firmly established a norm has to be to qualify as a customary international law norm. Cf. Sosa v. Alvarez-Machain, 542 U.S. 692, 124 S.Ct. 2739, 159 L.Ed.2d 718 (2004).10

62 But here, the content of customary international law is quite evident. Material support for terrorism was not a recognized violation of the international law of war as of 2001 (or even today, for that matter). As we have noted, the Geneva Conventions and the Hague Convention do not prohibit material support for terrorism. The 1998 Rome Statute of the International Criminal Court, which catalogues an extensive list of international war crimes, makes no mention of material support for terrorism. See Rome Statute of the International Criminal Court, July 17, 1998, 2187 U.N.T.S. 90. Nor does the Statute of the International Tribunal for the Former Yugoslavia, the Statute of the International Tribunal for Rwanda, or the Statute of the Special Court for Sierra Leone. See Statute of the International Tribunal for the Former Yugoslavia, adopted by S.C. Res. 827, U.N. Doc. S/RES/827 (1993), reprinted in 32 I.L.M. 1159, 1192; Statute of the International Tribunal for Rwanda, adopted by S.C. Res. 955, U.N. Doc. S/RES/955 (1994), reprinted in 33 I.L.M. 1598, 1602 (includes terrorism itself as a crime); Statute of the Special Court for Sierra Leone art. 3(d), Jan. 16, 2002, 2178 U.N.T.S. 138 (same). Nor have any international tribunals exercising common-law-type power determined that material support for terrorism is an international-law war crime.

(. . .)

64 In short, neither the major conventions on the law of war nor prominent modern international tribunals nor leading international-law experts have identified material support for terrorism as a war crime. Perhaps most telling, before this case, no person has ever been tried by an international-law war crimes tribunal for material support for terrorism.

The case is interesting because it reveals the strong position of customary international law as a basis for criminal responsibility in the US legal system. The fact that any retroactive application of the Military Commissions Act would infringe the *nullum crimen* principle could be 'repaired' by the direct application of international (customary) law. However, the Court of Appeal did not find that 'material support of terrorism' was a war crime under international law, not at the time of commission, nor in 2012. The court indicated that 'aiding and abetting' of terrorism could qualify as a war crime (when committed during an armed conflict), but Hamdan had not been charged with aiding and abetting. In his concurring opinion, Judge Ginsburg wryly observed that Hamdan would not be able to benefit from this judgment, as he had long since been transferred to Yemen.

Public Prosecutor (on behalf of Behram (Hussein) and ors) v Arklöf (Jackie), Judgment, Case No B 4084-04, ILDC 633 (SE 2006), 18th December 2006, Sweden

The Swedish national Jackie Arklöf went to the Balkans in 1993 and served in a military unit of the Croatian Council of Defence. On his return, he was accused of and stood trial for having committed war crimes in a non-international armed conflict. The relevant question was whether criminal responsibility for war crimes could be imposed on the basis of a reference in a domestic penal code to customary international law.

The circumstances of the case related to a non-international armed conflict. The threshold requirement concerning the intensity of the conflict was also reached. Hence, the only applicable treaty-based provisions were Common Article 3 of the Geneva Conventions, 1949 and Additional Protocol II concerning non-international armed conflicts. In addition, several rules in international humanitarian law were applicable in the case on the basis of custom. Rules that were considered to have customary status in non-international armed conflicts included Article 18 of the Geneva Convention relative to the Treatment of Prisoners of War (12 August 1949) 75 UNTS 135, entered into force 21 October 1950 ('Geneva Convention III'), Articles 33, 78, and 95 of Geneva Convention relative to the

> Protection of Civilian Persons in Time of War (12 August 1949) 75 UNTS 287, entered into force 21 October 1950 ('Geneva Convention IV') and the grave breaches provisions in Article 130 of Geneva Convention III, Article 147 of Geneva Convention IV, and Additional Protocol I, Article 85. (paragraphs 124-39).
>
> Most of the counts were proven, and Jackie Arklöf was found guilty on counts concerning violence to life and person, humiliating and degrading treatment, torture (Common Article 3 and Article 4 of Additional Protocol II), unlawful confinement (Article 78 of Geneva Convention IV), employment of prisoners in work of humiliating and degrading character (Article 95 of Geneva Convention IV), inadequate care of prisoners, (Article 5 of Additional Protocol II), forced movements of civilians (Article 17 of Additional Protocol II), disrespecting the protection of women (Article 76 of Additional Protocol I), and pillage (Article 133 of Geneva Convention IV and Article 4 of Additional Protocol II). These provisions constituted customary international law, were applicable in both international and internal armed conflicts, and provided the basis for criminal responsibility. Criminal responsibility for war crimes could be imposed on the basis of a reference in a domestic penal code to customary international law. (paragraphs 138, 142-63).

The Swedish court thus applied customary international law, in the cloak of domestic law, as an adequate basis for criminal conviction. In this respect, the commentator observed:

> 'The judgment was interesting in two respects. First, the Swedish legal system had traditionally been described as dualist—where international law and, more specifically, treaties were mainly implemented through transformation, but also through incorporation. As the Swedish Penal Code illustrates, [. . .] parts of customary law could be incorporated into Swedish law by reference (*renvoi*). Second, Sweden, like many other states, subscribed to the principle of legality, at the core of which were the requirements on specificity, non-retroactivity, foreseeability, and accessibility of the law. Chapter 22, section 6, provided that a violation of "a generally recognized principle or tenet relating to international humanitarian law concerning armed conflicts" constituted a crime. This provision and the present case brought to the fore questions about foreseeability and accessibility of the law, as illustrated by the fact that the court based part of Arklöf's criminal responsibility on customary principles. For example, with reference to an ICRC study on customary international humanitarian law, the court included unlawful confinement among the acts constituting war crimes in a non-international armed conflict'.[7]

Military Prosecutor v Massaba (Blaise Bongi), Criminal trial judgment and accompanying civil action for damages, RP No 018/2006, RMP No 242/PEN/06, ILDC 387 (CD 2006), 24th March 2006, Congo, The Democratic Republic of the; Ituri; Military Tribunal

On 24 October 2005, Blaise Massaba, a captain in the Congolese army, and a group of soldiers under his command, arrested five pupils and stole goods belonging to civilians at various locations in Ituri, a district in eastern DRC. Later that same day, Blaise Massaba ordered his soldiers to shoot the victims on the pretext that the pupils were members of the armed militias in eastern DRC. The soldiers obeyed and shot the victims and buried their corpses.

The military prosecutor of the Military Tribunal of Ituri instituted criminal proceedings against Blaise Massaba. He was charged with the war crimes of willful killing and pillaging, as provided for in Article 8(2)(b)(xvi) and 8(2)(a)(i), respectively, of the Rome Statute of the

7 M Klamberg, Analysis, *Public Prosecutor (on behalf of Behram (Hussein) and ors) v Arklöf (Jackie)*, ILDC 633 (SE 2006) A2.

International Criminal Court and the Congolese military penal code. The DRC had ratified the Rome Statute in 2002.

61 Whereas, by a referral decision of the Garrison Military Public Prosecutor, two charges falling under the jurisdiction of the International Criminal Court have been referred to the Military Tribunal of the Ituri Garrison; the charges were war crimes such as are provided for in Article 8(2)(b)(xvi) and Article 77 on the one hand, and, on the other, in Article 8(2)(a)(i) and Article 77 of the Rome Statute of the International Criminal Court of 17 July 1998;

62 Whereas, this Statute applies to the crimes of genocide, crimes against humanity and war crimes committed since 1 July 2002, but not to the crimes of aggression until such time as these are defined;

63 Whereas, the Democratic Republic of Congo ratified this statute by Decree-Law no 0013/002 of 30 March 2002;

64 Whereas, Articles 161–175 of the Military Penal Code of 18 November 2002, Law no 024/2002, provide for the crimes of genocide, crimes against humanity and war crimes;

65 Whereas, in consequence, the subject matter competence of the International Criminal Court is not exclusive, not only by virtue of the principles of complementarity and subsidiarity of that court in relation to national courts, but in the sense that a reading of the Statute shows that national courts are preferred to the ICC, which intervenes only on the conditions determined in that Statute;

66 Whereas, however, the Congolese national legislation, in this case the Military Penal Code of 18 November 2002, in force since 30 March 2003, contains a glaring omission in that it does not sanction war crimes, for which there is no penalty;

67 Whereas, clearly, the Congolese legislator had absolutely no intention of allowing this atrocious crime to go unpunished, having recognised its great gravity by ratifying the Rome Statute of the International Criminal Court;

68 Whereas, consequently, the failure to penalise this crime is in fact a purely accidental error (see Articles 173–175 of Law no 024/2002 of 18 November 2002 providing for war crimes, an omission that has led certain Congolese military criminal law experts, in particular Frank Mulenda, to declare that the crime of genocide, crimes against humanity and war crimes provided for by the Military Penal Code have no relation to the Rome Statute; consequently, jurisdiction in this particular case is not essentially based on the recognition of these serious crimes by the Military Penal Code);

69 Whereas, according to Article 2 of the Military Penal Code, "no offence may be punished by a penalty that had not been laid down by the law before the offence was committed";

70 In this case, this national law has never laid down a penalty for war crimes, not even by the mechanism of referral;

71 Whereas, in these conditions, there is good reason for seeking to bridge these gaps in the national legislation by relying on the Rome Statute of the International Criminal Court ratified by the DRC, in order better to attain the Congolese legislator's objective of having war crimes punished by national military courts (see point VII of the preamble to Laws 023 and 024/2002 of 18 November 2002 in the Official Journal of the RDC, in its special issue of 30 March 2003);

72 Article 215 of the DRC constitution promulgated on 18 February 2006 stipulates that "legally concluded international treaties and agreements shall, once published, have an authority superior to that of the laws, provided that each treaty or agreement is applied by the other party";

73 For this reason, in its interlocutory judgment in case RP no 086/05, RMP 279/GMZ/WAB/2005, delivered on 12 January 2006, the Military Tribunal of the Mbandaka Garrison, to which a case concerning crimes against humanity provided for in Article 166 of the Military Penal Code had been referred, decided to investigate and try this charge in accordance with the provisions and penalties of the Rome Statute, which it deemed to be more clearly defined, better suited in that, unlike the Military Penal Code, it contains mechanisms to protect the rights of victims, and less severe in the penalties imposed in that it does not recognise the death penalty;

74 These reasons justify the public prosecutor in this case who, in his official capacity, has referred to the Rome Statute. The ratification of the Statute by the DRC makes it part of the legal fabric of the law of the Democratic Republic of Congo, by virtue of legal monism with primacy accorded to international law, in this instance the ICC Statute, which inspired the introduction into the Military Penal Code of the crimes falling within the competence of the Statute;

Courts of the DRC have, on several occasions, displayed an open and receptive attitude towards international (criminal) law. The monist system, as embodied by Article 215 of the DRC constitution, enables courts to apply self-executing norms of international law directly, superseding any conflicting national statutes. In the case under scrutiny, the military court applied the Rome Statute in order to fill the gaps in domestic law. In other judgments, the courts simply ignored the Military Code, arguing that the Rome Statute contained more precise definitions, was more accommodating to the interests of the victims or provided for more lenient punishment.[8] It is questionable whether in these cases international law standards really conflicted with domestic law. After all, as long as domestic law does not prescribe the imposition of capital punishment, prosecutors and courts alike are allowed to resort to the more lenient standards under international law.

Supreme State Prosecutor v Ribičič (Mitja), Order on Whether to Open Pre-Trial Criminal Investigation, Ks 962/2006, ILDC 523 (SI 2006), 27th June 2006, Slovenia; Ljubljana; Regional Court

Eighty-six year old Ribičič was suspected of having ordered the murder of 217 people without trial while he was deputy head of the Slovenian branch of the Yugoslav communist secret service 'OZNA'. As the dreadful event had occurred in the aftermath of the Second World War, the legal issue before the court was whether crimes against the civilian population, criminalized in Article 374 of the Criminal Code, could also be committed in time of peace.

21 The disposition of Article 374 of the Penal Code of the Republic of Slovenia, before its amendments in 2004, defines war crimes against civil populations in the time of war, armed conflict or occupation; but, as was already stated, in this context of evaluation it is important to take into consideration the quoted Charter of the International Military Tribunal at Nuremberg and the Decree

8 cf *Ituri District Military Prosecutor v Kahwa Panga Mandro*, First Instant Decision, RMP No 227/PEN/2006; ILDC 524 (CD 2006), 2 August 2006 and *Mbandaka Garrison Military Prosecutor v Kahenga Mumbere et al* RP 086/005 12 January 2006; not published.

ratifying the Convention on the Non-Applicability of Statutory Limitations to War Crimes and Crimes Against Humanity. The quoted provisions on the one hand show that these two international treaties define the punishability of and the non-applicability of statutory limitations also for crimes against humanity which were committed in time of peace and on the other hand place themselves above provisions of national legal systems in the sense that they determine the punishability when such offences do not represent a violation of the national laws of the country in which the offence was committed. Here we should mention that the provision of Article 4 of the Convention on the Non-Applicability of Statutory Limitations to War Crimes and Crimes Against Humanity imposes the obligation on State Parties to adopt, in accordance with their own constitutional procedures, all legislative and other measures needed to ensure that the legislative and other provisions on statutory limitations do not apply to the prosecution and punishment of crimes under Article 1 and 2 of the Convention and that any such provisions on statutory limitation are nullified. The State Parties, one of which was the former Yugoslavia, and the Republic of Slovenia adopted the international treaties which were signed by Yugoslavia and which pertain to the Republic of Slovenia, which have therefore accepted the obligation that they will, also in the subsequent legislative provisions, enable the prosecution of criminal offences, including crimes against humanity as defined by the aforementioned international treaties.'

(...)

23 From the Convention for the Protection of Human Rights and Fundamental Freedoms and its additional Protocols, the Act of Ratification of which is published in the Official Gazette of the Republic of Slovenia—international treaties, No 7/1994, an exception to the principle of legality in Article 7 arises. Paragraph 1 of the mentioned provision states that no one shall be convicted of any offence committed by acting or refraining from acting that was not defined as a criminal offence under national or international law at the time that it was committed. Furthermore, a sentence higher than prescribed at the time the offence was committed shall not be pronounced. However paragraph 2 of the same Article states that the Article is not an obstacle for the trial and punishment of persons for committing an act or refraining from acting which at the time when it was committed was punishable under the general principles of law recognised by civilised nations. Mutatis mutandis provide the provisions of Article 15 of the International Covenant on Civil and Political Rights, the Act of Ratification of which was published in the Official Gazette of SFRY, No 7/1971. This provision in paragraph 1 states that no one shall be convicted of offences or omissions which were not defined as a criminal offence under national or international law at the time they were committed. Furthermore, a higher sentence than would be pronounced at the time the offence was committed shall not be pronounced. If legislation defines a lighter sentence for the offence committed the perpetrator shall benefit from it. Paragraph 2 of the same Article states that the provisions of this Article do not prevent anyone from being convicted of an offence or omission which was, at the time it was committed or refrained from, defined as punishable under the general principles of law recognised by civilised nations. In both cases we are dealing with international conventions which are part of the Slovenian legal system and are so applied.

(...)

24 The international community has therefore, by proceeding from protecting basic human rights (to life, personal freedom, equality, etc.), developed and amended international humanitarian law. With reference to the provisions on prosecution of such criminal offences, it allowed for exceptions to the principle of legality because of the realisations, which are included in the preambles to different international treaties, that these are important provisions which should ensure protection of these rights and that the protection of the rights of the victims of crimes against humanity and international law are even stronger than the principle of legality, but it has to be stated at the same time that this does not mean that the law, national or international, should not consider the rights of suspects. The International Covenant on Civil and Political Rights and the Convention for the Protection of Human Rights and Fundamental Freedoms, with additional Protocols, are international legal acts adopted at the level of the United Nations (the Covenant …) and the Council of Europe (the Convention …) which continue and complement what is written in the Martens clause (which, as already stated, appears in connection with laws of war, but international treaties also developed in the direction of proscribing crimes against humanity committed in time of peace). Therefore, this is confirmation of the fact that there exist some general principles of law recognised by civilised nations which allow for exceptions to the principle of legality.

(…)

27 From the judgment of the Constitutional Court of the Republic of Slovenia, ref. no. U-1-6/93, of 01 April 1994, invoked by the charges and by the Motion of the investigating judge, when it ruled upon the use of provisions from the Decree on War Courts of 05 May 1944, it can be concluded that in constitutional and legal practices in the Republic of Slovenia it is permitted to use as a legal source the principles of law recognised by civilised nations. From this ruling it arises that in the Republic of Slovenia the provisions of the Decree on War Courts of 05 May 1944 that are not used are those which were, already at the time of drafting and use of the Decree, in breach of the general principles of law as recognised by civilised nations and are also in breach of the Constitution of the Republic of Slovenia. Such a judgment by the Constitutional Court of the Republic of Slovenia is also an additional argument which even further convinces this Senate that those provisions of the international treaties which were adopted by acts of ratification and which establish exceptions to the principle of legality by invoking the general principles of law recognised by civilised nations are not in breach of the Constitution of the Republic of Slovenia.

(…)

32 In this case, the Constitutional Court of the Republic of Slovenia used the provision of paragraph 2 of Article 15 of the ratified International Covenant on Civil and Political Rights, as already quoted in the Explanation of the Decision by this Senate. At the time the judgment by the Constitutional Court of the Republic of Slovenia was issued, the European Convention for the Protection of Human Rights and Fundamental Freedoms was not yet ratified and nevertheless, the Constitutional Court of the Republic of Slovenia invoked the suitable formulation and logically the same provisions as in paragraph 3 of Article 7 of this Convention. The Constitutional Court of the Republic of Slovenia explicitly stated in point 20 of the Explanation that the aforementioned provision of the ratified international treaty (referring to the provision of paragraph 2, Article 15 of the

> International Covenant ...) are binding on Slovenia in accordance with Article 8 of its Constitution, and the general principles of law invoked in the ratified treaty as interpreted here by this Senate prohibit retroactive proscription of all other offences which are not the subject of the quoted international treaties. Therefore, it can be concluded that in some cases, as assessed by this Senate, including the alleged criminal offence, an exception to the principle of legality or a prohibition of retroactivity as described in the ratified international treaties may be considered permissible.

Although Slovenian criminal law recognized 'crimes against humanity' as a separate category at the time of the massacre, the national interpretation at that time followed the well-known Nuremberg limitation, requiring a temporal link with armed conflict. The application of the Criminal Code (as amended in 2004), which had abolished the limitation, therefore implied an expansion to the detriment of the accused, which would normally be precluded by the prohibition of retroactive application. The court had to rely on Articles 7(2) of the European Convention on Human Rights and 15(2) of the International Covenant on Civil and Political Rights which allowed an exception to such a prohibition if a trial and conviction could be predicated on 'general principles of international law recognized by all civilized nations'.

Erdal (Fehriye) v Council of Ministers (Ministerraad), Decision, Decision No 73/2005, ILDC 9 (BE 2005), 20th April 2005, Belgium; Constitutional Court

Belgium had refused the Turkish request for extradition of Fehriye Erdal, whose surrender was sought on the charge of possession of illegal arms, invoking the political offence exception. Alternatively, Belgium sought to prosecute Mrs Erdal for offences, mentioned in Article 2 of the European Convention on the Suppression of Terrorism, but the courts lacked the necessary—extraterritorial—jurisdiction. In order to remove that obstacle, the Belgian legislature adopted an Act granting the Belgian courts jurisdiction over the acts listed in Article 2 (Act of 13 March 2003), introducing Article 10(6) into the Preliminary Title of the Code of Criminal Procedure. By Article 379 of the Act of 22 December 2003, the legislature further declared Article 10(6) applicable to facts committed before its entry into force. The Act of 13 March 2003 became popularly known as the 'Erdal Act', because it had been adopted with a view to establishing jurisdiction over Erdal's offences committed in Turkey. Erdal filed an action for annulment of the Erdal Act with the Constitutional Court, arguing that Article 379 violated the principle of non-retroactivity of criminal law.

> The Law of 13 March 2003 does not create any new incriminations given that all the acts referred to in Article 2 of the European Convention on the Suppression of Terrorism were already punishable in themselves under Belgian criminal law, as demonstrated in the course of parliamentary proceedings (on this point, see *Parl. Doc.*, Chamber, 2000–2001, DOC 50–1179/001, pp. 5–7).
>
> Nonetheless, Article 10 (6) of the Preliminary Title of the Code of Criminal Procedure, insofar as it extends the extraterritorial competence of the Belgian courts, provides a legal basis for prosecution in Belgium. Whereas previously, there was no legal basis for prosecution nor therefore, *a fortiori*, for sanction of such acts in Belgium, following the law of 13 March 2003 this is now the case.
>
> As a result, the Law of 13 March 2003 must be considered as a provision of substantive criminal law.
>
> (...)
>
> B.8.1 Conformément à la jurisprudence de la Cour européenne des droits de l'homme, l'article 7 de la Convention européenne des droits de l'homme consacre le principe de légalité en matière pénale et interdit en particulier l'application rétroactive de la loi pénale lorsqu'elle joue en défaveur de l'intéressé (Kokkinakis

> c. Grèce, arrêt du 25 mai 1993, série A, n° 260-A, § 52; Coëme et autres c. Belgique, arrêt du 22 juin 2000, § 145). Il est ainsi requis qu'au moment où le prévenu a posé l'acte qui donne lieu aux poursuites et à la condamnation, une disposition législative existât qui rendait cet acte punissable (voy. Coëme et autres c. Belgique, *loc. cit.*, § 145).
>
> B.8.2 It emerges from the above that at the moment when the applicant is thought to have performed the acts of which she is suspected, there existed no legal basis according to which she could have been prosecuted and sentenced for these acts by the Belgian criminal courts.

The most interesting aspect of this case is that the Constitutional Court took the legal interests of the accused as point of reference and accordingly interpreted the prohibition of retroactive application of criminal law as also covering an extension of the scope of criminal jurisdiction. In an earlier decision the Supreme Court had accepted that an Act of Parliament could itself declare its application with retroactive effect. This was exactly what the Erdal Act did, as the commentator correctly observed. However, this construction did not find mercy in the eyes of the Constitutional Court.

Public Prosecutor's Office, de Lois (Graciela) (intervening) and ors (intervening) v Manzorro (Adolfo), Final Appeal Judgment, Case No 16/2005, Aranzadi JUR 2005/132318, ILDC 136 (ES 2005), 19th April 2005, Spain; National Court; Criminal Chamber

The case concerned criminal proceedings before the High Court (*Audiencia Nacional*) against Adolfo Scilingo, an Argentine officer alleged to have been involved in the unlawful detention, torture and elimination of alleged subversive persons during the Argentine military regime since 1976, for crimes against humanity. The prominent issue was whether crimes against humanity committed in Argentina in the late 1970s were punishable in the Spanish legal order, *inter alia*, by effect of customary international law.

> As mentioned earlier, the first and apparently most significant problem we will address for the application of the criminal provision contained in Article 607 bis of the PC relating to crimes against humanity is the fact that it was not valid at the time the acts in question were committed, due to its recent incorporation into Spanish law. In guaranteeing the principle of legality, Article 9(3) of the CE also refers to the principle of the non-retroactivity of the most favourable sanctions. Article 25 CE expressly states that "No person can be sentenced or sanctioned for actions or omissions that were not a crime at the time they occurred […] under legislation in force at the time". Thus, a number of problems arise relating to the principle of legality and categorisation of criminal laws: the retroactivity, certainty and predictability of the applicable criminal law.
>
> H3 The application to Scilingo of the norms penalizing crimes against humanity did not breach the principle of legality. Even considering that the Criminal Code did not penalize such crimes until October 2004, the crime already existed as a *ius cogens* norm of customary international law long before that date. Further, international custom was part of the Spanish legal order, and hence, the principle of *nullum crimen sine lege* was fully respected in this case. (paragraphs B.1-B.2 and B.4)

Scilingo was the first Spanish criminal case in which an accused stood trial for alleged commission of crimes against humanity. The High Court took the opportunity to deliver a much elaborated opinion in which it divulged a very friendly attitude towards international law. Customary international law did not have to be incorporated in the domestic legal order, but could autonomously serve as an adequate basis for prosecution.

Like many others, the ILDC commentator was critical:

> 'The High Court held that the principle of legality and *nullum crimen sine lege* did not require the existence of a domestic legislative provision prohibiting a certain conduct: to meet the standards of this principle, it held, it was sufficient that a rule of international law concerning the crime existed at the time when the alleged offence was committed. The court thus presented an interesting view of the principle of legality. It argued that it was not necessary for a customary rule of international law proscribing the conduct to be incorporated in national law (one misses in the judgment, in any case, a short explanation of the principles on the incorporation and status of international law in the Spanish legal order); if the conduct was criminalized on the international legal plane, there was already a rule of "law" on the matter so that the principle *nullum crimen sine lege* was respected. This point has also been criticized, as international law would have no sufficient precision to satisfy the principle of legality'.[9]

Movement Against Racism and for Peoples' Friendship v Aussaresses, Appeal judgment, Appeal no 02-80719, Decision no 122, ILDC 775 (FR 2003), 17th June 2003, France; Court of Cassation [Cass]; Criminal Division

In May 2001, French General Paul Aussaresses published a book entitled *Special Services, Algeria 1955–1957* (*Services spéciaux, Algérie 1955–1957* (Editions Perrin, Paris 2001)). As army intelligence service co-ordinator, he detailed, without remorse, all the tortures, arbitrary executions, and massacres of civilians he had ordered and participated in during the conflict in Algeria. Following these revelations, the Movement Against Racism and for Peoples' Friendship ('MRAP') filed a civil-party complaint against unnamed persons for crimes against humanity committed during the events in Algeria. Indirectly, they sought the repeal of the amnesty from which Aussaresses was benefiting.

The Court of Cassation was seized to answer the question whether prosecution and trial of Aussaresses could be predicated on either conventional or customary international law, qualifying his acts as crimes against humanity, or, alternatively whether the French Criminal Code of 1994 could be applied retroactively to that purpose.

> **17** That, the provisions of the Law of 26 December 1964 and those of the Statute of the International Military Tribunal at Nuremberg, annexed to the Agreement of London of 8 August 1945, only relate to the acts committed for the European Axis countries;
>
> (...)
>
> **18** That, furthermore, the principles of the legality of the offences and the penalties and the non-retroactivity of the more severe criminal law, contained in Articles 8 of the Declaration of the Rights of Man and the Citizen, 7-1 of the European Convention on Human Rights, 15-1 of the International Covenant on Civil and Political Rights, 111-3 and 112-1 of the Criminal Code, prevent Articles 211-1 to 212-3 of this Code penalising crimes against humanity that apply to acts committed before the date of their entry into force, 1 March 1994;
>
> (...)

9 L Paradell, B Montejo, Analysis, *Public Prosecutor's Office, de Lois (Graciela) (intervening) and ors (intervening) v Manzorro (Adolfo)*, ILDC 136 (ES 2005) A4, referring to A Gil Gil, 'The Flaws of the Scilingo Judgment' (2005) 3 *Journal of International Criminal Justice* 1082, 1086–1087.

> 19 That finally, international custom may not compensate the absence of the incriminating text by categorising the acts reported by the injured party as crimes against humanity;

None of the three efforts to thwart the French reading of the legality principle was successful. The Court of Cassation harboured a restrictive interpretation of conventional international law (Statute of the IMT), denying its applicability to the French-Algerian conflict. It stressed the prohibition of retroactive application as a natural and logic corollary of the legality principle. And finally, the court held that customary international law could not palliate the lack of explicit domestic provisions, making it abundantly clear that customary international law as such could never serve as an adequate legal basis for prosecution and conviction within the French legal order.

Bouterse (Desire), Re, Judgment on Appeal, Decision No LJN: AB1471, Case No HR 00749/01 CW 2323, NJ 2002, 559, ILDC 80 (NL 2001), 18th September 2001, Netherlands; Supreme Court [HR]

Protracted proceedings preceded the landmark decision of the Dutch Supreme Court on the question whether Surinam's former commander-in-chief Desi Bouterse could be prosecuted on the charge of having been involved in the 1982 December killings of fifteen prominent young Surinamese men who had criticized Bouterse's government. In the judgement the legal issues of direct application of international law, *nullum crimen*, and universal jurisdiction were strongly intertwined. In this part, the former aspects will be addressed.

> 4.5. The findings at 4.4 above mean that the unreserved prohibition of Article 16 of the Constitution and Article 1, paragraph 1, of the Criminal Code (incorporating the legality principle. HvdW), as referred to at 4.3 above, should not be applicable in cases where this would be incompatible with provisions of treaties or decisions of international organisations binding on all persons. However, neither the Convention against Torture and Other Cruel, Inhuman or Degrading Treatment or Punishment nor any other treaties or decisions of an international organisation applicable here contains a provision entailing an obligation to treat acts as referred to in the Torture Convention Implementation Act as punishable with retroactive effect.
>
> 4.6. It follows that the provisions of the Criminal Code applicable at the time when the offences that are the subject of the complaint were committed in 1982 may be applied to the offences in so far as they were envisaged and made punishable at the time, but also that Articles 1 and 2 of the Implementation Act may not be applied to such offences since this legislation did not come into force until 20 January 1989. It also follows from the above that in so far as the obligation to declare such offences as punishable with retroactive effect results from unwritten international law, the courts are not free to decide not to apply the Torture Convention Implementation Act (which does not provide for this) on account of the fact that it is contrary to unwritten international law. According to the parliamentary history of Article 94 of the Constitution, as recounted at 4.4 above, the framers of the Constitution did not wish to accept the application of unwritten international law if such application would conflict with national legal regulations.
>
> 4.7. In view of the above findings, it is not necessary to answer the question of whether the offences referred to by the Court of Appeal can be deemed to be offences within the meaning of Article 7 of the European Convention on Human Rights and Article 15 of the International Covenant on Civil and Political Rights, which provide that the rule referred to in the first paragraph of these provisions, namely that no one may be held guilty of any criminal offence on account of any act or omission which

did not constitute a criminal offence under national or international law at the time when it was committed, does not prevent the trial and punishment of anyone who commits an act or omission that constituted a criminal offence at the time of the act or omission in accordance with the general principles of law recognised by the community of nations.

(...)

6. Assessment of the third ground of appeal

6.1. This ground of appeal raises the question of whether the Netherlands has jurisdiction in relation to the relevant acts committed before the entry into force of the Torture Convention Implementation Act, in so far as such acts constituted criminal offences under the Criminal Code at the time when they were committed.

6.2. As regards the relevant offences of the Criminal Code, the jurisdiction rules of Articles 2-8 of the Criminal Code are applicable. These rules do not provide for jurisdiction in a case such as the present one, which involves—as it has been submitted—offences committed outside the Netherlands by a person not having Dutch nationality.

6.3. Neither in the Torture Convention Implementation Act nor elsewhere is retroactive effect given to the expansion in Article 5 of the Torture Convention Implementation Act of the jurisdiction rules as regards criminal offences under the Criminal Code, which also fulfil the definition of torture now provided for in the Torture Convention Implementation Act . Nor does the parliamentary history of this provision contain any basis for the granting of retroactive effect to the said Article 5, and indeed the parliamentary history as set out in the explanatory notes to the ground of appeal, at 59, could much more easily be interpreted as an indication to the contrary.

6.4. It is not necessary to answer whether a rule of unwritten international law exists on the basis of which the Netherlands has jurisdiction with retroactive effect with regard to the offences referred to in 6.3 because the courts, in accordance with the findings at 4.4–4.6 above, are not free to decide not to apply the national jurisdiction rules on account of conflict with unwritten international law.

The reasoning of the court was layered and rather complicated. The court started by taking the domestic provisions on the legality principle as point of reference. It conceded that international conventional law could trump these provisions, in view of the hierarchical supremacy of self-executing provisions of international conventions, but observed that the relevant provisions of the Torture Convention were not in force at the time of the December Killings, nor did the convention itself ordain its retroactive application. *Per argumentum a contrario*, customary international law did not supersede an Act of Parliament, so the alleged punishability of torture under customary international law was of no avail. Interestingly, the Dutch Supreme Court considered the retroactive application of expanded jurisdiction on the same par as the retroactive application of substantive criminal law, taking a similar approach as the Belgian courts in *Erdal v Council of Ministers* (ILDC 9 (BE 2005)).

United States v Smith (Thomas), Appeal Judgment, 18 US (5 Wheat.) 153 (1820), 5 L.Ed. 57 (1820), ILDC 1053 (US 1820), 2nd February 1820, United States; Supreme Court [US]

Thomas Smith seized a ship by violence, committed plunder and robbery on the sea, and was thereafter caught and charged with piracy. Piracy was punishable by death pursuant to an Act of Congress. For the definition of piracy, this Act simply referred to the law of nations. The legal issue that the Supreme Court had to decide was twofold: First, whether a statute that incorporated by reference international law regarding the criminal definition of piracy was consistent with the principle of legality. And next, whether the crime of piracy was defined by the law of nations with reasonable certainty.

> 2 The first point made at the bar is whether this enactment be a constitutional exercise of the authority delegated to Congress upon the subject of piracies. The Constitution declares that Congress shall have power "to define and punish piracies and felonies committed on the high seas, and offenses against the law of nations." The argument which has been urged on behalf of the prisoner is that Congress is bound to define, in terms, the offense of piracy, and is not at liberty to leave it to be ascertained by judicial interpretation. If the argument be well founded, it seems admitted by the counsel that it equally applies to the 8th section of the Act of Congress of 1790, ch. 9, which declares that robbery and murder committed on the high seas shall be deemed piracy, and yet, notwithstanding a series of contested adjudications on this section, no doubt has hitherto been breathed of its conformity to the Constitution.
>
> (...)
>
> 5 It is next to be considered whether the crime of piracy is defined by the law of nations with reasonable certainty. What the law of nations on this subject is may be ascertained by consulting the works of jurists writing professedly on public law, or by the general usage and practice of nations, or by judicial decisions recognizing and enforcing that law. There is scarcely a writer on the law of nations, who does not allude to piracy as a crime of a settled and determinate nature, and whatever may be the diversity of definitions in other respects, all writers concur in holding that robbery or forcible depredations upon the sea, *animo furandi,* is piracy. The same doctrine is held by all the great writers on maritime law in terms that admit of no reasonable doubt. The common law, too, recognizes and punishes piracy as an offense not against its own municipal code, but as an offense against the law of nations (which is part of the common law), as an offense against the universal law of society, a pirate being deemed an enemy of the human race. Indeed, until the statute of 28 Henry VIII, ch. 15, piracy was punishable in England only in the admiralty as a civil law offense, and that statute, in changing the jurisdiction, has been universally admitted not to have changed the nature of the offense. Sir Charles Hedges, in his charge at the admiralty sessions in the case of *Rex v. Dawson,* 5 State Trials, declared in emphatic terms that "piracy is only a sea term for robbery, piracy being a robbery committed within the jurisdiction of the admiralty." Sir Leoline Jenkins, too, on a like occasion, declared that "a robbery, when committed upon the sea, is what we call piracy," and he cited the civil law writers in proof. And it is manifest from the language of Sir William Blackstone in his comments on piracy that he considered the common law definition as distinguishable in no essential respect from that of the law of nations. So that whether we advert to writers on the common law or the maritime law or the law of nations, we shall find that they universally treat of piracy as an offense against the law of nations and that its true definition by that law is robbery upon the sea. And the general practice of all nations in punishing all persons, whether natives or foreigners, who have committed this offense against any persons whatsoever with whom they are in amity is a conclusive proof that the offense is supposed to depend not upon the particular provisions of any municipal code, but upon the law of nations, both for its definition and punishment. We have therefore no hesitation in declaring that piracy, by the law of nations, is robbery upon the sea, and that it is sufficiently and constitutionally defined by the fifth section of the act of 1819.
>
> (...)

> 7 It is to be certified to the circuit court that upon the facts stated, the case is piracy, as defined by the law of nations, so as to be punishable under the Act of Congress of the 3d of March, 1819.

In this classic case (the oldest in the collection of ILDC), the Supreme Court addressed quintessential aspects of the legality principle which naturally emerge whenever international law enters the scene. Is the law of nations accessible and sufficiently precise to be cognizable for the average citizen? The Supreme Court answered both questions in the affirmative. Probably, this decision was partially inspired by the consideration that pirates are not 'average citizens, but have historically been considered as *hostes humani generis*'.[10]

III. Substantive International Criminal Law

1. Genocide

Genocide is defined in Article II of the Convention on the Prevention and Punishment of the Crime of Genocide 1984 ('The Genocide Convention')[11] as any of the following acts committed with intent to destroy, in whole or in part, a national, ethnical, racial or religious group, as such:

(a) Killing members of the group;
(b) Causing serious bodily harm to members of the group;
(c) Deliberately inflicting on the group conditions of life calculated to bring about its physical destruction in whole or in part;
(d) Imposing measures intended to prevent births within the group;
(e) Forcibly transferring children of the group to another group.

This definition was adopted without change in the Statutes of the two ad hoc international criminal tribunals for the former Yugoslavia (ICTY)[12] and for Rwanda (ICTR)[13] and in the Rome Statute of the International Criminal Court (ICC).[14] The crime of genocide is also considered to be part of customary international law[15] and may in fact be a *jus cogens* crime. Although the subject of interpretation and application before the ICTY and the ICTR, there has been little consideration of the crime of genocide in domestic courts.

(a) Incitement to genocide

Canada (Minister of Citizenship and Immigration), League for Human Rights of B'nai Brith Canada (intervening) and ors (intervening) v Mugesera (Léon) and ors, Appeal to Supreme Court, 2005 SCC 40, [2005] 2 SCR 100, (2001) 254 DLR (4th) 200, ILDC 180 (CA 2005), 28th June 2005, Canada; Supreme Court [SCC]

Mugesera was accused of delivering an inflammatory speech to a meeting of Hutu's in 1992. He fled to Canada after an arrest warrant was issued against him in Rwanda. He achieved permanent residency status in Canada in 1993. On being informed of the existence of the arrest

10 *United States v Smith (Thomas)*, Appeal judgment, 18 US (5 Wheat) 153 (1820) 5 L Ed 57 (1820), ILDC 1053 (US 1820), 2nd February 1820, United States; Supreme Court [US].

11 Convention on the Prevention and Punishment of the Crime of Genocide (adopted 9 December 1948, entered into force 12 January 1951) 78 UNTS 277.

12 UNSC Res 827, Statute of the International Criminal Tribunal for the Former Yugoslavia (25 May 1993, as amended on 17 May 2002) UN Doc S/RES/827, Article 4(2).

13 UNSC Res 955, Statute of the International Criminal Tribunal for Rwanda (8 November 1994, as last amended on 13 October 2006) UN Doc S/RES/955, Article 2(2).

14 Rome Statute of the International Criminal Court (n 1) Article 6.

15 See *Reservations to the Convention on the Prevention and Punishment of the Crime of Genocide* (Advisory Opinion) [1951] ICJ Rep 15.

warrant, Canadian authorities sought to deport Mugesera back to Rwanda. His deportation was ordered by an immigration adjudicator. The decision was upheld by the Immigration and Refugee Board (Appeal Division) and the Federal Court (Trial Division) but overturned by the Federal Court of Appeal. The Supreme Court of Canada upheld the original decision to deport. Of particular interest were the findings of the Supreme Court in relation to the allegations of incitement to genocide and incitement to crimes against humanity.[16]

(2) Incitement to Genocide

81 The second offence that the Minister [of Citizenship and Immigration – Ed] alleges Mr. Mugesera committed in giving the speech is advocating or promoting genocide. We will now consider the elements of the offence and whether they are made out on the facts as found by Mr. Duquette (who wrote the main reasons for the IAD decision – Ed).

82 Genocide is a crime originating in international law. International law is thus called upon to play a crucial role as an aid in interpreting domestic law, particularly as regards the elements of the crime of incitement to genocide. Section 318(1) of the *Criminal Code* incorporates, almost word for word, the definition of genocide found in art. II of the *Genocide Convention*, and the Minister's allegation B makes specific reference to Rwanda's accession to the *Genocide Convention.* Canada is also bound by the *Genocide Convention.* In addition to treaty obligations, the legal principles underlying the *Genocide Convention* are recognized as part of customary international law: see International Court of Justice, Advisory Opinion of May 28, 1951, *Reservations to the Convention on the Prevention and Punishment of the Crime of Genocide*, I.C.J. Reports 1951, at p. 15. The importance of interpreting domestic law in a manner that accords with the principles of customary international law and with Canada's treaty obligations was emphasized in *Baker v. Canada (Minister of Citizenship and Immigration)*, [1999] 2 S.C.R. 817, at paras. 69–71. In this context, international sources like the recent jurisprudence of international criminal courts are highly relevant to the analysis.

(a) The Elements of Advocating Genocide

83 Section 318(1) of the *Criminal Code* proscribes the offence of advocating genocide: "Every one who advocates or promotes genocide is guilty of an indictable offence and liable to imprisonment for a term not exceeding five years." Genocide is defined as the act of killing members of an identifiable group or of deliberately inflicting conditions of life on an identifiable group calculated to bring about the physical destruction of that group, in whole or in part: subs. (2). Subsection (4), at the relevant time, defined an identifiable group as "any section of the public distinguished by colour, race, religion or ethnic origin". There is no Canadian jurisprudence dealing specifically with s. 318(1) of the *Criminal Code.*

(i) Is Proof of Genocide Required?

84 In *Prosecutor v. Akayesu*, 9 IHRR 608 (1998), the Trial Chamber of the International Criminal Tribunal for Rwanda ("ICTR") drew a distinction between the constituent elements of the crimes of complicity in genocide and incitement to genocide. In the case of a charge of complicity, the prosecution must prove that genocide has actually occurred. A charge of incitement to genocide, however, does not require proof that genocide has in fact happened:

16 Incitement to crimes against humanity will be discussed below in section III.2.

In the opinion of the Chamber, the fact that such acts are in themselves particularly dangerous because of the high risk they carry for society, even if they fail to produce results, warrants that they be punished as an exceptional measure. The Chamber holds that genocide clearly falls within the category of crimes so serious that direct and public incitement to commit such a crime must be punished as such, even where such incitement failed to produce the result expected by the perpetrator. [para. 562]

85 In the case of the allegation of incitement to genocide, the Minister does not need to establish a direct causal link between the speech and any acts of murder or violence. Because of its inchoate nature, incitement is punishable by virtue of the criminal act alone irrespective of the result. It remains a crime regardless of whether it has the effect it is intended to have: see also *Prosecutor v. Nahimana, Barayagwiza and Ngeze*, Case No. ICTR-99-52-T (Trial Chamber I) ("*Media Case*"), 3 December 2003, at para. 1029. The Minister is not required, therefore, to prove that individuals who heard Mr. Mugesera's speech killed or attempted to kill any members of an identifiable group.

(ii) The Criminal Act: Direct and Public Incitement

86 The criminal act requirement for incitement to genocide has two elements: the act of incitement must be direct and it must be public: *Akayesu*, Trial Chamber, at para. 559. See also art. III(c) of the *Genocide Convention*. The speech was public. We need only consider the meaning of the requirement that it be direct.

87 In *Akayesu*, the Trial Chamber of the ICTR held that the *direct element* "implies that the incitement assume a direct form and specifically provoke another to engage in a criminal act, and that more than mere vague or indirect suggestion goes to constitute direct incitement" (para. 557). The direct element of incitement "should be viewed in the light of its cultural and linguistic content" (para. 557). *Depending on the audience*, a particular speech may be perceived as direct in one country, and not so in another. The determination of whether acts of incitement can be viewed as direct necessarily focusses mainly on the issue of whether the persons for whom the message was intended immediately grasped the implication thereof (para. 558). The words used must be clear enough to be immediately understood by the intended audience. Innuendo and obscure language do not suffice.

(iii) The Guilty Mind for Direct and Public Incitement to Genocide

88 The guilty mind required for the crime of incitement to genocide is an "intent to directly prompt or provoke another to commit genocide" (*Akayesu*, Trial Chamber, at para. 560). It implies a desire on the part of the perpetrator to cause another to have the state of mind necessary to commit the acts enumerated in s. 318(2) of the *Criminal Code*. The person who incites must also have the specific intent to commit genocide: an intent to destroy in whole or in part any identifiable group, namely, any section of the public distinguished by colour, race, religion, or ethnic origin (s. 318(2) and (4) of the *Criminal Code*).

89 Intent can be inferred from the circumstances. Thus, the court can infer the genocidal intent of a particular act from the systematic perpetration of other culpable acts against the group; the scale of any atrocities that are committed and their general nature in a region or a country; or the fact that victims are deliberately and systematically targeted on account of their membership in a particular group while the members of other groups are left alone: *Akayesu*, Trial Chamber, at para. 523. A speech that is given in the context of a genocidal environment will have a heightened impact, and for this reason the environment in which a statement is made can be an indicator of the speaker's intent (*Media Case*, at para. 1022).

Although the case relates directly to the application of the immigration laws of Canada, this case has wider significance insofar as it addresses the substantive law of genocide (in particular, the matter of incitement to genocide). In determining whether the Immigration and Refugee Board (Appeal Division) (IAD) had correctly applied the law on genocide, the Supreme Court undertook an analysis of that law as contained in Section 318 of the Criminal Code (Canada).

On the specific question of incitement to genocide, the Supreme Court of Canada relied heavily on the jurisprudence of the ICTR, extensively citing the case of *Prosecutor v Akayesu*.[17] The limited assertion by the Supreme Court that: 'Genocide is a crime originating in international law […] In this context, international sources like the recent jurisprudence of international criminal courts are highly relevant to the analysis' is questionable given the fact that the jurisprudence of the ICTR does not in and of itself constitute a formal source of international law. Nevertheless, insofar as the relevant states are party to the Genocide Convention, and in light of the direct link between the ICTR Statute and the Genocide Convention highlighted above, it would seem that the jurisprudence of the ICTR is at least highly persuasive.

The analysis of incitement to genocide undertaken by the Supreme Court, although short, is clear and precise, bearing in mind that the court was concerned merely with the question of whether the IAD had correctly applied the law. Nevertheless, even in this context, the discussion of genocidal intent (the so-called *dolus specialis* of genocide) is rather limited. While the Supreme Court correctly acknowledges that the intent element of incitement to genocide requires not only 'an intent to directly promote or provoke another to commit genocide' but also the specific intent to commit genocide, it would have been beneficial had the Supreme Court provided further analysis of how that intent on behalf of Mugesera was present at the time he delivered his speech. Given the fact that the speech was delivered in 1992, some two years before the 1994 genocide in Rwanda, the need to evidence the specific intent to commit genocide on behalf of Mugesera was particularly important. The IAD found intent in the fact that Mugesera 'knew approximately 2,000 Tutsis had been killed since October 1, 1990', that 'the context leaves no doubt as to his intent' and that 'he intended specifically to provoke citizens against one another'. The Supreme Court held that 'the IAD came to the correct legal conclusion'.

(b) Complicity in genocide

Van Anraat Case, Public Prosecutor and Fifteen anonymous victims v Van Anraat, Case No 2200050906-2, Decision No LJN: BA4676, ILDC 753 (NL 2007), 9th May 2007, Netherlands; The Hague; Court of Appeal

Van Anraat was accused of supplying Thiodiglycol (a chemical solvent), also known as TGD, to the Iraqi regime from 1985 to 1988. The chemical was used by the Iraqi regime in the production of chemical weapons which were used during the war with Iran and against Kurdish citizens. Van Anraat was accused of complicity in genocide and with various violations of customary international law and violations of various provisions of the Geneva Convention as punishable under the Netherland's War Crimes Act. Von Anraat was acquitted of complicity in genocide.

> 7. In the judgment of the question whether it can be proven that the defendant is liable to punishment on account of the actions he is charged with in the present criminal proceedings, the following issues should be considered.
>
> A. Is it possible to deduct from the evidence whether the actions described in the indictment—concisely summarized—the air attacks with mustard gas carried out by the Iraqi regime (the perpetrators), were indeed the consequence of the intention (hereafter: the genocidal intention) to partially or totally destroy the Kurdish population group in (Northern) Iraq as such?

17 *The Prosecutor v Jean-Paul Akayesu*, ICTR-96-4-T, Trial Chamber 1, 2 September 1998.

B. Article 48 of the Penal Code stipulates inter alia that persons who intentionally provide the opportunity, means or information necessary to commit criminal offences are considered to be accessories to those crimes. From the text of this article follows that the intention of the accessory should be focussed on all component parts of the crime under consideration. Consequently the question that needs to be answered is the following: to what extent is the Dutch criminal court entitled to apply Dutch law in judging the requirement of intention in the present case and to what extent should it (also) consider the application of international criminal law?

C. (If the answer to question A would be affirmative,) was the purpose of the defendant (also) focussed on the—possible—genocidal intention of the perpetrators?

Re A. The Court considers that, in answering the question whether the perpetrators had a genocidal intention, other completed actions committed by the perpetrators against the population group involved should also be taken into account. Although the aforesaid population group does not appear as such in the indictment, they do come forward from documents in the case file, especially from the reports inserted under H 74 and H 75, which were drawn up by the Special Rapporteur of the Commission on Human Rights of the United Nations, Mr. Van der Stoel, even if these actions as such do not (all) fulfil the description of the crime referred to as genocide. From a number of documents, including the afore mentioned reports and statements in the case file, it appears that the offences put forward in the charges refer to the air attacks that were carried out partly during the so-called Anfal Campaign by or under the command of the perpetrators. Moreover, they show that those attacks, however horrifying and shocking they were, formed part of a considerably larger complex of many years of actions against the Kurds in the Northern Iraqi territory, which is mainly inhabited by the Kurdish population. Apparently these actions involved the systematic destruction of hundreds of Kurdish villages. Hundreds of thousands of Kurdish civilians were chased from their home towns and deported to other places and tens of thousands of Kurds were killed. In one of his reports, Van der Stoel described the policy that constituted the basis for the so-called Anfal Campaign, as a policy that without a doubt had the characteristics of a genocidal design.

In view of the said facts and circumstances, the Court believes that the actions taken by the perpetrators, in any case even the ones that have not been included in the charges, as outlined in the above, as to their nature at least produce strong indications that the leaders of the Iraqi regime, also regarding the actions that have been put down in the charges, let themselves be guided by a genocidal intention with regards to at least a substantial part of the Kurdish population group in (Northern) Iraq.

Nevertheless, the Court deems that a final judicial judgment regarding the important as well as internationally significant question whether certain actions by certain persons as mentioned in the charges should be designated as genocide, deserves a better motivated judgment (which should be based on conclusive evidence) than the one on which the Court was able to establish its observation.

The Court would like to point out in this respect that Mr. Van der Stoel, in his capacity as witness, stated that he based his reports on human rights violations in Iraq (H 74 and H 75), reports which in this case should be regarded as highly relevant, on "a large stream of documents, fourteen tons" while, except for some annexes to those reports, there are no documents in the case file from which the findings and conclusions of the Special Rapporteur can be directly deduced and that could serve as evidence in these criminal proceedings to prove the offence of genocide with a sufficient degree of certainty.

In view of the consideration following hereafter under C, the Court thinks that only these observations need to be stated, and that any other observations could only be qualified as 'unnecessarily'.

Re B. The international aspects of the case under consideration have given the Court cause for a focus on international criminal law, especially when answering the question whether the defendant had the legally required degree of intention in committing the offences that he has been charged with. In this respect the Court concludes that, especially regarding the question which degree of intention is required for a conviction on account of complicity in genocide, international criminal law is still in a stage of development and does not seem to have crystallized out completely. The main question, which has not yet been answered unanimously in all respects, is whether the accessory must have "known" that the perpetrator acted with a genocidal intention or that a lesser degree of intention is sufficient, compared to or similar to the conditional intention as accepted in the Dutch legal system, or in other words: willingly and knowingly accepting the reasonable chance that a certain consequence or a certain circumstance will occur. The Court wishes to add that it holds the opinion that the legal history of the International Crimes Act does not provide an unambiguous answer for this matter either. Seen the fact that a ruling by the Court on this matter—notwithstanding the circumstance that such a ruling could possibly make a contribution to the development of law —, in view of the following consideration could not produce more than an 'obiter dictum' which in the eyes of the Court does not fit in with the decision on the case concerned, the Court has decided to leave this question for what it is.

Re C. When answering the above mentioned question, it is important to focus on the circumstance whether especially those actions carried out by the perpetrators that have not been included in the charges contribute to the credibility of the fact that these perpetrators did have genocidal intentions.

The Court takes the grounds that the case file does not include enough facts and circumstances which, with a sufficient degree of certainty, could lead to the assumption that the defendant, before or during the time of his actions in any way had knowledge about those actions of the perpetrators that have not been included in the charges, neither that he could reasonably suspect that these would occur or had occurred, nor did it become apparent that the defendant, in those days, had any other relevant information from which he could have concluded the genocidal intention of the perpetrators. In this respect the Court has taken into account that, as appears from the documents, the Iraqi authorities kept their actions against the Kurds away from publicity as much as possible. (Consequently) even a number of Dutch ambassadors, who were assigned to Baghdad at that time, as evidenced by their statements, appeared to have had no knowledge about the things that were actually happening to the Kurds.

Based on the above, the Court has come to the conclusion that it has not been established with a sufficient degree of certainty that the defendant, before or during this actions, disposed of the information that could give him the knowledge that by acting the way he did, which actions he has been charged with in the present proceedings, he would be assisting the perpetrators in the fulfilment of this alleged genocidal intention, or that could have made him aware that he willingly and knowingly accepted that reasonable chance. Seen that this criteria of intention, which is regarded as minimal, (also from an international criminal law point of view) has not been met, the Court believes that it has not been legally and convincingly proven that his intentional act, not even in a conditional way, was also targeted at the genocidal intention of the perpetrators.

Therefore the defendant should be acquitted of the principle charge under count 1.

It is disappointing that, having established that there were 'strong indications that the leaders of the Iraqi regime […] let themselves be guided by a genocidal intention with regards to at least a substantial part of the Kurdish population group in (Northern) Iraq', the court was unwilling to conclude that a genocide had taken place during the Anfal campaign, citing the international significance of such a finding as a reason not to provide it. Furthermore, in relation to the question of international criminal law, in direct contrast to the position taken by the Canadian Supreme Court in *Mugesera*, the Hague Court of Appeal appeared to refuse even to consider the jurisprudence of the ICTY or ICTR noting merely that 'in relation to complicity in genocide, international criminal law is still in a stage of development and does not seem to have crystallized out completely'. In his ILDC commentary on the case, one of the co-authors of this chapter pointed out that: 'Under international criminal law it is generally acknowledged that "knowledge" suffices as the required *mens rea* of accomplices to genocide'.[18] A finding to this effect by the Hague Court of Appeal would have assisted in the 'crystallization' of the *mens rea* of complicity in genocide. The commentator, nevertheless, notes that: 'Possible ignorance of genocide did not rule out, however, that Van Anraat knew or had reason to know that the commodities he had delivered to the Iraqi regime would be converted into chemical weapons which would be employed against both the Iranian enemy and the Kurdish population'.[19] It is this knowledge which, when proven, led to Van Anraat's conviction of complicity in war crimes and his eventual imprisonment for a period of 17 years.

2. Crimes against humanity

Crimes Against Humanity were defined in Article 6(c) of the Nuremberg Charter as including '[m]urder, extermination, enslavement, deportation, and other inhumane acts committed against any civilian population, before or during the war, or persecutions on political, racial or religious grounds in execution of or in connection with any crime within the jurisdiction of the Tribunal, whether or not in violation of the domestic law of the country where perpetrated'. The link to armed conflict was maintained in Article 5 of the Statute of the ICTY but not in Article 3 of the ICTR Statute which introduced the notion of a 'widespread or systematic attack against any civilian population'. Both Tribunals extended the relevant actus reus to include torture and rape. The Statute of the International Criminal Court defines crimes against humanity in Article 7 and further extends the relevant acts to include, additionally, sexual slavery, enforced prostitution, forced pregnancy, enforced sterilization, or any other form of sexual violence of comparable gravity; enforced disappearances and the crime of apartheid.[20] Article 7(2) introduces a policy-element to the definition by defining an attack directed against any civilian population as meaning 'a course of conduct involving the multiple commission of acts referred to in paragraph 1 against any civilian population, pursuant to or in furtherance of a State or organizational policy to commit such attack'.[21]

Canada (Minister of Citizenship and Immigration), League for Human Rights of B'nai Brith Canada (intervening) and ors (intervening) v Mugesera (Léon) and ors, Appeal to Supreme Court, 2005 SCC 40, [2005] 2 SCR 100, (2001) 254 DLR (4th) 200, ILDC 180 (CA 2005), 28th June 2005, Canada; Supreme Court [SCC]

For a brief summary of the facts of this case, see section III1(a).

(a) The Criminal Act of a Crime Against Humanity

1. Counselling an Enumerated Act That Is Not Committed and Murder as a Crime Against Humanity

132 The first question raised on the facts of this appeal is whether the fact that Mr. Mugesera counselled the commission of murders that were not committed meets the

18 H van der Wilt, Analysis, *Van Anraat Case, Public Prosecutor and Fifteen anonymous victims v Van Anraat*, ILDC 753 (NL 2007) A3.

19 ibid, A4.

20 Rome Statute of the International Criminal Court (n 1) Article 7.

21 ibid, Article 7(2).

initial criminal act requirement for a crime against humanity. Section 7(3.77) of the *Criminal Code* provides that "counselling" an act listed in s. 7(3.76) will be sufficient to meet the requirement. Murder is one of the acts listed in s. 7(3.76). Mr. Duquette found, as a matter of fact, that Mr. Mugesera's speech counselled the commission of murders. His findings of fact are sufficient to conclude, as discussed above, that Mr. Mugesera satisfied both the physical and mental elements of the "underlying offence" of counselling a murder that is not committed.

133 This does not end our analysis, however. As we noted above, s. 7(3.76) expressly incorporates principles of customary international law into the domestic formulation of crimes against humanity. We must therefore go further and consider whether the prevailing principles of international law accord with our initial analysis. A review of the jurisprudence of the ICTY and the ICTR suggests that it does not.

134 The statutes of the ICTY and the ICTR (U.N. Doc. S/RES/827 (1993) and U.N. Doc. S/RES/955 (1994), respectively) do not use the word "counselling". This does not mean, however, that the decisions of these courts cannot be informative as to the requirements for counselling as a crime against humanity. Both statutes provide that persons who "instigate" the commission of a proscribed act may be liable under international law. This Court found in *Sharpe*, at para. 56, that counselling refers to active inducement or encouragement from an objective point of view. The ICTR has found that instigation "involves prompting another to commit an offence": *Akayesu*, Trial Chamber, at para. 482. The two terms are clearly related. As a result, we may look to the jurisprudence of the ICTY and the ICTR on instigation in determining whether counselling an offence that is not committed will be sufficient to satisfy the initial criminal act requirement for a crime against humanity under s. 7(3.76) of the *Criminal Code*.

135 In *Prosecutor v. Rutaganda*, Case No. ICTR-96-3-T (Trial Chamber I), 6 December 1999, the ICTR conducted a review of the jurisprudence of the ICTY and the ICTR on individual criminal responsibility. The ICTR found that instigation (other than of genocide) involves (1) direct and public incitement to commit a proscribed act; but (2) *only where it has led to the actual commission of the instigated offence*: para. 38; see also *Akayesu*, Trial Chamber, at para. 482. It should be noted that the second requirement does not mean that the offence would not have been committed "but for" the instigation. However, a sufficient causal link must be made out: *Prosecutor v. Kordic and Cerkez*, Case No. IT-95-14/2-T (ICTY, Trial Chamber III), 26 February 2001, at para. 387.

136 Mr. Duquette of the IAD was unable to find that the commission of murders had actually occurred as a result of Mr. Mugesera's counselling. An interpretation of ss. 7(3.76) and 7(3.77) of the *Criminal Code* in light of customary international law shows that Mr. Mugesera's counselling of murder was not sufficient to satisfy the initial criminal act requirement for a crime against humanity.

(...)

2. Speech That Incites Hatred and Persecution as a Crime Against Humanity

147 In *Keegstra*, this Court found that the harm in hate speech lies not only in the injury to the self-dignity of target group members but also in the credence that may be given to the speech, which may promote discrimination and even violence (p. 748). This finding suggests that hate speech always denies fundamental rights. The equality and the life, liberty and security of the person of target-group members cannot but be affected: see, e.g., *Prosecutor v. Ruggiu*, 39 ILM 1338 (ICTR, Trial Chamber I 2000), at para. 22. This denial of fundamental rights may, in particular instances, reach the level of a gross or blatant denial equal in gravity to the other acts enumerated in s. 7(3.76). This is particularly likely if the speech openly advocates extreme violence (such as murder or extermination) against the target group, but it may not be limited to such instances. In contrast to the case of counselling an enumerated violent act, whether the persecution actually results in the commission of acts of violence is irrelevant: *Media Case*, at para. 1073.

148 What then can be said of Mr. Mugesera's speech? Mr. Duquette found as a matter of fact that Mr. Mugesera's speech had incited hatred of Tutsi and of his political opponents (para. 335). This incitement included the encouragement of acts of extreme violence, such as extermination (para. 336). Keeping in mind that acts of persecution must be evaluated in context, Mr. Duquette's finding that Mr. Mugesera's speech occurred in a volatile situation characterized by rampant ethnic tensions and political instability which had already led to the commission of massacres is also compelling (paras. 335–38). A speech such as Mr. Mugesera's, which actively encouraged ethnic hatred, murder and extermination and which created in its audience a sense of imminent threat and the need to act violently against an ethnic minority and against political opponents, bears the hallmarks of a gross or blatant act of discrimination equivalent in severity to the other underlying acts listed in s. 7(3.76). The criminal act requirement for persecution is therefore met.

149 Having concluded that the criminal act requirement for persecution is made out, we must go on to consider whether the culpable mental element of persecution is made out. Mr. Duquette found that Mr. Mugesera had a discriminatory intent in delivering his speech (para. 335). He found that Mr. Mugesera targeted Tutsi and political opponents on the sole basis of ethnicity and political affiliation with the intent to compel his audience into action against these groups. The IAD's findings of fact thus amply support a finding that Mr. Mugesera not only committed the criminal act of persecution, but did so with the requisite discriminatory intent.

150 In sum, the criminal act requirement for a crime against humanity under ss. 7(3.76) and 7(3.77) of the *Criminal Code* contains two primary elements: (1) the accused has committed an underlying enumerated act; and (2) that act contravened international law. With respect to the first element, both the physical and mental elements of the underlying act must be made out. In the case at bar, there were two possible underlying acts: counselling of murder, and persecution by hate speech. For counselling of murder to be considered a crime against humanity under international law, murders must actually have been committed. Mr. Duquette's finding that no murders were proven to have resulted from the speech therefore precludes a finding that Mr. Mugesera counselled murder within the meaning of s. 7(3.76). The other possible underlying act, persecution, is a gross or blatant denial of fundamental rights on discriminatory grounds equal in severity to the other acts enumerated in s. 7(3.76). Hate speech, particularly when it advocates egregious acts of violence, may constitute persecution. In this case, it does.

(...)

157 A contentious issue raised by the "widespread or systematic attack" requirement is whether the attack must be carried out pursuant to a government policy or plan. Some scholars suggest that limiting crimes against humanity to attacks which implement a government policy is necessary due to the nature and scale of such crimes: see, e.g., Bassiouni, at pp. 243–46. Others point out that the existence of a government policy has never been required and suggest that crimes against humanity take on their international character simply by virtue of the existence of a widespread and systematic attack: see, e.g., Mettraux, at pp. 270–82.

158 The Appeals Chamber of the ICTY held in *Prosecutor v. Kunarac, Kovac and Vukovic* that there was no additional requirement for a state or other policy behind the attack: Case Nos. IT-96-23-A & IT-96-23/1-A, 12 June 2002, at para. 98. The Appeals Chamber acknowledged that the existence of such a policy might be useful in establishing that the attack was directed against a civilian population or that it was widespread or systematic (particularly the latter). However, the existence of a policy or plan would ultimately be useful only for evidentiary purposes and it does not constitute a separate element of the offence (para. 98). It seems that there is currently no requirement in customary international law that a policy underlie the attack, though we do not discount the possibility that customary international law may evolve over time so as to incorporate a policy requirement (see, e.g., art. 7(2)(*a*) of the *Rome Statute of the International Criminal Court*, A/CONF. 183/9, 17 July 1998).

159 Considering all these factors, was a widespread or systematic attack taking place when Mr. Mugesera gave his speech? With respect to whether the attack was widespread, Mr. Duquette found that, between October 1, 1990 and November 22, 1992, almost 2,000 Tutsi were massacred in Rwanda (para. 336). Mr. Duquette also found as a fact that in October 1990 approximately 8,000 people, 90 percent of them Tutsi, were falsely arrested on suspicion of complicity with the RPF (para. 26). The massacres occurred in various parts of the country and the number of victims grew to the thousands. This suggests a large-scale action directed against a multiplicity of victims.

The first point to note is that, as this is a case relating to deportation, the relevant Canadian immigration law does not require proof of the commission of a crime against humanity beyond reasonable doubt but, rather, requires that there be 'reasonable grounds to believe' that Mugesera committed such a crime. Nevertheless, in determining that question, the Supreme Court undertook a lengthy and detailed analysis of the *actus reus* and *mens rea* of incitement to commit a crime against humanity. The analysis is very clear and precise and the judgment will no doubt prove useful in developing the jurisprudence, both domestic and international, around the relevant issue.

As highlighted above in relation to the discussion of Mugesera's involvement in the incitement of the crime of genocide, the reliance by the court on the jurisprudence of the ICTY and ICTR as a means of interpreting a Canadian statutory provision is arguably controversial. Given that the relevant Canadian laws on crimes against humanity are derived from customary law and not from treaty, as was the case in relation to genocide, the reference by the Supreme Court to 'the expertise of these tribunals and the authority in respect of customary international law with which they are vested'[22] requires further explanation, particularly given the fact that the approach was utilized by the Supreme Court as a grounds for reconsidering its own approach to the jurisprudence of the ICTR in *R v Finta*.[23] Nevertheless, it is clear that the court did not apply this jurisprudence as constitutive of customary international law but rather as highly persuasive decisions that 'should not be disregarded lightly by Canadian courts applying domestic legal provisions [...] which expressly incorporate international law'.[24] This referential approach

22 *Canada (Minister of Citizenship and Immigration), League for Human Rights of B'nai Brith Canada (intervening) and ors (intervening) v Mugesera (Léon) and ors*, Appeal to Supreme Court, 2005 SCC 40, [2005] 2 SCR 100, (2001) 254 DLR (4th) 200, ILDC 180 (CA 2005), 28th June 2005, Canada; Supreme Court [SCC], para 126.

23 [1994] 1 SCR 701.

24 *Canada (Minister of Citizenship and Immigration) v Mugesera and others* (n 24) para 126.

to the jurisprudence of the ICTR may be welcomed by international criminal lawyers but it is an approach that may not be followed in other domestic courts.

The final matter worthy of note is the reference of the Supreme Court to the non-requirement of a state or other policy as an element of crimes against humanity, citing the decision of the ICTY in *Prosecutor v Kunarac, Kovac and Vukovic*.[25] This correctly reflects both Canadian law and the customary international law applicable at the time of the speech. Such a requirement is not found in the Statutes of either the ICTY or ICTR. The Supreme Court, however, acknowledges the existence of Article 7(2)(a) of the ICC Statute which requires that an act committed against any civilian population requires to be committed 'pursuant to or in furtherance of a state or organizational policy to commit such an attack'. This change in the definition of crimes against humanity might have resulted in a different decision in the present case had it been part of customary law at the time of the delivery of the speech by Mugesera.

Public Prosecutor's Office, de Lois (Graciela) (intervening) and ors (intervening) v Manzorro (Adolfo), Final Appeal Judgment, Case No 16/2005, Aranzadi JUR 2005/132318, ILDC 136 (ES 2005), 19th April 2005, Spain; National Court; Criminal Chamber

For a brief summary of the facts of this case see section II.

> 2. The definition of a crime against humanity in our Penal Code is based on the commission of a specific act, such as murder, bodily harm, illegal detention etc. (underlying crime) in the context of a general and systematic attack on the civilian population or part of the population, considering that in all cases the commission of such acts will be considered a crime against humanity: 1) Due to the victim's status as a member of a group or community persecuted for political, racial, national, ethnic, cultural, religious, sexual or other reasons universally recognised as unacceptable under international law; 2) In the context of an institutionalised regime of systematic oppression and domination by one racial group of one or more racial groups with the intention of perpetuating this regime.
>
> [...]
>
> 4. With regards to the elements that define a crime against humanity, the jurisprudence of the International Criminal Tribunal of the Former Yugoslavia, through various relevant judgments, has established a series of elements or points that define the crime and proof of the same, which due to their usefulness and applicability to this case we have listed below:
>
> 1) The crime must be committed directly against a civilian population. ICTY *Kunarac, Kovac and Vukovic* (Trial Chamber) 22.02.2001; (Appeals Chamber) 12.06.2002. par. 90.
> 2) The crime does not have to be committed against the whole population, but a sufficiently large number of the population (representative of the population) ICTY *Kunarac, Kovac and Vukovic*, (Appeals Chamber) 12.06.2002, par. 90.
> 3) The population must be predominantly civilian. ICTY *Kordic and Cerkez* (Trial Chamber) 26.02.2001, par. 180; *Naletilic and Martinovic*, (Trial Chamber) 31.03.2003, par. 235; *Jelisic*, (Trial Chamber) 14.12.1999, par. 54.
> 4) The presence of non-civilians does not deprive the population of its civilian status. *Prosecutor v. Kupreskic et al.* (Trial Chamber) 14.01.2000, par. 549.
> 5) An interpretation of the concept of a civilian population is made in broad terms. *Jelisic*, (Trial Chamber) 14.12.1999, par. 54; *Prosecutor v. Kupreskic et al.* (Trial Chamber) 14.01.2000, par. 547–549.

25 Case Nos IT-96-23-A and IT-96-23/1-A. See above, para 158.

6) Protection refers to any civilian population independent of whether or not it is the civilian population proper. *Vasilejevic*, (Trial Chamber) 29.11.2002, par. 33;

7) At present, the requirement of an attack on the civilian population means an act in accordance with policies of the State or a non-government organisation, but which exercises de facto political power.

7) The attack must be "widespread or systematic". *Kunarac, Kovac and Vukovic* (Trial Chamber) 22.02.2001, par. 431;

Widespread: *Kordic and Cerkez* (Trial Chamber) 26.02.2001, par. 179; *Blaskic* (Trial Chamber) 3.03.2000, par. 206; *Martinovic*, (Trial Chamber) 31.03.2003, par. 236.

Systematic: *Kunarac, Kovac and Vukovic*, (Appeals Chamber) 12.06.2002, par. 94; *Naletilic and Martinovic*, (Trial Chamber) 31.03.2003, par. 236; *Blaskic* (Trial Chamber) 3.03.2000, par. 203.

8) It is the attack that must be "widespread or systematic", not the acts of the defendant.

9) A single act can be considered a crime against humanity if it is in connection with a "widespread or systematic" attack. *Kordic and Cerkez* (Trial Chamber) 26.02.2001, par. 178; *Kupreskic et al.* (Trial Chamber) 14.01.2000, par. 550.

10) It must be remembered that there are many factors that determine when an attack is "widespread or systematic" and which can be inferred from the context.

11) Attacks must occur on a large scale or be systematic or happen within the framework of a policy or plan of the state, but the latter need not necessarily apply.

12) Intent. The author must have the aim or intention to commit the underlying crimes. *Vasilejevic*, (Trial Chamber) 29.11.2002, par. 37;

13) The motives of the defendant are irrelevant. *Kunarac, Kovac and Vukovic*, (Appeals Chamber) 12.06.2002, par. 103; *Tadic* (Appeals Chamber) 15.07.1999, par. 270–272; *Kordic and Cerkez* (Trial Chamber) 26.02.2001, par. 187.

14) Whether an act is directly against the civilian population or a specific person is irrelevant. What is relevant is that the attack, and not the specific acts of the defendant, is against a civilian population. *Kunarac, Kovac and Vukovic*, (Appeals Chamber) 12.06.2002, par. 103.

15) Discriminatory intent is only necessary for the crime of persecution. *Tadic* (Appeals Chamber) 15.07.1999, par. 283, 292, 305; *Kordic and Cerkez* (Trial Chamber) 26.02.2001, par. 186; *Blaskic* (Trial Chamber) 3.03.2000, par. 244, 260; *Todorovic* (Trial Chamber) 31.07.2001, par. 113.

16) Awareness: The author must be aware that (s)he is participating in a widespread or systematic attack. *Kunarac, Kovac and Vukovic*, (Appeals Chamber) 12.06.2002, par. 102, 410, *Tadic* (Appeals Chamber) 15.07.1999, par. 271; *Kordic and Cerkez* (Trial Chamber) 26.02.2001, par. 185; *Blaskic* (Trial Chamber) 3.03.2000, par. 244, 247); alternatively, (s)he must accept the risk that the acts are part of such an attack. *Vasilejevic*, (Trial Chamber) 29.11.2002, par. 37; *Blaskic* (Trial Chamber) 3.03.2000, par. 257; *Krnojelac* (Trial Chamber) 15.03.2002, par. 59.

The defendant must be aware of the attack and the connection between his/her acts and the context.

17) Knowledge of the details of the attack is not necessary. *Kunarac, Kovac and Vukovic*, (Appeals Chamber) 12.06.2002, par. 102; *Krnojelac* (Trial Chamber) 15.03.2002, par. 59.

18) The defendant need not necessarily approve of the context of the attack of which his/her acts form part. *Kordic and Cerkez* (Trial Chamber) 26.02.2001, par. 185.

19) This knowledge of the context can be inferred from the concurrence of a series of elements, such as awareness of the political context in which the attack occurs, the role or position of the defendant within the attack, his/her relationship with the political or military hierarchy, the scope, seriousness and nature of the acts committed, etc. *Blaskic* (Trial Chamber) 3.03.2000, par. 258–259.

20) In terms of underlying crimes, in the case of murder there is no need to produce a corpse in order for the crime to exist. *Krnojelac* (Trial Chamber) 15.03.2002, par. 326

As noted previously, the High Court divulged a highly friendly attitude towards international law. The same can be said of its attitude to the jurisprudence of the ICTY, which it cited abundantly and without discussion as to its applicability either in terms of its own legal status or indeed to the factual situation before the court. Nevertheless, the citation of this jurisprudence is meticulous and helpful leading the ILDC commentator to conclude that 'despite all its shortcomings, tenuous, and at times questionable reasoning, this decision constitutes a meritorious effort to bypass the defects of Spanish criminal law on crimes against humanity and to contribute to the fight against impunity'.[26] Similar use was made by the Canadian Supreme Court of the jurisprudence of both the ICTY and ICTR in *Mugesera.*

Prosecutor v Paulov (Karl-Leonhard), Cassation judgment, no 3-1-1-31-00, Official Gazette, Riigi Teataja-RT Part III 2000, 11, 118, ILDC 198 (EE 2000), 21st March 2000, Estonia; Supreme Court

Paulov was accused of killing three members of the Estonian resistance against Soviet occupation in 1945 and 1948. The status of the victims as members of a resistance force was at issue at all levels of the proceedings, as was the meaning and effect of Article 61 of the Estonian Criminal Code which purported to deal with crimes against humanity.

4. In order to distinguish crimes against humanity from other criminal offences one must proceed from the following. In case of a convention criminal offence the perpetrator does not deny derogatory value in itself. The perpetrator does not place himself outside the existing value system. In killing the victim he acknowledges human life as having value, and its inviolability, even though he finds justification for his own specific act. In case of crimes against humanity the perpetrator places himself for various reasons (first and foremost religious, national or ideological) outside of the belief system. He acts in the name of other purposes (e.g. ethnic cleansing) and the values under attack (life, health, physical inviolability) are for him worthless in the given context. The attack need not have been directed against the specific victim; it could have been directed at a random member of the group.

5. The fact that genocide was not delimited from other crimes against humanity caused the Põlva County Court at first to proceed from the offence of genocide, then to use in the reasons partly such characteristics typical of crimes against humanity which cannot be considered as genocide, only to return to the offence of genocide at the end. The appeal proceeded only from the offence of genocide, without distinguishing genocide from other crimes against humanity. Neither did the Circuit Court distinguish between these two crimes, noting that 'the acts described cannot be qualified as a crime against humanity since international agreements do not define the killing of a member of a group resisting an occupying regime as a crime against humanity'.

26 L Paradell, B Montejo, Analysis, *Public Prosecutor's Office, de Lois (Graciela) (intervening) and ors (intervening) v Manzorro (Adolfo)*, ILDC 136 (ES 2005) A12.

The Criminal Chamber of the Supreme Court emphasizes that '*a group initiating resistance against an occupying regime*' as noted the composition of Section 611 of the Estonian Criminal Code, is a feature of an offence of genocide, not of a crime against humanity.

6. According to the determination of the County Court and the Circuit Court K.–L. Paulov:

6.1 was an agent of the Soviet Security with special authorisations;

6.2 he acted according to orders, taking part in the physical extermination of individuals called bandit groups and single bandits;

6.3 during such operations he murdered A. Sibul and Alfred and Aksel Pärl.

Based on these factual circumstances, both courts have come to the conclusion that K.–L. Paulov is guilty of murdering the victims, whereat the Circuit Court made a specification and noted that pursuant to clause 1 of Article 50 of the Additional Protocols of 8 June 1977 to the Geneva Conventions of 12 August 1948 Relating to the Protection of Victims of International Armed Conflicts the victims have to be considered civilians

7. In the appeal in cassation only the concept of crimes against humanity is used and it is claimed that the victims hid in the forest as civilians to escape repression. The occupying powers, however, decided to deprive them of their right to fair trial and murder them, and so it is claimed that here a crime against humanity is involved.

8. The Supreme Court agrees with this last standpoint and notes that depriving an individual to their right to life and to fair trial could be qualified as a crime against humanity as stipulated in Article 6(c) of the Charter the Nuremberg International Military Tribunal. K.–L. Paulov committed the murders in the interest and knowledge of the occupying authorities and was aware that no criminal liability would follow from his actions pursuant to Article 136 of the Criminal Code of the Federal Russian Soviet Socialist Republic, which was applicable to the territory of the Estonian Soviet Socialist Republic at the time. Taking into account that neither the court of first instance, nor of the second instance, in deciding the application of Section 611 of the Criminal Code of Estonia clearly proceeded from the necessity of distinguishing between genocide and other crimes against humanity, the courts incorrectly applied subsection 1 of Section 39(2) of the Code of Criminal Court and Cassation Procedure by incorrectly interpreting the provision in question of the Criminal Code.

The various stages of this case evidence considerable confusion as to the different crimes of genocide, crimes against humanity and, indeed, war crimes. Even within the judgment of the Supreme Court, it is not entirely clear what the relevance of the discussion of genocide might be. Consequently, the suggestion that genocide is merely a sub-class of crimes against humanity should be resisted. Similarly, the case is deficient in terms of its discussion of the notion of widespread or systematic attack, which is overlooked in favour of a much lower threshold of attacking civilians hiding from repression. Nevertheless, the particular focus of the Estonian Supreme Court on the notion of humanity as a distinguishing factor in the identification of crimes against humanity is interesting.

3. War crimes

The term 'War Crimes' typically refers to serious violations of the body of law and customs of armed conflict, often referred to as international humanitarian law.[27] Prior to the Second World

27 See C Ryngaert, 'International Humanitarian Law' Chapter 13 in this volume.

War, there was a degree of acceptance that the intrinsic nature of war *necessarily* entailed a decline in the standards of human behaviour normally expected, to a degree that was necessary to reach the ultimate goal of victory. This ethos was arguably perpetuated by the difficulty of regulating breaches of international humanitarian law, and prosecuting individuals. Undoubtedly, the phrase *silent enim leges inter arma* (no law in war) is no longer accepted by the international community, as international humanitarian law attempts to govern behaviour during wartime. (There is, however, the perpetual problem of enforceability with respect to the laws of war during active hostilities.)

The Charter of the Nuremberg International Military Tribunal (NIMT) included the explicit definition of War Crimes as 'violations of the laws or customs of war. Such violations shall include, but not be limited to, murder, ill-treatment or deportation to slave labor or for any other purpose of civilian population of or in occupied territory, murder or ill-treatment of prisoners of war or persons on the seas, killing of hostages, plunder of public or private property, wanton destruction of cities, towns or villages, or devastation not justified by military necessity'.[28] In the judgment of the NIMT, it was stated that the crimes laid out in Article 6b of the Charter, 'were already recognised as war crimes under international law',[29] including by provisions of the Hague Regulations of 1907.[30]

The Geneva Conventions, which were responsive to the atrocities committed during the Second World War, do not refer to 'War Crimes' per se, but rather 'grave breaches':

'Art. 147. Grave breaches to which the preceding Article relates shall be those involving any of the following acts, if committed against persons or property protected by the present Convention: wilful killing, torture or inhuman treatment, including biological experiments, wilfully causing great suffering or serious injury to body or health, unlawful deportation or transfer or unlawful confinement of a protected person, compelling a protected person to serve in the forces of a hostile Power, or wilfully depriving a protected person of the rights of fair and regular trial prescribed in the present Convention, taking of hostages and extensive destruction and appropriation of property, not justified by military necessity and carried out unlawfully and wantonly.'[31]

International criminal law, in its relative modernity, has since been much more explicit regarding breaching the laws of war. The next substantial contributions came from the ICTY and ICTR, which confirmed the grave breaches provisions as part of customary international law through their non-exhaustive definitions in their Statutes.[32] The ICTY includes *customs* of war within its definition, whereas the ICTR refers solely to violations of Common Article 3 to the Geneva Conventions 1949 and Additional Protocol II 1977.

The ICC in contrast, however, includes an *exhaustive* list of fifty offences relating to war crimes. As such, it is by far the most detailed, and includes four main headings, primarily the grave breaches provisions of the Geneva Conventions 1949, followed by 'other serious violations

28 United Nations, Charter of the International Military Tribunal: Annex to the Agreement for the prosecution and punishment of the major war criminals of the European Axis ('London Agreement') (signed 8 August 1945) Article 6b.

29 Judicial Decision, International Military Tribunal (Nuremberg) 1st October 1946, see (1947) 41 *American Journal of International Law* 248.

30 Convention (IV) respecting the Laws and Customs of War on Land and its annex: Regulations concerning the Laws and Customs of War on Land (signed 18 October 1907, entered into force 26 January 1910) Articles 46, 50, 52, and 56.

31 Convention (IV) Relative to the Protection of Civilian Persons in Time of War (signed 12 August 1949, entered into force 21 October 1950) 75 UNTS 287, Article 147.

32 UNSC Res 827, Statute of the International Criminal Tribunal for the Former Yugoslavia (25 May 1993, as amended on 17 May 2002) UN Doc S/RES/827, Article 2; UNSC Res 955, Statute of the International Criminal Tribunal for Rwanda (8 November 1994, as last amended on 13 October 2006) UN Doc S/RES/955, Article 4.

of the laws and customs applicable in international armed conflict'. Also included, are serious violations of Common Article 3 to the Geneva Conventions in relation to *international* armed conflict, as well as other serious violations of the laws and customs of war regarding *non*-international armed conflict.[33] It is worth mentioning the wording of the first sentence of Article 8, which reads: 'The Court shall have jurisdiction in respect of war crimes in particular when committed as part of a plan or policy or as part of a large-scale commission of such crimes'. Unlike 'Crimes Against Humanity', there is in fact no scalar requirement for War Crimes, despite the use of the wording 'large-scale'. A *single* act which meets the requirements of a war crime, even when committed in isolation, is sufficient.

(a) Required nexus to armed conflict

Niyonteze and Military Prosecutor of the Military Tribunal of First instance 2 v Military Appeals Tribunal 1A, Cassation judgment, ILDC 349 (CH 2001), 27th April 2001, Switzerland; Military Supreme Court

This case concerned a Rwandan citizen residing in Geneva, Niyonteze, who was accused of committing acts during the civil war in his role as *bourgmestre* (mayor). In 1999, the Military Tribunal at First Instance found him to be guilty of, among various counts, homicide, and consequently sentenced him to life imprisonment. On appeal in 2000, the Military Appeals Tribunal reversed the judgment in part, but upheld Niyonteze's conviction of serious violations of Common Article 3 to the Geneva Conventions, and Article 4 of Additional Protocol to the Geneva Conventions 1949. Niyonteze then appealed to the Military Supreme Court; he argued that the acts he had committed were not breaches of international humanitarian law, as there was an insufficient link between those acts and the armed conflict that took place.

> 9. The defendant complains of a violation of criminal law (cf. Article 185 (1) (d) CPM), i.e. Articles 108 (3) CPM and 109 (1) CPM, Common Article 3 to the Geneva Conventions, Articles 146 and 147 of Geneva Convention IV and Article 4 of Additional Protocol II. He argues that the acts attributed to him (cf. supra paragraphs 6 and 7) do not fall within a link of close connection with the Rwanda conflict and consequently do not fulfill the objective conditions for him to be considered as the perpetrator of the aforementioned violations of international humanitarian law.
>
> (…)
>
> For Common Article 3 and Article 4 of Protocol to be applicable, it is still necessary, within the framework of Article 109 CPM—that these acts (and their perpetrator) are in a certain connective relationship with the armed conflict, because any attempt on a life in the territory of a country experiencing such a conflict would be covered by international humanitarian law. The Court of Appeal has found that this condition was met; the defendant contests this.
>
> (…)
>
> e) In the Rwandan institutional system, the mayor is considered an agent of the State. It is a prominent position, as the communities are few in number (145 communities in 1991, formed, for the most part, by 40,000 to 50,000 inhabitants, cf. Des Forges, op. cit., p. 55). If the mayor does not formally have any military attributes, it follows from the file that the defendant was normally accompanied by soldiers over whom he in fact exercised some authority. Both at the time of the meeting at Mont Mushubati and his visits to Kabgayi, he acted in his capacity as mayor or making use of the authority conferred on him by this appointment, by issuing instructions to those under him. His objective was to "support or initiate efforts of war", to use the terminology

33 Rome Statute of the International Criminal Court (n 1) Article 8(2)(a), (2)(b), (2)(c), and (2)(e).

> applied by the ICTR, in other words, to promote the causes and the objectives of the government in place aimed at the massacre of Tutsis and moderate Hutus.
>
> (...)
>
> It is clear on the one hand that the link between the offences committed at Mont Mushubati and Kabgayi, and the armed conflict is sufficient and, on the other hand, that as a result of his authority, and the manner in which he carried out his functions as mayor, the defendant met the required conditions for being found to be a perpetrator of the offences, under the scope of Common Article 3 and the provisions of Protocol II. The ground for appeal based on a violation of Article 109 CPM is consequently unfounded.

Although acknowledging that decisions of the ICTR do not constitute binding precedents, the Military Supreme Court draws heavily on the jurisprudence of the ICTR to establish that civilians can commit violations of Common Article 3 and of Additional Protocol II where a sufficient link is established between the individual and the relevant armed conflict. However, it is worth bearing in mind the opinion of the ILDC commentator, who noted that the Military Supreme Court could and should have gone further:

> 'One could greet the attempts of the Military Supreme Court to apply faithfully the key concepts of international criminal law and to pay careful attention in this regard to the case law of the ICTR. However, in this particular case, one should recognize that the Military Tribunal of First Instance and the Military Appeals Tribunal were, in fact, better inspired. For they had rightly considered that not only persons related to the armed forces, but every individual could be held responsible for violations of Common Article 3 and Additional Protocol II. Indeed, less than two months after the decision was rendered by the Military Supreme Court, the Appeals Chamber of the ICTR itself found that the Trial Chamber had erred on a point of law in restricting the application of Common Article 3 to a certain category of persons. (See Prosecutor v Akayesu, [§ 630–646]).'[34]

Prosecutor v Joseph M., Case numbers 09/750009-06 and 09/750007-07; 23th March 2009, Netherlands; District Court in The Hague, Criminal Law Section (not in ILDC)

On or around 13 April 1994, the defendant and others allegedly stopped an ambulance in Birogo, Rwanda, and killed two women occupants together with their children. Three days later he attacked Tutsi civilians who stayed at the Seventh Day Adventists Complex in Mugonero. He was also accused of the rape and murder of three other women as well as other offences. Although found guilty of committing acts of torture and sentenced to twenty years' imprisonment, the defendant was cleared of charges of war crimes due to the lack of a nexus between the crimes and the armed conflict in Rwanda.

> **20.** The Defendant has committed very serious violent crimes against the passengers of an ambulance.
>
> (...)
>
> **22.** Defendant threatened the passengers of the ambulance with an attack on their lives, physical violence, death, mutilation, cruel (inhumane) treatment and torture. He threatened Mrs. [witness 3] and Mr. [witness 4] with violence against their lives and with murder.
>
> (...)

---

34 C Bergmann, A Ziegler, Analysis, *Niyonteze and Military Prosecutor of the Military Tribunal of First instance 2 v Military Appeals Tribunal 1A*, ILDC 349 (CH 2001) A7.

> 23. Consequently the conclusion should be that the violent offences committed by the Defendant, both the ones against the passengers of the ambulance and against Mrs. [witness 3] and Mr. [witness 4], constitute gross violations of international humanitarian law, which result in individual criminal responsibility of the Defendant.
>
> Requirements for war crimes
>
> 25. Based on CA 3 and APII, and the interpretation given to these treaties by (international) case law it is concluded that an offence can only be classified as a war crime on the following conditions.
>
> (...)
>
> (4) There must be a close correlation between the indictable offence and the armed conflict, a concept named 'nexus' in (international) literature and case law. After all the intended object of penalisation of war crimes is to offer protection against crimes which are (closely) related to the war.
>
> (...)
>
> 65. The Court (...) recalls (that) the (...) intention of the penalisation of war crimes is to offer protection against the consequences of a war in a conflict between armed forces who are capable of fulfilling their obligations under international humanitarian law. It agrees that the explanation on this penalisation which was provided for by case law of the international tribunals has undoubtedly enlarged the scope of this penalisation, however without forgetting the intended interest of protection. Furthermore the Court is of the opinion that this case law, especially of the ICTR, has been formed in cases against accused who had a different status than the Defendant who is presently on trial and that the ICTR advocates to observe restraint regarding non-combatants, like the Defendant. In the opinion of the Court the sole circumstance that the armed conflict against the RPF provided the regime with an excuse for ethnic violence and the Defendant with a motive and a licence to commit his crimes, do not turn these criminal offences into war crimes. The connection between these crimes and the armed conflict, that was carried out at the same time by the RAF and the RPF, is too remote; in other words the required close relationship (the nexus) has not been established.
>
> 66. Consequently the Court acquits the Defendant of the criminal offences that he was charged with under the primary counts 1 and 3 of the indictment with case number 09/750009-06.

This decision is a challenging one for those seeking to bring an end to impunity for international crimes. On the face of it, it places a significant limitation on the extent of the war crimes regime as currently laid down in the ICC statute. On the other hand, the law does require a nexus between the conduct in question and a relevant armed conflict. The case provides a detailed and thorough analysis of the jurisprudence of both the ICTY and ICTR on the point at issue to conclude that in the circumstances of the case, there was not a sufficient nexus between the offences and the wider armed conflict.

It is worth noting that if offences were sufficiently widespread and systematic, they might have constituted crimes against humanity (or, indeed, genocide if the required *mens rea* is proven). Given that the defendant was ultimately convicted of torture, it is surprising that the case did not address crimes against humanity more directly. Nevertheless, the case does provide some interesting guidance to other courts facing the question of what is the required nexus between war crimes and an underlying armed conflict.

(b) Relationship between war crimes and domestic criminal law

Public Prosecutor v K, Judgment, Case No 02853/02 U, Decision No LJN: AF6988, NS 2004, 199, ILDC 142 (NL 2004), 7th May 2004, Netherlands; Supreme Court [HR]

This case concerned 'Mrs K', who was a leading figure in the Kurdish Labour Party, and the question of her extradition. It was argued by her Defence Counsel that her relevant acts were governed exclusively by international humanitarian law, which permitted the killing of enemy combatants. This meant, it was argued, that the double criminality requirement had not been met. The District Court of Amsterdam agreed on this point and declined the extradition request. The Supreme Court in the current case disagreed and allowed the extradition of Mrs K.

> **3.3.6.** The cited Common Article 3 of the Geneva Conventions, in brief and to the extent it is important here, forbids any party to an internal armed conflict from making attacks on the life of or committing physical violence upon people taking no active part in the hostilities. Both The Netherlands and Turkey are party to the Conventions.
>
> From the textual history of the aforesaid Article 3 it appears that the drafting of this provision resulted from the wish to have the rules on international armed conflict applicable to the humanitarian laws of war set as forth in the aforesaid Conventions, seen as essential to civilized Nations, applicable also to internal armed conflict. The goal was therefore the protection of the aforesaid people in case of an internal armed conflict and also to lay down a legal basis for humanitarian intervention by the International Red Cross or any other neutral international assistance organization, without having such intervention characterized as improper involvement in an internal matter of a State involved in the conflict. Article 3 contains minimum norms to which the parties in conflict must adhere with respect to the previously mentioned people, and are intended for their protection.
>
> **3.3.7.** The circumstance that the previously mentioned Article, which contains no obligation for the parties to the Conventions to make any actions criminal, does not apply in any way reduces the authority of the States involved to prosecute and punish any criminal offences committed by members of an armed oppositional group in connection with an internal armed conflict. Article 3 does not by its nature withhold its protection from attacks on the life of or physical violence upon any people other than those not taking an active part in the hostilities. This article does not legitimize such actions. It is an incorrect opinion that the humanitarian law of war applies exclusively to cases of an internal armed conflict, so that application of general criminal law is switched off. One of the questions to be distinguished from the preceding, moreover, is whether in this concrete instance there has been a political offence, in which case extradition must, for this reason, be declared inadmissible. This question is examined in 3.4 below.
>
> **3.3.8.** It follows from these considerations that the penalization of violations of the humanitarian law of war in internal armed conflicts under Article 6 of the International Crimes Act does not mean that these actions could not (also) be punishable under general criminal law and even less that other behaviour that might be carried out in the context of an internal armed conflict could not on that account be made punishable under general criminal law.
>
> **3.3.9.** Under Netherlands law the offences for which extradition is requested, are made punishable by Article 140 of the Criminal Code in connection with Article 289 and/or Article 303 of the Criminal Code. Under these provisions, the offences

> can be punished under Netherlands law with imprisonment of a maximum of at least one year. It is true that the requesting State has not given consideration to the corresponding criminal provisions specified in the cited Articles 289 and 303 of the Criminal Code, but it is general knowledge also that the behaviours punishable under these Articles are also punishable under the law of the requesting State with a punishment in the spirit of Article 2 first paragraph of the European Convention on Extradition and that this penalty provision extends to the protection of the same right as does the Netherlands penalty provision.
>
> **3.3.10.** It follows from the preceding that this satisfies the requirements with respect to double criminality within the meaning of Article 2 first paragraph of the European Convention on Extradition.

Although primarily concerned with questions of jurisdiction, in particular, the political offence exception, this case provides a useful discussion of the relationship between international criminal law relating to war crimes and domestic criminal law. The case makes clear that Common Article 3 does not override domestic criminal law in the case of non-international armed conflict. As one of the present authors made clear in his ILDC commentary:

> 'The Supreme Court's opinion that the conduct was not exclusively governed by international humanitarian law was interesting as it shed a light on the question whether states were allowed to exceed international provisions in the field of international criminal law. Apparently, the Court was of the opinion that states' hands were not completely tied by international law and that they had a certain measure of discretion to engage in further penalization on the basis of domestic criminal law. The Court itself, however, was cautious to restrict its view to the slightly elusive and immature body of standards applicable in non-international armed conflicts, as these did not contain explicit obligations to penalize certain acts. (paragraph 3.3.7) However, the 'grave breaches' provisions in the Geneva Conventions, which were applicable in international armed conflicts, precisely dictated state obligations in this respect and did not permit deviant state practice.'[35]

Public Prosecutor v F, First instance, Criminal procedure, LJN: BA9575, 09/750001-06, ILDC 797 (NL 2007), 25th June 2007, Netherlands; The Hague; District Court

'F' was a high-ranking officer in 'Khad-e-Nezami', the Afghan Military Intelligence Service. He was accused on two counts, the second of most relevance here, that he had superior responsibility for acts committed against two victims.

> **66** The District Court is of the opinion that at the time of the charged offences 'superior responsibility' for war crimes committed in a non-international armed conflict resulted from international customary law which was developed in the years following the Second World War. This judgment is also based upon the ruling pronounced by the Appeals Chamber of the ICTY in the case against Hadžihasanovic, which shows that the Appeals Chamber is of the opinion that already at the time of the conclusion of the two Additional Protocols to the Geneva Conventions in 1977, in relation to international as well as non-international armed conflicts, superior responsibility resulted from international customary law.
>
> **67** This position of the Court implies that the offences committed by the defendant during the indicted period can be judged according to article 9 of the Criminal Law in Wartime Act. This article should be explained according to international (customary) law regarding the so-called superior responsibility. This (automatically) means that

35 H van der Wilt, Analysis, *Public Prosecutor v K*, ILDC 142 (NL 2004) A2.

> the Court will also take into consideration the legal precedents of ad-hoc tribunals, also in as far as they require the fulfillment of the condition of 'effective command and control'.
>
> (...)
>
> **79** The defendant was one of the deputies to the Director of the Military Khad (Khad-e-Nezami), an organisation that in those days committed violations of human rights on a large scale, like torturing prisoners. It can be assumed that the defendant was closely involved in these practices. Nevertheless, it can not be established with adequate certainty, that the defendant was in a position to exercise effective command and control over the Head of the Investigation and Interrogation Department in all cases and under all circumstances. Although in the chain of command he was superior to [P4], there is still a lack of clarity about the fact whether the defendant was at any point in time in a position to exercise 'effective command and control' over the Military Khad as deputy to [P3] and likewise over the Investigation and Interrogation Department, a position that was undeniably held by [P3].
>
> **80** For that reason it cannot be excluded that the defendant was not in a position to take disciplinary action against the responsible persons for the acts of violence committed against the victims referred to in the charges. In other words: the Court is of the opinion that the question whether the defendant had 'effective control' cannot be answered affirmatively with a sufficient degree of certainty.
>
> **81** Therefore, the Court believes that one of the most important requirements necessary to be able to give an affirmative answer to the question whether the defendant carried 'superior responsibility' for the war crimes he is charged with, has not been fulfilled.
>
> **82** This can only lead to the conclusion that the defendant should be acquitted of the offences he was charged with under count 2.

This case is primarily concerned with the question of universal jurisdiction and the effect of an amnesty in the territorial state. The case did, however, briefly consider the question of superior responsibility and adopted the position of the ICTY that the law on superior responsibility applied equally in both international and non-international armed conflicts. In the present case, however, the court found that the defendant was not able to exercise effective command and control over the head of the Investigation and Interrogation Department in all cases and under all circumstances. Accordingly, the defendant was acquitted in relation to the charge that was dependent upon superior responsibility.

IV. Conclusion

As international criminal tribunals and the International Criminal Court can only prosecute and try a limited number of perpetrators of international crimes, law enforcement by domestic courts will remain of crucial importance. The preceding synopsis of case law demonstrates the varied attitudes of national courts. Some are prepared to apply (customary) international law freely in order to fill the gaps in national legislation. Others are far more reluctant to engage in such a dauntless interpretative exercise, as this would militate against the *nullum crimen sine lege* principle. Ultimately, this reflects the wide variety in legal systems' position on the direct applicability of international law.

International criminal law is still in its infancy. It is a relatively young body of normative standards. This implies that concepts and doctrines have not yet fully crystallized, leaving both international and domestic courts some margin of appreciation to further develop the law. The summary of case law shows that national courts are often inclined to conform to the interpretations of international criminal tribunals. However, when international case law is inconclusive or contradictory, national courts sometimes take the opportunity to develop their own opinions, thus contributing to the further elucidation of international criminal law. There is nothing wrong with that. International criminal tribunals do not enjoy a monopoly of interpretation in the realm of international criminal law. The contributions of national courts may plug some loopholes and strengthen the normative framework of an evolving body of law.

16

Amnesties

CLAUDIA MARTIN

I. Introduction

The perpetration of gross human rights violations in several Latin American countries and the impunity that followed in the aftermath of those violations triggered the need to explore avenues for redressing the victims and making the perpetrators accountable. Despite the fact that the regional human rights system was designed to establish the international responsibility of states and not the individual responsibility of the perpetrators, the Inter-American Commission (Commission) and Court of Human Rights (referred to as the Court or the Inter-American Court) were crucial in developing a normative framework which, translated into the domestic jurisdictions of states by municipal courts, led to the prosecution and punishment of the worst crimes and criminals. The relevance of the normative framework lies in the fact that it was developed with regard to crimes for which no other international tribunals, notably the International Criminal Court (referred to as the ICC), have jurisdiction to prosecute and as a result of the interaction between the international and the national jurisdictions.

The normative framework was construed around the state duty to investigate, identify, and punish heinous human rights violations developed initially by the Commission and later enriched by the case law of the Court. In spite of the fact that the principles of accountability may be applied to facts unaffected by the application of amnesty laws (for example, the situation prevailing in Colombia where the failure of the state to investigate is not related to an amnesty law), its overall impact and complexity can be more easily understood with regard to countries that have enacted these laws to prevent the punishment of serious human rights perpetrators.

II. The Jurisprudence of the Inter-American System on Amnesty Laws

The Commission was the first international organ to declare the incompatibility of an amnesty law with a human rights treaty, namely, the American Convention on Human Rights (ACHR).[1] In *Alicia Consuelo Herrera et al v Argentina*,[2] the Commission reviewed Laws 23,492 and 23,521, as well as Decree No 1002/89 in light of the ACHR to determine their compatibility with the rights enshrined in that regional convention. Law 23,492[3] (also known as the Full Stop Law) declared extinguished the crimes perpetrated by state agents during the military dictatorship and those carried out by armed groups and set a sixty-day deadline for closing the existing criminal proceedings. The law applied only against those who had not been ordered to appear before a court, were not declared *in absentia* or were not fugitives.

1 Inter-American Commission on Human Rights, *Case Alicia Consuelo Herrera et al v Argentina*, Report 28/92, Cases 10147, 10181, 10262, 10309, and 10311, 2 October 1992, Annual Report of the Inter-American Commission on Human Rights 1992–1993; *Hugo Leonardo de los Santos Mendoza et al v Uruguay*, Report 29/92, Cases 10,029, 10,036, 10,145, 10,305, 10,372, 10,373, 10,374, and 10,375, 2 October,1992, Annual Report of the Inter-American Commission on Human Rights 1992–1993; *Massacre Las Hojas v El Salvador*, Report 26/92, Case 10287, Annual Report of the Inter-American Commission on Human Rights 1992–1993.

2 *Case Alicia Consuelo Herrera et al v Argentina* (n 1).

3 Law 23,492, adopted on 24 December 1986.

Before the deadline elapsed, the Argentine judiciary issued orders to about 500 members of the security forces to appear before the courts. As a response to that situation, the Argentine Congress enacted Law 23,521[4] to prevent that those members of the security forces were prosecuted. Law 23,521 (also known as the Due Obedience Law) established a non-rebuttable presumption that members of the security forces accused of serious violations of human rights were acting under coercion and following superior orders and extinguished criminal liability for the perpetration of those crimes. Ultimately, Decree Law 1002/89[5] granted a pardon to members of the armed forces who were not benefiting from the previous laws. Law 23,521 was initially found constitutional by the Supreme Court of Argentina in 1987.[6] In 2005, the Argentine Supreme Court re-examined the laws and found them unconstitutional.[7]

The Commission concluded that the effects of the Argentine laws and decree was to dismiss the charges against the perpetrators of human rights violations and close any trials initiated by the judiciary, thereby leaving no legal avenue for the victims or their next of kin to seek redress through criminal prosecutions.[8] The Commission construed a legal theory according to which the denial of justice resulting from the application of the amnesty laws involved a violation of three provisions of the ACHR. First, since the victims in the Argentine legal system were authorized to join the criminal proceedings as a civil party, the Commission found that the laws prevented the victims from bringing a criminal action against those responsible for the violation of their rights, in violation of Article 8(1) of the ACHR, which ensures the right to a hearing by a competent, independent, and impartial court.[9] Similarly, the laws deprived the victims from their right to seek redress for the violation of their rights through a judicial remedy, as protected by Article 25 of the ACHR.[10] Finally, the Commission found that by enacting the amnesty laws, Argentina failed to ensure the rights protected in the ACHR as required by Article 1(1) of the ACHR. Article 1(1) provides for a state duty to prevent, investigate, and punish the violation of rights protected in the ACHR.[11] The scope of this obligation was developed in the seminal case of *Velásquez Rodríguez v Honduras*,[12] where the Court concluded that the breach of fundamental rights such as the right to life, personal integrity, and personal liberty triggered a state duty to immediately and thoroughly investigate, identify, and punish those responsible for the perpetration of human rights violations. The enactment of the amnesty laws obstructed the investigation and punishment of the perpetrators of human rights violations in Argentina and consequently the state failed to comply with the duties arising out of Article 1(1).

In *Hugo Leonardo de los Santos Mendoza et al v Uruguay*,[13] the Commission reviewed the compatibility of Law 15,848 with the ACHR Law 15,848[14] (also known as the 'Caducidad Law') declared that the state power to seek punishment for crimes perpetrated during the military dictatorship by members of the security forces was extinguished. A court hearing a case against a person accused of those crimes had to require the executive branch to determine whether the facts under investigation fell within the scope of the law, in which case the court had to

4 Law 23,521, adopted 4 June 1987.

5 Decree Law 1002/89, adopted 6 October 1989.

6 Supreme Court of Argentina, *Causa incoada en virtud del Decreto No 280/84 del Poder Ejecutivo Nacional*, 22 June 1987.

7 Supreme Court of Argentina, *Simón, Julio Héctor et al about illegitimate deprivation of liberty*, Appeal judgment, S 1767 XXXVIII, 14 June 2005.

8 *Case Alicia Consuelo Herrera et al v Argentina* (n 1) para 32.

9 ibid, paras 34–37.

10 ibid, para 39.

11 ibid, paras 40–41.

12 Inter-American Court of Human Rights, *Case of Velásquez Rodríguez v Honduras*, Merits, Judgment of 29 July 1988, Series C No 4.

13 *Hugo Leonardo de los Santos Mendoza et al v Uruguay* (n 1).

14 Law 15,848 [Ley de Caducidad de la Pretensión Punitiva del Estado], adopted on 22 December 1986.

dismiss them. The law was found constitutional by the Supreme Court of Uruguay in 1988 and approved by a national referendum called for that purpose pursuant to the provisions of the Uruguayan Constitution in 1989.[15] In October 2009 a plebiscite was held to determine whether the Caducidad Law had to be repealed, but it did not obtain the number of votes required to repeal it.[16] Law 15,848 was declared unconstitutional by the Supreme Court of Uruguay in several cases,[17] but in Uruguay the judgments declaring the unconstitutionality of a law are not of general application; they only apply to the case under analysis.[18] Consequently, the law remains in force.

In *Hugo Leonardo de los Santos Mendoza et al* the Commission concluded that the enactment of the law and its application prevented the victims and/or their next of kin from pursuing redress in a court of law for the human rights violations that affected them.[19] Thus, similar to the amnesty laws in Argentina, the Commission concluded that there was a violation of Articles 8(1), 25, and 1(1) of the ACHR.[20] Additionally, the Commission stated that the gravity of the crimes to which the law applied had to be considered because 'the social imperative of their clarification and investigation cannot be equated with that of a mere common crime'.[21]

Furthermore, in the cases reviewing the amnesty laws in Argentina and Uruguay, the Commission concluded that the payment of damages to the victims was not sufficient to redress the violations of their rights.[22] In both cases, the concerned states argued that the victims could still claim monetary compensation in spite of the application of the amnesty laws extinguishing the criminal liability of the perpetrators.[23] Notwithstanding the existence of additional measures of redress, the Commission still found that the criminal prosecution and punishment of the perpetrators of human rights violations was an essential component of the right to judicial protection that states could not disregard through the enactment of amnesty laws.[24] It is worth noting that historically the measures of redress awarded in Argentina had been more extensive than in Uruguay. Whereas Argentina established a truth commission-[25] and enacted laws to award monetary compensation to the victims of the military dictatorship,[26] Uruguay has failed

15 See G D Fernández, 'Uruguay' in J Arnold, J M Simon, and J Woischnick (eds), *Estado de derecho y delincuencia de Estado en América Latina. Una visión comparativa* (UNAM 2006) 264–65 http://www.bibliojuridica.org/libros/5/2116/12.pdf (last accessed 21 November 2017).

16 See Human Rights Watch, *Uruguay: Plebiscite Undermines Justice*, 27 October 2009 http://www.hrw.org/en/news/2009/10/27/uruguay-plebiscite-undermines-justice (last accessed 21 November 2017).

17 See in this regard *Sabalsagaray Curutchet, Blanca Stela*, Denuncia, Excepción de Inconstitucionalidad Arts 1, 3 y 4 de la Ley No 15.848, Ficha 97-397/2004, Sentencia 365/2009, 19 de octubre de 2009; *Organización de Derechos Humanos*, Denuncia, Excepción de Inconstitucionalidad Arts 1, 3 y 4 de la Ley No 15.848, Ficha IUE: 2-21986/2006, Sentencia 1525/2010, 29 de octubre de 2010, and *García Hernández, Amaral y otros*, Ficha 173-318/2006, 15 de diciembre de 2010.

18 Thus, the outcome of these judgments was that the Caducidad Law would not be applied to impede the prosecution of those responsible for the human rights violations perpetrated against the victims included in those cases.

19 *Hugo Leonardo de los Santos Mendoza et al v Uruguay* (n 1) para 39.

20 ibid, paras 46, 49, and 51.

21 ibid, para 38.

22 *Case Alicia Consuelo Herrera et al v Argentina* (n 1) para 51; *Hugo Leonardo de los Santos Mendoza et al v Uruguay* (n 1) para 53.

23 *Case Alicia Consuelo Herrera et al v Argentina* (n 1) para 26; *Hugo Leonardo de los Santos Mendoza et al v Uruguay* (n 1) para 11.

24 *Case Alicia Consuelo Herrera et al v Argentina* (n 1) para 51; *Hugo Leonardo de los Santos Mendoza et al v Uruguay* (n 1) para 53.

25 The National Commission on the Disappeared (CONADEP) was set up by President Raul Alfonsín on 15 December 1983. The final report of the CONADEP known as 'Nunca Mas' (Never Again) was released in September 1984.

26 See Laws 24,043, enacted on 23 December 1991 (granting economic compensation for civilians detained by a military court and those who remained in administrative detention upon orders of the executive power); Law 24,321, enacted on 6 August 1994 (providing that any person who has disappeared involuntarily from his or her home until 12/10/83 may be judicially declared 'absent by forced disappearance'); Law 24,411, enacted on

to investigate the facts that transpired during the military dictatorship to its full extent[27] and only provided compensation to a limited number of victims.[28]

Between 1996 and 1998, the Commission decided three complaints challenging the compatibility of the amnesty law in Chile. *Héctor Garay Hermosilla et al*,[29] *Juan Aniceto Meneses Reyes et al*,[30] and *Alfonso René Chanfeu Orayce*[31] related to the disappearance or extrajudicial execution of several victims and the subsequent impunity endured by the victims' next of kin. All the cases considered in the complaints were investigated by military courts and dismissed upon application of the amnesty law. In most of the cases the decision of the military courts was later confirmed by the Supreme Court of Chile. In contrast to Argentina and Uruguay, where the amnesty laws were enacted by a democratic Congress, in Chile the law was adopted by the military government led by Augusto Pinochet.[32] The Commission defined the amnesty law as a 'self-amnesty' because it was issued by a government to protect those in power and their collaborators from subsequent prosecutions regarding the egregious human rights violations that transpired during the military dictatorship.[33] Moreover, it concluded that the self-amnesty law lacked legitimacy because it was adopted by a regime that came to power by force and overthrew a democratic government.[34] Ultimately, the Commission found that the application of the self-amnesty law to the cases under analysis violated the

---

24 December 1994 (regulating the compensation that the next of kin of victims of forced disappearance were entitled to receive); and Law 25,914, enacted on 4 August 2004 (stipulating benefits for those born while their mothers were deprived from their liberty, or were arrested while under age due to their parents' detention) www.glin.gov (last accessed 21 November 2017).

27 On 9 August 2000, President Battle set up the National Commission for Peace to investigate the fate of the disappeared in Uruguay. This Commission did not have powers to investigate other human rights violations such as torture. The Commission presented its report on 10 April 2003. See in this regard J Errandonea, 'Justicia transicional en Uruguay' 47 *Revista IIDH* 13, 40–46. In 2015, President Tabaré Vásquez set up a Working Group on Truth and Justice within the executive branch. The Working Group, made up of seven members, is vested with the power to investigate the crimes against humanity perpetrated by state agents or others working under the color of law from 1968–1985, to collect all the existing information and create archives that can be used in prosecutions or other investigations initiated to satisfy the right to truth. Also, the Working Group will follow up on the implementation of domestic and international judgments regarding victims of those crimes, as well as the implementation of the reparations laws. See in this regard, A R Alves Nogueira and C P Carvalho, Panorama de Justicia Transicional en 2015, *Uruguay*, 169–70 http://olap.fder.edu.uy/wp-content/uploads/2015/06/Justic%CC%A7a-de-Transic%CC%A7a%CC%83o-e-Justicia-de-Transicion-WEB-FINAL.pdf (last accessed 21 November 2017). Also, see Presidential Decree of 19 May 2015 creating the Working Group https://medios.presidencia.gub.uy/tav_portal/2015/noticias/NO_P907/decreto.pdf (last accessed 6 March 2018).

28 See Fernández (n 15) 268; P Galain Palermo, *Uruguay*, in K Ambos, E Malarino, and G Elsner (eds), *Justicia de Transición: Informes de América Latina, Alemania, Italia y España* (Kondad Adenauer Stitfung 2009) 396. For subsequent developments in the area of reparations see UNHRC, 'Report of the Special Rapporteur on the promotion of truth, justice, reparation and guarantees of non-recurrence, P de Greiff, Mission to Uruguay' (2014) UN Doc A/HRC/27/56/Add.2, 12–13.

29 Inter-American Commission on Human Rights, *Héctor Garay Hermosilla et al v Chile*, Report 36/96, Case 10,843, 15 October 1996, Annual Report of the Inter-American Commission on Human Rights 1996.

30 Inter-American Commission on Human Rights, *Juan Aniceto Meneses Reyes et al v Chile*, Report 34/96, Cases 11,228, 11,229, 11,231, and 11,182, 15 October 1996, Annual Report of the Inter-American Commission on Human Rights 1996.

31 Inter-American Commission on Human Rights, *Alfonso René Chanfeau Orayce et al v Chile*, Report 25/98, Cases 11,505, 11,532, 11,541, 11,546, 11,549, 11569, 11,572, 11,573, 11,583, 11,585, 11,595, 11,652, 11,657, 11,675, and 11,705, 7 April 1998, Annual Report of the Inter-American Commission on Human Rights 1998.

32 Decree Law 2,191, enacted on 18 April 1978. For background information on the process of enactment of the amnesty law in Chile, see C Correa, 'El Decreto Ley de Amnistía: orígenes, aplicación y debate sobre su validez' in P Veloso (ed) *Justicia, Derechos Humanos y el Decreto de Amnistía* (PNUD 2010) 13–17.

33 *Héctor Garay Hermosilla et al v Chile* (n 29) paras 29–30; *Juan Aniceto Meneses Reyes et al v Chile* (n 30) paras 28-29; *Alfonso René Chanfeau Orayce et al v Chile* (n 31) paras 19-20.

34 *Héctor Garay Hermosilla et al v Chile* (n 29) paras 26–28; *Juan Aniceto Meneses Reyes et al v Chile* (n 30) paras 25-27; *Alfonso René Chanfeau Orayce et al v Chile* (n 31) paras 17–18.

rights to a fair trial and judicial protection under Articles 8(1) and 25 of the ACHR, as well as the duty to investigate and punish under Article 1(1) of the same treaty.[35] In the Chilean cases, the Commission incorporated an additional legal argument by concluding that the state's failure to derogate the self-amnesty law after the ACHR came into force for Chile involved the violation of the duty arising out of Article 2 of that treaty.[36] Article 2 provides that state parties to the ACHR undertake to adopt all the necessary measures to make the rights enshrined in that treaty effective. According to the Inter-American Court, Article 2 entails a state duty to derogate or amend any laws or measures that are in conflict with the full exercise of the rights protected by the ACHR.[37] Thus, Chile's failure to derogate the amnesty law after ratifying the ACHR and the absence of any adjustment in the state domestic laws to render the conventional rights effective in Chile constituted a breach of the obligation enshrined in Article 2.

Another issue developed by the Commission in the *Alfonso René Chanfeau Orayce et al* case was the articulation of the notion of the right to truth.[38] According to the Commission, Chile had an individual and collective duty to ensure the right of the victims' next of kin and society as a whole to know the truth regarding the serious violations of human rights that transpired in that country during the military dictatorship, as well as the identity of the perpetrators.[39] The Commission construed the right to truth from the obligations arising out of Articles 1(1), 8(1), 25, and 13 of the ACHR.[40] Similar to prior cases, the Commission concluded that the measures of reparation adopted by the state were not sufficient to meet the obligations established in the ACHR, in particular the duty to prosecute and punish the perpetrators of serious human rights violations.[41] Moreover, the Commission clearly stated that the investigations carried out by the Chilean Truth Commission[42] were not sufficient to afford protection to the victims' right to judicial protection and comply with the duty to ensure under Articles 25 and 1(1) of the ACHR.[43]

Lastly, the Commission reviewed the compatibility of the amnesty law enacted in El Salvador after the conclusion of the peace agreements that ended the armed conflict in that country with the ACHR. The amnesty law (also known as the General Amnesty Law for the Consolidation of Peace)[44] was enacted five days after the Truth Commission[45] created to investigate and report on the serious human rights violations that transpired during the armed conflict had issued its

35 *Héctor Garay Hermosilla et al v Chile* (n 29) paras 67, 72, 78; *Juan Aniceto Meneses Reyes et al v Chile* (n 30) paras 66, 71, 77; *Alfonso René Chanfeau Orayce et al v Chile* (n 31) paras 59, 65, 71.

36 *Héctor Garay Hermosilla et al v Chile* (n 29) para 93; *Juan Aniceto Meneses Reyes et al v Chile* (n 30) para 92; *Alfonso René Chanfeau Orayce et al v Chile* (n 31) para 84.

37 Inter-American Court of Human Rights, *International Responsibility for the Promulgation and Enforcement of Laws in Violation of the Convention*, Advisory Opinion No 14, Series A No 14, OC-14/94, 9 December 1994, para 39.

38 *Alfonso René Chanfeau Orayce et al v Chile* (n 31) para 39.

39 ibid, para 88.

40 ibid, para 85.

41 ibid, para 70.

42 On 25 April 1991, President Aylwin Azócar set up the National Commission for Truth and Reconciliation ('Comisión Rettig') to investigate the worst human rights violations perpetrated during the military dictatorship. The Commission released its report on 9 February 1991. Later, President Lagos set up the National Commission on Political Detention and Torture ('Comisión Valech') to document the cases of victims who were detained and torture for political reasons. This Commission started its work on 13 November 2003 and its final report was released on 28 November 2004.

43 *Alfonso René Chanfeau Orayce et al v Chile* (n 31) para 97.

44 Legislative Decree 486, enacted on 20 March 1993.

45 The creation of the Truth Commission in El Salvador was agreed as part of the UN-brokered peace agreements that ended the conflict in El Salvador. The Commission released a report 'Informe de la Comisión de la Verdad en El Salvador: De la Locura a la Esperanza' (Report of the Truth Commission for El Salvador: From Madness to Hope) on 1 April 1993.

report. The law granted full, absolute, and unconditional amnesty to all those who participated in the perpetration of political crimes, common crimes linked to political crimes and certain common crimes. The effects of the law were that convicted perpetrators were released and the pending cases were dismissed. Also, the law stated that cases brought with respect to crimes covered by the amnesty had to be dismissed *in limine* because the law extinguished the criminal liability of the alleged perpetrators. Finally, the law also extinguished the civil liability and prevented the victims from seeking damages.

In *Lucio Parada Cea et al v El Salvador*,[46] *Ignacio Ellacuría et al v El Salvador*,[47] and *Monsignor Oscar Arnulfo Romero y Galdámez v El Salvador*,[48] the Commission underlined that the crimes to which the amnesty law applied involved serious offences such as summary executions, torture, and forced disappearances.[49] Also, it stated that the seriousness of these crimes had triggered the adoption of special treaties enshrining principles to fight impunity such as the principle of universal jurisdiction and the inapplicability of a statute of limitations.[50] The Commission was referring in particular to the universal and regional convention on the prevention and punishment of torture, as well as the regional convention on forced disappearances of persons which enshrined the aforementioned principles.[51] Finally, the Commission concluded that the forced disappearance of persons is a crime against humanity and suggested that the state duty to investigate these crimes is broader than the obligation to investigate ordinary crimes.[52] The Commission's analysis in these cases introduces notions of international criminal law to articulate the theory that serious crimes cannot be treated as ordinary crimes. Thus, the duty to investigate these serious crimes and punish their perpetrators is so imperative that it justifies the involvement of courts beyond the domestic jurisdiction under the principle of universal jurisdiction or the non-application of well-established due process rights such as statutes of limitation to ensure that the perpetrators of those offences are not left unpunished. Ultimately, the Commission's approach reflects the need to lay a stronger legal foundation for the interpretation of the obligations arising under the ACHR in

46 Inter-American Commission on Human Rights, *Lucio Parada Cea et al v El Salvador*, Report No 1/99, Case 10,480, 27 January 1999, Annual Report of the Inter-American Commission on Human Rights 1998.

47 Inter-American Commission on Human Rights, *Ignacio Ellacuría et al v El Salvador*, Report No 136/99, Case 10,488, 22 December 1999, Annual Report of the Inter-American Commission on Human Rights 1999.

48 Inter-American Commission on Human Rights, *Monsignor Oscar Arnulfo Romero y Galdámez v El Salvador*, Report No 37/00, Case 11,481, 13 April 2000, Annual Report of the Inter-American Commission on Human Rights 1999.

49 *Lucio Parada Cea et al v El Salvador* (n 46) para 112; *Ignacio Ellacuría et al v El Salvador* (n 47) para 209; and *Monsignor Oscar Arnulfo Romero y Galdámez v El Salvador* (n 48) para 134.

50 *Lucio Parada Cea et al v El Salvador* (n 46) para 112; *Ignacio Ellacuría et al v El Salvador* (n 47) para 209; and *Monsignor Oscar Arnulfo Romero y Galdámez v El Salvador* (n 48) para 134. The Commission had made a similar statement in the *Alfonso René Chanfeau Orayce et al v Chile*. However, in that case the Commission did not analyze this issue at length. See *Alfonso René Chanfeau Orayce et al v Chile* (n 31) para 39.

51 Inter-American Convention to Prevent and Punish Torture (adopted 9 December 1985, entered into force 27 February 1987) OAS Treaties Series No 67; Convention Against Torture and Other Cruel, Inhuman or Degrading Treatment or Punishment (adopted 10 December 1984, entered into force 26 June 1987) 1465 UNTS 85; and Inter-American Convention on Forced Disappearances of Persons (adopted 9 June 1994, entered into force 28 March 1996) OAS Treaty Series No 68. The principle of universal jurisdiction is enshrined in Article 12 of the Inter-American Convention on Torture; Article 5 of the UN Convention Against Torture and Article IV of the Inter-American Convention on Forced Disappearances. Moreover, Article VII of the Inter-American Convention on Forced Disappearances states that the criminal prosecution of forced disappearances will not be subject to the application of statutes of limitation. However, the same Article provides that '[i]f there should be a norm of a fundamental character preventing application of the stipulation contained in the previous paragraph, the period of limitation shall be equal to that which applies to the gravest crime in the domestic laws of the corresponding State Party'.

52 In fact, the Commission stated that the 'social need to explain and investigate these crimes against humanity cannot be placed at the same level as mere civil crimes'. See, *inter alia*, *Lucio Parada Cea et al v El Salvador* (n 46) para 113.

light of the gravity of the offences involved. Despite the fact that the Truth Commission created in El Salvador issued an emblematic report naming the perpetrators of human rights violations, the Commission followed its prior case law stating that this type of processes were not sufficient to meet the obligations arising out of Article 1(1) of the ACHR.[53] Also, in the three cases the Commission found, in line with its prior case law, violations of Articles 2, 8(1), 25, and 1(1) of the ACHR for the failure to investigate the gross human rights violations perpetrated in El Salvador, as a result of the application of the amnesty law.[54] Additionally, the Commission found a violation of the right to truth and construed the scope of this right from a combined interpretation of Articles 1(1), 8(1), 25, and 13 of the ACHR.[55]

The principles of accountability developed by the Commission under the ACHR were later embraced and further expanded by the Inter-American Court. The first case decided by the Court involved the determination of the compatibility of the amnesty laws enacted in Peru during President Fujimori's administration and the ACHR.[56] In *Barrios Altos v Peru*,[57] the Court followed a similar approach to the Commission's.

Barrios Altos related to the extrajudicial execution of fifteen people by Peruvian state agents and the injury of four other individuals for their alleged connection to Shining Path (*Sendero Luminoso*). No serious investigation of these crimes was pursued until a civil prosecutor filed charges against several members of the National Intelligence Service. This investigation triggered the enactment of Law 26,479 exonerating members of the army, police force, and civilians who had violated human right from 1980 and 1985. The law came into effect immediately. The next day, a first instance court held the law inapplicable because it violated constitutional guarantees, and Peru's international obligations under the ACHR. This decision was appealed. Before public hearings on the constitutional issues started, the Peruvian congress adopted Amnesty Law No 26,492. This new law declared that the legality of the amnesty laws could not be reviewed by the judiciary and that their application was mandatory.

In *Barrios Altos*, the Court first concluded that amnesty provisions, statutes of limitations, or any other measures enacted or applied to prevent the investigation and punishment of those responsible for the perpetration of serious human rights violations such as torture, extra-judicial executions, or forced disappearances were incompatible with international human rights law principles.[58] Next, the Court held that the enactment of Laws No 26,479 and 26,492 prevented the victims' next of kin and the surviving victims from being heard by a judge, as established in Article 8(1) of the ACHR.[59] Peru also violated the right to judicial protection embodied in Article 25 and failed to comply with Article 1(1) by preventing the investigation, capture, prosecution, and conviction of those responsible for the events that occurred in *Barrios Altos*.[60] Furthermore, the adoption of the amnesty laws was incompatible

53 *Lucio Parada Cea et al v El Salvador* (n 46) para 145; *Ignacio Ellacuría et al v El Salvador* (n 47) paras 229–31; *Monsignor Oscar Arnulfo Romero y Galdámez v El Salvador* (n 48) para 150.

54 *Lucio Parada Cea et al v El Salvador* (n 46) paras 122, 128, 146; *Ignacio Ellacuría et al v El Salvador* (n 47) paras 196, 217, 220; *Monsignor Oscar Arnulfo Romero y Galdámez v El Salvador* (n 48) para 141.

55 *Lucio Parada Cea et al v El Salvador* (n 46) para 147; *Ignacio Ellacuría et al v El Salvador* (n 47) para 221; *Monsignor Oscar Arnulfo Romero y Galdámez v El Salvador* (n 48) para 142.

56 In two previous judgments in the *Case of Loayza Tamayo v Peru, Reparations and Costs*, Judgment of 27 November 1998, Series C No 42, and *Case of Castillo Paéz v Peru*, Reparations and Costs, Judgment of 27 November 1998, Series C No 43, the Court briefly analysed the implications of the amnesty laws for the victims' rights, but it was in the *Barrios Altos* judgment in which this tribunal had the historical opportunity to define the scope of the obligations to investigate and prosecute under Article 1(1) of the ACHR and its relationship to the victims' right to seek truth and justice in cases of gross violations of human rights.

57 Inter-American Court of Human Rights, *Case of Barrios Altos v Peru*, Merits, Judgment March 14, 2001, Series C No 75.

58 ibid, para 41.

59 ibid, para 42.

60 ibid.

with Article 2 of the ACHR because Peru failed to comply with the obligation not to enact domestic legislative measures that violated the rights protected in that treaty.[61] Ultimately, the Court concluded that given the incompatibility of the amnesty laws with the ACHR, those laws lacked legal effect and could not continue to be used to obstruct the investigation and punishment of those responsible for the human rights violations in the present case.[62] Most importantly, the Court concluded that the amnesty laws could neither be applied to other criminal proceedings in which the violation of non-derogable rights protected by the ACHR was investigated.[63] Through this legal conclusion, the Court gave its decision an *erga omnes* effect which was later adopted by certain domestic courts as the legal foundation to support a declaration of incompatibility of amnesty laws with the ACHR at the domestic jurisdiction.

The second relevant case decided by the Inter-American Court was *Almonacid Arellano et al v Chile*[64] in which the Court reviewed for the first time the compatibility of the Chilean self-amnesty law with the ACHR. *Almonacid Arellano et al* refers to the death of Luis Almonacid Arellano, an elementary education teacher, member of the Chilean Communist Party, and union leader who was murdered by members of the police after arresting him at his home on 16 September 1973. These events transpired in the city of Rancagua, Chile, a few days after a *coup d'état* had overthrown President Allende, and were carried out as part of the wide repression unleashed by the Pinochet military dictatorship against alleged opponents to the new regime. Though a criminal investigation was opened as a result of the murder of Mr Almonacid Arellano in 1973, the case was ultimately dismissed in September 1974 without ever having identified or punished the perpetrators. On April 18, 1978, the *de facto* government passed Decree Law No 2191 granting amnesty to perpetrators of criminal acts carried out from 11 September 1973, until 10 March 1978.[65] Some criminal acts were excluded from the application of the amnesty law.[66]

In 1992, the victim's wife requested the reopening of the case and brought charges against the two alleged perpetrators before a first instance court. In September 1996, the military jurisdiction requested the ordinary court to decline to exercise jurisdiction over the case on the basis that, at the time of the murder, the two alleged perpetrators were on active duty under military jurisdiction. Moreover, the military court stated that when Mr Almonacid Arellano was killed, there was in effect a state of siege, which should be construed as a state or time of war; thus, the military court had jurisdiction over the investigation of his murder. In December 1996, the Supreme Court of Chile confirmed the transfer of jurisdiction from the civilian courts to the military courts. In January 1997, the military courts ordered the dismissal and closing of the investigation upon application of the amnesty law, which was confirmed by the court martial. A motion for review filed with the Supreme Court was dismissed on the grounds that it was time-barred.

61 ibid.

62 ibid, para 44.

63 ibid.

64 Inter-American Court of Human Rights, *Case of Almonacid Arellano et al v Chile*, Preliminary Objections, Merits, Reparations and Costs, Judgment of 26 September 2006, Series C No 154.

65 Decree Law No 2191 states:

> Section 1 - Amnesty shall be granted to all individuals who performed illegal acts, whether as perpetrators, accomplices or accessories after the fact, during the state of siege in force from September 11, 1973 to March 10, 1978, provided they are not currently subject to legal proceedings or have been already sentenced.
> Section 2 - Amnesty shall be further granted to those individuals who, to the date of this Decree Law, have been sentenced by military courts, after September 11, 1973.

66 For example, robbery aggravated by violence or intimidation, rape, and embezzlement were excluded from the application of the amnesty law.

In addition to following the analysis developed by the Commission, the Court in *Almonacid Arellano* made a significant development in the articulation of new aspects of the principles of accountability. Particularly, the Court found for the first time that certain crimes committed in the context of a generalized and systematic attack against civilians amounted to crimes against humanity and therefore imposed upon the state a duty to investigate, prosecute, and punish the perpetrators.[67] This obligation cannot be overridden by the application of amnesty laws or similar domestic provisions excluding criminal liability for the perpetrators.[68] The Court held similarly in the *Miguel Castro-Castro Prison Case*[69] and in the *La Cantuta Case*.[70] As in *Barrios Altos*, the Court concluded that the amnesty law in Chile, which prevented the investigation of a crime against humanity, involved a violation of Articles 8(1), 25, 1(1), and 2 of the ACHR.[71]

In contrast to the Commission's views, the Court in *Barrios Altos* and *Almonacid Arellano* rejected the notion of the right to truth as an independent violation of human rights as construed by the Commission in its case law. The Court concluded that the right to truth is subsumed in the victims' right to obtain justice through the investigation and punishment of the perpetrators under Articles 1(1), 8, and 9 of the ACHR.[72]

The Court has decided three additional cases regarding the compatibility of amnesty laws with the ACHR. First, *Gomes Lund et al (Guerrilha do Araguaia) v Brazil*[73] refers to the torture and forced disappearance of seventy individuals perpetrated by the Brazilian armed forces as part of the operation to eradicate the Guerrilha do Araguaia between 1972–1975, during the military dictatorship in that country. The torture and disappearances of these individuals where never investigated due to the application of Amnesty Law No 6,683/79. On 29 April 2010, the Supreme Court of Brazil ruled in favor of the constitutionality of the amnesty law. The Court reiterated its prior case law regarding the incompatibility of the amnesty laws with the ACHR and found Brazil in violation of Articles 1(1), 8, 25, and 2 of that treaty.[74] Ultimately, the Court concluded that the amnesty law in Brazil had no legal effects and should not represent a legal obstacle for the prosecution of the perpetrators of forced disappearances in the present case.[75]

---

67 *Case of Almonacid Arellano et al v Chile* (n 64) paras 104, 110–11. In previous cases, the Court has stated that the practice of forced disappearances constituted a crime against humanity. However, the Court has never made a reasoned analysis finding a certain human rights violation under the ACHR a crime against humanity and the implications of that determination. In the *Gómez Palomino* case, for example, the Court indicated in a footnote that the Convention on Forced Disappearances considers the practice of forced disappearances a crime against humanity. See Inter-American Court of Human Rights, *Case of Gómez Palomino v Peru*, Judgment of 22 November 2005, Series C No 136, para 92. Additionally, the Court in *Serrano Cruz Sisters* and *Goiburú* held that a forced disappearance that is part of a pattern or practice of disappearances constitutes a crime against humanity. See Inter-American Court of Human Rights, *Case of the Serrano Cruz Sisters v El Salvador*, Preliminary Objections, Judgment of 23 November 2004, Series C No 118, para 103; *Case of Goiburú et al v Paraguay*, Merits, Reparations and Costs, Judgment of 22 September 2006, Series C No 153, para 82. Finally, although the Inter-American Commission and the petitioners argued that the extrajudicial executions perpetrated against members of an indigenous community in the *Plan de Sánchez Massacre* case constituted genocide, the Court refused to rule on that matter stating that it lacked jurisdiction *rationae materiae*. The Court, however, found that the massacre was part of a pattern of committing this kind of acts and therefore involved an aggravated international responsibility for the state. See Inter-American Court of Human Rights, *Case of the Plan de Sánchez Massacre v Guatemala*, Judgment of 29 April 2004, Series C No 105, para 51.

68 *Case of Almonacid Arellano et al v Chile* (n 64) para 114.

69 Inter-American Court of Human Rights, *Case of the Miguel Castro-Castro Prison v Peru*, Judgment of 25 November 2006, Series C No 160, paras 403–405.

70 Inter-American Court of Human Rights, *Case of La Cantuta v Peru*, Merits, Reparations and Costs, Judgment of 29 November 2006, Series C No 162, para 225.

71 *Case of Almonacid Arellano et al v Chile* (n 64) paras 122, 128–29.

72 ibid, para 148.

73 Inter-American Court of Human Rights, *Gomes Lund et al (Guerrilha do Araguaia) v Brazil*, Preliminary Objections, Merits, Reparations, and Costs, Judgment of 24 November 2010, Series C No 219.

74 ibid, paras 172–73.

75 ibid, para 174.

Secondly, *Juan Gelman, María Claudia Iruretagoyena de Gelman y María Macarena Gelman García Iruretagoyena v Uruguay*[76] relates to the forced disappearance of María Claudia Iruretagoyena de Gelman and the appropriation, and suppression of identity and nationality of her minor daughter in 1976. The facts that transpired in this case were never investigated and the perpetrators were not identified and punished as a result of the application of Amnesty Law 15,848, also known as the Caducidad Law, enacted by the democratic Congress of Uruguay and approved by the majority of the population in a referendum. The Court found that the prohibition of forced disappearances and the correlative duty to investigate and punish the perpetrators of these crimes were *jus cogens* norms which prevented states from applying rules such as amnesty laws to shield those responsible from criminal liability.[77] Consequently, the Court found that the Caducidad Law was incompatible with the ACHR and that Uruguay was responsible for the violation of Articles 1(1), 8, 25, and 2 of the same treaty.[78] The Court reiterated that the law had no legal effects and should not be used as an obstacle for the investigation, prosecution, and punishment of those responsible for the forced disappearance of the victims, the torture that they underwent, and the suppression of the identity of María Macarena Gelman García Iruretagoyena.[79]

Most recently, the Court has ruled on the compatibility of the amnesty law of El Salvador in the *Case of the Massacres of El Mozote and nearby places*.[80] This case involves the extrajudicial execution of more than 900 civilian victims, including men, women, and children, in the village of El Mozote, the canton of La Joya, the villages of Rancheria, Los Toriles, and Jocote Amarillo, as well as in the canton of Cerro Pando and in a cave in Cerro Ortiz, as part of an alleged counterinsurgency operation that was part of a 'scorched earth' policy planned and carried out by members of the Armed Forces of El Salvador. Before being killed the victims were illegally and arbitrarily deprived of their liberty and subjected to different forms of ill-treatment. Additionally, evidence shows that women in the village of El Mozote were raped by the perpetrators. Surviving victims were forced to leave the villages and lost all of their possessions. Even if the Truth Commission set up to investigate gross violations of human rights during the conflict in El Salvador exposed the Case of El Mozote and nearby villages, criminal prosecutions initiated to punish the perpetrators were interrupted in application of the 'Law of General Amnesty for the Consolidation of Peace', adopted in 1993. As stated above, this law required *in limine* termination of existing prosecutions, provided for a general amnesty to those involved in the conflict, including perpetrators of gross violations of human rights, and extinguished civil liability. In contrast to other amnesty cases reviewed by the Court, the facts that transpired in this case occurred in the framework of an internal armed conflict in El Salvador. In this regard, the Court rejected that the amnesty law was authorized by Article 6(5) of Protocol II to the Geneva Conventions because that provision encourages the application of amnesties to those who have taken part in the non-international armed conflict or who are deprived of liberty for reasons related to the armed conflict, but excludes as beneficiaries perpetrators of war crimes or crimes against humanity.[81]

The Court first found that the adoption of the amnesty law was contrary to the letter and spirit of the Peace Accords signed by the waging parties in that conflict, which envisioned the existence of a truth commission and criminal prosecutions for those involved in human rights

76 Inter-American Court of Human Rights, *Case Gelman v Uruguay*, Merits and Reparations, Judgment of 24 February 2011, Series C No 221.

77 ibid, para 183.

78 ibid, para 230.

79 ibid, para 232.

80 Inter-American Court of Human Rights, *Case of the Massacres of El Mozote and nearby places v El Salvador*, Merits, Reparations and Costs, Judgment of 25 October 2012, Series C No 252.

81 ibid, paras 285–87.

violations.[82] The language agreed upon in those accords, interpreted in light of the ACHR, shows a serious violation of the state's international obligation to investigate and punish the grave human rights violations and the breaches of international humanitarian law relating to the massacres of El Mozote and nearby places, by preventing the survivors and the victims' next of kin from accessing a court and receiving judicial protection, in light of Articles 8(1) and 25 of the ACHR.[83] Also, in line with its prior case law, the Court found violations to Articles 1(1) and 2 of that instrument as a result of the state's failure to respect and ensure the rights protected by the ACHR and adjust its domestic legislation to the obligations arising out of that treaty.[84] Once more in this judgment, the Court concluded that the law had no legal effects and should not be an obstacle for the criminal investigation of those involved in the perpetration of the gross human rights violations that transpired in this case or other similar cases.[85]

Interestingly, since the *Gomes Lund et al (Guerrilha do Araguaia)* case, the Court seems to have changed its interpretation with respect to the right to truth and has shown more willingness to relate it to the right to access to information, under Article 13 of the ACHR.[86] Certainly, in that case the petitioners had filed a domestic remedy requesting information on the place of burial of the victims and information on the military operations executed to eliminate the members of the group. The remedy was rejected by several courts, depriving the victims' next of kin from crucial information on their whereabouts and the facts that led to their disappearance. The Court followed a similar interpretation in *Gelman* and the *Mozote Massacre* cases.[87]

III. The Interaction between International and Domestic Courts in Applying the Principles of Accountability

The Commission's jurisprudence and the Court's findings in *Barrios Altos* triggered a complete new process of accountability in Latin America. As a result of the principles developed under the ACHR and other human rights treaties, domestic courts in several countries, including Argentina, Peru, Chile, Uruguay, and, most recently, El Salvador found the amnesty laws unconstitutional and/or ordered the reopening of criminal proceedings. Other countries have continued to face a debate on the compatibility of the amnesty laws with international human rights law such as is the case of Brazil (and Uruguay given the particularities of the domestic legal system).

Since the initial case law of the Inter-American organs on amnesty laws limited itself to articulate the duty to investigate and punish under the ACHR and other international human rights instruments, the domestic courts were left with the task of translating into domestic laws and procedures the actual implementation of those duties. As a result, the rationales to declare national amnesty laws unconstitutional and/or reopen the criminal investigations into gross human rights violations that occurred in the past were different depending on the country concerned, the legal culture, and the political environment in which the judgments were adopted. It is worth

82 ibid, para 292.

83 ibid, para 295.

84 ibid, para 296.

85 ibid.

86 *Gomes Lund et al (Guerrilha do Araguaia) v Brazil* (n 73) paras 200–02.

87 See, in this regard, *Case Gelman v Uruguay* (n 76) para 243; *Case of the Massacres of El Mozote and nearby places v El Salvador* (n 80) para 298. In its most recent cases on gross violations of human rights, the Court has acknowledged the autonomous nature of the right to truth, but has related it to the right to access to justice. See, in this regard, Inter-American Court of Human Rights, *Case of Peasant Community of Santa Barbara v Peru*, Preliminary Objections, Merits, Reparations, and Costs, Judgment of 1 September 2015, Series C No 299, paras 261–67; *Case of the Members of the village of Chichupac and neighboring communities of the Municipality of Rabinal v Guatemala*, Preliminary Objections, Merits, Reparations and Costs, Judgment of 30 November 2016, Series C No 328, paras 260–61.

mentioning that since the judgment in *Almonacid Arellano*, the Court has best articulated the duty to investigate and prosecute under the ACHR and offered more guidance to domestic courts as to the scope of those obligations. As will be noted in the following sections, the Court's jurisprudence at the same time has nurtured itself from the interpretations and legal approaches construed by domestic courts.[88]

The subsequent sections are representative of the different rationales followed by domestic courts when articulating international human rights obligations with domestic laws and principles. Overall, the approaches reproduced in the case law below show the struggle of domestic courts to develop a legal approach that would incorporate the inter-American human rights standards within an existing constitutional order. The outcome of those judgments has been in general praised by the human rights community but, in some cases, strongly criticized by other domestic constituencies, including those in the domestic criminal law area.

1. The permanent nature of the crime of forced disappearance

Sepúlveda (Juan Manuel Contreras), Re and ors, Action to annul, Rol No 517-2004, ILDC 394 (CL 2004), 17th December 2004, Chile; Supreme Court

Miguel Angel Sandoval was abducted by the Chilean secret police (*Dirección de Inteligencia Nacional*—DINA) operating during Augusto Pinochet's dictatorship on 7 January 1975. Investigations in the case were closed in 1976 after a *habeas corpus* to establish the whereabouts of the victim was rejected. They were later reopened in 1988, after democracy was reestablished in Chile, to identify and punish those responsible for the victim's disappearance, whose whereabouts were still unknown. In 1978, the military authorities enacted an amnesty law (*Decreto Ley* No 2191) that applied to crimes committed between 11 September 1973 and 10 March 1978. According to prior interpretations of Chilean courts, the amnesty law did not prevent the investigation of crimes alleged to have been committed in that period, but required judges to acquit those found responsible as authors and accomplices. In 2003, however, a court of first instance found that the amnesty law did not apply to the present case because Sandoval's whereabouts continued to be unknown and therefore the crime was a permanent and continuous one, which exceeded the time limit established by the amnesty law. The domestic court framed the crime as 'aggravated kidnapping' under the Chilean criminal code since Chile had not typified the crime of forced disappearance of persons at the time. The Court of Appeal affirmed the lower court's judgment based on the existence of an international duty to prosecute and punish crimes against humanity which prevented the application of an amnesty law to those allegedly responsible. The Supreme Court of Chile agreed.

> H2 There was no basis for annulling the decision of the Court of Appeal as there was no mistake in the identification of the applicable law. The applicable law was Article 141 of the Criminal Code, and the main argument for dismissing the application of the Amnesty Law was the continuous character of the crime, the commission of which could be assumed to have extended beyond the time limit established by the Amnesty Law insofar as the whereabouts of Mr Sandoval are still unknown.
>
> H3 The international norms and the international doctrine mentioned in the Court of Appeal's decision were included *obiter dictum* to stress the seriousness of the offence, but they had no influence on the *dispositif*. Therefore, the punishment applied to the persons involved in the commission the crime was based on the Criminal Code and not on international instruments.

88 See, *inter alia, Gomes Lund et al (Guerrilha do Araguaia) v Brazil* (n 73); *Case Gelman v Uruguay* (n 76).

H4 Common Article 3, Geneva Conventions, 1949 did not apply to the *coup d'etat* in Chile, and hence the Court of Appeal was correct in holding that the Geneva Conventions did not provide a basis for an international obligation to prosecute those responsible for the forced disappearance of persons.

Despite the judgment of the Supreme Court, it was not clear from the decision whether the rationale not to apply the amnesty law in the present case was based on international law obligations binding upon Chile or exclusively on domestic norms. Additionally, the Supreme Court judgment held that the amnesty law was not applicable to this case, but did not rule on its compatibility with international law. Even if the judgment in *Sandoval* was overruled in the case of the disappearances of *Ricardo Rioseco* and *Luis Cotal*,[89] subsequently the doctrine of the permanent nature of the crime of forced disappearance for justifying the non-application of the amnesty law was upheld in other cases.[90] Also, in those subsequent cases, the Supreme Court changed its position regarding the application of the Geneva Conventions to the period covered by the amnesty law and concluded that those treaties provided that persecution for the crime of forced disappearances could not be subject to a statute of limitation.[91] In *Episodio Rudy Cárcamo Ruiz*, the Supreme Court of Chile went even further as it characterized forced disappearance as a crime against humanity under international law and, as such, imprescriptible.[92] In all these cases, the domestic courts in Chile ruled on the non-application of a statute of limitation to the crimes under analysis to allow for its prosecution after the expiration of the amnesty law in March 10, 1978.

It is worth noting that the permanent nature of the crime of forced disappearance was used by the Inter-American Court in *Gomes Lund et al (Guerrilha do Araguaia)* to reject the argument that derogating the amnesty law in Brazil and reopening the criminal proceedings would involve a violation of the principle of legality and the prohibition of the retroactive application of the law.[93]

2. The direct application of international human rights law by domestic courts

As stated previously, in *Barrios Altos* the Court concluded that amnesty laws, statutes of limitations or other measures enacted to impede investigation into the violation of non-derogable rights such as the right to life and not to be subject to torture were incompatible with the ACHR. As a result, the amnesty laws in Peru were null and void and could not be applied to prevent the criminal investigation into the murders perpetrated in *Barrios Altos* or any other existing proceedings in Peru in which violations of similar rights were investigated. The Court's findings in *Barrios Altos* were later used by the Supreme Court of Argentina as one of the main foundations to declare the unconstitutionality of the amnesty laws in that country in the case of *Simón, Julio Héctor et al about illegitimate deprivation of liberty*.[94]

Simón (Julio Héctor) v Office of the Public Prosecutor, Appeal judgment, S. 1767. XXXVIII, ILDC 579 (AR 2005), 14th June 2005, Argentina; Supreme Court [CSJ]

On 28 November 1978, Julio Héctor Simón, along with other members of the Argentine Federal Police, kidnapped José Liborio Poblete, his wife Gertrudis Marta Hlaczik, and their daughter Claudia Victoria Poblete. They were taken to the detention centre *El Olimpo*, where

89 Supreme Court of Chile, Judgment of 4 August 2005, Rol 457-2005.

90 See, *inter alia*, Supreme Court of Chile, *Episodio Parral Case*, Judgment of 27 December 2007, Rol 3585-05; *Londres 38 Case*, Judgment of 4 February 2014, Rol 2182-98.

91 Supreme Court of Chile, *Episodio Parral Case*, Judgment of 27 December 2007, Rol 3585-05, para 17; *Londres 38 Case*, Judgment of 4 February 2014, Rol 2182-98, para 24.

92 Supreme Court of Chile, Judgment of 24 May 2012, Rol 288-2012, paras 32 and 33.

93 *Gomes Lund et al (Guerrilha do Araguaia) v Brazil* (n 73) para 179.

94 *Simón, Julio Héctor et al about illegitimate deprivation of liberty* (n 7).

Julio Simón and other officials tortured Poblete and Hlaczik. Poblete and Hlaczik were removed from detention in January 1979 and later disappeared. Claudia Poblete was taken from her parents while they were in detention and later delivered to Lieutenant Colonel Ceferino Landa and his wife, who changed her name and registered her as their daughter. On 6 March 2001, the first instance court held that there was sufficient evidence to charge Julio Simón and Juan Antonio Del Cerro with the kidnapping, torture, and subsequent disappearance of José Poblete and Gertrudis Hlaczik. The court held that the Full Stop Law (*Ley de Punto Final*), No 23.492, 23 December 1986 and the Law of Due Obedience (*Ley de Obediencia Debida*), No 23.521, 4 June 1987, which prevented the prosecution of Julio Simón and Juan Antonio del Cerro, violated several provisions of the ACHR and the International Covenant on Civil and Political Rights, among other human rights treaties, and were invalid. This decision was affirmed by the Federal Appeals Court for Criminal and Correctional Matters on 9 November 2001. The Supreme Court of Argentina agreed.

H1 Law No 23.521 was not applicable to Julio Simón's situation. This law was enacted by Congress with the purpose of validating the decision taken by the Executive Branch to grant amnesty to military and security personnel involved in crimes committed from 24 March 1976 to 26 September 1983. However, since that law had been adopted, until the present time, international human rights law had developed principles which prohibited states from adopting these types of laws to avoid prosecution of perpetrators of crimes against humanity.

H2 Pursuant to the amendments to its Constitution, Article 75(22) was incorporated, granting constitutional rank to a series of human rights treaties, including the ACHR and the ICCPR. By adopting this provision, Argentina assumed a series of duties under international law, which were of constitutional rank and limited the power of the state to prevent prosecutions for serious crimes. Insofar as the Amnesty Laws sought to leave unpunished grave violations of human rights, these laws were contrary to the ACHR and the ICCPR and were therefore unconstitutional.

H3 The jurisprudence of the Inter-American Court of Human Rights ('Inter-American Court') and the Inter-American Commission on Human Rights ('Inter-American Commission') constituted essential guidelines for the interpretation of the duties and obligations derived from the ACHR.

H4 According to the decision of the Inter-American Court in the *Case of Velásquez Rodríguez v Honduras*, Reparations and costs, IACHR Series C no 4; IHRL 1388 (IACHR 1989), 21 July 1989, states parties to the ACHR were obligated to prevent, investigate, and punish all violations of human rights protected by that treaty. As established by subsequent jurisprudence of the Inter-American Court, states parties were prohibited from establishing internal legal mechanisms that would prevent the state's compliance with its duty to prosecute and punish gross violations of human rights.

H5 In accordance with the conclusions of the Inter-American Commission in *Consuelo and ors v Argentina*, Report no 28/92, OEA/Ser. L/V/II.83, Inter-American Commission on Human Rights, 2 October 1992, the Amnesty Laws hindered the state's ability to prosecute serious human rights violations, and therefore violated Articles 1 (obligation to respect rights), 8 (right to a fair trial), and 25 of the ACHR (right to judicial protection), as well as Article 18 of the Declaration (right to a fair trial). In that case, the Commission had recommended that Argentina adopt all the necessary measures to clarify the facts and identify the perpetrators of human rights violations.

H6 However, the scope of Argentina's duties were not clear until the Inter-American Court issued its judgment in *Case of Barrios Altos v Peru*, Judgment, IACHR Series C no 87, 14 March 2001. In that case, the Court found that Peru's 'self-amnesty' laws, as well as other laws that sought to provide amnesty or prevent the investigation and punishment of those responsible for grave human rights violations, violated Article 8 (the right to a fair trial) and Article 25 (the right to judicial protection), in conjunction with Articles 1(1) (obligation to respect rights) and 2 of the ACHR (domestic legal effects). The Inter-American Court held that amnesty laws were incompatible with the spirit and letter of the ACHR, as they left victims defenceless and served to perpetuate the impunity of those responsible.

H7 Applying those conclusions to the case at hand, Argentina was obligated to abolish the laws in question, leave the laws without effect, and refuse to give effect to any invocation of the principle of legality or the prohibition against retroactive application of the law. Thus, any person who could have benefited from the Amnesty Laws was prevented from invoking the prohibition against retroactivity of a less favourable law and from claiming that the matter had been settled.

H8 As noted by the UN Committee on Human Rights in Concluding Observations on the Human Rights Committee, Argentina, UN Doc CCPR/C/79/Add.46, 5 April 1995, regarding Argentina's reports under Article 40 of the ICCPR, the Amnesty Laws were inconsistent with Argentina's duties under that treaty as they deprived victims of the right to an effective remedy in violation of Articles 2 and 9 of the ICCPR. Furthermore, pursuant to the Committee's Concluding Observations of the Human Rights Committee, Argentina, UN Doc CCPR/CO/70/ARG, 3 November 2000, the mere repeal of the laws for the future was insufficient; the violations of the rights protected in the ICCPR had to be punished and no statute of limitations could be applied.

Later, the Supreme Court of Guatemala reached a similar conclusion with regard to the domestic implementation of the judgment of the Inter-American Court in the *Case of the 'Las Dos Erres' Massacre v Guatemala*. In that case, the Inter-American Court had held that the application of the Law of National Reconciliation would violate the obligations arising out of the ACHR. In consequence, it ordered Guatemala not to apply the law and continue the prosecution of the alleged perpetrators of the massacre.[95] The criminal chamber of the Supreme Court of Guatemala concluded that the Court's judgment was self-executing and that the investigations had to continue, among other reasons, because of the impossibility of applying the Law of National Reconciliation.[96] Also, in 2015, an appellate court in Guatemala ruled that a 1986 amnesty law could not apply to international crimes, including genocide and crimes against humanity in the genocide case against former head of state Efrain Rios Montt.[97] In particular, the court concluded that Guatemala had ratified the 1949 Convention on the Prevention and Punishment of Genocide and accordingly has an international obligation to investigate, prosecute, and punish the perpetrators of genocide, in light of the constitutional status of international human rights treaties in that state.[98] Rios Montt still faces charges of genocide and crimes against humanity for the death of 1,771 Mayan Ixiles between March 1982 and August 1983.[99]

95 Inter-American Court of Human Rights, *Case of the 'Las Dos Erres' Massacre v Guatemala*, Judgment of 24 November 2009, Series C No 211, para 131.

96 Corte Suprema de Justicia, Cámara Penal, *Solicitud de ejecución de sentencia de la Corte Interamericana de Derechos Humanos de Derechos Humanos*, No MP001/2006/96951, 8 February 2010 http://www.corteidh.or.cr/tablas/r28570.pdf (last accessed 21 November 2017).

97 Sala Primera de la Corte de Apelaciones del Ramo Penal, Narcoactividad y Delitos contra el Ambiente, Proceedings 01076-2011-00015, 5 October 2015 http://www.bdh.org.gt/data/uploads/doc-direccion.pdf (last accessed 21 November 2017).

98 ibid, 13–14.

99 See, in this regard, J M Burt, 'Appeals Court Upholds Suspension of Ríos Montt Genocide Trial' *International Justice Monitor* (3 June 2016) https://www.ijmonitor.org/2016/06/appeals-court-upholds-suspension-of-rios-montt-genocide-trial/ (last accessed 21 November 2017).

Furthermore, Chilean courts have also resorted to international human rights norms binding upon that state and the jurisprudence of the Inter-American system to rule on the non-applicability of the amnesty law in that country.[100]

Even if the judgment in the *Simón* case was celebrated in the human rights community, there was an extensive debate in legal circles regarding the reasoning followed by the court to declare the amnesty laws unconstitutional. A number of experts and legal observers in Argentina criticized the conclusions of the court directly applying the jurisprudence of the Inter-American Court in *Barrios Altos* because the factual context and the legal issues raised in that case were different from the Argentine situation. Furthermore, legal experts contested the court's conclusion, rejecting the application of the constitutional principle of legality in light of the state's duty to prosecute those responsible for gross human rights violations developed in the jurisprudence of the Inter-American system.[101]

Also, the Supreme Court judgment holding that the amnesty laws in Argentina were unconstitutional as a result of the application of international human rights law and case law was not accepted by all the Justices of that Tribunal. For example, Justice Fayt dissented in strong terms.

> H23 Article 27 of the Constitution, which required all treaties to which Argentina entered to be in conformity with the principles of the Constitution, prohibited the application of any treaty that allowed for the retroactive application of penal law, since this was contrary to the principle of legality recognized by Article 18 of the Constitution.
>
> H24 Though the 1994 reform of the Constitution provided international human rights treaties with constitutional rank, those treaties did not prevail over constitutional principles of public law, which were of first order in the constitutional hierarchy. International treaties must only complement the Constitution and could never prevent the application of its provisions.
>
> H25 The Inter-American Court's decision in *Barrios Altos* was not applicable to the issues in Julio Simón's case because the Peruvian auto-amnesty laws differed from the laws at issue here, both in their origin and their effect. First, the Peruvian law was a self-amnesty law enacted to expunge the criminal responsibility of those who were in power, whereas the Amnesty Laws were proposed by a democratically elected government and voted by an elected Congress to reach a peaceful reconciliation with the past. Secondly, while the Peruvian self-amnesty resulted in complete impunity, the laws under consideration did not prevent that those who did not fall within their scope of application were prosecuted. Finally, the Peruvian laws violated the right of the victims' family to the truth, while the Amnesty Laws did not hinder the victims' next of kin to learn what had transpired. It was a grave error to declare unconstitutional the Amnesty Laws based on the Inter-American Court's interpretations in a case totally dissimilar to the case in question.

Similarly, the constitutional chamber of the Supreme Court of El Salvador rejected the claimant's request to find the amnesty law in that country unconstitutional on the basis of the human rights treaties of which El Salvador was a party. In 2016, however, the same court overruled

100 See, *inter alia*, Supreme Court of Chile, *Carlos Prats Case*, Judgment of 8 July 2010, Rol 2596-09; *Londres 38 Case* (n 90) Rol 2182-98; J Flores A and R Gonzalez Perez, Judgment of 27 February 2015, Rol 22343-2014.

101 For some aspects of this debate in Spanish, see L Filippini, 'Algunos problemas de la aplicación del derecho internacional de los derechos humanos en el fallo Simón de la Corte Suprema argentina' in M Reed Hurtado (ed), *Judicialización de Crímenes de Sistema—Estudios de caso y análisis comparado* (Centro Internacional para la Justicia Transicional 2008) 467–511; and A M Vítolo, *La posibilidad de perdonar a los responsables de cometer crímenes de lesa humanidad*, Anales de la Academia Nacional de Ciencias Morales y Políticas, 5–64 (Institutos 2007) https://www.ancmyp.org.ar/user/files/V%C3%ADtoloseparata.pdf (last accessed 21 November 2017).

that judgment and found the amnesty law unconstitutional on the basis of the international human rights and international humanitarian law obligations of the state. The two judgments follow.

Castro Duarte and ors v Legislative Assembly of El Salvador and ors, Application for Constitutional Review, 24-97/21-98, ILDC 1458 (SV 2000), 26th September 2000, El Salvador; Supreme Court of Justice [CSJ]

The General Amnesty Act for the Consolidation of Peace was adopted on March 20, 1993, five days after the publication of the report adopted by the Commission on the Truth from El Salvador. The amnesty law granted a full, absolute, and unconditional amnesty to those individuals who had participated in any way in the commission of political or common crimes in which the number of persons involved was no less than 20 during the conflict that transpired in that country. Claimants challenged the constitutionality of the amnesty law arguing that it breached Articles 1(1), 2, and 25(1) of the ACHR. Also, they argued that the ACHR was an integral part of the constitution since it complemented its content in human rights matters. They asserted that the ACHR, along with the constitution, formed a 'constitutionality block'. Furthermore, petitioners argued that the amnesty laws indirectly violated other human rights treaties, including the Convention on the Prevention and Punishment of the Crime of Genocide, the Convention against Torture and Other Cruel, Inhuman or Degrading Treatment or Punishment and the Inter-American Convention to Prevent and Punish Torture.

> H2 Although it was undeniable that human rights treaties complemented and developed the content of rights and freedoms enshrined in the Constitution, that situation did not imply, in any way, that those treaties were an integral part of the Constitution, nor that those instruments were deemed part of a constitutionality block.
>
> H3 Article 246 of the Constitution explicitly established the supreme character of the Constitution, stating that it would prevail over any other domestic law. Article 145 of the Constitution forbade the state from signing or ratifying any treaty whose terms were in contradiction with the Constitution unless reservations to those contradictory dispositions were made. Article 149 of the Constitution established the facility for submitting a treaty to judicial review or declaring it unconstitutional.
>
> H4 The fact that human rights treaties complemented and developed rights and freedoms enshrined in the Constitution did not presuppose, in any way, a normative fusion between those corpuses of law, nor an expansion of the parameter of constitutionality.
>
> H5 In El Salvador, human rights treaties, as well as other domestic laws, specified the content and scope of the rights and freedoms enshrined in the Constitution, particularly in those cases in which it was deemed necessary to expand the content and scope of those rights and freedoms in order to enhance the Constitution's protection and assurance.
>
> H6 This implied that human rights treaties were not supposed to be deemed as mere technical references without binding effects within the Salvadorian legal framework, but as the law of the land for the people under the jurisdiction of the state. To affirm the contrary would be to disregard Article 144 of the Constitution, which stipulated the binding effects of all international treaties. This Article established that the treaties concluded between El Salvador and other states or international organizations constituted the law of the land, from the moment those treaties entered into force.
>
> H7 In those cases in which a right or a freedom presumably violated was not expressly enshrined in the Constitution, it was not especially necessary for a petitioner to invoke a violation of a human rights treaty. This respected the fact that the Constitution

contained several normative values from which a wide array of rights and freedoms inherent to human dignity could be derived. However, it did not imply that human rights treaties could not be invoked in order to complement or develop those rights or freedoms which had derived from the normative values included in the Constitution.

H8 In El Salvador, the protection and assurance of rights and freedoms incorporated in international human rights treaties was not restricted to constitutional processes, nor limited to the Constitutional Chamber of the Supreme Court of Justice. All judges from all jurisdictions within El Salvador, when exercising their powers, were compelled to protect and ensure the rights and freedoms enshrined in human rights treaties, since they constituted the law of the land from the moment of entry into force, and, therefore had binding effects within the state.

H9 The legal framework of El Salvador did not contemplate the existence of a constitutionality block. The purpose of an application for constitutional review was to guarantee the conformity of the whole Salvadorian legal framework with the Constitution and not with those treaties ratified by the state, no matter what their nature might be.

[…]

H11 Although Article 144 of the Constitution established that in the event of a conflict between a treaty and a domestic law the treaty would prevail, the facility for determining the existence of a conflict between both laws was outside the sphere of competence of the Constitutional Chamber when dealing with an application for constitutional review. In this type of constitutional process, the parameter of control was always the Constitution and not laws hierarchically inferior to it, whatever their nature may be.

H12 The Amnesty Act was in conformity with the Constitution.

H13 The petition for the application for constitutional review based specifically on a possible contradiction between the human rights treaties invoked and the Amnesty Act was dismissed.

H14 It was beyond the sphere of competence of the Constitutional Chamber to determine the possible existence of an incompatibility between Articles 1 and 4 of the Amnesty Act and Articles 1(1), 2, and 25(1) of the ACHR; Articles 1, 2, 3, and 4 of the Genocide Convention; Articles 1, 2, and 4 of the Torture Convention; and Articles 1, 2, 3, 4, 5, and 6 of the Inter-American Torture Convention.

Re General Amnesty Act for the Consolidation of Peace, Cuellar Martínez et al., Application for constitutional review, 44-2013/145-2013, 13th July 2016, ILDC 2808

Claimants presented a general challenge to the General Amnesty Act for the Consolidation of Peace of 1993, alleging that it is unconstitutional on several accounts. First, they argued that the adoption of a wide, absolute and unconditional amnesty violates the principle of complementarity between the Constitution and Articles 1.1 and 2 of the American Convention on Human Rights (ACHR), 2.2 of the International Covenant on Civil and Political Rights (ICCPR) and Article 4 of Protocol II to the Geneva Conventions which provide for the duties to respect and ensure human rights and prohibit the application of amnesty laws to crimes against humanity and war crimes. Secondly, they alleged that the amnesty law also breaches the complementary between the Constitution and Articles 1.1 and 2 of the ACHR as it prevents victims of gross violations of human rights from obtaining reparations.

H1 Amnesties are a legitimate means to facilitate transitions from wartime to peace and to start the reconciliation process, as noted in Article 6.5 of the Second Protocol to the Geneva Conventions (which El Salvador ratified in 1978). However, this provision provides that even the broadest possible amnesty can never be absolute and unconditional. Broad, absolute amnesties are obstacles to achieving justice. Therefore, the 1993 Law's is unconstitutional due to its broad scope and inconsistency with El Salvador's international obligations as a state party to the ACHR, the ICCPR and the Protocol II to the Geneva Conventions

H2 The Amnesty Law should not have protected those who committed crimes against humanity and war crimes. In doing so, the Law violated the rights of victims impacted by those crimes, rights held under the American Convention on Human Rights (ACHR), the International Covenant on Civil and Political Rights (ICCPR), and Convention Against Torture (CAT).

H3 The United Nations (UN) and Organization of American States (OAS) do not explicitly mention amnesties in their charters. However, these bodies do require that states uphold their treaty obligations to protect fundamental human rights. The human rights at issue here are fundamental, non-derogable ius cogens norms. The ACHR (articles 4, 5, 6), ICCPR (articles 4, 6, 7), CAT, International Convention for the Protection of All Persons, and the Inter-American Convention on Forced Disappearances recognize fundamental rights to life, personal physical integrity, and protection from torture that the 1993 Amnesty Law jeopardizes.

H4 The Inter-American Court (IACHR) has found certain kinds of amnesty laws incompatible with international law and states' international obligations, including the 1993 Amnesty Law in the *Mozote Massacre case v. El Salvador*. Some states wrongly use certain amnesties to evade their responsibility to investigate, sanction and bring perpetrators to justice.

H5 As set out and defined in the Rome Statute, war crimes and crimes against humanity are non-derogable, ius cogens norms susceptible to universal jurisdiction.

H6 The 1993 Amnesty Law will remain viable, but will no longer cover crimes against humanity and war crimes (articles 1 and 4 are unconstitutional, invalid). The 1992 National Reconciliation Law will regain its validity, as it excludes these crimes from the amnesty, notably excluding those persons and crimes that were investigated by the Truth Commission for their participation in the war (articles 2, 3, 4, 5, 7 unconstitutional, invalid).

H7 Due to the unconstitutionality of the 1993 Amnesty law, the statute of limitations cannot be invoked as a defence to the crimes that the amnesty covered but should not have. The statute of limitations cannot start running if it was impossible for victims of these grave violations of human rights to access the courts. This also means that in securing justice for these crimes, the law will apply retroactively.

A similar situation, but with a reversed outcome, transpired in the case of Uruguay. Initially, the duties to investigate and punish articulated by the Commission and the Court's jurisprudence were important elements in *Sabalsagaray Curutchet, Blanca Stela Maris—case of Nibia Sabalsagaray*, where the Supreme Court made extensive consideration of those standards to declare the amnesty law unconstitutional and order the reopening of criminal proceedings against alleged perpetrators of human rights violations during the military regime.[102] Interestingly, in a subsequent case the Supreme Court of Uruguay shifted its interpretation regarding the application of international human rights law by domestic courts.[103] It ruled that the jurisprudence of the

102 *Sabalsagaray Curutchet, Blanca Stela* (n 17). See also in this regard, *Organización de Derechos Humanos, Denuncia, Excepción de Inconstitucionalidad Arts. 1, 3 y 4 de la Ley No 15.848* (n 17), and *García Hernández, Amaral y otros* (n 17).

103 Supreme Court of Uruguay, *M L, J F F, O, Denuncia, Excepción de Inconstitucionalidad, Arts. 1, 2 y 3 de la Ley Nro. 18.831*, IUE 2–109971/2011.

Inter-American Court was not binding upon the domestic courts of that country and that, while human rights treaties were part of the domestic order, the constitution prevailed over them. The case related to the constitutional review of Law 18,831 which was adopted after the Court ruled on the *Gelman* case already discussed before. As stated, in *Gelman* the Court concluded that the amnesty law in Uruguay was incompatible with the ACHR and ordered Uruguay to adjust its domestic legislation to the international obligations arising out of that treaty.[104] First, Law 18,831 reestablished the state's power to prosecute those who perpetrated gross violations of human rights during the military regime in that country, an authority which had been curtailed by the so called Caducity Law.[105] Secondly, it provided that the crimes committed during the dictatorship were not covered by statutes of limitation.[106] Finally, it characterized such human rights violations as crimes against humanity.[107] The Supreme Court found that the last two aspects covered by Law 18,831 were unconstitutional under the Constitution of Uruguay and rejected the application of the interpretations of the Inter-American Court stating that the persecution of crimes against humanity is not subject to a statute of limitations and that access to justice for the victims of those crimes cannot not be prevented by an amnesty law.[108] The Supreme Court also concluded that the judgment in *Gelman* was not directly applicable to the analysis of this case.[109]

3. The application of international humanitarian law and the grave breaches provisions

After the *coup d'état* that overthrew the constitutional government in Chile on 11 September 1973, the military authorities that took power adopted Decree No 5 on the basis of the alleged situation of internal commotion in which the country was immersed and the need to combat the actions perpetrated against the integrity of the members of the armed forces, the police, and the population. Article 1 of Decree 5 provided that the existing situation had to be framed as a 'time of war' for purposes of the application of the military code rules and related legislation. Later, on 11 September 1974, the military authorities passed Decree No 641 authorizing the use of military courts and the application of military laws and penalties, permitted only in times of war, due to the existence of a situation of internal commotion created by 'seditious or rebellious forces that are organized or about to be organized, either in the open or clandestinely'. Some courts and authors considered that the adoption of that legislation and the declaration of the state of war triggered the application of Common Article 3 of the Geneva Conventions to the period covered by the amnesty laws. Even if it was not clear that the situation in itself should be characterized as an internal armed conflict, the proponents of this legal approach considered that it was a contradiction that the military government justified the use of military courts and the imposition of martial laws on the existence of a situation of war, but rejected the punishment that international humanitarian law established for those who violated its principles and rules. This legal approach was followed by lower and appeal courts in a number of cases and was later applied by the Supreme Court in the extrajudicial execution of Manuel Tomás Rojas.

---

104 *Case Gelman v Uruguay* (n 76) para 232.

105 Law 18,331, *Pretensión Punitiva del Estado Restablecimiento para los Delitos Cometidos en Aplicación del Terrorismo de Estado hasta el 1º de Marzo de 1985*, Article 1 https://legislativo.parlamento.gub.uy/temporales/leytemp3821350.htm (last accessed 24 November 2017).

106 ibid, Article 2.

107 ibid, Article 3.

108 For an analysis of the judgment see F Michelini, *Reflections on Uruguayan Law No 18831 a Year After Its Enactment* https://www.wcl.american.edu/hrbrief/20/3michelini.pdf (last accessed 24 November 2017).

109 *M L, J F F, O, Denuncia, Excepción de Inconstitucionalidad, Arts. 1, 2 y 3 de la Ley Nro. 18.831* (n 103). For the reaction of the Inter-American Court to this judgment, see Inter-American Court of Human Rights, *Case of Gelman v Uruguay*, Monitoring Compliance with Judgment, Order of the Inter-American Court of Human Rights of 20 March 2013, available only in Spanish http://www.corteidh.or.cr/cf/Jurisprudencia2/busqueda_supervision_cumplimiento.cfm?lang=en (last accessed 24 November 2017).

Re Víctor Raúl Pinto, Re, Pinto (Víctor Raúl) v Relatives of Tomás Rojas, Decision on Annulment, Case No 3125-04, ILDC 1093 (CL 2007), 13th March 2007, Chile; Supreme Court

The present case refers to the extrajudicial execution of Mario Tomás Rojas, a political prisoner who was detained in a prisoners' camp in the village of Chena, on 7 December 1973. Víctor Raúl Pinto, who was claiming the application of the amnesty law in the case, was a young officer at the time and the only one among the alleged perpetrators who was identified. The court of first instance applied the amnesty law and the Court of Appeals affirmed. Rojas' next of kin filed a remedy to annul the lower courts' judgments before the Supreme Court.

> H3 The obligation to prosecute those individually responsible for crimes against humanity was established in the 1949 Geneva Conventions, ratified by Chile in 1950, and promulgated in the Official Gazette in 1951. At the time of Manuel Rojas' death, a non-international armed conflict was taking place in Chile. Therefore, Common Article 3 of the Geneva Conventions was applicable to the persons involved in the conflict.
>
> H4 Manuel Rojas' execution constituted a grave breach of Article 147 of the Fourth Geneva Convention. Since Article 146 of the Convention established an absolute obligation to impose individual criminal responsibility, it prohibited the operation of amnesty laws in cases of grave breaches of the Geneva Conventions.
>
> H5 The state's obligation to protect individuals taking part in an armed conflict in its territory involved the duty not to take measures promoting crimes against humanity or promoting impunity for the prospective offenders.
>
> H6 The court of appeals erred when it invoked the Protocol Additional to the Geneva Conventions of 12 August 1949 relating to the Protection of Victims of Non-International Armed Conflicts (8 June 1977) 1125 UNTS 609, entered into force 7 December 1979 ('Protocol II'), in support of the admissibility of amnesties during non-international armed conflicts. Article 6(5) of Protocol II was meant to benefit the losing party and to prevent the application of criminal law to those who took arms in a non-international armed conflict, who could not benefit from the prisoner of war status, and who, at the end of the conflict, were still in the hands of the party that controlled state power. Amnesties therefore could not be applied to war crimes committed by the state's own officials.
>
> H7 With regard to the possible objection that the Geneva Conventions could not be applied as they had been promulgated before the enactment of the Amnesty Law, in this case, it was not possible to apply the maxim *lex posterior derogat [legi priori]*. In Chile, treaties possessed supra-legal hierarchy and therefore must be applied even against validly passed statutes. Furthermore, according to Article 5 of the Constitution, 1980 (Chile) human rights treaties possessed constitutional primacy.
>
> H8 Recognizing the power of the state to delete war crimes committed by state agents through the enactment of amnesties and using international humanitarian law for this purpose would make humanitarian law irrelevant.
>
> H9 The Amnesty Law amounted to an act of self absolution, prohibited by Article 148 of the Fourth Geneva Convention.
>
> H10 The prohibition against committing crimes against humanity had been established by customary international law and by *ius cogens*. According to the international law of human rights, crimes against humanity were not subject to statutes of limitation, to amnesties, or to circumstances precluding responsibility. Customary international law, being part of the domestic law of Chile, also prevailed over domestic legislation.

Even if the jurisprudence on this issue has not been consistent, the Supreme Court of Chile and other lower courts have concluded in subsequent cases that the Geneva Conventions applied to the situation that transpired in Chile between 1973 and 1978. In this regard, they have used the principles of international humanitarian law to affirm that the gross human rights violations perpetrated during that period constituted crimes against humanity, or even crimes of war. From that characterization they have upheld the non-applicability of a statute of limitation and have sustained that the perpetrators of those crimes must be investigated and punished accordingly.[110]

It is worth noting that the Constitutional Court of South Africa reached an opposite conclusion when characterizing whether the Geneva Conventions applied to the struggle that took place in that country during the apartheid era. In contrast to Chile, the constitution of South Africa contemplated the adoption of an amnesty law as part of the efforts of pacification and reconciliation for past human rights violations that occurred in the country before the 1990s.

AZAPO case, Azanian People's Organization ('AZAPO') and ors v President of South Africa and ors, Direct access to the Constitutional Court, CCT 17/96, [1996] ZACC 16, 1996 (4) SA 671 (CC), 1996 (8) BCLR 1015, ILDC 648 (ZA 1996), 25th July 1996, South Africa; Constitutional Court [CC]

The 1993 constitution of South Africa included in the epilogue a provision for granting amnesty by statutory means in respect of acts and offences associated with political objectives and committed in the course of the conflicts of the past. As a result, the South African parliament adopted the Promotion of National Unity and Reconciliation Act, 95-34, 26 July 1995 to promote national unity and reconciliation, by establishing as complete a picture as possible of the causes, nature, and extent of gross human rights violations committed by either side during the apartheid years. For this purpose, a Truth and Reconciliation Commission was established. Section 20(7) of the Reconciliation Act provided that the granting of amnesty extinguished civil or criminal proceedings of the amnesty holder. The Azanian People's Organization (AZAPO) and others challenged the Reconciliation Act on constitutional basis. Also, they argued that under the Geneva Conventions, South Africa was under an international obligation to prosecute those responsible for gross human rights violations, rendering section 20(7) of the Reconciliation Act legally invalid. The Constitutional Court of South Africa rejected the challenges.

> [1] For decades South African history has been dominated by a deep conflict between a minority which reserved for itself all control over the political instruments of the state and a majority who sought to resist that domination. Fundamental human rights became a major casualty of this conflict as the resistance of those punished by their denial was met by laws designed to counter the effectiveness of such resistance. The conflict deepened with the increased sophistication of the economy, the rapid acceleration of knowledge and education and the ever increasing hostility of an international community steadily outraged by the inconsistency which had become manifest between its own articulated ideals after the Second World War and the official practices which had become institutionalised in South Africa through laws enacted to give them sanction and teeth by a Parliament elected only by a privileged minority. The result was a debilitating war of internal political dissension and confrontation, massive expressions of labour militancy, perennial student unrest, punishing international economic isolation, widespread dislocation in crucial areas of national endeavour, accelerated levels of armed conflict and a dangerous combination of anxiety, frustration and anger among expanding proportions of the populace. The legitimacy of law itself was deeply wounded as the country haemorrhaged dangerously in the face of this tragic conflict which had begun to traumatise the entire nation.

110 See, *inter alia, Episodio Rudy Cárcamo Ruiz* (n 92); *Londres 38 Case* (n 90).

[2] During the eighties it became manifest to all that our country with all its natural wealth, physical beauty and human resources was on a disaster course unless that conflict was reversed. It was this realisation which mercifully rescued us in the early nineties as those who controlled the levers of state power began to negotiate a different future with those who had been imprisoned, silenced, or driven into exile in consequence of their resistance to that control and its consequences. Those negotiations resulted in an interim Constitution committed to a transition towards a more just, defensible and democratic political order based on the protection of fundamental human rights. It was wisely appreciated by those involved in the preceding negotiations that the task of building such a new democratic order was a very difficult task because of the previous history and the deep emotions and indefensible inequities it had generated; and that this could not be achieved without a firm and generous commitment to reconciliation and national unity. It was realised that much of the unjust consequences of the past could not ever be fully reversed. It might be necessary in crucial areas to close the book on that past.

.....

[24] What emerges from the experience of these and other countries that have ended periods of authoritarian and abusive rule, is that there is no single or uniform international practice in relation to amnesty. Decisions of states in transition, taken with a view to assisting such transition, are quite different from acts of a state covering up its own crimes by granting itself immunity. In the former case, it is not a question of the governmental agents responsible for the violations indemnifying themselves, but rather, one of a constitutional compact being entered into by all sides, with former victims being well-represented, as part of an ongoing process to develop constitutional democracy and prevent a repetition of the abuses.

[25] Mr Soggot contended on behalf of the applicants that the state was obliged by international law to prosecute those responsible for gross human rights violations and that the provisions of section 20(7) which authorised amnesty for such offenders constituted a breach of international law. We were referred in this regard to the provisions of article 49 of the first Geneva Convention for the Amelioration of the Condition of the Wounded and Sick in Armed Forces in the Field, article 50 of the second Geneva Convention for the Amelioration of the Condition of Wounded, Sick and Shipwrecked Members of Armed Forces at Sea, article 129 of the third Geneva Convention relative to the Treatment of Prisoners of War and article 146 of the fourth Geneva Convention relative to the Protection of Civilian Persons in Time of War. The wording of all these articles is exactly the same and provides as follows:

> "The High Contracting Parties undertake to enact any legislation necessary to provide effective penal sanctions for persons committing, or ordering to be committed, any of the grave breaches ..."

defined in the instruments so as to include, inter alia, wilful killing, torture or inhuman treatment and wilfully causing great suffering or serious injury to body or health. They add that each High Contracting Party shall be under an obligation to search for persons alleged to have committed such grave breaches and shall bring such persons, regardless of their nationality, before its own courts.

[26] The issue which falls to be determined in this Court is whether section 20(7) of the Act is inconsistent with the Constitution. If it is, the enquiry as to whether or not international law prescribes a different duty is irrelevant to that determination. International law and the contents of international treaties to which South Africa might or might not be a party at any particular time are, in my view, relevant only in

the interpretation of the Constitution itself, on the grounds that the lawmakers of the Constitution should not lightly be presumed to authorise any law which might constitute a breach of the obligations of the state in terms of international law. International conventions and treaties do not become part of the municipal law of our country, enforceable at the instance of private individuals in our courts, until and unless they are incorporated into the municipal law by legislative enactment.

…

[28] The exact terms of the relevant rules of public international law contained in the Geneva Conventions relied upon on behalf of the applicants would therefore be irrelevant if, on a proper interpretation of the Constitution, section 20(7) of the Act is indeed authorised by the Constitution, but the content of these Conventions in any event do not assist the case of the applicants.

[29] In the first place it is doubtful whether the Geneva Conventions of 1949 read with the relevant Protocols thereto apply at all to the situation in which this country found itself during the years of the conflict to which I have referred.

[30] Secondly, whatever be the proper ambit and technical meaning of these Conventions and Protocols, the international literature in any event clearly appreciates the distinction between the position of perpetrators of acts of violence in the course of war (or other conflicts between states or armed conflicts between liberation movements seeking self-determination against colonial and alien domination of their countries), on the one hand, and their position in respect of violent acts perpetrated during other conflicts which take place within the territory of a sovereign state in consequence of a struggle between the armed forces of that state and other dissident armed forces operating under responsible command, within such a state on the other. In respect of the latter category, there is no obligation on the part of a contracting state to ensure the prosecution of those who might have performed acts of violence or other acts which would ordinarily be characterised as serious invasions of human rights. On the contrary, article 6(5) of Protocol II to the Geneva Conventions of 1949 provides that

> "[a]t the end of hostilities, the authorities in power shall endeavour to grant the broadest possible amnesty to persons who participated in the armed conflict, or those deprived of their liberty for reasons related to the armed conflict, whether they are interned or detained."

[31] The need for this distinction is obvious. It is one thing to allow the officers of a hostile power which has invaded a foreign state to remain unpunished for gross violations of human rights perpetrated against others during the course of such conflict. It is another thing to compel such punishment in circumstances where such violations have substantially occurred in consequence of conflict between different formations within the same state in respect of the permissible political direction which that state should take with regard to the structures of the state and the parameters of its political policies and where it becomes necessary after the cessation of such conflict for the society traumatised by such a conflict to reconstruct itself. The erstwhile adversaries of such a conflict inhabit the same sovereign territory. They have to live with each other and work with each other and the state concerned is best equipped to determine what measures may be most conducive for the facilitation of such reconciliation and reconstruction. That is a difficult exercise which the nation within such a state has to perform by having regard to its own peculiar history, its complexities, even its contradictions and its emotional and institutional traditions. What role punishment should play in respect of erstwhile acts of criminality in such a situation is part of the complexity. …

The agonies of a nation seeking to reconcile the tensions between justice for those wronged during conflict, on the one hand, and the consolidation of the transition to a nascent democracy, on the other, has also been appreciated by other international commentators. It is substantially for these reasons that amnesty clauses are not infrequent in international agreements concluded even after a war between different states.

> "Amnesty clauses are frequently found in peace treaties and signify the will of the parties to apply the principle of tabula rasa to past offences, generally political delicts such as treason, sedition and rebellion, but also to war crimes. As a sovereign act of oblivion, amnesty may be granted to all persons guilty of such offences or only to certain categories of offenders."

[32] Considered in this context, I am not persuaded that there is anything in the Act and more particularly in the impugned section 20(7) thereof, which can properly be said to be a breach of the obligations of this country in terms of the instruments of public international law relied on by Mr Soggot. The amnesty contemplated is not a blanket amnesty against criminal prosecution for all and sundry, granted automatically as a uniform act of compulsory statutory amnesia. It is specifically authorised for the purposes of effecting a constructive transition towards a democratic order. It is available only where there is a full disclosure of all facts to the Amnesty Committee and where it is clear that the particular transgression was perpetrated during the prescribed period and with a political objective committed in the course of the conflicts of the past. That objective has to be evaluated having regard to the careful criteria listed in section 20(3) of the Act, including the very important relationship which the act perpetrated bears in proportion to the object pursued.

4. Gross human rights violations as crimes against humanity under customary law and the *jus cogens* obligation to prosecute them

Several concurring justices in the *Simón Case* noted that the crimes perpetrated in this case, which were covered by the Argentine amnesty laws, could be characterized as crimes against humanity and were forbidden by international law at the time these offences were perpetrated.[111] At least one Justice found that the norms requiring punishment for crimes against humanity have attained the status of *jus cogens* and have been in force since immemorial times.[112]

The Supreme Court of Argentina had previously followed a similar analysis in *Chile v Arancibia Clavel*,[113] where it concluded that Argentina was legally obliged to investigate and prosecute the alleged perpetrators of human rights because they were crimes against humanity and, as such, were not subject to the application of a statute of limitations.

Chile v Arancibia Clavel (Enrique Lautaro), Appeal Judgment, Case No 259, A 533 XXXVIII, ILDC 1082 (AR 2004), 24th August 2004, Argentina; Supreme Court [CSJ]

Enrique Lautaro Arancibia Clavel was a member of an external unit of the DINA (*Dirección de Inteligencia Nacional*) whose main function was to persecute political opponents to the Pinochet regime who were exiled in Argentina. He was accused of forming part of a group of people involved in the kidnapping, torture and murder of several individuals, including the killing of Carlos José Santiago Prats, a former Commander in Chief of the Armed Forces of Chile during the Allende administration, and his wife. The Supreme Court of Argentina found that the crime of forming part of an association (*asociación ilícita*) to perpetrate crimes against humanity was in itself a crime against humanity. One of the concurring members of

111 See, *inter alia, Simón, Julio Héctor et al about illegitimate deprivation of liberty* (n 7).

112 ibid, para 40.

113 *Chile v Arancibia Clavel*, Appeal judgment, Case No 259, A533 XXXVIII, 24 August 2004.

the court considered that the crime of forming part of an illicit association was similar to the crime of conspiracy in the common law tradition.

> 28) This Convention [Convention on the Non-Applicability of Statutory Limitations to War Crimes and Crimes Against Humanity] only confirms imprescriptibility which involves the recognition of a rule that is already in existence (ius cogens) as part of customary international law. In this way, the prohibition on the retroactive application of criminal law is not violated, but rather a principle of customary international law is reaffirmed as being already in existence at the time of the commission of the acts.
>
> ....
>
> 31) At the time of the acts, the Argentine State had already contributed to the formation of international custom in favour of the imprescriptibility of crimes against humanity (see Decisions: 318:2148, opinion of Judge Bossert, recital 88 et seq.).
>
> 32) In accordance with the above, and as part of this evolution of international human rights law, it could be said that the Convention on the Non-Applicability of Statutory Limitations to War Crimes and Crimes Against Humanity merely represented the codification of principles already in force in our State as part of the international community.
>
> 33) As a result, the acts for which Arancibia Clavel was sentenced were already prohibited under international law at the time they were committed. Consequently, the Convention cannot be applied retroactively; rather, this was already the rule as a consequence of international custom in force since the 1960s, by which Argentina was bound.
>
> 34) Considering that at the time the facts under investigation were perpetrated they characterized crimes against humanity under international human rights law binding upon the Argentine state, as a natural consequence these facts must be inexorable subject to trial and are not subject to a statute of limitations, as it was established in Decisions: 318:2148.
>
> 35) This conclusion was held by the Inter-American Court of Human Rights when it stated "This Court considers that all amnesty provisions, provisions on prescription and the establishment of measures designed to eliminate responsibility are inadmissible, because they are intended to prevent the investigation and punishment of those responsible for serious human rights violations such as torture, extrajudicial, summary or arbitrary execution and forced disappearance, all of them prohibited because they violate non-derogable rights recognized by international human rights law ... the said laws lack legal effect and may not continue to obstruct the investigation of the grounds on which this case is based or the identification and punishment of those responsible, nor can they have the same or a similar impact with regard to other cases that have occurred in Peru" (Case of *Barrios Altos v Peru*, Merits, Series C no 75, 14 March 2001).
>
> 36) By virtue of the said precedent, given that the Argentine State has assumed under the Inter-American legal order not only an obligation to respect human rights, but also an obligation to guarantee the said rights: "In principle, the State is liable for any violation of rights recognised in the Convention committed by an act of a government authority or persons acting with powers held as a result of their official status. Nevertheless, these are not the only situations in which a State is obliged to prevent, investigate and punish violations of human rights; nor are these the only circumstances in which the responsibility of the State could be compromised as a result of a violation of these rights. Indeed, a crime that violates human rights which is initially

> not attributable to a State, for example, because it is the work of an individual or because the author of the said crime has not been identified, can give rise to the international responsibility of the State, not as a result of this fact per se but owing to the lack of due diligence exercised in preventing or dealing with the violation under the terms stipulated in the Convention" (ICtHR, *Velázquez Rodríguez* case, decision of 29 July 1988, recital 172, Series C No. 4).
>
> The said decision clearly established the obligation of the State to structure the government apparatus, in all areas involving the exercise of government power, in such a way that its institutions can ensure respect for human rights, including the obligation to prevent, investigate and punish all violations of rights recognised in the Convention. From this point of view, the application of the provisions of domestic law on prescription constitutes a violation of the obligation of the State to pursue and punish and, consequently, entails its international responsibility (see ICtHR, *Barrios Altos* case, decision of 14 March 2001, recital 41, Series C No. 75; *Trujillo Oroza vs. Bolivia* case—reparations, decision of 27 February 2002, recital 106, Series C No. 92; *Benavides Cevallos* case, enforcement of sentence, decision of 9 September 2003, recitals 6 and 7).
>
> 37) In light of the above considerations, it should be stated that the act which gave rise to the sentence imposed on Arancibia Clavel for conspiracy constitutes a crime against humanity and is therefore imprescriptible.

The Inter-American Court followed a similar analysis in the *Case of Almonacid Arellano v Chile*. The Court concluded that the extrajudicial execution of Almonacid Arellano was part of a generalized and systematic practice by the military authorities in Chile to attack sectors of the civilian population considered opponents to the regime and thus constituted a crime against humanity.[114] The Court reasoned that murder was considered a crime against humanity in the 1945 Charter of the Nuremberg Tribunal, even if at the time a war nexus was required.[115] The scope of crimes against humanity and the binding nature under international law of the principles recognized by the Charter of the Nuremberg Tribunal and its judgments were subsequently confirmed by Resolution 95(I) of the General Assembly and the International Law Commission, which in 1950 formulated the Principles of International Law Recognized in the Charter of the Nuremberg Tribunal and in the judgment of the tribunal.[116] Moreover, the Court acknowledged that subsequent international practice has defined crimes against humanity as certain inhuman acts, including murder, committed in a context of a generalized or systematic attack against civilians, perpetrated during both peace and war times.[117] Ultimately, the Court concluded that this international law rule was binding upon states by the time Almonacid Arellano was killed by state officials in September 1973.[118] Since the murder of the victim was perpetrated within a framework of generalized and systematic repression, which resulted in the execution and disappearance of more than 3,000 victims, Almonacid Arellano's deprivation of life constitutes a crime against humanity under international law.[119]

Secondly, the Court concluded that the prohibition of crimes against humanity has attained the level of *jus cogens* and, consequently, there is an obligation to punish such crimes pursuant to general principles of international law.[120] In the case of the ACHR, Article 1(1) of that treaty provides that '[s]tates must prevent, investigate and punish all violations of the rights recognized

114 *Case of Almonacid Arellano et al v Chile* (n 64) para 104.
115 ibid, para 96.
116 ibid, para 98.
117 ibid, para 96.
118 ibid.
119 ibid, para 103.
120 ibid, para 99.

by the Convention and, at the same time, guarantee the reinstatement, if possible, of the violated rights, and as the case may be, the reparation of the damage caused due to the violation of human rights'.[121] The Court stated that it is apparent from international practice and the case law of this tribunal, especially the *Barrios Altos* case,[122] that the adoption and enforcement of amnesty laws prevents compliance with the duty to punish the perpetrators of crimes against humanity and, as a result, amnesty laws are not applicable to those crimes under current international law.[123]

Next, the Court found that the Chilean law granted amnesty to perpetrators of certain crimes against humanity, including murder,[124] and therefore was incompatible with the obligations arising out of the ACHR and engaged the international responsibility of the state.[125] Moreover, the Court stated that given its nature, the amnesty law 'does not have any legal effect and cannot remain as an obstacle for the investigation of the facts inherent to the instant case, or for the identification and punishment of those responsible thereof'.[126] Finally, it concluded that under the duty arising out of Article 2, which imposes a legislative obligation to revise any domestic laws or practices that are in breach of the ACHR, Chile must effectively repeal the amnesty law.[127] The Court acknowledged that the law was a self-amnesty passed by a military regime to prevent the prosecution of its members; however, it concluded that since the ratification of the ACHR in 1990, the state has maintained in force this legislation in absolute breach of the rights protected by that treaty.[128] Even if the amnesty law has not been applied by domestic courts in recent times, keeping the laws in the legislative body of the state is contrary to the wording and spirit of the ACHR and thereby a breach of Article 2 of that instrument.[129]

The Court indicated that when the legislative power fails to set aside laws that are contrary to the ACHR, the judiciary still must respect the duty to ensure arising out of Article 1(1) of that treaty.[130] Domestic courts must exercise a sort of 'conventionality control' between domestic laws and practices and the ACHR.[131] To avoid engaging the international responsibility of the state, domestic courts must ensure that those laws and practices are not in breach of the ACHR, in which case they must refrain from enforcing them.[132] In accomplishing that control, domestic courts must take into account both the ACHR and the case law of the Court when interpreting the scope of the provisions of that treaty.[133] In the case under analysis, the domestic courts failed to carry out such control and applied the amnesty laws, which had the effect of closing the investigation; consequently, the trial and punishment of the perpetrators of Almonacid Arellano's murder was not pursued.[134] As a result, the victims' rights to judicial protection and a fair trial protected by Articles 8 and 25 of the ACHR were violated.[135] Similarly, the state failed to respect the general obligation enshrined in Article 1(1), according to which the state must investigate, identify, and punish the perpetrators of human rights violations.[136] This is even more important in

121 ibid, para 110.
122 *Case of Barrios-Altos v Peru* (n 57).
123 *Case of Almonacid Arellano et al v Chile* (n 64) paras 110–14.
124 Though not a part of the case under analysis, the Court also considered that the Chilean amnesty law could not be applied to prevent the investigation of other crimes against humanity such as forced disappearance and torture.
125 *Case of Almonacid Arellano et al v Chile* (n 64) para 119.
126 ibid.
127 ibid, para 121.
128 ibid.
129 ibid.
130 ibid, para 123.
131 ibid, para 124.
132 ibid, para 123.
133 ibid, para 124
134 ibid, para 126.
135 ibid, para 128.
136 ibid.

cases such as the one under analysis which involves the perpetration of crimes against humanity. The Court also found that the transfer of the case to the military jurisdiction constituted an additional violation of Article 8(1) since the state failed to afford the victims their right to be heard by a competent, independent, and impartial tribunal.[137]

Also, the Supreme Court of Argentina in *Mazzeo et al* concluded that a Presidential Decree granting pardon to high-ranking members of the armed forces who were not covered by the amnesty laws was unconstitutional because the crimes of which the perpetrators were accused were crimes against humanity under customary international law and the state was under an obligation to prosecute and punish those responsible.

Riveros v Office of the Public Prosecutor, Recourse of cassation and unconstitutionality, M 2333 XLII, ILDC 1084 (AR 2007), 13th July 2007, Argentina; Supreme Court [CSJ]

On 7 October 1989, the President of Argentina issued Decree 1002/89 granting a pardon to a group of high-ranking military and security officials who were being investigated for their alleged participation in crimes—murder, torture, cruel and inhuman treatment, serious bodily harm, and violation of domicile—committed during the so-called 'Dirty War'. Santiago Omar Riveros was one of them. A group of victims challenged the constitutionality of the pardons in the criminal proceedings instituted against Mr Riveros before a federal court, but this claim was dismissed. The Supreme Court confirmed the dismissal. The constitutionality of Decree 1002/89 was challenged again in a subsequent case against Riveros. In November 2004, the Federal Court of First Instance upheld the action and declared the unconstitutionality of the decree. The National Court of Criminal Cassation agreed. Santiago Riveros filed an extraordinary remedy before the Supreme Court arguing that: (i) the Supreme Court had already affirmed the constitutionality of the presidential decree; (ii) the Supreme Court's judgment was *res judicata*; (iii) neither the constitution nor the international human rights treaties incorporated therein prohibited pardons of sentence regarding crimes against humanity; and (iv) the acts allegedly committed by him did not amount to crimes against humanity.

H1 The acts underlying the present case constituted crimes against humanity.

H2 Under international law, states were duty bound to investigate, prosecute, and punish individuals responsible for serious human rights violations.

H3 The prohibition of the commission of crimes against humanity was *jus cogens* and, thus, non-derogable.

H4 The prohibition of the commission by state officials of crimes against humanity and the duty to punish those responsible for such crimes were part of conventional and customary law at the relevant time, and were reaffirmed in the American Convention on Human Rights (22 November 1969) 1144 UNTS 123, entered into force 18 July 1978 ('ACHR') and the International Covenant on Civil and Political Rights (16 December 1966) 999 UNTS 171, entered into force 23 March 1976 ('ICCPR').

H5 All Argentinean courts should have interpreted the ACHR in light of the jurisprudence of the Inter-American Court of Human Rights ('IACHR').

H6 According to the IACHR, the states parties to the ACHR were obliged to investigate violations of the ACHR, establish legal responsibilities, provide victims with effective remedies, and identify and punish the intellectual authors of human rights violations, with no exceptions.

H7 The Preamble and Article 4(2) of the Convention Against Torture and Other Cruel, Inhuman or Degrading Treatment or Punishment (10 December 1984) 1465 UNTS 85, entered into force 26 June 1987 obliged states parties to investigate and

137 ibid, para 133.

punish individuals allegedly responsible for torture. This treaty came into force for Argentina before the adoption of Decree 1002/89.

H8 Crimes against humanity were not subject to statutes of limitations—*Chile v Arancibia Clavel,* Appeal judgment, Case no 259, A 533 XXXVIII; ILDC 1082 (AR 2004), 24 August 2004 ('*Chile v Clavel*').

H9 Victims of serious human rights violations had the right to learn the truth about the facts which resulted in such violations and had a fundamental role to play in investigatory proceedings of such violations.

H10 Regardless of whether pardons may be granted to persons being investigated or prosecuted, they should not be granted if the crimes investigated were crimes against humanity, or if the international obligation to investigate and punish such crimes would be violated. Moreover, pardons granted to persons convicted of crimes against humanity violated the international obligation to impose appropriate sentences for such crimes.

H11 Decree 1002/89 was contrary to *jus cogens,* the ACHR, and the ICCPR. It violated the duties to investigate, prosecute, and punish crimes against humanity, as well as the victims' right to an effective remedy to discover the truth about such crimes.

In recent years, the Supreme Court of Chile has consistently ruled that certain crimes perpetrated during the dictatorship are crimes against humanity under customary international law and that there is a *jus cogens* obligation to prosecute and punish such perpetrators. These obligations cannot be obliterated by application of the amnesty law. These rulings have been influenced by the judgment of the Inter-American Court in the *Almonacid Arellano* case.

The Vergara Toledo brothers case, Vergara Toledo v Ambler Hinojosa and ors, Action to annul, Case No 7.089-09, ILDC 1946 (CL 2010), 4th August 2010, Chile; Supreme Court

In 1985, Eduardo and Rafael Vergara Toledo, members of a leftist political party, were executed by members of the police (*carabineros*). A military court ordered the proceedings against the perpetrators closed. In 2003, the Supreme Court reopened the case on the grounds that there was new evidence. A special judge was appointed, who later found that the evidence had been manipulated and one of the victims had been shot from a short distance in the back of the head. The accused policemen alleged that the charges against them should be dismissed on the basis of the principle of *res judicata* or double jeopardy and/or because the statute of limitations for the offence had expired.

H1 After 1973, Chile had effectively functioned under a "state of emergency" declared by the government. Even though the situation was not one of "non-international armed conflict," it was not dissimilar. Clear evidence of this was that freedom of speech was restricted, information was controlled, and part of the population was prosecuted in a systematic way for their political beliefs.

H2 Legal ideas evolved with time. The Geneva Convention for the Amelioration of the Condition of the Wounded and Sick in Armed Forces in the Field (12 August 1949) 75 UNTS 35, entered into force 21 October 1950, Geneva Convention for the Amelioration of the Condition of Wounded, Sick and Shipwrecked Members of Armed Forces at Sea (12 August 1949) 75 UNTS 81, entered into force 21 October 1950, Geneva Convention Relative to the Protection of Civilian Persons in Time of War (12 August 1949) 75 UNTS 287, entered into force 21 October 1950 (collectively, the "Geneva Conventions"), and the Protocol Additional to the Geneva Conventions of 12 August 1949, and relating to the Protection of Victims of Non-International Armed Conflicts (Protocol II) (8 June 1977) 1125 UNTS 609, entered into force 7 December 1979 had not considered that scenario, but now the idea of crimes against humanity had been updated by *ius cogens* and some treaty provisions. These included, for instance, Article 1(b) of the United Nations Convention on the Non-Applicability of Statutory Limitations to War Crimes and Crimes Against Humanity (16 December 1968) 73 UNTS 754, entered into force 11 November 1970, Article 7 of the Rome Statute of the International Criminal Court (1 July 1998) UN Doc A/CONF 183/9, entered into force 1 July 2002 ("Rome Statute"), and Article 7 of the Statute of the International Criminal Tribunal for Rwanda, UN Doc S/RES/955, UN Security Council 1994. Those instruments recognized that crimes against humanity could be committed during peacetime. The facts of this case fit perfectly within those concepts, and humanitarian law and international criminal law provisions were applicable.

H3 Because the underlying facts of this case – the execution of two political activists by the police in a context of massive human rights abuses – could be labelled as crime against humanity, the statute of limitations did not apply because of the Geneva Conventions and several treaties that were not yet ratified by Chile, but whose provisions were *ius cogens* norms at the time the crime was perpetrated.

H4 Regarding double jeopardy, the investigation that was carried out had not been rigorous enough and the military judge lacked impartiality.

H5 Chile was under an obligation to prosecute civil servants who had committed crimes against humanity.

H6 Hugo Dolmestch J, in a dissenting opinion: The facts could not be qualified as crimes against humanity because the historical context could not fit within the description of internal conflict provided by international law. Consequently, limitations applied to the situation and they could even cover deficient investigations.

5. The duty to investigate and prosecute in cases of 'fraudulent res judicata'

In *Almonacid Arellano*, the Inter-American Court ordered Chile to ensure that the amnesty law be left without legal effect so that it does not continue to hinder the investigation of Almonacid Arellano's murder or other similar violations of human rights perpetrated in Chile during the military regime.[138] Additionally, it ordered the state to set aside any judgments issued by the military courts in violation of rights protected by the ACHR and refer the investigation to a civilian court, which should identify the perpetrators of the victim's murder and apply the appropriate sanctions.[139] The Court held that the state cannot invoke the application of a statute of limitations, the principle of non-retroactivity of criminal laws, or the *ne bis in idem* (double jeopardy) principle to avoid pursuing a criminal investigation.[140] First, crimes against humanity are neither susceptible to the application of amnesty laws nor subject to a statute of limitations.[141] Though Chile has not ratified the Convention on the Non-Applicability of Statutory Limitations to War Crimes and Crimes against Humanity, which states that crimes against humanity are not subject to a statute of limitations, this principle has become a *jus cogens* norm which must be respected by that state as an imperative rule of international law.[142] Secondly, the *ne bis in idem* principle is not an absolute right and can consequently be restricted under certain circumstances, including: 1) when the court that heard the case and decided on a dismissal or acquittal of the alleged perpetrators intended to shield the persons charged from criminal responsibility; 2) when the criminal proceedings were

138 *Case of Almonacid Arellano et al v Chile* (n 64) para 145.
139 ibid, paras 146–47.
140 ibid, para 151.
141 ibid, para 152.
142 ibid, para 153.

not conducted independently, impartially, or in accordance with due process principles; or 3) when there was no actual intention of bringing the alleged perpetrators to justice. In those cases, according to the court, the judgment rendered 'produces an "apparent" or "fraudulent" *res judicata*'.[143] Moreover, in cases in which new information is made available regarding the identity of perpetrators of crimes against humanity, the investigations must be reopened, even if the case ended with an acquittal of those perpetrators.[144] The Court held that 'the dictates of justice, the rights of the victims, and the spirit and the wording of the American Convention supersedes the protection of the *ne bis in idem* principle'.[145] In *Almonacid Arellano*, two of the stated conditions were met.[146] First, the investigation was not carried out by an independent and impartial tribunal.[147] Secondly, an amnesty law was applied with the intention of excluding the criminal responsibility of the perpetrators of the victim's murder.[148] Thus, the Court found that the state could not argue that the application of a statute of limitations or the principles of non-retroactivity of criminal laws or *ne bis in idem* justify the failure to prosecute and punish the perpetrators of the victim's murder. The Court followed a similar conclusion, *inter alia*, in *La Cantuta v Peru*,[149] *Gomes Lund et al (Guerrilha do Araguaia) v Brazil*,[150] *Gelman v Uruguay*,[151] and *Massacres of El Mozote and nearby places v El Salvador*.[152]

In the case of *Mazzeo et al*, following the Court's interpretation in *Almonacid Arellano*, the Supreme Court of Argentina concluded that the principles of *res judicata* and *ne bis in idem* were not absolute rights and were subject to exceptions in cases in which it was clear that a domestic court acquitted an alleged perpetrator only with the purpose of shielding the perpetrator from criminal liability.

Riveros v Office of the Public Prosecutor, Recourse of cassation and unconstitutionality, M 2333 XLII, ILDC 1084 (AR 2007), 13th July 2007, Argentina; Supreme Court [CSJ]

For facts see above section III.4.

> H12 The *res judicata* principle, implicitly recognized by the Constitution and laid down in Article 8(4) of the ACHR and Article 14(7) of the ICCPR, was subject to exceptions. It could not be applied if the sentence had not been preceded by due process, and fraudulent sentences could be revised.
>
> H13 The *res judicata* principle aimed at safeguarding the *ne bis in idem* principle, whose purpose was to protect the individual against the state by preventing the latter, with all its resources and powers, to repeatedly attempt to convict the former of an alleged offence. Both principles were closely related as to their object and purpose.
>
> H14 Under international humanitarian law, both principles were interpreted by axiological analysis. International criminal courts could exercise their jurisdiction over individuals that had been tried by national courts, provided that the specific conditions laid down in their statutes were met.
>
> H15 The *ne bis in idem* principle was not an absolute human right. The justifications for the application of the two principles at the domestic level were not compelling where crimes against humanity were at stake. The international legal instruments that

143 ibid, para 154.
144 ibid.
145 ibid.
146 ibid, para 155.
147 ibid.
148 ibid.
149 *La Cantuta v Peru* (n 70) para 226.
150 *Gomes Lund et al (Guerrilha do Araguaia) v Brazil* (n 73) para 256.
151 *Gelman v Uruguay* (n 76) paras 253–54.
152 *Massacres of El Mozote and nearby places v El Salvador* (n 80) para 319.

dealt with crimes against humanity, as well as those that imposed duties to investigate, prosecute, and punish those responsible, did not admit statutes of limitations, amnesties, or any other measure that may frustrate punishment. Decree 1002/89 was thus unconstitutional.

Similarly, the Constitutional Court of Peru in the *Salazar Monroe case* applied the *Barrios Altos* case to declare without effect the acquittal of one of the members of the so called 'Colina Group' that participated in the murders of the victims in the aforementioned case.[153] The Constitutional Court concluded that the scope of the duty to investigate and punish articulated in *Barrios Altos* required not only depriving of effect the outcome of proceedings in which the amnesty laws were applied, but also other practices or procedural steps whose purpose was to shield the perpetrators of heinous crimes from being punished.[154] Thus, the resolution dismissing the claimant's charges in *Salazar Monroe* was also found without effect because the criminal proceeding in which he was investigated did not intend to effectively establish his guilt, but shield him from being convicted.[155] Moreover, the resolution was not issued by an independent and impartial court because the case was tried and decided by a military court.[156] Ultimately, since the resolution dismissing the claimant's charges was found null and void, the initiation of a second criminal proceeding against the claimant in the ordinary jurisdiction did not violate the principles of *res judicata* and *ne bis in idem*.[157] The Constitutional Court of Peru followed a similar reasoning in the *Martin Rivas* case[158] which involved another member of the 'Colina Group' who participated in the disappearances of the students at La Cantuta University.

Martin Rivas v Constitutional and Social Chamber of the Supreme Court, Appeal judgment, 679-2005-PA/TC, ILDC 960 (PE 2007), 2nd March 2007, Peru; Constitutional Court

The appellant requests an injunction against the Supreme Council of Military Justice, alleging violations of his right to due process, res judicata, amnesty and the principle of legal certainty, in order to render null and void: a) the resolution dated 17 October 2001, which annuls—in accordance with amnesty law 26479—the resolution that led to the closure of his case, and b) the resolution dated 13 October 2003, which declares the annulment sought against the resolution dated 17 October 2001 inadmissible. The appellant states that in 1995, the Sala de Guerra granted him amnesty for events relating to the *La Cantuta* case (Case 157-V-93). This measure was referred to the review chamber for military justice, the same chamber that had approved the closure of the case. Nevertheless, on 17 October 2001 the respondent reopened the case, annulling the enforceable judgment that had ordered its closure and, later, rejected the appeal for annulment filed by the appellant.

In the appeal, the appellant alleges that the resolutions handed down by the court of the Supreme Council of Military Justice contravene amnesty laws (Laws 26479 and 26492), as well as the American Convention on Human Rights and Additional Protocol II to the Geneva Conventions Relating to Non-international Armed Conflicts. In addition, he states that according to the jurisprudence of the Inter-American Court of Human Rights in the *Castillo Petruzzi et al* case, the inevitable conclusion is that the American Convention on Human Rights cannot suppress or limit the right of the Peruvian state to grant amnesty, particularly if the

153 Constitutional Court of Peru, *Julio Rolando Salazar Monroe*, Case No 03938-2007-PA/TC, Judgment of 5 November 2007.

154 ibid, para 32.

155 ibid, paras 45–53.

156 ibid, para 44.

157 ibid, para 54.

158 Constitutional Court of Peru, *Martin Rivas v Constitutional and Social Chamber of the Supreme Court*, Appeal judgment, Case No 679-2005-PA/TC, 2 March 2007.

Constitutional Tribunal itself declared as inadmissible the claim of unconstitutionality filed against various Articles in amnesty laws.

> 1. The objective of the claim is to render null and void the resolutions handed down by the Supreme Council of Military Justice on 13 October 2003 and 17 October 2001 whereby, in accordance with Amnesty Laws 26479 and 26492, the resolution that closed the investigation into the events surrounding case no. 157-V-93 was annulled. The appellant contends that his constitutional rights to res judicata, legal certainty, due process and amnesty (*sic*) have been violated.
>
> 28. [...] Nor can amnesty laws be passed in opposition to international obligations derived from international human rights treaties and agreements ratified by the Peruvian State. The ability of human rights treaties to limit amnesty laws in material terms is based on Article 55 and Final and Transitory Provision IV of the Constitution. According to the former, treaties and agreements become part of domestic law upon ratification and, therefore, are binding on the public authorities. According to the latter, treaties are used to delimit the scope of fundamental rights guaranteed in the Constitution.
>
> 29. Based on treaties and international jurisprudence concerning human rights, it is possible to identify the fundamental rights definitively guaranteed by laws that could be compromised by the passing of an amnesty law (i.e. the right to the legal protection of rights and the right to truth). This is the case both when a decision is made regarding the powers conferred by the law on its bearer and when a declaration is made regarding the kind of interference with the law that is prohibited.
>
> 30. The obligations assumed by the Peruvian State with the ratification of human rights treaties include the obligation to guarantee rights that, under international law, cannot be repealed and in respect of which the State has made an international commitment to sanction their violation. In view of the mandate contained in Article V of the Preliminary Title of the Code of Constitutional Procedure, one turns to the treaties that have given material form to the absolute proscription of crimes for which, under international law, amnesty cannot be given since they contravene the minimum standards governing the protection of human dignity.
>
> 33. In the ambit of the regional system for the protection of human rights, the Inter-American Court has emphasised that
>
>> " ... all amnesty provisions, provisions on prescription and the establishment of measures designed to eliminate responsibility are inadmissible, because they are intended to prevent the investigation and punishment of those responsible for serious human rights violations such as torture, extrajudicial, summary or arbitrary execution and forced disappearance, all of them prohibited because they violate non-derogable rights recognized by international human rights law."
>
> 35. The first question, namely whether or not these laws are compatible with international human rights law and the Constitution, is not an issue that should be resolved in isolation, but rather in terms of the integration thereof. This applies insofar as it is necessary to understand international law as a law of integration based on the international responsibility of States. Thus, in light of this responsibility, neither the automatic derogation of domestic laws, in the event of a conflict with their international obligations, nor ignorance of the said obligations on a domestic level is postulated, but rather the harmonisation and integration thereof.
>
> 36. Thus, it is not appropriate to assume a dualist view of the primacy of international law over domestic law and vice versa; rather, what is required is a solution

based on integration and the construction of jurisprudence in the area of the relationship between the Inter-American System of Human Rights and domestic constitutional law. [. . .]

43. From the above, it can be inferred that the Inter-American Court of Human Rights has declared that the abovementioned amnesty laws do not have legal force and therefore the ruling has general force. Accordingly, the said ruling is applicable not only to the events that led to the *Barrios Altos* case, but also to cases in which its application acted as a bar to the prosecution of serious violations of rights recognised in the American Convention, such as the *La Cantuta* case.

50. Therefore, since the said amnesty laws have no legal force, the court has ruled that decisions of a judicial nature handed down with a view to the protection of the said laws do not constitute constitutional res judicata and, therefore, the right recognised in Article 139 (paragraph 13) of the Constitution has not been affected.

58. Accordingly, it should be pointed out that although the Legislature has the power to grant amnesty, i.e. pardon crimes committed by particular individuals, which has the effect of res judicata, Article 102 (paragraph 6) and Article 139 (paragraph 13) of the Constitution state that this does not mean that Congress can seek refuge in amnesty laws for crimes against humanity, such as kidnapping, torture and summary execution; therefore, the legitimacy of the Constitution rests on the defence of individuals and respect for human dignity as the supreme objectives of society and the state, in accordance with Article 1 of the Constitution.

60. By virtue thereof, the court is of the view that amnesty laws 26479 and 26492 are null and void and have no legal force *ab initio*. Thus, judgments handed down to guarantee immunity for human rights violations committed by members of the *Grupo Colina* are also null and void. As judgments that have been annulled, they do not constitute constitutional res judicata guaranteed by Articles 102 (paragraph 6) and 139 (paragraph 13) of the Constitution, inasmuch as there is no conformity with the intended order of values, constitutional principles and fundamental rights enshrined in the Constitution.

6. The duty to investigate and prosecute and the proportionality of the punishment

The appropriateness of granting amnesty in exchange for national reconciliation or peace in the case of armed conflict has been at the core of the debate in all the countries that faced the challenge to resolve domestic violence. Argentina, Uruguay, Brazil, Peru, and El Salvador, among others, have based their decisions to grant amnesty to the perpetrators of gross violations of human rights on the need to ensure a peaceful transition after years of violence and turmoil. The need to strike a balance between these two competing interests, namely the rights of victims to seek justice and the conditions to ensure the transition to a democratic government, was a fundamental argument of the Constitutional Court of South Africa when deciding on the constitutionality of that country's amnesty law. Similarly, it has been cited by the Supreme Court of Brazil as one of the most central rationales to uphold the constitutionality of the amnesty law in that country.[159] In recent years, however, an evolution in the debate on transitional justice has taken domestic and international tribunals and organs to conclude that the need to restore peace cannot be an obstacle to ensure the rights of human rights victims to truth and justice. Evidence of that evolution can be seen in the reasoning of the majority in the *Simon* case as well as in the judgment of the Supreme Court of Uruguay in *Sabalsagaray Curutchet, Blanca Stela*,[160]

159 Supremo Tribunal Federal, *Acción de Incumplimiento de Precepto Fundamental No 153*, 29 April 2010.
160 *Sabalsagaray Curutchet, Blanca Stela* (n 17).

and most recently in the judgment of the Constitutional Chamber of the Supreme Court of El Salvador declaring the unconstitutionality of the amnesty law in that country.[161] In light of the understanding under current international law that the duty to investigate and punish cannot be eroded or limited in exchange for reconciliation and peace, some states have sought alternative formulas to the punishment that the alleged perpetrators of crimes against humanity or war crimes would have received under ordinary legislation. The case of the Colombian Law on Justice and Peace appears to be, at least in theory, an example of such a new development in the debate on amnesty laws and punishment.

Gallón Giraldo and 104 others representing themselves or non-governmental organizations v Ministry of Interior and Justice and ors, Constitutional Complaint, Judgment No C-370/2006, File D-6032, ILDC 660 (CO 2006), 18th May 2006, Colombia; Constitutional Court

In 2002 Colombia negotiated with the paramilitary groups the demobilization of about 31,000 of their members, including sixty of their top leaders. As part of the negotiations, the issue of granting amnesty to some of the members of the paramilitary groups, specifically those who were responsible for committing serious crimes of international concern, was considered and debated. On 25 July 2005, the Colombian Congress enacted Law 975 (Law on Justice and Peace). The Law on Justice and Peace comprised two main parts. The first set out the criminal procedure applicable to members of illegal armed groups that were accused of committing serious crimes under domestic and international law and established the conditions under which members of these groups could benefit from an alternative punishment (five to eight years in prison). These conditions included, *inter alia*, to fully confess their crimes, depose their weapons, enter into a peace agreement, stop their interference in public affairs, release the people they had kidnapped, and contribute to finding the victims of forced disappearance. The second part of the law related to the rights of victims to truth, justice, and reparation. The constitutionality of the Law on Justice and Peace was challenged alleging that it violated the right to justice because minimum human rights standards and *jus cogens* norms were not respected, in particular the prohibition on committing crimes against humanity and war crimes, and the holding of perpetrators accountable. In addition, claimants argued that the benefit of alternative punishment was disproportionate, as excessive benefits were granted to members of paramilitary groups without imposing any strict obligations with respect to truth, reparation, and non-repetition. The Constitutional Court of Colombia upheld the constitutionality of the law.

H1 The international community has acknowledged that in pursuance of the goal of achieving peace in society, justice may be subject to certain flexibilities. However, during the transitional stage, states must not forget their obligations under international law to respect human rights, to investigate any violation committed, to hold accountable those responsible, and to repair victims' suffering.

H2 International law contains guidelines and obligations that states should follow with respect to the rights of truth, justice, and reparation, even during the transitional stage to peace. These are contained in various instruments of human rights; in judgments of the Inter-American Court of Human Rights; and in decisions of other human rights bodies.

H3 In order to determine whether the Law on Justice and Peace complied with Colombia's obligations under international and domestic law, a balancing test was used to weigh conflicting rights with the aim of harmonizing them, or determining which should prevail. This was the appropriate method, because achieving stable and

161 See *General Amnesty Act for the Consolidation of Peace, Cuellar Martínez et al, Application for constitutional review*, 44-2013/145-2013, 13 July 2016.

lasting peace might require certain restrictions on the value of and right to justice. However, peace is not an absolute value and the rights of victims to justice should not be underestimated.

H4 The benefit of an alternative punishment (five to eight years in prison) established under the Law on Justice and Peace did not constitute a system of impunity. The Law did not grant any amnesties or pardons because it did not terminate or forbid criminal investigations against those who might have committed crimes, nor did it permit the suspension of punishment resulting from a criminal process.

H5 The benefit of alternative punishment provided under Article 3 of the Law on Justice and Peace consisted of suspending the execution of a specific punishment in a sentence and imposing an alternative punishment in return for the beneficiary's contribution to the achievement of peace; collaboration with justice; reparation of the victims; and adequate re-socialization. This was one of the measures that could be taken with the aim of achieving peace. The Law was found to be in accordance with the Constitution, 1991 (Colombia) and with international standards as it did not affect the right to justice in a disproportionate manner.

H6 The benefits of alternative punishment granted by the Law on Justice and Peace to members of illegal armed groups could only be conferred on those who had fully satisfied the victims' rights to truth, by confessing, completely and faithfully, all the crimes in which they had participated as members of the illegal groups. This included providing information about the fate of disappeared persons. Dealing with crimes of international concern, such as massacres, mass kidnappings, murders, disappearances, bombing of towns, and massive recruitment of children, among others, required the state to adopt mechanisms that completely and faithfully satisfied the rights of victims and society to truth, while at the same time respected the rights of the accused and the prohibition against self-incrimination.

H7 Victims or others affected by the crimes could access the criminal investigation file from the beginning of the investigation, in order to exercise their rights to truth, justice and reparation. Timely access to the file allowed victims and their relatives to collaborate with the Office of the Prosecutor in its duty to investigate thoroughly.

H8 Colombia's obligation to investigate and prosecute human rights violations was an element of the right to justice according to international law. Relevant instruments, such as the American Convention on Human Rights (22 November 1969) 1144 UNTS 123, entered into force 18 July 1978 and the Principles for the Protection and Promotion of Human Rights through Action to Combat Impunity, E/CN.4/Sub.2/1997/20/Rev.1, annex II, showed that states must conduct investigations in an exhaustive, serious, and diligent manner and within reasonable time to guarantee due diligence and effectiveness. The short investigation terms provided under the Law on Justice and Peace did not disproportionately affect the right to justice, as the investigation would still be conducted in an effective manner.

H9 The right to reparation, even in processes of transitional justice, required that the perpetrators of serious crimes compensate victims with their own assets for the damage that they have caused. According to international law, such reparation is an essential condition for guaranteeing the rights of victims and to combat impunity. Exempting the perpetrators of serious crimes from civil responsibility would amount to an amnesty. The state had a subsidiary obligation to compensate only if it was found responsible for having committed crimes or if the perpetrator's assets were insufficient.

It is worth noting that the Inter-American Court has not expressly ruled on the compatibility of the Law on Peace and Justice with the ACHR. In the cases of the *Mapiripán Massacre* and the *Ituango Massacre*, the Court limited itself to reiterate its constant jurisprudence that no domestic legal provision, including amnesty provisions, can prevent a state from complying with the duty to investigate and punish those responsible for human rights violations under Article 1(1) of the ACHR.[162] In the *Case of the Rochela Massacre*, the Court stated in general that 'with regard to the principle of proportionality of the punishment, the Court deems it appropriate to emphasize that the punishment which the state assigns to the perpetrator of illicit conduct should be proportional to the rights recognized by law and the culpability with which the perpetrated acted, which in turn should be established as a function of the nature and gravity of the events. The punishment should be the result of a judgment issued by a judicial authority. Moreover, in identifying the appropriate punishment, the reasons for the punishment should be determined. With regard to the principle of lenity based upon the existence of an earlier more lenient law, this principle should be harmonized with the principle of proportionality of punishment, such that criminal justice does not become illusory. Every element which determines the severity of the punishment should correspond to a clearly identifiable objective and be compatible with the Convention'.[163] In the end, however, the Court did not rule on whether the alternative punishment established by the Law on Peace and Justice was compatible with the ACHR. The Court followed a similar approach in subsequent cases, including in *Manuel Cepeda Vargas v Colombia*[164] and the *Case of the Afro-descendant communities displaced from the Cacarica River Basin (Operation Genesis) v Colombia*.[165]

Since 2007, in the case of *Juan Luis Rivera Matus*, the Supreme Court of Chile has also developed a legal interpretation to reduce the punishment of those convicted of crimes against humanity perpetrated during the dictatorship in that country.[166] In subsequent years, this interpretation was upheld in several cases including the disappearance of the priest *Antonio Llido*, where the Supreme Court, after reaffirming that such crime constituted a crime against humanity and could not be subject to a statute of limitations, held that a partial statutory limitation applied to reduce the punishment of those convicted in the case.[167] A similar approach was followed in another renowned case involving the murder of the former Chief of the Chilean Army, Carlos Prats and his wife. Human rights experts in Chile have criticized this approach arguing that it violates the duty to investigate, prosecute, and punish arising out of international human rights treaties that required that the punishment for crimes against humanity be proportional to the gravity of the crime.[168]

---

162 Inter-American Court of Human Rights, *Case of the Mapiripán Massacre v Colombia*, Merits, Reparations and Costs, Judgment of September 15, 2005, Series C No 134, paras 303–04; *Case of the Ituango Massacres v Colombia*, Preliminary Objections, Merits, Reparations and Costs, Judgment of 1 July 2006, Series C No 148, para 402.

163 Inter-American Court of Human Rights, *Case of the Rochela Massacre v Colombia*, Merits, Reparations and Costs, Judgment of 11 May 2005, Series C No 163, paras 195–96.

164 Inter-American Court of Human Rights, *Case of Manuel Cepeda Vargas v Colombia*, Preliminary Objections, Merits, Reparations and Costs, Judgment of 26 May 2010, Series C No 213, paras 150, 153, and 166.

165 Inter-American Court of Human Rights, *Case of the Afro-descendant communities displaced from the Cacarica River Basin (Operation Genesis) v Colombia*, Preliminary Objections, Merits, Reparations and Costs, Judgment of 20 November 2013, Series C No 270, para 390. In this last case, however, the Court seems more inclined to accept the investigations carried out in the context of the Law 975 (Law on Justice and Peace). See in this regard paras 391–93 of the judgment.

166 Supreme Court of Chile, *Episodio Juan Luis Rivera Matus*, Rol 3808-2006, Judgment of 30 July 2007.

167 Supreme Court of Chile, *Episodio Antonio Llido Mengual*, Rol 8939/2009, Judgment of 30 August 2010.

168 See, *inter alia*, K Fernandez Neira and P Sferrazza Taibi, 'La aplicación de la prescripción gradual del delito en las causas sobre violaciones de derechos humanos' (2009) 7 *Estudios Constitucionales* 1, 299–330; I González Ramírez, S Malamud Herrera, M Soledad Fuentealba Martínez, and F Pardo Montenegro, 'La media prescripción frente al delito de desaparición forzada de personas, ¿incumplimiento de la normativa internacional en materia de crímenes de lesa humanidad?' (2014) 10 *Revista Direito GV* 1, 321–46.

Episodio "Carlos Prats," Appeal Judgment to the Supreme Court, Rol N° 2596-09, Judgment of July 8, 2010, ILDC 2807

On 30 September 1974, General Carlos Prats was murdered by a car bomb, along with his wife Sofia Cuthbert. General Prats was the former Interior minister and Commander-in-Chief of the Chilean Army. He went into voluntary exile to Argentina immediately after the *coup d'état* that overthrew President Allende. Further investigations proved that the National Intelligence Directorate (Chilean Secret Police), under Juan Manuel Guillermo Contreras' direction, was involved in the planning and execution of the acts. Moreover, Juan Manuel Guillermo Contreras, Raul Iturriaga Neumman, Jorge Iturriaga Neumman, Pedro Espinoza Bravo, Jose Zara Holguer, Maraiana Callejas Honores, Michael Townley, Cristoph George Willike Floel, Juan Morales Salgado, and Reginaldo Valdes Alarcon were part of a criminal organization opposing the political regime through a systemic practice of terror and violence. This criminal organization, headed by Juan Manuel Guillermo Contreras, planned and committed the arbitrarily execution of General Prats and Ms Cuthbert in Buenos Aires. The first instance court convicted the accused and the Court of Appeals affirmed. Defendants appealed against that judgment arguing, *inter alia*, that the statute of limitations had run out with respect to the crimes of which they were charged and that they were covered by Amnesty Law 2.191. Alternatively, they alleged that Article 103 of the Chilean Criminal Code should apply to reduce their convictions. This provision establishes that '[i]f the guilty party comes forward or is found before the statutory limitation for the criminal proceeding or the penalty has expired, but half of that time period has already elapsed, in either case, in considering such limitations, the tribunal shall recognize that fact as amounting to two or more mitigating circumstances and not as an aggravating factor, and shall apply the rules contained in Articles 65, 66, 67, and 68,[169] either in imposing the sentence, or to reduce the one already imposed'.[170] The Supreme Court characterized the crimes perpetrated in this case as crimes against humanity and concluded that the international obligations of Chile imposed a duty to investigate and punish those crimes. Moreover, crimes against humanity are not subject to statutes of limitation under international law.

> H1 The principle of non-applicability of statutes of limitation to crimes against humanity does not restrict the application of the "partial lapse of the statutory time period" (media prescripción) or "partial statutory limitation" (prescripción gradual), as the latter involves only a mere reduction of the punishment. While the application of a statute of limitation extinguishes the criminal liability and prohibits the application of any punishment, the "partial lapse of the statutory time period" or "partial statutory limitation" only reduces the quantum of the punishment, which subsists albeit in a modified manner.
>
> H2 The existence of the rule of "partial lapse of the statutory time period" or "partial statutory limitation" is justified in the social need of preventing the indefinite application of criminal norms that create a situation of uncertainty for the alleged perpetrator, who is not clear whether criminal liability may be applied to him or not. However, this rule has not the purpose of perpetuating impunity, particularly in cases of crimes against humanity.
>
> H3 The rule of "partial lapse of the statutory time period" or "partial statutory limitation" has not been extensively contemplated in other liberal states, but it has been in existence in the criminal laws of Chile since the inception of the criminal code. Moreover, as a rule of *ordre public* it must be applied by courts regardless of

---

169 These Articles regulate the extent of the punishment as applicable to different crimes.

170 Inter-American Commission on Human Rights, *Juan Luis Rivera Matus et al v Chile*, Report on admissibility No 58/16, Petitions 1275-94 B and 1566-08, OEA/Ser.L/V/II.159, doc 67, 6 December 2016, para 14.

> whether or not it was requested by the accused in a case. In contrast to the principle of non-applicability of statutes of limitation to crimes against humanity, the rule of "partial lapse of the statutory time period" or "partial statutory limitation" is not prohibited by international law.
>
> H4 Taken into account the crimes for which the accused are charged, namely deprivation of life and illicit association, the statute of limitation would have started to run fifteen years after the perpetration of such crimes. On the other hand, for the application of the rule of "partial lapse of the statutory time period" or "partial statutory limitation" half of that time must have elapsed. Thus, in the case of aggravated murder seven and a half years must have passed for the rule to apply. Since the crimes in the present case were perpetrated in 1974, that period has elapsed in excess.

Interestingly, the Supreme Court in these cases ruled that the gross violations of human rights characterized crimes against humanity and were therefore imprescriptible. However, the court still took into account the date from which the statute of limitations would start running in order to calculate the time from which the rule of 'partial lapse of the statutory time period' or 'partial statutory limitation' would become applicable. Once the court concluded that such rule applied, it considerably reduced the extent of the punishment that convicted perpetrators of crimes against humanity would receive. Eventually, the Supreme Court stopped applying the rule of 'partial lapse of the statutory time period' or 'partial statutory limitation' to enforced disappearance cases starting with the case of *Rudy Cárcamo Ruiz* in 2012 on the basis that this was a permanent crime until the whereabouts of the victim were established.[171] However, at least one of the chambers of the Supreme Court has continued to follow this approach in cases regarding extrajudicial executions and torture.[172]

The application of the rule of 'partial lapse of the statutory time period' or 'partial statutory limitation' was challenged by the Human Rights Committee in 2014 in the Concluding Observations issued after the periodic review of Chile before that body.[173] Specifically, the Committee recommended Chile to repeal or amend Article 103 of the Criminal Code to make it compatible with the provisions of the International Covenant on Civil and Political Rights.[174] It stated that Chile 'should continue its concerted efforts to investigate all human rights violations proactively and to ensure that the perpetrators are identified, prosecuted and given appropriate penalties that are in proportion to the gravity of their offences'.[175]

Similarly, the Inter-American Commission in 2016 declared admissible the case of *Juan Luis Rivera Matus* and thirteen other cases involving a multiplicity of victims in which the Supreme Court of Chile had applied the rule of 'partial lapse of the statutory time period' or 'partial statutory limitation' to reduce the punishment of the perpetrators of gross human rights violations.[176] Petitioners argued that 'the obligations to impose penalties was violated because the benefits applied signified that the guilty parties were allowed to remain largely unpunished, and that by applying partially mitigating circumstances and giving weight to the passage of time, the state infringed its obligations to respect and ensure the free and full exercise of rights recognized by the Convention'.[177] The Commission concluded that there was a colorable claim of violations of

---

171 *Episodio Rudy Cárcamo Ruiz* (n 92).

172 For a detailed analysis on this issue see Instituto Nacional de Derechos Humanos de Chile, *Informe Anual 2015: Situación de los Derechos Humanos en Chile*, 218–20 http://bibliotecadigital.indh.cl/handle/123456789/875 (last accessed 24 November 2017).

173 ibid, 219.

174 UNHRC, 'Concluding observations on the sixth periodic report of Chile' (2014) UN Doc CCPR/C/CHL/CO/6, para 8.

175 ibid.

176 *Juan Luis Rivera Matus et al v Chile* (n 170).

177 ibid, para 18.

Articles 8 and 25 of the ACHR for the failure to ensure the victims or their next of kin access to justice and an effective remedy, Article 5 of the ACHR for the suffering underwent by the victims' next of kin, all in relation to Articles 1.1 and 2 of the same instrument.[178] Also, the Commission suggested that the application of the rule of 'partial lapse of the statutory time period' or 'partial statutory limitation' could be incompatible with the prohibition against applying statutory limitations in cases of crimes against humanity.[179]

The issue regarding the reduction of the punishment for convicted perpetrators of crimes against humanity was again brought to the forefront in a recent judgment of the Supreme Court of Argentina in the case of *Luis Muiña*, who was convicted for the kidnapping and subsequent torture of five victims in a public hospital in Buenos Aires in 1976.[180] The principle invoked by the Supreme Court in this case to reduce the conviction of Muiña was the so called '2x1 rule'. This rule, which was in effect from 1994 and 2001, established that after two years of pretrial detention, each day spent in prison without a firm conviction could be counted as two days toward a person's sentence.[181] This rule had never been applied to the perpetrators of crimes against humanity before.[182] Moreover, the rule was neither in effect when the crimes perpetrated by Muiña occurred nor when he was deprived of his liberty.[183] The judgment caused an extensive outcry in the legal community that triggered the adoption of a law by Congress barring the application of the 2x1 rule to perpetrators of crimes against humanity.[184] Also, lower courts, including the Court of Criminal Cassation have rejected its application in subsequent judgments.[185]

IV. Conclusion

This chapter shows that twenty-five years after the Commission decided the first cases declaring the incompatibility of amnesty laws with the ACHR in Argentina and Uruguay, the normative framework developed by the Inter-American Human Rights organs has had a demonstrable impact in the prosecution and punishment of the worst human rights crimes and perpetrators in the region. The normative framework was construed around the state duty to investigate, identify, and punish heinous human rights violations in light of Articles 8, 25, 1(1), and 2 of the ACHR.

The principles of accountability developed by the Commission under the ACHR were later embraced and further expanded by the Court. The first case decided by the Court involved the determination of the compatibility of the amnesty laws enacted in Peru during President Fujimori's administration and the ACHR. In *Barrios Altos v Peru*, the Court followed a similar approach to the Commission's. Subsequently, one after the other, the Court found that the amnesty laws in Chile, Uruguay, Brazil, and, most recently, El Salvador were also incompatible with the ACHR. Domestic courts in Argentina found the amnesty laws in that country incompatible with the ACHR on the basis of the jurisprudence of the Court.

---

178 ibid, para 131.

179 ibid.

180 Supreme Court of Argentina, *Recurso de hecho deducido por la defensa de Luis Muiña en la causa Bignone, Reynaldo Benito Antonio y otro s/recurso extraordinario*, 3 May 2017.

181 See, *inter alia*, CEJIL, *La justicia argentina se equivoca con el 2x1 para crímenes contra la humanidad* (9 May 2017) https://www.cejil.org/es/justicia-argentina-se-equivoca-2x1-crimenes-contra-humanidad (last accessed 24 November 2017).

182 ibid.

183 ibid.

184 See, Inter-American Commission on Human Rights, *IACHR Expresses Concern over Argentine Supreme Court Decision*, 15 May 2017, http://www.oas.org/en/iachr/media_center/PReleases/2017/060.asp accessed 24 November 2017.

185 See, *inter alia*, Cámara Federal de Casación Penal, *Riveros, Santiago Omar s/recurso de casación*, Expte N° FSM 493/2008/TO1/4/1/CFC4 del registro de la Sala II, 9 June 2017.

The relevance of the normative framework lies on the fact that it was developed in regard to crimes for which no other international tribunals, notably the ICC, have jurisdiction to prosecute and as a result of the interaction between the international and the national jurisdictions. Had it not been for the normative framework built by the human organs of the Inter-American System, the accountability process that has taken place in Latin America would probably not have happened.

Certainly, the initial case law of the Inter-American organs on amnesty laws was limited to articulate the duty to investigate and punish under the ACHR and other international human rights instruments, leaving domestic courts with the task of translating into domestic laws and procedures the actual implementation of those duties. As a result, the legal rationales used to find amnesty laws unconstitutional and/or reopen criminal investigations into gross human rights violations that occurred in the past were different depending on the country concerned, the legal culture and the political environment in which the judgments were adopted. As this chapter shows some of these rationales arguably overstretched the interpretations of domestic and international principles and triggered extensive criticism from practitioners and academics alike. Others consolidated existing principles such as the notion of crimes against humanity and expanded them to situations that were not covered before. It is worth mentioning that starting with *Almonacid Arellano*, the Inter-American Court has best articulated the duty to investigate and prosecute under the ACHR and offered more guidance to domestic courts as to the scope of those obligations. Moreover, since *Gomes Lund et al (Guerrilha do Araguaia)* and *Gelman*, the Court's jurisprudence has nurtured itself from the interpretations and legal approaches construed by domestic courts.

Overall, the approaches reproduced in this chapter show the struggle of the domestic jurisdictions to develop a legal approach that would incorporate the inter-American human rights standards within an existing constitutional order. In spite of the consolidated jurisprudence on amnesty laws in the Inter-American System, several challenges remain in the region regarding its consistent application. First, there is still resistance to its application in some countries, including Brazil and Uruguay. Secondly, it is not clear whether the judgment of the Court in *El Mozote* and the subsequent judgment of the Constitutional Court of El Salvador declaring the unconstitutionality of the amnesty law will trigger much awaited prosecutions for those involved in the perpetration of crimes against humanity and war crimes during the armed conflict that transpired in that country. Thirdly, the judgment of the Supreme Court of Argentina in the *Luis Muiña* case and the application of the 2x1 rule shows that, even in those countries in which the case law seems to be more consolidated, there is the risk of setbacks. Finally, the new peace accord in Colombia and the imminent establishment of a special jurisdiction for peace may create new challenges for the interpretation and application of the principles of accountability developed by the organs of the Inter-American Human Rights System. Ultimately, it will be the task of civil society organizations, the Commission and the Court, as well as like-minded domestic courts, to ensure that twenty five years of jurisprudence on amnesty laws continues to be applied in the countries of the region.

17

Economic and Social Rights

ARISTOTELES CONSTANTINIDES

I. Introduction

In contemporary international law all human rights are regarded as indivisible, interdependent and interrelated.[1] They are still, however, classified in various categories.[2] A pertinent distinction is between civil and political rights (such as the rights to life, integrity and liberty of the person, the right to a fair trial, the freedoms of thought, expression, religion, association, etc) and economic, social and cultural rights (such as the rights to work, to form and join trade unions and to strike, the rights to education, health and social security, the right to an adequate standard of living, including the rights to food, water and adequate housing, the right to take part in cultural life, etc), which are all enshrined in the Universal Declaration of Human Rights (UDHR).[3]

Although the initial idea was to include all these rights in a single legally binding human rights treaty,[4] the Cold War divide made it impossible to draw up a universal human rights convention inclusive of all rights recognized in the UDHR. Many Western states insisted on dividing the UDHR rights in two different treaties. They contended that—unlike civil and political rights—economic, social and cultural rights were non-enforceable and non-justiciable programmatic rights.[5] Even though they did not seriously resist international legal recognition of socio-economic rights,[6] many of them treat(ed) them as important statements of public policy goals rather than individual legal claims.[7] They conceived human rights as legally enforceable individual rights based on the model of the European Convention on Human Rights (ECHR),[8] which was adopted by the Council of Europe in 1950 and included only civil rights.

Despite the resistance of socialist states, this approach eventually prevailed and led to the adoption in 1966 of two separate treaties, the International Covenant on Civil and Political Rights (ICCPR)[9] and the International Covenant on Economic, Social and Cultural Rights (ICESCR).[10] The two covenants are respectively monitored by the Human Rights Committee

---

1 UNGA, 'Vienna Declaration and Programme of Action' (12 July 1993) UN Doc A/CONF.157/23, para 5.

2 See T van Boven, 'Categories of Rights' in D Moeckli, S Shah, and S Sivakumaran (eds), *International Human Rights Law* (2nd edn, OUP 2014) 143–56.

3 UNGA, 'Universal Declaration of Human Rights' UNGA Res 217 A (III) (10 December 1948) UN Doc A/RES/3/217 A.

4 UNGA Res 421 (V) (4 December 1950) UN Doc A/RES/421(V).

5 M Nowak, *Introduction to the International Human Rights Regime* (Martinus Nijhoff 2003) 78–79.

6 Indeed, virtually all Western states became parties to the ICESCR, except for the US, which signed the Covenant in 1977 but has yet to ratify it. For an explanation of the US position see D Forsythe, 'The United States and International Economic Rights: Law, Social Reality, and Political Choice' in S Hertel and L Minkler (eds), *Economic Rights: Conceptual, Measurement, and Policy Issues* (CUP 2007) 310–24.

7 J Donnelly, 'The West and Economic Rights' in S Hertel and L Minkler (eds), *Economic Rights: Conceptual, Measurement, and Policy Issues* (CUP 2007) 37, 42.

8 European Convention for the Protection of Human Rights and Fundamental Freedoms, as amended by Protocols Nos 11 and 14 (signed 4 November 1950, entered into force 3 September 1953) ETS 5.

9 International Covenant on Civil and Political Rights (adopted 16 December 1966, entered into force 23 March 1976) 999 UNTS 171.

10 International Covenant on Economic, Social and Cultural Rights (adopted 16 December 1966, entered into force 3 January 1976) 993 UNTS 3.

and the Committee on Economic, Social and Cultural Rights (CESCR).[11] These expert bodies adopt non-binding General Comments on issues of general nature as well as on specific rights, which interpret, clarify, and specify the content of rights and the scope of the Covenant obligations. The Human Rights Committee was also given the competence from the outset to examine individual complaints against violations of the ICCPR.[12] A similar mechanism for the ICESCR was only adopted in 2009 and entered into force in 2013.

The International Bill of Rights (that is, the UDHR along with the two Covenants) was supplemented with numerous universal and regional human rights treaties. Some of them focus on specific rights, while other focus on specific categories of persons. The European and American regional systems have adopted separate treaties on economic, social and cultural rights,[13] whereas the African Charter on Human and Peoples' Rights includes the full range of human rights without differentiating as to the nature of obligations to fulfil them. Significantly, the African Charter has made all rights, including socio-economic rights, subject to the individual complaints procedure and the African Commission on Human and Peoples' Rights has held that 'no right in the African Charter cannot be made effective'.[14]

This is not a unique statement. The Supreme Court of India has been a pioneer in treating socio-economic rights as justiciable by interpreting the right to life in Article 21 of the Indian constitution broadly as encompassing, among others, the rights to health, food, and shelter. Other courts in the Indian subcontinent and elsewhere have followed a similar approach.[15] Economic, social and cultural rights are protected in dozens of national constitutions and are frequently given effect by the respective national judiciaries. International jurisprudence on socio-economic rights being rather scant, the case law of domestic courts is even more pertinent for the determination and enforcement of (international legal rules on) socio-economic rights than it is for civil and political rights, which are routinely enforced by numerous international (*vide* regional) courts and quasi-judicial bodies.

It seems then that the controversy over the nature of economic, social and cultural rights as human rights belongs largely to the past, especially since the solemn pronouncements in the Vienna Declaration of Human Rights, which was adopted by consensus in 1993. The last couple of decades have witnessed a resurgence of interest and new or renewed thinking and emphasis on socio-economic rights.[16] There remains, however, a considerable difference in the legal

11 Unlike the Human Rights Committee which was provided in the ICCPR, the CESCR was only established in 1987 following Resolution 1985/17 of the UN Economic and Social Council, which is another indication that ICESCR rights were initially considered as non-enforceable and thus unworthy of monitoring.

12 This competence could only be exercised against those states that became parties to an additional protocol, which was adopted in 1966 and entered into force ten years later.

13 European Social Charter (adopted 18 October 1961, entered into force 26 February 1965) CETS No 035; Additional Protocol to the American Convention on Human Rights in the Area of Economic, Social and Cultural Rights (Protocol of San Salvador) (adopted 17 November 1988, entered into force 16 November 1999) OAS Treaty Series No 69 (1988) reprinted in Basic Documents Pertaining to Human Rights in the Inter-American System OEA/Ser L V/II.82 Doc 6 Rev 1 at 67 (1992).

14 African Commission on Human and Peoples' Rights, *The Social and Economic Rights Action Center and the Center for Economic and Social Rights v Nigeria*, Comm No 155/96, 27 October 2001, para 68.

15 See, eg, *Asare and Three Other Individuals v Ga West District Assembly and Attorney General*, Decision of the High Court of Justice, Suit no AP 36/2007, ILDC 1488 (GH 2008), 2nd May 2008, Ghana [gh], where the Ghanaian High Court interpreted the right to life in the Constitution of Ghana to include, *inter alia*, the right to adequate nutrition and shelter by reference to decisions of the African Commission and the Supreme Court of India.

16 Among the burgeoning academic literature see, eg, B Ramcharan, *Judicial Protection of Economic, Social and Cultural Rights* (Martinus Nijhoff 2005); F Coomans (ed), *Justiciability of Economic and Social Rights: Experiences from Domestic Systems* (Intersentia 2006); V Gauri and D Brinks (eds), *Courting Social Justice: Judicial Enforcement of Social and Economic Rights in the Developing World* (CUP 2008); D Barak-Erez and A Gross (eds), *Exploring Social Rights: Between Theory and Practice* (Hart Publishing 2011).

provisions on the nature of states parties' obligations under the two Covenants. While Article 2 of the ICCPR provides for an immediate obligation of states parties to respect and ensure civil and political rights to all individuals in their territory and subject to their jurisdiction, the parallel Article 2 of the ICESCR provides for the progressive realization of the Covenant's rights by states parties, by taking steps, individually and through international assistance and co-operation, to the maximum of their available resources. In addition, there still exist different perceptions on the justiciability and enforceability of socio-economic rights and the self-executing character of the ICESCR, in view of the varying legal and judicial cultures across the world and the various approaches towards judicial review and separation of powers.

The present chapter aims to shed light on these controversies and developments by focusing on the burgeoning case law of domestic courts, which testifies to a steady shift towards accepting the justiciability of economic, social and cultural rights. The first section presents cases relating to the nature and scope of state obligations under the ICESCR in the context of claims for the violation of specific rights recognized in the Covenant. The picture portrayed is neither black nor white. The second section focuses on specific economic and social rights. Some cases concern group action addressing systemic problems, while others concern individual claims.

The decisions presented in this chapter are a representative sample of domestic case law on socio-economic rights. There are many more and their number is increasing. The main criterion for the selection is their reference to and reliance on international human rights law (mostly the ICESCR) for deciding the case.

II. The Legal Nature of Obligations Arising from the ICESCR

A and B v Government of the Canton of Zurich, Appeal against a Regulation of 15 September 1999 adopted by the Canton of Zurich on the Tuition at Schools of Higher Education, Case No 2P.273/1999, BGE 126 I 242, ILDC 350 (CH 2000), 22nd September 2000, Switzerland; Federal Supreme Court [BGer]

The applicants claimed that a Regulation introducing registration and tuition fees for attending a school of tertiary education level (the *Technikum Winterthur*)—the attendance of which used to be free—violated Article 13(2)(b) (on secondary education) and Article 13(2)(c) (on higher education) of the ICESCR. In deciding the case, the Swiss Federal Supreme Court had to consider whether the provisions of the ICESCR were self-executing and could thus be invoked by individuals before the Swiss courts.

> 2 c) Subject to certain exceptions, the International Covenant on Economic, Social and Cultural Rights (ICESCR) is not regarded in the jurisprudence of the Federal Court of Justice as directly applicable. As the Federal Court stated in its basic decision 120 Ia 1 C. 5c pp. 11 et seq., its Arts. 6 to 15 contain a list of economic, social and cultural rights, the full realisation of which each Contracting State is obliged to observe, exhausting all its opportunities and by all suitable means, especially by legislative measures and through international aid and cooperation (cf. Article 2 (1)). The international law obligations assumed by Switzerland under this Covenant are consequently of a programmatic nature; the provisions of the Treaty are not directed at the individual—contrary to the directly applicable guarantees of the [ICCPR], to which Switzerland also acceded at the same time—but (primarily) at the Parliaments of the Contracting States, which must regard them as a guideline for their activities [...] The Federal Council and Parliament have consequently assumed that the provisions of the ICESCR essentially grant the individual no subjective or legally enforceable rights, apart from a few exceptions, that the citizen could invoke before Swiss administrative and legal authorities [...].

d) As far as the provision of Article 13 (2) c. of the ICESCR now in question is concerned, the Federal Court clearly denied its direct applicability, insofar as Contracting States are obliged to make university education accessible "to all, on the basis of capacity, by every appropriate means, and in particular by the progressive introduction of free education". The Federal Court held that no claim to individual rights to a particular admission procedure or to a particular limitation or reduction in any fees could be derived from this provision; it should be made clear to the national parliament when, by what means and within what period, it should achieve the objective stated in Article 13 (2) c., to the extent that it regards the requirement concerned as not already met (BGE 120 Ia 1 C. 5d pp. 12–13).

There is no reason for departing from this Statement. It is not as such questioned by the petitioners. The only point can be whether Article 13 (2) c. (or b.) of the Covenant also has enforceable, directly applicable substance insofar as it prevents the national parliament from increasing or reintroducing charges, because this will mean a step back from the recognised constitutional objective. [. . .]

e) However, in BGE 120 Ia 1 c. 5d p. 13, which addresses the admissibility of increasing university fees, the Federal Court itself considered the provisions of Article 13 (2) c. of the ICESCR as too unspecific in this regard. The actual object of the provision was to make university education available to everyone in accordance with his abilities, irrespective of his financial ability to pay. The choice of "suitable means" had been put to Parliament; the "particular" gradual dispensing of tuition was mentioned as only one possible way. As the typical tuition fees in Switzerland form merely a fraction of the total cost of living of students, a simple reduction in fees or even a full tuition waiver would not secure access to the university for financially indigent students; this obstacle could only be removed by granting bursaries. The Parliament therefore had substantial discretion as to what means it would adopt to achieve the objectives set out in Article 13 (2) c. of the ICESCR and as to how it intended to reconcile these resources. The individual was unable to rely on this provision because it lacked the necessary specificity. It was, moreover, clearly directed only at Parliament, which—irrespective of its specific nature—excluded its enforcement by Constitutional Objection under Article 84 (1) c. Constitution from the start.

g) [. . .] The ICESCR contains no provisions as to how it must be implemented in the domestic order [. . .]. The question at issue is therefore how obligations of treaty law undertaken must be executed and whether and to what extent the provisions of this Covenant can be invoked within a state as "self-executing" by an individual in connection with an individual objection procedure [. . .]. In addition, there is no competent treaty body for the ICESCR at international level that could specify authoritatively the individual obligations and claims in a specific case under this Covenant. The ICCPR provides—in addition to an obligatory reporting system—both for an optional (applicable to Switzerland) State Objections procedure and for an optional (not applicable to Switzerland) Individual Objections procedure. In contrast, the ICESCR, as an international implementing instrument, refers only to the reporting system, i.e. examination of reports to be submitted periodically by the Contracting States, which may result in comments and recommendations by the Social Committee. While these opinions are important to the interpretation and development of the law, they do not have any directly binding nature [. . .].

3.— Article 13 (2) (b) and (c) of the ICESCR do not contain, as will be shown, any enforceable guarantees concerning rights of the individual, that might be invoked in the present case on the basis of Article 84 (1) c. Constitution by Constitutional Objection.

> b) The tuition fees newly payable by students of the former *Technikum Winterthur* cannot be properly understood separated from the other arrangements for university education. They can only be considered in conjunction with the measures mentioned. [...] The introduction of an exemption from tuition fees for all state universities would certainly comply with the requirements of Article 13 (2) (b) and (c) of the ICESCR, but a step of this kind would hardly be materially justifiable under the existing fee regulations in comparison to similar institutions (universities) in Switzerland. Retaining such a privilege for simply one individual branch of a university (the former *Technikum Winterthur*) would in turn be open to question from the perspective of legal uniformity. The additional burden resulting from the new uniform fee regulations for part of the student body of the institution can therefore be perfectly justified, even if these regulations run counter to the requirements of Article 13 (2) (b) and (c) of the ICESCR (progressive introduction of exemption from tuition for higher technical and university education).
>
> [...] Whether the introduction of tuition fees for students at the *Technikum Winterthur* is a step back in achieving the objectives of the Covenant, in breach of Article 13 (2) (c) or (b) of the ICESCR, or whether the disadvantage faced by these students with regard to fees—which is not practically unlawful under the Covenant [...]—is offset by other improvements in educational policy, may well form a subject of a reporting procedure under Arts. 16 et seq. of the ICESCR. However, on account of the lack of specificity of the testing scale and because the totality of measures introduced in the sphere of universities (including the forecasts of their actual effect) should be included in a proper assessment; the question lacks the necessary judicial basis (cf. C. 2b) to form the subject of a constitutional objection under the rights of the individual in accordance with Article 84 (1) c. Constitution. Therefore, there is no need to consider the documents subsequently submitted by the petitioners concerning Switzerland's report on the implementation of Article 13 (2) (c) of the ICESCR and the related opinions of the UN bodies concerned.

This elaborate decision is representative of the traditional 'Western' viewpoint that the obligations deriving from the ICESCR, and in particular Article 13(2)(b) and (c) on the right to education, are of a programmatic nature and not self-executing because they are too unspecific and allow states substantial discretion as to the choice of means to implement them.[17] As will be seen in many other cases discussed in this chapter, this general and unqualified statement no longer represents the predominant view. Many other courts have been more attentive to the approach of the Committee on Economic, Social and Cultural Rights, which has affirmed the justiciability of the rights contained in the ICESCR. Interestingly, one of the court's arguments was the lack of an individual complaint procedure in the ICESCR, which is, however, no longer the case, thus further weakening the soundness of this approach. As to the question of progressive realization, the court referred to the 'lack of specificity of the testing scale' but also—and this was arguably more convincing—the need to make a proper assessment based on the totality of the measures that were introduced. Overall, however, as also noted by the ILDC reporters, 'one could legitimately argue that Article 13(2)(b) and 13(2)(c) were able to be directly invoked before Swiss courts for opposing the introduction of fees for the former Technikum Winterthur'.[18]

17 See also *DD v HDP Compensation Fund for Family Allowances*, Appeal judgment, Cass No S 06 0105 F/2008; ILDC 1114 (BE 2008), 26 May 2008, Court of Cassation, where the Belgian Court of Cassation, in line with Belgian jurisprudence, summarily denied any direct effect to the ICESCR provisions, by simply restating the text of the provisions and by referring to Article 2(1) of the covenant, without any further analysis. P de Man, Analysis, *DD v HDP Compensation Fund for Family Allowances*, ILDC 1114 (BE 2008) A2.

18 C Bergmann and A Ziegler, Analysis, *A and B v Government of the Canton of Zurich*, ILDC 350 (CH 2000) A5.

In *Imposition of general tuition fees for higher education, Students' Union of the University of Paderborn v University of Paderborn,*[19] which involved similar facts (tuition fees introduced in 2006 in the German federal state of North Rhine-Westphalia) and legal issues, the court refrained from deciding on whether Article 13(2)(c) of the ICESCR was self-executing.[20]

Government of South Africa and ors v Grootboom, Appeal to Constitutional Court, [2000] ZACC 19, 2001 (1) SA 46, 2000 (11) BCLR 1169 (CC), ILDC 285 (ZA 2000), 4th October 2000, South Africa; Constitutional Court [CC]

Mrs Grootboom and a large group of adult and children squatters were evicted from the vacant privately owned land they had occupied and they ended up camping on a sports field at Wallacedene, in Western Cape, South Africa. They sought relief from the High Court under sections 26 (right of access to adequate housing) and 28 (children's right to basic shelter) of the South African Constitution. The High Court held that the respondent governmental bodies had taken reasonable measures to address the problem of housing within scarce resources but had failed in their obligations to provide shelter for the children. Upon appeal, one of the issues before the Constitutional Court was the scope of the state's obligations regarding adequate housing, including a minimum core obligation to which both the adults and children would be entitled. The 'minimum core' argument was put forward by the *amici curiae* and was based on the interpretation of Article 2(1) of the ICESCR by the CESCR in its General Comment 3.

> [20] While the justiciability of socio-economic rights has been the subject of considerable jurisprudential and political debate, the issue of whether socio-economic rights are justiciable at all in South Africa has been put beyond question by the text of our Constitution as construed in the Certification judgment […]:
>
> > "[T]hese rights are, at least to some extent, justiciable. […] [M]any of the civil and political rights entrenched in the [constitutional text before this Court for certification in that case] will give rise to similar budgetary implications without compromising their justiciability. The fact that socio-economic rights will almost inevitably give rise to such implications does not seem to us to be a bar to their justiciability. At the very minimum, socio-economic rights can be negatively protected from improper invasion."
>
> […] The question is therefore not whether socio-economic rights are justiciable under our Constitution, but how to enforce them in a given case. This is a very difficult issue which must be carefully explored on a case-by-case basis. […]
>
> **ii) The relevant international law and its impact**
>
> [29] The obligations undertaken by states parties to the Covenant are monitored by the United Nations Committee on Economic, Social and Cultural Rights (the committee). The *amici* relied on the relevant general comments issued by the committee concerning the interpretation and application of the Covenant, and argued that these general comments constitute a significant guide to the interpretation of section 26. In particular they argued that in interpreting this section, we should adopt an approach similar to that taken by the committee in paragraph 10 of general comment 3 issued in 1990, in which the committee found that socio-economic rights contain a minimum core:

19 *Imposition of general tuition fees for higher education, Students' Union of the University of Paderborn v University of Paderborn*, Appeal judgment, 6 C 16/08, ILDC 1556 (DE 2009), 29 April 2009, Germany; Federal Administrative Court [BVerwG].

20 B Brodkorb, Analysis, *Imposition of general tuition fees for higher education, Students' Union of the University of Paderborn v University of Paderborn*, ILDC 1556 (DE 2009) A8.

"10 On the basis of the extensive experience gained by the Committee, as well as by the body that preceded it, over a period of more than a decade of examining States parties' reports the Committee is of the view that minimum core obligation to ensure the satisfaction of, at the very least, minimum essential levels of each of the rights is incumbent upon every State party. Thus, for example, a State party in which any significant number of individuals is deprived of essential foodstuffs, of essential primary health care, of basic shelter and housing, or of the most basic forms of education, is *prima facie*, failing to discharge its obligations under the Covenant. If the Covenant were to be read in such a way as not to establish such a minimum core obligation, it would be largely deprived of its raison d'etre. By the same token, it must be noted that any assessment as to whether a State has discharged its minimum core obligation must also take account of resource constraints applying within the country concerned. Article 2(1) obligates each State party to take the necessary steps "to the maximum of its available resources". In order for a State party to be able to attribute its failure to meet at least its minimum core obligations to a lack of available resources it must demonstrate that every effort has been made to use all resources that are at its disposition in an effort to satisfy, as a matter of priority, those minimum obligations."

[30] [...] A state party must demonstrate that every effort has been made to use all the resources at its disposal to satisfy the minimum core of the right. However, it is to be noted that the general comment does not specify precisely what that minimum core is.

[31] [...] Minimum core obligation is determined generally by having regard to the needs of the most vulnerable group that is entitled to the protection of the right in question. It is in this context that the concept of minimum core obligation must be understood in international law.

[32] It is not possible to determine the minimum threshold for the progressive realisation of the right of access to adequate housing without first identifying the needs and opportunities for the enjoyment of such a right. These will vary according to factors such as income, unemployment, availability of land and poverty. [...] All this illustrates the complexity of the task of determining a minimum core obligation for the progressive realisation of the right of access to adequate housing without having the requisite information on the needs and the opportunities for the enjoyment of this right. The committee developed the concept of minimum core over many years of examining reports by reporting states. This Court does not have comparable information.

[33] [...] There are difficult questions relating to the definition of minimum core in the context of a right to have access to adequate housing, in particular whether the minimum core obligation should be defined generally or with regard to specific groups of people. As will appear from the discussion below, the real question in terms of our Constitution is whether the measures taken by the state to realise the right afforded by section 26 are reasonable. There may be cases where it may be possible and appropriate to have regard to the content of a minimum core obligation to determine whether the measures taken by the state are reasonable. However, even if it were appropriate to do so, it could not be done unless sufficient information is placed before a court to enable it to determine the minimum core in any given context. In this case, we do not have sufficient information to determine what would comprise the minimum core obligation in the context of our Constitution. It is not in any event necessary to decide whether it is appropriate for a court to determine in the first instance the minimum core content of a right.

[34] […] Subsection (1) [of section 26] aims at delineating the scope of the right. It is a right of everyone including children. Although the subsection does not expressly say so, there is, at the very least, a negative obligation placed upon the state and all other entities and persons to desist from preventing or impairing the right of access to adequate housing. […]

[36] […] The poor are particularly vulnerable and their needs require special attention. It is in this context that the relationship between sections 26 and 27 and the other socio-economic rights is most apparent. If under section 27 the state has in place programmes to provide adequate social assistance to those who are otherwise unable to support themselves and their dependants, that would be relevant to the state's obligations in respect of other socio-economic rights.

Reasonable legislative and other measures

[…]

[41] The measures must establish a coherent public housing programme directed towards the progressive realisation of the right of access to adequate housing within the state's available means. The programme must be capable of facilitating the realisation of the right. The precise contours and content of the measures to be adopted are primarily a matter for the legislature and the executive. […] A court considering reasonableness will not enquire whether other more desirable or favourable measures could have been adopted, or whether public money could have been better spent. The question would be whether the measures that have been adopted are reasonable. […]

[43] In determining whether a set of measures is reasonable, it will be necessary to consider housing problems in their social, economic and historical context and to consider the capacity of institutions responsible for implementing the programme. […] A programme that excludes a significant segment of society cannot be said to be reasonable. […]

[44] […] To be reasonable, measures cannot leave out of account the degree and extent of the denial of the right they endeavour to realise. Those whose needs are the most urgent and whose ability to enjoy all rights therefore is most in peril, must not be ignored by the measures aimed at achieving realisation of the right. […] If the measures, though statistically successful, fail to respond to the needs of those most desperate, they may not pass the test.

Progressive realisation of the right

[45] […] The term "progressive realisation" shows that it was contemplated that the right could not be realised immediately. […] [A]ccessibility should be progressively facilitated: legal, administrative, operational and financial hurdles should be examined and, where possible, lowered over time. Housing must be made more accessible not only to a larger number of people but to a wider range of people as time progresses. The phrase is taken from international law and Article 2.1 of the Covenant in particular. The committee has helpfully analysed this requirement in the context of housing as follows:

> "Nevertheless, the fact that realization over time, or in other words progressively, is foreseen under the Covenant should not be misinterpreted as depriving the obligation of all meaningful content. It is on the one hand a necessary flexibility device, reflecting the realities of the real world and the difficulties involved for any country in ensuring full realization of economic, social and cultural rights. On the other hand, the phrase must be read in the light of the overall objective, indeed the raison d'être, of the Covenant which is to establish clear obligations for States

parties in respect of the full realization of the rights in question. It thus imposes an obligation to move as expeditiously and effectively as possible towards that goal. Moreover, any deliberately retrogressive measures in that regard would require the most careful consideration and would need to be fully justified by reference to the totality of the rights provided for in the Covenant and in the context of the full use of the maximum available resources."

Although the committee's analysis is intended to explain the scope of states parties' obligations under the Covenant, it is also helpful in plumbing the meaning of "progressive realisation" in the context of our Constitution. The meaning ascribed to the phrase is in harmony with the context in which the phrase is used in our Constitution and there is no reason not to accept that it bears the same meaning in the Constitution as in the document from which it was so clearly derived.

Within available resources

[46] The third defining aspect of the obligation to take the requisite measures is that the obligation does not require the state to do more than its available resources permit. This means that both the content of the obligation in relation to the rate at which it is achieved as well as the reasonableness of the measures employed to achieve the result are governed by the availability of resources. […]

[66] […] The nationwide housing programme falls short of obligations imposed upon national government to the extent that it fails to recognise that the state must provide for relief for those in desperate need. They are not to be ignored in the interests of an overall programme focussed on medium and long-term objectives. It is essential that a reasonable part of the national housing budget be devoted to this, but the precise allocation is for national government to decide in the first instance.

[99] The following order is made:

1. The appeal is allowed in part.
2. […] It is declared that:
   (a) Section 26(2) of the Constitution requires the state to devise and implement within its available resources a comprehensive and coordinated programme progressively to realise the right of access to adequate housing.
   (b) The programme must include reasonable measures such as, but not necessarily limited to, those contemplated in the Accelerated Managed Land Settlement Programme, to provide relief for people who have no access to land, no roof over their heads, and who are living in intolerable conditions or crisis situations.
   (c) As at the date of the launch of this application, the state housing programme in the area of the Cape Metropolitan Council fell short of compliance with the requirements in paragraph (b), in that it failed to make reasonable provision within its available resources for people in the Cape Metropolitan area with no access to land, no roof over their heads, and who were living in intolerable conditions or crisis situations.

This landmark judgment is among the most cited and influential decisions of domestic courts on socio-economic rights. It was not the first pronouncement of the Constitutional Court of South Africa in favour of justiciability. The first case was *Soobramoney*,[21] which however had linked socio-economic rights with available resources and followed a deferential approach to the government. *Grootboom* was more elaborate and made more extensive use of international law. This was done within the constitutional context of South Africa but with some reference to the

21 *Soobramoney v Minister of Health KwaZulu Natal*, 1997 (12) BCLR 1696 (CC) 8.

ICESCR and the CESCR's General Comments, although South Africa was not a party to the covenant at the time (it became a party in 2015); its courts have, however, a constitutional duty to consider international law when interpreting the constitution.[22]

Grootboom was both hailed and criticized. It was hailed for its outcome and for illustrating that it is feasible to judicially enforce social rights, thus providing a showcase for other domestic courts. It was criticized, *inter alia*, for employing the concept of reasonableness in a rather administrative law fashion instead of a proper application of the minimum core, as the latter has been articulated by the CESCR.[23] There were concerns that the indeterminate standard of reasonableness failed to give (sufficient) effect to the obligation for timely implementation. It was also feared that applicants would not be entitled to any tangible relief as a matter of individual right; the government policies would rather be judicially tested against the standard of reasonableness and, when found to fall short thereof, the court would (merely) order the state to revise existing policies or devise reasonable ones for the progressive realization of the rights within available resources.

Grootboom had a major impact on South Africa's housing policy but there were also problems regarding implementation and enforcement. Some of these problems could have been overcome if the court's order had included some form of supervision over the (reasonableness of the) government measures taken in implementation of the judgment. Indeed, once the obstacle of justiciability is overcome, implementation and enforcement present major challenges in cases involving socio-economic rights, especially in developing countries.

Minister of Health and ors v Treatment Action Campaign [TAC] and ors, Appeal to Constitutional Court, 2002 CCT 8/02, [2002] ZACC 15, 2002 (5) SA 721, (2002) 10 BCLR 1033, ILDC 517 (ZA 2002), 5th July 2002, South Africa; Constitutional Court [CC]

The respondents in this case were groups and members of civil society concerned with the treatment of people with HIV/AIDS. They brought a case before the High Court arguing that the restriction on the availability of Nevirapine—an anti-retroviral medicine proven to reduce mother-to-child transmission of HIV—to selected pilot sites in the public health sector, was in breach of the constitutional rights of everyone to have access to health care services (section 27(1) of the South African constitution) and of the right of children to basic health care services (section 28(1)(c) of the constitution). They also argued that the government programme for the prevention of mother-to-child transmission of HIV at birth was inadequate. The High Court found that the government's policy was unreasonable and ordered the government to make Nevirapine more widely available and also to develop an effective and comprehensive national programme for HIV prevention. The relief granted was a form of supervisory jurisdiction. Upon appeal before the Constitutional Court, the government, *inter alia*, raised separation of powers concerns, whereas the *amici curiae* argued that section 27(1) of the constitution established a minimum core to which everyone is entitled.

> **Enforcement of socio-economic rights**
>
> [. . .]
>
> [25] The question in the present case [. . .] is not whether socio-economic rights are justiciable. Clearly they are. The question is whether the applicants have shown that the measures adopted by the government to provide access to health care services for HIV-positive mothers and their newborn babies fall short of its obligations under the Constitution.

22 W Kaguongo, Analysis, *Government of South Africa and ors v Grootboom*, ILDC 285 (ZA 2000) A2.

23 See, eg, D Bilchitz, 'Giving Socio-economic Rights Teeth: The Minimum Core and Its Importance' (2002) 119 *South African Law Journal* 484; J Dugard, 'Judging the Judges: Towards an Appropriate Role for the Judiciary in South Africa's Transformation' (2007) 20 *Leiden Journal of International Law* 965, 975.

Minimum core

[26] [...] It was contended that section 27(1) of the Constitution establishes an individual right vested in everyone. This right, so the contention went, has a minimum core to which every person in need is entitled. The concept of "minimum core" was developed by the United Nations Committee on Economic, Social and Cultural Rights [...].

[34] [...] [T]he socio-economic rights of the Constitution should not be construed as entitling everyone to demand that the minimum core be provided to them. Minimum core was thus treated as possibly being relevant to reasonableness under s 26(2), and not as a self-standing right conferred on everyone under s 26(1).

[35] [...] It is impossible to give everyone access even to a "core" service immediately. All that is possible, and all that can be expected of the state, is that it act reasonably to provide access to the socio-economic rights identified in sections 26 and 27 on a progressive basis. [...]

[36] The state is obliged to take reasonable measures progressively to eliminate or reduce the large areas of severe deprivation that afflict our society. [...] As the Bill of Rights indicates, their function in respect of socio-economic rights is directed towards ensuring that legislative and other measures taken by the state are reasonable. [...]

[37] It should be borne in mind that in dealing with such matters the courts are not institutionally equipped to make the wide-ranging factual and political enquiries necessary for determining what the minimum-core standards called for by the first and second *amici* should be, nor for deciding how public revenues should most effectively be spent. There are many pressing demands on the public purse. [...]

[38] Courts are ill-suited to adjudicate upon issues where court orders could have multiple social and economic consequences for the community. The Constitution contemplates rather a restrained and focused role for the courts, namely, to require the state to take measures to meet its constitutional obligations and to subject the reasonableness of these measures to evaluation. Such determinations of reasonableness may in fact have budgetary implications, but are not in themselves directed at rearranging budgets. In this way the judicial, legislative and executive functions achieve appropriate constitutional balance.

[39] We therefore conclude that section 27(1) of the Constitution does not give rise to a self-standing and independent positive right enforceable irrespective of the considerations mentioned in section 27(2).

Considerations relevant to reasonableness

[67] The policy of confining nevirapine to research and training sites fails to address the needs of mothers and their newborn children who do not have access to these sites. It fails to distinguish between the evaluation of programmes for reducing mother-to-child transmission and the need to provide access to health care services required by those who do not have access to the sites.

[70] In dealing with these questions it must be kept in mind that this case concerns particularly those who cannot afford to pay for medical services. To the extent that government limits the supply of nevirapine to its research sites, it is the poor outside the catchment areas of these sites who will suffer. There is a difference in the positions of those who can afford to pay for services and those who cannot. State policy must take account of these differences.

Evaluation of the policy to limit nevirapine to research and training sites

[80] [. . .] A potentially lifesaving drug was on offer and where testing and counselling facilities were available it could have been administered within the available resources of the state without any known harm to mother or child. In the circumstances we agree with the finding of the High Court that the policy of government in so far as it confines the use of nevirapine to hospitals and clinics which are research and training sites constitutes a breach of the state's obligations under section 27(2) read with section 27(1)(a) of the Constitution.

The powers of the courts

[98] [. . .] All arms of government should be sensitive to and respect this separation [of powers]. This does not mean, however, that courts cannot or should not make orders that have an impact on policy.

[99] [. . .] Where state policy is challenged as inconsistent with the Constitution, courts have to consider whether in formulating and implementing such policy the state has given effect to its constitutional obligations. If it should hold in any given case that the state has failed to do so, it is obliged by the Constitution to say so. In so far as that constitutes an intrusion into the domain of the executive, that is an intrusion mandated by the Constitution itself. [. . .] Even simple declaratory orders against government or organs of state can affect their policy and may well have budgetary implications. Government is constitutionally bound to give effect to such orders whether or not they affect its policy and has to find the resources to do so.

[106] [. . .] Where a breach of any right has taken place, including a socio-economic right, a court is under a duty to ensure that effective relief is granted. The nature of the right infringed and the nature of the infringement will provide guidance as to the appropriate relief in a particular case. Where necessary this may include both the issuing of a mandamus and the exercise of supervisory jurisdiction.

[107] An examination of the jurisprudence of foreign jurisdictions on the question of remedies shows that courts in other countries also accept that it may be appropriate, depending on the circumstances of the particular case, to issue injunctive relief against the state. [. . .]

Relief

[125] It is essential that there be a concerted national effort to combat the HIV/AIDS pandemic. The government has committed itself to such an effort. We have held that its policy fails to meet constitutional standards because it excludes those who could reasonably be included where such treatment is medically indicated to combat mother–to–child transmission of HIV. That does not mean that everyone can immediately claim access to such treatment, although the ideal [. . .] is to achieve that goal. Every effort must, however, be made to do so as soon as reasonably possible. The increases in the budget to which we have referred will facilitate this.

[129] The order made by the High Court included a structural interdict requiring the appellants to revise their policy and to submit the revised policy to the court to enable it to satisfy itself that the policy was consistent with the Constitution. [. . .] We do not consider, however, that orders should be made in those terms unless this is necessary. The government has always respected and executed orders of this Court. There is no reason to believe that it will not do so in the present case.

This decision was a follow-up to and a confirmation of *Grootboom*. There was less outright discussion of international law than one might have expected. Nevertheless, as noted by the

ILDC reporter, several issues that arose in this case are relevant to international law: the minimum core of socio-economic rights, their justiciability, and the remedies to be granted.[24] Justiciability was readily reaffirmed based on previous established jurisprudence. Regarding the minimum core, the court followed its approach in *Grootboom* and read the relevant constitutional provisions as not entitling individuals to be provided with health care services by the state as a matter of subjective right; rather, everyone was entitled to require the state to adopt reasonable measures for the progressive realization of the right to ensure access to health care services for everyone.[25]

As to the remedies, the court rejected the government's argument that it could only issue a declaratory order because any other order would upset the separation of powers. Among other arguments, the court pointed to judgments from foreign jurisdictions where courts had issued other than merely declaratory orders, such as mandatory and structural injunctions. While asserting its right to issue such remedies and maintain supervisory jurisdiction over the follow-up measures of the executive, the court opted for not doing so in the case at hand. Even though this judgment shared similar criticism as *Grootboom*,[26] the practical outcome was outstanding and led to improved living conditions for thousands of poor and vulnerable people.[27]

President of Slovakia v National Council of Slovakia and Ministry of Justice (intervening), Constitutional review, PL ÚS 3/04, ILDC 1208 (SK 2006), 30th March 2006, Slovakia

Based on a constitutional provision, the President of Slovakia requested the Constitutional Court to review the conformity of certain provisions of the 2003 Act on Assistance in Material Needs with, *inter alia*, Article 11(1) of the ICESCR. The president argued that some of the benefits granted to low-income families in material need could not ensure a dignified standard of living as required by the Covenant. The respondent National Council of Slovakia argued that the amounts of the benefits for families in material need had been fixed at six different levels, depending on the type and size of households, and that fixing the given amounts of benefits did not violate the international obligations of Slovakia under the ICESCR.

> H1 The economic, social, and cultural rights in question were of a programmatic nature in so far as each state party to the ICESCR undertook to take all possible steps to the maximum of its available resources, with a view to achieving progressively the full realization of the rights recognized in the ICESCR by all appropriate means (Article 2(1) of the ICESCR). Article 11(1) of the ICESCR, which required the state parties to take appropriate steps to ensure the realization of the right of everyone to an adequate standard of living for himself and his family, was likewise of a programmatic nature. The substantive provisions of the ICESCR (Articles 6, 7, 8 and 9) did not set out any strict limits or quantitative aims to be reached at national level, as this would have contradicted the programmatic nature of the economic, social, and cultural rights. The progress in realization of the rights depended on the economic situation in each country. In fact, their realization could vary in the same country depending on the economic development in different time periods (eg, long-lasting economic recession, or strategic orientation of the national economy).

24 W Kaguongo, Analysis, *Minister of Health and ors v Treatment Action Campaign [TAC] and ors*, ILDC 517 (ZA 2002) A1.

25 ibid, A3.

26 See, eg, D Davis, 'Socio-Economic Rights: The Promise and Limitation: The South African Experience' in D Barak-Erez and A Gross (eds), *Exploring Social Rights: Between Theory and Practice* (Hart Publishing 2011) 193, 200–02.

27 L Forman, 'What Future for the Minimum Core? Contextualising the Implications of South African Socio-economic Rights Jurisprudence for the International Human Right to Health' in J Harrington and M Stuttaford (eds), *Global Health and Human Rights: Legal and Philosophical Perspectives* (Routledge 2010) 62, 75.

H2 Article I§10 of the Act, which established different benefits for different family situations or different groups of people (eg single-parent families, childless families, families with varying numbers of children), provided some of them with less than the official basic benefit of 1,450 Slovak koruna. The ICESCR did not fix the level at which the average standard of living needed to be maintained or how such a standard of living had to be attained and the state parties were likewise free to establish the criteria to assess it. Neither Article 11 of the ICESCR nor any other provisions of the ICESCR set out a financial (or another type of) qualification of the realization of economic, social, and cultural rights. The ICESCR did not contain non-derogable rights and, according to the general rule, 'the State may subject such rights only to such limitations as are determined by law only in so far as this may be compatible with the nature of these rights and solely for the purpose of promoting the general welfare in a democratic society.' The legislative limitations in Article I§10 of the Act were therefore compatible with the ICESCR.

H3 Judge Bárány, dissenting: The programmatic nature of the ICESCR rights did not mean that the ICESCR represented only a political declaration. It represented a fully fledged international treaty on human rights, which imposed on Slovakia specific international obligations.

H4 It was true that the ICESCR did not require a state party to maintain a specific standard of living as this depended on the economic situation in each country. Yet, in the context of the national system of the social measures that aimed to ensure dignified and civilized standard of living in Slovakia, state benefits granted to individuals who were in material need had been objectively fixed at such a low level that it could not sufficiently accommodate the very basic needs of individuals and were thus clearly incompatible with the right of everyone to 'an adequate standard of living' and to 'the continuous improvement of living conditions' guaranteed by Article 11(1) of the ICESCR.

H5 There was no economic pressure or other catastrophe that would justify the fact that such low benefits were established with respect to the individuals living at the poverty line. In this respect, General Comment no 7, UN Committee on Economic, Social and Cultural Rights, had to be taken into account.

H6 General Comment on Article 2(1) of the ICESCR, which contained the key interpretation of the nature of the obligations of state parties, required that 'any deliberately retrogressive measures in that regard would require the most careful consideration and would need to be fully justified by reference to the totality of the rights provided for in the Covenant and in the context of the full use of the maximum available resources'. There was, however, neither careful consideration nor justification when adopting Article I§10 of the Act and this provision was thus incompatible with Article 11(1) in conjunction with Article 2(1) of the ICESCR.

This decision illustrates the difficulties in determining the exact content and scope of socio-economic rights in specific cases and engaging in judicial review of implementing legislation. The majority could not identify any clear standard to do so in the ICESCR and relied on the programmatic nature of its obligations to deny such review. On the contrary, the dissenting judge, guided by the General Comments of the CESCR, found that the very low state benefits to the most in need were incompatible with the right of everyone to an adequate standard of living and to 'the continuous improvement of living conditions' guaranteed by Article 11(1) of the Covenant. Indeed, most of the decisions considering economic and social rights as justiciable refer to the General Comments of the CESCR—despite and irrespective of their non-binding nature—in a quest to give the obligations under the covenant a (more) specific content, which would allow their judicial review.

Kenya v Minister for Home Affairs and ors, *ex parte* Sitamze, First Instance, Civil Case 1652 of 2004, (2008) eKLR, ILDC 1094 (KE 2007), 18th April 2007, Kenya; Nairobi; High Court

Mr Sitamze, a Cameroonian national, was licensed to register a company in Kenya, which was managed successfully by his Kenyan wife. His application for a work permit that would have allowed him to stay and work in Kenya was, however, rejected on grounds of national security. He then sought an order of *mandamus* to compel, *inter alia*, the Minister of Home Affairs to issue him a work permit. One of his arguments was that the minister's refusal was a denial of his right to work under Article 6(2) of the ICESCR.

> 53 [...] [S]ince Kenya is a State that is a party to the [ICESCR], the Court must rise to the occasion in addressing, recognizing and giving remedies under the Covenant. To give effect to the human rights provided for under the International Covenant on Economic, Social and Cultural Rights, 1966, the Court should interpret the Constitution generously to reflect a dynamic and progressive society. [...]
>
> 65 In this case, I think it is apt to restate the State obligation as regards economic, social and cultural Rights. The treatment which States owe to non-nationals (and nationals) under (ICESCR) have been conceptualized as covering three levels of state obligations:
>
> - the duty to respect
> - the duty to protect
> - the duty to fulfill
>
> 66 The obligation to respect requires the State to abstain from interfering with the freedom of the individual. The obligation to protect requires the State to prevent other individuals from interfering with the rights of the individual. The obligation to fulfill requires the State to take necessary measures to ensure satisfaction of the needs of the individual that cannot be secured by the personal efforts of that individual alone. The latter obligation is central to economic, social and cultural rights and is the basis of the State's duty to progressively realize the rights of the ICESCR.
>
> 67 [...] Work might not exist for everyone but shall progressively become a State obligation to provide directly or by creating an enabling environment. No doubt, the State party cannot frustrate a non-national or a national who has created work for himself and others as in this case, because she would be in breach of (ICESCR) and as expounded herein also in breach of the Constitution. In situations such as set out in the facts where the applicant has created employment the State obligation is both to respect and protect the right to work.
>
> 71 [...] [I]n so far as the Covenant Rights are not inconsistent with the Constitution the Court has a duty to recognise them and apply them where appropriate, as Kenya as a member State has specific obligations under the Covenant which obligations, in turn, demand both judicial interpretation, and in some cases judicial remedies. It follows therefore the Covenant's Rights cannot be said to be outside the Court's role or mandate and in my view they are justiciable. [...]
>
> 73 Thus, despite the fact that many states especially the developing states face many economic and social problems, the rights expressed in the Covenant have been and remain a legal tool, aimed at achieving a steady improvement in the living conditions of the people in each state regardless of the means and resources available. A State's ability to direct its policy to achieving even the barest minimum in satisfying the covenant rights is necessary. [...] The ICESCR rights constitute in my view foundational values under s 1 and s 1A of the Constitution quite apart from constituting international State obligations for Kenya. [...] Granted that in practice most

> (ICESCR) rights demand both administrative action and remedies, this does not oust the Court's role.
>
> 74 The reality on the ground is that, the Covenant's rights entail both a legal duty of immediate enforcement to achieve the basic minimum (subject to resource availability) and an allowance for progressive realization of the rights which cannot be immediately enforced due to resource constraints for example in developing countries.
>
> 77 It is therefore evident that the Covenant Rights apply to both national and non-nationals pursuant to [Article 2 of the ICESCR]. Thus under [that provision] Kenya would be perfectly entitled to regulate the issue of work permits by law and she has a margin of appreciation, that has to take into account the needs of her nationals and also take into account the national interest including security concerns. A non national such as the applicant cannot properly argue that the right is absolute because it is subject to the margin of appreciation accorded to each State and also subject to the national interest including security concerns. The need to comply with the requirements of the Immigration laws and regulations is embraced by the Article.
>
> 78 Finally on justiciability of the Covenants Rights it is pertinent to observe that whereas in many cases administrative remedies are contemplated as the effective remedies, where a (ICESCR) Covenant right cannot be made fully effective without some role of the judiciary, judicial remedies would still be necessary and the courts must be involved.
>
> 79 Turning to the facts of the case before me I find that it would not be right for Kenya to discriminate against a non national where he has created legitimate employment for himself and his family but where there are national security concerns—the Respondent would be entitled to decline issue a work permit or to renew or extend the same. Such a rejection would in my view not constitute a violation of the Covenant's right to work or any constitutional foundational value and in particular the right to work and the right to family life.

Economic, social and cultural rights, including the right to work, were not enshrined in the Bill of Rights of the Kenyan constitution. The court ruled, however, that they could be enforceable under the constitution to give effect to Kenya's obligations under the ICESCR. This was remarkable since, as noted by the ILDC reporter, Kenya followed the dualist model.[28] The court made an extensive analysis of the nature and extent of state obligations under the covenant, also towards non-nationals. It eventually dismissed the case by relying on a classified document that considered the applicant as a threat to national security.

Cuzco Bar Association and ors v Congress of the Republic, Original Petition, Case No 050-2004-A1/TC, 004-2005-P1/TC, 007-2005-P1/TC, 009-2005-P1/TC, ILDC 679 (PE 2005), 3rd June 2005, Peru; Constitutional Court

The petitioners claimed that the Pension Reform Laws introduced by Peru in 2004 deprived them of rights acquired under previous laws and violated the right to pension, the right to social security, and other fundamental rights protected by the constitution and international treaties. This was indeed a retrogressive measure and the principle of progressive realization was at issue. The state responded that by introducing pension cuts to a minority of privileged pensioners the new laws aimed to benefit the majority of pensioners and thus better accord with the principle of social equality.

> 49. [...] There is no doubt it will take some time for economic, social and cultural rights to be realized in full. In its General Comment no. 3, the United Nations

28 K O Otieno, Analysis, *Kenya v Minister for Home Affairs and ors*, ILDC 1094 (KE 2007) A1–A2.

> Committee on Economic, Social and Cultural Rights stipulates that this does not constitute denial of the fact that said principle "[…] must be interpreted in light of the overall objective […] which is to establish clear obligations for States parties in respect of the full realization of the rights in question. It thus imposes an obligation to move as expeditiously and effectively as possible towards that goal. Moreover, any deliberately retrogressive measures in that regard would require the most careful consideration and would need to be fully justified by reference to the totality of the rights provided for in the Covenant and in the context of the full use of the maximum available resources."
>
> The progressivity principle implies that among the various options open to the legislator to regulate the exercise of said rights, "[…] in principle, political powers have banned the choice of suppositions of unreasonable regulations and selecting suppositions of regulations that amount to a reversal in the enjoyment of current economic, social and cultural rights."
>
> While this international provision does not constitute a binding mandate for the State given its soft law status, it does lead to the conclusion (reasonable in light of the principle of the legal parallelism of forms) that the progressivity principle is not absolute.
>
> On the other hand, it should be remembered that it is a purely objective principle and not subjective; as a result, the reform being questioned, which affects a group of pensioners not representative in quantitative terms in relation to social security, is not unconstitutional per se. If provision has been made for the objective and proportional reduction in the pensions of the minority along the lines of equity with the right to a pension in accordance with the principle of human dignity for the majority, the progressivity principle will not be affected.
>
> As a result, there is no infringement of this principle when an attempt is made to obtain justice and equality between pensioners under the protection of a democratic concept of common justice. A minority of pensioners cannot benefit at the expense of the majority of pensioners.
>
> 88. […] Nevertheless, the fact that realization over time, or in other words progressively, "is foreseen under the Covenant should not be misinterpreted as depriving the obligation of all meaningful content. On the one hand, a flexibility device is necessary, reflecting the realities of the real world and the difficulties faced by any country in ensuring full realization of economic, social and cultural rights. On the other hand, the phrase must be interpreted in light of the overall objective (indeed the raison d'être) of the Covenant, which is to establish clear obligations for States parties in respect of the full realization of the rights in question", since minimum obligations are not eliminated "as a result of limitations on resources, obligations to monitor the extent of the realization, or more especially of the non-realization, of economic, social and cultural rights, and to devise strategies and programmes for their promotion."

This decision articulated and made a convincing application of the principle of 'progressive realization' (or progressivity), which is central to the implementation of the rights recognized in the ICESCR. The pension cuts to privileged pensioners were obviously a retrogressive measure but one that aimed at bringing justice by equalizing a discriminatory pension system.[29] The court referred to 'objective and proportional reduction […] along the lines of equity', thus giving the contours of a permissible disregard of progressivity. Besides, as noted by the court with reference to the relevant General Comment 3 CESCR, the principle of progressive realization was not absolute.

---

29 E Salmón Gárate, Analysis, *Cuzco Bar Association and ors v Congress of the Republic*, ILDC 679 (PE 2005) A2–A3.

III. Economic and Social Rights in the Case Law of Domestic Courts

1. Right to education

Sánchez v Ceballos, Application for constitutional review, Decision no C-376-10, ILDC 2124 (CO 2010), 19th May 2010, Colombia; Constitutional Court

This case was about free primary education in Colombia. The plaintiffs filed a constitutional claim arguing that Colombia's national education law was not in conformity with international human rights law by allowing for the option to charge tuition fees on primary education.

H5 According to the international law of human rights, the content and scope of Colombia's international obligations to guarantee the right to education varied depending on the level of education concerned. This was derived from the international provisions that cited differentiated treatment for primary, secondary, and higher education, depending on economic accessibility to education. According to binding international standards, Colombia had an obligation to ensure the right of access to primary education for all children, and also to ensure that it was free of charge. (paragraph 4)

H7 The content of the obligation of the right to education had been corroborated by the CESCR, particularly through General Comment No 11 and General Comment No 13, and reports of the former Special Rapporteur of the United Nations Right to Education. Those documents concluded unequivocally that while primary education should be free for everyone, state parties had the duty to implement free secondary and higher education gradually. (paragraph 4)

H8 Through interpreting Articles 44 and 67 of the Constitution harmoniously with the relevant human rights treaties signed by Colombia, the Constitutional Court had held that education was a fundamental right of all persons under 18. (paragraph 5.2)

H9 The Constitutional Court had reiterated the principle of free education and had indicated that the charging of tuition fees by educational institutions could stand as a barrier to both access and continuity for children in the education system. It had recognized that international instruments pointed out the duty of progressive introduction of free education for secondary and higher education, and while it had not made explicit reference to these instruments, it had protected free education at the primary level. (paragraph 6)

H10 According to the hermeneutic rule contained in Article 93 of the Constitution, the interpretation of the right to education […] had to be carried out 'in accordance with international human rights treaties ratified by Colombia'. […] That interpretive rule was particularly relevant when the normative content of a superior rule was ambiguous, or apparently contradicted the principles or relevant provisions of those treaties. (paragraph 8.2.1)

H11 Free basic primary education was integral to the content of the human rights treaties ratified by Colombia […] […] That was a minimum, enforceable, and immediate obligation upon states, while the progressive mechanism was intended for ensuring access to secondary and higher levels of education. (paragraph 8.2.2)

H12 […] The recovery of tuition fees was incompatible with the principle of universal free education at the primary level, which was a clear and immediate obligation for the state; those charges might be compatible with Colombia's obligation to progressively implement free secondary and higher education, as long as it made reference to the capacity of individuals or families to pay in a reasonable manner. (paragraph 8.2.4)

The Constitutional Court of Colombia made an exemplary use and application of international human rights law in this case, including the pertinent General Comments issued by the CESCR, to interpret the relevant provisions of the Colombian constitution, and rightly concluded that, unlike secondary and higher education, free primary education was an unequivocal and immediately enforceable obligation of the state. Identical findings were made in another judgment of the Constitutional Court of Colombia issued on the same day.[30]

Western Cape Forum for Intellectual Disability v Government of South Africa and Government of the Province of the Western Cape (joining), Final judgment, Case no 18678/2007, ILDC 1847 (ZA 2010), 11th November 2010, South Africa; Western Cape; Cape Town; Western Cape High Court [WC-HC]

The applicant Forum represented over 150 non-governmental organizations (NGOs) providing care for children with severe and profound intellectual disabilities. In South Africa's Western Cape, such children were not admitted to any state schools and the only education available to them was at special care centres run by such NGOs. Children who could not have access to them received no education at all. The NGOs received some financial support from the state, which was, however, less than the support given for the education of children who attended mainstream schools. The applicant complained that this policy infringed the rights of those children to education, equality, and human dignity.

> [20] The need to provide fully for mentally or physically disabled children is recognised world-wide. The United Nations Convention on the Rights of the Child states in article 23
>
> > "a mentally or physically disabled child should enjoy a full and decent life, in conditions which ensure dignity, promote self-reliance and facilitate the child's active participation in the community."
> >
> > Article 28 confirms the right to education. [. . .]
>
> [21] The African Charter on the Rights and Welfare of the Child provides in Article 11(1) and (2)(a) that
>
> > "[e]very child shall have the right to an education" and "[t]he education of the child shall be directed to . . . the promotion and development of the child's personality, talents and mental and physical abilities to their fullest potential . . ." [. . .]
>
> [23] Closer to home is the Convention on the Rights of Persons with Disabilities and its optional protocol which were ratified by South Africa on 30 November 2007. [. . .]
> Article 24 of the Convention provides
>
> "1. States Parties recognize the right of persons with disabilities to education. [. . .]
> 2. In realizing this right, States Parties shall ensure that:
>   (a) Persons with disabilities are not excluded from the general education system on the basis of disability, and that children with disabilities are not excluded from free and compulsory primary education, or from secondary education, on the basis of disability;
>   (b) Persons with disabilities can access an inclusive, quality and free primary education and secondary education on an equal basis with others in the communities in which they live;
>
> [. . .]

30 *Castillo and Hoyos, Ministry of National Education (intervening) and ors (intervening) v General Attorney of Colombia*, Individual constitutional complaint, Decision Number C-376/10, ILDC 1839 (CO 2010), 19 May 2010, Constitutional Court.

> 4. In order to help ensure the realization of this right, States Parties shall take appropriate measures to employ teachers, including teachers with disabilities, who are qualified in sign language and/or Braille, and to train professionals and staff who work at all levels of education. Such training shall incorporate disability awareness and the use of appropriate augmentative and alternative modes, means and formats of communication, educational techniques and materials to support persons with disabilities."
>
> [24] Inasmuch as the state currently cooperates with and relies on organisations such as the applicant to provide education for mentally disabled children, it must be borne in mind that this does not relieve the state from its constitutional obligation. [. . .]
>
> [25] A case in point is that of *O'Donoghue* which was heard in the Irish High Court where the court held that the failure of a government to provide 'primary education' in the context of the Irish Constitution for Intellectually Disabled Children was in breach of the constitution. [. . .]
>
> [26] The defence that the respondents are unable to afford further expenditure on education and that the government's failure to do so is justifiable for its rational connection to a legitimate government purpose is in my view misplaced. [. . .] In any event, the reliance on a rational connection to a legitimate government purpose does not address the issue as to why the affected children have been singled out for manifestly less favourable treatment than others and why any shortage in funds is not imposed on all children, including the affected ones. [. . .] I am accordingly of the view that the appellant has established that the rights of the affected children to receive a basic education are being infringed.

This case exemplified how the international legal framework and comparative sources on the rights of children with disabilities were successfully invoked with a view to informing the interpretation of the constitution and rectifying a structural problem facing children with disabilities in South Africa. Significantly, the order issued by the court included a structural interdict, which is a far-reaching form of relief requiring the state to devise and implement a plan of action overseen by the court to remedy the violation. The High Court has generally been more prone to using this remedy in socio-economic rights cases than the Constitutional Court.[31] The government, however, did not eventually appeal the court's decision and the verdict thus became final.

Another interesting case on the right of children with disabilities to education is *Peña Delgado (on behalf of Viña Peña) v Coomeva EPS* of the Constitutional Court of Colombia.[32] Based on the UN Disability Convention and General Comment 5 of the CESCR, the court affirmed that 'disability was no longer considered as a disease but as a reality that has always existed' and observed that 'this change in perspective had led to a transformation of language to refer to these facts. This clarification of language to consider the circumstances of disability not only helped to overcome other problems transcending disability but also to bring about a change in the perspective of society'.[33] With respect to education, the court clarified that:

> H2 Persons with disabilities had the right to access 'inclusive' education, which meant the ability to enjoy education in regular classrooms. This possibility should have been considered the general rule, and special education should have been regarded as the last option, to be considered an exception. As to the importance of an inclusive education policy, one could have observed the development of domestic legislation, human rights treaties concerning persons with disabilities, and their impact on constitutional jurisprudence, as well as some examples of the development of that policy in other countries. (paragraph 5.6.2.2)

31 C Mbazira, *Litigating Socio-economic Rights in South Africa* (Pretoria University Law Press 2009) 165–66.

32 *Peña Delgado (on behalf of Viña Peña) v Coomeva EPS*, Constitutional petition, No 974/2010, ILDC 1840 (CO 2010), 30 November 2010, Constitutional Court.

33 ibid, para 5.6.1.

2. Right to health

Flores and ors v Southern Peru Copper Corporation, Appeal Judgment, Docket No 02-9008, 414 F.3d 233 (2d Cir. 2003), ILDC 303 (US 2003), 29th August 2003, United States; Court of Appeals (2nd Circuit) [2d Cir]

The plaintiffs were residents of Ilo in Peru and brought personal injury claims in the United States (US) under the Alien Tort Statute, based on severe lung diseases and respiratory illnesses allegedly caused by the emissions from the defendant's industrial activities. They contended that the pollution caused by the defendant corporation constituted an offence under customary law because it violated their right to life and their right to health.

> 54. As an initial matter, we hold that the asserted "right to life" and "right to health" are insufficiently definite to constitute rules of customary international law. [...]
>
> 55. Far from being "clear and unambiguous," the statements relied on by plaintiffs to define the rights to life and health are vague and amorphous. For example, the statements that plaintiffs rely on to define the rights to life and health include the following:
>
>> Everyone has the right to a standard of living adequate for the health and well-being of himself and of his family [...]. Universal Declaration of Human Rights, Art. 25 [...].
>>
>> The States Parties to the present Covenant recognize the right of everyone to the enjoyment of the highest attainable standard of physical and mental health. International Covenant on Economic, Social and Cultural Rights, Art. 12 [...].
>>
>> Human beings are ... entitled to a healthy and productive life in harmony with nature. Rio Declaration on Environment and Development ("Rio Declaration"), United Nations Conference on Environment and Development, Rio de Janeiro, Brazil, June 13, 1992, Principle 1 [...].
>
> 56. These principles are boundless and indeterminate. They express virtuous goals understandably expressed at a level of abstraction needed to secure the adherence of States that disagree on many of the particulars regarding how actually to achieve them. [...] Similarly, the exhortation that all people are entitled to the "highest attainable standard of physical and mental health," [Art. 12 ICESCR] proclaims only nebulous notions that are infinitely malleable.
>
> 57. In support of plaintiffs' argument that the statements and instruments discussed above are part of customary international law, plaintiffs attempt to underscore the universality of the principles asserted by pointing out that they "contain *no limitations as to how or by whom these rights may be violated.*" [...] (emphasis added). However, this assertion proves too much; because of the conceded absence of any "limitations" on these "rights," they do not meet the requirement of our law that rules of customary international law be clear, definite, and unambiguous.
>
> 58. For the foregoing reasons, plaintiffs have failed to establish the existence of a customary international law "right to life" or "right to health."

The court's conclusion that there is no right to health under international customary law was in line with the case law of US courts on the right to health as well as with the overall US approach to social rights.[34] It was followed some years later in *Calcaño Pallano and ors v AES Corporation*

34 C Lee, Analysis, *Flores and ors v Southern Peru Copper Corporation*, ILDC 303 (US 2003) A3. See also *Doe and ors, United States (intervening) and ors (intervening) v State of Texas and ors*, Merits, 501 F Supp 544 (SD Tex 1980), ILDC 1977 (US 1980), 21 July 1980, United States; Texas; District Court for the Southern District of Texas [SD Tex], para 194, where the court held that 'the right to education, while it represents an important international goal, has not acquired the status of customary international law'. The court's conclusion was based on the interstate nature of international law.

and ors.[35] This conclusion is rather controversial today since the prevailing view in international law seems to be that the right to health, and social rights more generally, being part of the international bill of rights, are considered as customary law.[36]

RJSA, widow of R (on behalf of GRS in the capacity of official guardian) v Peruvian Superior Court, Appeal to the Constitutional Court, No 3081-2007-PA/TC, ILDC 969 (PE 2007), 9th November 2007, Peru; Constitutional Court

The petitioner brought a suit on behalf of her daughter who suffered from paranoid schizophrenia, claiming that her discharge from a public rehabilitation centre was in breach of her daughter's right to health in view of inadequate available care outside the centre.

H3 In order to understand the scope of the right to health, it was necessary to interpret the Constitution in light of the pertinent international instruments to which Peru was party. The means Peru employed to protect such rights had to comply with its obligations under the ICESCR and the Inter-American Convention on the Elimination of All Forms of Discrimination Against Persons with Disabilities […], among others. (paragraphs 21-35, 43)

H4 Compliance with international obligations in the area of economic, social and cultural rights should not be measured by the amount of the national budget ascribed to those obligations, but by the real attitude of the government so that individuals enjoyed the progressive development of their rights. (paragraph 43)

H5 The right to health was holistic, encompassing both mental and physical well-being. (paragraphs 17-18)

H6 The duty on the part of the state to ensure the highest level of physical and mental health did not require a guarantee of good health, but rather the highest level of well-being possible given an individual's particular circumstance, according to Article 10 of the Additional Protocol to the American Convention on Human Rights in the Area of Economic, Social and Cultural Rights […]. (paragraph 29)

H7 The constitutional right to health, according to what had been established in international human rights law, encompassed not only a negative but also a positive obligation on behalf of the state: a concept necessary for the right to actually be fulfilled, especially where the beneficiaries of those rights were subjects from vulnerable groups. (paragraphs 19-20)

H8 Given the intimate connection between the right to life and the right to health, recognized under both domestic and international law, a lack of economic resources could not justify denying a person health care in such a way that his or her right to life became threatened. (paragraph 23)

H9 The right to mental health in international human rights law was focused on achieving the rehabilitation, independence, and social inclusion of the person suffering the disability. (paragraph 34)

H10 The lack of budget and its centralized nature (carried out mostly in Lima) were examples of the violation of Peru's international commitments related to the protection of the human right to health. (paragraph 43)

---

35 Consolidated trial judgment, CA No N10C-04-054, ILDC 1830 (US 2011), 15th July 2011, Superior Court [Del Super], para 66.

36 cf O de Schutter, *International Human Rights Law* (2nd edn, CUP 2014) 63. See also A Gross, 'The Right to Health in an Era of Privatisation and Globalisation: National and International Perspectives' in D Barak-Erez and A Gross (eds), *Exploring Social Rights: Between Theory and Practice* (Hart Publishing 2011) 289, 295.

H11 A patient's discharge must always take place after considering the family's situation and evaluating whether those conditions would contribute to the full recovery of the patient, once out of the hospital. The discharge in this case, therefore, violated GRS's fundamental right to health, as there had been a failure to consider that she would not receive the adequate long-term medical care necessary due to her caregiver's physical and socio-economic limitations. (paragraphs 55, 64-65)

H12 The discharge was void and EsSalud was ordered to provide GRS with indefinite hospitalization and medical treatment. (paragraph 65)

In view of the constitutional duty to interpret constitutional rights and freedoms in compliance with international human rights law, the Constitutional Court of Peru engaged in a lengthy discussion of the pertinent aspects of international law applicable to Peru on the right to (physical and mental) health. This included numerous non-binding instruments. Indeed, this decision stands out in terms of the large number (25) of international instruments cited. As noted by the ILDC reporter, the discussion of international law was used rather to criticize the legislature for failing to ensure compliance with Peru's international obligations than as justification for the outcome of the case at hand, which was based on pragmatic considerations rather than the mechanical application of international law.[37]

Naz Foundation and Voices against 377 (joining) v Government of National Capital Territory of Delhi, Joint Action Council, Kannur (intervening) and BP Singhal (intervening) and Union of India (joining), Appeal decision, WP(C) No 7455/2001, ILDC 1849 (IN 2009), 2nd July 2009, India; National Capital Territory; New Delhi

The petitioner, an Indian NGO committed to HIV/AIDS intervention and prevention, filed a public interest litigation challenging the constitutionality of section 377 of the Indian Penal Code (IPC), which criminalized any homosexual sexual act. One of the arguments was that section 377 infringed the right to health, as embodied in Article 21 of the constitution of India which protected the right to life, and was a serious impediment to successful public health interventions and significantly impaired HIV/AIDS prevention efforts and access to treatment.

SECTION 377 IPC AS AN IMPEDIMENT TO PUBLIC HEALTH

61. Article 12 of the International Covenant on Economic, Social and Cultural Rights makes it obligatory on the "State to fulfill everyone's right to the highest attainable standard of health." The Supreme Court of India interpreting Article 21 of the Indian Constitution in the light of Article 12 of the Covenant held that the right to health inhered in the fundamental right to life under Article 21. [. . .]

63. General Comment No.14 (2000) [E/C.12/2000/4; 11 August 2000] on Article 12 of the International Covenant on Economic, Social and Cultural Rights states that right to health is not to be understood as a right to be healthy. The right to health contains both freedoms and entitlements. The freedoms include the right to control one's health and body, including sexual reproductive freedom, and the right to be free from interference, such as the right to be free from torture, non-consensual medical treatment and experimentation. By contrast, the entitlements include the right to a system of health, protection which provides equality of opportunity for people to enjoy the highest attainable level of health. It further states:

37 E Salmón Gárate, Analysis, *RJSA, widow of R (on behalf of GRS in the capacity of official guardian) v Peruvian Superior Court*, ILDC 969 (PE 2007) A4.

> "Non-discrimination and equal treatment. By virtue of article 2.2 and article 3, the Covenant proscribes any discrimination in access to health care and underlying determinants of health, as well as to means and entitlements for their procurement, on the grounds of race, colour, sex, language, religion, political or other opinion, national or social origin, property, birth, physical or mental disability, health status (including HIV/AIDS), sexual orientation and civil, political, social or other status, which has the intention or effect of nullifying or impairing the equal enjoyment or exercise of the right to health. The Committee stresses that many measures, such as most strategies and programmes designed to eliminate health-related discrimination, can be pursued with minimum resource implications through the adoption, modification or abrogation of legislation or the dissemination of information…" [para 18]
> 64. The 2001 UN General Assembly Special Session (UNGASS) Declaration of Commitment on HIV/AIDS, held on 25-27 June, 2001, adopted by all UN Member States emphasized the importance of "addressing the needs of those at the greatest risk of, and most vulnerable to, new infection as indicated by such factors as ... sexual practices." In 2005, 22 governments from different regions along with representatives of non-governmental organisations and people living with HIV as members of the UNAIDS governing board, called for the development of programmes targeted at key affected groups and populations, including men who have sex with men, describing this as "one of the essential policy actions for HIV prevention". [UNAIDS (2005) Intensifying HIV Prevention, Geneva, Joint United Nations Programme on HIV/AIDS]. Since then, country and regional consultations have confirmed that the stigma, discrimination and criminalisation faced by men who have sex with men are major barriers to the movement for universal access to HIV prevention, treatment, care and support. [United Nations A/60/737 Assessment by UNAIDS to the General Assembly on Scaling up HIV Prevention, Treatment, Care and Support, March 24, 2006]. […]

The court made extensive reference to international and comparative legal and other sources in a 'uniquely powerful example of cosmopolitan constitutional borrowing',[38] as evidence for the connection between discrimination against homosexual men and the increased risk of HIV infection, to inform the interpretation of domestic (constitutional) law and held that section 377 IPC violated Articles 14 (equality before the law), 15 (prohibition of discrimination), and 21 (right to life) of the constitution.

In a disappointing setback, that verdict was overturned by the Supreme Court of India in *Suresh Kumar Koushal v NAZ Foundation*,[39] where the court stressed the value of judicial restraint in a constitutional democracy and passed the responsibility for decriminalizing homosexuality to the legislature.[40] In concluding that section 377 IPC did not violate any constitutional provisions, the court also commented on the extensive reliance of the High Court on foreign judgments: 'Though these judgments shed considerable light on various aspects of this right (concerning gay people) and are informative in relation to the plight of sexual minorities, we feel that they cannot be applied blindfolded for deciding the constitutionality of the law enacted by the Indian legislature'.[41] In February 2016, the Supreme Court decided to reopen the case and re-examine its 2013 judgment.

---

38 R Raman, Analysis, *Naz Foundation and Voices against 377 (joining) v Government of National Capital Territory of Delhi, Joint Action Council, Kannur (intervening) and BP Singhal (intervening) and Union of India (joining)*, ILDC 1849 (IN 2009) A4.

39 Civil Appeal No 10972 of 2013, 11 December 2013.

40 Y Naik, *Homosexuality in the Jurisprudence of the Supreme Court of India* (Springer 2017) 91.

41 *Suresh Kumar Koushal v NAZ Foundation* (n 39) para 52.

Laxmi Mandal v Deen Dayal Harinagar Hospital & Ors, WP(C) Nos 8853 of 2008, High Court of Delhi, 4 June 2010 (not in ILDC)

The sad facts and the issues raised in this case concerned the systemic failure of the maternal healthcare scheme of India, which has one of the highest rates of maternal mortality in the world. The petition was brought on behalf of two women living below the poverty line: one was living under a tree and delivered a child there in full public view, and the other—from a scheduled or 'untouchable' caste—died after repeatedly being denied adequate maternal healthcare, although she was entitled to free hospital treatment.

> 19. [T]hese petitions focus on two inalienable survival rights that form part of the right to life. One is the right to health, which would include the right to access government (public) health facilities and receive a minimum standard of treatment and care. In particular this would include the enforcement of the reproductive rights of the mother and the right to nutrition and medical care of the newly born child and continuously thereafter till the age of about six years. The other facet is the right to food which is seen as integral to the right to life and right to health.
>
> 20. The right to health forming an inalienable component of the right to life under Article 21 of the Constitution has been settled in two important decisions of the Supreme Court: *Pt. Parmanand Katara v. Union of India* (1989) 4 SCC 286 and *Paschim Banga Khet Majoor Samiti v. State of West Bengal* (1996) 4 SCC 37. The orders in the *PUCL Case* are a continuation of the efforts of the Supreme Court at protecting and enforcing the right to health of the mother and the child and underscoring the interrelatedness of those rights with the right to food. This is consistent with the international human rights law which is briefly discussed hereafter.
>
> 21. Article 25 of the Universal Declaration of Human Rights, which is considered as having the force of customary international law, declares: [. . .]
>
> 22. The International Covenant on Economic, Social and Cultural Rights (ICESCR), which has been ratified by India, spells out in greater detail the various facets of the broad right to health. Articles 10 and 12 of the ICESCR which are relevant in this context, read as under: [. . .]
>
> 23. The Committee on Economic Social and Cultural Rights has in its General Comment No. 14 of 2000 on the right to health under the ICESCR explained the scope of the rights as under:
>
>> '[. . .] 11. The Committee interprets the right to health, as defined in article 12.1, as an inclusive right extending not only to timely and appropriate health care but also to the underlying determinants of health, such as access to safe and potable water and adequate sanitation, an adequate supply of safe food, nutrition and housing, healthy occupational and environmental conditions, and access to health-related education and information, including on sexual and reproductive health. A further important aspect is the participation of the population in all health-related decision-making at the community, national and international levels. . . .
>>
>> 14. "The provision for the reduction of the stillbirth rate and of infant mortality and for the healthy development of the child" (art. 12.2 (a)) may be understood as requiring measures to improve child and maternal health, sexual and reproductive health services, including access to family planning, pre- and post-natal care, emergency obstetric services and access to information, as well as to resources necessary to act on that information.'

> 24. The reproductive rights of women have been accorded recognition, and the obligations of States have been spelt out in the Convention on the Elimination of all Forms of Discrimination Against Women (CEDAW) which is another international convention ratified by India. The relevant provisions of the CEDAW in this context are: Article 12 […] Article 14 […]
>
> 25. The Child Rights Convention (CRC) which has also been ratified by India delineates the rights of the newly born and the young child thus: Article 24 […] Article 27 […]
>
> 26. International human rights norms as contained in the Conventions which have been ratified by India are binding on India to the extent they are not inconsistent with the domestic law norms. The Protection of Human Rights Act, 1993 (PHRA) recognises that the above Conventions are now part of the Indian human rights law. […]
> 27. The orders in the *PUCL Case* implicitly recognize and enforce the fundamental right to life under Article 21 of the Constitution of the child and the mother. This includes the right to health, reproductive health and the right to food. In effect, the Supreme Court has spelt out what the "minimum core" of the right to health and food is, and also spelt out, consistent with international human rights law, the "obligations of conduct" and the "obligations of result" of the Union of India, the States and the UTs. While recognizing the indivisibility of civil rights and social and economic rights, the Supreme Court has made them enforceable in courts of law by using the device of a "continuing mandamus." On their part, the High Courts in this country would be obligated to carry forth the mandate of the orders of the Supreme Court to ensure the implementation of those orders within the States and UTs. This then forms the background to this Court's intervention in these petitions.

The court relied largely on international law to identify and criticize the shortcomings of the Indian maternal healthcare scheme and issued general directions towards its improvement and overhaul. Interestingly, in this respect, it held that Article 25 of the UDHR was customary law. It also ordered the award of compensation and other forms of reparation to the surviving mother and the families of both victims. However, despite the usage of relevant international rules by Indian courts with a view to effectuating social change in that context, this case also shows the gap that so often exists between the law that protects women's economic and social rights and its actual (non-)implementation, especially in cases compounded by discrimination and poverty.

3. Right to social security

ISSSTESON case, Final award on jurisdiction, merits and damages, ILDC 1466 (MX 2009), 18th March 2009, Mexico; Supreme Court of Justice of the Nation

This case concerned a Mexican public employee who was required to prove that he was in good health in order to be affiliated as a member of the social security system. He claimed that this requirement (under Article 6 of the Medical Services By-Laws of the 'ISSSTESON', that is, the office of the Security and Social Services of the Mexican state of Sonora's Employees Institute) was unconstitutional and violated his rights to health and social security. His *amparo* lawsuit—a special procedure for alleged human rights violations—was denied and he filed a petition to the Supreme Court.

> H1 The right to social security could be ascribed to Mexico's legal system from Articles 22 and 25 of the UDHR, Article XVI of the American Declaration, Article 9 of the ICESCR, and Article 9 of the Protocol of San Salvador. The statement by the Committee on Economic, Social and Cultural Rights, General Comment No 19, dedicated to the right to social security, could not be ignored.

H2 The legal sources of international origin that detailed the substance of the fundamental right to health were Article 25 of the UDHR, Article XI of the American Declaration, Article 12 of the ICESCR, Article 10 of the Protocol of San Salvador, and General Comment No 14.

H3 The ILO Convention Concerning Minimum Standards of Social Security ('ILO Convention 102') was also pertinent.

H4 Article 123(B) of the [Mexican Constitution] established the fundamental principles of social rights, which sought the preservation of the working class based on conditions of minimal dignity, including access to medical services. In that order, the right to have access to medical services provided by the social security system arose from the sole condition of being a state employee, without needing to prove any further conditions.

H5 Thus, when Article 6 of the ISSSTESON's Medical Services By-Laws made the access to medical services provided by the social security system conditional on proving good health, it violated the right to social security envisaged in Article 123(B) of the Constitution, interpreted under Mexico's international human rights obligations.

H7 Article 6 of the ISSSTESON's Medical Services By-Laws also violated the right to health envisaged in Article 4 of the Constitution, interpreted under Mexico's international human rights obligations, when it established as a prerequisite the need to prove good health, because the right to health is a social right and it involves not only the right to be healthy, but the possibility to access, in equitable conditions, health services in any case and under any circumstances. It entailed a correlated obligation of the state to promote laws that guaranteed access to appropriate health services.

This was another successful vindication of social rights based on constitutional provisions as interpreted in light of Mexico's international obligations under the ICESCR and other international legal sources.

Cuzco Bar Association and ors v Congress of the Republic, Original Petition, Case No 050-2004-A1/TC, 004-2005-P1/TC, 007-2005-P1/TC, 009-2005-P1/TC, ILDC 679 (PE 2005), 3rd June 2005, Peru; Constitutional Court

70. [...] "[...] social security is considered not only an essential component of integrated systems for social protection, but a fundamental human right. This is recognised in various international human rights instruments formally ratified by Peru."

76. [...] [The right to a pension] is a material realisation of the right to life, in view of the principle of indivisibility of fundamental rights and constitutional *objectives* designed to protect human dignity [...].

In this way, our Constitution incorporates the promotion of a dignified quality of life among its citizens as a genuine legal obligation that at the same time contains a well-defined option in favour of a qualitative model of the State in which people are its ontological assumption, a model that expressly rejects a form of mere quantitative social and economic development.

In this way, the fundamental right to a pension allows pensioners to live in dignified conditions. [...]

98. [...] In the *Case of Five Pensioners vs. Peru*, Judgment of 28 February 2003 [...] "(...) the Inter-American Court of Human Rights indicated that the right to a pension constitutes an acquired right inasmuch as this is expressly recognised in the Peruvian Constitution and, to the extent that it had been incorporated in the pensioners' total assets, was thus subject to protection through the right to property under

article 21 of the Covenant. The opinion of the Inter-American Court of Human Rights is shared, and expressly adopted, by the Peruvian constitutional court, which on numerous occasions has identified the right to a pension with the right to property." [...]

99. [...] [T]he essential content of the fundamental right to a pension consists of the right to receive a pension, the right not to be arbitrarily deprived of the said pension and the right to a minimum living pension.

[...] [T]here is no suggestion that the prohibition on the balancing of pensions with remuneration under the reform law will affect the essential content of the fundamental right to a pension, since balancing is not part of that content but rather non-essential content; [...]

103. "... [...] The balancing of pensions with the remuneration of active employees is not part of any international covenant or of the doctrinarian principles governing social security such that it can be treated as a fundamental right or central nucleus of the right.

105. [...] The Constitution must at least require the State to provide a minimum subsistence income, protected as essential content, so that individuals can enjoy a dignified quality of life thereby trying to ensure material equality. For this purpose, protection of the right to a dignified quality of life should be an obligation incumbent on the State that must be met at all stages of the lives of its citizens.

This decision made an extensive analysis of the meaning and scope of the right to social security as protected by the constitution of Peru and informed by the jurisprudence of the Inter-American Court of Human Rights and the General Comments of the CESCR. The Constitutional Court of Peru did share the view of the IACtHR on identifying the right to a pension with the right to property but, significantly, it determined through its own analysis that a pension was distinct from property based on several differing characteristics.[42] The court also held that the right to social security under the ICESCR did not include balancing of pensions with the remuneration of active employees. This was crucial in reaching the conclusion that the pension reform in Peru was not unconstitutional.

State Social Security Institute v Organization of the Disabled in Iceland, Appeal judgment, Case no 125/2000 (Supreme Court), H 2000 4480, ILDC 68 (IS 2000), 19th December 2000, Iceland; Supreme Court

The Organization of the Disabled in Iceland claimed that the curtailment of social security payments to disabled persons, based on the income of their spouse, violated the constitutionally protected right to minimum social benefits, which was rooted in the relevant international obligations of Iceland and should be construed accordingly.

17 [...] According to Paragraph 1 of Article 76 of the Constitution [...] the law shall guarantee for everyone the necessary assistance in case of sickness, invalidity, infirmity by reason of old age, unemployment and similar circumstances. The commentary [...] made particular note that it was assumed that more detailed rules on social assistance of this nature would be established by law and that the provision set the condition that rules ensuring such assistance must exist. In this respect, particular attention was brought to Articles 12 and 13 of the European Social Charter ratified by Iceland on 15 January 1976, [...] and Articles 11 and 12 of the [ICESCR], ratified by Iceland on 22 August 1979 [...]. Parties to the first convention undertake to *i.a.* establish or maintain social securities or maintain them at a satisfactory level at least equal to that required for the ratification of the ILO

42 E Salmón Gárate, Analysis, *Cuzco Bar Association and ors v Congress of the Republic*, ILDC 679 (PE 2005) A8.

Convention No. 102 Concerning Minimum Standards of Social Security. Article 67 of this Convention establishes the rules that this minimum must fulfil and states that no curtailments may be made except in the case of substantial additional amounts. The second convention involves *i.a.* that the parties to the Covenant recognise the right of everyone to an adequate standard of living for himself/herself and his/her family.

25. [. . .] [I]t is within the authority of the legislator to set the limits, on which the disability pension and income supplement shall be based, provided that they fulfil other provisions of the Constitution and can be construed in light of international legal obligations that the Icelandic government has undertaken. [. . .]

26 As stated earlier, it must be seen that Paragraph 1 of Article 76 of the Constitution involves basic rights that are based on individuals. Notwithstanding the scope of the general legislature to evaluate how these minimum rights should be determined, the courts cannot avoid taking a position on whether such evaluation was in accordance with the principles of the Constitution. In light of the arrangement of the rights of disability pensioners pursuant to the Social Security Act and the consequences that they can actually have on individuals, this arrangement cannot be seen to ensure them the minimum rights inherent in the above Constitutional provision, in the manner that they are able to enjoy the human rights that Article 65 of the Constitution provides them with, insofar as the provision can be understood in Icelandic legislation, cf. Article 26 of the ICCPR, ratified by Iceland on 22 August 1979 and Article 9 of the ICESCR. In accordance with the above, the claim of the counter-appellant for the recognition that the income supplements of married disability pensioners could not be curtailed from 1 January 1999 [. . .], is recognised.

This was another decision where the ICESCR and other relevant treaties influenced the outcome of the case by informing the interpretation of the corresponding constitutional rights. In doing so, the Supreme Court of Iceland exercised judicial review of the relevant legislation, even though it recognized that the legislature had the primary competence to evaluate how minimum rights should be determined.

Drēziņš and ors v Parliament of Latvia and Cabinet of Ministers (intervening), Request for constitutional review, Case no 2009-43-01, ILDC 2144 (LV 2009), Latvian Herald, no 201 (4187), 21st December 2009, Latvia

The applicants were Latvian pensioners who challenged the constitutionality of the 2009 Law on State Pension and State Allowance Disbursement, which was adopted as part of a deal with international creditors in order to reduce the budget deficit. The law provided for cuts of 10 per cent to the amount received by current pensioners and 70 per cent to the pensions of future pensioners. The petitioners claimed that the law breached, *inter alia*, the principle of legitimate expectations and the right to social security protected by the constitution of Latvia and Article 9 of the ICESCR. The Latvian parliament (*Saeima*) argued that the cuts were an urgent measure to improve the declining Latvian economy and were a condition of the international creditors for granting a loan to Latvia.

20. [. . .] When ascertaining the nature of the fundamental rights established by the Constitution, one should also take into account the international commitments that Latvia has undertaken in the area of human rights. The international regulations of human rights and the practice of their application at the level of constitutional rights serve as interpretative means for determining the nature and scope of the principles of judicial state and fundamental rights as far as they do not lead to the restriction of the fundamental rights provided by the Constitution [. . .].

Thus, Article 9 of the International Covenant on Economic, Social and Cultural Rights (hereinafter – the Covenant) prescribes that the States that are Parties to the Covenant recognise the right of everyone to social security, including social insurance. Admittedly, the European Convention for the Protection of Human Rights and Fundamental Freedoms (hereinafter – the Convention) does not contain provisions analogous to the content of Article 109 of the Constitution. Nevertheless, the European Court of Human Rights (hereinafter – ECtHR) adjudicates the matters pertaining to social security and social assistance in the light of property rights as they are interpreted in Protocol 1, Article 1 of the Convention […]. [T]he decrease of pension disbursement amount prescribed in the impugned legal provisions should also be considered in the context of principles derived from Article 1 of the Constitution and Protocol 1, Article 1 of the Convention, taking into account both the protection of property rights provided therein and the Latvian system of pension financing.

27.2. […] The main challenge of the pension system is to ensure its sustainability. The UN Committee on Economic, Social and Cultural Rights has also affirmed that social security scheme should be sustainable, especially with respect to pensions – to guarantee that both the current and future generations would be able to enact their rights to pension (*see […] General Comment No. 19. The right to social security, E/C.12/GC/19 4 February 2008, para. 11*). […] However, the economic situation in the State, or the need to reduce the budget deficit, in the absence of other legitimate ends, cannot serve as an overarching justification for the State to restrict the rights previously granted to persons.

28. […] The Limburg Principles – developed for the implementation of the Covenant in 1986 – stipulate that measures must be taken without delay and using all the necessary means in order to guarantee the respective rights at least at a minimum level, irrespective of the development level of a country. […] The laws that restrict the enactment of any social rights cannot be unjust or discriminatory (*see Limburg Principles on the Implementation of the International Covenant on Economic, Social and Cultural Rights, U.N. Commission on Human Rights, U.N. ESCOR, 43d Sess., U.N. Doc. E/CN.4/1987/17*). Even if a country has a substantial deficiency of financial resources, it is obliged to protect the weakest members of the society (*see […] General Comment No.3. The nature of States parties obligations, E/1991/23 14 December 1990, para. 12; […] General Comment No. 6. The economic, social and cultural rights of older persons, E/1996/22 8 December 1995, para. 17*).

29.2. […] The task of the Court is to determine whether the impugned provisions are reasonable and harmonised, whether the State possesses the resources needed for their implementation, whether the provisions are balanced, flexible and bring about short-term or long-term satisfaction of needs as well as whether these provisions are transparent and have been made public […].

30.1. […] The Constitutional Court has not received any information attesting that the international creditors stipulated the adoption of the impugned provisions as a prerequisite for granting the loan. The […] measures pertaining to the reduction of pension disbursements, are to be characterised as an action of the State with the aim to reduce the budget expenditures and, consequently, to be eligible for the international loan.

[…] The Constitutional Court maintained that the conceptual decision with respect to the receipt of the international loan and terms and conditions thereof is to be deemed as an important and significant matter of State and public life, and that, in compliance with the procedure established by the Constitution, it had

> to be decided by the legislator itself. [...] [T]hese decisions cannot replace the rights established by the Constitution [...]. Therefore, the international commitments assumed by the Cabinet of Ministers cannot by themselves serve as an argument for the restriction of the fundamental rights established by Article 109 of the Constitution.
>
> 30.2. In order to ascertain whether there were less restricting means at the disposal of the legislator, the Constitutional Court had to determine whether the legislator had considered possible alternatives to the impugned provisions.
>
> The ECtHR has indicated that public interests also in the context of decrease of pension or other comparable disbursements leave broad freedom of action to the legislator. The Court must respect this freedom of action – unless it is evident that the legislator's action has no reasonable justification (*see the ECtHR Judgment in the Case Moskal v. Poland, Application No. 10373/05, 15 September 2009, para. 61*).
>
> 30.2.2. The Constitutional Court concluded that neither the Cabinet of Ministers, nor the Saeima had carried out objective and well-weighed analysis neither regarding the consequences of the adoption of the impugned provisions, nor regarding other, less restrictive means for the attainment of the legitimate end. [...] Therefore, the impugned provisions do not comply with Article 109 of the Constitution.
>
> 31. The Constitutional Court pointed out that even if the State reduces the pension disbursement amounts for a period of time in the situation of rapid economic recession, there is still a definite body of fundamental rights that the State is not entitled to derogate from. In this context, it is essential to determine whether the rights of pension recipients to social security have been infringed according to substance (*see ECtHR Judgment in Case Kjartan Ásmundsson v. Iceland, Application no. 60669/00, passed on 30 March 2005, para. 39*). [...] States should secure, within limits, a standard of worthwhile human life and opportunity to take active part in the state, public, social and cultural life to all elderly people [...].
>
> 31.2. [...] The UN Committee on Economic, Social and Cultural Rights has described the duty of the State to guarantee the availability of social security at least at a minimum level. In the cases when state, considering the resources at its disposal, is incapable to ensure this minimum level to all the risk groups, it should specify the groups that need special protection, and social security should be provided for these groups (*see General Comment No. 19, para. 59*).

This was the first decision issued in the aftermath of the 2008 financial crisis challenging austerity measures, in a remarkable gradual change of attitude by highest courts in Europe towards engaging in judicial review of legislation interfering with socio-economic rights even in times of economic hardship, when the options available to the legislature and the executive were admittedly restricted, even more so, given the strong international pressure to adopt such measures. In its elaborate judgment, the Constitutional Court of Latvia ruled that the constitutional right to social security, interpreted in accordance with Latvia's international obligations under the ICESCR and the ECHR, should prevail. The court made extensive reference to General Comments of the CESCR, the case law of the European Court of Human Rights (ECtHR), and even the *Limburg* principles elaborated by a group of eminent scholars. The court insisted in the protection of the weakest members of the society and ruled that the executive and the legislature should have carried out an impact assessment of the measures and should have investigated whether less restrictive measures could have attained the same objectives.

4. Right to adequate standard of living

(a) *Right to adequate housing*

Jaftha and van Rooyen v Schoeman and ors, Appeal decision, CCT74/03, [2004] ZACC 25, ILDC 1846 (ZA 2004), 2005 (2) SA 140 (CC), 2005 (1) BCLR 78 (CC), 8th October 2004, South Africa; Constitutional Court [CC]

The two applicants were unemployed and poor women who had borrowed small amounts of money from private individuals. Although they paid some instalments they fell back on their debts, which had escalated owing to interest and other costs. Their houses were sold in execution of their outstanding debts by operation of sections 66 and 67 of the Magistrates' Courts Act 1944. They challenged these provisions before the Cape High Court and, upon appeal, before the Constitutional Court of South Africa as being contrary to Article 26 of the constitution, which recognized the right to adequate housing.

The right to adequate housing in international law

[23] Although the concept of adequate housing was briefly discussed in *Government of the Republic of South Africa and Others v Grootboom and Others* this Court has yet to consider it in any detail. This subject has however been dealt with by the United Nations Committee on Economic, Social and Cultural Rights (the Committee) in the context of the International Covenant on Economic, Social and Cultural Rights, 1966 (the Covenant). In terms of section 39(1)(b) of the Constitution, this Court must consider international law when interpreting the Bill of Rights. Therefore, guidance may be sought from international instruments that have considered the meaning of adequate housing.

[24] Article 11(1) of the Covenant reads as follows:

> "The States Parties to the present Covenant recognize the right of everyone to an adequate standard of living for himself and his family, including *adequate food, clothing and housing*, and to the continuous improvement of living conditions.
>
> The States Parties will take appropriate steps to ensure the realization of this right, recognizing to this effect the essential importance of international co-operation based on free consent." (Emphasis added.)

In its General Comment 4, the Committee, giving content to article 11(1) of the Covenant, emphasised the need not to give the right to housing a restrictive interpretation and to see it as "the right to live somewhere in security, peace and dignity". The position of the Committee reflects the view adopted by this Court in *Grootboom*, that the right to dignity is inherently linked with socio-economic rights. It is important, for the purposes of this case, to point to the Committee's recognition that "the concept of adequacy is particularly significant in relation to the right to housing". While acknowledging that adequacy "is determined in part by social, economic, cultural, climatic, ecological and other factors", it has identified "certain aspects of the right that must be taken into account for this purpose in any particular context." Of relevance is the focus on security of tenure. The Committee points out that security of tenure takes many forms, not just ownership, but that "all persons should possess a degree of security of tenure which guarantees legal protection against forced eviction, harassment and other threats."

[31] [...] [T]he appellants, in their claim, distinguish between the positive and the negative aspects of the right to housing. They argue that it is the negative aspect of the right which has been violated. [...] The appellants argue that the positive obligations are clearly subject to progressive realisation but that it would make no sense to say the same of the negative ones. In this case the appellants already have their homes and the state has a duty to protect their right of access to adequate housing. The availability of state resources is not an issue.

[33] The appellants are indeed correct.

[42] The interests of creditors must not be overlooked. There might be circumstances where, notwithstanding the relatively small amount of money owed, the creditor's advantage in execution outweighs the harm caused to the debtor. […]

[43] However, it is clear that there will be circumstances in which it will be unjustifiable to allow execution […] because the advantage that attaches to a creditor who seeks execution will be far outweighed by the immense prejudice and hardship caused to the debtor.

[52] […] [S]ection 66(1)(a) of [Magistrates' Courts Act 1944, allowing execution against the immovable property of debtors without judicial oversight in certain cases] is overbroad and constitutes a violation of section 26(1) of the Constitution to the extent that it allows execution against the homes of indigent debtors, where they lose their security of tenure. [It] is not justifiable and cannot be saved to the extent that it allows for such executions where no countervailing considerations in favour of the creditor justify the sales in execution.

This was the first South African case to elaborate on the right to adequate housing. The court once again made extensive reference to Article 11(1) of the ICESCR and General Comment 4 of the CESCR by operation of section 39(1)(b) of the constitution, which requires South African courts to consider international law when interpreting the Bill of Rights. Most importantly, the court's finding that the eviction of the applicants impinged upon the negative aspect of the right to adequate housing is yet another illustration that social rights may have direct effect and are not inherently non-justiciable. Thus, their implementation does not necessarily depend upon the availability of financial resources.

Corporation of the City of Victoria and Attorney General of British Columbia (intervening) v Adams and ors and British Columbia Civil Liberties Association (intervening), First instance judgment, 2008 BCSC 1363, ILDC 1843 (CA 2008), 14th October 2008, Canada; British Columbia; Supreme Court [BCSC]

The defendants were homeless and were sleeping overnight in parks, which was prohibited under the City of Victoria's Parks Regulation bylaws. They claimed that the bylaws and the operational policy of the City's police in enforcing them violated their rights under section 7 of the Canadian Charter of Rights and Freedoms (Charter) which provides that 'everyone has the right to life, liberty and security of the person and the right not to be deprived thereof except in accordance with the principles of fundamental justice'. In examining whether the claim fell within this provision, the court addressed the relevance to be given to Canada's international obligations.

[85] Canada is a party to several international human rights instruments which recognize adequate housing as a fundamental right. The Universal Declaration of Human Rights […] at Article 25(1) states:

> Everyone has the right to a standard of living adequate for the health and well-being of himself and of his family, including food, clothing, housing and medical care and necessary social services, and the right to security in the event of unemployment, sickness, disability, widowhood, old age or other lack of livelihood in circumstances beyond his control.

[87] Similarly, Article 11.1 of the International Covenant on Economic, Social, and Cultural Rights […] declares:

> The States Parties to the present Covenant recognize the right of everyone to an adequate standard of living for himself and his family, including adequate food, clothing and housing, and to the continuous improvement of living conditions. The States Parties will take appropriate steps to ensure the realization of this right,

recognizing to this effect the essential importance of international co-operation based on free consent.

[88] Article 2.1 of the Covenant outlines the obligation of each state party to the Covenant to take steps, "to the maximum of [its] available resources, with a view to achieving progressively the full realization of the rights recognized in the present Covenant".

[89] The United Nations has determined that all persons should possess a degree of security of housing tenure that guarantees legal protection against forced eviction and that forced eviction constitutes a gross violation of human rights. The United Nations affirmed that security of tenure takes a variety of forms, including informal settlements, such as occupation of land or property. In its General Comment No. 4 on Article 11.1 of the Covenant, the Committee on Economic, Social and Cultural Rights 6th session, U.N. Doc. E/1992/23, annex III (1991) at 114 recognized at para. 18:

> [T]hat instances of forced eviction are *prima facie* incompatible with the requirements of the Covenant and can only be justified in the most exceptional circumstances, and in accordance with the relevant principles of international law. [emphasis in original]

[90] Although Article 11.1 of the Covenant is perhaps the most comprehensive and significant expression of the obligation of states to recognize adequate housing as a basic and fundamental human right, there are also a wide variety of other international covenants and declarations that establish the different dimensions of the right to adequate housing and enshrine it as a fundamental principle of international law.

[91] The United Nations Conference on Human Settlements (Habitat II), 3-14 June, 1996, which produced the Habitat Agenda, U.N. Doc. A/Conf. 165/14 (June 14, 1996) addressed "adequate shelter for all" as a theme of global importance. [. . .]

[98] The federal government has expressed the view that s. 7 of the Charter must be interpreted in a manner consistent with Canada's obligations under the Covenant to not deprive persons of the basic necessities of life, in its response to a question from the Committee on Economic, Social, and Cultural Rights. [. . .]

[99] [. . .] [T]he federal government gave the following answer at Question 53:

> The Supreme Court of Canada has stated that section 7 of the Charter may be interpreted to include the rights protected under the Covenant (see decision of *Slaight Communications v. Davidson* [1989] 1 S.C.R. 1038). *The Supreme Court has also held section 7 as guaranteeing that people are not to be deprived of basic necessities* (see decision of *Irwin Toy v. A. -G. Québec*, [1989] 1 S.C.R. 927). *The Government of Canada is bound by these interpretations of section 7 of the Charter.* [Emphasis added]

[100] I conclude that while the various international instruments do not form part of the domestic law of Canada, they should inform the interpretation of the Charter and in this case, the scope and content of s. 7.

The court found that the bylaws violated section 7 of the Canadian Charter. This decision is interesting and significant for various reasons: it was issued by a court of a 'Western' country; since the Canadian Charter does not explicitly enshrine any socio-economic rights, the court in effect considered the right to adequate housing as component of the right to life, liberty and security of the person in a manner reminiscent of courts in developing countries, most notably India; the various international instruments referred to in the decision, including non-legally binding ones, were used to inform the interpretation of the Charter, which is a well-established practice in Canadian jurisprudence. Upon appeal, the Court of Appeal for British Columbia largely upheld this decision and ruled that the trial judge did not improperly intrude into the policy decisions of elected officials in finding the bylaw provisions as unconstitutional since it was left to the City to consider alternative solutions in the context of its own legislative policies.[43] Importantly, no issue was raised regarding the trial court's use of international instruments as an aid to interpreting the Charter since it was held that such use, especially in respect of section 7 of the Charter, was well-established in Canadian case law.[44]

Singh and ors v Government of Delhi, through Secretary, Public Works Department, National Capital Territory of Delhi and Municipal Corporation of Delhi, through Additional Commissioner, Slum & Jhuggie Jhomprie Department (joining), Final judgment, WP(C) No 8904/2009, WP(C) No 7735/2007, WP(C) No 7317/2009, WP(C) No 9246/2009, ILDC 2108 (IN 2010), 2010 Indlaw DEL 592, 2010 (168) DLT 218, 11th February 2010, India; National Capital Territory; New Delhi; High Court

The petitioners were slum dwellers whose settlements were demolished by the government ahead of the 2010 Commonwealth Games in New Delhi. They claimed that their denial of relocation and relocation assistance was in breach of their right to shelter.

> **International Conventions**
>
> 27. International concern over the world housing situation has been expressed by Governments themselves in numerous international declarations, conventions and agreements.
>
> [. . .]
>
> 32. The Covenant indicates that priority should be given to social welfare and the level of effort should increase over time. These obligations apply to any State that has ratified the Covenant regardless of the State's economic resources. Of course, the States would devise their own steps for the realization of these rights in accordance with their own resources. India has signed and ratified this Covenant and the State is under an obligation to give effect to its provisions.
>
> 33. The General Comment 7 dated 20th May 1997 on the right to adequate housing (Article 11.1) by the Commission on Economic, Social and Cultural rights reads as follows:
>
>> "(1) In its General Comment No.4, (1991), the Committee observed that all persons should possess a degree of security of tenure which guarantees legal protection against forced eviction, harassment and other threats. It concluded that forced evictions are prima facie incompatible with the requirement of the Covenant. [. . .]"
>
> 34. The recognized importance of the right to housing over time has led to its ratification and reinforcement through other international declarations, conventions and conferences, in which more precise and complex objectives have been developed. Of these declarations, special note should be made of The Habitat I Vancouver Declaration (1976), the International Year of the Homeless (1987).
>
> **Special Rapporteur's Guidelines on Relocation of Displaced**
>
> 35. Annexure-I of the Report of the Special Rapporteur on Adequate Housing lays down basic principles and guidelines on development based evictions and displacement. Insofar as relocation of the displaced is concerned, the guidelines provide:
>
>> "52. The Government and any other parties responsible for providing just compensation and sufficient alternative accommodation, or restitution when feasible,

43 *Victoria (City) v Adams*, 2009 BCCA 563, paras 10, 194–95.

44 L Clarke, Analysis, *Corporation of the City of Victoria and Attorney General of British Columbia (intervening) v Adams and ors and British Columbia Civil Liberties Association (intervening)*, ILDC 1843 (CA 2008) A2.

must do so immediately upon the eviction, except in cases of force majeure. At a minimum, regardless of the circumstances and without discrimination, competent authorities shall ensure that evicted persons or groups, especially those who are unable to provide for themselves, have safe and secure access to: (a) essential food, potable water and sanitation; (b) basic shelter and housing; (c) appropriate clothing; (d) essential medical services; (e) livelihood sources; (f) fodder for livestock and access to common property resources previously depended upon; and (g) education for children and childcare facilities. States should also ensure that members of the same extended family or community are not separated as a result of evictions. [. . .]
55. Identified relocation sites must fulfil the criteria for adequate housing according to international human rights law. [. . .]

58. Persons, groups or communities affected by an eviction should not suffer detriment to their human rights, including their right to the progressive realization of the right to adequate housing. This applies equally to host communities at relocation sites."

UN Committee's Observations on India

36. The UN Committee on Economic, Social and Cultural Rights in May, 2008, in its Concluding Observations on India, called upon the Indian government to address the issue of rising homelessness, including the need for disaggregated data on the homeless. In particular, it mentioned:

[. . .]

71. The Committee recommends that the State party take immediate measures to effectively enforce laws and regulations prohibiting displacement and forced evictions, and ensure that persons evicted from their homes and lands be provided with adequate compensation and/or offered alternative accommodation, in accordance with the guidelines adopted by the Committee in its General Comment No. 7 on forced evictions (1997). The Committee also recommends that, prior to implementing development and urban renewal projects, sporting events and other similar activities, the State party should undertake open, participatory and meaningful consultations with affected residents and communities. In this connection, the Committee draws the attention of the State party to its General Comment No. 4 on the right to adequate housing (1991) and further requests the State party to provide information in its next periodic report on progress achieved in this regard, including disaggregated statistics relating to forced evictions.

Right to Shelter—Constitutional Perspectives

37. In a catena of decisions, the Supreme Court has enlarged the meaning of life under Article 21 of the Constitution to include within its ambit, the right to shelter.

[. . .]

55. We find no difficulty in the context of the present case, and in the light of the jurisprudence developed by our Supreme Court and the High Court in the cases referred to earlier, to require the respondents to engage meaningfully with those who are sought to be evicted. It must be remembered that the MPD-2021 clearly identifies the relocation of slum dwellers as one of the priorities for the government. Spaces have been earmarked for housing of the economically weaker sections. The government will be failing in its statutory and constitutional obligation if it fails to identify spaces equipped infrastructurally with the civic amenities that can ensure a decent living to those being relocated prior to initiating the moves for eviction.

> 57. [...] It is the State's constitutional and statutory obligation to ensure that if the jhuggi dweller is forcibly evicted and relocated, such jhuggi dweller is not worse off. The relocation has to be a meaningful exercise consistent with the rights to life, livelihood and dignity of such jhuggi dweller.
>
> **Conclusion**
>
> 62. It is declared that:
>
> (i) The decision of the respondents holding that the petitioners are [...] not entitled to relocation, is hereby declared as illegal and unconstitutional.
>
> (ii) In terms of the extant policy for relocation of jhuggi dwellers, which is operational in view of the orders of the Supreme Court, the cases of the petitioners will be considered for relocation.
>
> (iii) Within a period of four months from today, each of those eligible among the petitioners, in terms of the above relocation policy, will be granted an alternative site as per MPD-2021 subject to proof of residence prior to cut-off date. This will happen in consultation with each of them in a 'meaningful' manner, as indicated in this judgment.
>
> (iv) The State agencies will ensure that basic civic amenities, consistent with the rights to life and dignity of each of the citizens in the jhuggies, are available at the site of relocation.

This was another far-reaching Indian decision, in which the High Court of Delhi made extensive use of the ICESCR as well as non-binding sources to inform its interpretation of the right to shelter, which is protected within the ambit of the right to life under India's constitution and jurisprudence. The court directed the government to follow procedures both prior to and after the slum demolitions. In effect, these procedures were in accord with the Basic Principles and Guidelines on Development-based Evictions and Displacement of the UN Special Rapporteur on adequate housing and in compliance with the CESCR's Concluding Observations on India, which were both reproduced in the judgment in considerable length.

(b) Right to water

Mazibuko and ors v City of Johannesburg and ors, First instance decision, Case No 06/13865, [2008] ZAGPHC 128, ILDC 973 (ZA 2008), 30th April 2008, South Africa; Gauteng; Johannesburg; South Gauteng High Court [GPJ-HC]

The applicants were residents of Phiri, a township around Soweto in Johannesburg. They challenged the water policies introduced by the City of Johannesburg in 2004 as being unreasonable and falling short of providing sufficient water, which was guaranteed in section 27(1) of the South African constitution (one of the few constitutions to do so). Under the new system, once the amount of free water had been used, the water supply would be cut off and account holders would only be ensured a water supply if they bought prepaid water credits. The respondents argued, *inter alia*, that they were not obliged to provide free basic water to the poor, but that they were obliged to provide basic water at a fee. The High Court made an extensive analysis of the right to water in international law and found in favour of the applicants and instructed the city to revise its policy.

> [36] General Comment No. 15 (2002) of the United Nations Committee on Economic, Social and Cultural Rights' Twenty-ninth Session, Geneva 11–29 November 2002 ("*General Comment No. 15*") emphasises, amongst others, the following aspects to the right to water: availability and accessibility. Availability means that the water supply must not only be sufficient for each person for personal and domestic use but must also be continuous. Accessibility means both physical and economic accessibility on a non-discriminatory basis. The effect is that the right to water must be accessible equally to

the rich as well as to the poor and to the most vulnerable members of the population. It is in this context, that the State is under an obligation to provide the poor with the necessary water and water facilities on a non-discriminatory basis.

[37] In terms of paragraph 18 of General Comment No. 15 the State has a constant and continuing duty to the progressive realization of the right to water. Retrogressive measures taken by the State with regard to the right to water are prohibited. If such retrogressive measures are taken, the *onus* is on the State to prove that such retrogressive measures are justified with reference to the totality of the rights provided for in the Covenant. The State is obliged to respect, protect and fulfil the right to water.

[38] Article 24 of The Convention on the Rights of the Child ("*CRC*") contains an obligation on the State to fully implement the right of children to attain the highest possible standard of health and to combat disease through the provision of adequate food and drinking water. Article 14 of the African Convention on the Rights of the Child("*ACRC*") also has an identical obligation on the State.

[39] Article 16 of the African Charter on Human and Peoples' Rights guarantees the right to enjoy the best attainable standard of both physical and mental health. Failure by the State to supply basic services, such as safe drinking water and electricity, has been found by the African Commission to be violation of the article.

[40] Seen against the background of international law, decisions of the various international institutions and the similar language used in the Bill of Rights as that used in the various international instruments, the State is obliged to provide free basic water to the poor.

[41] Against this background, I am unable to appreciate the contention of the respondents that they are under no obligation to provide basic water to the poor. Their obligation is to ensure that every person has both physical and economic access to water. Their contention to the contrary is incongruent with their actions. The third respondent's promulgation of the Water Services Act and its Regulations as well as the respondents' water policies and its various adaptations, all point in the direction of compliance with the provisions of section 27(2) of the Constitution: the progressive realization of the right of access to sufficient water as well as compliance with the provisions of section 7(2) of the Constitution: the obligation not only to respect, protect but to promote and fulfil the rights contained in the Bill of Rights.

[44] Again to determine whether the Regulation falls short in providing sufficient water, it is instructive to determine what the international law regards as sufficient water.

[45] Under international law there is no express right to water. Article 25 of the Universal Declaration of Human Rights provides that everyone has the right to a standard of living adequate for health and well-being. In terms of CESCR, the right to water falls within the category of guarantees essential for securing an adequate standard of living. According to CESCR, the quantity of water available to each person must correspond with the World Health Organisation ("*WHO*") guidelines.

[46] WHO guidelines quantifies basic access to water as 25 litres per person per day. This is regarded as the lowest level to maintain life over the short term. This basic access assures consumptions while hygiene, being for hand washing and basic food hygiene, is not assured. There is a possibility that hygiene may be assured. However, laundry and bathing is difficult to assure unless water is carried out of source. According to the Human Development Report 2006 published by the United Nations Development Programme 20 litres per day is sufficient water per person.

[47] Regulation 3(b) provides for a *minimum* (my emphasis) quantity of potable water of 25 litres per person per day or 6 kilolitres per household per month. The Regulation clearly stipulates the minimum quantity of water per person per day.

[126] As pointed out above, the 25 litres per person per month or 6 kilolitres per household per month is the minimum quantity of water set by Regulation 3(b) of the National Standards Regulations. The respondents are, in terms of section 27(2), obliged to provide more than the minimum if its residents' needs so demand and they are able, within their available resources, to do so.

[133] [...] I do not understand the Constitutional Court to be rejecting the core minimum as part of our law.

[181] [...] It is undeniable that the applicants need more water than the 25 litres per person per day and that the respondents are able, within their available resources to meet this need. The respondents' provision of 25 litres per person per day is unreasonable. It appears that the respondents are able to provide 50 litres per person per day without restraining its capacity on water and its financial resources.

183.5 The City of Johannesburg alternatively Johannesburg Water (Pty) Ltd is ordered to provide each applicant and other similarly placed residents of Phiri Township with —

183.5.1 free basic water supply of 50 litres per person per day and

183.5.2 the option of a metered supply installed at the cost of the City of Johannesburg.

The key finding of the High Court, which was upheld by the Court of Appeal, was the quantification of the content of the right to water by specifying a minimum quantity of 'sufficient water' within the meaning of the constitution. This approach gave effect to the minimum core standard, as elaborated by the CESCR, which was extensively invoked in the judgment. This approach had been however disavowed by the Constitutional Court. Indeed, the judgments of the High Court and the Court of Appeal were overturned by the Constitutional Court, which reaffirmed its previous jurisprudence and stuck to the reasonableness approach.[45] In the words of the Constitutional Court, '[the] argument [...] that the Court should adopt a quantified standard determining the content of the right [...] must fail for the same reasons that the minimum core argument failed in *Grootboom* and *Treatment Action Campaign No 2*'.[46] The Constitutional Court found that the city's detailed account and constant review of the project and the measures taken in favour of those with the lowest incomes complied with the standard of reasonableness and thus ruled that neither the city's water policy nor the introduction of pre-paid water meters in Phiri were in violation of the constitution.[47]

NV Waterleiding Maatschappij Limburg v Anonymous, Appeal judgment, HD 200 018 358, LJN: BL6583, ILDC 1694 (NL 2010), 2nd March 2010, Netherlands

This was an appeal decision by the Den Bosch Court of Appeal against a judgment of the District Court of Maastricht,[48] which had found that closing off the water supply of a defaulting client constituted a breach of that person's right to water, as distilled from the right to an adequate standard of living and the right to health contained in Articles 11 and 12 of the ICESCR. This was found, notably, because the defaulting client was dependent on the regional monopolist, the Waterworks Company Limburg, for enjoyment of his right to water.[49]

H1 The human right to water as inferred from Articles 11 and 12 of the ICESCR did not entail an absolute right to water, in the sense that it would be without payment.

---

45 *Mazibuko and ors v City of Johannesburg and ors*, Appeal to Constitutional Court, Case CCT 39/09, [2009] ZACC 28, 8 October 2009, Constitutional Court.

46 ibid, para 56.

47 ibid, paras 168–69.

48 *Waterworks Company Limburg v Anonymous*, First instance judgment, LJN: BD5759, 294698 CV EXPL 08-4233, 25 June 2008.

49 *NV Waterleiding Maatschappij Limburg v Anonymous*, Appeal judgment, HD 200 018 358, LJN: BL6583, ILDC 1694 (NL 2010), 2 March 2010, Netherlands, F2.

> From General Comment No 15 it was clear that the right to water meant 'sufficient, safe, acceptable, physically accessible and affordable water for personal and domestic uses'. According to the CESCR Committee, economic accessibility entailed that '[w]ater, and water facilities and services, must be affordable for all. The direct and indirect costs and charges associated with securing water must be affordable, and must not compromise or threaten the realization of other Covenant rights', but not that water should be free.
>
> H2 The question as to whether Articles 11 and 12 of the ICESCR were directly effective under Dutch law according to Article 93 of the Constitution of the Netherlands could be left aside, since closing off the water supply in case of defaulting payment did not constitute a breach of the human right to water as inferred from those Articles.

As noted by the ILDC reporter, the Court of Appeal took an altogether different approach from that of the District Court.[50] It emphasized that the right to water did not entail a right to free water and reasoned that closing off the water supply of a defaulting client did not therefore come within the scope of the human right to water. Thus, the court did not address the question of whether it was permissible under international human rights law to cut off the water supply and, thereby, any access of a defaulting client to the minimum essential amount of water in order to enforce payment. In any case, it is remarkable that the court's reasoning on the affordability, rather than on the free availability of water, was based on the reference to 'affordable' water in General Comment 15 of the CESCR.

Matsipane Mosetlhanyane and Ors v The Attorney General, Appeal judgment, Civil Appeal No. CACLB-074-10, Botswana, 27 January 2011 (not in ILDC)

The applicants were members of the Basarwa community of Botswana. The community had been evicted from the Central Kalahari Game Reserve (CKGR) and was resettled in 2006 following a decision of the High Court of Botswana, which had found their previous eviction unconstitutional. The applicants claimed the right to have access to water for domestic uses from an existing and/or a new borehole(s) in the reserve at their own expense. They appealed against the decision of the High Court, which had dismissed their application. One of the submissions before the Court of Appeal was that the government's refusal to allow them the use of boreholes for domestic purposes amounted to degrading treatment.

> 19. It is appropriate to stress that in the exercise of a value judgment [of whether a person has been subjected to inhuman or degrading treatment], the Court is entitled to have regard to international consensus on the importance of access to water. Reference to two important documents will suffice:
>
> > (1) On 20 January 2003, the United Nations Committee on Economic, Social and Cultural Rights submitted a report on what it termed Substantive Issues Arising in the Implementation of the International Covenant on Economic, Social and Cultural Rights. In its introduction it stated the following:
> >
> > > "Water is a limited natural resource and a public good fundamental for life and health. The human right to water is indispensable for leading a life in human dignity. It is a prerequisite for the realization of other human rights ... "
> >
> > In paragraph 16(d) of the Report the Committee said the following:
>
> 16. Whereas the right to water applies to everyone, States parties should give special attention to those individuals and groups who have traditionally faced

50 R de Haan, Analysis, *NV Waterleiding Maatschappij Limburg v Anonymous*, ILDC 1694 (NL 2010) A1.

difficulties in exercising this right, including women, children, minority groups, indigenous peoples, refugees, asylum seekers, internally displaced persons, migrant workers, prisoners and detainees. In particular, States parties should take steps to ensure that:

> (d) Indigenous peoples' access to water resources on their ancestral lands is protected from encroachment and unlawful pollution. States should provide resources for indigenous peoples to design, deliver and control their access to water;
>
> (2) On July 2010, the United Nations General Assembly recognised the right to safe and clean drinking water as a fundamental human right that is essential for the full enjoyment of life and all human rights. Accordingly, the UN General Assembly called upon States:
>
>> "(b) To ensure full transparency of the planning and implementation process in the provision of safe drinking water and sanitation and the active, free and meaningful participation of the concerned local communities and relevant stakeholders."

The Court of Appeal held that allowing the applicants to live in the CKGR without the right to abstract water other than from plants amounted to degrading treatment and was unconstitutional. It ruled that the applicants had the right to recommission boreholes for domestic purposes at their own expense. This ruling made it feasible and meaningful for the Basawra community to resettle and live in the CKGR. In terms of international law and the right to water, this was the first decision to refer to the landmark UN General Assembly Resolution 64/292 on the human right to water and sanitation, which had been adopted a few months before the judgment was issued. Referring to both this Resolution and General Comment 15 of the CESCR was crucial in integrating the socio-economic rights framework in the jurisprudence and legal framework of Botswana, which did not formally recognize economic and social rights in its constitution. The court used the civil rights framework (the prohibition of degrading treatment) to advance socio-economic rights in this case. Lastly, it is noteworthy that the applicants did not argue and thus the court did not rule on the state's obligation to provide water at the government's expense.

5. Right to work, labour rights, and trade union rights

Health Services and Support-Facilities Subsector Bargaining Association and ors, Attorney General of Ontario (intervening) and ors (intervening) v Province of British Columbia, Final Appeal, Docket No 30554, 2007 SCC 27, (2007) 2 SCR 391, (2007) 283 DLR (4th) 40, [2007] 7 WWR 191, (2007) 157 CRR (2d) 21, (2007) 65 BCLR (4th) 201, ILDC 857 (CA 2007), 8th June 2007, Canada; Supreme Court [SCC]

The applicant trade unions and workers challenged the legislation introduced by Canada's province of British Columbia in 2002 on reforming the health and social services sectors, which, *inter alia*, gave employers considerable flexibility in organizing relations with their employees and precluded meaningful collective bargaining on some issues. The applicants argued that the new law violated the right to freedom of association under section 2(d) of the Canadian Charter of Rights and Freedoms (Charter). The trial and appeals courts rejected their arguments by relying on the case law of the Supreme Court of Canada that collective bargaining was not a Charter-protected activity. Before the Supreme Court the applicants argued, *inter alia*, that international human rights law could be used to interpret the scope of section 2(d) of the Charter as including certain aspects of the right to collective bargaining.

> 70 Canada's adherence to international documents recognizing a right to collective bargaining supports recognition of the right in s. 2(*d*) of the *Charter*. As Dickson C.J. observed in the *Alberta Reference*, at p. 349, the *Charter* should be presumed to

provide at least as great a level of protection as is found in the international human rights documents that Canada has ratified.

72 The *ICESCR*, the *ICCPR* and *Convention No. 87* extend protection to the functioning of trade unions in a manner suggesting that a right to collective bargaining is part of freedom of association. The interpretation of these conventions, in Canada and internationally, not only supports the proposition that there is a right to collective bargaining in international law, but also suggests that such a right should be recognized in the Canadian context under s. 2(*d*).

73 Article 8, para. (1)(*c*) of the *ICESCR* guarantees the "right of trade unions to function freely subject to no limitations other than those prescribed by law and which are necessary in a democratic society in the interests of national security or public order or for the protection of the rights and freedoms of others." This Article allows the "free functioning" of trade unions to be regulated, but not legislatively abrogated […]. Since collective bargaining is a primary function of a trade union, it follows that Article 8 protects a union's freedom to pursue this function freely.

74 Similarly, Article 22, para. 1 of the *ICCPR* states that "[e]veryone shall have the right to freedom of association with others, including the right to form and join trade unions for the protection of his interests." Paragraph 2 goes on to say that no restriction may be placed on the exercise of this right, other than those necessary in a free and democratic society for reasons of national security, public safety, public order, public health or the protection of the rights of others. This Article has been interpreted to suggest that it encompasses both the right to form a union and the right to collective bargaining: *Concluding Observations of the Human Rights Committee Canada*, U.N. Doc. CCPR/C/79/Add.105 (1999).

75 *Convention No. 87* has also been understood to protect collective bargaining as part of freedom of association. Part I of the Convention, entitled "Freedom of Association", sets out the rights of workers to freely form organizations which operate under constitutions and rules set by the workers and which have the ability to affiliate internationally. […]

76 *Convention No. 87* has been the subject of numerous interpretations by the ILO's Committee on Freedom of Association, Committee of Experts and Commissions of Inquiry. […] While not binding, they shed light on the scope of s. 2(*d*) of the *Charter* as it was intended to apply to collective bargaining […].

77 A recent review by ILO staff summarized a number of principles concerning collective bargaining. Some of the most relevant principles in international law are summarized in the following terms (see B. Gernigon, A. Odero and H. Guido, "ILO principles concerning collective bargaining" (2000), 139 *Intern'l Lab. Rev.* 33, at pp. 51–52):

A. The right to collective bargaining is a fundamental right endorsed by the members of the ILO in joining the Organization, which they have an obligation to respect, to promote and to realize, in good faith (ILO Declaration on Fundamental Principles and Rights at Work and its Follow-up).

…

D. The purpose of collective bargaining is the regulation of terms and conditions of employment, in a broad sense, and the relations between the parties.

…

H. The principle of good faith in collective bargaining implies recognizing representative organizations, endeavouring to reach an agreement, engaging in genuine and constructive negotiations, avoiding unjustified delays in negotiation and mutually respecting the commitments entered into, taking into account the results of negotiations in good faith.

I. In view of the fact that the voluntary nature of collective bargaining is a fundamental aspect of the principles of freedom of association, collective bargaining may not be imposed upon the parties and procedures to support bargaining must, in principle, take into account its voluntary nature; moreover, the level of bargaining must not be imposed unilaterally by law or by the authorities, and it must be possible for bargaining to take place at any level.

J. It is acceptable for conciliation and mediation to be imposed by law in the framework of the process of collective bargaining, provided that reasonable time limits are established. However, the imposition of compulsory arbitration in cases where the parties do not reach agreement is generally contrary to the principle of voluntary collective bargaining and is only admissible: [cases of essential services, administration of the State, clear deadlock, and national crisis].

K. Interventions by the legislative or administrative authorities which have the effect of annulling or modifying the content of freely concluded collective agreements, including wage clauses, are contrary to the principle of voluntary collective bargaining. These interventions include: the suspension or derogation of collective agreements by decree without the agreement of the parties; the interruption of agreements which have already been negotiated; the requirement that freely concluded collective agreements be renegotiated; the annulment of collective agreements; and the forced renegotiation of agreements which are currently in force. Other types of intervention, such as the compulsory extension of the validity of collective agreements by law are only admissible in cases of emergency and for short periods.

L. Restrictions on the content of future collective agreements ... are admissible only in so far as such restrictions are preceded by consultations with the organizations of workers and employers and fulfil the following conditions: [restrictions are exceptional measures; of limited duration; include protection for workers' standards of living]. [...]

78 The fact that a global consensus on the meaning of freedom of association did not crystallize in the *Declaration on Fundamental Principles and Rights at Work*, 6 IHRR 285 (1999), until 1998 does not detract from its usefulness in interpreting s. 2(*d*) of the *Charter*. For one thing, the Declaration was made on the basis of interpretations of international instruments, such as *Convention No. 87*, many of which were adopted by the ILO prior to the advent of the *Charter* and were within the contemplation of the framers of the *Charter*. For another, the *Charter*, as a living document, grows with society and speaks to the current situations and needs of Canadians. Thus Canada's *current* international law commitments and the current state of international thought on human rights provide a persuasive source for interpreting the scope of the *Charter*.

79 In summary, international conventions to which Canada is a party recognize the right of the members of unions to engage in collective bargaining, as part of the protection for freedom of association. [...]

> 168 […] We conclude that ss. 6(2), 6(4) and 9 of the Act are unconstitutional. However, we suspend this declaration for a period of 12 months to allow the government to address the repercussions of this decision. […]

The practice of the Supreme Court of Canada to refer to international law to inform the interpretation of the Canadian Charter was strengthened in this decision by the presumption that the rights protected in the Charter should be considered to be at least as comprehensive as their international law equivalents.[51] In the case at hand, this presumption and the extensive reference to relevant international instruments and their interpretation by international bodies resulted in overruling earlier case law and recognizing that section 2(d) of the Charter included a right to bargain collectively.

Public Prosecution of Egypt v Aldian Mustafa and Others, Decision on merit, No 4190/86 Ozbekia (121 Koli Shamal), ILDC 1483 (EG 1987), 16th April 1987, Egypt; Cairo; State Security Emergency Court

The defendants were national rail workers who had gone on strike demanding the improvement of their work conditions and wages. Their strike caused the disruption of rail services and considerable losses to the national rail company and others. They were arrested and charged with a range of offences, including breach of Article 124 of Egypt's 1973 Penal Code, which made it a crime if three or more workers collectively left their line of work or refused to carry out their duties for the purpose of securing a mutual gain. The defence challenged the criminalization of the strike in light of Egypt's ratification of the ICESCR, which recognized the right to strike in Article 8(d).

> H1 Although Article 8(d) of the ICESCR stated that the right to strike should be exercised in conformity with the laws of a particular country, this could not be used by a national authority to prohibit the exercise of this right, as otherwise any state could invoke its domestic arrangements to violate its international obligation.
>
> H3 Article 1(4) of the ICESCR provided that states should gradually implement the rights enshrined in the ICESCR. However, the right to strike did not fall in the category of rights that required gradual realization. States did not need to mobilize certain resources or wait for international assistance to ensure workers' enjoyment of the right to strike.
>
> H4 […] As Article 124 of the Penal Code, which prohibited the action of going on strike, clearly contradicted the right to strike as guaranteed by Article 8(d) of the ICESCR, it must be declared null and void.
>
> H5 The legitimate exercise of the right to strike was permissible. Acts such as agreements to go on strike and refusal to carry out duties were manifestations of the right to strike and thus permissible, or otherwise the right to strike would be meaningless.
>
> H6 The provision in the Penal Code criminalizing the act of going on strike was repealed by the adoption and publication of the ICESCR. Therefore the act of going on strike was legal. The accused persons were not guilty.

In this far-reaching and brave decision, an article of the Egyptian Penal Code was declared null and void because it conflicted with the right to strike as enshrined in Article 8(d) of the ICESCR.[52] If anything, this decision shows the emancipatory potential of the ICESCR, which can become a powerful tool for introducing welcome societal changes in the hands of daring judges.

---

51 G MacNeil, Analysis, *Health Services and Support-Facilities Subsector Bargaining Association and ors, Attorney General of Ontario (intervening) and ors (intervening) v Province of British Columbia*, ILDC 857 (CA 2007) A3.

52 See N Algheitta, Analysis, *Public Prosecution of Egypt v Aldian Mustafa and Others*, ILDC 1483 (EG 1987) A5.

Kav La'Oved (Worker's Hotline) Association and ors v Israel and ors, Original petition to the High Court of Justice, HCJ 4542/02, ILDC 382 (IL 2006), 30th March 2006, Israel; Supreme Court; Supreme Court as High Court of Justice

The petitioners, seven Israeli NGOs, challenged Israel's 'tying down policy' of employment of migrant workers, which prevented them from terminating their jobs and working for different employers and made them vulnerable to further abuses. The petitioners argued that this policy was a serious breach of the migrant workers' rights to freedom of occupation and human dignity, which are protected under the Israeli Basic Law and international law. The state defended the legality and reasonableness of this policy in light of the necessity to limit and monitor migration for employment into Israel and to prevent adverse effects on Israeli employees.

> 35. It would not be out of place to note that the individual's right to undertake employment freely and voluntarily is also anchored in international law. The International Covenant on Economic, Social and Cultural Rights (Treaties 31, 1037, at p. 205), which was signed and ratified by Israel on 3 October 1991, provides as follows in Article 6:
>
> > "1. The States Parties to the present Covenant recognize the right to work, which includes the right of everyone to the opportunity to gain his living by work which he freely chooses or accepts, and will take appropriate steps to safeguard this right."
>
> For the right to choose work "freely" see also: The Universal Declaration on Human Rights, Article 23(1); the International Covenant on Civil and Political Rights, Article 8; the European Social Charter, Part I, Article 1; The American Declaration on Human Rights and Obligations, Article 14. […]
>
> Article 7 of the International Covenant on Economic, Social and Cultural Rights provides further that:
>
> > The States Parties to the present Covenant recognize the right of everyone to the enjoyment of just and favourable conditions of work which ensure, in particular:
> >
> > (a) Remuneration which provides all workers, as a minimum, with:
> >
> > (i) Fair wages and equal remuneration for work of equal value without distinction of any kind …
> >
> > (ii) A decent living for themselves and their families in accordance with the provisions of the present Covenant;
> >
> > (b) Safe and healthy working conditions;
> >
> > (c) Equal opportunity for everyone to be promoted in his employment to an appropriate higher level, subject to no considerations other than those of seniority and competence;
> >
> > (d) Rest, leisure and reasonable limitation of working hours and periodic holidays with pay, as well as remuneration for public holidays.
>
> In addition, Convention No. 97 on Migrant Workers […] of the International Labour Organization (hereinafter: the "Convention on Migrant Workers"), which was signed and ratified by Israel on 30 March 1953, provides, in Article 6, that:
>
> 1. Each Member for which this Convention is in force undertakes to apply, without discrimination in respect of nationality, race, religion or sex, to immigrants lawfully within its territory, treatment no less favourable than that which it applies to its own nationals in respect of the following matters:
>
> > (a) in so far as such matters are regulated by law or regulations, or are subject to the control of administrative authorities —
> >
> > (i) remuneration, including family allowances where these form part of remuneration, hours of work, overtime arrangements, holidays with pay,

restrictions on home work, minimum age for employment, apprenticeship and training, women's work and the work of young persons;

(ii) membership of trade unions and enjoyment of the benefits of collective bargaining; …

36. These conventions have not been absorbed into our internal legal system via legislation. Prima facie, therefore, they do not create an obligation in this regard. However, the obligations in these conventions might have taken on a customary nature [citation omitted] and […] they, therefore, have become "part of the law of the land, subject to any Israeli legislation that makes contradictory provisions" (HCJ 785/87 Afo v. Commander of IDF, P.D. 42(2) 4, 35). However, since the Petitioners did not focus their claims in international law, and to the extent to which such law must be applied to the question that requires our ruling, and since we have not been asked to rule on the status of these obligations, we shall not hammer nails into this issue […].

37. Either way, everyone agrees that by virtue of the "presumption of compliance" between internal law and the provisions of international law, we are required to interpret statutes—as well as powers acquired by government authorities—in a manner which complies with the provisions of international law […]. Thus, the power acquired by the Minister of the Interior "to prescribe conditions for the grant of a visa or residence permit" is restricted and limited, inter alia, by the right available to any person "to gain his living by work which he freely chooses or accepts"; by the right available to any individual to enjoy "just and favourable conditions of work" and by the principal of non-discrimination between citizen workers and workers from foreign countries, which is anchored in the Convention on Migrant Workers (for the principle of non-discrimination regarding restrictions on employment of workers, see also Recommendation 86 of the International Labour Organization attached to the Convention on Migrant Workers—Migration for Employment Recommendation (Revised) 1949, Article 16).

39. In summary, my conclusion is that the tying-down policy harms the human right to dignity and the human right to liberty that are protected by the Basic Law. Human dignity is wanting due to the harm that the tying-down policy causes to the individual's freedom of action, and autonomy of will. The right to liberty, on the other hand, is harmed due to removal of the option from the individual to choose the identity of the person entering into a labour contract with him, and due to the fact that the person is compelled, due to the act of dismissal being combined with severe consequential harm, to work in the service of another, against his will. These harsh results are entirely foreign to the basic principles which lie at the foundation of our legal system.

62. Therefore, the tying-down policy, which is expressed by making the residency permit given to a foreign worker who comes to Israel conditional upon working for a specific employer, and which applies, in its current format, in the fields of agriculture, nursing and industry, is harmful to fundamental rights. The harm caused by this policy is not proportionate. The operative expression of this conclusion is that the Minister of the Interior may not make a residency permit given to foreign workers contingent upon the aforesaid condition. As a result, it is the Respondents' obligation to formulate a new employment arrangement which is balanced and proportionate with respect to foreign workers in these areas of employment, which will not be based on tying workers arriving in Israel to a single employer, and which will not tie the act of dismissal to any sanction, including loss of status in Israel.

This was another decision that shows the potential of international law in the field of economic and social rights, even in cases where the relevant conventions are not part of domestic law and the plaintiffs do not argue their case on the basis of international law. The Supreme Court of Israel made use of the 'presumption of compliance' between domestic law and international law and referred extensively to the right to work and labour rights in international law even though, as noted by the ILDC reporter, this was not necessary to reach its conclusions.[53]

Vishaka v State of Rajasthan, Initial decision, No 3011 of 1997, ILDC 442 (IN 1997), 13th August 1997, India; Supreme Court

The petitioners were social activists and NGOs and brought a class action aiming to bring about gender equality, prevent sexual harassment of women in work places, and fill related gaps in Indian legislation. The petition followed an incident of alleged gang rape of a female social worker in a village of Rajasthan, which was the subject matter of separate criminal proceedings. They argued that such incidents infringed numerous rights of women recognized in the Indian constitution and international treaties binding upon India.

> 7. In the absence of domestic law occupying the field, to formulate effective measures to check the evil of sexual harassment of working women at all work places, the contents of international Conventions and norms are significant for the purpose of interpretation of the guarantee of gender equality, right to work with human dignity in Arts. 14, 15, 19 (1) (g) and 21 of the Constitution and the safeguards against sexual harassment implicit therein. Any International Convention not inconsistent with the fundamental rights and in harmony with its spirit must be read into these provisions to enlarge the meaning and content thereof, to promote the object of the constitutional guarantee. [...]
>
> 10. Gender equality includes protection from sexual harassment and right to work with dignity, which is a universally recognised basic human right. The common minimum requirement of this right has received global acceptance. The International Conventions and norms are, therefore, of great significance in the formulation of the guidelines to achieve this purpose.
>
> 11. The obligation of this Court under Art. 32 of the Constitution for the enforcement of these fundamental rights in the absence of legislation must be viewed along with the role of judiciary envisaged in the Beijing Statement of Principles of the Independence of the judiciary in the LAWASIA region. [...]
>
> 12. Some provisions in the Convention on the Elimination of All Forms of Discrimination against Women, of significance in the present context are [Article 11 paragraph 1 (a) on the right to work and (f)] the right to protection of health and to safety in working conditions, including the safeguarding of the function of reproduction [and] Article 24: State Parties undertake to adopt all necessary measures at the national level aimed at achieving the full realization of the rights recognised in the present Convention.
>
> 13. The general recommendations of CEDAW in this context in respect of Art. 11 are:
>
> "Violence and equality in employment:
>
> 22. Equality in employment can be seriously impaired when women are subjected to gender specific violence, such as sexual harassment in the work place.

53 T Kritzman, Analysis, *Kav La'Oved (Worker's Hotline) Association and ors v Israel and ors*, ILDC 382 (IL 2006) A3.

23. Sexual harassment includes such unwelcome sexually determined behavior as physical contacts and advances, sexually coloured remarks, showing pornography and sexual demands, whether by words or actions. Such conduct can be humiliating and may constitute a health and safety problem; it is discriminatory when the woman has reasonable grounds to believe that her objection would disadvantage her in connection with her employment, including recruiting or promotion, or when it creates a hostile working environment. Effective complaints procedures and remedies, including compensation, should be provided."

14. The Government of India has ratified the above resolution on June 25, 1993 with some reservations which are not material in the present context. At the Fourth World Conference on Women in Beijing, the Government of India has also made an official commitment, inter alia, to formulate and operationalize a national policy on women which will continuously guide and inform action at every level and in every sector; to set up a Commission for Women to act as a public defender of women's human rights; to institutionalise a national level mechanism to monitor the implementation of the Platform for Action. We have, therefore, no hesitation in placing reliance on the above for the purpose of construing the nature and ambit of constitutional guarantee of gender equality in our Constitution.

This was a landmark decision concerning the rights of working women in India and particularly their legal protection from sexual harassment at work, which entailed the violation of various human rights. In the absence of any domestic legislation, the Supreme Court of India resorted to the relevant provisions of the CEDAW and related documents with a view to bringing gender justice and equality in the workplace. Significantly, the court laid down guidelines and norms, including a definition of sexual harassment, the duties of employers for the prevention of sexual harassment of working women, and the rights and remedies of victims. Again, however, the gap between the law and the reality in workplaces in India and elsewhere is huge.

IV. Conclusion

The decisions in this chapter are a representative sample testifying to a gradual change in international and comparative law during the last decades towards an ever-growing acceptance of the justiciability of socio-economic rights. Admittedly, some domestic courts still deny their justiciability but such a blunt denial has become increasingly less tenable in view of the powerful justification of justiciability that has been put forward by the CESCR and espoused by numerous domestic courts in both the Global South and the North.

Interestingly as well, in most cases the courts were less concerned—if at all—with the (non-)self-executing character of the ICESCR but employed the Covenant and the General Comments of the CESCR to inform the interpretation of socio-economic rights recognized in national constitutions.[54] What is more, courts in Canada, India, and Kenya have used the Covenant and even the General Comments to recognize or give effect to socio-economic rights, even though such rights were not explicitly enshrined in their constitutions. Furthermore, a considerable number of decisions in this chapter resulting from strategic or public interest litigation have also illustrated the emancipatory potential of socio-economic rights, as interpreted in the light of relevant international law, to address systemic problems and bring about significant societal changes, especially in developing countries. That said, the gap between recognition of such

54 See also M Kanetake and A Nollkaemper, 'The Application of Informal International Instruments Before Domestic Courts' (2014) 46 *George Washington International Law Review* 765, 775–77.

rights in international and domestic law and jurisprudence and their actual enforcement is an ever-present one.

Indeed, the main conceptual and practical challenges that lie ahead regarding economic and social rights in international law pertain less to their legal nature as justiciable human rights (this, however, does remain a challenge in some—mainly 'Western'—states) than to the extent of their content, practical application, and enforcement in concrete national contexts. Such challenges are best exemplified in the rich jurisprudence of South African courts and their much-criticized preference of the reasonableness approach over that of the minimum core.

The manufacturer's authorised representative in the EU for product
safety is Oxford University Press España S.A. of El Parque Empresarial
San Fernando de Henares, Avenida de Castilla, 2 - 28830 Madrid
(www.oup.es/en or product.safety@oup.com). OUP España S.A. also acts
as importer into Spain of products made by the manufacturer.
Printed and bound by CPI Group (UK) Ltd, Croydon, CR0 4YY
15/09/2026
02217466-0001